The Literature of America: Nineteenth Century

Irving Howe

Hunter College

Richard M. Ludwig
Princeton University
Consulting Editor in American Literature

McGRAW-HILL BOOK COMPANY

New York   *St. Louis*   *San Francisco*   *Düsseldorf*
London   *Mexico*   *Panama*   *Sydney*   *Toronto*

The Literature of America: Nineteenth Century

This book was set in Primer
by Monotype Composition Company, Inc.,
and printed on permanent paper
and bound by Quinn & Boden Company, Inc.
The designer was Barbara Ellwood.
The editors were Robert Fry, Cheryl Kupper, and David Dunham.
Les Kaplan supervised the production.

The Literature of America: Nineteenth Century

Library of Congress Catalog Card Number 75–115153

1 2 3 4 5 6 7 8 9 0   QBQB   7 9 8 7 6 5 4 3 2 1 0

Acknowledgments

HENRY ADAMS, Letters "To Charles Francis Adams, Jr.," "To John Gorham Palfrey," and "To William James" from *Letters of Henry Adams*, edited by Worthington Chauncy Ford. "American Ideals" from *History of the United States of America during the Administration of Thomas Jefferson.* Chapter 1, "Quincy," Chapter 17, "President Grant," Chapter 22, "Chicago," and Chapter 25, "The Dynamo and the Virgin," from *The Education of Henry Adams.* Copyright 1946 by Charles F. Adams. Reprinted by permission of Houghton Mifflin Company.

RICHARD HENRY DANA, JR., Chapter 15 from *Two Years Before the Mast*, published by Houghton Mifflin Company.

EMILY DICKINSON, "Success Is Counted Sweetest," "Exultation Is the Going," "What Inn Is This," "Safe In Their Alabaster Chambers," "Wild Nights! Wild Nights!" "There's a Certain Slant of Light," "I Felt a Funeral in My Brain," "The Soul Selects Her Own Society," "It Might Be Lonelier," "Much Madness is Divinest Sense," "This Is My Letter to the World," "I Heard a Fly Buzz When I Died," "It Was Not Death, For I Stood Up," "I Started Early, Took My Dog," "The Heart Asks Blessing First," "Our Journey Had Advanced," "Pain Has an Element of Blank," "Because I Could Not Stop for Death," "A Light Exists in Spring," "The Missing All Prevented Me," "At Half-past Three a Single Bird," "The Last Night That She Lived," "After a Hundred Years," "Great Streets of Silence Led Away," "As Imperceptibly as Grief," "There Came a Wind Like a Bugle," and "My Life Closed Twice Befor Its Close" are reprinted by permission of the publishers and the Trustees of Amherst College from Thomas H. Johnson, Editor, *The Poems of Emily Dickinson*, Cambridge, Mass.: The Belknap Press of Harvard University Press, Copyright, 1951, 1955, by the President and Fellows of Harvard College. "After Great Pain a Formal Feeling Comes," copyright 1929, © 1957 by Mary L. Hampson from *The Complete Poems of Emily Dickinson*, edited by Thomas H. Johnson, by permission of Little, Brown and Co.

SARAH ORNE JEWETT, "The Hilton's Holiday," from *The Best Stories of Sarah Orne Jewett*, published by Houghton Mifflin Company.

FREDERICK GODDARD TUCKERMAN, "Thin Little Leaves of Wood Fern, Ribbed and Toothed," "And Change with Hurried Hand Has Swept These Scenes," "Under the Mountain, as When First I Knew," "Not the Round Natural World, Not the Deep Mind" and "An Upper Chamber in a Darkened House" from *The Complete Poems of Frederick Goddard Tuckerman*, edited by N. Scott Momaday. Copyright © 1965 by Oxford University Press, Inc. Reprinted by permission. "Nor, Though She Seems to Cast with Backward Hand" by Frederick Goddard Tuckerman from *Complete Poems of Frederick Goddard Tuckerman (The Sonnets of F. G. Tuckerman).* Copyright 1931 by Alfred Knopf, 1959 by Witter Bynner. Reprinted by permission of Random House, Inc. "The Cricket" from *The Complete Poems of Frederick Goddard Tuckerman.* Copyright 1950 by Margaret Tuckerman Clark. Reprinted by permission of The Cummington Press.

Preface

How is this anthology different from all other anthologies of nineteenth-century American literature? The question can properly be asked by teachers who may teach it and students who may study it, and a few simple and candid answers are probably in order. To be totally different from other anthologies would be, of course, disastrous. There are classic texts in American literature that every anthologist must and wants to include. Emerson's essays, some Hawthorne stories, Whitman's "Song of Myself," one or two of Melville's short novels—these are mandatory. But once an editor goes beyond such classical texts, he faces a series of choices, some of them very difficult and all revealing his tacit judgments.

The once-dominant Brahmin poets—Longfellow, Holmes, Lowell—still appear, in this anthology, in part because of their historical importance and in part because some of their work remains interesting; but there can be no blinking the fact that during the last few decades a revolution in judgment concerning their work has taken place. They no longer occupy the dominant position they once did, a displacement with which I largely concur. It seems unlikely that they will ever again be seen as central figures in American writing.

Certain other writers, however, are included who rarely, if ever, appear in anthologies of American literature. I have chosen liberally from the poetry of Jones Very and Frederick Tuckerman, two distinguished American poets who have only recently begun to receive their due. I have included selections from such Civil War memoirists as Generals Grant and Sherman, as well as Mrs. Chestnut, each of whom is a master of narrative or social evocation. I have taken pleasure in using some selections from the autobiographies of Frederick Douglass, not merely because I share the opinion that it is time black writers gained recognition but because Douglass seems to me a splendid writer. And I have included an entire section of writings from the great nineteenth-century American historians, on the assumption that their work has distinct literary value. All of these selections add up to a considerable sum by way of innovation; a good many are not to be found in any other anthology of American literature.

The traditional arrangement of American literature anthologies has been to treat the Civil War as a half-way point. But the three-volume anthology of which the present volume is a part has been organized on the contrasting premise that the traditional arrangement no longer works. The achievement of twentieth-century American writing is so considerable that it simply cannot be treated as something to be tacked on to post-Civil-War nineteenth-century American literature.

There remains the problem of how to approach the literature of the past, whether historically or critically, as accumulated evidence of human experience or as works of the imagination that can be read as if contemporaneous. So baldly stated, the choice is unpalatable. Serious teachers and students will want to see the poetry of Whitman as both expression of the nineteenth-century American ethos and autonomous works of literature; they will want to read Twain, Melville, and Thoreau as both ancestors and contemporaries. Still, the study of literature is a historical discipline in at least two senses: a novel or a poem should be related, tactfully and carefully, to the social history of the time in which it was composed, and it should be seen as an event within the evolving history of literature itself. Hence, in my judgment, it is not really possible to grasp the whole of a literature by studying only its major figures; mountains take on their grandeur only by comparison to plateaus and plains and valleys.

Finally, a word to the student: the end of literature is, I believe, pleasure—the pleasure of intellectual and emotional growth, the pleasure of sharing insights with powerful minds, the pleasure of discovering the visions of life that great writers have left us. I would not claim that every piece in this book is likely to yield pleasure: some of them you may not like and some you may find of little more than historical value. But the bulk of this anthology has been designed with the purpose of yielding its readers pleasure. The editor hopes it will.

IRVING HOWE

Contents

37

General Introduction

I

America began as an idea of Europe. Even before Columbus sailed the ocean, and certainly for centuries later, the hope kept surging through European society that a newly discovered land would bring a newly created life, free of ancient hatreds and traditions. "In the beginning all the world was America," wrote the English philosopher John Locke, strikingly expressing the European feeling that America was somehow equivalent to, or a recreation of, a primal state of innocence. Early in the sixteenth century, Thomas More located his *Utopia* in the New World. The early-eighteenth-century poem of Bishop George Berkeley would be repeatedly quoted by later American writers as foretelling the mission of this new civilization:

In happy climes, the seat of innocence,
   Where nature guides and virtue rules;
Where men shall not impose for truth and sense
   The pedantry of courts and schools,

There shall be sung another golden age.
   The rise of empires and of arts,
The good and great, inspiring epic rage,
   The wisest heads and noblest hearts.

*   *   *

Westward the course of empire takes its way;
   The first four acts already past,
A fifth shall close the drama with the day—
   Time's noblest offspring in the last.

Late in the eighteenth century, as a new wave of romantic feeling swept across a Europe grown weary of its own sophistication, America came to be looked upon as the home of the "noble savage." For many cultivated Europeans, especially those of liberal and/or romantic outlook, America became a kind of "anti-Europe," a projection of the deep need to escape from the tyrannies of the past and to gain for mankind that most precious of opportunities: a second chance. In the early nineteenth century, the German philosopher Hegel wrote:

America is the land of the future, where, in the times ahead of us, the burden of the old world's history shall reveal itself. . . . It is the land of desire for all those who are weary of the historical lumber-room of Europe. Napoleon is reported to have said: "Cette vieille Europe m'ennuie." It is for America to abandon the ground on which hitherto the history of the world has unfolded itself.

In one way or another, these high and perhaps impossible expectations were held by many of the Europeans who came here—driven by exalted religious visions, lured by some scheme for new secular freedoms, or merely hungering after quick profits from a buccaneering raid. Once the colonists gained their independence and set themselves up as a sovereign nation led by a remarkably talented group of men, the dream that on these untainted shores would occur humanity's new beginning flared still more brightly.

Yet problems and paradoxes beset the culture of the young nation from the very outset. In the early nineteenth century, the United States contained a striking mixture of old and new cultures, inherited and improvised systems of value. The very people who yearned for a fresh start on North American soil had brought with them the heritage of the past; the very people who hoped to create a new Eden bore the marks and stains of the world they wished to leave behind. The pioneers who kept pushing beyond the edge of civilized settlement might seem almost a new breed of men slipping back into a rough primitivism, but they were also the sons and grandsons of Europe, who spoke her languages, worshiped by her faiths, and lived according to the Old World morality that had developed over the centuries.

Still in its merest infancy, the United States was testing out republican institutions at a time when there were few historical models to go by. Yet in European settlements established in North America for over two and a half centuries, a new culture—or perhaps more accurately, a cluster of loosely connected regional cultures—had gradually developed. This culture depended in part on European sources, but it also bore the imprint of the New World. It drew partly upon the traditions of English Protestantism and European humanism, but it also reflected the fact that this land where settlers had established their colonies had been bereft of a recorded history for all those centuries of Indians, forests, and silence. The settlers had come from a world in which the accumulations of history were thick with accomplishment, blood, shame, and glory; they entered a world where the human imagination found itself alone, uncrowded, and overawed by sheer space.

Europe and America, past and present, tradition and improvisation— this juxtaposition and mingling of cultural elements formed perhaps the central fact in the literary life of the young nation as it entered the nineteenth century. Americans were beginning to create a new idiom out of the shrewd turnings and dry understatements of Yankee speech, the dialect of Negro slaves, the raciness and chest-thumping bravado of Western talk, the jumbled accents and special vocabularies of European immigrants (between fifty and sixty million people would come to the United States in the nineteenth century). Yet most Americans spoke the English of Shakespeare, Milton, and Swift, still a significant index of the depth of their bond to the Old World.

It was with a peculiar kind of self-consciousness that our writers and critics in the early nineteenth century brooded over the possibility of creating a literature that would, in some fundamental revelation of value and tone, be "distinctively American"—a literature that might even justify the extravagant claims that publicists and journalists were already making for it. On the one hand, the essays and lectures of the time struggled earnestly to decree, almost overnight, a democratic culture in the United States that would put to shame all those aristocratic and decadent Europeans. For this was a time of bloated self-congratulation in American letters, a time marked by a cultural chauvinism which sought to glorify the minor provincial scribblers who would be forgotten in a few years. On the other hand, more thoughtful Americans felt an uncertainty, even anxiety, as to whether our writers could possibly escape the overwhelming influence of English literature at a time when many and perhaps most literate persons in Boston, New York, and Philadelphia still looked to the old country for intellectual and cultural sustenance.

In 1818, a British writer expressed the condescension felt by many Englishmen: "Why should Americans write books, when a six weeks' passage brings them, in their own tongue, our sense, science and genius, in bales and hogsheads? Prairies, steam-boats, grist-mills are their natural objects for centuries to come." In 1820, the English wit Sidney Smith asked: "In the four quarters of the globe, who reads an American book? Or goes to an American play? Or looks at an American picture or statue?" And in truth, when they were not smarting over such slights, Americans had to admit to themselves that American literature was still a frail achievement, perhaps interesting to relatives and neighbors but amateurish and trivial when held up against the achievements of Europe. Thus Margaret Fuller, a friend of Emerson's, articulated in the early 1840s a thought that scores of other Americans had either anticipated or would soon repeat:

It does not follow because many books are written by persons born in America that there exists an American literature. Books which imitate or represent the thought and life of Europe do not constitute an American literature. Before such can exist, *an original idea must animate this nation* and fresh currents of life must call into life fresh thoughts along its shores. [Italics added]

II

Here we are, then, suddenly thrust into the United States of 1835, as
observers acutely interested in the growth of a new and "distinctively American" literature. What main forces—both as heritage of
the past and condition of the present—might crucially affect the
work of American novelists and poets? We can at least explore the
main avenue that would lead to a satisfactory answer.

The Memory of the Puritans.   Before the Founding Fathers appeared
to lead the colonists through the Revolution and on to the establishment of the new Republic of the United States, the most serious and
accomplished group of American thinkers flourished among the
Puritan divines of New England. To contemporary Americans the
term *Puritan* has come to suggest repression, prudishness, and
meanness of spirit. Such elements did no doubt play a part in the
thought and feeling of seventeenth- and eighteenth-century New
England, but it would be absurd to suppose that they characterized
the whole region or always went unchallenged. As it arose in England, Puritanism was essentially a theological doctrine strongly
influenced by the ideas of John Calvin; as it developed in New
England, it was not only a theological doctrine but an entire style
of life which enabled the beleaguered settlers to bind together their
communities by ties of common faith.

In its earlier, undiluted versions, New England Puritanism propounded
fierce and rigorous doctrine. The Puritans accepted Calvin's dictum
that some men are chosen or "elected" for heavenly salvation,
others doomed to eternal damnation quite apart from whether or
not they performed good works on this earth. Man, argued Calvin,
is at heart so depraved, so stained with sin, that nothing within his
own powers can possibly earn his salvation—only God's freely offered
grace, a token of infinite love, can secure a place for anyone among
those predestined to be saved. To us in the twentieth century, this
view seems a likely inducement to passivity and despair. Yet history
makes amply clear that the impact of Calvinism upon its followers
was quite the opposite: it encouraged self-assurance, strength of
character, worldly activism; it encouraged them to suppose—no one
could entirely *know*—that they *were* among the elect and to behave
as if God had indeed taken them to His bosom. Such behavior might
lead to the sin of pride, as the Puritans well knew, and it cannot be
said that this was a sin they all managed to avoid. But it could also
lead to an intense moral seriousness, an exalted view of religious
obligation, and a severe, unrelenting self-scrutiny by means of which
both to test one's claim to be among the chosen and to put down
one's pride.

George Santayana, the distinguished philosopher who wrote in the
New England of a later era, has written about doctrinal Calvinism

with a mixture of irony and respect that seems very much to the point. Calvinism asserts

that sin exists, that sin is punished, and that it is beautiful that sin should exist to be punished. The heart of Calvinism is therefore divided between its tragic concern at its own miserable condition, and tragic exultation about the universe at large. . . . Human nature, it feels, is totally depraved; to have the instincts and motives that we necessarily have is a great scandal, and we must suffer for it; but that scandal is requisite, since otherwise the serious importance of being as we ought to be would not have been vindicated.

As it developed in seventeenth- and eighteenth-century New England, Puritanism signified a theological-cultural outlook that encouraged a moral intensity which sometimes soured into fanaticism. A high-minded creed, it taught men to be constantly concerned with the drama of salvation—the whole of human existence came to be seen as a battlefield upon which the forces of good and evil warred eternally. It declared work a virtue, along with thrift. It applauded worldly success, provided that no immoralities were committed along the way. It was, in short, a world view that fused strict religious obedience with bourgeois industriousness. And in New England, away from the fleshpots of the Old World, it hoped to create "a new Heaven and Earth."

By the early nineteenth century, Puritanism had largely exhausted itself, and gradually it gave way to the rationalistic moralism of the prosperous and conservative Unitarian church. The Unitarians retained the strict morality of the Puritan conscience, but the stark sense of sin and the high religious fervor died out. Life had become easier, and prosperity softened the grandsons of the Puritans. As Unitarian leader William Ellery Channing wrote: "In our judgment of professed Christians we are guided more by their temper and lives than by any peculiarities of opinion"—a dismissal which the appalled Puritan divines would have deemed rank heresy. And as Henry Adams wrote in his *History of the United States during the Administrations of Thomas Jefferson and James Madison* (1889–1891):

Under the influence of Channing and his friends, human nature was adorned with virtues hardly suspected before, and with hopes of perfection on earth altogether strange to theology. The Church then charmed. The worth of man became under Channing's teachings a source of pride and joy, with such insistence as to cause his hearers to recall, almost with a sense of relief, that the Saviour himself had been content to regard them only as of more value than many sparrows.

For all its moral earnestness, however, Unitarianism represented a spiritual thinning-out, a loss of religious energy after the rigors and exaltations of Puritanism. But for the writers beginning to work in the 1830s and 1840s, Puritanism, the world view of their grand-fathers—saints and inquisitors, men of will and spirit—still exerted a powerful hold on the imagination. If young writers like Hawthorne and Melville could no longer accept in any literal way the theology of "original sin," they still felt the impressiveness, even the heroism, of the crusty old New Englanders. This was especially true for Hawthorne, the first great American novelist, about whom Austin Warren has aptly remarked: ". . . his deepest mind, the mind out of which he wrote his most characteristic tales and novels, was the ancestral mind, the mind upon which the curse had been laid, the haunted mind; his imaginative world was the world of witches, the Quakers, the Puritans—the seventeenth century New England in which his ancestors had enacted such conspicuous roles." Compar-ing the writings of the Unitarian ministers with the Puritan divines, Hawthorne stressed

the difference between the cold, lifeless, vaguely liberal clergymen of our day, and the narrow but earnest cushion-thumper of puritanical times. On the whole, I prefer the last-mentioned variety of the black-coated tribe.

For a young writer like Hawthorne looking to the American past for usable subjects, Puritanism had the tremendous value of treating human experience as inherently and inescapably dramatic: Puri-tanism, with its horizons of election and damnation, its ceaseless struggles between good and evil, its insistence that nothing, not even the most obscure corner of man's psyche, could be exempt from the blot of sinfulness. In its absolutist moral distinctions, Puritanism reduced human existence to a timeless allegory, thereby contributing obliquely to the taste for symbolism of writers like Hawthorne and Melville. The Puritan outlook also provided a crude but powerful psychology according to which the true believer must always keep inspecting and questioning his inner motives. To the Puritan, man perched forever on the brink of peril; the devil worked forever busily; existence was forever endangered. For writers like Emerson, Hawthorne, and Melville this seemingly sterile view of life provided a powerful force, both historical and intellectual in nature, that they could struggle *against*. These writers were no longer Puritans themselves; indeed, they were reacting against the beliefs of their ancestors; yet precisely insofar as they were both appalled and fascinated by it, Puritanism helped to shape their work. Tradi-tions against which writers—and indeed all men—rebel can be far more influential than the opinions they proclaim. And for a great many poets and novelists of the nineteenth century—not only Hawthorne, Melville, and Twain, but Cooper, Emerson, and Emily Dickinson—the enormous shadow of the Puritan past, at once grand and repellent, embodying the rightness of moral judgment and the brutality of moral righteousness, long held sway over their imaginations.

The Molding of National Consciousness. The early decades of the United States were remarkable for the rapidity and assurance with which the institutions of the country were built up. The Constitution had set general guidelines and limitations, but it could not, of course, provide detailed answers to such problems as how the branches of the government were to function, or how the country should behave in the international arena, or how the relations between federal and state agencies would be regulated.

Yet without too much strain, the basic characteristics of the American system were established within four or five decades. A Bill of Rights—the single greatest political achievement of this country—was attached to the Constitution. The powers of the executive were defined, enlarged, and consolidated. The cabinet system was perfected. The two-party system, though not the parties we know today, came into being. A powerful creed of judicial authority, growing up under the guidance of Chief Justice Marshall, soon gave birth to the practice of judicial review.

The country grew in size and prospered economically. In 1839, a writer for the influential magazine *The Democratic Review* could declare with some justice that in half a century the United States had achieved "a progress in all the substantial elements of national grandeur which is believed to have had scarce a parallel in the annals of mankind." The territory of the Union had increased threefold; the population had quadrupled, from less than four million to about sixteen million. The national debt had been paid off. And the national revenue, boasted *The Democratic Review,* had increased to the point where there was a surplus of "some twenty or thirty millions of dollars yearly, instead of only three or four millions, as at first."

The most spectacular sign of national growth was the steady expansion throughout the nineteenth century of the frontier westward. New states were regularly created. Farmers whose soil had eroded, city artisans who saw no future at home, middle-class Easterners in search of adventure, wealth, freedom—all moved westward, taking advantage of government policies that allotted lands cheaply to those who promised to settle them. A growing world market for grain, a steadily rising rate of immigration from Europe, and the improvement of the federal road system—all enabled the nation to keep expanding westward.

This American consolidation went beyond the mere matters of government institutions and economic prosperity. The symbols which bind a people together in collective life and faith—slogans ("I have not yet begun to fight"), flags (the stars and stripes), animal totems (the eagle)—were quickly improvised. At first the symbolic figure for the United States had been Brother Jonathan, but after the war of 1812 it became Uncle Sam. The Founding Fathers were raised to a quasimythical status, and George Washington was surrounded with a halo of sanctity. Under the guidance of the great dictionary compiler Noah Webster, a feeling sprang up that, while Americans used the same language as the English did, they were slowly transforming it into a new, an American, language: "Great Britain," wrote Webster, "whose children we are, and whose language we speak, should no longer be *our* standard." As he compiled his dictionaries, he deliberately included locutions unique to American experience and declared his pride in these signs that a new experience was creating a new language.

Less tangibly but at least as important, a sentiment of American nationalism also began to grow. At its least attractive, this nationalism manifested itself in narrow chauvinism and provincialism, crude boasting about native achievements, and happy ignorance of the rich European past. Henry Adams, in his previously cited *History*, had some sharp words to say about "the mass of Americans" who "knew little of the difficulties which surrounded a complex society":

The Duc de Liancourt, like many critics, was struck by this ignorance. Among other instances, he met with one in the person of a Pennsylvania miller, Thomas Lea, "a sound American patriot, persuading himself that nothing good is done, and that no one has any brains, except in America; that the wit, the imagination, the genius of Europe are already in decrepitude. . . ." In the year 1796 the House of Representatives debated whether to insert in the Reply to the President's Speech a passing remark that the nation was "the freest and most enlightened in the world"—a nation as yet in swaddling clothes, which had neither literature, arts, sciences, nor history; nor even enough nationality to be sure it was a nation.

At its impressive best, however, American nationalism represented an effort to raise the ideal of democracy to a collective myth, a semireligious faith. America has been ordained to set an example for the rest of the world in tolerance, freedom, and order: she would prove an "asylum for the oppressed"; she would justify through word and deed that optimistic vision of humanity glimpsed by early-nineteenth-century Europe, often as delineated in Romantic poetry and fiction. And much of the most valuable, certainly the most fresh and indigenous, poetry and fiction to be written in the United States—that of Melville, Twain, and Whitman—derives from this reverential feeling for democracy.

Between the vision of democracy and the American penchant for an unqualified individualism, certain tensions, even severe conflicts, were bound to develop. One historian of nineteenth-century America, Henry Bamford Parkes, has cogently remarked on this problem:

> By liberating men from social restraints and encouraging them to seek the fulfillment of their desires and ideals through the conquest of the wilderness, the civilization of America had produced contradictory tendencies. The hope that had gradually taken shape in America was that of a society characterized by a universal freedom and equality in which all men could live without frustration and without fear. But this hope could not be realized unless it permeated men's minds and guided their actions with the compulsive power of a religion. Americans must not only talk democracy; they must feel and act as democrats. But meanwhile individual Americans had acquired an energy and confidence of the will that too often resulted in an unrestrained drive toward domination and exploitation, in spiritual as well as in material things. And in proportion as they acquired power and privilege, they were inclined to repudiate American ideals and to turn back to the European doctrines of order, authority and class hierarchy.

This conflict between the democratic outlook and the impulse to an unrestrained and often predatory individualism would be dramatized as a central theme in Herman Melville's *Moby Dick,* a prose epic that is one of the most distinctively "American" works of fiction in our whole literary history. But in the actual experience of most Americans living in the 1830s and 1840s, it was not yet a conflict they felt very deeply or acutely. A few decades later the growth of the young nation—its increasing urbanization, industrialization, and commercialization—would bring about a sharp collision between its dominant social institutions and the social and moral ideals inherited from the Founding Fathers. But in the early 1800s the United States still largely conformed—with the significant exceptions of a few Northern cities and the Southern plantation system based on slave labor—to the Jeffersonian image of a nation resting on an independent yeomanry and happily free of those large urban concentrations that, in Jefferson's view, could only bring corruption and class conflict. The vision of America that had flourished in the heroic Revolutionary age could still stir the great mass of Americans, the same vision which had been expressed with classical eloquence by Hector St. John de Crèvecoeur, a French immigrant turned American farmer, in his superb letters about life in the New World. America, he said, is not composed, as Europe is, of

> great lords who possess everything, and of a herd of people who have nothing. Here are no aristocratic families, no courts, no kings, no bishops,

no ecclesiastical dominion, no invisible power giving to a few a very visible one; no great manufacturers employing thousands, no great refinement of luxury. . . . We are the most perfect society now existing in the world. Here man is free as he ought to be.

The ideal America so glowingly evoked by Crèvecoeur is essentially a Jeffersonian America, and during the Jacksonian and immediate post-Jacksonian years it had some genuine connection with the realities of American experience. In the 1830s small independent farmers still comprised a large portion of the American population. The economy was still, for the most part, preindustrial. The population was still largely homogeneous in character, and the problems that would later be created by large-scale immigration were not yet in view. The culture was still marked by a dependence on English sources, models, and styles. The example of the Founding Fathers— men revered for their wisdom and nobility—still molded the hopes and expectations of most Americans. It was therefore possible for Henry Adams, writing half a century later, to say that

except for Negro slavery, [early-nineteenth-century America] was sound and healthy in every part. Stripped for the hardest work, every muscle firm and elastic, every ounce of brain ready for use, and not a trace of superfluous flesh on his nervous and supple body, the American stood in the world as a new order. [Italics added]

The tone here is rhapsodic, all the more remarkable in a writer as caustic as Adams usually is; but what today strikes us most violently is the qualifying phrase in italic. For in retrospect it seems clear that, as regards both American history and American literature, the phrase, "except for Negro slavery," must loom far larger than Adams supposed.

The issue of slavery had troubled some Americans from their colonial beginnings. Back in the mid-seventeenth century the Quakers had repudiated slavery and freed their slaves. Other Christian sects had done the same. With the founding of the United States, the fundamental ambivalence—or let us rather say, the deep national shame—regarding slavery was codified in the Constitution. The Constitution does not even mention slavery, using instead the genteel euphemism "persons held in service or labor." But despite this evasion and the distaste some of the Founding Fathers sincerely felt toward slavery, the Constitution also allowed the states to add three-fifths of the slaves to the whole number of free persons in apportioning Congressional representation, thereby laying the basis for the political strength of the slaveowning states. No wonder the Abolitionist leader Wendell Phillips would say about the Founding Fathers: " I love these men; I hate their work. I respect their memory; I reject their deeds."

The three-fifths rule was followed by Eli Whitney's invention of the cotton gin in 1793, which made both possible and profitable the large-scale manufacture of cotton through the use of Negro slave labor and thereby gave the plantation owners a new stake in the "peculiar institution." What followed in American life during the first half of the nineteenth century has been vividly described by the historian Dwight Dumond:

It was now possible to make enormous profits by growing cotton with slave labor in the vast interior region of the Southern states. Within a decade after the Constitution, the development of the Black Belt and Cotton Kingdom had begun. Profits from slave breeding ended the flutter of doubts in Virginia and Maryland. The plantation owners did not emancipate their slaves. Instead, their plantations grounds took the place of Africa as the breeding ground for labor, and the interstate slave trade carried their produce to market as the African slave trade had done. All the original slave states of the South could not supply the swelling demand for slaves in the Black Belt. Slavery, in all parts of the South, was developing from a labor device into a system—an economic system, a social system, a system of racial adjustment, the basis of extraordinary political power, and the source of an increasingly comprehensive social philosophy. In this system, slaves (3,500,000 by 1860) were denied opportunity to cultivate intellectual and moral progress; denied incentive to develop creative talents; robbed of dignity and self-esteem. Society deprived the slave, so far as possible, of all human attributes, then argued a natural inferiority from the artificial inferiority it had created. Slaveholding thus confirmed the notion of Negro inferiority, as well as the practice of exploitation, and projected both into an interminable future. No admission of the evil was now made, no anticipation of its extinction was countenanced.

From the vantage point of our own time we can see that slavery was not merely an inhumane institution, both as it allowed the master to be all-powerful and as it reduced the slaves to utter powerlessness; it was also profoundly corrupting in its effects on American culture and character, especially insofar as it led to convictions of racial supremacy, ranging from the brute hatred of the redneck, to the casuistry of theologians justifying bondage through Biblical quotations, and on to the pseudoscholarship of intellectuals defending the "peculiar institution." Long after slavery was abolished, its ghastly heritage of racism survived.

For several decades before the Civil War it was extremely dangerous for anyone to speak in the South against slavery, and even in the North the antislavery movement, known as Abolitionism, suffered frequent physical attack and personal slander, both from mobs and public officials. A debate—passionate, unyielding, beyond compromise—raged through the country over the social and moral permissibility of slavery. In the West there were frequent conflicts, sometimes erupting into open violence, between those who wanted the new states to be free and those who wanted to import slaves. Southern apologists broadened their claims for slavery, declaring that the ownership of men was not only right for their region but good for the entire country; one influential extremist, George Fitzhugh, went so far as to say in 1854 that slavery was "a form, and the very best form, of socialism." In the North almost all the leading American writers saw the antislavery issue as a moral crusade involving the fate of the nation. Walt Whitman wrote in 1856, "You young men! American mechanics, farmers, boatmen, manufacturers, and all work-people of South, the same as North! You are either to abolish slavery, or it will abolish you!"

Here is the most terrible paradox of American experience. Everything in the foreground of American life during the 1830s and 1840s might seem cheerful and sunny, but behind the scenes was the moral poison of chattel slavery. The very land that had been celebrated as the new paradise for all mankind, the second garden of Eden, was the embittered captive of an ancient sin. The period in our history that seems in retrospect the most attractive and egalitarian was also the one during which the stain of slavery spread across the nation.

A *Culture of Regions.*   National consolidation may have been the dominant political trend in nineteenth-century America, but culturally, nationalism was still more a program than a reality, more a hope than an achievement. The cultural life of most Americans in the 1830s and 1840s for example, was still shaped at least as much by region—especially if it were New England or the South— as by national citizenship. Between the residents of Massachusetts and those of Georgia little community of literary tastes or intellectual assumption was perceptible. Each region had slowly developed a cultural style distinctively its own, and out of these styles had grown up, or soon would grow up, folk and popular expressions, ranging from oral story telling to humble dramatics, and schools of regional writing, sometimes limited to "local color" but often presenting shrewd and realistic genre pictures of local experience.

Some of the great American writers who began to publish at this time can usefully be regarded as having begun their careers, in some sense, as regional writers. They began by writing about ways of life peculiar to demarcated geographical areas: Hawthorne, in his early sketches of New England manners, and Twain, in his early tales and anecdotes about the "old Southwest." At first heavily stressing traits of conduct and speech that seemed unique to their regions, they went beyond local notation to create fiction that could seem significant to people of any place or country.

In the 1830s and 1840s, however, regionalism was still the dominant fact about American culture. Indeed, the very frequency and shrillness of the calls issued for the creation of a national—an American—culture gave ample proof of the persistence of regionalism. Few Americans were strongly aware of participating in a new and integrated national culture. To be sure, national magazines had appeared by this time; books circulated throughout the country; the work of a very few writers was recognized, here and abroad, as American. But these were signs of striving, not of realization. Nor did the regionalism of American writing result primarily from difficulties of communicating between one section of the country and another. For the most part, the regional or provincial stamp of our cultural life was the product of inexperience, the hesitations of writers who found it easier to annotate charmingly or shrewdly local ways of life than to capture imaginatively whatever made both Americans and Europeans regard the United States as a new experience in the life of Western man.

During the second half of the nineteenth century, regionalism underwent a change. It settled into a natural outlet for writers with modest talents or for writers who satisfied a popular nostalgia for local styles of life that were beginning to disappear. Some of the functions that regional writing assumed in the nineteenth century were of a kind that journalism performs for us now: sketches of local events, descriptions of character types who flourish in this place or that occupation, a kind of impressionistic rendering as "news" of the way some Americans lived in their neck of the woods and others cavorted down the road.

For the sake of convenience, the growth of regional cultures can be divided into three periods or phases:

1 *Folk* material: legends, stories, caricatures, jokes, aphorisms, turns of phrase.
2 Popular *semiliterary* writings in magazines, newspaper sketches, and also various kinds of semiprofessional entertainments. These may be written by individuals for publication or worked up by local groups for presentation, but they do not display much cultural ambition or pretension.
3 *Literary* works composed by professional writers but limited, either by choice or lack of talent, to the life and manners of a particular region.

Thus, in New England there had grown up the popular image of the Yankee, shrewd, taciturn, an "aboriginal character," as Constance

Rourke puts it in her fine book *American Humour*, "sprung suddenly, long-sided and nimble, from the gray rocks of his native soil." In 1830, for example, a minor writer named Seba Smith began writing brief sketches about a character named Jack Downing, who both displayed predictable Yankee traits and sometimes indulged in barbed social criticism. From 1847 to 1848 James Russell Lowell, a more serious writer, published the *Biglow Papers*, a long series of poems in which he used some of the same kinds of material—local dialect, shrewd country speech, idiosyncratic traits of New England character—in a more sophisticated way.

Development from the first of these categories of regional culture to the last was by no means straight and unwavering; neither history in general nor literary history in particular moves in so simple a way. The actuality was probably closer to a simultaneous jumble of all three. But slowly, and after a good many false starts, an authentic literary use of American experience and American speech came into being here. "The first real postulate of an original literature," James Russell Lowell shrewdly remarked, "is that a people should use their language instinctively and unconsciously, as if it were a lively part of their growth and personality, not as the mere torpid boon of education. . . ." And once this did begin to happen, it became possible for the major American writers, especially Mark Twain, to transform regional language into the medium, and regional custom into the matter, of great literature.

One of the richest of these regional cultures was that of the "old Southwest,"—Tennessee, Georgia, Alabama, Louisiana, Mississippi, Arkansas, and Missouri. The very designation underscores the fact that its dominant cultural materials drew not upon plantation life but upon the experience of the frontier. The main achievement of the old Southwest was its humor—free-ranging, lusty, anecdotal— and behind that humor hovered the legends of the backwoodsmen: Mike Fink, the river man, and Davy Crockett, the hunter and backwoods oracle, whom Constance Rourke has called the "minor deities whom men create in their own image and magnify to magnify themselves."

Most of the writers who composed humorous stories in the old Southwest were not really professional writers, but lawyers, editors, journalists, and riverboat captains who put down in simple but often pungent language stories they had heard or had heard and then elaborated. Like Mark Twain later on, they wrote with one eye cocked toward the East, and many of their sketches appeared in *The Spirit of the Times*, a lively and popular sports weekly published in New York between 1831 and 1861. They wished to interpret their region for the cultured folk in Boston and New York, while at the same time employing rough dialect that might repel those same cultured Easterners. Their writing generally took two styles: a stiff, lifeless, eighteenth-century English that they had been taught to regard as "fine prose," and a tangy local dialect, sometimes recorded so faithfully (as in George Harris's stories about the rascal Sut Lovingood) that we now find it hard to read. Just as the imitation of the balanced periods and elaborate rhythms of neoclassical prose made a good deal of early-nineteenth-century American writing seem insipid, so the effort to capture every twist and turn of regional dialect made the work of the humorists seem idiosyncratic. The humorists of the old Southwest approached but did not reach that easy yet stylized, colloquial yet eloquent, prose which Mark Twain would perfect and many later writers and critics would come to regard as the distinctive American style.

Often the writers of the old Southwest wrote about rogue heroes and tricksters, rough-and-tumble frontier figures like Simon Suggs, whose most memorable remark sums up a whole side of American experience: "It is good to be shifty in a new country." Their language was, at its best, racy and alive: "The feller looked as slunk in the face as a baked apple." They were keen at observing rednecks, horse traders, braggarts, heroes of zest, energy, and shrewdness—as in what is perhaps the best book of old Southwest humor, Augustus Longstreet's *Georgia Scenes*. As one American critic, George Woodberry, has neatly summed up their work: "It was as if all the world had gone on a picaresque journey . . . and at the chance roundup for nightly rest and refreshment fell to telling what, and especially whom, they had met with."

In the end, however, these writers matter for still another reason: they prepared the way for Mark Twain.

An American Literature? Through most of the nineteenth century, cultivated Americans continued to discuss not only whether there could or should be a distinctively national literature, but more important, such related questions as what materials of native experience could this literature be drawn from and which forms and styles could it employ or improvise in order to realize its distinctiveness?

At least until the Civil War, and probably for some time afterward, Boston was looked upon as the cultural capital of the country. Here were the centers of publishing, the theorists of religion, the greatest American university, and those amiable and dignified figures who have since been described, perhaps a bit unfairly, as the poets and essayists of the "Genteel Tradition." The kind of writing favored in Boston—the work of men like Henry Wadsworth Longfellow, James Russell Lowell, and Oliver Wendell Holmes—set a tone of earnest provincialism, conventional decorum, and polite and sometimes clever observation. True, each of these writers did try to capture something of the American experience: Longfellow, in his narrative poems about Hiawatha and Evangeline; Lowell, in his satiric dialect poem, *Biglow Papers;* Holmes, in his light verse and fiction. But they could discover neither a vocabulary nor a set of literary conventions nor a group of imagined characters through which to dramatize what was new, unruly, and vivid in American life. For all its modest charms and cultivation, the work of these writers now seems pale, bookish, innocuous; it neither engages the mind nor stirs the emotions. In their own day they were greatly admired, perhaps because a provincial culture, in its wish to emulate European models, tends to overemphasize refinement and to become what T. S. Eliot later described as "overcivilized." Certainly they were esteemed far higher than writers such as Whitman and Melville whom we now think of as among our nineteenth-century masters, and for a good many decades later their poems and essays formed standard fare in high-school literature courses. But despite some recent critical efforts to patch up their reputations, it seems unlikely they will ever again be read with any deep or spontaneous interest. Minor writers of a particular historical moment, big frogs in what Edgar Allan Poe, sneering at Boston, called "Frogpondium," Longfellow, Holmes, and Lowell failed to engage fully—to say nothing of lustily or angrily or dangerously— with the American experience. Or as Barrett Wendell, a critic writing at about the turn of the century, put it: their writing is "a record of the national inexperience," displaying "its refinement of temper, conscientious sense of form, and instinctive disregard for actual fact."

A "record of the national inexperience"—the phrase may indeed signify the failure they shared with many nineteenth-century American writers trying to discover how they could, or if they could, relate themselves to the life of their country. The complaint that for the novelist or poet American experience is too thin, too lacking in historical depth and social richness, sounds repeatedly throughout the century.

James Fenimore Cooper wrote:

The . . . obstacle against which American literature has to contend is in the poverty of materials. There is scarcely an ore which contributes to the wealth of the author that is found here in veins as rich as in Europe. There are no annals for the historian; no follies (beyond the most vulgar and commonplace) for the dramatist; no obscure fictions for the writer of romance; no gross and hardy offenses against decorum for the moralist; nor any of the rich artificial auxiliaries of poetry. . . . There is no

costume for the peasant (there is scarcely a peasant at all), no wig for
the judge, no baton for the general, no diadem for the chief magistrate.
The darkest ages of their history are illuminated by the light of truth;
the utmost efforts of their chivalry are limited by the laws of God; and
even the deeds of their sages and heroes are to be sung in a language
that would differ but little from a version of the ten commandments.

And Nathaniel Hawthorne:

No author, without a trial, can conceive of the difficulty of writing a
romance about a country where there is no shadow, no antiquity, no
mystery, no picturesque and gloomy wrong, nor anything but a commonplace prosperity, in broad and simple daylight, as is happily the case
with my dear native land . . . Romance and poetry, ivy, lichens, and wall-
flowers, need ruin to make them grow.

And later Henry James, in his biography of Hawthorne:

One might enumerate the items of high civilization, as it exists in other
countries, which are absent from the texture of American life, until it
should be a wonder to know what was left. No State, in the European
sense of the word, and indeed barely a specific national name. No sovereign, no court, no personal loyalty, no aristocracy, no church, no clergy,
no army, no diplomatic service, no country gentlemen, no palaces, no
castles, nor manors, nor old country houses, nor parsonages, nor thatched
cottages, nor ivied ruins; no cathedrals, nor abbeys, nor little Norman
churches . . . no literature, no novels, no museums, no pictures, no political society, no sporting class. . . .

Why did these matter? Because, James goes on to say, it takes
"an accumulation of history and custom . . . to form a suggestion
for the novelist."

These remarks all add up to an explanation of the difficulty of writing
the kind of social novel that flourished in nineteenth-century
Europe, the novel resting upon detailed contrasts of manners among
sharply defined and contending classes, upon elaborations of intrigue in settled and complex societies, and upon the relationship
between a lower-class or disadvantaged outsider and the hostile or
decadent culture of a sophisticated European city. Yet, as Philip
Rahv has shrewdly noticed, a central weakness inheres in all these
arguments:

What is wrong is the tacit assumption that the ingredients [of literature]
are of a fixed kind, given once and for all. . . . Is it not more to the point
to acknowledge that the genuinely new and venturesome in literary art
emerges from a fresh selection of the materials at hand, from an assimila-
tion, that is, to imaginative forms of that which life newly offers but
which the conventions of past literature are too rigid to let through?

That there were indeed new deposits of material to be mined in American life was recognized by such early-nineteenth-century American writers as Washington Irving, James Fenimore Cooper, and Nathaniel Hawthorne. In a few charming stories, Irving drew upon the legendary material of Dutch New York. Cooper, on a much larger scale, created in his Leatherstocking Tales a legendary narrative embodying the sense of America as virgin land and the West as the locale of an unspoiled Eden. Both these writers failed, Irving in his mild and minor way and Cooper in his stiff and major way, through an inability to develop a style that would break away from the heavy conventions of eighteenth-century English prose and thereby achieve an "organic" relation to the new material. Hawthorne, the first major American novelist, did his best work in recreating Puritan New England as a setting for his allegories and dramas of troubled conscience. He drew a great deal upon local historical accounts and regional memories, but even he had often to employ a formalistic and sluggish Augustan prose, a style borrowed from the eighteenth-century English prose masters and, as it may now seem to us, not sufficiently integrated with his matter.

To cite these instances is to begin indicating the ways in which nineteenth-century American literature did find its own voice. In fiction, as Hawthorne remarked in the preface to *The House of the Seven Gables,* American writers turned instinctively toward the romance rather than the novel. What is the difference? The novel, wrote Hawthorne, "is presumed to aim at a very minute fidelity, not merely to the possible, but to the probable and ordinary course of man's experience." Consider how rarely in nineteenth-century American fiction we find the standard subjects, themes, and settings of the European novel: emotional conflicts and moral problems in the relationships between the sexes (*Anna Karenina, Madame Bovary*); a young man from the provinces trapped between social idealism and worldly ambition in a corrupt city (*The Red and the Black, Great Expectations*); the horror of industrial and urban society as it destroys human beings (*Hard Times, Germinal*). By comparison to the European, American fiction tends to be symbolic, metaphysical, set in imaginative realms of possibility rather than recognizable social locales. A whaling ship in pursuit of a white whale; an old trapper alone on the prairie; a boy and a Negro slave adrift on a raft—these are not the customary settings or subjects of the English or Continental novel. As Richard Chase remarks, American fiction in the nineteenth century is less concerned with familiar social reality and less caught up with the conventions of realism:

The romance, following distantly the medieval example, feels free to render reality in less volume and detail. It tends to prefer action to character, and action will be freer in a romance than in a novel, encountering, as it were, less resistance from reality. . . . The characters, probably two-dimensional types, will not be completely related to each other or to society or to the past. Human beings will on the whole be shown in ideal relation—that is, they will share emotions only after these have become abstract or symbolic. . . .

In American romances it will not matter much what class people come from, and where the novelist would arouse our interest in a character by exploring his origin, the romancer will probably do so by enveloping it in mystery . . . The plot we may expect to be highly colored. Astonishing events may occur, and these are likely to have a symbolic or ideological, rather than a realistic, plausibility. Being less committed to the immediate rendition of reality than the novel, the romance will more freely veer toward mythic, allegorical and symbolistic forms.

Of course, none of this suggests that simply because American experience contained large elements of historical novelty, American literature had therefore to abandon all traditional forms and pretend that nothing significant or worth imitating had ever been written. Such notions have indeed recurred throughout our literary history, but that does not make them any the less nonsensical. Of innovation, experiment, adaptation to new circumstances and subjects there has been no end in our prose and poetry; yet by its very nature, literature must always draw upon its past, and whether American writers have known or acknowledged it, they have drawn upon and formed a line of continuity with European literature. Both the fundamentals of Christian belief which shaped American culture and the romantic revolt against Christian orthodoxy which is so striking a feature in the work of our major nineteenth-century writers, have innumerable ties with European experience, European thinkers, European books. Hawthorne would be impossible without Spenser and Bunyan; Melville without Shakespeare and Milton; even so distinctively American a poet as Emily Dickinson without Donne.

Between Mark Twain and Herman Melville, the two great innovators in mid-nineteenth-century American fiction, the tone and limits of American prose style in the coming century were largely set. Twain worked with the spoken language as he remembered it from childhood, sometimes rendering the vernacular with absolute fidelity and more often raising it to pungent heights of stylization. The line of stylistic innovation that runs through Sherwood Anderson, Gertrude Stein, and Ernest Hemingway in twentieth-century American fiction has its origins in Twain's best work. His language is at once colloquial and pure, gritty and poetic, drawn from the humorists of the old Southwest and the great tradition of English prose. Melville, in *Moby Dick,* helped to create another tradition of American prose style which in our time has been most brilliantly developed by William Faulkner. At its best, Melville's prose ranged from an affectionate and humorous rendering of plebeian speech, the democratic poetry in the dialog of Ishmael and Queequeg, to a highly elaborate and philosophical rhetoric, as if tragic oratory were mixed with religious meditation and raised to a pitch of virtuosity. Melville also owed a good deal to English models, especially Shakespeare and Milton, but finally, the style he worked out was quite his own, fitted both to a New England whaling boat with a conglomerate crew and to a symbolic journey undertaken by Americans obsessed with reaching beyond mere physical appearances.

If we glance but for a moment at nineteenth-century American poetry, we see that the two major figures, Walt Whitman and Emily Dickinson, also diverged from the traditional lines of English poetry, both from eighteenth-century neoclassicism and from nineteenth-century romanticism. Whitman broke away almost entirely from traditional metrics, basing his lines not on a fixed number of beats or syllables but on the principle of cadence, a rolling phrase or clause forming both a rhythmic unit and a unit of speech or declamation:

> *Smile, O voluptuous cool-breathed earth!*
> *Earth of the slumbering and liquid trees!*
> *Earth of departed sunset—earth of the mountains misty-topt!*
> *Earth of the vitreous pour of the full moon just tinged with blue!*
> *Earth of shine and dark mottling the tide of the river!*
> *Earth of the limpid grey of clouds brighter and clearer for my sake!*
> *Far-swooping elbowed earth—rich apple-blossomed earth!*
> *Smile, for your lover comes.*

Whitman introduced into his poetry catalogs of American objects and places, lists of affection and desire; he democratized poetry and roughed it up, tearing it away from the forms and formalism of traditional English verse and pushing it well on the way toward what we have since come to call free verse.

Emily Dickinson, by contrast, wrote cryptic and crabbed, oracular and telegraphic little poems, with something of the tart understatement and sly perception of New England within or behind them:

> *My life closed twice before its close;*
> *It yet remains to see*
> *If Immortality unveil*
> *A third event to me,*

So huge, so hopeless to conceive,
As these that twice befell.
Parting is all we know of heaven,
And all we need of hell.

Where Whitman was expansive and enclosing, Emily Dickinson was fanatically compressive. Both, as the English critic A. C. Ward has remarked with but a slight amount of exaggeration, wrote "as though no one had written poetry before." The remark is both praise and criticism, a tribute to freshness and an attack upon eccentricity.

In the discussions of American literature as a unique expression which went on throughout the nineteenth century—and indeed go on to this very day—more than innovations of form and technique were at stake.

What fascinated literary observers most deeply was the presumed spiritual distinctiveness of American writing, those qualities of mind and feeling that would set off our literature from all others. We shall say more about this in a little while, but here it would be useful to quote from the shrewdest of all commentators on this subject, Alexis de Tocqueville, who in 1835 published *Democracy in America,* the greatest of all social studies of the new land. In a democracy, wrote de Tocqueville, there would be "a motley multitude whose intellectual wants" are endlessly varied. "These new votaries of the pleasures of mind have not all received the same education; they do not resemble their fathers; nay, they perpetually differ from themselves, for they live in a state of incessant change of place, feelings and fortunes. The mind of each is therefore unattached to that of his fellows by tradition or common habits. . . ."

What kind of literature can then arise in such a loose and fluid society?

Literature in democratic ages can never present, as it does in the periods of aristocracy, an aspect of order, regularity, science, and art; its form, on the contrary, will ordinarily be slighted, sometimes despised. Style will frequently be fantastic, incorrect, overburdened and loose, almost always vehement and bold. Authors will aim at rapidity of execution more than at perfection of detail . . . there will be more wit than erudition, more imagination than profundity; and literary performances will bear marks of an untutored and rude vigor of thought. . . . The object of authors . . . will be to stir the passions more than to charm the taste.

To speak of American literature as if it were all of a piece, as if it were without internal variety, conflict, and change, would be foolish. But insofar as we can isolate the major characteristics of our literature, it seems clear that its two greatest periods—that of mid-nineteenth-century Romanticism, the "American Renaissance," ex-

emplified in the work of Emerson, Whitman, and Melville, and that
of twentieth-century "modernism," exemplified in the work of Hart
Crane, Ernest Hemingway, William Carlos Williams, and William
Faulkner—do conform astonishingly to de Tocqueville's analysis.

American literature establishes its own tradition of rebelliousness: it
is steadily concerned with testing the farthest reaches to which
individualism—an individualism assertive, willed, and often self-
destructive—can be driven. It sees man not so much as a member
of society, either conforming to or revolting against its norms, but
as a solitary figure, seeking to discover his essential being in the
spaces of a new world, often overcome with a terrible loneliness
and giving way to a profound despair. In the work of Twain, Melville, Whitman, and even, a bit later, Henry James, the self is pitted
against society; unadjusted man against a recalcitrant social order;
a pure vision of human possibility against the discovery that even
in this new world many of the sins and crimes of the old one are
being reenacted. At least until the last two decades of the nineteenth century, the typical hero of American fiction is a loner who
embodies natural virtues, and his test is usually the difficulty,
perhaps impossibility, of maintaining these virtues in the social
world.

In American literature the authority of the great classical figures of
European poetry and fiction tends to break down, sometimes to be
violently denied. Our major figures forever engage in both thematic
and formal experimentation: Whitman turns away from traditional
metrics and improvises a cadenced "free" verse, Melville abandons
the limits of the traditional social novel and improvises in *Moby
Dick* a prose epic that must be read, at least in part, as a work of
symbolism, and almost all the major mid-nineteenth-century American writers—especially Melville, Whitman, and Twain—shake off
the regularities and proprieties of English prose style to experiment
with risky juxtapositions and bold mixtures of "low" colloquialism
and "high" oratorical eloquence. Sometimes these experiments degenerate into mere provincial crankiness and eccentricity: hardly
an American writer of the time escapes occasional drops into incoherence and obscurity. But at best it leads to brilliant innovations
in both prose and poetry, works of literature which strike directly
to the essence of human suffering and ecstacy.

Little concerned with models of formal decorum, seeking restlessly for
new subjects and structures by means of which to capture the
"new-ness" of American experience, our nineteenth-century masters
seem always to be starting out afresh, imaginative journeyers into
the freedom and terror of a new world. The social "thickness" embodied in the novels of George Eliot, the Parisian sophistication

reflected in the novels of Stendhal and Balzac, the richness of human community to be found in the fiction of Tolstoy—all this barely appears in American literature, especially that composed before Henry James. The high polish, richness of mythic allusion, brilliant craftsmanship in technique, and moral traditionalism to be found in the poetry of, say, seventeenth-century England—all this barely appears in American literature, especially that composed before the twentieth century. But in the work of our great nineteenth-century figures there is something else: a direct symbolic or philosophical penetration to man's condition as he stands in the New World, relatively unencumbered by social relationships, historical memories, and conventional decorums.

This thumbnail description of American writing will obviously not apply to some periods in our literature or to many individual novelists and poets; it is of almost no use, for example, in trying to understand the realistic novelists who make their appearance toward the end of the nineteenth and the beginning of the twentieth centuries. Perhaps the reason we tend to think along the lines just sketched is that the great figures of American romanticism—Emerson, Thoreau, Melville, and Whitman—loom so large in our literature. There has also been a strong inclination during the years since the Second World War to seek out whatever is "unique" in American literature, perhaps because we have become very self-conscious about America as a historical power. It might therefore be useful to remember that in literary history, innovation is possible only against a background of tradition and that what we regard as special to American writing must finally be placed within the continuity of Western culture.

III

All through the 1840s and 1850s there had been gathering in American society a series of social and political tensions which, in their sum, made the Civil War (1861 to 1865) seem all but unavoidable. North and South represented two cultures, two ways of life and standards of value: if not, as fanatics might say, a conflict between absolute good and absolute evil, then a conflict in which most of our major writers, despising the very idea of slavery, aligned themselves with the North. The Civil War also represented a clash between two modes of economy, an expanding and increasingly urban industrialism which rested on free labor as against a plantation agrarianism resting on black slavery. During the two or three decades before the war broke out, the conflict between regions took several forms: economically, Northern industrialists pressed for tariffs to be placed on the manufactures which the South imported cheaply from England; politically, decisions had to be made in Congress about whether the new Western states would be free or slave (a string of compromises, rapidly improvised, as rapidly collapsed); and legally, the South, through its major spokesman John C. Calhoun, proclaimed the doctrine of states rights according to which any state could veto federal legislation, while the North insisted on the supremacy of the federal government.

The Civil War was the first modern war in the history of Western mankind. It was the first to be fought mainly by civilians rather than professional soldiers; the first to be fought by massive armies and in which large-scale massacre proved a path to victory; the first in which victory would finally depend on a supremacy of industrial resources. Through the minds of many Americans—one can see this in the novels and poems of the next several decades—the war sent a chill of horror. For it destroyed, perhaps forever, the dream of a peaceful and pastoral America that would somehow be exempt from the bloodletting of European history. If this country could be torn apart by fratricide, then there was no reason to suppose that any of the other historical sins and crimes of Europe would necessarily be avoided here. And yet—such is the terrible irony of history—the Civil War did bring to an end the abominable institution of slavery, even if complete equality and freedom would remain a distant prospect for American Negroes.

A turning point had been reached: every thoughtful American knew this. In *The Gilded Age* (1873) Mark Twain and Charles Dudley Warner wrote: ". . . the eight years in America from 1860 to 1868 uprooted institutions that were centuries old, changed the politics of a people, transformed the social life of half the century, and wrought so profoundly upon the entire national character that the influence cannot be measured short of two or three generations." A few years later Henry James, in his study of Hawthorne, wrote that the war had persuaded Americans that ". . . the world is a more complicated place than it had hitherto seemed, the future more treacherous, success more difficult." James was right: a greyness of spirit, a profound sense of weariness, comes over American culture in the years after the war. Lewis Mumford, a cultural historian writing in our own time, has summarized this sense of change and dismay:

On one side the Golden Day, the period of an Elizabethan daring on the sea, of a well-balanced adjustment of farm and factory in the East, of a thriving regional culture operating through the lecture-lyceum and the provincial college. . . . When the curtain rose on the post-bellum scene, this old America was for all practical purposes abolished.

Now such statements exaggerate some, if only because violence had already left its mark on America before the Civil War and urban industrialism had made its appearance too. But it cannot be disputed that among cultivated Americans the feeling was strong that, unavoidable as the Civil War may have been and desirable as some of its results surely were, American society had now turned in an unfamiliar and puzzling direction.

The literary effects were slow in coming, and in any case, the ten or fifteen years after the Civil War were not—in terms of published writing—exactly brilliant. Melville wrote his angular and anguished war poems during the years of the fighting, though by now he had scarcely an audience left. Whitman wrote his tender poems of wartime suffering and then subsided into relatively minor work. And in the next several decades some of the leading generals, like Grant and Sherman, published memoirs of the war that were remarkably vivid and well written. The first major novel about the war, however, did not appear until 1895, when a brilliant young writer named Stephen Crane published *The Red Badge of Courage*.

Though barren for literature, the years immediately following the Northern victory were marked by a tremendous economic expansion. "The Gilded Age," "the Age of the Robber Barons," "the Age of the Great Barbecue"—these are some of the unflattering designations that cultural historians have given to the 1870s and 1880s. During these years American society took on the major characteristics of industrial capitalism: a large-scale concentration of wealth and power in a few hands, the growth of enormous personal fortunes, the use of technology and science for industrial development, bitter clashes between corporations and newly organized workers.

Abraham Lincoln himself had foreseen these developments and the problems they would bring:

I see in the near future a crisis arising that unnerves me and causes me to tremble for the safety of my country. By a result of the war, corporations have been enthroned, and an era of corruption in high places will follow, and the money power of the country will endeavor to prolong its reign by working upon the prejudices of the people, until all wealth is aggregated in a few hands and the Republic is destroyed.

Economic and technological changes were amazingly rapid. Between 1865 and 1900 railroad mileage in the United States increased from thirty-five thousand to two hundred thousand. Built with the sweat of underpaid immigrant labor, and made possible by generous federal subsidies in the form of land grants, the railroads helped create a unified national economy. Between 1865 and 1878 United

States internal investment in manufactures increased from 1½ billion dollars to 3 billion dollars. In 1864 the Bessemer process for the making of steel was introduced, and by 1879 the production of steel in the United States had reached 925,000 tons. Similar developments took place in the meat-packing industry—the spread of railroads, the invention of refrigeration—and in the production of oil. Clothes began to be mass- and machine-manufactured, cheaply and in bright colors. Within the major industries, the factory system—involving careful division of labor, the breakdown of work into relatively simple tasks, strict supervision of employees by foremen, and the rationalization of production in accordance with "scientific" precepts—became more and more prevalent. Together with these developments went the growth of a modern communications industry, first through the telegraph (1844) and then the telephone (1876). And even the countryside experienced a trend toward mechanization and concentration, with the family farm slowly being replaced by commercial agriculture requiring investments in mechanical equipment beyond the capacity of many small farmers.

A new class of millionaires arose—the Carnegies in steel, the Rockefellers in oil, the Fricks in coal. Some, later to be called the "Robber Barons," were unscrupulous speculators in stock manipulations. The number of millionaires increased from a mere handful in the early 1860s to more than 4,000 by the early 1890s. A sense of the business methods and morals of the period is suggested by the historian Allan Nevins in *The Emergence of Modern America:*

The most lurid light upon the rudimentary commercial morals of the period and the legal defenselessness of the public was that thrown by the great railway freebooters, whose operations were well launched before Grant took office. Daniel Drew, Jay Gould and Cornelius Vanderbilt, three New Yorkers, battled with an unscrupulousness previously unknown in American finance. All three men had risen from the humblest estate to positions of financial might. . . . Drew was born on a small farm in Putnam County, where he began life as a cattle drover; Gould, the son of a farmer in Delaware County, was successively a clerk in a country store, a surveyor and a tanner; while Vanderbilt, a native of Staten Island, had gained his first capital by running a ferry to Manhattan. Drew, now a very old man but as energetic and unscrupulous as ever, was no better than a sharper though he maintained a snuffling piety. Whenever he had been unusually fortunate in plucking trustful men, he salved his conscience by a grant to some philanthropic object; it was he who founded the Drew Theological Seminary in New Jersey with promised gifts totaling a million, most of which was never delivered. Gould was a coldhearted corruptionist who never hesitated to debauch a newspaper, prostitute a legislature or make city officials his pawns. As for Vanderbilt (called "the

Commodore" from his success in building boats), he maintained an air of high respectability and public spirit, but he never forgot his pocket interests.

Vanderbilt's effort in the late sixties to wrest control of the Erie from Drew and Drew's associate, Gould, brought on a veritable battle of the giants in which all thought of public rights and all considerations of decency were lost. The "Commodore" played a lone hand. Drew not only relied heavily upon the cunning Gould, but enlisted also the extraordinary figure known as "Jim" Fisk. Fisk had begun his career as a peddler in Vermont, had been the manager of an itinerant circus and had finally made a profitable place for himself among the New York stock gamblers. He became distinguished as a fat, flashy, boastful voluptuary who kept a harem of mistresses, maintained a costly opera house, and lived a life of gilded luxury. This triumvirate not only outplayed Vanderbilt, but employed methods that shocked the whole nation as a revelation of business corruption run wild.

From Europe, especially the Slavic and east European countries, there came vast numbers of immigrants. They poured into the new industrial cities in the East and Midwest, ready to work hard for low wages in order to get a start in the New World. Inevitably, bitter and violent strikes broke out, such as the country had never seen before, and large-scale trade-union organization began, first in the craft-oriented Knights of Labor and then in the more inclusive American Federation of Labor.

Great cities, bursting with slums and corruption, sprang up. In 1860 only one-sixth of the American population lived in cities, but by 1900 the percentage had dramatically increased to one-third. In twenty years, between 1880 and 1900, the population of Chicago tripled, from half a million to a million and a half. All the blights of urban life with which Americans of our own time are only too familiar, began to make their appearance in these years: crime, juvenile delinquency, prostitution, oppression of the poor.

American society, even in the 1870s and 1880s, was not without its social critics, men who kept pointing, often vainly, to the growth of economic injustice and the lowered tone of public life. In addition to social reformers, the more aristocratic intellectuals, of whom Henry Adams was the most distinguished example, felt a growing despair over the quality of American society: its corruption, its vulgarity, its crass materialism, its indulgence in a fatuous and superficial "optimism," and its turn toward the pernicious doctrines of Social Darwinism, according to which human life is organized on an analogy to that of the jungle, and men inevitably find themselves caught up in a cutthroat struggle in which only the "fittest" (often the richest) survive.

In the far West, as the Indians were steadily beaten back and deprived of their rights, the land was being finally settled—the last stage of a great sweep of social migration. By 1890 the frontier was gone. The country had been completely, if sparsely, settled, and the hope for a new start in the West, by now a deeply ingrained part of American mythology, could no longer prompt thousands of Easterners to uproot themselves each year. Yet the frontier has remained a powerful force in our cultural life, growing all the stronger in our shared nostalgic fantasies (the Western movie, the cowboy hero) as it has ceased to be a practical solution to our problems in reality.

Meanwhile, after the brief period of Reconstruction, during which federal authority was directly exerted in the Southern states and the former slaves enjoyed a measure of political freedom, the South gradually reestablished a more subtle, though by no means benevolent, version of its old racial hierarchy. Terror was frequently used against the Negroes; relations were improved with the federal government (which by the late 1870s had abandoned whatever slight intention it had of helping the former slaves gain economic independence); and as a result, the remnants of the old plantation class, together with a new class of commercial parasites and predators, reconsolidated political power in the South. Between the end of the war and 1900, the Southern states enacted a series of Jim Crow laws enforcing segregation quite as rigidly as—and sometimes with greater brutality than—it had enforced slavery itself.

For American writers and intellectuals, indeed for all thoughtful Americans, this was a depressing time. They felt the values of the older Jeffersonian America slipping away and the values of the new industrial America proving brutish and corrupt. "Wherever men of cultivation looked," writes the historian Richard Hofstadter, "they found themselves facing hostile forces and an alien mentality." There emerged a "peculiarly American underground of frustrated aristocrats, a type of genteel reformer whose very existence dramatized the alienation of education and intellect from significant political and economic power." Somewhat later, after the turn of the century, this revulsion from the grossness of the new American ruling classes would be expressed with a witty fastidiousness in *The Education of Henry Adams*. More immediately, during the 1870s and 1880s, other writers responded with open disgust and silent dismay. Mark Twain publicly lashed out against the vulgarities of commercialism, frequently succumbed to them himself, and then ricocheted to a misanthropic pessimism. Melville shrank into virtual anonymity, quite forgotten by American readers and clearly not at ease in a world he had so uncannily anticipated in his book *The Confidence-Man*. Among our major writers only Walt Whitman, aging into the serenity of a native saint, tried directly to cope with the problem of American society. In his lengthy essay *Democratic Vistas* he remained stubbornly, even heroically, faithful to the democratic and egalitarian ideal.

Whitman lashed out in two directions, first against those intellectuals who had withdrawn into aristocratic notions of culture and looked down their noses at "the mob," and then against those who had succumbed to the corruptions of the marketplace. It was the latter who drew his main attention, for it was they who now seemed the more immediate and larger threat. "Everywhere in shop, street, church, theatre, barroom, official chair are pervading flippancy and vulgarity, low cunning, infidelity;" everywhere "the depraving influences of riches just as much as poverty, the absence of all high ideals of character." As against the sterile gentility of the Brahmins and the "optimistic" mindlessness of those who aligned themselves with the new industrial society, Whitman advanced a vision of "the People" as a source of strength and value, "the People" from whom there might yet come "a sublime and serious Religious Democracy." As against the cult of "individualism, which isolated" men from other men, he spoke for "adhesiveness or love, that fuses, ties and aggregates." As against the paleface writings of Boston and "the mean flat average" of the popular writers of the moment, he proposed a vigorous democratic culture in which men would cultivate independent tastes, reading would be "not a half-sleep but ... a gymnast's struggle," and the United States yet become "a nation of supple and athletic minds."

Moving these words still are; but the truth is that Whitman failed to answer the question of how and whether this vision could be realized—perhaps because no answer existed. A democratic culture in which men would be both equal and independent, fraternal and strong-minded—yes. But how could that culture flourish, how could it so much as survive, in a world ruled by money and brute force? The estrangement of the artist from commercial society which has become a commonplace of twentieth-century life, Whitman foresaw and disliked; but he had no solution for the problems that gave rise to this estrangement. His noble voice would echo through the following decades and inspire other critics of our culture, but the perplexities with which he grappled in *Democratic Vistas* he could not finally cope with. Nor, for that matter, has anyone else.

In the two decades that followed the Civil War, the major American writers went their own and often lonely ways. Emily Dickinson, living in Amherst and all but deaf to mundane American society, wrote her poems and kept the bulk of them in manuscript; Mark Twain wrote his novels and stories; Herman Melville, the works of his old age, mostly short fiction; and Whitman, the occasional

minor poems of his declining years. What was popular, and to some
extent new, during these years was the work of several groups of
regional writers who have since been lumped under the heading of
"local color." In the South, the West, and New England the local-
color writers sought to depict—sometimes to exploit for purposes
of romantic sentimentalism—the distinctive traits of regional society and culture. (For further comments on local-color writers, see
page 806.) The best of these writers, like Sarah Orne Jewett in
New England, made their local observation into a foundation for
a strong realism dealing with the life of common people. In the
Midwest there arose a number of writers, limited in talent but serious and honest in intent, who wrote about farm and small-town
life with an unprecedented astringency: Ed Howe in *The Story of
a Country Town,* Joseph Kirkland in *Zury: The Meanest Man in
Spring County,* Hamlin Garland in *Main Traveled Roads.* Grim and
often depressing reports of disillusionment with farm and small-
town life in the Midwest, such books tried primarily to dispel the
genteel deceits of popular writing and the ingrained self-deceptions
of popular mythology in late-nineteenth-century America. They
focused on the moral parochialism, the psychic repressiveness, and
the social injustices of agrarian America; they were concerned,
above all, to tell a bitter truth about the meanness and deprivation
of that part of American life which was most often romanticized;
they expressed the desire of sensitive young men to break loose
from their provincial origins and find some principle of humaneness with which to look back upon their younger years. Some of
these books now seem more interesting as social reportage than as
imaginative literature; but they had a distinct importance as pioneer
efforts in the turn to realism which became the central fact about
American writing during the 1880s and 1890s.

One literary historian, Bernard Bowron, has keenly described some of
the forces in American culture which led serious writers to turn
toward a socially critical and harshly worded realism:

Disenchantment is a great power for realism; and, as a somewhat younger
generation of writers took the measure of rural America, they found less
and less reason to idealize it. It had been all very well for Jefferson, in
his remote world, to declare that "those who work in the earth are the
chosen people of God . . . whose breasts He has made His peculiar deposit
for substantial and genuine virtues." But Jefferson . . . had not lived to
see the countryside put under bondage to the cities. In post Civil-War
America . . . technology had shifted the political and cultural axis of our
civilization. As the "Lord of the Soil" lost his potency as folk hero, the
urban tycoon stepped in to take his place. The farmer was now only a
hick, a hayseed; even his sons deserted him for the richer possibilities

of city life. The westward movement was reversing itself. One response to this tremendous social fact was the nostalgia of the local color regionalists. A more significant one was the regionalism of disillusion. Men like Ed Howe, Hamlin Garland, Harold Frederic—thoroughly ambivalent about their own rural origins—tried to examine their regions in the light of the altered social perspective. . . .

Clearly, their disillusion with the agrarian myth struck very deep. It was not just a question of whether the American farmer was more or less prosperous and content than he was supposed to be. What was at issue, rather, was an entire way of life, now losing its power over the mind as the world of cities superseded it. . . .

It was the particular importance of the novelist William Dean Howells that he served as a cultural link between the older and the newer America. He was the friend of Mark Twain, the prose elegist of pastoral America, and the friend of Henry James, the novelist who would bridge the gap between New England innocence and European sophistication. Howells had grown up in agrarian Ohio and later remembered his youth with a fond nostalgia, but he wrote most of his realistic novels about the life of Americans in the cities. He depicted the gradual decline of old-fashioned, individualist businessmen when assaulted by unscrupulous operators, the violence of conflict between worker and employer, the ways in which life in the city came increasingly to resemble a jungle where ". . . the fierce struggle for survival, with the stronger life persisting . . . seemed . . . lawless, goodless." A benign and mild figure himself, closer in temperament to the simplicities he had left behind than to the bewildering problems he now felt obliged to confront, Howells embodied in his own career the transition of American literature from a realism of agrarian disillusion to a realism of urban dismay. (Further discussion of realism in American writing and the idea of literary realism itself can be found on pages 808–810.)

The century ends with Stephen Crane's harshly realistic *Maggie,* a novel about a tenement girl's fall into prostitution and suicide, intended, as Crane wrote, "to show that environment is a tremendous thing in the world and frequently shapes lives regardless. . . ." After *Maggie,* Crane went ahead to write *The Red Badge of Courage,* a great novel about men in the Civil War, which is realistic in temper but more artful in method than those techniques we usually associate with the term "realism."

Howells and Crane had made their contribution; Henry James would continue writing until the First World War; Theodore Dreiser would soon appear on the literary scene. The way lay clear for the beginning of twentieth-century American writing.

IV

Any literature as far-ranging as that of nineteenth-century America must clearly have a wide diversity of themes, preoccupations, techniques, and forms. Suppose, however, we ask ourselves by way of conclusion: Can we discover, at whatever risk of simplification, a major unifying theme or preoccupation in nineteenth-century American literature? Even to attempt this, we must put aside the new realistic writings of the 1880s and 1890s and concentrate instead on the work of those who wrote before the Civil War or whose careers span both the pre- and post-Civil War periods.

For many of our writers in the first half of the nineteenth century, and for some, like Mark Twain, in the second half, America as a collective experience signified the possibility of a new start for humanity, paradise regained. The wilderness and sometimes the frontier appeared to writers like Cooper and Twain (and in our own century, to a writer like Faulkner) as source and scene of mobility, freedom, innocence. Once society developed, it tended to hollow out these values. And not one or another form of society, not a better or worse society, but the very idea of society itself was regarded with skepticism and distaste.

This myth—it lies deeply imbedded in our fictions and legends—borrows credence from the hold of the frontier on our national life. A myth of space, it recalls a time when men could measure their independence by their physical distance from one another. It is a myth that records the secret voice of a society regretting its own existence.

Inescapably the settling of the wilderness was a violation. For a short time afterward a precarious balance could still be established between the natural and the social—a balance which might preserve a margin of paradise. But the pioneer equilibrium could not last for long, and soon the wilderness was gone. So, too, was the possibility of an independent and self-sustained life: paradise had been lost, again.

This on the level of myth—that is, those deepest attitudes, stories, and legends which, in their sum, animate a culture. But on the level of history, things are very different. The Founding Fathers of the United States were hard-headed and realistic men who set about creating a state that would protect their social interests while at the same time avoiding tyranny, both aristocratic and popular. As they went at the task of state-making, they grasped the need to reconcile a wide range of conflicting interests in a society which, precisely because it was a society, could yield only limited satisfactions.

They worked into the Constitution a series of balances, which to this very day inhibit both the direct expression of the popular will and the tendencies toward autocratic usurpation. It is a system which rests on the premise that the best way to ensure stable social conditions and provide adequate protection of human rights is through a politics of countervailing coalitions. In the *Federalist* papers James Madison stated the philosophical premise behind this system of government with classical precision:

Ambition must be made to counteract ambition. . . . It may be a reflection on human nature that such devices should be necessary to control the abuses of government. But what is government itself but the greatest of all reflections on human nature? If men were angels, no government would be necessary. . . . In framing a government which is to be administered by men over men, the great difficulty lies in this: you must first enable the government to control the governed; and in the next place oblige it to control itself.

Now the question we encounter is this: Could the principles upon which the American government was founded and the expectations that had arisen with the beginning of American settlement be at all reconciled? Can one bring together the worldly realism of the *Federalist* papers with the edenic nostalgia expressed by so many nineteenth-century writers? That this conflict was a real one, and so regarded by the principle actors, may be seen in a caustic passage Hamilton wrote for the *Federalist* papers:

Reflections of this kind [in behalf of a balance of power] may have trifling weight with men who hope to see realized in America the halcyon scenes of the poetic or fabulous age; but to those who believe we are likely to experience a common portion of the vicissitudes and calamities which have fallen to the lot of other nations . . . etc., etc.

During the 1820s and 1830s, many Americans must have felt that a harmonious relation between institutions and desires was indeed possible. Soon enough, everything changed. With time, it became clear that America was trapped in a conflict between its guiding institutions (better though these might seem than any other within sight or memory) and its guiding myth (poignant as this would seem in its absolute unrealizability). And from this conflict there have followed enormous consequences.

Classical European literature often displays an extratemporal dimension—its urge to transcendence breaks past the cramped social horizons and crowded spaces of an old world, to create itself anew in the guise of an ideal future, a heavenly prospect sanctioned by Christianity and thereby removed from the paltriness of time. But at least until the idea of America takes hold of the European

imagination there is, for Europeans, no place else to go. Locked
into space, they can only transfer their hopes to a time beyond time.
Their escape is vertical.

In nineteenth-century American literature the wish to break past the
limits of the human condition manifests itself through images of
space. Our characteristic fictions chart journeys not so much in
order to get their heroes out of America but to transport the idea
of America into a new and undefiled space. The urge to transcendence appears in our fictions as accounts of men who move away,
past frontiers and borders, into the "territory" or out to sea, in
order to preserve their images of possibility. For the enticements of
space offer the hope—perhaps only a delusion—of a new beginning: so that, for a time, an individual hero can be seen as reenact-
ing, within or beyond the society, the myth upon which the society
rests but which it has not been able to fulfill. In America this new
start is seen not so much in terms of an improvement or a reorder-
ing of the social structure, but as a leap wholly beyond the edge of
society—a wistful ballet of transcendence.

Now many critics have noticed these elements in our literature, and
have usefully discussed them in terms of an Adamic myth, a wish
to return to innocence, a nostalgia for the purity we never had. Or
they have seen in our writing a wish to escape the guilt brought
on by the defilement of the countryside; to put down the burdens
of success, family, and women; and to be done with the whole idea
of society and sink back into a state of primal fraternity: blood
brothers on the raft, the hunting ground, the lonely river—everyone
(black, red, and white) in common friendliness.

Let us see what happens, however, if we accept this approach to nineteenth-century American literature and then somewhat shift its
terms. Let us see what happens if we acknowledge the cogency of
interpreting many of our major poems and fictions as releasing
a hunger for a state of nature not yet soiled by history and commerce; if we further agree that troubled responses to sexuality and
perhaps a wish to discard the threat of mature sexual life in behalf
of a fellowship of innocents are involved in these poems and fictions; and if we then look at them in political terms.

It is a special kind of politics that is here at stake: not primarily the
usual struggles for power among contending classes within a fixed
society; nor the study of the mechanics of power as employed by a
stable ruling class; nor even the dynamics of party maneuvering;
but rather a politics concerned with the *idea* of society itself, a
politics that dares consider—wonderful question—whether society
is good and—still more wonderful—whether society is necessary.
The paradox of it all is that a literature which on any manifest
level is not really political at all, a literature which has little to tell

us about the social surface and instead reaches for the psychic and metaphysical depths of man, should nevertheless be precisely the literature to raise the most fundamental problems in political theory: what is the rationale for society, the justification for the state?

And if we agree for a moment—as a limited perspective—so to regard nineteenth-century American literature, we discover running through it a strong if subterranean current of anarchism.

Not anarchism as the political movement known to nineteenth-century Europe: a movement with an established ideology and a spectrum of emphases ranging from populism to terrorism. That kind of thing has meant very little in the United States. We have in mind something else: anarchism as a social vision arising spontaneously and with the greatest urgency from the conditions of preindustrial American culture: anarchism as a bias of the American imagination in terms of its deepest, which is perhaps to say, its most frustrated yearnings.

Anarchism here signifies a vision of a human community beyond the calculation of good and evil; beyond the need for the state as an apparatus of law and suppression; beyond the yardsticks of moral measurement; beyond the need, in fact, for the constraints of authority. It envisages a community of autonomous persons, each secure in his own being and aware of his own mind. Anarchism here signifies a collective wish to refuse the contaminations of history, precisely at the point where the nation's history begins to seem oppressive and irreversible. The anarchist vision coursing through nineteenth-century American literature speaks for a wish to undo or unravel restrictions which violate the deepest myth of the very society which has felt the necessity of establishing these restrictions. What is novel here is the assumption that because of our blessed locale we could find space—a little beyond the border, further past the shore—in which to return, backward and free, to a stateless fraternity, so that the very culture created on the premise of mankind's second chance would, in failing that chance, yet allow its people a series of miniature recurrences.

The oppressive system of laws, what Melville would later call the "forms" in *Billy Budd,* gives way to the self-ordering discipline of persons in a fraternal relationship. While this relationship is seen as enabled by, and perhaps only possible within, the arena of an unsullied nature, it is not so much the thought of pastorale which excites our major nineteenth-century writers as it is a vision of human ease, brotherhood, and comradeship being fulfilled within the pastoral setting. And thereby the problem of authority, perhaps the most difficult that can be faced in political thought, is—at least on the imaginative plane—simply dissolved: which to some of us may seem a solution as inadequate as it is entrancing.

The dream of paradise is lodged deep in the imaginations of our nineteenth-century American writers, as in those of almost all sensitive
Americans of the time. Yet they live in a society Madison helped to
form, Jackson to reform, and the expansion of American business
to transform. The conviction that injustice and vulgarity grow
stronger during the nineteenth century is shared by many of our
writers—a conviction, finally, that an America is being created
which frustrates both the dream of a new Eden and the political
idea of a democracy resting upon sturdy, independent citizens.
Neither in practice nor thought can our writers find a way of dealing with this sense of disenchantment, if only because the country
with which they become disenchanted has itself been the object of
enormous expectations. In their bitterness with the social reality
and their tacit recognition that they cannot really affect its course,
American writers seek to get around or to "transcend" the intracta-
bility of what they encounter. Whatever they cannot change
head-on, they will now turn away from, clinging meanwhile to that
anarchic vision which seems all the more beautiful as it reaches
into the distance of lost possibilities. And thereby they create an
ideal place of the imagination—precarious, transient, unstained—
which speaks far more eloquently to the inner desires of our collective life than it can represent or cope with its coarse actualities.

Is this not a paradigm of *Huckleberry Finn*, as Mark Twain turned
from the torments of slavery and all it represents to the idyll of
Nigger Jim and Huck on the raft? If American literature in the
nineteenth century seldom succeeds in depicting with any complexity or directness the rough textures of social life, it nevertheless
has an enormous relevance to our moral life.

This vision first appears with imaginative strength in James Fenimore
Cooper's fiction. Like Hawthorne after him, Cooper was deeply
conservative in his thought, and some of his novels are meant to
defend privileges of the Upstate New York landowners. But together with this conscious bias there can be detected in Cooper's
fiction a yearning for a state of social comeliness which he saw
embodied in the life of the Indians and, more persuasively, in the
habits of his culture hero, Natty Bumppo.

Cooper's anarchist vision appears as a substratum of feeling, a cluster
of wistful images, picturesque set-pieces and mythic figures. It is a
vision that breaks past his pompous style, as if meant to shatter
his conservative opinions. In Cooper's fiction the Indian tribes are
never burdened with government, in the sense of a centralized
authority commanding force against its own citizens. Within the
tribe, the essential unit of social life is the family, in many respects
a more powerful unit than the tribe itself. Military service is voluntary, and when the braves go on the warpath, they act out of their

own free will. As Cooper portrays it—and historical accuracy need not concern us for a moment—the life of the Indians can be severely bound by tradition, rites, concepts of honor, and limitations of mind, but it is not subject to the institutional authority and the social regulations we associate with the state. With Natty Bumppo, the Deerslayer and Pathfinder, Cooper identifies more openly, for in Natty his conservative and anarchist impulses find a genuine harmony. Natty brings together a refined version of civilized decorum and the purity of natural man—indeed, it is precisely the unlikelihood of this mixture which makes him so poignant a figure. Propertyless as a matter of principle and self-governing through ascetic training, Natty is a monk of the woods living in a fraternal closeness with Chingachgook, his Indian companion, at ease with the natural world and apart from social crowding and hypocrisy. Natty is the American at once free from historical sophistication and primitivist degradation; he bears out D. H. Lawrence's remark that the Leatherstocking Tales are "a wish-fulfillment, a kind of yearning myth." In Natty self and society are at peace; or better yet, society becomes absorbed into self, in a truce of composure. Natty lives out the anarchist idyll of a life so beautifully attuned to its own inner needs and thereby so lucidly harmonious with the external world that there is need for neither rules nor restraints.

In *Huckleberry Finn* the anarchist motif reaches its greatest if least explicit embodiment. When Huck and Nigger Jim are alone on that indispensable raft (itself so wonderful a symbol of the isolation, purity, and helplessness upon which the anarchist vision rests), they set up a communal order transcending in value the charms of their personal friendliness. They create a community of equals, because a community goes beyond the mere *idea* of equality. The idea of equality is enforced by a state and requires that, unavoidable violations apart, fixed norms and regulations be imposed on persons of varying needs and powers. The community of equals is established by persons and involves a delicate adjustment, moment by moment, to the desires each perceives in the other.

The community of the raft is a community of friends, quietly competent at the tasks facing them: tasks of self-preservation and self-ordering. The impulse to freedom embodied in the escape of Huck and Nigger Jim is a freedom that cannot be confined to, or even adequately described in, social terms. It comes into spontaneous existence, and not as a matter of status obligation, or legal right. It exists as an active relationship, a shared capacity for sympathetic identification with the natural world, which is seen neither as inherently good nor inherently bad but as a resource which those with the proper sense of reverence can tap. Or it can be a sympathetic identification with other men, which is seen in the novel as something to be learned, so that the learning becomes a way of moving past mere learning and received morality. Huck's education is a kind of education, perhaps the only kind, that matters: an education of the emotions. And on the raft his emotions are freed because he knows that *they*—the people of the town, the figures of judgment, the men of authority, the agents of the state—are away. As every reader notices, Huck Finn does not reach a conceptual grasp of the problem of slavery: what, come to think of it, would be so remarkable in his decision to help Nigger Jim gain freedom if he, Huck, concluded that it was the right thing to do? As a decent American boy, he would then be under moral obligation to offer his help. What is remarkable about Huck's decision is that he makes it in violation of norms he accepts, so that it becomes a triumph of nature over culture, impulse over convention, anarchic fraternity over registered authority. It is, for Huck, a matter of *friendliness*. And in a state of friendliness, men—at least in nineteenth-century American fiction—do not need society. Yet, precisely because he does not understand practically the problem he has surmounted spiritually, Huck is also helpless before it: he may not need society, but society wants him.

As long as Huck and Nigger Jim can float upon that blessed raft there is no need for fixed measurements of right and wrong, good and evil. When Huck and Nigger Jim achieve their moments of fraternal union, we are transported to a kind of ecstasy, a muted rapture enabling them to rise beyond the calculations of morality. One is reminded of the Hasidic legend which has it that if you move upward step by step on the ladder of morality you will in the end break loose and float away into a buoying space.

Yet Twain was too shrewd a writer and too troubled a man to compose a mere idyll. The precarious community of friends established on the raft is threatened at almost every moment. It is invaded by alien figures, the Duke and the Dauphin, who are presented in terms of comedy but whose significance is steadily felt to be ominous. To the extent that Huck and Nigger Jim overcome them, and also fend off assaults from enemies both on the river and from the shore, it is partly as a triumph of their innocence, the innocence of friends, and partly as a triumph of shrewdness, Huck's shrewd social personality which upon need he quickly reestablishes.

Huck is a figure at once fixed and amorphous, recognizable and anonymous. On the raft he sheds his mask—perhaps one might even say, his skin—of personality; everything which a human being absorbs or introjects from his society. The more comfortable he feels, the less individual he seems; for he blends into a state of passive receptivity; he is no longer a demarcated character but a

current of experience. The self grows harmonious with its surroundings; it exists as awareness and caress rather than wariness and
will. Between Huck and Jim there develops an I-Thou relationship,
a sentience so keen that for a few moments the whole American
self-violation seems blotted out and we live in the rapture of idyll,
the America that might have been, the paradise of anarchy. On the
river Huck's personality is always in process of dissolution, for
there he can leave behind both anxiety and shrewdness and ease
himself into repose and contemplation. On the land Huck chooses
the masquerades of personality, or more accurately, he knows that
he must choose them. He adopts a variety of names, sometimes
passing himself off as Tom Sawyer, the commonplace American
boy, and sometimes as the less-than-beatific, riverside Huck Finn.
Even on land he is very fine, an admirable moral figure. But on the
raft he has no need for disguise, no burden of personality, no
strategy of shrewdness. In the community of friends, lawless and
stateless, there are story telling, amiable philosophizing about Sol-
lermun the King, eating, sleeping, and keeping loose.

It cannot last. For all the while Twain is making certain that we remember paradise consists of a few rickety boards nailed together;
that the raft contains a run-away slave worth a sizable number of
dollars; that violence and corruption threaten at every bend of the
shore; and that the paradisial journey is a drift southward, deeper
and deeper into the darkness of slavery. The anarchic enclave must
disintegrate under the pressure of the world, and perhaps, in the
end, contribute to conservative resignation. Before the world itself,
Huck and Nigger Jim are helpless. At one and the same time they
represent the power of transcendence, of rising above the crippling
grasp of society, and the pitiable vulnerability of a boy and a slave
who try to evade the authority of that society. Between these two
extremes is there not a causal relationship, one in which our most
splendid yearnings come out of our most utter impotence?

The clash between anarchic yearning and fixed authority leads both
to the marvellously open and spacious quality of nineteenth-century
American writing and to the choked misanthropy that so often
follows. For writers caught up with the utopian vision it is particularly hard, as they grow older, to find those modulated resolutions
that characterize the classical European writers. Our literature is
schizoid, flaring to ecstasy and falling into misanthropy, but rarely
passing at the middle level of social engagement and realism. The
American myth, of which the anarchic vision is one mode, exerts
too great a hold upon our nineteenth-century masters; and then,
as it shatters itself upon the shores of reality, there follows a disenchantment beyond bearing. Where the traditional treatment of
society in the English novel occurs in terms of class adjustments,

contained conflicts, even class revolutions—all within the shared assumption of the inescapability of social authority and visible power—the American imagination, at its deepest level, keeps calling into question the idea of society itself. And as the nation moves irrevocably into the modern world, what can that come to but absolute despair?

In no other Western culture of the past two centuries, to my knowledge, has so much attention been paid to and so many demands expressed for the "creation of values." When one comes to think of it, that is really extraordinary. The literatures of Europe either sustain traditional values or enlarge upon revolutionary values; but both are seen as inseparable from the social order in which the writer writes and the reader reads. In our culture we have made the unprecedented demand upon writers that they create values quite apart from either tradition or insurgency. What we have often meant by this is that they establish a realm of values apart from the setting of actual life, that they become priests of the possible in a world of shrinking possibilities. We ask them to discover, out of their desperate clarity, a vision which we can cherish and cherish perhaps in direct proportion to our knowledge that we will not—or cannot—live by it. The result is that every now and again we strike off a fiction of such transparent powers it sends the world into enchantment but also that we deny ourselves the possibilities of a hard realism in both our literature and our politics. Yet, within our literature, the anarchic impulse—together with the accompanying moral ultimatism and apolitical politics—remains enormously powerful, and even those who grow skeptical about its value must grant that it still has a notable imaginative thrust.

In our world, the vision of a society of true friends living in composed affability and fraternity is one that must bring the writer to a ferocious impasse. For when that always entrancing voice calls once more, "Come back to the raft ag'in, Huck honey," the reply of the age is, "You can't go home again."

An endless dialectic in our life and our literature, this clash between anarchy and authority. It courses through the work of many of our major nineteenth-century American writers—Cooper, Twain, Melville most of all—and its influence can be felt in many of our twentieth-century writers as well. Abstractly considered, this clash between the dream of anarchic bliss and the need commonly felt for social authority may be beyond resolution. But in the greatest of our writers it is embodied, dramatized, celebrated, and mourned with an urgency of desire which marks the distinctiveness of our culture and our literature.

New York Writers: Romantics and Literati

Introduction

In the first several decades of the nineteenth century there began to appear an indigenous American literature, or at least an American literature striving to be indigenous. During the years between, say, 1800 and 1840 there took place a large-scale expansion of magazine publishing, an increase in the number of books imported from Europe, the rise of publishing firms specializing in handsome sets of native authors, and the creation of copyright arrangements which gave American writers a certain amount of financial protection.

New England remained the center of serious and traditional literary culture, first in the genteel conservatism and moral earnestness of the Unitarian church and Harvard scholarship during the opening two decades of the century and then in the cultural-philosophical revolt led by Ralph Waldo Emerson (both discussed in later section introductions). Meanwhile, in the 1820s and 1830s, New York City, already the mercantile capital of the country and a town embodying the rough practical vitality of the new nation, began to play an increasingly important cultural role. Here was the beginning of a new urbanism, not the gentle and genteel life of Boston, but a commercial center full of noise, bustle, and energy. Here were published magazines, and here gathered little groups of writers, most of them important only for the moment, that satisfied tastes less earnest and somewhat more worldly than those to which the New Englanders appealed.

The three literary men most respected at the time—Washington Irving, William Cullen Bryant, James Fenimore Cooper—were all, to one or another extent, associated with New York. In 1833 an influential magazine called *The Knickerbocker* was started in New York; it published Irving, Cooper, Bryant, Longfellow, Hawthorne—almost a roll-call of the talent then available. Four years later an even more influential journal began, *The Democratic Review*, in which the prominent writers of the day could find a hearing. American writers, it is true, were still paid rather meagerly; their reputations at home still depended too much on what their compatriots heard about their reception by English critics; but at least they were now published in journals of fair to large circulation, and at least discussion was under way on the nature and merits of this new writing.

Seen in retrospect, much of this writing was wildly overestimated. It had to be. Americans wanted to step into the glories of culture as quickly and easily as they had already plunged into the turbulence of history. Like over-anxious mothers touting child prodigies, they huffed and they puffed over delicate lady poets, genteel provincial essayists, derivative minor story tellers. There was not yet present in this country a serious literary public which could make critical discriminations or judge the work of local figures by the exacting standards of world literature. There was not yet present—at least until the appearance of Edgar Allan Poe—a skilled professional critic who went beyond the comfortable provincialism of Atlantic seaboard culture. The atmosphere in the country was benign, amiable, and self-approving: it felt good in 1820 or 1830 to be an American (at least if your skin was white), and for a while American literary people were not inclined to be strict with one another.

Soon enough, all this began to change. In 1845 a young New England writer named James Russell Lowell, then still in his twenties, wrote a shrewd appreciation of another American writer, Edgar Allan Poe, then in his thirties. Though a bit fussy in style, the opening paragraph of Lowell's essay shows that the more serious writers of these years were beginning to make the critical discounts that would later become standard:

The situation of American literature is anomalous. It has no center, or, if it have, it is like that of the sphere of Hermes. It is divided into many systems, each revolving round its several suns, and often presenting to the rest only the faint glimmer of a milk-and-watery way. Our capital city, unlike London or Paris, is not a great central heart, from which life and vigor radiate to the extremeties, but resembles more an isolated umbilicus, stuck down as near as may be to the center of the land, and seeming rather to tell a legend of former usefulness than to serve any present need. Boston, New York, Philadelphia, each has it literature almost more distinct than those of the different dialects of Germany; and the Young Queen of the West has also one of her own, of which some articulate rumor barely has reached us dwellers by the Atlantic. Meanwhile, a great babble is kept up concerning a national literature, and the country, having delivered itself of the ugly likeness of a paint-bedaubed, filthy savage, smilingly dandles the rag baby upon her maternal knee, as if it were veritable flesh and blood, and would grow timely to bone and sinew.

Three years later Lowell published his long verse commentary on American writing, *A Fable for Critics*, which contained numerous shrewd estimates—some of them direct hits—of his contemporaries. It also contained a passage full of good sense about the problem that kept forever agitating American writers at this time, the relation of the fledgling native literature to that of England:

There are truths you Americans need to be told,
And it never'll refute them to swagger and scold;
John Bull, looking o'er the Atlantic, in choler
At your aptness for trade, says you worship the dollar,
But to scorn such eye-dollar-try's what very few do,

And John goes to that church as often as you do.
No matter what John says, don't try to outcrow him,
'Tis enough to go quietly on and outgrow him;
Like most fathers, Bull hates to see Number One
Displacing himself in the mind of his son,
And detests the same faults in himself he'd neglected
When he sees them again in his child's glass reflected;
To love one another you're too like by half;
If he is a bull, you're a pretty stout calf,
And tear your own pasture for naught but to show
What a nice pair of horns you're beginning to grow.

The sharpest, if also most eccentric and bilious, critical intelligence of the time was that of Edgar Allan Poe. The first American critic to apply to our local writers standards developed through a reading of the major European poets, he was also the first to study the work of our writers in close textual detail, foregoing vague grandiosities and examining instead particular stanzas and passages; the first to shrug off the slack amiability of the dominant culture and to write as if literary judgments were matters of utmost importance; and the first to argue against the "didactic heresy" in literature (the notion that poems and fictions are written in order to bring about moral improvement) and to insist that literature was its own justification for being. In notable essays on Longfellow and Hawthorne he attacked New England culture: he was respectful toward both writers, acknowledging their talents, but charged Longfellow with subordinating his poetic powers to a sluggish moralism and Hawthorne with weakening his great imaginative gift by succumbing to the moral rigidities of allegory. A fierce polemicist, often rude, indifferent to both personal feelings and clique allegiances, Poe raced in to do battle against what he regarded as vanity, back scratching, ignorance, and provincial self-satisfaction. Often he was wrong, and his general principles of criticism do not stand up as well as many of his particular judgments; but a new professionalism, a new standard of seriousness, was introduced into American life when he spoke out:

Among all the *pioneers* of American literature, whether prose or poetical, there is *not one* whose productions have not been much overrated by his countrymen. But this fact is more especially obvious in respect to such of these pioneers as are no longer living; nor is it a fact of so deeply transcendental a nature as only to be accounted for by the Emersons and Alcotts. In the first place, we have but to consider that gratitude, surprise, and a species of hyper-patriotic triumph have been blended, and finally confounded with mere admiration, or appreciation, in respect to the labors of our earlier writers; and, in the second place, that Death has thrown his customary veil of the sacred over these commingled feelings, forbidding them, in a measure, to be *now* separated or subjected to analysis.

What Poe raged against, finally, was the cozy provincialism of American literary culture during the 1830s and 1840s: the provincialism of a culture that made things too comfortable for itself, that found it agreeable to snuggle into the role of junior cousin to the British. Even the three American writers most honored in the 1820s and 1830s—Irving, Bryant, and Cooper—were in important ways provincial figures, though one of them, Cooper, had an original and perhaps major talent. It was the strength of all three, but again especially Cooper, that they saw the need for turning to native materials, native scenes, native experiences: what sense would it make to have writers participating in a promising new historical experience who did little more than imitate the giants of English literature? Yet all of them betray the constricting influences of a provincial New York, or Atlantic, culture, which in turn must to a considerable extent be defined by its dependence on English models. All of them, though Cooper least, tended to regard the American setting as merely "picturesque," that is, a charming or vivid background for minor literary effects; they had not yet worked out an indigenous style or a fully absorbed involvement with their native land. Irving borrowed heavily, and obviously, from the essayistic style of such eighteenth-century English writers as Goldsmith and Addison; Bryant leaned heavily on the romantic nature poems of Wordsworth; and Cooper showed strong traces of Sir Walter Scott's historical romances.

One test of the future of American literature lay in the discussion of what might constitute an appropriate American style—or (since it really makes little sense to speak of an American style as if it were a collective obligation binding on all writers) what might constitute an appropriate *range* of styles for the American writers beginning to work in the first few decades of the nineteenth century. A number of influences, or shaping cultural pressures, were at work. One of these, perhaps the dominant one, was the neoclassic style of eighteenth-century England: stately, formal, impersonal, latinate, and clearly the mark of a highly developed, traditional culture. Another was the native American passion for oratory: the Fourth of July oration, tending to become more and more florid and pompous, or the kind of political address for which Daniel Webster became famous, a lengthy overview of American destiny with full excursions into religion, ancient tyranny, European corruption, and associated matters. At a time when communications were poor and transportation difficult, the political address became an important social and cultural occasion: farmers and townspeople flocked to listen from long distances, drawn by the prospect of education, entertainment, and conviviality. Naturally enough, this heavy oratorical manner found its way into American prose. Still another style coming into favor was a rude and rough simulacrum of regional dialects, anticipating the local-color writers who would soon become important in American literature. One hostile critic, Joseph Dennie, satirically characterized this style as "the militia style . . . a vile alloy of provincial idioms and colloquial barbarism." In any case, the more sensitive writers and critics saw clearly that their uncertain cultural identity was reflected in an uncertain style. Washington Irving humorously described the American Muse as "a pawnbroker's widow, with rings on every finger, and loaded with borrowed and hetereogeneous finery."

By the 1830s, however, a trend grew toward refusing the borrowed formalism of the neoclassic style. In England itself that style had been shaken and then broken by the romantic revolution; and in America writers were gradually moving toward a prose—though not yet a poetry—that seemed freer of English constraints and more harmoniously related to the native conditions of life.

It has become customary for literary historians and critics to speak of the writers who appear in this section as largely influenced by English and Continental romanticism. The term *romanticism* is one that critics and historians despair of defining with any degree of precision, yet find indispensible because it does point to a large-scale revolution in feeling and sensibility which began toward the late eighteenth century in Europe and then swept through the first half of the nineteenth century. Briefly and schematically put, cultural romanticism suggests at least some or all of the following: a rejection of the rationalist mentality that had dominated eighteenth-century England, and still lingered among the New England Unitarians, and a conviction that true knowledge came from the heart, by insight and intuition; a stress upon the sanctity and endless interest of the individual ("If the single man plant himself indomitably on the instincts and there abide," wrote Emerson, "the huge world will come round to him"); a search for the principle of godhead or transcendence within man's soul rather than as a force or being externalized in some inaccessible distance; a preoccupation with inner, subjective feelings, lovingly and sometimes narcissistically explored; a belief in the creative powers of the human imagination; a persuasion that nature not only was intrinsically beautiful but could serve as a spiritual resource, suggesting a purity of form to contrast with the artificial corruptions of society, and a purity of content which might serve to replace lapsed religious beliefs; an enthusiasm for ordinary people, the natural or common man; and sometimes a fondness for picturesque effects, Gothic chiaroscuro, medieval ruins. In short, English and Continental romanticism signified a rebellion of the ego, an upsurge of enthusiasm for what was felt to be unfettered life as against rigid dogmas and conventions. Transported to the United States, romanticism often underwent a sea change: it became a little pale, and somehow it even grew moralistic.

Now it would be a mistake to suppose that all the writers included in this section were equally affected by the winds of romanticism. Irving remained an essentially eighteenth-century sensibility, though he did share in the romantic fondness for the quaint, the picturesque, and for local color. Bryant in his poetry was drawn to the natural scene, but he showed little of the emotional agitation, the *Sturm und Drang* (storm and stress), of the English romantic poets. Cooper projected a romantic vision of a lonely, pure-souled, and mythic figure in the hero of his Leatherstocking Tales, Natty Bumppo, but his own opinions were decidedly conservative. Of all these early nineteenth-century American writers Poe was the most unreservedly romantic: uninterested in ordinary social life, utterly at odds with any impulse to literary realism, drawn to the strange and the perverse in his subject matter, and convinced that the function of the writer was not to imitate the familiar social world but to project the hidden qualities of his inner life.

WASHINGTON IRVING (1783–1859)

*Washington Irving was America's first internationally acclaimed man
of letters, as well as the most popular writer in the United States
during the first two or three decades of the nineteenth century—an
estimate that time has steadily, if gently, deflated. He was born
into a well-to-do New York family, in which the precepts of Presbyterian morality and commercial shrewdness ruled together, but
he paid little attention to either, preferring instead the pleasant
social and mild cultural life of provincial New York during the
years of his youth. While still young he went abroad for reasons of
health; later, he would spend many years in England, where his
personal charm and amiable literary productions won him many
friends. When the family business failed in 1818, he began to depend on literature for his livelihood—and though literature, at least
in this respect, would fail many other, and greater, American
writers, it did not fail him. During the last quarter of his life
Irving was prosperous and greatly honored, even to the point of
serving for a time as American Ambassador to Spain; but the quality of his work kept declining.*

*Irving's first major success, at the age of twenty-six, was a burlesque of
New York Dutch history,* Knickerbocker's History of New York, *in
which he caught once and for all the literary tone that would so
please his contemporaries. Satirical but kindly, he made fun of
the old New York burghers, but so gently that the grandsons of
those burghers enjoyed every minute of it. Irving's finest work can
be found in* The Sketch Book of Geoffrey Crayon, Gent., *which he
published a decade after the* History. *It consists of a series of
familiar essays and sketches located both in English and American
settings. Irving continued to publish a good many other works in a
wide variety of forms and styles, some satiric, some playfully
humorous, others aspiring to serious historical scholarship, but
almost all marked by a characteristic geniality and picturesqueness
of tone.*

*What pleased both English and American audiences was Irving's gen-
tlemanly manner, both as man and writer. The English graciously
accepted him as a minor master, a worthy if dependent follower
of the eighteenth-century essayistic tradition of Addison and Goldsmith; the Americans were gratified that, at a time when Europeans
often accused them of being culturally uncouth, one of their own
could produce such polished work and gain the respect of the "home
country." Even during his lifetime, however, there were dissenting
voices. Poe, with his characteristic sharpness, wrote: "Irving is
much overrated, and a nice distinction might be drawn between his
just and his surreptitious and adventitious reputation—between*

what is due to the pioneer solely, and what to the writer." The British novelist, Maria Edgeworth, remarked testily that in Irving "the workmanship surpasses the work. There is too much care and cost bestowed on petty objects."

From the distance of a century and a half later, it is hard not to agree with such verdicts. A good part of what Irving wrote is no more than amiable and superficial journalism; a good part of it seems uninteresting because we do not take very readily to his affectation of gentlemanly mellowness, gentlemanly mildness, and gentlemanly melancholy. Irving seldom tried to go beyond the picturesque, and of all literary manners that is perhaps the one most likely to fade. Yet a work like Knickerbocker's History *is valuable as a reflection of the easy good nature—sometimes, not always, distinguishable from mere provincial complacence—that Americans displayed during the first years of the Republic, that historical moment when the trials of the Revolution were behind the young nation but the troubles of the pre-Civil War years not yet felt.*

The best of Irving's work consists of a few stories such as "Rip Van Winkle" in which he reaches deeply into folk sources and experiences. Though the bare outlines of the plot of "Rip Van Winkle" come from a German story, Irving successfully transplanted them in an American setting, so that one can place this story, as well as "The Legend of Sleepy Hollow," among the first pieces of fiction to be located in and to draw from the materials of colonial American life.

FURTHER READING

The definitive biography is Stanley Williams' *The Life of Washington Irving* (1935). The chapter on Irving in V. L. Parrington's *Main Currents in American Thought,* II (1927) is somewhat caustic but interesting; more amiable is Van Wyck Brooks' *The World of Washington Irving* (1944).

FROM **A History of New York**
by Diedrich Knickerbocker *(1809)*

*Chapter 4   Containing Further Particulars of the Golden Age, and
What Constituted a Fine Lady and Gentleman in the Days of
Walter the Doubter*

In this dulcet period of my history, when the beauteous island of
Manna-hata presented a scene, the very counterpart of those glowing
pictures drawn of the golden reign of Saturn, there was, as I have
before observed, a happy ignorance, an honest simplicity prevalent
among its inhabitants, which, were I even able to depict, would be but
little understood by the degenerate age for which I am doomed to write.
Even the female sex, those arch innovators upon the tranquility, the
honesty, and gray-beard customs of society, seemed for a while to conduct themselves with incredible sobriety and comeliness.

Their hair, untortured by the abominations of art, was scrupulously
pomatumed back from their foreheads with a candle, and covered with
a little cap of quilted calico, which fitted exactly to their heads. Their
petticoats of linsey-woolsey were striped with a variety of gorgeous
dyes,—though I must confess these gallant garments were rather short,
scarce reaching below the knee; but then they made up in the number,
which generally equalled that of the gentleman's small-clothes; and
what is still more praiseworthy, they were all of their own manufacture,—of which circumstance, as may well be supposed, they were not
a little vain.

These were the honest days in which every woman staid at home,
read the Bible, and wore pockets,—ay, and that too of a goodly size,
fashioned with patchwork into many curious devices, and ostentatiously
worn on the outside. These, in fact, were convenient receptacles, where
all good housewives carefully stored away such things as they wished
to have at hand; by which means they often came to be incredibly
crammed; and I remember there was a story current, when I was a
boy, that the lady of Wouter Van Twiller once had occasion to empty
her right pocket in search of a wooden ladle, when the contents filled
a couple of corn-baskets, and the utensil was discovered lying among
some rubbish in one corner;—but we must not give too much faith
to all these stories, the anecdotes of those remote periods being very
subject to exaggeration.

Besides these notable pockets, they likewise wore scissors and pincushions suspended from their girdles by red ribands, or, among the
more opulent and showy classes, by brass, and even silver chains,—
indubitable tokens of thrifty housewives, and industrious spinsters. I
cannot say much in vindication of the shortness of the petticoats; it
doubtless was introduced for the purpose of giving the stockings a
chance to be seen, which were generally of blue worsted, with magnifi-

cent red clocks,—or, perhaps, to display a well-turned ankle, and a neat, though serviceable foot, set off by a high-heeled leathern shoe, with a large and splendid silver buckle. Thus we find that the gentle sex in all ages have shown the same disposition to infringe a little upon the laws of decorum, in order to betray a lurking beauty, or gratify an innocent love of finery.

From the sketch here given, it will be seen that our good grand-mothers differed considerably in their ideas of a fine figure from their scantily dressed descendants of the present day. A fine lady, in those times, waddled under more clothes, even on a fair summer's day, than would have clad the whole bevy of a modern ball-room. Nor were they the less admired by the gentlemen in consequence thereof. On the contrary, the greatness of a lover's passion seemed to increase in proportion to the magnitude of its object,—and a voluminous damsel, arrayed in a dozen of petticoats, was declared by a Low-Dutch sonneteer of the province to be radiant as a sunflower, and luxuriant as a full-blown cabbage. Certain it is, that in those days the heart of a lover could not contain more than one lady at a time; whereas the heart of a modern gallant has often room enough to accommodate half a dozen. The reason of which I conclude to be, that either the hearts of the gentle-men have grown larger, or the persons of the ladies smaller: this, however, is a question for physiologists to determine.

But there was a secret charm in these petticoats, which, no doubt, entered into the consideration of the prudent gallants. The wardrobe of a lady was in those days her only fortune; and she who had a good stock of petticoats and stockings was as absolutely an heiress as is a Kamchatka damsel with a store of bear-skins, or a Lapland belle with a plenty of reindeer. The ladies, therefore, were very anxious to display these powerful attractions to the greatest advantage; and the best rooms in the house, instead of being adorned with caricatures of dame Nature, in water-colors and needle-work, were always hung round with abundance of homespun garments, the manufacture and the property of the females,—a piece of laudable ostentation that still prevails among the heiresses of our Dutch villages.

The gentlemen, in fact, who figured in the circles of the gay world in these ancient times, corresponded, in most particulars, with the beauteous damsels whose smiles they were ambitious to deserve. True it is, their merits would make but a very inconsiderable impression upon the heart of a modern fair: they neither drove their curricles, nor sported their tandems, for as yet those gaudy vehicles were not even dreamt of; neither did they distinguish themselves by their brilliancy at the table, and their consequent rencontres with watchmen, for our forefathers were of too pacific a disposition to need those guardians of the night, every soul throughout the town being sound asleep before nine o'clock. Neither did they establish their claims to gentility at the expense of their tailors, for as yet those offenders against the pockets of society, and the tranquillity of all aspiring young gentlemen, were unknown in New Amsterdam; every good housewife made the clothes of her husband and family, and even the goede vrouw [good wife] of Van Twiller himself thought it no disparagement to cut out her husband's linsey-woolsey galligaskins.

Not but what there were some two or three youngsters who manifested the first dawning of what is called fire and spirit; who held all labor in contempt; skulked about docks and market-places; loitered in the sunshine; squandered what little money they could procure at hustle-cap and chuck-farthing; swore, boxed, fought cocks, and raced their neighbors' horses; in short, who promised to be the wonder, the talk, and abomination of the town, had not their stylish career been unfortunately cut short by an affair of honor with a whipping-post.

Far other, however, was the truly fashionable gentleman of those days: his dress, which served for both morning and evening, street and drawing-room, was a linsey-woolsey coat, made, perhaps, by the fair hands of the mistress of his affections, and gallantly bedecked with abundance of large brass buttons; half a score of breeches heightened the proportions of his figure; his shoes were decorated by enormous copper buckles: a low-crowned broad-rimmed hat overshadowed his burly visage; and his hair dangled down his back in a prodigious queue of eel-skin.

Thus equipped, he would manfully sally forth, with pipe in mouth, to besiege some fair damsel's obdurate heart,—not such a pipe, good reader, as that which Acis did sweetly tune in praise of his Galatea, but one of true Delft manufacture, and furnished with a charge of fragrant tobacco. With this would he resolutely set himself down before the fortress, and rarely failed, in the process of time, to smoke the fair enemy into a surrender, upon honorable terms.

Such was the happy reign of Wouter Van Twiller, celebrated in many a long-forgotten song as the real golden age, the rest being nothing but counterfeit copper-washed coin. In that delightful period, a sweet and holy calm reigned over the whole province. The burgomaster smoked his pipe in peace; the substantial solace of his domestic cares, after her daily toils were done, sat soberly at the door, with her arms crossed over her apron of snowy white, without being insulted with ribald street-walkers or vagabond boys,—those unlucky urchins who do so infest our streets, displaying, under the roses of youth, the thorns and briers of iniquity. Then it was that the lover with ten breeches, and the damsel with petticoats of half a score, indulged in all the innocent endearments of virtuous love, without fear and without reproach; for what had that virtue to fear, which was defended by a shield of good linsey-woolseys, equal at least to the seven bull-hides of the invincible Ajax?

Ah, blissful and never to be forgotten age! when everything was better than it has ever been since, or ever will be again,—when Buttermilk Channel was quite dry at low water,—when the shad in the Hudson were all salmon,—and when the moon shone with a pure and resplendent whiteness, instead of that melancholy yellow light which is the consequence of her sickening at the abominations she every night witnesses in this degenerate city.

Happy would it have been for New Amsterdam could it always have existed in this state of blissful ignorance and lowly simplicity; but, alas! the days of childhood are too sweet to last! Cities, like men, grow out of them in time, and are doomed alike to grow into the bustle, the cares, and miseries of the world. Let no man congratulate himself, when he beholds the child of his bosom or the city of his birth increasing in magnitude and importance,—let the history of his own life teach him the dangers of the one, and this excellent little history of Manna-hata convince him of the calamities of the other.

Rip Van Winkle (1819)

A Posthumous Writing of Diedrich Knickerbocker

> *By Woden,[1] God of Saxons,*
> *From whence comes Wensday, that is Wodensday.*
> *Truth is a thing that ever I will keep*
> *Unto thylke day in which I creep into*
> *My sepulchre—*
>
> CARTWRIGHT[2]

(The following Tale was found among the papers of the late Diedrich Knickerbocker, an old gentleman of New York, who was very curious in the Dutch history of the province, and the manners of the descendants from its primitive settlers. His historical researches, however, did not lie so much among books as among men; for the former are lamentably scanty on his favorite topics; whereas he found the old burghers, and still more their wives, rich in that lengendary lore, so invaluable to true history. Whenever, therefore, he happened upon a genuine Dutch family, snugly shut up in its low-roofed farmhouse, under a spreading sycamore, he looked upon it as a little clasped volume of black-letter, and studied it with the zeal of a book-worm.

The result of all these researches was a history of the province during the reign of the Dutch governors, which he published some years since. There have been various opinions as to the literary character of his work, and, to tell the truth, it is not a whit better than it

---

[1] Germanic god of war.
[2] Taken from William Cartwright, *The Ordinary* (1651).

should be. Its chief merit is its scrupulous accuracy, which indeed was a little questioned on its first appearance, but has since been completely established; and it is now admitted into all historical collections, as a book of unquestionable authority.

The old gentleman died shortly after the publication of his work, and now that he is dead and gone, it cannot do much harm to his memory to say that his time might have been much better employed in weightier labors. He, however, was apt to ride his hobby his own way; and though it did now and then pick up the dust a little in the eyes of his neighbors, and grieve the spirit of some friends, for whom he felt the truest deference and affection; yet his errors and follies are remembered "more in sorrow than in anger," and it begins to be suspected, that he never intended to injure or offend. But however his memory may be appreciated by critics, it is still held dear by many folk, whose good opinion is well worth having; particularly by certain biscuit-bakers, who have gone so far as to imprint his likeness on their new-year cakes; and have thus given him a chance for immortality, almost equal to the being stamped on a Waterloo Medal, or a Queen Anne's Farthing.)

Whoever has made a voyage up the Hudson must remember the Kaatskill mountains. They are a dismembered branch of the great Appalachian family, and are seen away to the west of the river, swelling up to a noble height, and lording it over the surrounding country. Every change of season, every change of weather, indeed, every hour of the day, produces some change in the magical hues and shapes of these mountains, and they are regarded by all the good wives, far and near, as perfect barometers. When the weather is fair and settled, they are clothed in blue and purple, and print their bold outlines on the clear evening sky; but, sometimes, when the rest of the landscape is cloudless, they will gather a hood of gray vapors about their summits, which, in the last rays of the setting sun, will glow and light up like a crown of glory.

At the foot of these fairy mountains, the voyager may have described the light smoke curling up from a village, whose shingle-roofs gleam among the trees, just where the blue tints of the upland melt away into the fresh green of the nearer landscape. It is a little village, of great antiquity, having been founded by some of the Dutch colonists, in the early times of the province, just about the beginning of the government of the good Peter Stuyvestant (may he rest in peace!), and there were some of the houses of the original settlers standing within a few years, built of small yellow bricks brought from Holland, having latticed windows and gable fronts, surmounted with weathercocks.

In that same village, and in one of these very houses (which, to tell the precise truth, was sadly time-worn and weather-beaten), there lived many years since, while the country was yet a province of Great Britain, a simple good-natured fellow, of the name of Rip Van Winkle. He was a descendant of the Van Winkles who figured so gallantly in the chivalrous days of Peter Stuyvestant, and accompanied him to the siege of Fort Christina. He inherited, however, but little of the martial character of his ancestors. I have observed that he was a simple good-natured man; he was, moreover, a kind neighbor, and an obedient hen-pecked husband. Indeed, to the latter circumstance might be owing that meekness of spirit which gained him such universal popularity; for those men are most apt to be obsequious and conciliating abroad, who are under the discipline of shrews at home. Their tempers, doubtless, are rendered pliant and malleable in the fiery furnace of domestic tribulation; and a curtain lecture is worth all the sermons in the world for teaching the virtues of patience and long-suffering. A termagant wife may, therefore, in some respects, be considered a tolerable blessing; and if so, Rip Van Winkle was thrice blessed.

Certain it is, that he was a great favorite among all the good wives of the village, who, as usual, with the amiable sex, took his part in all family squabbles; and never failed, whenever they talked those matters over in their evening gossipings, to lay all the blame on Dame Van Winkle. The children of the village, too, would shout with joy whenever he approached. He assisted at their sports, made their playthings, taught them to fly kites and shoot marbles, and told them long stories of ghosts, witches, and Indians. Whenever he went dodging about the village, he was surrounded by a troop of them, hanging on his skirts, clambering on his back, and playing a thousand tricks on him with impunity; and not a dog would bark at him throughout the neighborhood.

The great error in Rip's composition was an insuperable aversion to all kinds of profitable labor. It could not be from the want of assiduity or perseverance; for he would sit on a wet rock, with a rod as long and heavy as a Tartar's lance, and fish all day without a murmur, even though he should not be encouraged by a single nibble. He would carry a fowling-piece on his shoulder for hours together, trudging through woods and swamps, and up hill and down dale, to shoot a few squirrels or wild pigeons. He would never refuse to assist a neighbor even in the roughest toil, and was a foremost man at all country frolics for husking Indian corn, or building stone-fences; the women of the village, too, used to employ him to run their errands, and to do such little odd jobs as their less obliging husbands would not do for them. In a word Rip was ready to attend to anybody's business but his own; but as to doing family duty, and keeping his farm in order, he found it impossible.

In fact, he declared it was of no use to work on his farm; it was the most pestilent little piece of ground in the whole country; everything about it went wrong, and would go wrong, in spite of him. His fences were continually falling to pieces; his cow would either go astray, or get among the cabbages; weeds were sure to grow quicker in his fields than anywhere else; the rain always made a point of setting in just as he had some outdoor work to do; so that though his patrimonial estate had dwindled away under his management, acre by acre, until there was little more left than a mere patch of Indian corn and potatoes, yet it was the worst conditioned farm in the neighborhood.

His children, too, were as ragged and wild as if they belonged to nobody. His son Rip, an urchin begotten in his own likeness, promised to inherit the habits, with the old clothes of his father. He was generally seen trooping like a colt at his mother's heels, equipped in a pair of his father's cast-off galligaskins,[3] which he had much ado to hold up with one hand, as a fine lady does her train in bad weather.

Rip Van Winkle, however, was one of those happy mortals, of foolish, well-oiled dispositions, who take the world easy, eat white bread or brown, whichever can be got with least thought or trouble, and would rather starve on a penny than work for a pound. If left to himself, he would have whistled life away in perfect contentment; but his wife kept continually dinning in his ears about his idleness, his carelessness, and the ruin he was bringing on his family. Morning, noon, and night, her tongue was incessantly going, and every thing he said or did was sure to produce a torrent of household eloquence. Rip had but one way of replying to all lectures of the kind, and that, by frequent use, had grown into a habit. He shrugged his shoulders, shook his head, cast up his eyes, but said nothing. This, however, always provoked a fresh volley from his wife; so that he was fain to draw off his forces, and take to the outside of the house—the only side which, in truth, belongs to a hen-pecked husband.

Rip's sole domestic adherent was his dog Wolf, who was as much hen-pecked as his master; for Dame Van Winkle regarded them as companions in idleness, and even looked upon Wolf with an evil eye, as the cause of his master's going so often astray. True it is, in all points of spirit befitting an honorable dog, he was as courageous an animal as ever scoured the woods—but what courage can withstand the everduring and all-besetting terrors of a woman's tongue? The moment Wolf entered the house his crest fell, his tail drooped to the ground, or curled between his legs, he sneaked about with a gallows air, casting many a sidelong glance at Dame Van Winkle, and at the least flourish of a broomstick or ladle, he would fly to the door with yelping precipitation.

Times grew worse and worse with Rip Van Winkle as years of matrimony rolled on; a tart temper never mellows with age, and a sharp tongue is the only edged tool that grows keener with constant use. For a long while he used to console himself, when driven from home, by frequenting a kind of perpetual club of the sages, philosophers, and other idle personages of the village; which held its sessions on a bench before a small inn, designated by a rubicund portrait of His Majesty George the Third. Here they used to sit in the shade through a long lazy

[3] Knee breeches.

summer's day, talking listlessly over village gossip, or telling endless sleepy stories about nothing. But it would have been worth any statesman's money to have heard the profound discussions that sometimes took place, when by chance an old newspaper fell into their hands from some passing traveller. How solemnly they would listen to the contents, as drawled out by Derrick Van Bummel, the schoolmaster, a dapper learned little man, who was not to be daunted by the most gigantic word in the dictionary; and how sagely they would deliberate upon public events some months after they had taken place.

The opinions of this junto were completely controlled by Nicholas Vedder, a patriarch of the village, and landlord of the inn, at the door of which he took his seat from morning till night, just moving sufficiently to avoid the sun and keep in the shade of a large tree; so that the neighbors could tell the hour by his movements as accurately as by a sun-dial. It is true he was rarely heard to speak, but smoked his pipe incessantly. His adherents, however (for every great man has his adherents), perfectly understood him, and knew how to gather his opinions. When any thing that was read or related displeased him, he was observed to smoke his pipe vehemently, and to send forth short, frequent and angry puffs; but when pleased, he would inhale the smoke slowly and tranquilly, and emit it in light and placid clouds; and sometimes, taking the pipe from his mouth, and letting the fragrant vapor curl about his nose, would gravely nod his head in token of perfect approbation.

From even this stronghold the unlucky Rip was at length routed by his termagant wife, who would suddenly break in upon the tranquility of the assemblage and call the members all to naught; nor was that august personage, Nicholas Vedder himself, sacred from the daring tongue of this terrible virago, who charged him outright with encouraging her husband in habits of idleness.

Poor Rip was at last reduced almost to despair; and his only alternative, to escape from the labor of the farm and clamor of his wife, was to take gun in hand and stroll away into the woods. Here he would sometimes seat himself at the foot of a tree, and share the contents of his wallet with Wolf, with whom he sympathized as a fellow-sufferer in persecution. "Poor Wolf," he would say, "thy mistress leads thee a dog's life of it; but never mind, my lad, whilst I live thou shalt never want a friend to stand by thee!" Wolf would wag his tail, look wistfully in his master's face, and if dogs can feel pity I verily believe he reciprocated the sentiment with all his heart.

In a long ramble of the kind on a fine autumnal day, Rip had unconsciously scrambled to one of the highest parts of the Kaatskill mountains. He was after his favorite sport of squirrel shooting, and the still solitudes had echoed and re-echoed with the reports of his gun. Panting and fatigued, he threw himself, late in the afternoon, on a green knoll, covered with mountain herbage, that crowned the brow of a precipice.

From an opening between the trees he could overlook all the lower country for many a mile of rich woodland. He saw at a distance the lordly Hudson, far, far below him, moving on its silent but majestic course, with the reflection of a purple cloud, or the sail of a lagging bark, here and there sleeping on its glassy bosom, and at last losing itself in the blue highlands.

On the other side he looked down into a deep mountain glen, wild, lonely, and shagged, the bottom filled with fragments from the impending cliffs, and scarcely lighted by the reflected rays of the setting sun. For some time Rip lay musing on this scene; evening was gradually advancing; the mountains began to throw their long blue shadows over the valleys; he saw that it would be dark long before he could reach the village, and he heaved a heavy sigh when he thought of encountering the terrors of Dame Van Winkle.

As he was about to descend, he heard a voice from a distance, hallooing, "Rip Van Winkle! Rip Van Winkle!" He looked round, but could see nothing but a crow winging its solitary flight across the mountain. He thought his fancy must have deceived him, and turned again to descend, when he heard the same cry through the still evening air; "Rip Van Winkle! Rip Van Winkle!"—at the same time Wolf bristled up his back, and giving a low growl, skulked to his master's side, looking fearfully down into the glen. Rip now felt a vague apprehension stealing over him; he looked anxiously in the same direction, and perceived a strange figure slowly toiling up the rocks, and bending under the weight of something he carried on his back. He was surprised to see any human being in this lonely and unfrequented place, but supposing it to be some one of the neighborhood in need of his assistance, he hastened down to yield it.

On nearer approach he was still more surprised at the singularity of the stranger's appearance. He was a short square-built old fellow, with thick bushy hair, and a grizzled beard. His dress was of the antique Dutch fashion—a cloth jerkin strapped round the waist—several pair of breeches, the outer one of ample volume, decorated with rows of buttons down the sides, and bunches at the knees. He bore on his shoulder a stout keg, that seemed full of liquor, and made signs for Rip to approach and assist him with the load. Though rather shy and distrustful of this new acquaintance, Rip complied with his usual alacrity; and mutually relieving one another, they clambered up a narrow gully, apparently the dry bed of a mountain torrent. As they ascended, Rip every now and then heard long rolling peals, like distant thunder, that seemed to issue out of a deep ravine, or rather cleft, between lofty rocks, toward which their rugged path conducted. He paused for an instant, but supposing it to be the muttering of one of those transient thunder-showers which often take place in mountain heights, he proceeded. Passing through the ravine, they came to a hollow, like a small amphitheatre, surrounded by perpendicular precipices, over the brinks of which impending trees shot their branches, so that you only caught glimpses of the azure sky and the bright evening cloud. During the whole time Rip and his companion had labored on in silence; for though the former marvelled greatly what could be the object of carrying a keg of liquor up this wild mountain, yet there was something strange and incomprehensible about the unknown, that inspired awe and checked familiarity.

On entering the amphitheatre, new objects of wonder presented themselves. On a level spot in the centre was a company of odd-looking personages playing at nine-pins. They were dressed in a quaint outlandish fashion; some wore short doublets, others jerkins, with long knives in their belts, and most of them had enormous breeches, of similar style with that of the guide's. Their visages, too, were peculiar: one had a large head, broad face, and small piggish eyes: the face of another seemed to consist entirely of nose, and was surmounted by a white sugar-loaf hat, set off with a little red cock's tail. They all had beards, of various shapes and colors. There was one who seemed to be the commander. He was a stout old gentleman, with a weather-beaten countenance; he wore a laced doublet, broad belt and hanger, high crowned hat and feather, red stockings, and high-heeled shoes, with roses in them. The whole group reminded Rip of the figures in an old Flemish painting, in the parlor of Dominie Van Shaick, the village parson, and which had been brought over from Holland at the time of the settlement.

What seemed particularly odd to Rip was, that though these folks were evidently amusing themselves, yet they maintained the gravest faces, the most mysterious silence, and were, withal, the most melancholy party of pleasure he had ever witnessed. Nothing interrupted the stillness of the scene but the noise of the balls, which, whenever they were rolled, echoed along the mountains like rumbling peals of thunder.

As Rip and his companion approached them, they suddenly desisted from their play, and stared at him with such fixed statue-like gaze, and such strange, uncouth, lacklustre countenances, that his heart turned within him, and his knees smote together. His companion now emptied the contents of the keg into large flagons, and made signs to him to wait upon the company. He obeyed with fear and trembling; they quaffed the liquor in profound silence, and then returned to their game.

By degrees Rip's awe and apprehension subsided. He even ventured, when no eye was fixed upon him, to taste the beverage, which he found had much of the flavor of excellent Hollands. He was naturally a thirsty soul, and was soon tempted to repeat the draught. One taste provoked another; and he reiterated his visits to the flagon so often that at length his senses were overpowered, his eyes swam in his head, his head gradually declined, and he fell into a deep sleep.

On waking, he found himself on the green knoll whence he had first seen the old man of the glen. He rubbed his eyes—it was a bright sunny morning. The birds were hopping and twittering among the bushes, and the eagle was wheeling aloft, and breasting the pure mountain breeze. "Surely," thought Rip, "I have not slept here all night." He recalled the occurrences before he fell asleep. The strange man with a keg of liquor—the mountain ravine—the wild retreat among the rocks—the wobegone party at ninepins—the flagon—"Oh! that flagon! that wicked flagon!" thought Rip—"what excuse shall I make to Dame Van Winkle!"

He looked round for his gun, but in place of the clean well-oiled fowling-piece, he found an old firelock lying by him, the barrel incrusted with rust, the lock falling off, and the stock worm-eaten. He now suspected that the grave roysters of the mountain had put a trick upon him, and, having dosed him with liquor, had robbed him of his gun. Wolf, too, had disappeared, but he might have strayed away after a squirrel or partridge. He whistled after him and shouted his name, but all in vain; the echoes repeated his whistle and shout, but no dog was to be seen.

He determined to revisit the scene of the last evening's gambol, and if he met with any of the party, to demand his dog and gun. As he rose to walk, he found himself stiff in the joints, and wanting in his usual activity. "These mountain beds do not agree with me," thought Rip, "and if this frolic should lay me up with a fit of the rheumatism, I shall have a blessed time with Dame Van Winkle." With some difficulty he got down into the glen: he found the gully up which he and his companion had ascended the preceding evening; but to his astonishment a mountain stream was now foaming down it, leaping from rock to rock, and filling the glen with babbling murmurs. He, however, made shift to scramble up its sides, working his toilsome way through thickets of birch, sassafras, and witchhazel, and sometimes tripped up or entangled by the wild grapevines that twisted their coils or tendrils from tree to tree, and spread a kind of network in his path.

At length he reached to where the ravine had opened through the cliffs to the amphitheatre; but no traces of such opening remained. The rocks presented a high impenetrable wall over which the torrent came tumbling in a sheet of feathery foam, and fell into a broad deep basin, black from the shadows of the surrounding forest. Here, then, poor Rip was brought to a stand. He again called and whistled after his dog; he was only answered by the cawing of a flock of idle crows, sporting high in air about a dry tree that overhung a sunny precipice; and who, secure in their elevation, seemed to look down and scoff at the poor man's perplexities. What was to be done? the morning was passing away, and Rip felt famished for want of his breakfast. He grieved to give up his dog and gun; he dreaded to meet his wife; but it would not do to starve among the mountains. He shook his head, shouldered the rusty firelock, and, with a heart full of trouble and anxiety, turned his steps homeward.

As he approached the village he met a number of people, but none whom he knew, which somewhat surprised him, for he had thought himself acquainted with every one in the country round. Their dress, too, was of a different fashion from that to which he was accustomed. They all stared at him with equal marks of surprise, and whenever they cast their eyes upon him, invariably stroked their chins. The constant recurrence of this gesture induced Rip, involuntarily, to do the same, when, to his astonishment, he found his beard had grown a foot long!

He had now entered the skirts of the village. A troop of strange children ran at his heels, hooting after him, and pointing at his gray beard. The dogs, too, not one of which he recognized for an old acquaintance, barked at him as he passed. The very village was altered; it was larger and more populous. There were rows of houses which he had never seen before, and those which had been his familiar haunts had disappeared. Strange names were over the doors—strange faces at the windows—every thing was strange. His mind now misgave him; he began to doubt whether both he and the world around him were not bewitched. Surely this was his native village, which he had left but the day before. There stood the Kaatskill mountains—there ran the silver Hudson at a distance—there was every hill and dale precisely as it had always been—Rip was sorely perplexed—"That flagon last night," thought he, "has addled my poor head sadly!"

It was with some difficulty that he found the way to his own house, which he approached with silent awe, expecting every moment to hear the shrill voice of Dame Van Winkle. He found the house gone to decay— the roof fallen in, the windows shattered, and the doors off the hinges. A half-starved dog that looked like Wolf was skulking about it. Rip called him by name, but the cur snarled, showed his teeth, and passed on. This was an unkind cut indeed—"My very dog," sighed poor Rip, "has forgotten me!"

He entered the house, which, to tell the truth, Dame Van Winkle had always kept in neat order. It was empty, forlorn, and apparently abandoned. This desolateness overcame all his connubial fears—he called loudly for his wife and children—the lonely chambers rang for a moment with his voice, and then all again was silence.

He now hurried forth, and hastened to his old resort, the village inn—but it too was gone. A large rickety wooden building stood in its place, with great gaping windows, some of them broken and mended with old hats and petticoats, and over the door was painted, "The Union Hotel, by Jonathan Doolittle." Instead of the great tree that used to shelter the quiet little Dutch inn of yore, there now was reared a tall naked pole, with something on the top that looked like a red nightcap, and from it was fluttering a flag, on which was a singular assemblage of stars and stripes—all this was strange and incomprehensible. He recognized on the sign, however, the ruby face of King George, under which he had smoked so many a peaceful pipe; but even this was singularly metamorphosed. The red coat was changed for one of blue and buff, a sword was held in the hand instead of a sceptre, the head was decorated with a cocked hat, and underneath was painted in large characters, GENERAL WASHINGTON.

There was, as usual, a crowd of folk about the door, but none that Rip recollected. The very character of the people seemed changed. There was a busy, bustling, disputatious tone about it, instead of the accustomed phlegm and drowsy tranquility. He looked in vain for the sage Nicholas Vedder, with his broad face, double chin, and fair long pipe, uttering clouds of tobacco-smoke instead of idle speeches; or Van Brummel, the schoolmaster, doling forth the contents of an ancient newspaper. In place of these, a lean, bilious-looking fellow, with his pockets full of handbills, was haranguing vehemently about rights of citizens—elections—members of congress—liberty—Bunker's Hill— heroes of seventy-six—and other words, which were a perfect Babylonish jargon to the bewildered Van Winkle.

The appearance of Rip, with his long grizzled beard, his rusty fowling piece, his uncouth dress, and an army of women and children at his heels, soon attracted the attention of the tavern politicians. They crowded round him, eyeing him from head to foot with great curiosity. The orator bustled up to him, and, drawing him partly aside, inquired "on which side he voted?" Rip stared in vacant stupidity. Another short but busy little fellow pulled him by the arm, and, rising on tiptoe, inquired in his ear, "Whether he was Federal or Democrat?" Rip was equally at a loss to comprehend the question; when a knowing, self-important old gentleman, in a sharp cocked hat, made his way through the crowd, putting them to the right and left with his elbows as he passed, and planting himself before Van Winkle, with one arm akimbo, the other resting on his cane, his keen eyes and sharp hat penetrating, as it were, into his very soul, demanded in an austere tone, "what brought him to the election with a gun on his shoulder, and a mob at his heels, and whether he meant to breed a riot in the village?"—"Alas! gentlemen," cried Rip, somewhat dismayed, "I am a poor quiet man, a native of the place, and a loyal subject of the king, God bless him!"

Here a general shout burst from the by-standers—"A tory! a tory! a spy! a refugee! hustle him! away with him!" It was with great difficulty that the self-important man in the cocked hat restored order; and, having assumed a tenfold austerity of brow, demanded again of the unknown culprit, what he came there for, and whom he was seeking? The poor man humbly assured him that he meant no harm, but merely came there in search of some of his neighbors, who used to keep about the tavern.

"Well—who are they?—name them."

Rip bethought himself a moment, and inquired, "Where's Nicholas Vedder?"

There was a silence for a little while, when an old man replied, in a thin piping voice, "Nicholas Vedder! why, he is dead and gone these eighteen years! There was a wooden tombstone in the churchyard that used to tell all about him, but that's rotten and gone too."

"Where's Brom Dutcher?"

"Oh, he went off to the army in the beginning of the war; some say he was killed at the storming of Stony Point—others say he was drowned in a squall at the foot of Antony's Nose. I don't know—he never came back again."

"Where's Van Bummel, the schoolmaster?"

"He went off to the wars too, was a great militia general, and is now in congress."

Rip's heart died away at hearing of these sad changes in his home and friends, and finding himself thus alone in the world. Every answer puzzled him too, by treating of such enormous lapses of time, and of matters which he could not understand: war—congress—Stony Point;—he had no courage to ask after any more friends, but cried out in despair, "Does nobody here know Rip Van Winkle?"

"Oh, Rip Van Winkle!" exclaimed two or three, "Oh, to be sure! that's Rip Van Winkle yonder, leaning against the tree."

Rip looked, and beheld a precise counterpart of himself, as he went up the mountain: apparently as lazy, and certainly as ragged. The poor fellow was now completely confounded. He doubted his own identity, and whether he was himself or another man. In the midst of his bewilderment, the man in the cocked hat demanded who he was, and what was his name?

"God knows," exclaimed he, at his wit's end; "I'm not myself—I'm somebody else—that's me yonder—no—that's somebody else got into my shoes—I was myself last night, but I fell asleep on the mountain, and they've changed my gun, and every thing's changed, and I'm changed, and I can't tell what's my name, or who I am!"

The by-standers began now to look at each other, nod, wink significantly, and tap their fingers against their foreheads. There was a whisper, also, about securing the gun, and keeping the old fellow from doing mischief, at the very suggestion of which the self-important man in the cocked hat retired with some precipitation. At this critical moment a fresh comely woman pressed through the throng to get a peep at the gray-bearded man. She had a chubby child in her arms, which, frightened at his looks, began to cry. "Hush, Rip," cried she, "hush, you little fool; the old man won't hurt you." The name of the child, the air of the mother, the tone of her voice, all awakened a train of recollection in his mind. "What is your name, my good woman?" asked he.

"Judith Gardenier."

"And your father's name?"

"Ah, poor man, Rip Van Winkle was his name, but it's twenty years since he went away from home with his gun, and never has been heard of since—his dog came home without him; but whether he shot himself, or was carried away by the Indians, nobody can tell. I was then but a little girl."

Rip had but one question more to ask; but he put it with a faltering voice:

"Where's your mother?"

"Oh, she too had died but a short time since; she broke a blood-vessel in a fit of passion at a New-England peddler."

There was a drop of comfort, at least, in this intelligence. The honest man could contain himself no longer. He caught his daughter and her child in his arms. "I am your father!" cried he—"Young Rip Van Winkle once—old Rip Van Winkle now!—Does nobody know poor Rip Van Winkle?"

All stood amazed, until an old woman, tottering out from among the crowd, put her hand to her brow, and peering under it in his face for a moment, exclaimed, "Sure enough! it is Rip Van Winkle—it is himself! Welcome home again, old neighbor—Why, where have you been these twenty long years?"

Rip's story was soon told, for the whole twenty years had been to him but as one night. The neighbors stared when they heard it; some were seen to wink at each other, and put their tongues in their cheeks: and the self-important man in the cocked hat, who, when the alarm was over, had returned to the field, screwed down the corners of his mouth, and shook his head—upon which there was a general shaking of the head throughout the assemblage.

It was determined, however, to take the opinion of old Peter Vanderdonk, who was seen slowly advancing up the road. He was a descendant of the historian of that name, who wrote one of the earliest accounts of the province. Peter was the most ancient inhabitant of the village, and well versed in all the wonderful events and traditions of the neighborhood. He recollected Rip at once, and corroborated his story in the most satisfactory manner. He assured the company that it was a fact, handed down from his ancestor the historian, that the Kaatskill mountains had always been haunted by strange beings. That it was affirmed that the great Hendrick Hudson, the first discoverer of the river and country, kept a kind of vigil there every twenty years, with his crew of the Half-moon; being permitted in this way to revisit the scenes of his enterprise, and keep a guardian eye upon the river, and the great city called by his name. That his father had once seen them in their old Dutch dresses playing at nine-pins in a hollow of the mountain; and that he himself had heard, one summer afternoon, the sound of their balls, like distant peals of thunder.

To make a long story short, the company broke up, and returned to the more important concerns of the election. Rip's daughter took him home to live with her; she had a snug, well-furnished house, and a stout cheery farmer for a husband, whom Rip recollected for one of the urchins that used to climb upon his back. As to Rip's son and heir, who was the ditto of himself, seen leaning against the tree, he was employed to work on the farm; but evinced an hereditary disposition to attend to any thing else but his business.

Rip now resumed his old walks and habits; he soon found many of his former cronies, though all rather the worse for the wear and tear of time; and preferred making friends among the rising generation, with whom he soon grew into great favor.

Having nothing to do at home, and being arrived at that happy age when a man can be idle with impunity, he took his place once more on the bench at the inn door, and was reverenced as one of the patriarchs of the village, and a chronicle of the old times "before the war." It was some time before he could get into the regular track of gossip, or could be made to comprehend the strange events that had taken place during his torpor. How that there had been a revolutionary war—that the country had thrown off the yoke of old England—and that, instead of being a subject of His Majesty George the Third, he was now a free citizen of the United States. Rip, in fact, was no politician; the changes of states and empires made but little impression on him; but there was one species of despotism under which he had long groaned, and that was—petticoat government. Happily that was at an end; he had got his neck out of the yoke of matrimony, and could go in and out whenever he pleased, without dreading the tyranny of Dame Van Winkle. Whenever her name was mentioned, however, he shook his head, shrugged his shoulders, and cast up his eyes; which might pass either for an expression of resignation to his fate, or joy at his deliverance.

He used to tell his story to every stranger that arrived at Mr. Doolittle's hotel. He was observed, at first, to vary on some points every time he told it, which was, doubtless, owing to his having so recently awaked. It at last settled down precisely to the tale I have related, and not a man, woman, or child in the neighborhood, but knew it by heart. Some always pretended to doubt the reality of it, and insisted that Rip had been out of his head, and that this was one point on which he always remained flighty. The old Dutch inhabitants, however, almost universally gave it full credit. Even to this day they never hear a thunderstorm of a summer afternoon about the Kaatskill, but they say Hendrick Hudson and his crew are at their game of ninepins; and it is a common wish of all hen-pecked husbands in the neighborhood, when life hangs heavy on their hands, that they might have a quieting draught out of Rip Van Winkle's flagon.

The Legend of Sleepy Hollow (1820)

Found among the Papers of the Late Diedrich Knickerbocker

> *A pleasing land of drowsy head it was,*
> *Of dreams that wave before the half-shut eye;*
> *And of gay castles in the clouds that pass,*
> *For ever flushing round a summer sky.*
> CASTLE OF INDOLENCE[1]

In the bosom of one of those spacious coves which indent the eastern shore of the Hudson, at that broad expansion of the river denominated by the ancient Dutch navigators the Tappan Zee, and where they always prudently shortened sail, and implored the protection of St. Nicholas when they crossed, there lies a small market-town or rural port, which by some is called Greensburgh, but which is more generally and properly known by the name of Tarry Town. This name was given, we are told, in former days, by the good housewives of the adjacent country, from the inveterate propensity of their husbands to linger about the village tavern on market days. Be that as it may, I do not vouch for the fact, but merely advert to it, for the sake of being precise and authentic. Not far from this village, perhaps about two miles, there is a little valley, or rather lap of land, among high hills, which is one of the quietest places in the whole world. A small brook glides through it, with just murmur enough to lull one to repose; and the occasional whistle of a quail, or tapping of a woodpecker, is almost the only sound that ever breaks in upon the uniform tranquillity.

I recollect that, when a stripling, my first exploit in squirrel-shooting was in a grove of tall wallnut-trees that shades one side of the valley. I had wandered into it at noon time, when all nature is peculiarly quiet, and was startled by the roar of my own gun, as it broke the Sabbath stillness around, and was prolonged and reverberated by the angry echoes. If ever I should wish for a retreat, whither I might steal from the world and its distractions, and dream quietly away the remnant of a troubled life, I know of none more promising than this little valley.

From the listless repose of the place, and the peculiar character of its inhabitants, who are descendants from the original Dutch settlers, this sequestered glen has long been known by the name of SLEEPY HOLLOW, and its rustic lads are called the Sleepy Hollow Boys throughout all the neighboring country. A drowsy, dreamy influence seems to hang over the land, and to pervade the very atmosphere. Some say that the place was bewitched by a high German doctor, during the early days of the settlement; others, that an old Indian chief, the prophet or

---

[1] A poem by James Thomson (1748).

wizard of his tribe, held his powwows there before the country was discovered by Master Hendrick Hudson. Certain it is, the place still continues under the sway of some witching power, that holds a spell over
the minds of the good people, causing them to walk in a continual
reverie. They are given to all kinds of marvellous beliefs; are subject to
trances and visions; and frequently see strange sights, and hear music
and voices in the air. The whole neighborhood abounds with local tales,
haunted spots, and twilight superstitions; stars shoot and meteors glare
oftener across the valley than in any other part of the country, and the
nightmare, with her whole nine fold, seems to make it the favorite
scene of her gambols.

The dominant spirit, however, that haunts this enchanted region,
and seems to be commander-in-chief of all the powers of the air, is the
apparition of a figure on horseback without a head. It is said by some
to be the ghost of a Hessian trooper, whose head had been carried away
by a cannon-ball, in some nameless battle during the revolutionary war;
and who is ever and anon seen by the country folk, hurrying along in
the gloom of night, as if on the wings of the wind. His haunts are not
confined to the valley, but extend at times to the adjacent roads, and
especially to the vicinity of a church at no great distance. Indeed, certain
of the most authentic historians of those parts, who have been careful
in collecting and collating the floating facts concerning this spectre,
allege that the body of the trooper, having been buried in the church-
yard, the ghost rides forth to the scene of battle in nightly quest of his
head; and that the rushing speed with which he sometimes passes along
the Hollow, like a midnight blast, is owing to his being belated, and in
a hurry to get back to the church-yard before daybreak.

Such is the general purport of this legendary superstition, which
has furnished materials for many a wild story in that region of shadows;
and the spectre is known, at all the country firesides, by the name of
the Headless Horseman of Sleepy Hollow.

It is remarkable that the visionary propensity I have mentioned is
not confined to the native inhabitants of the valley, but is unconsciously
imbibed by every one who resides there for a time. However wide awake
they may have been before they entered that sleepy region, they are sure,
in a little time, to inhale the witching influence of the air, and begin
to grow imaginative—to dream dreams, and see apparitions.

I mention this peaceful spot with all possible laud; for it is in such
little retired Dutch valleys, found here and there embosomed in the
great State of New-York, that population, manners, and customs, remain fixed; while the great torrent of migration and improvement,
which is making such incessant changes in other parts of this restless
country, sweeps by them unobserved. They are like those little nooks
of still water which border a rapid stream; where we may see the straw
and bubble riding quietly at anchor, or slowly revolving in their mimic
harbor, undisturbed by the rush of the passing current. Though many

years have elapsed since I trod the drowsy shades of Sleepy Hollow, yet I question whether I should not still find the same trees and the same families vegetating in its sheltered bosom.

In this by-place of nature, there abode, in a remote period of American history, that is to say, some thirty years since, a worthy wight of the name of Ichabod Crane; who sojourned, or, as he expressed it, 'tarried,' in Sleepy Hollow, for the purpose of instructing the children of the vicinity. He was a native of Connecticut; a State which supplies the Union with pioneers for the mind as well as for the forest, and sends forth yearly its legions of frontier woodsmen and country schoolmasters. The cognomen of Crane was not inapplicable to his person. He was tall, but exceedingly lank, with narrow shoulders, long arms and legs, hands that dangled a mile out of his sleeves, feet that might have served for shovels, and his whole frame most loosely hung together. His head was small, and flat at top, with huge ears, large green glassy eyes, and a long snipe nose, so that it looked like a weather-cock, perched upon his spindle neck, to tell which way the wind blew. To see him striding along the profile of a hill on a windy day, with his clothes bagging and fluttering about him, one might have mistaken him for the genius of famine descending upon the earth, or some scarecrow eloped from a cornfield.

His school-house was a low building of one large room, rudely constructed of logs; the windows partly glazed, and partly patched with leaves of old copy-books. It was most ingeniously secured at vacant hours, by a withe twisted in the handle of the door, and stakes set against the window shutters; so that, though a thief might get in with perfect ease, he would find some embarrassment in getting out; an idea most probably borrowed by the architect, Yost Van Houten, from the mystery of an eel-pot. The school-house stood in a rather lonely but pleasant situation, just at the foot of a woody hill, with a brook running close by, and a formidable birch tree growing at one end of it. From hence the low murmur of his pupils' voices, conning over their lessons, might be heard in a drowsy summer's day, like the hum of a bee-hive; interrupted now and then by the authoritative voice of the master, in the tone of menace or command; or, peradventure, by the appalling sound of the birch, as he urged some tardy loiterer along the flowery path of knowledge. Truth to say, he was a conscientious man, and ever bore in mind the golden maxim, 'Spare the rod and spoil the child.'—Ichabod Crane's scholars certainly were not spoiled.

I would not have it imagined, however, that he was one of those cruel potentates of the school, who joy in the smart of their subjects; on the contrary, he administered justice with discrimination rather than severity; taking the burthen off the backs of the weak, and laying it on those of the strong. Your mere puny stripling, that winced at the least flourish of the rod, was passed by with indulgence; but the claims of justice were satisfied by inflicting a double portion on some little, tough, wrong-headed, broad-skirted Dutch urchin, who sulked and swelled and grew dogged and sullen beneath the birch. All this he called 'doing his duty by their parents'; and he never inflicted a chastisement without following it by the assurance, so consolatory to the smarting urchin, that 'he would remember it, and thank him for it the longest day he had to live.'

When school hours were over, he was even the companion and playmate of the larger boys; and on holiday afternoons would convoy some of the smaller ones home, who happened to have pretty sisters, or good housewives for mothers, noted for the comforts of the cupboard. Indeed it behooved him to keep on good terms with his pupils. The revenue arising from his school was small, and would have been scarcely sufficient to furnish him with daily bread, for he was a huge feeder, and though lank, had the dilating powers of an anaconda; but to help out his maintenance, he was, according to country custom in those parts, boarded and lodged at the houses of the farmers, whose children he instructed. With these he lived successively a week at a time; thus going the rounds of the neighborhood, with all his worldly effects tied up in a cotton handkerchief.

That all this might not be too onerous on the purses of his rustic patrons, who are apt to consider the costs of schooling a grievous burden, and school-masters as mere drones, he had various ways of rendering himself both useful and agreeable. He assisted the farmers occasionally in the lighter labors of their farms; helped to make hay; mended the fences; took the horses to water; drove the cows from pasture; and cut wood for the winter fire. He laid aside, too, all the dominant dignity and absolute sway with which he lorded it in his little empire, the school, and became wonderfully gentle and ingratiating. He found favor in the eyes of the mothers, by petting the children, particularly the youngest; and like the lion bold, which whilom so magnanimously the lamb did hold, he would sit with a child on one knee, and rock a cradle with his foot for whole hours together.

In addition to his other vocations, he was the singing-master of the neighborhood, and picked up many bright shillings by instructing the young folks in psalmody. It was a matter of no little vanity to him, on Sundays, to take his station in front of the church gallery, with a band of chosen singers; where, in his own mind, he completely carried away the palm from the parson. Certain it is, his voice resounded far above all the rest of the congregation; and there are peculiar quavers still to be heard in that church, and which may even be heard half a mile off, quite to the opposite side of the mill-pond, on a still Sunday morning, which are said to be legitimately descended from the nose of Ichabod Crane. Thus, by divers little make-shifts in that ingenious way which is commonly denominated 'by hook and by crook', the worthy pedagogue got on tolerably enough, and was thought, by all who understood nothing of the labor of headwork, to have a wonderfully easy life of it.

The schoolmaster is generally a man of some importance in the female circle of a rural neighborhood; being considered a kind of idle gentlemanlike personage, of vastly superior taste and accomplishments to the rough country swains, and, indeed, inferior in learning only to the parson. His appearance, therefore, is apt to occasion some little stir at the tea-table of a farmhouse, and the addition of a supernumerary dish of cakes or sweetmeats, or, peradventure, the parade of a silver tea-pot. Our man of letters, therefore, was peculiarly happy in the smiles of all the country damsels. How he would figure among them in the church-yard, between services on Sundays! gathering grapes for them from the wild vines that over-run the surrounding trees; reciting for their amusement all the epitaphs on the tombstones; or sauntering, with a whole bevy of them, along the banks of the adjacent mill-pond; while the more bashful country bumpkins hung sheepishly back, envying his superior elegance and address.

From his half itinerant life, also, he was a kind of travelling gazette, carrying the whole budget of local gossip from house to house; so that his appearance was always greeted with satisfaction. He was, moreover, esteemed by the women as a man of great erudition, for he had read several books quite through, and was a perfect master of Cotton Mather's history of New-England Witchcraft,[2] in which, by the way, he most firmly and potently believed.

He was, in fact, an odd mixture of small shrewdness and simple credulity. His appetite for the marvellous, and his powers of digesting it, were equally extraordinary; and both had been increased by his residence in this spellbound region. No tale was too gross or monstrous for his capacious swallow. It was often his delight, after his school was dismissed in the afternoon, to stretch himself on the rich bed of clover, bordering the little brook that whimpered by his school-house, and there con over old Mather's direful tales, until the gathering dusk of the evening made the printed page a mere mist before his eyes. Then, as he wended his way, by swamp and stream and awful woodland, to the farmhouse where he happened to be quartered, every sound of nature, at that witching hour, fluttered his excited imagination: the moan of the whip-poor-will[3] from the hill-side; the boding cry of the tree-toad, that harbinger of a storm; the dreary hooting of the screech-owl, or the sudden rustling in the thicket of birds frightened from their roost. The fire-flies, too, which sparkled most vividly in the darkest places, now and then startled him, as one of uncommon brightness would stream across his path; and if, by chance, a huge blockhead of a beetle came winging his blundering flight against him, the poor varlet was ready to

[2] This is not an actual work by Cotton Mather. The reference is to one of his *Memorable Providences* (1689) or to *Wonders of the Invisible World* (169).

[3] The whip-poor-will is a bird which is only heard at night. It receives its name from its note, which is thought to resemble those words.

give up the ghost, with the idea that he was struck with a witch's token. His only resource on such occasions, either to drown thought, or drive away evil spirits, was to sing psalm tunes;—and the good people of Sleepy Hollow, as they sat by their doors of an evening, were often filled with awe, at hearing his nasal melody, 'in linked sweetness long drawn out,' floating from the distant hill, or along the dusky road.

Another of his sources of fearful pleasure was, to pass long winter evenings with the old Dutch wives, as they sat spinning by the fire, with a row of apples roasting and spluttering along the hearth, and listen to their marvellous tales of ghosts and goblins, and haunted fields, and haunted brooks, and haunted bridges, and haunted houses, and particularly of the headless horseman, or galloping Hessian of the Hollow, as they sometimes called him. He would delight them equally by his anecdotes of witchcraft, and of the direful omens and portentous sights and sounds in the air, which prevailed in the earlier times of Connecticut; and would frighten them wofully with speculations upon comets and shooting stars; and with the alarming fact that the world did absolutely turn round, and that they were half the time topsy-turvy!

But if there was a pleasure in all this, while snugly cuddling in the chimney corner of a chamber that was all of a ruddy glow from the crackling wood fire, and where, of course, no spectre dared to show his face, it was dearly purchased by the terrors of his subsequent walk homewards. What fearful shapes and shadows beset his path amidst the dim and ghastly glare of a snowy night!—With what wistful look did he eye every trembling ray of light streaming across the waste fields from some distant window!—How often was he appalled by some shrub covered with snow, which, like a sheeted spectre, beset his very path!— How often did he shrink with curdling awe at the sound of his own steps on the frosty crust beneath his feet; and dread to look over his shoulder, lest he should behold some uncouth being tramping close behind him!—and how often was he thrown into complete dismay by some rushing blast, howling among the trees, in the idea that it was the Galloping Hessian on one of his nightly scourings!

All these, however, were mere terrors of the night, phantoms of the mind that walk in darkness; and though he had seen many spectres in his time, and been more than once beset by Satan in divers shapes, in his lonely perambulations, yet daylight put an end to all these evils; and he would have passed a pleasant life of it, in despite of the devil and all his works, if his path had not been crossed by a being that causes more perplexity to mortal man than ghosts, goblins, and the whole race of witches put together, and that was—a woman.

Among the musical disciples who assembled, one evening in each week, to receive his instructions in psalmody, was Katrina Van Tassel, the daughter and only child of a substantial Dutch farmer. She was a blooming lass of fresh eighteen; plump as a partridge; ripe and melting and rosy cheeked as one of her father's peaches, and universally famed, not merely for her beauty, but her vast expectations. She was withal a little of a coquette, as might be perceived even in her dress, which was a mixture of ancient and modern fashions, as most suited to set off her charms. She wore the ornaments of pure yellow gold, which her great-great-grandmother had brought over from Saardam[4]; the tempting stomacher of the olden time; and withal a provokingly short petticoat, to display the prettiest foot and ankle in the country round.

Ichabod Crane had a soft and foolish heart towards the sex; and it is not to be wondered at, that so tempting a morsel soon found favor in his eyes; more especially after he had visited her in her paternal mansion. Old Baltus Van Tassel was a perfect picture of a thriving, contented, liberal-hearted farmer. He seldom, it is true, sent either his eyes or his thoughts beyond the boundaries of his own farm; but within those every thing was snug, happy, and well-conditioned. He was satisfied with his wealth, but not proud of it; and piqued himself upon the hearty abundance, rather than the style in which he lived. His stronghold was situated on the banks of the Hudson, in one of those green, sheltered, fertile nooks, in which the Dutch farmers are so fond of nestling. A great elm-tree spread its broad branches over it; at the foot of which bubbled up a spring of the softest and sweetest water, in a little well, formed of a barrel; and then stole sparkling away through the grass, to a neighboring brook, that bubbled along among alders and dwarf willows. Hard by the farmhouse was a vast barn, that might have served for a church; every window and crevice of which seemed bursting forth with the treasures of the farm; the flail was busily resounding within it from morning to night; swallows and martins skimmed twittering about the eaves; and rows of pigeons, some with one eye turned up, as if watching the weather, some with their heads under their wings, or buried in their bosoms, and others swelling, and cooing, and bowing about their dames, were enjoying the sunshine on the roof. Sleek unwieldy porkers were grunting in the repose and abundance of their pens; whence sallied forth, now and then, troops of sucking pigs, as if to snuff the air. A stately squadron of snowy geese were riding in an adjoining pond, convoying whole fleets of ducks; regiments of turkeys were gobbling through the farmyard, and guinea fowls fretting about it, like ill-tempered housewives, with their peevish discontented cry. Before the barn door strutted the gallant cock, that pattern of a husband, a warrior, and a fine gentleman, clapping his burnished wings, and crowing in the pride and gladness of his heart—sometimes tearing up the earth with his feet, and then generously calling his ever-hungry family of wives and children to enjoy the rich morsel which he had discovered.

The pedagogue's mouth watered, as he looked upon this sumptuous promise of luxurious winter fare. In his devouring mind's eye, he pic-

---

[4] A village in Holland.

tured to himself every roasting-pig running about with a pudding in his belly, and an apple in his mouth; the pigeons were snugly put to bed in a comfortable pie, and tucked in with a coverlet of crust; the geese were swimming in their own gravy; and the ducks pairing cosily in dishes, like snug married couples, with a decent competency of onion sauce. In the porkers he saw carved out the future sleek side of bacon, and juicy relishing ham; not a turkey but he beheld daintily trussed up, with its gizzard under its wing, and, peradventure, a necklace of savory sausages; and even bright chanticleer himself lay sprawling on his back, in a side-dish, with uplifted claws, as if craving that quarter which his chivalrous spirit disdained to ask while living.

As the enraptured Ichabod fancied all this and as he rolled his great green eyes over the fat meadow-lands, the rich fields of wheat, of rye, of buckwheat, and Indian corn, and the orchards burthened with ruddy fruit, which surrounded the warm tenement of Van Tassel, his heart yearned after the damsel who was to inherit these domains, and his imagination expanded with the idea, how they might be readily turned into cash, and the money invested in immense tracts of wild land, and shingle palaces in the wilderness. Nay, his busy fancy already realized his hopes, and presented to him the blooming Katrina, with a whole family of children, mounted on the top of a wagon loaded with household trumpery, with pots and kettles dangling beneath; and he beheld himself bestriding a pacing mare, with a colt at her heels, setting out for Kentucky, Tennessee, or the Lord knows where.

When he entered the house the conquest of his heart was complete. It was one of those spacious farmhouses, with high-ridged, but lowly-sloping roofs, built in the style handed down from the first Dutch settlers; the low projecting eaves forming a piazza along the front, capable of being closed up in bad weather. Under this were hung flails, harness, various utensils of husbandry, and nets for fishing in the neighboring river. Benches were built along the sides for summer use; and a great spinning-wheel at one end, and a churn at the other, showed the various uses to which this important porch might be devoted. From this piazza the wondering Ichabod entered the hall, which formed the centre of the mansion and the place of usual residence. Here, rows of resplendent pewter, ranged on a long dresser, dazzled his eyes. In one corner stood a huge bag of wool ready to be spun; in another a quantity of linsey-woolsey just from the loom; ears of Indian corn, and strings of dried apples and peaches, hung in gay festoons along the walls, mingled with the gaud of red peppers; and a door left ajar gave him a peep into the best parlor, where the claw-footed chairs, and dark mahogany tables, shone like mirrors; and irons, with their accompanying shovel and tongs, glistened from their covert of asparagus tops; mock-oranges and conch-shells decorated the mantel-piece; strings of various colored birds' eggs were suspended above it: a great ostrich egg was hung from the centre of the room, and a corner cupboard, knowingly left open, displayed immense treasures of old silver and well-mended china.

From the moment Ichabod laid his eyes upon these regions of delight, the peace of his mind was at an end, and his only study was how to gain the affections of the peerless daughter of Van Tassel. In this enterprise, however, he had more real difficulties than generally fell to the lot of a knight-errant of yore, who seldom had any thing but giants, enchanters, fiery dragons, and such like easily-conquered adversaries, to contend with; and had to make his way merely through gates of iron and brass, and walls of adamant, to the castle keep, where the lady of his heart was confined; all which he achieved as easily as a man would carve his way to the centre of a Christmas pie; and then the lady gave him her hand as a matter of course. Ichabod, on the contrary, had to win his way to the heart of a country coquette, beset with a labyrinth of whims and caprices, which were for ever presenting new difficulties and impediments; and he had to encounter a host of fearful adversaries of real flesh and blood, the numerous rustic admirers, who beset every portal to her heart; keeping a watchful and angry eye upon each other, but ready to fly out in the common cause against any new competitor.

Among these the most formidable was a burly, roaring, roystering blade, of the name of Abraham, or, according to the Dutch abbreviation, Brom Van Brunt, the hero of the country round, which rang with his feats of strength and hardihood. He was broad-shouldered and double-jointed, with short curly black hair, and a bluff, but not unpleasant countenance, having a mingled air of fun and arrogance. From his Herculean frame and great powers of limb, he had received the nick-name of BROM BONES, by which he was universally known. He was famed for great knowledge and skill in horsemanship, being as dexterous on horseback as a Tartar. He was foremost at all races and cock-fights; and, with the ascendency which bodily strength acquires in rustic life, was the umpire in all disputes, setting his hat on one side, and giving his decisions with an air and tone admitting of no gainsay or appeal. He was always ready for either a fight or a frolic; but had more mischief than ill-will in his composition; and, with all his overbearing roughness, there was a strong dash of waggish good humor at bottom. He had three or four boon companions, who regarded him as their model, and at the head of whom he scoured the country, attending every scene of feud or merriment for miles round. In cold weather he was distinguished by a fur cap, surmounted with a flaunting fox's tail; and when the folks at a country gathering descried this well-known crest at a distance, whisking about among a squad of hard riders, they always stood by for a squall. Sometimes his crew would be heard dashing along past the farmhouses at midnight, with whoop and halloo, like a troop of Don Cossacks; and the old dames, startled out of their sleep, would listen for a moment till the hurry-scurry had clattered by, and then exclaim, 'Ay, there goes Brom Bones and his gang!' The neighbors looked upon him with a mixture of awe, admiration, and good-will; and when any madcap prank, or rustic brawl, occurred in the vicinity, always shook their heads, and warranted Brom Bones was at the bottom of it.

This rantipole [5] hero had for some time singled out the blooming Katrina for the object of his uncouth gallantries, and though his amorous toyings were something like the gentle caresses and endearments of a bear, yet it was whispered that she did not altogether discourage his hopes. Certain it is, his advances were signals for rival candidates to retire, who felt no inclination to cross a lion in his amours; insomuch, that when his horse was seen tied to Van Tassel's paling, on a Sunday night, a sure sign that his master was courting, or, as it is termed, 'sparking,' within all other suitors passed by in despair, and carried the war into other quarters.

Such was the formidable rival with whom Ichabod Crane had to contend, and, considering all things, a stouter man than he would have shrunk from the competition, and a wiser man would have despaired. He had, however, a happy mixture of pliability and perseverance in his nature; he was in form and spirit like a supplejack—yielding, but tough; though he bent, he never broke; and though he bowed beneath the slightest pressure, yet, the moment it was away—jerk! he was erect, and carried his head as high as ever.

To have taken the field openly against his rival would have been madness; for he was not a man to be thwarted in his amours, any more than that stormy lover, Achilles. Ichabod, therefore, made his advances in a quiet and gently-insinuating manner. Under cover of his character of singing-master, he made frequent visits at the farmhouse; not that he had any thing to apprehend from the meddlesome interference of parents, which is so often a stumbling-block in the path of lovers. Balt Van Tassel was an easy indulgent soul; he loved his daughter better even than his pipe, and, like a reasonable man and an excellent father, let her have her way in every thing. His notable little wife, too, had enough to do to attend to her housekeeping and manage her poultry; for, as she sagely observed, ducks and geese are foolish things, and must be looked after, but girls can take care of themselves. Thus while the busy dame bustled about the house, or plied her spinning-wheel at one end of the piazza, honest Balt would sit smoking his evening pipe at the other, watching the achievements of a little wooden warrior, who, armed with a sword in each hand, was most valiantly fighting the wind on the pinnacle of the barn. In the meantime, Ichabod would carry on his suit with the daughter by the side of the spring under the great elm, or sauntering along in the twilight, that hour so favorable to the lover's eloquence.

I profess not to know how women's hearts are wooed and won. To

---

[5] A rare word meaning wild.

me they have always been matters of riddle and admiration. Some seem
to have but one vulnerable point, or door of access; while others have a
thousand avenues, and may be captured in a thousand different ways.
It is a great triumph of skill to gain the former, but a still greater proof
of generalship to maintain possession of the latter, for the man must
battle for his fortress at every door and window. He who wins a thousand common hearts is therefore entitled to some renown; but he who
keeps undisputed sway over the heart of a coquette, is indeed a hero.
Certain it is, this was not the case with the redoubtable Brom Bones;
and from the moment Ichabod Crane made his advances, the interests
of the former evidently declined; his horse was no longer seen tied at
the palings on Sunday nights, and a deadly feud gradually arose between him and the preceptor of Sleepy Hollow.

Brom, who had a degree of rough chivalry in his nature, would fain
have carried matters to open warfare, and have settled their pretensions
to the lady, according to the mode of those most concise and simple
reasons, the knights-errant of yore—by single combat; but Ichabod was
too conscious of the superior might of his adversary to enter the lists
against him: he had overheard a boast of Bones, that he would 'double
the schoolmaster up, and lay him on a shelf of his own school-house;'
and he was too wary to give him an opportunity. There was something
extremely provoking in this obstinately pacific system; it left Brom no
alternative but to draw upon the funds of rustic waggery in his disposition, and to play off boorish practical jokes upon his rival. Ichabod
became the object of whimsical persecution to Bones, and his gang of
rough riders. They harried his hitherto peaceful domains; smoked out
his singing school, by stopping up the chimney; broke into the school-
house at night, in spite of its formidable fastenings of withe and window stakes, and turned every thing topsy-turvy: so that the poor schoolmaster began to think all the witches in the country held their meetings
there. But what was still more annoying, Brom took all opportunities of
turning him into ridicule in presence of his mistress, and had a scoundrel dog whom he taught to whine in the most ludicrous manner, and
introduced as a rival of Ichabod's to instruct her in psalmody.

In this way matters went on for some time, without producing any
material effect on the relative situation of the contending powers. On
a fine autumnal afternoon, Ichabod, in pensive mood, sat enthroned on
a lofty stool whence he usually watched all the concerns of his little
literary realm. In his hand he swayed a ferule, that sceptre of despotic
power; the birch of justice reposed on three nails, behind the throne, a
constant terror to evil doers; while on the desk before him might be
seen sundry contraband articles and prohibited weapons, detected upon
the persons of idle urchins; such as half-munched apples, popguns,
whirligigs, fly-cages, and whole legions of rampant little paper game-
cocks. Apparently there had been some appalling act of justice recently
inflicted, for his scholars were all busily intent upon their books, or slyly

whispering behind them with one eye kept upon the master; and a kind of buzzing stillness reigned throughout the school-room. It was suddenly interrupted by the appearance of a Negro, in tow-cloth jacket and trowsers, a round-crowned fragment of a hat, like the cap of Mercury,[6] and mounted on the back of a ragged, wild, half-broken colt, which he managed with a rope by way of halter. He came clattering up to the school door with an invitation to Ichabod to attend a merry-making or 'quilting frolic', to be held that evening at Mynheer Van Tassel's; and having delivered his message with that air of importance, and effort at fine language, which a Negro is apt to display on petty embassies of the kind, he dashed over the brook, and was seen scampering away up the hollow, full of the importance and hurry of his mission.

All was now bustle and hubbub in the late quiet school-room. The scholars were hurried through their lessons, without stopping at trifles; those who were nimble skipped over half with impunity, and those who were tardy, had a smart application now and then in the rear, to quicken their speed, or help them over a tall word. Books were flung aside without being put away on the shelves, inkstands were overturned, benches thrown down, and the whole school was turned loose an hour before the usual time; bursting forth like a legion of young imps, yelping and racketing about the green, in joy at their early emancipation.

The gallant Ichabod now spent at least an extra half hour at his toilet, brushing and furbishing up his best, and indeed only suit of rusty black, and arranging his looks by a bit of broken looking-glass, that hung up in the school-house. That he might make his appearance before his mistress in the true style of a cavalier, he borrowed a horse from the farmer with whom he was domiciliated, a choleric old Dutchman, of the name of Hans Van Ripper, and, thus gallantly mounted, issued forth, like a knight-errant in quest of adventures. But it is meet I should, in the true spirit of romantic story, give some account of the looks and equipments of my hero and his steed. The animal he bestrode was a broken-down plough-horse, that had outlived almost every thing but his viciousness. He was gaunt and shagged, with a ewe neck and a head like a hammer; his rusty mane and tail were tangled and knotted with burrs; one eye had lost its pupil, and was glaring and spectral; but the other had the gleam of a genuine devil in it. Still he must have had fire and mettle in his day, if we may judge from the name he bore of Gunpowder. He had, in fact, been a favorite steed of his master's, the choleric Van Ripper, who was a furious rider, and had infused, very probably, some of his own spirit into the animal; for, old and broken-down as he looked, there was more of the lurking devil in him than in any young filly in the country.

Ichabod was a suitable figure for such a steed. He rode with short stirrups, which brought his knees nearly up to the pommel of the

[6] A winged hat, symbol of speed as messenger of the Greek gods.

saddle; his sharp elbows stuck out like grasshoppers'; he carried his whip perpendicularly in his hand, like a sceptre, and, as his horse jogged on, the motion of his arms was not unlike the flapping of a pair of wings. A small wool hat rested on the top of his nose, for so his scanty strip of forehead might be called; and the skirts of his black coat fluttered out almost to the horse's tail. Such was the appearance of Ichabod and his steed, as they shambled out of the gate of Hans Van Ripper, and it was altogether such an apparition as is seldom to be met with in broad daylight.

It was, as I have said, a fine autumnal day, the sky was clear and serene, and nature wore that rich and golden livery which we always associate with the idea of abundance. The forests had put on their sober brown and yellow, while some trees of the tenderer kind had been nipped by the frosts into brilliant dyes of orange, purple, and scarlet. Streaming files of wild ducks began to make their appearance high in the air; the bark of the squirrel might be heard from the groves of beech and hickory nuts, and the pensive whistle of the quail at intervals from the neighbouring stubble-field.

The small birds were taking their farewell banquets. In the fulness of their revelry, they fluttered, chirping and frolicking, from bush to bush, and tree to tree, capricious from the very profusion and variety around them. There was the honest cock-robin, the favorite game of stripling sportsmen, with its loud querulous note; and the twittering blackbirds flying in sable clouds; and the golden-winged woodpecker, with his crimson crest, his broad black gorget, and splendid plumage; and the cedar bird, with its red-tipt wings and yellow-tipt tail, and its little monteiro cap of feathers; and the blue jay, that noisy coxscomb, in his gay light-blue coat and white under-clothes; screaming and chattering, nodding and bobbing and bowing, and pretending to be on good terms with every songster of the grove.

As Ichabod jogged slowly on his way, his eye, ever open to every symptom of culinary abundance, ranged with delight over the treasures of jolly autumn. On all sides he beheld vast store of apples; some hanging in oppressive opulence on the trees; some gathered into baskets and barrels for the market; others heaped up in rich piles for the cider-press. Farther on he beheld great fields of Indian corn, with its golden ears peeping from their leafy coverts, and holding out the promise of cakes and hasty pudding; and the yellow pumpkins lying beneath them, turning up their fair round bellies to the sun, and giving ample prospects of the most luxurious of pies; and anon he passed the fragrant buckwheat fields, breathing the odor of the bee-hive, and as he beheld them, soft anticipation stole over his mind of dainty slapjacks, well buttered, and garnished with honey or treacle, by the delicate little dimpled hand of Katrina Van Tassel.

Thus feeding his mind with many sweet thoughts and 'sugar suppositions,' he journeyed along the sides of a range of hills which look out upon some of the goodliest scenes of the mighty Hudson. The sun gradually wheeled his broad disk down into the west. The wide bosom of the Tappan Zee lay motionless and glassy, excepting that here and there a gentle undulation waved and prolonged the blue shadow of the distant mountain. A few amber clouds floated in the sky, without a breath of air to move them. The horizon was of a fine golden tint, changing gradually into a pure apple green, and from that into the deep blue of the mid-heaven. A slanting ray lingered on the woody crests of the precipices that overhung some parts of the river, giving greater depth to the dark-gray and purple of their rocky sides. A sloop was loitering in the distance, dropping slowly down with the tide, her sail hanging uselessly against the mast; and as the reflection of the sky gleamed along the still water, it seemed as if the vessel was suspended in the air.

It was toward evening that Ichabod arrived at the castle of the Heer Van Tassel, which he found thronged with the pride and flower of the adjacent country. Old farmers, a spare leathern-faced race, in homespun coats and breeches, blue stockings, huge shoes, and magnificent pewter buckles. Their brisk withered little dames, in close crimped caps, long-waisted short-gowns, homespun petticoats, with scissors and pincushions, and gay calico pockets hanging on the outside. Buxom lasses, almost as antiquated as their mothers, excepting where a straw hat, a fine ribbon or perhaps a white frock, gave symptoms of city innovation. The sons, in short square-skirted coats with rows of stupendous brass buttons, and their hair generally queued in the fashion of the times, especially if they could procure an eel-skin for the purpose, it being esteemed, throughout the country, as a potent nourisher and strengthener of the hair.

Brom Bones, however, was the hero of the scene, having come to the gathering on his favorite steed Daredevil, a creature, like himself, full of mettle and mischief, and which no one but himself could manage. He was, in fact, noted for preferring vicious animals, given to all kinds of tricks, which kept the rider in constant risk of his neck, for he held a tractable well-broken horse as unworthy of a lad of spirit.

Fain would I pause to dwell upon the world of charms that burst upon the enraptured gaze of my hero, as he entered the state parlor of Van Tassel's mansion. Not those of the bevy of buxom lasses, with their luxurious display of red and white: but the ample charms of a genuine Dutch country tea-table, in the sumptuous time of autumn. Such heaped-up platters of cakes of various and almost indescribable kinds, known only to experienced Dutch housewives! There was the doughty doughnut, the tenderer oly koek, and the crisp and crumbling cruller; sweet cakes and short cakes, ginger cakes and honey cakes, and the whole family of cakes. And then there were apple pies and peach pies and pumpkin pies; besides slices of ham and smoked beef; and moreover delectable dishes of preserved plums, and peaches, and pears, and quinces; not to mention broiled shad and roasted chickens; together with bowls of milk and cream, all mingled higgledy-piggledy, pretty much as I have enumerated them, with the motherly tea-pot sending up its clouds of vapor from the midst—Heaven bless the mark! I want breath and time to discuss this banquet as it deserves, and am too eager to get on with my story. Happily, Ichabod Crane was not in so great a hurry as his historian, but did ample justice to every dainty.

He was a kind and thankful creature, whose heart dilated in proportion as his skin was filled with good cheer; and whose spirits rose with eating as some men's do with drink. He could not help, too, rolling his large eyes round him as he ate, and chuckling with the possibility that he might one day be lord of all this scene of almost unimaginable luxury and splendor. Then, he thought, how soon he'd turn his back upon the old school-house; snap his fingers in the face of Hans Van Ripper, and every other niggardly patron, and kick any itinerant pedagogue out of doors that should dare to call him comrade!

Old Baltus Van Tassel moved about among his guests with a face dilated with content and good humor, round and jolly as the harvest moon. His hospitable attentions were brief, but expressive, being confined to a shake of the hand, a slap on the shoulder, a loud laugh, and a pressing invitation to 'fall to, and help themselves.'

And now the sound of the music from the common room, or hall, summoned to the dance. The musician was an old grayheaded Negro, who had been the itinerant orchestra of the neighborhood for more than half a century. His instrument was as old and battered as himself. The greater part of the time he scraped on two or three strings, accompanying every movement of the bow with a motion of the head; bowing almost to the ground, and stamping with his foot whenever a fresh couple were to start.

Ichabod prided himself upon his dancing as much as upon his vocal powers. Not a limb, not a fibre about him was idle; and to have seen his loosely hung frame in full motion, and clattering about the room, you would have thought Saint Vitus himself, that blessed patron of the dance, was figuring before you in person. He was the admiration of all the Negroes; who having gathered, of all ages and sizes, from the farm and the neighborhood, stood forming a pyramid of shining black faces at every door and window, gazing with delight at the scene, rolling their white eye-balls, and showing grinning rows of ivory from ear to ear. How could the flogger of urchins be otherwise than animated and joyous? the lady of his heart was his partner in the dance, and smiling graciously in reply to all his amorous oglings; while Brom Bones, sorely smitten with love and jealousy, sat brooding by himself in one corner.

When the dance was at an end, Ichabod was attracted to a knot of the sager folks, who, with old Van Tassel, sat smoking at one end of the piazza, gossiping over former times, and drawing out long stories about the war.

This neighborhood, at the time of which I am speaking, was one of those highly-favored places which abound with chronicle and great men. The British and American line had run near it during the war; it had, therefore, been the scene of marauding, and infested with refugees, cow-boys, and all kinds of border chivalry. Just sufficient time had elapsed to enable each story-teller to dress up his tale with a little becoming fiction, and, in the indistinctness of his recollection, to make himself the hero of every exploit.

There was the story of Doffue Martling, a large blue-bearded Dutchman, who had nearly taken a British frigate with an old iron nine-pounder from a mud breastwork, only that his gun burst at the sixth discharge. And there was an old gentleman who shall be nameless, being too rich a mynheer to be lightly mentioned, who, in the battle of Whiteplains, being an excellent master of defence, parried a musket ball with a small sword, insomuch that he absolutely felt it whiz round the blade, and glance off at the hilt: in proof of which, he was ready at any time to show the sword, with the hilt a little bent. There were several more that had been equally great in the field, not one of whom but was persuaded that he had a considerable hand in bringing the war to a happy termination.

But all these were nothing to the tales of ghosts and apparitions that succeeded. The neighborhood is rich in legendary treasures of the kind. Local tales and superstitions thrive best in these sheltered long-settled retreats; but are trampled under foot by the shifting throng that forms the population of most of our country places. Besides, there is no encouragement for ghosts in most of our villages, for they have scarcely had time to finish their first nap, and turn themselves in their graves, before their surviving friends have travelled away from the neighborhood; so that when they turn out at night to walk their rounds, they have no acquaintance left to call upon. This is perhaps the reason why we so seldom hear of ghosts except in our long-established Dutch communities.

The immediate cause, however, of the prevalence of supernatural stories in these parts, was doubtless owing to the vicinity of Sleepy Hollow. There was a contagion in the very air that blew from that haunted region; it breathed forth an atmosphere of dreams and fancies infecting all the land. Several of the Sleepy Hollow people were present at Van Tassel's, and, as usual, were doling out their wild and wonderful legends. Many dismal tales were told about funeral trains, and mourning cries and wailings heard and seen about the great tree where the unfortunate Major André [7] was taken, and which stood in the neighborhood. Some mention was made also of the woman in white, that haunted the dark glen at Raven Rock, and was often heard to shriek on winter nights before a storm, having perished there in the snow. The

[7] Captured during the American Revolution with plans of West Point and proof that Benedict Arnold had committed treason.

chief part of the stories, however, turned upon the favorite spectre of
Sleepy Hollow, the headless horseman, who had been heard several
times of late, patrolling the country; and, it was said, tethered his horse
nightly among the graves in the churchyard.

The sequestered situation of this church seems always to have made
it a favorite haunt of troubled spirits. It stands on a knoll, surrounded
by locust-trees and lofty elms, from among which its decent, whitewashed walls shine modestly forth, like Christian purity beaming
through the shades of retirement. A gentle slope descends from it to a
silver sheet of water, bordered by high trees, between which, peeps may
be caught at the blue hills of the Hudson. To look upon its grass-grown
yard, where the sunbeams seem to sleep so quietly, one would think that
there at least the dead might rest in peace. On one side of the church
extends a wide woody dell, along which raves a large brook among
broken rocks and trunks of fallen trees. Over a deep black part of the
stream, not far from the church, was formerly thrown a wooden bridge;
the road that led to it, and the bridge itself, were thickly shaded by
overhanging trees, which cast a gloom about it, even in the daytime;
but occasioned a fearful darkness at night. This was one of the favourite haunts of the headless horseman; and the place where he was most
frequently encountered. The tale was told of old Brouwer, a most
heretical disbeliever in ghosts, how he met the horseman returning from
his foray into Sleepy Hollow, and was obliged to get up behind him;
how they galloped over bush and brake, over hill and swamp, until they
reached the bridge; when the horseman suddenly turned into a skeleton,
threw old Brouwer into the brook, and sprang away over the tree-tops
with a clap of thunder.

This story was immediately matched by a thrice marvellous adventure of Brom Bones, who made light of the galloping Hessian as an
arrant jockey. He affirmed that, on returning one night from the neighboring village of Sing Sing, he had been overtaken by this midnight
trooper; that he had offered to race with him for a bowl of punch, and
should have won it too, for Daredevil beat the goblin horse all hollow,
but, just as they came to the church-bridge, the Hessian bolted, and
vanished in a flash of fire.

All these tales, told in that drowsy undertone with which men talk
in the dark, the countenances of the listeners only now and then receiving a casual gleam from the glare of a pipe, sank deep in the mind of
Ichabod. He repaid them in kind with large extracts from his invaluable
author, Cotton Mather, and added many marvellous events that had
taken place in his native State of Connecticut, and fearful sights which
he had seen in his nightly walks about Sleepy Hollow.

The revel now gradually broke up. The old farmers gathered together
their families in their wagons, and were heard for some time rattling
along the hollow roads, and over the distant hills. Some of the damsels
mounted on pillions behind their favorite swains, and their light-hearted

laughter, mingling with the clatter of hoofs, echoed along the silent woodlands, sounding fainter and fainter until they gradually died away—and the late scene of noise and frolic was all silent and deserted. Ichabod only lingered behind, according to the custom of country lovers, to have a tête-à-tête with the heiress; fully convinced that he was now on the high road to success. What passed at this interview I will not pretend to say, for in fact I do not know. Something, however, I fear me, must have gone wrong, for he certainly sallied forth, after no very great interval, with an air quite desolate and chop-fallen.—Oh these women! these women! Could that girl have been playing off any of her coquettish tricks?—Was her encouragement of the poor pedagogue all a mere sham to secure her conquest of his rival?—Heaven only knows, not I!—Let it suffice to say, Ichabod stole forth with the air of one who had been sacking a hen-roost, rather than a fair lady's heart. Without looking to the right or left to notice the scene of rural wealth, on which he had so often gloated, he went straight to the stable, and with several hearty cuffs and kicks, roused his steed most uncourteously from the comfortable quarters in which he was soundly sleeping, dreaming of mountains of corn and oats, and whole valleys of timothy and clover.

It was the very witching time of night that Ichabod, heavy-hearted and crest-fallen, pursued his travel homewards, along the sides of the lofty hills which rise above Tarry Town, and which he had traversed so cheerily in the afternoon. The hour was as dismal as himself. Far below him, the Tappan Zee spread its dusky and indistinct waste of waters, with here and there the tall mast of a sloop, riding quietly at anchor under the land. In the dead hush of midnight, he could even hear the barking of the watch dog from the opposite shore of the Hudson; but it was so vague and faint as only to give an idea of his distance from this faithful companion of man. Now and then, too, the long-drawn crowing of a cock, accidentally awakened, would sound far, far off, from some farmhouse away among the hills—but it was like a dreaming sound in his ear. No signs of life occurred near him, but occasionally the melancholy chirp of a cricket, or perhaps the guttural twang of a bull-frog, from a neighboring marsh, as if sleeping uncomfortably, and turning suddenly in his bed.

All the stories of ghosts and goblins that he had heard in the afternoon, now came crowding upon his recollection. The night grew darker and darker; the stars seemed to sink deeper in the sky, and driving clouds occasionally hid them from his sight. He had never felt so lonely and dismal. He was, moreover, approaching the very place where many of the scenes of the ghost stories had been laid. In the centre of the road stood an enormous tulip-tree, which towered like a giant above all the other trees of the neighborhood, and formed a kind of landmark. Its limbs were gnarled, and fantastic, large enough to form trunks for ordinary trees, twisting down almost to the earth, and rising again into the air. It was connected with the tragical story of the unfortunate André, who had been taken prisoner hard by; and was universally known by the name of Major André's tree. The common people regarded it with a mixture of respect and superstition, partly out of sympathy for the fate of its ill-starred namesake, and partly from the tales of strange sights and doleful lamentations told concerning it.

As Ichabod approached this fearful tree, he began to whistle; he thought his whistle was answered—it was but a blast sweeping sharply through the dry branches. As he approached a little nearer, he thought he saw something white, hanging in the midst of the tree—he paused and ceased whistling; but on looking more narrowly, perceived that it was a place where the tree had been scathed by lightning, and the white wood laid bare. Suddenly he heard a groan—his teeth chattered and his knees smote against the saddle: it was but the rubbing of one huge bough upon another, as they were swayed about by the breeze. He passed the tree in safety, but new perils lay before him.

About two hundred yards from the tree a small brook crossed the road, and ran into a marshy and thickly-wooded glen, known by the name of Wiley's swamp. A few rough logs, laid side by side, served for a bridge over this stream. On that side of the road where the brook entered the wood, a group of oaks and chestnuts, matted thick with wild grapevines, threw a cavernous gloom over it. To pass this bridge was the severest trial. It was at this identical spot that the unfortunate André was captured, and under the covert of those chestnuts and vines were the sturdy yeomen concealed who surprised him. This has ever since been considered a haunted stream, and fearful are the feelings of the schoolboy who has to pass it alone after dark.

As he approached the stream, his heart began to thump; he summoned up, however, all his resolution, gave his horse half a score of kicks in the ribs, and attempted to dash briskly across the bridge; but instead of starting forward, the perverse old animal made a lateral movement, and ran broadside against the fence. Ichabod, whose fears increased with the delay, jerked the reins on the other side, and kicked lustily with the contrary foot: it was all in vain; his steed started, it is true, but it was only to plunge to the opposite side of the road into a thicket of brambles and alder bushes. The schoolmaster now bestowed both whip and heel upon the starveling ribs of old Gunpowder, who dashed forward, snuffling and snorting, but came to a stand just by the bridge, with a suddenness that had nearly sent his rider sprawling over his head. Just at this moment a plashy tramp by the side of the bridge caught the sensitive ear of Ichabod. In the dark shadow of the grove, on the margin of the brook, he beheld something huge, misshapen, black and towering. It stirred not, but seemed gathered up in the gloom, like some gigantic monster ready to spring upon the traveller.

The hair of the affrighted pedagogue rose upon his head with terror. What was to be done? To turn and fly was now too late; and besides, what chance was there of escaping ghost or goblin, if such it was, which could ride upon the wings of the wind? Summoning up, therefore, a show of courage, he demanded in stammering accents— 'Who are you?' He received no reply. He repeated his demand in a still more agitated voice. Still there was no answer. Once more he cudgelled the sides of the inflexible Gunpowder, and, shutting his eyes, broke forth with involuntary fervor into a psalm tune. Just then the shadowy object of alarm put itself in motion, and, with a scramble and a bound, stood at once in the middle of the road. Though the night was dark and dismal, yet the form of the unknown might now in some degree be ascertained. He appeared to be a horseman of large dimensions, and mounted on a black horse of powerful frame. He made no offer of molestation or sociability, but kept aloof on one side of the road, jogging along on the blind side of old Gunpowder, who had now got over his fright and waywardness.

Ichabod, who had no relish for this strange midnight companion, and bethought himself of the adventure of Brom Bones with the Galloping Hessian, now quickened his steed, in hopes of leaving him behind. The stranger, however, quickened his horse to an equal pace. Ichabod pulled up, and fell into a walk, thinking to lag behind—the other did the same. His heart began to sink within him; he endeavoured to resume his psalm tune, but his parched tongue clove to the roof of his mouth, and he could not utter a stave. There was something in the moody and dogged silence of this pertinacious companion, that was mysterious and appalling. It was soon fearfully accounted for. On mounting a rising ground, which brought the figure of his fellow-traveller in relief against the sky, gigantic in height, and muffled in a cloak, Ichabod was horror-struck, on perceiving that he was headless!—but his horror was still more increased, on observing that the head, which should have rested on his shoulders, was carried before him on the pommel of the saddle: his terror rose to desperation; he rained a shower of kicks and blows upon Gunpowder, hoping, by a sudden movement, to give his companion the slip—but the spectre started full jump with him. Away then they dashed, through thick and thin; stones flying, and sparks flashing at every bound. Ichabod's flimsy garments fluttering in the air, as he stretched his long lank body away over his horse's head, in the eagerness of his flight.

They had now reached the road which turns off to Sleepy Hollow; but Gunpowder, who seemed possessed with a demon, instead of keeping up it, made an opposite turn, and plunged headlong down hill to the left. This road leads through a sandy hollow, shaded by trees for about a quarter of a mile, where it crosses the bridge famous in goblin story, and just beyond swells the green knoll on which stands the white-washed church.

As yet the panic of the steed had given his unskilful rider an apparent advantage in the chase; but just as he had got half way through the hollow, the girths of the saddle gave way, and he felt it slipping from under him. He seized it by the pommel, and endeavored to hold it firm, but in vain; and had just time to save himself by clasping old Gunpowder round the neck, when the saddle fell to the earth, and he heard it trampled under foot by his pursuer. For a moment the terror of Hans Van Ripper's wrath passed across his mind—for it was his Sunday saddle; but this was no time for petty fears; the goblin was hard on his haunches; and (unskilful rider that he was!) he had much ado to maintain his seat; sometimes slipping on one side, sometimes on another, and sometimes jolted on the high ridge of his horse's backbone, with a violence that he verily feared would cleave him asunder.

An opening in the trees now cheered him with the hopes that the church bridge was at hand. The wavering reflection of a silver star in the bosom of the brook told him that he was not mistaken. He saw the walls of the church dimly glaring under the trees beyond. He recollected that the place where Brom Bones's ghostly competitor had disappeared. 'If I can but reach that bridge,' thought Ichabod, 'I am safe.' Just then he heard the black steed panting and blowing close behind him; he even fancied that he felt his hot breath. Another convulsive kick in the ribs, and old Gunpowder sprang upon the bridge; he thundered over the resounding planks; he gained the opposite side; and now Ichabod cast a look behind to see if his pursuer should vanish, according to rule, in a flash of fire and brimstone. Just then he saw the goblin rising in his stirrups, and in the very act of hurling his head at him. Ichabod endeavored to dodge the horrible missile, but too late. It encountered his cranium with a tremendous crash—he was tumbled headlong into the dust, and Gunpowder, the black steed, and the goblin rider, passed by like a whirlwind.

The next morning the old horse was found without his saddle, and with the bridle under his feet, soberly cropping the grass at his master's gate. Ichabod did not make his appearance at breakfast—dinner-hour came, but no Ichabod. The boys assembled at the school-house, and strolled idly about the banks of the brook; but no schoolmaster. Hans Van Ripper now began to feel some uneasiness about the fate of poor Ichabod, and his saddle. An inquiry was set on foot, and after diligent investigation they came upon his traces. In one part of the road leading to the church was found the saddle trampled in the dirt; the tracks of horses' hoofs deeply dented in the road, and evidently at furious speed, were traced to the bridge, beyond which, on the bank of a broad part of the brook, where the water ran deep and black, was found the hat of the unfortunate Ichabod, and close beside it a shattered pumpkin.

The brook was searched, but the body of the schoolmaster was not to be discovered. Hans Van Ripper, as executor of his estate, examined the bundle which contained all his worldly effects. They consisted of two shirts and a half; two stocks for the neck; a pair or two of worsted stockings; an old pair of corduroy small-clothes; a rusty razor; a book of psalm tunes, full of dogs' ears; and a broken pitch-pipe. As to the books and furniture of the school-house, they belonged to the community, excepting Cotton Mather's History of Witch-craft, a New England Almanac, and a book of dreams and fortune-telling; in which last was a foolscap much scribbled and blotted in several fruitless attempts to make a copy of verses in honor of the heiress of Van Tassel. These magic books and the poetic scrawl were forthwith consigned to the flames by Hans Van Ripper; who from that time forward determined to send his children no more to school; observing, that he never knew any good come of this same reading and writing. Whatever money the schoolmaster possessed, and he had received his quarter's pay but a day or two before, he must have had about his person at the time of his disappearance.

The mysterious event caused much speculation at the church on the following Sunday. Knots of gazers and gossips were collected in the church-yard, at the bridge, and at the spot where the hat and pumpkin had been found. The stories of Brouwer, of Bones, and a whole budget of others, were called to mind; and when they had diligently considered them all, and compared them with the symptoms of the present case, they shook their heads, and came to the conclusion that Ichabod had been carried off by the galloping Hessian. As he was a bachelor, and in nobody's debt, nobody troubled his head any more about him. The school was removed to a different quarter of the hollow, and another pedagogue reigned in his stead.

It is true, an old farmer, who had been down to New-York on a visit several years after, and from whom this account of the ghostly adventure was received, brought home the intelligence that Ichabod Crane was still alive; that he had left the neighborhood, partly through fear of the goblin and Hans Van Ripper, and partly in mortification at having been suddenly dismissed by the heiress; that he had changed his quarters to a distant part of the country; had kept school and studied law at the same time, had been admitted to the bar, turned politician, electioneered, written for the newspapers, and finally had been made a justice of the Ten Pound Court. Brom Bones too, who, shortly after his rival's disappearance, conducted the blooming Katrina in triumph to the altar, was observed to look exceedingly knowing whenever the story of Ichabod was related, and always burst into a hearty laugh at the mention of the pumpkin; which led some to suspect that he knew more about the matter than he chose to tell.

The old country wives, however, who are the best judges of these matters, maintain to this day that Ichabod was spirited away by supernatural means; and it is a favorite story often told about the neighborhood round the winter evening fire. The bridge became more than ever an object of superstitious awe, and that may be the reason why the road has been altered of late years, so as to approach the church by the border of the mill-pond. The school-house being deserted, soon fell to decay, and was reported to be haunted by the ghost of the unfortunate pedagogue; and the plough boy, loitering homeward of a still summer evening, has often fancied his voice at a distance, chanting a melancholy psalm tune among the tranquil solitudes of Sleepy Hollow.

Postscript, Found in the Handwriting of Mr. Knickerbocker

The preceding Tale is given, almost in the precise words in which I heard it related at a Corporation meeting of the ancient city of Manhattoes, at which were present many of its sagest and most illustrious burghers. The narrator was a pleasant, shabby, gentlemanly old fellow, in pepper-and-salt clothes, with a sadly humorous face; and one whom I strongly suspected of being poor,—he made such efforts to be entertaining. When his story was concluded, there was much laughter and approbation, particularly from two or three deputy aldermen, who had been asleep the greater part of the time. There was, however, one tall, dry-looking old gentleman, with beetling eyebrows, who maintained a grave and rather severe face throughout: now and then folding his arms, inclining his head, and looking down upon the floor, as if turning a doubt over in his mind. He was one of your wary men, who never laugh, but upon good grounds—when they have reason and the law on their side. When the mirth of the rest of the company had subsided, and silence was restored, he leaned one arm on the elbow of his chair, and sticking the other akimbo, demanded, with a slight, but exceedingly sage motion of the head, and contraction of the brow, what was the moral of the story, and what it went to prove?

The story-teller, who was just putting a glass of wine to his lips, as a refreshment after his toils, paused for a moment, looked at his inquirer with an air of infinite deference, and, lowering the glass slowly to the table, observed, that the story was intended most logically to prove:—

'That there is no situation in life but has its advantages and pleasures—provided we will but take a joke as we find it:

'That, therefore, he that runs races with goblin troopers is likely to have rough riding of it.

'Ergo, for a country schoolmaster to be refused the hand of a Dutch heiress, is a certain step to high preferment, in the state.'

The cautious old gentleman knit his brows tenfold closer after this explanation, being sorely puzzled by the ratiocination of the syllogism; while, methought, the one in pepper-and-salt eyed him with something of a triumphant leer. At length he observed, that all this was very well, but still he thought the story a little on the extravagant—there were one or two points on which he had his doubts.

'Faith, sir,' replied the story-teller, 'as to that matter, I don't believe one half of it myself.'

WILLIAM CULLEN BRYANT (1794–1878)

Bryant grew up in a milieu that can in many ways be regarded as "characteristically American": a small town in western Massachusetts, still devout and conservative, clinging to the Calvinist faith and the simple life. His father was a country doctor, his mother a descendent of John and Priscilla Alden. In his outlook and his writing, Bryant bears the stamp of the young nation as it moves away from the earlier Puritan heritage and toward a more worldly native liberalism.

When Bryant's father took an early version of "Thanatopsis" to the North American Review, a leading magazine of the day, its editor protested, "No one on this side of the Atlantic is capable of writing such verse!" Even after the poem appeared in 1817, and a volume of Bryant's early poems had come out four years later, he was forced to continue his law practice in Great Barrington, Massachusetts; the writing of poetry hardly seemed a likely way to earn a living. In 1852 he received an offer, however, to edit the New York Review and Atheneum Magazine, and he then moved to New York City.

For the remaining years of his long life, Bryant occupied a distinguished place in American literary and journalistic life. In 1829 he became editor of the influential newspaper, the New York Evening Post, and remained with it until his death. He was a consistent spokesman for liberalism, upholding the right of collective bargaining, pleading for abolition of slavery, and contributing to the cultural life of the city. As an editor Bryant exemplified the ideal of disinterested public service which flourished among our intellectuals during the nineteenth century.

Bryant's reputation as a poet, once very high, has declined over the decades. The handful of his poems still likely to strike modern readers as first-rate have notable virtues: they are written in an unaffected and often elevated diction which breaks decisively from the latinate heaviness and pseudo-Augustan pomposities affected by earlier American poets; they reveal a genuine feeling for, and capacity to represent, the American landscape, its distinctive hues and tones, its hush of newness; and they express a world outlook of disciplined stoicism which merits respect even from those who cannot yield agreement. Matthew Arnold, the great late-nineteenth-century English critic, felt that "To a Waterfowl" was the finest lyric of its length in English, and if that now seems an overstatement, the poem nevertheless survives as a fine instance of the style of restrained romanticism Bryant developed in his early years.

His faults became more noticeable as he grew older: a tendency toward prolixity, with lines that gravely, sluggishly limp along but rarely startle or delight; an increasing gentility of sentiment, the kind of stock "high-mindedness" school teachers and obedient pupils used to associate with poetry; and a weakness for the vague sublime, a rhetoric promising more than it delivers. In Bryant's verse one can see the joined influences of eighteenth-century neoclassicism and nineteenth-century romanticism, but only rarely with the intellectual firmness of the former or the emotional fire of the latter. James Russell Lowell, in his A Fable for Critics, *put the case sharply against Bryant: ". . . Bryant, as quiet, as cool, and as dignified/ As a smooth, silent iceberg, that never is ignified." But Lowell also remarked that Bryant was the one poet of early-nineteenth-century America who knew "how much grace, strength and dignity lie in Repose." His handful of distinguished poems are marked by gentleness and purity of language, and in the house of literature there ought always to be some space for the writer of quiet voice.*

FURTHER READING

William Cullen Bryant: Representative Selections (1935) has a helpful introduction by its editor, Tremaine McDowell. A standard work is H. H. Peckham, *Gotham Yankee: A Biography of William Cullen Bryant* (1951).

Thanatopsis (1817, 1821)

        To him who in the love of Nature holds
Communion with her visible forms, she speaks
A various language; for his gayer hours
She has a voice of gladness, and a smile
And eloquence of beauty, and she glides
Into his darker musings, with a mild
And healing sympathy, that steals away
Their sharpness, ere he is aware. When thoughts
Of the last bitter hour come like a blight
Over thy spirit, and sad images   10
Of the stern agony, and shroud, and pall,
And breathless darkness, and the narrow house,
Make thee to shudder, and grow sick at heart,—
Go forth, under the open sky, and list
To Nature's teachings, while from all around—

Earth and her waters, and the depths of air,—
Comes a still voice—
     Yet a few days, and thee
The all-beholding sun shall see no more
In all his course; nor yet in the cold ground,
Where thy pale form was laid, with many tears,   20
Nor in the embrace of ocean, shall exist
Thy image. Earth, that nourished thee, shall claim
Thy growth, to be resolved to earth again,
And, lost each human trace, surrendering up
Thine individual being, shalt thou go
To mix forever with the elements,
To be a brother to the insensible rock
And to the sluggish clod, which the rude swain
Turns with his share, and treads upon. The oak
Shall send his roots abroad, and pierce they mould. 30

  Yet not to thine eternal resting-place
Shalt thou retire alone, nor couldst thou wish
Couch more magnificent. Thou shalt lie down
With patriarchs of the infant world, with kings,
The powerful of the earth, the wise, the good,
Fair forms, and hoary seers of ages past,
All in one mighty sepulchre. The hills
Rock-ribbed and ancient as the sun, the vales
Stretching in pensive quietness between;
The venerable woods—rivers that move   40
In majesty, and the complaining brooks
That make the meadows green; and, poured round all,
Old Ocean's gray and melancholy waste,—
Are but the solemn decorations all
Of the great tomb of man. The golden sun,
The planets, all the infinite host of heaven,
Are shining on the sad abodes of death,
Through the still lapse of ages. All that tread
The globe are but a handful to the tribes
That slumber in its bosom.—Take the wings 50
Of morning, pierce the Barcan wilderness,[1]
Or lose thyself in the continuous woods
Where rolls the Oregon, and hears no sound,
Save his own dashings—yet the dead are there:
And millions in those solitudes, since first
The flight of years began, have laid them down
In their last sleep—the dead reign there alone.
So shalt thou rest, and what if thou withdraw

[1] An old name for the eastern portion of Libya.

In silence from the living, and no friend
Take note of thy departure? All that breathe   *60*
Will share thy destiny. The gay will laugh
When thou are gone, the solemn brood of care
Plod on, and each one as before will chase
His favorite phantom; yet all these shall leave
Their mirth and their employments, and shall come
And make their bed with thee. As the long train
Of ages glide away, the sons of men,
The youth in life's green spring, and he who goes
In the full strength of years, matron and maid,
The speechless babe, and the gray-headed man—   *70*
Shall one by one be gathered to thy side,
By those, who in their turn shall follow them.

    So live, that when thy summons comes to join
The innumerable caravan, which moves
To that mysterious realm, where each shall take
His chamber in the silent halls of death,
Thou go not, like the quarry-slave at night,
Scourged to his dungeon, but, sustained and soothed
By an unfaltering trust, approach thy grave,
Like one who wraps the drapery of his couch   *80*
About him, and lies down to pleasant dreams.

To a Waterfowl (1818)

    Whither, 'midst falling dew,
While glow the heavens with the last steps of day,
Far, through their rosy depths, dost thou pursue
    Thy solitary way?

    Vainly the fowler's eye
Might mark thy distant flight, to do thee wrong,
As, darkly seen against the crimson sky,
    Thy figure floats along.

    Seek's thou the plashy brink
Of weedy lake, or marge of river wide,   *10*
Or where the rocking billows rise and sink
    On the chafed ocean side?

    There is a Power, whose care
Teaches thy way along that pathless coast,—
The desert and illimitable air,
    Lone wandering, but not lost.

All day thy wings have fann'd,
At that far height, the cold thin atmosphere;
Yet stoop not, weary, to the welcome land,
    Though the dark night is near.   20

And soon that toil shall end,
Soon shalt thou find a summer home, and rest,
And scream among thy fellows; reeds shall bend,
    Soon, o'er thy sheltered nest.

Thou'rt gone, the abyss of heaven
Hath swallowed up thy form, yet, on my heart
Deeply hath sunk the lesson thou hast given,
    And shall not soon depart.

He, who, from zone to zone,
Guides through the boundless sky thy certain flight,   30
In the long way that I must trace alone,
    Will lead my steps aright.

An Indian at the Burial-place of His Fathers (1824)

It is the spot I came to seek—
    My father's ancient burial-place,
Ere from these vales, ashamed and weak,
    Withdrew our wasted race.
It is the spot—I know it well—
Of which our old traditions tell.

For here the upland bank sends out
    A ridge toward the river-side;
I know the shaggy hills about,
    The meadows smooth and wide,   10
The plains, that, toward the southern sky,
Fenced east and west by mountains lie.

A white man, gazing on the scene,
    Would say a lovely spot was here,
And praise the lawns, so fresh and green,
    Between the hills so sheer.
I like it not—I would the plain
Lay in its tall old groves again.

The sheep are on the slopes around,
    The cattle in the meadows feed,   20

And laborers turn the crumbling ground,
    Or drop the yellow seed,
And prancing steeds, in trappings gay,
Whirl the bright chariot o'er the way.

Methinks it were a nobler sight
    To see these vales in woods arrayed,
Their summits in the golden light,
    Their trunks in grateful shade,
And herds of deer that bounding go
O'er hills and prostrate trees below.   *30*

And then to mark the lord of all,
    The forest hero, trained to wars,
Quivered and plumed, and lithe and tall,
    And seamed with glorious scars,
Walk forth, amid his reign, to dare
The wolf, and grapple with the bear.

This bank, in which the dead were laid,
    Was sacred when its soil was ours;
Hither the silent Indian maid
    Brought wreaths of beads and flowers,   *40*
And the gray chief and gifted seer
Worshipped the god of thunders here.

But now the wheat is green and high
    On clods that hid the warrior's breast,
And scattered in the furrows lie
    The weapons of his rest;
And there, in the loose sand, is thrown
Of his large arm the mouldering bone.

Ah, little thought the strong and brave
    Who bore their lifeless chieftain forth—   *50*
Or the young wife that weeping gave
    Her first-born to the earth,
That the pale race, who waste us now,
Among their bones should guide the plough.

They waste us—ay—like April snow
    In the warm noon, we shrink away;
And fast they follow, as we go
    Toward the setting day—
Till they shall fill the land, and we
Are driven into the Western sea.   *60*

But I behold a fearful sign,
    To which the white men's eyes are blind;

Their race may vanish hence, like mine,
    And leave no trace behind,
Save ruins o'er the region spread,
And the white stones above the dead.

Before these fields were shorn and tilled,
    Full to the brim our rivers flowed;
The melody of waters filled
    The fresh and boundless wood;   70
And torrents dashed and rivulets played,
And fountains spouted in the shade.

Those grateful sounds are heard no more,
    The springs are silent in the sun;
The rivers, by the blackened shore,
    With lessening current run;
The realm our tribes are crushed to get
May be a barren desert yet.

The Prairies (1833)

These are the gardens of the Desert, these
The unshorn fields, boundless and beautiful,
For which the speech of England has no name—
The Prairies. I behold them for the first,
And my heart swells, while the dilated sight
Takes in the encircling vastness. Lo! they stretch
In airy undulations, far away,
As if the Ocean, in his gentlest swell,
Stood still, with all his rounded billows fixed,
And motionless forever. Motionless?—   10
No—they are all unchained again. The clouds
Sweep over with their shadows, and, beneath,
The surface rolls and fluctuates to the eye; [1]
Dark hollows seem to glide along and chase
The sunny ridges. Breezes of the South!
Who toss the golden and the flame-like flowers,
And pass the prairie-hawk [2] that, poised on high,

---

[1] The prairies of the West, with an undulating surface, *rolling prairies*, as they were called, present to the unaccustomed eye a singular spectacle when the shadows of the clouds are passing rapidly over them. The face of the ground seems to fluctuate and toss like billows of the sea. *Au.*

[2] I have seen the prairie-hawk balancing himself in the air for hours together, apparently over the same spot; probably watching his prey. *Au.*

Flaps his broad wings, yet moves not—ye have played
Among the palms of Mexico and vines
Of Texas, and have crisped the limpid brooks   20
That from the fountains of Sonora [3] glide
Into the calm Pacific—have ye fanned
A nobler or a lovelier scene than this?
Man hath no part in all this glorious work:
The hand that built the firmament hath heaved
And smoothed these verdant swells, and sown their slopes
With herbage, planted them with island-groves,
And hedged them round with forests. Fitting floor
For this magnificent temple of the sky—
With flowers whose glory and whose multitude   30
Rival the constellations! The great heavens
Seem to stoop down upon the scene in love,—
A nearer vault, and of a tenderer blue,
Than that which bends above our Eastern hills.

As o'er the verdant waste I guide my steed,
Among the high rank grass that sweeps his sides
The hollow beating of his footstep seems
A sacrilegious sound. I think of those
Upon whose rest he tramples. Are they here—
The dead of other days?—and did the dust   40
Of these fair solitudes once stir with life
And burn with passion? Let the mighty mounds
That overlook the rivers, or that rise
In the dim forest crowded with old oaks,
Answer. A race, that long has passed away,
Built them; a disciplined and populous race
Heaped, with long toil, the earth, while yet the Greek
Was hewing the Pentelicus [4] to forms
Of symmetry, and rearing on its rock
The glittering Parthenon. These ample fields   50
Nourished their harvests,[5] here their herds were fed,
When haply by their stalls the bison lowed,
And bowed his manèd shoulder to the yoke.
All day this desert murmured with their toils,
Till twilight blushed, and lovers walked, and wooed
In a forgotten language, and old tunes,

[3] State in northwestern Mexico.

[4] Mountains north of Athens, in which white marble is quarried.

[5] The size and extent of the mounds in the valley of the Mississippi indicate the existence, at a remote period, of a nation once populous and laborious, and therefore probably subsisting by agriculture. *Au.*

From instruments of unremembered form,
Gave the soft winds a voice. The red-man came—
The roaming hunter-tribes, warlike and fierce,
And the mound-builders vanished from the earth.   60
The solitude of centuries untold
Has settled where they dwelt. The prairie-wolf
Hunts in their meadows, and his fresh-dug den
Yawns by my path. The gopher mines the ground
Where stood their swarming cities. All is gone;
All—save the piles of earth that hold their bones,
The platforms where they worshipped unknown gods,
The barriers which they builded from the soil
To keep the foe at bay—till o'er the walls
The wild beleaguers broke, and, one by one,   70
The strongholds of the plain were forced, and heaped
With corpses. The brown vultures of the wood
Flocked to those vast uncovered sepulchres,
And sat, unscared and silent, at their feast.
Haply some solitary fugitive,
Lurking in marsh and forest, till the sense
Of desolation and of fear became
Bitterer than death, yielded himself to die.
Man's better nature triumphed then. Kind words
Welcomed and soothed him; the rude conquerors [6]   80
Seated the captive with their chiefs; he chose
A bride among their maidens, and at length
Seemed to forget—yet ne'er forgot—the wife
Of his first love, and her sweet little ones,
Butchered, amid their shrieks, with all his race.

    Thus change the forms of being. Thus arise
Races of living things, glorious in strength,
And perish, as the quickening breath of God
Fills them, or is withdrawn. The red-man, too,
Has left the blooming wilds he ranged so long,   90
And, nearer to the Rocky Mountains, sought
A wilder hunting-ground. The beaver builds
No longer by these streams, but far away,
On waters whose blue surface ne'er gave back
The white man's face—among Missouri's Springs,
And pools whose issues swell the Oregon—
He rears his little Venice. In these plains

[6] Instances are not wanting of generosity like this among the North American Indians toward a captive or survivor of a hostile tribe on which the greatest cruelties
had been exercised. *Au.*

The bison feeds no more. Twice twenty leagues
Beyond remotest smoke of hunter's camp,
Roams the majestic brute, in herds that shake   *100*
The earth with thundering steps—yet here I meet
His ancient footprints stamped beside the pool.

    Still this great solitude is quick with life.
Myriads of insects, gaudy as the flowers
They flutter over, gentle quadrupeds,
And birds, that scarce have learned the fear of man,
Are here, and sliding reptiles of the ground,
Startlingly beautiful. The graceful deer
Bounds to the wood at my approach. The bee,
A more adventurous colonist than man,   *110*
With whom he came across the eastern deep,
Fills the savannas with his murmurings,
And hides his sweets, as in the golden age,
Within the hollow oak. I listen long
To his domestic hum, and think I hear
The sound of that advancing multitude
Which soon shall fill these deserts. From the ground
Comes up the laugh of children, the soft voice
Of maidens, and the sweet and solemn hymn
Of Sabbath worshippers. The low of herds   *120*
Blends with the rustling of the heavy grain
Over the dark brown furrows. All at once
A fresher wind sweeps by, and breaks my dream,
And I am in the wilderness alone.

The Battle-field (1837)

Once this soft turf, this rivulet's sands,
    Were trampled by a hurrying crowd,
And fiery hearts and armèd hands
    Encountered in the battle-cloud.

Ah! never shall the land forget
    How gushed the life-blood of her brave—
Gushed, warm with hope and courage yet,
    Upon the soil they fought to save.

Now all is calm, and fresh, and still;
    Alone the chirp of flitting bird,   *10*
And talk of children on the hill,
    And bell of wandering kine, are heard.

No solemn host goes trailing by
    The black-mouthed gun and staggering wain;
Men start not at the battle-cry,
    Oh, be it never heard again!

Soon rested those who fought; but thou
    Who minglest in the harder strife
For truths which men receive not now,
    Thy warfare only ends with life.   20

A friendless warfare! lingering long
    Through weary day and weary year,
A wild and many-weaponed throng
    Hang on thy front, and flank, and rear.

Yet nerve thy spirit to the proof,
    And blench not at thy chosen lot.
The timid good may stand aloof,
    The sage may frown—yet faint thou not.

Nor heed the shaft too surely cast,
    The foul and hissing bolt of scorn;   30
For with thy side shall dwell, at last,
    The victory of endurance born.

Truth, crushed to earth, shall rise again;
    Th' eternal years of God are hers;
But Error, wounded, writhes in pain,
    And dies among his worshippers.

Yea, though thou lie upon the dust,
    When they who helped thee flee in fear,
Die full of hope and manly trust,
    Like those who fell in battle here.   40

Another hand thy sword shall wield,
    Another hand the standard wave,
Till from the trumpet's mouth is pealed
    The blast of triumph o'er thy grave.

The Tides (1860)

The moon is at her full, and, riding high,
    Floods the calm fields with light;
The airs that hover in the summer-sky
    Are all asleep to-night.

There comes no voice from the great woodlands round
    That murmured all the day;
Beneath the shadow of their boughs the ground
    Is not more still than they.

But ever heaves and moans the restless Deep;
    His rising tides I hear,   10
Afar I see the glimmering billows leap;
    I see them breaking near.

Each wave springs upward, climbing toward the fair
    Pure light that sits on high—
Springs eagerly, and faintly sinks, to where
    The mother-waters lie.

Upward again it swells; the moonbeams show
    Again its glimmering crest;
Again it feels the fatal weight below,
    And sinks, but not to rest.   20

Again and yet again; until the Deep
    Recalls his brood of waves;
And, with a sullen moan, abashed, they creep
    Back to his inner caves.

Brief respite! they shall rush from that recess
    With noise and tumult soon,
And fling themselves, with unavailing stress,
    Up toward the placid moon.

O restless Sea, that, in thy prison here,
    Dost struggle and complain;   30
Through the slow centuries yearning to be near
    To that fair orb in vain;

The glorious source of light and heat must warm
    Thy billows from on high,
And change them to the cloudy trains that form
    The curtain of the sky.

Then only may they leave the waste of brine
    In which they welter here,
And rise above the hills of earth, and shine
    In a serener sphere.   40

JAMES FENIMORE COOPER (1789–1851)

Raised in the frontier settlement of Cooperstown, New York, where his father was judge, political leader, and a wealthy landowner ruling his tenants with an iron hand, Cooper came to know, while still a youth, both the lure of the frontier and the aristocratic pretensions his father represented. At thirteen he was sent to Yale, from which he was expelled three years later for rowdiness, and then he spent five years at sea as both sailor and officer. These two experiences— life along the frontier and life at sea, both of them major temptations for young Americans in the early nineteenth century—would form decisive influences on Cooper's work as a writer. His first successful novel, The Spy *(1821), is a somewhat awkward attempt to incorporate elements of American experience into a stock romance; his next novel,* The Pioneers *(1823), is a significant step forward, since we meet in its pages Cooper's great hero Natty Bumppo. Though not planned as such,* The Pioneers *turned out to be the first, in point of composition, of the Leatherstocking Tales. Over the next twenty years Cooper wrote four more volumes in this series, extending the story of Natty backward into his youth (*The Deerslayer, *1841) and forward into old age (*The Prairie, *1827).*

To educate his children and economize on his expenditures, Cooper lived in Europe from 1826 to 1833. Though he now lost the popular following he had built up at home, he continued doggedly to write until his death—a vast body of work including more than thirty novels, volumes of travel, history, and social criticism, as well as numerous political tracts. Cooper's reputation in his homeland has been erratic, but in Europe, especially during the nineteenth century, he was enormously admired and widely read.

Even those literary critics who dismiss Cooper's fiction will usually grant his importance as an analyst and critic of American institutions. Formally his position may not seem impressive—at first glance it may appear to be no more than a crusty defense of conservative privileges. But his social views require a more careful scrutiny.

When Cooper wrote with an eye toward Europe, he presented himself as a staunch American defending democracy as the best of all possible systems; when he wrote with an eye toward his countrymen, he posed as a quarrelsome descendent of the Federalists who feared the rise of the plebeian masses and had serious reservations about democracy. Strongly conservative in formal opinion, Cooper believed in the value of a natural elite or rural aristocracy as a class that could provide a democratic society with moral leadership and keep it from degenerating into rule by the mob. Strongly egalitarian in his deeper emotions, Cooper shared the faith of his countrymen that a unique historical experiment was being conducted on these shores.

"It takes a first class aristocrat," he wrote, "to make a first class Democrat." Like Jefferson somewhat earlier, he felt that the best guarantee of liberty lay in the existence of a strong class of independent landowning farmers. Whatever the rightness or wrongness of Cooper's formal views, his position gave him one great advantage— a certain distance from the unchallenged pieties of his day. His social criticism, still cogent in our own time, thereby offered sharp insights into the danger he saw that democracy might create a mediocre culture reducing everything to a dull conformity.

Critical opinion about Cooper as novelist has varied radically over the years. His faults as a writer of fiction are glaring: plots that creak and groan from an excess of intrigue, melodrama, coincidence, and complication; women characters, or as he humorlessly calls them, "females," who are lifeless beyond bearing and virtuous beyond credence; a prolixity of language that can become infuriating. Perhaps his greatest difficulty as a novelist is this: he was the first American writer to seize, in a large and comprehensive way, on distinctively American subject matter, but he could not develop a style that would be appropriate to this discovery. As a result he often wrote about Indians, pioneers, and the woods in an orotund, latinate prose which muffles the freshness of his observations.

In the nineteenth century the attack on Cooper's novels was led by Mark Twain, in a famous burlesque called "Fenimore Cooper's Literary Offenses." Twain charged that Cooper violated the most elementary of literary requirements, that ". . . the personages in a tale shall be alive, except in the case of corpses, and that always the reader shall be able to tell the corpses from the others. But this detail has been overlooked in the Deerslayer *tale."*

Regarded as a realistic novelist, Cooper is an easy target. None of his books is free of that stuffy rhetoric which Twain took such pleasure in ridiculing; all of them, even the best of the Leatherstocking Tales, are badly marred by soap-opera situations and romantic posturings. Yet in the last several decades there has developed a school of literary criticism that makes large claims for Cooper, seeing him as the first American writer who evoked, in the stories about Natty Bumppo and his Indian companion Chingachgook, the great myth of our culture—the myth of a fraternal union between white and nonwhite men which would be in the starkest moral contrast to the actualities of American society; the myth of a relaxed freedom in the uncleared spaces beyond and in opposition to our social arrangements; the myth of a good and simple life, uncompetitive and un-

ambitious, under the stars, in the silence of the woods and sharing in the peacefulness of nature. (For a further discussion of this theme, see section IV of the General Introduction.)

That this myth should first have been developed on a large scale by a writer who consciously held ideas favoring social hierarchy and class privilege is something of an anomaly. In a penetrating criticism of his fiction, D. H. Lawrence wrote about these two sides of Cooper:

Fenimore, lying in his Louis Quatorze hotel in Paris, passionately musing about Natty Bumppo and the pathless forest, and mixing his imagination with the Cupids and Butterflies on the painted ceiling, while Mrs. Cooper was struggling with her latest gown in the next room. . . .

Men live by lies.

In actuality, Fenimore loved the genteel continent of Europe, and waited gasping for the newspapers to praise his WORK.

In another actuality he loved the tomahawking continent of America, and imagined himself Natty Bumppo.

His actual desire was to be: Monsieur Fenimore Cooper, le grand écrivain américain.

His innermost wish was to be: Natty Bumppo.

Now Natty and Fenimore, arm-in-arm, are an odd couple.

You can see Fenimore: blue coat, silver buttons, silver-and-diamond buckle shoes, ruffles.

You see Natty Bumppo: a grizzled, uncouth old renegade, with gaps in his old teeth and a drop on the end of his nose.

But Natty was Fenimore's great wish: his wishfulfillment.

Cooper's large gifts, as a narrator of mythic tales more than as a social novelist, come through in the Leatherstocking series. His central figures (not the subsidiary ones) are quite as alive as Twain said they should be. Natty himself, whom Lawrence brilliantly described as a saint with a gun, takes on a larger-than-life dimension, somewhat like a Don Quixote or an Odysseus, those permanent inhabitants of the human imagination who seem to step out of the books in which they first appeared and to take on an independent life. The sense of early America—the hush of the endless forests, the solitude of its handful of inhabitants, the charms of a life at once paradisial and civilized, the threat of violence represented by the savages—all this appears in Cooper's fiction with imaginative force and magnitude. Cooper had a fine pictorial imagination, and some *of his best writing consists of static yet very beautiful set-pieces in which he paints verbal pictures—they seem to come almost framed—of the New World.*

Cooper does not lend himself very well to anthologizing, since his best work is expansive, requiring a large canvas. He is hard, perhaps impossible, to excerpt. The selections that follow may, nevertheless, show a few of his gifts and lead readers to his major books.

FURTHER READING

James Franklin Beard has edited two volumes of *The Letters and Journals of James Fenimore Cooper* (1960) and is at work on what may be the definitive biography. A good introduction is James Grossman, *James Fenimore Cooper* (1949). Important studies appear in Richard Chase, *The American Novel and Its Tradition* (1957); Yvor Winters, *In Defense of Reason* (1947); Marius Bewley, *The Eccentric Design* (1959); and of course, D. H. Lawrence, *Studies in Classic American Literature* (1924).

FROM *The Prairie* (1827)[1]

Chapter 32

. . . Then it was, as Abiram appeared, pale, terrified, and tottering beneath a load of detected guilt, that the younger members of the family were first apprized that he still belonged to the class of the living. A general and superstitious impression had spread among them that his crime had been visited by a terrible retribution from Heaven, and they now gazed at him, as at a being who belonged rather to another world, than as a mortal, who like themselves had still to endure the last agony, before the great link of human existence could be broken. The criminal himself appeared to be in a state in which the most sensitive and startling terror was singularly combined with total

[1] Chapter 32 of *The Prairie* shows Cooper at the peak of his art as a novelist. *The Prairie*, in terms of internal events, is the last of the Leatherstocking series, in which Natty Bumppo is shown as an old man ready to die. As if to balance off and complicate his view of Natty as the agent of a freedom located in the natural world and beyond the corruptions of civilization, Cooper introduces into *The Prairie* a powerfully drawn character, Ishmael Bush, who also moves beyond the demands of civilization but who represents the negative side of Natty's creed. Ishmael is a squatter and outlaw, yet in chapter 32 he takes the law into his own hands, meting out judgment against his wife's brother for having killed Ishmael's son.

physical apathy. The truth was, that while his person had been numbed by the shock, his susceptibility to apprehension kept his agitated mind in unrelieved distress. When he found himself in the open air, he looked about him, in order to gather, if possible, some evidences of his future fate from the countenances of those who were gathered round. Seeing every where grave but composed features, and meeting in no eye any expression that threatened immediate violence, the miserable man began to revive, and, by the time he was seated in the wagon, his artful faculties were beginning to plot the expedients of parrying the just resentment of his kinsmen, or, if these should fail him, the means of escaping from a punishment that his forebodings told him would be terrible.

Throughout the whole of these preparations Ishmael had rarely spoken. A gesture, or a glance of the eye, had served to indicate his pleasure to his sons, and with these simple methods of communication, all parties appeared perfectly content. When the signal was made to proceed, the squatter threw his rifle into the hollow of his arm, and his axe across his shoulder, taking the lead as usual. Esther had buried herself in the wagon which contained her daughters; the young men took their customary places among the cattle, or nigh the teams, and the whole proceeded, at their ordinary, dull, but unremitted gait.

For the first time in many a day, the squatter turned his back towards the setting sun. The route he held was in the direction of the settled country, and the manner in which he moved sufficed to tell his children, who had learned to read their father's determinations in his mien, that their journey on the prairie was shortly to have an end. Still nothing else transpired for hours, that might denote the existence of any sudden or violent revolution in the purposes or feelings of Ishmael. During all that time he marched alone, keeping a few hundred rods in front of his teams, seldom giving any sign of extraordinary excitement. Once or twice, indeed, his huge figure was seen standing on the summit of some distant swell, with the head bent towards the earth, as he leaned on his rifle; but then these moments of intense thought were rare and of short continuance. The train had long thrown its shadows towards the east before any material alteration was made in the disposition of their march. Water-courses were waded, plains were passed, and rolling ascents risen and descended, without producing the smallest change. Long practised in the difficulties of that peculiar species of travelling in which he was engaged, the squatter avoided the more impracticable obstacles of their route by a sort of instinct, invariably inclining to the right or left in season, as the formation of the land, the presence of trees, or the signs of rivers forewarned him of the necessity of such movements.

At length the hour arrived when charity to man and beast required a temporary suspension of labour. Ishmael chose the required spot with all his customary sagacity. The regular formation of the country, such as it has been described in the earlier pages of our book, had long been interrupted by a more unequal and broken surface. There were, it is true, in general, the same wide and empty wastes, the same rich and extensive bottoms, and that wild and singular combination of swelling fields and of nakedness, which gives that region the appearance of an ancient country, incomprehensibly stripped of its people and their dwellings. But these distinguishing features of the rolling prairies had long been interrupted by irregular hillocks, occasional masses of rock, and broad belts of forest.

Ishmael chose a spring, that broke out of the base of a rock some forty or fifty feet in elevation, as a place well suited to the wants of his herds. The water moistened a small swale that lay beneath the spot, which yielded, in return for the fecund gift a scanty growth of grass. A solitary willow had taken root in the alluvion, and profiting by its exclusive possession of the soil, the tree had sent up its stem far above the crest of the adjacent rock, whose peaked summit had once been shadowed by its branches. But its loveliness had gone with the mysterious principle of life. As if in mockery of the meagre show of verdure that the spot exhibited, it remained a noble and solemn monument of former fertility. The larger, ragged and fantastic branches still obtruded themselves abroad, while the white and hoary trunk stood naked and tempest-riven. Not a leaf, nor a sign of vegetation was to be seen about it. In all things it proclaimed the frailty of existence and the fulfilment of time.

Here Ishmael, after making the customary signal for the train to approach, threw his vast frame upon the earth, and seemed to muse on the deep responsibility of his present situation. His sons were not long in arriving, for the cattle no sooner scented the food and water than they quickened their pace, and then succeeded the usual bustle and avocations of a halt.

The impression made by the scene of that morning was not so deep or lasting on the children of Ishmael and Esther, as to induce them to forget the wants of nature. But while the sons were searching among their stores, for something substantial to appease their hunger, and the younger fry were wrangling about their simple dishes, the parents of the unnurtured family were far differently employed.

When the squatter saw that all, even to the reviving Abiram, were busy in administering to their appetites, he gave his downcast partner a glance of his eye, and withdrew towards a distant roll of the land, which bounded the view towards the east. The meeting of the pair, in this naked spot, was like an interview held above the grave of their murdered son. Ishmael signed to his wife to take a seat beside him on a fragment of rock, and then followed a space, during which neither seemed disposed to speak.

"We have journeyed together long, through good and bad," Ishmael at length commenced; "much have we had to try us, and some bitter cups have we been made to swallow, my woman; but nothing like this has ever before lain in my path."

"It is a heavy cross for a poor, misguided, and sinful woman to bear!" returned Esther, bowing her head to her knees, and partly concealing her face in her dress. "A heavy and a burdensome weight is this to be laid upon the shoulders of a sister and a mother!"

"Ay; therein lies the hardship of the case. I had brought my mind to the punishment of that houseless trapper, with no great strivings, for the man had done me few favours, and God forgive me if I suspected him wrongfully of much evil! This is, however, bringing shame in at one door of my cabin, in order to drive it out at the other. But shall a son of mine be murdered, and he who did it go at large?—the boy would never rest!"

"Oh, Ishmael, we pushed the matter far! Had little been said, who would have been the wiser? Our consciences might then have been quiet."

"Eest'er," said the husband, turning on her a reproachful but still a dull regard, "the hour has been, my woman, when you thought another hand had done this wickedness?"

"I did, I did! the Lord gave me the feeling, as a punishment for my sins! but his mercy was not slow in lifting the veil; I looked into the book, Ishmael, and there I found the words of comfort."

"Have you that book at hand, woman; it may happen to advise in such a dreary business."

Esther fumbled in her pocket and was not long in producing the fragment of a bible, which had been thumbed and smoke-dried till the print was nearly illegible. It was the only article, in the nature of a book, that was to be found among the chattels of the squatter, and it had been preserved by his wife, as a melancholy relic of more prosperous, and possibly of more innocent days. She had long been in the habit of resorting to it, under the pressure of such circumstances as were palpably beyond human redress, though her spirit and resolution rarely needed support under those that admitted of reparation through any of the ordinary means of reprisal. In this manner Esther had made a sort of convenient ally of the word of God; rarely troubling it for counsel, however, except when her own incompetency to avert an evil was too apparent to be disputed. We shall leave casuists to determine how far she resembled any other believers in this particular, and proceed directly with the matter before us.

"There are many awful passages in these pages, Ishmael," she said, when the volume was opened, and the leaves were slowly turning under her finger, "and some there ar' that teach the rules of punishment."

Her husband made a gesture for her to find one of those brief rules of conduct, which have been received among all Christian nations as the direct mandates of the Creator, and which have been found so just, that even they, who deny their high authority, admit their wisdom. Ishmael listened with grave attention, as his companion read all those verses, which her memory suggested, and which were thought applicable to the situation in which they found themselves. He made her show him the words, which he regarded with a sort of strange reverence. A resolution once taken was usually irrevocable, in one who was moved with so much difficulty. He put his hand upon the book, and closed the pages himself, as much as to apprize his wife that he was satisfied. Esther, who so well knew his character, trembled at the action, and casting a glance at his steady but contracting eye, she said—

"And yet, Ishmael, my blood, and the blood of my children, is in his veins! cannot mercy be shown?"

"Woman," he answered sternly, "when we believed, that miserable old trapper had done this deed, nothing was said of mercy!"

Esther made no reply, but folding her arms upon her breast, she sat silent and thoughtful for many minutes. Then she once more turned her anxious gaze upon the countenance, of her husband, where she found all passion and care apparently buried in the coldest apathy. Satisfied now, that the fate of her brother was sealed, and possibly conscious how well he merited the punishment that was meditated, she no longer thought of mediation. No more words passed between them. Their eyes met for an instant, and then both arose and walked in profound silence towards the encampment.

The squatter found his children expecting his return, in the usual listless manner with which they awaited all coming events. The cattle were already herded, and the horses in their gears, in readiness to proceed so soon as he should indicate that such was his pleasure. The children were already in their proper vehicle, and, in short, nothing delayed the departure but the absence of the parents of the wild brood.

"Abner," said the father, with the deliberation with which all his proceedings were characterized, "take the brother of your mother from the wagon, and let him stand on the 'arth."

Abiram issued from his place of concealment, trembling, it is true, but far from destitute of hopes, as to his final success in appeasing the just resentment of his kinsman. After throwing a glance around him, with the vain wish of finding a single countenance in which he might detect a solitary gleam of sympathy, he endeavoured to smother those apprehensions, that were by this time reviving in all their original violence, by forcing a sort of friendly communication between himself and the squatter—

"The beasts are getting jaded, brother," he said; "and as we have made so good a march already, is it not time to 'camp. To my eye you may go far, before a better place than this is found to pass the night in."

"'Tis well you like it. Your tarry here ar' likely to be long. My sons, draw nigh and listen. Abiram White," he added, lifting his cap, and speaking with a solemnity and steadiness, that rendered even his dull mien imposing, "you have slain my first-born, and according to the laws of God and man must you die!"

The kidnapper started at this terrible and sudden sentence, with the terror that one would exhibit who unexpectedly found himself in the grasp of a monster, from whose power there was no retreat. Although filled with the most serious forebodings of what might be his lot, his courage had not been equal to look his danger in the face, and with the deceitful consolation, with which timid tempers are apt to conceal their desperate condition from themselves, he had rather courted a treacherous relief in his cunning, than prepared himself for the worst.

"Die!" he repeated in a voice, that scarcely issued from his chest; "a man is surely safe among his friends!"

"So thought my boy," returned the squatter, motioning for the team, that contained his wife and the girls, to proceed, as he very coolly examined the priming of his piece. "By the rifle did you destroy my son, and it is fit and just that you meet your end by the same weapon."

Abiram stared about him with a gaze that, for the moment, bespoke an unsettled reason. He even laughed, as if he would not only persuade himself but others that what he heard was some pleasantry, intended to try his nerves. But no where did his frightful merriment meet with an answering echo. All around was solemn and still. The visages of his nephews were excited, but cold towards him, and that of his former confederate frightfully determined. This very steadiness of mien was a thousand times more alarming and hopeless than any violence could have proved. The latter might possibly have touched his spirit and awakened resistance, but the former threw him entirely on the feeble resources of himself.

"Brother," he said, in a hurried, unnatural whisper, "did I hear you?"

"My words are plain, Abiram White; you have done murder, and for the same must you die!"

"Where is Esther? sister, sister, will you leave me! Oh! Sister! do you hear my call?"

"I hear one speak from the grave!" returned the husky tones of Esther, as the wagon passed the spot where the criminal stood. "It is the voice of my first-born, calling aloud for justice! God have mercy, God have mercy on your soul!"

The team slowly pursued its route, and the deserted Abiram now found himself deprived of the smallest vestige of hope. Still he could not summon fortitude to meet his death, and had not his limbs refused to aid him, he would yet have attempted to fly. Then, by a sudden revolution from hope to utter despair, he fell upon his knees, and commenced a prayer, in which cries for mercy to God and to his kinsman were wildly and blasphemously mingled. The sons of Ishmael turned

away in horror at the disgusting spectacle, and even the stern nature
of the squatter began to bend before such abject misery.

"May that, which you ask of Him, be granted," he said; "but a father
can never forget a murdered child."

He was answered by the most humble appeals for time. A week, a
day, an hour, were each implored, with an earnestness commensurate
to the value they receive, when a whole life is compressed into their
short duration. The squatter was troubled, and at length he yielded in
part to the petitions of the criminal. His final purpose was not altered,
though he changed the means; "Abner," he said, "mount the rock and
look on every side, that we may be sure none are nigh."

While his nephew was obeying this order, gleams of reviving hope
were seen shooting across the quivering features of the kidnapper. The
report was favourable, nothing having life, the retiring teams excepted,
was to be seen. A messenger was, however, coming from the latter, in
great apparent haste. Ishmael awaited its arrival. He received from the
hands of one of his wondering and frighted girls a fragment of that
book, which Esther had preserved with so much care. The squatter
beckoned the child away, and placed the leaves in the hands of the
criminal.

"Eest'er has sent you this," he said, "that, in your last moments, you
may remember God."

"Bless her, bless her! a good and kind sister has she been to me!
But time must be given, that I may read; time, my brother, time!"

"Time shall not be wanting. You shall be your own executioner, and
this miserable office shall pass away from my hands."

Ishmael proceeded to put his new resolution in force. The immediate apprehensions of the kidnapper were quieted, by an assurance that
he might yet live for days, though his punishment was inevitable. A
reprieve, to one as abject and wretched as Abiram, temporarily produced the same effects as a pardon. He was even foremost in assisting
in the appalling arrangements, and of all the actors, in that solemn
tragedy, his voice alone was facetious and jocular.

A thin shelf of the rock projected beneath one of the ragged arms
of the willow. It was many feet from the ground, and admirably adapted
to the purpose which, in fact, its appearance had suggested. On this
little platform was the criminal placed, his arms bound at the elbows
behind his back, beyond the possibility of liberation, with a proper cord
leading from his neck to the limb of the tree. The latter was so placed,
that when suspended the body could find no foot-hold. The fragment of
the bible was placed in his hands, and he was there left to seek his
consolation as he might from its pages.

"And now, Abiram White," said the squatter, when his sons had
descended from completing this arrangement, "I give you a last and
solemn asking. Death is before you in two shapes. With this rifle can

your misery be cut short, or by that cord, sooner or later, must you meet your end."

"Let me yet live! Oh, Ishmael, you know not how sweet life is, when the last moment draws so nigh!"

"'Tis done;" said the squatter motioning for his assistants to follow the herds and teams. "And now, miserable man, that it may prove a consolation to your end, I forgive you my wrongs and leave you to your God."

Ishmael then turned and pursued his way across the plain at his ordinary sluggish and ponderous gait. Though his head was bent a little towards the earth, his inactive mind did not prompt him to cast a look behind. Once, indeed, he thought he heard his name called, in tones that were a little smothered, but they failed to make him pause.

At the spot where he and Esther had conferred he reached the boundary of the visible horizon from the rock. Here he stopped, and ventured a glance in the direction of the place he had just quitted. The sun was near dipping into the plains beyond, and its last rays lighted the naked branches of the willow. He saw the ragged outline of the whole drawn against the glowing heavens, and he even traced the still upright form of the being he had left to his misery. Turning the roll of the swell he proceeded with the feelings of one, who had been suddenly and violently separated from a recent confederate, forever.

Within a mile the squatter overtook his teams. His sons had found a place suited to the encampment for the night, and merely awaited his approach to confirm their choice. Few words were necessary to express his acquiescence. Every thing passed in a silence more general and remarkable than ever. The chidings of Esther were not heard among her young, or if heard, they were more in the tones of softened admonition than in her usual upbraiding key.

No questions nor explanations passed between the husband and his wife. It was only as the latter was about to withdraw among her children, for the night, that the former saw her taking a furtive look at the pan of his rifle. Ishmael bade his sons seek their rest, announcing his intention to look to the safety of the camp in person. When all was still, he walked out upon the prairie, with a sort of sensation that he found his breathing among the tents too straitened. The night was well adapted to heighten the feelings, which had been created by the events of the day.

The wind had risen with the moon, and it was occasionally sweeping over the plain, in a manner that made it not difficult for the sentinel to imagine that strange and unearthly sounds were mingling in the blast. Yielding to the extraordinary impulses of which he was the subject, he cast a glance around to see that all were slumbering in security, and then he strayed towards the swell of land already mentioned. Here the squatter found himself at a point that commanded a view to the east and to the west. Light fleecy clouds were driving before the moon, which was cold and watery, though there were moments, when its placid rays were shed from clear blue fields, seeming to soften objects to its own mild loveliness.

For the first time, in a life of so much wild adventure, Ishmael felt a keen sense of solitude. The naked prairies began to assume the forms of illimitable and dreary wastes, and the rushing of the wind sounded like the whisperings of the dead. It was not long before he thought a shriek was borne past him on a blast. It did not sound like a call from earth, but it swept frightfully through the upper air, mingled with the hoarse accompaniment of the wind. The teeth of the squatter were compressed, and his huge hand grasped the rifle, as though it would crush the metal like paper. Then came a lull, a fresher blast, and a cry of horror that seemed to have been uttered at the very portals of his ears. A sort of echo burst involuntarily from his own lips, as men will often shout under unnatural excitement, and throwing his rifle across his shoulder, he proceeded towards the rock with the strides of a giant.

It was not often that the blood of Ishmael moved at the rate with which the fluid circulates in the veins of ordinary men; but now he felt it ready to gush from every pore in his body. The animal was aroused in his most latent energies. Ever as he advanced he heard those shrieks, which sometimes seemed ringing among the clouds, and sometimes passed so nigh as to appear to brush the earth. At length there came a cry, in which there could be no delusion, or to which the imagination could lend no horror. It appeared to fill each cranny of the air, as the visible horizon is often charged to fulness by one dazzling flash of the electric fluid. The name of God was distinctly audible, but it was awfully and blasphemously blended with sounds that may not be repeated. The squatter stopped, and for a moment he covered his ears with his hands. When he withdrew the latter, a low and husky voice at his elbow asked in smothered tones—

"Ishmael, my man, heard ye nothing?"

"Hist!" returned the husband, laying a powerful arm on Esther, without manifesting the smallest surprise at the unlooked-for presence of his wife. "Hist, woman! if you have the fear of Heaven be still!"

A profound silence succeeded. Though the wind rose and fell as before, its rushing was no longer mingled with those fearful cries. The sounds were imposing and solemn, but it was the solemnity and majesty of nature in its solitude.

"Let us go on," said Esther; "all is hushed."

"Woman, what has brought you here?" demanded her husband, whose blood had returned into its former channels, and whose thoughts had already lost a portion of their excitement.

"Ishmael, he murdered our first-born, but it is not meet that the son of my mother should lie upon the ground like the carrion of a dog!"

"Follow;" returned the squatter again grasping his rifle, and striding towards the rock. The distance was still considerable, and their approach, as they drew nigh the place of execution, was moderated by awe. Many minutes had passed, before they reached a spot where they might distinguish the outlines of the dusky objects.

"Where have you put the body?" whispered Esther. "See, here are pick and spade, that a brother of mine may sleep in the bosom of the earth!"

The moon broke from behind a mass of clouds, and the eye of the woman was enabled to follow the finger of Ishmael. It pointed to a human form swinging in the wind, beneath the ragged and shining arm of the willow. Esther bent her head and veiled her eyes from the sight. But Ishmael drew nigher, and long contemplated his work in awe, though not in compunction. The leaves of the sacred book were scattered on the ground, and even a fragment of the shelf had been displaced by the kidnapper in his agony. But all was now in the stillness of death. The grim and convulsed countenance of the victim was at times brought full into the light of the moon, and again as the wind lulled, the fatal rope drew a dark line across its bright disk. The squatter raised his rifle, with extreme care, and fired. The cord was cut and the body came lumbering to the earth, a heavy and insensible mass.

Until now Esther had not moved nor spoken. But her hand was not slow to assist in the labour of the hour. The grave was soon dug. It was instantly made to receive its miserable tenant. As the lifeless form descended, Esther, who sustained the head, looked up into the face of her husband with an expression of anguish, and said—

"Ishmael, my man, it is very terrible! I cannot kiss the corpse of my father's child!"

The squatter laid his broad hand on the bosom of the dead, and said—

"Abiram White, we all have need of mercy; from my soul do I forgive you! may God in Heaven have pity on your sins!"

The woman bowed her face, and imprinted her lips long and fervently on the pallid forehead of her brother. After this came the falling clods and all the solemn sounds of filling a grave. Esther lingered on her knees, and Ishmael stood uncovered while the woman muttered a prayer. All was then finished.

On the following morning the teams and herds of the squatter were seen pursuing their course towards the settlements. As they approached the confines of society, the train was blended among a thousand others. Though some of the numerous descendants of this peculiar pair, were reclaimed from their lawless and semi-barbarous lives, the principals of the family, themselves, were never heard of more.

FROM **The American Democrat** (1838)

An Aristocrat and a Democrat

We live in an age when the words aristocrat and democrat are much used, without regard to the real significations. An aristocrat is one of a few who possess the political power of a country; a democrat, one of the many. The words are also properly applied to those who entertain notions favorable to aristocratical or democratical forms of government. Such persons are not necessarily either aristocrats or democrats in fact, but merely so in opinion. Thus a member of a democratical government may have an aristocratical bias, and vice versa.

To call a man who has the habits and opinions of a gentleman, an aristocrat from that fact alone, is an abuse of terms and betrays ignorance of the true principles of government, as well as of the world. It must be an equivocal freedom under which every one is not the master of his own innocent acts and associations; and he is a sneaking democrat indeed who will submit to be dictated to, in those habits over which neither law nor morality assumes a right of control.

Some men fancy that a democrat can only be one who seeks the level, social, mental and moral, of the majority, a rule that would at once exclude all men of refinement, education, and taste from the class. These persons are enemies of democracy, as they at once render it impracticable. They are usually great sticklers for their own associations and habits, too, though unable to comprehend any of a nature that are superior. They are, in truth, aristocrats in principle, though assuming a contrary pretension, the groundwork of all their feelings and arguments being self. Such is not the intention of liberty, whose aim is to leave every man to be the master of his own acts; denying hereditary honors, it is true, as unjust and unnecessary, but not denying the inevitable consequences of civilization.

The law of God is the only rule of conduct in this, as in other matters. Each man should do as he would be done by. Were the question put to the greatest advocate of indiscriminate association, whether he would submit to have his company and habits dictated to him, he would be one of the first to resist the tyranny; for they who are the most rigid in maintaining their own claims in such matters, are usually the loudest in decrying those whom they fancy to be better off than themselves. Indeed, it may be taken as a rule in social intercourse, that he who is the most apt to question the pretensions of others is the most conscious of the doubtful position he himself occupies; thus establishing the very claims he affects to deny, by letting his jealousy of it be seen. Manners, education, and refinement, are positive things, and they bring with them innocent tastes which are productive of high enjoyments; and it is as unjust to deny their possessors their indulgence as it would be to insist on the less fortunate's passing the time they would rather devote to athletic amusements, in listening to operas for which they have no relish, sung in a language they do not understand.

All that democracy means, is as equal a participation in rights as is practicable; and to pretend that social equality is a condition of popular institutions is to assume that the latter are destructive of civilization, for, as nothing is more self-evident than the impossibility of raising all men to the highest standard of tastes and refinement, the alternative would be to reduce the entire community to the lowest. The whole embarrassment on this point exists in the difficulty of making men comprehend qualities they do not themselves possess. We can all perceive the difference between ourselves and our inferiors, but when it comes to a question of the difference between us and our superiors, we fail to appreciate merits of which we have no proper conceptions. In face of this obvious difficulty, there is the safe and just governing rule, already mentioned, or that of permitting every one to be the undisturbed judge of his own habits and associations, so long as they are innocent and do not impair the rights of others to be equally judges for themselves. It follows, that social intercourse must regulate itself, independently of institutions, with the exception that the latter, while they withheld no natural, bestow no factitious advantages beyond those which are inseparable from the rights of property, and general civilization.

In a democracy, men are just as free to aim at the highest attainable places in society, as to attain the largest fortunes; and it would be clearly unworthy of all noble sentiment to say that the grovelling competition for money shall alone be free, while that which enlists all the liberal acquirements and elevated sentiments of the race, is denied the democrat. Such an avowal would be at once a declaration of the inferiority of the system, since nothing but ignorance and vulgarity could be its fruits.

The democratic gentleman must differ in many essential particulars from the aristocratical gentleman, though in their ordinary habits and tastes they are virtually identical. Their principles vary; and, to a slight degree, their deportment accordingly. The democrat, recognizing the right of all to participate in power, will be more liberal in his general sentiments, a quality of superiority in itself; but in conceding this much to his fellow man, he will proudly maintain his own independence of vulgar domination as indispensable to his personal habits. The same principles and manliness that would induce him to depose a royal despot would induce him to resist a vulgar tyrant.

There is no more capital, though more common error, than to suppose him an aristocrat who maintains his independence of habits; for democracy asserts the control of the majority, only in matters of law, and not in matters of custom. The very object of the institution is the utmost practicable personal liberty, and to affirm the contrary would be sacrificing the end to the means.

An aristocrat, therefore, is merely one who fortifies his exclusive privileges by positive institutions, and a democrat, one who is willing to admit of a free competition in all things. To say, however, that the last supposes this competition will lead to nothing is an assumption that means are employed without any reference to an end. He is the purest democrat who best maintains his rights, and no rights can be dearer to a man of cultivation than exemptions from unseasonable invasions on his time by the coarse minded and ignorant.

Preface to the Leatherstocking Tales (1850)

This series of Stories, which has obtained the name of *The Leather-Stocking Tales,* has been written in a very desultory and inartificial manner. The order in which the several books appeared was essentially different from that in which they would have been presented to the world, had the regular course of their incidents been consulted. In *The Pioneers,* the first of the series written, the Leather-Stocking is represented as already old, and driven from his early haunts in the forest, by the sound of the axe, and the smoke of the settler. *The Last of the Mohicans,* the next book in the order of publication, carried the readers back to a much earlier period in the history of our hero, representing him as middle-aged, and in the fullest vigor of manhood. In *The Prairie,* his career terminates, and he is laid in his grave. There, it was originally the intention to leave him, in the expectation that, as in the case of the human mass, he would soon be forgotten. But a latent regard for this character induced the author to resuscitate him in *The Pathfinder,* a book that was not long after succeeded by *The Deerslayer,* thus completing the series as it now exists.

While the five books that have been written were originally published in the order mentioned, that of the incidents, insomuch as they are connected with the career of their principal character, is, as has been stated, very different. Taking the life of the Leather-Stocking as a guide, *The Deerslayer* should have been the opening book, for in that work he is seen just emerging into manhood; to be succeeded by *The Last of the Mohicans, The Pathfinder, The Pioneers,* and *The Prairie.* This arrangement embraces the order of events, though far from being that in which the books at first appeared. *The Pioneers* was published in 1822; *The Deerslayer* in 1841; making the interval between them nineteen years. Whether these progressive years have had a tendency to lessen the value of the last-named book by lessening the native fire of its author, or of adding somewhat in the way of improved taste and a more matured judgment, is for others to decide.

If anything from the pen of the writer of these romances is at all to outlive himself, it is, unquestionably, the series of *The Leather-Stock-*

ing Tales. To say this, is not to predict a very lasting reputation for the series itself, but simply to express the belief it will outlast any, or all, of the works from the same hand.

It is undeniable that the desultory manner in which *The Leather-Stocking Tales* were written, has, in a measure, impaired their harmony, and otherwise lessened their interest. This is proved by the fate of the two books last published, though probably the two most worthy an enlightened and cultivated reader's notice. If the facts could be ascertained, it is probable the result would show that of all those (in America, in particular) who have read the three first books of the series, not one in ten has a knowledge of the existence even of the two last. Several causes have tended to produce this result. The long interval of time between the appearance of *The Prairie* and that of *The Pathfinder,* was itself a reason why the later books of the series should be overlooked. There was no longer novelty to attract attention, and the interest was materially impaired by the manner in which events were necessarily anticipated, in laying the last of the series first before the world. With the generation that is now coming on the stage this fault will be partially removed by the edition contained in the present work, in which the several tales will be arranged solely in reference to their connexion with each other.

The author has often been asked if he had any original in his mind, for the character of Leather-Stocking. In a physical sense, different individuals known to the writer in early life, certainly presented themselves as models, through his recollections; but in a moral sense this man of the forest is purely a creation. The idea of delineating a character that possessed little of civilization but its highest principles as they are exhibited in the uneducated, and all of savage life that is not incompatible with these great rules of conduct, is perhaps natural to the situation in which Natty was placed. He is too proud of his origin to sink into the condition of the wild Indian, and too much a man of the woods not to imbibe as much as was at all desirable, from his friends and companions. In a moral point of view it was the intention to illustrate the effect of seed scattered by the way side. To use his own language, his 'gifts' were 'white gifts,' and he was not disposed to bring on them discredit. On the other hand, removed from nearly all the temptations of civilized life, placed in the best associations of that which is deemed savage, and favorably disposed by nature to improve such advantages, it appeared to the writer that his hero was a fit subject to represent the better qualities of both conditions, without pushing either to extremes.

There was no violent stretch of the imagination, perhaps, in supposing one of civilized associations in childhood, retaining many of his earliest lessons amid the scenes of the forest. Had these early impressions, however, not been sustained by continued, though casual connexion with men of his own color, if not of his own caste, all our information goes to show he would soon have lost every trace of his origin. It is believed that sufficient attention was paid to the particular circumstances in which this individual was placed to justify the picture of his qualities that has been drawn. The Delawares early attracted the attention of missionaries, and were a tribe unusually influenced by their precepts and example. In many instances they became Christians, and cases occurred in which their subsequent lives gave proof of the efficacy of the great moral changes that had taken place within them.

A leading character in a work of fiction has a fair right to the aid which can be obtained from a poetical view of the subject. It is in this view, rather than in one more strictly circumstantial, that Leather-Stocking has been drawn. The imagination has no great task in portraying to itself a being removed from the every-day inducements to err, which abound in civilized life, while he retains the best and simplest of his early impressions; who sees God in the forest; hears him in the winds; bows to him in the firmament that o'ercanopies all; submits to his sway in a humble belief of his justice and mercy; in a word, a being who finds the impress of the Deity in all the works of nature, without any of the blots produced by the expedients, and passion, and mistakes of man. This is the most that has been attempted in the character of Leather-Stocking. Had this been done without any of the drawbacks of humanity, the picture would have been, in all probability, more pleasing than just. In order to preserve the *vraisemblable*, therefore, traits derived from the prejudices, tastes, and even the weaknesses of his youth, have been mixed up with these higher qualities and longings, in a way, it is hoped, to represent a reasonable picture of human nature, without offering to the spectator a 'monster of goodness'.

It has been objected to these books that they give a more favorable picture of the red man than he deserves. The writer apprehends that much of this objection arises from the habits of those who have made it. One of his critics, on the appearance of the first work in which Indian character was portrayed, objected that its 'characters were Indians of the school of Heckewelder, rather than of the school of nature'. These words quite probably contain the substance of the true answer to the objection. Heckewelder was an ardent, benevolent missionary, bent on the good of the red man, and seeing in him one who had the soul, reason, and characteristics of a fellow-being. The critic is understood to have been a very distinguished agent of the government, one very familiar with Indians, as they are seen at the councils to treat for the sale of their lands, where little or none of their domestic qualities come in play, and where, indeed, their evil passions are known to have the fullest scope. As just would it be to draw conclusions of the general state of American society from the scenes of the capital, as to suppose that the negotiating of one of these treaties is a fair picture of Indian life.

It is the privilege of all writers of fiction, more particularly when their works aspire to the elevation of romances, to present the *beau-idéal* of their characters to the reader. This it is which constitutes poetry, and to suppose that the red man is to be represented only in the squalid misery or in the degraded moral state that certainly more or less belongs to his condition, is, we apprehend, taking a very narrow view of an author's privileges. Such criticism would have deprived the world of even Homer.

JOHN JAMES AUDUBON (1785–1851)

The son of a French naval officer, Audubon was born in Santo Domingo and spent most of his life in travels that took him from the American wilderness to publishing houses in Europe. While his wife supported herself and their two sons by working as a governess, Audubon ranged over the North American continent, sketching its birds and writing in his journals a record of the people he met and places he visited. With the publication, in 1827 to 1838, of his major work, The Birds of North America, *his fame spread throughout the world.*

Audubon rarely appears in collections of American literature, and he is rarely thought of as a literary man. Yet his writing merits attention not merely because he provides authoritative information, but also because he is able to write strong expository prose, at once exact and vivid. Audubon was that rare creature, a man of scientific distinction who also wrote as well as, if not better than, most professional literary people of his day. Students who do not plan on literary careers but would like to write precisely and evocatively might more usefully study the style of a man like Audubon than the styles of our major novelists and poets. The latter most of us could never emulate; the former provides a usable model.

FURTHER READING

Francis Hobart Herrick's *Audubon the Naturalist: A History of His Life and Times* (1917); Donald C. Peattie's *Audubon's America* (1940); Howard Corning's edition of the *Journals of J. J. Audubon, Made During His Trip to New Orleans in 1820–21* (1929).

FROM *The Ornithological Biography* (1831–1839)

The Ohio

To render more pleasant the task which you have imposed upon yourself, of following an author through the mazes of descriptive ornithology, permit me, kind reader, to relieve the tedium which may be apt now and then to come upon you, by presenting you with occasional descriptions of the scenery and manners of the land which has furnished the objects that engage your attention. The natural features of that land are not less remarkable than the moral character of her inhabitants; and I cannot find a better subject with which to begin, than one of those magnificent rivers that roll the collected waters of her extensive territories to the ocean.

When my wife, my eldest son (then an infant), and myself were returning from Pennsylvania to Kentucky, we found it expedient, the waters being unusually low, to provide ourselves with a *skiff*, to enable us to proceed to our abode at Henderson. I purchased a large, commodious, and light boat of that denomination. We procured a mattress, and our friends furnished us with ready prepared viands. We had two stout Negro rowers, and in this trim we left the village of Shippingport, in expectation of reaching the place of our destination in a very few days.

It was in the month of October. The autumnal tints already decorated the shores of that queen of rivers, the Ohio. Every tree was hung with long and flowing festoons of different species of vines, many loaded with clustered fruits of varied brilliancy, their rich bronzed carmine mingling beautifully with the yellow foliage, which now predominated over the yet green leaves, reflecting more lively tints from the clear stream than ever landscape painter portrayed or poet imagined.

The days were yet warm. The sun had assumed the rich and glowing hue, which at that season produces the singular phenomenon called there the "Indian Summer." The moon had rather passed the meridian of her grandeur. We glided down the river, meeting no other ripple of the water than that formed by the propulsion of our boat. Leisurely we moved along, gazing all day on the grandeur and beauty of the wild scenery around us.

Now and then, a large cat-fish rose to the surface of the water in pursuit of a shoal of fry, which starting simultaneously from the liquid element, like so many silvery arrows, produced a shower of light, while the pursuer with open jaws seized the stragglers, and, with a splash of the tail, disappeared from our view. Other fishes we heard uttering beneath our bark a rumbling noise, the strange sounds of which we discovered to proceed from the white perch, for on casting our net from the bow we caught several of that species, when the noise ceased for a time.

Nature, in her varied arrangements, seems to have felt a partiality towards this portion of our country. As the traveller ascends or descends the Ohio, he cannot help remarking that alternately, nearly the whole length of the river, the margin, on one side, is bounded by lofty hills and a rolling surface, while on the other, extensive plains of the richest alluvial land are seen as far as the eye can command the view. Islands of varied size and form rise here and there from the bosom of the water, and the winding course of the stream frequently brings you to places, where the idea of being on a river of great length changes to that of floating on a lake of moderate extent. Some of these islands are of considerable size and value; while others, small and insignificant, seem as if intended for contrast, and as serving to enhance the general interest of the scenery. These little islands are frequently overflowed during great *freshets* or floods, and receive at their heads prodigious heaps of drifted timber. We foresaw with great concern the alteration that cultivation would soon produce along those delightful banks.

As night came, sinking in darkness the broader portions of the river, our minds became affected by strong emotions, and wandered far beyond the present moments. The tinkling of bells told us that the cattle which bore them were gently roving from valley to valley in search of food, or returning to their distant homes. The hooting of the Great Owl, or the muffled noise of its wings as it sailed smoothly over the stream, were matters of interest to us; so was the sound of the boatman's horn, as it came winding more and more softly from afar. When daylight returned, many songsters burst forth with echoing notes, more and more mellow to the listening ear. Here and there the lonely cabin of a squatter struck the eye, giving note of commencing civilization. The crossing of the stream by a deer foretold how soon the hills would be covered with snow.

Many sluggish flat-boats we overtook and passed: some laden with produce from the different head-waters of the small rivers that pour their tributary streams into the Ohio; others, of less dimensions, crowded with emigrants from distant parts, in search of a new home. Purer pleasures I never felt; nor have you, reader, I ween, unless indeed you have felt the like, and in such company.

The margins of the shores and of the river were at this season amply supplied with game. A Wild Turkey, a Grouse, or a Blue-winged Teal, could be procured in a few moments; and we fared well, for, whenever we pleased, we landed, struck up a fire, and provided as we were with the necessary utensils, procured a good repast.

Several of these happy days passed, and we neared our home, when, one evening, not far from Pigeon Creek (a small stream which runs into the Ohio, from the State of Indiana), a loud and strange noise was heard, so like the yells of Indian warfare, that we pulled at our oars, and made for the opposite side as fast and as quietly as possible. The sounds increased, we imagined we heard cries of "murder;" and as we knew that some depredations had lately been committed in the country by dissatisfied parties of Aborigines, we felt for a while extremely uncomfortable. Ere long, however, our minds became more calmed and we plainly discovered that the singular uproar was produced by an enthusiastic set of Methodists, who had wandered thus far out of the common way, for the purpose of holding one of their annual camp meetings, under the shade of a beech forest. Without meeting with any other interruption, we reached Henderson, distant from Shippingport by water about two hundred miles.

When I think of these times, and call back to my mind the grandeur and beauty of those almost uninhabited shores; when I picture to myself the dense and lofty summits of the forest, that everywhere spread along the hills, and overhung the margins of the stream, unmolested by the axe of the settler; when I know how dearly purchased the safe navigation of that river has been by the blood of many worthy Virginians; when I see that no longer any Aborigines are to be found there, and that the vast herds of elks, deer and buffaloes which one pastured on these hills and in these valleys, making for themselves great roads to the several salt-springs, have ceased to exist; when I reflect that all this grand portion of our Union, instead of being in a state of nature, is now more or less covered with villages, farms, and towns, where the din of hammers and machinery is constantly heard; that the woods are fast disappearing under the axe by day, and the fire by night; that hundreds of steam-boats are gliding to and fro, over the whole length of the majestic river, forcing commerce to take root and to prosper at every spot; when I see the surplus population of Europe coming to assist in the destruction of the forest, and transplanting civilization into its darkest recesses;—when I remember that these extraordinary changes have all taken place in the short period of twenty years, I pause, wonder, and, although I know all to be fact, can scarcely believe its reality.

Whether these changes are for the better or for the worse, I shall not pretend to say; but in whatever way my conclusions may incline, I feel with regret that there are on record no satisfactory accounts of the state of that portion of the country, from the time when our people first settled in it. This has not been because no one in America is able to accomplish such an undertaking. Our Irvings and our Coopers have proved themselves fully competent for the task. It has more probably been because the changes have succeeded each other with such rapidity, as almost to rival the movements of their pen. However, it is not too late yet; and I sincerely hope that either or both of them will ere long furnish the generations to come with those delightful descriptions which they are so well qualified to give, of the original state of a country that has been so rapidly forced to change her form and attire under the influence of increasing population. Yes; I hope to read, ere I close my earthly career, accounts from those delightful writers of the progress of civilization in our western country. They will speak of the Clarks, the Croghans, the Boons, and many other men of great and daring enterprise. They will analyze, as it were, into each component part, the country as it once existed, and will render the picture, as it ought to be, immortal.

The Prairie

On my return from the Upper Mississippi, I found myself obliged to cross one of the wide Prairies, which, in that portion of the United States vary the appearance of the country. The weather was fine, all around me was as fresh and blooming as if it had just issued from the bosom of nature. My knapsack, my gun, and my dog, were all I had for baggage and company. But, although well moccasined, I moved slowly along, attracted by the brilliancy of the flowers, and the gambols of the fawns around their dams, to all appearance as thoughtless of danger as I felt myself.

My march was of long duration; I saw the sun sinking beneath the horizon long before I could perceive any appearance of woodland, and nothing in the shape of man had I met with that day. The track which I followed was only an old Indian trace, and as darkness overshadowed the prairie, I felt some desire to reach at least a copse, in which I might lie down to rest. The Night-hawks were skimming over and around me, attracted by the buzzing wings of the beetles which form their food, and the distant howling of wolves gave me some hope that I should soon arrive at the skirts of some woodland.

I did so, and almost at the same instant a fire-light attracting my eye, I moved towards it, full of confidence that it proceeded from the camp of some wandering Indians. I was mistaken:—I discovered by its glare that it was from the hearth of a small log cabin, and that a tall figure passed and repassed between it and me, as if busily engaged in household arrangements.

I reached the spot, and presenting myself at the door, asked the tall figure, which proved to be a woman, if I might take shelter under her roof for the night. Her voice was gruff, and her attire negligently thrown about her. She answered in the affirmative. I walked in, took a wooden stool, and quietly seated myself by the fire. The next object that attracted my notice was a finely formed young Indian, resting his head between his hands, with his elbows on his knees. A long bow rested against the log wall near him, while a quantity of arrows and two or three raccoon skins lay at his feet. He moved not; he apparently breathed not. Accustomed to the habits of the Indians, and knowing that they pay little attention to the approach of civilized strangers (a circumstance which in some countries is considered as evincing the apathy of their character), I addressed him in French, a language not unfrequently partially known to the people in that neighborhood. He raised his head, pointed to one of his eyes with his finger, and gave me a significant glance with the other. His face was covered with blood. The fact was, that an hour before this, as he was in the act of discharging an arrow at a raccoon in the top of a tree, the arrow had split upon the cord, and sprung back with such violence into his right eye as to destroy it for ever.

Feeling hungry, I inquired what sort of fare I might expect. Such a thing as a bed was not to be seen, but many large untanned bear and buffalo hides lay piled in a corner. I drew a fine time-piece from my breast, and told the woman that it was late, and that I was fatigued. She had espyed my watch, the richness of which seemed to operate upon her feelings with electric quickness. She told me that there was plenty of venison and jerked buffalo meat, and that on removing the ashes I should find a cake. But my watch had struck her fancy, and her curiosity had to be gratified by an immediate sight of it. I took off the gold chain that secured it from around my neck, and presented it to her. She was all ecstasy, spoke of its beauty, asked me its value, and put the chain round her brawny neck, saying how happy the possession of such a watch should make her. Thoughtless, and, as I fancied myself, in so retired a spot, secure, I paid little attention to her talk or her movements. I helped my dog to a good supper of venison, and was not long in satisfying the demands of my own appetite.

The Indian rose from his seat, as if in extreme suffering. He passed and repassed me several times, and once pinched me on the side so violently, that the pain nearly brought forth an exclamation of anger. I looked at him. His eye met mine; but his look was so forbidding, that it struck a chill into the more nervous part of my system. He again seated himself, drew his butcher-knife from its greasy scabbard, examined its edge, as I would do that of a razor suspected dull, replaced it, and again taking his tomahawk from his back, filled the pipe of it with tobacco, and sent me expressive glances whenever our hostess chanced to have her back towards us.

Never until that moment had my senses been awakened to the danger which I now suspected to be about me. I returned glance for glance to my companion, and rested well assured that, whatever enemies I might have, he was not of their number.

I asked the woman for my watch, wound it up, and under pretence of wishing to see how the weather might probably on the morrow, took up my gun, and walked out of the cabin. I slipped a ball into each barrel, scraped the edges of my flints, renewed the primings, and returning to the hut, gave a favourable account of my observations. I took a few bearskins, made a pallet of them, and calling my faithful dog to my side, lay down, with my gun close to my body, and in a few minutes was, to all appearance, fast asleep.

A short time had elapsed, when some voices were heard, and from the corner of my eyes I saw two athletic youths making their entrance, bearing a dead stag on a pole. They disposed of their burden, and asking for whisky, helped themselves freely to it. Observing me and the wounded Indian, they asked who I was, and why the devil that rascal (meaning the Indian, who, they knew, understood not a word of English) was in the house. The mother—for so she proved to be, bade them speak less loudly, made mention of my watch, and took them to a corner, where a conversation took place, the purport of which it required little shrewdness in me to guess. I tapped my dog gently. He moved his tail, and with indescribable pleasure I saw his fine eyes alternately fixed on me and raised towards the trio in the corner. I felt that he perceived danger in my situation. The Indian exchanged a last glance with me.

The lads had eaten and drunk themselves into such condition, that I already looked upon them as *hors de combat;* and the frequent visits of the whisky bottle to the ugly mouth of their dam I hoped would soon reduce her to a like state. Judge of my astonishment, reader, when I saw this incarnate fiend take a large carving-knife, and go to the grindstone to whet its edge. I saw her pour the water on the turning machine, and watched her working away with the dangerous instrument, until the sweat covered every part of my body, in despite of my determination to defend myself to the last. Her task finished, she walked to her reeling sons, and said, "There, that'll soon settle him! Boys, kill yon ————, and then for the watch."

I turned, cocked my gun-locks silently, touched my faithful companion, and lay ready to start up and shoot the first who might attempt my life. The moment was fast approaching, and that night might have been my last in this world, had not Providence made preparations for my rescue. All was ready. The infernal hag was advancing slowly, probably contemplating the best way of despatching me, whilst her sons should be engaged with the Indian. I was several times on the eve of rising and shooting her on the spot:—but she was not to be punished thus. The door was suddenly opened, and there entered two stout travellers, each with a long rifle on his shoulder. I bounced up on my feet, and making them most heartily welcome, told them how well it was for me that they should have arrived at that moment. The tale was told in a minute. The drunken sons were secured, and the woman, in spite of her defence and vociferations, shared the same fate. The Indian fairly danced with joy, and gave us to understand that, as he could not sleep for pain, he would watch over us. You may suppose we slept much less than we talked. The two strangers gave me an account of their once having been themselves in a somewhat similar situation. Day came, fair and rosy, and with it the punishment of our captives.

They were now quite sobered. Their feet were unbound, but their arms were still securely tied. We marched them into the woods off the road, and having used them as Regulators were wont to use such delinquents, we set fire to the cabin, gave all the skins and implements to the young Indian warrior, and proceeded, well pleased, towards the settlements.

During upwards of twenty-five years, when my wanderings extended to all parts of our country, this was the only time at which my life was in danger from my fellow creatures. Indeed, so little risk do travellers run in the United States, that no one born there ever dreams of any to be encountered on the road; and I can only account for this occurrence by supposing that the inhabitants of the cabin were not Americans.

Will you believe, reader, that not many miles from the place where this adventure happened, and where fifteen years ago, no habitation belonging to civilized man was expected, and very few ever seen, large roads are now laid out, cultivation has converted the woods into fertile fields, taverns have been erected, and much of what we Americans call comfort is to be met with. So fast does improvement proceed in our abundant and free country.

JAMES KIRKE PAULDING (1778–1860)

Paulding was a native of Putnam County, New York, and collaborated with Washington Irving in publishing a humorous periodical, Salmagundi: Or the Whim-whams and Opinions of Launcelot Langstaff, Esq., and Others, *in 1807 to 1808. His later works include attacks on English despotism and Sir Walter Scott's romantic fiction, all reflecting his intense American patriotism and Jacksonian egalitarianism. A play,* The Lion of the West *(1831), made him a popular success, and he depicted frontier scenes with a certain vividness in two novels,* The Dutchman's Fireside *(1831) and* Westward Ho! *(1832). In addition to being a literary man, Paulding occupied an important place in the politics of his day and served as Secretary of the Navy under President Van Buren (1831 to 1841).*

In the history of American literature Paulding is a decidedly minor figure, but his Letters from the South *are notable first for revealing the way in which a Northerner, predisposed to hostility toward the South, is gradually charmed by its customs, and then for the journalistic ease with which he brings "news" of one region to another. In the early nineteenth century, when communications were far less efficient than they are today, one of the functions of literary men was to describe the life of one region for readers of another.*

FURTHER READING

Paulding's son William wrote his father's *Literary Life* in 1867; A. L. Herold published a study, *James Kirke Paulding: Versatile American* (1926); V. L. Parrington has a sympathetic section in *Main Currents of American Thought,* II (1927).

FROM *Letters from the South* (*1835*)

One of the first things that strikes a northern man, who flounders into Virginia, or either of the more southern states, loaded with a pack of prejudices as large as a pedler's is, that he has, all life long, been under a very mistaken notion of the state of their manners. So, at least, it fared with me, who, you know, had a singular antipathy to gouging, and mint-juleps, the latter of which I have, however, pretty nearly got over. Before I had been long in this part of the world, I discovered, to my great surprise, that the people were very much like other folks, only a little more hospitable; and it is now my settled opinion, notwithstanding all counter authorities, that a civil, honest, well-meaning man, like myself, may traverse the southern states, mountains and all, without being either obliged to fight, without special reason, or put up with insults from any body. Every day's experience, in short, convinces me, that the people of our part of the world have been much misled by the idle tales of travelling pedlers, sent out to buy tobacco and cotton, or by the unneighbourly arts of men, knowing better, but misrepresenting for party purposes.

"Ould Virginia," which, according to the proverb, "never tires," has come in for a full share of this ignorant or interested obloquy; for it seems that her sister states have never been brought to forgive her, for not only producing a Washington, but, with an indecorous kind of prodigality, furnishing three or four other presidents in succession. This has scandalized the other states desperately; for each one, as a matter of course, thinks itself entitled to give a president in time, even though it may have so happened that it never produced a man whose talents and opportunities qualified him for that high station. However I may lament this misfortune of poor Virginia, I don't think she is so very much to blame for producing a succession of such distinguished men, and hold, that we of the north are, in duty bound, to forgive her, provided she promise never to do so again. But, whether she does or not, I will confess to you, that such is my want of the true local *amor patria*, that, provided we get good presidents, I care not what state they come from; since, somehow or other, I have taken up an old notion, that whether a man be born east, west, north, or south, provided he is born within the limits of our country, he is still an American; and, that the attempt to put in claims to the presidency distinct from merit and talents, originated in the petty ambition of grovelling politicians, who could never expect to gain distinction, except by pampering the vanity of their constituents at home.

Be this as it may, I think it is much to be wished, that the people of the various divisions of the United States were a little more acquainted with each other, for, I am satisfied, they would be the better friends for it. At present, like the tenants of one of those amazing high houses in Edinburgh, that accommodate several families, though living, as it were, under the same roof, they have scarcely a speaking acquaintance. The impressions, which they long since took upon trust, with respect to each other, from ignorant or ill-natured travellers, interested in deceiving or sporting with their credulity; the stories of horseracing, drinking, and gouging, on one hand, and of tricking and witch-burning on the other, that have passed current for a century or more, are still received as pictures of existing manners, though even, at any time, they were of rare occurrence, and very many of these practices are altogether extinct. The changes which succeed each other, in this chameleon country, more rapidly than in any other part of the world, have, it would seem, passed unmarked and unrecorded, while the good people still continue to believe and tremble. The impressions of the natives here, with respect to those of the eastward, are still tinctured with the remembrance of witch-burnings; and not a pious dame in our northern parts, that would not compound for her son coming back with one eye left, from an excursion into the back parts of the southern states.

Such foolish prejudices are worthy of honest John Bull, who, from time immemorial, has believed that his neighbours, the French, eat frogs, and are destitute of religion, as well as of every manly and womanly virtue. But our people, who all read, and write, and think, and reason—some right—others wrong, ought to be ashamed of themselves, to believe so badly of their countrymen and neighbours. It is a foolish absurdity, ever the product of national folly, or national antipathy, to assert, that cotemporary and neighbouring people, having the same lights of religion, living under similar laws, and enjoying, equally, the advantages of education, should be so essentially different in morals. They may differ, it is true, in manners; but there is no philosophical reason for their exhibiting a contrast of morals, or that one should be so much wiser and better than the other. I believe, if we place them fairly in comparison, with no interest to allure us astray, and no antipathies to tempt us from the truth, we shall find, that an inferiority in one point will be met by a superiority in another; that, though they may differ in various respects, there is no general disparity; and that, on the whole, the scale remains equally balanced. There are two distinct classes of faults in the world; one open, palpable, and offensive; the other secret, sly, and hypocritical. Those who commit the former, are worse than they seem; and those who indulge in the latter, are not half so good as they appear. The former are offenders against decency and the laws of man; the latter against virtue and the Divinity. . . .

That Richmond will increase rapidly in exact proportion to the increase of population and agriculture in the range of country watered by James river and its branches, I have no doubt. But I do doubt whether either the one or other will increase, at least for a very long time, in a way to realize the anticipations entertained by many people here. The Atlantic states, except such as possess a back territory equal, or nearly equal, in fertility and in natural advantages, to the western states, and those which will from time to time grow out of the Mississippi and Missouri territories, will not hereafter increase in a ratio corresponding with their previous growth. The more active and enterprising—the people who partake of youth, enterprise, and hardihood, and who increase the actual productions of the earth by their labours, are looking more and more to the west, "over the hills and far away." It is in that direction the tide which knows no ebb, will continue to flow, till the great vacuum is filled up, when, possibly, a reaction will take place, and people re-emigrate to the back-woods of the Atlantic coast. The prospect of exchanging a little exhausted farm, for one ten times as large, where the labours and privations of a few years are repaid by the sweets of independence to themselves and their children, will allure many of the young ones of the east, to the land of promise in the west.

The people of the United States partake, in no small degree, of the habits of their predecessors, the aborigines, who, when they have exhausted one hunting-ground, pull up stakes, and incontinently march off to another, four or five hundred miles off, where game is plenty. So with honest brother Jonathan. When he has eaten up every thing around him, and worked his land to skin and bone, and when his house is just on the point of tumbling about his ears; instead of taking the trouble of restoring the one, or rebuilding the other, he abandons both; and packing up his moveables, consisting of his wife and chubby boys, in a wagon, whistles himself to the banks of the Ohio, the Illinois, or the Missouri,—all one to him. Here he builds him a log cabin,—and his axe is like the whirlwind, which levels the tallest trees of the forest in a twinkling. By-and-by he puts an addition to his cabin; and last of all, builds him a stately house, and becomes a judge, a general, or a member of congress,—for our people are jacks of all trades, and the same man can turn his hand or his head to any thing.

It is easy to perceive the effects that will result, and which in part have already resulted, from this habit of emigration, for which our people are distinguished. The most hardy, active, industrious children of the elder states, who have little or no birth-right at home,—who have sagacity to perceive the advantages, and courage to encounter the difficulties of so long a journey, go where the land is cheap, and labour repaid with abundance. Those who remain behind, will consist of a sober, regular race, forming a very useful ingredient in our mixed population; possessing, perhaps, more of the elegances, but less of the solid independence of life; and who will make as good citizens, but not as good soldiers, as the hardy emigrants to the *new countries*. They will increase, perhaps, the manufactures of the country; but probably the produce of the land, which is the consequence of well-directed industry, will not increase in equal proportion, so long as there remains such a field for enterprise in the western world. . . .

By-and-by, Kentucky, Tennessee, and Ohio, will be old states, increasing indeed in population, but by no means in comparison with their former ratio. They, in time, will become the parents of new states, far in the wilderness, and the current of emigration will continue to flow, till it reaches the shores of another Atlantic in the west. Old DANIEL BOON is still the file-leader. He was the first settler of Kentucky, which soon grew too populous for him; and by regular emigrations he has reached the Missouri, which he is now following up to the Rocky Mountains. If he lives, he will, I have little doubt, get to the mouth of Columbia river, and there, perhaps, sit down, like another Alexander of Macedon, and weep, because there are no more worlds to—*settle.*

This is a true travelling letter. I began at Richmond, and ended at the mouth of the Columbia river; a tolerable journey enough. In my next I will try to set you down somewhere nearer home, if possible; perhaps on the top of the Blue Ridge, if I can get thus far. Good by. . . .

RICHARD HENRY DANA, JR. (1815–1882)

The senior Dana, a Boston literary critic, was an ardent champion of romanticism, but the writings of his son show none of the extravagance characteristic of the father. While studying at Harvard, Dana strained his eyes and, to recover his health, shipped out as a sailor on a two-year voyage. Reentering Harvard in 1836, he graduated at the head of his class and taught there for a time. In 1840 he published an account of his voyage, Two Years before the Mast, *a book that would remain popular for decades to come.*

In later life Dana worked as a lawyer, and his steady concern for the rights of American seamen, then subjected to miserable conditions and outrageous tyranny, soon made him known as the "sailor's lawyer," a role that appears to have been as morally rewarding as it was financially damaging.

Two Years before the Mast *is a vivid personal narrative; the prose is muscular, and the outlook testifies to the humaneness of early-nineteenth-century New Englanders. Dana's book anticipates the sea works of Herman Melville, who was obviously influenced by* Two Years before the Mast *but who added a metaphysical depth and poetic range beyond the capacities of the earlier writer. The section here reprinted has an equivalent in Melville's* White Jacket *(1850), which describes similar brutalities in the United States Navy and helped persuade the Congress to abolish flogging.*

FURTHER READING

Charles Francis Adams, Jr., published a two-volume biography, *Richard Henry Dana* (1891). A later study is Samuel Shapiro, *Richard Henry Dana* (1961). A brief estimate of Dana can be found in Bliss Perry's *The Praise of Folly and Other Papers* (1923) and Van Wyck Brooks's *The Flowering of New England* (1936).

FROM *Two Years before the Mast* (1840)

Chapter 15

For several days the captain seemed very much out of humor. Nothing went right, or fast enough for him. He quarrelled with the cook, and threatened to flog him for throwing wood on deck, and had a dispute with the mate about reeving a Spanish burton; the mate saying that he was right, and had been taught how to do it by a man *who was a sailor!* This the captain took in dudgeon, and they were at swords' points at once. But his displeasure was chiefly turned against a large, heavy-moulded fellow from the Middle States, who was called Sam. This man hesitated in his speech, was rather slow in his motions, and was only a tolerably good sailor, but usually seemed to do his best; yet the captain took a dislike to him, thought he was surly and lazy, and "if you once give a dog a bad name,"—as the sailor-phrase is,—"he may as well jump overboard." The captain found fault with everything this man did, and hazed him for dropping a marline-spike from the main-yard, where he was at work. This, of course, was an accident, but it was set down against him. The captain was on board all day Friday, and everything went on hard and disagreeably. "The more you drive a man, the less he will do," was as true with us as with any other people. We worked late Friday night, and were turned-to early Saturday morning. About ten o'clock the captain ordered our new officer, Russell, who by this time had become thoroughly disliked by all the crew, to get the gig ready to take him ashore. John, the Swede, was sitting in the boat alongside, and Mr. Russell and I were standing by the main hatchway, waiting for the captain, who was down in the hold, where the crew were at work, when we heard his voice raised in violent dispute with somebody, whether it was with the mate or one of the crew I could not tell, and then came blows and scuffling. I ran to the side and beckoned to John, who came aboard, and we leaned down the hatchway, and though we could see no one, yet we knew that the captain had the advantage, for his voice was loud and clear:—

"You see your condition! You see your condition! Will you ever give me any more of your *jaw?*" No answer; and then came wrestling and heaving, as though the man was trying to turn him. "You may as well keep still, for I have got you," said the captain. Then came the question, "Will you ever give me any more of your jaw?"

"I never gave you any, sir," said Sam; for it was his voice that we heard, though low and half choked.

"That's not what I ask you. Will you ever be impudent to me again?"

"I never have been, sir," said Sam.

"Answer my question, or I'll make a spread eagle of you! I'll flog you, by G——d."

"I'm no negro slave," said Sam.

"Then I'll make you one," said the captain; and he came to the hatchway, and sprang on deck, threw off his coat, and, rolling up his sleeves, called out to the mate: "Seize that man up, Mr. Amerzene! Seize him up! Make a spread eagle of him! I'll teach you all who is master aboard!"

The crew and officers followed the captain up the hatchway; but it was not until after repeated orders that the mate laid hold of Sam, who made no resistance, and carried him to the gangway.

"What are you going to flog that man for, sir?" said John, the Swede, to the captain.

Upon hearing this, the captain turned upon John; but, knowing him to be quick and resolute, he ordered the steward to bring the irons, and, calling upon Russell to help him, went up to John.

"Let me alone," said John. "I'm willing to be put in irons. You need not use any force"; and, putting out his hands, the captain slipped the irons on, and sent him aft to the quarter-deck. Sam, by this time, was *seized up*, as it is called, that is, placed against the shrouds, with his wrists made fast to them, his jacket off, and his back exposed. The captain stood on the break of the deck, a few feet from him, and a little raised, so as to have a good swing at him, and held in his hand the end of a thick, strong rope. The officers stood round, and the crew grouped together in the waist. All these preparations made me feel sick and almost faint, angry and excited as I was. A man—a human being, made in God's likeness—fastened up and flogged like a beast! A man, too, whom I had lived with, eaten with, and stood watch with for months, and knew so well! If a thought of resistance crossed the minds of any of the men, what was to be done? Their time for it had gone by. Two men were fast, and there were left only two men besides Stimson and myself, and a small boy of ten or twelve years of age; and Stimson and I would not have joined the men in a mutiny, as they knew. And then, on the other side, there were (beside the captain) three officers, steward, agent, and clerk, and the cabin supplied with weapons. But beside the numbers, what is there for sailors to do? If they resist, it is mutiny; and if they succeed, and take the vessel, it is piracy. If they ever yield again, their punishment must come; and if they do not yield, what are they to be for the rest of their lives? If a sailor resist his commander, he resists the law, and piracy or submission is his only alternative. Bad as it was, they saw it must be borne. It is what a sailor ships for. Swinging the rope over his head, and bending his body so as to give it full force, the captain brought it down upon the poor fellow's back. Once, twice,—six times. "Will you ever give me any more of your jaw?" The man writhed with pain, but said not a word. Three times more. This was too much, and he muttered something which I could not hear; this brought as many more as the man could stand, when the captain ordered him to be cut down, and to go forward.

"Now for you," said the captain, making up to John, and taking his irons off. As soon as John was loose, he ran forward to the forecastle. "Bring that man aft!" shouted the captain. The second mate, who had been in the forecastle with these men the early part of the voyage, stood still in the waist, and the mate walked slowly forward; but our third officer, anxious to show his zeal, sprang forward over the windlass, and laid hold of John; but John soon threw him from him. The captain stood on the quarter-deck, bareheaded, his eyes flashing with rage, and his face as red as blood, swinging the rope, and calling out to his officers: "Drag him aft!—Lay hold of him! I'll *sweeten* him!" &c., &c. The mate now went forward, and told John quietly to go aft; and he, seeing resistance vain, threw the blackguard third mate from him, said he would go aft of himself, that they should not drag him, and went up to the gangway and held out his hands; but as soon as the captain began to make him fast, the indignity was too much, and he struggled; but, the mate and Russell holding him, he was soon seized up. When he was made fast, he turned to the captain, who stood rolling up his sleeves and getting ready for the blow, and asked him what he was to be flogged for. "Have I ever refused my duty, sir? Have you ever known me to hang back, or to be insolent, or not to know my work?"

"No," said the captain, "it is not that that I flog you for; I flog you for your interference, for asking questions."

"Can't a man ask a question here without being flogged?"

"No," shouted the captain; "nobody shall open his mouth aboard this vessel but myself," and began laying the blows upon his back, swinging half round between each blow, to give it full effect. As he went on, his passion increased, and he danced about the deck, calling out, as he swung the rope: "If you want to know what I flog you for, I'll tell you. It's because I like to do it!—because I like to do it!—It suits me! That's what I do it for!"

The man writhed under the pain until he could endure it no longer, when he called out, with an exclamation more common among foreigners than with us: "O Jesus Christ! O Jesus Christ!"

"Don't call on Jesus Christ," shouted the captain; *"he can't help you. Call on Frank Thompson!* He's the man! He can help you! Jesus Christ can't help you now!"

At these words, which I never shall forget, my blood ran cold. I could look on no longer. Disgusted, sick, I turned away, and leaned over the rail, and looked down into the water. A few rapid thoughts, I don't know what,—our situation, a resolution to see the captain punished when we got home,—crossed my mind; but the falling of the blows and the cries of the man called me back once more. At length they ceased, and, turning round, I found that the mate, at a signal from the captain, had cast him loose. Almost doubled up with pain, the man walked slowly forward, and went down into the forecastle. Every one else stood still at his post, while the captain, swelling with rage, and with the importance of his achievement, walked the quarter-deck, and at each turn, as he came forward, calling out to us: "You see your condition! You see where I've got you all, and you know what to expect!"—"You've been mistaken in me; you didn't know what I was! Now you know what I am!"—"I'll make you toe the mark, every soul of you, or I'll flog you all, fore and aft, from the boy up!"—"You've got a driver over you! Yes, a *slave-driver,—a nigger-driver!* I'll see who'll tell me he isn't a NIGGER slave!" With this and the like matter, equally calculated to quiet us, and to allay any apprehensions of future trouble, he entertained us for about ten minutes, when he went below. Soon after, John came aft, with his bare back covered with stripes and wales in every direction, and dreadfully swollen, and asked the steward to ask the captain to let him have some salve, or balsam, to put upon it. "No," said the captain, who heard him from below; "tell him to put his shirt on; that's the best thing for him, and pull me ashore in the boat. Nobody is going to lay-up on board this vessel." He then called to Mr. Russell to take those two men and two others in the boat, and pull him ashore. I went for one. The two men could hardly bend their backs, and the captain called to them to "give way," "give way!" but, finding they did their best, he let them alone. The agent was in the stern sheets, but during the whole pull—a league or more—not a word was spoken. We landed; the captain, agent, and officer went up to the house, and left us with the boat. I, and the man with me, stayed near the boat, while John and Sam walked slowly away, and sat down on the rocks. They talked some time together, but at length separated, each sitting alone. I had some fears of John. He was a foreigner, and violently tempered, and under suffering; and he had his knife with him, and the captain was to come down alone to the boat. But nothing happened; and we went quietly on board. The captain was probably armed, and if either of them had lifted a hand against him, they would have had nothing before them but flight, and starvation in the woods of California, or capture by the soldiers and Indians, whom the offer of twenty dollars would have set upon them.

After the day's work was done, we went down into the forecastle, and ate our plain supper; but not a word was spoken. It was Saturday night; but there was no song,—no "sweethearts and wives." A gloom was over everything. The two men lay in their berths, groaning with pain, and we all turned in, but, for myself, not to sleep. A sound coming now and then from the berths of the two men showed that they were awake, as awake they must have been, for they could hardly lie in one posture long; the dim, swinging lamp shed its light over the dark hole in which we lived, and many and various reflections and purposes coursed through my mind. I had no apprehension that the captain would try to lay a hand on me; but our situation, living under a tyranny, with an ungoverned, swaggering fellow administering it; of the character of the country we were in; the length of the voyage; the uncertainty attending our return to America; and then, if we should return, the prospect of obtaining justice and satisfaction for these poor men; and I vowed that, if God should ever give me the means, I would do something to redress the grievances and relieve the sufferings of that class of beings with whom my lot had so long been cast.

EDGAR ALLAN POE (1809–1849)

The story of Poe's life is ghastly enough to have been written by Poe himself. It is a story of bizarre relationships, personal wretchedness, physical and psychological self-destruction; a story of a man endowed with large gifts, a man courageous in defending his esthetic principles, but also morbid, perhaps a little mad, in the exultation of his pride. Poe seems in his own life to have wanted to achieve that "unity of effect" which he praised in literature: an effect of romantic agony, exceptional suffering, perhaps heroic suicide.

He was born to traveling actors. The father disappeared when the child was one year old, and the mother died before he was three. Edgar was then taken into the home of John Allan, a wealthy Richmond merchant, but was never legally adopted. This was a relationship guaranteed to create trouble: the boy was spoiled, yet he had always to be aware that he lived with the Allans on sufferance; he could never take for granted his comfort or security. Throughout his life, and in much of his work, Poe would display the psychology of the orphan, of all those who feel themselves to be discarded.

All his life Poe was inclined to look for solace in women either motherly and reassuring or very young and childlike. Two such relationships marked his youth, one with the mother of a school friend and the other with a girl whose parents forced her to drop him. It was the pattern, as W. H. Auden unkindly but accurately remarks, of "an unmanly sort of man whose love-life seems to have been largely confined to crying in laps and playing house."

In 1826 Poe entered the University of Virginia, but because of gambling debts and drinking his foster-father soon withdrew him. This led to another fierce quarrel, whereupon Poe left the Allans, went to Boston, and there published his first book, Tamerlane and Other Poems (1827). He then spent two years as an enlisted man in the army, and in 1829 he issued a second volume of poems, Al Aaraaf, Tamerlane, and Other Poems. Neither book brought him the recognition he craved nor the income he needed. In 1830 he entered West Point, again supported by Allan, but disliking the place, he got himself dismissed through a premeditated piece of insubordination. Now, the break with Allan became final.

For the rest of his life Poe was trapped between poverty and panic. He never earned enough, either as writer or editor, to escape extreme financial worries, and there were times when he was simply underfed. In 1831 he moved to his Baltimore relatives, Mrs. Maria Clemm and her daughter Virginia, and published a third volume, Poems, again with little recognition. He now tried consciously to adapt his work to commercial necessities—mostly by writing popular tales of terror. He met with some success. In 1832 he published a number of such stories; in 1833 he won a literary prize of 100 dollars; and thereafter he found employment editing various journals, jobs usually terminated because of his irascibility and drinking. Nevertheless, by about 1835 Poe began to attract considerable attention: his criticism was sharply written and obviously of a higher level than anything else then being done, and he was an editor of considerable resourcefulness.

In 1836 Poe married his thirteen-year-old cousin, Virginia Clemm. Taking his child bride with him, Poe now moved to New York City where he tried his hand at free-lance literary work; then, in 1838, he went to Philadelphia, where a period of relative prosperity followed. But by 1844 he was back in New York, and again there were editorships, quarrels, poverty. Three years later, when Poe was in one of his worst financial crises, his young wife died of tuberculosis.

The rest is disaster. Poe drank too much, and alcohol in even small quantities disarranged him radically. He was frequently ill, physically and perhaps mentally. He exhausted himself in quests for feminine solace. In 1849 he was found drunk on a Baltimore street, and a few days later he died in a hospital.

Literary people have never agreed about Poe as poet, story writer, and critic. Major poets like William Butler Yeats and Alfred Tennyson praised him. The French symbolists, especially Baudelaire and Mallarmé, looked upon him as their master. But Emerson called him "the jingle man," Lowell declared him to be "three-fifths genius and two-fifths sheer fudge," and Whitman wrote that his verses *"belong among the electric lights of imaginative literature, brilliant and dazzling, but with no heat." This split in judgment, often reflecting a larger disagreement about the nature and ends of literature itself, has continued into our own day. At the least, no critic or reader seems merely lukewarm toward Poe.*

His basic opinions and attitudes differed strikingly from those of most important nineteenth-century American writers. He had little interest in orthodox theology or the heterodox religion of the time. He was openly contemptuous of democracy and social reform. He sneered at the common man who was frequently the object of nineteenth-century adoration. He endorsed the institution of slavery. He had no feeling for humanitarian causes or ideals. Perhaps to compensate for his own origins and insecurities, Poe struck the pose of Southern aristocrat—with more violence and venom than a true aristocrat might consider it proper to employ. Yet it would be a mistake to suppose that, because he was so sharply at odds with the dominant intellectual style of his day, Poe was somehow a "sport" in American culture, an oddity requiring special explanation. For there has always been a tradition, at least since Poe himself, of extreme estheticism, even preciosity, in our culture; always a tradition of fastidious revulsion from the commonness of our life.

Poe's aristocratic posture had one positive consequence: it enabled him to shake loose from the moralistic didacticism that afflicted most literary discussion at the time and to insist that literature should be valued in its own right. He was the first important American writer who saw literature as an end in itself, requiring no moral, religious, or political justification. Repeatedly he attacked what he called "the didactic heresy," that is, the notion that literature has the task of teaching certain moral doctrines. He tried, however narrowly, to examine a literary work by literary standards, with a coldly dispassionate and expert eye. For his time and place, this was a revolutionary innovation and, historically speaking, more important than the specific doctrines Poe advanced in his criticism.

These doctrines speak for an extreme version of romanticism and are more than a little dubious. A poem, he wrote in 1831,

> is opposed to a work of science by having, for its immediate object, pleasure not truth; to romance, by having, for its object, an indefinite instead of a definite pleasure . . . to which end music is an essential, since the comprehension of sweet sound is our most indefinite conception.

Poe believed that "a long poem does not exist. I maintain that the phrase, 'a long poem,' is a flat contradiction in terms." He thought of the poem, seldom to be more than 100 lines in length, as a way of producing "sensations which bewilder while they enthrall—and

*which would not so enthrall if they did not bewilder." In short, he
took an irrationalist and—his opponents would charge—an ob-
scurant view of poetry: the poem would cast a spell of some
"magical" sort; and toward this end it required what he called "unity
of effect," that is, one overwhelming impression created through
sonority of sound, repetition of phrases, and rhythmic incantation.
Like the more extreme European romantics, he hoped thereby to be
able to enter a state of short-lived excitement in which a supernal
beauty, free of the imperfections of the world and flesh, could be
glimpsed. And also in accordance with more extreme romantic
notions, Poe felt that the proper tone of poetry is melancholic, and
its best subject, the death of a beautiful woman:*

> *I asked myself—"Of all melancholy topics, what, according to the uni-
> versal understanding of mankind, is the most melancholy?" Death—was
> the obvious reply. "And when," I said, "is this most melancholy of topics
> most poetical?" From what I have already explained . . . the answer . . .
> is obvious—"When it most closely allies itself to Beauty": the death,
> then, of a beautiful woman is, unquestionably, the most poetical topic in
> the world—and equally is it beyond doubt that the lips best suited for
> such topic are those of a bereaved lover.*

*Few serious poets or critics would subscribe today to such notions. By
his own private declaration, Poe simply denied the title of "poetry"
to most of the poems, great, good, and commonplace, ever written.
He reduced poetry to a form of irrationalist incantation, a sort of
metrical turning on, deprived of the moral substance and intellectual richness that, at its best, it had always had. Right enough in
arguing against the didactic heresy, he confused the objection to
moralist preaching with a denial of moral content and significance
in poetry. The critic Yvor Winters has stated some of the other
objections to Poe's view of poetry:*

> *Poe's very conception of poetic unity is one of mood, or emotion; . . . he
> regards the existence of mood to be governed by narrow mechanical
> rules—in other words, exaltation of spirit is merely a form of nervous
> excitement. The word* effect *is here used as elsewhere as a synonym for*
> impression; *artistic unity is described specifically as totality of effect.
> There appears to be no awareness whatever of that comprehensive act
> of the spirit, in part intellectual, whereby we understand and remember*
> Paradise Lost *as a whole, seize the whole intention with intellect and
> with memory, and, plunging into any passage, experience that passage
> in relationship to the whole, an act in which the emotional element,
> since it is involved in and supported by the rational understanding, rises
> superior to mechanical necessity.*

*Poe's own poetry suffers from the kinds of faults that follow from his
theories. His poems are sometimes haunting in their strangeness*

and wierdness, but too often they seem merely mechanical in rhythm, vaguely portentous in significance; and they rarely tempt a close or a second reading. Remarkable figure that he was, Poe now can hardly be supposed one of our major poets.

His stories, by common consent, hold up somewhat better than his poems. In a letter written in 1835 Poe describes the qualities he prefers in short fiction as "the ludicrous heightened into the grotesque; the fearful coloured into the horrible; the witty exaggerated into the burlesque; the singular wrought out into the strange and mystical." It was with elements of the grotesque and the horrible that Poe worked best, the kind of fiction called Gothic. Gothic usually is a mode of fiction that tries to create effects of the frightful and perverse; it is set in ruined castles and abbeys, with groaning windows, numerous spiders, and regular ghosts; it is populated with wilting and doomed aristocrats stricken with rare diseases, or with evil but beautiful heroes wantonly torturing innocent heroines (butterflies on the wrack), or with evil but beautiful heroines sucking the lifeblood out of their victims (the vampire theme); and its general purport is to suggest a violation of traditional values, a celebration of such unsanctioned impulses as sadism, masochism, necrophilia, and so forth. The tone of Poe's Gothic stories has been vividly described by Van Wyck Brooks:

> *Since the days of the alchemists no one has produced more than Poe the effects of damnation, no one has been more conscious of being damned. In his pages the breath of life never stirs; crimes occur which do not reverberate in the human conscience, there is laughter which has no sound, there is weeping without tears, there is beauty without love, there is love without children, trees grow which bear no fruit, flowers which have no fragrance—it is a silent world, cold, blasted, moon-struck, sterile, a devil's heath. Only a sensation of intolerable remorse pervades it.*

Yet, for all their melodramatic excess, gimcrack settings, and florid language, the best of Poe's stories are impressive. Their terror, as he said, is "not of Germany, but of the soul." Through worn and often crude devices, they project conditions of psychic nightmare. Nor does Poe mean these stories, as recent interpreters would have it, as visions of abnormality. For him the distinction between normal and the abnormal barely exists, and he shows no interest in therapeutic possibilities. His cult of damnation and death strikes him not as a perversity to be explained, but as a reality to be endured. With the lucidity of detachment, he tries to present externalized structures of terror, the chasm of nothingness in our souls which is the ultimate source of horror. His stories, said Baudelaire, show "absurdity installing itself in the intellect, and governing it with a crushing logic."

FURTHER READING

George E. Woodberry's 1885 biography, *The Life of Edgar Allan Poe,* was revised in 1909 and is still worth attention; it has been factually corrected in Arthur Quinn's *Edgar Allan Poe: A Critical Biography* (1941). The brilliant, historically important, if overly enthusiastic, writings of Baudelaire appear in *Baudelaire on Poe* (1952), edited by Lois and Francis E. Hyslop, Jr. Interesting criticism appears in Edward H. Davidson's *Poe: a Critical Study* (1957); Harry Levin's *The Power of Blackness* (1958); Patrick Quinn, *The French Face of Edgar Poe* (1957).

To Helen (1831)

Helen, thy beauty is to me
   Like those Nicéan barks of yore,
That gently, o'er a perfumed sea,
   The weary, way-worn wanderer bore
   To his own native shore.

On desperate seas long wont to roam,
   Thy hyacinth hair, thy classic face,
Thy Naiad airs have brought me home
   To the glory that was Greece,
And the grandeur that was Rome.   10

Lo! in yon brilliant window-niche
   How statue-like I see thee stand,
   The agate lamp within thy hand!
Ah, Psyche, from the regions which
   Are Holy Land!

The City in the Sea (1831)

Lo! Death has reared himself a throne
In a strange city lying alone
Far down within the dim West,
Where the good and the bad and the worst and the best
Have gone to their eternal rest.
There shrines and palaces and towers
(Time-eaten towers that tremble not!)
Resemble nothing that is ours.
Around, by lifting winds forgot,

Resignedly beneath the sky   10
The melancholy waters lie.

No rays from the holy heaven come down
On the long night-time of that town;
But light from out the lurid sea
Streams up the turrets silently—
Gleams up the pinnacles far and free—
Up domes—up spires—up kingly halls—
Up fanes—up Babylon-like walls—
Up shadowy long-forgotten bowers
Of sculptured ivy and stone flowers—   20
Up many and many a marvellous shrine
Whose wreathéd friezes intertwine
The viol, the violet, and the vine.
Resignedly beneath the sky
The melancholy waters lie.
So blend the turrets and shadows there
That all seem pendulous in air,
While from a proud tower in the town
Death looks gigantically down.

There open fanes and gaping graves   30
Yawn level with the luminous waves;
But not the riches there that lie
In each idol's diamond eye—
Not the gaily-jewelled dead
Tempt the waters from their bed;
For no ripples curl, alas!
Along that wilderness of glass—
No swellings tell that winds may be
Upon some far-off happier sea—
No heavings hint that winds have been   40
On seas less hideously serene.

But lo, a stir is in the air!
The wave—there is a movement there!
As if the towers had thrust aside,
In slightly sinking, the dull tide—
As if their tops had feebly given
A void within the filmy Heaven.
The waves have now a redder glow—
The hours are breathing faint and low—
And when, amid no earthly moans,   50
Down, down that town shall settle hence,
Hell, rising from a thousand thrones,
Shall do it reverence.

The Sleeper (1831)

At midnight, in the month of June,
I stand beneath the mystic moon.
An opiate vapor, dewy, dim,
Exhales from out her golden rim,
And, softly dripping, drop by drop,
Upon the quiet mountain top,
Steals drowsily and musically
Into the universal valley.
The rosemary nods upon the grave;
The lily lolls upon the wave;   10
Wrapping the fog about its breast,
The ruin moulders into rest;
Looking like Lethe, see! the lake
A conscious slumber seems to take,
And would not, for the world, awake.
All Beauty sleeps!—and lo! where lies
Irene, with her Destinies!

Oh, lady bright! can it be right—
This window open to the night?
The wanton airs, from the tree-top,   20
Laughingly through the lattice drop—
The bodiless airs, a wizard rout,
Flit through thy chamber in and out,
And wave the curtain canopy
So fitfully—so fearfully—
Above the close and fringéd lid
'Neath which thy slumb'ring soul lies hid,
That, o'er the floor and down the wall,
Like ghosts the shadows rise and fall!

Oh, lady dear, hast thou no fear?   30
Why and what art thou dreaming here?
Sure thou art come o'er far-off seas,
A wonder to these garden trees!
Strange is thy pallor! strange thy dress!
Strange, above all, thy length of tress,
And this all solemn silentness!

The lady sleeps! Oh, may her sleep,
Which is enduring, so be deep!
Heaven have her in its sacred keep!
This chamber changed for one more holy,   40
This bed for one more melancholy,
I pray to God that she may lie

Forever with unopened eye,
While the pale sheeted ghosts go by!

My love, she sleeps! Oh, may her sleep,
As it is lasting, so be deep!
Soft may the worms about her creep!
Far in the forest, dim and old,
For her may some tall vault unfold—
Some vault that oft hath flung its black   50
And wingéd panels fluttering back,
Triumphant, o'er the crested palls,
Of her grand family funerals—

Some sepulchre, remote, alone,
Against whose portal she hath thrown,
In childhood, many an idle stone—
Some tomb from out whose sounding door
She ne'er shall force an echo more,
Thrilling to think, poor child of sin!
It was the dead who groaned within.   60

Israfel *(1831)*

In Heaven a spirit doth dwell
     "Whose heart-strings are a lute";
None sing so wildly well
As the angel Israfel,[1]
And the giddy stars (so legends tell),
Ceasing their hymns, attend the spell
     Of his voice, all mute.

Tottering above
     In her highest noon,
     The enamoured moon   10
Blushes with love,
     While, to listen, the red levin[2]
     (With the rapid Pleiads,[3] even,
     Which were seven,)
     Pauses in Heaven.

1 And the angel Israfel, [whose heart-strings are a lute, and] who has the sweetest
voice of all God's creatures. *Koran.*
2 Lightning.
3 A group of stars.

And they say (the starry choir
    And the other listening things)
That Israfeli's fire
Is owing to that lyre
    By which he sits and sings—   20
The trembling living wire
    Of those unusual strings.

But the skies that angel trod,
    Where deep thoughts are a duty,
Where Love's a grown-up God,
    Where the Houri glances are
Imbued with all the beauty
    Which we worship in a star.

Therefore, thou art not wrong,
    Israfeli, who despisest   30
An unimpassioned song;
To thee the laurels belong,
    Best bard, because the wisest!
Merrily live, and long!

The ecstasies above
    With thy burning measures suit—
Thy grief, thy joy, thy hate, thy love,
    With the fervour of thy lute—
    Well may the stars be mute!

Yes, Heaven is thine; but this   40
    Is a world of sweets and sours;
    Our flowers are merely—flowers,
And the shadow of thy perfect bliss
    Is the sunshine of ours.

If I could dwell
Where Israfel
    Hath dwelt, and he where I,
He might not sing so wildly well
    A mortal melody,
While a bolder note than this might swell   50
    From my lyre within the sky.

The Raven *(1845)*

Once upon a midnight dreary, while I pondered, weak and weary,
Over many a quaint and curious volume of forgotten lore—
While I nodded, nearly napping, suddenly there came a tapping,
As of some one gently rapping, rapping at my chamber door.
"'Tis some visitor," I muttered, "tapping at my chamber door—
    Only this and nothing more."

Ah, distinctly I remember it was in the bleak December;
And each separate dying ember wrought its ghost upon the floor.
Eagerly I wished the morrow;—vainly I had sought to borrow
From my books surcease of sorrow—sorrow for the lost Lenore—   10
For the rare and radiant maiden whom the angels name Lenore—
    Nameless *here* for evermore.

And the silken, sad, uncertain rustling of each purple curtain
Thrilled me—filled me with fantastic terrors never felt before;
So that now, to still the beating of my heart, I stood repeating
"'Tis some visitor entreating entrance at my chamber door—
Some late visitor entreating entrance at my chamber door;—
    This it is and nothing more."

Presently my soul grew stronger; hesitating then no longer,
"Sir," said I, "or Madam, truly your forgiveness I implore;   20
But the fact is I was napping, and so gently you came rapping,
And so faintly you came tapping, tapping at my chamber door,
That I scarce was sure I heard you"—here I opened wide the
    door;—
    Darkness there and nothing more.

Deep into that darkness peering, long I stood there wondering,
    fearing,
Doubting, dreaming dreams no mortal ever dared to dream before;
But the silence was unbroken, and the stillness gave no token,
And the only word there spoken was the whispered word,
    "Lenore!"
This I whispered, and an echo murmured back the word "Lenore!"
    Merely this and nothing more.   30

Back into the chamber turning, all my soul within me burning,
Soon again I heard a tapping somewhat louder than before.
"Surely," said I, "surely that is something at my window lattice;
Let me see, then, what thereat is, and this mystery explore—
Let my heart be still a moment and this mystery explore;—
    'Tis the wind and nothing more!"

Open here I flung the shutter, when, with many a flirt and flutter
In there stepped a stately Raven of the saintly days of yore.
Not the least obeisance made he; not a minute stopped or stayed
     he;
But, with mien of lord or lady, perched above my chamber door—   40
Perched upon a bust of Pallas [1] just above my chamber door—
     Perched, and sat, and nothing more.

Then this ebony bird beguiling my sad fancy into smiling,
By the grave and stern decorum of the countenance it wore,
"Though thy crest be shorn and shaven, thou," I said, "art sure no
     craven,
Ghastly grim and ancient Raven wandering from the Nightly
     shore—
Tell me what thy lordly name is on the Night's Plutonian shore!"
     Quoth the Raven, "Nevermore."

Much I marvelled this ungainly fowl to hear discourse so plainly,
Though its answer little meaning—little relevancy bore;   50
For we cannot help agreeing that no living human being
Ever yet was blessed with seeing bird above his chamber door—
Bird or beast upon the sculptured bust above his chamber door,
     With such name as "Nevermore."

But the Raven, sitting lonely on the placid bust, spoke only
That one word, as if his soul in that one word he did outpour.
Nothing farther then he uttered—not a feather then he fluttered—
Till I scarcely more than muttered "Other friends have flown
     before—
On the morrow *he* will leave me, as my hopes have flown before."
     Then the bird said "Nevermore."   60

Startled at the stillness broken by reply so aptly spoken,
"Doubtless," said I, "what it utters is its only stock and store
Caught from some unhappy master whom unmerciful Disaster
Followed fast and followed faster till his songs one burden bore—
Till the dirges of his Hope that melancholy burden bore
     Of 'Never—nevermore.' "

But the Raven still beguiling all my fancy into smiling,
Straight I wheeled a cushioned seat in front of bird, and bust and
     door;
Then, upon the velvet sinking, I betook myself to linking
Fancy unto fancy, thinking what this ominous bird of yore—   70

[1] Pallas Athene, goddess of wisdom.

What this grim, ungainly, ghastly, gaunt, and ominous bird of
  yore
 Meant in croaking "Nevermore."

This I sat engaged in guessing, but no syllable expressing
To the fowl whose fiery eyes now burned into my bosom's core;
This and more I sat divining, with my head at ease reclining
On the cushion's velvet lining that the lamplight gloated o'er,
But whose velvet violet lining with the lamplight gloating o'er,
  She shall press, ah, nevermore!

Then, methought, the air grew denser, perfumed from an unseen
  censer
Swung by Seraphim whose foot-falls tinkled on the tufted floor.   *80*
"Wretch," I cried, "thy God hath lent thee—by these angels he
  hath sent thee
Respite—respite and nepenthe from thy memories of Lenore;
Quaff, oh quaff this kind nepenthe [2] and forget this lost Lenore!"
  Quoth the Raven "Nevermore."

"Prophet!" said I, "thing of evil! prophet still, if bird or devil!—
Whether Tempter sent, or whether tempest tossed thee here
  ashore,
Desolate yet all undaunted, on this desert land enchanted—
On this home by Horror haunted—tell me truly, I implore—
Is there—*is* there balm in Gilead?—tell me—tell me, I implore!"
  Quoth the Raven "Nevermore."   *90*

"Prophet!" said I, "thing of evil!—prophet still, if bird or devil!
By that Heaven that bends above us—by that God we both
  adore—
Tell this soul with sorrow laden if, within the distant, Aidenn,
It shall clasp a sainted maiden whom the angels name Lenore—
Clasp a rare and radiant maiden whom the angels name Lenore."
  Quoth the Raven "Nevermore."

"Be that word our sign of parting, bird or fiend!" I shrieked,
  upstarting—
"Get thee back into the tempest and the Night's Plutonian shore!
Leave no black plume as a token of that lie thy soul hath spoken!
Leave my loneliness unbroken!—quit the bust above my door!   *100*
Take thy beak from out my heart, and take thy form from off my
  door!"
  Quoth the Raven "Nevermore."

---

[2] A drink supposed to end sorrow.

And the Raven, never flitting, still is sitting, *still* is sitting
On the pallid bust of Pallas just above my chamber door;
And his eyes have all the seeming of a demon's that is dreaming,
And the lamp-light o'er him streaming throws his shadow on the
      floor;
And my soul from out that shadow that lies floating on the floor
    Shall be lifted—nevermore!

Ulalume: A Ballad (1847)

The skies they were ashen and sober;
    The leaves they were crispéd and sere—
    The leaves they were withering and sere;
It was night, in the lonesome October
    Of my most immemorial year:
It was hard by the dim lake of Auber,[1]
    In the misty mid region of Weir—
It was down by the dank tarn of Auber,
    In the ghoul-haunted woodland of Weir.

Here once, through an alley Titanic,   10
    Of cypress, I roamed with my Soul—
    Of cypress, with Psyche, my Soul.
These were days when my heart was volcanic
    As the scoriac[2] rivers that roll—
    As the lavas that restlessly roll
Their sulphurous currents down Yaanek
    In the ultimate climes of the Pole—
That groan as they roll down Mount Yaanek
    In the realms of the Boreal[3] Pole.

Our talk had been serious and sober,   20
    But our thoughts they were palsied and sere—
    Our memories were treacherous and sere;
For we knew not the month was October,
    And we marked not the night of the year
    (Ah, night of all nights in the year!)—
We noted not the dim lake of Auber
    (Though once we had journey down here)—

[1] This name, like Weir and Yaanek, was apparently invented by Poe.
[2] Volcanic.
[3] Northern.

Remembered not the dank tarn of Auber,
    Nor the ghoul-haunted woodland of Weir.

And now, as the night was senescent   *30*
    And star-dials pointed to morn—
    As the star-dials hinted of morn—
At the end of our path a liquescent
    And nebulous lustre was born,
Out of which a miraculous crescent
    Arose with a duplicate horn—
Astarte's [4] bediamonded crescent
    Distinct with its duplicate horn.

And I said: "She is warmer than Dian; [5]
    She rolls through an ether of sighs—   *40*
    She revels in a region of sighs.
She has seen that the tears are not dry on
    These cheeks, where the worm never dies,
And has come past the stars of the Lion, [6]
    To point us the path to the skies—
    To the Lethean [7] peace of the skies—
Come up, in despite of the Lion,
    To shine on us with her bright eyes—
Come up through the lair of the Lion,
    With love in her luminous eyes."   *50*

But Psyche, uplifting her finger
    Said: "Sadly this star I mistrust—
    Her pallor I strangely mistrust:
Ah, hasten!—ah, let us not linger!
    Ah, fly!—let us fly!—for we must."
In terror she spoke, letting sink her
    Wings till they trailed in the dust—
In agony sobbed, letting sink her
    Plumes till they trailed in the dust—
    Till they sorrowfully trailed in the dust.   *60*

I replied: "This is nothing but dreaming:
    Let us on by this tremulous light!
    Let us bathe in this crystalline light!
Its Sibyllic splendor is beaming
    With Hope and in Beauty to-night!
    See!—it flickers up the sky through the night!

[4] Goddess of love.

[5] Goddess of the moon, suggesting chaste love.

[6] Constellation of Leo, danger.

[7] Lethe, legendary river, suggests forgetfulness.

Ah, we safely may trust to its gleaming,
    And be sure it will lead us aright—
We safely may trust to a gleaming,
    That cannot but guide us aright,   70
    Since it flickers up to Heaven through the night."

Thus I pacified Psyche and kissed her,
    And tempted her out of her gloom—
    And conquered her scruples and gloom;
And we passed to the end of the vista,
    But we stopped by the door of a tomb—
    By the door of a legended tomb;
And I said: "What is written, sweet sister,
    On the door of this legended tomb?"
    She replied: "Ulalume—Ulalume!—   80
    'Tis the vault of thy lost Ulalume!"

Then my heart it grew ashen and sober
    As the leaves that were crispéd and sere—
    As the leaves that were withering and sere;
And I cried: "It was surely October
    On *this* very night of last year
    That I journeyed—I journeyed down here!—
    That I brought a dread burden down here—
    On this night of all nights in the year,
    Ah, what demon has tempted me here?   90
Well I know, now, this dim lake of Auber—
    This misty mid region of Weir—
Well I know, now, this dank tarn of Auber,
    This ghoul-haunted woodland of Weir."

Said we, then—the two, then: "Ah can it
    Have been that woodlandish ghouls—
    The pitfull, the merciful ghouls—
To bar up our way and to ban it
    From the secret that lies in these wolds—
    From the thing that lies hidden in these wolds—   100
Have drawn up the spectre of a planet
    From the limbo of lunary souls—
This sinfully scintillant planet
    From the Hell of the planetary souls?

Ligeia *(1838, 1845)*

And the will therein lieth, which dieth not. Who knoweth the mysteries of the will, with its vigor? For God is but a great will pervading all things by nature of its intentness. Man doth not yield himself to the angels, nor unto death utterly, save only through the weakness of his feeble will. *Joseph Glanvill*

I cannot, for my soul, remember how, when, or even precisely where, I first became acquainted with the lady Ligeia. Long years have since elapsed, and my memory is feeble through much suffering. Or, perhaps, I cannot *now* bring these points to mind, because, in truth, the character of my beloved, her rare learning, her singular yet placid cast of beauty, and the thrilling and enthralling eloquence of her low musical language, made their way into my heart by paces so steadily and stealthily progressive that they have been unnoticed and unknown. Yet I believe that I met her first and most frequently in some large, old, decaying city near the Rhine. Of her family—I have surely heard her speak. That it is of a remotely ancient date cannot be doubted. Ligeia! Ligeia! Buried in studies of a nature more than all else adapted to deaden impressions of the outward world, it is by that sweet word alone—by Ligeia—that I bring before mine eyes in fancy the image of her who is no more. And now, while I write, a recollection flashes upon me that I have *never known* the paternal name of her who was my friend and my betrothed, and who became the partner of my studies, and finally the wife of my bosom. Was it a playful charge on the part of my Ligeia? or was it a test of my strength of affection, that I should institute no inquiries upon this point? or was it rather a caprice of my own—a wildly romantic offering on the shrine of the most passionate devotion? I but indistinctly recall the fact itself—what wonder that I have utterly forgotten the circumstances which originated or attended it? And, indeed, if ever that spirit which is entitled *Romance*—if ever she, the wan and the misty-winged *Ashtophet* of idolatrous Egypt, presided, as they tell, over marriages ill-omened, then most surely she presided over mine.

There is one dear topic, however, on which my memory fails me not. It is the *person* of Ligeia. In stature she was tall, somewhat slender, and, in her latter days, even emaciated. I would in vain attempt to portray the majesty, the quiet ease of her demeanor, or the incomprehensible lightness and elasticity of her footfall. She came and departed as a shadow. I was never made aware of her entrance into my closed study save by the dear music of her low sweet voice, as she placed her marble hand upon my shoulder. In beauty of face no maiden ever equalled her. It was the radiance of an opium-dream—an airy and spirit-lifting vision more wildly divine than the phantasies which hovered about the slumbering souls of the daughters of Delos. Yet her

features were not of that regular mould which we have been falsely
taught to worship in the classical labors of the heathen. "There is no
exquisite beauty," say Bacon, Lord Verulam, speaking truly of all the
forms and *genera* of beauty, "without some *strangeness* in the proportion." Yet, although I saw that the features of Ligeia were not of a
classic regularity—although I perceived that her loveliness was indeed
"exquisite," and felt that there was much of "strangeness" pervading it,
yet I have tried in vain to detect the irregularity and to trace home my
own perception of "the strange." I examined the contour of the lofty and
pale forehead—it was faultless—how cold indeed that word when
applied to a majesty so divine!—the skin rivalling the purest ivory, the
commanding extent and repose, the gentle prominence of the regions
above the temples; and then the raven-black, the glossy, the luxuriant
and naturally-curling tresses, setting forth the full force of the Homeric
epithet, "hyacinthine!" I looked at the delicate outlines of the nose—
and nowhere but in the graceful medallions of the Hebrews had I beheld a similar perfection. There were the same luxurious smoothness
of surface, the same scarcely perceptible tendency to the aquiline, the
same harmoniously curved nostrils speaking the free spirit. I regarded
the sweet mouth. Here was indeed the triumph of all things heavenly—
the magnificent turn of the short upper lip—the soft, voluptuous slumber of the under—the dimples which sported, and the color which
spoke—the teeth glancing back, with a brilliancy almost startling, every
ray of the holy light which fell upon them in her serene and placid yet
most exultingly radiant of all smiles. I scrutinized the formation of
the chin—and, here too, I found the gentleness of breadth, the softness
and the majesty, the fulness and the spirituality, of the Greek—the
contour which the god Apollo revealed but in a dream, to Cleomenes,
the son of the Athenian. And then I peered into the large eyes of Ligeia.

For eyes we have no models in the remotely antique. It might have
been, too, that in these eyes of my beloved lay the secret to which Lord
Verulam alludes. They were, I must believe, far larger than the ordinary eyes of our own race. They were even fuller than the fullest of
the gazelle eyes of the tribe of the valley of Nourjahad. Yet it was only
at intervals—in moments of intense excitement—that this peculiarity
became more than slightly noticeable in Ligeia. And at such moments
was her beauty—in my heated fancy thus it appeared perhaps—the
beauty of beings either above or apart from the earth—the beauty of
the fabulous Houri of the Turk. The hue of the orbs was the most
brilliant of black, and, far over them, hung jetty lashes of great length.
The brows, slightly irregular in outline, had the same tint. The "strangeness," however, which I found in the eyes, was of a nature distinct
from the formation, or the color, or the brilliancy of the features, and
must, after all, be referred to the *expression*. Ah, word of no meaning!
behind whose vast latitude of mere sound we intrench our ignorance
of so much of the spiritual. The expression of the eyes of Ligeia! How

for long hours have I pondered upon it! How have I, through the whole
of a midsummer night, struggled to fathom it! What was it—that something more profound than the well of Democritus—which lay far within
the pupils of my beloved? What *was* it? I was possessed with a passion
to discover. Those eyes! those large, those shining, those divine orbs!
they became to me twin stars of Leda, and I to them devoutest of
astrologers.

There is no point, among the many incomprehensible anomalies of
the science of mind, more thrillingly exciting than the fact—never, I
believe, noticed in the schools—that in our endeavors to recall to
memory something long forgotten, we often find ourselves *upon the
very verge* of remembrance, without being able, in the end, to remember. And thus how frequently, in my intense scrutiny of Ligeia's eyes,
have I felt approaching the full knowledge of their expression—felt it
approaching—yet not quite be mine—and so at length entirely depart!
And (strange, oh strangest mystery of all!) I found, in the commonest
objects of the universe, a circle of analogies to that expression. I mean
to say that, subsequently to the period when Ligeia's beauty passed into
my spirit, there dwelling as in a shrine, I derived, from many existences
in the material world, a sentiment such as I felt always aroused, within
me, by her large and luminous orbs. Yet not the more could I define
that sentiment, or analyze, or even steadily view it. I recognized it, let
me repeat, sometimes in the survey of a rapidly growing vine—in the
contemplation of a moth, a butterfly, a chrysalis, a stream of running
water. I have felt it in the ocean; in the falling of a meteor. I have felt
it in the glances of unusually aged people. And there are one or two
stars in heaven—(one especially, a star of the sixth magnitude, double
and changeable, to be found near the large star in Lyra) in a telescopic
scrutiny of which I have been made aware of the feeling. I have been
filled with it by certain sounds from stringed instruments, and not unfrequently by passages from books. Among innumerable other instances,
I well remember something in a volume of Joseph Glanvill, which (perhaps merely from its quaintness—who shall say?) never failed to inspire me with the sentiment;—"And the will therein lieth which dieth
not. Who knoweth the mysteries of the will, with its vigor? For God is
but a great will pervading all things by nature of its intentness. Man
doth not yield him to the angels, nor unto death utterly, save only
through the weakness of his feeble will."

Length of years and subsequent reflection, have enabled me to trace,
indeed, some remote connection between this passage in the English
moralist and a portion of the character of Ligeia. An *intensity* in
thought, action, or speech, was possibly, in her, a result, or at least
an index, of that gigantic volition which, during our long intercourse,
failed to give other and more immediate evidence of its existence. Of
all the women whom I have ever known, she, the outwardly calm, the
ever-placid Ligeia, was the most violently a prey to the tumultuous

vultures of stern passion. And of such passion I could form no estimate, save by the miraculous expansion of those eyes which at once so delighted and appalled me—by the almost magical melody, modulation, distinctness, and placidity of her very low voice—and by the fierce energy (rendered doubly effective by contrast with her manner of utterance) of the wild words which she habitually uttered.

I have spoken of the learning of Ligeia: it was immense—such as I have never known in woman. In the classical tongues was she deeply proficient, and as far as my own acquaintance extended in regard to the modern dialects of Europe, I have never known her at fault. Indeed upon any theme of the most admired, because simply the most abstruse of the boasted erudition of the academy, have I *ever* found Ligeia at fault? How singularly—how thrillingly, this one point in the nature of my wife has forced itself, at this late period only, upon my attention! I said her knowledge was such as I have never known in woman—but where breathes the man who has traversed, and successfully, *all* the wide areas of moral, physical, and mathematical science? I saw not then what I now clearly perceive, that the acquisitions of Ligeia were gigantic, were astounding; yet I was sufficiently aware of her infinite supremacy to resign myself, with a child-like confidence, to her guidance through the chaotic world of metaphysical investigation at which I was most busily occupied during the earlier years of our marriage. With how vast a triumph—with how vivid a delight—with how much of all that is ethereal in hope—did I *feel,* as she bent over me in studies but little sought—but less known—that delicious vista by slow degrees expanding before me, down whose long, gorgeous, and all untrodden path, I might at length pass onward to the goal of a wisdom too divinely precious not to be forbidden!

How poignant, then, must have been the grief with which, after some years, I beheld my well-grounded expectations take wings to themselves and fly away! Without Ligeia I was but as a child groping benighted. Her presence, her readings alone, rendered vividly luminous the many mysteries of the transcendentalism in which we were immersed. Wanting the radiant lustre of her eyes, letters, lambent and golden, grew duller than Saturnian lead. And now those eyes shone less and less frequently upon the pages over which I pored. Ligeia grew ill. The wild eyes blazed with a too—too glorious effulgence; the pale fingers became of the transparent waxen hue of the grave; and the blue veins upon the lofty forehead swelled and sank impetuously with the tides of the most gentle emotion. I saw that she must die—and I struggled desperately in spirit with the grim Azrael. [1] And the struggles of the passionate wife were, to my astonishment, even more energetic than my own. There had been much in her stern nature to impress me with the belief that, to her, death would have come without its terrors;

[1] The angel of death.

but not so. Words are impotent to convey any just idea of the fierceness of resistance with which she wrestled with the Shadow. I groaned in anguish at the pitiable spectacle. I would have soothed—I would have reasoned; but, in the intensity of her wild desire for life,—for life— *but* for life—solace and reason were alike the uttermost of folly. Yet not until the last instance, amid the most convulsive writhings of her fierce spirit, was shaken the external placidity of her demeanor. Her voice grew more gentle—grew more low—yet I would not wish to dwell upon the wild meaning of the quietly uttered words. My brain reeled as I hearkened entranced, to a melody more than mortal—to assumptions and aspirations which mortality had never before known.

That she loved me I should not have doubted; and I might have been easily aware that, in a bosom such as hers, love would have reigned no ordinary passion. But in death only was I fully impressed with the strength of her affection. For long hours, detaining my hand, would she pour out before me the overflowing of a heart whose more than passionate devotion amounted to idolatry. How had I deserved to be so blessed by such confessions?—how had I deserved to be so cursed with the removal of my beloved in the hour of my making them? But upon this subject I cannot bear to dilate. Let me say only, that in Ligeia's more than womanly abandonment to a love, alas! all unmerited, all unworthily bestowed, I at length recognized the principle of her longing with so wildly earnest a desire, for the life which was now fleeing so rapidly away. It is this wild longing—it is this eager vehemence of desire for life—*but* for life—that I have no power to portray—no utterance capable of expressing.

At high noon of the night in which she departed, beckoning me peremptorily, to her side, she bade me repeat certain verses composed by herself not many days before. I obeyed her.—They were these:—

Lo! 'tis a gala night
    Within the lonesome latter years!
An angel throng, bewinged, bedight
    In veils, and drowned in tears,
Sit in a theatre, to see
    A play of hopes and fears,
While the orchestra breathes fitfully
    The music of the spheres.

Mimes, in the form of God on high,
    Mutter and mumble low,
And hither and thither fly;
    Mere puppets they, who come and go
At bidding of vast formless things
    That shift the scenery to and fro,
Flapping from out their Condor wings
    Invisible Wo!

That motley drama!—oh, be sure
   It shall not be forgot!
With its Phantom chased for evermore,
   By a crowd that seize it not,
Through a circle that ever returneth in
   To the self-same spot,
And much of Madness and more of Sin
   And Horror the soul of the plot.

But see, amid the mimic rout,
   A crawling shape intrude!
A blood-red thing that writhes from out
   The scenic solitude!
It writhes!—it writhes!—with mortal pangs
   The mimes become its food,
And the seraphs sob at vermin fangs
   In human gore imbued.

Out—out are the lights—out all!
   And over each quivering form,
The curtain, a funeral pall,
   Comes down with the rush of a storm,
And the angels, all pallid and wan,
   Uprising, unveiling, affirm
That the play is the tragedy, "Man,"
   And its hero the Conqueror Worm.

"O God!" half shrieked Ligeia, leaping to her feet and extending her arms aloft with a spasmodic movement, as I made an end of these lines—"O God! O Divine Father!—shall these things be undeviatingly so?—shall this Conqueror be not once conquered? Are we not part and parcel in Thee? Who—who knoweth the mysteries of the will with its vigor? Man doth not yield him to the angels, *nor unto death utterly,* save only through the weakness of his feeble will."

And now, as if exhausted with emotion, she suffered her white arms to fall, and returned solemnly to her bed of death. And as she breathed her last sighs, there came mingled with them a low murmur from her lips. I bent to them my ear, and distinguished, again, the concluding words of the passage in Glanvill—"*Man doth not yield him to the angels, nor unto death utterly, save only through the weakness of his feeble will.*"

She died;—and I, crushed into the very dust with sorrow, could no longer endure the lonely desolation of my dwelling in the dim and decaying city by the Rhine. I had no lack of what the world calls wealth. Ligeia had brought me far more, very far more than ordinarily falls to the lot of mortals. After a few months, therefore, of weary and aimless wandering, I purchased, and put in some repair, an abbey, which

I shall not name, in one of the wildest and least frequented portions of
fair England. The gloomy and dreary grandeur of the building, the
almost savage aspect of the domain, the many melancholy and time-
honored memories connected with both, had much in unison with the
feelings of utter abandonment which had driven me into that remote
and unsocial region of the country. Yet although the external abbey,
with its verdant decay hanging about it, suffered but little alteration,
I gave way, with a child-like perversity, and perchance with a faint hope
of alleviating my sorrows, to a display of more than regal magnificence
within.—For such follies, even in childhood, I had imbibed a taste, and
now they came back to me as if in the dotage of grief. Alas, I feel how
much even of incipient madness might have been discovered in the
gorgeous and fantastic draperies, in the solemn carvings of Egypt, in
the wild cornices and furniture, in the Bedlam patterns of the carpets
of tufted gold! I had become a bounden slave in the trammels of opium,
and my labors and orders had taken a coloring from my dreams. But
these absurdities I must not pause to detail. Let me speak only of that
one chamber, ever accursed, whither, in a moment of mental alienation,
I led from the altar as my bride—as the successor of the unforgotten
Ligeia—the fair-haired and blue-eyed Lady Rowena Trevanion, of
Tremaine.

There is no individual portion of the architecture and decoration of
that bridal chamber which is not now visibly before me. Where were
the souls of the haughty family of the bride, when, through thirst of
gold, they permitted to pass the threshold of an apartment *so* bedecked,
a maiden and a daughter so beloved? I have said that I minutely remember the details of the chamber—yet I am sadly forgetful on topics
of deep moment—and here there was no system, no keeping, in the
fantastic display, to take hold upon the memory. The room lay in a high
turret of the castellated abbey, was pentagonal in shape, and of capacious size. Occupying the whole southern face of the pentagon was the
sole window—an immense sheet of unbroken glass from Venice—a
single pane, and tinted of a leaden hue, so that the rays of either the
sun or moon passing through it, fell with a ghastly lustre on the objects
within. Over the upper portion of this huge window, extended the
trellis-work of an aged vine, which clambered up the massy walls of
the turret. The ceiling, of gloomy-looking oak, was excessively lofty,
vaulted, and elaborately fretted with the wildest and most grotesque
specimens of a semi-Gothic, semi-Druidical device. From out the most
central recess of this melancholy vaulting, depended, by a single chain
of gold with long links, a huge censer of the same metal, Saracenic in
pattern, and with many perforations so contrived that there writhed
in and out of them, as if endued with a serpent vitality, a continual
succession of parti-colored fires.

Some few ottomans and golden candelabra, of Eastern figure, were
in various stations about—and there was the couch, too—the bridal

couch—of an Indian model, and low, and sculptured of solid ebony, with a pall-like canopy above. In each of the angles of the chamber stood on end a gigantic sarcophagus of black granite, from the tombs of the kings over against Luxor, with their aged lids full of immemorial sculpture. But in the draping of the apartment lay, alas! the chief phantasy of all. The lofty walls, gigantic in height—even unproportionably so—were hung from summit to foot, in vast folds, with a heavy and massive-looking tapestry—tapestry of a material which was found alike as a carpet on the floor, as a covering for the ottomans and the ebony bed, as a canopy for the bed and as the gorgeous volutes of the curtains which partially shaded the window. The material was the richest cloth of gold. It was spotted all over, at irregular intervals, with arabesque figures, about a foot in diameter, and wrought upon the cloth in patterns of the most jetty black. But these figures partook of the true character of the arabesque only when regarded from a single point of view. By a contrivance now common, and indeed traceable to a very remote period of antiquity, they were made changeable in aspect. To one entering the room, they bore the appearance of simple monstrosities; but upon a farther advance, this appearance gradually departed; and step by step, as the visiter moved his station in the chamber, he saw himself surrounded by an endless succession of the ghastly forms which belong to the superstition of the Norman, or arise in the guilty slumbers of the monk. The phantasmagoric effect was vastly heightened by the artificial introduction of a strong continual current of wind behind the draperies—giving a hideous and uneasy animation to the whole.

In halls such as these—in a bridal chamber such as this—I passed, with the Lady of Tremaine, the unhallowed hours of the first month of our marriage—passed them with but little disquietude. That my wife dreaded the fierce moodiness of my temper—that she shunned me and loved me but little—I could not help perceiving; but it gave me rather pleasure than otherwise. I loathed her with a hatred belonging more to demon than to man. My memory flew back, (oh, what intensity of regret!) to Ligeia, the beloved, the august, the beautiful, the entombed. I revelled in recollections of her purity, of her wisdom, of her lofty, her ethereal nature, of her passionate, her idolatrous love. Now, then, did my spirit fully and freely burn with more than all the fires of her own. In the excitement of my opium dreams (for I was habitually fettered in the shackles of the drug) I would call aloud upon her name, during the silence of the night, or among the sheltered recesses of the glens by day, as if, through the wild eagerness, the solemn passion, the consuming ardor of my longing for the departed, I could restore her to the pathways she had abandoned—ah, *could* it be forever?—upon the earth.

About the commencement of the second month of the marriage, the Lady Rowena was attacked with sudden illness, from which her recovery was slow. The fever which consumed her rendered her nights uneasy; and in her perturbed state of half-slumber, she spoke of sounds, and of

motions, in and about the chamber of the turret, which I concluded had
no origin save in the distemper of her fancy, or perhaps in the phantasmagoric influences of the chamber itself. She became at length convalescent—finally well. Yet but a brief period elapsed, ere a second
more violent disorder again threw her upon a bed of suffering; and
from this attack her frame, at all times feeble, never altogether recovered. Her illnesses were, after this epoch, of alarming character, and of
more alarming recurrence, defying alike the knowledge and the great
exertions of her physicians. With the increase of the chronic disease
which had thus, apparently, taken too sure hold upon her constitution
to be eradicated by human means, I could not fail to observe a similar
increase in the nervous irritation of her temperament, and in her
excitability by trivial causes of fear. She spoke again, and now more
frequently and pertinaciously, of the sounds—of the slight sounds—
and of the unusual motions among the tapestries, to which she had
formerly alluded.

One night, near the closing in of September, she pressed this distressing subject with more than usual emphasis upon my attention. She
had just awakened from an unquiet slumber, and I had been watching,
with feelings half of anxiety, half of vague terror, the workings of her
emaciated countenance. I sat by the side of her ebony bed, upon one of
the ottomans of India. She partly arose, and spoke, in an earnest low
whisper, of sounds which she *then* heard, but which I could not hear—
of motions which she *then* saw, but which I could not perceive. The
wind was rushing hurriedly behind the tapestries, and I wished to show
her (what, let me confess it, I could not *all* believe) that those almost
inarticulate breathings, and those very gentle variations of the figures
upon the wall, were but the natural effects of that customary rushing
of the wind. But a deadly pallor, overspreading her face, had proved to
me that my exertions to reassure her would be fruitless. She appeared
to be fainting, and no attendants were within call. I remembered where
was deposited a decanter of light wine which had been ordered by her
physicians, and hastened across the chamber to procure it. But, as I
stepped beneath the light of the censer, two circumstances of a startling
nature attracted my attention. I had felt that some palpable although
invisible object had passed lightly by my person; and I saw that there
lay upon the golden carpet, in the very middle of the rich lustre thrown
from the censer, a shadow—a faint, indefinite shadow of angelic
aspect—such as might be fancied for the shadow of a shade. But I was
wild with the excitement of an immoderate dose of opium, and heeded
these things but little, nor spoke of them to Rowena. Having found the
wine, I recrossed the chamber, and poured out a gobletful, which I held
to the lips of the fainting lady. She had now partially recovered, however, and took the vessel herself, while I sank upon an ottoman near
me, with my eyes fastened upon her person. It was then that I became
distinctly aware of a gentle foot-fall upon the carpet, and near the

couch; and in a second thereafter, as Rowena was in the act of raising the wine to her lips, I saw, or may have dreamed that I saw, fall within the goblet, as if from some invisible spring in the atmosphere of the room, three or four large drops of a brilliant and ruby colored fluid. If this I saw—not so Rowena. She swallowed the wine unhesitatingly, and I forbore to speak to her of a circumstance which must, after all, I considered, have been but the suggestion of a vivid imagination, rendered morbidly active by the terror of the lady, by the opium, and by the hour.

Yet I cannot conceal it from my own perception that, immediately subsequent to the fall of the ruby-drops, a rapid change for the worse took place in the disorder of my wife; so that, on the third subsequent night, the hands of her menials prepared her for the tomb, and on the fourth, I sat alone, with her shrouded body, in that fantastic chamber which had received her as my bride.—Wild visions, opium-engendered, flitted, shadowlike, before me. I gazed with unquiet eye upon the sarcophagi in the angles of the room, upon the varying figures of the drapery, and upon the writhing of the parti-colored fires in the censer overhead. My eyes then fell, as I called to mind the circumstances of a former night, to the spot beneath the glare of the censer where I had seen the faint traces of the shadow. It was there, however, no longer; and breathing with greater freedom, I turned my glances to the pallid and rigid figure upon the bed. Then rushed upon me a thousand memories of Ligeia—and then came back upon my heart, with the turbulent violence of a flood, the whole of that unutterable wo with which I had regarded *her* thus enshrouded. The night waned; and still, with a bosom full of bitter thoughts of the one only and supremely beloved, I remained gazing upon the body of Rowena.

It might have been midnight, or perhaps earlier, or later, for I had taken no note of time, when a sob, low, gentle, but very distinct, startled me from my revery.—I *felt* that it came from the bed of ebony—the bed of death. I listened in an agony of superstitious terror—but there was no repetition of the sound. I strained my vision to detect any motion in the corpse—but there was not the slightest perceptible. Yet I could not have been deceived. I *had* heard the noise, however faint, and my soul was awakened within me. I resolutely and perseveringly kept my attention riveted upon the body. Many minutes elapsed before any circumstance occurred tending to throw light upon the mystery. At length it became evident that a slight, a very feeble, and barely noticeable tinge of color had flushed up within the cheeks, and along the sunken small veins of the eyelids. Through a species of unutterable horror and awe, for which the language of mortality has no sufficiently energetic expression, I felt my heart cease to beat, my limbs grow rigid where I sat. Yet a sense of duty finally operated to restore my self-possession. I could no longer doubt that we had been precipitate in our preparations—that Rowena still lived. It was necessary that some immediate exertion be made; yet the turret was altogether apart from the portion of the abbey tenanted by the servants—there were none within call— I had no means of summoning them to my aid without leaving the room for many minutes—and this I could not venture to do. I therefore struggled alone in my endeavors to call back the spirit still hovering. In a short period it was certain, however, that a relapse had taken place; the color disappeared from both eyelid and cheek, leaving a wanness even more than that of marble; the lips became doubly shrivelled and pinched up in the ghastly expression of death; a repulsive clamminess and coldness overspread rapidly the surface of the body; and all the usual rigorous stiffness immediately supervened. I fell back with a shudder upon the couch from which I had been so startlingly aroused, and again gave myself up to passionate waking visions of Ligeia.

An hour thus elapsed when (could it be possible?) I was a second time aware of some vague sound issuing from the region of the bed. I listened—in extremity of horror. The sound came again—it was a sigh. Rushing to the corpse, I saw—distinctly saw—a tremor upon the lips. In a minute afterward they relaxed, disclosing a bright line of the pearly teeth. Amazement now struggled in my bosom with the profound awe which had hitherto reigned there alone. I felt that my vision grew dim, that my reason wandered; and it was only by a violent effort that I at length succeeded in nerving myself to the task which duty thus once more had pointed out. There was now a partial glow upon the forehead and upon the cheek and throat; a perceptible warmth pervaded the whole frame; there was even a slight pulsation at the heart. The lady *lived;* and with redoubled ardor I betook myself to the task of restoration. I chafed and bathed the temples and the hands, and used every exertion which experience, and no little medical reading, could suggest. But in vain. Suddenly, the color fled, the pulsation ceased, the lips resumed the expression of the dead, and, in an instant afterward, the whole body took upon itself the icy chilliness, the livid hue, the intense rigidity, the sunken outline, and all the loathsome peculiarities of that which has been, for many days, a tenant of the tomb.

And again I sunk into visions of Ligeia—and again, (what marvel that I shudder while I write?) *again* there reached my ears a low sob from the region of the ebony bed. But why shall I minutely detail the unspeakable horrors of that night? Why shall I pause to relate how, time after time, until near the period of the gray dawn, this hideous drama of revivification was repeated; how each terrific relapse was only into a sterner and apparently more irredeemable death; how each agony wore the aspect of a struggle with some invisible foe; and how each struggle was succeeded by I know not what of wild change in the personal appearance of the corpse? Let me hurry to a conclusion.

The greater part of the fearful night had worn away, and she who had been dead once again stirred—and now more vigorously than hitherto, although arousing from a dissolution more appalling in its utter hopelessness than any. I had long ceased to struggle or to move, and remained sitting rigidly upon the ottoman, a helpless prey to a whirl of violent emotions, of which extreme awe was perhaps the least terrible, the least consuming. The corpse, I repeat, stirred, and now more vigorously than before. The hues of life flushed up with unwonted energy into the countenance—the limbs relaxed—and, save that the eyelids were yet pressed heavily together, and that the bandages and draperies of the grave still imparted their charnel character to the figure, I might have dreamed that Rowena had indeed shaken off, utterly, the fetters of Death. But if this idea was not, even then, altogether adopted, I could at least doubt no longer, when, arising from the bed, tottering, with feeble steps, with closed eyes, and with the manner of one bewildered in a dream, the thing that was enshrouded advanced boldly and palpably into the middle of the apartment.

I trembled not—I stirred not—for a crowd of unutterable fancies connected with the air, the stature, the demeanor of the figure, rushing hurriedly through my brain, had paralyzed—had chilled me into stone. I stirred not—but gazed upon the apparition. There was a mad disorder in my thoughts—a tumult unappeasable. Could it, indeed, be the *living* Rowena who confronted me? Could it, indeed, be Rowena *at all*— the fair-haired, the blue-eyed Lady Rowena Trevanion of Tremaine? Why, *why* should I doubt it? The bandage lay heavily about the mouth—but then might it not be the mouth of the breathing Lady of Tremaine? And the cheeks—there were the roses as in her noon of life—yes, these might indeed be the fair cheeks of the living Lady of Tremaine. And the chin, with its dimples, as in health, might it not be hers?—but *had she then grown taller since her malady?* What inexpressible madness seized me with that thought? One bound, and I had reached her feet! Shrinking from my touch, she let fall from her head, unloosened, the ghastly cerements which had confined it, and there streamed forth into the rushing atmosphere of the chamber huge masses of long and dishevelled hair; *it was blacker than the raven wings of midnight!* And now slowly opened *the eyes* of the figure which stood before me. "Here then, at least," I shrieked aloud, "can I never—can I never be mistaken—these are the full, and the black, and the wild eyes—of my lost love—of the Lady—of the LADY LIGEIA."

The Fall of the House of Usher (1839)

Son cœur est un luth suspendu;
Sitôt qu'on le touche il résonne.[1]
                        De Béranger

During the whole of a dull, dark, and soundless day in the autumn of the year, when the clouds hung oppressively low in the heavens, I had been passing alone, on horseback, through a singularly dreary tract of country, and at length found myself, as the shades of the evening drew on, within view of the melancholy House of Usher. I know not how it was—but, with the first glimpse of the building, a sense of insufferable gloom pervaded my spirit. I say insufferable; for the feeling was unrelieved by any of that half-pleasurable, because poetic, sentiment with which the mind usually receives even the sternest natural images of the desolate or terrible. I looked upon the scene before me—upon the mere house, and the simple landscape features of the domain—upon the bleak walls—upon the vacant eye-like windows—upon a few rank sedges—and upon a few white trunks of decayed trees—with an utter depression of soul which I can compare to no earthly sensation more properly than to the after-dream of the reveller upon opium—the bitter lapse into every-day life—the hideous dropping off of the veil. There was an iciness, a sinking, a sickening of the heart—an unredeemed dreariness of thought which no goading of the imagination could torture into aught of the sublime. What was it—I paused to think—what was it that so unnerved me in the contemplation of the House of Usher? It was a mystery all insoluble; nor could I grapple with the shadowy fancies that crowded upon me as I pondered. I was forced to fall back upon the unsatisfactory conclusion, that while, beyond doubt, there *are* combinations of very simple natural objects which have the power of thus affecting us, still the analysis of this power lies among considerations beyond our depth. It was possible, I reflected, that a mere different arrangement of the particulars of the scene, of the details of the picture, would be sufficient to modify, or perhaps to annihilate its capacity for sorrowful impression; and, acting upon this idea, I reigned my horse to the precipitous brink of a black and lurid tarn that lay in unruffled lustre by the dwelling, and gazed down—but with a shudder even more thrilling than before—upon the remodelled and inverted images of the gray sedge, and the ghastly tree-stems, and the vacant and eye-like windows.

Nevertheless, in this mansion of gloom I now proposed to myself a sojourn of some weeks. Its proprietor, Roderick Usher, had been one of my boon companions in boyhood; but many years had elapsed since our last meeting. A letter, however, had lately reached me in a distant part of the country—a letter from him—which, in its wildly importunate

---

[1] His heart is a suspended lute/Which quivers when it is touched.

nature, had admitted of no other than a personal reply. The MS. gave evidence of nervous agitation. The writer spoke of acute bodily illness— of a mental disorder which oppressed him—and of an earnest desire to see me, as his best and indeed his only personal friend, with a view of attempting, by the cheerfulness of my society, some alleviation of his malady. It was the manner in which all this, and much more, was said—it was the apparent *heart* that went with his request—which allowed me no room for hesitation; and I accordingly obeyed forthwith what I still considered a very singular summons.

Although, as boys, we had been even intimate associates, yet I really knew little of my friend. His reserve had been always excessive and habitual. I was aware, however, that his very ancient family had been noted, time out of mind, for a peculiar sensibility of temperament, displaying itself, through long ages, in many works of exalted art, and manifested, of late, in repeated deeds of munificent yet unobtrusive charity, as well as in a passionate devotion to the intricacies, perhaps even more than to the orthodox and easily recognizable beauties, of musical science. I had learned, too, the very remarkable fact, that the stem of the Usher race, all time-honoured as it was, had put forth, at no period, any enduring branch; in other words, that the entire family lay in the direct line of descent, and had always, with very trifling and very temporary variation, so lain. It was this deficiency, I considered, while running over in thought the perfect keeping of the character of the premises with the accredited character of the people, and while speculating upon the possible influence which the one, in the long lapse of centuries, might have exercised upon the other—it was this deficiency, perhaps, of collateral issue, and the consequent undeviating transmission, from sire to son, of the patrimony with the name, which had, at length, so identified the two as to merge the original title of the estate in the quaint and equivocal appellation of the "House of Usher"— an appellation which seemed to include, in the minds of the peasantry who used it, both the family and the family mansion.

I have said that the sole effect of my somewhat childish experiment—that of looking down within the tarn—had been to deepen the first singular impression. There can be no doubt that the consciousness of the rapid increase of my superstition—for why should I not so term it?—served mainly to accelerate the increase itself. Such, I have long known, is the paradoxical law of all sentiments having terror as a basis. And it might have been for this reason only, that, when I again uplifted my eyes to the house itself, from its image in the pool, there grew in my mind a strange fancy—a fancy so ridiculous, indeed, that I but mention it to show the vivid force of the sensations which oppressed me. I had so worked upon my imagination as really to believe that about the whole mansion and domain there hung an atmosphere peculiar to themselves and their immediate vicinity—an atmosphere which had no affinity with the air of heaven, but which had reeked up from the decayed trees, and the gray wall, and the silent tarn—a pestilent and mystic vapour, dull, sluggish, faintly discernible, and leaden-hued.

Shaking off from my spirit what *must* have been a dream, I scanned more narrowly the real aspect of the building. Its principal feature seemed to be that of an excessive antiquity. The discoloration of ages had been great. Minute fungi overspread the whole exterior, hanging in a fine tangled web-work from the eaves. Yet all this was apart from any extraordinary dilapidation. No portion of the masonry had fallen; and there appeared to be a wild inconsistency between its still perfect adaptation of parts, and the crumbling condition of the individual stones. In this there was much that reminded me of the specious totality of old woodwork which has rotted for long years in some neglected vault, with no disturbance from the breath of the external air. Beyond this indication of extensive decay, however, the fabric gave little token of instability. Perhaps the eye of a scrutinizing observer might have discovered a barely perceptible fissure, which, extending from the roof of the building in front, made its way down the wall in a zigzag direction, until it became lost in the sullen waters of the tarn.

Noticing these things, I rode over a short causeway to the house. A servant in waiting took my horse, and I entered the Gothic archway of the hall. A valet, of stealthy step, thence conducted me, in silence, through many dark and intricate passages in my progress to the *studio* of his master. Much that I encountered on the way contributed, I know not how, to heighten the vague sentiments of which I have already spoken. While the objects around me—while the carvings of the ceilings, the sombre tapestries of the walls, the ebon blackness of the floors, and the phantasmagoric armorial trophies which rattled as I strode, were but matters to which, or to such as which, I had been accustomed from my infancy—while I hesitated not to acknowledge how familiar was all this—I still wondered to find how unfamiliar were the fancies which ordinary images were stirring up. On one of the staircases, I met the physician of the family. His countenance, I thought, wore a mingled expression of low cunning and perplexity. He accosted me with trepidation and passed on. The valet now threw open a door and ushered me into the presence of his master.

The room in which I found myself was very large and lofty. The windows were long, narrow, and pointed, and at so vast a distance from the black oaken floor as to be altogether inaccessible from within. Feeble gleams of encrimsoned light made their way through the trellissed panes, and served to render sufficiently distinct the more prominent objects around; the eye, however, struggled in vain to reach the remoter angles of the chamber, or the recesses of the vaulted and fretted ceiling. Dark draperies hung upon the walls. The general furniture was profuse, comfortless, antique, and tattered. Many books and musical instruments lay scattered about, but failed to give any vitality to the scene. I felt that I breathed an atmosphere of sorrow. An air of stern, deep, and irredeemable gloom hung over and pervaded all.

Upon my entrance, Usher arose from a sofa on which he had been lying at full length, and greeted me with a vivacious warmth which had much in it, I at first thought, of an overdone cordiality—of the constrained effort of the *ennuyé* man of the world. A glance, however, at his countenance convinced me of his perfect sincerity. We sat down; and for some moments, while he spoke not, I gazed upon him with a feeling half of pity, half of awe. Surely, man had never before so terribly altered, in so brief a period, as had Roderick Usher! It was with difficulty that I could bring myself to admit the identity of the wan being before me with the companion of my early boyhood. Yet the character of his face had been at all times remarkable. A cadaverousness of complexion; an eye large, liquid, and luminous beyond comparison; lips somewhat thin and very pallid, but of a surpassingly beautiful curve; a nose of a delicate Hebrew model, but with a breadth of nostril unusual in similar formations; a finely moulded chin, speaking, in its want of prominence, of a want of moral energy; hair of a more than web-like softness and tenuity; these features, with an inordinate expansion above the regions of the temple, made up altogether a countenance not easily to be forgotten. And now in the mere exaggeration of the prevailing character of these features, and of the expression they were wont to convey, lay so much of change that I doubted to whom I spoke. The now ghastly pallor of the skin, and the now miraculous lustre of the eye, above all things startled and even awed me. The silken hair, too, had been suffered to grow all unheeded, and as, in its wild gossamer texture, it floated rather than fell about the face, I could not, even with effort, connect its Arabesque expression with any idea of simple humanity.

In the manner of my friend I was at once struck with an incoherence—an inconsistency; and I soon found this to arise from a series of feeble and futile struggles to overcome an habitual trepidancy—an excessive nervous agitation. For something of this nature I had indeed been prepared, no less by his letter, than by reminiscences of certain boyish traits, and by conclusions deduced from his peculiar physical conformation and temperament. His action was alternately vivacious and sullen. His voice varied rapidly from a tremulous indecision (when the animal spirits seemed utterly in abeyance) to that species of energetic concision—that abrupt, weighty, unhurried, and hollow-sounding enunciation—that leaden, self-balanced, and perfectly modulated guttural utterance, which may be observed in the lost drunkard, or the irreclaimable eater of opium, during the periods of his most intense excitement.

It was thus that he spoke of the object of my visit, of his earnest desire to see me, and of the solace he expected me to afford him. He entered, at some length, into what he conceived to be the nature of his malady. It was, he said, a constitutional and a family evil, and one for which he despaired to find a remedy—a mere nervous affection, he immediately added, which would undoubtedly soon pass off. It displayed itself in a host of unnatural sensations. Some of these, as he detailed them, interested and bewildered me; although, perhaps, the terms and the general manner of their narration had their weight. He suffered much from a morbid acuteness of the senses; the most insipid food was alone endurable; he could wear only garments of certain texture; the odours of all flowers were oppressive; his eyes were tortured by even a faint light; and there were but peculiar sounds, and these from stringed instruments, which did not inspire him with horror.

To an anomalous species of terror I found him a bounden slave. "I shall perish," said he, "I *must* perish in this deplorable folly. Thus, thus, and not otherwise, shall I be lost. I dread the events of the future, not in themselves, but in their results. I shudder at the thought of any, even the most trivial, incident, which may operate upon this intolerable agitation of soul. I have, indeed, no abhorrence of danger, except in its absolute effect—in terror. In this unnerved—in this pitiable condition—I feel that the period will sooner or later arrive when I must abandon life and reason together, in some struggle with the grim phantasm, FEAR."

I learned, moreover, at intervals, and through broken and equivocal hints, another singular feature of his mental condition. He was enchained by certain superstitious impressions in regard to the dwelling which he tenanted, and whence, for many years, he had never ventured forth—in regard to an influence whose suppositious force was conveyed in terms too shadowy here to be re-stated—an influence which some peculiarities in the mere form and substance of his family mansion had, by dint of long sufferance, he said, obtained over his spirit—an effect which the *physique* of the gray walls and turrets, and of the dim tarn into which they all looked down, had, at length, brought about upon the *morale* of his existence.

He admitted, however, although with hesitation, that much of the peculiar gloom which thus afflicted him could be traced to a more natural and far more palpable origin—to the severe and long-continued illness—indeed to the evidently approaching dissolution—of a tenderly beloved sister, his sole companion for long years, his last and only relative on earth. "Her decease," he said, with a bitterness which I can never forget, "would leave him (him, the hopeless and the frail) the last of the ancient race of the Ushers." While he spoke, the lady Madeline (for so was she called) passed slowly through a remote portion of the apartment, and, without having noticed my presence, disappeared. I regarded her with an utter astonishment not unmingled with dread; and yet I found it impossible to account for such feelings. A sensation of stupor oppressed me, as my eyes followed her retreating steps. When a door, at length, closed upon her, my glance sought instinctively and eagerly the countenance of the brother—but he had buried his face in his hands, and I could only perceive that a far more than ordinary wanness had overspread the emaciated fingers through which trickled many passionate tears.

The disease of the lady Madeline had long baffled the skill of her physicians. A settled apathy, a gradual wasting away of the person, and frequent although transient affections of a partially cataleptical character were the unusual diagnosis. Hitherto she had steadily borne up against the pressure of her malady, and had not betaken herself finally to bed; but on the closing in of the evening of my arrival at the house, she succumbed (as her brother told me at night with inexpressible agitation) to the prostrating power of the destroyer; and I learned that the glimpse I had obtained of her person would thus probably be the last I should obtain—that the lady, at least while living, would be seen by me no more.

For several days ensuing, her name was unmentioned by either Usher or myself: and during this period I was busied in earnest endeavours to alleviate the melancholy of my friend. We painted and read together, or I listened, as if in a dream, to the wild improvisations of his speaking guitar. And thus, as a closer and still closer intimacy admitted me more unreservedly into the recesses of his spirit, the more bitterly did I perceive the futility of all attempt at cheering a mind from which darkness, as if an inherent positive quality, poured forth upon all objects of the moral and physical universe in one unceasing radiation of gloom.

I shall ever bear about me a memory of the many solemn hours I thus spent alone with the master of the House of Usher. Yet I should fail in any attempt to convey an idea of the exact character of the studies, or of the occupations, in which he involved me, or led me the way. An excited and highly distempered ideality threw a sulphureous lustre over all. His long improvised dirges will ring forever in my ears. Among other things, I hold painfully in mind a certain singular perversion and amplification of the wild air of the last waltz of Von Weber. From the paintings over which his elaborate fancy brooded, and which grew, touch by touch, into vaguenesses at which I shuddered the more thrillingly, because I shuddered knowing not why;—from these paintings (vivid as their images now are before me) I would in vain endeavour to educe more than a small portion which should lie within the compass of merely written words. By the utter simplicity, by the nakedness of his designs, he arrested and overawed attention. If ever mortal painted an idea, that mortal was Roderick Usher. For me at least, in the circumstances then surrounding me, there arose out of the pure abstractions which the hypochondriac contrived to throw upon his canvas, an intensity of intolerable awe, no shadow of which felt I ever yet in the contemplation of the certainly glowing yet too concrete reveries of Fuseli.

One of the phantasmagoric conceptions of my friend, partaking not
so rigidly of the spirit of abstraction, may be shadowed forth, although
feebly, in words. A small picture presented the interior of an immensely
long and rectangular vault or tunnel, with low walls, smooth, white,
and without interruption or device. Certain accessory points of the design served well to convey the idea that this excavation lay at an exceeding depth below the surface of the earth. No outlet was observed in
any portion of its vast extent, and no torch or other artificial source of
light was discernible; yet a flood of intense rays rolled throughout, and
bathed the whole in a ghastly and inappropriate splendour.

I have just spoken of that morbid condition of the auditory nerve
which rendered all music intolerable to the sufferer, with the exception
of certain effects of stringed instruments. It was, perhaps, the narrow
limits to which he thus confined himself upon the guitar which gave
birth, in great measure, to the fantastic character of his performances.
But the fervid *facility* of his *impromptus* could not be so accounted for.
They must have been, and were, in the notes, as well as in the words
of his wild fantasias (for he not unfrequently accompanied himself
with rhymed verbal improvisations), the result of that intense mental
collectedness and concentration to which I have previously alluded as
observable only in particular moments of the highest artificial excitement. The words of one of these rhapsodies I have easily remembered.
I was, perhaps, the more forcibly impressed with it as he gave it, because, in the under or mystic current of its meaning, I fancied that I
perceived, and for the first time, a full consciousness on the part of
Usher of the tottering of his lofty reason upon her throne. The verses,
which were entitled "The Haunted Palace," ran very nearly, if not
accurately, thus:

I

In the greenest of our valleys,
  By good angels tenanted,
Once a fair and stately palace—
  Radiant palace—reared its head.
In the monarch Thought's dominion—
  It stood there!
Never seraph spread a pinion
  Over fabric half so fair.

II

Banners yellow, glorious, golden,
  On its roof did float and flow
(This—all this—was in the olden
  Time long ago)
And every gentle air that dallied,
  In that sweet day,
Among the ramparts plumed and pallid,
  A winged odour went away.

III

Wanderers in that happy valley
*   Through two luminous windows saw*
Spirits moving musically
*   To a lute's well-tuned law,*
Round about a throne, where sitting
*   (Porphyrogene!)*
In state his glory well befitting,
*   The ruler of the realm was seen.*

IV

And all with pearl and ruby glowing
*   Was the fair palace door,*
Through which came flowing, flowing, flowing
*   And sparkling evermore,*
A troop of Echoes whose sweet duty
*   Was but to sing,*
In voices of surpassing beauty,
*   The wit and wisdom of their king.*

V

But evil things, in robes of sorrow,
*   Assailed the monarch's high estate;*
(Ah, let us mourn, for never morrow
*   Shall dawn upon him, desolate!)*
And, round about his home, the glory
*   That blushed and bloomed*
Is but a dim-remembered story
*   Of the old time entombed.*

VI

And travellers now within that valley,
*   Through the red-litten windows see*
Vast forms that move fantastically
*   To a discordant melody;*
While, like a rapid ghastly river,
*   Through the pale door,*
A hideous throng rush out forever,
*   And laugh—but smile no more.*

I well remember that suggestions arising from this ballad, led us into a train of thought, wherein there became manifest an opinion of Usher's which I mention not so much on account of its novelty, (for other men have thought thus,) as on account of the pertinacity with which he maintained it. This opinion, in its general form, was that of the sentience of all vegetable things. But, in his disordered fancy, the idea had assumed a more daring character, and trespassed, under certain conditions, upon the kingdom of inorganization. I lack words to express the full extent, or the earnest *abandon* of his persuasion. The belief, however, was connected (as I have previously hinted) with the gray stones of the home of his forefathers. The conditions of the sentence had been here, he imagined, fulfilled in the method of collocation of these stones—in the order of their arrangement, as well as in that of the many *fungi* which overspread them, and of the decayed trees which stood around—above all, in the long undisturbed endurance of this arrangement, and in its reduplication in the still waters of the tarn. Its evidence—the evidence of the sentience—was to be seen, he said (and I here started as he spoke), in the gradual yet certain condensation of an atmosphere of their own about the waters and the walls. The result was discoverable, he added, in that silent yet importunate and terrible influence which for centuries had moulded the destinies of his family, and which made *him* what I now saw him—what he was. Such opinions need no comment, and I will make none.

Our books—the books which, for years, had formed no small portion of the mental existence of the invalid—were, as might be supposed, in strict keeping with this character of phantasm. We pored together over such works as the Ververt et Chartreuse of Gresset; the Belphegor of Machiavelli; the Heaven and Hell of Swedenborg; the Subterranean Voyage of Nicholas Klimm of Holberg; the Chiromancy of Robert Flud, of Jean D'Indaginé, and of De la Chambre; the Journey into the Blue Distance of Tieck; and the City of the Sun of Campanella. One favourite volume was a small octavo edition of the *Directorium Inquisitorum,* by the Dominican Eymeric de Gironne; and there were passages in Pomponius Mela, about the old African Satyrs and Œgipans, over which Usher would sit dreaming for hours. His chief delight, however, was found in the perusal of an exceedingly rare and curious book in quarto Gothic—the manual of a forgotten church—the *Vigiliœ Mortuorum secundum Chorum Ecclesiœ Maguntinœ.*

I could not help thinking of the wild ritual of this work, and of its probable influence upon the hypochondriac, when, one evening, having informed me abruptly that the lady Madeline was no more, he stated his intention of preserving her corpse for a fortnight, (previously to its final interment,) in one of the numerous vaults within the main walls of the building. The worldly reason, however, assigned for this singular proceeding, was one which I did not feet at liberty to dispute. The brother had been led to his resolution (so he told me) by consideration of the unusual character of the malady of the deceased, of certain obtrusive and eager inquiries on the part of her medical men, and of the remote and exposed situation of the burial-ground of the family. I will not deny that when I called to mind the sinister countenance of the person whom I met upon the staircase, on the day of my arrival at the house, I had no desire to oppose what I regarded as at best but a harmless, and by no means an unnatural, precaution.

At the request of Usher, I personally aided him in the arrangements for the temporary entombment. The body having been encoffined, we two alone bore it to its rest. The vault in which we placed it (and which had been so long unopened that our torches, half smothered in its oppressive atmosphere, gave us little opportunity for investigation) was small, damp, and entirely without means of admission for light; lying, at great depth, immediately beneath that portion of the building in which was my own sleeping apartment. It had been used, apparently, in remote feudal times, for the worst purposes of a donjon-keep, and, in later days, as a place of deposit for powder, or some other highly combustible substance, as a portion of its floor, and the whole interior of a long archway through which we reached it, were carefully sheathed with copper. The door, of massive iron, had been also, similarly protected. Its immense weight caused an unusually sharp grating sound, as it moved upon its hinges.

Having deposited our mournful burden upon tressels within this region of horror, we partially turned aside the yet unscrewed lid of the coffin, and looked upon the face of the tenant. A striking similitude between the brother and sister now first arrested my attention; and Usher, divining, perhaps, my thoughts, murmured out some few words from which I learned that the deceased and himself had been twins, and that sympathies of a scarcely intelligible nature had always existed between them. Our glances, however, rested not long upon the dead—for we could not regard her unawed. The disease which had thus entombed the lady in the maturity of youth, had left, as usual in all maladies of a strictly cataleptical character, the mockery of a faint blush upon the bosom and the face, and that suspiciously lingering smile upon the lip which is so terrible in death. We replaced and screwed down the lid, and, having secured the door of iron, made our way, with toil, into the scarcely less gloomy apartments of the upper portion of the house.

And now, some days of bitter grief having elapsed, an observable change came over the features of the mental disorder of my friend. His ordinary manner had vanished. His ordinary occupations were neglected or forgotten. He roamed from chamber to chamber with hurried, unequal, and objectless step. The pallor of his countenance had assumed, if possible, a more ghastly hue—but the luminousness of his eye had utterly gone out. The once occasional huskiness of his tone was heard no more; and a tremulous quaver, as if of extreme terror, habitually characterized his utterance. There were times, indeed, when I thought his unceasingly agitated mind was labouring with some oppressive secret, to divulge which he struggled for the necessary courage. At times, again, I was obliged to resolve all into the mere inexplicable vagaries of madness, for I beheld him gazing upon vacancy for long hours, in an attitude of the profoundest attention, as if listening to some imaginary sound. It was no wonder that his condition terrified—that it infected me. I felt creeping upon me, by slow yet certain degrees, the wild influences of his own fantastic yet impressive superstitions.

It was, especially, upon retiring to bed late in the night of the seventh or eighth day after the placing of the lady Madeline within the donjon, that I experienced the full power of such feelings. Sleep came not near my couch—while the hours waned and waned away. I struggled to reason off the nervousness which had dominion over me. I endeavoured to believe that much, if not all of what I felt, was due to the bewildering influence of the gloomy furniture of the room—of the dark and tattered draperies, which, tortured into motion by the breath of a rising tempest, swayed fitfully to and fro upon the walls, and rustled uneasily about the decorations of the bed. But my efforts were fruitless. An irrepressible tremour gradually pervaded my frame; and, at length, there sat upon my very heart an incubus of utterly causeless alarm. Shaking this off with a gasp and a struggle, I uplifted myself upon the pillows, and, peering earnestly within the intense darkness of the chamber, hearkened—I know not why, except that an instinctive spirit prompted me—to certain low and indefinite sounds which came, through the pauses of the storm, at long intervals, I knew not whence. Overpowered by an intense sentiment of horror, unaccountable yet unendurable, I threw on my clothes with haste, (for I felt that I should sleep no more during the night,) and endeavoured to arouse myself from the pitiable condition into which I had fallen, by pacing rapidly to and fro through the apartment.

I had taken but few turns in this manner, when a light step on an adjoining staircase arrested my attention. I presently recognised it as that of Usher. In an instant afterward he rapped, with a gentle touch, at my door, and entered, bearing a lamp. His countenance was, as usual, cadaverously wan—but, moreover, there was a species of mad hilarity in his eyes—an evidently restrained *hysteria* in his whole demeanour. His air appalled me—but anything was preferable to the solitude which I had so long endured, and I even welcomed his presence as a relief.

"And you have not seen it?" he said abruptly, after having stared about him for some moments in silence—"you have not then seen it?— but, stay! you shall." Thus speaking, and having carefully shaded his lamp, he hurried to one of the casements, and threw it freely open to the storm.

The impetuous fury of the entering gust nearly lifted us from our feet. It was, indeed, a tempestuous yet sternly beautiful night, and one wildly singular in its terror and its beauty. A whirlwind had apparently collected its force in our vicinity; for there were frequent and violent alterations in the direction of the wind; and the exceeding density of the clouds (which hung so low as to press upon the turrets of the house) did not prevent our perceiving the life-like velocity with which they flew careering from all points against each other, without passing away into the distance. I say that even their exceeding density did not prevent our perceiving this—yet we had no glimpse of the moon or stars—nor was there any flashing forth of the lightning. But the under surfaces of the huge masses of agitated vapour, as well as all terrestrial objects immediately around us, were glowing in the unnatural light of a faintly luminous and distinctly visible gaseous exhalation which hung about and enshrouded the mansion.

"You must not—you shall not behold this!" said I, shuddering, to Usher, as I led him, with a gentle violence, from the window to a seat. "These appearances, which bewilder you, are merely electrical phenomena not uncommon—or it may be that they have their ghastly origin in the rank miasma of the tarn. Let us close this casement;—the air is chilling and dangerous to your frame. Here is one of your favourite romances. I will read, and you shall listen;—and so we will pass away this terrible night together."

The antique volume which I had taken up was the "Mad Trist" of Sir Launcelot Canning; but I had called it a favourite of Usher's more in sad jest than in earnest; for, in truth, there is little in its uncouth and unimaginative prolixity which could have had interest for the lofty and spiritual ideality of my friend. It was, however, the only book immediately at hand; and I indulged a vague hope that the excitement which now agitated the hypochondriac, might find relief (for the history of mental disorder is full of similar anomalies) even in the extremness of the folly which I should read. Could I have judged, indeed, by the wild overstrained air of vivacity with which he hearkened, or apparently hearkened, to the words of the tale, I might well have congratulated myself upon the success of my design.

I had arrived at that well-known portion of the story where Ethelred, the hero of the Trist, having sought in vain for peaceable admission into the dwelling of the hermit, proceeds to make good an entrance by force. Here, it will be remembered, the words of the narrative run thus:

"And Ethelred, who was by nature of a doughty heart, and who was now mighty withal, on account of the powerfulness of the wine which he had drunken, waited no longer to hold parley with the hermit, who, in sooth, was of an obstinate and maliceful turn, but, feeling the rain upon his shoulders, and fearing the rising of the tempest, uplifted his mace outright, and, with blows, made quickly room in the plankings of the door for his gauntleted hand; and now pulling therewith sturdily, he so cracked, and ripped, and tore all asunder, that the noise of the dry and hollow-sounding wood alarumed and reverberated throughout the forest."

At the termination of this sentence I started and, for a moment, paused; for it appeared to me (although I at once concluded that my excited fancy had deceived me)—It appeared to me that, from some very remote portion of the mansion, there came, indistinctly, to my ears, what might have been, in its exact similarity of character, the echo (but a stifled and dull one certainly) of the very cracking and ripping sound which Sir Launcelot had so particularly described. It was, beyond doubt, the coincidence alone which had arrested my attention;

for, amid the rattling of the sashes of the casements, and the ordinary commingled noises of the still increasing storm, the sound, in itself, had nothing, surely, which should have interested or disturbed me. I continued the story:

"But the good champion Ethelred, now entering within the door, was sore enraged and amazed to perceive no signal of the maliceful hermit; but, in the stead thereof, a dragon of a scaly and prodigious demeanour, and of a fiery tongue, which sate in guard before a palace of gold, with a floor of silver; and upon the wall there hung a shield of shining brass with this legend enwritten—

Who entereth herein, a conqueror hath bin;
Who slayeth the dragon, the shield he shall win.

And Ethelred uplifted his mace, and struck upon the head of the dragon, which fell before him, and gave up his pesty breath, with a shriek so horrid and harsh, and withal so piercing, that Ethelred had fain to close his ears with his hands against the dreadful noise of it, the like whereof was never before heard."

Here again I paused abruptly, and now with a feeling of wild amazement—for there could be no doubt whatever that, in this instance, I did actually hear (although from what direction it proceeded I found it impossible to say) a low and apparently distant, but harsh, protracted, and most unusual screaming or grating sound—the exact counterpart of what my fancy had already conjured up for the dragon's unnatural shriek as described by the romancer.

Oppressed, as I certainly was, upon the occurrence of this second and most extraordinary coincidence, by a thousand conflicting sensations, in which wonder and extreme terror were predominant, I still retained sufficient presence of mind to avoid exciting, by any observation, the sensitive nervousness of my companion. I was by no means certain that he had noticed the sounds in question; although, assuredly, a strange alteration had, during the last few minutes, taken place in his demeanour. From a position fronting my own, he had gradually brought round his chair, so as to sit with his face to the door of the chamber; and thus I could but partially perceive his features, although I saw that his lips trembled as if he were murmuring inaudibly. His head had dropped upon his breast—yet I knew that he was not asleep, from the wide and rigid opening of the eye as I caught a glance of it in profile. The motion of his body, too, was at variance with this idea— for he rocked from side to side with a gentle yet constant and uniform sway. Having rapidly taken notice of all this, I resumed the narrative of Sir Launcelot, which thus proceeded:

"And now, the champion, having escaped from the terrible fury of the dragon, bethinking himself of the brazen shield, and of the breaking up of the enchantment which was upon it, removed the carcass from out of the way before him, and approached valorously over the

silver pavement of the castle to where the shield was upon the wall;
which in sooth tarried not for his full coming, but fell down at his feet
upon the silver floor, with a mighty great and terrible ringing sound."

No sooner had these syllables passed my lips, than—as if a shield
of brass had indeed, at the moment, fallen heavily upon a floor of
silver—I became aware of a distinct, hollow, metallic, and clangorous,
yet apparently muffled, reverberation. Completely unnerved, I leaped
to my feet; but the measured rocking movement of Usher was undisturbed. I rushed to the chair in which he sat. His eyes were bent fixedly
before him, and throughout his whole countenance there reigned a
stony rigidity. But, as I placed my hand upon his shoulder, there came
a strong shudder over his whole person; a sickly smile quivered about
his lips; and I saw that he spoke in a low, hurried, and gibbering murmur, as if unconscious of my presence. Bending closely over him, I at
length drank in the hideous import of his words.

"Not hear it?—yes, I hear it, and *have* heard it. Long—long—
long—many minutes, many hours, many days, have I heard it—yet I
dared not—oh, pity me, miserable wretch that I am!—I dared not—I
dared not speak! *We have put her living in the tomb!* Said I not that
my senses were acute? I *now* tell you that I heard her first feeble
movements in the hollow coffin. I heard them—many, many days ago—
yet I dared not—I *dared not speak!* And now—to-night—Ethelred—
ha! ha!—the breaking of the hermit's door, and the death-cry of the
dragon, and the clangour of the shield—say, rather, the rending of her
coffin, and the grating of the iron hinges of her prison, and her struggles
within the coppered archway of the vault! Oh whither shall I fly? Will
she not be here anon? Is she not hurrying to upbraid me for my haste?
Have I not heard her footstep on the stair? Do I not distinguish that
heavy and horrible beating of her heart? MADMAN!"—here he sprang
furiously to his feet, and shrieked out his syllables, as if in the effort
he were giving up his soul—"MADMAN! I TELL YOU THAT SHE NOW
STANDS WITHOUT THE DOOR!"

As if in the superhuman energy of his utterance there had been
found the potency of a spell, the huge antique panels to which the
speaker pointed threw slowly back, upon the instant, their ponderous
and ebony jaws. It was the work of the rushing gust—but then without
those doors there DID stand the lofty and enshrouded figure of the lady
Madeline of Usher. There was blood upon her white robes, and the
evidence of some bitter struggle upon every portion of her emaciated
frame. For a moment she remained trembling and reeling to and fro
upon the threshold, then, with a low moaning cry, fell heavily inward
upon the person of her brother, and in her violent and now final death-
agonies, bore him to the floor a corpse, and a victim to the terrors he
had anticipated.

From that chamber, and from that mansion, I fled aghast. The
storm was still abroad in all its wrath as I found myself crossing the old

causeway. Suddenly there shot along the path a wild light, and I turned to see whence a gleam so unusual could have issued; for the vast house and its shadows were alone behind me. The radiance was that of the full, setting, and blood-red moon, which now shone vividly through that once barely discernible fissure, of which I have before spoken as extending from the roof of the building, in a zigzag direction, to the base. While I gazed, this fissure rapidly widened—there came a fierce breath of the whirlwind—the entire orb of the satellite burst at once upon my sight—my brain reeled as I saw the mighty walls rushing asunder—there was a long tumultuous shouting sound like the voice of a thousand waters—and the deep and dank tarn at my feet closed sullenly and silently over the fragments of the "HOUSE OF USHER."

The Man of the Crowd (1840, 1845)

Ce grand malheur, de ne pouvoir être seul.[1]
     La Bruyère

It was well said of a certain German book that *"es lässt sich nicht lesen"*—it does not permit itself to be read. There are some secrets which do not permit themselves to be told. Men die nightly in their beds, wringing the hands of ghostly confessors, and looking them piteously in the eyes—die with despair of heart and convulsion of throat, on account of the hideousness of mysteries which will not *suffer themselves* to be revealed. Now and then, alas, the conscience of man takes up a burden so heavy in horror that it can be thrown down only into the grave. And thus the essence of all crime is undivulged.

Not long ago, about the closing in of an evening in autumn, I sat at the large bow window of the D—— Coffee-House in London. For some months I had been ill in health, but was now convalescent, and, with returning strength, found myself in one of those happy moods which are so precisely the converse of *ennui*—moods of the keenest appetency, when the film from the mental vision departs—the ἀχλὺς ἣ πρὶν ἐπῆεν [2]—and the intellect, electrified, surpasses as greatly its every-day condition, as does the vivid yet candid reason of Leibnitz, the mad and flimsy rhetoric of Gorgias. Merely to breathe was enjoyment; and I derived positive pleasure even from many of the legitimate sources of pain. I felt a calm but inquisitive interest in every thing. With a cigar in my mouth and a newspaper in my lap, I had been amusing myself for the greater part of the afternoon, now in poring over advertisements, now in observing the promiscuous company in the room, and now in peering through the smoky panes into the street.

---

[1] This great disaster, not to be able to be alone.

[2] The mist that was on it.

This latter is one of the principal thoroughfares of the city, and had been very much crowded during the whole day. But, as the darkness came on, the throng momently increased; and, by the time the lamps were well lighted, two dense and continuous tides of population were rushing past the door. At this particular period of the evening I had never before been in a similar situation, and the tumultuous sea of human heads filled me, therefore, with a delicious novelty of emotion. I gave up, at length, all care of things within the hotel, and became absorbed in contemplation of the scene without.

At first my observations took an abstract and generalizing turn. I looked at the passengers in masses, and thought of them in their aggregate relations. Soon, however, I descended to details, and regarded with minute interest the innumerable varieties of figure, dress, air, gait, visage, and expression of countenance.

By far the greater number of those who went by had a satisfied business-like demeanor, and seemed to be thinking only of making their way through the press. Their brows were knit, and their eyes rolled quickly; when pushed against by fellow-wayfarers they evinced no symptom of impatience, but adjusted their clothes and hurried on. Others, still a numerous class, were restless in their movements, had flushed faces, and talked and gesticulated to themselves, as if feeling in solitude on account of the very denseness of the company around. When impeded in their progress, these people suddenly ceased muttering, but redoubled their gesticulations, and awaited, with an absent and overdone smile upon the lips, the course of the persons impeding them. If jostled, they bowed profusely to the jostlers, and appeared overwhelmed with confusion.—There was nothing very distinctive about these two large classes beyond what I have noted. Their habiliments belonged to that order which is pointedly termed the decent. They were undoubtedly noblemen, merchants, attorneys, tradesmen, stock-jobbers —the Eupatrids [3] and the common-places of society—men of leisure and men actively engaged in affairs of their own—conducting business upon their own responsibility. They did not greatly excite my attention.

The tribe of clerks was an obvious one; and here I discerned two remarkable divisions. There were the junior clerks of flash houses— young gentlemen with tight coats, bright boots, well-oiled hair, and supercilious lips. Setting aside a certain dapperness of carriage, which may be termed *deskism* for want of a better word, the manner of these persons seemed to me an exact facsimile of what had been the perfection of *bon ton* about twelve or eighteen months before. They wore the cast-off graces of the gentry;—and this, I believe, involves the best definition of the class.

The division of the upper clerks of staunch firms, or of the "steady old fellows," it was not possible to mistake. These were known by their

[3] Greek nobles.

coats and pantaloons of black or brown, made to sit comfortably, with white cravats and waistcoats, broad solid-looking shoes, and thick hose or gaiters.—They had all slightly bald heads, from which the right ears, long used to pen-holding, had an odd habit of standing off on end. I observed that they always removed or settled their hats with both hands, and wore watches, with short gold chains of a substantial and ancient pattern. Theirs was the affectation of respectability;—if indeed there be an affectation so honorable.

There were many individuals of dashing appearance, whom I easily understood as belonging to the race of swell pick-pockets, with which all great cities are infested. I watched these gentry with much inquisitiveness, and found it difficult to imagine how they should ever be mistaken for gentlemen by gentlemen themselves. Their voluminousness of wristband, with an air of excessive frankness, should betray them at once.

The gamblers, of whom I descried not a few, were still more easily recognisable. They wore every variety of dress, from that of the desperate thimble-rig bully, with velvet waistcoat, fancy neckerchief, gilt chains, and filigreed buttons, to that of the scrupulously inornate clergyman than which nothing could be less liable to suspicion. Still all were distinguished by a certain sodden swarthiness of complexion, a filmy dimness of eye, and pallor and compression of lip. There were two other traits, moreover, by which I could always detect them;—a guarded lowness of tone in conversation, and a more than ordinary extension of the thumb in a direction at right angles with the fingers.—Very often, in company with these sharpers, I observed an order of men somewhat different in habits, but still birds of a kindred feather. They may be defined as the gentlemen who live by their wits. They seem to prey upon the public in two battalions—that of the dandies and that of the military men. Of the first grade the leading features are long locks and smiles; of the second, frogged coats and frowns.

Descending in the scale of what is termed gentility, I found darker and deeper themes for speculation. I saw Jew peddlers, with hawk eyes flashing from countenances whose every other feature wore only an expression of abject humility; sturdy professional street beggars scowling upon mendicants of a better stamp, whom despair alone had driven forth into the night for charity; feeble and ghastly invalids, upon whom death had placed a sure hand, and who sidled and tottered through the mob, looking every one beseechingly in the face, as if in search of some chance consolation, some lost hope; modest young girls returning from long and late labor to a cheerless home, and shrinking more tearfully than indignantly from the glances of ruffians, whose direct contact, even, could not be avoided; women of the town of all kinds and of all ages—the unequivocal beauty in the prime of her womanhood, putting one in mind of the statue in Lucian, with the surface of Parian marble, and the interior filled with filth—the loathsome and utterly lost leper in rags—the wrinkled, bejewelled and paint-begrimed beldame, making a last effort at youth—the mere child of immature form, yet, from long association, an adept in the dreadful coquetries of her trade, and burning with a rabid ambition to be ranked the equal of her elders in vice; drunkards innumerable and indescribable—some in shreds and patches, reeling, inarticulate, with bruised visage and lack-lustre eyes—some in whole although filthy garments, with a slightly unsteady swagger, thick sensual lips, and hearty-looking rubicund faces—others clothed in materials which had once been good, and which even now were scrupulously well brushed—men who walked with a more than naturally firm and springy step, but whose countenances were fearfully pale, whose eyes were hideously wild and red, and who clutched with quivering fingers, as they strode through the crowd, at every object which came within their reach; beside these, pie-men, porters, coal-heavers, sweeps; organ-grinders, monkey-exhibitors and ballad-mongers, those who vended with those who sang; ragged artizans and exhausted laborers of every description, and all full of a noisy and inordinate vivacity which jarred discordantly upon the ear, and gave an aching sensation to the eye.

As the night deepened, so deepened to me the interest of the scene; for not only did the general character of the crowd materially alter (its gentler features retiring in the gradual withdrawal of the more orderly portion of the people, and its harsher ones coming out into bolder relief, as the late hour brought forth every species of infamy from its den,) but the rays of the gas-lamps, feeble at first in their struggle with the dying day, had now at length gained ascendancy, and threw over every thing a fitful and garish lustre. All was dark yet splendid—as that ebony to which has been likened the style of Tertullian.

The wild effects of the light enchained me to an examination of individual faces; and although the rapidity with which the world of light flitted before the window, prevented me from casting more than a glance upon each visage, still it seemed that, in my then peculiar mental state, I could frequently read, even in that brief interval of a glance, the history of long years.

With my brow to the glass, I was thus occupied in scrutinizing the mob, when suddenly there came into view a countenance (that of a decrepid old man, some sixty-five or seventy years of age,)—a countenance which at once arrested and absorbed my whole attention, on account of the absolute idiosyncrasy of its expression. Any thing even remotely resembling that expression I had never seen before. I well remember that my first thought, upon beholding it, was that Retszch, had he viewed it, would have greatly preferred it to his own pictural incarnations of the fiend. As I endeavored, during the brief minute of my original survey, to form some analysis of the meaning conveyed, there arose confusedly and paradoxically within my mind, the ideas of vast mental power, of caution, of penuriousness, of avarice, of coolnes, of malice, of blood-thirstiness, of triumph, of merriment, of excessive terror, of intense—of supreme despair. I felt singularly aroused, startled, fascinated. "How wild a history," I said to myself, "is written within that bosom!" Then came a craving desire to keep the man in view—to know more of him. Hurriedly putting on an overcoat, and seizing my hat and cane, I made my way into the street, and pushed through the crowd in the direction which I had seen him take; for he had already disappeared. With some little difficulty I at length came within sight of him, approached, and followed him closely, yet cautiously, so as not to attract his attention.

I had now a good opportunity of examining his person. He was short in stature, very thin, and apparently very feeble. His clothes, generally, were filthy and ragged; but as he came, now and then, within the strong glare of a lamp, I perceived that his linen, although dirty, was of beautiful texture; and my vision deceived me, or, through a rent in a closely-buttoned and evidently second-handed *roquelaire* [4] which enveloped him, I caught a glimpse both of a diamond and of a dagger. These observations heightened my curiosity, and I resolved to follow the stranger whithersoever he should go.

It was now fully night-fall, and a thick humid fog hung over the city, soon ending in a settled and heavy rain. This change of weather had an odd effect upon the crowd, the whole of which was at once put into new commotion, and overshadowed by a world of umbrellas. The waver, the jostle, and the hum increased in a tenfold degree. For my own part I did not much regard the rain—the lurking of an old fever in my system rendering the moisture somewhat too dangerously pleasant. Tying a handerchief about my mouth, I kept on. For half an hour the old man held his way with difficulty along the great thoroughfare; and I here walked close at his elbow through fear of losing sight of him. Never once turning his head to look back, he did not observe me. By and bye he passed into a cross street, which, although densely filled with people, was not quite so much thronged as the main one he had quitted. Here a change in his demeanor became evident. He walked more slowly and with less object than before—more hesitatingly. He crossed and re-crossed the way repeatedly, without apparent aim; and the press was still so thick, that, at every such movement, I was obliged to follow him closely. The street was a narrow and long one, and his course lay within it for nearly an hour, during which the passengers had gradually diminished to about that number which is ordinarily seen at noon on Broadway near the park—so vast a difference is there between a London populace and that of the most frequented American city. A second turn brought us into a square, brilliantly lighted, and overflowing with life. The old manner of the stranger re-appeared. His chin fell upon his breast, while his eyes rolled wildly from under his knit brows, in every

---

[4] A coat.

direction, upon those who hemmed him in. He urged his way steadily and perseveringly. I was surprised, however, to find, upon his having made the circuit of the square, that he turned and retraced his steps. Still more was I astonished to see him repeat the same walk several times—once nearly detecting me as he came round with a sudden movement.

In this exercise he spent another hour, at the end of which we met with far less interruption from passengers than at first. The rain fell fast; the air grew cool; and the people were retiring to their homes. With a gesture of impatience, the wanderer passed into a by-street comparatively deserted. Down this, some quarter of a mile long, he rushed with an activity I could not have dreamed of seeing in one so aged, and which put me to much trouble in pursuit. A few minutes brought us to a large and busy bazaar, with the localities of which the stranger appeared well acquainted, and where his original demeanor again became apparent, as he forced his way to and fro, without aim, among the host of buyers and sellers.

During the hour and a half, or thereabouts, which we passed in this place, it required much caution on my part to keep him within reach without attracting his observation. Luckily I wore a pair of caoutchouc [5] over-shoes, and could move about in perfect silence. At no moment did he see that I watched him. He entered shop after shop, priced nothing, spoke no word, and looked at all objects with a wild and vacant stare. I was now utterly amazed at his behaviour, and firmly resolved that we should not part until I had satisfied myself in some measure respecting him.

A loud-toned clock struck eleven, and the company were fast deserting the bazaar. A shop-keeper, in putting up a shutter, jostled the old man, and at the instant I saw a strong shudder come over his frame. He hurried into the street, looked anxiously around him for an instant, and then ran with incredible swiftness through many crooked and people-less lanes, until we emerged once more upon the great thoroughfare whence we had started—the street of the D—— Hotel. It no longer wore, however, the same aspect. It was still brilliant with gas; but the rain fell fiercely, and there were few persons to be seen. The stranger grew pale. He walked moodily some paces up the once populous avenue, then, with a heavy sigh, turned in the direction of the river, and, plunging through a great variety of devious ways, came out, at length, in view of one of the principal theatres. It was about being closed, and the audience were thronging from the doors. I saw the old man gasp as if for breath while he threw himself amid the crowd; but I thought that the intense agony of his countenance had, in some measure, abated. His head again fell upon his breast; he appeared as I had seen him at first. I observed that he now took the course in which had gone the

[5] A kind of rubber.

greater number of the audience—but, upon the whole, I was at a loss to comprehend the waywardness of his actions.

As he proceeded, the company grew more scattered, and his old uneasiness and vacillation were resumed. For some time he followed closely a party of some ten or twelve roisterers; but from this number one by one dropped off, until three only remained together, in a narrow and gloomy lane little frequented. The stranger paused, and, for a moment, seemed lost in thought; then, with every mark of agitation, pursued rapidly a route which brought us to the verge of the city, amid regions very different from those we had hitherto traversed. It was the most noisome quarter of London, where every thing wore the worst impress of the most deplorable poverty, and of the most desperate crime. By the dim light of an accidental lamp, tall, antique, worm-eaten, wooden tenements were seen tottering to their fall, in directions so many and capricious that scarce the semblance of a passage was discernible between them. The paving-stones lay at random, displaced from their beds by the rankly growing grass. Horrible filth festered in the dammed-up gutters. The whole atmosphere teemed with desolation. Yet, as we proceeded, the sounds of human life revived by sure degrees, and at length large bands of the most abandoned of a London populace were seen reeling to and fro. The spirits of the old man again flickered up, as a lamp which is near its death-hour. Once more he strode onward with elastic tread. Suddenly a corner was turned, a blaze of light burst upon our sight, and we stood before one of the huge suburban temples of Intemperance—one of the palaces of the fiend, Gin.

It was now nearly day-break; but a number of wretched inebriates still pressed in and out of the flaunting entrance. With a half shriek of joy the old man forced a passage within, resumed at once his original bearing, and stalked backward and forward, without apparent object, among the throng. He had not been thus long occupied, however, before a rush to the doors gave token that the host was closing them for the night. It was something even more intense than despair that I then observed upon the countenance of the singular being whom I had watched so pertinaciously. Yet he did not hesitate in his career, but, with a mad energy, retraced his steps at once, to the heart of the mighty London. Long and swiftly he fled, while I followed him in the wildest amazement, resolute not to abandon a scrutiny in which I now felt an interest all-absorbing. The sun arose while we proceeded, and, when we had once again reached that most thronged mart of the populous town, the street of the D—— Hotel, it presented an appearance of human bustle and activity scarcely inferior to what I had seen on the evening before. And here, long, amid the momently increasing confusion, did I persist in my pursuit of the stranger. But, as usual, he walked to and fro, and during the day did not pass from out the turmoil of that street. And, as the shades of the second evening came on, I grew wearied unto death, and, stopping fully in front of the wanderer, gazed

at him steadfastly in the face. He noticed me not, but resumed his
solemn walk, while I, ceasing to follow, remained absorbed in contemplation. "This old man," I said at length, "is the type and the genius
of deep crime. He refuses to be alone. *He is the man of the crowd.* It
will be in vain to follow; for I shall learn no more of him, nor of his
deeds. The worst heart of the world is a grosser book than the 'Hortulus
Animæ,'[6] and perhaps it is but one of the great mercies of God that
'es lässt sich nicht lesen.'"[7]

The Purloined Letter (1845)

Nil sapientiae odiosius acumine nimio.
                    Seneca

At Paris, just after dark one gusty evening in the autumn of 18——,
I was enjoying the twofold luxury of meditation and a meerschaum, in
company with my friend C. Auguste Dupin, in his little back library, or
bookcloset, *au troisième, No. 33, Rue Dunôt, Faubourg St. Germain.*
For one hour at least we had maintained a profound silence; while each,
to any casual observer, might have seemed intently and exclusively
occupied with the curling eddies of smoke that oppressed the atmosphere of the chamber. For myself, however, I was mentally discussing
certain topics which had formed matter for conversation between us
at an earlier period of the evening; I mean the affair of the Rue Morgue,
and the mystery attending the murder of Marie Rogêt. I looked upon
it, therefore, as something of a coincidence, when the door of our apartment was thrown open and admitted our old acquaintance, Monsieur
G——, the Prefect of the Parisian police.

We gave him a hearty welcome; for there was nearly half as much
of the entertaining as of the contemptible about the man, and we had
not seen him for several years. We had been sitting in the dark, and
Dupin now arose for the purpose of lighting a lamp, but sat down again,
without doing so, upon G——'s saying that he had called to consult us,
or rather to ask the opinion of my friend, about some official business
which had occasioned a great deal of trouble.

"If it is any point requiring reflection," observed Dupin, as he fore-
bore to enkindle the wick, "we shall examine it to better purpose in the
dark."

"That is another of your odd notions," said the Prefect, who had a
fashion of calling every thing "odd" that was beyond his comprehension,
and thus lived amid an absolute legion of "oddities."

[6] The *Hortulus Animæ cum Oratiunculis Aliquibus Superadditis* of Grünninger. Au.
[7] Doesn't allow itself to be read.

---

[1] Nothing is more odious to good sense than too much cleverness.

"Very true," said Dupin, as he supplied his vistor with a pipe, and rolled towards him a comfortable chair.

"And what is the difficulty now?" I asked. "Nothing more in the assassination way, I hope?"

"Oh no; nothing of that nature. The fact is, the business is *very* simple indeed, and I make no doubt that we can manage it sufficiently well ourselves; but then I thought Dupin would like to hear the details of it, because it is so excessively *odd.*"

"Simple and odd," said Dupin.

"Why, yes; and not exactly that, either. The fact is, we have all been a good deal puzzled because the affair *is* so simple, and yet baffles us altogether."

"Perhaps it is the very simplicity of the thing which puts you at fault," said my friend.

"What nonsense you *do* talk!" replied the Prefect, laughing heartily.

"Perhaps the mystery is a little *too* plain," said Dupin.

"Oh, good heavens! who ever heard of such an idea?"

"A little *too* self-evident."

"Ha! ha! ha!—ha! ha! ha!—ho! ho! ho!"—roared our visitor, profoundly amused, "oh, Dupin, you will be the death of me yet!"

"And what, after all, *is* the matter on hand? I asked.

"Why, I will tell you," replied the Prefect, as he gave a long, steady, and contemplative puff, and settled himself in his chair, "I will tell you in a few words; but, before I begin, let me caution you that this is an affair demanding the greatest secrecy, and that I should most probably lose the position I now hold, were it known that I confided it to any one."

"Proceed," said I.

"Or not," said Dupin.

"Well, then; I have received personal information, from a very high quarter, that a certain document of the last importance has been purloined from the royal apartments. The individual who purloined it is known; this beyond a doubt; he was seen to take it. It is known, also, that it still remains in his possession."

"How is this known?" asked Dupin.

"It is clearly inferred," replied the Prefect, "from the nature of the document, and from the non-appearance of certain results which would at once arise from its passing *out* of the robber's possession;—that is to say, from his employing it as he must design in the end to employ it."

"Be a little more explicit," I said.

"Well, I may venture so far as to say that the paper gives its holder a certain power in a certain quarter where such power is immensely valuable." The Prefect was fond of the cant of diplomacy.

"Still I do not quite understand," said Dupin.

"No? Well; the disclosure of the document to a third person who shall be nameless would bring in question the honor of a personage of most exalted station; and this fact gives the holder of the document an ascendancy over the illustrious personage whose honor and peace are so jeopardized."

"But this ascendancy," I interposed, "would depend upon the robber's knowledge of the loser's knowledge of the robber. Who would dare—"

"The thief," said G——, "is the Minister D——, who dares all things, those unbecoming as well as those becoming a man. The method of the theft was not less ingenious than bold. The document in question—a letter, to be frank—had been received by the personage robbed while alone in the royal *boudoir*. During its perusal she was suddenly interrupted by the entrance of the other exalted personage from whom especially it was her wish to conceal it. After a hurried and vain endeavor to thrust it in a drawer, she was forced to place it, open as it was, upon a table. The address, however, was uppermost, and, the contents thus unexposed, the letter escaped notice. At this juncture enters the Minister D——. His lynx eye immediately perceives the paper, recognizes the handwriting of the address, observes the confusion of the personage addressed, and fathoms her secret. After some business transactions, hurried through in his ordinary manner, he produces a letter somewhat similar to the one in question, opens it, pretends to read it, and then places it in close juxtaposition to the other. Again he converses, for some fifteen minutes, upon the public affairs. At length, in taking leave, he takes also from the table the letter to which he had no claim. Its rightful owner saw, but, of course, dared not call attention to the act, in the presence of the third personage who stood at her elbow. The Minister decamped; leaving his own letter—one of no importance—upon the table."

"Here, then," said Dupin to me, "you have precisely what you demand to make the ascendancy complete—the robber's knowledge of the loser's knowledge of the robber."

"Yes," replied the Prefect; "and the power thus attained has, for some months past, been wielded, for political purposes, to a very dangerous extent. The personage robbed is more thoroughly convinced, every day, of the necessity of reclaiming her letter. But this, of course, cannot be done openly. In fine, driven to despair, she has committed the matter to me."

"Than whom," said Dupin, amid a perfect whirlwind of smoke, "no more sagacious agent could, I suppose, be desired, or even imagined."

"You flatter me," replied the Prefect; "but it is possible that some such opinion may have been entertained."

"It is clear," said I, "as you observe, that the letter is still in possession of the Minister; since it is this possession, and not any employment of the letter, which bestows the power. With the employment the power departs."

"True," said G——; "and upon this conviction I proceeded. My first care was to make thorough search of the Minister's hotel; and here my

chief embarrassment lay in the necessity of searching without his knowledge. Beyond all thing, I have been warned of the danger which would
result from giving him reason to suspect our design."

"But," said I, "you are quite *au fait* in these investigations. The
Parisian police have done this thing often before."

"Oh yes; and for this reason I did not despair. The habits of the
Minister gave me, too, a great advantage. He is frequently absent from
home all night. His servants are by no means numerous. They sleep at
a distance from their master's apartment, and, being chiefly Neapolitans,
are readily made drunk. I have keys, as you know, with which I can
open any chamber or cabinet in Paris. For three months a night has not
passed, during the greater part of which I have not been engaged,
personally, in ransacking the D—— Hôtel. My honor is interested, and,
to mention a great secret, the reward is enormous. So I did not abandon
the search until I had become fully satisfied that the thief is a more
astute man than myself. I fancy that I have investigated every nook and
corner of the premises in which it is possible that the paper can be
concealed."

"But is it not possible," I suggested, "that although the letter may
be in the possession of the Minister, as it unquestionably is, he may
have concealed it elsewhere than upon his own premises?"

"This is barely possible," said Dupin. "The present peculiar condition
of affairs at court, and especially of those intrigues in which D—— is
known to be involved, would render the instant availability of the document—its susceptibility of being produced at a moment's notice—a
point of nearly equal importance with its possession."

"It's susceptibility of being produced?" said I.

"That is to say, of being *destroyed*," said Dupin.

"True," I observed; "the paper is clearly then upon the premises.
As for its being upon the person of the Minister, we may consider that
as out of the question."

"Entirely," said the Prefect. "He has been twice waylaid, as if by
footpads, and his person rigorously searched under my own inspection."

"You might have spared yourself this trouble," said Dupin. "D——,
I presume, is not altogether a fool, and, if not, must have anticipated
these waylayings, as a matter of course."

"Not *altogether* a fool," said G——, "but then he's a poet, which
I take to be only one remove from a fool."

"True," said Dupin, after a long and thoughtful whiff from his
meerschaum, "although I have been guilty of certain doggerel myself."

"Suppose you detail," said I, "the particulars of your search."

"Why the fact is, we took our time, and we searched *every where*.
I have had long experience in these affairs. I took the entire building,
room by room; devoting the nights of a whole week to each. We examined, first, the furniture of each apartment. We opened every possible
drawer; and I presume you know that, to a properly trained police

agent, such a thing as a *secret* drawer is impossible. Any man is a dolt who permits a 'secret' drawer to escape him in a search of this kind. The thing is *so* plain. There is a certain amount of bulk—a space—to be accounted for in every cabinet. Then we have accurate rules. The fiftieth part of a line could not escape us. After the cabinets we took the chairs. The cushions we probed with the fine long needles you have seen me employ. From the tables we removed the tops."

"Why so?"

"Sometimes the top of a table, or other similarly arranged piece of furniture, is removed by the person wishing to conceal an article; then the leg is excavated, the article deposited within the cavity, and the top replaced. The bottoms and tops of bed-posts are employed in the same way."

"But could not the cavity be detected by sounding?" I asked.

"By no means, if, when the article is deposited, a sufficient wadding of cotton be placed around it. Besides, in our case, we were obliged to proceed without noise."

"But you could not have removed—you could not have taken to pieces *all* articles of furniture in which it would have been possible to make a deposit in the manner you mention. A letter may be compressed into a thin spiral roll, not differing much in shape or bulk from a large knitting-needle, and in this form it might be inserted into the rung of a chair, for example. You did not take to pieces all the chairs?"

"Certainly not; but we did better—we examined the rungs of every chair in the hotel, and, indeed, the jointings of every description of furniture, by the aid of a most powerful microscope. Had there been any traces of recent disturbance we should not have failed to detect it instantly. A single grain of gimlet-dust, for example, would have been as obvious as an apple. Any disorder in the glueing—any unusual gaping in the joints—would have sufficed to insure detection."

"I presume you looked to the mirrors, between the boards and the plates, and you probed the beds and the bed-clothes, as well as the curtains and carpets."

"That of course; and when we had absolutely completed every particle of the furniture in this way, then we examined the house itself. We divided its entire surface into compartments, which we numbered, so that none might be missed; then we scrutinized each individual square inch throughout the premises, including the two houses immediately adjoining, with the microscope, as before."

"The two houses adjoining!" I exclaimed; "you must have had a great deal of trouble."

"We had; but the reward offered is prodigious."

"You include the *grounds* about the houses?"

"All the grounds are paved with brick. They gave us comparatively little trouble. We examined the moss between the bricks, and found it undisturbed."

"You looked among D——'s papers, of course, and into the books of the library?"

"Certainly; we opened every package and parcel; we not only opened every book, but we turned over every leaf in each volume, not contenting ourselves with a mere shake, according to the fashion of some of our police officers. We also measured the thickness of every book-*cover,* with the most accurate admeasurement, and applied to each the most jealous scrutiny of the miscroscope. Had any of the bindings been recently meddled with, it would have been utterly impossible that the fact should have escaped observation. Some five or six volumes, just from the hands of the binder, we carefully probed, longitudinally, with the needles."

"You explored the floors beneath the carpets?"

"Beyond doubt. We removed every carpet, and examined the boards with the microscope."

"And the paper on the walls?"

"Yes."

"You looked into the cellars?"

"We did."

"Then," I said, "you have been making a miscalculation, and the letter is *not* upon the premises, as you supposed."

"I fear you are right there," said the Prefect. "And now, Dupin, what would you advise me to do?"

"To make a thorough re-search of the premises."

"That is absolutely needless," replied G——. "I am not more sure that I breathe than I am that the letter is not at the Hôtel."

"I have no better advice to give you," said Dupin. "You have, of course, an accurate description of the letter?"

"Oh yes!"—And here the Prefect, producing a memorandum-book, proceeded to read aloud a minute account of the internal, and especially of the external appearance of the missing document. Soon after finishing the perusal of this description, he took his departure, more entirely depressed in spirits than I had ever know the good gentleman before.

In about a month afterwards he paid us another visit, and found us occupied very nearly as before. He took a pipe and a chair and entered into some ordinary conversation. At length I said,—

"Well, but G——, what of the purloined letter? I presume you have at last made up your mind that there is no such thing as overreaching the Minister?"

"Confound him, say I—yes; I made the re-examination, however, as Dupin suggested—but it was all labor lost, as I knew it would be."

"How much was the reward offered, did you say?" asked Dupin.

"Why, a very geat deal—a *very* liberal reward—I don't like to say how much, precisely; but one thing I *will* say, that I wouldn't mind giving my individual check for fifty thousand francs to any one who could obtain me that letter. The fact is, it is becoming of more and more importance every day; and the reward has been lately doubled. If it were trebled, however, I could do no more than I have done."

"Why, yes," said Dupin, drawlingly, between the whiffs of his meerschaum, "I really—think, G——, you have not exerted yourself— to the utmost in this matter. You might—do a little more, I think, eh?"

"How?"—in what way?"

"Why—puff, puff—you might—puff, puff—employ counsel in the matter, eh?—puff, puff, puff. Do you remember the story they tell of Abernethy!"

"No; hang Abernethy!"

"To be sure! hang him and welcome. But, once upon a time, a certain rich miser conceived the design of sponging upon this Abernethy for a medical opinion. Getting up, for this purpose, an ordinary conversation in a private company, he insinuated his case to his physician, as that of an imaginary individual.

"'We will suppose,' said the miser, 'that his symptoms are such and such; now, doctor, what would *you* have directed him to take?'"

"'Take!' said Abernethy, 'why, take *advice*, to be sure.'"

"But," said the Prefect, a little discomposed, "I am *perfectly* willing to take advice, and to pay for it. I would *really* give fifty thousand francs to any one who would aid me in the matter."

"In that case," replied Dupin, opening a drawer, and producing a check-book, "you may as well fill me up a check for the amount mentioned. When you have signed it, I will hand you the letter."

I was astounded. The Prefect appeared absolutely thunder-stricken. For some minutes he remained speechless and motionless, looking incredulously at my friend with open mouth, and eyes that seemed starting from their sockets; then, apparently recovering himself in some measure, he seized a pen, and after several pauses and vacant stares, finally filled up and signed a check for fifty thousand francs, and handed it across the table to Dupin. The latter examined it carefully and deposited it in his pocket-book; then, unlocking an *escritoire*, took thence a letter and gave it to the Prefect. This functionary grasped it in a perfect agony of joy, opened it with a trembling hand, cast a rapid glance at its contents, and then, scrambling and struggling to the door, rushed at length unceremoniously from the room and from the house, without having uttered a syllable since Dupin had requested him to fill up the check.

When he had gone, my friend entered into some explanations.

"The Parisian police," he said, "are exceedingly able in their way. They are persevering, ingenious, cunning, and thoroughly versed in the knowledge which their duties seem chiefly to demand. Thus, when G—— detailed to us his mode of searching the premises at the Hôtel D——, I felt entire confidence in his having made a satisfactory investigation—so far as his labors extended."

"So far as his labors extended?" said I.

"Yes," said Dupin. "The measures adopted were not only the best of their kind, but carried out to absolute perfection. Had the letter been deposited with the range of their search, these fellows would, beyond a question, have found it."

I merely laughed—but he seemed quite serious in all that he said.

"The measures, then," he continued, "were good in their kind, and well executed; their defect lay in their being inapplicable to the case, and to the man. A certain set of highly ingenious resources are, with the Prefect, a sort of Procrustean bed, to which he forcibly adapts his designs. But he perpetually errs by being too deep or too shallow, for the matter in hand; and many a schoolboy is a better reasoner than he. I knew one about eight years of age, whose success at guessing in the game of 'even and odd' attracted universal admiration. This game is simple, and is played with marbles. One player holds in his hand a number of these toys, and demands of another whether that number is even or odd. If the guess is right, the guesser wins one; if wrong, he loses one. The boy to whom I allude won all the marbles of the school. Of course he had some principle of guessing; and this lay in mere observation and admeasurement of the astuteness of his opponents. For example, an arrant simpleton is his opponent, and, holding up his closed hand, asks, 'are they even or odd?' Our schoolboy replies, 'odd,' and loses; but upon the second trial he wins, for he then says to himself, 'the simpleton had them even upon the first trial, and his amount of cunning is just sufficient to make him have them odd upon the second; I will therefore guess odd';—he guesses odd, and wins. Now, with a simpleton a degree above the first, he would have reasoned thus: 'This fellow finds that in the first instance I guessed odd, and, in the second, he will propose to himself upon the first impulse, a simple variation from even to odd, as did the first simpleton; but then a second thought will suggest that this is too simple a variation, and finally he will decide upon putting it even as before. I will therefore guess even';—he guesses even, and wins. Now this mode of reasoning in the schoolboy, whom his fellows termed 'lucky,'—what, in its last analysis, is it?"

"It is merely," I said, "an identification of the reasoner's intellect with that of his opponent."

"It is," said Dupin; "and, upon inquiring of the boy by what means he effected the *thorough* identification in which his success consisted, I received answer as follows: 'When I wish to find out how wise, or how stupid, or how good, or how wicked is any one, or what are his thoughts at the moment, I fashion the expression of my face, as accurately as possible, in accordance with the expression of his, and then wait to see what thoughts or sentiments arise in my mind or heart, as if to match or correspond with the expression.' This response of the schoolboy lies at the bottom of all the spurious profundity which has been attributed to Rochefoucauld, to La Bougive, to Machiavelli, and to Campanella."

"And the identification," I said, "of the reasoner's intellect with that of his opponent, depends, if I understand you aright, upon the accuracy with which the opponent's intellect is admeasured."

"For its practical value it depends upon this," replied Dupin; "and the Prefect and his cohort fail so frequently, first, by default of this identification, and, secondly, by ill-admeasurement, or rather through non-admeasurement of the intellect with which they are engaged. They consider only their *own* ideas of ingenuity; and, in searching for anything hidden, advert only to the modes in which *they* would have hidden it. They are right in this much—that their own ingenuity is a faithful representative of that of *the mass;* but when the cunning of the individual felon is diverse in character from their own, the felon foils them, of course. This always happens when it is above their own, and very usually when it is below. They have no variation of principle in their investigations; at best, when urged by some unusual emergency—by some extraordinary reward—they extend or exaggerate their old modes of *practice*, without touching their principles. What, for example, in this case of D——, has been done to vary the principle of action? What is all this boring, and probing, and sounding, and scrutinizing with the microscope, and dividing the surface of the building into registered square inches—what is it all but an exaggeration *of the application* of the one principle or set of principles of search, which are based upon the one set of notions regarding human ingenuity, to which the Prefect, in the long routine of his duty, has been accustomed? Do you not see he has taken it for granted that *all* men proceed to conceal a letter—not exactly in a gimlet-hole bored in a chair-leg—but, at least, in *some* out-of-the-way hole or corner suggested by the same tenor of thought which would urge a man to secrete a letter in a gimlet-hole bored in a chair-leg? And do you not see also, that such *recherchés* nooks for concealment are adopted only for ordinary occasions, and would be adopted only by ordinary intellects; for, in all cases of concealment, a disposal of the article concealed—a disposal of it in this *recherché* manner—is, in the very first instance, presumable and presumed; and thus its discovery depends, not at all upon the acumen, but altogether upon the mere care, patience, and determination of the seekers; and where the case is of importance—or, what amounts to the same thing in the policial eyes, when the reward is of magnitude,—the qualities in question have *never* been known to fail? You will now understand what I meant in suggesting that, had the purloined letter been hidden any where within the limits of the Prefect's examination—in other words, had the principle of its concealment been comprehended within the principles of the Prefect—its discovery would have been a matter altogether beyond question. This functionary, however, has been thoroughly mystified; and the remote source of his defeat lies in the supposition that the Minister is a fool, because he has acquired renown as a poet. All fools are poets; this the Prefect *feels;* and he is merely guilty of a *non distributio medii*[2] in thence inferring that all poets are fools."

"But is this really the poet?" I asked. "There are two brothers, I know; and both have attained reputation in letters. The Minister I believe has written learnedly on the Differential Calculus. He is a mathematician, and no poet."

"You are mistaken; I know him well; he is both. As poet *and* mathematician, he would reason well; as mere mathematician, he could not have reasoned at all, and thus would have been at the mercy of the Prefect."

"You surprise me," I said, "by these opinions, which have been contradicted by the voice of the world. You do not mean to set at naught the well-digested idea of centuries. The mathematical reason has long been regarded as *the* reason *par excellence.*"

" '*Il y a à parier,*' " replied Dupin, quoting from Chamfort, " '*que toute idée publique, toute convention reçue, est une sottise, car elle a convenu au plus grand nombre.*'[3] The mathematicians, I grant you, have done their best to promulgate the popular error to which you allude, and which is none the less an error for its promulgation as truth. With an art worthy a better cause, for example, they have insinuated the term 'analysis' into application to algebra. The French are the originators of this particular deception; but if a term is of any importance— if words derive any value from applicability—then 'analysis' conveys 'algebra' about as much as, in Latin, '*ambitus*' implies 'ambition,' '*religio*' 'religion,' or '*homines honesti*' a set of *honorable* men."

"You have a quarrel on hand, I see," said I, "with some of the algebraists of Paris; but proceed."

"I dispute the availability, and thus the value, of that reason which is cultivated in any especial form other than the abstractly logical. I dispute, in particular, the reason educed by mathematical study. The mathematics are the science of form and quantity; mathematical reasoning is merely logic applied to observation upon form and quantity. The great error lies in supposing that even the truths of what is called *pure* algebra, are abstract or general truths. And this error is so egregious that I am confounded at the universality with which it has been received. Mathematical axioms are *not* axioms of general truth. What is true of *relation*—of form and quantity—is often grossly false in regard to morals, for example. In this latter science it is very usually *un*true that the aggregated parts are equal to the whole. In chemistry also the axiom fails. In the consideration of motive it fails; for two motives, each of a given value, have not, necessarily, a value when united, equal to

[2] Undistributed middle.

[3] I'll bet that every popular idea, every set convention, is an idiocy, because it has suited the majority.

the sum of their values apart. There are numerous other mathematical truths which are only truths within the limits of *relation*. But the mathematician argues, from his *finite truths*, through habit, as if they were of an absolutely general applicability—as the world indeed imagines them to be. Bryant, in his very learned 'Mythology,' mentions an analogous source of error, when he says that 'although the Pagan fables are not believed, yet we forget ourselves continually, and make inferences from them as existing realities.' With the algebraists, however, who are Pagans themselves, the 'Pagan fables' *are* believed, and the inferences are made, not so much through lapse of memory, as through an unaccountable addling of the brains. In short, I never yet encountered the mere mathematician who could be trusted out of equal roots, or one who did not clandestinely hold it as a point of his faith that $x^2 + px$ was absolutely and unconditionally equal to q. Say to one of these gentlemen, by way of experiment, if you please, that you believe occasions may occur where $x^2 + px$ is *not* altogether equal to q, and, having made him understand what you mean, get out of his reach as speedily as convenient, for, beyond doubt, he will endeavor to knock you down.

"I mean to say," continued Dupin, while I merely laughed at his last observations, "that if the Minister had been no more than a mathematician, the Prefect would have been under no necessity of giving me this check. I knew him, however, as both mathematician and poet, and my measures were adapted to his capacity, with reference to the circumstances by which he was surrounded. I knew him as a courtier, too, and as a bold *intriguant*. Such a man, I considered, could not fail to be aware of the ordinary policial modes of action. He could not have failed to anticipate—and events have proved that he did not fail to anticipate—the waylayings to which he was subjected. He must have foreseen, I reflected, the secret investigations of his premises. His frequent absences from home at night, which were hailed by the Prefect as certain aids to his success, I regarded only as *ruses,* to afford opportunity for thorough search to the police, and thus the sooner to impress them with the conviction to which G——, in fact, did finally arrive— the conviction that the letter was not upon the premises. I felt, also, that the whole train of thought, which I was at some pains in detailing to you just now, concerning the invariable principal of policial action in searches for articles concealed—I felt that this whole train of thought would necessarily pass through the mind of the Minister. It would imperatively lead him to despise all the ordinary *nooks* of concealment. *He* could not, I reflected, be so weak as not to see that the most intricate and remote recess of his hotel would be as open as his commonest closets to the eyes, to the probes, to the gimlets, and to the microscopes of the Prefect. I saw, in fine, that he would be driven, as a matter of course, to *simplicity*, if not deliberately induced to it as a matter of choice. You will remember, perhaps, how desperately the Prefect laughed when I suggested, upon our first interview, that it was just possible this mystery troubled him so much on account of its being so *very* self-evident."

"Yes," said I, "I remember his merriment well. I really thought he would have fallen into convulsions."

"The material world," continued Dupin, "abounds with the very strict analogies to the immaterial; and thus some color of truth has been given to the rhetorical dogma, that metaphor, or simile, may be made to strengthen an argument, as well as to embellish a description. The principle of the *vis inertiœ*,[4] for example, seems to be identical in physics and metaphysics. It is not more true in the former, that a large body is with more difficulty set in motion than a smaller one, and that its subsequent *momentum* is commensurate with this difficulty, than it is, in the latter, that intellects of the vaster capacity, while more forcible, more constant, and more eventful in their movements than those of inferior grade, are yet the less readily moved, and more embarrassed and full of hesitation in the first few steps of their progress. Again: have you ever noticed which of the street signs, over the shop doors, are the most attractive of attention?"

"I have never given the matter a thought," I said.

"There is a game of puzzles," he resumed, "which is played upon a map. One party playing requires another to find a given word—the name of town, river, state or empire—any word, in short, upon the motely and perplexed surface of the chart. A novice in the game generally seeks to embarrass his opponents by giving them the most minutely lettered names; but the adept selects such words as stretch, in large characters, from one end of the chart to the other. These, like the over-largely lettered signs and placards of the street, escape observation by dint of being excessively obvious; and here the physical oversight is precisely analogous with the moral inapprehension by which the intellect suffers to pass unnoticed those considerations which are too obtrusively and too palpably self-evident. But this is a point, it appears, somewhat above or beneath the understanding of the Prefect. He never once thought it probable, or possible, that the Minister had deposited the letter immediately beneath the nose of the whole world, by way of best preventing any portion of that world from perceiving it.

"But the more I reflected upon the daring, dashing, and discriminating ingenuity of D——; upon the fact that the document must always have been *at hand*, if he intended to use it to good purpose; and upon the decisive evidence, obtained by the Prefect, that it was not hidden within the limits of that dignitary's ordinary search—the more satisfied I became that, to conceal this letter, the Minister had resorted to the comprehensive and sagacious expedient of not attempting to conceal it at all.

---

[4] Force of inertia.

"Full of these ideas, I prepared myself with a pair of green spectacles, and called one fine morning, quite by accident, at the Ministerial
hotel. I found G—— at home, yawning, lounging, and dawdling, as
usual, and pretending to be in the last extremity of *ennui*. He is, perhaps, the most really energetic human being now alive—but that is only
when nobody sees him.

"To be even with him, I complained of my weak eyes, and lamented
the necessity of the spectacles, under cover of which I cautiously and
thoroughly surveyed the apartment, while seemingly intent only upon
the conversation of my host.

"I paid especial attention to a large writing-table near which he sat,
and upon which lay confusedly some miscellaneous letters and other
papers, with one or two musical instruments and a few books. Here,
however, after a long and very deliberate scrutiny, I saw nothing to
excite particular suspicion.

"At length my eyes, in going the circuit of the room, fell upon a
trumpery filigree card-rack of pasteboard, that hung dangling by a dirty
blue ribbon, from a little brass knob just beneath the middle of the
mantel-piece. In this rack, which had three or four compartments, were
five or six visiting cards and a solitary letter. This last was much soiled
and crumpled. It was torn nearly in two, across the middle—as if a
design, in the first instance, to tear it entirely up as worthless, had been
altered, or stayed, in the second. It had a large black seal, bearing the
D—— cipher *very* conspicuously, and was addressed, in a diminutive
female hand, to D——, the Minister, himself. It was thrust carelessly,
and even, as it seemed, contemptuously, into one of the upper divisions
of the rack.

"No sooner had I glanced at this letter, than I concluded it to be
that of which I was in search. To be sure, it was, to all appearance,
radically different from the one of which the Prefect had read us so
minute a description. Here the seal was large and black, with the
D—— cipher; there it was small and red, with the ducal arms of the
S—— family. Here, the address, to the Minister, was diminutive and
feminine; there the superscription, to a certain royal personage, was
markedly bold and decided; the size alone formed a point of correspondence. But, then, the *radicalness* of these differences, which was
excessive; the dirt; the soiled and torn condition of the paper, so inconsistent with the *true* methodical habits of D——, and so suggestive of
a design to delude the beholder into an idea of the worthlessness of the
document;—these things, together with the hyperobtrusive situation of
this document, full in the view of every visitor, and thus exactly in
accordance with the conclusions to which I had previously arrived;
these things, I say, were strongly corroborative of suspicion, in one who
came with the intention to suspect.

"I protracted my visit as long as possible, and, while I maintained
a most animated discussion with the Minister, on a topic which I knew

well had never failed to interest and excite him, I kept my attention
really riveted upon the letter. In this examination, I committed to
memory its external appearance and arrangement in the rack; and also
fell, at length, upon a discovery which set at rest whatever trivial doubt
I might have entertained. In scrutinizing the edges of the paper, I observed them to be more *chafed* than seemed necessary. They presented
the *broken* appearance which is manifested when a stiff paper, having
been once folded and pressed with a folder, is refolded in a reversed
direction, in the same creases or edges which had formed the original
fold. This discovery was sufficient. It was clear to me that the letter
had been turned, as a glove, inside out, re-directed, and resealed. I bade
the Minister good morning, and took my departure at once, leaving a
gold snuff-box upon the table.

"The next morning I called for the snuff-box, when we resumed,
quite eagerly, the conversation of the preceding day. While thus engaged, however, a loud report, as if of a pistol, was heard immediately
beneath the windows of the hotel, and was succeeded by a series of
fearful screams, and the shouting of a mob. D—— rushed to a casement, threw it open, and looked out. In the meantime, I stepped to the
card-rack, took the letter, and put it in my pocket, and replaced it by a
fac-simile (so far as regards externals), which I had carefully prepared
at my lodgings; imitating the D—— cipher, very readily, by means of a
seal formed of bread.

"The disturbance in the street had been occasioned by the frantic
behavior of a man with a musket. He had fired it among a crowd of
women and children. It proved, however, to have been without ball,
and the fellow was suffered to go his way as a lunatic or a drunkard.
When he had gone, D—— came from the window, whither I had followed him immediately upon securing the object in view. Soon afterwards I bade him farewell. The pretended lunatic was a man in my
own pay."

"But what purpose had you," I asked, "in replacing the letter by a
fac-simile? Would it not have been better, at the first visit, to have
seized it openly, and departed?"

"D——," replied Dupin, "is a desperate man, and a man of nerve.
His hotel, too, is not without attendants devoted to his interests. Had I
made the wild attempt you suggest, I might never have left the Ministerial presence alive. The good people of Paris might have heard of me
no more. But I had an object apart from these considerations. You
know my political prepossessions. In this matter, I act as a partisan of
the lady concerned. For eighteen months the Minister has had her in
his power. She has now him in hers—since, being unaware that the
letter is not in his possession, he will proceed with his exactions as if
it was. Thus will he inevitably commit himself, at once, to his political
destruction. His downfall, too, will not be more precipitate than awk-

ward. It is all very well to talk about the *facilis descensus Averni*[5]; but in all kinds of climbing, as Catalani said of singing, it is far more easy to get up than to come down. In the present instance I have no sympathy—at least no pity—for him who descends. He is that *monstrum horrendum*,[6] an unprincipled man of genius. I confess, however, that I should like very well to know the precise character of his thoughts, when, being defied by her whom the Prefect terms 'a certain personage,' he is reduced to opening the letter which I left for him in the card-rack."

"How? did you put any thing particular in it?"

"Why—it did not seem altogether right to leave the interior blank— that would have been insulting. D——, at Vienna once, did me an evil turn, which I told him, quite good-humoredly, that I should remember. So, as I knew he would feel some curiosity in regard to the identity of the person who had outwitted him, I thought it a pity not to give him a clue. He is well acquainted with my MS., and I just copied into the middle of the blank sheet the words—

> —*Un dessein si funeste,*
> *S'il n'est digne d'Atrée, est digne de Thyeste.*[7]

They are to be found in Crébillon's Atrée.' "

FROM **Review of Nathaniel Hawthorne's
Twice-told Tales** (1842)

In defense of allegory (however or for whatever object employed) there is scarcely one respectable word to be said. Its best appeals are made to the fancy—that is to say, to our sense of adaptation, not of matters proper, but of matters improper for the purpose, of the real with the unreal; having never more of intelligible connection than has something with nothing, never half so much of effective affinity as has the substance for the shadow. The deepest emotion aroused within us by the happiest allegory, *as* allegory, is a very, very imperfectly satisfied sense of the writer's ingenuity in overcoming a difficulty we should have preferred his not having attempted to overcome. The fallacy of the idea that allegory, in any of its moods, can be made to enforce a truth, that metaphor, for example, may illustrate as well as embellish an argument, could be promptly demonstrated; the converse of the supposed fact might be shown, indeed, with very little trouble; but these are topics foreign to my present purpose. One thing is clear, that if allegory ever establishes a fact, it is by dint of overturning a fiction. Where the

---

[5] Facile descent to Hades.

[6] Horrendous monster.

[7] A plan so deadly is worthy of Thyestes, if not of Atreus.

suggested meaning runs through the obvious one in a *very* profound undercurrent, so as never to interfere with the upper one without our own volition, so as never to show itself unless *called* to the surface, there only, for the proper uses of fictitious narrative, is it available at all. Under the best circumstances, it must always interfere with that unity of effect which, to the artist, is worth all the allegory in the world. Its vital injury, however, is rendered to the most vitally important point in fiction—that of earnestness or verisimilitude. That *The Pilgrim's Progress* is a ludicrously overrated book, owing its seeming popularity to one or two of those accidents in critical literature which by the critical are sufficiently well understood, is a matter upon which no two thinking people disagree; but the pleasure derivable from it, in any sense, will be found in the direct ratio of the reader's capacity to smother its true purpose, in the direct ratio of his ability to keep the allegory out of sight, or of his *in*ability to comprehend it. Of allegory properly handled, judiciously subdued, seen only as a shadow or by suggestive glimpses, and making its nearest approach to truth in a not obtrusive and therefore not unpleasant *appositeness,* the *Undine* of De La Motte Foqué is the best, and undoubtedly a very remarkable specimen.

The obvious causes, however, which have prevented Mr. Hawthorne's *popularity* do not suffice to condemn him in the eyes of the few who belong properly to books, and to whom books, perhaps, do not quite so properly belong. These few estimate an author, not as do the public, altogether by what he does, but in great measure—indeed, even in the greatest measure—by what he evinces a capability of doing. In this view, Hawthorne stands among literary people in America much in the same light as did Coleridge in England. The few, also, through a certain warping of the taste, which long pondering upon books as books merely never fails to induce, are not in condition to view the errors of a scholar as errors altogether. At any time these gentlemen are prone to think the public not right rather than an educated author wrong. But the simple truth is that the writer who aims at impressing the people is *always* wrong when he fails in forcing that people to receive the impression. How far Mr. Hawthorne has addressed the people at all, is, of course, not a question for me to decide. His books afford strong internal evidence of having been written to himself and his particular friends alone. . . .

A skillful literary artist has constructed a tale. If wise, he has not fashioned his thoughts to accommodate his incidents; but having conceived, with deliberate care, a certain unique or single *effect* to be wrought out, he then invents such incidents—he then combines such events as may best aid him in establishing this preconceived effect. If his very intitial sentence tend not to the outbringing of this effect, then he has failed in his first step. In the whole composition there should be no word written, of which the tendency, direct or indirect, is not to the one pre-established design. And by such means, with such care and skill, a picture is at length painted which leaves in the mind of him who contemplates it with a kindred art, a sense of the fullest satisfaction. The idea of the tale has been presented unblemished, because undisturbed; and this is an end unattainable by the novel. Undue brevity is just as exceptionable here as in the poem; but undue length is yet more to be avoided.

We have said that the tale has a point of superiority even over the poem. In fact, while the *rhythm* of this latter is an essential aid in the development of the poem's highest idea—the idea of the Beautiful—the artificialities of this rhythm are an inseparable bar to the development of all points of thought or expression which have their basis in *Truth*. But Truth is often, and in very great degree, the aim of the tale. Some of the finest tales are tales of ratiocination. Thus the field of this species of composition, if not in so elevated a region on the mountain of Mind, is a tableland of far vaster extent than the domain of the mere poem. Its products are never so rich, but infinitely more numerous, and more appreciable by the mass of mankind. The writer of the prose tale, in short, may bring to his theme a vast variety of modes or inflections of thought and expression (the ratiocinative, for example, the sarcastic, or the humorous)—which are not only antagonistical to the nature of the poem, but absolutely forbidden by one of its most peculiar and indispensable adjuncts; we allude, of course, to rhythm. It may be added, here, *par parenthèse,* that the author who aims at the purely beautiful in a prose tale is laboring at a great disadvantage. For Beauty can be better treated in the poem. Not so with terror, or passion, or horror, or a multitude of such other points. And here it will be seen how full of prejudice are the usual animadversions against those *tales of effect,* many fine examples of which were found in the earlier numbers of *Blackwood*. The impressions produced were wrought in a legitimate sphere of action, and constituted a legitimate although sometimes an exaggerated interest. They were relished by every man of genius: although there were found many men of genius who condemned them without just ground. The true critic will but demand that the design intended be accomplished, to the fullest extent, by the means most advantageously applicable.

We have very few American tales of real merit—we may say, indeed, none, with the exception of *The Tales of a Traveller* of Washington Irving, and these *Twice-Told Tales* of Mr. Hawthorne. Some of the pieces of Mr. John Neal abound in vigor and originality; but, in general, his compositions of this class are excessively diffuse, extravagant, and indicative of an imperfect sentiment of Art. Articles at random are, now and then, met with in our periodicals which might be advantageously compared with the best effusions of the British magazines; but, upon the whole, we are far behind our progenitors in this department of literature.

Of Mr. Hawthorne's *Tales* we would say, emphatically, that they belong to the highest region of Art—an Art subservient to genius of a very lofty order. We had supposed, with good reason for so supposing, that he had been thrust into his present position by one of the impudent cliques which beset our literature, and whose pretensions it is our full purpose to expose at the earliest opportunity; but we have been most agreeably mistaken. We know of few compositions which the critic can more honestly commend than these *Twice-Told Tales*. As Americans, we feel proud of the book.

Mr. Hawthorne's distinctive trait is invention, creation, imagination, originality—a trait which, in the literature of fiction, is positively worth all the rest. But the nature of the originality, so far as regards its manifestation in letters, is but imperfectly understood. The inventive or original mind as frequently displays itself in novelty of *tone* as in novelty of matter. Mr. Hawthorne is original in *all* points. . . .

I must hasten to conclude this paper with a summary of Mr. Hawthorne's merits and demerits.

He is peculiar and not original—unless in those detailed fancies and detached thoughts which his want of general originality will deprive of the appreciation due to them, in preventing them from ever reaching the public eye. He is infinitely too fond of allegory, and can never hope for popularity so long as he persists in it. This he will not do, for allegory is at war with the whole tone of his nature, which disports itself never so well as when escaping from the mysticism of his *Goodman Browns* and *White Old Maids* into the hearty, genial, but still Indian-summer sunshine of his *Wakefields* and *Little Annie's Rambles*. Indeed, his spirit of "metaphor run mad" is clearly imbibed from the phalanx and phalanstery atmosphere in which he has been so long struggling for breath. He has not half the material for the exclusiveness of authorship that he possesses for its universality. He has the purest style, the finest taste, the most available scholarship, the most delicate humor, the most touching pathos, the most radiant imagination, the most consummate ingenuity; and with these varied good qualities he has done *well* as a mystic. But is there any one of these qualities which should prevent his doing doubly as well in a career of honest, upright, sensible, prehensible, and comprehensible things? Let him mend his pen, get a bottle of visible ink, come out from the Old Manse, cut Mr. Alcott, hang (if possible) the editor of the *Dial*, and throw out of the window to the pigs all his odd numbers of the *North American Review*.

FROM *The Philosophy of Composition* (1846)

There is a radical error, I think, in the usual mode of constructing a story. Either history affords a thesis—or one is suggested by an incident of the day—or, at best, the author sets himself to work in the combination of striking events to form merely the basis of his narrative—designing, generally, to fill in with description, dialogue, or autorial comment, whatever crevices of fact, or action, may, from page to page, render themselves apparent.

I prefer commencing with the consideration of an *effect*. Keeping originality *always* in view—for he is false to himself who ventures to dispense with so obvious and so easily attainable a source of interest—I say to myself, in the first place, "Of the innumerable effects, or impressions, of which the heart, the intellect, or (more generally) the soul is susceptible, what one shall I, on the present occasion, select?" Having chosen a novel, first, and secondly, a vivid effect, I consider whether it can be best wrought by incident or tone—whether by ordinary incidents and peculiar tone, or the converse, or by peculiarity both of incident and tone—afterward looking about me (or rather within) for such combinations of event, or tone, as shall best aid me in the construction of the effect.

I have often thought how interesting a magazine paper might be written by any author who would—that is to say who could—detail, step by step, the processes by which any one of his compositions attained its ultimate point of completion. Why such a paper has never been given to the world, I am much at a loss to say—but, perhaps, the autorial vanity has had more to do with the omission than any one other cause. Most writers—poets in especial—prefer having it understood that they compose by a species of fine frenzy—an ecstatic intuition—and would positively shudder at letting the public take a peep behind the scenes, at the elaborate and vacillating crudities of thought—at the true purposes seized only at the last moment—at the innumerable glimpses of idea that arrived not at the maturity of full view—at the fully matured fancies discarded in despair as unmanageable—at the cautious selections and rejections—at the painful erasures and interpolations—in a word, at the wheels and pinions—the tackle for scene-shifting—the step-ladders and demon-traps—the cock's feathers, the red paint and the black patches, which, in ninety-nine cases out of the hundred, constitute the properties of the literary *histrio*.

I am aware, on the other hand, that the case is by no means common, in which an author is at all in condition to retrace the steps by which his conclusions have been attained. In general, suggestions, having arisen pell-mell, are pursued and forgotten in a similar manner. . . .

Let us dismiss, as irrelevant to the poem, *per se*, the circumstance—or say the necessity—which, in the first place, gave rise to the intention of composing *a* poem that should suit at once the popular and the critical taste.

We commence, then, with this intention.

The initial consideration was that of extent. If any literary work is too long to be read at one sitting, we must be content to dispense with the immensely important effect derivable from unity of impression—for, if two sittings be required, the affairs of the world interfere, and everything like totality is at once destroyed. But since, *ceteris paribus,* no poet can afford to dispense with *anything* that may advance his design, it but remains to be seen whether there is, in extent, any advantage to counterbalance the loss of unity which attends it. Here I say no, at once. What we term a long poem is, in fact, merely a succession of brief ones—that is to say, of brief poetical effects. It is needless to demonstrate that a poem is such, only inasmuch as it intensely excites, by elevating, the soul; and all intense excitements are, through a psychal necessity, brief. For this reason, at least one half of the *Paradise Lost* is essentially prose—a succession of poetical excitements interspersed, *inevitably,* with corresponding depressions—the whole being deprived, through the extremeness of its length, of the vastly important artistic element, totality, or unity, of effect.

It appears evident, then, that there is a distinct limit, as regards length, to all works of literary art—the limit of a single sitting—and that, although in certain classes of prose composition, such as *Robinson Crusoe* (demanding no unity), this limit may be advantageously overpassed, it can never properly be overpassed in a poem. Within this limit, the extent of a poem may be made to bear mathematical relation to its merit—in other words, to the excitement or elevation—again in other words, to the degree of the true poetical effect which it is capable of inducing; for it is clear that the brevity must be in direct ratio of the intensity of the intended effect: —this, with one proviso—that a certain degree of duration is absolutely requisite for the production of any effect at all.

Holding in view these considerations, as well as that degree of excitement which I deemed not above the popular, while not below the critical, taste, I reached at once what I conceived the proper *length* for my intended poem—a length of about one hundred lines. It is, in fact, a hundred and eight.

My next thought concerned the choice of an impression, or effect, to be conveyed: and here I may as well observe that, throughout the construction, I kept steadily in view the design of tendering the work *universally* appreciable. I should be carried too far out of my immediate topic were I to demonstrate a point upon which I have repeatedly insisted, and which, with the poetical, stands not in the slightest need of demonstration—the point, I mean, that Beauty is the sole legitimate province of the poem. A few words, however, in elucidation of my real meaning, which some of my friends have evinced a disposition to misrepresent. That pleasure which is at once the most intense, the most elevating, and the most pure, is, I believe, found in the contemplation of the beautiful. When, indeed, men speak of Beauty, they mean, precisely, not a quality, as is supposed, but an effect—they refer, in short, just to that intense and pure elevation of *soul*—*not* of intellect, or of heart—upon which I have commented, and which is experienced in consequence of contemplating "the beautiful." Now I designate Beauty as the province of the poem, merely because it is an obvious rule of Art that effects should be made to spring from direct causes—that objects should be attained through means best adapted for their attainment— no one as yet having been weak enough to deny that the peculiar elevation alluded to is *most readily* attained in the poem. Now the object Truth, or the satisfaction of the intellect, and the object Passion, or the excitement of the heart, are, although attainable, to a certain extent, in poetry, far more readily attainable in prose. Truth, in fact, demands a precision, and Passion a *homeliness* (the truly passionate will comprehend me) which are absolutely antagonistic to that Beauty which, I maintain, is the excitement, or pleasurable elevation, of the soul. It by no means follows from any thing here said, that passion, or even truth, may not be introduced, and even profitably introduced, into a poem— for they may serve in elucidation, or aid the general effect, as do discords in music, by contrast—but the true artist will always contrive, first, to tone them into proper subservience to the predominant aim, and, secondly, to enveil them, as far as possible, in that Beauty which is the atmosphere and the essence of the poem.

Regarding, then, Beauty as my province, my next question referred to the *tone* of its highest manifestation—and all experience has shown that this tone is one of *sadness*. Beauty of whatever kind, in its supreme development, invariably excites the sensitive soul to tears. Melancholy is thus the most legitimate of all the poetical tones.

FROM ***The Poetic Principle*** (1850)

. . . I hold that a long poem does not exist. I maintain that the phrase, "a long poem," is simply a flat contradiction in terms.

I need scarcely observe that a poem deserves its title only inasmuch as it excites, by elevating the soul. The value of the poem is in the ratio of this elevating excitement. But all excitements are, through a psychal necessity, transient. That degree of excitement which would entitle a poem to be so called at all, cannot be sustained throughout a composition of any great length. After the lapse of half an hour, at the very utmost, it flags—fails—a revulsion ensues—and then the poem is, in effect, and in fact, no longer such.

There are, no doubt, many who have found difficulty in reconciling the critical dictum that the "Paradise Lost" is to be devoutly admired throughout, with the absolute impossibility of maintaining for it, during perual, the amount of enthusiasm which that critical dictum would demand. This great work, in fact, is to be regarded as poetical only when, losing sight of that vital requisite in all works of Art, Unity, we view it merely as a series of minor poems. If, to preserve its Unity— its totality of effect or impression—we read it (as would be necessary) at a single sitting, the result is but a constant alternation of excitement and depression. After a passage of what we feel to be true poetry, there follows, inevitably, a passage of platitude which no critical pre-judgment can force us to admire; but if, upon completing the work, we read it again, omitting the first book—that is to say, commencing with the second—we shall be surprised at now finding that admirable which we before condemned—that damnable which we had previously so much admired. It follows from all this that the utimate, aggregate, or absolute effect of even the best epic under the sun, is a nullity: and this is precisely the fact.

In regard to the Iliad, we have, if not positive proof, at least very good reason, for believing it intended as a series of lyrics; but, granting the epic intention, I can say only that the work is based in an imperfect sense of Art. The modern epic is, of the supposititious ancient model, but an inconsiderate and blindfold imitation. But the day of these artistic anomalies is over. If, at any time, any very long poem were popular in reality, which I doubt, it is at least clear that no very long poem will ever be popular again.

That the extent of a poetical work is, *ceteris paribus* [other things being equal], the measure of its merit, seems undoubtedly, when we thus state it, a proposition sufficiently absurd—yet we are indebted for it to the Quarterly Reviews. Surely there can be nothing in mere size, abstractly considered—there can be nothing in mere bulk, so far as a volume is concerned, which has so continuously elicited admiration from these saturnine pamphlets! A mountain, to be sure, by the mere sentiment of physical magnitude which it conveys, does impress us with a sense of the sublime—but no man is impressed after *this* fashion by the material grandeur of even "The Columbiad." Even the Quarterlies have not instructed us to be so impressed by it. As yet, they have not insisted on our estimating Lamartine by the cubic foot, or Pollok by the pound—but what else are we to infer from their continued prating about "sustained effort"? If, by "sustained effort," any little gentleman has accomplished an epic, let us frankly commend him for the effort—if this indeed be a thing commendable—but let us forbear praising the epic on the effort's account. It is to be hoped that common sense, in the time to come, will prefer deciding upon a work of Art, rather by the impression it makes—by the effect it produces—than by the time it took to impress the effect, or by the amount of "sustained effort" which had been found necessary in effecting the impression. The fact is, that perseverance is one thing and genius quite another—nor can all the Quarterlies in Christendom confound them. By-and-by, this proposition, with many which I have just been urging, will be received as self-evident. In the meantime, by being generally condemned as falsities, they will not be essentially damaged as truths.

On the other hand, it is clear that a poem may be improperly brief. Undue brevity degenerates into mere epigrammatism. A very short poem, while now and then producing a brilliant or vivid, never produces a profound or enduring effect. There must be the steady pressing down of the stamp upon the wax. . . .

While the epic mania—while the idea that, to merit in poetry, prolixity is indispensable—has for some years past been gradually dying out of the public mind by mere dint of its own absurdity—we find it succeeded by a heresy too palpably false to be long tolerated, but one which, in the brief period it has already endured, may be said to have accomplished more in the corruption of our Poetical Literature than all its other enemies combined. I allude to the heresy of The Didactic. It has been assumed, tacitly and avowedly, directly and indirectly, that the ultimate object of all Poetry is Truth. Every poem, it is said, should inculcate a moral; and by this moral is the poetical merit of the work to be adjudged. We Americans especially have patronized this happy idea; and we Bostonians, very especially, have developed it in full. We have taken it into our heads that to write a poem simply for the poem's sake, and to acknowledge such to have been our design, would be to confess ourselves radically wanting in the true Poetic dignity and force:—but the simple fact is, that would we but permit ourselves to look into our own souls, we should immediately there discover that under the sun there neither exists nor can exist any work more thoroughly dignified—more supremely noble than this very poem—this poem *per se*, this poem which is a poem and nothing more—this poem written solely for the poem's sake.

With as deep a reverence for the True as ever inspired the bosom of man, I would nevertheless limit, in some measure, its modes of inculcation. I would limit to enforce them. I would not enfeeble them by dissipation. The demands of Truth are severe. She has no sympathy with the myrtles. All *that* which is so indispensable in Song is precisely all that with which she has nothing whatever to do. It is but making her a flaunting paradox to wreathe her in gems and flowers. In enforcing a truth, we need severity rather than efflorescence of language. We must be simple, precise, terse. We must be cool, calm, unimpassioned. In a word, we must be in that mood which, as nearly as possible, is the exact converse of the poetical. *He* must be blind indeed who does not perceive the radical and chasmal differences between the truthful and the poetical modes of inculcation. He must be theory-mad beyond redemption who, in spite of these differences, shall still persist in attempting to reconcile the obstinate oils and waters of Poetry and Truth.

Dividing the world of mind into its three most immediately obvious distinctions, we have the Pure Intellect, Taste, and the Moral Sense. I place Taste in the middle, because it is just this position which, in the mind, it occupies. It holds intimate relations with either extreme; but from the Moral Sense is separated by so faint a difference that Aristotle has not hesitated to place some of its operations among the virtues themselves. Nevertheless, we find the offices of the trio marked with a sufficient distinction. Just as the Intellect concerns itself with Truth, so Taste informs us of the Beautiful while the Moral Sense is regardful of Duty. Of this latter, while Conscience teaches the obligation, and Reason the expediency, Taste contents herself with displaying the charms:—waging war upon Vice solely on the ground of her deformity, her disproportion, her animosity to the fitting, to the appropriate, to the harmonious, in a word, to Beauty.

An immortal instinct, deep within the spirit of man, is thus plainly a sense of the Beautiful. This it is which administers to his delight in the manifold forms, and sounds, and odors, and sentiments, amid which he exists. And just as the lily is repeated in the lake, or the eyes of Amaryllis in the mirror, so is the mere oral or written repetition of these forms, and sounds, and colors, and odors, and sentiments, a duplicate source of delight. But this mere repetition is not poetry. He who shall simply sing, with however glowing enthusiasm, or with however vivid a truth of description, of the sights, and sounds, and odors, and colors, and sentiments, which greet him in common with all mankind—he, I say, has yet failed to prove his divine title. There is still a something in the distance which he has been unable to attain. We have still a thirst unquenchable, to allay which he has not shown us the crystal springs. This thirst belongs to the immortality of Man. It is at once a consequence and an indication of his perennial existence. It is the desire of the moth for the star. It is no mere appreciation of the Beauty before us—but a wild effort to reach the Beauty above. Inspired by an ecstatic prescience of the glories beyond the grave, we struggle by multiform combinations among the things and thoughts of Time, to attain a portion of that Loveliness whose very elements, perhaps, appertain to eternity alone. And thus when by Poetry—or when by Music, the most entrancing of the Poetic moods—we find ourselves melted into tears— we weep then—not as the Abbate Gravina supposes—through excess of pleasure, but through a certain, petulant, impatient sorrow at our inability to grasp now, wholly, here on earth, at once and forever, those divine and rapturous joys, of which through the poem or through the music, we attain to but brief and indeterminate glimpses.

The struggle to apprehend the supernal Loveliness—this struggle, on the part of souls fittingly constituted—has given to the world all that which it (the world) has ever been enabled at once to understand and to feel as poetic.

The Poetic Sentiment, of course, may develop itself in various modes—in Painting, in Sculpture, in Architecture, in the Dance—very especially in Music—and very peculiarly, and with a wide field, in the composition of the Landscape Garden. Our present theme, however, has regard only to its manifestation in words. And here let me speak briefly on the topic of rhythm. Contenting myself with the certainty that Music, in its various modes of metre, rhythm, and rhyme, is of so vast a moment in Poetry as never to be wisely rejected—is so vitally important an adjunct that he is simply silly who declines its assistance, I will not now pause to maintain its absolute essentiality. It is in Music, perhaps, that the soul most nearly attains the great end for which, when inspired by the Poetic Sentiment, it struggles—the creation of supernal Beauty. It may be, indeed, that here this sublime end is, now and then, attained in fact. We are often made to feel, with a shivering delight, that from an earthly harp are stricken notes which cannot have been unfamiliar to the angels. And thus there can be little doubt that in the union of Poetry with Music in its popular sense, we shall find the widest field for the Poetic development. The old Bards and Minne-singers had advantages which we do not possess—and Thomas Moore, singing his own songs, was, in the most legitimate manner, perfecting them as poems.

To recapitulate, then:—I would define, in brief, the Poetry of Words as The Rhythmical Creation of Beauty. Its sole arbiter is Taste. With the Intellect or with the Conscience, it has only collateral relations. Unless incidentally, it has no concern whatever either with Duty or with Truth.

A few words, however, in explanation. That pleasure which is at once the most pure, the most elevating, and the most intense, is derived, I maintain, from the contemplation of the Beautiful. In the contemplation of Beauty we alone find it possible to attain that pleasurable elevation, or excitement, of the soul, which we recognize as the Poetic Sentiment, and which is so easily distinguished from Truth, which is the satisfaction of the Reason, or from Passion, which is the excitement of the heart. I make Beauty, therefore—using the word as inclusive of the sublime—I make Beauty the province of the poem, simply because it is an obvious rule of Art that effects should be made to spring as directly as possible from their causes:—no one as yet having been weak enough to deny that the peculiar elevation in question is at least most readily attainable in the poem. It by no means follows, however, that the incitements of Passion, or the precepts of Duty, or even the lessons of Truth, may not be introduced into a poem, and with advantage; for they may subserve, incidentally, in various ways, the general purposes of the work:—but the true artist will always contrive to tone them down in proper subjection to that Beauty which is the atmosphere and the real essence of the poem. . . .

Thus, although in a very cursory and imperfect manner, I have endeavored to convey to you my conception of the Poetic Principle. It has been my purpose to suggest that, while this Principle itself is strictly and simply the Human Aspiration for Supernal Beauty, the manifestation of the Principle is always found in an elevating excitement of the Soul—quite independent of that passion which is the intoxication of the Heart—or of that Truth which is the satisfaction of the Reason. For in regard to Passion, alas! its tendency is to degrade, rather than to elevate the Soul. Love, on the contrary—Love—the true, the divine Eros—the Uranian, as distinguished from the Dionaean Venus—is unquestionably the purest and truest of all poetical themes. And in regard to Truth—if, to be sure, through the attainment of a truth, we are led to perceive a harmony where none was apparent before, we experience, at once, the true poetical effect—but this effect is referable to the harmony alone, and not in the least degree to the truth which merely served to render the harmony manifest.

New England Writers: Brahmins and Mystics

Introduction

Throughout most of the nineteenth century, New England was commonly regarded as the cultural center of the United States, and Boston as the cultural center of New England. As one might expect, New England had a considerable variety of literary work—from genteel light verse to brooding mystical poetry, from jocular light essays to opaque philosophical discussions; and the writing that now seems most valuable to us was not always highly regarded, or even known, during the time it was being composed. But about one thing there can hardly be disagreement: in the eyes of most Americans, and especially those who lived on the northern part of the Atlantic seaboard, Boston was the cultural capital of the nation.

The culture of nineteenth-century Boston (which, for our purposes, includes Cambridge) has been a matter for sharp debate among our literary historians, and over the last several decades there have been several shifts of opinion. Readers now in their later years will remember that during their school days Longfellow, Holmes, and Lowell were taught—and had to be memorized!—not merely as major writers but as native sages representing the fulfillment of American culture. During the thirties a sharp revision of opinion began: the culture of nineteenth-century Boston came to be looked upon as feeble, timid, and washed-out; it had reached decrepitude without having passed through vigor. Our literary historians and critics now exalted the work of other nineteenth-century New England writers: Thoreau, Hawthorne, and Melville. V. L. Parrington, perhaps the most influential literary historian to reflect the "progressive" outlook of the twenties and thirties, spoke of Boston culture with undisguised contempt:

> The essence of the genteel tradition was a refined ethicism, that professed to discover the highest virtue in shutting one's eyes to disagreeable fact, and the highest law of convention. Gone were the franker days . . . when a wit might find his choicest *bons mots* in the bottom of his cups. Coarseness had given way to refinement. It was the romanticism of Brahmin culture, with all Falstaffian vulgarity deleted, and every smutch of the natural man bleached out in the pure sunshine of manners. It was Victorianism of a more maidenly purity than the English strain, so carefully filtered by passing through the close Puritan mesh that the smallest impurities were removed. The first of literary commandments was the commandment of reticence. Literature was conceived of as belonging to the library and drawing-room, and it must observe the drawing-room amenities. Only a vulgarian would lug a spade there. Any venture into realism was likely to prove libidinous, and surely to be common.

In turn, this judgment of Boston culture became the standard one in our schools and colleges, so much so that Longfellow and Holmes seemed figures to be mocked rather than read. It was easy to poke fun at the values of a James Russell Lowell when he said, ". . . better to be a good fellow than a good poet. . . ." And it was easy to quote from Emerson who lived a few (crucial) miles away in Concord: "If Socrates were here, we could go and talk with him; but Longfellow, we cannot go and talk with; there is a palace, and servants, and a row of bottles of different coloured wines, and wine glasses, and fine coats."

During the mid-1950s, however, still another revision of opinion began concerning nineteenth-century Boston culture, in part because the conservative mood of the fifties found the tone of Boston congenial and in part because some critics became uneasy about the new orthodoxy of judgment. Literary historians and critics began to turn back to nineteenth-century Boston with an eye less jaundiced and less "Jeffersonian" than Parrington's. In the mid-sixties there appeared an interesting book by an English critic, Martin Green, *The Problem of Boston,* which had a long-overdue friendly word for the cultural atmosphere in which men like Longfellow and Holmes had worked. The rehabilitation proposed by Green was, however, only partial, for though he rejected attitudes of easy superiority toward the Boston Brahmins and found much to admire in the intellectual life of the city, he had to acknowledge that the poetry and prose of its once-esteemed figures must still seem faded to readers of our day.

Large portions of American society and culture in the early nineteenth century might be described as rough, unpolished, and even vulgar; but the society and culture of Boston, marked by the complacence of provincialism, had already entered a stage of overrefinement. (Perhaps this was one reason that other sections of the country, uneasily aware that their social and cultural arrangements were still crude, were inclined to be so respectful toward Boston.) With its established wealth, its philanthropy, its numerous cultural institutions, its earnestness of mind, and its "possession" of Harvard University, Boston seemed to provide an ideal atmosphere for distinguished literary work. It was characterized by seriousness; it was dedicated to high literary standards; it kept one eye nervously but intelligently cocked toward the culture of Europe; it avoided the low-brow and chauvinist bravado of other regions in the United States; it honored its writers; and it even provided them with a good literary market. Martin Green has brought together in his book impressive evidence of the ways in which Boston provided support for libraries, symphonies, lectures series, museums, and universities, a record no other American city can match. A distinguished twentieth-century Bostonian, the historian Samuel Eliot Morison, has written:

> When a [Boston] family had accumulated a certain fortune, instead of trying to build it up still further, to become a Rockefeller or Carnegie or Huntington and then perhaps discharge its debt to society by some great foundation, it would step out of business or finance and try to accomplish something in literature, education, medical research, the arts, or public service. Generally one or two members of the family continued in business, to look after the family securities and enable the creative brothers or cousins to carry on without the handicap of poverty. Of course there were families like that in other cities, but in Boston there were so many of them as to constitute a recognized way of life.

And the American novelist William Dean Howells, who grew up as a farm boy in mid-nineteenth-century Ohio and came to Boston as a young man hoping to begin a literary career, would remember its atmosphere with gratitude:

> Elsewhere we literary folk are apt to be such a common lot . . . we arrive from all sorts of holes and corners of the earth, remote, obscure . . . but at Boston we were of ascertained and noted origin, and a good part of us dropped from the skies. Instead of holding horses before the doors of theatres; or capping verses at the plough-tail . . . or sleeping in doorways or under the arches of bridges; or serving as apothecaries' 'prentices—we were good society from the beginning. I think this was none the worse for us, and it was vastly the better for good society.

If, then, Boston was a city benevolently inclined toward culture and even willing to subsidize it with a generosity unmatched anywhere else in the country, the question that unavoidably follows is this: Why was the culture of Boston, in the words of the American historian Richard Hofstadter, "so light, so chatty, so cozily humorous, so genial, so sunny, so pompous at times, so damnably superficial?" Boston, as Martin Green concedes, "excluded from its literature the telling of deeply personal truths; those truths which reveal the non-social self, or the non-social aspects of relationships and states of being, aspects so painful or so obscure as to be useless, even detrimental, to consider the conduct of one's social (which here includes much of moral) life." The writers of Boston did not dig, they did not dare, they were too safe. One of Boston's leading cultural lights, Charles Eliot Norton, wrote in a letter of 1887: "I wonder whether you would agree with me that the set of men of letters . . . whom we have known, is a good deal the best that the world has seen; not the greatest, perhaps, but the pleasantest to live with. . . . There are no such liars as Pope, or cynics as Swift, or vulgarians as Gay, or sycophants as Young, or mockers as Sterne. . . ." Indeed there were not; but then neither were there any poets as brilliant as Pope or satirists as powerful as Swift or novelists as inventive as Sterne. The writers of Boston were too much at home with themselves and their little world, too relaxed in their amiable pleasantness for the risks involved in great literature.

Have we then come full-circle, back to the kind of assault Parrington launched? Not quite. The graciousness, charm, and sincerity of the Boston writers should be recognized, not simply dismissed as insufficiently realistic; the limited achievements of the Boston writers deserve a measure of honor, for they are more than, or not always, genteelly evasive; and their commitment to social decency and affability is not to be sneered at. In the end, however, it seems unlikely that Longfellow and Holmes will ever again reign as major figures in American literature or that the tradition and style we associate with them will ever again be regarded as a model for writers to come. Some changes in literary taste prove to be permanent.

With the passage of time, the glory of Boston has faded, and by common critical consent the writing undertaken in the 1820s, 1840s, and 1850s in the neighborhood town of Concord is now regarded as far more important, indeed as the first major flowering of American literature. The Concord writers are accordingly presented and discussed in the following section, "The American Renaissance."

A number of interesting New England writers outside the Boston and Concord schools pretty much went their own way. John Greenleaf Whittier, the self-educated Quaker poet who dealt with rural simplicities, homely moral certainties, and regional vignettes; Jones Very, friend and contemporary of Emerson but, in his intense Christian mysticism, at the opposite spiritual pole from Emerson; and Frederick Tuckerman, also somewhat under Emerson's influence but finally a poet who cannot be conveniently placed in any group—these writers, of varying interest and accomplishment, belong to the world of nineteenth-century New England literature quite as much as the Boston, the Concord, or any other group.

HENRY WADSWORTH LONGFELLOW (1807–1882)

*The rise and fall of Longfellow's reputation is one of the most fasci-
nating episodes in the history of literary taste in America.*

During the nineteenth century Longfellow was unquestionably the most
popular American poet, both at home and abroad. He was translated into most European languages. He won the admiration of
distinguished literary figures in England. And even during the first
several decades of the twentieth century he was the one American
poet most ordinary people in this country admired. Few Americans
now beyond middle age are unlikely to have missed a struggle in
their high school years with Longfellow's lengthy narrative poems,
"The Courtship of Miles Standish" and "Evangeline."

After the First World War, with the rise of literary modernism and the
new poetry associated with such figures as T. S. Eliot, Wallace
Stevens, and E. E. Cummings, a sharp revision of opinion occurred
among most literary people, if not yet most school teachers. Longfellow came to be sneered at and dismissed as a sugary sentimentalist, a preacher of obvious morals, a spokesman for Victorian gentility. Only in recent years has there been some effort, notably in a
fine critical biography by Newton Arvin, to provide a balanced
judgment, usually as an acknowledgment that Longfellow's earlier
reputation was wildly inflated but also that moderate admiration
is due some of his poems.

Longfellow was born in Portland, Maine, where his father was a prosperous judge. The family had deep roots in the American past,
Longfellow's mother being a descendent of John and Priscilla Alden.
After graduating from Bowdoin College, Longfellow spent three
years in Europe studying foreign languages and literatures. In
1834 he was appointed to the chair of modern languages at Harvard, which he kept for twenty fruitful years, resigning only to
devote himself fully to his own writing. Longfellow impressed his
contemporaries with his bookishness and contemplative serenity,
but in reality his life was somewhat more troubled: he faced the
agonies attendant on the death of his first wife and a long struggle
before he could persuade his second one to marry him. Affluent,
cultivated, and at ease in the world of Boston letters, Longfellow
not only wrote voluminously; he played a valuable role in bringing
European traditions and masterpieces, often through felicitous
translations, to an American public now more ready for a somewhat
larger portion of world culture than it had been earlier in the
century.

*Simply as a literary technician, Longfellow was highly accomplished.
He imported into English, not always with success, metrical*

schemes from a variety of European languages, ranging from the Finnish to the German. His verse is marked by a consistent melodiousness. And, within the limitations of Brahmin culture, he was an eminently serious man. Yet it is hard, by now, to avoid the judgment that many of his poems, especially the longer ones, are commonplace in matter and tedious in execution. Many start with a simple narrative in which stock figures, barely chiaroscuroed in their moral traits, are flatly presented; word cameos of the picturesque setting are systematically inserted; and then an earnest, upright, but usually quite commonplace, moral is tacked on at the end. Only seldom is Longfellow genuinely intent upon penetrating beneath the surface of accepted moralism and conventional goodwill. Only seldom does he try to grapple with the complexities of experience or the ambiguities of language. His poetry has few rough edges, and his mind, few personal strengths. A film of tepid amiability hangs over his work.

But the notion that he is merely a stuffed owl meant to lull middle-class readers into complacency, or some devil wishing to multiply the torments of school children, is really an oversimplification. Longfellow's range of sympathies can be wider than his detractors allow; he was more than a genteel Bostonian making pretty tracings on the tissue paper of culture; he knew something about suffering and frustration. A poem like "The Jewish Cemetery at Newport" is notable for its quietly achieved historical pathos and its quietly felicitous phrasing. A poem like "In the Churchyard at Cambridge" displays, as I. A. Richards has said, "a social, urbane, highly cultivated, self-confident, temperate and easy kind of humour." Perhaps the solution to the Longfellow problem is to read him mostly in his smaller pieces, and in small doses. Posterity may yet save him from the excesses of fame.

FURTHER READING

Lawrance Thompson, *Young Longfellow* (1938); Edward Wagenknecht, *Longfellow, A Full-length Portrait* (1955); Newton Arvin, *Longfellow: His Life and Work* (1963).

The Fire of Drift-wood (1849)

Devereaux Farm, Near Marblehead

We sat within the farm-house old,
    Whose windows, looking o'er the bay,
Gave to the sea-breeze damp and cold
    An easy entrance, night and day.

Not far away we saw the port,
    The strange, old-fashioned, silent town,
The lighthouse, the dismantled fort,
    The wooden houses, quaint and brown.

We sat and talked until the night,
    Descending, filled the little room;   10
Our faces faded from the sight,
    Our voices only broke the gloom.

We spake of many a vanished scene,
    Of what we once had thought and said,
Of what had been, and might have been,
    And who was changed, and who was dead;

And all that fills the hearts of friends,
    When first they feel, with secret pain,
Their lives thenceforth have separate ends,
    And never can be one again;   20

The first slight swerving of the heart,
    That words are powerless to express,
And leave it still unsaid in part,
    Or say it in too great excess.

The very tones in which we spake
    Had something strange, I could but mark;
The leaves of memory seemed to make
    A mournful rustling in the dark.

Oft died the words upon our lips,
    As suddenly, from out the fire   30
Built of the wreck of stranded ships,
    The flames would leap and then expire.

And, as their splendor flashed and failed,
    We thought of wrecks upon the main,
Of ships dismasted, that were hailed
    And sent no answer back again.

The windows, rattling in their frames,
    The ocean, roaring up the beach,
The gusty blast, the bickering flames,
    All mingled vaguely in our speech;   40

Until they made themselves a part
    Of fancies floating through the brain,
The long-lost ventures of the heart,
    That send no answers back again.

O flames that glowed! O hearts that yearned!
    They were indeed too much akin,
The drift-wood fire without that burned,
    The thoughts that burned and glowed within.

In the Churchyard at Cambridge (1851)

In the village churchyard she lies,
Dust is in her beautiful eyes,
    No more she breathes, nor feels, nor stirs;
At her feet and at her head
Lies a slave to attend the dead,
    But their dust is white as hers.

Was she, a lady of high degree,
So much in love with the vanity
    And foolish pomp of this world of ours?
Or was it Christian charity,   10
And lowliness and humility,
    The richest and rarest of all dowers?

Who shall tell us? No one speaks;
No color shoots into those cheeks,
    Either of anger or of pride,
At the rude question we have asked;
Nor will the mystery be unmasked
    By those who are sleeping at her side.

Hereafter?—And you think to look
On the terrible pages of that Book   20
    To find her failings, faults and errors?
Ah, you will then have other cares,
In your own shortcomings and despairs,
    In your own secret sins and terrors!

The Jewish Cemetery at Newport (1852)

How strange it seems! These Hebrews in their graves,
    Close by the street of this fair seaport town,
Silent beside the never-silent waves,
    At rest in all this moving up and down!

The trees are white with dust, that o'er their sleep
    Wave their broad curtains in the south-wind's breath,
While underneath these leafy tents they keep
    The long, mysterious Exodus of Death.

And these sepulchral stones, so old and brown,
    That pave with level flags their burial-place,   10
Seem like the tablets of the Law, thrown down
    And broken by Moses at the mountain's base.

The very names recorded here are strange,
    Of foreign accent, and of different climes;
Alvares and Rivera interchange
    With Abraham and Jacob of old times.

"Blessed be God, for he created Death!"
    The mourners said, "and Death is rest and peace;"
Then added, in the certainty of faith,
    "And giveth Life that nevermore shall cease."   20

Closed are the portals of their Synagogue,
    No Psalms of David now the silence break,
No Rabbi reads the ancient Decalogue
    In the grand dialect the Prophets spake.

Gone are the living, but the dead remain,
    And not neglected; for a hand unseen,
Scattering its bounty, like a summer rain,
    Still keeps their graves and their remembrance green.

How came they here? What burst of Christian hate,
    What persecution, merciless and blind,   30
Drove o'er the sea—that desert desolate—
    These Ishmaels and Hagars [1] of mankind?

They lived in narrow streets and lanes obscure,
    Ghetto and Judenstrass, [2] in mirk and mire;
Taught in the school of patience to endure
    The life of anguish and the death of fire.

[1] Gen. 16:21. Hagar was a concubine of Abraham and was driven into the desert with Ishmael, the son she had by Abraham.
[2] Segregated Jewish quarters in European cities.

All their lives long, with the unleavened bread,
 And bitter herbs of exile and its fears,
The wasting famine of the heart they fed,
 And slaked its thirst with marah of their tears. *40*

Anathema maranatha!³ was the cry
 That rang from town to town, from street to street:
At every gate the accursed Mordecai⁴
 Was mocked and jeered, and spurned by Christian feet.

Pride and humiliation hand in hand
 Walked with them through the world where'er they went;
Trampled and beaten were they as the sand,
 And yet unshaken as the continent.

For in the background figures vague and vast
 Of patriarchs and of prophets rose sublime, *50*
And all the great traditions of the Past
 They saw reflected in the coming time.

And thus forever with reverted look
 The mystic volume of the world they read,
Spelling it backward, like a Hebrew book,
 Till life became a Legend of the Dead.

But ah! what once has been shall be no more!
 The groaning earth in travail and in pain
Brings forth its races, but does not restore,
 And the dead nations never rise again. *60*

My Lost Youth *(1855)*

Often I think of the beautiful town
 That is seated by the sea;
Often in thought go up and down
The pleasant streets of that dear old town,
 And my youth comes back to me.
  And a verse of a Lapland song
  Is haunting my memory still:
  "A boy's will is the wind's will,
And the thoughts of youth are long, long thoughts."

I can see the shadowy lines of its trees, *10*
 And catch, in sudden gleams,

³ A curse, see I Cor. 16:22.
⁴ Cousin of Queen Esther, see Book of Esther.

The sheen of the far-surrounding seas,
And islands that were the Hesperides [1]
     Of all my boyish dreams.
          And the burden of that old song,
          It murmurs and whispers still:
     "A boy's will is the wind's will,
And the thoughts of youth are long, long thoughts."

I remember the black wharves and the slips,
     And the sea-tides tossing free;   20
And Spanish sailors with bearded lips,
And the beauty and mystery of the ships,
     And the magic of the sea.
          And the voice of that wayward song
          Is singing and saying still:
     "A boy's will is the wind's will,
And the thoughts of youth are long, long thoughts."

I remember the bulwarks by the shore,
     And the fort upon the hill;
The sunrise gun, with its hollow roar,   30
The drum-beat repeated o'er and o'er,
     And the bugle wild and shrill.
          And the music of that old song
          Throbs in my memory still:
     "A boy's will is the wind's will,
And the thoughts of youth are long, long thoughts."

I remember the sea-fight far away,
     How it thundered o'er the tide!
And the dead captains, as they lay
In their graves, o'erlooking the tranquil bay   40
     Where they in battle died.
          And the sound of that mournful song
          Goes through me with a thrill:
     "A boy's will is the wind's will,
And the thoughts of youth are long, long thoughts."

I can see the breezy dome of groves,
     The shadows of Deering's Woods;
And the friendships old and the early loves
Come back with a Sabbath sound, as of doves
     In quiet neighborhoods.   50
          And the verse of that sweet old song,
          It flutters and murmurs still:

[1] Beautiful gardens in Greek legend where golden apples grow.

"A boy's will is the wind's will,
And the thoughts of youth are long, long thoughts."

I remember the gleams and glooms that dart
    Across the school-boy's brain;
The song and the silence in the heart,
That in part are prophecies, and in part
    Are longings wild and vain.
        And the voice of that fitful song   60
        Sings on, and is never still:
"A boy's will is the wind's will,
And the thoughts of youth are long, long thoughts."

There are things of which I may not speak;
    There are dreams that cannot die;
There are thoughts that make the strong heart weak,
And bring a pallor into the cheek,
    And a mist before the eye.
        And the words of that fatal song
        Come over me like a chill: 70
"A boy's will is the wind's will,
And the thoughts of youth are long, long thoughts."

Strange to me now are the forms I meet
    When I visit the dear old town;
But the native air is pure and sweet,
And the trees that o'ershadow each well-known street,
    As they balance up and down,
        Are singing the beautiful song,
        Are sighing and whispering still:
"A boy's will is the wind's will,   80
And the thoughts of youth are long, long thoughts."

And Deering's Woods are fresh and fair,
    And with joy that is almost pain
My heart goes back to wander there,
And among the dreams of the days that were,
    I find my lost youth again.
        And the strange and beautiful song,
        The groves are repeating it still:
"A boy's will is the wind's will,
And the thoughts of youth are long, long thoughts."   90

The Tide Rises, the Tide Falls (1880)

The tide rises, the tide falls,
The twilight darkens, the curlew calls;
Along the sea-sands damp and brown
The traveller hastens toward the town,
    And the tide rises, the tide falls.

Darkness settles on roofs and walls,
But the sea, the sea in the darkness calls;
The little waves, with their soft, white hands,
Efface the footprints in the sands,
    And the tide rises, the tide falls.   10

The morning breaks; the steeds in their stalls
Stamp and neigh, as the hostler calls;
The day returns, but nevermore
Returns the traveller to the shore,
    And the tide rises, the tide falls.

OLIVER WENDELL HOLMES (1809–1894)

*Harvard formed the inner, and Boston the outer, center from which
evolved the many vocations of Oliver Wendell Holmes: teacher,
scientist, physician, lecturer, and writer. He was a lively man, with
a gift for amusing talk; he wrote with facility and polish, as befits
that "harmless, untitled, inoffensive aristocracy" to which he gave
the title of Boston Brahmins. (For further discussion of this literary
group, see the introduction to this section.)*

*After studying medicine in Paris for two years, Holmes returned to
graduate from Harvard in 1836. He was professor of anatomy at
Harvard for thirty-five years and dean of the medical school from
1847 to 1853; he became famous during his lifetime as wit, story
teller, versifier, and man of letters; he kept publishing books
throughout his life, most notably* The Autocrat of the Breakfast
Table *(1858), a collection of informal papers, and* Elsie Venner
(1861), a novel.

*Though once admired as the epitome of refined Boston culture, Holmes's
reputation has declined. His chatty essays now seem too imitative of
English coffee-house talk, but without the underlying intellectual
substance present in that talk at its best. His poetry, mostly light
and society verse, is ephemeral when not flat, and forgettable when
still amusing. Holmes is important in the history of American cul-*

*ture, if only because Boston itself is so important; but it seems
unlikely he will ever again hold the high place he once enjoyed in
American letters.*

FURTHER READING

S. I. Hayakawa and H. M. Jones edited *Oliver Wendell Holmes: Representative Selections* (1939) with an informative introduction. Eleanor Tilton's *Amiable Autocrat* (1947) is a recent biography.

The Last Leaf (1831)

I saw him once before,
As he passed by the door,
   And again
The pavement stones resound
As he totters o'er the ground
   With his cane.

They say that in his prime,
Ere the pruning-knife of Time
   Cut him down,
Not a better man was found   10
By the Crier on his round
   Through the town.

But now he walks the streets,
And he looks at all he meets
   Sad and wan,
And he shakes his feeble head,
That it seems as if he said,
   "They are gone."

The mossy marbles rest
On the lips that he has prest   20
   In their bloom,
And the names he loved to hear
Have been carved for many a year
   On the tomb.

My grandmamma has said—
Poor old lady, she is dead
   Long ago—
That he had a Roman nose,
And his cheek was like a rose
   In the snow.   30

But now his nose is thin,
And it rests upon his chin
    Like a staff,
And a crook is in his back,
And a melancholy crack
    In his laugh.

I know it is a sin
For me to sit and grin
    At him here;
But the old three-cornered hat,
And the breeches, and all that,   40
    Are so queer!

And if I should live to be
The last leaf upon the tree
    In the spring,
Let them smile, as I do now,
At the old forsaken bough
    Where I cling.

The Deacon's Masterpiece (1858)

Or, the Wonderful "One-hoss Shay": A Logical Story

Have you heard of the wonderful one-hoss shay,
That was built in such a logical way
It ran a hundred years to a day,
And then, of a sudden, it—ah, but stay,
I'll tell you what happened without delay,
Scaring the parson into fits,
Frightening people out of their wits,—
Have you ever heard of that, I say?

Seventeen hundred and fifty-five.
Georgius Secundus was then alive,—   10
Snuffy old drone from the German hive.
That was the year when Lisbon-town
Saw the earth open and gulp her down,
And Braddock's army was done so brown,[1]
Left without a scalp to its crown.
It was on the terrible Earthquake-day
That the Deacon finished the one-hoss shay.

[1] British general badly defeated by American troops in an ambush during the Revolution.

Now in building of chaises, I tell you what,
There is always *somewhere* a weakest spot,—
In hub, tire, felloe, in spring or thill,   20
In panel, or crossbar, or floor, or sill,
In screw, bolt, thoroughbrace,—lurking still,
Find it somewhere you must and will,—
Above or below, or within or without,—
And that's the reason, beyond a doubt,
That a chaise *breaks down*, but doesn't *wear out.*
But the Deacon swore (as Deacons do,
With an "I dew vum," or an "I tell *yeou*")
He would build one shay to beat the taown
'N' the keountry 'n' all the kentry raoun';   30
It should be so built that it *couldn'* break daown;
"Fur," said the Deacon, "'t's mighty plain
Thut the weakes' place mus' stan' the strain;
'N' the way t' fix it, uz I maintain,
        Is only jest
T' make that place uz strong uz the rest."

So the Deacon inquired of the village folk
Where he could find the strongest oak,
That couldn't be split nor bent nor broke,—
That was for spokes and floors and sills;   40
He sent for lancewood to make the thills;
The crossbars were ash, from the straightest trees,
The panels of white-wood, that cuts like cheese,
But lasts like iron for things like these;
The hubs of logs from the "Settler's ellum,"—
Last of its timber,—they couldn't sell 'em,

Never an axe had seen their chips,
And the wedges flew from between their lips,
Their blunt ends frizzled like celery-tips;
Step and prop-iron, bolt and screw,   50
Spring, tire, axle, and linchpin too,
Steel of the finest, bright and blue;
Thoroughbrace bison-skin, thick and wide;
Boot, top, dasher, from tough old hide
Found in the pit when the tanner died.
That was the way he "put her through."
"There!" said the Deacon, "naow she'll dew!"

Do! I tell you, I rather guess
She was a wonder, and nothing less!
Colts grew horses, beards turned gray,   60
Deacon and deaconess dropped away,

Children and grandchildren—where were they?
But there stood the stout old one-hoss shay
As fresh as on Lisbon-earthquake-day!

EIGHTEEN HUNDRED;—it came and found
The Deacon's masterpiece strong and sound.
Eighteen hundred increased by ten;—
"Hahnsum kerridge" they called it then.
Eighteen hundred and twenty came;—
Running as usual; much the same.   70
Thirty and forty at last arrive,
And then come fifty, and FIFTY-FIVE.

Little of all we value here
Wakes on the morn of its hundredth year
Without both feeling and looking queer.
In fact, there's nothing that keeps its youth,
So far as I know, but a tree and truth.
(This is a moral that runs at large;
Take it.—You're welcome.—No extra charge.)

FIRST OF NOVEMBER,—the Earthquake-day,—   80
There are traces of age in the one-hoss shay,
A general flavor of mild decay,
But nothing local, as one may say.
There couldn't be,—for the Deacon's art
Had made it so like in every part
That there wasn't a chance for one to start.
For the wheels were just as strong as the thills,
And the floor was just as strong as the sills,
And the panels just as strong as the floor,
And the whipple-tree neither less nor more,   90
And the back crossbar as strong as the fore,
And spring and axle and hub *encore*.
And yet, *as a whole*, it is past a doubt
In another hour it will be *worn out!*

First of November, 'Fifty-five!
This morning the parson takes a drive.
Now, small boys, get out of the way!
Here comes the wonderful one-hoss shay,
Drawn by a rat-tailed, ewe-necked bay.
"Huddup!" said the parson.—Off went they.   100
The parson was working his Sunday's text,—
Had go to *fifthly*, and stopped perplexed
At what the—Moses—was coming next.
All at once the horse stood still,
Close by the meet'n'-house on the hill.

First a shiver, and then a thrill,
Then something decidedly like a spill,—
And the parson was sitting upon a rock,
At half past nine by the meet'n'-house clock—
Just the hour of the Earthquake shock! *110*
What do you think the parson found,
When he got up and stared around?
The poor old chaise in a heap or mound,
As if it had been to the mill and ground!
You see, of course, if you're not a dunce,
How it went to pieces all at once,—
All at once, and nothing first,—
Just as bubbles do when they burst.

End of the wonderful one-hoss shay.
Logic is logic. That's all I say. *120*

My Aunt (*1831*)

My aunt! my dear unmarried aunt!
    Long years have o'er her flown;
Yet still she strains the aching clasp
    That binds her virgin zone;
I know it hurts her,—though she looks
    As cheerful as she can;
Her waist is ampler than her life,
    For life is but a span.

My aunt! my poor deluded aunt!
    Her hair is almost gray; *10*
Why will she train that winter curl
    In such a spring-like way?
How can she lay her glasses down,
    And say she reads as well,
When, through a double convex lens,
    She just makes out to spell?

Her father—grandpapa! forgive
    This erring lip its smiles—
Vowed she should make the finest girl
    Within a hundred miles; *20*
He sent here to a stylish school;
    'Twas in her thirteenth June;
And with her, as the rules required,
    "Two towels and a spoon."

They braced my aunt against a board,
    To make her straight and tall;
They laced her up, they starved her down,
    To make her light and small;
They pinched her feet, they singed her hair,
    They screwed it up with pins;—   *30*
O never mortal suffered more
    In penance for her sins.

So, when my precious aunt was done,
    My grandsire brought her back;
(By daylight, lest some rabid youth
    Might follow on the track;)
"Ah!" said my grandsire, as he shook
    Some powder in his pan,
"What could this lovely creature do
    Against a desperate man!"   *40*

Alas! nor chariot, nor barouche,
    Nor bandit cavalcade,
Tore from the trembling father's arms
    His all-accomplished maid.
For her how happy had it been!
    And Heaven had spared to me
To see one sad, ungathered rose
    On my ancestral tree.

JAMES RUSSELL LOWELL (1819–1891)

Lowell was the youngest in the central literary trio of the Boston Brahmins which also included Longfellow and Holmes, and he was the most versatile and facile writer among them. Yet, for reasons that have lately begun to interest historians of American literature, he is the one whose work seems most to have faded.

James Russell Lowell was born into a distinguished Cambridge family. He went, of course, to Harvard, but soon abandoned his idea of becoming a lawyer and instead turned to journalism shortly after his graduation in 1840. That same year he met Maria White, an enthusiastic Abolitionist whom he married in 1844. The publication, in 1848, of Poems, The Vision of Sir Launfal, A Fable for Critics, *and* The Biglow Papers *quickly and spectacularly established him as a leading poet and critic in the environs of Harvard.*

In 1857 Lowell joined Longfellow and Whittier to establish the Atlantic Monthly, *for some years to be the country's most distinguished*

*magazine. He became its first and genuinely distinguished editor.
From 1855 to 1866 he was also professor of modern languages at
Harvard, having taken over the chair Longfellow had vacated. In
1877 he began still another career as a diplomat, first as Minister
to Spain and then as Minister to England, where he greatly pleased
Queen Victoria.*

Hardly an aspect of nineteenth-century American cultural life escaped
the energy or inspection of Lowell. As a young man he was an
ardent Democrat and Abolitionist. In his middle years he became
a solid pillar of the Boston cultural world: editor of its major journals, arbiter of its most refined tastes, spokesman for its dominant
values. In old age he grew more conservative, remarking once that
after all his travels throughout the world he still found Cambridge,
Massachusetts, "the best society I ever saw."

Lowell tried his hand at almost everything in literature, except prose
fiction. He could write earnest odes, satiric poems, dialect verse,
and literary essays. He was quick with a phrase, nimble with a pun,
handy with an allusion, and skillful with a literary characterization,
as in his couplet about Whittier,

A fervour of mind which knows no separation
'Twixt simple excitement and pure inspiration.

or in his sentence about Thoreau, whom he respected but did not
like: "Thoreau watched Nature like a detective who is to go upon
the stand."

Some of The Biglow Papers still crackle; more creak. His poems now
seem too mellifluous, untroubled, mild. His essays are highly
polished and highly knowledgeable; they are not to be disdained.
Yet little of his work reaches the level of the truly distinguished.
Indeed, Lowell as a figure, or a problem, now seems more interesting than the work he did. He polished his mind, and his style, into
a glazed bookishness which never was sufficient for the composing
of first-rate books.

FURTHER READING

Leon Howard, *Victorian Knight-errant: The Early career of James Russell Lowell* (1952); Martin Duberman, *James Russell Lowell* (1966).

FROM **The Biglow Papers, First Series** (1848)

No. 1: A Letter from Mr. Ezekiel Biglow of Jaalam to the Hon. Joseph T. Buckingham, Editor of the Boston Courier, Inclosing a Poem of His Son, Mr. Hosea Biglow

Jaylem, June 1846.
Mister Eddyter:—Our Hosea wuz down to Boston last week, and he see a cruetin Sarjunt a struttin round as popler as a hen with 1 chicking, with 2 fellers a drummin and fifin arter him like all nater. the sarjunt he thout Hosea hedn't gut his i teeth cut cos he looked a kindo's though he'd jest com down, so he cal'lated to hook him in, but Hosy woodn't take none o' his sarse for all he hed much as 20 Rooster's tales stuck onto his hat and eenamost enuf brass a bobbin up and down on his shoulders and figureed onto his coat and trousis, let alone wut nater hed sot in his featers, to make a 6 pounder out on.

wal, Hosea he com home considerabal riled, and arter I'd gone to bed I heern Him a thrashin round like a short-tailed Bull in fli-time. The old Woman ses she to me ses she, Zekle, ses she, our Hosee's gut the chollery or suthin anuther ses she, don't you Bee skeered, ses I, he's oney amaking pottery. . . .

If you print 'em I wish you'd jest let folks know who hosy's father is, cos my ant Keziah used to say it's nater to be curus ses she, she aint livin though and he's a likely kind o' lad.

Ezekiel Biglow.

Thrash away, you'll *hev* to rattle
　On them kittle-drums o' yourn,—
'Tain't a knowin' kind o' cattle
　Thet is ketched with moldy corn;
Put in stiff, you fifer feller,
　Let folks see how spry you be,—
Guess you'll toot till you are yeller
　'Fore you git ahold o' me!

Thet air flag's a leetle rotten,
　Hope it ain't your Sunday's best;—　　10
Fact! it takes a sight o' cotton
　To stuff out a soger's chest:
Sence we farmers hev to pay fer't,
　Ef you must wear humps like these,
Sposin' you should try salt hay fer't,
　It would du ez slick ez grease.

'Twouldn't suit them Southun fellers,
　They're a dreffle graspin' set,
We must ollers blow the bellers
　Wen they want their irons het;　　20

May be it's all right ez preachin',
    But *my* narves it kind o' grates,
Wen I see the overreachin'
    O' them nigger-drivin' States.

Them thet rule us, them slave-traders,
    Haint they cut a thunderin' swarth,
(Helped by Yankee renegaders,)
    Thru the vartu o' the North!
We begin to think it's nater
    To take sarse an' not be riled;—   30
Who'd expect to see a tater
    All on eend at bein' biled?

Ez fer war, I call it murder,—
    There you hev it plain an' flat;
I don't want to go no furder
    Than my Testyment fer that;
God hez sed so plump an' fairly,
    It's ez long ez it is broad,
An' you've gut to git up airly
    Ef you want to take in God.   40

'Taint your eppyletts an' feathers
    Make the thing a grain more right;
'Taint afollerin' your bell-wethers
    Will excuse ye in His sight;
Ef you take a sword an' dror it,
    An' go stick a feller thru,
Guv'ment aint to answer for it,
    God'll send the bill to you.

Wut's the use o' meetin'-goin'
    Every Sabbath, wet or dry,   50
Ef it's right to go amowin'
    Feller-men like oats an' rye?
I dunno but whut it's pooty
    Trainin' round in bobtail coats,—
But it's curus Christian dooty
    This 'ere cuttin' folks's throats.

They may talk o' Freedom's airy
    Tell they're pupple in the face,—
It's a grand gret cemetary
    Fer the barthrights of our race;   60
They jest want this Californy
    So's to lug new slave-states in
To abuse ye, an' to scorn ye,
    An' to plunder ye like sin.

Aint it cute to see a Yankee
    Take sech everlastin' pains,
All to git the Devil's thankee,
    Helpin' on 'em weld their chains?
Wy, it's jest ez clear ez figgers,
    Clear ez one an' one make two,   70
Chaps thet make black slaves o' niggers
    Want to make wite slaves o' you.

Tell ye jest the eend I've come to
    Arter cipherin' plaguy smart,
An' it makes a handy sum, tu,
    Any gump could larn by heart;
Laborin' man an' laborin' woman
    Hev one glory an' one shame,
Ev'y thin' thet's done inhuman
    Injers all on 'em the same.   80

'Taint by turnin' out to hack folks
    You're agoin' to git your right,
Nor by lookin' down on black folks
    Coz you're put upon by wite;
Slavery aint o' nary color,
    'Taint the hide thet makes it wus,
All it keers fer in a feller
    'S jest to make him fill its pus.

Want to tackle *me* in, du ye?
    I expect you'll hev to wait;   90
Wen cold lead puts daylight thru ye
    You'll begin to kal'late;
'Spose the crows wun't fall to pickin'
    All the carkiss from your bones,
Coz you helped to give a lickin'
    To them poor half-Spanish drones?

Jest go home an' ask our Nancy
    Wether I'd be sech a goose
Ez to jine ye,—guess you'd fancy
    The etarnal bung was loose!   100
She wants me fer home consumption,
    Let alone the hay's to mow,—
Ef you're arter folks o' gumption,
    You've a darned long row to hoe.

Take them editors thet's crowin'
    Like a cockerel three months old,—
Don't ketch any on 'em goin',
    Though they *be* so blasted bold;

Aint they a prime lot o' fellers?
    'Fore they think on't guess they'll sprout,   *110*
(Like a peach thet's got the yellers)
    With the meanness bustin' out.

Wal, go 'long to help 'em stealin'
    Bigger pens to cram with slaves,
Help the men thet's ollers dealin'
    Insults on your father's graves;
Help the strong to grind the feeble,
    Help the many agin the few,
Help the men thet call your people
    Witewashed slaves an' peddlin' crew!   *120*

Massachusetts, God forgive her,
    She's akneelin' with the rest,
She thet ough' to ha' clung ferever
    In her grand old eagle-nest;
She thet ough' to stand so fearless
    W'ile the wracks are round her hurled,
Holdin' up a beacon peerless
    To the oppressed of all the world!

Ha'n't they sold your colored seamen?
    Ha'n't they made your env'ys w'iz?   *130*
Wut'll make ye act like free men?
    Wut'll git your dander riz?
Come, I'll tell ye wut I'm thinkin'
    Is our dooty in this fix,
They'd ha' done 't ez quick ez winkin'
    In the days o' seventy-six.

Clang the bells in every steeple,
    Call all true men to disown
The tradoocers of our people,
    The enslavers o' their own;   *140*
Let our dear old Bay State proudly
    Put the trumpet to her mouth,
Let her ring this messidge loudly
    In the ears of all the South: —

'I'll return ye good fer evil
    Much ez we frail mortils can,
But I won't go help the Devil
    Makin' man the cus o' man;
Call me coward, call me traiter,
    Jest ez suits your mean idees,—   *150*

Here I stand a tyrant-hater,
 An' the friend o' God an' Peace!'

Ef I'd *my* way I hed ruther
 We should go to work an' part,—
They take one way, we take t'other,—
 Guess it wouldn't break my heart;
Man hed ough' to put asunder
 Them thet God has noways jined;
An' I shouldn't gretly wonder
 Ef there's thousands o' my mind.   160

FROM **A Fable for Critics** (1848)

 ... 'There comes Emerson first, whose rich words, every one,
Are like gold nails [1] in temples to hang trophies on,
Whose prose is grand verse, while his verse, the Lord knows,
Is some of it pr— No, 'tis not even prose;
I'm speaking of meters; some poems have welled
From those rare depths of soul that have ne'er been excelled;
They're not epics, but that doesn't matter a pin,
In creating, the only hard thing's to begin;
A grass-blade's no easier to make than an oak;
If you've once found the way, you've achieved the grand stroke; 10
In the worst of his poems are mines of rich matter,
But thrown in a heap with a crash and a clatter;
Now it is not one thing nor another alone
Makes a poem, but rather the general tone,
The something pervading, uniting the whole,
The before unconceived, unconceivable soul,
So that just in removing this trifle or that, you
Take away, as it were, a chief limb of the statue;
Roots, wood, bark, and leaves singly perfect may be,
But, clapt hodge-podge together, they don't make a tree. 20

 'But, to come back to Emerson (whom, by the way,
I believe we left waiting),—his is, we may say,
A Greek head on right Yankee shoulders, whose range
Has Olympus for one pole, for t'other the Exchange;
He seems, to my thinking (although I'm afraid
The comparison must, long ere this, have been made),

---

[1] Eccles. 12:11. "The words of the wise are as ... nails fastened by the masters of assemblies. ..."

A Plotinus-Montaigne,[2] where the Egyptian's gold mist
And the Gascon's shrewd wit cheek-by-jowl coexist;
All admire, and yet scarcely six converts he's got
To I don't (nor they either) exactly know what;   30
For though he builds glorious temples, 'tis odd
He leaves never a doorway to get in a god.
'Tis refreshing to old-fashioned people like me
To meet such a primitive Pagan as he,
In whose mind all creation is duly respected
As parts of himself—just a little projected;
And who's willing to worship the stars and the sun,
A convert to—nothing but Emerson.
So perfect a balance there is in his head,
That he talks of things sometimes as if they were dead;   40
Life, nature, love, God, and affairs of that sort,
He looks at as merely ideas; in short,
As if they were fossils stuck round in a cabinet,
Of such vast extent that our earth's a mere dab in it;
Composed just as he is inclined to conjecture her,
Namely, one part pure earth, ninety-nine parts pure lecturer;
You are filled with delight at his clear demonstration,
Each figure, word, gesture, just fits the occasion,
With the quiet precision of science he'll sort 'em,
But you can't help suspecting the whole a *post mortem.* . . .   50

　'There is Hawthorne, with genius so shrinking and rare
That you hardly at first see the strength that is there;
A frame so robust, with a nature so sweet,
So earnest, so graceful, so lithe and so fleet,
Is worth a descent from Olympus to meet;
'Tis as if a rough oak that for ages had stood,
With his gnarled bony branches like ribs of the wood,
Should bloom, after cycles of struggle and scathe,
With a single anemone trembly and rathe;
His strength is so tender, his wildness so meek,   60
That a suitable parallel sets one to seek,—
He's a John Bunyan Fouqué,[3] a Puritan Tieck;[4]
When Nature was shaping him, clay was not granted

2 Plotinus (3d century A.D.), a neoplatonic philosopher; Michel de Montaigne
(1553–1592), a French skeptical moralist. The suggestion here is that Emerson
combines traits of the two, idealism and skepticism.
3 John Bunyan (1628–1688), author of *Pilgrim's Progress;* Baron de la Motte Fouqué
(1777–1843), author of fanciful romances. The suggestion here is that Hawthorne
combines the allegory of one with the romance of the other.
4 Lüdwig Tieck (1773–1853), German romantic writer.

For making so full-sized a man as she wanted,
So, to fill out her model, a little she spared
From some finer-grained stuff for a woman prepared,
And she could not have hit a more excellent plan
For making him fully and perfectly man.
The success of her scheme gave her so much delight,
That she tried it again, shortly after, in Dwight;[5]   70
Only, while she was kneading and shaping the clay,
She sang to her work in her sweet childish way,
And found, when she'd put the last touch to his soul,
That the music had somehow got mixed with the whole.

    'Here's Cooper, who's written six volumes to show
He's as good as a lord; well, let's grant that he's so;
If a person prefer that description of praise,
Why, a coronet's certainly cheaper than bays;
But he need take no pains to convince us he's not
(As his enemies say) the American Scott.[6]   80
Choose any twelve men, and let C. read aloud
That one of his novels of which he's most proud,
And I'd lay any bet that, without ever quitting
Their box, they'd be all, to a man, for acquitting.
He has drawn you one character, though, that is new,
One wildflower he's plucked that is wet with the dew
Of this fresh Western world, and, the thing not to mince,
He has done naught but copy it ill ever since;
His Indians, with proper respect be it said,
Are just Natty Bumppo,[7] daubed over with red,   90
And his very Long Toms[8] are the same useful Nat,
Rigged up in duck pants and a sou'wester hat
(Though once in a Coffin, a good chance was found
To have slipped the old fellow away underground).
All his other men figures are clothes upon sticks,
The *dernière chemise* of a man in a fix
(As a captain besieged, when his garrison's small,
Sets up caps upon poles to be seen o'er the wall);
And the women he draws from one model don't vary,
All sappy as maples and flat as a prairie.   100
When a character's wanted, he goes to the task
As a cooper would do in composing a cask;
He picks out the staves, of their qualities heedful,

[5] John Sullivan Dwight (1813–1893), American composer.
[6] Sir Walter Scott (1771–1832), Scottish historical novelist.
[7] Hero of Cooper's Leatherstocking series.
[8] Long Tom Coffin, a character in Cooper's *The Pilot* (1823).

Just hoops them together as tight as is needful,
And, if the best fortune should crown the attempt, he
Has made at the most something wooden and empty.

'Don't suppose I would underrate Cooper's abilities;
If I thought you'd do that, I should feel very ill at ease;
The men who have given to *one* character life
And objective existence are not very rife;   110
You may number them all, both prose writers and singers,
Without overrunning the bounds of your fingers,
And Natty won't go to oblivion quicker
Than Adams the parson or Primrose the vicar,[9]

'There is one thing in Cooper I like, too, and that is
That on manners he lectures his countrymen gratis;
Not precisely so either, because, for a rarity,
He is paid for his tickets in unpopularity.
Now he may overcharge his American pictures,
But you'll grant there's a good deal of truth in his strictures;   120
And I honor the man who is willing to sink
Half his present repute for the freedom to think,
And, when he has thought, be his cause strong or weak,
Will risk t'other half for the freedom to speak,
Caring naught for what vengeance the mob has in store,
Let that mob be the upper ten thousand or lower. . . .

'There are one or two things I should just like to hint,
For you don't often get the truth told you in print;
The most of you (this is what strikes all beholders)
Have a mental and physical stoop in the shoulders;   130
Though you ought to be free as the winds and the waves,
You've the gait and the manners of runaway slaves;
Though you brag of your New World, you don't half believe in it;
And as much of the Old as is possible weave in it;
Your goddess of freedom, a tight, buxom girl,
With lips like a cherry and teeth like a pearl,
With eyes bold as Herë's, and hair floating free,
And full of the sun as the spray of the sea,
Who can sing at a husking or romp at a shearing,
Who can trip through the forests alone without fearing,   140
Who can drive home the cows with a song through the grass,
Keeps glancing aside into Europe's cracked glass,
Hides her red hands in gloves, pinches up her lithe waist,
And makes herself wretched with transmarine taste;

[9] Parson Adams, lovable figure in Henry Fielding's *Joseph Andrews* (1742); Primrose is a verbose character in Oliver Goldsmith's *The Vicar of Wakefield* (1766).

She loses her fresh country charm when she takes
Any mirror except her own rivers and lakes.

   'You steal Englishmen's books and think Englishmen's thought,
With their salt on her tail your wild eagle is caught;
Your literature suits its each whisper and motion
To what will be thought of it over the ocean;   *150*
The cast clothes of Europe your statesmanship tries
And mumbles again the old blarneys and lies;—
Forget Europe wholly, your veins throb with blood,
To which the dull current in hers is but mud;
Let her sneer, let her say your experiment fails,
In her voice there's a tremble e'en now while she rails,
And your shore will soon be in the nature of things
Covered thick with gilt driftwood of castaway kings,
Where alone, as it were in a Longfellow's *Waif,*
Her fugitive pieces will find themselves safe.   *160*
O my friends, thank your god, if you have one, that he
'Twixt the Old World and you set the gulf of a sea;
Be strong-backed, brown-handed, upright as your pines,
By the scale of a hemisphere shape your designs,
Be true to yourselves and this new nineteenth age,
As a statue by Powers, or a picture by Page,
Plow, sail, forge, build, carve, paint, make all over new,
To your own New-World instincts contrive to be true,
Keep your ears open wide to the Future's first call,
Be whatever you will, but yourselves first of all,   *170*
Stand fronting the dawn on Toil's heaven-scaling peaks,
And become my new race of more practical Greeks.—
Hem! your likeness at present, I shudder to tell o't,
Is that you have your slaves, and the Greek had his helot.'

JOHN GREENLEAF WHITTIER (1807–1892)

*The son of poor and pious New England Quakers, John Greenleaf
   Whittier came as close as any nineteenth-century American poet
   could to embodying the virtues traditionally associated with preindustrial American life: independence, frugality, simplicity, and
   moral rectitude. His education as a boy was irregular, mostly
   through intervals of schooling between chores on the farm. The
   few books in his father's house he read over and over again, especially the Bible and the basic texts of the Quakers. At fifteen he
   came across the poems of Robert Burns, the Scottish folk or folk-
   like poet who composed in the vernacular and made the lives of the*

peasants one of his main subjects. Burns, recalled Whittier, was the first poet he ever read and ". . . it had a lasting influence on me."

As a young man Whittier worked on Boston and Hartford newspapers, but his earnest idealism could hardly be satisfied by a routine newspaper career. He threw himself into the antislavery crusade, editing a number of Abolitionist journals, writing poems and pamphlets in behalf of the slaves, and risking his life before enraged mobs. After the war he settled down to a quiet life in New England and published in 1867 his charming idyll, Snow-Bound, a vast popular success. His last years were full of honors.

Whittier's poems seem an answer to Emerson's call for a poetry of "the near, the low, the common." He writes about ordinary farmers, commonplace events at home, the virtues of hard work, an uncomplicated faith in God. His poetic limitations are as transparent as his moral strengths. He yields himself much too easily to an insistent and threadbare didacticism; he has almost no ironic distance from his own beliefs; he slides comfortably into the sentimental; and his verse has a way of clopping along, like a well-broken horse on a familiar country road. Yet his handful of living poems, in their moral ruggedness and homely sweetness, now strike one as more vital than the work of his contemporaries in Boston, the Longfellow-Holmes-Lowell group. He remains a small figure in our literature, but the real thing.

The poems that follow illustrate his divergent interests. "Telling the Bees" is a country narrative. "Ichabod" is a political poem for which Whittier supplied the following note:

This poem was the outcome of the surprise and grief and forecast of evil consequences which I felt on reading the seventh of March [1850] speech of Daniel Webster in support of the "compromise" and the Fugitive Slave Bill. No partisan or personal enmity dictated it. On the contrary my admiration of the splendid personality and intellectual power of the great senator was never stronger than when I laid down his speech, and in one of the saddest moments of my life penned my protest. . . .

FURTHER READING

John B. Pickard, *John Greenleaf Whittier: An Introduction and Inter-pretation* (1961); Lewis Leary, *John Greenleaf Whittier* (1961).

Telling the Bees (1857)

Here is the place; right over the hill
    Runs the path I took;
You can see the gap in the old wall still,
    And the stepping-stones in the shallow brook.

There is the house, with the gate red-barred,
    And the poplars tall;
And the barn's brown length, and the cattle-yard,
    And the white horns tossing above the wall.

There are the beehives ranged in the sun;
    And down by the brink
Of the brook are her poor flowers, weed-o'errun,   10
    Pansy and daffodil, rose and pink.

A year has gone, as the tortoise goes,
    Heavy and slow;
And the same rose blows, and the same sun glows,
    And the same brook sings of a year ago.

There's the same sweet clover-smell in the breeze;
    And the June sun warm
Tangles his wings of fire in the trees,   20
    Setting, as then, over Fernside farm.

I mind me how with a lover's care
    From my Sunday coat
I brushed off the burrs, and smoothed my hair,
    And cooled at the brookside my brow and throat.

Since we parted, a month had passed,—
    To love, a year;
Down through the beeches I looked at last
    On the little red gate and the well-sweep near.

I can see it all now,—the slantwise rain   30
    Of light through the leaves,
The sundown's blaze on her window-pane,
    The bloom of her roses under the eaves.

Just the same as a month before,—
    The house and the trees,
The barn's brown gable, the vine by the door,—
    Nothing changed but the hives of bees.

Before them, under the garden wall,
    Forward and back,
Went drearily singing the chore-girl small,   40
    Draping each hive with a shred of black.

Trembling, I listened: the summer sun
    Had the chill of snow;
For I knew she was telling the bees of one
    Gone on the journey we all must go!

Then I said to myself, "My Mary weeps
    For the dead to-day:
Haply her blind old grandsire sleeps
    The fret and the pain of his age away."

But her dog whined low; on the door-way sill,   *50*
    With his cane to his chin,
The old man sat; and the chore-girl still
    Sung to the bees stealing out and in.

And the song she was singing ever since
    In my ear sounds on:—
"Stay at home, pretty bees, fly not hence!
    Mistress Mary is dead and gone!"

Ichabod (1850)[1]

So fallen! so lost! the light withdrawn
    Which once he wore!
The glory from his gray hairs gone
    Forevermore!

Revile him not, the Tempter hath
    A snare for all;
And pitying tears, not scorn and wrath,
    Befit his fall!

Oh, dumb be passion's stormy rage,
    When he who might   *10*
Have lighted up and led his age,
    Falls back in night.

Scorn! would the angels laugh, to mark
    A bright soul driven,
Fiend-goaded, down the endless dark,
    From hope and heaven!

Let not the land once proud of him
    Insult him now,

[1] Sam. 4:21. "And she named him Ichabod, saying, the glory is departed from Israel."

Nor brand with deeper shame his dim,
    Dishonered brow.   20

But let its humbled sons, instead,
    From sea to lake,
A long lament, as for the dead,
    In sadness make.

Of all we loved and honored, naught
    Save power remains;
A fallen angel's pride of thought,
    Still strong in chains.

All else is gone; from those great eyes
    The soul has fled: 30
When faith is lost, when honor dies,
    The man is dead!

Then pay the reverence of old days
    To his dead fame;
Walk backward, with averted gaze,
    And hide the shame!

JONES VERY (1813–1880)

Religious feelings, religious sentiments, religious memories are every-
where to be seen in nineteenth-century American writing; but
strictly orthodox Christian belief can be found in the work of only
one significant poet of the time, the mystic Jones Very. During his
lifetime Very published a volume of his writings which won the
praise of Bryant, Emerson, and Hawthorne. But despite the appear-
ance of two collections of his work a few years after his death,
Very's name all but disappeared from our literary histories and
anthologies. He was "rediscovered" in a vigorous essay which the
critic Yvor Winters wrote in 1938.

Born in Salem, Massachusetts, Very taught school there to earn enough
money to go to Harvard College and then Harvard Divinity School.
For a short time he worked as a tutor of Greek at Harvard, before
being licensed as a Unitarian minister and beginning to preach.
(Unitarianism in the nineteenth century was a roomy and hospitable
denomination permitting a Calvinist like Very to speak his mind
on religious matters without interference.) Very's outer life was
uneventful. Shy and retiring, in closer relation to heaven than to
earth, he lived in Salem, except for a brief period when he was

committed to an asylum in Somerville, Massachusetts. Objecting, Ralph Waldo Emerson said that Very was "profoundly sane."

Emerson sympathized with Very's attempts to communicate the experience of religious ecstasy and himself edited Very's first book, Essays and Poems, *in 1839. Though the two men were friendly, they were radically different. As Yvor Winters has pungently remarked, "Very's poems bear witness unanswerably that he had the [religious] experience which Emerson merely recommends." Very seems genuinely to have believed that his poems were dictated by a higher power, and it was to that power that he wished to submit himself unconditionally. He is the only important nineteenth-century American poet in whom the experience of mysticism— communion with God through love, ecstasy, and contemplation, without the medium of human reason—is a major theme. And he is the only American poet of the nineteenth century in whom the state of beatitude, or perfect blessedness, can sometimes be glimpsed. It is no wonder that his contemporaries compared Very's poetry to that of such seventeenth-century English devotional poets as George Herbert and Henry Vaughan.*

Restricted though it is in scope and rigid in doctrine, Very's best poetry is strikingly powerful. The language is fiercely controlled, and the substance, intensely serious. Though not richly metaphorical, or as playfully ingenious as the work of the seventeenth-century "metaphysical" poets, Very's poetry now and again achieves a kind of luminous rapture by means of which the experience of mysticism becomes accessible to those who can never have known it themselves.

FURTHER READING

The two recent substantial critical works are, William Bartlett, *Jones Very: Emerson's "Brave Saint"* (1942), and Edwin Gittleman, *Jones Very: The Effective Years* (1967).

Enoch (1838)

I looked to find a man who walked with God,
Like the translated patriarch of old;—
Though gladdened millions on his footstool trod,
Yet none with Him did such sweet converse hold.
I heard the wind in low complaint go by
That none its melodies like him could hear;—

Day unto day spoke wisdom from on high,
Yet none like David turned a willing ear:
God walked alone, unhonored, through the earth.
For Him no heart-built temple open stood;   *10*
The soul, forgetful of her nobler birth,
Had hewn Him lofty shrines of stone and wood,
And left unfinished, and in ruins still,
The only temple He delights to fill.

The Lost *(1839)*

The fairest day that ever yet has shone,
Will be when thou the day within shalt see;
The fairest rose that ever yet has blown,
When thou the flower thou lookest on shalt be.
But thou art far away among Time's toys;
Thyself the day thou lookest for in them,
Thyself the flower that now thine eye enjoys,
But wilted now thou hang'st upon thy stem.
The bird thou hearest on the budding tree,
Thou hast made sing with thy forgotten voice;   *10*
But when it swells again to melody,
The song is thine in which thou wilt rejoice;
And thou new risen 'midst these wonders live,
That now to them dost all thy substance give.

The Dead *(1839)*

I see them,—crowd on crowd they walk the earth,
Dry leafless trees no autumn wind laid bare;
And in their nakedness find cause for mirth,
And all unclad would winter's rudeness dare;
No sap doth through their clattering branches flow,
Whence springing leaves and blossoms bright appear;
Their hearts the living God have ceased to know
Who gives the spring-time to th' expectant year.
They mimic life, as if from Him to steal
His glow of health to paint the livid cheek;   *10*
They borrow words for thoughts they cannot feel,
That with a seeming heart their tongue may speak;
And in their show of life more dead they live
Than those that to the earth with many tears they give.

Today (1839)

I live but in the present,—where art thou?
Hast thou a home in some past, future year?
I call to thee from every leafy bough,
But thou art far away and canst not hear.

Each flower lifts up its red or yellow head,
And nods to thee as thou art passing by:
Hurry not on, but stay thine anxious tread,
And thou shalt live with me, for there am I.

The stream that murmurs by thee,—heed its voice,
Nor stop thine ear; 'tis I that bid it flow;   10
And thou with its glad waters shalt rejoice,
And of the life I live within them know.

And hill, and grove, and flowers, and running stream,
When thou dost live with them shall look more fair;
And thou awake as from a cheating dream,
The life today with me and mine to share.

Thy Brother's Blood (1839)

I have no brother. They who meet me now
Offer a hand with their own wills defiled,
And, while they wear a smooth, unwrinkled brow,
Know not that Truth can never be beguiled.
Go wash the hand that still betrays thy guilt;—
Before the Spirit's gaze what stain can hide?
Abel's red blood upon the earth is spilt,
And by thy tongue it cannot be denied.
I hear not with the ear,—the heart doth tell
Its secret deeds to me untold before;   10
Go, all its hidden plunder quickly sell,
Then shalt thou cleanse thee from thy brother's gore,
Then will I take thy gift;—that bloody stain
Shall not be seen upon thy hand again.

The Created *(1883)*

There is naught for thee by thy haste to gain;
'Tis not the swift with me that win the race;
Through long endurance of delaying pain,
Thine opened eye shall see thy Father's face;
Nor here nor there, where now thy feet would turn,
Thou wilt find Him who ever waits for thee;
But let obedience quench desires that burn,
And where thou art thy Father too will be.
Behold! as day by day the spirit grows,
Thou see'st by inward light things hid before;   *10*
Till what God is, thyself, His image shows;
And thou wilt wear the robe that first thou wore,
When bright with radiance from his forming hand,
He saw the lord of all His creatures stand.

The Hand and Foot *(1883)*

The hand and foot that stir not, they shall find
Sooner than all the rightful place to go:
Now in their motion free as roving wind,
Though first no snail so limited and slow;
I mark them full of labor all the day,
Each active motion made in perfect rest;
They cannot from their path mistaken stray,
Though 't is not theirs, yet in it they are blest;
The bird has not their hidden track found out,
The cunning fox though full of art he be;   *10*
It is the way unseen, the certain route,
Where ever bound, yet thou art ever free;
The path of Him, whose perfect law of love
Bids spheres and atoms in just order move.

The New Man *(1886)*

The hands must touch and handle many things,
The eyes long waste their glances all in vain;
The feet course still in idle, mazy rings,
Ere man himself, the lost, shall back regain
The hand that ever moves, the eyes that see,
While day holds out his shining lamp on high,

And, strait as flies the honey-seeking bee,
Direct the feet to unseen flowers they spy;
These, when they come, the man revealed from heaven,
Shall labor all the day in quiet rest   10
And find at eve the covert duly given,
Where with the bird they find sweet sleep and rest,
That shall their wasted strength to health restore,
And bid them seek with morn the hills and fields once more.

FREDERICK GODDARD TUCKERMAN (1821–1873)

Almost forgotten and certainly neglected, Tuckerman was a contemporary and neighbor of the New England transcendentalists, but sharply different from them in outlook and style. During his lifetime he published a single volume, Poems, *in 1860; he won a modest recognition, mostly through private letters of praise from Hawthorne, Emerson, and Longfellow. Living in near isolation in the Berkshires, Tuckerman seems not to have cared about getting into print the work he composed after 1860; he was genuinely the kind of poet who writes to himself; and once dead, he passed into obscurity. His work is not to be found in the great majority of anthologies, nor is it mentioned in most of our literary histories.*

About Tuckerman himself not much is known. The son of a wealthy merchant, he was graduated from Harvard with a law degree but chose not to practice. He retired to western Massachusetts where, equipped with telescope and herbarium, he lived as a country gentleman distinguished by a semiprofessional interest in science. In 1847 he married, happily; ten years later his wife died after childbirth; and from this blow Tuckerman seems never to have recovered.

A good part of Tuckerman's work consists of narrative and reflective poems, some of them derivative of the romantics, most of them too long and limp, few of them remarkable. His distinguished writing — and it is a puzzle that in a country which has not really had a surplus of distinguished poets, he should have been all but forgotten — is to be found in his sonnets and in a long poem called "The Cricket." His work is strikingly different from most American poetry of his time. Tuckerman had no interest in blending the roles of poet and prophet, no temptation to employ his writing as a platform from which to rise to a condition of transport, whether traditionally Christian or romantically pantheistic. He had no taste for the soaring line, the inflated pronouncement, the inflammation of selfhood which Emerson was drawn to and Whitman practiced; he was incapable of the mystic exaltation of Jones Very or the gnomic compressions of Emily Dickinson. All these contemporaries, whatever their other differences, were linked by a desire somehow to achieve union with a transcendent principle, in part because they found ordinary life insufficient.

Tuckerman, by contrast, wrote from a sharp endowment of common-sense and realism. Like anyone raised in nineteenth-century New England, he felt the gradual slipping-away of God as a personal trouble; but he never tried to force his way into religious belief or bludgeon his soul into ecstacy. In the sonnets and "The Cricket" he writes out of a hard awareness of human limitation: he does not confuse himself with the cosmos, the trees, or the spiritual ether. He is not a soul on the lookout for mergers, nor does he care to mythicize himself in behalf of poetry. His even-voiced and quiet verse meditations, though marred by an occasional breakdown of syntax and archaism of diction, are realistic in psychology and moral tone. His characteristic topics—the burden and value of grief, the way in which emotional distance enables a proper inspection of the world, the pressures of boredom tempting one to sink into insentience—are all treated as elements of common experience. Emerson may have courted Nature, but Tuckerman observed carefully the local phenomena of nature. Tuckerman keeps returning to the experience of duality between the perceiving self and the perceived world—an experience that seemed to him so basic to the human situation that no theory could undo it.

A poetry of observation, dwelling mainly on the pleasures and qualities of sensuous appearance, gives way in Tuckerman's work to a poetry of meditation, dwelling mainly on the sensibility of loss and decline. Tuckerman's fondness for the theme of depletion, the voice in minor key, can become tiresome if his sonnets are read in bulk. But at his best, when he fuses the meditative and descriptive modes, when he brings together a ruminative speaker and a setting of closely observed phenomena, he is a poet of great moral seriousness and verbal refinement. Whatever the cause for his long neglect, it is time for reparations.

FURTHER READING

Witter Bynner wrote a lengthy introduction to his *Sonnets of Frederick Goddard Tuckerman* (1931), and Samuel Golden added more material in his *Frederick Goddard Tuckerman: An American Sonneteer* (1952). The most reliable edition of, as well as the most authoritative introduction to, Tuckerman's work appears in N. Scott Momaday, *The Complete Poems of Frederick Tuckerman* (1965).

Thin Little Leaves of Wood Fern, Ribbed and Toothed (1931)

Thin little leaves of wood fern, ribbed and toothed,
Long curved sail needles of the green pitch pine,
With common sandgrass, skirt the horizon line,
And over these the incorruptible blue!
Here let me gently lie and softly view
All world asperities, lightly touched and smoothed
As by his gracious hand, the great Bestower.
What though the year be late? some colors run
Yet through the dry, some links of melody.
Still let me be, by such, assuaged and soothed   10
And happier made, as when, our schoolday done,
We hunted on from flower to frosty flower,
Tattered and dim, the last red butterfly,
Or the old grasshopper molasses-mouthed.

And Change with Hurried Hand Has Swept These Scenes (1860)

And change with hurried hand has swept these scenes:
The woods have fallen, across the meadow-lot
The hunter's trail and trap-path is forgot,
And fire has drunk the swamps of evergreens;
Yet for a moment let my fancy plant
These autumn hills again: the wild dove's haunt,
The wild deer's walk. In golden umbrage shut,
The Indian river runs, Quonecktacut!
Here, but a lifetime back, where falls tonight
Behind the curtained pane a sheltered light   10
On buds of rose or vase of violet
Aloft upon the marble mantel set,
Here in the forest-heart, hung blackening
The wolfbait on the bush beside the spring.

Under the Mountain, as When First I Knew *(1860)*

Under the mountain, as when first I knew
Its low dark roof and chimney creeper-twined,
The red house stands; and yet my footsteps find,
Vague in the walks, waste balm and feverfew.
But they are gone: no soft-eyed sisters trip
Across the porch or lintels; where, behind,
The mother sat, sat knitting with pursed lip.
The house stands vacant in its green recess,
Absent of beauty as a broken heart.
The wild rain enters, and the sunset wind   10
Sighs in the chambers of their loveliness
Or shakes the pane—and in the silent noons
The glass falls from the window, part by part,
And ringeth faintly in the grassy stones.

Not the Round Natural World, Not the Deep Mind *(1860)*

Not the round natural world, not the deep mind,
The reconcilement holds: the blue abyss
Collects it not; our arrows sink amiss
And but in Him may we our import find.
The agony to know, the grief, the bliss
Of toil, is vain and vain: clots of the sod
Gathered in heat and haste and flung behind
To blind ourselves and others, what but this
Still grasping dust and sowing toward the wind?
No more thy meaning seek, thine anguish plead,   10
But leaving straining thought and stammering word,
Across the barren azure pass to God:
Shooting the void in silence like a bird,
A bird that shuts his wings for better speed.

Nor, Though She Seem to Cast with Backward Hand *(1931)*

Nor, though she seem to cast with backward hand
Strange measure, sunny cold or cloudy heat,
Or break with stamping rain the farmer's wheat,
Yet in such waste no waste the soul descries,
Intent to glean by barrenest sea and land.
For whoso waiteth, long and patiently,
Will see a movement stirring at his feet—
If he but wait nor think himself much wise.
Nay, from the mind itself a glimpse will rest
Upon the dark; summoning from vacancy   10
Dim shapes about his intellectual lamp,
Calling these in and causing him to see;
As the night-heron waking in the swamp
Lights up the pools with her phosphoric breast.

An Upper Chamber in a Darkened House *(1860)*

An upper chamber in a darkened house,
Where, ere his footsteps reached ripe manhood's brink,
Terror and anguish were his lot to drink;
I cannot rid the thought nor hold it close
But dimly dream upon that man alone:
Now through autumn clouds most softly pass,
The cricket chides beneath the doorstep stone
And greener than the season grows the grass.
Nor can I drop my lids nor shade my brows,
But there he stands beside the lifted sash;   10
And with a swooning of the heart, I think
Where the black shingles slope to meet the boughs
And, shattered on the roof like smallest snows,
The tiny petals of the mountain ash.

The Cricket (1950)

I

The humming bee purrs softly o'er his flower;
    From lawn and thicket
The dogday locust singeth in the sun
    From hour to hour:
Each has his bard, and thou, ere day be done,
    Shalt have no wrong.
So bright that murmur mid the insect crowd,
Muffled and lost in bottom-grass, or loud
    By pale and picket:
Shall I not take to help me in my song   10
    A little cooing cricket?

II

The afternoon is sleepy; let us lie
Beneath these branches whilst the burdened brook,
Muttering and moaning to himself, goes by;
And mark our minstrel's carol whilst we look
Toward the faint horizon swooning blue.
    Or in a garden bower,
Trellised and trammeled with deep drapery
    Of hanging green,
    Light glimmering through—   20
There let the dull hop be
Let bloom, with poppy's dark refreshing flower:
Let the dead fragrance round our temples beat,
Stunning the sense to slumber, whilst between
The falling water and fluttering wind
    Mingle and meet,
    Murmur and mix,
No few faint pipings from the glades behind,
    Or alder-thicks:
But louder as the day declines,   30
From tingling tassel, blade, and sheath,
Rising from nets of river vines,
    Winrows and ricks,
    Above, beneath,
    At every breath,
At hand, around, illimitably
Rising and falling like the sea,
    Acres of cricks!

III

Dear to the child who hears the rustling voice
Cease at his footstep, though he hears thee still,   40
Cease and resume with vibrance crisp and shrill,
Thou sittest in the sunshine to rejoice.
Night lover too; bringer of all things dark
And rest and silence; yet thou bringest to me
Always that burthen of the unresting Sea,
The moaning cliffs, the low rocks blackly stark;
These upland inland fields no more I view,
But the long flat seaside beach, the wild seamew,
     And the overturning wave!
Thou bringest too, dim accents from the grave   50
To him who walketh when the day is dim,
Dreaming of those who dream no more of him,
With edged remembrances of joy and pain;
And heyday looks and laughter come again:
Forms that in happy sunshine lie and leap,
With faces where but now a gap must be,
Renunciations, and partitions deep
And perfect tears, and crowning vacancy!
And to thy poet at the twilight's hush,
No chirping touch of lips with tittering blush,   60
But wringing arms, hearts wild with love and woe,
Closed eyes, and kisses that would not let go!

IV

So wert thou loved in that old graceful time
     When Greece was fair,
While god and hero hearkened to thy chime;
     Softly astir
Where the long grasses fringed Cayster's lip;
Long-drawn, with shimmering sails of swan and ship,
     And ship and swan;
     Or where   70
     Reedy Eurotas ran.
Did that low warble teach thy tender flute
     Xenaphyle?
Its breathings mild? say! did the grasshopper
Sit golden in thy purple hair
     O Pasammathe?
     Or wert thou mute,
Grieving for Pan amid the alders there?
And by the water and along the hill

That thirsty tinkle in the herbage still, 80
Though the lost forest wailed to horns of Arcady?

V
Like the Enchanter old—
Who sought mid the dead water's weeds and scum
For evil growths beneath the moonbeam cold,
    Or mandrake or dorcynium;
And touched the leaf that opened both his ears,
So that articulate voices now he hears
In cry of beast, or bird, or insect's hum,—
Might I but find thy knowledge in thy song!
    That twittering tongue, 90
Ancient as light, returning like the years.
    So might I be,
Unwise to sing, thy true interpreter
Through denser stillness and in sounder dark,
Than ere thy notes have pierced to harrow me.
    So might I stir
    The world to hark
    To thee my lord and lawgiver,
    And cease my quest:
Content to bring thy wisdom to the world; 100
Content to gain at last some low applause,
    Now low, now lost
Like thine from mossy stone, amid the stems and straws,
    Or garden gravemound tricked and dressed—
    Powdered and pearled
    By stealing frost—
In dusky rainbow beauty of euphorbias!
For larger would be less indeed, and like
The ceaseless simmer in the summer grass
To him who toileth in the windy field, 110
    Or where the sunbeams strike,
Naught in innumerable numerousness.
    So might I much possess,
    So much must yield;
But failing this, the dell and grassy dike,
The water and the waste shall still be dear,
And all the pleasant plots and places
    Where thou hast sung, and I have hung
    To ignorantly hear.
Then Cricket, sing thy song! or answer mine! 120
Thine whispers blame, but mine has naught but praises.

It matters not. Behold! the autumn goes,
    The shadow grows,
The moments take hold of eternity;
Even while we stop to wrangle or repine
    Our lives are gone—
    Like thinnest mist,
Like yon escaping color in the tree;
Rejoice! rejoice! whilst yet the hours exist—
Rejoice or mourn, and let the world swing on   130
Unmoved by cricket song of thee or me.

The American Renaissance

Introduction

The first great period in American literature came in New England and, to a lesser extent, New York during the two decades before the Civil War. Emerson, Thoreau, Hawthorne, Melville, and Whitman: these writers, comprising what the literary historian F. O. Matthiessen has called "the American Renaissance," produced a body of poetry, fiction, and essays which can hold its own by comparison with the masterpieces of nineteenth-century Europe. What links these writers is that each, in his highly individual way, succeeded in representing and transfiguring American experience. In their work the problems of a democratic literature—the literature reflecting a new kind of society and thereby, perhaps, a new kind of human being—reach both statement and solution. And all of them are related, as advocates, disciples, and even antagonists, with a vague but powerful religious-ethical movement known as transcendentalism.

In 1836 a group of writers and intellectuals, calling themselves the Transcendental Club, began to meet in Concord, Massachusetts. Lively, serious, and talented, these young people discussed religion, philosophy, and literature; their leading figure, Ralph Waldo Emerson, had been a Unitarian minister but had found it impossible to subscribe to a fixed Christian theology. Between 1840 and 1844 the transcendentalists published *The Dial*, one of the most distinguished intellectual journals this country has ever had. Comprising a sort of genteel bohemia—what other kind could there be in nineteenth-century New England?—the transcendentalists helped create the conditions for the first major outburst of American literature. Their ideas were vague—religious conviction dissolving into idealist sentiment. Their language was airy and imprecise. But they came at the right moment; they stirred up a whirl of thought and feeling; they made it seem exciting to be alive, to be an American, to be a writer.

From their Puritan ancestors they inherited a habit of thinking in symbols, an inclination to sustained self-scrutiny, and a belief in the claims of the personal will. From the English romantics, especially Coleridge and Carlyle, they took over the philosophy of idealism which declared spirit or mind to be the source and guide of matter, and intuition a mode of knowledge superior to reason. From the Hindu philosophers, especially the Bhagavad-Ghita, they borrowed a smattering of mysticism. And all of these wisps and strands of thought were bound together by the Puritan heritage of moralism and the American impulse toward optimism. Strictly speaking, it was an intellectual mish-mash; but it roused spirits and quickened hearts.

Simply as a religious-philosophical outlook, transcendentalism resists easy summary. It came to its moment of influence after a period in which the dominant religious creed of New England was Unitarianism, a form of liberal Protestant belief which placed a heavy stress on moral virtue, personal sobriety, and a rational approach to both the story of Christ and the burdens of humanity. (A common joke had it that to be a Unitarian you had only to believe in "the fatherhood of God, the brotherhood of Man, and the neighborhood of Boston.") Decent men who reflected in the style of their thought, and even in the style of their sermons, the growing stability and prosperity of commercial New England, the Unitarian ministers pushed Christianity about as far as it could go toward a rationalistic ethic while remaining a religion at all.

The young transcendentalists, by contrast, wanted a religion without a church, without formally ordained ministers, without dogma, and almost without doctrine. Reflecting in these opinions the anarcho-democratic bias of early-nineteenth-century America, they urged, in Emerson's words, that it was the task of spiritual leaders to ". . . cast behind you all conformity, and acquaint men at first hand with Deity." This necessarily meant to abandon all notions of scriptural infallibility, even of scriptural authority, and to reduce ministers to the level of all other men, to whom revelations of divinity might or might not come. Everything would now rest upon personal intuition, personal insight, personal faith. Emerson and his friends raised the *I* to a quasi-divine status, so that man—in what amounted to a restatement of an old Christian heresy—would now be seen not merely as being like God but as participating in the godhead, that is, sharing directly in the substance of divinity. For those brought up in a secular age, this may seem a very fine distinction; but for those to whom religion still mattered, it was of the first importance.

As against scriptural authority, the claims of the learned, and the uses of reason, transcendentalism said that each man could discover truth within himself, through flashes of intuition, through achieving a harmonious relationship with nature, and through heeding the promptings of his unconscious. Emerson and his friends were usually willing to admit that man gained a kind of knowledge through the uses of his senses; but they believed that there was also a knowledge, and probably a superior kind of knowledge, to be reached by *transcending* the senses. In religion, the equivalent to this philosophic view was the effort to establish a direct communion between the soul and God, a communion that need not be mediated through priests and holy books. In ethics, the corollary was a belief in the inherent worth of man, his essential and original goodness. The vision of life held by the transcendentalists verged on the pantheistic belief that God is everywhere present, suffusing each animate creature and perhaps even each inanimate object—a God utterly different from the unattainable and distant figure the Puritans had credited. For the transcendentalists, the physical world became the outer mask or system of symbols for an inner world of spiritual values, all pointing to an ultimate and perfect harmony between nature and man.

What transcendentalism finally represented was one of those way-stations between religion, on the one hand, and ethics and esthetics, on the other—the kind of way-station that was created throughout the nineteenth century in Europe as a consequence of the breakdown of orthodox Christian belief. The God of the New or Old Testament had begun to fade, perhaps He was no longer there; yet the universe was still filled with His benevolent spirit. Each individual, triumphant in his powers and potentialities, could single-handedly reach the divine secret, and not necessarily through painful thought or disciplined submission, but by opening himself directly to the "Over-Soul," that nebulous portion of divinity in which all men shared or could share.

This outlook was profoundly optimistic; it was staunchly democratic and, to some extent, Jacksonian; it preserved the sentiments and values of Christianity while discarding its dogmas and rituals; and it was superbly attuned to the needs of nineteenth-century Americans who wished for a creed that might exalt their sense that to be born in this country and at this time signified a kind of special destiny. As George Hochfield, in an essay on transcendentalism, has remarked:

The portrait of the self-reliant man, the follower of his conscience, the divinely inspired democratic individual, which is passionately delineated in the writings of the whole Transcendentalist group, helped to create and identify an American type that seems to have become a permanent element of the national life. . . .

What the young men who came of age in the 1820s and 1830s . . . felt most deeply was that a radically new world was taking shape around them, requiring for its comprehension and its fulfillment a new vision of man. . . . If one may attribute, for the sake of definition, a single overriding motive to the Transcendentalist group, it was no less than the creation of a new literature, the literature, in a word, of democracy. Democracy had already taken political shape in America, and the democratic ideals of equality and liberty were already deeply implanted in the American spirit, but the inmost meaning of democracy—its new conception of the nature of man, his place in the world, and his relation to the divine—had hardly been thought about as yet. . . .

[In discovering the power or faculty which the nineteenth century called Reason but which we call intuition, that is, the power or faculty which can give man direct and immediate access to supersensual knowledge], the Transcendentalists discovered their mission, which was to elaborate the meaning of democracy as a new unfolding of the human spirit ... [Thereby, they] both divinized man and endowed him with a dynamic and expansive energy.

In short, the transcendentalists developed and expressed the world outlook which would serve the major American writers of the mid-nineteenth century both as a guide to follow and—for a few skeptics like Hawthorne—a force to resist.

It was in "The American Scholar," first given as the Phi Beta Kappa address at Harvard in 1837, that Emerson put forward, in its most fundamental and lasting form, the idea of a distinctively American literature which, for him and his friends, was a concrete outcome of their philosophical notions. The value of daily experience, the need for a vibrant and organic connection between words and objects, the unity of physical phenomenon and spiritual meaning, the desire to forge a literary subject out of American common experience and a literary vocabulary out of American colloquial speech—all are celebrated in "The American Scholar," and celebrated with great eloquence:

I embrace the common, I explore and sit at the feet of the familiar, the low. Give me insight into today, and you may have the antique and future worlds. What would we really know the meaning of? The meal in the firkin; the milk in the pan; the ballad in the street; the news of the boat; the glance of the eye; the form and the gait of the body;—show me the ultimate reason of these matters; show me the sublime presence of the highest spiritual cause lurking, as always it does lurk, in these suburbs and extremities of nature; let me see every trifle bristling with the polarity that ranges it instantly on an eternal law; and the shop, the plough, and the ledger referred to the like cause by which light undulates and the poets sing;—and the world lies no longer a dull miscellany and lumber-room, but has form and order; there is no trifle, there is no puzzle, but one design unites and animates the farthest pinnacle and the lowest trench.

Emerson is the major spokesman, the theoretician, of the transcendentalist period; his influence upon American culture has been incalculable. Thoreau, though knottier in temperament and more tough-minded in manner than Emerson, shared many of his beliefs and exemplified them in both his style of life and his style as a prose writer. Hawthorne, while a neighbor of Emerson and a curious spectator of the somewhat cranky world of New England idealism, stands as a polar opposite: he resists Emersonian ideas, he suspects

and dislikes them, yet as a contemporary he is forced to pay attention to them—and that, too, is a kind of tribute. Whitman is
profoundly influenced by Emerson, and in his major poems he
secularizes the notions of transcendentalism, removing them almost
entirely from their theological casing. The relation of Melville to
transcendentalism is, finally, very complex and a matter of dispute:
it is clear that, at least in his earlier work, up to and including
Moby Dick, he was fascinated by transcendentalist spiritualism.
Some of his critics believe, however, that in *Moby Dick,* as also in
his later works, there is a turning away from Emerson's beliefs
and the development of a more tragic, a darker, a less "accepting"
view of human existence.

In any case, what matters most is not doctrine itself, nor even the
extent to which these individual writers accepted portions of it, but
the fact that transcendentalism brought together in stirring form
many of the central ideas and sentiments of the age, stimulating
our major nineteenth-century writers to go their own ways and
develop their own visions of the fate of man in the New World,
the problems of the citizen in the new democracy. What should
matter to the reader and student of American literature is not so
much the doctrines of transcendentalism themselves but the ways
in which these doctrines released the imaginative energies of our
writers and played a role, either as catalyst or force to resist, in the
creation of great works like *The Scarlet Letter, Moby Dick, Walden,*
and *Song of Myself.*

RALPH WALDO EMERSON (1803–1882)

One fact about Emerson seems beyond dispute: he was the most influential American writer of the nineteenth century. If you look into the work of American poets and novelists as various as Thoreau, Melville, Whitman, Robert Frost, Edwin Arlington Robinson, Wallace Stevens and Norman Mailer, you will find the mark of Emerson. To this day the slant and surge of Emerson's thought survives among many Americans, including some who have not read him or would scorn him if they did. Many of the ideas popular on the American campus during the 1960s, especially among student dissidents, owe at least a partial debt to Emerson.

Which leads us to a second fact: American students do not take readily to Emerson's essays and poems and are often inclined to dismiss them as obscure, vague, or irrelevant. Emerson was not the kind of writer who would have cared for captive audiences; he would have wanted either to be read with intensity of response—enthusiasm and/or denunciation—or not read at all.

What then can we make of this apparent contradiction: a writer of enormous cultural influence who fails to arouse much enthusiasm? For that matter, what can we make of Emerson at all?

He came from several generations of New England ministers. His grandfather was a minister at Concord who blessed the local farmers starting the American Revolution. His father, pastor of the First Church, Unitarian, of Boston, died in 1811, leaving a widow and four sons in circumstances of poverty. Nevertheless, because of Mrs. Emerson's hard work and strength of character, all the Emerson boys went to Harvard, and Ralph Waldo graduated in 1821. For a time he taught uneasily in a girls' school to help his brothers through Harvard; then, in 1825, he attended the Harvard Divinity School and was licensed the following year for the ministry. In 1829 he became associate pastor of the Second Church of Boston and married the lovely young Ellen Tucker. But neither his peace of mind nor his personal happiness lasted long. Two years later his wife died, and in 1832 he felt obliged to resign his pastorate because he could not in good conscience administer the rite of the Last Supper. In his sermon of farewell one can already hear the characteristic Emersonian voice:

It is my desire, in the office of a Christian minister, to do nothing which I cannot do with my whole heart. Having said this, I have said all. I have no hostility to this institution [the Lord's Supper]; I am only stating my want of sympathy with it.

His "want of sympathy" extended beyond this particular ritual. Emerson moved away completely from Christian dogmas, rites, and institutions—though not from its morality—and he retained a strong sense of religiosity, but it is by no means clear that he continued to believe in the Christian God. He was now entering on the adventure, frequent among nineteenth-century intellectuals, of a purely personal religious experience.

Still under thirty, Emerson went to Europe and talked with leading writers of the time—Coleridge, Wordsworth, Landor, Carlyle— absorbing the philosophy of German idealism from its English adherents. In 1833 he was back in America and, in 1834, he settled in Concord, where he bought a house and two acres of land. He married a second time and began his lifelong career as lecturer, writer, and editor.

In 1836 Emerson published his first book, Nature, *a major statement of the transcendentalist creed, as well as a first approximation of his aphoristic style of exposition. The little book was quietly received, but in the two years that followed Emerson achieved national fame as an intellectual spokesman for "the newness" (as it was then called). First came his Phi Beta Kappa address at Harvard, "The American Scholar," in 1837, with its stirring call for an independent and indigenous American culture; then came his Divinity School Address in 1838, in which he broke completely with all versions of orthodox theology and quite scandalized his audience. With the publication of his* Essays, First Series *(1841) and* Essays, Second Series *(1844), Emerson consolidated his reputation.*

Between 1842 and 1844 Emerson served as editor of The Dial, *the journal of the transcendentalists and probably the most famous literary magazine ever published in this country. He had also begun to spend a good deal of time on the lecture circuit to supplement the income left him after his first wife's death and also to develop his ideas before growing audiences.*

Though a spokesman for the intellectual radicals of his day—radical more with regard to moral and philosophical than to political issues—Emerson kept aloof from the slavery controversies of the 1830s and 1840s. His justification is easy to understand but hard to accept: he had "quite other slaves to free than those Negroes, to wit, imprisoned spirits, imprisoned thoughts." But as the struggle reached its climax, Emerson could not remain silent, and when Daniel Webster, New England's leading politician, supported the Fugitive Slave Law in 1850, Emerson denounced him: "The word liberty in the mouth of Mr. Webster sounds like the word love in the mouth of a courtezan." The law itself Emerson called "a filthy enactment." In 1859 he came publicly to the support of John Brown.

Emerson accomplished his major writing mostly in the years between 1836 and 1860; afterward he lived quietly in Concord as a respected figure, aware that his creative powers had declined. The essays he wrote—the main source of his fame—derived from two sources: first, the journals he kept throughout his lifetime, and second, the lectures he gave during his prime years, themselves often put together from passages in the journals and then edited and reworked for publication. He was a tidy New Englander who saved scraps and pieces of writing to weave into new compositions.

Emerson's influence has been enormous, not only on Americans, but also on Europeans (Marcel Proust, for example). Yet it is not at all easy to put one's finger on precisely the element in his work that has drawn so many readers to him. His formal philosophy of transcendentalism was a pastiche of European idealism and romanticism, with a chastening touch of Puritan moralism and an exotic bit of Hindu mysticism thrown in. Transcendentalism as such (see pages 261–265) can hardly have been the main reason for Emerson's influence, since others have held similar—and if you wish, equally nebulous—ideas, only to be soon forgotten. Emerson did come onto the American scene at the right time, bringing to full expression the moods of intellectual and religious heterodoxy that were gathering in the country. Despite a certain coolness of manner, he was a charismatic figure, at least among the writers of his day and the lyceum audiences. His personality was neither flamboyant nor overpowering, but it seems nevertheless to have been magnetic. And he was, of course, a very forceful writer in his somewhat gnomic way. All of these factors—his sense of timing, his personality, his prose style—contributed to his success as cultural spokesman, yet none seems likely to have been crucial.

Examined rigorously and coldly, the way one might examine the propositions of a formal philosopher, Emerson's writings constitute a mass of contradictions. He was quite aware of this: "I write anecdotes of the intellect; a sort of Farmer's Almanac of mental moods." Mental moods are notoriously changeable, and those of Emerson were especially so. He demands that the reader keep hopping with him, unsystematically, from insight to insight, notion to notion. Yet some threads of consistency run through his lectures, essays, and poems. He was in rebellion against the formalism and logic of the eighteenth-century rationalists; against the dark moral views of the Puritan forefathers; against the literary strictness of the English neoclassical writers; against the moral calculus of the utilitarian philosophers; in short, against the "materialism" and "scientism" of much modern thought. At a time when it had come to seem that humanity must live increasingly under the domination of external and impersonal laws—whether laws of the cosmos or society, God or the state, even logic or rhetoric—Emerson insisted upon the possibility, no, the sanctity, of freedom. He insisted upon the freedom of the individual man who creates himself afresh during the course of his experience, the individual man who shares in the universal current of divinity (what Emerson called "the Over-Soul") and is yet a unique personality. "In all my lectures," he wrote, "I have taught one doctrine, namely, the infinitude of the private man." And in this celebration of the individual, Emerson favored the active virtues—energy, power, genius—all of them almost indistinguishable, as he saw it, from one another.

The crucial phrase here is, of course, "the infinitude of the private man," and it is crucial because it is deeply ambiguous. It can refer to a profound inner development of character, the growth that comes from reflection, deep feeling, and virtuous action; or it can refer to an ethic that justifies the crudities of financial acquisition, the barbarities of the exploiters of nature and man. It can speak for the highest or the lowest in our experience—and Emerson, to be candid, did not always trouble to keep the distinction clear. He could write with notable force about men in their actual circumstances: "Things are in the saddle/And ride mankind." Or:

Stand in State Street and see the heads and the gait and gestures of the men; they are doomed ghosts going under Judgement all day long.

And then he could write, in a spirit one finds hard to describe as anything but philistine, that "Money . . . is, in its effects and laws, as beautiful as roses. Property keeps the accounts of the world, and is always moral." No wonder Henry James, Sr., declared himself astonished by Emerson's "unconsciousness of evil."

Such contradictions apart—and they are many—Emerson's word was the exhilarating, sometimes intoxicating message that each man, famous or obscure, rich or poor, has enormous potentialities, since in each of us there is both a portion of the godhead and (perhaps therefore) a unique personality. He taught that men could maintain a relationship to divinity that is wholly personal, without the intercession of institution or belief, and often resting on no more than the fragile support of intuition. The world is sparked with divinity; the divine principle fills everything alive; and men, by opening themselves and discovering the beautiful in the ordinary, can link themselves to, can become akin to, the divine. (The current expression might be "tune in.")

The language in which Emerson put these notions—"The highest revelation is that God is in every man"—may be distant from that of our own day. But a great deal that is happening in America, both on and off the campus, is very close in spirit to Emerson.

He believed, as John Jay Chapman wrote, that "The soul and the cosmos were somehow related, and related so intimately that the cosmos might be regarded as a sort of projection or diagram of the soul." Or more precisely, again in Chapman's words,

The fancy that the good, the true, the beautiful—all things of which we instinctively approve—are somehow connected together and are really one thing; that our appreciation of them is in its essence the recognition of a law; that this law, in fact all law and the very idea of law, is a mere subjective experience; and that hence any external sequence which we coordinate and name, like the law of gravity, is really intimately connected with our moral nature—this fancy . . . Emerson adopted as a corner stone of his thought.

A "fancy" it may be, but it profoundly responded to the needs and profoundly captured the imagination of democratic man. It gave him a Weltanschauung, *a world outlook, enabling him to sanctify the ordinary and elevate the humble. It made possible the divinization of democracy. It can be heard, in a different idiom, on the lips of young people today who may never have heard of Emerson or find it hard to read him.*

"I embrace the common," *he wrote in one of his great passages,*

I explore and sit at the feet of the familiar, the low. . . . What would we really know the meaning of? The meal in the firkin; the milk in the pan; the ballad in the street; the news of the boat; the glance of the eye; the form and gait of the body.

And in his journals for 1840 he turned to language with the same perspective:

The language of the street is always strong. What can describe the folly and emptiness of scolding like the word jawing? *I feel too the force of the double negative, though clean contrary to our grammar rules. And I confess to some pleasure from the stinging rhetoric of a rattling oath in the mouth of truckmen and teamsters. How laconic and brisk it is by the side of the* North American Review. *Cut these words and they would bleed; they are vascular and alive; they walk and run.*

Emerson seemed to free mankind—nineteenth-century democratic, bustling, optimistic mankind—for endless possibilities and endless conquests. He celebrated the powers of the commonplace and its divinity too. He provided a creed appropriate to the time and the place, and then Walt Whitman transposed it into the poetry of Leaves of Grass. He shook off, once and for all, the seeming gloom of Original Sin and all the other heavy dispensations of the Puritans; he gave Americans a green light, for their best and their worst impulses—and a blessing too.

Did it then matter very much that he contradicted himself? On one side of Emerson's thought stands, for example, the idea of self-reliance, both in its serious and corrupted forms. "Nature never rhymes her children, nor makes two men alike." On the other side, *there is the Emerson who could write as if individuality were insignificant besides the shared depths of divinity:*

The study of many individuals leads us to an elemental region wherein the individual is lost.... All that respects the individual is temporary and prospective, like the individual himself, who is ascending out of his limits into a catholic existence.

How can these passages be reconciled? Emerson's most cogent critic of recent times, Newton Arvin, offers an answer:

He will never be understood by readers who fail to take it in that he is a consciously "dialectical" thinker—one, that is, who holds that contradiction is inherent in experience itself, that the natural order is through and through paradoxical.... This truth is what he calls ... Polarity: "The fact of two poles," he says, "of two forces ... is universal, and each force by its own activity develops the other." ... The most comprehensive and abstract manifestation of the principle of Polarity was for Emerson, as for Plato, the antithesis of Unity and Variety, the One and the Many....

Will this explanation do? The reader will have to decide for himself. Some of Emerson's critics have felt, as Marcus Cunliffe remarks, that "the notion of polarity seduced him," making it much too easy to claim to reconcile opposites and contradictions. Contradiction, adds Cunliffe,

faces him at every turn. How to reconcile good with evil, the individual with society, the rival claims of nonconformity with neighborliness, scholarship with intuition, the need to be up and doing with the equally imperative need to sit down and think? The charge against him is not that he sought to resolve these problems, but that he missed their serious implications by erecting contradiction into a system.

Whoever does try to fathom the depths and measure the contradictions of Emerson's thought will have to expose himself to a writer of remarkable powers of persuasion. The essays, with their startling mixture of high-flown philosophical speculation and down-to-earth colloquialism, follow the patterns of oratory. They should be read as if a forceful but restrained speaker were delivering an address— the thought should then come through more clearly. Emerson spoke in aphorisms, riddles, epigrams, and proverbs. His language is richly metaphorical, his sentences often stand out like raisins in a cake, and only those who remain fast in their rationalism—or rationality?—are likely to resist him.

FURTHER READING

The full-scale standard biography is Ralph L. Rusk, *The Life of Ralph Waldo Emerson* (1949). Frederic Carpenter's *Emerson Handbook*

(1953) is a useful guide to biography and criticism. Among other recent studies worth consulting are: Sherman Paul, *Emerson's Angle of Vision: Man and Nature in American Experience* (1952); Stephen E. Whicher, *Freedom and Fate: An Inner Life of Ralph Waldo Emerson* (1953); and Vivian Hopkins, *Spires of Form: A Study of Emerson's Aesthetic Theory* (1951).

Concord Hymn *(1837)*

Sung at the Completion of the Battle Monument, July 4, 1837

By the rude bridge that arched the flood,
    Their flag to April's breeze unfurled,
Here once the embattled farmers stood
    And fired the shot heard round the world.

The foe long since in silence slept;
    Alike the conqueror silent sleeps;
And Time the ruined bridge has swept
    Down the dark stream which seaward creeps.

On this green bank, by this soft stream,
    We set to-day a votive stone;   10
That memory may their deed redeem,
    When, like our sires, our sons are gone.

Spirit, that made those heroes dare
    To die, and leave their children free,
Bid Time and Nature gently spare
    The shaft we raise to them and thee.

The Problem *(1840)*

I like a church; I like a cowl;
I love a prophet of the soul;
And on my heart monastic aisles
Fall like sweet strains, or pensive smiles;
Yet not for all his faith can see
Would I that cowlèd churchman be.

Why should the vest on him allure,
Which I could not on me endure?

Not from a vain or shallow thought
His awful Jove young Phidias [1] brought;   *10*
Never from lips of cunning fell
The thrilling Delphic oracle;
Out from the heart of nature rolled
The burdens of the Bible old;
The litanies of nations came,
Like the volcano's tongue of flame,
Up from the burning core below—
The canticles of love and woe:
The hand that rounded Peter's dome [2]
And groined the aisles of Christian Rome   *20*
Wrought in a sad sincerity;
Himself from God he could not free;
He builded better than he knew;—
The conscious stone to beauty grew.

Know'st thou what wove yon woodbird's nest
Of leaves, and feathers from her breast?
Or how the fish outbuilt her shell,
Painting with morn each annual cell?
Or how the sacred pine-tree adds
To her old leaves new myriads?   *30*
Such and so grew these holy piles,
Whilst love and terror laid the tiles.
Earth proudly wears the Parthenon,
As the best gem upon her zone,
And Morning opes with haste her lids
To gaze upon the Pyramids;
O'er England's abbeys bends the sky,
As on its friends, with kindred eye;
For out of Thought's interior sphere
These wonders rose to upper air;   *40*
And Nature gladly gave them place,
Adopted them into her race,
And granted them an equal date
With Andes and with Ararat.

These temples grew as grows the grass;
Art might obey, but not surpass.
The passive Master lent his hand
To the vast soul that o'er him planned;
And the same power that reared the shrine
Bestrode the tribes that knelt within.   *50*

[1] Greek sculptor (fifth century B.C.) who did a statue of Zeus.
[2] Michelangelo (1475–1564) designed the dome of St. Peter's Cathedral in Rome.

Ever the fiery Pentecost
Girds with one flame the countless host,
Trances the heart through chanting choirs,
And through the priest the mind inspires.
The word unto the prophet [3] spoken
Was writ on tables yet unbroken;
The word by seers or sibyls told,
In groves of oak, or fanes of gold,
Still floats upon the morning wind,
Still whispers to the willing mind.   60
One accent of the Holy Ghost
The heedless world hath never lost.
I know what say the fathers wise—
The Book itself before me lies,
Old *Chrysostom*, best Augustine,[4]
And he who blent both in his line,
The younger *Golden Lips* or mines,
Taylor,[5] the Shakspeare of divines.
His words are music in my ear,
I see his cowlèd portrait dear;   70
And yet, for all his faith could see,
I would not the good bishop be.

Compensation *(1841)*

I

The wings of Time are black and white,
Pied with morning and with night.
Mountain tall and ocean deep
Trembling balance duly keep.
In changing moon and tidal wave
Glows the feud of Want and Have.
Gauge of more and less through space,
Electric star or pencil plays,
The lonely Earth amid the balls
That hurry through the eternal halls,   10
A makeweight flying to the void,
Supplemental asteroid,

---

[3] A reference to Moses and the Commandments (Exod. 32:34).
[4] John of Antioch (A.D. 347–407), a church father, was called Chrysostum, which means golden lips; St. Augustine (A.D. 354–430), author of *The City of God*.
[5] Jeremy Taylor (1613–1667), an English clergyman.

Or compensatory spark,
Shoots across the neutral Dark.

II

Man's the elm, and Wealth the vine;
Stanch and strong the tendrils twine:
Though the frail ringlets thee deceive,
None from its stock that vine can reave.
Fear not, then, thou child infirm,
There's no god dare wrong a worm;   20
Laurel crowns cleave to deserts,
And power to him who power exerts.
Hast not thy share? On wingéd feet,
Lo! it rushes thee to meet;
And all that Nature made thy own,
Floating in air or pent in stone,
Will rive the hills and swim the sea,
And, like thy shadow, follow thee.

Grace *(1842)*

How much, preventing God! how much I owe
To the defenses thou hast round me set:
Example, custom, fear, occasion slow,—
These scornèd bondmen were my parapet.
I dare not peep over this parapet,
To gauge with glance the roaring gulf below,
The depths of sin to which I had descended,
Had not these me against myself defended.

Give All To Love *(1847)*

Give all to love;
Obey thy heart;
Friends, kindred, days,
Estate, good-fame,
Plans, credit and the Muse,—
Nothing refuse.

'Tis a brave master;
Let it have scope:

Follow it utterly,
Hope beyond hope: *10*
High and more high
It dives into noon,
With wing unspent,
Untold intent;
But it is a god,
Knows its own path
And the outlets of the sky.

It was never for the mean;
It requireth courage stout.
Souls above doubt,   *20*
Valor unbending,
It will reward,—
They shall return
More than they were,
And every ascending.

Leave all for love;
Yet, hear me, yet,
One word more thy heart behoved,
One pulse more of firm endeavor,
Keep thee today,   *30*
Tomorrow, forever,
Free as an Arab
Of thy beloved.

Cling with life to the maid;
But when the surprise,
First vague shadow of surmise
Flits across her bosom young,
Of a joy apart from thee,
Free be she, fancy-free;
Nor thou detain her vesture's hem,   *40*
Nor the palest rose she flung
From her summer diadem.

Though thou loved her as thyself,
As a self of purer clay,
Though her parting dims the day,
Stealing grace from all alive;
Heartily know,
When half-gods go,
The gods arrive.

Ode Inscribed to W. H. Channing (1847)[1]

Though loath to grieve
The evil time's sole patriot,
I cannot leave
My honied thought
For the priest's cant,
Or statesman's rant.

If I refuse
My study for their politique,
Which at the best is trick,
The angry Muse   10
Puts confusion in my brain.

But who is he that prates
Of the culture of mankind,
Of better arts and life?
Go, blindworm, go,
Behold the famous States
Harrying Mexico[2]
With rifle and with knife!

Or who, with accent bolder,
Dare praise the freedom-loving mountaineer?   20
I found by thee, O rushing Contoocook![3]
And in thy valleys, Agiochook![4]
The jackals of the negro-holder.

The God who made New Hampshire
Taunted the lofty land
With little men;
Small bat and wren
House in the oak:
If earth-fire cleave
The upheaved land, and bury the folk,   30
The southern crocodile would grieve.
Virtue palters; Right is hence;
Freedom praised, but hid;
Funeral eloquence
Rattles the coffin-lid.

[1] Emerson wrote this poem in response to the urgings of reformers like the Reverend William Henry Channing that he take an active part in the antislavery movement.

[2] Emerson, Thoreau, and many other American writers strongly opposed, as an unjust adventure, the war with Mexico (1846–1848).

[3] New Hampshire river.

[4] Indian name for White Mountains.

What boots thy zeal,
O glowing friend,
That would indignant rend
The northland from the south?
Wherefore? to what good end?   *40*
Boston Bay and Bunker Hill
Would serve things still;
Things are of the snake.

The horseman serves the horse,
The neatherd serves the neat,[5]
The merchant serves the purse,
The eater serves his meat;
'T is the day of the chattel,
Web to weave, and corn to grind;
Things are in the saddle,   *50*
And ride mankind.

There are two laws discrete,
Not reconciled—
Law for man, and law for thing;
The last builds town and fleet,
But it runs wild,
And doth the man unking.

'T is fit the forest fall,
The steep be graded,
The mountain tunnelled,   *60*
The sand shaded,
The orchard planted,
The glebe tilled,
The prairie granted,
The steamer built.

Let man serve law for man;
Live for friendship, live for love,
For truth's and harmony's behoof;
The state may follow how it can,
As Olympus follows Jove.   *70*

     Yet do not I implore
The wrinkled shopman to my sounding woods;
Nor bid the unwilling senator
Ask votes of thrushes in the solitudes.
Every one to his chosen work;
Foolish hands may mix and mar;

---

[5] Cattle.

Wise and sure the issues are.
Round they roll till dark is light,
Sex to sex, and even to odd;
The over-god   80
Who marries Right to Might,
Who peoples, unpeoples,
He who exterminates
Races by stronger races,
Black by white faces,
Knows to bring honey
Out of the lion;
Grafts gentlest scion
On pirate and Turk.

The Cossack eats Poland,   90
Like stolen fruit;
Her last noble is ruined,
Her last poet mute:
Straight, into double band
The victors divide;
Half for freedom strike and stand;
The astonished Muse finds thousands at her side.

Days (1857)

Daughters of Time, the hypocritic Days,
Muffled and dumb like barefoot dervishes,
And marching single in an endless file,
Bring diadems and fagots in their hands.
To each they offer gifts after his will,
Bread, kingdoms, stars, and sky that holds them all.
I, in my pleached garden, watched the pomp,
Forgot my morning wishes, hastily
Took a few herbs and apples, and the Day
Turned and departed silent. I, too late,   10
Under her solemn fillet saw the scorn.

Terminus (1867)[1]

It is time to be old
To take in sail:
The god of bounds,
Came to me in his fatal rounds
And said: "No more!
No farther spread
Thy broad ambitious branches and thy root.
Fancy departs: no more invent;
Contract thy firmament
To compass of a tent.   10
There's not enough for this and that,
Make thy option which of two;
Economize the failing river,
Not the less revere the Giver;
Leave the many and hold the few.
Timely wise, accept the terms,
Soften the fall with wary foot;
Still plan and smile,
And, fault[2] of novel germs,
Mature the unfallen fruit.   20
Curse, if thou wilt, thy sires,
Bad husbands[3] of their fires,
Who, when they gave thee breath,
Failed to bequeath
The needful sinew stark as once,
The Baresark[4] marrow to thy bones,
But left a legacy of ebbing veins,
Inconstant heat and nerveless reins;
Amid the Muses left thee deaf and dumb,
Amid the gladiators halt and numb."   30

As the bird trims her to the gale,
I trim myself to the storm of time;
I man the rudder, reef the sail,
Obey the voice at eve obeyed at prime:
"Lowly faithful, banish fear,
Right onward drive unharmed;
The port, well worth the cruise, is near,
And every wave is charmed."

[1] God of boundaries in Roman mythology; here also suggesting termination, end of life.

[2] In the absence of.

[3] Economizers.

[4] Great warrior in Norse mythology.

Climacteric *(Posthumous)*

I am not wiser for my age,
Nor skilful by my grief;
Life loiters at the book's first page,—
Ah! could we turn the leaf.

Nahant *(Posthumous)*

All day the waves assailed the rock,
    I heard no church-bell chime,
The sea-beat scorns the minster clock
    And breaks the glass of Time.

Self-reliance *(1841)*

"Ne te quæsiveris extra."[1]

*Man is his own star; and the soul that can
Render an honest and a perfect man,
Commands all light, all influence, all fate;
Nothing to him falls early or too late.
Our acts our angels are, or good or ill,
Our fatal shadows that walk by us still.
Epilogue to Beaumont and Fletcher's
Honest Man's Fortune*

*Cast the bantling on the rocks,
Suckle him with the she-wolf's teat,
Wintered with the hawk and fox,
Power and speed be hands and feet.*

I read the other day some verses written by an eminent painter which were original and not conventional. The soul always hears an admonition in such lines, let the subject be what it may. The sentiment they instil is of more value than any thought they may contain. To believe your own thought, to believe that what is true for you in your private heart is true for all men—that is genius. Speak your latent conviction, and it shall be the universal sense; for the inmost in due time becomes the outmost, and our first thought is rendered back to us by

[1] Do not seek yourself outside of yourself (*Persuis' Satires*). In his *Journals*, 3:337, Emerson paraphrases: Thou art sufficient unto thyself.

the trumpets of the Last Judgment. Familiar as the voice of the mind is to each, the highest merit we ascribe to Moses, Plato and Milton is that they set at naught books and traditions, and spoke not what men, but what *they* thought. A man should learn to detect and watch that gleam of light which flashes across his mind from within, more than the lustre of the firmament of bards and sages. Yet he dismisses without notice his thought, because it is his. In every work of genius we recognize our own rejected thoughts; they come back to us with a certain alienated majesty. Great works of art have no more affecting lesson for us than this. They teach us to abide by our spontaneous impression with good-humored inflexibility then most when the whole cry of voices is on the other side. Else to-morrow a stranger will say with masterly good sense precisely what we have thought and felt all the time, and we shall be forced to take with shame our own opinion from another.

There is a time in every man's education when he arrives at the conviction that envy is ignorance; that imitation is suicide; that he must take himself for better for worse as his portion; that though the wide universe is full of good, no kernel of nourishing corn can come to him but through his toil bestowed on that plot of ground which is given to him to till. The power which resides in him is new in nature, and none but he knows what that is which he can do, nor does he know until he has tried. Not for nothing one face, one character, one fact, makes much impression on him, and another none. This sculpture in the memory is not without preëstablished harmony. The eye was placed where one ray should fall, that it might testify of that particular ray. We but half express ourselves, and are ashamed of that divine idea which each of us represents. It may be safely trusted as proportionate and of good issues, so it be faithfully imparted, but God will not have his work made manifest by cowards. A man is relieved and gay when he has put his heart into his work and done his best; but what he has said or done otherwise shall give him no peace. It is a deliverance which does not deliver. In the attempt his genius deserts him; no muse befriends; no invention, no hope.

Trust thyself: every heart vibrates to that iron string. Accept the place the divine providence has found for you, the society of your contemporaries, the connection of events. Great men have always done so, and confided themselves childlike to the genius of their age, betraying their perception that the absolutely trustworthy was seated at their heart, working through their hands, predominating in all their being. And we are now men, and must accept in the highest mind the same transcendent destiny; and not minors and invalids in a protected corner, not cowards fleeing before a revolution, but guides, redeemers and benefactors, obeying the Almighty effort and advancing on Chaos and the Dark.

What pretty oracles nature yields us on this text in the face and behavior of children, babes, and even brutes! That divided and rebel mind, that distrust of a sentiment because our arithmetic has computed the strength and means opposed to our purpose, these have not. Their mind being whole, their eye is a yet unconquered; and when we look in their faces we are disconcerted. Infancy conforms to nobody; all conform to it; so that one babe commonly makes four or five out of the adults who prattle and play to it. So God has armed youth and puberty and manhood no less with its own piquancy and charm, and made it enviable and gracious and its claims not to be put by, if it will stand by itself. Do not think the youth has no force, because he cannot speak to you and me. Hark! in the next room his voice is sufficiently clear and emphatic. It seems he knows how to speak to his contemporaries. Bashful or bold then, he will know how to make us seniors very unnecessary.

The nonchalance of boys who are sure of a dinner, and would disdain as much as a lord to do or say aught to conciliate one, is the healthy attitude of human nature. A boy is in the parlor what the pit is in the playhouse; independent, irresponsible, looking out from his corner on such people and facts as pass by, he tries and sentences them on their merits, in the swift, summary way of boys, as good, bad, interesting, silly, eloquent, troublesome. He cumbers himself never about consequences, about interests; he gives an independent, genuine verdict. You must court him; he does not court you. But the man is as it were clapped into jail by his consciousness. As soon as he has once acted or spoken with *éclat* he is a committed person, watched by the sympathy or the hatred of hundreds, whose affections must now enter into his account. There is no Lethe for this. Ah, that he could pass again into his neutrality! Who can thus avoid all pledges and, having observed, observe again from the same unaffected, unbiased, unbribable, unaffrighted innocence—must always be formidable. He would utter opinions on all passing affairs, which being seen to be not private but necessary, would sink like darts into the ear of men and put them in fear.

These are the voices which we hear in solitude, but they grow faint and inaudible as we enter into the world. Society everywhere is in conspiracy against the manhood of every one of its members. Society is a joint-stock company, in which the members agree, for the better securing of his bread to each shareholder, to surrender the liberty and culture of the eater. The virtue in most request is conformity. Self-reliance is its aversion. It loves not realities and creators, but names and customs.

Whoso would be a man, must be a nonconformist. He who would gather immortal palms must not be hindered by the name of goodness, but must explore if it be goodness. Nothing is at last sacred but the integrity of your own mind. Absolve you to yourself, and you shall have the suffrage of the world. I remember an answer which when quite young I was prompted to make to a valued adviser who was wont to importune me with the dear old doctrines of the church. On my saying, "What have I to do with the sacredness of traditions, if I live wholly from within?" my friend suggested—"But these impulses may be from below, not from above." I replied, "They do not seem to me to be such; but if I am the Devil's child, I will live then from the Devil." No law can be sacred to me but that of my nature. Good and bad are but names very readily transferable to that or this; the only right is what is after my constitution; the only wrong what is against it. A man is to carry himself in the presence of all opposition as if every thing were titular and ephemeral but he. I am ashamed to think how easily we capitulate to badges and names, to large societies and dead institutions. Every decent and well-spoken individual affects and sways me more than is right. I ought to go upright and vital, and speak the rude truth in all ways. If malice and vanity wear the coat of philanthropy, shall that pass? If an angry bigot assumes this bountiful cause of Abolition, and comes to me with his last news from Barbadoes, why should I not say to him, 'Go love thy infant; love thy wood-chopper; be good-natured and modest; have that grace; and never varnish your hard, uncharitable ambition with this incredible tenderness for black folk a thousand miles off. Thy love afar is spite at home.' Rough and graceless would be such greeting, but truth is handsomer than the affection of love. Your goodness must have some edge to it—else it is none. The doctrine of hatred must be preached, as the counteraction of the doctrine of love, when that pules and whines. I shun father and mother and wife and brother when my genius calls me. I would write on the lintels of the door-post, *Whim*. I hope it is somewhat better than whim at last, but we cannot spend the day in explanation. Expect me not to show cause why I seek or why I exclude company. Then again, do not tell me, as a good man did to-day, of my obligation to put all poor men in good situations. Are they *my* poor? I tell thee, thou foolish philanthropist, that I grudge the dollar, the dime, the cent I give to such men as do not belong to me and to whom I do not belong. There is a class of persons to whom by all spiritual affinity I am bought and sold; for them I will go to prison if need be; but your miscellaneous popular charities; the education at college of fools; the building of meeting-houses to the vain end to which many now stand; alms to sots, and the thousand-fold Relief Societies; though I confess with shame I sometimes succumb and give the dollar, it is a wicked dollar, which by and by I shall have the manhood to withhold.

Virtues are, in the popular estimate, rather the exception than the rule. There is the man *and* his virtues. Men do what is called a good action, as some piece of courage or charity, much as they would pay a fine in expiation of daily non-appearance on parade. Their works are done as an apology or extenuation of their living in the world—as invalids and the insane pay a high board. Their virtues are penances. I do not wish to expiate, but to live. My life is for itself and not for a spectacle. I much prefer that it should be of a lower strain, so it be genuine and equal, than that it should be glittering and unsteady. I wish it to be sound and sweet, and not to need diet and bleeding. I ask primary evidence that you are a man, and refuse this appeal from the man to his actions. I know that for myself it makes no difference whether I do or forbear those actions which are reckoned excellent. I cannot consent to pay for a privilege where I have intrinsic right. Few and mean as my gifts may be, I actually am, and do not need for my own assurance or the assurance of my fellows any secondary testimony.

What I must do is all that concerns me, not what the people think. This rule, equally arduous in actual and in intellectual life, may serve for the whole distinction between greatness and meanness. It is the harder because you will always find those who think they know what is your duty better than you know it. It is easy in the world to live after the world's opinion; it is easy in solitude to live after our own; but the great man is he who in the midst of the crowd keeps with perfect sweetness the independence of solitude.

The objection to conforming to usages that have become dead to you is that it scatters your force. It loses your time and blurs the impression of your character. If you maintain a dead church, contribute to a dead Bible-society, vote with a great party either for the government or against it, spread your table like base housekeepers—under all these screens I have difficulty to detect the precise man you are: and of course so much force is withdrawn from your proper life. But do your work, and I shall know you. Do your work, and you shall reinforce yourself. A man must consider what a blind-man's-buff is this game of conformity. If I know your sect I anticipate your argument. I hear a preacher announce for his text and topic the expediency of one of the institutions of his church. Do I not know beforehand that not possibly can he say a new and spontaneous word? Do I not know that with all this ostentation of examining the grounds of the institution he will do no such thing? Do I not know that he is pledged to himself not to look but at one side, the permitted side, not as a man, but as a parish minister? He is a retained attorney, and these airs of the bench are the emptiest affectation. Well, most men have bound their eyes with one or another handkerchief, and attached themselves to some one of these communities of opinion. This conformity makes them not false in a few particulars, authors of a few lies, but false in all particulars. Their every truth is not quite true. Their two is not the real two, their four not the real four; so that every word they say chagrins us and we know not where to begin to set them right. Meantime nature is not slow to equip us in the prison-uniform of the party to which we adhere. We come to wear one cut of face and figure, and acquire by degrees the gentlest asinine expression. There is a mortifying experience in particular, which does not fail to wreak itself also in the general history; I mean "the foolish face of praise," the forced smile which we put on in company where we do not feel at ease, in answer to conversation which does not interest us. The muscles, not spontaneously moved but moved by a low usurping wilfulness, grow tight about the outline of the face, with the most disagreeable sensation.

For nonconformity the world whips you with its displeasure. And therefore a man must know how to estimate a sour face. The by-standers look askance on him in the public street or in the friend's parlor. If this aversion had its origin in contempt and resistance like his own he might well go home with a sad countenance; but the sour faces of the multitude, like their sweet faces, have no deep cause, but are put on and off as the wind blows and a newspaper directs. Yet is the discontent of the multitude more formidable than that of the senate and the college. It is easy enough for a firm man who knows the world to brook the rage of the cultivated classes. Their rage is decorous and prudent, for they are timid, as being very vulnerable themselves. But when to their feminine rage the indignation of the people is added, when the ignorant and the poor are aroused, when the unintelligent brute force that lies at the bottom of society is made to growl and mow, it needs the habit of magnanimity and religion to treat it godlike as a trifle of no concernment.

The other terror that scares us from self-trust is our consistency; a reverence for our past act or word because the eyes of others have no other data for computing our orbit than our past acts, and we are loth to disappoint them.

But why should you keep your head over your shoulder? Why drag about this corpse of your memory, lest you contradict somewhat you have stated in this or that public place? Suppose you should contradict yourself; what then? It seems to be a rule of wisdom never to rely on your memory alone, scarcely even in acts of pure memory, but to bring the past for judgment into the thousand-eyed present, and live ever in a new day. In your metaphysics you have denied personality to the Deity, yet when the devout motions of the soul come, yield to them heart and life, though they should clothe God with shape and color. Leave your theory, as Joseph his coat in the hand of the harlot, and flee.

A foolish consistency is the hobgoblin of little minds, adored by little statesmen and philosophers and divines. With consistency a great soul has simply nothing to do. He may as well concern himself with his shadow on the wall. Speak what you think now in hard words and to-morrow speak what to-morrow thinks in hard words again, though it contradict every thing you said to-day.—'Ah, so you shall be sure to be misunderstood.'—Is it so bad then to be misunderstood? Pythagoras was misunderstood, and Socrates, and Jesus, and Luther, and Copernicus, and Galileo, and Newton, and every pure and wise spirit that ever took flesh. To be great is to be misunderstood.

I suppose no man can violate his nature. All the sallies of his will are rounded in by the law of his being, as the inequalities of Andes and Himmaleh are insignificant in the curve of the sphere. Nor does it matter how you gauge and try him. A character is like an acrostic or

Alexandrian stanza; read it forward, backward, or across, it still spells the same thing. In this pleasing contrite wood-life which God allows me, let me record day by day my honest thought without prospect or retrospect, and, I cannot doubt, it will be found symmetrical, though I mean it not and see it not. My book should smell of pines and resound with the hum of insects. The swallow over my window should inter-weave that thread or straw he carries in his bill into my web also. We pass for what we are. Character teaches above our wills. Men imagine that they communicate their virtue or vice only by overt actions, and do not see that virtue or vice emit a breath every moment.

There will be an agreement in whatever variety of actions, so they be each honest and natural in their hour. For of one will, the actions will be harmonious, however unlike they seem. These varieties are lost sight of at a little distance, at a little height of thought. One tendency unites them all. The voyage of the best ship is a zigzag line of a hundred tacks. See the line from a sufficient distance, and it straightens itself to the average tendency. Your genuine action will explain itself and will explain your other genuine actions. Your conformity explains nothing. Act singly, and what you have already done singly will justify you now. Greatness appeals to the future. If I can be firm enough to-day to do right and scorn eyes, I must have done so much right before as to defend me now. Be it how it will, do right now. Always scorn appearances and you always may. The force of character is cumulative. All the foregone days of virtue work their health into this. What makes the majesty of the heroes of the senate and the field, which so fills the imagination? The consciousness of a train of great days and victories behind. They shed a united light on the advancing actor. He is attended as by a visible escort of angels. That is it which throws thunder into Chatham's voice,[2] and dignity into Washington's port, and America into Adams's eye. Honor is venerable to us because it is no ephemera. It is always ancient virtue. We worship it to-day because it is not of to-day. We love it and pay it homage because it is not a trap for our love and homage, but is self-dependent, self-derived, and therefore of an old immaculate pedi-gree, even if shown in a young person.

I hope in these days we have heard the last of conformity and con-sistency. Let the words be gazetted and ridiculous henceforward. Instead of the gong for dinner, let us hear a whistle from the Spartan fife. Let us never bow and apologize more. A great man is coming to eat at my house. I do not wish to please him; I wish that he should wish to please me. I will stand here for humanity, and though I would make it kind, I would make it true. Let us affront and reprimand the smooth medi-ocrity and squalid contentment of the times, and hurl in the face of custom and trade and office, the fact which is the upshot of all history, that there is a great responsible Thinker and Actor working wherever

2 William Pitt, Earl of Chatham (1708–1778), English statesman.

a man works; that a true man belongs to no other time or place, but is the centre of things. Where he is, there is nature. He measures you and all men and all events. Ordinarily, every body in society reminds us of somewhat else, or of some other person. Character, reality, reminds you of nothing else; it takes place of the whole creation. The man must be so much that he must make all circumstances indifferent. Every true man is a cause, a country, and an age; requires infinite spaces and numbers and time fully to accomplish his design; and posterity seem to follow his steps as a train of clients. A man Cæsar is born, and for ages after we have a Roman Empire. Christ is born, and millions of minds so grow and cleave to his genius that he is confounded with virtue and the possible of man. An institution is the lengthened shadow of one man; as, Monachism,[3] of the Hermit Antony; the Reformation, of Luther; Quakerism, of Fox; Methodism, of Wesley; Abolition, of Clarkson.[4] Scipio,[5] Milton called "the height of Rome"; and all history resolves itself very easily into the biography of a few stout and earnest persons.

Let a man then know his worth, and keep things under his feet. Let him not peep or steal, or skulk up and down with the air of a charity-boy, a bastard, or an interloper in the world which exists for him. But the man in the street, finding no worth in himself which corresponds to the force which built a tower or sculptured a marble god, feels poor when he looks on these. To him a palace, a statue, or a costly book have an alien and forbidding air, much like a gay equipage, and seem to say like that, "Who are you, Sir?" Yet they all are his, suitors for his notice, petitioners to his faculties that they will come out and take possession. The picture waits for my verdict; it is not to command me, but I am to settle its claims to praise. That popular fable of the sot who was picked up dead-drunk in the street, carried to the duke's house, washed and dressed and laid in the duke's bed, and, on his waking, treated with all obsequious ceremony like the duke, and assured that he had been insane, owes its popularity to the fact that it symbolizes so well the state of man, who is in the world a sort of sot, but now and then wakes up, exercises his reason and finds himself a true prince.

Our reading is mendicant and sycophantic. In history our imagination plays us false. Kingdom and lordship, power and estate, are a gaudier vocabulary than private John and Edward in a small house and common day's work; but the things of life are the same to both; the sum total of both is the same. Why all this deference to Alfred and Scanderbeg and Gustavus?[6] Suppose they were virtuous; did they wear out virtue? As great a stake depends on your private act to-day as fol-

3 Monasticism, founded by St. Anthony (c. A.D. 250–350).

4 Thomas Clarkson (1760–1846), English antislavery leader.

5 Roman general in second century B.C. who destroyed Carthage.

6 Alfred the Great (849–901), Saxon King; Scanderbeg: national hero of Albania (1403–1468) who opposed the Turks; Gustavus Adolphus (1594–1632) Swedish king who led the Protestant cause in Thirty Years' War.

lowed their public and renowned steps. When private men shall act with original views, the lustre will be transferred from the actions of kings to those of gentlemen.

The world has been instructed by its kings, who have so magnetized the eyes of nations. It has been taught by this colossal symbol the mutual reverence that is due from man to man. The joyful loyalty with which men have everywhere suffered the king, the noble, or the great proprietor to walk among them by a law of his own, make his own scale of men and things and reverse theirs, pay for benefits not with money but with honor, and represent the law in his person, was the hieroglyphic by which they obscurely signified their consciousness of their own right and comeliness, the right of every man.

The magnetism which all original action exerts is explained when we inquire the reason of self-trust. Who is the Trustee? What is the aboriginal Self, on which a universal reliance may be grounded? What is the nature and power of that science-baffling star, without parallax, without calculable elements, which shoots a ray of beauty even into trivial and impure actions, if the least mark of independence appear? The inquiry leads us to that source, at once the essence of genius, of virtue, and of life, which we call Spontaneity or Instinct.[7] We denote this primary wisdom as Intuition, whilst all later teachings are tuitions. In that deep force, the last fact behind which analysis cannot go, all things find their common origin. For the sense of being which in calm hours rises, we know not how, in the soul, is not diverse from things, from space, from light, from time, from man, but one with them and proceeds obviously from the same source whence their life and being also proceed. We first share the life by which things exist and afterwards see them as appearances in nature and forget that we have shared their cause. Here is the fountain of action and of thought. Here are the lungs of that inspiration which giveth man wisdom and which cannot be denied without impiety and atheism. We lie in the lap of immense intelligence, which makes us receivers of its truth and organs of its activity. When we discern justice, when we discern truth, we do nothing of ourselves, but allow a passage to its beams. If we ask whence this comes, if we seek to pry into the soul that causes, all philosophy is at fault. Its presence or its absence is all we can affirm. Every man discriminates between the voluntary acts of his mind and his involuntary perceptions, and knows that to his involuntary perceptions a perfect faith is due. He may err in the expression of them, but he knows that these things are so, like day and night, not to be disputed. My wilful actions and acquisitions are but roving; the idlest reverie, the faintest

---

[7] Concerning this difficult term, Newton Arvin, an Emerson scholar, has remarked: ". . . a misunderstood and perhaps infelicitous term here. Emerson means by it, however, not, as has been unintelligently maintained, mere biological or animal drive, but an innate power of spiritual insight which is not and cannot be the product of any teaching. . . ."

native emotion, command my curiosity and respect. Thoughtless people contradict as readily the statement of perceptions as of opinions, or rather much more readily; for they do not distinguish between perception and notion. They fancy that I choose to see this or that thing. But perception is not whimsical, but fatal. If I see a trait, my children will see it after me, and in course of time all mankind—although it may chance that no one has seen it before me. For my perception of it is as much a fact as the sun.

The relations of the soul to the divine spirit are so pure that it is profane to seek to interpose helps. It must be that when God speaketh he should communicate, not one thing, but all things; should fill the world with his voice; should scatter forth light, nature, time, souls, from the centre of the present thought; and new date and new create the whole. Whenever a mind is simple and receives a divine wisdom, old things pass away—means, teachers, texts, temples fall; it lives now, and absorbs past and future into the present hour. All things are made sacred by relation to it—one as much as another. All things are dissolved to their centre by their cause, and in the universal miracle petty and particular miracles disappear. If therefore a man claims to know and speak of God and carries you backward to the phraseology of some old mouldered nation in another country, in another world, believe him not. Is the acorn better than the oak which is its fulness and completion? Is the parent better than the child into whom he has cast his ripened being? Whence then this worship of the past? The centuries are conspirators against the sanity and authority of the soul. Time and space are but physiological colors which the eye makes, but the soul is light: where it is, is day; where it was, is night; and history is an impertinence and an injury if it be any thing more than a cheerful apologue or parable of my being and becoming.

Man is timid and apologetic; he is no longer upright; he dares not say 'I think,' 'I am,' but quotes some saint or sage. He is ashamed before the blade of grass or the blowing rose. These roses under my window make no reference to former roses or to better ones; they are for what they are; they exist with God to-day. There is no time to them. There is simply the rose; it is perfect in every moment of its existence. Before a leaf-bud has burst, its whole life acts; in the full-blown flower there is no more; in the leafless root there is no less. Its nature is satisfied and it satisfies nature in all moments alike. But man postpones or remembers; he does not live in the present, but with reverted eye laments the past, or, heedless of the riches that surround him, stands on tiptoe to foresee the future. He cannot be happy and strong until he too lives with nature in the present, above time.

This should be plain enough. Yet see what strong intellects dare not yet hear God himself unless he speak the phraseology of I know not what David, or Jeremiah, or Paul. We shall not always set so great a price on a few texts, on a few lives. We are like children who repeat by rote the sentences of grandames and tutors, and, as they grow older, of the men of talents and character they chance to see—painfully recollecting the exact words they spoke; afterwards, when they come into the point of view which those had who uttered these sayings, they understand them and are willing to let the words go; for at any time they can use words as good when occasion comes. If we live truly, we shall see truly. It is as easy for the strong man to be strong, as it is for the weak to be weak. When we have new perception, we shall gladly disburden the memory of its hoarded treasures as old rubbish. When a man lives with God, his voice shall be as sweet as the murmur of the brook and the rustle of the corn.

And now at last the highest truth on this subject remains unsaid; probably cannot be said; for all that we say is the far-off remembering of the intuition. That thought by what I can now nearest approach to say it, is this. When good is near you, when you have life in yourself, it is not by any known or accustomed way; you shall not discern the footprints of any other; you shall not see the face of man; you shall not hear any name; the way, the thought, the good, shall be wholly strange and new. It shall exclude example and experience. You take the way from man, not to man. All persons that ever existed are its forgotten ministers. Fear and hope are alike beneath it. There is somewhat low even in hope. In the hour of vision there is nothing that can be called gratitude, nor properly joy. The soul raised over passion beholds identity and eternal causation, perceives the self-existence of Truth and Right, and calms itself with knowing that all things go well. Vast spaces of nature, the Atlantic Ocean, the South Sea; long intervals of time, years, centuries, are of no account. This which I think and feel underlay every former state of life and circumstances, as it does underlie my present, and what is called life and what is called death.

Life only avails, not the having lived. Power ceases in the instant of repose; it resides in the moment of transition from a past to a new state, in the shooting of the gulf, in the darting to an aim. This one fact the world hates; that the soul *becomes;* for that forever degrades the past, turns all riches to poverty, all reputation to a shame, confounds the saint with the rogue, shoves Jesus and Judas equally aside. Why then do we prate of self-reliance? Inasmuch as the soul is present there will be power not confident but agent. To talk of reliance is a poor external way of speaking. Speak rather of that which relies because it works and is. Who has more obedience than I masters me, though he should not raise his finger. Round him I must revolve by the gravitation of spirits. We fancy it rhetoric when we speak of eminent virtue. We do not yet see that virtue is Height, and that a man or a company of men, plastic and permeable to principles, by the law of nature must overpower and ride all cities, nations, kings, rich men, poets, who are not.

This is the ultimate fact which we so quickly reach on this, as on every topic, the resolution of all into the ever-blessed ONE. Self-existence is the attribute of the Supreme Cause, and it constitutes the measure of good by the degree in which it enters into all lower forms. All things real are so by so much virtue as they contain. Commerce, husbandry, hunting, whaling, war, eloquence, personal weight, are somewhat, and engage my respect as examples of its presence and impure action. I see the same law working in nature for conservation and growth. Power is, in nature, the essential measure of right. Nature suffers nothing to remain in her kingdoms which cannot help itself. The genesis and maturation of a planet, its poise and orbit, the bended tree recovering itself from the strong wind, the vital resources of every animal and vegetable, are demonstrations of the self-sufficing and therefore self-relying soul.

Thus all concentrates: let us not rove; let us sit at home with the cause. Let us stun and astonish the intruding rabble of men and books and institutions by a simple declaration of the divine fact. Bid the invaders take the shoes from off their feet, for God is here within. Let our simplicity judge them, and our docility to our own law demonstrate the poverty of nature and fortune beside our native riches.

But now we are a mob. Man does not stand in awe of man, nor is his genius admonished to stay at home, to put itself in communication with the internal ocean, but it goes abroad to beg a cup of water of the urns of other men. We must go alone. I like the silent church before the service begins, better than any preaching. How far off, how cool, how chaste the persons look, begirt each one with a precinct or sanctuary! So let us always sit. Why should we assume the faults of our friend, or wife, or father, or child, because they sit around our hearth, or are said to have the same blood? All men have my blood and I all men's. Not for that will I adopt their petulance or folly, even to the extent of being ashamed of it. But your isolation must not be mechanical, but spiritual, that is, must be elevation. At times the whole world seems to be in conspiracy to importune you with emphatic trifles. Friend, client, child, sickness, fear, want, charity, all knock at once at thy closet door and say—'Come out unto us.' But keep thy state; come not into their confusion. The power men possess to annoy me I give them by a weak curiosity. No man can come near me but through my act. "What we love that we have, but by desire we bereave ourselves of the love."

If we cannot at once rise to the sanctities of obedience and faith, let us at least resist our temptations; let us enter into the state of war and wage. Thor[8] and Woden,[9] courage and constancy, in our Saxon breasts. This is to be done in our smooth times by speaking the truth. Check this lying hospitality and lying affection. Live no longer to the expectation of these deceived and deceiving people with whom we converse.

[8] Norse god of war.
[9] Scandinavian pagan god.

Say to them, 'O father, O mother, O wife, O brother, O friend, I have lived with you after appearances hitherto. Henceforward I am the truth's. Be it known unto you that henceforward I obey no law less than the eternal law. I will have no covenants but proximities. I shall endeavor to nourish my parents, to support my family, to be the chaste husband of one wife—but these relations I must fill after a new and unprecedented way. I appeal from your customs. I must be myself. I cannot break myself any longer for you, or you. If you can love me for what I am, we shall be the happier. If you cannot, I will still seek to deserve that you should. I will not hide my tastes or aversions. I will so trust that what is deep is holy, that I will do strongly before the sun and moon whatever inly rejoices me and the heart appoints. If you are noble, I will love you; if you are not, I will not hurt you and myself by hypocritical attentions. If you are true, but not in the same truth with me, cleave to your companions; I will seek my own. I do this not selfishly but humbly and truly. It is alike your interest, and mine, and all men's, however long we have dwelt in lies, to live in truth. Does this sound harsh to-day? You will soon love what is dictated by your nature as well as mine, and if we follow the truth it will bring us out safe at last.'— But so may you give these friends pain. Yes, but I cannot sell my liberty and my power, to save their sensibility. Besides, all persons have their moments of reason, when they look out into the region of absolute truth; then will they justify me and do the same thing.

The populace think that your rejection of popular standards is a rejection of all standard, and mere antinomianism;[10] and the bold sensualist will use the name of philosophy to gild his crimes. But the law of consciousness abides. There are two confessionals, in one or the other of which we must be shriven. You may fulfil your round of duties by clearing yourself in the *direct,* or in the *reflex* way. Consider whether you have satisfied your relations to father, mother, cousin, neighbor, town, cat and dog—whether any of these can upbraid you. But I may also neglect this reflex standard and absolve me to myself. I have my own stern claims and perfect circle. It denies the name of duty to many offices that are called duties. But if I can discharge its debts it enables me to dispense with the popular code. If any one imagines that this law is lax, let him keep its commandment one day.

And truly it demands something godlike in him who has cast off the common motives of humanity and has ventured to trust himself for a taskmaster. High be his heart, faithful his will, clear his sight, that he may in good earnest be doctrine, society, law, to himself, that a simple purpose may be to him as strong as iron necessity is to others!

If any man consider the present aspects of what is called by distinction *society,* he will see the need of these ethics. The sinew and

10 The doctrine that a Christian flooded by the influx of divine grace is free to set aside the moral law.

heart of man seem to be drawn out, and we are become timorous, desponding whimperers. We are afraid of truth, afraid of fortune, afraid of death, and afraid of each other. Our age yields no great and perfect persons. We want men and women who shall renovate life and our social state, but we see that most natures are insolvent, cannot satisfy their own wants, have an ambition out of all proportion to their practical force and do lean and beg day and night continually. Our housekeeping is mendicant, our arts, our occupations, our marriages, our religion we have not chosen, but society has chosen for us. We are parlor soldiers. We shun the rugged battle of fate, where strength is born.

If our young men miscarry in their first enterprises they lose all heart. If the young merchant fails, men say he is *ruined.* If the finest genius studies at one of our colleges and is not installed in an office within one year afterwards in the cities or suburbs of Boston or New York, it seems to his friends and to himself that he is right in being disheartened and in complaining the rest of his life. A sturdy lad from New Hampshire or Vermont, who in turn tries all the professions, who *teams it, farms it, peddles,* keeps a school, preaches, edits a newspaper, goes to Congress, buys a township, and so forth, in successive years, and always like a cat falls on his feet, is worth a hundred of these city dolls. He walks abreast with his days and feels no shame in not 'studying a profession,' for he does not postpone his life, but lives already. He has not one chance, but a hundred chances. Let a Stoic open the resources of man and tell men they are not leaning willows, but can and must detach themselves; that with the exercise of self-trust, new powers shall appear; that a man is the word made flesh, born to shed healing to the nations; that he should be ashamed of our compassion, and that the moment he acts from himself, tossing the laws, the books, idolatries and customs out of the window, we pity him no more but thank and revere him; and that teacher shall restore the life of man to splendor and make his name dear to all history.

It is easy to see that a greater self-reliance must work a revolution in all the offices and relations of men; in their religion; in their education; in their pursuits; their modes of living; their association; in their property; in their speculative views.

I

In what prayers do men allow themselves! That which they call a holy office is not so much as brave and manly. Prayer looks abroad and asks for some foreign addition to come through some foreign virtue, and loses itself in endless mazes of natural and supernatural, and mediatorial and miraculous. Prayer that craves a particular commodity, anything less than all good, is vicious. Prayer is the contemplation of the facts of life from the highest point of view. It is the soliloquy of a beholding and jubilant soul. It is the spirit of God pronouncing his works good. But prayer as a means to effect a private end is meanness and theft. It supposes dualism and not unity in nature and consciousness. As soon as the man is at one with God, he will not beg. He will then see prayer in all action. The prayer of the farmer kneeling in his field to weed it, the prayer of the rower kneeling with the stroke of his oar, are true prayers heard throughout nature, though for cheap ends. Caratach, in Fletcher's "Bonduca," when admonished to inquire the mind of the god Audate, replies—

His hidden meaning lies in our endeavors;
Our valors are our best gods.

Another sort of false prayers are our regrets. Discontent is the want of self-reliance: it is infirmity of will. Regret calamities if you can thereby help the sufferer; if not, attend your own work and already the evil begins to be repaired. Our sympathy is just as base. We come to them who weep foolishly and sit down and cry for company, instead of imparting to them truth and health in rough electric shocks, putting them once more in communication with their own reason. The secret of fortune is joy in our hands. Welcome evermore to gods and men is the self-helping man. For him all doors are flung wide; him all tongues greet, all honors crown, all eyes follow with desire. Our love goes out to him and embraces him because he did not need it. We solicitously and apologetically caress and celebrate him because he held on his way and scorned our disapprobation. The gods love him because men hated him. "To the persevering mortal," said Zoroaster,[11] "the blessed Immortals are swift."

As men's prayers are a disease of the will, so are their creeds a disease of the intellect. They say with those foolish Israelites, 'Let not God speak to us, lest we die. Speak thou, speak any man with us, and we will obey.' [12] Everywhere I am hindered of meeting God in my brother, because he has shut his own temple doors and recites fables merely of his brother's, or his brother's brother's God. Every new mind is a new classification. If it prove a mind of uncommon activity and power, a Locke, a Lavoisier, a Hutton, a Bentham, a Fourier,[13] it imposes its classification on other men, and lo! a new system. In proportion to the depth of the thought, and so to the number of the objects it touches and brings within reach of the pupil, is his complacency. But chiefly is this apparent in creeds and churches, which are also classifications of some

[11] Founder of ancient Persian religion.

[12] Paraphrased from Exodus 20:19.

[13] John Locke (1632–1704), English philosopher; Antoine Lavoisier (1743–1894), French chemist; James Hutton (1726–1797), English geologist; Jeremy Bentham (1748–1832), English philosopher; Francois Fourier (1772–1837), French utopian socialist.

powerful mind acting on the elemental thought of duty and man's relation to the Highest. Such is Calvinism, Quakerism, Swedenborgism. The
pupil takes the same delight in subordinating every thing to the new
terminology as a girl who has just learned botany in seeing a new earth
and new seasons thereby. It will happen for a time that the pupil will
find his intellectual power has grown by the study of his master's mind.
But in all unbalanced minds the classification is idolized, passes for the
end and not for a speedily exhaustible means, so that the walls of the
system blend to their eye in the remote horizon with the walls of the
universe; the luminaries of heaven seem to them hung on the arch their
master built. They cannot imagine how you aliens have any right to
see—how you can see; 'It must be somehow that you stole the light
from us.' They do not yet perceive that light, unsystematic, indomitable,
will break into any cabin, even into theirs. Let them chirp awhile and
call it their own. If they are honest and do well, presently their neat
new pinfold will be too strait and low, will crack, will lean, will rot and
vanish, and the immortal light, all young and joyful, million-orbed,
million-colored, will beam over the universe as on the first morning.

II

It is for want of self-culture that the superstition of Travelling,
whose idols are Italy, England, Egypt, retains its fascination for all
educated Americans. They who made England, Italy, or Greece venerable in the imagination, did so by sticking fast where they were, like
an axis of the earth. In manly hours we feel that duty is our place. The
soul is no traveller; the wise man stays at home, and when his necessities, his duties, on any occasion call him from his house, or into foreign lands, he is at home still and shall make men sensible by the
expression of his countenance that he goes, the missionary of wisdom
and virtue, and visits cities and men like a sovereign and not like an
interloper or a valet.

I have no churlish objection to the circumnavigation of the globe
for the purposes of art, of study, and benevolence, so that the man is
first domesticated, or does not go abroad with the hope of finding somewhat greater than he knows. He who travels to be amused, or to get
somewhat which he does not carry, travels away from himself, and
grows old even in youth among old things. In Thebes, in Palmyra, his
will and mind have become old and dilapidated as they. He carries ruins
to ruins.

Travelling is a fool's paradise. Our first journeys discover to us the
indifference of places. At home I dream that at Naples, at Rome, I can
be intoxicated with beauty and lose my sadness. I pack my trunk, embrace my friends, embark on the sea and at last wake up in Naples,
and there beside me is the stern fact, the sad self, unrelenting, identical,
that I fled from. I seek the Vatican and the palaces. I affect to be intoxi-

cated with sights and suggestions, but I am not intoxicated. My giant goes with me wherever I go.

III

But the rage of travelling is a symptom of a deeper unsoundness affecting the whole intellectual action. The intellect is vagabond, and our system of education fosters restlessness. Our minds travel when our bodies are forced to stay at home. We imitate; and what is imitation but the travelling of the mind? Our houses are built with foreign taste; our shelves are garnished with foreign ornaments; our opinions, our tastes, our faculties, lean, and follow the Past and the Distant. The soul created the arts wherever they have flourished. It was in his own mind that the artist sought his model. It was an application of his own thought to the thing to be done and the conditions to be observed. And why need we copy the Doric or the Gothic model? Beauty, convenience, grandeur of thought and quaint expression are as near to us as to any, and if the American artist will study with hope and love the precise thing to be done by him, considering the climate, the soil, the length of the day, the wants of the people, the habit and form of the government, he will create a house in which all these will find themselves fitted, and taste and sentiment will be satisfied also.

Insist on yourself; never imitate. Your own gift you can present every moment with the cumulative force of a whole life's cultivation; but of the adopted talent of another you have only an extemporaneous half possession. That which each can do best, none but his Maker can teach him. No man yet knows what it is, nor can, till that person has exhibited it. Where is the master who could have taught Shakspeare? Where is the master who could have instructed Franklin, or Washington, or Bacon, or Newton? Every great man is a unique. The Scipionism of Scipio is precisely that part he could not borrow. Shakspeare will never be made by the study of Shakspeare. Do that which is assigned you, and you cannot hope too much or dare too much. There is at this moment for you an utterance brave and grand as that of the colossal chisel of Phidias, or trowel of the Egyptians, or the pen of Moses or Dante, but different from all these. Not possibly will the soul, all rich, all eloquent, with thousand-cloven tongue, deign to repeat itself; but if you can hear what these patriarchs say, surely you can reply to them in the same pitch of voice; for the ear and the tongue are two organs of one nature. Abide in the simple and noble regions of thy life, obey thy heart, and thou shalt reproduce the Foreworld again.

IV

As our Religion, our Education, our Art look abroad, so does our spirit of society. All men plume themselves on the improvement of society, and no man improves.

Society never advances. It recedes as fast on one side as it gains on the other. It undergoes continual changes; it is barbarous, it is civilized, it is christianized, it is rich, it is scientific; but this change is not amelioration. For every thing that is given something is taken. Society acquires new arts and loses old instincts. What a contrast between the well-clad, reading, writing, thinking American, with a watch, a pencil and a bill of exchange in his pocket, and the naked New Zealander, whose property is a club, a spear, a mat and an undivided twentieth of a shed to sleep under! But compare the health of the two men and you shall see that the white man has lost his aboriginal strength. If the traveller tell us truly, strike the savage with a broad-axe and in a day or two the flesh shall unite and heal as if you struck the blow into soft pitch, and the same blow shall send the white to his grave.

The civilized man has built a coach, but has lost the use of his feet. He is supported on crutches, but lacks so much support of muscle. He has a fine Geneva watch, but he fails of the skill to tell the hour by the sun. A Greenwich nautical almanac he has, and so being sure of the information when he wants it, the man in the street does not know a star in the sky. The solstice he does not observe; the equinox he knows as little; and the whole bright calendar of the year is without a dial in his mind. His note-books impair his memory; his libraries overload his wit; the insurance-office increases the number of accidents; and it may be a question whether machinery does not encumber; whether we have not lost by refinement some energy, by a Christianity, entrenched in establishments and forms, some vigor of wild virtue. For every Stoic was a Stoic; but in Christendom where is the Christian?

There is no more deviation in the moral standard than in the standard of height or bulk. No greater men are now than ever were. A singular equality may be observed between the great men of the first and of the last ages; nor can all the science, art, religion, and philosophy of the nineteenth century avail to educate greater men than Plutarch's heroes, three or four and twenty centuries ago. Not in time is the race progressive. Phocion,[14] Socrates, Anaxagoras,[15] Diogenes,[16] are great men, but they leave no class. He who is really of their class will not be called by their name, but will be his own man, and in his turn the founder of a sect. The arts and inventions of each period are only its costume and do not invigorate men. The harm of the improved machinery may compensate its good. Hudson and Behring[17] accomplished so much in their fishing-boats as to astonish Parry[18] and Franklin, whose

[14] Greek philosopher (402?–317 B.C.).

[15] Greek philosopher (500–428 B.C.).

[16] Greek philosopher (412?–323 B.C.).

[17] Vitus Jonassen Bering (1681–1741), Danish navigator after whom Bering Sea is named.

[18] Sir William Edward Parry (1790–1855), English explorer of the Arctic.

equipment exhausted the resources of science and art. Galileo, with an opera-glass, discovered a more splendid series of celestial phenomena than any one since. Columbus found the New World in an undecked boat. It is curious to see the periodical disuse and perishing of means and machinery which were introduced with loud laudation a few years or centuries before. The great genius returns to essential man. We reckoned the improvements of the art of war among the triumphs of science, and yet Napoleon conquered Europe by the bivouac, which consisted of falling back on naked valor and disencumbering it of all aids. The Emperor held it impossible to make a perfect army, says Las Cases,[19] "without abolishing our arms, magazines, commissaries and carriages, until, in imitation of the Roman custom, the soldier should receive his supply of corn, grind it in his hand-mill and bake his bread himself."

Society is a wave. The wave moves onward, but the water of which it is composed does not. The same particle does not rise from the valley to the ridge. Its unity is only phenomenal. The persons who make up a nation to-day, next year die, and their experience dies with them.

And so the reliance on Property, including the reliance on governments which protect it, is the want of self-reliance. Men have looked away from themselves and at things so long that they have come to esteem the religious, learned and civil institutions as guards of property, and they deprecate assaults on these, because they feel them to be assaults on property. They measure their esteem of each other by what each has, and not by what each is. But a cultivated man becomes ashamed of his property, out of new respect for his nature. Especially he hates what he has if he see that it is accidental—came to him by inheritance, or gift, or crime; then he feels that it is not having; it does not belong to him, has no root in him and merely lies there because no revolution or no robber takes it away. But that which a man is, does always by necessity acquire; and what the man acquires, is living property, which does not wait the beck of rulers, or mobs, or revolutions, or fire, or storm, or bankruptcies, but perpetually renews itself wherever the man breathes. "Thy lot or portion of life," said the Caliph Ali, "is seeking after thee; therefore be at rest from seeking after it." Our dependence on these foreign goods leads us to our slavish respect for numbers. The political parties meet in numerous conventions; the greater the concourse and with each new uproar of announcement, The delegation from Essex! The Democrats from New Hampshire! The Whigs of Maine! the young patriot feels himself stronger than before by a new thousand of eyes and arms. In like manner the reformers summon conventions and vote and resolve in multitude. Not so, O friends! will the God deign to enter and inhabit you, but by a method precisely the reverse. It is only as a man puts off all foreign support

19 French official (1766–1842) who wrote a famous book on Napoleon's last days.

and stands alone that I see him to be strong and to prevail. He is weaker by every recruit to his banner. Is not a man better than a town? Ask nothing of men, and, in the endless mutation, thou only firm column must presently appear the upholder of all that surrounds thee. He who knows that power is inborn, that he is weak because he has looked for good out of him and elsewhere, and, so perceiving, throws himself unhesitatingly on his thought, instantly rights himself, stands in the erect position, commands his limbs, works miracles; just as a man who stands on his feet is stronger than a man who stands on his head.

So use all that is called Fortune. Most men gamble with her, and gain all, and lose all, as her wheel rolls. But do thou leave as unlawful these winnings, and deal with Cause and Effect, the chancellors of God. In the Will work and acquire, and thou hast chained the wheel of Chance, and shall sit hereafter out of fear from her rotations. A political victory, a rise of rents, the recovery of your sick or the return of your absent friend, or some other favorable event raises your spirits, and you think good days are preparing for you. Do not believe it. Nothing can bring you peace but yourself. Nothing can bring you peace but the triumph of principles.

The American Scholar *(1837)*[1]

Mr. President and Gentlemen:

I greet you on the recommencement of our literary year. Our anniversary is one of hope, and, perhaps, not enough of labor. We do not meet for games of strength or skill, for the recitation of histories, tragedies, and odes, like the ancient Greeks; for parliaments of love and poesy, like the Troubadours; nor for the advancement of science, like our contemporaries in the British and European capitals. Thus far, our holiday has been simply a friendly sign of the survival of the love of letters amongst a people too busy to give to letters any more. As such it is precious as the sign of an indestructible instinct. Perhaps the time is already come when it ought to be, and will be, something else; when the sluggard intellect of this continent will look from under its iron lids and fill the postponed expectation of the world with something better than the exertions of mechanical skill. Our day of dependence, our long apprenticeship to the learning of other lands, draws to a close. The millions that around us are rushing into life, cannot always be fed on

---

[1] Oration delivered before the Phi Beta Kappa Society, at Cambridge, August 31, 1837. Oliver Wendell Holmes said: "This grand oration was our intellectual Declaration of Independence .... the young men went from it as if a prophet had been proclaiming to them, 'Thus saith the Lord.'"

the sere remains of foreign harvests. Events, actions arise, that must be sung, that will sing themselves. Who can doubt that poetry will revive and lead in a new age, as the star in the constellation Harp, which now flames in our zenith, astronomers announce, shall one day be the pole-star for a thousand years?

In this hope I accept the topic which not only usage but the nature of our association seem to prescribe to this day—the AMERICAN SCHOLAR. Year by year we come up hither to read one more chapter of his biography. Let us inquire what light new days and events have thrown on his character and his hopes.

It is one of those fables which out of an unknown antiquity convey an unlooked-for wisdom, that the gods, in the beginning, divided Man into men, that he might be more helpful to himself: just as the hand was divided into fingers, the better to answer its end.

The old fable covers a doctrine ever new and sublime; that there is One Man—present to all particular men only partially, or through one faculty; and that you must take the whole society to find the whole man. Man is not a farmer, or a professor, or an engineer, but he is all. Man is priest, and scholar, and statesman, and producer, and soldier. In the *divided* or social state these functions are parcelled out to individuals, each of whom aims to do his stint of the joint work, whilst each other performs his. The fable implies that the individual, to possess himself, must sometimes return from his own labor to embrace all the other laborers. But, unfortunately, this original unit, this fountain of power, has been so distributed to multitudes, has been so minutely subdivided and peddled out, that it is spilled into drops, and cannot be gathered. The state of society is one in which the members have suffered amputation from the trunk, and strut about so many walking monsters—a good finger, a neck, a stomach, an elbow, but never a man.

Man is thus metamorphosed into a thing, into many things. The planter, who is Man sent out into the field to gather food, is seldom cheered by any idea of the true dignity of his ministry. He sees his bushel and his cart, and nothing beyond, and sinks into the farmer, instead of Man on the farm. The tradesman scarcely ever gives an ideal worth to his work, but is ridden by the routine of his craft, and the soul is subject to dollars. The priest becomes a form; the attorney a statute-book; the mechanic a machine; the sailor a rope of the ship.

In this distribution of functions the scholar is the delegated intellect. In the right state he is *Man Thinking*. In the degenerate state, when the victim of society, he tends to become a mere thinker, or still worse, the parrot of other men's thinking.

In this view of him, as Man Thinking, the theory of his office is contained. Him Nature solicits with all her placid, all her monitory pictures; him the past instructs; him the future invites. Is not indeed every man a student, and do not all things exist for the student's behoof? And, finally, is not the true scholar the only true master? But the old

oracle said, "All things have two handles: beware of the wrong one."
In life, too often, the scholar errs with mankind and forfeits his privilege. Let us see him in his school, and consider him in reference to the
main influences he receives.

I

The first in time and the first in importance of the influences upon
the mind is that of nature. Every day, the sun; and, after sunset, Night
and her stars. Ever the winds blow; ever the grass grows. Every day,
men and women, conversing—beholding and beholden. The scholar is
he of all men whom this spectacle most engages. He must settle its value
in his mind. What is nature to him? There is never a beginning, there
is never an end, to the inexplicable continuity of this web of God, but
always circular power returning into itself. Therein it resembles his own
spirit, whose beginning, whose ending, he never can find—so entire, so
boundless. Far too as her splendors shine, system on system shooting
like rays, upward, downward, without centre, without circumference—
in the mass and in the particle, Nature hastens to render account of
herself to the mind. Classification begins. To the young mind every
thing is individual, stands by itself. By and by, it finds how to join two
things and see in them one nature; then three, then three thousand;
and so, tyrannized over by its own unifying instinct, it goes on tying
things together, diminishing anomalies, discovering roots running under
ground whereby contrary and remote things cohere and flower out from
one stem. It presently learns that since the dawn of history there has
been a constant accumulation and classifying of facts. But what is
classification but the perceiving that these objects are not chaotic, and
are not foreign, but have a law which is also a law of the human mind?
The astronomer discovers that geometry, a pure abstraction of the
human mind, is the measure of planetary motion. The chemist finds
proportions and intelligible method throughout matter; and science is
nothing but the finding of analogy, identity, in the most remote parts.
The ambitious soul sits down before each refractory fact; one after
another reduces all strange constitutions, all new powers, to their class
and their law, and goes on forever to animate the last fibre of organization, the outskirts of nature, by insight.

Thus to him, to this schoolboy under the bending dome of day, is
suggested that he and it proceed from one root; one is leaf and one is
flower; relation, sympathy, stirring in every vein. And what is that root?
Is not that the soul of his soul? A thought too bold; a dream too wild.
Yet when this spiritual light shall have revealed the law of more earthly
natures—when he has learned to worship the soul, and to see that the
natural philosophy that now is, is only the first gropings of its gigantic
hand, he shall look forward to an ever expanding knowledge as to a
becoming creator. He shall see that nature is the opposite of the soul,

answering to it part for part. One is seal and one is print. Its beauty is the beauty of his own mind. Its laws are the laws of his own mind. Nature then becomes to him the measure of his attainments. So much of nature as he is ignorant of, so much of his own mind does he not yet possess. And, in fine, the ancient precept, "Know thyself," and the modern precept, "Study nature," become at last one maxim.

II

The next great influence into the spirit of the scholar is the mind of the Past—in whatever form, whether of literature, of art, of institutions, that mind is inscribed. Books are the best type of the influence of the past, and perhaps we shall get at the truth—learn the amount of this influence more conveniently—by considering their value alone.

The theory of books is noble. The scholar of the first age received into him the world around; brooded thereon; gave it the new arrangement of his own mind, and uttered it again. It came into him life; it went out from him truth. It came to him short-lived actions; it went out from him immortal thoughts. It came to him business; it went from him poetry. It was dead fact; now, it is quick thought. It can stand, and it can go. It now endures, it now flies, it now inspires. Precisely in proportion to the depth of mind from which it issued, so high does it soar, so long does it sing.

Or, I might say, it depends on how far the process had gone, of transmuting life into truth. In proportion to the completeness of the distillation, so will the purity and imperishableness of the product be. But none is quite perfect. As no air-pump can by any means make a perfect vacuum, so neither can any artist entirely exclude the conventional, the local, the perishable from his book, or write a book of pure thought, that shall be as efficient, in all respects, to a remote posterity, as to contemporaries, or rather to the second age. Each age, it is found, must write its own books; or rather, each generation for the next succeeding. The books of an older period will not fit this.

Yet hence arises a grave mischief. The sacredness which attaches to the act of creation, the act of thought, is transferred to the record. The poet chanting was felt to be a divine man: henceforth the chant is divine also. The writer was a just and wise spirit: henceforward it is settled the book is perfect; as love of the hero corrupts into worship of his statue. Instantly the book becomes noxious: the guide is a tyrant. The sluggish and perverted mind of the multitude, slow to open to the incursions of Reason, having once so opened, having once received this book, stands upon it, and makes an outcry if it is disparaged. Colleges are built on it. Books are written on it by thinkers, not by Man Thinking; by men of talent, that is, who start wrong, who set out from accepted dogmas, not from their own sight of principles. Meek young men grow up in libraries, believing it their duty to accept the views which

Cicero, which Locke, which Bacon, have given; forgetful that Cicero, Locke, and Bacon were only young men in libraries when they wrote these books.

Hence, instead of Man Thinking, we have the bookworm. Hence the book-learned class, who value books, as such; not as related to nature and the human constitution, but as making a sort of Third Estate with the world and the soul. Hence the restorers of readings, the emendators, the bibliomaniacs of all degrees.

Books are the best of things, well used; abused, among the worst. What is the right use? What is the one end which all means go to effect? They are for nothing but to inspire. I had better never see a book than to be warped by its attraction clean out of my own orbit, and made a satellite instead of a system. The one thing in the world, of value, is the active soul. This every man is entitled to; this every man contains within him, although in almost all men obstructed and as yet unborn. The soul active sees absolute truth and utters truth, or creates. In this action it is genius; not the privilege of here and there a favorite, but the sound estate of every man. In its essence it is progressive. The book, the college, the school of art, the institution of any kind, stop with some past utterance of genius. This is good, say they—let us hold by this. They pin me down. They look backward and not forward. But genius looks forward: the eyes of man are set in his forehead, not in his hindhead: man hopes: genius creates. Whatever talents may be, if the man create not, the pure efflux of the Deity is not his; cinders and smoke there may be, but not yet flame. There are creative manners, there are creative actions, and creative words; manners, actions, words, that is, indicative of no custom or authority, but springing spontaneous from the mind's own sense of good and fair.

On the other part, instead of being its own seer, let it receive from another mind its truth, though it were in torrents of light, without periods of solitude, inquest, and self-recovery, and a fatal disservice is done. Genius is always sufficiently the enemy of genius by over-influence. The literature of every nation bears me witness. The English dramatic poets have Shakspearized now for two hundred years.

Undoubtedly there is a right way of reading, so it be sternly subordinated. Man Thinking must not be subdued by his instruments. Books are for the scholar's idle times. When he can read God directly, the hour is too precious to be wasted in other men's transcripts of their readings. But when the intervals of darkness come, as come they must—when the sun is hid and the stars withdraw their shining—we repair to the lamps which were kindled by their ray, to guide our steps to the East again, where the dawn is. We hear, that we may speak. The Arabian proverb says, "A fig tree, looking on a fig tree, becometh fruitful."

It is remarkable, the character of the pleasure we derive from the best books. They impress us with the conviction that one nature wrote and the same reads. We read the verses of one of the great English

poets, of Chaucer, of Marvell, of Dryden, with the most modern joy—
with a pleasure, I mean, which is in great part caused by the abstraction of all *time* from their verses. There is some awe mixed with the
joy of our surprise, when this poet, who lived in some past world, two
or three hundred years ago, says that which lies close to my own soul,
that which I also had well-nigh thought and said. But for the evidence
thence afforded to the philosophical doctrine of the identity of all minds,
we should suppose some preëstablished harmony, some foresight of
souls that were to be, and some preparation of stores for their future
wants, like the fact observed in insects, who lay up food before death
for the young grub they shall never see.

I would not be hurried by any love of system, by any exaggeration
of instincts, to underrate the Book. We all know, that as the human
body can be nourished on any food, though it were boiled grass and
the broth of shoes, so the human mind can be fed by any knowledge.
And great and heroic men have existed who had almost no other information than by the printed page. I only would say that it needs a strong
head to bear that diet. One must be an inventor to read well. As the
proverb says, "He that would bring home the wealth of the Indies, must
carry out the wealth of the Indies." There is then creative reading as
well as creative writing. When the mind is braced by labor and invention, the page of whatever book we read becomes luminous with manifold allusion. Every sentence is doubly significant, and the sense of our
author is as broad as the world. We then see, what is always true, that
as the seer's hour of vision is short and rare among heavy days and
months, so is its record, perchance, the least part of his volume. The
discerning will read, in his Plato or Shakspeare, only that least part—
only the authentic utterances of the oracles; all the rest he rejects, were
it never so many times Plato's and Shakspeare's.

Of course there is a portion of reading quite indispensable to a wise
man. History and exact science he must learn by laborious reading.
Colleges, in like manner, have their indispensable office—to teach elements. But they can only highly serve us when they aim not to drill, but
to create; when they gather from far every ray of various genius to their
hospitable halls, and by the concentrated fires, set the hearts of their
youth on flame. Thought and knowledge are natures in which apparatus
and pretension avail nothing. Gowns and pecuniary foundations, though
of towns of gold, can never countervail the least sentence or syllable of
wit. Forget this, and our American colleges will recede in their public
importance, whilst they grow richer every year.

III

There goes in the world a notion that the scholar should be a
recluse, a valetudinarian—as unfit for any handiwork or public labor
as a penknife for an axe. The so-called "practical men" sneer at specu-

lative men, as if, because they speculate or *see*, they could do nothing. I have heard it said that the clergy—who are always, more universally than any other class, the scholars of their day—are addressed as women; that the rough, spontaneous conversation of men they do not hear, but only a mincing and diluted speech. They are often virtually disfranchised; and indeed there are advocates for their celibacy. As far as this is true of the studious classes, it is not just and wise. Action is with the scholar subordinate, but it is essential. Without it he is not yet man. Without it thought can never ripen into truth. Whilst the world hangs before the eye as a cloud of beauty, we cannot even see its beauty. Inaction is cowardice, but there can be no scholar without the heroic mind. The preamble of thought, the transition through which it passes from the unconscious to the conscious, is action. Only so much do I know, as I have lived. Instantly we know whose words are loaded with life, and whose not.

The world—this shadow of the soul, or *other me*—lies wide around. Its attractions are the keys which unlock my thoughts and make me acquainted with myself. I run eagerly into this resounding tumult. I grasp the hands of those next me, and take my place in the ring to suffer and to work, taught by an instinct that so shall the dumb abyss be vocal with speech. I pierce its order; I dissipate its fear; I dispose of it within the circuit of my expanding life. So much only of life as I know by experience, so much of the wilderness have I vanquished and planted, or so far have I extended my being, my dominion. I do not see how any man can afford, for the sake of his nerves and his nap, to spare any action in which he can partake. It is pearls and rubies to his discourse. Drudgery, calamity, exasperation, want, are instructors in eloquence and wisdom. The true scholar grudges every opportunity of action past by, as a loss of power. It is the raw material out of which the intellect moulds her splendid products. A strange process too, this by which experience is converted into thought, as a mulberry leaf is converted into satin. The manufacture goes forward at all hours.

The actions and events of our childhood and youth are now matters of calmest observation. They lie like fair pictures in the air. Not so with our recent actions—with the business which we now have in hand. On this we are quite unable to speculate. Our affections as yet circulate through it. We no more feel or know it than we feel the feet, or the hand, or the brain of our body. The new deed is yet a part of life—remains for a time immersed in our unconscious life. In some contemplative hour it detaches itself from the life like a ripe fruit, to become a thought of the mind. Instantly it is raised, transfigured; the corruptible has put on incorruption. Henceforth it is an object of beauty, however base its origin and neighborhood. Observe too the impossibility of antedating this act. In its grub state, it cannot fly, it cannot shine, it is a dull grub. But suddenly, without observation, the selfsame thing unfurls beautiful wings, and is an angel of wisdom. So is there no fact, no event, in our private history, which shall not, sooner or later, lose its adhesive, inert form, and astonish us by soaring from our body into the empyrean. Cradle and infancy, school and playground, the fear of boys, and dogs, and ferrules, the love of little maids and berries, and many another fact that once filled the whole sky, are gone already; friend and relative, profession and party, town and country, nation and world, must also soar and sing.

Of course, he who has put forth his total strength in fit actions has the richest return of wisdom. I will not shut myself out of this globe of action, and transplant an oak into a flowerpot, there to hunger and pine; nor trust the revenue of some single faculty, and exhaust one vein of thought, much like those Savoyards, who, getting their livelihood by carving shepherds, shepherdesses, and smoking Dutchmen, for all Europe, went out one day to the mountain to find stock, and discovered that they had whittled up the last of their pine trees. Authors we have, in numbers, who have written out their vein, and who, moved by a commendable prudence, sail for Greece or Palestine, follow the trapper into the prairie, or ramble round Algiers, to replenish their merchantable stock.

If it were only for a vocabulary, the scholar would be covetous of action. Life is our dictionary. Years are well spent in country labors; in town; in the insight into trades and manufactures; in frank intercourse with many men and women; in science; in art; to the one end of mastering in all their facts a language by which to illustrate and embody our perceptions. I learn immediately from any speaker how much he has already lived, through the poverty or the splendor of his speech. Life lies behind us as the quarry from whence we get tiles and copestones for the masonry of to-day. This is the way to learn grammar. Colleges and books only copy the language which the field and the workyard made.

But the final value of action, like that of books, and better than books, is that it is a resource. That great principle of Undulation in nature, that shows itself in the inspiring and expiring of the breath; in desire and satiety; in the ebb and flow of the sea; in day and night; in heat and cold; and, as yet more deeply ingrained in every atom and every fluid, is known to us under the name of Polarity—these "fits of easy transmission and reflection," as Newton called them, are the law of nature because they are the law of spirit.

The mind now thinks, now acts, and each fit reproduces the other. When the artist has exhausted his materials, when the fancy no longer paints, when thoughts are no longer apprehended and books are a weariness—he has always the resources to *live*. Character is higher than intellect. Thinking is the function. Living is the functionary. The stream retreats to its source. A great soul will be strong to live, as well as strong to think. Does he lack organ or medium to impart his truths? He can still fall back on this elemental force of living them. This is a total act.

Thinking is a partial act. Let the grandeur of justice shine in his affairs. Let the beauty of affection cheer his lowly roof. Those "far from fame", who dwell and act with him, will feel the force of his constitution in the doings and passages of the day better than it can be measured by any public and designed display. Time shall teach him that the scholar loses no hour which the man lives. Herein he unfolds the sacred germ of his instinct, screened from influence. What is lost in seemliness is gained in strength. Not out of those on whom systems of education have exhausted their culture, comes the helpful giant to destroy the old or to build the new, but out of unhandselled [2] savage nature; out of terrible Druids and Berserkers come at last Alfred and Shakspeare.

I hear therefore with joy whatever is beginning to be said of the dignity and necessity of labor to every citizen. There is virtue yet in the hoe and the spade, for learned as well as for unlearned hands. And labor is everywhere welcome; always we are invited to work; only be this limitation observed, that a man shall not for the sake of wider activity sacrifice any opinion to the popular judgments and modes of action.

I have now spoken of the education of the scholar by nature, by books, and by action. It remains to say somewhat of his duties.

They are such as become Man Thinking. They may all be comprised in self-trust. The office of the scholar is to cheer, to raise, and to guide men by showing them facts amidst appearances. He plies the slow, unhonored, and unpaid task of observation. Flamsteed and Herschel,[3] in their glazed observatories, may catalogue the stars with the praise of all men, and the results being splendid and useful, honor is sure. But he, in his private observatory, cataloguing obscure and nebulous stars of the human mind, which as yet no man has thought of as such—watching days and months sometimes for a few facts; correcting still his old records; must relinquish display and immediate fame. In the long period of his preparation he must betray often an ignorance and shiftlessness in popular arts, incurring the disdain of the able who shoulder him aside. Long he must stammer in his speech; often forego the living for the dead. Worse yet, he must accept—how-often!—poverty and solitude. For the ease and pleasure of treading the old road, accepting the fashions, the education, the religion of society, he takes the cross of making his own, and, of course, the self-accusation, the faint heart, the frequent uncertainty and loss of time, which are the nettles and tangling vines in the way of the self-relying and self-directed; and the state of virtual hostility in which he seems

---

[2] A rare word suggesting something like *unequipped* or *unprovided for.*

[3] John Flamsteed (1646–1719), English astronomer; Sir Frederick William Herschel (1738–1822), German astronomer, or his English son, Sir John Herschel (1792–1871), also a famous astronomer.

to stand to society, and especially to educated society. For all this loss and scorn, what offset? He is to find consolation in exercising the highest functions of human nature. He is one who raises himself from private considerations and breathes and lives on public and illustrious thoughts. He is the world's eye. He is the world's heart. He is to resist the vulgar prosperity that retrogrades ever to barbarism, by preserving and communicating heroic sentiments, noble biographies, melodious verse, and the conclusions of history. Whatsoever oracles the human heart, in all emergencies, in all solemn hours, has uttered as its commentary on the world of actions—these he shall receive and impart. And whatsoever new verdict Reason from her inviolable seat pronounces on the passing men and events of to-day—this he shall hear and promulgate.

These being his functions, it becomes him to feel all confidence in himself, and to defer never to the popular cry. He and he only knows the world. The world of any moment is the merest appearance. Some great decorum, some fetish of a government, some ephemeral trade, or war, or man, is cried up by half mankind and cried down by the other half, as if all depended on this particular up or down. The odds are that the whole question is not worth the poorest thought which the scholar has lost in listening to the controversy. Let him not quit his belief that a popgun is a popgun, though the ancient and honorable of the earth affirm it to be the crack of doom. In silence, in steadiness, in severe abstraction, let him hold by himself; add observation to observation, patient of neglect, patient of reproach, and bide his own time— happy enough if he can satisfy himself alone that this day he has seen something truly. Success treads on every right step. For the instinct is sure, that prompts him to tell his brother what he thinks. He then learns that in going down into the secrets of his own mind he has descended into the secrets of all minds. He learns that he who has mastered any law in his private thoughts, is master to that extent of all men whose language he speaks, and of all into whose language his own can be translated. The poet, in utter solitude remembering his spontaneous thoughts and recording them, is found to have recorded that which men in crowded cities find true for them also. The orator distrusts at first the fitness of his frank confessions, his want of knowledge of the persons he addresses, until he finds that he is the complement of his hearers; that they drink his words because he fulfils for them their own nature; the deeper he dives into his privatest, secretest presentiment, to his wonder he finds this is the most acceptable, most public, and universally true. The people delight in it; the better part of every man feels, This is my music; this is myself.

In self-trust all the virtues are comprehended. Free should the scholar be—free and brave. Free even to the definition of freedom, "without any hindrance that does not arise out of his own constitution." Brave; for fear is a thing which a scholar by his very function puts

behind him. Fear always springs from ignorance. It is a shame to him
if his tranquillity, amid dangerous times, arise from the presumption
that like children and women his is a protected class; or if he seek a
temporary peace by the diversion of his thoughts from politics or vexed
questions, hiding his head like an ostrich in the flowering bushes, peeping into microscopes, and turning rhymes, as a boy whistles to keep
his courage up. So is the danger a danger still; so is the fear worse.
Manlike let him turn and face it. Let him look into its eye and search
its nature, inspect its origin—see the whelping of this lion—which lies
no great way back; he will then find in himself a perfect comprehension
of its nature and extent; he will have made his hands meet on the other
side, and can henceforth defy it and pass on superior. The world is his
who can see through its pretension. What deafness, what stone-blind
custom, what overgrown error you behold is there only by sufferance—
by your sufferance. See it to be a lie, and you have already dealt it its
mortal blow.

Yes, we are the cowed—we the trustless. It is a mischievous notion
that we are come late into nature; that the world was finished a long
time ago. As the world was plastic and fluid in the hands of God, so
it is ever to so much of his attributes as we bring to it. To ignorance
and sin, it is flint. They adapt themselves to it as they may; but in
proportion as a man has any thing in him divine, the firmament flows
before him and takes his signet and form. Not he is great who can alter
matter, but he who can alter my state of mind. They are the kings of
the world who give the color of their present thought to all nature and
all art, and persuade men by the cheerful serenity of their carrying the
matter, that this thing which they do is the apple which the ages have
desired to pluck, now at last ripe, and inviting nations to the harvest.
The great man makes the great thing. Wherever Macdonald sits, there
is the head of the table. Linnæus [4] makes botany the most alluring of
studies, and wins it from the farmer and the herb-woman; Davy, chemistry; and Cuvier, fossils. [5] The day is always his who works in it with
serenity and great aims. The unstable estimates of men crowd to him
whose mind is filled with a truth, as the heaped waves of the Atlantic
follow the moon.

For this self-trust, the reason is deeper than can be fathomed—
darker than can be enlightened. I might not carry with me the feeling
of my audience in stating my own belief. But I have already shown
the ground of my hope, in adverting to the doctrine that man is one.
I believe man has been wronged; he has wronged himself. He has
almost lost the light that can lead him back to his prerogatives. Men
are become of no account. Men in history, men in the world of to-day,

[4] Carolus Linnaeus (1707–1778), Swedish botanist.
[5] Sir Humphry Davy (1778–1829), English chemist; Georges Leopold Cuvier (1769–
1832), French naturalist.

are bugs, are spawn, and are called "the mass" and "the herd." In a century, in a millennium, one or two men; that is to say, one or two approximations to the right state of every man. All the rest behold in the hero or the poet their own green and crude being—ripened; yes, and are content to be less, so *that* may attain to its full stature. What a testimony, full of grandeur, full of pity, is borne to the demands of his own nature, by the poor clansman, the poor partisan, who rejoices in the glory of his chief. The poor and the low find some amends to their immense moral capacity, for their acquiescence in a political and social inferiority. They are content to be brushed like flies from the path of a great person, so that justice shall be done by him to that common nature which it is the dearest desire of all to see enlarged and glorified. They sun themselves in the great man's light, and feel it to be their own element. They cast the dignity of man from their down-trod selves upon the shoulders of a hero, and will perish to add one drop of blood to make that great heart beat, those giant sinews combat and conquer. He lives for us, and we live in him.

Men, such as they are, very naturally seek money or power; and power because it is as good as money—the "spoils," so called, "of office." And why not? for they aspire to the highest, and this, in their sleep-walking, they dream is highest. Wake them and they shall quit the false good and leap to the true, and leave governments to clerks and desks. This revolution is to be wrought by the gradual domestication of the idea of Culture. The main enterprise of the world for splendor, for extent, is the upbuilding of a man. Here are the materials strewn along the ground. The private life of one man shall be a more illustrious monarchy, more formidable to its enemy, more sweet and serene in its influence to its friend, than any kingdom in history. For a man, rightly viewed, comprehendeth the particular natures of all men. Each philosopher, each bard, each actor has only done for me, as by a delegate, what one day I can do for myself. The books which once we valued more than the apple of the eye, we have quite exhausted. What is that but saying that we have come up with the point of view which the universal mind took through the eyes of one scribe; we have been that man, and have passed on. First, one, then another, we drain all cisterns, and waxing greater by all these supplies, we crave a better and more abundant food. The man has never lived that can feed us ever. The human mind cannot be enshrined in a person who shall set a barrier on any one side to this unbounded, unboundable empire. It is one central fire, which, flaming now out of the lips of Etna, lightens the capes of Sicily, and now out of the throat of Vesuvius, illuminates the towers and vineyards of Naples. It is one light which beams out of a thousand stars. It is one soul which animates all men.

But I have dwelt perhaps tediously upon this abstraction of the Scholar. I ought not to delay longer to add what I have to say of nearer reference to the time and to this country.

Historically, there is thought to be a difference in the ideas which predominate over successive epochs, and there are data for marking the genius of the Classic, of the Romantic, and now of the Reflective or Philosophical age. With the views I have intimated of the oneness or the identity of the mind through all individuals, I do not much dwell on these differences. In fact, I believe each individual passes through all three. The boy is a Greek; the youth, romantic; the adult, reflective. I deny not, however, that a revolution in the leading idea may be distinctly enough traced.

Our age is bewailed as the age of Introversion. Must that needs be evil? We, it seems, are critical; we are embarrassed with second thoughts; we cannot enjoy any thing for hankering to know whereof the pleasure consists; we are lined with eyes; we see with our feet; the time is infected with Hamlet's unhappiness—

Sicklied o'er with the pale cast of thought.

It is so bad then? Sight is the last thing to be pitied. Would we be blind? Do we fear lest we should outsee nature and God, and drink truth dry? I look upon the discontent of the literary class as a mere announcement of the fact that they find themselves not in the state of mind of their fathers, and regret the coming state as untried; as a boy dreads the water before he has learned that he can swim. If there is any period one would desire to be born in, is it not the age of Revolution; when the old and the new stand side by side and admit of being compared; when the energies of all men are searched by fear and by hope; when the historic glories of the old can be compensated by the rich possibilities of the new era? This time, like all times, is a very good one, if we but know what to do with it.

I read with some joy of the auspicious signs of the coming days, as they glimmer already through poetry and art, through philosophy and science, through church and state.

One of these signs is the fact that the same movement which effected the elevation of what was called the lowest class in the state, assumed in literature a very marked and as benign an aspect. Instead of the sublime and beautiful, the near, the low, the common, was explored and poetized. That which had been negligently trodden under foot by those who were harnessing and provisioning themselves for long journeys into far countries, is suddenly found to be richer than all foreign parts. The literature of the poor, the feelings of the child, the philosophy of the street, the meaning of household life, are the topics of the time. It is a great stride. It is a sign—is it not?—of new vigor when the extremities are made active, when currents of warm life run into the hands and the feet. I ask not for the great, the remote, the romantic; what is doing in Italy or Arabia; what is Greek art, or Provençal minstrelsy; I embrace the common, I explore and sit at the feet of the familiar, the low. Give me insight into to-day, and you may have the antique and future worlds. What would we really know the meaning of? The meal in the firkin; the milk in the pan; the ballad in the street; the news of the boat; the glance of the eye; the form and the gait of the body; show me the ultimate reason of these matters; show me the sublime presence of the highest spiritual cause lurking, as always it does lurk, in these suburbs and extremities of nature; let me see every trifle bristling with the polarity that ranges it instantly on an eternal law; and the shop, the plough, and the ledger referred to the like cause by which light undulates and poets sing; and the world lies no longer a dull miscellany and lumber-room, but has form and order; there is no trifle, there is no puzzle, but one design unites and animates the farthest pinnacle and the lowest trench.

This idea has inspired the genius of Goldsmith, Burns, Cowper, and, in a newer time, of Goethe, Wordsworth, and Carlyle. This idea they have differently followed and with various success. In contrast with their writing, the style of Pope, of Johnson, of Gibbon, looks cold and pedantic. This writing is blood-warm. Man is surprised to find that things near are not less beautiful and wondrous than things remote. The near explains the far. The drop is a small ocean. A man is related to all nature. This perception of the worth of the vulgar is fruitful in discoveries. Goethe, in this very thing the most modern of the moderns, has shown us, as none ever did, the genius of the ancients.

There is one man of genius who has done much for this philosophy of life, whose literary value has never yet been rightly estimated; I mean Emanuel Swedenborg.[6] The most imaginative of men, yet writing with the precision of a mathematician, he endeavored to engraft a purely philosophical Ethics on the popular Christianity of his time. Such an attempt of course must have difficulty which no genius could surmount. But he saw and showed the connection between nature and the affections of the soul. He pierced the emblematic or spiritual character of the visible, audible, tangible word. Especially did his shade-loving muse hover over and interpret the lower parts of nature; he showed the mysterious bond that allies moral evil to the foul material forms, and has given in epical parables a theory of insanity, of beasts, of unclean and fearful things.

Another sign of our times, also marked by an analogous political movement, is the new importance given to the single person. Every thing that tends to insulate the individual—to surround him with barriers of natural respect, so that each man shall feel the world is his, and man shall treat with man as a sovereign state with a sovereign state—tends to true union as well as greatness. "I learned," said the melancholy Pestalozzi,[7] "that no man in God's wide earth is either willing or able to help any other man." Help must come from the bosom

[6] Emanuel Swedenborg (1688–1772), Swedish mystical writer.
[7] Johann Pestalozzi (1746–1827), Swiss educational theorist.

alone. The scholar is that man who must take up into himself all the ability of the time, all the contributions of the past, all the hopes of the future. He must be an university of knowledges. If there be one lesson more than another which should pierce his ear, it is, The world is nothing, the man is all; in yourself is the law of all nature, and you know not yet how a globule of sap ascends; in yourself slumbers the whole of Reason; it is for you to know all; it is for you to dare all. Mr. President and Gentlemen, this confidence in the unsearched might of man belongs, by all motives, by all prophecy, by all preparation, to the American Scholar. We have listened too long to the courtly muses of Europe. The spirit of the American freeman is already suspected to be timid, imitative, tame. Public and private avarice make the air we breathe thick and fat. The scholar is decent, indolent, complaisant. See already the tragic consequence. The mind of this country, taught to aim at low objects, eats upon itself. There is no work for any but the decorous and the complaisant. Young men of the fairest promise, who begin life upon our shores, inflated by the mountain winds, shined upon by all the stars of God, find the earth below not in unison with these, but are hindered from action by the disgust which the principles on which business is managed inspire, and turn drudges, or die of disgust, some of them suicides. What is the remedy? They did not yet see, and thousands of young men as hopeful now crowding to the barriers for the career do not yet see, that if the single man plant himself indomitably on his instincts, and there abide, the huge world will come round to him. Patience—patience; with the shades of all the good and great for company; and for solace the perspective of your own infinite life; and for work the study and the communication of principles, the making those instincts prevalent, the conversion of the world. Is it not the chief disgrace in the world, not to be an unit; not to be reckoned one character; not to yield that peculiar fruit which each man was created to bear, but to be reckoned in the gross, in the hundred, or the thousand, of the party, the section, to which we belong; and our opinion predicted geographically, as the north, or the south? Not so, brothers and friends—please God, ours shall not be so. We will walk on our own feet; we will work with our own hands; we will speak our own minds. The study of letters shall be no longer a name for pity, for doubt, and for sensual indulgence. The dread of man and the love of man shall be a wall of defence and a wreath of joy around all. A nation of men will for the first time exist, because each believes himself inspired by the Divine Soul which also inspires all men.

The Poet (1844)[1]

A moody child and wildly wise
Pursued the game with joyful eyes,
Which chose, like meteors, their way,
And rived the dark with private ray:
They overleapt the horizon's edge,
Searched with Apollo's privilege;
Through man, and woman, and sea, and star
Saw the dance of nature forward far;
Through worlds, and races, and terms, and times
Saw musical order, and pairing rhymes.

Olympian bards who sung
  Divine ideas below,
Which always find us young,
  And always keep us so.[2]

Those who are esteemed umpires of taste are often persons who have acquired some knowledge of admired pictures or sculptures, and have an inclination for whatever is elegant; but if you inquire whether they are beautiful souls, and whether their own acts are like fair pictures, you learn that they are selfish and sensual. Their cultivation is local, as if you should rub a log of dry wood in one spot to produce fire, all the rest remaining cold. Their knowledge of the fine arts is some study of rules and particulars, or some limited judgment of color or form, which is exercised for amusement or for show. It is a proof of the shallowness of the doctrine of beauty as it lies in the minds of our amateurs, that men seem to have lost the perception of the instant dependence of form upon soul. There is no doctrine of forms in our philosophy. We were put into our bodies, as fire is put into a pan to be carried about; but there is no accurate adjustment between the spirit and the organ, much less is the latter the germination of the former. So in regard to other forms, the intellectual men do not believe in any essential dependence of the material world on thought and volition. Theologians think it a pretty air-castle to talk of the spiritual meaning of a ship or a cloud, of a city or a contract, but they prefer to come again to the solid ground of historical evidence; and even the poets are contented with a civil and conformed manner of living, and to write

[1] This powerful and extremely influential essay, with its stress on the creative imagination and the poet's "dream power," as well as its significant anticipations of aspects of literary symbolism, is Emerson's main esthetic statement. It is also the central statement of literary romanticism in American criticism. The essay is drawn from a series of lectures Emerson gave in 1841 to 1842, though by the time of its publication it was thoroughly reworked.

[2] The poem is Emerson's own.

poems from the fancy, at a safe distance from their own experience. But the highest minds of the world have never ceased to explore the double meaning, or shall I say the quadruple or the centuple of much more manifold meaning, of every sensuous fact; Orpheus, Empedocles, Heraclitus, Plato, Plutarch, Dante, Swedenborg,[3] and the masters of sculpture, picture and poetry. For we are not pans and barrows, nor ever porters of the fire and torch-bearers, but children of the fire, made of it, and only the same divinity transmuted and at two or three removes, when we know least about it. And this hidden truth, that the fountains whence all this river of Time and its creatures floweth are intrinsically ideal and beautiful, draws us to the consideration of the nature and functions of the Poet, or the man of Beauty; to the means and materials he uses, and to the general aspect of the art in the present time.

The breadth of the problem is great, for the poet is representative. He stands among partial men for the complete man, and apprises us not of his wealth, but of the common wealth. The young man reveres men of genius, because, to speak truly, they are more himself than he is. They receive of the soul as he also receives, but they more. Nature enhances her beauty, to the eye of loving men, from their belief that the poet is beholding her shows at the same time. He is isolated among his contemporaries by truth and by his art, but with this consolation in his pursuits, that they will draw all men sooner or later. For all men live by truth and stand in need of expression. In love, in art, in avarice, in politics, in labor, in games, we study to utter our painful secret. The man is only half himself, the other half is his expression.

Notwithstanding this necessity to be published, adequate expression is rare. I know not how it is that we need an interpreter, but the great majority of men seem to be minors, who have not yet come into possession of their own, or mutes, who cannot report the conversation they have had with nature. There is no man who does not anticipate a supersensual utility in the sun and stars, earth and water. These stand and wait to render him a peculiar service. But there is some obstruction or some excess of phlegm in our constitution, which does not suffer them to yield the due effect. Too feeble fall the impressions of nature on us to make us artists. Every touch should thrill. Every man should be so much an artist that he could report in conversation what had befallen him. Yet, in our experience, the rays or appulses have sufficient force to arrive at the senses, but not enough to reach the quick and compel the reproduction of themselves in speech. The poet is the person in

[3] Orpheus, a legendary Greek figure, whose lyre was supposed to charm animals; Empedocles, a Greek philosopher who claimed prophetic powers; Heraclitus, a Greek philosopher; Swedenborg, a Swedish mystic discussed in the final section of Emerson's essay, "The American Scholar." What all these figures seem to have in common is that they saw the material world in terms of spiritual meanings and signs.

whom these powers are in balance, the man without impediment, who sees and handles that which others dream of, traverses the whole scale of experience, and is representative of man, in virtue of being the largest power to receive and to impart.

For the universe has three children, born at one time, which re-appear under different names in every system of thought, whether they be called cause, operation and effect; or, more poetically, Jove, Pluto, Neptune; or, theologically, the Father, the Spirit and the Son; but which we will call here the Knower, the Doer and the Sayer. These stand respectively for the love of truth, for the love of good, and for the love of beauty. These three are equal. Each is that which he is, essentially, so that he cannot be surmounted or analyzed, and each of these three has the power of the others latent in him and his own, patent.

The poet is the sayer, the namer, and represents beauty. He is a sovereign, and stands on the center. For the world is not painted or adorned, but is from the beginning beautiful; and God has not made some beautiful things, but Beauty is the creator of the universe. There-fore the poet is not any permissive potentate, but is emperor in his own right. Criticism is infested with a cant of materialism, which assumes that manual skill and activity is the first merit of all men, and dis-parages such as say and do not, overlooking the fact that some men, namely poets, are natural sayers, sent into the world to the end of expression, and confounds them with those whose province is action but who quit it to imitate the sayers. But Homer's words are as costly and admirable to Homer as Agamemnon's victories are to Agamemnon. The poet does not wait for the hero or the sage, but, as they act and think primarily, so he writes primarily what will and must be spoken, reckoning the others, though primaries also, yet, in respect to him, secondaries and servants; as sitters or models in the studio of a painter, or as assistants who bring building-materials to an architect.

For poetry was all written before time was, and whenever we are so finely organized that we can penetrate into that region where the air is music, we hear those primal warblings and attempt to write them down, but we lose ever and anon a word or a verse and substitute some-thing of our own, and thus miswrite the poem. The men of more deli-cate ear write down these cadences more faithfully, and these tran-scripts, though imperfect, become the songs of the nations. For nature is as truly beautiful as it is good, or as it is reasonable, and must as much appear as it must be done, or be known. Words and deeds are quite indifferent modes of the divine energy. Words are also actions, and actions are a kind of words.

The sign and credentials of the poet are that he announces that which no man foretold. He is the true and only doctor; [4] he knows and tells; he is the only teller of news, for he was present and privy to the

---

[4] That is, teacher.

appearance which he describes. He is a beholder of ideas and an utterer of the necessity and causal. For we do not speak now of men of poetical talents, or of industry and skill in meter, but of the true poet. I took part in a conversation the other day concerning a recent writer of lyrics,[5] a man of subtle mind, whose head appeared to be a music-box of delicate tunes and rhythms, and whose skill and command of language we could not sufficiently praise. But when the question arose whether he was not only a lyrist but a poet, we were obliged to confess that he is plainly a contemporary, not an eternal man. He does not stand out of our low limitations, like a Chimborazo[6] under the line, running up from a torrid base through all the climates of the globe, with belts of the herbage of every latitude on its high and mottled sides; but this genius is the landscape-garden of a modern house, adorned with fountains and statues, with well-bred men and women standing and sitting in the walks and terraces. We hear, through all the varied music, the ground-tone of conventional life. Our poets are men of talents who sing, and not the children of music. The argument is secondary, the finish of the verses is primary.

For it is not meters, but a meter-making argument that makes a poem,—a thought so passionate and alive that like the spirit of a plant or an animal it has an architecture of its own, and adorns nature with a new thing. The thought and the form are equal in the order of time, but in the order of genesis the thought is prior to the form. The poet has a new thought; he has a whole new experience to unfold; he will tell us how it was with him, and all men will be the richer in his fortune. For the experience of each new age requires a new confession, and the world seems always waiting for its poet. I remember when I was young how much I was moved one morning by tidings that genius had appeared in a youth who sat near me at table. He had left his work and gone rambling none knew whither, and had written hundreds of lines, but could not tell whether that which was in him was therein told; he could tell nothing but that all was changed,—man, beast, heaven, earth and sea. How gladly we listened! how credulous! Society seemed to be compromised. We sat in the aurora of a sunrise which was to put out all the stars. Boston seemed to be at twice the distance it had the night before, or was much farther than that. Rome,—what was Rome? Plutarch and Shakespeare were in the yellow leaf,[7] and Homer no more should be heard of. It is much to know that poetry has been written this very day, under this very roof, by your side. What! that wonderful spirit has not expired! These stony moments are still

[5] Apparently Tennyson.

[6] A mountain in Ecuador.

[7] An echo of *Macbeth*, 5:3, 22–23: "My way of life is fall'n into the sere, the yellow leaf."

sparkling and animated! I had fancied that the oracles were all silent, and nature had spent her fires; and behold! all night, from every pore, these fine auroras have been streaming. Every one has some interest in the advent of the poet, and no one knows how much it may concern him. We know that the secret of the world is profound, but who or what shall be our interpreter, we know not. A mountain ramble, a new style of face, a new person, may put the key into our hands. Of course the value of genius to us is in the veracity of its report. Talent may frolic and juggle; genius realizes and adds. Mankind in good earnest have availed so far in understanding themselves and their work, that the foremost watchman on the peak announces his news. It is the truest word ever spoken, and the phrase will be the fittest, most musical, and the unerring voice of the world for that time.

All that we call sacred history attests that the birth of a poet is the principal event in chronology. Man, never so often deceived, still watches for the arrival of a brother who can hold him steady to a truth until he has made it his own. With what joy I begin to read a poem which I confide in as an inspiration! And now my chains are to be broken; I shall mount above these clouds and opaque airs in which I live,—opaque, though they seem transparent,—and from the heaven of truth I shall see and comprehend my relations. That will reconcile me to life and renovate nature, to see trifles animated by a tendency, and to know what I am doing. Life will no more be a noise; now I shall see men and women, and know the signs by which they may be discerned from fools and satans. This day shall be better than my birthday: then I became an animal; now I am invited into the science of the real. Such is the hope, but the fruition is postponed. Oftener it falls that this winged man, who will carry me into the heaven, whirls me into mists, then leaps and frisks about with me as it were from cloud to cloud, still affirming that he is bound heavenward; and I, being myself a novice, am slow in perceiving that he does not know the way into the heavens, and is merely bent that I should admire his skill to rise like a fowl or a flying fish, a little way from the ground or the water; but the all-piercing, all-feeding and ocular air of heaven that man shall never inhabit. I tumble down again soon into my old nooks, and lead the life of exaggerations as before, and have lost my faith in the possibility of any guide who can lead me thither where I would be.

But, leaving these victims of vanity, let us, with new hope, observe how nature, by worthier impulses, has insured the poet's fidelity to his office of announcement and affirming, namely by the beauty of things, which becomes a new and higher beauty when expressed. Nature offers all her creatures to him as a picture-language. Being used as a type, a second wonderful value appears in the object, far better than its old value; as the carpenter's stretched cord, if you hold your ear close enough, is musical in the breeze. "Things more excellent than every image," says Jamblichus,[8] "are expressed through images." Things admit of being used as symbols because nature is a symbol, in the whole, and in every part. Every line we can draw in the sand has expression; and there is no body without its spirit or genius. All form is an effect of character; all condition, of the quality of the life; all harmony, of health; and for this reason a perception of beauty should be sympathetic, or proper only to the good. The beautiful rests on the foundations of the necessary. The soul makes the body, as the wise Spenser teaches: —

So every spirit, as it is more pure,
And hath in it the more of heavenly light,
So it the fairer body doth procure
To habit in, and it more fairly dight,
With cheerful grace and amiable sight.
For, of the soul, the body form doth take,
For soul is form, and doth the body make.[9]

Here we find ourselves suddenly not in a critical speculation but in a holy place, and should go very warily and reverently. We stand before the secret of the world, there where Being passes into Appearance and Unity into Variety.

The Universe is the externization of the soul. Wherever the life is, that bursts into appearance around it. Our science is sensual,[10] and therefore superficial. The earth and the heavenly bodies, physics and chemistry, we sensually treat, as if they were self-existent; but these are the retinue of that Being we have. "The mighty heaven," said Proclus,[11] "exhibits, in its transfigurations, clear images of the splendor of intellectual perceptions; being moved in conjunction with the unapparent periods of intellectual natures." Therefore science always goes abreast with the just elevation of the man, keeping step with religion and metaphysics; or the state of science is an index of our self-knowledge. Since every thing in nature answers to a moral power, if any phenomenon remains brute and dark it is because the corresponding faculty in the observer is not yet active.

No wonder then, if these waters be so deep, that we hover over them with a religious regard. The beauty of the fable proves the importance of the sense; to the poet, and to all others; or, if you please, every man is so far a poet as to be susceptible of these enchantments of nature; for all men have the thoughts whereof the universe is the celebration. I find that the fascination resides in the symbol. Who loves nature? Who does not? Is it only poets, and men of leisure and cultiva-

---

[8] A neoplatonic philosopher (fourth century A.D.).

[9] Lines 127–133 from "An Hymn in Honor of Beautie" by Edmund Spencer.

[10] Meaning materialistic, naturalistic.

[11] A neoplatonic philosopher (fifth century A.D.).

tion, who live with her? No; but also hunters, farmers, grooms and butchers, though they express their affection in their choice of life and not in their choice of words. The writer wonders what the coachman or the hunter values in riding, in horses and dogs. It is not superficial qualities. When you talk with him he holds these at as slight a rate as you. His worship is sympathetic; he has no definitions, but he is commanded in nature by the living power which he feels to be there present. No imitation or playing of these things would content him; he loves the earnest of the north wind, of rain, of stone and wood and iron. A beauty not explicable is dearer than a beauty which we can see to the end of. It is nature the symbol, nature certifying the supernatural, body overflowed by life which he worships with coarse but sincere rites.

The inwardness and mystery of this attachment drive men of every class to the use of emblems. The schools of poets and philosophers are not more intoxicated with their symbols than the populace with theirs. In our political parties, compute the power of badges and emblems. See the great ball [12] which they roll from Baltimore to Bunker Hill! In the political processions, Lowell goes in a loom, and Lynn in a shoe, and Salem in a ship.[13] Witness the cider-barrel, the log-cabin, the hickory-stick, the palmetto, and all the cognizances of party.[14] See the power of national emblems. Some stars, lilies, leopards, a crescent, a lion, an eagle, or other figure which came into credit God knows how, on an old rag of bunting, blowing in the wind on a fort at the ends of the earth, shall make the blood tingle under the rudest or the most conventional exterior. The people fancy they hate poetry, and they are all poets and mystics!

Beyond this universality of the symbolic language, we are apprised of the divineness of this superior use of things, whereby the world is a temple whose walls are covered with emblems, pictures and commandments of the Deity,—in this, that there is no fact in nature which does not carry the whole sense of nature; and the distinctions which we make in events and in affairs, of low and high, honest and base, disappear when nature is used as a symbol. Thought makes everything fit for use. The vocabulary of an omniscient man would embrace words and images excluded from polite conversation. What would be base, or even obscene, to the obscene, becomes illustrious, spoken in a new connection of thought. The piety of the Hebrew prophets purges their grossness. The circumcision is an example of the power of poetry to raise the low and offensive. Small and mean things serve as well as great

---

[12] In the presidential election of 1840, these were used by the Whigs in campaigning for Harrison.

[13] Three cities in Massachusetts; Lowell, known for textile industry; Lynn, for shoe factories; and Salem, for shipping.

[14] The cider barrel and the log cabin were used by the Whigs as political symbols; the hickory stick and the palmetto were used by the Democrats.

symbols. The meaner the type by which a law is expressed, the more
pungent it is, and the more lasting in the memories of men; just as we
choose the smallest box or case in which any needful utensil can be
carried. Bare lists of words are found suggestive to an imaginative and
excited mind, as it is related of Lord Chatham[15] that he was accustomed to read in Bailey's Dictionary when he was preparing to speak
in Parliament. The poorest experience is rich enough for all the purposes of expressing thought. Why covet a knowledge of new facts? Day
and night, house and garden, a few books, a few actions, serve us as
well as would all trades and all spectacles. We are far from having
exhausted the significance of the few symbols we use. We can come to
use them yet with a terrible simplicity. It does not need that a poem
should be long. Every word was once a poem. Every new relation is a
new word. Also we use defects and deformities to a sacred purpose, so
expressing our sense that the evils of the world are such only to the
evil eye. In the old mythology, mythologists observe, defects are ascribed
to divine natures, as lameness to Vulcan, blindness to Cupid, and the
like,—to signify exuberances.[16]

For as it is dislocation and detachment from the life of God that
makes things ugly, the poet, who re-attaches things to nature and the
Whole,—re-attaching even artificial things and violation of nature, to
nature, by a deeper insight,—disposes very easily of the most disagreeable facts. Readers of poetry see the factory-village and the railway,
and fancy that the poetry of the landscape is broken up by these; for
these works of art are not yet consecrated in their reading; but the poet
sees them fall within the great Order not less than the beehive or the
spider's geometrical web. Nature adopts them very fast into her vital
circles, and the gliding train of cars she loves like her own. Besides, in
a centered mind, it signifies nothing how many mechanical inventions
you exhibit. Though you add millions, and never so surprising, the fact
of mechanics has not gained a grain's weight. The spiritual fact remains
unalterable, by many or by few particulars; as no mountain is of any
appreciable height to break the curve of the sphere. A shrewd country-
boy goes to the city for the first time, and the complacent citizen is not
satisfied with his little wonder. It is not that he does not see all the fine
houses and know that he never saw such before, but he disposes of
them as easily as the poet finds place for the railway. The chief value
of the new fact is to enhance the great and constant fact of Life, which
can dwarf any and every circumstance, and to which the belt of
wampum and the commerce of America are alike.

The world being thus put under the mind for verb and noun, the
poet is he who can articulate it. For though life is great, and fascinates
and absorbs; and though all men are intelligent of the symbols through

---

[15] William Pitt (1708–1778), English statesman, famous as orator.
[16] Great abundance.

which it is named; yet they cannot originally use them. We are symbols and inhabit symbols; workmen, work, and tools, words and things, birth and death, all are emblems; but we sympathize with the symbols, and being infatuated with the economical uses of things, we do not know that they are thoughts. The poet, by an ulterior intellectual perception, gives them a power which makes their old use forgotten, and puts eyes and a tongue into every dumb and inanimate object. He perceives the independence of the thought on the symbol, the stability of the thought, the accidency [17] and fugacity [18] of the symbol. As the eyes of Lyncaeus [19] were said to see through the earth, so the poet turns the world to glass, and shows us all things in their right series and procession. For through that better perception he stands one step nearer to things, and sees the flowing or metamorphosis; perceives that thought is multiform; that within the form of every creature is a force compelling it to ascend into a higher form; and following with his eyes the life, uses the forms which express that life, and so his speech flows with the flowing of nature. All the facts of the animal economy, sex, nutriment, gestation, birth, growth, are symbols of the passage of the world into the soul of man, to suffer there a change and reappear a new and higher fact. He uses forms according to the life, and not according to the form. This is true science. The poet alone knows astronomy, chemistry, vegetation and animation, for he does not stop at these facts, but employs them as signs. He knows why the plain or meadow of space was strown with these flowers we call suns and moons and stars; why the great deep is adorned with animals, with men, and gods; for in every word he speaks he rides on them as the horses of thought.

By virtue of this science the poet is the Namer or Language-maker, naming things sometimes after their appearance, sometimes after their essence, and giving to every one its own name and not another's, thereby rejoicing the intellect, which delights in detachment or boundary. The poets made all the words, and therefore language is the archives of history, and, if we must say it, a sort of tomb of the muses. For though the origin of most of our words is forgotten, each word was at first a stroke of genius, and obtained currency because for the moment it symbolized the world to the first speaker and to the hearer. The etymologist finds the deadest word to have been once a brilliant picture. Language is fossil poetry. As the limestone of the continent consists of infinite masses of the shells of animalcules, so language is made up of images or tropes, which now, in their secondary use, have long ceased to remind us of their poetic origin. But the poet names the thing because he sees it, or comes one step nearer to it than any other. This expression or naming is not art, but a second nature, grown out of the first,

[17] Of an accidental character.
[18] Instability.
[19] The most sharp-sighted of the Argonauts in Greek mythology.

as a leaf out of a tree. What we call nature is a certain self-regulated motion or change; and nature does all things by her own hands, and does not leave another to baptize her but baptizes herself; and this through the metamorphosis again. I remember that a certain poet[20] described it to me thus: —

Genius is the activity which repairs the decays of things, whether wholly or partly of a material and finite kind. Nature, through all her kingdoms, insures herself. Nobody cares for planting the poor fungus; so she shakes down from the gills of one agaric countless spores, any one of which, being preserved, transmits new billions of spores tomorrow or next day. The new agaric of this hour has a chance which the old one had not. This atom of seed is thrown into a new place, not subject to the accidents which destroyed its parent two rods off. She makes a man; and having brought him to ripe age, she will no longer run the risk of losing this wonder at a blow, but she detaches from him a new self, that the kind may be safe from accidents to which the individual is exposed. So when the soul of the poet has come to ripeness of thought, she detaches and sends away from it its poems or songs,—a fearless, sleepless, deathless progeny, which is not exposed to the accidents of the weary kingdom of time; a fearless, vivacious offspring, clad with wings (such was the virtue of the soul out of which they came) which carry them fast and far, and infix them irrecoverably into the hearts of men. These wings are the beauty of the poet's soul. The songs, thus flying immortal from their mortal parent, are pursued by clamorous flights of censures, which swarm in far greater numbers and threaten to devour them; but these last are not winged. At the end of a very short leap they fall plump down and rot, having received from the souls out of which they came no beautiful wings. But the melodies of the poet ascend and leap and pierce into the deeps of infinite time.

So far the bard taught me, using his freer speech. But nature has a higher end, in the production of new individuals, than security, namely *ascension*, or the passage of the soul into higher forms. I knew in my younger days the sculptor who made the statue of the youth which stands in the public garden. He was, as I remember, unable to tell directly what made him happy or unhappy, but by wonderful indirections he could tell. He rose one day, according to his habit, before the dawn, and saw the morning break, grand as the eternity out of which it came, and for many days after, he strove to express this tranquillity, and lo! his chisel had fashioned out of marble the form of a beautiful youth, Phosphorus,[21] whose aspect is such that it said all persons who look on it become silent. The poet also resigns himself to his mood, and that thought which agitated him is expressed, but *alter idem*,[22] in a manner totally new. The expression is organic, or the new

[20] A self-masquerade; Emerson himself.
[21] Greek; the morning star.
[22] Latin; "the same, yet different."

type which things themselves take when liberated. As, in the sun, objects paint their images on the retina of the eye, so they, sharing the aspiration of the whole universe, tend to paint a far more delicate copy of their essence in his mind. Like the metamorphosis of things into higher organic forms is their change into melodies. Over everything stands its daemon or soul, and, as the form of the thing is reflected by the eye, so the soul of the thing is reflected by a melody. The sea, the mountain-ridge, Niagara, and every flower-bed, pre-exist, or super-exist, in pre-cantations,[23] which sail like odors in the air, and when any man goes by with an ear sufficiently fine, he overhears them and endeavors to write down the notes without diluting or depraving them. And herein is the legitimation of criticism, in the mind's faith that the poems are a corrupt version of some text in nature with which they ought to be made to tally. A rhyme in one of our sonnets should not be less pleasing than the iterated nodes of a seashell, or the resembling difference of a group of flowers. The pairing of the birds is an idyl, not tedious as our idyls are; a tempest is a rough ode, without falsehood or rant; a summer, with its harvest sown, reaped and stored, is an epic song, subordinating how many admirably executed parts. Why should not the symmetry and truth that modulate these, glide into our spirits, and we participate the invention of nature?

This insight, which expresses itself by what is called Imagination, is a very high sort of seeing, which does not come by study, but by the intellect being where and what it sees; by sharing the path or circuit of things through forms, and so making them translucid to others. The path of things is silent. Will they suffer a speaker to go with them? A spy they will not suffer; a lover, a poet, is the transcendency of their own nature,—him they will suffer. The condition of true naming, on the poet's part, is his resigning himself to the divine *aura* which breathes through forms, and accompanying that.

It is a secret which every intellectual man quickly learns, that beyond the energy of his possessed and conscious intellect he is capable of a new energy (as of an intellect doubled on itself), by abandonment to the nature of things; that beside his privacy of power as an individual man, there is a great public power on which he can draw, by unlocking, at all risks, his human doors, and suffering the ethereal tides to roll and circulate through him; then he is caught up into the life of the Universe, his speech is thunder, his thought is law, and his words are universally intelligible as the plants and animals. The poet knows that he speaks adequately then only when he speaks somewhat wildly, or "with the flower of the mind"; not with the intellect used as an organ, but with the intellect released from all service and suffered to take its direction from its celestial life; or as the ancients were wont to express themselves, not with intellect alone but with the intellect inebriated by

[23] Prophetic incantations.

nectar. As the traveler who has lost his way throws his reins on his horse's neck and trusts to the instinct of the animal to find his road, so must we do with the divine animal who carries us through this world. For if in any manner we can stimulate this instinct, new passages are opened for us into nature; the mind flows into and through things hardest and highest, and the metamorphosis is possible.

This is the reason why bards love wine, mead, narcotics, coffee, tea, opium, the fumes of sandalwood and tobacco, or whatever other procurers of animal exhilaration. All men avail themselves of such means as they can, to add this extraordinary power to their normal powers; and to this end they prize conversation, music, pictures, sculpture, dancing, theaters, traveling, war, mobs, fires, gaming, politics or love, or science, or animal intoxication,—which are several coarser or finer *quasi*-mechanical substitutes for the true nectar, which is the ravishment of the intellect by coming nearer to the fact. These are auxiliaries to the centrifugal tendency of a man, to his passage out into free space, and they help him to escape the custody of that body in which he is pent up, and of that jail-yard of individual relations in which he is enclosed. Hence a great number of such as were professionally expressers of Beauty, as painters, poets, musicians and actors, have been more than others wont to lead a life of pleasure and indulgence; all but the few who received the true nectar; and, as it was a spurious mode of attaining freedom, as it was an emancipation not into the heavens but into the freedom of baser places, they were punished for that advantage they won, by a dissipation and deterioration. But never can any advantage be taken of nature by a trick. The spirit of the world, the great calm presence of the Creator, comes not forth to the sorceries of opium or of wine. The sublime vision comes to the pure and simple soul in a clean and chaste body. That is not an inspiration, which we owe to narcotics, but some counterfeit excitement and fury. Milton says [24] that the lyric poet may drink wine and live generously, but the epic poet, he who shall sing of the gods and their descent unto men, must drink water out of a wooden bowl. For poetry is not "Devil's wine," but God's wine. It is with this as it is with toys. We fill the hands and nurseries of our children with all manner of dolls, drums and horses; withdrawing their eyes from the plain face and sufficing objects of nature, the sun and moon, the animals, the water and stones, which should be their toys. So the poet's habit of living should be set on a key so low that the common influences should delight him. His cheerfulness should be the gift of the sunlight; the air should suffice for his inspiration, and he should be tipsy with water. That spirit which suffices quiet hearts, which seems to come forth to such from every dry knoll of sere grass, from every pine stump and half-imbedded stone on which the

[24] In *Elegia VI*, a Latin poem.

dull March sun shines, comes forth to the poor and hungry, and such as are of simple taste. If thou fill thy brain with Boston and New York, with fashion and covetousness, and wilt stimulate thy jaded senses with wine and French coffee, thou shalt find no radiance of wisdom in the lonely waste of the pine woods.

If the imagination intoxicates the poet, it is not inactive in other men. The metamorphosis excites in the beholder an emotion of joy. The use of symbols has a certain power of emancipation and exhilaration for all men. We seem to be touched by a wand which makes us dance and run about happily, like children. We are like persons who come out of a cave or cellar into the open air. This is the effect on us of tropes, fables, oracles and all poetic forms. Poets are thus liberating gods. Men have really got a new sense, and found within their world another world, or nest of worlds; for, the metamorphosis once seen, we divine that it does not stop. I will not now consider how much this makes the charm of algebra and the mathematics, which also have their tropes, but it is felt in every definition; as when Aristotle defines *space* to be an immovable vessel in which things are contained;—or when Plato defines a *line* to be a flowing point; or *figure* to be a bound of solid; and many the like. What a joyful sense of freedom we have when Vitruvius [25] announces the old opinion of artists that no architect can build any house well who does not know something of anatomy. When Socrates, in Charmides,[26] tells us that the soul is cured of its maladies by certain incantations, and that these incantations are beautiful reasons, from which temperance is generated in souls; when Plato calls the world an animal, and Timaeus [27] affirms that the plants also are animals; or affirms a man to be a heavenly tree, growing with his root, which is his head, upward; and, as George Chapman, following him, writes,

So in our tree of man whose nervie root
Springs in his top;—

when Orpheus speaks of hoariness as "that white flower which marks extreme old age"; when Proclus calls the universe the statue of the intellect; when Chaucer, in his praise of "Gentilesse," compares good blood in mean condition to fire, which, though carried to the darkest house betwixt this and the mount of Caucasus, will yet hold its natural office and burn as bright as if twenty thousand men did it behold; when John saw, in the Apocalypse, the ruin of the world through evil, and the stars fall from heaven as the fig tree casteth her untimely fruit; when Aesop reports the whole catalogue of common daily rela-

[25] A Roman author (first century B.C.).
[26] A dialog by Plato.
[27] A dialog by Plato.

tions through the masquerade of birds and beasts; [28]—we take the cheerful hint of the immortality of our essence and its versatile habit and escapes, as when the gypsies say of themselves "it is in vain to hang them, they cannot die."

The poets are thus liberating gods. The ancient British bards had for the title of their order, "Those who are free throughout the world." They are free, and they make free. An imaginative book renders us much more service at first, by stimulating us through its tropes, than afterward when we arrive at the precise sense of the author. I think nothing is of any value in books excepting the transcendental and extraordinary. If a man is inflamed and carried away by his thought, to that degree that he forgets the authors and the public and heeds only this one dream which holds him like an insanity, let me read his paper, and you may have all the arguments and histories and criticism. All the value which attaches to Pythagoras, Paracelsus, Cornelius Agrippa, Cardan, Kepler, Swedenborg, Schelling, Oken,[29] or any other who introduces questionable facts into his cosmogony, as angels, devils, magic, astrology, palmistry, mesmerism, and so on, is the certificate we have of departure from routine, and that here is a new witness. That also is the best success in conversation, the magic of liberty, which puts the world like a ball in our hands. How cheap even the liberty then seems; how mean to study, when an emotion communicates to the intellect the power to sap and upheave nature; how great the perspective! nations, times, systems, enter and disappear like threads in tapestry of large figure and many colors; dream delivers us to dream, and while the drunkenness lasts we will sell our bed, our philosophy, our religion, in our opulence.

There is good reason why we should prize this liberation. The fate of the poor shepherd, who, blinded and lost in the snowstorm, perishes in a drift within a few feet of his cottage door, is an emblem of the state of man. On the brink of the waters of life and truth, we are miserably dying. The inaccessibleness of every thought but that we are in, is wonderful. What if you come near to it; you are as remote when you are nearest as when you are farthest. Every thought is also a prison; every heaven is also a prison. Therefore we love the poet, the inventor, who in any form, whether in an ode or in an action or in looks and behavior, has yielded us a new thought. He unlocks our chains and admits us to a new scene.

This emancipation is dear to all men, and the power to impart it, as it must come from greater depth and scope of thought, is a measure

[28] A string of quotations and references: "So in our tree . . . ," from the dedication of Chapman's *Homer;* Orpheus, legendary Greek poet; Proclus, fifth century neoplatonist; Chaucer, in the Wife of Bath's Tale, lines 283–289; John, in Rev. 4:13. [29] This somewhat whimsical list brings together philosophers, scientists, alchemists, and quacks.

of intellect. Therefore all books of the imagination endure, all which ascend to that truth that the winter sees nature beneath him, and uses it as his exponent. Every verse or sentence possessing this virtue will take care of its own immortality. The religions of the world are the ejaculations of a few imaginative men.

But the quality of the imagination is to flow, and not to freeze. The poet did not stop at the color or the form, but read their meaning; neither may he rest in this meaning, but he makes the same objects exponents of his new thought. Here is the difference betwixt the poet and the mystic, that the last nails a symbol to one sense, which was a true sense for a moment, but soon becomes old and false. For all symbols are fluxional; all language is vehicular and transitive, and is good, as ferries and horses are, for conveyance, not as farms and houses are, for homestead. Mysticism consists in the mistake of an accidental and individual symbol for an universal one. The morning-redness happens to be the favorite meteor to the eyes of Jacob Behmen,[30] and comes to stand to him for truth and faith; and, he believes, should stand for the same realities to every reader. But the first reader prefers as naturally the symbol of a mother and child, or a gardener and his bulb, or a jeweler polishing a gem. Either of these, or of a myriad more, are equally good to the person to whom they are significant. Only they must be held lightly, and be very willingly translated into the equivalent terms which others use. And the mystic must be steadily told,—All that you say is just as true without the tedious use of that symbol as with it. Let us have a little algebra, instead of this trite rhetoric,— universal signs, instead of these village symbols,—and we shall both be gainers. The history of hierarchies seems to show that all religious error consisted in making the symbol too stark and solid, and was at last nothing but an excess of the organ of language.

Swedenborg, of all men in the recent ages, stands eminently for the translator of nature into thought. I do not know the man in history to whom things stood so uniformly for words. Before him the metamorphosis continually plays. Everything on which his eye rests, obeys the impulses of moral nature. The figs become grapes whilst he eats them. When some of his angels affirmed a truth, the laurel twig which they held blossomed in their hands. The noise which at a distance appeared like gnashing and thumping, on coming nearer was found to be the voice of disputants. The men in one of his visions, seen in heavenly light, appeared like dragons, and seemed in darkness; but to each other they appeared as men, and when the light from heaven shone into their cabin, they complained of the darkness, and were compelled to shut the window that they might see.

There was this perception in him which makes the poet or seer an

---

[30] A German mystic (1575–1624), from whom Emerson might claim an intellectual line of descent.

object of awe and terror, namely that the same man or society of men
may wear one aspect to themselves and their companions, and a different aspect to higher intelligences. Certain priests, whom he describes
as conversing very learnedly together, appeared to the children who
were at some distance, like dead horses; and many the like misappear-
ances. And instantly the mind inquires whether these fishes under the
bridge, yonder oxen in the pasture, those dogs in the yard, are immutably fishes, oxen and dogs, or only so appear to me, and perchance
to themselves appear upright men; and whether I appear as a man to
all eyes. The Brahmins and Pythagoras propounded the same question,
and if any poet has witnessed the transformation he doubtless found
it in harmony with various experiences. We have all seen changes as
considerable in wheat and caterpillars. He is the poet and shall draw
us with love and terror, who sees through the flowing vest the firm
nature, and can declare it.

I look in vain for the poet whom I describe. We do not wish sufficient plainness or sufficient profoundness address ourselves to life, nor
dare we chaunt our own times and social circumstance. If we filled the
day with bravery, we should not shrink from celebrating it. Time and
nature yield us many gifts, but not yet the timely man, the new religion, the reconciler, whom all things await. Dante's praise is that he
dared to write his autobiography in colossal cipher, or into universality.
We have had no genius in America, with tyrannous eye, which knew
the value of our incomparable materials, and saw, in the barbarism
and materialism of the times, another carnival of the same gods whose
picture he so much admires in Homer; then in the Middle Age; then in
Calvinism. Banks and tariffs, the newspaper and caucus, Methodism
and Unitarianism, are flat and dull to dull people, but rest on the same
foundations of wonder as the town of Troy and the temple of Delphi,[31]
and are as swiftly passing away. Our log-rolling, our stumps and their
politics, our fisheries, our Negroes and Indians, our boats and our
repudiations, the wrath of rogues and the pusillanimity of honest men,
the northern trade, the southern planting, the western clearing, Oregon
and Texas, are yet unsung. Yet America is a poem in our eyes; its
ample geography dazzles the imagination, and it will not wait long for
meters. If I have not found that excellent combination of gifts in my
countrymen which I seek, neither could I aid myself to fix the idea of
the poet by reading now and then in Chalmers's collection[32] of five
centuries of English poets. These are wits more than poets, though
there have been poets among them. But when we adhere to the ideal
of the poet, we have our difficulties even with Milton and Homer. Milton
is too literary, and Homer too literal and historical.

[31] The temple containing the oracle of Apollo.
[32] Alexander Chalmers (1759–1834) edited a collection of English poets in twenty-
one volumes that were published in 1810.

But I am not wise enough for a national criticism, and must use the old largeness a little longer, to discharge my errand from the muse to the poet concerning his art.

Art is the path of the creator to his work. The paths or methods are ideal and eternal, though few men ever see them; not the artist himself for years, or for a lifetime, unless he come into the conditions. The painter, the sculptor, the composer, the epic rhapsodist, the orator, all partake one desire, namely to express themselves symmetrically and abundantly, not dwarfishly and fragmentarily. They found or put themselves in certain conditions, as, the painter and sculptor before some impressive human figures; the orator into the assembly of the people; and the others in such scenes as each has found exciting to his intellect; and each presently feels the new desire. He hears a voice, he sees a beckoning. Then he is apprised, with wonder, what herds of daemons hem him in. He can no more rest; he says, with the old painter, "By God it is in me and must go forth of me." He pursues a beauty, half seen, which flies before him. The poet pours out verses in every solitude. Most of the things he says are conventional, no doubt; but by and by he says something which is original and beautiful. That charms him. He would say nothing else but such things. In our way of talking we say "That is yours, this is mine"; but the poet knows well that it is not his; that it is as strange and beautiful to him as to you; he would fain hear the like eloquence at length. Once having tasted this immortal ichor,[33] he cannot have enough of it, and as an admirable creative power exists in these intellections, it is of the last importance that these things get spoken. What a little of all we know is said! What drops of all the sea of our science are baled up! and by what accident it is that these are exposed, when so many secrets sleep in nature! Hence the necessity of speech and song; hence these throbs and heart-beatings in the orator, at the door of the assembly, to the end namely that thought may be ejaculated as Logos, or Word.

Doubt not, O poet, but persist. Say "It is in me, and shall out." Stand there, balked and dumb, stuttering and stammering, hissed and hooted, stand and strive, until at last rage draw out of thee that *dream-power* which every night shows thee is thine own; a power transcending all limit and privacy, and by virtue of which a man is the conductor of the whole river of electricity. Nothing walks, or creeps, or grows, or exists, which must not in turn arise and walk before him as exponent of his meaning. Comes he to that power, his genius is no longer exhaustible. All the creatures by pairs and by tribes pour into his mind as into a Noah's ark, to come forth again to people to a new world. This is like the stock of air for our respiration or for the combustion of our fire-

[33] In Greek mythology, the blood of the gods. Emerson's editors have speculated that he meant the word as a synonym for nectar, the drink of the gods, or ambrosia, their food.

place; not a measure of gallons, but the entire atmosphere if wanted. And therefore the rich poets, as Homer, Chaucer, Shakespeare, and Raphael, have obviously no limits to their works except the limits of their lifetime, and resemble a mirror carried through the street, ready to render an image of every created thing.

O poet! a new nobility is conferred in groves and pastures, and not in castles or by the sword-blade any longer. The conditions are hard, but equal. Thou shalt leave the world, and know the muse only. Thou shalt not know any longer the times, customs, graces, politics, or opinions of men, but shall take all from the muse. For the time of towns is tolled from the world by funereal chimes, but in nature the universal hours are counted by succeeding tribes of animals and plants, and by growth of joy on joy. God wills also that thou abdicate a manifold and duplex life, and that thou be content that others speak for thee. Others shall be thy gentlemen and shall represent all courtesy and worldly life for thee; others shall do the great and resounding actions also. Thou shalt lie close hid with nature, and canst not be afforded to the Capitol or the Exchange. The world is full of renunciations and apprenticeships, and this is thine; thou must pass for a fool and a churl for a long season. This is the screen and sheath in which Pan has protected his well-beloved flower, and thou shalt be known only to thine own, and they shall console thee with tenderest love. And thou shalt not be able to rehearse the names of thy friends in thy verse, for an old shame before the holy ideal. And this is the reward; that the ideal shall be real to thee, and the impressions of the actual world shall fall like summer rain, copious, but not troublesome to thy invulnerable essence. Thou shalt have the whole land for thy park and manor, the sea for thy bath and navigation, without tax and without envy; the woods and the rivers thou shalt own, and thou shalt possess that wherein others are only tenants and boarders. Thou true land-lord! sea-lord! air-lord! Wherever snow falls or water flows or birds fly, wherever day and night meet in twilight, wherever the blue heaven is hung by clouds or sown with stars, wherever are forms with transparent boundaries, wherever are outlets into celestial space, wherever is danger, and awe, and love,— there is Beauty, plenteous as rain, shed for thee, and though thou shouldst walk the world over, thou shalt not be able to find a condition inopportune or ignoble.

HENRY DAVID THOREAU (1817–1862)

He was born protestant. He declined to give up his large ambition of knowledge and action for any narrow craft or calling, aiming at a much more comprehensive calling, the art of living well. If he slighted and defied the opinions of others, it was only that he was more intent to reconcile his practise with his own belief. . . .

He was bred to no profession; he never married; he lived alone; he never went to church; he never voted; he refused to pay a tax to the State; he ate no flesh, he drank no wine, he never knew the use of tobacco; and though a naturalist, he used neither trap nor gun. . . . He had no talent for wealth, and knew how to be poor without the least hint of squalor or inelegance. . . .

His senses were acute, his frame well-knit and hardy, his hands strong and skillful in the use of tools. . . . He could pace sixteen rods more accurately than another man could measure them with rod and chain. He could find his path in the woods at night, he said, better by his feet than by his eyes. . . . He was a good swimmer, runner, skater, boatman. . . . And the relation of body to mind was still finer than we have indicated. He said he wanted every stride his legs made. The length of his walk uniformly made the length of his writing. If shut up in the house he did not write at all.

These sentences come from Emerson's essay on Thoreau, first spoken as an oration after Thoreau's death. Briefly and beautifully, they say almost everything that needs to be said for Thoreau. Almost everything that needs to be said against him appears in a sentence by the philosopher Alfred North Whitehead:

The self-sufficient independent man, with his peculiar property which concerns no one else, is a concept without any validity for modern civilization.

Henry David Thoreau was born in Concord, and there, except for brief trips of exploration, he lived the whole of his life. As he remarked with his usual mixture of asperity and playfulness: "I have never gotten over my surprise that I should have been born into the most estimable place in all the world, and in the very nick of time too." In 1837 he was graduated from Harvard College—graduated, his biographers often add, "without distinction." Yet Thoreau would show himself, even in his most bucolic or recalcitrant moments, a highly educated man, steeped in English poetry and with a wide knowledge of ancient and modern languages. Harvard seems to have done more for him than he cared to acknowledge.

Once out of Harvard, he spent a number of years as what the world calls a drifter. He helped his brother run a school for a while. He *worked with his family manufacturing pencils at home. He began, in the manner of Emerson, to keep a journal. He did odd jobs in Concord, repairing and painting houses. For a time he lived with the Emersons as a sort of combined handyman and disciple. During the early 1840s he wrote essays for* The Dial. *And he tried giving lectures, though he would never be as popular on the lyceum circuit as Emerson was.*

Thoreau's true work in life was the nurturing of his consciousness, a little through relations with other people in Concord, a little more through reading, but mostly through the days he spent in the natural world. What Emerson spoke about, he did; what Emerson preached, he realized. He knew the woods and streams, the birds and animals, as neighbors, almost as friends. Weighted with a heavier portion of Yankee common sense, his prose was seldom as rhapsodic as Emerson's; he was a good deal more dry and laconic than Emerson; but he truly experienced the Emersonian idea of nature as the tangible evidence of divinity. His journals and passages in Walden *suggest that in his moments of aliveness—and in his youth these were frequent—Thoreau could reach the Over-Soul simply by taking a walk. A complicated man searching for simplicity yet skeptical enough to refuse simple-minded primitivism, Thoreau could live with blazing intensity the life of quiet observation and reflection to which both Emerson and he were devoted.*

In one of his pieces Thoreau wrote:

> *Every creature is better alive than dead, men and moose and pine-trees.... It is the living spirit of the tree, not its spirit of turpentine, with which I sympathize, and which heals my cuts. It is as immortal as I am, and perchance will go to as high a heaven, there to tower above me still.*

When James Russell Lowell accepted for the Atlantic Monthly *the essay in which this passage appears, he cut the last sentence, apparently feeling it was too fanciful or transcendental for his readers. Thoreau was angry, and rightly so, for he had said precisely what he meant.*

Only July 4, 1845, he began his famous stay at Walden Pond—not as a hermit or as a scientific naturalist but as a man who wanted, he says in a marvelous passage in Walden, *"to live deliberately, to front only the essential facts of life...." He spent slightly more than two years at Walden, and when he left, it was "for as good a reason as I went there. Perhaps it seemed to me that I had several more lives to live and could not spare any more time for that one." Never a recluse, he received visitors, he went home for weekends, he worked six weeks a year doing odd jobs in Concord. "There is no reason,"* he once said, "why the scholar who professes to be a little wiser than the mass of men, should not do his work in the ditch occasionally, and by means of his superior wisdom make much less suffice for him."

In 1846, while still at Walden, Thoreau was arrested for refusing to pay the poll tax, and he spent a night in the Concord jail. It was an experience, he remarked, "novel and interesting enough." An anonymous relative or friend paid the tax and Thoreau left jail in the morning, thereby preventing him from trying to challenge the constitutionality of slavery in the courts. Shortly after this incident— at the time a local curiosity, later to be known throughout the world—Thoreau read a paper to his fellow townsmen entitled "The Relation of the Individual to the States." He published it in 1849. Civil Disobedience, as the essay would come to be known, attracted little attention at the time, but it has since become a major document in pacifist and anarchist thought, deeply influencing both Tolstoi and Gandhi.

In 1849 Thoreau published his first book, A Week on the Concord and Merrimack Rivers, which foreshadowed that organic fusion of travel observation and moral reflection he would achieve in Walden. The book sold a mere 200 copies, and four years later the publisher shipped the remainder to Thoreau. "I have now a library of nearly nine hundred volumes," he noted in his journal, "over seven hundred of which I wrote myself."

Notwithstanding his extreme individualism, Thoreau became active during the 1850s in the antislavery crusade. He helped a number of escaped slaves reach freedom in Canada. He spoke eloquently at an Abolitionist convention in 1854. When John Brown, the antislavery leader, organized an armed uprising at Harpers Ferry in 1859, Thoreau spoke in his behalf. After Brown's death, the Concord selectmen refused to approve a service for him; Thoreau went to the town hall and rang the bell himself.

Thoreau was dead before his forty-fifth birthday from the tuberculosis he had carried throughout his life. When an aunt inquired if he had made his peace with God, he answered: "I have never quarreled with him."

The essential quest controlling Thoreau's life and work was to discover, perhaps define, the conditions of human freedom. Throughout most of his life, though somewhat less so toward the end, he looked upon freedom as almost an absolute state of being, which might be reached by the man who shook off convention and torpor and succeeded in penetrating to the roots of his own self. Freedom he saw first of all as the shaking off of external social restraints—the re-

*straints of government, family, and even friendship. But this was
only a negative freedom, the kind that made true freedom possible.
True freedom Thoreau regarded as a condition of maximum self-
realization: that state in which man is most closely and keenly
linked to his natural environment, that condition of harmony in
which the physical and spiritual are united, that mixture of intense
responsiveness and relaxed ease which constitutes the highest form
of consciousness. Thoreau's freedom was asocial, perhaps antisocial;
it did not depend, except as a necessary preliminary, on collective
effort or effective government; it was a state of being—perhaps a
romantic equivalent to the religious condition of beatitude—which
each man had to reach for himself. Or as he once wrote:*

*The best and bravest deed is that which the whole man—heart, lungs,
hands, fingers and toes—at any time prompts. . . . This is the meaning
of integrity; this is to be an integer, and not a fraction.*

*The last phrase; "not a fraction," is crucial. It suggests that in his own
Yankee style Thoreau was expressing one of the major concerns of
nineteenth-century thinkers, a concern shared by men as different
from one another, and from him, as Carlyle and Marx. He was
objecting to the increasing depersonalization of men who have to
work in factories or offices; he was objecting to the reduction of
men to their social role or economic function. As F. O. Matthiessen
has remarked:*

*He objected to the division of labor since it divided the worker, not
merely the work, and reduced him from a man to an operative. . . . The
root of his hatred of the division of labor was that it destroyed the potential balance of his agrarian world, one of the main ideals of which was
the union of labor and culture.*

*The ideal by which Thoreau lived was that of the independent crafts-
man: independent in circumstance, independent in mind. He tried
first to achieve this condition for himself, but not merely for himself; he saw himself as a possible instance—instance, more than
example—in the experiment of living. And while he did not pretend
to tell other men how to live, he was convinced that no effort at
self-discovery could be successful if it did not include a radical discarding of the trappings of civilization. "Wherever a man goes," he
wrote in* Walden, *"men will pursue and paw him with their dirty
institutions, and if they can, constrain him to belong to their
desperate odd-fellow society." The solution he urged was "simplicity,
simplicity, simplicity." "Let your affairs be as two or three, and not
a hundred or a thousand; instead of a million count half a dozen,
and keep your accounts on your thumb nail."*

*Everything in Thoreau leads, finally, inward. His political anarchism,
his devotion to skill in work and craft, his rapt involvement with*

*the natural world—all are avenues to the enlargement of conscious-
ness. Thoreau wanted his life to be a series of rebirths, each time
escaping boredom and routine. A thrifty New Englander inhabits
his skin, refusing to "waste" any portion or moment of life, trying
to extract as much moral and psychic profit as possible.*

*Thoreau's creed has had an enormous appeal for Americans, almost in
direct proportion to our fear that it is unrealizable. Indeed, the more
we may feel that his invitation to simplicity comes at least a century too late, the more powerful will be the sentiments of nostalgia
it evokes.*

*Subjected to hard scrutiny, Thoreau's views may not prove as pleasing
as his uncritical apologists make out. What he failed to notice, or
remark upon, was the costs that were inseparable from his choices.
Never having married, he did not have to put Walden to the test
of diapers; having no children, he found it relatively easy to keep
his accounts on his thumbnail. To insist that men "front only the
essential facts of life" is splendid, but what if Thoreau's way of
doing so impresses other men as a scanting of the richest emotional
and sensual experiences of life? Thoreau could withdraw from his
community without paying too high a price, first because Concord
was tolerant of local deviants and second because it was only a mile
away from Walden, so that when he wanted good conversation he
could wander back and talk to Emerson. Thoreau knew very little
about the problems of living as a free individual—if one can do so
at all—in the world of industrialism: he found ways of subsisting
that simply are not available to most men. And he cared very little
about the problem of maintaining a democratic society since, rather
selfishly, he assumed its existence. His plea for civil disobedience
remains powerful, an indispensable corrective to the abuses and
tyrannies that can occur even when majorities rule and minorities
are free to protest. But he failed to consider the possibility that a
democratic society might be threatened if most of its members
insisted that they too would systematically put conscience above
law and individual will above community agreement. On this matter
he can approach cynicism:*

> *I quietly declare war with the State, after my fashion, though I will
> still make use and get what advantage of her I can, as is usual in such
> cases.*

*That Thoreau was driven to civil disobedience is a grave indictment of
the society of his day; that he was able to proclaim it freely is a
significant tribute to American democracy.*

*Thoreau's greatest strength, certainly his greatest interest for us here,
is as a writer. He is a master of English prose, not only of the*

American nineteenth century, but of all time. His prose is muscular, knotty, vivid, pulsing. Each sentence crackles with the energy of a strong mind and the precision of an expert craftsman. He admired the kind of writer who "was satisfied with giving an exact description of things as they appeared to him. . . ." He scorned writers who used "torpid words, wooden or lifeless words, such words as 'humanity,' which have a paralysis in their tales." His style has sometimes been described as conversational, but that is not at all an exact description of the way he wrote. Conversation—just listen to it sometimes—is loose, sloppy, and wasteful. Thoreau's prose is tight, precise, and economical. His sentences are painstakingly constructed; he clearly worked hard to make them right. Those who speak of his conversational style may actually mean that he abandoned, like Emerson before him, the latinate style that earlier American writers had copied from eighteenth-century England— though Thoreau, as a rule, wrote better than Emerson, with greater color and idiomatic force.

Here is a famous Thoreau sentence, the first half of which, at least, seems a source of Hemingway's prose style:

As I came home through the woods with my string of fish, trailing my pole, it being now quite dark, I caught a glimpse of a woodchuck, stealing across my path, and felt a strange thrill of savage delight, and was strongly tempted to seize and devour him raw; not that I was hungry then, except for that wildness which he represented.

Here are a few of his sentences, cited by Emerson as examples of Thoreau's "literary excellence:"

Some circumstantial evidence is very strong, as when you find a trout in the milk.

The youth gets together his materials to build a bridge to the moon, or perchance a palace or temple on the earth, and, at length, the middle aged man concludes to build a woodshed with them.

How can we expect a harvest of thought who have not had a seed-time of character?

I put on some hemlock-boughs, and the rich salt cracking of their leaves was like mustard to the ear, the crackling of uncountable regiments. Dead trees love the fire.

The writing here is not conversational, nor does it, as in Twain's prose, employ the vernacular. Thoreau uses short, concrete words, frequent prepositional phrases, and a kind of aphoristic paradox to knit together feeling and thought. In Walden, his masterpiece, the sentences build up into a firm organic structure, shaped according to

*the rhythm of the year and the perception of the man who lives in
alert harmony with it.*

FURTHER READING

The standard biography is Henry Seidel Canby, *Thoreau* (1939), sup-
plemented in some respects by Walter Harding, *Thoreau: Man of
Concord* (1960). A fine critical appreciation appears in F. O.
Matthiessen, *American Renaissance* (1941). Sherman Paul's *The
Shores of America: Thoreau's Inward Exploration* (1958) studies
his mind and art.

Civil Disobedience (1849)

I heartily accept the motto, "That government is best which governs
least"; and I should like to see it acted up to more rapidly and systematically. Carried out, it finally amounts to this, which also I believe—
"That government is best which governs not at all"; and when men are
prepared for it, that will be the kind of government which they will
have. Government is at best but an expedient; but most governments
are usually, and all governments are sometimes, inexpedient. The objections which have been brought against a standing army, and they are
many and weighty, and deserve to prevail, may also at last be brought
against a standing government. The standing army is only an arm of
the standing government. The government itself, which is only the
mode which the people have chosen to execute their will, is equally
liable to be abused and perverted before the people can act through it.
Witness the present Mexican war, the work of comparatively a few
individuals using the standing government as their tool; for, in the
outset, the people would not have consented to this measure.

This American government—what is it but a tradition, though a
recent one, endeavoring to transmit itself unimpaired to posterity, but
each instant losing some of its integrity? It has not the vitality and
force of a single living man; for a single man can bend it to his will. It
is a sort of wooden gun to the people themselves. But it is not the less
necessary for this; for the people must have some complicated machinery or other, and hear its din, to satisfy that idea of government which
they have. Governments show thus how successfully men can be imposed on, even impose on themselves, for their own advantage. It is
excellent, we must all allow. Yet this government never of itself
furthered any enterprise, but by the alacrity with which it got out of
its way. *It* does not keep the country free. *It* does not settle the West. *It*
does not educate. The character inherent in the American people has
done all that has been accomplished; and it would have done some-

what more, if the government had not sometimes got in its way. For government is an expedient by which men would fain succeed in letting one another alone; and, as has been said, when it is most expedient, the governed are most let alone by it. Trade and commerce, if they were not made of india-rubber, would never manage to bounce over the obstacles which legislators are continually putting in their way; and, if one were to judge these men wholly by the effects of their actions and not partly by their intentions, they would deserve to be classed and punished with those mischievous persons who put obstructions on the railroads.

But, to speak practically and as a citizen, unlike those who call themselves no-government men, I ask for, not at once no government, but *at once* a better government. Let every man make known what kind of government would command his respect, and that will be one step toward obtaining it.

After all, the practical reason why, when the power is once in the hands of the people, a majority are permitted, and for a long period continue, to rule is not because they are most likely to be in the right, nor because this seems fairest to the minority, but because they are physically the strongest. But a government in which the majority rule in all cases cannot be based on justice, even as far as men understand it. Can there not be a government in which majorities do not virtually decide right and wrong, but conscience?—in which majorities decide only those questions to which the rule of expediency is applicable? Must the citizen ever for a moment, or in the least degree, resign his conscience to the legislator? Why has every man a conscience, then? I think that we should be men first, and subjects afterward. It is not desirable to cultivate a respect for the law, so much as for the right. The only obligation which I have a right to assume is to do at any time what I think right. It is truly enough said that a corporation has no conscience; but a corporation of conscientious men is a corporation *with* a conscience. Law never made men a whit more just; and, by means of their respect for it, even the well-disposed are daily made the agents of injustice. A common and natural result of an undue respect for law is, that you may see a file of soldiers, colonel, captain, corporal, privates, powder-monkeys, and all, marching in admirable order over hill and dale to the wars, against their wills, ay, against their common sense and consciences, which makes it very steep marching indeed, and produces a palpitation of the heart. They have no doubt that it is a damnable business in which they are concerned; they are all peaceably inclined. Now, what are they? Men at all? or small movable forts and magazines, at the service of some unscrupulous man in power? Visit the Navy Yard, and behold a marine, such a man as an American government can make, or such as it can make a man with its black arts—a mere shadow and reminiscence of humanity, a man laid out

alive and standing, and already, as one may say, buried under arms
with funeral accompaniments, though it may be,

Not a drum was heard, not a funeral note,
*   As his corse to the rampart we hurried;*
Not a soldier discharged his farewell shot
*   O'er the grave where our hero we buried.*[1]

The mass of men serve the state thus, not as men mainly, but as
machines, with their bodies. They are the standing army, and the
militia, jailers, constables, *posse comitatus,* etc. In most cases there is
no free exercise whatever of the judgment or of the moral sense; but
they put themselves on a level with wood and earth and stones; and
wooden men can perhaps be manufactured that will serve the purpose
as well. Such command no more respect than men of straw or a lump
of dirt. They have the same sort of worth only as horses and dogs. Yet
such as these even are commonly esteemed good citizens. Others—as
most legislators, politicians, lawyers, ministers, and office-holders—serve
the state chiefly with their heads; and, as they rarely make any moral
distinctions, they are as likely to serve the devil, without *intending* it,
as God. A very few—as heroes, patriots, martyrs, reformers in the great
sense, and *men*—serve the state with their consciences also, and so
necessarily resist it for the most part; and they are commonly treated
as enemies by it. A wise man will only be useful as a man, and will
not submit to be "clay," and "stop a hole to keep the wind away,"[2] but
leave that office to his dust at least:

I am too high-born to be propertied,
To be a secondary at control,
Or useful serving-man and instrument
To any sovereign state throughout the world.[3]

He who gives himself entirely to his fellow men appears to them
useless and selfish; but he who gives himself partially to them is
pronounced a benefactor and philanthropist.

How does it become a man to behave toward this American government today? I answer, that he cannot without disgrace be associated
with it. I cannot for an instant recognize that political organization as
my government which is the *slave's* government also.

All men recognize the right of revolution; that is, the right to refuse
allegiance to, and to resist, the government, when its tyranny or its
inefficiency are great and unendurable. But almost all say that such is

[1] The opening lines of "Burial of Sir John Moore at Corunna," by the Irish
clergyman-poet Charles Wolfe (1791–1823).
[2] Shakespeare, *Hamlet,* 5:1; 236–37.
[3] Shakespeare, *King John,* 5:2; 79–82.

not the case now. But such was the case, they think, in the Revolution of '75. If one were to tell me that this was a bad government because it taxed certain foreign commodities brought to its ports, it is most probable that I should not make an ado about it, for I can do without them. All machines have their friction; and possibly this does enough good to counterbalance the evil. At any rate, it is a great evil to make a stir about it. But when the friction comes to have its machine, and oppression and robbery are organized, I say, let us not have such a machine any longer. In other words, when a sixth of the population of a nation which has undertaken to be the refuge of liberty are slaves, and a whole country is unjustly overrun and conquered by a foreign army, and subjected to military law, I think that it is not too soon for honest men to rebel and revolutionize. What makes this duty the more urgent is the fact that the country so overrun is not our own, but ours is the invading army.

Paley,[4] a common authority with many on moral questions, in his chapter on the "Duty of Submission to Civil Government," resolves all civil obligation into expediency; and he proceeds to say that "so long as the interest of the whole society requires it, that is, so long as the established government cannot be resisted or changed without public inconveniency, it is the will of God . . . that the established government be obeyed—and no longer. This principle being admitted, the justice of every particular case of resistance is reduced to a computation of the quantity of the danger and grievance on the one side, and of the probability and expense of redressing it on the other." Of this, he says, every man shall judge for himself. But Paley appears never to have contemplated those cases to which the rule of expediency does not apply, in which a people, as well as an individual, must do justice, cost what it may. If I have unjustly wrested a plank from a drowning man, I must restore it to him though I drown myself. This, according to Paley, would be inconvenient. But he that would save his life, in such a case, shall lose it. This people must cease to hold slaves, and to make war on Mexico, though it cost them their existence as a people.

In their practice, nations agree with Paley; but does anyone think that Massachusetts does exactly what is right at the present crisis?

A drab of state, a cloth-o'-silver slut,
To have her train borne up, and her soul trail in the dirt.

Practically speaking, the opponents to a reform in Massachusetts are not a hundred thousand politicians at the South, but a hundred thousand merchants and farmers here, who are more interested in commerce and agriculture than they are in humanity, and are not prepared to do justice to the slave and to Mexico, *cost what it may.* I quarrel not

---

[4] William Paley (1743–1805), British philosopher, author of *Principles of Moral and Political Philosophy* (1785).

with far-off foes, but with those who, near at home, co-operate with, and do the biding of, those far away, and without whom the latter would be harmless. We are accustomed to say, that the mass of men are unprepared; but improvement is slow, because the few are not materially wiser or better than the many. It is not so important that many should be as good as you, as that there be some absolute goodness somewhere; for that will leaven the whole lump. There are thousands who are *in opinion* opposed to slavery and to the war, who yet in effect do nothing to put an end to them; who, esteeming themselves children of Washington and Franklin, sit down with their hands in their pockets, and say that they know not what to do, and do nothing; who even postpone the question of freedom to the question of free trade, and quietly read the prices-current along with the latest advices from Mexico, after dinner, and, it may be, fall asleep over them both. What is the price-current of an honest man and patriot today? They hesitate, and they regret, and sometimes they petition; but they do nothing in earnest and with effect. They will wait, well disposed, for others to remedy the evil, that they may no longer have it to regret. At most, they give only a cheap vote, and a feeble countenance and Godspeed, to the right, as it goes by them. There are nine hundred and ninety-nine patrons of virtue to one virtuous man. But it is easier to deal with the real possessor of a thing than with the temporary guardian of it.

All voting is a sort of gaming, like checkers or backgammon, with a slight moral tinge to it, a playing with right and wrong, with moral questions; and betting naturally accompanies it. The character of the voters is not staked. I cast my vote, perchance, as I think right; but I am not vitally concerned that that right should prevail. I am willing to leave it to the majority. Its obligation, therefore, never exceeds that of expediency. Even voting *for the right* is *doing* nothing for it. It is only expressing to men feebly your desire that it should prevail. A wise man will not leave the right to the mercy of chance, nor wish it to prevail through the power of the majority. There is but little virtue in the action of masses of men. When the majority shall at length vote for the abolition of slavery, it will be because they are indifferent to slavery, or because there is but little slavery left to be abolished by their vote. *They* will then be the only slaves. Only *his* vote can hasten the abolition of slavery who asserts his own freedom by his vote.

I hear of a convention to be held at Baltimore, or elsewhere, for the selection of a candidate for the Presidency, made up chiefly of editors, and men who are politicians by profession; but I think, what is it to any independent, intelligent, and respectable man what decision they may come to? Shall we not have the advantage of his wisdom and honesty, nevertheless? Can we not count upon some independent votes? Are there not many individuals in the country who do not attend conventions? But no: I find that the respectable man, so called, has immediately drifted from his position, and despairs of his country, when his country has more reason to despair of him. He forthwith adopts one of the candidates thus selected as the only *available* one, thus proving that he is himself *available* for any purposes of the demagogue. His vote is of no more worth than that of any unprincipled foreigner or hireling native, who may have been bought. O for a man who is a *man*, and, as my neighbor says, has a bone in his back which you cannot pass your hand through! Our statistics are at fault: the population has been returned too large. How many *men* are there to a square thousand miles in this country? Hardly one. Does not America offer any inducement for men to settle here? The American has dwindled into an Odd Fellow—one who may be known by the development of his organ of gregariousness, and a manifest lack of intellect and cheerful self-reliance; whose first and chief concern, on coming into the world, is to see that the almshouses are in good repair; and, before yet he has lawfully donned the virile garb, to collect a fund for the support of the widows and orphans that may be; who, in short, ventures to live only by the aid of the Mutual Insurance company, which has promised to bury him decently.

It is not a man's duty, as a matter of course, to devote himself to the eradication of any, even the most enormous, wrong; he may still properly have other concerns to engage him; but it is his duty, at least, to wash his hands of it, and, if he gives it no thought longer, not to give it practically his support. If I devote myself to other pursuits and contemplations, I must first see, at least, that I do not pursue them sitting upon another man's shoulders. I must get off him first, that he may pursue his contemplations too. See what gross inconsistency is tolerated. I have heard some of my townsmen say, "I should like to have them order me out to help put down an insurrection of the slaves, or to march to Mexico—see if I would go"; and yet these very men have each, directly by their allegiance, and so indirectly, at least, by their money, furnished a substitute. The soldier is applauded who refuses to serve in an unjust war by those who do not refuse to sustain the unjust government which makes the war; is applauded by those whose own act and authority he disregards and sets at naught; as if the state were penitent to that degree that it hired one to scourge it while it sinned, but not to that degree that it left off sinning for a moment. Thus, under the name of Order and Civil Government, we are all made at last to pay homage to and support our own meanness. After the first blush of sin comes its indifference; and from immoral it becomes, as it were, *un*moral, and quite unnecessary to that life which he have made.

The broadest and most prevalent error requires the most disinterested virtue to sustain it. The slight reproach to which the virtue of patriotism is commonly liable, the noble are most likely to incur. Those who, while they disapprove of the character and measures of a government, yield to it their allegiance and support are undoubtedly its most conscientious supporters, and so frequently the most serious obstacles to reform. Some are petitioning the State to dissolve the Union, to disregard the requisitions of the President. Why do they not dissolve it themselves—the union between themselves and the State—and refuse to pay their quota into its treasury? Do not they stand in the same relation to the State that the State does to the Union? And have not the same reasons prevented the State from resisting the Union which have prevented them from resisting the State?

How can a man be satisfied to entertain an opinion merely, and enjoy *it*? Is there any enjoyment in it, if his opinion is that he is aggrieved? If you are cheated out of a single dollar by your neighbor, you do not rest satisfied with knowing that you are cheated, or with saying that you are cheated, or even with petitioning him to pay you your due; but you take effectual steps at once to obtain the full amount, and see that you are never cheated again. Action from principle, the perception and the performance of right, changes things and relations; it is essentially revolutionary, and does not consist wholly with anything which was. It not only divides States and churches, it divides families; ay, it divides the *individual*, separating the diabolical in him from the divine.

Unjust laws exist: shall we be content to obey them, or shall we endeavor to amend them, and obey them until we have succeeded, or shall we transgress them at once? Men generally, under such a government as this, think that they ought to wait until they have persuaded the majority to alter them. They think that, if they should resist, the remedy would be worse than the evil. But it is the fault of the government itself that the remedy *is* worse than the evil. *It* makes it worse. Why is it not more apt to anticipate and provide for reform? Why does it not cherish its wise minority? Why does it cry and resist before it is hurt? Why does it not encourage its citizens to be on the alert to point out its faults, and *do* better than it would have them? Why does it always crucify Christ, and excommunicate Copernicus and Luther, and pronounce Washington and Franklin rebels?

One would think, that a deliberate and practical denial of its authority was the only offence never contemplated by government; else, why has it not assigned its definite, its suitable and proportionate, penalty? If a man who has no property refuses but once to earn nine shillings for the State, he is put in prison for a period unlimited by any law that I know, and determined only by the discretion of those who placed him there; but if he should steal ninety times nine shillings from the State, he is soon permitted to go at large again.

If the injustice is part of the necessary friction of the machine of government, let it go, let it go: perchance it will wear smooth—certainly the machine will wear out. If the injustice has a spring, or a pulley, or a rope, or a crank, exclusively for itself, then perhaps you may consider whether the remedy will not be worse than the evil; but if it is of such a nature that it requires you to be the agent of injustice to another, then, I say, break the law. Let your life be a counter-friction to stop the machine. What I have to do is to see, at any rate, that I do not lend myself to the wrong which I condemn.

As for adopting the ways which the State has provided for remedying the evil, I know not of such ways. They take too much time, and a man's life will be gone. I have other affairs to attend to. I came into this world, not chiefly to make this a good place to live in, but to live in it, be it good or bad. A man has not everything to do, but something; and because he cannot do *everything*, it is not necessary that he should do *something* wrong. It is not my business to be petitioning the Governor or the Legislature any more than it is theirs to petition me; and if they should not hear my petition, what should I do them? But in this case the State has provided no way: its very Constitution is the evil. This may seem to be harsh and stubborn and unconciliatory; but it is to treat with the utmost kindness and consideration the only spirit that can appreciate or deserves it. So is all change for the better, like birth and death, which convulse the body.

I do not hesitate to say, that those who call themselves Abolitionists should at once effectually withdraw their support, both in person and property, from the government of Massachusetts, and not wait till they constitute a majority of one, before they suffer the right to prevail through them. I think that it is enough if they have God on their side, without waiting for that other one. Moreover, any man more right than his neighbors constitutes a majority of one already.

I meet this American government, or its representative, the State government, directly, and face to face, once a year—no more—in the person of its tax-gatherer; this is the only mode in which a man situated as I am necessarily meets it; and it then says distinctly, Recognize me; and the simplest, the most effectual, and, in the present posture of affairs, the indispensablest mode of treating with it on this head, of expressing your little satisfaction with and love for it, is to deny it then. My civil neighbor, the tax-gatherer, is the very man I have to deal with—for it is, after all, with men and not with parchment that I quarrel—and he has voluntarily chosen to be an agent of the government. How shall he ever know well what he is and does as an officer of the government, or as a man, until he is obliged to consider whether he shall treat me, his neighbor, for whom he has respect, as a neighbor and well-disposed man, or as a maniac and disturber of the peace, and see if he can get over this obstruction to his neighborliness without a ruder and more impetuous thought or speech corresponding with his action. I know this well, that if one thousand, if one hundred, if ten men whom I could name—if ten *honest* men only—ay, if *one* HONEST man, in this State of Massachusetts, *ceasing to hold slaves*, were actually to withdraw from this copartnership, and be locked up in the county jail therefor, it would be the abolition of slavery in America. For it matters not how small the beginning may seem to be: what is once well done is done forever. But we love better to talk about it: that we say is our mission. Reform keeps many scores of newspapers in its service, but not one man. If my esteemed neighbor, the State's ambassador,[5] who will devote his days to the settlement of the question of human rights in the Council Chamber, instead of being threatened with the prisons of Carolina, were to sit down the prisoner of Massachusetts, that State which is so anxious to foist the sin of slavery upon her sister— though at present she can discover only an act of inhospitality to be the ground of a quarrel with her—the Legislature would not wholly waive the subject the following winter.

Under a government which imprisons any unjustly, the true place for a just man is also a prison. The proper place today, the only place which Massachusetts has provided for her freer and less desponding spirits, is in her prisons, to be put out and locked out of the State by her own act, as they have already put themselves out by their principles. It is there that the fugitive slave, and the Mexican prisoner on parole, and the Indian come to plead the wrongs of his race should find them; on that separate, but more free and honorable, ground, where the State places those who are not *with* her, but *against* her—the only house in a slave State in which a free man can abide with honor. If any think that their influence would be lost there, and their voices no longer afflict the ear of the State, that they would not be as an enemy within its walls, they do not know by how much truth is stronger than error, nor how much more eloquently and effectively he can combat injustice who has experienced a little in his own person. Cast your whole vote, not a strip of paper merely, but your whole influence. A minority is powerless while it conforms to the majority; it is not even a minority then; but it is irresistible when it clogs by its whole weight. If the alternative is to keep all just men in prison, or give up war and salvery, the State will not hesitate which to choose. If a thousand men were not to pay their tax-bills this year, that would not be a violent and bloody measure, as it would be to pay them, and enable the State to commit violence and shed innocent blood. This is, in fact, the definition of a peaceable revolution, if any such is possible. If the tax-gatherer, or any other public officer, asks me, as one has done, "But what shall I do?" my answer is, "If you really wish to do anything, resign your office. When the subject has refused allegiance, and the officer has resigned his office, then the revolution is accomplished. But even suppose blood should flow. Is there not a sort of blood shed when the conscience is wounded? Through this wound a man's real manhood and immortality flow out, and he bleeds to an everlasting death. I see this blood flowing now.

I have contemplated the imprisonment of the offender, rather than the seizure of his goods—though both will serve the same purpose—

[5] Samuel Hoar (1778–1856) of Concord, sent to Charleston, S.C., to represent Negro seamen from Massachusetts threatened with enslavement.

because they who assert the purest right, and consequently are most dangerous to a corrupt State, commonly have not spent much time in accumulating property. To such the State renders comparatively small service, and a slight tax is wont to appear exorbitant, particularly if they are obliged to earn it by special labor with their hands. If there were one who lived wholly without the use of money, the State itself would hesitate to demand it of him. But the rich man—not to make any invidious comparison—is always sold to the institution which makes him rich. Absolutely speaking, the more money, the less virtue; for money comes between a man and his objects, and obtains them for him; and it was certainly no great virtue to obtain it. It puts to rest many questions which he would otherwise be taxed to answer; while the only new question which it puts is the hard but superfluous one, how to spend it. Thus his moral ground is taken from under his feet. The opportunities of living are diminished in proportion as what are called the "means" are increased. The best thing a man can do for his culture when he is rich is to endeavor to carry out those schemes which he entertained when he was poor. Christ answered the Herodians according to their condition. "Show me the tribute-money," said he— and one took a penny out of his pocket—if you use money which has the image of Caesar on it, and which he has made current and valuable, that is, *if you are men of the State*, and gladly enjoy the advantages of Caesar's government, then pay him back some of his own when he demands it. "Render therefore to Caesar that which is Caesar's, and to God those things which are God's"—leaving them no wiser than before as to which was which; for they did not wish to know.

When I converse with the freest of my neighbors, I perceive that, whatever they may say about the magnitude and seriousness of the question, and their regard for the public tranquillity, the long and the short of the matter is, that they cannot spare the protection of the existing government, and they dread the consequences to their property and families of disobedience to it. For my own part, I should not like to think that I ever rely on the protection of the State. But, if I deny the authority of the State when it presents its tax bill, it will soon take and waste all my property, and so harass me and my children without end. This is hard. This makes it impossible for a man to live honestly, and at the same time comfortably, in outward respects. It will not be worth the while to accumulate property; that would be sure to go again. You must hire or squat somewhere, and raise but a small crop, and eat that soon. You must live within yourself, and depend upon yourself always tucked up and ready for a start, and not have many affairs. A man may grow rich in Turkey even, if he will be in all respects a good subject of the Turkish government. Confucius said: "If a state is governed by the principles of reason, poverty and misery are subjects of shame; if a state is not governed by the principles of reason, riches and honors are the subjects of shame." No: until I want the protection of

Massachusetts to be extended to me in some distant Southern port, where my liberty is endangered, or until I am bent solely on building up an estate at home by peaceful enterprise, I can afford to refuse allegiance to Massachusetts, and her right to my property and life. It costs me less in every sense to incur the penalty of disobedience to the State than it would to obey. I should feel as if I were worth less in that case.

Some years ago, the State met me in behalf of the Church, and commanded me to pay a certain sum toward the support of a clergyman whose preaching my father attended, but never I myself. "Pay," it said, "or be locked up in the jail." I declined to pay. But, unfortunately, another man saw fit to pay it. I did not see why the schoolmaster should be taxed to support the priest, and not the priest the schoolmaster; for I was not the State's schoolmaster, but I supported myself by voluntary subscription. I did not see why the lyceum should not present its tax bill, and have the State to back its demand, as well as the Church. However, at the request of the selectmen, I condescended to make some such statement as this in writing: "Know all men by these presents, that I, Henry Thoreau, do not wish to be regarded as a member of any incorporated society which I have not joined." This I gave to the town clerk; and he has it. The State, having thus learned that I did not wish to be regarded as a member of that church, has never made a like demand on me since; though it said that it must adhere to its original presumption that time. If I had known how to name them, I should then have signed off in detail from all the societies which I never signed on to; but I did not know where to find a complete list.

I have paid no poll-tax for six years. I was put into a jail once on this account, for one night; and, as I stood considering the walls of solid stone, two or three feet thick, the door of wood and iron, a foot thick, and the iron grating which strained the light, I could not help being struck with the foolishness of that institution which treated me as if I were mere flesh and blood and bones, to be locked up. I wondered that it should have concluded at length that this was the best use it could put me to, and had never thought to avail itself of my services in some way. I saw that, if there was a wall of stone between me and my townsmen, there was a still more difficult one to climb or break through before they could get to be as free as I was. I did not for a moment feel confined, and the walls seemed a great waste of stone and mortar. I felt as if I alone of all my townsmen had paid my tax. They plainly did not know how to treat me, but behaved like persons who are underbred. In every threat and in every compliment there was a blunder; for they thought that my chief desire was to stand the other side of that stone wall. I could not but smile to see how industriously they locked the door on my meditations, which followed them out again without let or hindrance, and *they* were really all that was dangerous. As they could not reach me, they had resolved to punish my body; just as boys, if they cannot come at some person against whom they have a spite, will abuse his dog. I saw that the State was half-witted, that it was timid as a lone woman with her silver spoons, and that it did not know its friends from its foes, and I lost all my remaining respect for it, and pitied it.

Thus the State never intentionally confronts a man's sense, intellectual or moral, but only his body, his senses. It is not armed with superior wit or honesty, but with superior physical strength. I was not born to be forced. I will breathe after my own fashion. Let us see who is the strongest. What force has a multitude? They only can force me who obey a higher law than I. They force me to become like themselves. I do not hear of *men* being *forced* to live this way or that by masses of men. What sort of life were that to live? When I meet a government which says to me, "Your money or your life," why should I be in haste to give it my money? It may be in a great strait, and not know what to do: I cannot help that. It must help itself; do as I do. It is not worth the while to snivel about it. I am not responsible for the successful working of the machinery of society. I am not the son of the engineer. I perceive that, when an acorn and a chestnut fall side by side, the one does not remain inert to make way for the other, but both obey their own laws, and spring and grow and flourish as best they can, till one, perchance, overshadows and destroys the other. If a plant cannot live according to its nature, it dies; and so a man.

The night in prison was novel and interesting enough. The prisoners in their shirtsleeves were enjoying a chat and the evening air in the doorway, when I entered. But the jailer said, "Come, boys, it is time to lock up"; and so they dispersed, and I heard the sound of their steps returning into the hollow apartments. My room-mate was introduced to me by the jailer as "a first-rate fellow and a clever man." When the door was locked, he showed me where to hang my hat, and how he managed matters there. The rooms were whitewashed once a month; and this one, at least, was the whitest, most simply furnished, and probably the neatest apartment in the town. He naturally wanted to know where I came from, and what brought me there; and, when I had told him, I asked him in my turn how he came there, presuming him to be an honest man, of course; and, as the world goes, I believe he was. "Why," said he, "they accuse me of burning a barn; but I never did it." As near as I could discover, he had probably gone to bed in a barn when drunk, and smoked his pipe there; and so a barn was burnt. He had the reputation of being a clever man, had been there some three months waiting for his trial to come on, and would have to wait as much longer; but he was quite domesticated and contented, since he got his board for nothing, and thought that he was well treated.

He occupied one window, and I the other; and I saw that if one stayed there long, his principal business would be to look out the window. I had soon read all the tracts that were left there, and examined where former prisoners had broken out, and where a grate had been sawed off, and heard the history of the various occupants of that room; for I found that even here there was a history and a gossip which never circulated beyond the walls of the jail. Probably this is the only house in the town where verses are composed, which are afterward printed in a circular form, but not published. I was shown quite a long list of verses which were composed by some young men who had been detected in an attempt to escape, who avenged themselves by singing them.

I pumped my fellow-prisoner as dry as I could, for fear I should never see him again; but at length he showed me which was my bed, and left me to blow out the lamp.

It was like traveling into a far country, such as I had never expected to behold, to lie there for one night. It seemed to me that I never had heard the town clock strike before, nor the evening sounds of the village; for we slept with the windows open, which were inside the grating. It was to see my native village in the light of the Middle Ages, and our Concord was turned into a Rhine stream, and visions of knights and castles passed before me. They were the voices of old burghers that I heard in the streets. I was an involuntary spectator and auditor of whatever was done and said in the kitchen of the adjacent village inn— a wholly new and rare experience to me. It was a closer view of my native town. I was fairly inside of it. I never had seen its institutions before. This is one of its peculiar institutions; for it is a shire town. I began to comprehend what its inhabitants were about.

In the morning, our breakfasts were put through the hole in the door, in small oblong-square tin pans, made to fit, and holding a pint of chocolate, with brown bread, and an iron spoon. When they called for the vessels again, I was green enough to return what bread I had left; but my comrade seized it, and said that I should lay that up for lunch or dinner. Soon after he was let out to work at haying in a neighboring field, whither he went every day, and would not be back till noon; so he bade me good-day, saying that he doubted if he should see me again.

When I came out of prison—for some one interfered, and paid that tax—I did not perceive that great changes had taken place on the common, such as he observed who went in a youth and emerged a tottering and gray-headed man; and yet a change had to my eyes come over the scene—the town, and State, and country—greater than any that mere time could effect. I saw yet more distinctly the State in which I lived. I saw to what extent the people among whom I lived could be trusted as good neighbors and friends; that their friendship was for summer weather only; that they did not greatly propose to do right; that they were a distinct race from me by their prejudices and superstitions, as the Chinamen and Malays are; that in their sacrifices to humanity they ran no risks, not even to their property; that after all they were not so noble but they treated the thief as he had treated them, and hoped, by a certain outward observance and a few prayers, and by walking in a particular straight though useless path from time to time, to save their souls. This may be to judge my neighbors harshly; for I believe that many of them are not aware that they have such an institution as the jail in their village.

It was formerly the custom in our village, when a poor debtor came out of jail, for his acquaintances to salute him, looking through their fingers, which were crossed to represent the grating of a jail window, "How do ye do?" My neighbors did not thus salute me, but first looked at me, and then at one another, as if I had returned from a long journey. I was put into jail as I was going to the shoemaker's to get a shoe which was mended. When I was let out the next morning, I proceeded to finish my errand, and, having put on my mended shoe, joined a huckleberry party, who were impatient to put themselves under my conduct; and in half an hour—for the horse was soon tackled—was in the midst of a huckleberry field, on one of our highest hills, two miles off, and then the State was nowhere to be seen.

This is the whole history of "My Prisons." [6]

I have never declined paying the highway tax, because I am as desirous of being a good neighbor as I am of being a bad subject; and as for supporting schools, I am doing my part to educate my fellow-countrymen now. It is for no particular item in the tax bill that I refuse to pay it. I simply wish to refuse allegiance to the State, to withdraw and stand aloof from it effectually. I do not care to trace the course of my dollar, if I could, till it buys a man or a musket to shoot one with—the dollar is innocent—but I am concerned to trace the effects of my allegiance. In fact, I quietly declare war with the State, after my fashion, though I will still make what use and get what advantage of her I can, as is usual in such cases.

If others pay the tax which is demanded of me, from a sympathy with the State, they do but what they have already done in their own case, or rather they abet injustice to a greater extent than the State requires. If they pay the tax from a mistaken interest in the individual taxed, to save his property, or prevent his going to jail, it is because they have not considered wisely how far they let their private feelings interfere with the public good.

This, then, is my position at present. But one cannot be too much on his guard in such a case, lest his action be biased by obstinacy or an undue regard for the opinions of men. Let him see that he does only what belongs to himself and to the hour.

I think sometimes, Why, this people mean well, they are only ignorant; they would do better if they knew how: why give your neighbors

[6] *Le Mie Prigioni,* a record of his imprisonment in Austria by the Italian patriot Silvio Pellico (1789–1854).

this pain to treat you as they are not inclined to? But I think again, This is no reason why I should do as they do, or permit others to suffer much greater pain of a different kind. Again, I sometimes say to myself, When many millions of men, without heat, without ill will, without personal feeling of any kind, demand of you a few shillings only, without the possibility, such is their constitution, of retracting or altering their present demand, and without the possibility, on your side, of appeal to any other millions, why expose yourself to this overwhelming brute force? You do not resist cold and hunger, the winds and the waves, thus obstinately; you quietly submit to a thousand similar necessities. You do not put your head into the fire. But just in proportion as I regard this as not wholly a brute force, but partly a human force, and consider that I have relations to those millions as to so many millions of men, and not of mere brute or inanimate things, I see that appeal is possible, first and instantaneously, from them to the Maker of them, and, secondly, from them to themselves. But if I put my head deliberately into the fire, there is no appeal to fire or to the Maker of fire, and I have only myself to blame. If I could convince myself that I have any right to be satisfied with men as they are, and to treat them accordingly, and not according, in some respects, to my requisitions and expectations of what they and I ought to be, then, like a good Mussulman and fatalist, I should endeavor to be satisfied with things as they are, and say it is the will of God. And, above all, there is this difference between resisting this and a purely brute or natural force, that I can resist this with some effect; but I cannot expect, like Orpheus, to change the nature of the rocks and trees and beasts.

I do not wish to quarrel with any man or nation. I do not wish to split hairs, to make fine distinctions, or set myself up as better than my neighbors. I seek rather, I may say, even an excuse for conforming to the laws of the land. I am but too ready to conform to them. Indeed, I have reason to suspect myself on this head; and each year, as the tax-gatherer comes round, I find myself disposed to review the acts and position of the general and State governments, and the spirit of the people, to discover a pretext for conformity.

We must affect our country as our parents,
And if at any time we alienate
Our love or industry from doing it honor,
We must respect effects and teach the soul
Matter of conscience and religion,
And not desire of rule or benefit.

I believe that the State will soon be able to take all my work of this sort out of my hands, and then I shall be no better a patriot than my fellow-countrymen. Seen from a lower point of view, the Constitution, with all its faults, is very good; the law and the courts are very respectable; even this State and this American government are, in many respects, very admirable, and rare things, to be thankful for, such as a great many have described them; but seen from a point of view a little higher, they are what I have described them; seen from a higher still, and the highest, who shall say what they are, or that they are worth looking at or thinking of at all?

However, the government does not concern me much, and I shall bestow the fewest possible thoughts on it. It is not many moments that I live under a government, even in this world. If a man is thought-free, fancy-free, imagination-free, that which *is not* never for a long time appearing *to be* to him, unwise rulers or reformers cannot fatally interrupt him.

I know that most men think differently from myself; but those whose lives are by profession devoted to the study of these or kindred subjects content me as little as any. Statesmen and legislators, standing so completely within the institution, never distinctly and nakedly behold it. They speak of moving society, but have no resting-place without it. They may be men of a certain experience and discrimination, and have no doubt invented ingenious and even useful systems, for which we sincerely thank them; but all their wit and usefulness lie within certain not very wide limits. They are wont to forget that the world is not governed by policy and expediency. Webster never goes behind government, and so cannot speak with authority about it. His words are wisdom to those legislators who contemplate no essential reform in the existing government; but for thinkers, and those who legislate for all time, he never once glances at the subject. I know of those whose serene and wise speculations on this theme would soon reveal the limits of his mind's range and hospitality. Yet, compared with the cheap professions of most reformers, and the still cheaper wisdom and eloquence of politicians in general, his are almost the only sensible and valuable words, and we thank Heaven for him. Comparatively, he is always strong, original, and, above all, practical. Still, his quality is not wisdom, but prudence. The lawyer's truth is not Truth, but consistency or a consistent expediency. Truth is always in harmony with herself, and is not concerned chiefly to reveal the justice that may consist with wrong-doing. He well deserves to be called, as he has been called, the Defender of the Constitution. There are really no blows to be given by him but defensive ones. He is not a leader, but a follower. His leaders are the men of '87. "I have never made an effort," he says, "and never propose to make an effort; I have never countenanced an effort, and never mean to countenance an effort, to disturb the arrangement as originally made, by which the various States came into the Union." Still thinking of the sanction which the Constitution gives to slavery, he says, "Because it was a part of the original compact—let it stand." Notwithstanding his special acuteness and ability, he is unable to take a fact out of its merely political relations, and behold it as it lies absolutely to be disposed of by the intellect—what, for instance, it behooves a man to do here in America today with regard to slavery—but ventures, or is driven, to make some such desperate answer as the following, while professing to speak absolutely, and as a private man—from which what new and singular code of social duties might be inferred? "The manner," says he, "in which the governments of those States where slavery exists are to regulate it is for their own consideration, under their responsibility to their constituents, to the general laws of propriety, humanity, and justice, and to God. Associations formed elsewhere, springing from a feeling of humanity, or any other cause, have nothing whatever to do with it. They have never received any encouragement from me, and they never will." [7]

They who know of no purer sources of truth, who have traced up its stream no higher, stand, and wisely stand, by the Bible and the Constitution, and drink at it there with reverence and humility; but they who behold where it comes trickling into this lake or that pool, gird up their loins once more, and continue their pilgrimage toward its fountainhead.

No man with a genius for legislation has appeared in America. They are rare in the history of the world. There are orators, politicians, and eloquent men, by the thousand; but the speaker has not yet opened his mouth to speak who is capable of settling the much-vexed questions of the day. We love eloquence for its own sake, and not for any truth which it may utter, or any heroism it may inspire. Our legislators have not yet learned the comparative value of free trade and of freedom, of union, and of rectitude, to a nation. They have no genius or talent for comparatively humble questions of taxation and finance, commerce and manufactures and agriculture. If we were left solely to the wordy wit of legislators in Congress for our guidance, uncorrected by the seasonable experience and the effectual complaints of the people, America would not long retain her rank among the nations. For eighteen hundred years, though perchance I have no right to say it, the New Testament has been written; yet where is the legislator who has wisdom and practical talent enough to avail himself of the light which it sheds on the science of legislation?

The authority of government, even such as I am willing to submit to—for I will cheerfully obey those who know and can do better than I, and in many things even those who neither know nor can do so well— is still an impure one: to be strictly just, it must have the sanction and consent of the governed. It can have no pure right over my person and property but what I concede to it. The progress from an absolute to a limited monarchy, from a limited monarchy to a democracy, is a progress toward a true respect for the individual. Even the Chinese philosopher was wise enough to regard the individual as the basis of the empire. Is a democracy, such as we know it, the last improvement

[7] These extracts have been inserted since the lecture was read. *Au.*

possible in government? Is it not possible to take a step further towards recognizing and organizing the rights of man? There will never be a really free and enlightened State until the State comes to recognize the individual as a higher and independent power, from which all its own power and authority are derived, and treats him accordingly. I please myself with imagining a State at last which can afford to be just to all men, and to treat the individual with respect as a neighbor; which even would not think it inconsistent with its own repose if a few were to live aloof from it, not meddling with it, nor embraced by it, who fulfilled all the duties of neighbors and fellow men. A State which bore this kind of fruit, and suffered it to drop off as fast as it ripened, would prepare the way for a still more perfect and glorious State, which also I have imagined, but not yet anywhere seen.

FROM **Walden** *(1854)*

2   *Where I Lived, and What I Lived For*

At a certain season of our life we are accustomed to consider every spot as the possible site of a house. I have thus surveyed the country on every side within a dozen miles of where I live. In imagination I have bought all the farms in succession, for all were to be bought, and I knew their price. I walked over each farmer's premises, tasted his wild apples, discoursed on husbandry with him, took his farm at his price, at any price, mortgaging it to him in my mind; even put a higher price on it,—took everything but a deed of it,—took his word for his deed, for I dearly love to talk,—cultivated it, and him too to some extent, I trust, and withdrew when I had enjoyed it long enough, leaving him to carry it on. This experience entitled me to be regarded as a sort of real-estate broker by my friends. Wherever I sat, there I might live, and the landscape radiated from me accordingly. What is a house but a *sedes,* a seat?—better if a country seat. I discovered many a site for a house not likely to be soon improved, which some might have thought too far from the village, but to my eyes the village was too far from it. Well, there I might live, I said; and there I did live, for an hour, a summer and a winter life; saw how I could let the years run off, buffet the winter through, and see the spring come in. The future inhabitants of this region, wherever they may place their houses, may be sure that they have been anticipated. An afternoon sufficed to lay out the land into orchard, wood-lot, and pasture, and to decide what fine oaks or pines should be left to stand before the door, and whence each blasted tree could be seen to the best advantage; and then I let it lie, fallow perchance, for a man is rich in proportion to the number of things which he can afford to let alone.

My imagination carried me so far that I even had the refusal of several farms,—the refusal was all I wanted,—but I never got my fingers burned by actual possession. The nearest that I came to actual possession was when I bought the Hollowell place, and had begun to sort my seeds, and collected materials with which to make a wheelbarrow to carry it on or off with; but before the owner gave me a deed of it, his wife—every man has such a wife—changed her mind and wished to keep it, and he offered me ten dollars to release him. Now, to speak the truth, I had but ten cents in the world, and it surpassed my arithmetic to tell, if I was that man who had ten cents, or who had a farm, or ten dollars, or all together. However, I let him keep the ten dollars and the farm too, for I had carried it far enough; or rather, to be generous, I sold him the farm for just what I gave for it, and, as he was not a rich man, made him a present of ten dollars, and still had my ten cents, and seeds, and materials for a wheelbarrow left. I found thus that I had been a rich man without any damage to my poverty. But I retained the landscape, and I have since annually carried off what it yielded without a wheelbarrow. With respect to landscapes,—

I am monarch of all I survey,
My right there is none to dispute.[1]

I have frequently seen a poet withdraw, having enjoyed the most valuable part of a farm, while the crusty farmer supposed that he had got a few wild apples only. Why, the owner does not know it for many years when a poet has put his farm in rhyme, the most admirable kind of invisible fence, has fairly impounded it, milked it, skimmed it, and got all the cream, and left the farmer only the skimmed milk.

The real attractions of the Hollowell farm, to me, were: its complete retirement, being about two miles from the village, half a mile from the nearest neighbor, and separated from the highway by a broad field; its bounding on the river, which the owner said protected it by its fogs from frosts in the spring, though that was nothing to me; the gray color and ruinous state of the house and barn, and the dilapidated fences, which put such an interval between me and the last occupant; the hollow and lichen-covered apple tree, gnawed by rabbits, showing what kind of neighbors I should have; but above all, the recollection I had of it from my earliest voyages up the river, when the house was concealed behind a dense grove of red maples, through which I heard the housedog bark. I was in haste to buy it, before the proprietor finished getting out some rocks, cutting down the hollow apple trees, and grubbing up some young birches which had sprung up in the pasture, or, in short, had made any more of his improvements. To enjoy these advantages I was ready to carry it on; like Atlas, to take the world on

[1] From "Verses Supposed to be Written by Alexander Selkirk" by William Cowper (1731–1800).

my shoulders,—I never heard what compensation he received for that,—and do all those things which had no other motive or excuse but that I might pay for it and be unmolested in my possession of it; for I knew all the while that it would yield the most abundant crop of the kind I wanted, if I could only afford to let it alone. But it turned out as I have said.

All that I could say, then, with respect to farming on a large scale—I have always cultivated a garden—was, that I had had my seeds ready. Many think that seeds improve with age. I have no doubt that time discriminates between the good and the bad; and when at last I shall plant, I shall be less likely to be disappointed. But I would say to my fellows, once for all, As long as possible live free and uncommitted. It makes but little difference whether you are committed to a farm or the county jail.

Old Cato,[2] whose "De Re Rustica" is my "Cultivator," says,—and the only translation I have seen makes sheer nonsense of the passage,—"When you think of getting a farm turn it thus in your mind, not to buy greedily; nor spare your pains to look at it, and do not think it enough, to go round it once. The oftener you go there the more it will please you, if it is good." I think I shall not buy greedily, but go round and round it as long as I live, and be buried in it first, that it may please me the more at last.

The present was my next experiment of this kind, which I purpose to describe more at length, for convenience putting the experience of two years into one. As I have said, I do not propose to write an ode to dejection, but to brag as lustily as chanticleer in the morning, standing on his roost, if only to wake my neighbors up.

When first I took up my abode in the woods, that is, began to spend my nights as well as days there, which, by accident, was on Independence Day, or the Fourth of July, 1845, my house was not finished for winter, but was merely a defence against the rain, without plastering or chimney, the walls being of rough, weather-stained boards, with wide chinks, which made it cool at night. The upright white hewn studs and freshly planed door and window casings gave it a clean and airy look, especially in the morning, when its timbers were saturated with dew, so that I fancied that by noon some sweet gum would exude from them. To my imagination it retained throughout the day more or less of this auroral character, reminding me of a certain house on a mountain which I had visited a year before. This was an airy and unplastered cabin, fit to entertain a travelling god, and where a goddess might trail her garments. The winds which passed over my dwelling were such as sweep over the ridges of mountains, bearing the broken strains, or celestial parts only, of terrestrial music. The morning wind forever blows, the poem of creation is uninterrupted; but few are the ears that hear it. Olympus is but the outside of the earth everywhere.

2 Marcus Cato (234–149 B.C.), a Roman patriot.

The only house I had been the owner of before, if I except a boat, was a tent, which I used occasionally when making excursions in the summer, and this is still rolled up in my garret; but the boat, after passing from hand to hand, has gone down the stream of time. With this more substantial shelter about me, I had made some progress toward settling in the world. This frame, so slightly clad, was a sort of crystallization around me, and reacted on the builder. It was suggestive somewhat as a picture in outlines. I did not need to go outdoors to take the air, for the atmosphere within had lost none of its freshness. It was not so much within-doors as behind a door where I sat, even in the rainiest weather. The Harivansa [3] says "An abode without birds is like a meat without seasoning." Such was not my abode, for I found myself suddenly neighbor to the birds; not by having imprisoned one, but having caged myself near them. I was not only nearer to some of those which commonly frequent the garden and the orchard, but to these wilder and more thrilling songsters of the forest which never, or rarely, serenade a villager,—the wood thrush, the veery, the scarlet tanager, the field sparrow, the whip-poor-will, and many others.

I was seated by the shore of a small pond, about a mile and a half south of the village of Concord and somewhat higher than it, in the midst of an extensive wood between that town and Lincoln, and about two miles south of that our only field known to fame, Concord Battle Grounds; but I was so low in the woods that the opposite shore, half a mile off, like the rest, covered with wood, was my most distant horizon. For the first week, whenever I looked out on the pond it impressed me like a tarn high up on the side of a mountain, its bottom far above the surface of other lakes, and, as the sun arose, I saw it throwing off its nightly clothing of mist, and here and there, by degrees, its soft ripples or its smooth reflecting surface was revealed, while the mists, like ghosts, were stealthily withdrawing in every direction into the woods, as at the breaking up of some nocturnal conventicle. The very dew seemed to hang upon the trees later into the day than usual, as on the sides of mountains.

This small lake was of most value as a neighbor in the intervals of a gentle rain-storm in August, when, both air and water being perfectly still, but the sky overcast, mid-afternoon had all the serenity of evening, and the wood thrush sang around, and was heard from shore to shore. A lake like this is never smoother than at such a time; and the clear portion of the air above it being shallow and darkened by clouds, the water, full of light and reflections, becomes a lower heaven itself so much the more important. From a hill-top near by, where the wood had been recently cut off, there was a pleasant vista southward across the pond, through a wide indentation in the hills which form the shore there, where their opposite sides sloping toward each other suggested a stream flowing out in that direction through a wooded

[3] A fifth-century Sanskrit poem.

valley, but stream there was none. That way I looked between and over
the near green hills to some distant and higher ones in the horizon,
tinged with blue. Indeed, by standing on tiptoe I could catch a glimpse
of some of the peaks of the still bluer and more distant mountain
ranges in the northwest, those true-blue coins from heaven's own mint,
and also of some portion of the village. But in other directions, even
from this point, I could not see over or beyond the woods which surrounded me. It is well to have some water in your neighborhood, to
give buoyancy to and float the earth. One value even of the smallest
well is, that when you look into it you see that earth is not continent
but insular. This is as important as that it keeps butter cool. When I
looked across the pond from this peak toward the Sudbury meadows,
which in time of flood I distinguished elevated perhaps by a mirage in
their seething valley, like a coin in a basin, all the earth beyond the
pond appeared like a thin crust insulated and floated even by this small
sheet of intervening water, and I was reminded that this on which I
dwelt was but *dry land.*

Though the view from my door was still more contracted, I did
not feel crowded or confined in the least. There was pasture enough
for my imagination. The low shrub oak plateau to which the opposite
shore arose stretched away toward the prairies of the West and the
steppes of Tartary, affording ample room for all the roving families of
men. "There are none happy in the world but beings who enjoy freely
a vast horizon,"—said Damodara, when his herds required new and
larger pastures.

Both place and time were changed, and I dwelt nearer to those
parts of the universe and to those eras in history which had most
attracted me. Where I lived was as far off as many a region viewed
nightly by astronomers. We are wont to imagine rare and delectable
places in some remote and more celestial corner of the system, behind
the constellation of Cassiopeia's Chair, far from noise and disturbance.
I discovered that my house actually had its site in such a withdrawn,
but forever new and unprofaned, part of the universe. If it were worth
the while to settle in those parts near to the Pleiades or the Hyades, to
Aldebaran or Altair, then I was really there, or at an equal remoteness
from the life which I had left behind, dwindled and twinkling with as
fine a ray to my nearest neighbor, and to be seen only in moonless
nights by him. Such was that part of creation where I had squatted;—

There was a shepherd that did live,
    And held his thoughts as high
As were the mounts whereon his flocks
    Did hourly feed him by.

What should we think of the shepherd's life if his flocks always wandered to higher pastures than his thoughts?

Every morning was a cheerful invitation to make my life of equal simplicity, and I may say innocence, with Nature herself. I have been as sincere a worshipper of Aurora as the Greeks. I got up early and bathed in the pond; that was a religious exercise, and one of the best things which I did. They say that characters were engraven on the bathing tub of King Tching-thang to this effect: "Renew thyself completely each day; do it again, and again, and forever again." I can understand that. Morning brings back the heroic ages. I was as much affected by the faint hum of a mosquito making its invisible and unimaginable tour through my apartment at earliest dawn, when I was sitting with door and windows open, as I could be by any trumpet that ever sang of fame. It was Homer's requiem; itself an Iliad and Odyssey in the air, singing its own wrath and wanderings. There was something cosmical about it; a standing advertisement, till forbidden, of the everlasting vigor and fertility of the world. The morning, which is the most memorable season of the day, is the awakening hour. Then there is least somnolence in us; and for an hour, at least, some part of us awakes which slumbers all the rest of the day and night. Little is to be expected of that day, if it can be called a day, to which we are not awakened by our Genius, but by the mechanical nudgings of some servitor, are not awakened by our own newly acquired force and aspirations from within, accompanied by the undulations of celestial music, instead of factory bells, and a fragrance filling the air—to a higher life than we fell asleep from; and thus the darkness bear its fruit, and prove itself to be good, no less than the light. That man who does not believe that each day contains an earlier, more sacred, and auroral hour than he has yet profaned, has despaired of life, and is pursuing a descending and darkening way. After a partial cessation of his sensuous life, the soul of man, or its organs rather, are reinvigorated each day, and his Genius tries again what noble life it can make. All memorable events, I should say, transpire in morning time and in a morning atmosphere. The Vedas[4] say, "All intelligences awake with the morning." Poetry and art, and the fairest and most memorable of the actions of men, date from such an hour. All poets and heroes, like Memnon, are the children of Aurora, and emit their music at sunrise. To him whose elastic and vigorous thought keeps pace with the sun, the day is a perpetual morning. It matters not what the clocks say or the attitudes and labors of men. Morning is when I am awake and there is a dawn in me. Moral reform is the effort to throw off sleep. Why is it that men give so poor an account of their day if they have not been slumbering? They are not such poor calculators. If they had not been overcome with drowsiness, they would have performed something. The millions are awake enough for physical labor; but only one in a million is awake enough for effective intellectual exertion, only one in a hundred millions to a poetic or divine life. To be awake is to be alive. I have never

4 Sacred Hindu books.

yet met a man who was quite awake. How could I have looked him in the face?

We must learn to reawaken and keep ourselves awake, not by mechanical aids, but by an infinite expectation of the dawn, which does not forsake us in our soundest sleep. I know of no more encouraging fact than the unquestionable ability of man to elevate his life by a conscious endeavor. It is something to be able to paint a particular picture, or to carve a statue, and so to make a few objects beautiful; but it is far more glorious to carve and paint the very atmosphere and medium through which we look, which morally we can do. To affect the quality of the day, that is the highest of arts. Every man is tasked to make his life, even in its details, worthy of the contemplation of his most elevated and critical hour. If we refused, or rather used up, such paltry information as we get, the oracles would distinctly inform us how this might be done.

I went to the woods because I wished to live deliberately, to front only the essential facts of life, and see if I could not learn what it had to teach, and not, when I came to die, discover that I had not lived. I did not wish to live what was not life, living is so dear; nor did I wish to practise resignation, unless it was quite necessary. I wanted to live deep and suck out all the marrow of life, to live so sturdily and Spartanlike as to put to rout all that was not life, to cut a broad swath and shave close, to drive life into a corner, and reduce it to its lowest terms, and, if it proved to be mean, why then to get the whole and genuine meanness of it, and publish its meanness to the world; or if it were sublime, to know it by experience, and be able to give a true account of it in my next excursion. For most men, it appears to me, are in a strange uncertainty about it, whether it is of the devil or of God, and have *somewhat hastily* concluded that it is the chief end of man here to "glorify God and enjoy him forever."

Still we live meanly, like ants; though the fable tells us that we were long ago changed into men; like pygmies we fight with cranes; it is error upon error, and clout upon clout, and our best virtue has for its occasion a superfluous and evitable wretchedness. Our life is frittered away by detail. An honest man has hardly need to count more than his ten fingers, or in extreme cases he may add his ten toes, and lump the rest. Simplicity, simplicity, simplicity! I say, let your affairs be as two or three, and not a hundred or a thousand; instead of a million count half a dozen, and keep your accounts on your thumb-nail. In the midst of this chopping sea of civilized life, such are the clouds and storms and quicksands and thousand-and-one items to be allowed for, that a man has to live, if he would not founder and go to the bottom and not make his port at all, by dead reckoning, and he must be a great calculator indeed who succeeds. Simplify, simplify. Instead of three meals a day, if it be necessary eat but one; instead of a hundred dishes, five; and reduce other things in proportion. Our life is like a German

Confederacy, made up of petty states, with its boundary forever fluctuating, so that even a German cannot tell you how it is bounded at any moment. The nation itself, with all its so-called internal improvements, which, by the way are all external and superficial, is just such an unwieldly and overgrown establishment, cluttered with furniture and tripped up by its own traps, ruined by luxury and heedless expense, by want of calculation and a worthy aim, as the million households in the land; and the only cure for it, as for them, is in a rigid economy, a stern and more than Spartan simplicity of life and elevation of purpose. It lives too fast. Men think that it is essential that the *Nation* have commerce, and export ice, and talk through a telegraph, and ride thirty miles an hour, without a doubt, whether *they* do or not; but whether we should live like baboons or like men, is a little uncertain. If we do not get out sleepers,[5] and forge rails, and devote days and nights to the work, but go to tinkering upon our *lives* to improve *them*, who will build railroads? And if railroads are not built, how shall we get to heaven in season? But if we stay at home and mind our business, who will want railroads? We do not ride on the railroad; it rides upon us. Did you ever think what those sleepers are that underlie the railroad? Each one is a man, an Irishman, or a Yankee man. The rails are laid on them, and they are covered with sand, and the cars run smoothly over them. They are sound sleepers, I assure you. And every few years a new lot is laid down and run over; so that, if some have the pleasure of riding on a rail, others have the misfortune to be ridden upon. And when they run over a man that is walking in his sleep, a supernumerary sleeper in the wrong position, and wake him up, they suddenly stop the cars, and make a hue and cry about it, as if this were an exception. I am glad to know that it takes a gang of men for every five miles to keep the sleepers down and level in their beds as it is, for this is a sign that they may sometime get up again.

Why should we live with such hurry and waste of life? We are determined to be starved before we are hungry. Men say that a stitch in time saves nine, and so they take a thousand stitches to-day to save nine to-morrow. As for *work*, we haven't any of any consequence. We have the Saint Vitus' dance, and cannot possibly keep our heads still. If I should only give a few pulls at the parish bell-rope, as for a fire, that is, without setting the bell, there is hardly a man on his farm in the outskirts of Concord, notwithstanding that press of engagements which was his excuse so many times this morning, nor a boy, nor a woman, I might almost say, but would forsake all and follow that sound, not mainly to save property from the flames, but, if we will confess the truth, much more to see it burn, since burn it must, and we, be it known, did not set it on fire,—or to see it put out, and have a hand in it, if that is done as handsomely; yes, even if it were the parish church

[5] Railroad ties.

itself. Hardly a man takes a half-hour's nap after dinner, but when he wakes he holds up his head and asks, "What's the news?" as if the rest of mankind had stood his sentinels. Some give directions to be waked every half-hour, doubtless for no other purpose; and then, to pay for it, they tell what they have dreamed. After a night's sleep the news is as indispensable as the breakfast. "Pray tell me anything new that has happened to a man anywhere on this globe,"—and he reads it over his coffee and rolls, that a man has had his eyes gouged out this morning on the Wachito River; never dreaming the while that he lives in the dark unfathomed mammoth cave of this world, and has but the rudiment of an eye himself.

For my part, I could easily do without the post office. I think that there are very few important communications made through it. To speak critically, I never received more than one or two letters in my life—I wrote this some years ago—that were worth the postage. The penny-post is, commonly, an institution through which you seriously offer a man that penny for his thoughts which is so often safely offered in jest. And I am sure that I never read any memorable news in a newspaper. If we read of one man robbed, or murdered, or killed by accident, or one house burned, or one vessel wrecked, or one steamboat blown up, or one cow run over on the Western Railroad, or one mad dog killed, or one lot of grasshoppers in the winter,—we never need read of another. One is enough. If you are acquainted with the principle, what do you care for a myriad instances and applications? To a philosopher all *news*, as it is called, is gossip, and they who edit and read it are old women over their tea. Yet not a few are greedy after this gossip. There was such a rush, as I hear, the other day at one of the offices to learn the foreign news by the last arrival, that several large squares of plate glass belonging to the establishment were broken by the pressure,—news which I seriously think a ready wit might write a twelvemonth, or twelve years, beforehand with sufficient accuracy. As for Spain, for instance, if you know how to throw in Don Carlos and the Infanta, and Don Pedro and Seville and Granada, from time to time in the right proportions,—they may have changed the names a little since I saw the papers,—and serve up a bullfight when other entertainments fail, it will be true to the letter, and give us as good an idea of the exact state or ruin of things in Spain as the most succinct and lucid reports under this head in the newspapers: and as for England, almost the last significant scrap of news from that quarter was the revolution of 1649; and if you have learned the history of her crops for an average year, you never need attend to that thing again, unless your speculations are of a merely pecuniary character. If one may judge who rarely looks into the newspapers, nothing new does ever happen in foreign parts, a French revolution not excepted.

What news! how much more important to know what that is which was never old! "Kieou-he-yu [6] (great dignitary of the state of Wei) sent a man to Khoung-tseu to know his news. Khoung-tseu caused the messenger to be seated near him, and question him in these terms: What is your master doing? The messenger answered with respect: My master desires to diminish the number of his faults, but he cannot come to the end of them. The messenger being gone, the philosopher remarked: What a worthy messenger! What a worthy messenger!" The preacher, instead of vexing the ears of drowsy farmers on their day of rest at the end of the week,—for Sunday is the fit conclusion of an ill-spent week, and not the fresh and brave beginning of a new one,—with this one other draggle-tail of a sermon, should shout with thundering voice, "Pause! Avast! Why so seeming fast, but deadly slow?"

Shams and delusions are esteemed for soundest truths, while reality is fabulous. If men would steadily observe realities only, and not allow themselves to be deluded, life, to compare it with such things as we know, would be like a fairy tale and the Arabian Nights' Entertainments. If we respected only what is inevitable and has a right to be, music and poetry would resound along the streets. When we are unhurried and wise, we perceive that only great and worthy things have any permanent and absolute existence, that petty fears and petty pleasures are but the shadow of the reality. This is always exhilarating and sublime. By closing the eyes and slumbering, and consenting to be deceived by shows, men establish and confirm their daily life of routine and habit everywhere, which still is built on purely illusory foundations. Children, who play life, discern its true law and relations more clearly than men, who fail to live it worthily, but who think that they are wiser by experience, that is, by failure. I have read in a Hindoo book, that "there was a king's son, who, being expelled in infancy from his native city, was brought up by a forester, and, growing up to maturity in that state, imagined himself to belong to the barbarous race with which he lived. One of his father's ministers having discovered him, revealed to him what he was, and the misconception of his character was removed, and he knew himself to be a prince. So soul," continues the Hindoo philosopher, "from the circumstances in which it is placed, mistakes its own character, until the truth is revealed to it by some holy teacher, and then it knows itself to be *Brahme*." I perceive that we inhabitants of New England live this mean life that we do because our vision does not penetrate the surface of things. We think that that *is* which *appears* to be. If a man should walk through this town and see only the reality, where, think you, would the "Mill-dam" [7] go to? If he should give us an account of the realities he beheld there, we should not recognize the place in his description. Look at a meeting-house, or a court-house, or

[6] From Analects of Confucius.

[7] Concord had previously been a mill town, and the dam a place where its citizens congregated.

a jail, or a shop, or a dwelling-house, and say what that thing really is before a true gaze, and they would all go to pieces in your account of them. Men esteem truth remote, in the outskirts of the system, behind the farthest star, before Adam and after the last man. In eternity there is indeed something true and sublime. But all these times and places and occasions are now and here. God himself culminates in the present moment, and will never be more divine in the lapse of all the ages. And we are enabled to apprehend at all what is sublime and noble only by the perpetual instilling and drenching of the reality that surrounds us. The universe constantly and obediently answers to our conceptions; whether we travel fast or slow, the track is laid for us. Let us spend our lives in conceiving then. The poet or the artist never yet had so fair and noble a design but some of his posterity at least could accomplish it.

Let us spend one day as deliberately as Nature, and not be thrown off the track by every nutshell and mosquito's wing that falls on the rails. Let us rise early and fast, or break fast, gently and without perturbation; let company come and let company go, let the bells ring and the children cry,—determined to make a day of it. Why should we knock under and go with the stream? Let us not be upset and over-whelmed in that terrible rapid and whirlpool called a dinner, situated in the meridian shallows. Weather this danger and you are safe, for the rest of the way is down hill. With unrelaxed nerves, with morning vigor, sail by it, looking another way, tied to the mast like Ulysses. If the engine whistles, let it whistle till it is hoarse for its pains. If the bell rings, why should we run? We will consider what kind of music they are like. Let us settle ourselves, and work and wedge our feet downward through the mud and slush of opinion, and prejudice, and tradition, and delusion, and appearance, that alluvion which covers the globe, through Paris and London, through New York and Boston and Concord, through Church and State, through poetry and philosophy and religion, till we come to a hard bottom and rocks in place, which we can call *reality*, and say, This is, and no mistake; and then begin, having a point d'appui, below freshet and frost and fire, a place where you might found a wall or a state, or set a lamp-post safely, or perhaps a gauge, not a Nilometer,[8] but a Realometer, that future ages might know how deep a freshet of shams and appearances had gathered from time to time. If you stand right fronting and face to face to a fact, you will see the sun glimmer on both its surfaces, as if it were a cimeter, and feel its sweet edge dividing you through the heart and marrow, and so you will happily conclude your mortal career. Be it life or death, we crave only reality. If we are really dying, let us hear the rattle in our throats and feel cold in the extremities; if we are alive, let us go about our business.

Time is but the stream I go a-fishing in. I drink at it; but while I drink I see the sandy bottom and detect how shallow it is. Its thin

---

[8] A device for measuring the rise and fall of the Nile in antiquity.

current slides away, but eternity remains. I would drink deeper; fish in the sky, whose bottom is pebbly with stars. I cannot count one. I know not the first letter of the alphabet. I have always been regretting that I was not as wise as the day I was born. The intellect is a cleaver; it discerns and rifts its way into the secret of things. I do not wish to be any more busy with my hands than is necessary. My head is hands and feet. I feel all my best faculties concentrated in it. My instinct tells me that my head is an organ for burrowing, as some creatures use their snout and fore paws, and with it I would mine and burrow my way through these hills. I think that the richest vein is somewhere hereabouts; so by the divining-rod and thin rising vapors I judge; and here I will begin to mine.

5   *Solitude*

This is a delicious evening, when the whole body is one sense, and imbibes delight through every pore. I go and come with a strange liberty in Nature, a part of herself. As I walk along the stony shore of the pond in my shirt-sleeves, though it is cool as well as cloudy and windy, and I see nothing special to attract me, all the elements are unusually congenial to me. The bullfrogs trump to usher in the night, and the note of the whip-poor-will is borne on the rippling wind from over the water. Sympathy with the fluttering alder and poplar leaves almost takes away my breath; yet, like the lake, my serenity is rippled but not ruffled. These small waves raised by the evening wind are as remote from storm as the smooth reflecting surface. Though it is now dark, the wind still blows and roars in the wood, the waves still dash, and some creatures lull the rest with their notes. The repose is never complete. The wildest animals do not repose, but seek their prey now; the fox, and skunk, and rabbit, now roam the fields and woods without fear. They are Nature's watchmen,—links which connect the days of animated life.

When I return to my house I find that visitors have been there and left their cards, either a bunch of flowers, or a wreath of evergreen, or a name in pencil on a yellow walnut leaf or a chip. They who come rarely to the woods take some little piece of the forest into their hands to play with by the way, which they leave, either intentionally or accidentally. One has peeled a willow wand, woven it into a ring, and dropped it on my table. I could always tell if visitors had called in my absence, either by the bended twigs or grass, or the print of their shoes, and generally of what sex or age or quality they were by some slight trace left, as a flower dropped, or a bunch of grass plucked and thrown away, even as far off as the railroad, half a mile distant, or by the lingering odor of a cigar or pipe. Nay, I was frequently notified of the passage of a traveller along the highway sixty rods off by the scent of his pipe.

There is commonly sufficient space about us. Our horizon is never quite at our elbows. The thick wood is not just at our door, nor the pond, but somewhat is always clearing, familiar and worn by us, appropriated and fenced in some way, and reclaimed from Nature. For what reason have I this vast range and circuit, some square miles of unfrequented forest, for my privacy, abandoned to me by men? My nearest neighbor is a mile distant, and no house is visible from any place but the hill-tops within half a mile of my own. I have my horizon bounded by woods all to myself; a distant view of the railroad where it touches the pond on the one hand, and of the fence which skirts the woodland road on the other. But for the most part it is as solitary where I live as on the prairies. It is as much Asia or Africa as New England. I have, as it were, my own sun and moon and stars, and a little world all to myself. At night there was never a traveller passed my house, or knocked at my door, more than if I were the first or last man; unless it were in the spring, when at long intervals some came from the village to fish for pouts,—they plainly fished much more in the Walden Pond of their own natures, and baited their hooks with darkness,—but they soon retreated, usually with light baskets, and left "the world to darkness and to me," and the black kernel of the night was never profaned by any human neighborhood. I believe that men are generally still a little afraid of the dark, though the witches are all hung, and Christianity and candles have been introduced.

Yet I experienced sometimes that the most sweet and tender, the most innocent and encouraging society may be found in any natural object, even for the poor misanthrope and most melancholy man. There can be no very black melancholy to him who lives in the midst of nature and has his senses still. There was never yet such a storm but it was Æolian music to a healthy and innocent ear. Nothing can rightly compel a simple and brave man to a vulgar sadness. While I enjoy the friendship of the seasons I trust that nothing can make life a burden to me. The gentle rain which waters my beans and keeps me in the house to-day is not drear and melancholy, but good for me too. Though it prevents my hoeing them, it is of far more worth than my hoeing. If it should continue so long as to cause the seeds to rot in the ground and destroy the potatoes in the low lands, it would still be good for the grass on the uplands, and, being good for the grass, it would be good for me. Sometimes, when I compare myself with other men, it seems as if I were more favored by the gods than they, beyond any deserts that I am conscious of; as if I had a warrant and surety at their hands which my fellows have not, and were especially guided and guarded. I do not flatter myself, but if it be possible they flatter me. I have never felt lonesome, or in the least oppressed by a sense of solitude, but once, and that was a few weeks after I came to the woods, when, for an hour, I doubted if the near neighborhood of man was not essential to a serene and healthy life. To be alone was something unpleasant. But I was at the same time conscious of a light insanity in my mood, and seemed to foresee my recovery. In the midst of a gentle rain while these thoughts prevailed, I was suddenly sensible of such sweet and beneficent society in Nature, in the very pattering of the drops, and in every sound and sight around my house, an infinite and unaccountable friendliness all at once like an atmosphere sustaining me, as made the fancied advantages of human neighborhood insignificant, and I have never thought of them since. Every little pine needle expanded and swelled with sympathy and befriended me. I was so distinctly made aware of the presence of something kindred to me, even in scenes which we are accustomed to call wild and dreary, and also that the nearest of blood to me and humanest was not a person nor a villager, that I thought no place could ever be strange to me again.—

Mourning untimely consumes the sad;
Few are their days in the land of the living,
Beautiful daughter of Toscar.[10]

Some of my pleasantest hours were during the long rainstorms in the spring or fall, which confined me to the house for the afternoon as well as the forenoon, soothed by their ceaseless roar and felting; when an early twilight ushered in a long evening in which many thoughts had time to take root and unfold themselves. In those driving northeast rains which tried the village houses so, when the maids stood ready with mop and pail in front entries to keep the deluge out, I sat behind my door in my little house, which was all entry, and thoroughly enjoyed its protection. In one heavy thunder-shower the lightning struck a large pitch pine across the pond, making a very conspicuous and perfectly regular spiral groove from top to bottom, an inch or more deep, and four or five inches wide, as you would groove a walking-stick. I passed it again the other day, and was struck with awe on looking up and beholding that mark, now more distinct than ever, where a terrific and resistless bolt came down out of the harmless sky eight years ago. Men frequently say to me, "I should think you would feel lonesome down there, and want to be nearer to folks, rainy and snowy days and nights especially." I am tempted to reply to such,—This whole earth which we inhabit is but a point in space. How far apart, think you, dwell the two most distant inhabitants of yonder star, the breadth of whose disk cannot be appreciated by our instruments? Why should I feel lonely? Is not our planet in the Milky Way? This which you put seems to me not to be the most important question. What sort of space is that which separates a man from his fellows and makes him solitary? I have found that no exertion of the legs can bring two minds much nearer to one another. What do we want most to dwell near to? Not to many men surely, the depot, the post-office, the bar-room, the meeting-house, the

[10] Taken from the pseudo-epic poems of "Ossian."

school-house, the grocery, Beacon Hill, or the Five Points, where men most congregate, but to the perennial source of our life, whence in all our experience we have found that to issue, as the willow stands near the water and sends out its roots in that direction. This will vary with different natures, but this is the place where a wise man will dig his cellar. . . . I one evening overtook one of my townsmen, who has accumulated what is called "a handsome property,"—though I never got a *fair* view of it,—on the Walden road, driving a pair of cattle to market, who inquired of me how I could bring my mind to give up so many of the comforts of life. I answered that I was very sure I liked it passably well; I was not joking. And so I went home to my bed, and left him to pick his way through the darkness and the mud to Brighton,—or Bright-town,—which place he would reach some time in the morning.

Any prospect of awakening or coming to life to a dead man makes indifferent all times and places. The place where that may occur is always the same, and indescribably pleasant to all our senses. For the most part we allow only outlying and transient circumstances to make our occasions. They are, in fact, the cause of our distraction. Nearest to all things is that power which fashions their being. *Next* to us the grandest laws are continually being executed. *Next* to us is not the workman whom we have hired, with whom we love so well to talk, but the workman whose work we are.

"How vast and profound is the influence of the subtle powers of Heaven and of Earth!"

"We seek to perceive them, and we do not see them; we seek to hear them, and we do not hear them; identified with the substance of things, they cannot be separated from them."

"They cause that in all the universe men purify and sanctify their hearts, and clothe themselves in their holiday garments to offer sacrifices and oblations to their ancestors. It is an ocean of subtle intelligences. They are everywhere, above us, on our left, on our right; they environ us on all sides."

We are the subjects of an experiment which is not a little interesting to me. Can we not do without the society of our gossips a little while under these circumstances,—have our own thoughts to cheer us? Confucius says truly, "Virtue does not remain as an abandoned orphan; it must of necessity have neighbors."

With thinking we may be beside ourselves in a sane sense. By a conscious effort of the mind we can stand aloof from actions and their consequences; and all things, good and bad, go by us like a torrent. We are not wholly involved in Nature. I may be either the driftwood in the stream, or Indra in the sky looking down on it. I *may* be affected by a theatrical exhibition; on the other hand, I *may not* be affected by an actual event which appears to concern me much more. I only know myself as a human entity; the scene, so to speak, of thoughts and affections; and am sensible of a certain doubleness by which I can stand as remote from myself as from another. However intense my experience, I am conscious of the presence and criticism of a part of me, which, as it were, is not a part of me, but spectator, sharing no experience, but taking note of it, and that is no more I than it is you. When the play, it may be the tragedy, of life is over, the spectator goes his way. It was a kind of fiction, a work of the imagination only, so far as he was concerned. This doubleness may easily make us poor neighbors and friends sometimes.

I find it wholesome to be alone the greater part of the time. To be in company, even with the best, is soon wearisome and dissipating. I love to be alone. I never found the companion that was so companionable as solitude. We are for the most part more lonely when we go abroad among men than when we stay in our chambers. A man thinking or working is always alone, let him be where he will. Solitude is not measured by the miles of space that intervene between a man and his fellows. The really diligent student in one of the crowded hives of Cambridge College is as solitary as a dervis in the desert. The farmer can work alone in the field or the woods all day, hoeing or chopping, and not feel lonesome, because he is employed; but when he comes home at night he cannot sit down in a room alone, at the mercy of his thoughts, but must be where he can "see the folks," and recreate, and, as he thinks, remunerate himself for his day's solitude; and hence he wonders how the student can sit alone in the house all night and most of the day without ennui and "the blues;" but he does not realize that the student, though in the house, is still at work in *his* field, and chopping in *his* woods, as the farmer in his, and in turn seeks the same recreation and society that the latter does, though it may be a more condensed form of it.

Society is commonly too cheap. We meet at very short intervals, not having had time to acquire any new value for each other. We meet at meals three times a day, and give each other a new taste of that old musty cheese that we are. We have had to agree on a certain set of rules, called etiquette and politeness, to make this frequent meeting tolerable and that we need not come to open war. We meet at the post-office, and at the sociable, and about the fireside every night; we live thick and are in each other's way, and stumble over one another, and I think that we thus lose some respect for one another. Certainly less frequency would suffice for all important and hearty communications. Consider the girls in a factory,—never alone, hardly in their dreams. It would be better if there were but one inhabitant to a square mile, as where I live. The value of a man is not in his skin, that we should touch him.

I have heard of a man lost in the woods and dying of famine and exhaustion at the foot of a tree, whose loneliness was relieved by the grotesque visions with which, owing to bodily weakness, his diseased imagination surrounded him, and which he believed to be real. So also, owing to bodily and mental health and strength, we may be continually cheered by a like but more normal and natural society, and come to know that we are never alone.

I have a great deal of company in my house; especially in the morning, when nobody calls. Let me suggest a few comparisons, that some one may convey an idea of my situation. I am no more lonely than the loon in the pond that laughs so loud, or than Walden Pond itself. What company has that lonely lake, I pray? And yet it has not the blue devils, but the blue angels in it, in the azure tint of its waters. The sun is alone, except in thick weather, when there sometimes appear to be two, but one is a mock sun. God is alone,—but the devil, he is far from being alone; he sees a great deal of company; he is legion. I am no more lonely than a single mullein or dandelion in a pasture, or a bean leaf, or sorrel, or a horse-fly, or a bumblebee. I am no more lonely than the Mill Brook, or a weathercock, or the north star, or the south wind, or an April shower, or a January thaw, or the first spider in a new house.

I have occasional visits in the long winter evenings, when the snow falls fast and the wind howls in the wood, from an old settler and original proprietor, who is reported to have dug Walden Pond, and stoned it, and fringed it with pine woods; who tells me stories of old time and of new eternity; and between us we manage to pass a cheerful evening with social mirth and pleasant views of things, even without apples or cider,—a most wise and humorous friend, whom I love much, who keeps himself more secret than ever did Goffe or Whalley; and though he is thought to be dead, none can show where he is buried. An elderly dame, too, dwells in my neighborhood, invisible to most persons, in whose odorous herb garden I love to stroll sometimes, gathering simples and listening to her fables; for she has a genius of unequalled fertility, and her memory runs back farther than mythology, and she can tell me the original of every fable, and on what fact every one is founded, for the incidents occurred when she was young. A ruddy and lusty old dame, who delights in all weathers and seasons, and is likely to outlive all her children yet.

The indescribable innocence and beneficence of Nature,—of sun and wind and rain, of summer and winter,—such health, such cheer, they afford forever! and such sympathy have they ever with our race, that all Nature would be affected, and the sun's brightness fade, and the winds would sigh humanely, and the clouds rain tears, and the woods shed their leaves and put on mourning in midsummer, if any man should ever for a just cause grieve. Shall I not have intelligence with the earth? Am I not partly leaves and vegetable mould myself?

What is the pill which will keep us well, serene, contented? Not my or thy great-grandfather's, but our great-grandmother Nature's universal, vegetable, botanic medicines, by which she has kept herself young always, outlived so many old Parrs in her day, and fed her health with their decaying fatness. For my panacea, instead of one of those quack vials of a mixture dipped from Acheron and the Dead Sea, which come out of those long shallow black-schooner looking wagons which we sometimes see made to carry bottles, let me have a draught of undiluted morning air. Morning air! If men will not drink of this at the fountain-head of the day, why, then, we must even bottle up some and sell it in the shops, for the benefit of those who have lost their subscription ticket to morning time in this world. But remember, it will not keep quite till noon-day even in the coolest cellar, but drive out the stopples long ere that and follow westward the steps of Aurora. I am no worshipper of Hygeia, who was the daughter of that old herb-doctor Æsculapius, and who is represented on monuments holding a serpent in one hand, and in the other a cup out of which the serpent sometimes drinks; but rather of Hebe, cup-bearer to Jupiter, who was the daughter of Juno and wild lettuce, and who had the power of restoring gods and men to the vigor of youth. She was probably the only thoroughly sound-conditioned, healthy, and robust young lady that ever walked the globe, and wherever she came it was spring.

11 Higher Laws

As I came home through the woods with my string of fish, trailing my pole, it being now quite dark, I caught a glimpse of a woodchuck stealing across my path, and felt a strange thrill of savage delight, and was strongly tempted to seize and devour him raw; not that I was hungry then, except for that wildness which he represented. Once or twice, however, while I lived at the pond, I found myself ranging the woods, like a half-starved hound, with a strange abandonment, seeking some kind of venison which I might devour, and no morsel could have been too savage for me. The wildest scenes had become unaccountably familiar. I found in myself, and still find, an instinct toward a higher, or, as it is named, spiritual life, as do most men, and another toward a primitive rank and savage one, and I reverence them both. I love the wild not less than the good. The wildness and adventure that are in fishing still recommended it to me. I like sometimes to take rank hold on life and spend my day more as the animals do. Perhaps I have owed to this employment and to hunting, when quite young, my closest acquaintance with Nature. They early introduce us to and detain us in scenery with which otherwise, at that age, we should have little acquaintance. Fishermen, hunters, wood-choppers, and others, spending their lives in the fields and woods, in a peculiar sense a part of Nature themselves, are often in a more favorable mood for observing her, in the intervals of their pursuits, than philosophers or poets even, who approach her with expectation. She is not afraid to exhibit herself to them. The traveller on the prairie is naturally a hunter, on the head waters of the Missouri and Columbia a trapper, and at the Falls of St.

Mary a fisherman. He who is only a traveller learns things at second-hand and by the halves, and is poor authority. We are most interested when science reports what those men already know practically or instinctively, for that alone is a true *humanity*, or account of human experience.

They mistake who assert that the Yankee has few amusements, because he has not so many public holidays, and men and boys do not play so many games as they do in England, for here the more primitive but solitary amusements of hunting, fishing, and the like have not yet given place to the former. Almost every New England boy among my contemporaries shouldered a fowling-piece between the ages of ten and fourteen; and his hunting and fishing grounds were not limited, like the preserves of an English nobleman, but were more boundless even than those of a savage. No wonder, then, that he did not oftener stay to play on the common. But already a change is taking place, owing, not to an increased humanity, but to an increased scarcity of game, for perhaps the hunter is the greatest friend of the animals hunted, not excepting the Humane Society.

Moreover, when at the pond, I wished sometimes to add fish to my fare for variety. I have actually fished from the same kind of necessity that the first fishers did. Whatever humanity I might conjure up against it was all factitious, and concerned my philosophy more than my feelings. I speak of fishing only now, for I had long felt differently about fowling, and sold my gun before I went to the woods. Not that I am less humane than others, but I did not perceive that my feelings were much affected. I did not pity the fishes nor the worms. This was habit. As for fowling, during the last years that I carried a gun my excuse was that I was studying ornithology, and sought only new or rare birds. But I confess that I am now inclined to think that there is a finer way of studying ornithology than this. It requires so much closer attention to the habits of the birds, that, if for that reason only, I have been willing to omit the gun. Yet notwithstanding the objection on the score of humanity, I am compelled to doubt if equally valuable sports are ever substituted for these; and when some of my friends have asked me anxiously about their boys, whether they should let them hunt, I have answered, yes,—remembering that it was one of the best parts of my education,—*make* them hunters, though sportsmen only at first, if possible, mighty hunters at last, so that they shall not find game large enough for them in this or any vegetable wilderness,—hunters as well as fishers of men. Thus far I am of the opinion of Chaucer's nun, who

yave not of the text a pulled hen
That saith that hunters ben not holy men.[11]

There is a period in the history of the individual, as of the race, when

[11] From the Prologue to *The Canterbury Tales*.

the hunters are the "best men," as the Algonquins called them. We cannot but pity the boy who has never fired a gun; he is no more humane, while his education has been sadly neglected. This was my answer with respect to those youths who were bent on this pursuit, trusting that they would soon outgrow it. No humane being, past the thoughtless age of boyhood, will wantonly murder any creature which holds its life by the same tenure that he does. The hare in its extremity cries like a child. I warn you, mothers, that my sympathies do not always make the usual *philanthropic* distinctions.

Such is oftenest the young man's introduction to the forest, and the most original part of himself. He goes thither at first as a hunter and fisher, until at last, if he has the seeds of a better life in him, he distinguishes his proper objects, as a poet or naturalist it may be, and leaves the gun and fish-pole behind. The mass of men are still and always young in this respect. In some countries a hunting parson is no uncommon sight. Such a one might make a good shepherd's dog, but is far from being the Good Shepherd. I have been surprised to consider that the only obvious employment, except wood-chopping, ice-cutting, or the like business, which ever to my knowledge detained at Walden Pond for a whole half-day any of my fellow-citizens, whether fathers or children of the town, with just one exception, was fishing. Commonly they did not think that they were lucky, or well paid for their time, unless they got a long string of fish, though they had the opportunity of seeing the pond all the while. They might go there a thousand times before the sediment of fishing would sink to the bottom and leave their purpose pure; but no doubt such a clarifying process would be going on all the while. The Governor and his Council faintly remember the pond, for they went a-fishing there when they were boys; but now they are too old and dignified to go a-fishing, and so they know it no more forever. Yet even they expect to go to heaven at last. If the legislature regards it, it is chiefly to regulate the number of hooks to be used there; but they know nothing about the hook of hooks with which to angle for the pond itself, impaling the legislature for a bait. Thus, even in civilized communities, the embryo man passes through the hunter stage of development.

I have found repeatedly, of late years, that I cannot fish without falling a little in self-respect. I have tried it again and again. I have skill at it, and, like many of my fellows, a certain instinct for it, which revives from time to time, but always when I have done I feel that it would have been better if I had not fished. I think that I do not mistake. It is a faint intimation, yet so are the first streaks of morning. There is unquestionably this instinct in me which belongs to the lower orders of creation; yet with every year I am less a fisherman, though without more humanity or even wisdom; at present I am no fisherman at all. But I see that if I were to live in a wilderness I should again be tempted to become a fisher and hunter in earnest. Beside, there is something essentially unclean about this diet and all flesh, and I began to see where housework commences, and whence the endeavor, which costs so much, to wear a tidy and respectable appearance each day, to keep the house sweet and free from all ill odors and sights. Having been my own butcher and scullion and cook, as well as the gentleman for whom the dishes were served up, I can speak from an unusually complete experience. The practical objection to animal food in my case was its uncleanness; and besides, when I had caught and cleaned and cooked and eaten my fish, they seemed not to have fed me essentially. It was insignificant and unnecessary, and cost more than it came to. A little bread or a few potatoes would have done as well, with less trouble and filth. Like many of my contemporaries, I had rarely for many years used animal food, or tea, or coffee, etc.; not so much because of any ill effects which I had traced to them, as because they were not agreeable to my imagination. The repugnance to animal food is not the effect of experience, but is an instinct. It appeared more beautiful to live low and fare hard in many respects; and though I never did so, I went far enough to please my imagination. I believe that every man who has ever been earnest to preserve his higher or poetic faculties in the best condition has been particularly inclined to abstain from animal food, and from much food of any kind. It is a significant fact, stated by entomologists,—I find it in Kirby and Spence,—that "some insects in their perfect state, though furnished with organs of feeding, make no use of them;" and they lay it down as "a general rule, that almost all insects in this state eat much less than in that of larvæ. The voracious caterpillar when transformed into a butterfly . . . and the gluttonous maggot when become a fly" content themselves with a drop or two of honey or some other sweet liquid. The abdomen under the wings of the butterfly still represents the larva. This is the tidbit which tempts his insectivorous fate. The gross feeder is a man in the larva state; and there are whole nations in that condition, nations without fancy or imagination, whose vast abdomens betray them.

It is hard to provide and cook so simple and clean a diet as will not offend the imagination; but this, I think, is to be fed when we feed the body; they should both sit down at the same table. Yet perhaps this may be done. The fruits eaten temperately need not make us ashamed of our appetites, nor interrupt the worthiest pursuits. But put an extra condiment into your dish, and it will poison you. It is not worth the while to live by rich cookery. Most men would feel shame if caught preparing with their own hands precisely such a dinner, whether of animal or vegetable food, as is every day prepared for them by others. Yet till this is otherwise we are not civilized, and, if gentlemen and ladies, are not true men and women. This certainly suggests what change is to be made. It may be vain to ask why the imagination will not be reconciled to flesh and fat. I am satisfied that it is not. Is it not a reproach that man is a carnivorous animal? True, he can and does live, in a great measure, by preying on other animals; but this is a miserable way,—as any one who will go to snaring rabbits, or slaughtering lambs, may learn,—and he will be regarded as a benefactor of his race who shall teach man to confine himself to a more innocent and wholesome diet. Whatever my own practice may be, I have no doubt that it is a part of the destiny of the human race, in its gradual improvement, to leave off eating animals, as surely as the savage tribes have left off eating each other when they came in contact with the more civilized.

If one listens to the faintest but constant suggestions of his genius, which are certainly true, he sees not to what extremes, or even insanity, it may lead him; and yet that way, as he grows more resolute and faithful, his road lies. The faintest assured objection which one healthy man feels will at length prevail over the arguments and customs of mankind. No man ever followed his genius till it misled him. Though the result were bodily weakness, yet perhaps no one can say that the consequences were to be regretted, for these were a life in conformity to higher principles. If the day and the night are such that you greet them with joy, and life emits a fragrance like flowers and sweet-scented herbs, is more elastic, more starry, more immortal,—that is your success. All nature is your congratulation, and you have cause momentarily to bless yourself. The greatest gains and values are farthest from being appreciated. We easily come to doubt if they exist. We soon forget them. They are the highest reality. Perhaps the facts most astounding and most real are never communicated by man to man. The true harvest of my daily life is somewhat as intangible and indescribable as the tints of morning or evening. It is a little star-dust caught, a segment of the rainbow which I have clutched.

Yet, for my part, I was never unusually squeamish; I could sometimes eat a fried rat with a good relish, if it were necessary. I am glad to have drunk water so long, for the same reason that I prefer the natural sky to an opium-eater's heaven. I would fain keep sober always; and there are infinite degrees of drunkenness. I believe that water is the only drink for a wise man; wine is not so noble a liquor; and think of dashing the hopes of a morning with a cup of warm coffee, or of an evening with a dish of tea! Ah, how low I fall when I am tempted by them! Even music may be intoxicating. Such apparently slight causes destroyed Greece and Rome, and will destroy England and America. Of all ebriosity, who does not prefer to be intoxicated by the air he breathes? I have found it to be the most serious objection to coarse labors long continued, that they compelled me to eat and drink coarsely also. But to tell the truth, I find myself at present somewhat less particular in these respects. I carry less religion to the table, ask no blessing; not because I am wiser than I was, but, I am obliged to confess, because, however much it is to be regretted, with years I have grown more coarse and indifferent. Perhaps these questions are entertained only in youth, as most believe of poetry. My practice is "nowhere," my opinion is here. Nevertheless I am far from regarding myself as one of those privileged ones to whom the Ved refers when it says, that "he who has true faith in the Omnipresent Supreme Being may eat all that exists," that is, is not bound to inquire what is his food, or who prepares it; and even in their case it is to be observed, as a Hindoo commentator has remarked, that the Vedant limits this privilege to "the time of distress."

Who has not sometimes derived an inexpressible satisfaction from his food in which appetite had no share? I have been thrilled to think that I owed a mental perception to the commonly gross sense of taste, that I have been inspired through the palate, that some berries which I had eaten on a hillside had fed my genius. "The soul not being mistress of herself," says Thseng-tseu,[12] "one looks, and one does not see; one listens, and one does not hear; one eats, and one does not know the savor of food." He who distinguishes the true savor of his food can never be a glutton; he who does not cannot be otherwise. A puritan may go to his brown-bread crust with as gross an appetite as ever an alderman to his turtle. Not that food which entereth into the mouth defileth a man, but the appetite with which it is eaten. It is neither the quality nor the quantity, but the devotion to sensual savors; when that which is eaten is not a viand to sustain our animal, or inspire our spiritual life, but food for the worms that possess us. If the hunter has a taste for mud-turtles, muskrats, and other such savage tidbits, the fine lady indulges a taste for jelly made of a calf's foot, or for sardines from over the sea, and they are even. He goes to the mill-pond, she to her preserve-pot. The wonder is how they, how you and I, can live this slimy, beastly life, eating and drinking.

Our whole life is startlingly moral. There is never an instant's truce between virtue and vice. Goodness is the only investment that never fails. In the music of the harp which trembles round the world it is the insisting on this which thrills us. The harp is the travelling patterer for the Universe's Insurance Company, recommending its laws, and our little goodness is all the assessment that we pay. Though the youth at last grows indifferent, the laws of the universe are not indifferent, but are forever on the side of the most sensitive. Listen to every zephyr for some reproof, for it is surely there, and he is unfortunate who does not hear it. We cannot touch a string or move a stop but the charming moral transfixes us. Many an irksome noise, go a long way off, is heard as music, a proud, sweet satire on the meanness of our lives.

We are conscious of an animal in us, which awakens in proportion as our higher nature slumbers. It is reptile and sensual, and perhaps cannot be wholly expelled; like the worms which, even in life and health, occupy our bodies. Possibly we may withdraw from it, but never

[12] Chinese philosopher (fourth century B.C).

change its nature. I fear that it may enjoy a certain health of its own; that we may be well, yet not pure. The other day I picked up the lower jaw of a hog, with white and sound teeth and tusks, which suggested that there was an animal health and vigor distinct from the spiritual. This creature succeeded by other means than temperance and purity. "That in which men differ from brute beasts," says Mencius,[13] "is a thing very inconsiderable; the common herd lose it very soon; superior men preserve it carefully." Who knows what sort of life would result if we had attained to purity? If I knew so wise a man as could teach me purity I would go to seek him forthwith. "A command over our passions, and over the external senses of the body, and good acts, are declared by the Ved to be indispensable in the mind's approximation to God." Yet the spirit can for the time pervade and control every member and function of the body, and transmute what in form is the grossest sensuality into purity and devotion. The generative energy, which, when we are loose, dissipates and makes us unclean, when we are continent invigorates and inspires us. Chastity is the flowering of man; and what are called Genius, Heroism, Holiness, and the like, are but various fruits which succeed it. Man flows at once to God when the channel of purity is open. By turns our purity inspires and our impurity casts us down. He is blessed who is assured that the animal is dying out in him day by day, and the divine being established. Perhaps there is none but has cause for shame on account of the inferior and brutish nature to which he is allied. I fear that we are such gods or demigods only as fauns and satyrs, the divine allied to beasts, the creatures of appetite, and that, to some extent, our very life is our disgrace.—

How happy's he who hath due place assigned
To his beasts and disafforested his mind!

.   .   .

    Can use his horse, goat, wolf, and ev'ry beast,
And is not ass himself to all the rest!
Else man not only is the herd of swine,
But he's those devils too which did incline
Them to a headlong rage, and made them worse.[14]

All sensuality is one, though it takes many forms; all purity is one. It is the same whether a man eat, or drink, or cohabit, or sleep sensually. They are but one appetite, and we only need to see a person do any one of these things to know how great a sensualist he is. The impure can neither stand nor sit with purity. When the reptile is attacked at one mouth of his burrow, he shows himself at another. If you would be chaste, you must be temperate. What is chastity? How shall a man know if he is chaste? He shall not know it. We have heard of this virtue,

[13] Chinese thinker (third century B.C.?).
[14] From John Donne, "Letter to Sir Edward Hebert at Iulyers."

but we know not what it is. We speak conformably to the rumor which we have heard. From exertion come wisdom and purity; from sloth ignorance and sensuality. In the student sensuality is a sluggish habit of mind. An unclean person is universally a slothful one, one who sits by a stove, whom the sun shines on prostrate, who reposes without being fatigued. If you would avoid uncleanness, and all the sins, work earnestly, though it be at cleaning a stable. Nature is hard to overcome, but she must be overcome. What avails it that you are Christian, if you are not purer than the heathen, if you deny yourself no more, if you are not more religious? I know of many systems of religion esteemed heathenish whose precepts fill the reader with shame, and provoke him to new endeavors, though it be to the performance of rites merely.

I hesitate to say these things, but it is not because of the subject,— I care not how obscene my *words* are,—but because I cannot speak of them without betraying my impurity. We discourse freely without shame of one form of sensuality, and are silent about another. We are so degraded that we cannot speak simply of the necessary functions of human nature. In earlier ages, in some countries, every function was reverently spoken of and regulated by law. Nothing was too trivial for the Hindoo lawgiver, however offensive it may be to modern taste. He teaches how to eat, drink, cohabit, void excrement and urine and the like, elevating what is mean, and does not falsely excuse himself by calling these things trifles.

Every man is the builder of a temple, called his body, to the god he worships, after a style purely his own, nor can he get off by hammering marble instead. We are all sculptors and painters, and our material is our own flesh and blood and bones. Any nobleness begins at once to refine a man's features, any meanness or sensuality to imbrute them.

John Farmer sat at his door one September evening, after a hard day's work, his mind still running on his labor more or less. Having bathed, he sat down to re-create his intellectual man. It was a rather cool evening, and some of his neighbors were apprehending a frost. He had not attended to the train of his thoughts long when he heard some one playing on a flute, and that sound harmonized with his mood. Still he thought of his work; but the burden of his thought was, that though this kept running in his head, and he found himself planning and contriving it against his will, yet it concerned him very little. It was no more than the scurf of his skin, which was constantly shuffled off. But the notes of the flute came home to his ears out of a different sphere from that he worked in, and suggested work for certain faculties which slumbered in him. They gently did away with the street, and the village, and the state in which he lived. A voice said to him,—Why do you stay here and live this mean moiling life, when a glorious existence is possible for you? Those same stars twinkle over other fields than these.—

But how to come out of this condition and actually migrate thither? All that he could think of was to practise some new austerity, to let his mind descend into his body and redeem it, and treat himself with ever increasing respect.

12   Brute Neighbors

Sometimes I had a companion in my fishing, who came through the village to my house from the other side of the town, and the catching of the dinner was as much a social exercise as the eating of it.

Hermit. I wonder what the world is doing now. I have not heard so much as a locust over the sweet-fern these three hours. The pigeons are all asleep upon their roosts,—no flutter from them. Was that a farmer's noon horn which sounded from beyond the woods just now? The hands are coming in to boiled salt beef and cider and Indian bread. Why will men worry themselves so? He that does not eat need not work. I wonder how much they have reaped. Who would live there where a body can never think for the barking of Bose? And oh, the housekeeping! to keep bright the devil's door-knobs, and scour his tubs this bright day! Better not keep a house. Say, some hollow tree; and then for morning calls and dinner-parties! Only a woodpecker tapping. Oh, they swarm; the sun is too warm there; they are born too far into life for me. I have water from the spring, and a loaf of brown bread on the shelf.—Hark! I hear a rustling of the leaves. Is it some ill-fed village hound yielding to the instinct of the chase? or the lost pig which is said to be in these woods, whose tracks I saw after the rain? It comes on apace; my sumachs and sweetbriers tremble.—Eh, Mr. Poet, is it you? How do you like the world to-day?

Poet. See those clouds; how they hang! That's the greatest thing I have seen to-day. There's nothing like it in old paintings, nothing like it in foreign lands,—unless when we were off the coast of Spain. That's a true Mediterranean sky. I thought, as I have my living to get, and have not eaten to-day, that I might go a-fishing. That's the true industry for poets. It is the only trade I have learned. Come, let's along.

Hermit. I cannot resist. My brown bread will soon be gone. I will go with you gladly soon, but I am just concluding a serious meditation. I think that I am near the end of it. Leave me alone, then, for a while. But that we may not be delayed, you shall be digging the bait meanwhile. Angleworms are rarely to be met with in these parts, where the soil was never fattened with manure; the race is nearly extinct. The sport of digging the bait is nearly equal to that of catching the fish, when one's appetite is not too keen; and this you may have all to yourself to-day. I would advise you to set in the spade down yonder among the ground-nuts, where you see the johnswort waving. I think that I may warrant you one worm to every three sods you turn up, if you look well in among the roots of the grass, as if you were weeding. Or, if you choose to go farther, it will not be unwise, for I have found the increase of fair bait to be very nearly as the squares of the distances.

Hermit alone. Let me see; where was I? Methinks I was nearly in this frame of mind; the world lay about at this angle. Shall I go to heaven or a-fishing? If I should soon bring this meditation to an end, would another so sweet occasion be likely to offer? I was as near being resolved into the essence of things as ever I was in my life. I fear my thoughts will not come back to me. If it would do any good, I would whistle for them. When they make us an offer, is it wise to say, We will think of it? My thoughts have left no track, and I cannot find the path again. What was it that I was thinking of? It was a very hazy day. I will just try these three sentences of Confutsee;[15] they may fetch that state about again. I know not whether it was the dumps or a budding ecstasy. Mem. There never is but one opportunity of a kind.

Poet. How now, Hermit, is it too soon? I have got just thirteen whole ones, beside several which are imperfect or undersized; but they will do for the smaller fry; they do not cover up the hook so much. Those village worms are quite too large; a shiner may make a meal off one without finding the skewer.

Hermit. Well, then, let's be off. Shall we to the Concord? There's good sport there if the water be not too high.

Why do precisely these objects which we behold make a world? Why has man just these species of animals for his neighbors; as if nothing but a mouse could have filled this crevice? I suspect that Pilpay & Co.[16] have put animals to their best use, for they are all beasts of burden, in a sense, made to carry some portion of our thoughts.

The mice which haunted my house were not the common ones, which are said to have been introduced into the country, but a wild native kind not found in the village. I sent one to a distinguished naturalist, and it interested him much. When I was building, one of these had its nest underneath the house, and before I had laid the second floor, and swept out the shavings, would come out regularly at lunch time and pick up the crumbs at my feet. It probably had never seen a man before; and it soon became quite familiar, and would run over my shoes and up my clothes. It could readily ascend the sides of the room by short impulses, like a squirrel, which it resembled in its motions. At length, as I leaned with my elbow on the bench one day, it ran up my clothes, and along my sleeve, and round and round the paper which held my dinner, while I kept the latter close, and dodged and played at bopeep with it; and when at last I held still a piece of cheese between my thumb and finger, it came and nibbled it, sitting

[15] Confucius.
[16] An Arabic fabulist (eighth century).

in my hand, and afterward cleaned its face and paws, like a fly, and walked away.

A phœbe soon built in my shed, and a robin for protection in a pine which grew against the house. In June the partridge (*Tetrao umbellus*), which is so shy a bird, led her brood past my windows, from the woods in the rear to the front of my house, clucking and calling to them like a hen, and in all her behavior proving herself the hen of the woods. The young suddenly disperse on your approach, at a signal from the mother, as if a whirlwind had swept them away, and they so exactly resemble the dried leaves and twigs that many a traveller has placed his foot in the midst of a brood, and heard the whir of the old bird as she flew off, and her anxious calls and mewing, or seen her trail her wings to attract his attention, without suspecting their neighborhood. The parent will sometimes roll and spin round before you in such a dishabille, that you cannot, for a few moments, detect what kind of creature it is. The young squat still and flat, often running their heads under a leaf, and mind only their mother's directions given from a distance, nor will your approach make them run again and betray themselves. You may even tread on them, or have your eyes on them for a minute, without discovering them. I have held them in my open hand at such a time, and still their only care, obedient to their mother and their instinct, was to squat there without fear or trembling. So perfect is this instinct, that once, when I had laid them on the leaves again, and one accidentally fell on its side, it was found with the rest in exactly the same position ten minutes afterward. They are not callow like the young of most birds, but more perfectly developed and precocious even than chickens. The remarkably adult yet innocent expressions of their open and serene eyes is very memorable. All intelligence seems reflected in them. They suggest not merely the purity of infancy, but a wisdom clarified by experience. Such an eye was not born when the bird was, but is coeval with the sky it reflects. The woods do not yield another such a gem. The traveller does not often look into such a limpid well. The ignorant or reckless sportsman often shoots the parent at such a time, and leaves these innocents to fall a prey to some prowling beast or bird, or gradually mingle with the decaying leaves which they so much resemble. It is said that when hatched by a hen they will directly disperse on some alarm, and so are lost, for they never hear the mother's call which gathers them again. These were my hens and chickens.

It is remarkable how many creatures live wild and free though secret in the woods, and still sustain themselves in the neighborhood of towns, suspected by hunters only. How retired the otter manages to live here! He grows to be four feet long, as big as a small boy, perhaps without any human being getting a glimpse of him. I formerly saw the raccoon in the woods behind where my house is built, and probably still heard their whinnering at night. Commonly I rested an hour or two in the shade at noon, after planting, and ate my lunch, and read a little by a spring which was the source of a swamp and of a brook, oozing from under Brister's Hill, half a mile from my field. The approach to this was through a succession of descending grassy hollows, full of young pitch pines, into a larger wood about the swamp. There, in a very secluded and shaded spot, under a spreading white pine, there was yet a clean, firm sward to sit on. I had dug out the spring and made a well of clear gray water, where I could dip up a pailful without roiling it, and thither I went for this purpose almost every day in mid-summer, when the pond was warmest. Thither, too, the woodcock led her brood, to probe the mud for worms, flying but a foot above them down the bank, while they ran in a troop beneath; but at last, spying me, she would leave her young and circle round and round me, nearer and nearer till within four or five feet, pretending broken wings and legs, to attract my attention, and get off her young, who would already have taken up their march, with faint, wiry peep, single file through the swamp, as she directed. Or I heard the peep of the young when I could not see the parent bird. There too the turtle doves sat over the spring, or fluttered from bough to bough of the soft white pines over my head; or the red squirrel, coursing down the nearest bough, was particularly familiar and inquisitive. You only need sit still long enough in some attractive spot in the woods that all its inhabitants may exhibit themselves to you by turns.

I was witness to events of a less peaceful character. One day when I went out to my wood-pile, or rather my pile of stumps, I observed two large ants, the one red, the other much larger, nearly half an inch long, and black, fiercely contending with one another. Having once got hold they never let go, but struggled and wrestled and rolled on the chips incessantly. Looking farther, I was surprised to find that the chips were covered with such combatants, that it was not a *duellum*, but a *bellum*, a war between two races of ants, the red always pitted against the black, and frequently two red ones to one black. The legions of these Myrmidons [17] covered all the hills and vales in my wood-yard, and the ground was already strewn with the dead and dying, both red and black. It was the only battle which I have ever witnessed, the only battle-field I ever trod while the battle was raging; internecine war; the red republicans on the one hand, and the black imperialists on the other. On every side they were engaged in deadly combat, yet without any noise that I could hear, and human soldiers never fought so resolutely. I watched a couple that were fast locked in each other's embraces, in a little sunny valley amid the chips, now at noonday prepared to fight till the sun went down, or life went out. The smaller red champion had fastened himself like a vise to his adversary's front, and through all the tumblings on that field never for an instant ceased to gnaw at one of

[17] Legendary followers of Achilles.

his feelers near the root, having already caused the other to go by the board; while the stronger black one dashed him from side to side, and, as I saw on looking nearer, had already divested him of several of his members. They fought with more pertinacity than bulldogs. Neither manifested the least disposition to retreat. It was evident that their battle-cry was "Conquer or die." In the meanwhile there came along a single red ant on the hillside of this valley, evidently full of excitement, who either had despatched his foe, or had not yet taken part in the battle; probably the latter, for he had lost none of his limbs; whose mother had charged him to return with his shield or upon it. Or perchance he was some Achilles, who had nourished his wrath apart, and had now come to avenge or rescue his Patroclus. He saw this unequal combat from afar,—for the blacks were nearly twice the size of the red,—he drew near with rapid pace till he stood on his guard within half an inch of the combatants; then, watching his opportunity, he sprang upon the black warrior, and commenced his operations near the root of his right fore leg, leaving the foe to select among his own members; so there were three united for life, as if a new kind of attraction had been invented which put all other locks and cements to shame. I should not have wondered by this time to find that they had their respective musical bands stationed on some eminent chip, and playing their national airs the while, to excite the slow and cheer the dying combatants. I was myself excited somewhat even as if they had been men. The more you think of it, the less the difference. And certainly there is not the fight recorded in Concord history, at least, if in the history of America, that will bear a moment's comparison with this, whether for the numbers engaged in it, or for the patriotism and heroism displayed. For numbers and for carnage it was an Austerlitz or Dresden.[18] Concord fight! Two killed on the patriots' side, and Luther Blanchard wounded! Why here every ant was a Buttrick,[19]—"Fire! for God's sake fire!"—and thousands shared the fate of Davis and Hosmer.[20] There was not one hireling there. I have no doubt that it was a principle they fought for, as much as our ancestors, and not to avoid a threepenny tax on their tea; and the results of this battle will be as important and memorable to those whom it concerns as those of the battle of Bunker Hill, at least.

I took up the chip on which the three I have particularly described were struggling, carried it into my house, and placed it under a tumbler on my window-sill, in order to see the issue. Holding a microscope to the first-mentioned red ant, I saw that, though he was assiduously gnawing at the near fore leg of his enemy, having severed his remaining feeler, his own breast was all torn away, exposing what vitals he

[18] Places where Napoleon won large-scale victories in 1805 and 1813.
[19] Major in command at battle of Concord.
[20] Killed at Concord.

had there to the jaws of the black warrior, whose breastplate was apparently too thick for his to pierce; and the dark carbuncles of the sufferer's eyes shone with ferocity such as war only could excite. They struggled half an hour longer under the tumbler, and when I looked again the black soldier had severed the heads of his foes from their bodies, and the still living heads were hanging on either side of him like ghastly trophies at his saddle-bow, still apparently as firmly fastened as ever, and he was endeavoring with feeble struggles, being without feelers and with only the remnant of a leg, and I know not how many other wounds, to divest himself of them; which at length, after half an hour or more, he accomplished. I raised the glass, and he went off over the window-sill in that crippled state. Whether he finally survived that combat, and spent the remainder of his days in some Hôtel des Invalides, I do not know; but I thought that his industry would not be worth much thereafter. I never learned which party was victorious, nor the cause of the war; but I felt for the rest of that day as if I had had my feelings excited and harrowed by witnessing the struggle, the ferocity and carnage, of a human battle before my door.

Kirby and Spence tell us that the battles of ants have long been celebrated and the date of them recorded, though they say that Huber is the only modern author who appears to have witnessed them. "Æneas Sylvius," say they, "after giving a very circumstantial account of one contested with great obstinacy by a great and small species on the trunk of a pear tree," adds that " 'this action was fought in the pontificate of Eugenius the Fourth, in the presence of Nicholas Pistoriensis, an eminent lawyer, who related the whole history of the battle with the greatest fidelity.' A similar engagement between great and small ants is recorded by Olaus Magnus, in which the small ones, being victorious, are said to have buried the bodies of their own soldiers, but left those of their giant enemies a prey to the birds. This event happened previous to the expulsion of the tyrant Christiern the Second from Sweden." The battle which I witnessed took place in the Presidency of Polk, five years before the passage of Webster's Fugitive-Slave Bill.

Many a village Bose, fit only to course a mud-turtle in a victualling cellar, sported his heavy quarters in the woods, without the knowledge of his master, and ineffectually smelled at old fox burrows and woodchucks' holes; led perchance by some slight cur which nimbly threaded the wood, and might still inspire a natural terror in its denizens;— now far behind his guide, barking like a canine bull toward some small squirrel which had treed itself for scrutiny, then, cantering off, bending the bushes with his weight, imagining that he is on the track of some stray member of the jerbilla family. Once I was surprised to see a cat walking along the stony shore of the pond, for they rarely wander so far from home. The surprise was mutual. Nevertheless the most domestic cat, which has lain on a rug all her days, appears quite at home in the woods, and, by her sly and stealthy behavior, proves herself more

native there than the regular inhabitants. Once, when berrying, I met
with a cat with young kittens in the woods, quite wild, and they all,
like their mother had their backs up and were fiercely spitting at me. A
few years before I lived in the woods there was what was called a
"winged cat" in one of the farmhouses in Lincoln nearest the pond, Mr.
Gilian Baker's. When I called to see her in June, 1842, she was gone
a-hunting in the woods, as was her wont (I am not sure whether it was
a male or female, and so use the more common pronoun), but her mistress told me that she came into the neighborhood a little more than a year
before, in April, and was finally taken into their house, that she was of
a dark brownish-gray color, with a white spot on her throat, and white
feet, and had a large bushy tail like a fox; that in the winter the fur
grew thick and flatted out along her sides, forming strips ten or twelve
inches long by two and a half wide, and under her chin like a muff,
the upper side loose, the under matted like felt, and in the spring these
appendages dropped off. They gave me a pair of her "wings," which I
keep still. There is no appearance of a membrane about them. Some
thought it was part flying squirrel or some other wild animal, which is
not impossible, for, according to naturalists, prolific hybrids have been
produced by the union of the marten and domestic cat. This would
have been the right kind of cat for me to keep, if I had kept any; for
why should not a poet's cat be winged as well as his horse?

In the fall the loon (*Colymbus glacialis*) came, as usual, to moult
and bathe in the pond, making the woods ring with his wild laughter
before I had risen. At rumor of his arrival all the Mill-dam sportsmen
are on the alert, in gigs and on foot, two by two and three by three,
with patent rifles and conical balls and spy-glasses. They come rustling
through the woods like autumn leaves, at least ten men to one loon.
Some station themselves on this side of the pond, some on that, for the
poor bird cannot be omnipresent; if he dive here he must come up
there. But now the kind October wind rises, rustling the leaves and
rippling the surface of the water, so that no loon can be heard or seen,
though his foes sweep the pond with spy-glasses, and make the woods
resound with their discharges. The waves generously rise and dash
angrily, taking sides with all water-fowl, and our sportsmen must beat
a retreat to town and shop and unfinished jobs. But they were too often
successful. When I went to get a pail of water early in the morning I
frequently saw this stately bird sailing out of my cove within a few rods.
If I endeavored to overtake him in a boat, in order to see how he would
manœuvre, he would dive and be completely lost, so that I did not discover him again, sometimes, till the latter part of the day. But I was
more than a match for him on the surface. He commonly went off in a
rain.

As I was paddling along the north shore one very calm October
afternoon, for such days especially they settle on to the lakes, like the
milkweed down, having looked in vain over the pond for a loon, sud-

denly one, sailing out from the shore toward the middle a few rods in front of me, set up his wild laugh and betrayed himself. I pursued with a paddle and he dived, but when he came up I was nearer than before. He dived again, but I miscalculated the direction he would take, and we were fifty rods apart when he came to the surface this time, for I had helped to widen the interval; and again he laughed long and loud, and with more reason than before. He manœuvred so cunningly that I could not get within half a dozen rods of him. Each time, when he came to the surface, turning his head this way and that, he coolly surveyed the water and the land, and apparently chose his course so that he might come up where there was the widest expanse of water and at the greatest distance from the boat. It was surprising how quickly he made up his mind and put his resolve into execution. He led me at once to the widest part of the pond, and could not be driven from it. While he was thinking one thing in his brain, I was endeavoring to divine his thought in mine. It was a pretty game, played on the smooth surface of the pond, a man against a loon. Suddenly your adversary's checker disappears beneath the board, and the problem is to place yours nearest to where his will appear again. Sometimes he would come up unexpectedly on the opposite side of me, having apparently passed directly under the boat. So long-winded was he and so unweariable, that when he had swum farthest he would immediately plunge again, nevertheless; and then no wit could divine where in the deep pond, beneath the smooth surface, he might be speeding his way like a fish, for he had time and ability to visit the bottom of the pond in its deepest part. It is said that loons have been caught in the New York lakes eighty feet beneath the surface, with hooks set for trout,—though Walden is deeper than that. How surprised must the fishes be to see this ungainly visitor from another sphere speeding his way amid their schools! Yet he appeared to know his course as surely under water as on the surface, and swam much faster there. Once or twice I saw a ripple where he approached the surface, just put his head out to reconnoitre, and instantly dived again. I found that it was as well for me to rest on my oars and wait his reappearing as to endeavor to calculate where he would rise; for again and again, when I was straining my eyes over the surface one way, I would suddenly be startled by his unearthly laugh behind me. But why, after displaying so much cunning, did he invariably betray himself the moment he came up by that loud laugh? Did not his white breast enough betray him? He was indeed a silly loon, I thought. I could commonly hear the splash of the water when he came up, and so also detected him. But after an hour he seemed as fresh as ever, dived as willingly, and swam yet farther than at first. It was surprising to see how serenely he sailed off with unruffled breast when he came to the surface, doing all the work with his webbed feet beneath. His usual note was this demoniac laughter, yet somewhat like that of a water-fowl; but occasionally, when he had balked me most successfully and come up a long way off, he uttered a long-drawn unearthly howl, probably more like that of a wolf than any bird; as when a beast puts his muzzle to the ground and deliberately howls. This was his loon-ing,—perhaps the wildest sound that is ever heard here, making the woods ring far and wide. I concluded that he laughed in derision of my efforts, confident of his own resources. Though the sky was by this time overcast, the pond was so smooth that I could see where he broke the surface when I did not hear him. His white breast, the stillness of the air, and the smoothness of the water were all against him. At length, having come up fifty rods off, he uttered one of those prolonged howls, as if calling on the god of loons to aid him, and immediately there came a wind from the east and rippled the surface, and filled the whole air with misty rain, and I was impressed as if it were the prayer of the loon answered, and his god was angry with me; and so I left him disappearing far away on the tumultuous surface.

For hours, in fall days, I watched the ducks cunningly tack and veer and hold the middle of the pond, far from the sportsman; tricks which they will have less need to practise in Louisiana bayous. When compelled to rise they would sometimes circle round and round and over the pond at a considerable height, from which they could easily see to other ponds and the river, like black motes in the sky; and, when I thought they had gone off thither long since, they would settle down by a slanting flight of a quarter of a mile on to a distant part which was left free; but what beside safety they got by sailing in the middle of Walden I do not know, unless they love its water for the same reason that I do.

18   Conclusion

To the sick the doctors wisely recommend a change of air and scenery. Thank Heaven, here is not all the world. The buckeye does not grow in New England, and the mocking-bird is rarely heard here. The wild goose is more of a cosmopolite than we; he breaks his fast in Canada, takes a luncheon in the Ohio, and plumes himself for the night in a southern bayou. Even the bison, to some extent, keeps pace with the seasons, cropping the pastures of the Colorado only till a greener and sweeter grass awaits him by the Yellowstone. Yet we think that if rail fences are pulled down, and stone walls piled up on our farms, bounds are henceforth set to our lives and our fates decided. If you are chosen town clerk, forsooth, you cannot go to Tierra del Fuego [21] this summer: but you may go to the land of infernal fire nevertheless. The universe is wider than our views of it.

Yet we should oftener look over the tafferel of our craft, like curious passengers, and not make the voyage like stupid sailors picking oakum.

[21] Archipelago at southern end of South America.

The other side of the globe is but the home of our correspondent. Our voyaging is only great-circle sailing, and the doctors prescribe for diseases of the skin merely. One hastens to southern Africa to chase the giraffe; but surely that is not the game he would be after. How long, pray, would a man hunt giraffes if he could? Snipes and woodcocks also may afford rare sport; but I trust it would be nobler game to shoot one's self.—

Direct your eye right inward, and you'll find
A thousand regions in your mind
Yet undiscovered. Travel them, and be
Expert in home-cosmography.

What does Africa,—what does the West stand for? Is not our own interior white on the chart? black though it may prove, like the coast, when discovered. Is it the source of the Nile, or the Niger, or the Mississippi, or a Northwest Passage around this continent, that we would find? Are these the problems which most concern mankind? Is Franklin [22] the only man who is lost, that his wife should be so earnest to find him? Does Mr. Grinnell know where he himself is? Be rather the Mungo Park,[23] the Lewis and Clark [24] and Frobisher,[25] of your own streams and oceans; explore your own higher latitudes,—with ship-loads of preserved meats to support you, if they be necessary; and pile the empty cans sky-high for a sign. Were preserved meats invented to preserve meat merely? Nay, be a Columbus to whole new continents and worlds within you, opening new channels, not of trade, but of thought. Every man is the lord of a realm beside which the earthly empire of the Czar is but a petty state, a hummock left by the ice. Yet some can be patriotic who have no *self*-respect, and sacrifice the greater to the less. They love the soil which makes their graves, but have no sympathy with the spirit which may still animate their clay. Patriotism is a maggot in their heads. What was the meaning of that South-Sea Exploring Expedition, with all its parade and expense, but an indirect recognition of the fact that there are continents and seas in the moral world to which every man is an isthmus or an inlet, yet unexplored by him, but that it is easier to sail many thousand miles through cold and storm and cannibals, in a government ship, with five hundred men and boys to assist one, than it is to explore the private sea, the Atlantic and Pacific Ocean of one's being alone.—

Erret, et extremos alter, scrutetur Iberos
Plus habet hic vitae, plus habet ille viae.

[22] Sir John Franklin (1786–1847), English explorer.
[23] British explorer (1771–1806).
[24] Merriwether Lewis (1774–1809) and William Clark (1770–1838), American explorers, sought land route to Pacific.
[25] English explorer (1535–1594), sailed the Arctic.

Let them wander and scrutinize the outlandish Australians.
I have more of God, they more of the road.

It is not worth the while to go round the world to count the cats in
Zanzibar. Yet do this even till you can do better, and you may perhaps
find some "Symmes' Hole" by which to get at the inside at last. England
and France, Spain and Portugal, Gold Coast and Slave Coast, all front
on this private sea; but no bark from them has ventured out of sight
of land, though it is without doubt the direct way to India. If you would
learn to speak all tongues and conform to the customs of all nations,
if you would travel farther than all travellers, be naturalized in all
climes, and cause the Sphinx to dash her head against a stone, even
obey the precept of the old philosopher, and Explore thyself. Herein
are demanded the eye and the nerve. Only the defeated and deserters
go to the wars, cowards that run away and enlist. Start now on that
farthest western way, which does not pause at the Mississippi or the
Pacific, nor conduct toward a wornout China or Japan, but leads on
direct, a tangent to this sphere, summer and winter, day and night,
sun down, moon down, and at last earth down too.

It is said that Mirabeau [26] took to highway robbery "to ascertain
what degree of resolution was necessary in order to place one's self in
formal opposition to the most sacred laws of society." He declared that
"a soldier who fights in the ranks does not require half so much courage
as a foot-pad,"—"that honor and religion have never stood in the way
of a well-considered and firm resolve." This was manly, as the world
goes; and yet it was idle, if not desperate. A saner man would have
found himself often enough "in formal opposition" to what are deemed
"the most sacred laws of society," through obedience to yet more sacred
laws, and so have tested his resolution without going out of his way.
It is not for a man to put himself in such an attitude to society, but to
maintain himself in whatever attitude he find himself through obedience to the laws of his being, which will never be one of opposition to
a just government, if he should chance to meet with such.

I left the woods for as good a reason as I went there. Perhaps it
seemed to me that I had several more lives to live, and could not spare
any more time for that one. It is remarkable how easily and insensibly
we fall into a particular route, and make a beaten track for ourselves.
I had not lived there a week before my feet wore a path from my door
to the pond-side; and though it is five or six years since I trod it, it is
still quite distinct. It is true, I fear, that others may have fallen into it,
and so helped to keep it open. The surface of the earth is soft and
impressible by the feet of men; and so with the paths which the mind
travels. How worn and dusty, then, must be the highways of the world,
how deep the ruts of tradition and conformity! I did not wish to take a
cabin passage, but rather to go before the mast and on the deck of

26 Comte Honoré de Mirabeau (1749–1791), major figure in French Revolution.

the world, for there I could best see the moonlight amid the mountains. I do not wish to go below now.

I learned this, at least, by my experiment: that if one advances confidently in the direction of his dreams, and endeavors to live the life which he has imagined, he will meet with a success unexpected in common hours. He will put some things behind, will pass an invisible boundary; new, universal, and more liberal laws will begin to establish themselves around and within him; or the old laws be expanded, and interpreted in his favor in a more liberal sense, and he will live with the license of a higher order of beings. In proportion as he simplifies his life, the laws of the universe will appear less complex, and solitude will not be solitude, nor poverty poverty, nor weakness weakness. If you have built castles in the air, your work need not be lost; that is where they should be. Now put the foundations under them.

It is a ridiculous demand which England and America make, that you shall speak so that they can understand you. Neither men nor toadstools grow so. As if that were important, and there were not enough to understand you without them. As if Nature could support but one order of understandings, could not sustain birds as well as quadrupeds, flying as well as creeping things, and *hush* and *whoa*, which Bright can understand, were the best English. As if there were safety in stupidity alone. I fear chiefly lest my expression may not be *extra-vagant* enough, may not wander far enough beyond the narrow limits of my daily experience, so as to be adequate to the truth of which I have been convinced. *Extra vagance!* it depends on how you are yarded. The migrating buffalo, which seeks new pastures in another latitude, is not extravagant like the cow which kicks over the pail, leaps the cowyard fence, and runs after her calf, in milking time. I desire to speak somewhere *without* bounds; like a man in a waking moment, to men in their waking moments; for I am convinced that I cannot exaggerate enough even to lay the foundation of a true expression. Who that has heard a strain of music feared then lest he should speak extravagantly any more forever? In view of the future or possible, we should live quite laxly and undefined in front, our outlines dim and misty on that side; as our shadows reveal an insensible perspiration toward the sun. The volatile truth of our words should continually betray the inadequacy of the residual statement. Their truth is instantly *translated;* its literal monument alone remains. The words which express our faith and piety are not definite; yet they are significant and fragrant like frankincense to superior natures.

Why level downward to our dullest perception always, and praise that as common sense? The commonest sense is the sense of men asleep, which they express by snoring. Sometimes we are inclined to class those who are once-and-a-half-witted with the half-witted, because we appreciate only a third part of their wit. Some would find fault with the morning red, if they ever got up early enough. "They pretend," as I hear, "that the verses of Kabir have four different senses, illusion, spirit, intellect, and the exotic doctrine of the Vedas;" but in this part of the world it is considered a ground for complaint if a man's writings admit of more than one interpretation. While England endeavors to cure the potato-rot, will not any endeavor to cure the brain-rot, which prevails so much more widely and fatally?

I do not suppose that I have attained to obscurity, but I should be proud if no more fatal fault were found with my pages on this score than was found with the Walden ice. Southern customers objected to its blue color, which is the evidence of its purity, as if it were muddy, and preferred to Cambridge ice, which is white, but tastes of weeds. The purity men love is like the mists which envelop the earth, and not like the azure ether beyond.

Some are dinning in our ears that we Americans, and moderns generally, are intellectual dwarfs compared with the ancients, or even the Elizabethan men. But what is that to the purpose? A living dog is better than a dead lion. Shall a man go and hang himself because he belongs to the race of pygmies, and not be the biggest pygmy that he can? Let every one mind his own business, and endeavor to be what he was made.

Why should we be in such desperate haste to succeed and in such desperate enterprises? If a man does not keep pace with his companions, perhaps it is because he hears a different drummer. Let him step to the music which he hears, however measured or far away. It is not important that he should mature as soon as an apple tree or an oak. Shall he turn his spring into summer? If the condition of things which we were made for is not yet, what were any reality which we can substitute? We will not be shipwrecked on a vain reality. Shall we with pains erect a heaven of blue glass over ourselves, though when it is done we shall be sure to gaze still at the true ethereal heaven far above, as if the former were not?

There was an artist in the city of Kouroo who was disposed to strive after perfection. One day it came into his mind to make a staff. Having considered that in an imperfect work time is an ingredient, but into a perfect work time does not enter, he said to himself, It shall be perfect in all respects, though I should do nothing else in my life. He proceeded instantly to the forest for wood, being resolved that it should not be made of unsuitable material; and as he searched for and rejected stick after stick, his friends gradually deserted him, for they grew old in their works and died, but he grew not older by a moment. His singleness of purpose and resolution, and his elevated piety, endowed him, without his knowledge, with perennial youth. As he made no compromise with Time, Time kept out of his way, and only sighed a distance because he could not overcome him. Before he had found a stock in all respects suitable the city of Kouroo was a hoary ruin, and he sat on one of its mounds to peel the stick. Before he had given it the proper shape the dynasty of the Candahars [27] was at an end, and with the point of the stick he wrote the name of the last of that race in the sand, and then resumed his work. By the time he had smoothed and polished the staff Kalpa [28] was no longer the pole-star; and ere he had put on the ferule and the head adorned with precious stones, Brahma [29] had awoke and slumbered many times. But why do I stay to mention these things? When the finishing stroke was put to his work, it suddenly expanded before the eyes of the astonished artist into the fairest of all the creations of Brahma. He had made a new system in making a staff, a world with full and fair proportions; in which, though the old cities and dynasties had passed away, fairer and more glorious ones had taken their places. And now he saw by the heap of shavings still fresh at his feet, that, for him and his work, the former lapse of time had been an illusion, and that no more time had elapsed than is required for a single scintillation from the brain of Brahma to fall on and inflame the tinder of a mortal brain. The material was pure, and his art was pure; how could the result be other than wonderful?

No face which we can give to a matter will stead us so well at last as the truth. This alone wears well. For the most part, we are not where we are, but in a false position. Through an infirmity of our natures, we suppose a case, and put ourselves into it, and hence are in two cases at the same time, and it is doubly difficult to get out. In sane moments we regard only the facts, the case that is. Say what you have to say, not what you ought. Any truth is better than make-believe. Tom Hyde, the tinker, standing on the gallows, was asked if he had anything to say. "Tell the tailors," said he, "to remember to make a knot in their thread before they take the first stitch." His companion's prayer is forgotten.

However mean your life is, meet it and live it; do not shun it and call it hard names. It is not so bad as you are. It looks poorest when you are richest. The fault-finder will find faults even in paradise. Love your life, poor as it is. You may perhaps have some pleasant, thrilling, glorious hours, even in a poor-house. The setting sun is reflected from the windows of the alms-house as brightly as from the rich man's abode; the snow melts before its door as early in the spring. I do not see but a quiet mind may live as contentedly there, and have as cheering thoughts, as in a palace. The town's poor seem to me often to live the most independent lives of any. Maybe they are simply great enough to receive without misgiving. Most think that they are above being supported by the town; but it oftener happens that they are not above supporting themselves by dishonest means, which should be more disreputable. Cultivate poverty like a garden herb, like sage. Do not trouble

[27] A city in Afghanistan.

[28] For Hindus, a day and a night of Brahma; 4,320,000,000 solar years.

[29] A Hindu god.

yourself much to get new things, whether clothes or friends. Turn the old; return to them. Things do not change; we change. Sell your clothes and keep your thoughts. God will see that you do not want society. If I were confined to a corner of a garret all my days, like a spider, the world would be just as large to me while I had my thoughts about me. The philosopher said: "From an army of three divisions one can take away its general, and put it in disorder; from the man the most abject and vulgar one cannot take away his thought." Do not seek so anxiously to be developed, to subject yourself to many influences to be played on; it is all dissipation. Humility like darkness reveals the heavenly lights. The shadows of poverty and meanness gather around us, "and lo! creation widens to our view." We are often reminded that if there were bestowed on us the wealth of Crœsus, our aims must still be the same, and our means essentially the same. Moreover, if you are restricted in your range by poverty, if you cannot buy books and newspapers, for instance, you are but confined to the most significant and vital experiences; you are compelled to deal with the material which yields the most sugar and the most starch. It is life near the bone where it is sweetest. You are defended from being a trifler. No man loses ever on a lower level by magnanimity on a higher. Superfluous wealth can buy superfluities only. Money is not required to buy one necessary of the soul.

I live in the angle of a leaden wall, into whose composition was poured a little alloy of bell-metal. Often, in the repose of my mid-day, there reaches my ears a confused *tintinnabulum* from without. It is the noise of my contemporaries. My neighbors tell me of their adventures with famous gentlemen and ladies, what notabilities they met at the dinner-table; but I am no more interested in such things than in the contents of the Daily Times. The interest and the conversation are about costumes and manners chiefly; but a goose is a goose still, dress it as you will. They tell me of California and Texas, of England and the Indies, of the Hon. Mr. —— of Georgia or Massachusetts, all transient and fleeting phenomena, till I am ready to leap from their court-yard like the Mameluke bey. I delight to come to my bearings,—not walk in procession with pomp and parade, in a conspicuous place, but to walk even with the Builder of the universe, if I may,—not live in this restless, nervous, bustling, trivial Nineteenth Century, but stand or sit thoughtfully while it goes by. What are men celebrating? They are all on a committee of arrangements, and hourly expect a speech from somebody. God is only the president of the day, and Webster is his orator. I love to weigh, to settle, to gravitate toward that which most strongly and rightfully attracts me;—not hang by the beam of the scale and try to weigh less,—not suppose a case, but take the case that is; to travel the only path I can, and that on which no power can resist me. It affords me no satisfaction to commence to spring an arch before I have got a solid foundation. Let us not play at kittly-benders. There is a solid bottom everywhere. We read that the traveller asked the boy if the swamp before him had a hard bottom. The boy replied that it had. But presently the traveller's horse sank in up to the girths, and he observed to the boy, "I thought you said that this bog had a hard bottom." "So it has," answered the latter, "but you have not got half way to it yet." So it is with the bogs and quicksands of society; but he is an old boy that knows it. Only what is thought, said, or done at a certain rare coincidence is good. I would not be one of those who will foolishly drive a nail into mere lath and plastering; such a deed would keep me awake nights. Give me a hammer, and let me feel for the furring. Do not depend on the putty. Drive a nail home and clinch it so faithfully that you can wake up in the night and think of your work with satisfaction,—a work at which you would not be ashamed to invoke the Muse. So will help you God, and so only. Every nail driven should be as another rivet in the machine of the universe, you carrying on the work.

Rather than love, than money, than fame, give me truth. I sat at a table where were rich food and wine in abundance, an obsequious attendance, but sincerity and truth were not; and I went away hungry from the inhospitable board. The hospitality was as cold as the ices. I thought that there was no need of ice to freeze them. They talked to me of the age of the wine and the fame of the vintage; but I thought of an older, a newer, and purer wine, of a more glorious vintage, which they had not got, and could not buy. The style, the house and grounds and "entertainment" pass for nothing with me. I called on the king, but he made me wait in his hall, and conducted like a man incapacitated for hospitality. There was a man in my neighborhood who lived in a hollow tree. His manners were truly regal. I should have done better had I called on him.

How long shall we sit in our porticoes practising idle and musty virtues, which any work would make impertinent? As if one were to begin the day with long-suffering, and hire a man to hoe his potatoes; and in the afternoon go forth to practise Christian meekness and charity with goodness aforethought! Consider the China pride and stagnant self-complacency of mankind. This generation inclines a little to congratulate itself on being the last of an illustrious line; and in Boston and London and Paris and Rome, thinking of its long descent, it speaks of its progress in art and science and literature with satisfaction. There are the Records of the Philosophical Societies, and the public Eulogies of *Great Men!* It is the good Adam contemplating his own virtue. "Yes, we have done great deeds, and sung divine songs, which shall never die,"—that is, as long as *we* can remember them. The learned societies and great men of Assyria,—where are they? What youthful philosophers and experimentalists we are! There is not one of my readers who has yet lived a whole human life. These may be but the spring months in the life of the race. If we have had the seven-years' itch, we have not seen the seventeen-year locust yet in Concord. We are acquainted with a mere pellicle of the globe on which we live. Most have not delved six feet beneath the surface, nor leaped as many above it. We know not where we are. Beside, we are sound asleep nearly half our time. Yet we esteem ourselves wise, and have an established order on the surface. Truly, we are deep thinkers, we are ambitious spirits! As I stand over the insect crawling amid the pine needles on the forest floor, and endeavoring to conceal itself from my sight, and ask myself why it will cherish those humble thoughts, and hide its head from me who might, perhaps, be its benefactor, and impart to its race some cheering information, I am reminded of the greater Benefactor and Intelligence that stands over me the human insect.

There is an incessant influx of novelty into the world, and yet we tolerate incredible dulness. I need only suggest what kind of sermons are still listened to in the most enlightened countries. There are such words as joy and sorrow, but they are only the burden of a psalm, sung with a nasal twang, while we believe in the ordinary and mean. We think that we can change our clothes only. It is said that the British Empire is very large and respectable, and that the United States are a first-rate power. We do not believe that a tide rises and falls behind every man which can float the British Empire like a chip, if he should ever harbor it in his mind. Who knows what sort of seventeen-year locust will next come out of the ground? The government of the world I live in was not framed, like that of Britain, in after-dinner conversations over the wine.

The life in us is like the water in the river. It may rise this year higher than man has ever known it, and flood the parched uplands; even this may be the eventful year, which will drown out all our muskrats. It was not always dry land where we dwell. I see far inland the banks which the stream anciently washed, before science began to record its freshets. Everyone has heard the story which has gone the rounds of New England, of a strong and beautiful bug which came out of the dry leaf of an old table of apple-tree wood, which had stood in a farmer's kitchen for sixty years, first in Connecticut, and afterward in Massachusetts—from an egg deposited in the living tree many years earlier still, as appeared by counting the annual layers beyond it; which was heard gnawing out for several weeks, hatched perchance by the heat of an urn. Who does not feel his faith in a resurrection and immortality strengthened by hearing of this? Who knows what beautiful and winged life, whose egg has been buried for ages under many concentric layers of woodenness in the dead dry life of society, deposited at first in the alburnum of the green and living tree, which has been gradually converted into the semblance of its well-seasoned tomb,—heard perchance gnawing out now for years by the astonished family

of man, as they sat round the festive board,—may unexpectedly come
forth from amidst society's most trivial and handselled furniture, to
enjoy its perfect summer life at last!

I do not say that John or Jonathan will realize all this; but such is
the character of that morrow which mere lapse of time can never make
to dawn. The light which puts out our eyes is darkness to us. Only
that day dawns to which we are awake. There is more day to dawn.
The sun is but a morning star.

NATHANIEL HAWTHORNE (1804–1864)

*New England history and the annals of the Hawthorne family run along
parallel lines. William Hathorne (Nathaniel added the w to the
name) arrived in Massachusetts with Governor Winthrop in 1630,
and his son John served as a judge in the Salem witchcraft trials
of 1692. Nathaniel's father was a New England sea captain whose
ship went down off Surinam while Nathaniel was still a boy.*

*After attending Bowdoin College, where he distinguished himself in
composition, Hawthorne returned to Salem to begin what he would
later call his "twelve dark years." These years of reading, writing,
and solitary rumination formed the prolonged training in the craft
of the first major American novelist. In 1837 they came to an end
when Hawthorne published his collection of stories and sketches,
Twice-told Tales. That same year he became engaged to Sophia
Peabody and began to look for some way to earn a living. He spent
two years in a Boston customhouse, and another seven months in
the utopian community of Brook Farm—both environments were
uncongenial to him—and then, in 1842, he married and went to
live with his bride in Concord, Massachusetts.*

*His stories brought in little money, and he soon accepted a job as sur-
veyor in the Salem customhouse. When the Democrats lost the next
election, he was dismissed and again had to depend on his writing.
The publication of his first novel, The Scarlet Letter, in 1850 made
him a literary success, though neither this masterpiece nor the
lesser novels he wrote in subsequent years enabled him to support
his family.*

*From 1853 to 1857 Hawthorne served as United States consul at Liver-
pool, a post awarded to him by Franklin Pierce, a college friend
who had just been elected President of the United States. After this
prosperous interval came to an end, Hawthorne spent another year
in Italy, the country that would become the setting of his last completed novel, The Marble Faun. His final years, back in the United*

States, were difficult: he would begin novels, or "romances" as he chose to call them, but could not complete any.

Hawthorne's family life was conventional and happy; his external manner was reserved; his public views were conservative. All that was daring or original in his thought went into his literary work.

No portrait of Hawthorne, wrote Henry James, "is at all exact which fails to insist upon the constant struggle which must have gone on between his shyness and his desire to know something of life; between what may be called his evasive and inquisitive tendencies." The remark provides a clue not merely to Hawthorne, but also to a good many other nineteenth-century American writers who tried to find some sort of balance between the rival pressures of a strongly religious past and an increasingly secular present. In Hawthorne's work this jostling of "evasive" and "inquisitive" impulses, of the wish to retreat from, and the urge to plunge into, human experience, is especially strong. The opinions he expresses in his novels tend to be commonplace, but the images of moral experiment and sexuality he creates through his women characters are anything but commonplace. His prose can plod along in a competent but not very vital way, until suddenly, roused to emotion, he breaks into a pure and passionate lucidity. On one side of him, Hawthorne contented himself with lukewarm sketches and predictable moral sentiments; on the other side, he probed into the hidden recesses of the human psyche (or, as he would have said, the soul), especially those dim areas where conscience encounters intellect.

Throughout his life Hawthorne was caught up with what we might now call a crisis of religious belief—a crisis seldom acute but apparently chronic. Formally he was not a religious man, certainly not a church-goer. But religion, or at least the moral and emotional reverberations of religion, haunted him. He felt that the traditional insights of Calvinism concerning the nature of man were more truthful, struck more profoundly into the reality of our natures, than did liberal religion or liberal secularism. Hawthorne's acute moral sense had been largely detached from the traditional context of Puritan orthodoxy, but it had found little else in which to thrive; he was quite incapable of sharing in the radiant—sometimes, the radiantly fatuous—philosophical optimism that cheered transcendentalist neighbors in Concord. When the young Herman Melville reviewed Hawthorne's Mosses from an Old Manse, he shrewdly detected in Hawthorne "that Calvinistic sense of Innate Depravity and Original Sin, from whose visitations . . . no deeply thinking man is always and wholly free."

As a grandson of the Puritans, to whom all existence seemed to constitute a moral drama in which absolute good was pitted against absolute evil, Hawthorne was naturally inclined toward symbolic or quasi-symbolic kinds of fiction. All religious thought, insofar as it posits some invisible world behind, and better than, the visible one, encourages the symbolic imagination. Hawthorne's stories employ the literary form known as allegory, though seldom in an unmixed or pure way. Deriving from medieval Christian writing, traditional allegory presents a line of action which is clearly meant to serve as an equivalent to a parallel line of moral ideas; the characters tend to embody abstract and monolithic qualities (greed, hypocrisy, charity, goodness). The result is that in reading allegory we focus not on the depiction of a complex human situation in its own right but rather on the working-out of a set of fixed and familiar moral premises. In short, allegory subordinates the presented action or image to a scheme of morality. Now, Hawthorne's stories follow the tradition of allegory up to a point, but in the best ones he enriches this form with elements of doubt, complication, and ambiguity, mostly because he no longer possesses the religious certainty which is essential to pure allegory. Extremely clever in his quiet way, Hawthorne both employs and undercuts allegory, so that in stories like "Young Goodman Brown" and "The Minister's Black Veil" we get not the solid assurance and undoubting truth of Christian allegory, but a more problematic kind of fiction.

As a nineteenth-century American, Hawthorne could not acquiesce in Puritan dogma, but neither could he break free from the Puritan heritage. He did not see what the Puritans had seen, but he saw as the Puritans had seen. His mode of vision was traditional; the substance of what he saw, innovative. He felt that no matter how questionable "original sin" might be as doctrine, it touched upon a fundamental truth concerning human beings—and to that extent he was linked with the religious past. But he also found himself drawn to the rebels, the moral experimentalists, the women shaken by passionate desires whom he depicted in his novels and stories— and to that extent he anticipated the psychological speculations of the future. He believed in the reality, the pervasiveness, the inescapability of guilt as man's condition and curse, but also as a spur to reflection, consciousness, and self-growth. Thus, the true locale of Hawthorne's fiction, especially the stories, is not the external social world, not the complex of institutions and relationships we call society, but rather the inner moral and psychic life of the private individual, locked away from scrutiny by his fellows and often from scrutiny by himself. The dramas of Hawthorne's fiction are enacted on a middle ground between traditional Christian morality and modern secular psychology.

Among American writers Hawthorne was the first who turned to the history of his own region, not for vignettes of local eccentricity and *charm, but for that rich and encircling context of experience which, in his view, forms the backdrop of error and crime, the substance of sin, in human affairs. The past is inescapable, and sin is omnipresent. Man can transcend it only by accepting its reality, and in Hawthorne's stories this often means a withdrawal into isolation as a way to both penance and self-discovery. Plumbing the depths of the tainted self, the sinner-rebel finds resources of moral renewal, and then, chastened in his pride and more finely aware of his vulnerability, he reenters the human community. Isolation and reunion—these form the characteristic scheme of Hawthorne's stories. Sometimes, however, there are surprising twists and turns: pride reasserts itself, the self refuses correction, and the appearance of reunion is acted out, but not the reality.*

Hawthorne lived and wrote from the resources of doubt. A shy and sometimes rather sly skepticism courses through his work, as he recognizes that no scheme, Christian or post-Christian, can fully contain or explain the energies of human desire and perversity. Yet one cannot read his novels—this is somewhat less true for the stories—without seeing that in addition to the skeptic there is also a writer eager for experiment in personal life, so that at times his "inquisitive tendency" becomes a sheer hunger for experience. Hawthorne finds himself drawn to moral outlaws who dare what he himself never consciously desired to dare. This Hawthorne yearns for some great liberating transformation which will bring him, for the first time, into full vibrant life. His mind was sluggish, cold, rationalistic; his creative self, passionate, warmly receptive, even sensual. Whatever discomfort the clash between these two may have brought him personally, it proved to be the fructifying principle of his work.

FURTHER READING

The literature on Hawthorne is large and frequently stimulating. Books worth consulting include: Newton Arvin, *Hawthorne* (1929); Austin Warren, *Hawthorne: Representative Selections* (1934); Mark Van Doren, *Nathaniel Hawthorne* (1949); Hyatt H. Waggoner, *Hawthorne: A Critical Study* (1955); and especially D. H. Lawrence, *Studies in Classic American Literature* (1923).

Roger Malvin's Burial (1832)

One of the few incidents of Indian warfare naturally susceptible of the moonlight of romance was that expedition undertaken for the defence of the frontiers in the year 1725, which resulted in the well-remembered "Lovell's Fight." Imagination, by casting certain circumstances judicially into the shade, may see much to admire in the heroism of a little band who gave battle to twice their number in the heart of the enemy's country. The open bravery displayed by both parties was in accordance with civilized ideas of valor; and chivalry itself might not blush to record the deeds of one or two individuals. The battle, though so fatal to those who fought, was not unfortunate in its consequences to the country; for it broke the strength of a tribe and conduced to the peace which subsisted during several ensuing years. History and tradition are unusually minute in their memorials of their affair; and the captain of a scouting party of frontier men has acquired as actual a military renown as many a victorious leader of thousands. Some of the incidents contained in the following pages will be recognized, notwithstanding the substitution of fictitious names, by such as have heard, from old men's lips, the fate of the few combatants who were in a condition to retreat after "Lovell's Fight."

The early sunbeams hovered cheerfully upon the tree-tops, beneath which two weary and wounded men had stretched their limbs the night before. Their bed of withered oak leaves was strewn upon the small level space, at the foot of a rock, situated near the summit of one of the gentle swells by which the face of the country is there diversified. The mass of granite, rearing its smooth, flat surface fifteen or twenty feet above their heads, was not unlike a gigantic gravestone, upon which the veins seemed to form an inscription in forgotten characters. On a tract of several acres around this rock, oaks and other hard-wood trees had supplied the place of the pines, which were the usual growth of the land; and a young and vigorous sapling stood close beside the travellers.

The severe wound of the elder man had probably deprived him of sleep; for, so soon as the first ray of sunshine rested on the top of the highest tree, he reared himself painfully from his recumbent posture and sat erect. The deep lines of his countenance and the scattered gray of his hair marked him as past the middle age; but his muscular frame would, but for the effect of his wound, have been as capable of sustaining fatigue as in the early vigor of life. Languor and exhaustion now sat upon his haggard features; and the despairing glance which he sent forward through the depths of the forest proved his own conviction that his pilgrimage was at an end. He next turned his eyes to the companion who reclined by his side. The youth—for he had scarcely attained the years of manhood—lay, with his head upon his arm, in the embrace of an unquiet sleep, which a thrill of pain from his wounds seemed each moment on the point of breaking. His right hand grasped a musket; and, to judge from the violent action of his features, his slumbers were bringing back a vision of the conflict of which he was one of the few survivors. A shout—deep and loud in his dreaming fancy—found its way in an imperfect murmur to his lips; and, starting even at the slight sound of his own voice, he suddenly awoke. The first act of reviving recollection was to make anxious inquiries respecting the condition of his wounded fellow-traveller. The latter shook his head.

"Reuben, my boy," said he, "this rock beneath which we sit will serve for an old hunter's gravestone. There is many and many a long mile of howling wilderness before us yet; nor would it avail me anything if the smoke of my own chimney were but on the other side of that swell of land. The Indian bullet was deadlier than I thought."

"You are weary with our three days' travel," replied the youth, "and a little longer rest will recruit you. Sit you here while I search the woods for the herbs and roots that must be our sustenance; and, having eaten, you shall lean on me, and we will turn our faces homeward. I doubt not that, with my help, you can attain to some one of the frontier garrisons."

"There is not two days' life in me, Reuben," said the other, calmly, "and I will no longer burden you with my useless body, when you can scarcely support your own. Your wounds are deep and your strength is failing fast; yet, if you hasten onward alone, you may be preserved. For me there is no hope, and I will await death here."

"If it must be so, I will remain and watch by you," said Reuben resolutely.

"No, my son, no," rejoined his companion. "Let the wish of a dying man have weight with you; give me one grasp of your hand and get you hence. Think you that my last moments will be eased by the thought that I leave you to die a more lingering death? I have loved you like a father, Reuben; and at a time like this I should have something of a father's authority. I charge you to be gone that I may die in peace."

"And because you have been a father to me, should I therefore leave you to perish and to lie unburied in the wilderness?" exclaimed the youth. "No; if your end be in truth approaching, I will watch by you and receive your parting words. I will dig a grave here by the rock, in which, if my weakness overcome me, we will rest together; or, if Heaven gives me strength, I will seek my way home."

"In the cities and wherever men dwell," replied the other, "they bury their dead in the earth; they hide them from the sight of the living; but here, where no step may pass perhaps for a hundred years, wherefore should I not rest beneath the open sky, covered only by the oak leaves when the autumn winds shall strew them? And for a monument, here is this gray rock, on which my dying hand shall carve the name of Roger Malvin; and the traveller in days to come will know that here sleeps a hunter and a warrior. Tarry not, then, for a folly like this, but hasten away, if not for your own sake, for hers who will else be desolate."

Malvin spoke the last few words in a faltering voice, and their effect upon his companion was strongly visible. They reminded him that there were other and less questionable duties than that of sharing the fate of a man whom his death could not benefit. Nor can it be affirmed that no selfish feeling strove to enter Reuben's heart, though the consciousness made him more earnestly resist his companion's entreaties.

"How terrible to wait the slow approach of death in this solitude!" exclaimed he. "A brave man does not shrink in the battle; and, when friends stand round the bed, even women may die composedly; but here"—

"I shall not shrink even here, Reuben Bourne," interrupted Malvin. "I am a man of no weak heart, and, if I were, there is a surer support than that of earthly friends. You are young, and life is dear to you. Your last moments will need comfort far more than mine; and when you have laid me in the earth, and are alone, and night is settling on the forest, you will feel all the bitterness of the death that may now be escaped. But I will urge no selfish motive to your generous nature. Leave me for my sake, that, having said a prayer for your safety, I may have space to settle my account undisturbed by worldly sorrows."

"And your daughter,—how shall I dare to meet her eye?" exclaimed Reuben. "She will ask the fate of her father, whose life I vowed to defend with my own. Must I tell her that he travelled three days' march with me from the field of battle and that then I left him to perish in the wilderness? Were it not better to lie down and die by your side than to return safe and say this to Dorcas?"

"Tell my daughter," said Roger Malvin, "that, though yourself sore wounded, and weak, and weary, you led my tottering footsteps many a mile, and left me only at my earnest entreaty, because I would not have your blood upon my soul. Tell her that through pain and danger you were faithful, and that, if your lifeblood could have saved me, it would have flowed to its last drop; and tell her that you will be something dearer than a father, and that my blessing is with you both, and that my dying eyes can see a long and pleasant path in which you will journey together."

As Malvin spoke he almost raised himself from the ground, and the energy of his concluding words seemed to fill the wild and lonely forest with a vision of happiness; but, when he sank exhausted upon his bed of oak leaves, the light which had kindled in Reuben's eye was quenched. He felt as if it were both sin and folly to think of happiness at such a moment. His companion watched his changing countenance, and sought with generous art to wile him to his own good.

"Perhaps I deceive myself in regard to the time I have to live," he resumed. "It may be that, with speedy assistance, I might recover of my wound. The foremost fugitives must, ere this, have carried tidings of our fatal battle to the frontiers, and parties will be out to succor those in like condition with ourselves. Should you meet one of these and guide them hither, who can tell but that I may sit by my own fireside again?"

A mournful smile strayed across the features of the dying man as he insinuated that unfounded hope,—which, however, was not without its effect on Reuben. No merely selfish motive, nor even the desolate condition of Dorcas, could have induced him to desert his companion at such a moment—but his wishes seized on the thought that Malvin's life might be preserved, and his sanguine nature heightened almost to certainty the remote possibility of procuring human aid.

"Surely there is reason, weighty reason, to hope that friends are not far distant," he said, half aloud. "There fled one coward, unwounded, in the beginning of the fight, and most probably he made good speed. Every true man on the frontier would shoulder his musket at the news; and, though no party may range so far into the woods as this, I shall perhaps encounter them in one day's march. Counsel me faithfully," he added, turning to Malvin, in distrust of his own motives. "Were your situation mine, would you desert me while life remained?"

"It is now twenty years," replied Roger Malvin,—sighing, however, as he secretly acknowledged the wide dissimilarity between the two cases,—"it is now twenty years since I escaped with one dear friend from Indian captivity near Montreal. We journeyed many days through the woods, till at length overcome with hunger and weariness, my friend lay down and besought me to leave him; for he knew that, if I remained, we both must perish; and, with but little hope of obtaining succor, I heaped a pillow of dry leaves beneath his head and hastened on."

"And did you return in time to save him?" asked Reuben, hanging on Malvin's words as if they were to be prophetic of his own success.

"I did," answered the other. "I came upon the camp of a hunting party before sunset of the same day. I guided them to the spot where my comrade was expecting death; and he is now a hale and hearty man upon his own farm, far within the frontiers, while I lie wounded here in the depths of the wilderness."

This example, powerful in affecting Reuben's decision, was aided, unconsciously to himself, by the hidden strength of many another motive. Roger Malvin perceived that the victory was nearly won.

"Now, go, my son, and Heaven prosper you!" he said. "Turn not back with your friends when you meet them, lest your wounds and weariness overcome you; but send hitherward two or three, that may be spared, to search for me; and believe me, Reuben, my heart will be lighted with every step you take towards home." Yet there was, perhaps, a change both in his countenance and voice as he spoke thus; for, after all, it was a ghastly fate to be left expiring in the wilderness.

Reuben Bourne, but half convinced that he was acting rightly, at length raised himself from the ground and prepared himself for his departure. And first, though contrary to Malvin's wishes, he collected a stock of roots and herbs, which had been their only food during the last two days. This useless supply he placed within reach of the dying man, for whom, also, he swept together a bed of dry oak leaves. Then climbing to the summit of the rock, which on one side was rough and broken, he bent the oak sapling downward, and bound his handkerchief to the topmost branch. This precaution was not unnecessary to direct any who might come in search of Malvin; for every part of the rock, except its broad, smooth front, was concealed at a little distance by the dense undergrowth of the forest. The handkerchief had been the bandage of a wound upon Reuben's arm; and, as he bound it to the tree, he vowed by the blood that stained it that he would return, either to save his companion's life or to lay his body in the grave. He then descended, and stood, with downcast eyes, to receive Roger Malvin's parting words.

The experience of the latter suggested much and minute advice respecting the youth's journey through the trackless forest. Upon this subject he spoke with calm earnestness, as if he were sending Reuben to the battle or the chase while he himself remained secure at home, and not as if the human countenance that was about to leave him were the last he would ever behold. But his firmness was shaken before he concluded.

"Carry my blessing to Dorcas, and say that my last prayer shall be for her and you. Bid her to have no hard thoughts because you left me here,"—Reuben's heart smote him,—"for that your life would not have weighed with you if its sacrifice could have done me good. She will marry you after she has mourned a little while for her father; and Heaven grant you long and happy days, and may your children's children stand round your death bed! And, Reuben," added he, as the weakness of mortality made its way at last, "return, when your wounds are healed and your weariness refreshed,—return to this wild rock, and lay my bones in the grave, and say a prayer over them."

An almost superstitious regard, arising perhaps from the customs of the Indians, whose war was with the dead as well as the living, was paid by the frontier inhabitants to the rites of sepulture; and there are many instances of the sacrifice of life in the attempt to bury those who had fallen by the "sword of the wilderness." Reuben, therefore, felt the full importance of the promise which he most solemnly made to return and perform Roger Malvin's obsequies. It was remarkable that the latter, speaking his whole heart in his parting words, no longer endeavored to persuade the youth that even the speediest succor might avail to the preservation of his life. Reuben was internally convinced that he should see Malvin's living face no more. His generous nature would fain have delayed him, at whatever risk, till the dying scene were past; but the desire of existence and the hope of happiness had strengthened in his heart, and he was unable to resist them.

"It is enough," said Roger Malvin, having listened to Reuben's promise. "Go, and God speed you!"

The youth pressed his hand in silence, turned, and was departing. His slow and faltering steps, however, had borne him but a little way before Malvin's voice recalled him.

"Reuben, Reuben," said he, faintly; and Reuben returned and knelt down by the dying man.

"Raise me, and let me lean against the rock," was his last request. "My face will be turned towards home, and I shall see you a moment longer as you pass among the trees."

Reuben, having made the desired alteration in his companion's posture, again began his solitary pilgrimage. He walked more hastily at first than was consistent with his strength; for a sort of guilty feeling, which sometimes torments men in their most justifiable acts, caused him to seek concealment from Malvin's eyes; but after he had trodden far upon the rustling forest leaves he crept back, impelled by a wild and painful curiosity, and, sheltered by the earthy roots of an uptorn tree, gazed earnestly at the desolate man. The morning sun was unclouded, and the trees and shrubs imbibed the sweet air of the month of May; yet there seemed a gloom on Nature's face, as if she sympathized with mortal pain and sorrow. Roger Malvin's hands were uplifted in a fervent prayer, some of the words of which stole through the stillness of the woods and entered Reuben's heart, torturing it with an unutterable pang. They were the broken accents of a petition for his own happiness and that of Dorcas; and, as the youth listened, conscience, or something in its similitude, pleaded strongly with him to return and lie down again by the rock. He felt how hard was the doom of the kind and generous being whom he had deserted in his extremity. Death would come like the slow approach of a corpse, stealing gradually towards him through the forest, and showing its ghastly and motionless features from behind a nearer and yet a nearer tree. But such must have been Reuben's own fate had he tarried another sunset; and who shall impute blame to him if he shrink from so useless a sacrifice? As he gave a parting look, a breeze waved the little banner upon the sapling oak and reminded Reuben of his vow.

Many circumstances combined to retard the wounded traveller in his way to the frontiers. On the second day the clouds, gathering densely over the sky, precluded the possibility of regulating his course by the position of the sun; and he knew not but that every effort of his almost exhausted strength was removing him farther from the home he sought. His scanty sustenance was supplied by the berries and other spontaneous products of the forest. Herds of deer, it is true, sometimes bounded past him, and partridges frequently whirred up before his footsteps; but his ammunition had been expended in the fight, and he had no means of slaying them. His wounds, irritated by the constant exertion in which lay the only hope of life, wore away his strength and at intervals confused his reason. But, even in the wanderings of intellect, Reuben's young heart clung strongly to existence; and it was only through absolute incapacity of motion that he at last sank down beneath a tree, compelled there to await death.

In this situation he was discovered by a party who, upon the first intelligence of the fight, had been despatched to the relief of the survivors. They conveyed him to the nearest settlement, which chanced to be that of his own residence.

Dorcas, in the simplicity of the olden time, watched by the bedside of her wounded lover, and administered all those comforts that are in the sole gift of woman's heart and hand. During several days Reuben's recollection strayed drowsily among the perils and hardships through which he had passed, and he was incapable of returning definite answers to the inquiries with which many were eager to harass him. No authentic particulars of the battle had yet been circulated; nor could mothers, wives, and children tell whether their loved ones were detained by captivity or by the stronger chain of death. Dorcas nourished her apprehensions in silence till one afternoon when Reuben awoke from an unquiet sleep, and seemed to recognize her more perfectly than at any previous time. She saw that his intellect had become composed, and she could no longer restrain her filial anxiety.

"My father, Reuben?" she began; but the change in her lover's countenance made her pause.

The youth shrank as if with a bitter pain, and the blood gushed vividly into his wan and hollow cheeks. His first impulse was to cover his face; but, apparently with a desperate effort, he half raised himself and spoke vehemently, defending himself against an imaginary accusation.

"Your father was sore wounded in the battle, Dorcas; and he bade me not burden myself with him, but only to lead him to the lakeside, that he might quench his thirst and die. But I would not desert the old man in his extremity, and, though bleeding myself, I supported him; I gave him half my strength, and led him away with me. For three days we journeyed on together, and your father was sustained beyond my hopes, but, awaking at sunrise on the fourth day, I found him faint and exhausted; he was unable to proceed; his life had ebbed away fast; and"—

"He died!" exclaimed Dorcas, faintly.

Reuben felt it impossible to acknowledge that his selfish love of life had hurried him away before her father's fate was decided. He spoke not; he only bowed his head; and between shame and exhaustion, sank back and hid his face in the pillow. Dorcas wept when her fears were thus confirmed; but the shock, as it had been long anticipated, was on that account the less violent.

"You dug a grave for my poor father in the wilderness, Reuben?" was the question by which her filial piety manifested itself.

"My hands were weak; but I did what I could," replied the youth in a smothered tone. "There stands a noble tombstone above his head; and I would to Heaven I slept as soundly as he!"

Dorcas, perceiving the wildness of his latter words, inquired no further at the time; but her heart found ease in the thought that Roger Malvin had not lacked such funeral rites as it was possible to bestow. The tale of Reuben's courage and fidelity lost nothing when she communicated it to her friends; and the poor youth, tottering from his sick chamber to breathe the sunny air, experienced from every tongue the miserable and humiliating torture of unmerited praise. All acknowledged that he might worthily demand the hand of the fair maiden to whose father he had been "faithful unto death;" and, as my tale is not of love, it shall suffice to say that in the space of a few months Reuben became the husband of Dorcas Malvin. During the marriage ceremony the bride was covered with blushes, but the bridegroom's face was pale.

There was now in the breast of Reuben Bourne an incommunicable thought—something which he was to conceal most heedfully from her whom he most loved and trusted. He regretted, deeply and bitterly, the moral cowardice that had restrained his words when he was about to disclose the truth to Dorcas; but pride, the fear of losing her affection, the dread of universal scorn, forbade him to rectify this falsehood. He felt that for leaving Roger Malvin he deserved no censure. His presence, the gratuitous sacrifice of his own life, would have added only another and a needless agony to the last moments of the dying man; but concealment had imparted to a justifiable act much of the secret effect of guilt; and Reuben, while reason told him that he had done right, experienced in no small degree the mental horrors which punish the perpetrator of undiscovered crime. By a certain association of ideas, he at times almost imagined himself a murderer. For years, also, a thought would occasionally recur, which, though he perceived all its folly and extravagance, he had not power to banish from his mind. It was a haunting and torturing fancy that his father-in-law was yet sitting at the foot of the rock, on the withered forest leaves, alive, and awaiting his pledged assistance. These mental deceptions, however, came and went, nor did he ever mistake them for realities, but in the calmest and clearest moods of his mind he was conscious that he had a deep vow unredeemed, and that an unburied corpse was calling to him out of the wilderness. Yet such was the consequence of his prevarication that he could not obey the call. It was now too late to require the assistance of Roger Malvin's friends in performing his long-deferred sepulture; and superstitious fears, of which none were more more susceptible than the people of the outward settlements, forbade Reuben to go alone. Neither did he know where in the pathless and illimitable forest to seek that smooth and lettered rock at the base of which the body lay: his remembrance of every portion of his travel thence was indistinct, and the latter part had left no impression upon his mind. There was, however, a continual impulse, a voice audible only to himself, commanding him to go forth and redeem his vow; and he had a strange impression that, were he to make the trial, he would be led straight to Malvin's bones. But year after year that summons, unheard but felt, was disobeyed. His one secret thought became like a chain binding down his spirit and like a serpent gnawing into his heart; and he was transformed into a sad and downcast yet irritable man.

In the course of a few years after their marriage changes began to be visible in the external prosperity of Reuben and Dorcas. The only riches of the former had been his stout heart and strong arm; but the latter, her father's sole heiress, had made her husband master of a farm, under older cultivation, larger, and better stocked than most of the frontier establishments. Reuben Bourne, however, was a neglectful husbandman; and, while the lands of the other settlers became annually more fruitful, his deteriorated in the same proportion. The discouragements to agriculture were greatly lessened by the cessation of Indian war, during which men held the plough in one hand and the musket in the other, and were fortunate if the products of their dangerous labor were not destroyed, either in the field or in the barn, by the savage enemy. But Reuben did not profit by the altered condition of the country; nor can it be denied that his intervals of industrious attention to his affairs were but scantily rewarded with success. The irritability by which he had recently become distinguished was another cause of his declining prosperity, as it occasioned frequent quarrels in his unavoidable intercourse with the neighboring settlers. The results of these were innumerable lawsuits; for the people of New England, in the earliest stages and wildest circumstances of the country, adopted, whenever attainable, the legal mode of deciding their differences. To be brief, the world did not go well with Reuben Bourne; and, though not till many years after his marriage, he was finally a ruined man, with but one remaining expedient against the evil fate that had pursued him. He was to throw sunlight into some deep recess of the forest, and seek subsistence from the virgin bosom of the wilderness.

The only child of Reuben and Dorcas was a son, now arrived at the age of fifteen years, beautiful in youth, and giving promise of a glorious manhood. He was peculiarly qualified for, and already began to excel in, the wild accomplishments of frontier life. His foot was fleet, his aim true, his apprehension quick, his heart glad and high; and all who anticipated the return of Indian war spoke of Cyrus Bourne as a future leader in the land. The boy was loved by his father with a deep and silent strength, as if whatever was good and happy in his own nature had been transferred to his child, carrying his affections with it. Even Dorcas, though loving and beloved, was far less dear to him; for Reuben's secret thoughts and insulated emotions had gradually made him a selfish man, and he could no longer love deeply except where he saw or imagined some reflection or likeness of his own mind. In Cyrus he recognized what he had himself been in other days; and at intervals he seemed to partake of the boy's spirit, and to be revived with a fresh and happy life. Reuben was accompanied by his son in the expedition, for the purpose of selecting a tract of land and felling and burning the timber, which necessarily preceded the removal of the household goods. Two months of autumn were thus occupied, after which Reuben Bourne and his young hunter returned to spend their last winter in the settlements.

It was early in the month of May that the little family snapped asunder whatever tendrils of affections had clung to inanimate objects, and bade farewell to the few who, in the blight of fortune, called themselves their friends. The sadness of the parting moment had, to each of the pilgrims, its peculiar alleviations. Reuben, a moody man, and misanthropic because unhappy, strode onward with his usual stern brow and downcast eye, feeling few regrets and disdaining to acknowledge any. Dorcas, while she wept abundantly over the broken ties by which her simple and affectionate nature had bound itself to everything, felt that the inhabitants of her inmost heart moved on with her, and that all else would be supplied wherever she might go. And the boy dashed one teardrop from his eye, and thought of the adventurous pleasures of the untrodden forest.

Oh, who, in the enthusiasm of a daydream, has not wished that he were a wanderer in a world of summer wilderness, with one fair and gentle being hanging lightly on his arm? In youth his free and exulting step would know no barrier but the rolling ocean or the snow-topped mountains; calmer manhood would choose a home where Nature had strewn a double wealth in the vale of some transparent stream; and when hoary age, after long, long years of that pure life, stole on and found him there, it would find him the father of a race, the patriarch of a people, the founder of a mighty nation yet to be. When death, like the sweet sleep which we welcome after a day of happiness, came over him, his far descendants would mourn over the venerated dust. Enveloped by tradition in mysterious attributes, the men of future generations would call him godlike; and remote posterity would see him standing, dimly glorious, far up the valley of a hundred centuries.

The tangled and gloomy forest through which the personages of my tale were wandering differed widely from the dreamer's land of fantasy; yet there was something in their way of life that Nature asserted as her own, and the gnawing cares which went with them from the world were all that now obstructed their happiness. One stout and shaggy steed, the bearer of all their wealth, did not shrink from the added weight of Dorcas; although her hardy breeding sustained her, during the latter part of each day's journey, by her husband's side. Reuben and his son, their muskets on their shoulders and their axes slung behind them, kept an unwearied pace, each watching with a hunter's eye for the game that supplied their food. When hunger bade, they halted and prepared their meal on the bank of some unpolluted forest brook, which, as they knelt down with thirsty lips to drink, murmured a sweet unwillingness, like a maiden at love's first kiss. They slept beneath a hut of branches, and awoke at peep of light refreshed for the toils of another day. Dorcas and the boy went on joyously, and even Reuben's spirit shone at intervals with an outward gladness; but inwardly there was a cold, cold sorrow, which he compared to the snow-drifts lying deep in the glens and hollows of the rivulets while the leaves were brightly green above.

Cyrus Bourne was sufficiently skilled in the travel of the woods to observe that his father did not adhere to the course they had pursued in their expedition of the preceding autumn. They were now keeping farther to the north, striking out more directly from the settlements, and into a region of which savage beasts and savage men were as yet the sole possessors. The boy sometimes hinted his opinions upon the subject, and Reuben listened attentively, and once or twice altered the direction of their march in accordance with his son's counsel; but, having so done, he seemed ill at ease. His quick and wandering glances were sent forward, apparently in search of enemies lurking behind the tree trunks; and, seeing nothing there, he would cast his eyes backwards as if in fear of some pursuer. Cyrus, perceiving that his father gradually resumed the old direction, forbore to interfere; nor, though something began to weigh upon his heart, did his adventurous nature permit him to regret the increased length and the mystery of their way.

On the afternoon of the fifth day they halted, and made their simple encampment nearly an hour before sunset. The face of the country, for the last few miles, had been diversified by swells of land resembling huge waves of a petrified sea; and in one of the corresponding hollows, a wild and romantic spot, had the family reared their hut and kindled their fire. There is something chilling, and yet heart-warming, in the thought of these three, united by strong bands of love and insulated from all that breathe beside. The dark and gloomy pines looked down upon them, and, as the wind swept through their tops, a pitying sound was heard in the forest; or did those old trees groan in fear that men were come to lay the axe to their roots at last? Reuben and his son, while Dorcas made ready their meal, proposed to wander out in search of game, of which that day's march had afforded no supply. The boy, promising not to quit the vicinity of the encampment, bounded off with a step as light and elastic as that of the deer he hoped to slay; while his father, feeling a transient happiness as he gazed after him, was about to pursue an opposite direction. Dorcas, in the meanwhile, had seated herself near their fire of fallen branches, upon the mossgrown and mouldering trunk of a tree uprooted years before. Her employment, diversified by an occasional glance at the pot, now beginning to simmer over the blaze, was the perusal of the current year's Massachusetts Almanac, which, with the exception of an old blackletter Bible, comprised all the literary wealth of the family. None pay a greater regard to arbitrary divisions of time than those who are excluded from society; and Dorcas mentioned, as if the information were of importance, that it was now the twelfth of May. Her husband started.

"The twelfth of May! I should remember it well," muttered he, while many thoughts occasioned a momentary confusion in his mind. "Where am I? Whither am I wandering? Where did I leave him?"

Dorcas, too well accustomed to her husband's wayward moods to note any peculiarity of demeanor, now laid aside the almanac and addressed him in that mournful tone which the tender hearted appropriate to griefs long cold and dead.

"It was near this time of the month, eighteen years ago, that my poor father left this world for a better. He had a kind arm to hold his head and a kind voice to cheer him, Reuben, in his last moments; and the thought of the faithful care you took of him has comforted me many a time since. Oh, death would have been awful to a solitary man in a wild place like this!"

"Pray Heaven, Dorcas," said Reuben, in a broken voice,—"pray Heaven that neither of us three dies solitary and lies unburied in this howling wilderness!" And he hastened away, leaving her to watch the fire beneath the gloomy pines.

Reuben Bourne's rapid pace gradually slackened as the pang, unintentionally inflicted by the words of Dorcas, became less acute. Many strange reflections, however, thronged upon him; and, straying onward rather like a sleep walker than a hunter, it was attributable to no care of his own that his devious course kept him in the vicinity of the encampment. His steps were imperceptibly led almost in a circle; nor did he observe that he was on the verge of a tract of land heavily timbered, but not with pinetrees. The place of the latter was here supplied by oaks and other of the harder woods; and around their roots clustered a dense and bushy under-growth, leaving, however, barren spaces between the trees, thick strewn with withered leaves. Whenever the rustling of the branches or the creaking of the trunks made a sound, as if the forest were waking from slumber, Reuben instinctively raised the musket that rested on his arm, and cast a quick, sharp glance on every side; but, convinced by a partial observation that no animal was near, he would again give himself up to his thoughts. He was musing on the strange influence that had led him away from his premeditated course, and so far into the depths of the wilderness. Unable to penetrate to the secret place of his soul where his motives lay hidden, he believed that a supernatural voice had called him onward, and that a supernatural power had obstructed his retreat. He trusted that it was Heaven's intent to afford him an opportunity of expiating his sin; he hoped that he might find the bones so long unburied; and that, having laid the earth over them, peace would throw its sunlight into the sepulchre of his heart. From these thoughts he was aroused by a rustling in the forest at some distance from the spot to which he had wandered. Perceiving the motion of some object behind a thick veil of undergrowth, he fired, with the instinct of a hunter and the aim of a practised marksman. A low moan, which told his success, and by which even animals can express their dying agony, was unheeded by Reuben Bourne. What were the recollections now breaking upon him?

The thicket into which Reuben had fired was near the summit of a swell of land, and was clustered around the base of a rock, which, in the shape and smoothness of one of its surfaces, was not unlike a gigantic gravestone. As if reflected in a mirror, its likeness was in Reuben's memory. He even recognized the veins which seemed to form an inscription in forgotten characters: everything remained the same, except that a thick covert of bushes shrouded the lower part of the rock, and would have hidden Roger Malvin had he still been sitting there. Yet in the next moment Reuben's eye was caught by another change that time had effected since he last stood where he was now standing again behind the earthy roots of the uptorn tree. The sapling to which he had bound the bloodstained symbol of his vow had increased and strengthened into an oak, far indeed from its maturity, but with no mean spread of shadowy branches. There was one singularity observable in this tree which made Reuben tremble. The middle and lower branches were in luxurian life, and an excess of vegetation had fringed the trunk almost to the ground; but a blight had apparently stricken the upper part of the oak, and the very topmost bough was withered, sapless, and utterly dead. Reuben remembered how the little banner had fluttered on that topmost bough, when it was green and lovely, eighteen years before. Whose guilt had blasted it?

Dorcas, after the departure of the two hunters, continued her preparations for their evening repast. Her sylvan table was the moss-covered trunk of a large fallen tree, on the broadest part of which she had spread a snow-white cloth and arranged what were left of the bright pewter vessels that had been her pride in the settlements. It had a strange aspect, that one little spot of homely comfort in the desolate heart of Nature. The sunshine yet lingered upon the higher branches of the trees that grew on rising ground; but the shadows of evening had deepened into the hollow where the encampment was made, and the firelight began to redden as it gleamed up the tall trunks of the pines or hovered on the dense and obscure mass of foliage that circled round the spot. The heart of Dorcas was not sad; for she felt that it was better to journey in the wilderness with two whom she loved than to be a lonely woman in a crowd that cared not for her. As she busied herself in arranging seats of mouldering wood, covered with leaves, for Reuben and her son, her voice danced through the gloomy forest in the measure of a song that she had learned in youth. The rude melody, the production of a bard who won no name, was descriptive of a winter evening in a frontier cottage, when, secured from savage inroad by the high-piled snow-drifts, the family rejoiced by their own fireside. The whole song possessed the nameless charm peculiar to unborrowed thought, but four continually-recurring lines shone out from the rest like the blaze of the hearth whose joys they celebrated. Into them, working magic with a few simple words, the poet had instilled the very essence of domestic love and household happiness, and they were poetry and picture joined in one. As Dorcas sang, the walls of her forsaken home seemed to encircle her; she no longer saw the gloomy pines, nor heard the wind which still, as she began each verse, sent a heavy breath through the branches, and died away in a hollow moan from the burden of the song. She was aroused by the report of a gun in the vicinity of the encampment; and either the sudden sound, or her loneliness by the glowing fire, caused her to tremble violently. The next moment she laughed in the pride of a mother's heart.

"My beautiful young hunter! My boy has slain a deer!" she exclaimed, recollecting that in the direction whence the shot proceeded Cyrus had gone to the chase.

She waited a reasonable time to hear her son's light step bounding over the rustling leaves to tell of his success. But he did not immediately appear; and she sent her cheerful voice among the trees in search of him.

"Cyrus! Cyrus!"

His coming was still delayed; and she determined, as the report had apparently been very near, to seek for him in person. Her assistance, also, might be necessary in bringing home the venison which she flattered herself he had obtained. She therefore set forward, directing her steps by the long-past sound, and singing as she went, in order that the boy might be aware of her approach and run to meet her. From behind the trunk of every tree, and from every hiding-place in the thick foliage of the undergrowth, she hoped to discover the countenance of her son, laughing with the sportive mischief that is born of affection. The sun was now beneath the horizon, and the light that came down among the leaves was sufficiently dim to create many illusions in her expecting fancy. Several times she seemed indistinctly to see his face gazing out from among the leaves; and once she imagined that he stood beckoning to her at the base of a craggy rock. Keeping her eyes on this object, however, it proved to be no more than the trunk of an oak fringed to the very ground with little branches, one of which, thrust out farther than the rest, was shaken by the breeze. Making her way round the foot of the rock, she suddenly found herself close to her husband, who had approached in another direction. Leaning upon the butt of his gun, the muzzle of which rested upon the withered leaves, he was apparently absorbed in the contemplation of some object at his feet.

"How is this, Reuben? Have you slain the deer and fallen asleep over him?" exclaimed Dorcas, laughing cheerfully, on her first slight observation of his posture and appearance.

He stirred not, neither did he turn his eyes towards her; and a cold, shuddering fear, indefinite in its source and object, began to creep into her blood. She now perceived that her husband's face was ghastly pale, and his features were rigid, as if incapable of assuming any other expression than the strong despair which had hardened upon them. He gave not the slightest evidence that he was aware of her approach.

"For the love of Heaven, Reuben, speak to me!" cried Dorcas; and the strange sound of her own voice affrighted her even more than the dead silence.

Her husband started, stared into her face, drew her to the front of the rock, and pointed with his finger.

Oh, there lay the boy, asleep, but dreamless, upon the fallen forest leaves! His cheek rested upon his arm—his curled locks were thrown back from his brow—his limbs were slightly relaxed. Had a sudden weariness overcome the youthful hunter? Would his mother's voice arouse him? She knew that it was death.

"This broad rock is the gravestone of your near kindred, Dorcas," said her husband. "Your tears will fall at once over your father and your son."

She heard him not. With one wild shriek, that seemed to force its way from the sufferer's inmost soul, she sank insensible by the side of her dead boy. At that moment the withered topmost bough of the oak loosened itself in the stilly air, and fell in soft, light fragments upon the rock, upon the leaves, upon Reuben, upon his wife and child, and upon Roger Malvin's bones. Then Reuben's heart was stricken, and the tears gushed out like water from a rock. The vow that the wounded youth had made the blighted man had come to redeem. His sin was expiated,—the curse was gone from him; and in the hour when he had shed blood dearer to him than his own, a prayer, the first for years, went up to Heaven from the lips of Reuben Bourne.

My Kinsman, Major Molineux (1832)

After the kings of Great Britain had assumed the right of appointing the colonial governors, the measures of the latter seldom met with the ready and generous approbation which had been paid to those of their predecessors, under the original charters. The people looked with most jealous scrutiny to the exercise of power which did not emanate from themselves, and they usually rewarded their rulers with slender gratitude for the compliances by which, in softening their instructions from beyond the sea, they had incurred the reprehension of those who gave them. The annals of Massachusetts Bay will inform us, that of six governors in the space of about forty years from the surrender of the old charter, under James II., two imprisoned by a popular insurrection; a third, as Hutchinson [1] inclines to believe, was driven from the province by the whizzing of a musket-ball; a fourth, in the opinion of the same historian, was hastened to his grave by continual bickerings with the House of Representatives; and the remaining two, as well as their successors, till the Revolution, were favored with few and brief intervals of peaceful sway. The inferior members of the court party, in times of high political excitement, led scarcely a more desirable life. These remarks may serve as a preface to the following adventures, which chanced upon a summer night, not far from a hundred years ago. The reader, in order to avoid a long and dry detail of colonial affairs, is requested to dispense with an account of the train of circumstances that had caused much temporary inflammation of the popular mind.

It was near nine o'clock of a moonlight evening, when a boat crossed the ferry with a single passenger, who had obtained his conveyance at that unusual hour by the promise of an extra fare. While he stood on the landing-place, searching in either pocket for the means of fulfilling his agreement, the ferryman lifted a lantern, by the aid of which, and the newly risen moon, he took a very accurate survey of the stranger's figure. He was a youth of barely eighteen years, evidently country-bred, and now, as it should seem, upon his first visit to town. He was clad in a coarse gray coat, well worn, but in excellent repair; his under garments were durably constructed of leather, and fitted tight to a pair of serviceable and well-shaped limbs; his stockings of blue yarn were the incontrovertible work of a mother or a sister; and on his head was a three-cornered hat, which in its better days had perhaps sheltered the graver brow of the lad's father. Under his left arm was a heavy cudgel formed of an oak sapling, and retaining a part of the hardened root; and his equipment was completed by a wallet, not so abundantly stocked as to incommode the vigorous shoulders on which it hung. Brown, curly hair, well-shaped features, and bright, cheerful

---

[1] Thomas Hutchinson (1711–1780), last royal governor of Massachusetts.

eyes were nature's gifts, and worth all that art could have done for his adornment.

The youth, one of whose names was Robin, finally drew from his pocket the half of a little province bill of five shillings, which, in the depreciation in that sort of currency, did but satisfy the ferryman's demand, with the surplus of a sexangular piece of parchment, valued at three pence. He then walked forward into the town, with as light a step as if his day's journey had not already exceeded thirty miles, and with as eager an eye as if he were entering London city, instead of the little metropolis of a New England colony. Before Robin had proceeded far, however, it occurred to him that he knew not whither to direct his steps; so he paused, and looked up and down the narrow street, scrutinizing the small and mean wooden buildings that were scattered on either side.

"This low hovel cannot be my kinsman's dwelling," thought he, "nor yonder old house, where the moonlight enters at the broken casement; and truly I see none hereabouts that might be worthy of him. It would have been wise to inquire my way of the ferryman, and doubtless he would have gone with me, and earned a shilling from the Major for his pains. But the next man I meet will do as well."

He resumed his walk, and was glad to perceive that the street now became wider, and the houses more respectable in their appearance. He soon discerned a figure moving on moderately in advance, and hastened his steps to overtake it. As Robin drew nigh, he saw that the passenger was a man in years, with a full periwig of gray hair, a wide-skirted coat of dark cloth, and silk stockings rolled above his knees. He carried a long and polished cane, which he struck down perpendicularly before him at every step; and at regular intervals he uttered two successive hems, of a peculiarly solemn and sepulchral intonation. Having made these observations, Robin laid hold of the skirt of the old man's coat, just when the light from the open door and windows of a barber's shop fell upon both their figures.

"Good evening to you, honored sir," said he, making a low bow, and still retaining his hold of the skirt. "I pray you tell me whereabouts is the dwelling of my kinsman, Major Molineux."

The youth's question was uttered very loudly; and one of the barbers, whose razor was descending on a well-soaped chin, and another who was dressing a Ramillies wig, left their occupations, and came to the door. The citizen, in the mean time, turned a long-favored countenance upon Robin, and answered him in a tone of excessive anger and annoyance. His two sepulchral hems, however, broke into the very centre of his rebuke, with most singular effect, like a thought of the cold grave obtruding among wrathful passions.

"Let go my garment, fellow! I tell you, I know not the man you speak of. What! I have authority, I have—hem, hem—authority; and if this be the respect you show for your betters, your feet shall be brought acquainted with the stocks by daylight, tomorrow morning!"

Robin released the old man's skirt, and hastened away, pursued by an ill-mannered roar of laughter from the barber's shop. He was at first considerably surprised by the result of his question, but, being a shrewd youth, soon thought himself able to account for the mystery.

"This is some country representative," was his conclusion, "who has never seen the inside of my kinsman's door, and lacks the breeding to answer a stranger civilly. The man is old, or verily—I might be tempted to turn back and smite him on the nose. Ah, Robin, Robin! even the barber's boys laugh at you for choosing such a guide! You will be wiser in time, friend Robin."

He now became entangled in a succession of crooked and narrow streets, which crossed each other, and meandered at no great distance from the water-side. The smell of tar was obvious to his nostrils, the masts of vessels pierced the moonlight above the tops of the buildings, and the numerous signs, which Robin paused to read, informed him that he was near the centre of business. But the streets were empty, the shops were closed, and lights were visible only in the second stories of a few dwelling-houses. At length, on the corner of a narrow lane, through which he was passing, he beheld the broad countenance of a British hero swinging before the door of an inn, whence proceeded the voices of many guests. The casement of one of the lower windows was thrown back, and a very thin curtain permitted Robin to distinguish a party at supper, round a well-furnished table. The fragrance of the good cheer steamed forth into the outer air, and the youth could not fail to recollect that the last remnant of his travelling stock of provision had yielded to his morning appetite, and that noon had found and left him dinnerless.

"Oh, that a parchment three-penny might give me a right to sit down at yonder table!" said Robin, with a sigh. "But the Major will make me welcome to the best of his victuals; so I will even step boldly in, and inquire my way to his dwelling."

He entered the tavern, and was guided by the murmur of voices and the fumes of tobacco to the public-room. It was a long and low apartment, with oaken walls, grown dark in the continual smoke, and floor which was thickly sanded, but of no immaculate purity. A number of persons—the larger part of whom appeared to be mariners, or in some way connected with the sea—occupied the wooden benches, or leather-bottomed chairs, conversing on various matters, and occasionally lending their attention to some topic of general interest. Three or four little groups were draining as many bowls of punch, which the West India trade had long since made a familiar drink in the colony. Others, who had the appearance of men who lived by regular and laborious handicraft, preferred the insulated bliss of an unshared potation, and became more taciturn under its influence. Nearly all, in short, evinced a predilection for the Good Creature in some of its various shapes, for this is a vice to which, as Fast Day sermons [2] of a hundred years ago will testify, we have a long hereditary claim. The only guests to whom Robin's sympathies inclined him were two or three sheepish countrymen, who were using the inn somewhat after the fashion of a Turkish caravansary; they had gotten themselves into the darkest corner of the room, and heedless of the Nicotian [3] atmosphere, were supping on the bread of their own ovens, and the bacon cured in their own chimney-smoke. But though Robin felt a sort of brotherhood with these strangers, his eyes were attracted from them to a person who stood near the door, holding whispered conversation with a group of ill-dressed associates. His features were separately striking almost to grotesqueness, and the whole face left a deep impression on the memory. The forehead bulged out into a double prominence, with a vale between; the nose came boldly forth in an irregular curve, and its bridge was of more than a finger's breadth; the eyebrows were deep and shaggy, and the eyes glowed beneath them like fire in a cave.

While Robin deliberated of whom to inquire respecting his kinsman's dwelling, he was accosted by the innkeeper, a little man in a stained white apron, who had come to pay his professional welcome to the stranger. Being in the second generation from a French Protestant, he seemed to have inherited the courtesy of his parent nation; but no variety of circumstances was ever known to change his voice from the one shrill note in which he now addressed Robin.

"From the country, I presume, sir?" said he, with a profound bow. "Beg leave to congratulate you on your arrival, and trust you intend a long stay with us. Fine town here, sir, beautiful buildings, and much that may interest a stranger. May I hope for the honor of your commands in respect to supper?"

"The man sees a family likeness! the rogue has guessed that I am related to the Major!" thought Robin, who had hitherto experienced little superfluous civility.

All eyes were now turned on the country lad, standing at the door, in his worn three-cornered hat, gray coat, leather breeches, and blue yarn stockings, leaning on an oaken cudgel, and bearing a wallet on his back.

Robin replied to the courteous innkeeper, with such an assumption of confidence as befitted the Major's relative. "My honest friend," he said, "I shall make it a point to patronize your house on some occasion, when"—here he could not help lowering his voice—"when I may have more than a parchment three-pence in my pocket. My present business,"

[2] Sermons delivered by New England clergy on special days of penance.
[3] Pertaining to nicotine.

continued he, speaking with lofty confidence, "is merely to inquire my way to the dwelling of my kinsman, Major Molineux."

There was a sudden and general movement in the room, which Robin interpreted as expressing the eagerness of each individual to become his guide. But the innkeeper turned his eyes to a written paper on the wall, which he read, or seemed to read, with occasional recurrences to the young man's figure.

"What have we here?" said he, breaking his speech into little dry fragments. " 'Left the house of the subscriber, bounden servant, Hezekiah Mudge,—had on, when he went away, gray coat, leather breaches, master's third-best hat. One pound currency reward to whosoever shall lodge him in any jail of the providence.' Better trudge, boy; better trudge!"

Robin had begun to draw his hand towards the lighter end of the oak cudgel, but a strange hostility in every countenance induced him to relinquish his purpose of breaking the courteous innkeeper's head. As he turned to leave the room, he encountered a sneering glance from the bold-featured personage whom he had before noticed; and no sooner was he beyond the door, than he heard a general laugh, in which the innkeeper's voice might be distinguished, like the dropping of small stones into a kettle.

"Now, is it not strange," thought Robin, with his usual shrewdness,—"is it not strange that the confession of an empty pocket should outweigh the name of my kinsman, Major Molineux? Oh, if I had one of those grinning rascals in the woods, where I and my oak sapling grew up together, I would teach him that my arm is heavy though my purse be light!"

On turning the corner of the narrow lane, Robin found himself in a spacious street, with an unbroken line of lofty houses on each side, and a steepled building at the upper end, whence the ringing of a bell announced the hour of nine. The light of the moon, and the lamps from the numerous shop-windows, discovered people promenading on the pavement, and amongst them Robin had hoped to recognize his hitherto inscrutable relative. The result of his former inquiries made him unwilling to hazard another, in a scene of such publicity, and he determined to walk slowly and silently up the street, thrusting his face close to that of every elderly gentleman, in search of the Major's lineaments. In his progress, Robin encountered many gay and gallant figures. Embroidered garments of showy colors, enormous periwigs, gold-laced hats, and silver-hilted swords glided past him and dazzled his optics. Travelled youths, imitators of the European fine gentlemen of the period, trod jauntily along, half dancing to the fashionable tunes which they hummed, and making poor Robin ashamed of his quiet and natural gait. At length, after many pauses to examine the gorgeous display of goods in the shop-windows, and after suffering some rebukes for the impertinence of his scrutiny into people's faces, the Major's kinsman found himself near the steepled building, still unsuccessful in his search. As yet, however, he had seen only one side of the thronged street; so Robin crossed, and continued the same sort of inquisition down the opposite pavement, with stronger hopes than the philosopher seeking an honest man, but with no better fortune. He had arrived about midway towards the lower end, from which his course began, when he overheard the approach of some one who struck down a cane on the flag-stones at every step, uttering at regular intervals, two sepulchral hems.

"Mercy on us!" quoth Robin, recognizing the sound.

Turning a corner, which chanced to be close at his right hand, he hastened to pursue his researches in some other part of the town. His patience now was wearing low, and he seemed to feel more fatigue from his rambles since he crossed the ferry, than from his journey of several days on the other side. Hunger also pleaded loudly within him, and Robin began to balance the propriety of demanding, violently, and with lifted cudgel, the necessary guidance from the first solitary passenger whom he should meet. While a resolution to this effect was gaining strength, he entered a street of mean appearance, on either side of which a row of ill-built houses was straggling towards the harbor. The moonlight fell upon no passenger along the whole extent, but in the third domicile which Robin passed there was a half-opened door, and his keen glance detected a woman's garment within.

"My luck may be better here," said he to himself.

Accordingly, he approached the door, and beheld it shut closer as he did so; yet an open space remained, sufficing for the fair occupant to observe the stranger, without a corresponding display on her part. All that Robin could discern was a strip of scarlet petticoat, and the occasional sparkle of an eye, as if the moonbeams were trembling on some bright thing.

"Pretty mistress," for I may call her so with a good conscience, thought the shrewd youth, since I know nothing to the contrary,—"my sweet pretty mistress, will you be kind enough to tell me whereabouts I must seek the dwelling of my kinsman, Major Molineux?"

Robin's voice was plaintive and winning, and the female, seeing nothing to be shunned in the handsome country youth, thrust open the door, and came forth into the moonlight. She was a dainty little figure, with a white neck, round arms, and a slender waist, at the extremity of which her scarlet petticoat jutted out over a hoop, as if she were standing in a balloon. Moreover, her face was oval and pretty, her hair dark beneath the little cap, and her bright eyes possessed a sly freedom, which triumphed over those of Robin.

"Major Molineux dwells here," said this fair woman.

Now, her voice was the sweetest Robin had heard that night, yet he could not help doubting whether that sweet voice spoke Gospel truth.

He looked up and down the mean street, and then surveyed the house before which they stood. It was a small, dark edifice of two stories, the second of which projected over the lower floor, and the front apartment had the aspect of a shop for petty commodities.

"Now, truly, I am in luck," replied Robin, cunningly, "and so indeed is my kinsman, the Major, in having so pretty a housekeeper. But I prithee trouble him to step to the door; I will deliver him a message from his friends in the country, and then go back to my lodgings at the inn."

"Nay, the Major has been abed this hour or more," said the lady of the scarlet petticoat; "and it would be to little purpose to disturb him to-night, seeing his evening draught was of the strongest. But he is a kind-hearted man, and it would be as much as my life's worth to let a kinsman of his turn away from the door. You are the good old gentleman's very picture, and I could swear that was his rainy-weather hat. Also he has garments very much resembling those leather small-clothes. But come in, I pray, for I bid you hearty welcome in his name."

So saying, the fair and hospitable dame took our hero by the hand; and the touch was light, and the force was gentleness, and though Robin read in her eyes what he did not hear in her words, yet the slender-waisted woman in the scarlet petticoat proved stronger than the athletic country youth. She had drawn his half-willing footsteps nearly to the threshold, when the opening of a door in the neighborhood startled the Major's housekeeper, and, leaving the Major's kinsman, she vanished speedily into her own domicile. A heavy yawn preceded the appearance of a man, who, like the Moonshine of Pyramus and Thisbe, carried a lantern, needlessly aiding his sister luminary in the heavens. As he walked sleepily up the street, he turned his broad, dull face on Robin, and displayed a long staff, spiked at the end.

"Home, vagabond, home!" said the watchman, in accents that seemed to fall asleep as soon as they were uttered. "Home, or we'll set you in the stocks by peep of day!"

"This is the second hint of the kind," thought Robin. "I wish they would end my difficulties, by setting me there to-night."

Nevertheless, the youth felt an instinctive antipathy towards the guardian of midnight order, which at first prevented him from asking his usual question. But just when the man was about to vanish behind the corner, Robin resolved not to lose the opportunity, and shouted lustily after him,—

"I say, friend! will you guide me to the house of my kinsman, Major Molineux?"

The watchman made no reply, but turned the corner and was gone; yet Robin seemed to hear the sound of drowsy laughter stealing along the solitary street. At that moment, also, a pleasant titter saluted him from the open window above his head; he looked up, and caught the sparkle of a saucy eye; a round arm beckoned to him, and next he heard light footsteps descending the staircase within. But Robin, being of the household of a New England clergyman, was a good youth, as well as a shrewd one; so he resisted temptation, and fled away.

He now roamed desperately, and at random, through the town, almost ready to believe that a spell was on him, like that by which a wizard of his country had once kept three pursuers wandering, a whole winter night, within twenty paces of the cottage which they sought. The streets lay before him, strange and desolate, and the lights were extinguished in almost every house. Twice, however, little parties of men, among whom Robin distinguished individuals in outlandish attire, came hurrying along; but, though on both occasions, they paused to address him, such intercourse did not at all enlighten his perplexity. They did but utter a few words in some language of which Robin knew nothing, and perceiving his inability to answer, bestowed a curse upon him in plain English and hastened away. Finally, the lad determined to knock at the door of every mansion that might appear worthy to be occupied by his kinsman, trusting that perseverance would overcome the fatality that had hitherto thwarted him. Firm in this resolve, he was passing beneath the walls of a church, which formed the corner of two streets, when, as he turned into the shade of its steeple, he encountered a bulky stranger, muffled in a cloak. The man was proceeding with the speed of earnest business, but Robin planted himself full before him, holding the oak cudgel with both hands across his body as a bar to further passage.

"Halt, honest man, and answer me a question," said he, very resolutely. "Tell me, this instant, whereabouts is the dwelling of my kinsman, Major Molineux!"

"Keep your tongue between your teeth, fool, and let me pass!" said a deep, gruff voice, which Robin partly remembered. "Let me pass, or I'll strike you to earth!"

"No, no, neighbor!" cried Robin, flourishing his cudgel, and then thrusting its larger end close to the man's muffled face. "No, no, I'm not the fool you take me for, nor do you pass till I have an answer to my question. Whereabouts is the dwelling of my kinsman, Major Molineux?"

The stranger, instead of attempting to force his passage, stepped back into the moonlight, unmuffled his face, and stared full into that of Robin.

"Watch here an hour, and Major Molineux will pass by," said he.

Robin gazed with dismay and astonishment on the unprecedented physiognomy of the speaker. The forehead with its double prominence, the broad hooked nose, the shaggy eyebrows, and fiery eyes were those which he had noticed at the inn, but the man's complexion had undergone a singular, or, more properly, a twofold change. One side of the face blazed an intense red, while the other was black as midnight, the division line being in the broad bridge of the nose; and a mouth which seemed to extend from ear to ear was black or red, in contrast to the color of the cheek. The effect was as if two individual devils, a fiend of fire and a fiend of darkness, had united themselves to form this infernal visage. The stranger grinned in Robin's face, muffled his party-colored features, and was out of sight in a moment.

"Strange things we travellers see!" ejaculated Robin.

He seated himself, however, upon the steps of the church-door, resolving to wait the appointed time for his kinsman. A few moments were consumed in philosophical speculations upon the species of man who had just left him; but having settled this point shrewdly, rationally, and satisfactorily, he was compelled to look elsewhere for his amusement. And first he threw his eyes along the street. It was of more respectable appearance than most of those into which he had wandered; and the moon, creating, like the imaginative power, a beautiful strangeness in familiar objects, gave something of romance to a scene that might not have possessed it in the light of day. The irregular and often quaint architecture of the houses, some of whose roofs were broken into numerous little peaks, while others ascended, steep and narrow, into a single point, and others again were square; the pure snow-white of some of their complexions, the aged darkness of others, and the thousand sparklings, reflected from bright substances in the walls of many; these matters engaged Robin's attention for a while, and then began to grow wearisome. Next he endeavored to define the forms of distant objects, starting away, with almost ghostly indistinctness, just as his eye appeared to grasp them; and finally he took a minute survey of an edifice which stood on the opposite side of the street, directly in front of the church-door, where he was stationed. It was a large, square mansion, distinguished from its neighbors by a balcony, which rested on tall pillars, and by an elaborate Gothic window, communicating therewith.

"Perhaps this is the very house I have been seeking," thought Robin.

Then he strove to speed away the time, by listening to a murmur which swept continually along the street, yet was scarcely audible, except to an unaccustomed ear like his; it was a low, dull, dreamy sound, compounded of many noises, each of which was at too great a distance to be separately heard. Robin marvelled at this snore of a sleeping town, and marvelled more whenever its continuity was broken by now and then a distant shout, apparently loud where it originated. But altogether it was a sleep-inspiring sound, and, to shake off its drowsy influence, Robin arose, and climbed a window-frame, that he might view the interior of the church. There the moonbeams came trembling in, and fell down upon the deserted pews, and extended along the quiet aisles. A fainter yet more awful radiance was hovering around the pulpit, and one solitary ray had dared to rest upon the open page of the great Bible. Had nature, in that deep hour, become a worshipper in the house which man had builded? Or was that heavenly light the visible sanctity of the place,—visible because no earthly and impure feet were within the walls? The scene made Robin's heart shiver with a sensation of loneliness stronger than he had ever felt in the remotest depths of his native woods; so he turned away and sat down again before the door. There were graves around the church, and now an uneasy thought obtruded into Robin's breast. What if the object of his search, which had been so often and so strangely thwarted, were all the time mouldering in his shroud? What if his kinsman should glide through younder gate, and nod and smile to him in dimly passing by?

"Oh that any breathing thing were here with me!" said Robin.

Recalling his thoughts from this uncomfortable track, he sent them over forest, hill, and stream, and attempted to imagine how that evening of ambiguity and weariness had been spent by his father's household. He pictured them assembled at the door, beneath the tree, the great old tree, which had been spared for its huge twisted trunk and venerable shade, when a thousand leafy brethren fell. There, at the going down of the summer sun, it was his father's custom to perform domestic worship, that the neighbors might come and join with him like brothers of the family, and that the wayfaring man might pause to drink at that fountain, and keep his heart pure by freshening the memory of home. Robin distinguished the seat of every individual of the little audience; he saw the good man in the midst, holding the Scriptures in the golden light that fell from the western clouds; he beheld him close the book and all rise up to pray. He heard the old thanksgivings for daily mercies, the old supplications for their continuance, to which he had so often listened in weariness, but which were now among his dear remembrances. He perceived the slight inequality of his father's voice when he came to speak of the absent one; he noted how his mother turned her face to the broad and knotted trunk; how his elder brother scorned, because the beard was rough upon his upper lip, to permit his features to be moved; how the younger sister drew down a low hanging branch before her eyes; and how the little one of all, whose sports had hitherto broken the decorum of the scene, understood the prayer for her playmate, and burst into clamorous grief. Then he saw them go in at the door; and when Robin would have entered also, the latch tinkled into its place, and he was excluded from his home.

"Am I here, or there?" cried Robin, starting; for all at once, when his thoughts had become visible and audible in a dream, the long, wide, solitary street shone out before him.

He aroused himself, and endeavored to fix his attention steadily upon the large edifice which he had surveyed before. But still his mind kept vibrating between fancy and reality; by turns, the pillars of the balcony lengthened into the tall, bare stems of pines, dwindled down to human figures, settled again into their true shape and size, and then commenced a new succession of changes. For a single moment, when he deemed himself awake, he could have sworn that a visage—one which he seemed to remember, yet could not absolutely name as his kinsman's—was looking towards him from the Gothic window. A deeper sleep wrestled with and nearly overcame him, but fled at the sound of footsteps along the opposite pavement. Robin rubbed his eyes, discerned a man passing at the foot of the balcony, and addressed him in a loud, peevish, and lamentable cry.

"Hallo, friend! must I wait here all night for my kinsman, Major Molineux?"

The sleeping echoes awoke, and answered the voice; and the passenger, barely able to discern a figure sitting in the oblique shade of the steeple, traversed the street to obtain a nearer view. He was himself a gentleman in his prime, of open, intelligent, cheerful, and altogether prepossessing countenance. Perceiving a country youth, apparently homeless and without friends, he accosted him in a tone of real kindness, which had become strange to Robin's ears.

"Well, my good lad, why are you sitting here?" inquired he. "Can I be of service to you in any way?"

"I am afraid not, sir," replied Robin, despondingly; "yet I shall take it kindly, if you'll answer me a single question. I've been searching, half the night, for one Major Molineux; now, sir, is there really such a person in these parts, or am I dreaming?"

"Major Molineux! The name is not altogether strange to me," said the gentleman, smiling. "Have you any objection to telling me the nature of your business with him?"

Then Robin briefly related that his father was a clergyman, settled on a small salary, at a long distance back in the country, and that he and Major Molineux were brothers' children. The Major, having inherited riches, and acquired civil and military rank, had visited his cousin, in great pomp, a year or two before; had manifested much interest in Robin and an elder brother, and, being childless himself, had thrown out hints respecting the future establishment of one of them in life. The elder brother was destined to succeed to the farm which his father cultivated in the interval of sacred duties; it was therefore determined that Robin should profit by his kinsman's generous intentions, especially as he seemed to be rather the favorite, and was thought to possess other necessary endowments.

"For I have the name of being a shrewd youth," observed Robin, in this part of his story.

"I doubt not you deserve it," replied his new friend, good-naturedly; "but pray proceed."

"Well, sir, being nearly eighteen years old, and well grown, as you see," continued Robin, drawing himself up to his full height, "I thought it high time to begin in the world. So my mother and sister put me in handsome trim, and my father gave me half the remnant of his last year's salary, and five days ago I started for this place, to pay the Major a visit. But, would you believe it, sir! I crossed the ferry a little after dark, and have yet found nobody that would show me the way to his dwelling; only, an hour or two since, I was told to wait here, and Major Molineux would pass by."

"Can you describe the man who told you this?" inquired the gentleman.

"Oh, he was a very ill-favored fellow, sir," replied Robin, "with two great bumps on his forehead, a hook nose, fiery eyes; and, what struck me as the strangest, his face was of two different colors. Do you happen to know such a man, sir?"

"Not intimately," answered the stranger, "but I chanced to meet him a little time previous to your stopping me. I believe you may trust his word, and that the Major will very shortly pass through this street. In the mean time, as I have a singular curiosity to witness your meeting, I will sit down here upon the steps and bear you company."

He seated himself accordingly, and soon engaged his companion in animated discourse. It was but a brief continuance, however, for a noise of shouting, which had long been remotely audible, drew so much nearer that Robin inquired its cause.

"What may be the meaning of this uproar?" asked he. "Truly, if your town be always as noisy, I shall find little sleep while I am an inhabitant."

"Why, indeed, friend Robin, there do appear to be three or four riotous fellows abroad to-night," replied the gentleman. "You must not expect all the stillness of your native woods here in our streets. But the watch will shortly be at the heels of these lads and"—

"Ay, and set them in the stocks by peep of day," interrupted Robin, recollecting his own encounter with the drowsy lantern-bearer. "But, dear sir, if I may trust my ears, an army of watchmen would never make head against such a multitude of rioters. There were at least a thousand voices went up to make that one shout."

"May not a man have several voices, Robin, as well as two complexions?" said his friend.

"Perhaps a man may; but Heaven forbid that a woman should!" responded the shrewd youth, thinking of the seductive tones of the Major's housekeeper.

The sounds of a trumpet in some neighboring street now became so evident and continual, that Robin's curiosity was strongly excited. In addition to the shouts, he heard frequent bursts from many instruments of discord, and a wild and confused laughter filled up the intervals. Robin rose from the steps, and looked wistfully towards a point whither people seemed to be hastening.

"Surely some prodigious merry-making is going on," exclaimed he. "I have laughed very little since I left home, sir, and should be sorry to lose an opportunity. Shall we step round the corner by that darkish house, and take our share of the fun?"

"Sit down again, sit down, good Robin," replied the gentleman, laying his hand on the skirt of the gray coat. "You forget that we must wait here for your kinsman; and there is reason to believe that he will pass by, in the course of a very few moments."

The near approach of the uproar had now disturbed the neighborhood; windows flew open on all sides; and many heads, in the attire of the pillow, and confused by sleep suddenly broken, were protruded to the gaze of whoever had leisure to observe them. Eager voices hailed each other from house to house, all demanding the explanation, which not a soul could give. Half-dressed men hurried towards the unknown commotion, stumbling as they went over the stone steps that thrust themselves into the narrow footwalk. The shouts, the laughter, and the tuneless bray, the antipodes of music, came onwards with increasing din, till scattered individuals, and then denser bodies, began to appear round a corner at the distance of a hundred yards.

"Will you recognize your kinsman, if he passes in this crowd?" inquired the gentleman.

"Indeed, I can't warrant it, sir; but I'll take my stand here, and keep a bright lookout," answered Robin, descending to the outer edge of the pavement.

A mighty stream of people now emptied into the street, and came rolling slowly towards the church. A single horseman wheeled the corner in the midst of them, and close behind him came a band of fearful wind-instruments, sending forth a fresher discord now that no intervening buildings kept it from the ear. Then a redder light disturbed the moonbeams, and a dense multitude of torches shone along the street, concealing, by their glare, whatever object they illuminated. The single horseman, clad in a military dress, and bearing a drawn sword, rode onward as the leader, and, by his fierce and variegated countenance, appeared like war personified; the red of one cheek was an emblem of fire and sword; the blackness of the other betokened the mourning that attends them. In his train were wild figures in the Indian dress, and many fantastic shapes without a model, giving the whole march a visionary air, as if a dream had broken forth from some feverish brain, and were sweeping visibly through the midnight streets. A mass of people, inactive, except as applauding spectators, hemmed the procession in; and several women ran along the sidewalk, piercing the confusion of heavier sounds with their shrill voices of mirth or terror.

"The double-faced fellow has his eye upon me," muttered Robin, with an indefinite but an uncomfortable idea that he was himself to bear a part in the pageantry.

The leader turned himself in the saddle, and fixed his glance full upon the country youth, as the steed went slowly by. When Robin had freed his eyes from those fiery ones, the musicians were passing before him, and the torches were close at hand; but the unsteady brightness of the latter formed a veil which he could not penetrate. The rattling of wheels over the stones sometimes found its way to his ear, and confused traces of a human form appeared at intervals, and then melted into the vivid light. A moment more, and the leader thundered a command to halt: the trumpets vomited a horrid breath, and then held their peace; the shouts and laughter of the people died away, and there remained only a universal hum, allied to silence. Right before Robin's eyes was an uncovered cart. There the torches blazed the brightest, there the moon shone out like day, and there, in tar-and-feathery dignity, sat his kinsman, Major Molineux!

He was an elderly man, of large and majestic person, and strong, square features, betokening a steady soul; but steady as it was, his enemies had found means to shake it. His face was pale as death, and far more ghastly; the broad forehead was contracted in his agony, so that his eyebrows formed one grizzled line; his eyes were red and wild, and the foam hung white upon his quivering lip. His whole frame was agitated by a quick and continual tremor, which his pride strove to quell, even in those circumstances of overwhelming humiliation. But perhaps the bitterest pang of all was when his eyes met those of Robin; for he evidently knew him on the instant, as the youth stood witnessing the foul disgrace of a head grown gray in honor. They stared at each other in silence, and Robin's knees shook, and his hair bristled, with a mixture of pity and terror. Soon, however, a bewildering excitement began to seize upon his mind; the preceding adventures of the night, the unexpected appearance of the crowd, the torches, the confused din and the hush that followed, the spectre of his kinsman reviled by that great multitude,—all this, and, more than all, a perception of tremendous ridicule in the whole scene, affected him with a sort of mental inebriety. At that moment a voice of sluggish merriment saluted Robin's ears; he turned instinctively, and just behind the corner of the church stood the lantern-bearer, rubbing his eyes, and drowsily enjoying the lad's amazement. Then he heard a peal of laughter like the ringing of silvery bells; a woman twitched his arm, a saucy eye met his, and he saw the lady of the scarlet petticoat. A sharp, dry cachinnation appealed to his memory, and standing on tiptoe in the crowd, with his white apron over his head, he beheld the courteous little innkeeper. And lastly, there sailed over the heads of the multitude a great, broad laugh, broken in the midst by two sepulchral hems; thus, "Haw, haw, haw,—hem, hem,—haw, haw, haw, haw!"

The sound proceeded from the balcony of the opposite edifice, and thither Robin turned his eyes. In front of the Gothic window stood the old citizen, wrapped in a wide gown, his gray periwig exchanged for a nightcap, which was thrust back from his forehead, and his silk stockings hanging about his legs. He supported himself on his polished cane in a fit of convulsive merriment, which manifested itself on his solemn old features like a funny inscription on a tombstone. Then Robin seemed to hear the voices of the barbers, of the guests of the inn, and of all who had made sport of him that night. The contagion was spreading among the multitude, when all at once, it seized upon Robin, and he sent forth a shout of laughter that echoed through the street,—every man shook his sides, every man emptied his lungs, but Robin's shout was the loudest there. The cloud-spirits peeped from their silvery islands, as the congregated mirth went roaring up the sky! The Man in the Moon heard the far bellow. "Oho," quoth he, "the old earth is frolicsome to-night!"

When there was a momentary calm in that tempestuous sea of sound, the leader gave the sign, the procession resumed its march. On they went, like fiends that throng in mockery around some dead potentate, mighty no more, but majestic still in his agony. On they went, in counterfeited pomp, in senseless uproar, in frenzied merriment, trampling all on an old man's heart. On swept the tumult, and left a silent street behind.

"Well, Robin, are you dreaming?" inquired the gentleman, laying his hand on the youth's shoulder.

Robin started, and withdrew his arm from the stone post to which he had instinctively clung, as the living stream rolled by him. His cheek was somewhat pale, and his eye not quite as lively as in the earlier part of the evening.

"Will you be kind enough to show me the way to the ferry?" said he, after a moment's pause.

"You have, then, adopted a new subject of inquiry?" observed his companion, with a smile.

"Why, yes, sir," replied Robin, rather dryly. "Thanks to you, and to my other friends, I have at last met my kinsman, and he will scarce desire to see my face again. I begin to grow weary of a town life, sir. Will you show me the way to the ferry?"

"No, my good friend Robin,—not to-night, at least," said the gentleman. "Some few days hence, if you wish it, I will speed you on your journey. Or, if you prefer to remain with us, perhaps, as you are a shrewd youth, you may rise in the world without the help of your kinsman, Major Molineux."

Young Goodman Brown (1835)

Young Goodman [1] Brown came forth at sunset into the street at Salem village; but put his head back, after crossing the threshold, to exchange a parting kiss with his young wife. And Faith, as the wife was aptly named, thrust her own pretty head into the street, letting the wind play with the pink ribbons of her cap while she called to Goodman Brown.

"Dearest heart," whispered she, softly and rather sadly, when her lips were close to his ear, "prithee put off your journey until sunrise and sleep in your own bed to-night. A lone woman is troubled with such dreams and such thoughts that she's afeared of herself sometimes. Pray tarry with me this night, dear husband, of all nights in the year."

"My love and my Faith," replied young Goodman Brown, "of all nights in the year, this one night must I tarry away from thee. My journey, as thou callest it, forth and back again, must needs be done 'twixt now and sunrise. What, my sweet, pretty wife, dost thou doubt me already, and we but three months married?"

"Then God bless you!" said Faith, with the pink ribbons; "and may you find all well when you come back."

"Amen!" cried Goodman Brown. "Say thy prayers, dear Faith, and go to bed at dusk, and no harm will come to thee."

So they parted; and the young man pursued his way until, being about to turn the corner by the meeting-house, he looked back and saw the head of Faith still peeping after him with a melancholy air, in spite of her pink ribbons.

"Poor little Faith!" thought he, for his heart smote him. "What a wretch am I to leave her on such an errand! She talks of dreams, too. Methought as she spoke there was trouble in her face, as if a dream had warned her what work is to be done to-night. But no, no; 'twould kill her to think it. Well, she's a blessed angel on earth; and after this one night I'll cling to her skirts and follow her to heaven."

With this excellent resolve for the future, Goodman Brown felt himself justified in making more haste on his present evil purpose. He had taken a dreary road, darkened by all the gloomiest trees of the forest, which barely stood aside to let the narrow path creep through, and closed immediately behind. It was all as lonely as could be; and there is this peculiarity in such a solitude, that the traveller knows not who may be concealed by the innumerable trunks and the thick boughs overhead; so that with lonely footsteps he may yet be passing through an unseen multitude.

"There may be a devilish Indian behind every tree," said Goodman Brown to himself; and he glanced fearfully behind him as he added, "What if the devil himself should be at my very elbow!"

---

[1] A term used in New England for people in middle social positions.

His head being turned back, he passed a crook of the road, and, looking forward again, beheld the figure of a man, in grave and decent attire, seated at the foot of an old tree. He arose at Goodman Brown's approach and walked onward side by side with him.

"You are late, Goodman Brown," said he. "The clock of the Old South was striking as I came through Boston, and that is full fifteen minutes agone."

"Faith kept me back a while," replied the young man, with a tremor in his voice, caused by the sudden appearance of his companion, though not wholly unexpected.

It was now deep dusk in the forest, and deepest in that part of it where these two were journeying. As nearly as could be discerned, the second traveller was about fifty years old, apparently in the same rank of life as Goodman Brown, and bearing a considerable resemblance to him, though perhaps more in expression than features. Still they might have been taken for father and son. And yet, though the elder person was as simply clad as the younger, and as simple in manner too, he had an indescribable air of one who knew the world, and who would not have felt abashed at the governor's dinner table or in King William's court,[2] were it possible that his affairs should call him thither. But the only thing about him that could be fixed upon as remarkable was his staff, which bore the likeness of a great black snake, so curiously wrought that it might almost be seen to twist and wriggle itself like a living serpent. This, of course, must have been an ocular deception, assisted by the uncertain light.

"Come, Goodman Brown," cried his fellow-traveller, "this is a dull pace for the beginning of a journey. Take my staff, if you are so soon weary."

"Friend," said the other, exchanging his slow pace for a full stop, "having kept covenant by meeting thee here, it is my purpose now to return whence I came. I have scruples touching the matter thou wot'st of."

"Sayest thou so?" replied he of the serpent, smiling apart. "Let us walk on, nevertheless, reasoning as we go; and if I convince thee not thou shalt turn back. We are but a little way in the forest yet."

"Too far! too far!" exclaimed the goodman, unconsciously resuming his walk. "My father never went into the woods on such an errand, nor his father before him. We have been a race of honest men and good Christians since the days of the martyrs; and shall I be the first of the name of Brown that ever took this path and kept"—

"Such company, thou wouldst say," observed the elder person, interpreting his pause. "Well said, Goodman Brown! I have been as well acquainted with your family as with ever a one among the Puritans; and that's no trifle to say. I helped your grandfather, the

2 William III (1650–1702).

constable, when he lashed the Quaker woman [3] so smartly through the streets of Salem; and it was I that brought your father a pitch-pine knot, kindled at my own hearth, to set fire to an Indian village, in King Philip's war.[4] They were my good friends, both; and many a pleasant walk have we had along this path, and returned merrily after midnight. I would fain be friends with you for their sake."

"If it be as thou sayest," replied Goodman Brown, "I marvel they never spoke of these matters; or, verily, I marvel not, seeing that the least rumor of the sort would have driven them from New England. We are a people of prayer, and good works to boot, and abide no such wickedness."

"Wickedness or not," said the traveller with the twisted staff, "I have a very general acquaintance here in New England. The deacons of many a church have drunk the communion wine with me; the select-men of divers towns make me their chairman; and a majority of the Great and General Court are firm supporters of my interest. The governor and I, too—But these are state secrets."

"Can this be so?" cried Goodman Brown, with a stare of amazement at his undisturbed companion. "Howbeit, I have nothing to do with the governor and council; they have their own ways, and are no rule for a simple husbandman like me. But, were I to go on with thee, how should I meet the eye of that good old man, our minister, at Salem village? Oh, his voice would make me tremble both Sabbath day and lecture day."

Thus far the elder traveller had listened with due gravity; but now burst into a fit of irrepressible mirth, shaking himself so violently that his snake-like staff actually seemed to wriggle in sympathy.

"Ha! ha! ha!" shouted he again and again; then composing himself, "Well, go on, Goodman Brown, go on; but, prithee, don't kill me with laughing."

"Well, then, to end the matter at once," said Goodman Brown, considerably nettled, "there is my wife, Faith. It would break her dear little heart; and I'd rather break my own."

"Nay, if that be the case," answered the other, "e'en go thy ways, Goodman Brown. I would not for twenty old women like the one hobbling before us that Faith should come to any harm."

As he spoke he pointed his staff at a female figure on the path, in whom Goodman Brown recognized a very pious and exemplary dame, who had taught him his catechism in youth, and was still his moral and spiritual adviser, jointly with the minister and Deacon Gookin.

"A marvel, truly, that Goody Cloyse [5] should be so far in the wilder-

---

[3] Hawthorne's grandfather persecuted Quakers.
[4] Between New England colonists and Indians, in 1676.
[5] Sentenced to death for witchcraft in Salem in 1692.

ness at nightfall," said he. "But with your leave, friend, I shall take a cut through the woods until we have left this Christian woman behind. Being a stranger to you, she might ask whom I was consorting with and whither I was going."

"Be it so," said his fellow-traveller. "Betake you to the woods, and let me keep the path."

Accordingly the young man turned aside, but took care to watch his companion, who advanced softly along the road until he had come within a staff's length of the old dame. She, meanwhile, was making the best of her way, with singular speed for so aged a woman, and mumbling some indistinct words—a prayer, doubtless—as she went. The traveller put forth his staff and touched her withered neck with what seemed the serpent's tail.

"The devil!" screamed the pious old lady.

"Then Goody Cloyse knows her old friend?" observed the traveller, confronting her and leaning on his writhing stick.

"Ah, forsooth, and is it your worship indeed?" cried the good dame. "Yea, truly is it, and in the very image of my old gossip, Goodman Brown, the grandfather of the silly fellow that now is. But—would your worship believe it?—my broomstick hath strangely disappeared, stolen, as I suspect, by that unhanged witch, Goody Cory, and that, too, when I was all anointed with the juice of smallage, and cinquefoil, and wolf's bane"—

"Mingled with fine wheat and the fat of a new-born babe," said the shape of old Goodman Brown.

"Ah, your worship knows the recipe," cried the old lady, cackling aloud. "So, as I was saying, being all ready for the meeting, and no horse to ride on, I made up my mind to foot it; for they tell me there is a nice young man to be taken into communion to-night. But now your good worship will lend me your arm, and we shall be there in a twinkling.

"That can hardly be," answered her friend. "I may not spare you my arm, Goody Cloyse; but here is my staff, if you will."

So saying, he threw it down at her feet, where, perhaps, it assumed life, being one of the rods which its owner had formerly lent to the Egyptian magi. Of this fact, however, Goodman Brown could not take cognizance. He had cast up his eyes in astonishment, and, looking down again, beheld neither Goody Cloyse nor the serpentine staff, but his fellow-traveller alone, who waited for him as calmly as if nothing had happened.

"That old woman taught me my catechism," said the young man; and there was a world of meaning in this simple comment.

They continued to walk onward, while the elder traveller exhorted his companion to make good speed and persevere in the path, discoursing so aptly that his arguments seemed rather to spring up in the bosom of his auditor than to be suggested by himself. As they went, he plucked a branch of maple to serve for a walking stick, and began to strip it of the twigs and little boughs, which were wet with evening dew. The moment his fingers touched them they became strangely withered and dried up as with a week's sunshine. Thus the pair proceeded, at a good free pace, until suddenly, in a gloomy hollow of the road, Goodman Brown sat himself down on the stump of a tree and refused to go any farther.

"Friend," said he, stubbornly, "my mind is made up. Not another step will I budge on this errand. What if a wretched old woman do choose to go to the devil when I thought she was going to heaven: is that any reason why I should quit my dear Faith and go after her?"

"You will think better of this by and by," said his acquaintance, composedly. "Sit here and rest yourself a while; and when you feel like moving again, there is my staff to help you along."

Without more words, he threw his companion the maple stick, and was as speedily out of sight as if he had vanished into the deepening gloom. The young man sat a few moments by the roadside, applauding himself greatly, and thinking with how clear a conscience he should meet the minister in his morning walk, nor shrink from the eye of good old Deacon Gookin. And what calm sleep would be his that very night, which was to have been spent so wickedly, but so purely and sweetly now, in the arms of Faith! Amidst these pleasant and praise-worthy meditations, Goodman Brown heard the tramp of horses along the road, and deemed it advisable to conceal himself within the verge of the forest, conscious of the guilty purpose that had brought him thither, though now so happily turned from it.

On came the hoof tramps and the voices of the riders, two grave old voices, conversing soberly as they drew near. These mingled sounds appeared to pass along the road, within a few yards of the young man's hiding-place; but, owing doubtless to the depth of the gloom at that particular spot, neither the travellers nor their steeds were visible. Though their figures brushed the small boughs by the wayside, it could not be seen that they intercepted, even for a moment, the faint gleam from the strip of bright sky athwart which they must have passed. Goodman Brown alternately crouched and stood on tiptoe, pulling aside the branches and thrusting forth his head as far as he durst without discerning so much as a shadow. It vexed him the more, because he could have sworn, were such a thing possible, that he recognized the voices of the minister and Deacon Gookin, jogging along quietly, as they were wont to do, when bound to some ordination or ecclesiastical council. While yet within hearing, one of the riders stopped to pluck a switch.

"Of the two, reverend sir," said the voice like the deacons, "I had rather miss an ordination dinner than to-night's meeting. They tell me that some of our community are to be here from Falmouth and beyond, and others from Connecticut and Rhode Island, besides several of Indian powwows, who, after their fashion, know almost as much deviltry as the best of us. Moreover, there is a goodly young woman to be taken into communion."

"Mighty well, Deacon Gookin!" replied the solemn old tones of the minister. "Spur up, or we shall be late. Nothing can be done you know until I get on the ground."

The hoofs clattered again; and the voices, talking so strangely in the empty air, passed on through the forest, where no church had ever been gathered or solitary Christian prayed. Whither, then, could these holy men be journeying so deep into the heathen wilderness? Young Goodman Brown caught hold of a tree for support, being ready to sink down on the ground, faint and overburdened with the heavy sickness of his heart. He looked up to the sky, doubting whether there really was a heaven above him. Yet there was the blue arch, and the stars brightening in it.

"With heaven above and Faith below, I will yet stand firm against the devil!" cried Goodman Brown.

While he still gazed upward into the deep arch of the firmament and had lifted his hands to pray, a cloud, though no wind was stirring, hurried across the zenith and hid the brightening stars. The blue sky was still visible, except directly overhead, where this black mass of cloud was sweeping swiftly northward. Aloft in the air, as if from the depths of the cloud, came a confused and doubtful sound of voices. Once the listener fancied that he could distinguish the accents of towns-people of his own, men, and women, both pious and ungodly, many of whom he had met at the communion table, and had seen others rioting at the tavern. The next moment, so indistinct were the sounds, he doubted whether he had heard aught but the murmur of the old forest, whispering without a wind. Then came a stronger swell of those familiar tones, heard daily in the sunshine at Salem village, but never until now from a cloud of night. There was one voice of a young woman, uttering lamentations, yet with an uncertain sorrow, and entreating for some favor, which, perhaps, it would grieve her to obtain; and all the unseen multitude, both saints and sinners, seemed to encourage her onward.

"Faith!" shouted Goodman Brown, in a voice of agony and desperation; and the echoes of the forest mocked him, crying, "Faith! Faith!" as if bewildered wretches were seeking her all through the wilderness.

The cry of grief, rage, and terror was yet piercing the night, when the unhappy husband held his breath for a response. There was a scream, drowned immediately in a louder murmur of voices, fading into far-off laughter, as the dark cloud swept away, leaving the clear and silent sky above Goodman Brown. But something fluttered lightly down through the air and caught on the branch of a tree. The young man seized it, and beheld a pink ribbon.

"My Faith is gone!" cried he, after one stupefied moment. "There is no good on earth; and sin is but a name. Come, devil; for to thee is this world given."

And, maddened with despair, so that he laughed loud and long, did Goodman Brown grasp his staff and set forth again, at such a rate that he seemed to fly along the forest path rather than to walk or run. The road grew wilder and drearier and more faintly traced, and vanished at length, leaving him in the heart of the dark wilderness, still rushing onward with the instinct that guides mortal man to evil. The whole forest was peopled with frightful sounds—the creaking of the trees, the howling of wild beasts, and the yell of Indians; while sometimes the wind tolled like a distant church bell, and sometimes gave a broad roar around the traveller, as if all Nature were laughing him to scorn. But he was himself the chief horror of the scene, and shrank not from its other horrors.

"Ha! ha! ha!" roared Goodman Brown when the wind laughed at him. "Let us hear which will laugh loudest. Think not to frighten me with your deviltry. Come witch, come wizard, come Indian powwow, come devil himself, and here comes Goodman Brown. You may as well fear him as he fear you."

In truth, all through the haunted forest there could be nothing more frightful than the figure of Goodman Brown. On he flew among the black pines, brandishing his staff with frenzied gestures, now giving vent to an inspiration of horrid blasphemy, and now shouting forth such laughter as set all the echoes of the forest laughing like demons around him. The fiend in his own shape is less hideous than when he rages in the breast of man. Thus sped the demoniac on his course, until, quivering among the trees, he saw a red light before him, as when the felled trunks and branches of a clearing have been set on fire, and throw up their lurid blaze against the sky, at the hour of midnight. He paused, in a lull of the tempest that had driven him onward, and heard the swell of what seemed a hymn, rolling solemnly from a distance with the weight of many voices. He knew the tune; it was a familiar one in the choir of the village meeting-house. The verse died heavily away, and was lengthened by a chorus, not of human voices, but of all the sounds of the benighted wilderness pealing in awful harmony together. Goodman Brown cried out, and his cry was lost to his own ear by its unison with the cry of the desert.

In the interval of silence he stole forward until the light glared full upon his eyes. At one extremity of an open space, hemmed in by the dark wall of the forest, arose a rock, bearing some rude, natural resemblance either to an altar or a pulpit, and surrounded by four blazing pines, their tops aflame, their stems untouched, like candles at an evening meeting. The mass of foliage that had overgrown the summit of the rock was all on fire, blazing high into the night and fitfully illuminating the whole field. Each pendent twig and leafy festoon was in a blaze. As the red light arose and fell, a numerous congregation alternately shone forth, then disappeared in shadow, and again grew, as it were, out of the darkness, peopling the heart of the solitary woods at once.

"A grave and dark-clad company," quoth Goodman Brown.

In truth they were such. Among them, quivering to and fro between gloom and splendor, appeared faces that would be seen next day at the council board of the province, and others which, Sabbath after Sabbath, looked devoutly heavenward and benignantly over the crowded pews, from the holiest pupils in the land. Some affirm that the lady of the governor was there. At least there were high dames well known to her, and wives of honored husbands, and widows, a great multitude, and ancient maidens, all of excellent repute, and fair young girls, who trembled lest their mothers should espy them. Either the sudden gleams of light flashing over the obscure field bedazzled Goodman Brown, or he recognized a score of the church members of Salem village famous for their especial sanctity. Good old Deacon Gookin had arrived, and waited at the skirts of that venerable saint, his revered pastor. But, irreverently consorting with these grave, reputable, and pious people, these elders of the church, these chaste dames and dewy virgins, there were men of dissolute lives and women of spotted fame, wretches given over to all mean and filthy vice, and suspected even of horrid crimes. It was strange to see that the good shrank not from the wicked, nor were the sinners abashed by the saints. Scattered also among their pale-faced enemies were the Indian priests, or powwows, who had often scared their native forest with more hideous incantations than any known to English witchcraft.

"But where is Faith?" thought Goodman Brown; and, as hope came into his heart, he trembled.

Another verse of the hymn arose, a slow and mournful strain, such as the pious love, but joined to words which expressed all that our nature can conceive of sin, and darkly hinted at far more. Unfathomable to mere mortals is the lore of fiends. Verse after verse was sung; and still the chorus of the desert swelled between like the deepest tone of a mighty organ; and with the final peal of that dreadful anthem there came a sound, as if the roaring wind, the rushing streams, the howling beasts, and every other voice of the unconcerted wilderness were mingling and according with the voice of guilty man in homage to the prince of all. The four blazing pines threw up a loftier flame, and obscurely discovered shapes and visages of horror on the smoke wreaths above the impious assembly. At the same moment the fire on the rock shot redly forth and formed a glowing arch above its base, where now appeared a figure. With reverence be it spoken, the figure bore no slight similitude, both in garb and manner, to some grave divine of the New England churches.

"Bring forth the converts!" cried a voice that echoed through the field and rolled into the forest.

At the word, Goodman Brown stepped forth from the shadow of the trees and approached the congregation, with whom he felt a loathful brotherhood by the sympathy of all that was wicked in his heart. He could have well-nigh sworn that the shape of his own dead father beckoned him to advance, looking downward from a smoke wreath, while a woman, with dim features of despair, threw out her hand to warn him back. Was it his mother? But he had no power to retreat one step, nor to resist, even in thought, when the minister and good old Deacon Gookin seized his arms and led him to the blazing rock. Thither came also the slender form of a veiled female, led between Goody Cloyse, that pious teacher of the catechism, and Martha Carrier,[6] who had received the devil's promise to be queen of hell. A rampant hag was she. And there stood the proselytes beneath the canopy of fire.

"Welcome, my children," said the dark figure, "to the communion of your race. Ye have found thus young your nature and your destiny. My children, look behind you!"

They turned; and flashing forth, as it were, in a sheet of flame, the fiend worshippers were seen; the smile of welcome gleamed darkly on every visage.

"There," resumed the sable form, "are all whom ye have reverenced from youth. Ye deemed them holier than yourselves, and shrank from your own sin, contrasting it with their lives of righteousness and prayerful aspirations heavenward. Yet here are they all in my worshipping assembly. This night it shall be granted you to know their secret deeds: how hoary-bearded elders of the church have whispered wanton words to the young maids of their households; how many a woman, eager for widows' weeds, has given her husband a drink at bedtime and let him sleep his last sleep in her bosom; how beardless youths have made haste to inherit their fathers' wealth; and how fair damsels—blush not, sweet ones—have dug little graves in the garden, and bidden me, the sole guest to an infant's funeral. By the sympathy of your human hearts for sin ye shall scent out all the places—whether in church, bedchamber, street, field, or forest—where crime has been committed, and shall exult to behold the whole earth one stain of guilt, one mighty blood spot. Far more than this. It shall be yours to penetrate, in every bosom, the deep mystery of sin, the fountain of all wicked arts, and which inexhaustibly supplies more evil impulses than human power—

[6] Hanged as witch in Salem in 1692.

than my power at its utmost—can make manifest in deeds. And now, my children, look upon each other."

They did so; and, by the blaze of the hell-kindled torches, the wretched man beheld his Faith, and the wife her husband, trembling before that unhallowed altar.

"Lo, there ye stand, my children," said the figure, in a deep and solemn tone, almost sad with its despairing awfulness, as if his once angelic nature could yet mourn for our miserable race. "Depending upon one another's hearts, ye had still hoped that virtue were not all a dream. Now are ye undeceived. Evil is the nature of mankind. Evil must be your only happiness. Welcome again, my children, to the communion of your race."

"Welcome," repeated the fiend worshippers, in one cry of despair and triumph.

And there they stood, the only pair, as it seemed, who were yet hesitating on the verge of wickedness in this dark world. A basin was hollowed, naturally, in the rock. Did it contain water, reddened by the lurid light? or was it blood? or, perchance, a liquid flame? Herein did the shape of evil dip his hand and prepare to lay the mark of baptism upon their foreheads, that they might be partakers of the mystery of sin, more conscious of the secret guilt of others, both in deed and thought, than they could now be of their own. The husband cast one look at his pale wife, and Faith at him. What polluted wretches would the next glance show them to each other, shuddering alike at what they disclosed and what they saw!

"Faith! Faith!" cried the husband, "look up to heaven, and resist the wicked one."

Whether Faith obeyed he knew not. Hardly had he spoken when he found himself amid calm night and solitude, listening to a roar of the wind which died heavily away through the forest. He staggered against the rock, and felt it chill and damp; while a hanging twig, that had been all on fire, besprinkled his cheek with the coldest dew.

The next morning young Goodman Brown came slowly into the street of Salem village, staring around him like a bewildered man. The good old minister was taking a walk along the graveyard to get an appetite for breakfast and meditate his sermon, and bestowed a blessing, as he passed, on Goodman Brown. He shrank from the venerable saint as if to avoid an anathema. Old Deacon Gookin was at domestic worship, and the holy words of his prayer were heard through the open window. "What God doth the wizard pray to?" quoth Goodman Brown. Goody Cloyse, that excellent old Christian, stood in the early sunshine at her own lattice, catechizing a little girl who had brought her a pint of morning's milk. Goodman Brown snatched away the child as from the grasp of the fiend himself. Turning the corner by the meeting-house, he spied the head of Faith, with the pink ribbons, gazing anxiously forth, and bursting into such joy at sight of him that she skipped along the street and almost kissed her husband before the whole village. But Goodman Brown looked sternly and sadly into her face, and passed on without a greeting.

Had Goodman Brown fallen asleep in the forest and only dreamed a wild dream of a witch-meeting?

Be it so if you will; but, alas! it was a dream of evil omen for young Goodman Brown. A stern, a sad, a darkly meditative, a distrustful, if not a desperate man did he become from the night of that fearful dream. On the Sabbath day, when the congregation were singing a holy psalm, he could not listen because an anthem of sin rushed loudly upon his ear and drowned all the blessed strain. When the minister spoke from the pulpit with power and fervid eloquence, and, with his hand on the open Bible, of the sacred truths of our religion, and of saint-like lives and triumphant deaths, and of future bliss or misery unutterable, then did Goodman Brown turn pale, dreading lest the roof should thunder down upon the gray blasphemer and his hearers. Often, waking suddenly at midnight, he shrank from the bosom of Faith; and at morning or eventide, when the family knelt down at prayer, he scowled and muttered to himself, and gazed sternly at his wife, and turned away. And when he had lived long, and was borne to his grave a hoary corpse, followed by Faith, an aged woman, and children and grandchildren, a goodly procession, besides neighbors not a few, they carved no hopeful verse upon his tombstone, for his dying hour was gloom.

The Minister's Black Veil (1836)

A Parable [1]

The sexton stood in the porch of Milford meeting-house, pulling busily at the bell-rope. The old people of the village came stooping along the street. Children, with bright faces, tripped merrily beside their parents, or mimicked a graver gait, in the conscious dignity of their Sunday clothes. Spruce bachelors looked sidelong at the pretty maidens, and fancied that the Sabbath sunshine made them prettier than on week days. When the throng had mostly streamed into the porch, the

[1] Another clergyman in New England, Mr. Joseph Moody, of York, Maine, who died about eighty years since, made himself remarkable by the same eccentricity that is here related of the Reverend Mr. Hooper. In his case, however, the symbol had a different import. In early life he had accidentally killed a beloved friend; and from that day till the hour of his own death, he hid his face from men. *Au.*

sexton began to toll the bell, keeping his eye on the Reverend Mr. Hooper's door. The first glimpse of the clergyman's figure was the signal for the bell to cease its summons.

"But what has good Parson Hooper got upon his face?" cried the sexton in astonishment.

All within hearing immediately turned about, and beheld the semblance of Mr. Hooper, pacing slowly his meditative way towards the meeting-house. With one accord they started, expressing more wonder than if some strange minister were coming to dust the cushions of Mr. Hooper's pulpit.

"Are you sure it is our parson?" inquired Goodman Gray of the sexton.

"Of a certainty it is good Mr. Hooper," replied the sexton. "He was to have exchanged pulpits with Parson Shute, of Westbury; but Parson Shute sent to excuse himself yesterday, being to preach a funeral sermon."

The cause of so much amazement may appear sufficiently slight. Mr. Hooper, a gentlemanly person, of about thirty, though still a bachelor, was dressed with due clerical neatness, as if a careful wife had starched his band, and brushed the weekly dust from his Sunday's garb. There was but one thing remarkable in his appearance. Swathed about his forehead, and hanging down over his face, so low as to be shaken by his breath, Mr. Hooper had on a black veil. On a nearer view it seemed to consist of two folds of crape, which entirely concealed his features, except the mouth and chin, but probably did not intercept his sight, further than to give a darkened aspect to all living and inanimate things. With this gloomy shade before him, good Mr. Hooper walked onward, at a slow and quiet pace, stooping somewhat, and looking on the ground, as is customary with abstracted men, yet nodding kindly to those of his parishioners who still waited on the meeting-house steps. But so wonder-struck were they that his greeting hardly met with a return.

"I can't really feel as if good Mr. Hooper's face was behind that piece of crape," said the sexton.

"I don't like it," muttered an old woman, as she hobbled into the meeting-house. "He has changed himself into something awful, only by hiding his face."

"Our parson has gone mad!" cried Goodman Gray, following him across the threshold.

A rumor of some unaccountable phenomenon had preceded Mr. Hooper into the meeting-house, and set all the congregation astir. Few could refrain from twisting their heads towards the door; many stood upright, and turned directly about; while several little boys clambered upon the seats, and came down again with a terrible racket. There was a general bustle, a rustling of the women's gowns and shuffling of the men's feet, greatly at variance with that hushed repose which should attend the entrance of the minister. But Mr. Hooper appeared not to notice the perturbation of his people. He entered with an almost noise-less step, bent his head mildly to the pews on each side, and bowed as he passed his oldest parishioner, a white-haired great grandsire, who occupied an arm-chair in the centre of the aisle. It was strange to observe how slowly this venerable man became conscious of something singular in the appearance of his pastor. He seemed not fully to par-take of the prevailing wonder, till Mr. Hooper had ascended the stairs, and showed himself in the pulpit, face to face with his congregation, except for the black veil. That mysterious emblem was never once withdrawn. It shook with his measured breath, as he gave out the psalm; it threw its obscurity between him and the holy page, as he read the Scriptures; and while he prayed, the veil lay heavily on his uplifted countenance. Did he seek to hide it from the dread Being whom he was addressing?

Such was the effect of this simple piece of crape, that more than one woman of delicate nerves was forced to leave the meeting-house. Yet perhaps the pale-faced congregation was almost as fearful a sight to the minister, as his black veil to them.

Mr. Hooper had the reputation of a good preacher, but not an energetic one: he strove to win his people heavenward by mild, persua-sive influences, rather than to drive them thither by the thunders of the Word. The sermon which he now delivered was marked by the same characteristics of style and manner as the general series of his pulpit oratory. But there was something, either in the sentiment of the discourse itself, or in the imagination of the auditors, which made it greatly the most powerful effort that they had ever heard from their pastor's lips. It was tinged, rather more darkly than usual, with the gentle gloom of Mr. Hooper's temperament. The subject had reference to secret sin, and those sad mysteries which we hide from our nearest and dearest, and would fain conceal from our own consciousness, even forgetting that the Omniscient can detect them. A subtle power was breathed into his words. Each member of the congregation, the most innocent girl, and the man of hardened breast, felt as if the preacher had crept upon them, behind his awful veil, and discovered their hoarded iniquity of deed or thought. Many spread their clasped hands on their bosoms. There was nothing terrible in what Mr. Hooper said, at least, no violence; and yet, with every tremor of his melancholy voice, the hearers quaked. An unsought pathos came hand in hand with awe. So sensible were the audience of some unwonted attribute in their minister, that they longed for a breath of wind to blow aside the veil, almost believing that a stranger's visage would be discovered, though the form, gesture, and voice were those of Mr. Hooper.

At the close of the services, the people hurried out with indecorous confusion, eager to communicate their pent-up amazement, and con-scious of lighter spirits the moment they lost sight of the black veil.

Some gathered in little circles, huddled closely together, with their mouths all whispering in the centre; some went homeward alone, wrapt in silent meditation; some talked loudly, and profaned the Sabbath day with ostentatious laughter. A few shook their sagacious heads, intimating that they could penetrate the mystery; while one or two affirmed that there was no mystery at all, but only that Mr. Hooper's eyes were so weakened by the midnight lamp, as to require a shade. After a brief interval, forth came good Mr. Hooper also, in the rear of his flock. Turning his veiled face from one group to another, he paid due reverence to the hoary heads, saluted the middle aged with kind dignity as their friend and spiritual guide, greeted the young with mingled authority and love, and laid his hands on the little children's heads to bless them. Such was always his custom on the Sabbath day. Strange and bewildered looks repaid him for his courtesy. None, as on former occasions, aspired to the honor of walking by their pastor's side. Old Squire Saunders, doubtless by an accidental lapse of memory, neglected to invite Mr. Hooper to his table, where the good clergyman had been wont to bless the food, almost every Sunday since his settlement. He returned, therefore, to the parsonage, and, at the moment of closing the door, was observed to look back upon the people, all of whom had their eyes fixed upon the minister. A sad smile gleamed faintly from beneath the black veil, and flickered about his mouth, glimmering as he disappeared.

"How strange," said a lady, "that a simple black veil, such as any woman might wear on her bonnet, should become such a terrible thing on Mr. Hooper's face!"

"Something must surely be amiss with Mr. Hooper's intellects," observed her husband, the physician of the village. "But the strangest part of the affair is the effect of this vagary, even on a sober-minded man like myself. The black veil, though it covers only our pastor's face, throws its influence over his whole person, and makes him ghostlike from head to foot. Do you not feel it so?"

"Truly do I," replied the lady; "and I would not be alone with him for the world. I wonder he is not afraid to be alone with himself!"

"Men sometimes are so," said her husband.

The afternoon service was attended with similar circumstances. At its conclusion, the bell tolled for the funeral of a young lady. The relatives and friends were assembled in the house, and the more distant acquaintances stood about the door, speaking of the good qualities of the deceased, when their talk was interrupted by the appearance of Mr. Hooper, still covered with his black veil. It was now an appropriate emblem. The clergyman stepped into the room where the corpse was laid, and bent over the coffin, to take a last farewell of his deceased parishioner. As he stooped, the veil hung straight down from his forehead, so that, if her eyelids had not been closed forever, the dead maiden might have seen his face. Could Mr. Hooper be fearful of her glance, that he so hastily caught back the black veil? A person who watched the interview between the dead and living, scrupled not to affirm, that, at the instant when the clergyman's features were disclosed, the corpse had slightly shuddered, rustling the shroud and muslin cap, though the countenance retained the composure of death. A superstitious old woman was the only witness of this prodigy. From the coffin Mr. Hooper passed into the chamber of the mourners, and thence to the head of the staircase, to make the funeral prayer. It was a tender and heart-dissolving prayer, full of sorrow, yet so imbued with celestial hopes, that the music of a heavenly harp, swept by the fingers of the dead, seemed faintly to be heard among the saddest accents of the minister. The people trembled, though they but darkly understood him when he prayed that they, and himself, and all of mortal race, might be ready, as he trusted this young maiden had been, for the dreadful hour that should snatch the veil from their faces. The bearers went heavily forth, and the mourners followed, saddening all the street, with the dead before them, and Mr. Hooper in his black veil behind.

"Why do you look back?" said one in the procession to his partner.

"I had a fancy," replied she, "that the minister and the maiden's spirit were walking hand in hand."

"And so had I, at the same moment," said the other.

That night, the handsomest couple in Milford village were to be joined in wedlock. Though reckoned a melancholy man, Mr. Hooper had a placid cheerfulness for such occasions, which often excited a sympathetic smile where livelier merriment would have been thrown away. There was no quality of his disposition which made him more beloved than this. The company at the wedding awaited his arrival with impatience, trusting that the strange awe, which had gathered over him throughout the day, would now be dispelled. But such was not the result. When Mr. Hooper came, the first thing that their eyes rested on was the same horrible black veil, which had added deeper gloom to the funeral, and could portend nothing but evil to the wedding. Such was its immediate effect on the guests that a cloud seemed to have rolled duskily from beneath the black crape, and dimmed the light of the candles. The bridal pair stood up before the minister. But the bride's cold fingers quivered in the tremulous hand of the bridegroom, and her deathlike paleness caused a whisper that the maiden who had been buried a few hours before was come from her grave to be married. If ever another wedding were so dismal, it was that famous one where they tolled the wedding knell. After performing the ceremony, Mr. Hooper raised a glass of wine to his lips, wishing happiness to the new-married couple in a strain of mild pleasantry that ought to have brightened the features of the guests, like a cheerful gleam from the hearth. At that instant, catching a glimpse of his figure in the looking-glass, the black veil involved his own spirit in the horror with which it overwhelmed all others. His frame shuddered, his lips grew white, he spilt the untasted wine upon the carpet, and rushed forth into the darkness. For the Earth, too, had on her Black Veil.

The next day, the whole village of Milford talked of little else than Parson Hooper's black veil. That, and the mystery concealed behind it, supplied a topic for discussion between acquaintances meeting in the street, and good women gossiping at their open windows. It was the first item of news that the tavern-keeper told to his guests. The children babbled of it on their way to school. One imitative little imp covered his face with an old black handkerchief, thereby so affrighting his playmates that the panic seized himself, and he well-nigh lost his wits by his own waggery.

It was remarkable that all of the busybodies and impertinent people in the parish, not one ventured to put the plain question to Mr. Hooper, wherefore he did this thing. Hitherto, whenever there appeared the slightest call for such interference, he had never lacked advisers, nor shown himself averse to be guided by their judgment. If he erred at all, it was by so painful a degree of self-distrust, that even the mildest censure would lead him to consider an indifferent action as a crime. Yet, though so well acquainted with this amiable weakness, no individual among his parishioners chose to make the black veil a subject of friendly remonstrance. There was a feeling of dread, neither plainly confessed nor carefully concealed, which caused each to shift the responsibility upon another, till at length it was found expedient to send a deputation of the church, in order to deal with Mr. Hooper about the mystery, before it should grow into a scandal. Never did an embassy so ill discharge its duties. The minister received them with friendly courtesy, but became silent, after they were seated, leaving to his visitors the whole burden of introducing their important business. The topic, it might be supposed, was obvious enough. There was the black veil swathed round Mr. Hooper's forehead, and concealing every feature above his placid mouth, on which, at times, they could perceive the glimmering of a melancholy smile. But that piece of crape, to their imagination, seemed to hang down before his heart, the symbol of a fearful secret between him and them. Were the veil but cast aside, they might speak freely of it, but not till then. Thus they sat a considerable time, speechless, confused, and shrinking uneasily from Mr. Hooper's eye, which they felt to be fixed upon them with an invisible glance. Finally, the deputies returned abashed to their constituents, pronouncing the matter too weighty to be handled except by a council of the churches, if, indeed, it might not require a general synod.

But there was one person in the village unappalled by the awe with which the black veil had impressed all beside herself. When the deputies returned without an explanation, or even venturing to demand one, she, with the calm energy of her character, determined to chase away the strange cloud that appeared to be settling round Mr. Hooper, every moment more darkly than before. As his plighted wife, it should be her privilege to know what the black veil concealed. At the minister's first visit, therefore, she entered upon the subject with a direct simplicity, which made the task easier both for him and her. After he had seated himself, she fixed her eyes steadfastly upon the veil, but could discern nothing of the dreadful gloom that had so overawed the multitude: it was but a double fold of crape, hanging down from his forehead to his mouth, and slightly stirring with his breath.

"No," said she aloud, and smiling, "there is nothing terrible in this piece of crape, except that it hides a face which I am always glad to look upon. Come, good sir, let the sun shine from behind the cloud. First lay aside your black veil: then tell me why you put it on."

Mr. Hooper's smile glimmered faintly.

"There is an hour to come," said he, "when all of us shall cast aside our veils. Take it not amiss, beloved friend, if I wear this piece of crape till then."

"Your words are a mystery, too," returned the young lady. "Take away the veil from them, at least."

"Elizabeth, I will," said he, "so far as my vow may suffer me. Know, then, this veil is a type and a symbol, and I am bound to wear it ever, both in light and darkness, in solitude and before the gaze of multitudes, and as with strangers, so with my familiar friends. No mortal eye will see it withdrawn. This dismal shade must separate me from the world: even you, Elizabeth, can never come behind it!"

"What grievous affliction hath befallen you," she earnestly inquired, "that you should thus darken your eyes forever?"

"If it be a sign of mourning," replied Mr. Hooper, "I, perhaps, like most other mortals, have sorrows dark enough to be typified by a black veil."

"But what if the world will not believe that it is the type of an innocent sorrow?" urged Elizabeth. "Beloved and respected as you are, there may be whispers that you hide your face under the consciousness of secret sin. For the sake of your holy office, do away this scandal!"

The color rose into her cheeks as she intimated the nature of the rumors that were already abroad in the village. But Mr. Hooper's mildness did not forsake him. He even smiled again—that same sad smile, which always appeared like a faint glimmering of light, proceeding from the obscurity beneath the veil.

"If I hide my face for sorrow, there is cause enough," he merely replied; "and if I cover it for secret sin, what mortal might not do the same?"

And with this gentle, but unconquerable obstinacy did he resist all her entreaties. At length Elizabeth sat silent. For a few moments she appeared lost in thought, considering, probably, what new methods might be tried to withdraw her lover from so dark a fantasy, which, if it had no other meaning, was perhaps a symptom of mental disease. Though of a firmer character than his own, the tears rolled down her cheeks. But, in an instant, as it were, a new feeling took the place of sorrow: her eyes were fixed insensibly on the black veil, when, like a sudden twilight in the air, its terrors fell around her. She arose, and stood trembling before him.

"And do you feel it then, at last?" said he mournfully.

She made no reply, but covered her eyes with her hand, and turned to leave the room. He rushed forward and caught her arm.

"Have patience with me, Elizabeth!" cried he, passionately. "Do not desert me, though this veil must be between us here on earth. Be mine, and hereafter there shall be no veil over my face, no darkness between our souls! It is but a mortal veil—it is not for eternity! O! you know not how lonely I am, and how frightened, to be alone behind my black veil. Do not leave me in this miserable obscurity forever!"

"Lift the veil but once, and look me in the face," said she.

"Never! It cannot be!" replied Mr. Hooper.

"Then farewell!" said Elizabeth.

She withdrew her arm from his grasp, and slowly departed, pausing at the door, to give one long shuddering gaze, that seemed almost to penetrate the mystery of the black veil. But, even amid his grief, Mr. Hooper smiled to think that only a material emblem had separated him from happiness, though the horrors, which it shadowed forth, must be drawn darkly between the fondest of lovers.

From that time no attempts were made to remove Mr. Hooper's black veil, or, by a direct appeal, to discover the secret which it was supposed to hide. By persons who claimed a superiority to popular prejudice, it was reckoned merely an eccentric whim, such as often mingles with the sober actions of men otherwise rational, and tinges them all with its own semblance of insanity. But with the multitude, good Mr. Hooper was irreparably a bugbear. He could not walk the street with any peace of mind, so conscious was he that the gentle and timid would turn aside to avoid him, and that others would make it a point of hardihood to throw themselves in his way. The impertinence of the latter class compelled him to give up his customary walk at sunset to the burial ground; for when he leaned pensively over the gate, there would always be faces behind the gravestones, peeping at his black veil. A fable went the rounds that the stare of the dead people drove him thence. It grieved him, to the very depth of his kind heart, to observe how the children fled from his approach, breaking up their merriest sports, while his melancholy figure was yet afar off. Their instinctive dread caused him to feel more strongly than aught else, that a preternatural horror was interwoven with the threads of the black crape. In truth, his own antipathy to the veil was known to be so great, that he never willingly passed before a mirror, nor stopped to drink at a still fountain, lest, in its peaceful bosom, he should be affrighted by himself. This was what gave plausibility to the whispers, that Mr. Hooper's conscience tortured him for some great crime too horrible to be entirely concealed, or otherwise than so obscurely intimated. Thus, from beneath the black veil, there rolled a cloud into the sunshine, an ambiguity of sin or sorrow, which enveloped the poor minister, so that love or sympathy could never reach him. It was said that ghost and fiend consorted with him there. With self-shudderings and outward terrors, he walked continually in its shadow, groping darkly within his own soul, or gazing through a medium that saddened the whole world. Even the lawless wind, it was believed, respected his dreadful secret, and never blew aside the veil. But still good Mr. Hooper sadly smiled at the pale visages of the worldly throng as he passed by.

Among all its bad influences, the black veil had the one desirable effect, of making its wearer a very efficient clergyman. By the aid of his mysterious emblem—for there was no other apparent cause—he became a man of awful power over souls that were in agony for sin. His converts always regarded him with a dread peculiar to themselves, affirming, though but figuratively, that, before he brought them to celestial light, they had been with him behind the black veil. Its gloom, indeed, enabled him to sympathize with all dark affections. Dying sinners cried aloud for Mr. Hooper, and would not yield their breath till he appeared; though ever, as he stooped to whisper consolation, they shuddered at the veiled face so near their own. Such were the terrors of the black veil, even when Death had bared his visage! Strangers came long distances to attend service at his church, with the mere idle purpose of gazing at his figure, because it was forbidden them to behold his face. But many were made to quake ere they departed! Once, during Governor Belcher's administration, Mr. Hooper was appointed to preach the election sermon. Covered with his black veil, he stood before the chief magistrate, the council, and the representatives, and wrought so deep an impression, that the legislative measures of that year were characterized by all the gloom and piety of our earliest ancestral sway.

In this manner Mr. Hooper spent a long life, irreproachable in outward act, yet shrouded in dismal suspicions; kind and loving, though unloved, and dimly feared; a man apart from men, shunned in their health and joy, but ever summoned to their aid in mortal anguish. As years wore on, shedding their snows above his sable veil, he acquired a name throughout the New England churches, and they called him Father Hooper. Nearly all his parishioners, who were of mature age when he was settled, had been borne away by many a funeral: he had one congregation in the church, and a more crowded one in the churchyard; and having wrought so late into the evening, and done his work so well, it was now good Father Hooper's turn to rest.

Several persons were visible by the shaded candlelight, in the death chamber of the old clergyman. Natural connections he had none. But there was the decorously grave, though unmoved physician, seeking only to mitigate the last pangs of the patient whom he could not save. There were the deacons, and other eminently pious members of his church. There, also, was the Reverend Mr. Clark, of Westbury, a young and zealous divine, who had ridden in haste to pray by the bedside of the expiring minister. There was the nurse, no hired handmaiden of death, but one whose calm affection had endured thus long in secrecy, in solitude, amid the chill of age, and would not perish, even at the dying hour. Who, but Elizabeth! And there lay the hoary head of good Father Hooper upon the death pillow, with the black veil still swathed about his brow, and reaching down over his face, so that each more difficult gasp of his faint breath caused it to stir. All through life that piece of crape had hung between him and the world: it had separated him from cheerful brotherhood and woman's love, and kept him in that saddest of all prisons, his own heart; and still it lay upon his face, as if to deepen the gloom of his darksome chamber, and shade him from the sunshine of eternity.

For some time previous, his mind had been confused, wavering doubtfully between the past and the present, and hovering forward, as it were, at intervals, into the indistinctness of the world to come. There had been feverish turns, which tossed him from side to side, and wore away what little strength he had. But in his most convulsive struggles, and in the wildest vagaries of his intellect, when no other thought retained its sober influence, he still showed an awful solicitude lest the black veil should slip aside. Even if his bewildered soul could have forgotten, there was a faithful woman at his pillow, who, with averted eyes, would have covered that aged face, which she had last beheld in the comeliness of manhood. At length the death-stricken old man lay quietly in the torpor of mental and bodily exhaustion, with an imperceptible pulse, and breath that grew fainter and fainter, except when a long, deep, and irregular inspiration seemed to prelude the flight of his spirit.

The minister of Westbury approached the bedside.

"Venerable Father Hooper," said he, "the moment of your release is at hand. Are you ready for the lifting of the veil that shuts in time from eternity?"

Father Hooper at first replied merely by a feeble motion of his head; then, apprehensive, perhaps, that his meaning might be doubted, he exerted himself to speak.

"Yea," said he, in faint accents, "my soul hath a patient weariness until that veil be lifted."

"And is it fitting," resumed the Reverend Mr. Clark, "that a man so given to prayer, of such a blameless example, holy in deed and thought, so far as mortal judgment may pronounce; is it fitting that a father in the church should leave a shadow on his memory, that may seem to blacken a life so pure? I pray you, my venerable brother, let not this thing be! Suffer us to be gladdened by your triumphant aspect as you go to your reward. Before the veil of eternity be lifted, let me cast aside this black veil from your face!"

And thus speaking, the Reverend Mr. Clark bent forward to reveal the mystery of so many years. But, exerting a sudden energy, that made all the beholders stand aghast, Father Hooper snatched both his hands from beneath the bedclothes, and pressed them strongly on the black veil, resolute to struggle, if the minister of Westbury would contend with a dying man.

"Never!" cried the veiled clergyman. "On earth, never!"

"Dark old man!" exclaimed the affrighted minister, "with what horrible crime upon your soul are you now passing to the judgment?"

Father Hooper's breath heaved; it rattled in his throat; but, with a mighty effort, grasping forward with his hands, he caught hold of life, and held it back till he should speak. He even raised himself in bed; and there he sat, shivering with the arms of death around him, while the black veil hung down, awful, at that last moment, in the gathered terrors of a lifetime. And yet the faint, sad smile, so often there, now seemed to glimmer from its obscurity, and linger on Father Hooper's lips.

"Why do you tremble at me alone?" cried he, turning his veiled face round the circle of pale spectators. "Tremble also at each other! Have men avoided me, and women shown no pity, and children screamed and fled, only for my black veil? What, but the mystery which it obscurely typifies, has made this piece of crape so awful? When the friend shows his inmost heart to his friend; the lover to his best beloved; when man does not vainly shrink from the eye of his Creator, loathsomely treasuring up the secret of his sin; then deem me a monster, for the symbol beneath which I have lived, and die! I look around me, and, lo! on every visage a Black Veil!"

While his auditors shrank from one another, in mutual affright, Father Hooper fell back upon his pillow, a veiled corpse, with a faint smile lingering on the lips. Still veiled, they laid him in his coffin, and a veiled corpse they bore him to the grave. The grass of many years has sprung up and withered on that grave, the burial stone is moss-grown, and good Mr. Hooper's face is dust; but awful is still the thought that it mouldered beneath the Black Veil!

Ethan Brand (1850)[1]

A Chapter from an Abortive Romance

Bartram the lime-burner, a rough, heavy-looking man, begrimed with charcoal, sat watching his kiln at nightfall, while his little son played at building houses with the scattered fragments of marble, when, on the hill-side below them, they heard a roar of laughter, not mirthful, but slow, and even solemn, like a wind shaking the boughs of the forest.

"Father, what is that?" asked the little boy, leaving his play, and pressing betwixt his father's knees.

"Oh, some drunken man, I suppose," answered the lime-burner; "some merry fellow from the bar-room in the village, who dared not laugh loud enough within doors lest he should blow the roof of the house off. So here he is, shaking his jolly sides at the foot of Graylock."

"But, father," said the child, more sensitive than the obtuse, middle-aged clown, "he does not laugh like a man that is glad. So the noise frightens me!"

"Don't be a fool, child!" cried his father, gruffly. "You will never make a man, I do believe; there is too much of your mother in you. I have known the rustling of a leaf startle you. Hark! Here comes the merry fellow now. You shall see that there is no harm in him."

Bartram and his little son, while they were talking thus, sat watching the same lime-kiln that had been the scene of Ethan Brand's solitary and meditative life, before he began his search for the Unpardonable Sin. Many years, as we have seen, had now elapsed, since that portentous night when the IDEA was first developed. The kiln, however, on the mountain-side, stood unimpaired, and was in nothing changed since he had thrown his dark thoughts into the intense glow of its furnace, and melted them, as it were, into the one thought that took possession of his life. It was a rude, round, tower-like structure about twenty feet high, heavily built of rough stones, and with a hillock of earth heaped about the larger part of its circumference; so that the blocks and fragments of marble might be drawn by cart-loads, and thrown in at the top. There was an opening at the bottom of the tower,

---

[1] In Hawthorne's notebook for 1844 there is the following item: "The search of an investigator for the Unpardonable Sin;—he at last finds it in his own heart and practise." Another item for the same year: "... the Unpardonable Sin might consist in a want of love and reverence for the Human Soul; in consequence of which, the investigator pried into its dark depths, not with a hope or purpose of making it better, but from a cold philosophical curiosity,—content that it should be wicked in what ever kind or degree, and only desiring to study it out. Would not this, in other words, be the separation of the intellect from the heart?"

like an oven-mouth, but large enough to admit a man in a stooping posture, and provided with a massive iron door. With the smoke and jets of flame issuing from the chinks and crevices of this door, which seemed to give admittance into the hill-side, it resembled nothing so such as the private entrance to the infernal regions, which the shepherds of the Delectable Mountains [2] were accustomed to show to pilgrims.

There are many such lime-kilns in that tract of country, for the purpose of burning the white marble which composes a large part of the substance of the hills. Some of them, built years ago, and long deserted, with weeds growing in the vacant round of the interior, which is open to the sky, and grass and wildflowers rooting themselves into the chinks of the stones, look already like relics of antiquity, and may yet be overspread with the lichens of centuries to come. Others, where the lime-burner still feeds his daily and night-long fire, afford points of interest to the wanderer among the hills, who seats himself on a log of wood or a fragment of marble, to hold a chat with the solitary man. It is a lonesome, and, when the character is inclined to thought, may be an intensely thoughtful occupation; as it proved in the case of Ethan Brand, who had mused to such strange purpose, in days gone by, while the fire in this very kiln was burning.

The man who now watched the fire was of a different order, and troubled himself with no thoughts save the very few that were requisite to his business. At frequent intervals, he flung back the clashing weight of the iron door, and, turning his face from the insufferable glare, thrust in huge logs of oak, or stirred the immense brands with a long pole. Within the furnace were seen the curling and riotous flames, and the burning marble, almost molten with the intensity of heat; while without, the reflection of the fire quivered on the dark intricacy of the surrounding forest, and showed in the foreground a bright and ruddy little picture of the hut, the spring beside its door, the athletic and coal-begrimed figure of the lime-burner, and the half-frightened child, shrinking into the protection of his father's shadow. And when, again, the iron door was closed, then reappeared the tender light of the half-full moon, which vainly strove to trace out the indistinct shapes of the neighboring mountains; and, in the upper sky, there was a flitting congregation of clouds, still faintly tinged with the rosy sunset, though thus far down into the valley the sunshine had vanished long and long ago.

The little boy now crept still closer to his father, as footsteps were heard ascending the hill-side, and a human form thrust aside the bushes that clustered beneath the trees.

"Halloo! who is it?" cried the lime-burner, vexed at his son's timid-

[2] An allusion to Bunyan's *Pilgrim's Progress*.

ity, yet half infected by it. "Come forward, and show yourself, like a man, or I'll fling this chunk of marble at your head!"

"You offer me a rough welcome," said a gloomy voice, as the unknown man drew nigh. "Yet I neither claim nor desire a kinder one, even at my own fireside."

To obtain a distincter view, Bartram threw open the iron door of the kiln, whence immediately issued a gush of fierce light, that smote full upon the stranger's face and figure. To a careless eye there appeared nothing very remarkable in his aspect, which was that of a man in a coarse, brown, country-made suit of clothes, tall and thin, with the staff and heavy shoes of a wayfarer. As he advanced, he fixed his eyes—which were very bright—intently upon the brightness of the furnace, as if he beheld, or expected to behold, some object worthy of note within it.

"Good evening, stranger," said the lime-burner; "whence come you, so late in the day?"

"I come from my search," answered the wayfarer; "for, at last, it is finished."

"Drunk!—or crazy!" muttered Bartram to himself. "I shall have trouble with the fellow. The sooner I drive him away, the better."

The little boy, all in a tremble, whispered to his father, and begged him to shut the door of the kiln, so that there might not be so much light; for that there was something in the man's face which he was afraid to look at, yet could not look away from. And, indeed, even the lime-burner's dull and torpid sense began to be impressed by an indescribable something in that thin, rugged, thoughtful visage, with the grizzled hair hanging wildly about it, and those deeply sunken eyes, which gleamed like fires within the entrance of a mysterious cavern. But, as he closed the door, the stranger turned towards him, and spoke in a quiet, familiar way, that made Bartram feel as if he were a sane and sensible man, after all.

"Your task draws to an end, I see," said he. "This marble has already been burning three days. A few hours more will convert the stone to lime."

"Why, who are you?" exclaimed the lime-burner. "You seem as well acquainted with my business as I am myself."

"And well I may be," said the stranger; "for I followed the same craft many a long year, and here, too, on this very spot. But you are a new-comer in these parts. Did you never hear of Ethan Brand?"

"The man that went in search of the Unpardonable Sin?" asked Bartram, with a laugh.

"The same," answered the stranger. "He has found what he sought, and therefore he comes back again."

"What! then you are Ethan Brand himself?" cried the lime-burner, in amazement. "I am a newcomer here, as you say, and they call it eighteen years since you left the foot of Graylock. But, I can tell you, the good folks still talk about Ethan Brand, in the village yonder, and what a strange errand took him away from his lime-kiln. Well, and so you have found the Unpardonable Sin?"

"Even so!" said the stranger, calmly.

"If the question is a fair one," proceeded Bartram, "where might it be?"

Ethan Brand laid his finger on his own heart.

"Here!" replied he.

And then, without mirth in his countenance, but as if moved by an involuntary recognition of the infinite absurdity of seeking throughout the world for what was the closest of all things to himself, and looking into every heart, save his own, for what was hidden in no other breast, he broke into a laugh of scorn. It was the same slow, heavy laugh, that had almost appaled the lime-burner when it heralded the wayfarer's approach.

The solitary mountain-side was made dismal by it. Laughter, when out of place, mistimed, or bursting forth from a disordered state of feeling, may be the most terrible modulation of the human voice. The laughter of one asleep, even if it be a little child,—the madman's laugh,—the wild, screaming laugh of a born idiot,—are sounds that we sometimes tremble to hear, and would always willingly forget. Poets have imagined no utterance of fiends or hobgoblins so fearfully appropriate as a laugh. And even the obtuse lime-burner felt his nerves shaken, as this strange man looked inward at his own heart, and burst into laughter that rolled away into the night, and was indistinctly reverberated among the hills.

"Joe," said he to his little son, "scamper down to the tavern in the village, and tell the jolly fellows there that Ethan Brand has come back, and that he has found the Unpardonable Sin!"

The boy darted away on his errand, to which Ethan Brand made no objection, nor seemed hardly to notice it. He sat on a log of wood, looking steadfastly at the iron door of the kiln. When the child was out of sight, and his swift and light footsteps ceased to be heard treading first on the fallen leaves and then on the rocky mountain-path, the lime-burner began to regret his departure. He felt that the little fellow's presence had been a barrier between his guest and himself, and that he must now deal, heart to heart, with a man who, on his own confession, had committed the one only crime for which Heaven could afford no mercy. That crime, in its indistinct blackness, seemed to overshadow him. The lime-burner's own sins rose up within him, and made his memory riotous with a throng of evil shapes that asserted their kindred with the Master Sin, whatever it might be, which it was within the scope of man's corrupted nature to conceive and cherish. They were all of one family; they went to and fro between his breast and Ethan Brand's, and carried dark greetings from one to the other.

Then Bartram remembered the stories which had grown traditionary in reference to this strange man, who had come upon him like a shadow of the night, and was making himself at home in his old place, after so long absence, that the dead people, dead and buried for years, would have had more right to be at home, in any familiar spot, than he. Ethan Brand, it was said, had conversed with Satan himself in the lurid blaze of this very kiln. The legend had been matter of mirth here-tofore, but looked grisly now. According to this tale, before Ethan Brand departed on his search, he had been accustomed to evoke a fiend from the hot furnace of the lime-kiln, night after night, in order to confer with him about the Unpardonable Sin; the man and the fiend each laboring to frame the image of some mode of guilt which could neither be atoned for nor forgiven. And, with the first gleam of light upon the mountain-top, the fiend crept in at the iron door, there to abide the intensest element of fire until again summoned forth to share in the dreadful task of extending man's possible guilt beyond the scope of Heaven's else infinite mercy.

While the lime-burner was struggling with the horror of these thoughts, Ethan Brand rose from the log, and flung open the door of the kiln. The action was in such accordance with the idea in Bartram's mind, that he almost expected to see the Evil One issue forth, red-hot, from the raging furnace.

"Hold! hold!" cried he, with a tremulous attempt to laugh; for he was ashamed of his fears, although they overmastered him. "Don't, for mercy's sake, bring out your Devil now!"

"Man!" sternly replied Ethan Brand, "what need have I of the Devil? I have left him behind me, on my track. It is with such half-way sin-ners as you that he busies himself. Fear not, because I open the door, I do but act by old custom, and am going to trim your fire, like a lime-burner, as I was once."

He stirred the vast coals, thrust in more wood, and bent forward to gaze into the hollow prison-house of the fire, regardless of the fierce glow that reddened upon his face. The lime-burner sat watching him, and half suspected this strange guest of a purpose, if not to evoke a fiend, at least to plunge bodily into the flames, and thus vanish from the sight of man. Ethan Brand, however, drew quietly back, and closed the door of the kiln.

"I have looked," said he, "into many a human heart that was seven times hotter with sinful passions than yonder furnace is with fire. But I found not there what I sought. No, not the Unpardonable Sin!"

"What is the Unpardonable Sin?" asked the lime-burner; and then he shrank farther from his companion, trembling lest his question should be answered.

"It is a sin that grew within my own breast," replied Ethan Brand, standing erect, with a pride that distinguishes all enthusiasts of his stamp. "A sin that grew nowhere else! The sin of an intellect that triumphed over the sense of brotherhood with man and reverence for God, and sacrificed everything to its own mighty claims! The only sin that deserves a recompense of immortal agony! Freely, were it to do again, would I incur the guilt. Unshrinkingly I accept the retribution!"

"The man's head is turned," muttered the lime-burner to himself. "He may be a sinner like the rest of us,—nothing more likely,—but, I'll be sworn, he is a madman too."

Nevertheless, he felt uncomfortable at his situation, alone with Ethan Brand on the wild mountain-side, and was right glad to hear the rough murmur of tongues, and the footsteps of what seemed a pretty numerous party, stumbling over the stones and rustling through the underbrush. Soon appeared the whole lazy regiment that was wont to infest the village tavern, comprehending three or four individuals who had drunk flip beside the bar-room fire through all the winters, and smoked their pipes beneath the stoop through all the summers, since Ethan Brand's departure. Laughing boisterously, and mingling all their voices together in unceremonious talk, they now burst into the moon-shine and narrow streaks of firelight that illuminated the open space before the lime-kiln. Bartram set the door ajar again, flooding the spot with light, that the whole company might get a fair view of Ethan Brand, and he of them.

There, among other old acquaintances, was a once ubiquitous man, now almost extinct, but whom we were formerly sure to encounter at the hotel of every thriving village throughout the country. It was the stage-agent. The present specimen of the genus was a wilted and smoke-dried man, wrinkled and red-nosed, in a smartly cut, brown, bobtailed coat, with brass buttons, who, for a length of time unknown, had kept his desk and corner in the bar-room, and was still puffing what seemed to be the same cigar that he had lighted twenty years before. He had great fame as a dry joker, though, perhaps, less on account of any intrinsic humor than from a certain flavor of brandy-toddy and tobacco-smoke, which impregnated all his ideas and expressions, as well as his person. Another well-remembered, though strangely altered, face was that of Lawyer Giles, as people still called him in courtesy; an elderly ragamuffin, in his soiled shirt-sleeves and tow-cloth trousers. This poor fellow had been an attorney, in what he called his better days, a sharp practitioner, and in great vogue among the village litigants; but flip, and sling, and toddy, and cocktails, imbibed at all hours, morning, noon, and night, had caused him to slide from intellectual to various kinds and degrees of bodily labor, till at last, to adopt his own phrase, he slid into a soap-vat. In other words, Giles was now a soap-boiler, in a small way. He had come to be but the fragment of a human being, a part of one foot having been chopped off by an axe, and an entire hand torn away by the devilish grip of a steam-engine. Yet, though the corporeal hand was gone, a spiritual member remained; for, stretching forth the stump, Giles steadfastly averred that he felt an invisible thumb and fingers with as vivid a sensation as before the real ones were amputated. A maimed and miserable wretch he was; but one, nevertheless, whom the world could not trample on, and had no right to scorn, either in this or any previous stage of his misfortunes, since he had still kept up the courage and spirit of a man, asked nothing in charity, and with his one hand—and that the left one—fought a stern battle against want and hostile circumstances.

Among the throng, too, came another personage, who, with certain points of similarity to Lawyer Giles, had many more of difference. It was the village doctor; a man of some fifty years, whom, at an earlier period of his life, we introduced as paying a professional visit to Ethan Brand during the latter's supposed insanity. He was now a purple-visaged, rude, and brutal, yet half-gentlemanly figure, with something wild, ruined, and desperate in his talk, and in all the details of his gesture and manners. Brandy possessed this man like an evil spirit, and made him as surly and savage as a wild beast, and as miserable as a lost soul; but there was supposed to be in him such wonderful skill, such native gifts of healing, beyond any which medical science could impart, that society caught hold of him, and would not let him sink out of its reach. So, swaying to and fro upon his horse, and grumbling thick accents at the bedside, he visited all the sick-chambers for miles about among the mountain towns, and sometimes raised a dying man, as it were, by miracle, or quite as often, no doubt, sent his patient to a grave that was dug many a year too soon. The doctor had an everlasting pipe in his mouth, and, as somebody said, in allusion to his habit of swearing, it was always alight with hell-fire.

These three worthies pressed forward and greeted Ethan Brand each after his own fashion, earnestly inviting him to partake of the contents of a certain black bottle in which, as they averred, he would find something far better worth seeking for than the Unpardonable Sin. No mind, which has wrought itself by intense and solitary meditation into a high state of enthusiasm, can endure the kind of contact with low and vulgar modes of thought and feeling to which Ethan Brand was now subjected. It made him doubt—and, strange to say, it was a painful doubt—whether he had indeed found the Unpardonable Sin, and found it within himself. The whole question on which he had exhausted life, and more than life, looked like a delusion.

"Leave me," he said bitterly, "ye brute beasts, that have made yourselves so, shrivelling up your souls with fiery liquors! I have done with you. Years and years ago, I groped into your hearts and found nothing there for my purpose. Get ye gone!"

"Why, you uncivil scoundrel," cried the fierce doctor, "is that the way you respond to the kindness of your best friends? Then let me tell you the truth. You have no more found the Unpardonable Sin than yonder boy Joe has. You are but a crazy fellow,—I told you so twenty years ago,—neither better nor worse than a crazy fellow, and the fit companion of old Humphrey, here!"

He pointed to an old man, shabbily dressed, with long white hair, thin visage, and unsteady eyes. For some years past this aged person had been wandering about among the hills, inquiring of all travellers whom he met for his daughter. The girl, it seemed, had gone off with a company of circus-performers, and occasionally tidings of her came to the village, and fine stories were told of her glittering appearance as she rode on horseback in the ring, or performed marvellous feats on the tight-rope.

The white-haired father now approached Ethan Brand, and gazed unsteadily into his face.

"They tell me you have been all over the earth," said he, wringing his hands with earnestness. "You must have seen my daughter, for she makes a grand figure in the world, and everybody goes to see her. Did she send any word to her old father, or say when she was coming back?"

Ethan Brand's eye quailed beneath the old man's. That daughter, from whom he so earnestly desired a word of greeting, was the Esther of our tale, the very girl whom, with such cold and remorseless purpose, Ethan Brand had made the subject of a psychological experiment, and wasted, absorbed, and perhaps annihilated her soul, in the process.

"Yes," murmured he, turning away from the hoary wanderer, "it is no delusion. There is an Unpardonable Sin!"

While these things were passing, a merry scene was going forward in the area of cheerful light, beside the spring and before the door of the hut. A number of the youth of the village, young men and girls, had hurried up the hill-side, impelled by curiosity to see Ethan Brand, the hero of so many a legend familiar to their childhood. Finding nothing, however, very remarkable in his aspect,—nothing but a sunburnt wayfarer, in plain garb and dusty shoes, who sat looking into the fire as if he fancied pictures among the coals,—these young people speedily grew tired of observing him. As it happened, there was other amusement at hand. An old German Jew travelling with a diorama on his back, was passing down the mountain-road towards the village just as the party turned aside from it, and, in hopes of eking out the profits of the day, the showman had kept them company to the lime-kiln.

"Come, old Dutchman," cried one of the young men, "let us see your pictures, if you can swear they are worth looking at!"

"Oh yes, Captain," answered the Jew,—whether as a matter of courtesy or craft, he styled everybody Captain,—"I shall show you, indeed, some very superb pictures!"

So, placing his box in a proper position, he invited the young men and girls to look through the glass orifices of the machine, and proceeded to exhibit a series of the most outrageous scratchings and daubings, as specimens of the fine arts, that ever an itinerant showman had the face to impose upon his circle of spectators. The pictures were worn out, moreover, tattered, full of cracks and wrinkles, dingy with tobacco-smoke, and otherwise in a most pitiable condition. Some purported to be cities, public edifices, and ruined castles in Europe; others represented Napoleon's battles and Nelson's sea-fights; and in the midst of these would be seen a gigantic, brown, hairy hand,—which might have been mistaken for the Hand of Destiny, though, in truth, it was only the showman's,—pointing its forefinger to various scenes of the conflict, while its owner gave historical illustrations. When, with much merriment at its abominable deficiency of merit, the exhibition was concluded, the German bade little Joe put his head into the box. Viewed through the magnifying-glasses, the boy's round, rosy visage assumed the strangest imaginable aspect of an immense Titantic child, the mouth grinning broadly, and the eyes and every other feature overflowing with fun at the joke. Suddenly, however, that merry face turned pale, and its expression changed to horror, for this easily impressed and excitable child had become sensible that the eye of Ethan Brand was fixed upon him through the glass.

"You make the little man to be afraid, Captain," said the German Jew, turning up the dark and strong outline of his visage from his stooping posture. "But look again, and, by chance, I shall cause you to see somewhat that is very fine, upon my word!"

Ethan Brand gazed into the box for an instant, and then starting back, looked fixedly at the German. What had he seen? Nothing, apparently; for a curious youth, who had peeped in almost at the same moment, beheld only a vacant space of canvas.

"I remember you now," muttered Ethan Brand to the showman.

"Ah, Captain," whispered the Jew of Nuremburg, with a dark smile, "I find it to be a heavy matter in my showbox,—this Unpardonable Sin! By my faith, Captain, it has wearied my shoulders, this long day, to carry it over the mountain."

"Peace," answered Ethan Brand, sternly, "or get thee into the furnace yonder!"

The Jew's exhibition had scarcely concluded, when a great, elderly dog—who seemed to be his own master, as no person in the company laid claim to him—saw fit to render himself the object of public notice. Hitherto, he had shown himself a very quiet, well-disposed old dog, going round from one to another, and, by way of being sociable, offering his rough head to be patted by any kindly hand that would take so much trouble. But now, all of a sudden, this grave and venerable quadruped, of his own mere motion, and without the slightest suggestion from anybody else, began to run round after his tail, which, to heighten the absurdity of the proceeding, was a great deal shorter than it should have been. Never was seen such headlong eagerness in pursuit of an object that could not possibly be attained; never was heard such a tremendous outbreak of growling, snarling, barking, and snapping,—as if one end of the ridiculous brute's body were at deadly and most unforgivable enmity with the other. Faster and faster, round about went the cur; and faster and still faster fled the unapproachable brevity of his tail; and louder and fiercer grew his yells of rage and animosity; until, utterly exhausted, and as far from the goal as ever, the foolish old dog ceased his performance as suddenly as he had begun it. The next moment he was as mild, quiet, sensible, and respectable in his deportment, as when he first scraped acquaintance with the company.

As may be supposed, the exhibition was greeted with universal laughter, clapping of hands, and shouts of encore, to which the canine performer responded by wagging all that there was to wag of his tail, but appeared totally unable to repeat his very successful effort to amuse the spectators.

Meanwhile, Ethan Brand had resumed his seat upon the log, and moved, it might be, by a perception of some remote analogy between his own case and that of this self-pursuing cur, he broke into the awful laugh, which, more than any other token, expressed the condition of his inward being. From that moment, the merriment of the party was at an end; they stood aghast, dreading lest the inauspicious sound should be reverberated around the horizon, and that mountain would thunder it to mountain, and so the horror be prolonged upon their ears. Then, whispering one to another that it was late,—that the moon was almost down,—that the August night was growing chill,—they hurried homewards, leaving the lime-burner and little Joe to deal as they might with their unwelcome guest. Save for these three human beings, the open space on the hill-side was a solitude, set in a vast gloom of forest. Beyond that darksome verge, the firelight glimmered on the stately trunks and almost black foliage of pines, intermixed with the lighter verdure of sapling oaks, maples, and poplars, while here and there lay the gigantic corpses of dead trees, decaying on the leaf-strewn soil. And it seemed to little Joe—a timorous and imaginative child—that the silent forest was holding its breath until some fearful thing should happen.

Ethan Brand thrust more wood into the fire, and closed the door of the kiln, then looking over his shoulder at the lime-burner and his son, he bade, rather than advised, them to retire to rest.

"For myself, I cannot sleep," said he. "I have matters that it concerns me to meditate upon. I will watch the fire, as I used to do in the old time."

"And call the Devil out of the furnace to keep you company, I suppose," muttered Bartram, who had been making intimate acquaintance with the black bottle above mentioned. "But watch, if you like, and call as many devils as you like! For my part, I shall be all the better for a snooze. Come, Joe!"

As the boy followed his father into the hut, he looked back at the wayfarer, and the tears came into his eyes, for his tender spirit had an intuition of the bleak and terrible loneliness in which this man had enveloped himself.

When they had gone, Ethan Brand sat listening to the crackling of the kindled wood, and looking at the little spirits of fire that issued through the chinks of the door. These trifles, however, once so familiar, had but the slightest hold of his attention, while deep within his mind he was reviewing the gradual but marvellous change that had been wrought upon him by the search to which he had devoted himself. He remembered how the night dew had fallen upon him,—how the dark forest had whispered to him,—how the stars had gleamed upon him,— a simple and loving man, watching his fire in the years gone by; and ever musing as it burned. He remembered with what tenderness, with what love and sympathy for mankind, and what pity for human guilt and woe, he had first begun to contemplate those ideas which afterwards became the inspiration of his life; with what reverence he had then looked into the heart of man, viewing it as a temple originally divine, and, however desecrated, still to be held sacred by a brother; with what awful fear he had deprecated the success of his pursuit, and prayed that the Unpardonable Sin might never be revealed to him. Then ensued that vast intellectual development, which, in its progress, disturbed the counterpoise between his mind and heart. The Idea that possessed his life had operated as a means of education; it had gone on cultivating his powers to the highest point of which they were susceptible; it had raised him from the level of an unlettered laborer to stand on a star-lit eminence, whither the philosophers of the earth, laden with the lore of universities, might vainly strive to clamber after him. So much for the intellect! But where was the heart? That, indeed, had withered,—had contracted,—had hardened,—had perished! It had ceased to partake of the universal throb. He had lost his hold of the magnetic chain of humanity. He was no longer a brother-man, opening the chambers or the dungeons of our common nature by the key of holy sympathy, which gave him a right to share in all its secrets; he was now a cold observer, looking on mankind as the subject of his experiment, and, at length, converting man and woman to be his puppets, and pulling the wires that moved them to such degrees of crime as were demanded for his study.

Thus Ethan Brand became a fiend. He began to be so from the moment that his moral nature had ceased to keep the pace of improvement with his intellect. And now, as his highest effort and inevitable development,—as the bright and gorgeous flower, and rich, delicious fruit of his life's labor,—he had produced the Unpardonable Sin!

"What more have I to seek? what more to achieve?" said Ethan Brand to himself. "My task is done, and well done!"

Starting from the log with a certain alacrity in his gait and ascending the hillock of earth that was raised against the stone circumference of the lime-kiln, he thus reached the top of the structure. It was a space of perhaps ten feet across, from edge to edge, presenting a view of the upper surface of the immense mass of broken marble with which the kiln was heaped. All these innumerable blocks and fragments of marble were red-hot and vividly on fire, sending up great spouts of blue flame, which quivered aloft and danced madly, as within a magic circle, and sank and rose again, with continual and multitudinous activity. As the lonely man bent forward over this terrible body of fire, the blasting heat smote up against his person with a breath that, it might be supposed, would have scorched and shrivelled him up in a moment.

Ethan Brand stood erect, and raised his arms on high. The blue flames played upon his face, and imparted the wild and ghastly light which alone could have suited its expression; it was that of a fiend on the verge of plunging into his gulf of intensest torment.

"O Mother Earth," cried he, "who art no more my Mother, and into whose bosom this frame shall never be resolved! O mankind, whose brotherhood I have cast off, and trampled thy great heart beneath my feet! O stars of heaven, that shone on me of old, as if to light me onward and upward!—farewell all, and forever. Come, deadly element of Fire,—henceforth my familiar friend! Embrace me, as I do thee!"

That night the sound of a fearful peal of laughter rolled heavily through the sleep of the lime-burner and his little son; dim shapes of horror and anguish haunted their dreams, and seemed still present in the rude hovel, when they opened their eyes to the daylight.

"Up, boy, up!" cried the lime-burner, staring about him. "Thank Heaven, the night is gone, at last; and rather than pass such another, I would watch my lime-kiln, wide awake, for a twelvemonth. This Ethan Brand, with his humbug of an Unpardonable Sin, has done me no such mighty favor, in taking my place!"

He issued from the hut, followed by little Joe, who kept fast hold of his father's hand. The early sunshine was already pouring its gold upon the mountaintops, and though the valleys were still in shadow, they smiled cheerfully in the promise of the bright day that was hastening onward. The village, completely shut in by hills, which swelled away gently about it, looked as if it had rested peacefully in the hollow of the great hand of Providence. Every dwelling was distinctly visible; the little spires of the two churches pointed upwards, and caught a fore-glimmering of brightness from the sun-gilt skies upon their gilded weathercocks. The tavern was astir, and the figure of the old, smoke-dried stage-agent, cigar in mouth, was seen beneath the stoop. Old Graylock was glorified with a golden cloud upon his head. Scattered likewise over the breasts of the surrounding mountains, there were heaps of hoary mist, in fantastic shapes, some of them far down into the valley, others high up towards the summits, and still others, of the same family of mist or cloud, hovering in the gold radiance of the upper atmosphere. Stepping from one to another of the clouds that rested on the hills, and thence to the loftier brotherhood that sailed in air, it seemed almost as if a mortal man might thus ascend into the heavenly regions. Earth was so mingled with sky that it was a day-dream to look at it.

To supply that charm of the familiar and homely, which Nature so readily adopts into a scene like this, the stagecoach was rattling down the mountain-road, and the driver sounded his horn, while Echo caught up the notes, and intertwined them into a rich and varied and elaborate harmony, of which the original performer could lay claim to little share. The great hills played a concert among themselves, each contributing a strain of airy sweetness.

Little Joe's face brightened at once.

"Dear father," cried he, skipping cheerily to and fro, "that strange man is gone, and the sky and the mountains all seem glad of it!"

"Yes," growled the lime-burner, with an oath, "but he has let the fire go down, and no thanks to him if five hundred bushels of lime are not spoiled. If I catch the fellow here-abouts again, I shall feel like tossing him into the furnace!"

With his long pole in his hand, he ascended to the top of the kiln. After a moment's pause, he called to his son.

"Come up here, Joe!" said he.

So little Joe ran up the hillock, and stood by his father's side. The marble was all burnt into perfect, snow-white lime. But on its surface, in the midst of the circle,—snow-white too, and thoroughly converted into lime,—lay a human skeleton, in the attitude of a person who, after long toil, lies down to long repose. Within the ribs—strange to say— was the shape of a human heart.

"Was the fellow's heart made of marble?" cried Bartram, in some perplexity at this phenomenon. "At any rate, it is burnt into what looks like a special good lime, and, taking all the bones together, my kiln is half a bushel the richer for him."

So saying, the rude lime-burner lifted his pole, and, letting it fall upon the skeleton, the relics of Ethan Brand were crumbled into fragments.

FROM *Journals and Notebooks*

August 5th. Friday [1842]

A rainy day—a rainy day—and I do verily believe there is no sun-shine in this world, except what beams from my wife's eyes. At present, she has laid her strict command on me to take pen in hand; and, to ensure my obedience has banished me to the little ten-foot-square apart-ment, misnamed my study; but she must not be surprised, if .the dismal-ness of the day, and the dulness of my solitude, should be the prominent characteristics of what I write. And what is there to write about at all? Happiness has no succession of events; because it is a part of eternity; and we have been living in eternity, ever since we came to this old Manse. Like Enoch, we seem to have been translated to the other state of being, without having passed through death. Our spirits must have flitted away, unconsciously, in the deep and quiet rapture of some long embrace; and we can only perceive that we have cast off our mortal part, by the more real and earnest life of our spirits. Externally, our Paradise has very much the aspect of a pleasant old domicile, on earth. The antique house (for it looks antique, though it was created by Providence expressly for our use, and at the precise time when we wanted it) stands behind a noble avenue of Balm of Gilead trees; and when we chance to observe a passing traveller, through the sunshine and the shadow of this long avenue, his figure appears too dim and remote to disturb our sense of blissful seclusion. Few, indeed, are the mortals who venture within our sacred precincts. George Prescott—who has not yet grown earthly enough, I suppose, to be debarred from occasional visits to Paradise—comes daily to bring three pints of milk, from some ambrosial cow;—occasionally, also, he makes an offering of mortal flowers, at the shrine of a certain angelic personage. Mr. Emerson comes sometimes, and has been so far favored as to be feasted (with a gnome, yclept Ellery Channing) on our nectar and ambrosia. Mr. Thorow [sic] has twice listened to the music of the spheres, which, for our private convenience, we have packed into a musical box. Elizabeth Hoar (who is much more at home among spirits than among fleshly bodies) came hither a few times, merely to welcome us to the ethereal world; but latterly she has vanished into some other region of infinite space. One rash mortal, on the second Sunday after our arrival, obtruded himself upon us in a gig. There have since been three or four callers, who preposterously think that the courtesies of the lower world are to be responded to by people whose home is in Paradise. I must not forget to mention that the butcher comes twice or thrice a week; and we have so far improved upon the custom of Adam and Eve, that we generally furnish forth our feasts with a portion of some delicate calf or lamb, whose unspotted innocence entitles them to the happiness of becoming our sustenance. Would that my wife would permit me to record the ethereal dainties, that kind Heaven provided for us, on the first day of our arrival! Never, surely, was such food heard of on earth—at least, not by me. Well; the above mentioned persons are nearly all that have intruded into the hallowed shade of our avenue;—except, indeed, a certain sinner who came to bargain for the grass in our orchard, and another who came with a new cistern; for it is one of the drawbacks upon our Paradise, that it contains no water fit either to drink or to bathe in; so that the showers of Heaven have become, in good truth, a godsend. I wonder why Providence does not cause a clear, cold fountain to bubble up at our doorstep;—methinks it would not be unreasonable to pray for such a favor. At present, we are under the ridiculous necessity of sending to the outer world for water. Only imagine Adam trudging out of Paradise with a bucket in each hand, to get water to drink, or for Eve to bathe in! Intolerable! I shall absolutely think myself wronged, unless I find the aforesaid fountain bubbling at our doorstep, the next time I look out. In other respects, Providence has treated us pretty tolerably well; but here I shall expect something further to be done. Also, in the way of future favors, a kitten would be very acceptable. Animals (except, perhaps, a pig) seem never out of place, even in the most paradisaical spheres. And, by the bye, a young colt comes up our avenue, now and then, to crop the seldom trodden herbage; and so do a company of cows, whose sweet breath well repays us for the food which they obtain. There are likewise a few hens, whose quiet cluck is heard pleasantly about the house. A black dog sometimes stands at the farther extremity of the avenue, and looks wistfully towards the house; but when I whistle to him, he puts his tail between his legs, and trots away. Foolish dog!—if he had more faith, he should have bones enough.

August 8th. Monday [1842]

I wish I could give a description of our house; for it really has a character of its own—which is more than can be said of most edifices in these days. . . . Notwithstanding all we have done to modernize the old house, we seem scarcely to have disturbed its air of antiquity. It is evident that other wedded pairs have spent their honeymoons here, though none so happily as ourselves—that children have been born here, and people have grown old and died in these rooms and chambers; although, for our behoof, the same apartments have consented to look cheerful once again. Then there are dark closets, and strange nooks and corners, where the ghosts of former occupants might hide themselves in the day time, and stalk forth, when night conceals all our sacrilegious improvements. We have seen no apparitions, as yet; but we hear strange noises, especially in the kitchen; and, last night, my wife, while sitting in the parlor, heard a thumping and pounding, as of somebody at work in my study. Nay, if I mistake not (for I was half asleep when she told me) she heard a sound as of some person crumpling paper in his hand, in our very bed-chamber. This must have been old Doctor Ripley, with one of his sermons;—there is a whole chest full of them in the garret; but he need have no apprehensions of our disturbing them. I never saw the old patriarch myself;—which I regret, as I should have been glad to associate his venerable figure, at ninety years of age, with the house in which he dwelt.

Externally, the house presents the same appearance as in the Doctor's day. It had once a coat of white paint; but the storms and sunshine of many years have almost obliterated it, and produced a sober greyish hue, which entirely suits the antique form of the structure. To re-paint its venerable face would be a real sacrilege; it would look like old Doctor Ripley in a brown wig. I hardly know why it is that our cheerful and lightsome repairs and improvements, in the interior of the house, seem to be in perfectly good taste, though the heavy old beams, and high panelling of the walls, speak of ages gone by. But so it is;—the cheerful paper-hangings have the air of belonging to the old walls; and such modernisms as astral-lamps, card-vases, gilded Cologne bottles, silver taperstands, and bronze and alabaster card-vases, do not seem at all impertinent. It is thus that an aged man may keep his heart warm for new things and new friends, and often furnish himself anew with ideas, though it would not be graceful for him to attempt to suit his exterior to the passing fashions of the day.

Sept. 1st. Thursday [1842]

Mr. Thorow [*sic*] dined with us yesterday. He is a singular character—a young man with much of wild original nature still remaining in him; and so far as he is sophisticated, it is in a way and method of his own. He is as ugly as sin, long-nosed, queer-mouthed, and with uncouth and somewhat rustic, although courteous manners, corresponding very well with such an exterior. But his ugliness is of an honest and agreeable fashion, and becomes him much better than beauty. He was educated, I believe, at Cambridge, and formerly kept school in this town; but for two or three years back, he has repudiated all regular modes of getting a living, and seems inclined to lead a sort of Indian life among civilized men—an Indian life, I mean, as respects the absence of any systematic effort for a livelihood. He has been for sometime an inmate of Mr. Emerson's family; and, in requital, he labors in the garden, and performs such other offices as may suit him—being entertained by Mr. Emerson for the sake of what true manhood there is in him. Mr. Thorow [*sic*] is a keen and delicate observer of nature—a genuine observer, which, I suspect, is almost as rare a character as even an original poet; and Nature, in return for his love, seems to adopt him as her especial child, and shows him secrets which few others are allowed to witness. He is familiar with beast, fish, fowl, and reptile, and has strange stories to tell of adventures, and friendly passages with these lower brethren of mortality. Herb and flower, likewise, wherever they grow, whether in garden, or wild wood, are his familiar friends. He is also on intimate terms with the clouds, and can tell the portents of storms. It is a characteristic trait, that he has a great regard for the memory of the Indian tribes, whose wild life would have suited him so well; and strange to say, he seldom walks over a ploughed field without picking up an arrow-point, a spear-head, or other relic of the red men—as if their spirits willed him to be the inheritor of their simple wealth.

With all this he has more than a tincture of literature—a deep and true taste for poetry, especially the elder poets, although more exclusive than is desirable, like all other Transcendentalists, so far as I am acquainted with them. He is a good writer—at least, he has written one good article, a rambling disquisition on Natural History in the last Dial,—which, he says, was chiefly made up from journals of his own observations. Methinks this article gives a very fair image of his mind and character—so true, minute, and literal in observation, yet giving the spirit as well as letter of what he sees, even as a lake reflects its wooded banks, showing every leaf, yet giving the wild beauty of the whole scene;—then there are passages in the article of cloudy and dreamy metaphysics, partly affected, and partly the natural exhalations of his intellect;—and also passages where his thoughts seem to measure and attune themselves into spontaneous verse, as they rightfully may, since there is real poetry in him. There is a basis of good sense and moral truth, too, throughout the article, which also is a reflection of his character; for he is not unwise to think and feel, however imperfect in his own mode of action. On the whole, I find him a healthy and wholesome man to know.

After dinner (at which we cut the first water-melon and musk melon that our garden has ripened) Mr. Thorow [*sic*] and I walked up the bank of the river; and, at a certain point, he shouted for his boat. Forthwith, a young man paddled it across the river, and Mr. Thorow [*sic*] and I voyaged further up the stream, which soon became more beautiful than any picture, with its dark and quiet sheet of water, half shaded, half sunny, between high and wooded banks. The late rains have swollen the stream so much, that many trees are standing up to their knees, as it were, in the water; and boughs, which lately swung high in air, now dip and drink deep of the passing wave. As to the poor cardinals, which glowed upon the bank, a few days since, I could see only a few of their scarlet caps, peeping above the water. Mr. Thorow [*sic*] managed the boat so perfectly, either with two paddles or with one, that it seemed instinct [*sic*] with his own will, and to require no physical effort to guide it. He said that, when some Indians visited Concord a few years since, he found that he had acquired, without a teacher, their precise method of propelling and steering a canoe. Nevertheless, being in want of money, the poor fellow was desirous of selling the boat, of which he is so fit a pilot, and which was built by his own hands; so I agreed to give him his price (only seven dollars) and accordingly became possessor of the Musketaquid. I wish I could acquire the aquatic skill of its original owner at as a reasonable a rate.

Sept 2d. Friday [1842]

Yesterday afternoon, while my wife, and Louisa, and I, were gathering the windfallen apples in our orchard, Mr. Thorow [*sic*] arrived with the boat. The adjacent meadow being overflowed by the rise of the stream, he had rowed directly to the foot of the orchard, and landed at the bars, after floating over forty or fifty yards of water, where people were making hay, a week or two since. I entered the boat with him, in order to have the benefit of a lesson in rowing and paddling. My little wife, who was looking on, cannot feel very proud of her husband's proficiency. I managed, indeed, to propel the boat by rowing with two oars; but the use of the single paddle is quite beyond my present skill. Mr. Thorow [sic] had assured me that it was only necessary to will the boat to go in any particular direction, and she would immediately take that course, as if imbued with the spirit of the steersman. It may be so with him, but certainly not with me; the boat seemed to be bewitched, and turned its head to every point of the compass except the right one. He then took the paddle himself, and though I could observe nothing peculiar in his management of it, the Musketaquid immediately became as docile as a trained steed. I suspect that she has not yet transferred her affections from her old master to her new one. By and bye, when we are better acquainted, she will grow more tractable; especially after she shall have had the honor of bearing my little wife, who is loved by all things, living or inanimate. We propose to change her name from Musketaquid (the Indian name of Concord river, meaning the river of meadows) to the Pond Lily—which will be very beautiful and appropriate, as, during the summer season, she will bring home many a cargo of pond lilies from along the river's weedy shore. It is not very likely that I shall make such long voyages in her as Mr. Thorow [sic] has. He once followed our river down to the Merrimack, and thence, I believe, to Newburyport—a voyage of about eighty miles, in this little vessel.

April 8th. Saturday [1843]

Mr. Emerson came, with a sunbeam in his face; and we had as good a talk as I ever remember experiencing with him. My little wife, I know, will demand to know every word that was spoken; but she knows me too [well] to anticipate anything of the kind. He seemed fullest of Margaret Fuller, who he says, has risen perceptibly into a higher state, since their last meeting. He apotheosized her as the greatest woman, I believe, of ancient or modern times, and the one figure in the world worth considering. (There rings the supper bell.) . . . Next Mr. Thoreau was discussed, and his approaching departure; in respect to which we agreed pretty well; but Mr. Emerson appears to have suffered some inconveniency from his experience of Mr. Thoreau as an inmate. It may well be that such a sturdy and uncompromising person is fitter to meet occasionally in the open air, than to have as a permanent guest at table and fireside.

Preface To
The House of the Seven Gables *(1851)*

When a writer calls his work a Romance, it need hardly be observed
that he wishes to claim a certain latitude, both as to its fashion and
material, which he would not have felt himself entitled to assume had
he professed to be writing a Novel. The latter form of composition is
presumed to aim at a very minute fidelity, not merely to the possible,
but to the probable and ordinary course of man's experience. The
former—while, as a work of art, it must rigidly subject itself to laws,
and while it sins unpardonably so far as it may swerve aside from the
truth of the human heart—has fairly a right to present that truth under
circumstances, to a great extent, of the writer's own choosing or creation. If he thinks fit, also, he may so manage his atmospherical
medium as to bring out or mellow the lights and deepen and enrich the
the shadows of the picture. He will be wise, no doubt, to make a very
moderate use of the privileges here stated, and, especially, to mingle
the Marvellous rather as a slight, delicate, and evanescent flavor, than
as any portion of the actual substance of the dish offered to the public.
He can hardly be said, however, to commit a literary crime even if he
disregard this caution.

In the present work, the author has proposed to himself—but with
what success, fortunately, it is not for him to judge—to keep undeviatingly within his immunities. The point of view in which this tale
comes under the Romantic definition lies in the attempt to connect a
bygone time with the very present that is flitting away from us. It is a
legend prolonging itself, from an epoch now gray in the distance, down
into our own broad daylight, and bringing along with it some of its
legendary mist, which the reader, according to his pleasure, may either
disregard, or allow it to float almost imperceptibly about the characters
and events for the sake of a picturesque effect. The narrative, it may be,
is woven of so humble a texture as to require this advantage, and, at
the same time, to render it the more difficult of attainment.

Many writers lay very great stress upon some definite moral purpose, at which they profess to aim their works. Not to be deficient in
this particular, the author has provided himself with a moral,—the
truth, namely, that the wrong-doing of one generation lives into the successive ones, and, divesting itself of every temporary advantage, becomes a pure and uncontrollable mischief; and he would feel it a
singular gratification if this romance might effectively convince mankind—or, indeed, any one man—of the folly of tumbling down an
avalanche of ill-gotten gold, or real estate, on the heads of an unfortunate posterity, thereby to maim and crush them, until the accumulated
mass shall be scattered abroad in its original atoms. In good faith,
however, he is not sufficiently imaginative to flatter himself with the
slightest hope of this kind. When romances do really teach anything,

or produce any effective operation, it is usually through a far more subtile process than the ostensible one. The author has considered it hardly worth his while, therefore, relentlessly to impale the story with its moral as with an iron rod,—or, rather, as by sticking a pin through a butterfly,—thus at once depriving it of life, and causing it to stiffen in an ungainly and unnatural attitude. A high truth, indeed, fairly, finely, and skilfully wrought out, brightening at every step, and crowning the final development of a work of fiction, may add an artistic glory, but is never any truer, and seldom any more evident, at the last page than at the first.

The reader may perhaps choose to assign an actual locality to the imaginary events of this narrative. If permitted by the historical connection,—which, though slight, was essential to his plan,—the author would very willingly have avoided anything of this nature. Not to speak of other objections, it exposes the romance to an inflexible and exceedingly dangerous species of criticism, by bringing his fancy-pictures almost into positive contact with the realities of the moment. It has been no part of his object, however, to describe local manners, nor in any way to meddle with the characteristics of a community for whom he cherishes a proper respect and a natural regard. He trusts not to be considered as unpardonably offending by laying out a street that infringes upon nobody's private rights, and appropriating a lot of land which had no visible owner, and building a house of materials long in use for constructing castles in the air. The personages of the tale—though they give themselves out to be of ancient stability and considerable prominence—are really of the author's own making, or, at all events, of his own mixing; their virtues can shed no lustre, nor their defects redound, in the remotest degree, to the discredit of the venerable town of which they profess to be inhabitants. He would be glad, therefore, if—especially in the quarter to which he alludes—the book may be read strictly as a Romance, having a great deal more to do with the clouds overhead than with any portion of the actual soil of the County of Essex.

HERMAN MELVILLE (1819–1891)

A sudden drop from middle-class comfort to genteel poverty can prove a searing, indeed a traumatic, experience for a boy: it can deepen his sensibilities, arouse his humane feelings, complicate his relationships with other people. This pattern of boyhood trouble, bringing with it sudden insecurities and perceptions, can be found in the lives of a good many American writers, notably Hawthorne and Melville. Melville's father belonged to a well-established family of merchants and importers, yet by the time of Herman's birth, in New York City, the family was slipping into debt, and with the death of the father in 1832, the sons had to go to work. Herman clerked in his brother's store, worked on an uncle's farm, and despite his lack of formal education, taught school for a while. In 1839 he signed on as a seaman with a merchant ship; in 1841 he sailed on a whaler; and in 1844 he returned from the South Pacific to the United States on an American warship. If the much-abused category of "proletarian writer" has any meaning at all, then Herman Melville, who in his younger years worked with his hands to earn his bread, certainly was one.

His first book Typee *(1846) is based partly on his experiences in the South Seas, though it also contains imaginative material concerning the lure of primitivism as an escape from Calvinist and commercial New England. The book attracted favorable attention in the New York literary world and, like its jolly successor* Omoo *(1847), pleased a large public which thought of Melville as "a man who had lived among the cannibals."*

Married in 1847 to Elizabeth Shaw, the daughter of the chief justice of Massachusetts, Melville settled in New York City and wrote the allegorical romance—half metaphysics, half adventure—called Mardi *(1849). For reasons both good and bad, this exasperating but intelligent book lost Melville his audience: he was no longer the darling American gone among the cannibals to entertain the folks back home. In 1850, as a financial retrenchment, Melville moved his family to a farm near Pittsfield, Massachusetts. Nearby lived Nathaniel Hawthorne, whose stories Melville admired extravagantly, and the two writers became friends. In the older writer Melville found a sympathetic understanding he had never known before, and he poured out his heart to Hawthorne in a series of exuberant letters. They met often and talked, as Hawthorne dryly noted, "about time and eternity, things of this world and the next, and books and publishers, and all possible and impossible matters."* Moby Dick *(1851) was dedicated to Hawthorne, who sent a letter— unfortunately lost—which Melville described as "joy-giving and exultation-breeding." Their friendship was broken, or perhaps merely interrupted, when Hawthorne moved away.*

In 1856, however, during a recuperative journey Melville undertook in Europe, he met Hawthorne briefly in England, and they resumed their conversations. An unforgettable portrait of the Melville of this period has been left by Hawthorne in his notebooks:

Melville, as he always does, began to reason of Providence and futurity, and of everything that lies beyond human ken, and informed me that he had "pretty much made up his mind to be annihilated"; but still he does not seem to rest in that anticipation; and, I think, will never rest until he gets hold of a definite belief. It is strange how he persists ... in wandering to-and-fro over these deserts, as dismal and monotonous as the sand hills amid which we were sitting. He can neither believe nor be comfortable in his unbelief; and he is too honest and courageous not to try to do one or the other.... He has a very high and noble nature. ...

During the 1850s Melville still devoted most of his time to writing books and magazine pieces (his great stories "Bartleby the Scrivener" and "Benito Cereno" were published at this time). Pierre (1852), *an over-wrought narrative about an intellectually and sexually troubled young man;* Israel Potter (1855), *a vigorous adventure tale set in the years of the American Revolution; and* The Confidence-Man (1857), *a mordant philosophical fiction that shows Melville at his most despairing—all, in sharply different ways, are works of high interest. Yet none sold well or received much critical approval. Gradually Melville sank into obscurity.*

In 1863 he took his family to New York where, for almost twenty years, he worked as a customs inspector on the waterfront. He published very little during these years, a few volumes of barely noticed poetry, until, after his retirement in 1885, he turned to a more ambitious project and in the year of his death completed his great short novel Billy Budd.

About so richly complex a writer as Melville, perhaps the most interest-*ing literary figure this country has ever had, it would be foolhardy to offer a summary criticism in a few paragraphs. But it may be useful to provide a few introductory clues. Here are several passages from Melville himself:*

This great power of blackness in [Hawthorne] derives its force from its appeal to that Calvinistic sense of Innate Depravity and Original Sin, from whose visitations, in some shape or other, no deeply thinking mind is always and wholly free.

There is the grand truth about Hawthorne. He says No! in thunder; but the Devil himself cannot make him say yes. For all men who say yes, lie. I love all men that dive ... the whole corps of intellectual thought-divers that have been diving & coming up again with bloodshot eyes since the world began.

To produce a mighty book, you must choose a mighty theme. No great and enduring volume can ever be written on the flea. ...

Once he had gone beyond the mild sensuous abandonments and para-disial enticements of his first two books, Melville's mind was essentially a speculative one. It was a mind shaped by the crumbling but still powerful heritage of Cristianity, with its insistence, both theoretic and empiric, on the ineradicability of evil in the human soul.

It was a mind trained to ask the questions that had always been put by Christianity but no longer able to remain at peace with the answers of Christianity. And through the seriousness of struggling with a religious heritage, it was a mind drawn to the darkness of moral and psychological ambiguities. "Contradiction and alienation," writes Richard Chase, "are of the essence in Melville's view of life and in his art. He saw human experience and the moral world man constructs for himself, indeed he saw nature itself, as riven by contradictions that could never be satisfactorily reconciled. Although his pessimism was modified in later years, he characteristically saw life as the quest of the individual for the truth and moral harmony that would always elude him, and he saw this quest as alienating the individual from the world, society, and himself."

The stain of evil spreading like a cancer across man's psyche; the fear that the universe is neither creative nor destructive but merely a mass of neutral and indifferent matter; the thought that moral scrutiny may endanger moral navigation, with probings into the motives of conduct resulting in a dissolution of the boundaries between good and evil; the possibility that "all men who dive . . ." bring up not pearls of wisdom but flotsam of skepticism—such were among the speculations on which Melville built his fiction. Here we must employ mere dry husks of statement, but in his books he gave them a wonderfully pungent and playful dramatization. When Melville failed, as in Pierre, *he failed in a mighty way and with "a mighty theme," for he cared about the ultimate questions not as classroom riddles but as the very passions of our existence.*

Saying this, one ought quickly to add that Melville was a writer full of the juices of life, enormously charming, bubbling with playfulness, and warm with the comradeship of democracy. He responded, as no other American writer of his century, to the romantic fantasy of abandoning civilization, the primitivist urge to drop the burdens of work and conscience. He absorbed into his books the folk materials of his native country, its humor and legends and stories—the white whale had first appeared in an American tall tale. And he could break into a healthy wrath against the money-grubbing meanness, the crude and corrupt materialism of an expanding America; Captain Ahab, it is commonly agreed, represents among other things the ruthlessness of the willful American free enterpriser determined to conquer everything before him.

It was not merely questions and speculations that concerned Melville; it was the experience of sensitive and energetic men who lived out these questions and speculations. In all his books through Moby Dick, *and more indirectly, in most of those following it, Melville relied on a recurrent pattern of narrative. The main action is a journey, usually a journey at sea, for the sea symbolizes the un-known, the uncharted, the perilous, which all men, if they but knew it, want to approach. Melvillian in his fallen circumstances, his green inexperience, his philosophical questings, and his humane openness, a young man goes to sea. Partly an orphan cut off from the cradling support of family, partly an exile saying "No," if not yet "in thunder," to the ruling pieties of his society, and partly a pilgrim searching for both his true self and new possibilities of belief, this young man undertakes a journey depicted by Melville as a physical adventure, but obviously meant to suggest spiritual dis-coveries. Sometimes he discovers the watery contentment of the Polynesian shores, where he can bathe his bruised Calvinist soul and heal his bruised American body, so as to return to the Western world. Sometimes he discovers the horrors of the nineteenth-century city, as in the Liverpool visit in* Redburn *(1849). Sometimes he dis-covers the plebeian fraternity, but also the sodden brutalities, that order the life of his shipmates—men with whom he must first prove himself as one who claims no special privileges and is willing to work hard, and from whom he must later reestablish his separate-ness in order to continue his Ishmaelite journey. And sometimes he discovers, as in the encounter with Captain Ahab, the tempta-tions and fatalities, the grandeurs and miseries, of the human will, clenched into a false Prometheanism, determined to conquer every-thing from the natural world to the mysteries of the soul. On this journey the young Melvillian hero dies in order to be reborn; he undergoes an initiation into pain and fortitude and then discovers a kind of wisdom which consists in relaxing before the persistence of intellectual uncertainty, while opening his heart to his comrades in work and life. What he learns on this journey can be reassuring —the lesson of common humanity and fraternity. What he learns can also be frightening—the conclusion that existence bears no meaning and the white whale signifies neither good nor evil but only dumb matter.*

In telling these stories Melville did not really write, in any strict sense, novels at all. He was not bound by the limits of verisimilitude, that is, creating a recognizable facsimile of the recognizable social world; he was not bound by the traditions of the well-made story or novel, with its economy and coherence of structure. He worked toward "open forms," in which the process of emotional discovery would lead to increment and growth; he created prose epics, or epic romances in prose, with characters that are larger than life and sometimes more symbolic presences than familiar human beings. He mixed fact-laden accounts of whaling in Moby Dick *with phantasms of evil spirits and legendary sea creatures. And his lan-guage, too, is not the matter-of-fact, transparent prose we usually* find in the nineteenth-century novel. No American writer has ever commanded so gorgeous a rhetoric—by no means always under control—as has Melville. He could write a hard, efficient, gritty prose in the manner of Defoe, a prose making for swift narrative and a precise description of things. He could slip away into a prose of contemplative quiet, self-enclosed and musing, a silky murmuring of thought like the calm of a sea. And he could open up into a full-scale Elizabethan rhetoric, rich in simile and metaphor, exotic in reference, playful and witty in metaphysical conceit, sometimes grotesque in its leaps from factuality to exaltation, and, as in the great passage about the fast-fish and loose-fish in Moby Dick, reaching an orchestrated fullness of meaning and music.

It is impossible to grasp the greatness of Moby Dick except by reading it from the first page to the last. The two long stories of Melville that appear in this anthology represent him in a more somber mood than that which dominates his earlier work. "Bartleby the Scrivener" is a fable of suffering and alienation linking Melville to such twentieth-century writers as Kafka. Austere in language, detached in tone, it is nevertheless a story which emerges into an unspeakable pathos: it is hard to think of another fiction in our language that shows man in such final desolation and loss or which measures so utterly the cost and pain of the nay-sayer. "Benito Cereno" is a more complex but problematic piece of work, wonderfully wrought in its atmospheric effects, its accumulation of fear and horror. An innocent and guileful American, Captain Delano, is brought into a climax of relation with the evils and bestialities of Benito Cereno's ship: part of the effect depends on our ability to apprehend more quickly than Delano what it is that he encounters, but a larger share of the effect derives from the entanglement of cause and significance, the difficulty of assigning clear valuations to a complex human situation. Certain elements in the story, such as the role of the black slaves, have taken on a weight that Melville could not have anticipated; but its essential import is a subtle terror before the nature of men and their deeds.

FURTHER READING

The single best volume of Melville criticism, which also contains adequate biographical material, is Newton Arvin's *Herman Melville* (1950). Other useful studies include Charles Olson, *Call Me Ishmael* (1947); Richard Chase, *Herman Melville* (1949); R. W. B. Lewis, *The American Adam* (1955).

Letter to Nathaniel Hawthorne

Pittsfield, Wednesday morning.
[March [?], 1851]

My Dear Hawthorne,—

Concerning the young gentleman's shoes, I desire to say that a pair to fit him, of the desired pattern, cannot be had in all Pittsfield,—a fact which sadly impairs that metropolitan pride I formerly took in the capital of Berkshire. Henceforth Pittsfield must hide its head. However, if a pair of *bootees* will at all answer, Pittsfield will be very happy to provide them. Pray mention all this to Mrs. Hawthorne, and command me.

"The House of the Seven Gables: A Romance. By Nathaniel Hawthorne. One vol. 16mo, pp. 344." The contents of this book do not belie its rich, clustering, romantic title. With great enjoyment we spent almost an hour in each separate gable. This book is like a fine old chamber, abundantly, but still judiciously, furnished with precisely that sort of furniture best fitted to furnish it. There are rich hangings, wherein are braided scenes from tragedies! There is old china with rare devices, set out on the carved buffet; there are long and indolent lounges to throw yourself upon; there is an admirable side-board, plentifully stored with good viands; there is a smell as of old wine in the pantry; and finally, in one corner, there is a dark little black-letter volume in golden clasps, entitled "Hawthorne: A Problem." It has delighted us; it has piqued a reperusal; it has robbed us of a day, and made us a present of a whole year of thoughtfulness; it has bred great exhilaration and exultation with the remembrance that the architect of the Gables resides only six miles off, and not three thousand miles away, in England, say. We think the book, for pleasantness of running interest, surpasses the other works of the author. The curtains are more drawn; the sun comes in more; genialities peep out more. Were we to particularize what most struck us in the deeper passages, we would point out the scene where Clifford, for a moment, would fain throw himself forth from the window to join the procession; or the scene where the judge is left seated in his ancestral chair. Clifford is full of an awful truth throughout. He is conceived in the finest, truest spirit. He is no caricature. He is Clifford. And here we would say that, did circumstances permit, we should like nothing better than to devote an elaborate and careful paper to the full consideration and analysis of the purport and significance of what so strongly characterizes all of this author's writings. There is a certain tragic phase of humanity which, in our opinion, was never more powerfully embodied than by Hawthorne. We mean the tragedies of human thought in its own unbiased, native, and profounder workings. We think that into no recorded mind has the intense feeling of the usable truth ever entered more deeply than into this man's. By usable truth, we mean the apprehension of the absolute condition of present things as they strike the eye of the man who fears them not, though they do their worst to him,—the man who, like Russia or the British Empire, declares himself a sovereign nature (in himself) amid the powers of heaven, hell, and earth. He may perish; but so long as he exists he insists upon treating with all Powers upon an equal basis. If any of those other Powers choose to withhold certain secrets, let them; that does not impair my sovereignty in myself; that does not make me tributary. And perhaps, after all, there is *no* secret. We incline to think that the Problem of the Universe is like the Freemason's mighty secret, so terrible to all children. It turns out, at last, to consist in a triangle, a mallet, and an apron,— nothing more! We incline to think that God cannot explain His own secrets, and that He would like a little information upon certain points Himself. We mortals astonish Him as much as He us. But it is this *Being* of the matter; there lies the knot with which we choke ourselves. As soon as you say *Me,* a *God,* a *Nature,* so soon you jump off from your stool and hang from the beam. Yes, that word is the hangman. Take God out of the dictionary, and you would have Him in the street.

There is the grand truth about Nathaniel Hawthorne. He says No! in thunder; but the Devil himself cannot make him say *yes.* For all men who say *yes,* lie; and all men who say *no,*—why, they are in the happy condition of judicious, unincumbered travellers in Europe; they cross the frontiers into Eternity with nothing but a carpet-bag,—that is to say, the Ego. Whereas those *yes*-gentry, they travel with heaps of baggage, and, damn them! they will never get through the Custom House. What's the reason, Mr. Hawthorne, that in the last stages of metaphysics a fellow always falls to *swearing* so? I could rip an hour. You see, I began with a little criticism extracted for your benefit from the "Pittsfield Secret Review," and here I have landed in Africa.

Walk down one of these mornings and see me. No nonsense; come. Remember me to Mrs. Hawthorne and the children.

H. Melville.

P.S. The marriage of Phoebe with the daguerreotypist is a fine stroke, because of his turning out to be a *Maule.* If you pass Hepzibah's cent-shop, buy me a Jim Crow (fresh) and send it to be by Ned Higgins.

FROM *White-Jacket* (1850)

Chapter 33   A Flogging

If you begin the day with a laugh, you may, nevertheless, end it with a sob and a sigh.

Among the many who were exceedingly diverted with the scene between the Down Easter and the lieutenant, none laughed more heartily than John, Peter, Mark, and Antone—four sailors of the starboard watch. The same evening these four found themselves prisoners in the 'brig,' with a sentry standing over them. They were charged with violating a well-known law of the ship—having been engaged in one of those tangled, general fights sometimes occurring among sailors. They had nothing to anticipate but a flogging, at the captain's pleasure.

Toward evening of the next day, they were startled by the dread summons of the boatswain and his mates at the principal hatchway— a summons that ever sends a shudder through every manly heart in a frigate:

'*All hands witness punishment, ahoy!*'

The hoarseness of the cry, its unrelenting prolongation, its being caught up at different points, and sent through the lowermost depths of the ship; all this produces a most dismal effect upon every heart not calloused by long habituation to it.

However much you may desire to absent yourself from the scene that ensues, yet behold it you must; or, at least, stand near it you must; for the regulations enjoin the attendance of almost the entire ship's company, from the corpulent captain himself to the smallest boy who strikes the bell.

'*All hands witness punishment, ahoy!*'

To the sensitive seaman that summons sounds like a doom. He knows that the same law which impels it—the same law by which the culprits of the day must suffer; that by that very law he also is liable at any time to be judged and condemned. And the inevitableness of his own presence at the scene: the strong arm that drags him in view of the scourge, and holds him there till all is over: forcing upon his loathing eye and soul the sufferings and groans of men who have familiarly consorted with him, eaten with him, battled out watches with him— men of his own type and badge—all this conveys a terrible hint of the omnipotent authority under which he lives. Indeed, to such a man the naval summons to witness punishment carries a thrill, somewhat akin to what we may impute to the quick and the dead, when they shall hear the Last Trump, that is to bid them all arise in their ranks, and behold the final penalties inflicted upon the sinners of our race. . . .

Concerning the license with which many captains violate the express laws laid down by Congress for the government of the Navy, a glaring instance may be quoted. For upward of forty years there has been on the American Statute Book a law prohibiting a captain from inflicting, on his own authority, more than twelve lashes at one time, and for one offence. If more are to be given, the sentence must be passed by a court-martial. Yet, for nearly half a century, this law has been frequently, and with almost perfect impunity, set at naught: though of late, through the exertions of Bancroft and others, it has been much better observed than formerly; indeed, at the present day, it is generally respected. Still, while the *Neversink* was lying in a South American port, on the cruise now written of, the seamen belonging to another American frigate informed us that their captain sometimes inflicted, upon his own authority, eighteen and twenty lashes. It is worth while to state that this frigate was vastly admired by the shore ladies for her wonderfully neat appearance. One of her forecastle men told me that he had used up three jack-knives (charged to him on the books of the purser) in scraping the belaying-pins and the combings of the hatchways.

It is singular that while the lieutenants of the watch in American men-of-war so long usurped the power of inflicting corporal punishment with the colt, few or no similar abuses were known in the English Navy. And though the captain of an English armed ship is authorised to inflict, at his own discretion, *more* than a dozen lashes (I think three dozen), yet it is to be doubted whether, upon the whole, there is as much flogging at present in the English Navy as in the American. The chivalric Virginian, John Randolph of Roanoke, declared, in his place in Congress, that on board of the American man-of-war that carried him out Ambassador to Russia he had witnessed more flogging than had taken place on his own plantation of five hundred African slaves in ten years. Certain it is from what I have personally seen, that the English officers, as a general thing, seem to be less disliked by their crews than the American officers by theirs. The reason probably is, that many of them, from their station in life, have been more accustomed to social command; hence, quarter-deck authority sits more naturally on them. A coarse, vulgar man, who happens to rise to high naval rank by the exhibition of talents not incompatible with vulgarity, invariably proves a tyrant to his crew. It is a thing that American man-of-war's men have often observed, that the lieutenants from the Southern States, the descendants of the old Virginians, are much less severe, and much more gentle and gentlemanly in command, than the Northern officers, as a class.

According to the present laws and usages of the Navy, a seaman, for the most trivial alleged offences, of which he may be entirely innocent, must, without a trial, undergo a penalty the traces whereof he carries to the grave; for to a man-of-war's man's experienced eye the marks of a naval scourging with the 'cat' are through life discernible. And with these marks on his back, this image of his Creator must rise at the Last Day. Yet so untouchable is true dignity, that there are cases wherein to be flogged at the gangway is no dishonour; though, to abase and hurl down the last pride of some sailor who has piqued him, be sometimes the secret motive, with some malicious officer, in procuring him to be condemned to the lash. But this feeling of the innate dignity remaining untouched, though outwardly the body be scarred for the whole term of the natural life, is one of the hushed things, buried among the holiest privacies of the soul; a thing between a man's God and himself; and forever undiscernible by our fellow-men, who account *that* a degradation which seems so to the corporal eye. But what torments must that seaman undergo, who, while his back bleeds at the gangway, bleeds agonised drops of shame from his soul! Are we not justified in immeasurably denouncing this thing? Join hands with me, then; and, in the name of that Being in whose image the flogged sailor is made, let us demand of legislators, by what right they dare profane what God Himself accounts sacred.

Is it lawful for you to scourge a man that is a Roman? asks the intrepid Apostle, well knowing, as a Roman citizen, that it was not. And now, eighteen hundred years after, is it lawful for you, my countrymen, to scourge a man that is an American?—to scourge him round the world in your frigates?

It is to no purpose that you apologetically appeal to the general depravity of the man-of-war's man. Depravity in the oppressed is no apology for the oppressor; but rather an additional stigma to him, as being, in a large degree, the effect, and not the cause and justification of oppression.

Chapter 35   Flogging not Lawful

It is next to idle, at the present day, merely to denounce an iniquity. Be ours, then, a different task.

If there are any three things opposed to the genius of the American Constitution, they are these: irresponsibility in a judge, unlimited discretionary authority in an executive, and the union of an irresponsible judge and an unlimited executive in one person.

Yet by virtue of an enactment of Congress, all the commodores in the American Navy are obnoxious to these three charges, so far as concerns the punishment of the sailor for alleged misdemeanours not particularly set forth in the Articles of War.

Here is the enactment in question.

XXXII. *Of the Articles of War.*—'All crimes committed by persons belonging to the Navy, which are not specified in the foregoing articles, shall be punished according to the laws and customs in such cases at sea.'

This is the article that, above all others, puts the scourge into the hands of the captain, calls him to no account for its exercise, and furnishes him with an ample warrant for inflictions of cruelty upon the common sailor hardly credible to landsmen.

By this article the captain is made a legislator, as well as a judge and an executive. So far as it goes, it absolutely leaves to his discretion to decide what things shall be considered crimes, and what shall be the penalty; whether an accused person has been guilty of actions by him declared to be crimes; and how, when, and where the penalty shall be inflicted.

In the American Navy there is an everlasting suspension of the Habeas Corpus. Upon the bare allegation of misconduct, there is no law to restrain the captain from imprisoning a seaman, and keeping him confined at his pleasure. While I was in the *Neversink,* the captain of an American sloop of war, from undoubted motives of personal pique, kept a seaman confined in the brig for upward of a month.

Certainly the necessities of navies warrant a code for its government more stringent than the law that governs the land; but that code should conform to the spirit of the political institutions of the country that ordains it. It should not convert into slaves some of the citizens of a nation of freemen. Such objections cannot be urged against the laws of the Russian Navy (not essentially different from our own), because the laws of that Navy, creating the absolute one-man power in the captain, and vesting in him the authority to scourge, conform in spirit to the territorial laws of Russia, which is ruled by an autocrat, and whose courts inflict the *knout* upon the subjects of the land. But with us it is different. Our institutions claim to be based upon broad principles of political liberty and equality. Whereas, it would hardly affect one iota the condition on shipboard of an American man-of-war's man, were he transferred to the Russian Navy and made a subject of the Czar.

As a sailor, he shares none of our civil immunities; the law of our soil in no respect accompanies the national floating timbers grown thereon, and to which he clings as his home. For him our Revolution was in vain; to him our Declaration of Independence is a lie.

It is not sufficiently borne in mind, perhaps, that though the naval code comes under the head of the martial law, yet, in time of peace, and in the thousand questions arising between man and man on board ship, this code, to a certain extent, may not improperly be deemed municipal. With its crew of 800 or 1,000 men, a three-decker is a city on the sea. But in most of these matters between man and man, the captain, instead of being a magistrate, dispensing what the law promulgates, is an absolute ruler, making and unmaking law as he pleases.

It will be seen that the XXth of the Articles of War provides, that if any person in the Navy negligently perform the duties assigned him, he shall suffer such punishment as a court-martial shall adjudge; but if the offender be a private (common sailor), he may, at the discretion of the captain, be put in irons or flogged. It is needless to say, that in cases where an officer commits a trivial violation of this law, a court-martial is seldom or never called to sit upon his trial; but in the sailor's case he is at once condemned to the lash. Thus, one set of sea-citizens is exempted from a law that is hung in terror over others. What would landsmen think, were the State of New York to pass a law against some offence, affixing a fine as a penalty, and then add to that law a section restricting its penal operation to mechanics and day labourers, exempting all gentlemen with an income of one thousand dollars? Yet thus, in the spirit of its practical operation, even thus, stands a good part of the naval laws wherein naval flogging is involved.

But a law should be 'universal,' and include in its possible penal operations the very judge himself who gives decisions upon it; nay, the very judge who expounds it. Had Sir William Blackstone violated the laws of England, he would have been brought before the bar over which he had presided, and would there have been tried, with the counsel for the Crown reading to him, perhaps, from a copy of his own *Commentaries*. And should he have been found guilty, he would have suffered like the meanest subject, 'according to law.'

How is it in an American frigate? Let one example suffice. By the Articles of War, and especially by Article I., an American captain may, and frequently does, inflict a severe and degrading punishment upon a sailor, while he himself is forever removed from the possibility of undergoing the like disgrace; and, in all probability, from undergoing any punishment whatever, even if guilty of the same thing—contention with his equals, for instance—for which he punishes another. Yet both sailor and captain are American citizens.

Now, in the language of Blackstone, again, there is a law, 'coeval with mankind, dictated by God Himself, superior in obligation to any other, and no human laws are of any validity if contrary to this.' That law is the Law of Nature; among the three great principles of which Justinian includes 'that to every man should be rendered his due.' But we have seen that the laws involving flogging in the Navy do *not* render to every man his due, since in some cases they indirectly exclude the officers from any punishment whatever, and in all cases protect them from the scourge, which is inflicted upon the sailor. Therefore, according to Blackstone and Justinian, those laws have no binding force; and every American man-of-war's man would be morally justified in resisting the scourge to the uttermost; and, in so resisting, would be religiously justified in what would be judicially styled 'the act of mutiny' itself.

If, then, these scourging laws be for any reason necessary, make them binding upon all who of right come under their sway; and let us see an honest commodore, duly authorised by Congress, condemning to the lash a transgressing captain by the side of a transgressing sailor.

And if the commodore himself prove a transgressor, let us see one of his brother commodores take up the lash against *him,* even as the boatswain's mates, the navy executioners, are often called upon to scourge each other.

Or will you say that a Navy officer is a man, but that an American-born citizen, whose grandsire may have ennobled him by pouring out his blood at Bunker Hill—will you say that, by entering the service of his country as a common seaman, and standing ready to fight her foes, he thereby loses his manhood at the very time he most asserts it? Will you say that, by so doing, he degrades himself to the liability of the scourge, but if he tarries ashore in time of danger, he is safe from that indignity? All our linked states, all four continents of mankind, unite in denouncing such a thought.

We plant the question, then, on the topmost argument of all. Irrespective of incidental considerations, we assert that flogging in the Navy is opposed to the essential dignity of man, which no legislator has a right to violate; that it is oppressive, and glaringly unequal in its operations; that it is utterly repugnant to the spirit of our democratic institutions; indeed, that it involves a lingering trait of the worst times of a barbarous feudal aristocracy; in a word, we denounce it as religiously, morally, and immutably *wrong.*

No matter, then, what may be the consequences of its abolition; no matter if we have to dismantle our fleets, and our unprotected commerce should fall a prey to the spoiler; the awful admonitions of justice and humanity demand that abolition without procrastination; in a voice that is not to be mistaken, demand that abolition to-day. It is not a dollar-and-cent question of expediency; it is a matter of *right and wrong.* And if any man can lay his hand on his heart, and solemnly say that this scourging is right, let that man but once feel the lash on his own back, and in his agony you will hear the apostate call the seven heavens to witness that it is *wrong.* And, in the name of immortal manhood, would to God that every man who upholds this thing were scourged at the gangway till he recanted.

Bartleby the Scrivener *(1853)*

A Story of Wall Street

I am a rather elderly man. The nature of my avocations for the last thirty years has brought me into more than ordinary contact with what would seem an interesting and somewhat singular set of men, of whom as yet nothing that I know of has ever been written:—I mean the law-copyists or scriveners. I have known very many of them, professionally and privately, and if I pleased, could relate divers histories, at which good-natured gentlemen might smile, and sentimental souls might weep. But I waive the biographies of all other scriveners for a few passages in the life of Bartleby, who was a scrivener the strangest I ever saw or heard of. While of other law-copyists I might write the complete life, of Bartleby nothing of that sort can be done. I believe that no materials exist for a full and satisfactory biography of this man. It is an irreparable loss to literature. Bartleby was one of those beings of whom nothing is ascertainable, except from the original sources, and in his case those are very small. What my own astonished eyes saw of Bartleby, *that* is all I know of him, except, indeed, one vague report which will appear in the sequel.

Ere introducing the scrivener, as he first appeared to me, it is fit I make some mention of myself, my *employés*, my business, my chambers, and general surroundings; because some such description is indispensable to an adequate understanding of the chief character about to be presented.

Imprimis: I am a man who, from his youth upward, has been filled with a profound conviction that the easiest way of life is the best. Hence, though I belong to a profession proverbially energetic and nervous, even to turbulence, at times, yet nothing of that sort have I ever suffered to invade my peace. I am one of those unambitious lawyers who never addresses a jury, or in any way draws down public applause; but in the cool tranquillity of a snug retreat, do a snug business among rich men's bonds and mortgages and title-deeds. All who know me, consider me an eminently *safe* man. The late John Jacob Astor, a personage little given to poetic enthusiasm, had no hesitation in pronouncing my first grand point to be prudence; my next, method. I do not speak it in vanity, but simply record the fact, that I was not unemployed in my profession by the late John Jacob Astor; a name which, I admit, I love to repeat, for it hath a rounded and orbicular sound to it, and rings like unto bullion. I will freely add, that I was not insensible to the late John Jacob Astor's good opinion.

Some time prior to the period at which this little history begins, my avocations had been largely increased. The good old office, now extinct in the State of New York, of a Master in Chancery, had been conferred upon me. It was not a very arduous office, but very pleasantly remunerative. I seldom lose my temper; much more seldom indulge in dangerous indignation at wrongs and outrages; but I must be permitted to be rash here and declare, that I consider the sudden and violent abrogation of the office of Master in Chancery, by the new Constitution, as a —— premature act; inasmuch as I had counted upon a life-lease of the profits, whereas I only received those of a few short years. But this is by the way.

My chambers were upstairs at No. —— Wall Street. At one end they looked upon the white wall of the interior of a spacious sky-light shaft, penetrating the building from top to bottom. This view might

have been considered rather tame than otherwise, deficient in what
landscape painters call "life." But if so, the view from the other end
of my chambers offered, at least, a contrast, if nothing more. In that
direction my windows commanded an unobstructed view of a lofty
brick wall, black by age and everlasting shade; which wall required
no spy-glass to bring out its lurking beauties, but for the benefit of all
near-sighted spectators, was pushed up to within ten feet of my
window panes. Owing to the great height of the surrounding buildings,
and my chambers being on the second floor, the interval between this
wall and mine not a little resembled a huge square cistern.

At the period just preceding the advent of Bartleby, I had two persons as copyists in my employment, and a promising lad as an office-
boy. First, Turkey; second, Nippers; third, Ginger Nut. These may seem
names, the like of which are not usually found in the Directory. In
truth they were nicknames, mutually conferred upon each other by my
three clerks, and were deemed expressive of their respective persons
or characters. Turkey was a short, pursy Englishman of about my own
age, that is, somewhere not far from sixty. In the morning, one might
say, his face was of a fine florid hue, but after twelve o'clock,
meridian—his dinner hour—it blazed like a grate full of Christmas
coals; and continued blazing—but, as it were, with a gradual wane—
till 6 o'clock P.M. or thereabouts, after which I saw no more of the
proprietor of the face, which, gaining its meridian with the sun,
seemed to set with it, to rise, culminate, and decline the following day,
with the like regularity and undiminished glory. There are many
singular coincidences I have known in the course of my life, not the
least among which was the fact, that exactly when Turkey displayed
his fullest beams from his red and radiant countenance, just then,
too, at that critical moment, began the daily period when I considered
his business capacities as seriously disturbed for the remainder of
the twenty-four hours. Not that he was absolutely idle, or averse to
business then; far from it. The difficulty was, he was apt to be altogether too energetic. There was a strange, inflamed, flurried, flighty
recklessness of activity about him. He would be incautious in dipping
his pen into his inkstand. All his blots upon my documents, were
dropped there after twelve o'clock, meridian. Indeed, not only would
he be reckless and sadly given to making blots in the afternoon, but
some days he went further, and was rather noisy. At such times,
too, his face flamed with augmented blazonry, as if cannel coal
had been heaped on anthracite. He made an unpleasant racket with
his chair; spilled his sand-box; in mending his pens, impatiently
split them all to pieces, and threw them on the floor in a sudden
passion; stood up and leaned over his table, boxing his papers about
in a most indecorous manner, very sad to behold in an elderly man
like him. Nevertheless, as he was in many ways a most valuable
person to me, and all the time before twelve o'clock, meridian, was

the quickest, steadiest creature, too, accomplishing a great deal of work in a style not easy to be matched—for these reasons, I was willing to overlook his eccentricities, though indeed, occasionally, I remonstrated with him. I did this very gently, however, because, though the civilest, nay, the blandest and most reverential of men in the morning, yet in the afternoon he was disposed, upon provocation, to be slightly rash with his tongue, in fact, insolent. Now, valuing his morning services as I did, and resolving not to lose them— yet, at the same time, made uncomfortable by his inflamed ways after twelve o'clock; and being a man of peace, unwilling by my admonitions to call forth unseemly retorts from him—I took upon me, one Saturday noon (he was always worse on Saturdays), to hint to him, very kindly, that perhaps now that he was growing old, it might be well to abridge his labours; in short, he need not come to my chambers after twelve o'clock, but, dinner over, had best go home to his lodgings and rest himself till tea-time. But no; he insisted upon his afternoon devotions. His countenance became intolerably fervid, as he oratorically assured me—gesticulating, with a long ruler, at the other side of the room—that if his services in the morning were useful, how indispensable, then, in the afternoon?

"With submission, sir," said Turkey on this occasion, "I consider myself your right-hand man. In the morning I but marshal and deploy my columns; but in the afternoon I put myself at their head, and gallantly charge the foe, thus!"—and he made a violent thrust with the ruler.

"But the blots, Turkey," intimated I.

"True,—but, with submission, sir, behold these hairs! I am getting old. Surely, sir, a blot or two of a warm afternoon is not to be severely urged against grey hairs. Old age—even if it blot the page—is honourable. With submission, sir, we *both* are getting old."

This appeal to my fellow-feeling was hardly to be resisted. At all events, I saw that go he would not. So I made up my mind to let him stay, resolving, nevertheless, to see to it, that during the afternoon he had to do with my less important papers.

Nippers, the second on my list, was a whiskered, sallow, and, upon the whole, rather piratical-looking young man of about five and twenty. I always deemed him the victim of two evil powers— ambition and indigestion. The ambition was evidenced by a certain impatient of the duties of a mere copyist—an unwarrantable usurpation of strictly professional affairs, such as the original drawing up of legal documents. The indigestion seemed betokened in an occasional nervous testiness and grinning irritability, causing the teeth to audibly grind together over mistakes committed in copying; unnecessary maledictions, hissed, rather than spoken, in the heat of business; and especially by a continual discontent with the height of the table where he worked. Though of a very ingenious mechanical turn, Nippers could never get this table to suit him. He put chips under it, blocks of various sorts, bits of pasteboard, and at last went so far as to attempt an exquisite adjustment by final pieces of folded blotting-paper. But no invention would answer. If, for the sake of easing his back, he brought the table lid at a sharp angle well up toward his chin, and wrote there like a man using the steep roof of a Dutch house for his desk—then he declared that it stopped the circulation in his arms. If now he lowered the table to his waist-bands, and stooped over it in writing, then there was a sore aching in his back. In short, the truth of the matter was, Nippers knew not what he wanted. Or, if he wanted anything, it was to be rid of a scrivener's table altogether. Among the manifestations of his diseased ambition was a fondness he had for receiving visits from certain ambiguous-looking fellows in seedy coats, whom he called his clients. Indeed I was aware that not only was he, at times, considerable of a ward-politician, but he occasionally did a little business at the Justices' courts, and was not unknown on the steps of the Tombs. I have good reason to believe, however, that one individual who called upon him at my chambers, and who, with a grand air, he insisted was his client, was no other than a dun, and the alleged title-deed, a bill. But with all his failings, and the annoyances he caused me, Nippers, like his compatriot Turkey, was a very useful man to me; wrote a neat, swift hand; and, when he chose, was not deficient in a gentle-manly sort of deportment. Added to this, he always dressed in a gentlemanly sort of way; and so, incidentally, reflected credit upon my chambers. Whereas with respect to Turkey, I had much ado to keep him from being a reproach to me. His clothes were apt to look oily and smell of eating-houses. He wore his pantaloons very loose and baggy in summer. His coats were execrable; his hat not to be handled. But while the hat was a thing of indifference to me, inasmuch as his natural civility and deference, as a dependent Englishman, always led him to doff it the moment he entered the room, yet his coat was another matter. Concerning his coats, I reasoned with him; but with no effect. The truth was, I suppose, that a man with so small an income, could not afford to sport such a lustrous face and a lustrous coat at one and the same time. As Nippers once observed, Turkey's money went chiefly for red ink. One winter day I presented Turkey with a highly-respectable looking coat of my own, a padded grey coat, of a most comfortable warmth, and which buttoned straight up from the knee to the neck. I thought Turkey would appreciate the favour, and abate his rashness and obstreperousness of after-noons. But no. I verily believe that buttoning himself up in so downy and blanket-like a coat had a pernicious effect upon him; upon the same principle that too much oats are bad for horses. In fact, precisely as a rash, restive horse is said to feel his oats, so Turkey felt his coat. It made him insolent. He was a man whom prosperity harmed.

Though concerning the self-indulgent habits of Turkey I had my own private surmises, yet touching Nippers I was well persuaded that whatever might be his faults in other respects, he was, at least, a temperate young man. But, indeed, nature herself seemed to have been his vintner, and at his birth charged him so thoroughly with an irritable, brandy-like disposition, that all subsequent potations were needless. When I consider how, amid the stillness of my chambers, Nippers would sometimes impatiently rise from his seat, and stooping over his table, spread his arms wide apart, seize the whole desk, and move it, and jerk it, with a grim, grinding motion on the floor, as if the table were a perverse voluntary agent, intent on thwarting and vexing him; I plainly perceive that for Nippers, brandy and water were altogether superfluous.

It was fortunate for me that, owing to its peculiar cause—indigestion—the irritability and consequent nervousness of Nippers, were mainly observable in the morning, while in the afternoon he was comparatively mild. So that Turkey's paroxysms only coming on about twelve o'clock, I never had to do with their eccentricities at one time. Their fits relieved each other like guards. When Nipper's was on, Turkey's was off; and *vice versa*. This was a good natural arrangement under the circumstances.

Ginger Nut, the third on my list, was a lad some twelve years old. His father was a carman, ambitious of seeing his son on the bench instead of a cart, before he died. So he sent him to my office as student at law, errand boy, and cleaner and sweeper, at the rate of one dollar a week. He had a little desk to himself, but he did not use it much. Upon inspection, the drawer exhibited a great array of the shells of various sorts of nuts. Indeed, to this quick-witted youth the whole noble science of the law was contained in a nut-shell. Not the least among the employments of Ginger Nut, as well as one which he discharged with the most alacrity, was his duty as cake and apple purveyor for Turkey and Nippers. Copying law papers being proverbially a dry, husky sort of business, my two scriveners were fain to moisten their mouths very often with Spitzenbergs [1] to be had at the numerous stalls nigh the Custom House and Post Office. Also, they sent Ginger Nut very frequently for that peculiar cake—small, flat, round, and very spicy—after which he had been named by them. Of a cold morning, when business was but dull, Turkey would gobble up scores of these cakes, as if they were mere wafers—indeed they sell them at the rate of six or eight for a penny—the scrape of his pen blending with the crunching of the crisp particles in his mouth. Of all the fiery afternoon blunders and flurried rashness of Turkey, was his once moistening a ginger-cake between his lips, and clapping

[1] A variety of apple.

it on to a mortgage for a seal. I came within an ace of dismissing him then. But he mollified me by making an oriental bow and saying— "With submission, sir, it was generous of me to find you in stationary on my own account."

Now my original business—that of a conveyancer and title hunter, and drawer-up of recondite documents of all sorts—was considerably increased by receiving the master's office. There was now great work for scriveners. Not only must I push the clerks already with me, but I must have additional help. In answer to my advertisement, a motionless young man one morning stood upon my office threshold, the door being open, for it was summer. I can see that figure now—pallidly neat, pitiably respectable, incurably forlorn! It was Bartleby.

After a few words touching his qualifications, I engaged him, glad to have among my corps of copyists a man of so singularly sedate an aspect, which I thought might operate beneficially upon the flighty temper of Turkey, and the fiery one of Nippers.

I should have stated before that ground glass folding-doors divided my premises into two parts, one of which was occupied by my scriveners, the other by myself. According to my humour I threw open these doors, or closed them. I resolved to assign Bartleby a corner by the folding-doors, but on my side of them, so as to have this quiet man within easy call, in case any trifling thing was to be done. I placed his desk close up to a small side-window in that part of the room, a window which originally had afforded a lateral view of certain grimy back-yards and bricks, but which, owing to subsequent erections, commanded at present no view at all, though it gave some light. Within three feet of the panes was a wall, and the light came down from far above, between two lofty buildings, as from a very small opening in a dome. Still further to a satisfactory arrangement, I procured a high green folding screen, which might entirely isolate Bartleby from my sight, though not remove him from my voice. And thus, in a manner, privacy and society were conjoined.

At first Bartleby did an extraordinary quantity of writing. As if long famishing for something to copy, he seemed to gorge himself on my documents. There was no pause for digestion. He ran a day and night line, copying by sun-light and by candle-light. I should have been quite delighted with his application, had he been cheerfully industrious. But he wrote on silently, palely, mechanically.

It is, of course, an indispensable part of a scrivener's business to verify the accuracy of his copy, word by word. Where there are two or more scriveners in an office, they assist each other in this examination, one reading from the copy, the other holding the original. It is a very dull, wearisome, and lethargic affair. I can readily imagine that to some sanguine temperaments it would be altogether intolerable.

For example, I cannot credit that the mettlesome poet Byron would have contentedly sat down with Bartleby to examine a law document of, say five hundred pages, closely written in a crimpy hand.

Now and then, in the haste of business, it had been my habit to assist in comparing some brief document myself, calling Turkey or Nippers for this purpose. One object I had in placing Bartleby so handy to me behind the screen, was to avail myself of his services on such trivial occasions. It was on the third day, I think, of his being with me, and before any necessity had arisen for having his own writing examined, that, being much hurried to complete a small affair I had in hand, I abruptly called to Bartleby. In my haste and natural expectancy of instant compliance, I sat with my head bent over the original on my desk, and my right hand sideways, and somewhat nervously extended with the copy, so that immediately upon emerging from his retreat, Bartleby might snatch it and proceed to business without the least delay.

In this very attitude did I sit when I called to him, rapidly stating what it was I wanted him to do—namely, to examine a small paper with me. Imagine my surprise, nay, my consternation, when without moving from his privacy, Bartleby in a singularly mild, firm voice, replied, "I would prefer not to."

I sat awhile in perfect silence, rallying my stunned faculties. Immediately it occurred to me that my ears had deceived me, or Bartleby had entirely misunderstood my meaning. I repeated my request in the clearest tone I could assume. But in quite as clear a one came the previous reply, "I would prefer not to."

"Prefer not to," echoed I, rising in high excitement, and crossing the room with a stride. "What do you mean? Are you moon-struck? I want you to help me compare this sheet here—take it," and I thrust it toward him.

"I would prefer not to," said he.

I looked at him steadfastly. His face was leanly composed; his grey eye dimly calm. Not a wrinkle of agitation rippled him. Had there been the least uneasiness, anger, impatience or impertinence in his manner; in other words, had there been anything ordinarily human about him; doubtless I should have violently dismissed him from the premises. But as it was, I should have as soon thought of turning my pale plaster-of-paris bust of Cicero out of doors. I stood gazing at him awhile, as he went on with his own writing, and then reseated myself at my desk. This is very strange, thought I. What had one best do? But my business hurried me. I concluded to forget the matter for the present, preserving it for my future leisure. So calling Nippers from the other room, the paper was speedily examined.

A few days after this, Bartleby concluded four lengthy documents, being quadruplicates of a week's testimony taken before me in my High

Court of Chancery. It became necessary to examine them. It was an important suit, and great accuracy was imperative. Having all things arranged, I called Turkey, Nippers and Ginger Nut from the next room, meaning to place the four copies in the hands of my four clerks, while I should read from the original. Accordingly Turkey, Nippers and Ginger Nut had taken their seats in a row, each with his document in hand, when I called to Bartleby to join this interesting group.

"Bartleby! quick, I am waiting."

I heard a slow scrape of his chair legs on the uncarpeted floor, and soon he appeared standing at the entrance of his hermitage.

"What is wanted?" said he mildly.

"The copies, the copies," said I hurriedly. "We are going to examine them. There"—and I held toward him the fourth quadruplicate.

"I would prefer not to," he said, and gently disappeared behind the screen.

For a few moments I was turned into a pillar of salt, standing at the head of my seated column of clerks. Recovering myself, I advanced toward the screen, and demanded the reason for such extraordinary conduct.

"*Why* do you refuse?"

"I would prefer not to."

With any other man I should have flown outright into a dreadful passion, scorned all further words, and thrust him ignominiously from my presence. But there was something about Bartleby that not only strangely disarmed me, but in a wonderful manner touched and disconcerted me. I began to reason with him.

"These are your own copies we are about to examine. It is labour saving to you, because one examination will answer for your four papers. It is common usage. Every copyist is bound to help examine his copy. Is it not so? Will you not speak? Answer!"

"I prefer not to," he replied in a flute-like tone. It seemed to me that while I had been addressing him, he carefully revolved every statement that I made; fully comprehended the meaning; could not gainsay the irresistible conclusion; but, at the same time, some paramount consideration prevailed with him to reply as he did.

"You are decided, then, not to comply with my request—a request made according to common usage and common sense?"

He briefly gave me to understand that on that point my judgment was sound. Yes: his decision was irreversible.

It is not seldom the case that when a man is browbeaten in some unprecedented and violently unreasonable way, he begins to stagger in his own plainest faith. He begins, as it were, vaguely to surmise that, wonderful as it may be, all the justice and all the reason are on the other side. Accordingly, if any disinterested persons are present, he turns to them for some reinforcement for his own faltering mind.

"Turkey," said I, "what do you think of this? Am I not right?"

"With submission, sir," said Turkey, with his blandest tone, "I think that you are."

"Nippers," said I, "what do *you* think of it?"

"I think I should kick him out of the office."

(The reader of nice perceptions will here perceive that, it being morning, Turkey's answer is couched in polite and tranquil terms but Nipper's reply in ill-tempered ones. Or, to repeat a previous sentence, Nipper's ugly mood was on duty, and Turkey's off.)

"Ginger Nut," said I, willing to enlist the smallest suffrage in my behalf, "what do *you* think of it?"

"I think, sir, he's a little *luny*," replied Ginger Nut, with a grin.

"You hear what they say," said I, turning towards the screen, "come forth and do your duty."

But he vouchsafed no reply. I pondered a moment in sore perplexity. But once more business hurried me. I determined again to postpone the consideration of this dilemma to my future leisure. With a little trouble we made out to examine the papers without Bartleby, though at every page or two, Turkey deferentially dropped his opinion that this proceeding was quite out of the common; while Nippers, twitching in his chair with a dyspeptic nervousness, ground out between his set teeth occasional hissing maledictions against the stubborn oaf behind the screen. And for his (Nipper's) part, this was the first and the last time he would do another man's business without pay.

Meanwhile Bartleby sat in his hermitage, oblivious to everything but his own peculiar business there.

Some days passed, the scrivener being employed upon another lengthy work. His late remarkable conduct led me to regard his ways narrowly. I observed that he never went to dinner; indeed that he never went any where. As yet I had never of my personal knowledge known him to be outside of my office. He was a perpetual sentry in the corner. At about eleven o'clock though, in the morning, I noticed that Ginger Nut would advance towards the opening in Bartleby's screen, as if silently beckoned thither by a gesture invisible to me where I sat. The boy would then leave the office jingling a few pence, and reappear with a handful of ginger-nuts which he delivered in the hermitage, receiving two of the cakes for his trouble.

He lives, then, on ginger-nuts, thought I; never eats a dinner, properly speaking; he must be a vegetarian then; but no; he never eats even vegetables, he eats nothing but ginger-nuts. My mind then ran on in reveries concerning the probable effects upon the human constitution of living entirely on ginger-nuts. Ginger-nuts are so called because they contain ginger as one of their peculiar constituents, and the final flavouring one. Now what was ginger? A hot, spicy thing.

Was Bartleby hot and spicy? Not at all. Ginger, then, had no effect upon Bartleby. Probably he preferred it should have none.

Nothing so aggravates an earnest person as a passive resistance. If the individual so resisted be of a not inhumane temper, and the resisting one perfectly harmless in his passivity; then, in the better moods of the former, he will endeavour charitably to construe to his imagination what proves impossible to be solved by his judgment. Even so, for the most part, I regarded Bartleby and his ways. Poor fellow! thought I, he means no mischief; it is plain he intends no insolence; his aspect sufficiently evinces that his eccentricities are involuntary. He is useful to me. I can get along with him. If I turn him away, the chances are he will fall in with some less indulgent employer, and then he will be rudely treated, and perhaps driven forth miserably to starve. Yes. Here I can cheaply purchase a delicious self-approval. To befriend Bartleby; to humour him in his strange wilfulness, will cost me little or nothing, while I lay up in my soul what will eventually prove a sweet morsel for my conscience. But this mood was not invariable with me. The passiveness of Bartleby sometimes irritated me. I felt strangely goaded on to encounter him in new oppo-sition, to elicit some angry spark from him answerable to my own. But indeed I might as well have essayed to strike fire with my knuckles against a bit of Windsor soap. But one afternoon the evil impulse in me mastered me, and the following little scene ensued:

"Bartleby," said I, "when those papers are all copied, I will compare them with you."

"I would prefer not to."

"How? Surely you do not mean to persist in that mulish vagary?"

No answer.

I threw open the folding-doors near by, and turning upon Turkey and Nippers, exclaimed in an excited manner:

"He says, a second time, he won't examine his papers. What do you think of it, Turkey?"

It was afternoon, be it remembered. Turkey sat glowing like a brass boiler, his bald head steaming, his hands reeling among his blotted papers.

"Think of it?" roared Turkey; "I think I'll just step behind his screen, and black his eyes for him!"

So saying, Turkey rose to his feet and threw his arms into a pugilistic position. He was hurrying away to make good his promise, when I detained him, alarmed at the effect of incautiously rousing Turkey's combativeness after dinner.

"Sit down, Turkey," said I, "and hear what Nippers has to say. What do you think of it, Nippers? Would I not be justified in immedi-ately dismissing Bartleby?"

"Excuse me, that is for you to decide, sir. I think his conduct quite unusual, and indeed unjust, as regards Turkey and myself. But it may only be a passing whim."

"Ah," exclaimed I, "you have strangely changed your mind then— you speak very gently of him now."

"All beer," cried Turkey; "gentleness is effects of beer—Nippers and I dined together to-day. You see how gentle *I* am, sir. Shall I go and black his eyes?"

"You refer to Bartleby, I suppose. No, not to-day, Turkey," I replied; "pray, put up your fists."

I closed the doors, and again advanced towards Bartleby. I felt additional incentives tempting me to my fate. I burned to be rebelled against again. I remembered that Bartleby never left the office.

"Bartleby," said I, "Ginger Nut is away; just step round to the Post Office, won't you? (it was but a three minutes' walk), and see if there is anything for me."

"I would prefer not to."

"You *will* not?"

"I *prefer* not."

I staggered to my desk, and sat there in a deep study. My blind inveteracy returned. Was there any other thing in which I could procure myself to be ignominiously repulsed by this lean, penniless wight?—my hired clerk? What added thing is there, perfectly reasonable, that he will be sure to refuse to do?

"Bartleby!"

No answer.

"Bartleby," in a louder tone.

No answer.

"Bartleby," I roared.

Like a very ghost, agreeably to the laws of magical invocation, at the third summons, he appeared at the entrance of his hermitage.

"Go to the next room, and tell Nippers to come to me."

"I prefer not to," he respectfully and slowly said, and mildly disappeared.

"Very good, Bartleby," said I, in a quiet sort of serenely severe self-possessed tone, intimating the unalterable purpose of some terrible retribution very close at hand. At the moment I half intended something of the kind. But upon the whole, as it was drawing towards my dinner-hour, I thought it best to put on my hat and walk home for the day, suffering much from perplexity and distress of mind.

Shall I acknowledge it? The conclusion of this whole business was, that it soon became a fixed fact of my chambers, that a pale young scrivener, by the name of Bartleby, had a desk there; that he copied for me at the usual rate of four cents a folio (one hundred words); but he was permanently exempt from examining the work done by him, that duty being transferred to Turkey and Nippers, out of compliment doubtless to their superior acuteness; moreover, said Bartleby was never on any account to be despatched on the most trivial errand of any sort; and that even if entreated to take upon him such a matter, it was generally understood that he would prefer not to—in other words, that he would refuse point-blank.

As days passed on, I became considerably reconciled to Bartleby. His steadiness, his freedom from all dissipation, his incessant industry (except when he chose to throw himself into a standing revery behind his screen), his great stillness, his unalterableness of demeanour under all circumstances, made him a valuable acquisition. One prime thing was this,—*he was always there;*—first in the morning, continually through the day, and the last at night. I had a singular confidence in his honesty. I felt my most precious papers perfectly safe in his hands. Sometimes to be sure I could not, for the very soul of me, avoid falling into sudden spasmodic passions with him. For it was exceeding difficult to bear in mind all the time those strange peculiarities, privileges, and unheard of exemptions, forming the tacit stipulations on Bartleby's part under which he remained in my office. Now and then, in the eagerness of despatching pressing business, I would inadvertently summon Bartleby, in a short, rapid tone, to put his finger, say, on the incipient tie of a bit of red tape with which I was about compressing some papers. Of course, from behind the screen the usual answer, "I prefer not to," was sure to come; and then, how could a human creature with the common infirmities of our nature, refrain from bitterly exclaiming upon such perverseness—such unreasonableness. However, every added repulse of this sort which I received only tended to lessen the probability of my repeating the inadvertence.

Here it must be said, that according to the custom of most legal gentlemen occupying chambers in densely-populated law buildings, there were several keys to my door. One was kept by a woman residing in the attic, which person weekly scrubbed and daily swept and dusted my apartments. Another was kept by Turkey for convenience' sake. The third I sometimes carried in my own pocket. The fourth I knew not who had.

Now, one Sunday morning I happened to go to Trinity Church, to hear a celebrated preacher, and finding myself rather early on the ground, I thought I would walk round to my chambers for awhile. Luckily I had my key with me; but upon applying it to the lock, I found it resisted by something inserted from the inside. Quite surprised, I called out; when to my consternation a key was turned from within; and thrusting his lean visage at me, and holding the door ajar, the apparition of Bartleby appeared, in his shirt sleeves, and otherwise in a strangely tattered dishabille, saying quietly that he was sorry, but he was deeply engaged just then, and—preferred not admitting me at present. In a brief word or two, he moreover added, that perhaps I had better walk round the block two or three times, and by that time he would probably have concluded his affairs.

Now, the utterly unsurmised appearance of Bartleby, tenanting my law-chambers on a Sunday morning, with his cadaverously gentle-manly *nonchalance,* yet withal firm and self-possessed, had such a strange effect upon me, that incontinently I slunk away from my own door, and did as desired. But not without sundry twinges of impotent rebellion against the mild effrontery of this unaccountable scrivener. Indeed, it was his wonderful mildness chiefly, which not only disarmed me, but unmanned me, as it were. For I consider that one, for the time, is in a way unmanned when he tranquilly permits his hired clerk to dictate to him, and order him away from his own premises. Further-more, I was full of uneasiness as to what Bartleby could possibly be doing in my office in his shirt sleeves, and in an otherwise dismantled condition of a Sunday morning. Was anything amiss going on? Nay, that was out of the question. It was not to be thought of for a moment that Bartleby was an immoral person. But what could he be doing there—copying? Nay again, whatever might be his eccentricities, Bartleby was an eminently decorous person. He would be the last man to sit down to his desk in any state approaching to nudity. Besides, it was Sunday; and there was something about Bartleby that forbade the supposition that he would by any secular occupation violate the proprieties of the day.

Nevertheless, my mind was not pacified; and full of a restless curiosity, at last I returned to the door. Without hindrance I inserted my key, opened it, and entered. Bartleby was not to be seen. I looked round anxiously, peeped behind his screen; but it was very plain that he was gone. Upon more closely examining the place, I surmised that for an indefinite period Bartleby must have ate, dressed, and slept in my office, and that too without plate, mirror, or bed. The cushioned seat of a rickety old sofa in one corner bore the faint impress of a lean, reclining form. Rolled away under his desk, I found a blanket; under the empty grate, a blacking box and brush; on a chair, a tin basin, with soap and a ragged towel; in a newspaper a few crumbs of ginger-nuts and a morsel of cheese. Yes, thought I, it is evident enough that Bartleby has been making his home here, keeping bache-lor's hall all by himself. Immediately then the thought came sweeping across me, What miserable friendlessness and loneliness are here revealed! His poverty is great; but his solitude, how horrible! Think of it. Of a Sunday, Wall Street is deserted as Petra; [2] and every night of every day it is an emptiness. This building too, which of week-days hums with industry and life, at nightfall echoes with sheer vacancy,

[2] Ancient ruined city in Palestine.

and all through Sunday is forlorn. And here Bartleby makes his home; sole spectator of a solitude which he has seen all populous—a sort of innocent and transformed Marius [3] brooding among the ruins of Carthage!

For the first time in my life a feeling of overpowering stinging melancholy seized me. Before, I had never experienced aught but a non-unpleasing sadness. The bond of a common humanity now drew me irresistibly to gloom. A fraternal melancholy! For both I and Bartleby were sons of Adam. I remembered the bright silks and sparkling faces I had seen that day, in gala trim, swan-like sailing down the Mississippi of Broadway; and I contrasted them with the pallid copyist, and thought to myself, Ah, happiness courts the light, so we deem the world is gay; but misery hides aloof, so we deem that misery there is none. These sad fancyings—chimeras, doubtless, of a sick and silly brain—led on to other and more special thoughts, concerning the eccentricities of Bartleby. Presentiments of strange discoveries hovered round me. The scrivener's pale form appeared to me laid out, among uncaring strangers, in its shivering winding sheet.

Suddenly I was attracted by Bartleby's closed desk, the key in open sight left in the lock.

I mean no mischief, seek the gratification of no heartless curiosity, thought I; besides, the desk is mine, and its contents, too, so I will make bold to look within. Everything was methodically arranged, the papers smoothly placed. The pigeon holes were deep, and, removing the files of documents, I groped into their recesses. Presently I felt something there, and dragged it out. It was an old bandana handkerchief, heavy and knotted. I opened it, and saw it was a savings' bank. I now recalled all the quiet mysteries which I had noted in the man. I remembered that he never spoke but to answer; that though at intervals he had considerable time to himself, yet I had never seen him reading—no, not even a newspaper; that for long periods he would stand looking out, at his pale window behind the screen, upon the dead brick wall; I was quite sure he never visited any refectory or eating-house; while his pale face clearly indicated that he never drank beer like Turkey, or tea and coffee even, like other men; that he never went anywhere in particular that I could learn; never went out for a walk, unless indeed that was the case at present; that he had declined telling who he was, or whence he came, or whether he had any relatives in the world; that though so thin and pale, he never complained of ill health. And more than all, I remembered a certain unconscious air of pallid—how shall I call it?—of pallid haughtiness, say, or rather an austere reserve about him, which had positively awed me

[3] Gauius Marius (second century B.C.), Roman general banished for political reasons.

into my tame compliance with his eccentricities, when I had feared to ask him to do the slightest incidental thing for me, even though I might know, from his long-continued motionlessness, that behind his screen he must be standing in one of those dead-wall reveries of his.

Revolving all these things, and coupling them with the recently discovered fact that he made my office his constant abiding place and home, and not forgetful of his morbid moodiness; revolving all these things, a prudential feeling began to steal over me. My first emotions had been those of pure melancholy and sincerest pity; but just in proportion as the forlornness of Bartleby grew and grew to my imagination, did that same melancholy merge into fear, that pity into repulsion. So true it is, and so terrible, too, that up to a certain point the thought or sight of misery enlists our best affections; but, in certain special cases, beyond that point it does not. They err who would assert that invariably this is owing to the inherent selfishness of the human heart. It rather proceeds from a certain hopelessness of remedying excessive and organic ill. To a sensitive being, pity is not seldom pain. And when at last it is perceived that such pity cannot lead to effectual succour, common sense bids the soul be rid of it. What I saw that morning persuaded me that the scrivener was the victim of innate and incurable disorder. I might give alms to his body; but his body did not pain him; it was his soul that suffered, and his soul I could not reach.

I did not accomplish the purpose of going to Trinity Church that morning. Somehow, the things I had seen disqualified me for the time from church-going. I walked homeward, thinking what I would do with Bartleby. Finally, I resolved upon this:—I would put certain calm questions to him the next morning, touching his history, &c., and if he declined to answer them openly and unreservedly (and I suppose he would prefer not), then to give him a twenty dollar bill over and above whatever I might owe him, and tell him his services were no longer required; but that if in any other way I could assist him, I would be happy to do so, especially if he desired to return to his native place, wherever that might be, I would willingly help to defray the expenses. Moreover, if, after reaching home, he found himself at any time in want of aid, a letter from him would be sure of a reply.

The next morning came.

"Bartleby," said I, gently calling to him behind his screen.

No reply.

"Bartleby," said I, in a still gentler tone, "come here; I am not going to ask you to do anything you would prefer not to do—I simply wish to speak to you."

Upon this he noiselessly slid into view.

"Will you tell me, Bartleby, where you were born?"

"I would prefer not to."

"Will you tell me *anything* about yourself?"

"I would prefer not to."

"But what reasonable objection can you have to speak to me? I feel friendly towards you."

He did not look at me while I spoke, but kept his glance fixed upon my bust of Cicero, which, as I then sat, was directly behind me, some six inches above my head.

"What is your answer, Bartleby?" said I, after waiting a considerable time for a reply, during which his countenance remained immovable, only there was the faintest conceivable tremor of the white attenuated mouth.

"At present I prefer to give no answer," he said, and retired into his hermitage.

It was rather weak in me I confess, but his manner on this occasion nettled me. Not only did there seem to lurk in it a certain calm disdain, but his perverseness seemed ungrateful, considering the undeniable good usage and indulgence he had received from me.

Again I sat ruminating what I should do. Mortified as I was at his behaviour, and resolved as I had been to dismiss him when I entered my office, nevertheless I strangely felt something superstitious knocking at my heart, and forbidding me to carry out my purpose, and denouncing me for a villain if I dared to breathe one bitter word against this forlornest of mankind. At last, familiarly drawing my chair behind his screen, I sat down and said: "Bartleby, never mind then about revealing your history; but let me entreat you, as a friend, to comply as far as may be with the usages of this office. Say now you will help to examine papers to-morrow or next day: in short, say now that in a day or two you will begin to be a little reasonable: — say so, Bartleby."

"At present I would prefer not to be a little reasonable," was his mildly cadaverous reply.

Just then the folding-doors opened, and Nippers approached. He seemed suffering from an unusually bad night's rest, induced by severer indigestion than common. He overheard those final words of Bartleby.

"*Prefer not*, eh?" gritted Nippers—"I'd *prefer* him, if I were you, sir," addressing me—"I'd *prefer* him; I'd give him preferences, the stubborn mule! What is it, sir, pray, that he prefers not to do now?"

Bartleby moved not a limb.

"Mr. Nippers," said I, "I'd prefer that you would withdraw for the present."

Somehow, of late I had got into the way of involuntarily using this word "prefer" upon all sorts of not exactly suitable occasions. And I trembled to think that my contact with the scrivener had already and seriously affected me in a mental way. And what further and deeper aberration might it not yet produce? This apprehension had not been without efficacy in determining me to summary means.

As Nippers, looking very sour and sulky, was departing, Turkey blandly and deferentially approached.

"With submission, what word, sir?" asked Turkey, respecting about Bartleby here, and I think that if he would but prefer to take a quart of good ale every day, it would do much towards mending him, and enabling him to assist in examining his papers."

"So you have got the word, too," said I, slightly excited.

"With submission, what word, sir?" asked Turkey, respectfully crowding himself into the contracted space behind the screen, and by so doing, making me jostle the scrivener. "What word, sir?"

"I would prefer to be left alone here," said Bartleby, as if offended at being mobbed in his privacy.

"That's the word, Turkey," said I—*"that's* it."

"Oh, *prefer*? oh, yes—queer word. I never use it myself. But, sir, as I was saying, if he would but prefer—"

"Turkey," interrupted I, "you will please withdraw."

"Oh, certainly, sir, if you prefer that I should."

As he opened the folding-door to retire, Nippers at his desk caught a glimpse of me, and asked whether I would prefer to have a certain paper copied on blue paper or white. He did not in the least roguishly accent the word prefer. It was plain that it involuntarily rolled from his tongue. I thought to myself, surely I must get rid of a demented man, who already has in some degree turned the tongues, if not the heads, of myself and clerks. But I thought it prudent not to break the dismission at once.

The next day I noticed that Bartleby did nothing but stand at his window in his dead-wall revery. Upon asking him why he did not write, he said that he had decided upon doing no more writing.

"Why, how now? what next?" exclaimed I, "do no more writing?"

"No more."

"And what is the reason?"

"Do you not see the reason for yourself?" he indifferently replied.

I looked steadfastly at him, and perceived that his eyes looked dull and glazed. Instantly it occurred to me, that his unexampled diligence in copying by his dim window for the first few weeks of his stay with me might have temporarily impaired his vision.

I was touched. I said something in condolence with him. I hinted that, of course, he did wisely in abstaining from writing for a while, and urged him to embrace that opportunity of taking wholesome exercise in the open air. This, however, he did not do. A few days after this, my other clerks being absent, and being in a great hurry to despatch certain letters by the mail, I thought that, having nothing else earthly to do, Bartleby would surely be less inflexible than usual, and carry these letters to the Post Office. But he blankly declined. So, much to my inconvenience, I went myself.

Still added days went by. Whether Bartleby's eyes improved or not, I could not say. To all appearance, I thought they did. But when I asked him if they did, he vouchsafed no answer. At all events, he would do no copying. At last, in reply to my urgings, he informed me that he had permanently given up copying.

"What!" exclaimed I; "suppose your eyes should get entirely well— better than ever before—would you not copy then?"

"I have given up copying," he answered and slid aside.

He remained, as ever, a fixture in my chamber. Nay—if that were possible—he became still more of a fixture than before. What was to be done? He would do nothing in the office: why should he stay there? In plain fact, he had now become a millstone to me, not only useless as a necklace, but afflictive to bear. Yet I was sorry for him. I speak less than truth when I say that, on his own account, he occasioned me uneasiness. If he would but have named a single relative or friend, I would instantly have written, and urged their taking the poor fellow away to some convenient retreat. But he seemed alone, absolutely alone in the universe. A bit of wreckage in the mid-Atlantic. At length, necessities connected with my business tyrannized over all other considerations. Decently as I could, I told Bartleby that in six days' time he must unconditionally leave the office. I warned him to take measures, in the interval, for procuring some other abode. I offered to assist him in this endeavour, if he himself would but take the first step towards a removal. "And when you finally quit me, Bartleby," added I, "I shall see that you go away not entirely unprovided. Six days from this hour, remember."

At the expiration of that period, I peeped behind the screen, and lo! Bartleby was there.

I buttoned up my coat, balanced myself; advanced slowly towards him, touched his shoulder, and said, "The time has come; you must quit this place; I am sorry for you; here is money; but you must go."

"I would prefer not," he replied, with his back still towards me.

"You *must*."

He remained silent.

Now I had an unbounded confidence in this man's common honesty. He had frequently restored to me sixpences and shillings carelessly dropped upon the floor, for I am apt to be very reckless in such shirt-button affairs. The proceeding then which followed will not be deemed extraordinary.

"Bartleby," said I, "I owe you twelve dollars on account; here are thirty-two; the odd twenty are yours.—Will you take it?" and I handed the bills towards him.

But he made no motion.

"I will leave them here then," putting them under a weight on the table. Then taking my hat and cane and going to the door, I tranquilly turned and added—"After you have removed your things from these offices, Bartleby, you will of course lock the door—since every one is now gone for the day but you—and if you please, slip your key underneath the mat, so that I may have it in the morning. I shall not see you again; so good-bye to you. If hereafter in your new place of abode I can be of any service to you, do not fail to advise me by letter. Good-bye, Bartleby, and fare you well."

But he answered not a word; like the last column of some ruined temple, he remained standing mute and solitary in the middle of the otherwise deserted room.

As I walked home in a pensive mood, my vanity got the better of my pity. I could not but highly plume myself on my masterly management in getting rid of Bartleby. Masterly I call it, and such it must appear to any dispassionate thinker. The beauty of my procedure seemed to consist in its prefect quietness. There was no vulgar bullying, no bravado of any sort, no choleric hectoring, no striding to and fro across the apartment, jerking out vehement commands for Bartleby to bundle himself off with his beggarly traps. Nothing of the kind. Without loudly bidding Bartleby depart—as an inferior genius might have done—I assumed the ground that depart he must; and upon that assumption built all I had to say. The more I thought over my procedure, the more I was charmed with it. Nevertheless, next morning, upon awakening, I had my doubts,—I had somehow slept off the fumes of vanity. One of the coolest and wisest hours a man has, is just after he awakes in the morning. My procedure seemed as sagacious as ever,—but only in theory. How it would prove in practice—there was the rub. It was truly a beautiful thought to have assumed Bartleby's departure; but, after all, that assumption was simply my own, and none of Bartleby's. The great point was, not whether I had assumed that he would quit me, but whether he would prefer so to do. He was more a man of preferences than assumptions.

After breakfast, I walked down town, arguing the probabilities *pro* and *con*. One moment I thought it would prove a miserable failure, and Bartleby would be found all alive at my office as usual; the next moment it seemed certain that I should see his chair empty. And so I kept veering about. At the corner of Broadway and Canal Street, I saw quite an excited group of people standing in earnest conversation.

"I'll take odds he doesn't" said a voice as I passed.

"Doesn't go?—done!" said I, "put up your money."

I was instinctively putting my hand in my pocket to produce my own, when I remembered that this was an election day. The words I had overheard bore no reference to Bartleby, but to the success or non-success of some candidate for the mayoralty. In my intent frame of mind, I had, as it were, imagined that all Broadway shared in my excitement, and were debating the same question with me. I passed on, very thankful that the uproar of the street screened my momentary absent-mindedness.

As I had intended, I was earlier than usual at my office door. I stood listening for a moment. All was still. He must be gone. I tried the knob. The door was locked. Yes, my procedure had worked to a charm; he indeed must be vanished. Yet a certain melancholy mixed with this: I was almost sorry for my brilliant success. I was fumbling under the door mat for the key, which Bartleby was to have left there for me, when accidently my knee knocked against a panel, producing a summoning sound, and in response a voice came to me from within—"Not yet; I am occupied."

It was Bartleby.

I was thunderstruck. For an instant I stood like the man who, pipe in mouth, was killed one cloudless afternoon long ago in Virginia, by summer lightning; at his own warm open window he was killed, and remained leaning out there upon the dreamy afternoon, till some one touched him, and he fell.

"Not gone!" I murmured at last. But again obeying that wondrous ascendency which the inscrutable scrivener had over me—and from which ascendency, for all my chafing, I could not completely escape—I slowly went down stairs and out into the street, and while walking round the block, considered what I should next do in this unheard-of perplexity. Turn the man out by an actual thrusting I could not; to drive him away by calling him hard names would not do; calling in the police was an unpleasant idea; and yet, permit him to enjoy his cadaverous triumph over me,—this too I could not think of. What was to be done? or, if nothing could be done, was there anything further that I could *assume* in the matter? Yes, as before I had prospectively assumed that Bartleby would depart, so now I might retrospectively assume that departed he was. In the legitimate carrying out of this assumption, I might enter my office in a great hurry, and pretending not to see Bartleby at all, walk straight against him as if he were air. Such a proceeding would in a singular degree have the appearance of a home-thrust. It was hardly possible that Bartleby would withstand such an application of the doctrine of assumptions. But, upon second thought, the success of the plan seemed rather dubious. I resolved to argue the matter over with him again.

"Bartleby," said I, entering the office, with a quietly severe expression, "I am seriously displeased. I am pained, Bartleby. I had thought better of you. I had imagined you of such a gentlemanly organization, that in any delicate dilemma a slight hint would suffice—in short, an assumption; but it appears I am deceived. Why," I added, unaffectedly starting, "you have not even touched that money yet," pointing to it, just where I had left it the evening previous.

He answered nothing.

"Will you, or will you not, quit me?" I now demanded in a sudden passion, advancing close to him.

"I would prefer *not* to quit you," he replied, gently emphasizing the *not*.

"What earthly right have you to stay here? Do you pay any rent? Do you pay my taxes? Or is this property yours?"

He answered nothing.

"Are you ready to go on and write now? Are your eyes recovered? Could you copy a small paper for me this morning? or help examine a few lines? or step round to the Post Office? In a word, will you do any thing at all, to give a colouring to your refusal to depart the premises?"

He silently retired into his remitage.

I was now in such a state of nervous resentment that I thought it but prudent to check myself, at present, from further demonstrations. Bartleby and I were alone. I remembered the tragedy of the unfortunate Adams and the still more unfortunate Colt in the solitary office of the latter; and how poor Colt, being dreadfully incensed by Adams, and imprudently permitting himself to get wildly excited, was at unawares hurried into his fatal act—an act which certainly no man could possibly deplore more than the actor himself. Often it had occurred to me in my ponderings upon the subject, that had that altercation taken place in the public street, or at a private residence, it would not have terminated as it did. It was the circumstance of being alone in a solitary office, upstairs, of a building entirely unhallowed by humanizing domestic associations—an uncarpeted office, doubtless, of a dusty, haggard sort of appearance;—this it must have been, which greatly helped to enhance the irritable desperation of the hapless Colt.

But when this old Adam of resentment rose in me and tempted me concerning Bartleby, I grappled him and threw him. How? Why, simply by recalling the divine injunction: "A new commandment give I unto you, that ye love one another." Yes, this it was that saved me. Aside from higher considerations, charity often operates as a vastly wise and prudent principle—a great safeguard to its possessor. Men have committed murder for jealousy's sake, and anger's sake, and hatred's sake, and selfishness' sake, and spiritual pride's sake; but no man that ever I heard of, ever committed a diabolical murder for sweet charity's sake. Mere self-interest, then, if no better motive can be enlisted, should, especially with high-tempered men, prompt all beings to charity and philanthropy. At any rate, upon the occasion in question, I strove to drown my exasperated feelings toward the scrivener by benevolently construing his conduct. Poor fellow, poor fellow! thought I, he doesn't mean any thing; and besides, he has seen hard times, and ought to be indulged.

I endeavoured also immediately to occupy myself, and at the same time to comfort my despondency. I tried to fancy that in the course of the morning, at such time as might prove agreeable to him, Bartleby, of his own free accord, would emerge from his hermitage, and take up some decided line of march in the direction of the door. But no. Half-past twelve o'clock came; Turkey began to glow in the face, overturn his inkstand, and become generally ostreperous; Nippers abated down into quietude and courtesy; Ginger Nut munched his noon apple; and Bartleby remained standing at his window in one of his profoundest dead-wall reveries. Will it be credited? Ought I to acknowledge it? That afternoon I left the office without saying one further word to him.

Some days now passed, during which at leisure intervals I looked a little into "Edwards on the Will," and "Priestley on Necessity." Under the circumstances, those books induced a salutary feeling. Gradually I slid into the persuasion that these troubles of mine, touching the scrivener, had been all predestinated from eternity, and Bartleby was billeted upon me for some mysterious purpose of an all-wise Providence, which it was not for a mere mortal like me to fathom. Yes, Bartleby, stay there behind your screen, thought I; I shall persecute you no more; you are harmless and noiseless as any of these old chairs; in short, I never feel so private as when I know you are here. At least I see it, I feel it; I penetrate to the predestinated purpose of my life. I am content. Others may have loftier parts to enact; but my mission in this world, Bartleby, is to furnish you with office room for such period as you may see fit to remain.

I believe that this wise and blessed frame of mind would have continued with me had it not been for the unsolicited an uncharitable remarks obtruded upon me by my professional friends who visited the rooms. But thus it often is, that the constant friction of illiberal minds wears out at last the best resolves of the more generous. Though to be sure, when I reflected upon it, it was not strange that people entering my office should be struck by the peculiar aspect of the unaccountable Bartleby, and so be tempted to throw out some sinister observations concerning him. Sometimes an attorney having business with me, and calling at my office, and finding no one but the scrivener there, would undertake to obtain some sort of precise information from him touching my whereabouts; but without heeding his idle talk, Bartleby would remain standing immovable in the middle of the room. So, after contemplating him in that position for a time, the attorney would depart, no wiser than he came.

Also, when a Reference was going on, and the room full of lawyers and witnesses and business was driving fast, some deeply occupied legal gentleman present, seeing Bartleby wholly unemployed, would request him to run round to his (the legal gentleman's) office and fetch some papers for him. Thereupon, Bartleby would tranquilly

decline, and yet remain idle as before. Then the lawyer would give
a great stare, and turn to me. And what could I say? At last I was
made aware that all through the circle of my professional acquaintance, a whisper of wonder was running round, having reference to
the strange creature I kept at my office. This worried me very much.
And as the idea came upon me of his possibly turning out a long-
lived man, and keep occupying my chambers, and denying my authority; and perplexing my visitors; and scandalizing my professional
reputation; and casting a general gloom over the premises; keeping
soul and body together to the last upon his savings (for doubtless he
spent but half a dime a day), and in the end perhaps outlive me,
and claim possession of my office by right of his perpetual occupancy:
as all these dark anticipations crowded upon me more and more,
and my friends continually intruded their relentless remarks upon
the apparition in my room, a great change was wrought in me. I
resolved to gather all my faculties together, and for ever rid me of
this intolerable incubus. Ere revolving any complicated project, however, adapted to this end, I first simply suggested to Bartleby the
propriety of his permanent departure. In a calm and serious tone, I
commended the idea to his careful and mature consideration. But
having taken three days to meditate upon it, he apprised me that
his original determination remained the same; in short, that he still
preferred to abide with me.

What shall I do? I now said to myself, buttoning up my coat to the
last button. What shall I do? what ought I to do? what does conscience
say I *should* do with this man, or rather ghost? Rid myself of him, I
must; go, he shall. But how? You will not thrust him, the poor, pale,
passive mortal,—you will not thrust such a helpless creature out of
your door? you will not dishonour yourself by such cruelty? No, I will
not, I cannot do that. Rather would I let him live and die here, and
then mason up his remains in the wall. What then will you do? For
all your coaxing, he will not budge. Bribes he leaves under you own
paper-weight on your table; in short, it is quite plain that he prefers
to cling to you.

Then something sever, something unusual must be done. What!
surely you will not have him collared by a constable, and commit his
innocent pallor to the common jail? And upon what ground could you
procure such a thing to be done?—a vagrant, is he? What! he a
vagrant, a wanderer, who refuses to budge? It is because he will *not*
be a vagrant, then, that you seek to count him *as* a vagrant. That is
too absurd. No visible means of support: there I have him. Wrong
again: for indubitably he *does* support himself, and that is the only
unanswerable proof that any man can show of his possessing the
means so to do. No more then. Since he will not quit me, I must quit

him. I will change my offices; I will move elsewhere; and give him fair notice, that if I find him on my new premises I will then proceed against him as a common trespasser.

Acting accordingly, next day I thus addressed him: "I find these chambers too far from the City Hall; the air is unwholesome. In a word, I propose to remove my offices next week, and shall no longer require your services. I tell you this now, in order that you may seek another place."

He made no reply, and nothing more was said.

On the appointed day I engaged carts and men, proceeded to my chambers, and having but little furniture, everything was removed in a few hours. Throughout all, the scrivener remained standing behind the screen, which I directed to be removed the last thing. It was withdrawn; and being folded up like a huge folio, left him the motionless occupant of a naked room. I stood in the entry watching him a moment, while something from within me upbraided me.

I re-entered, with my hand in my pocket—and—and my heart in my mouth.

"Good-bye, Bartleby; I am going—good-bye, and God some way bless you; and take that," slipping something in his hand. But it dropped upon the floor and then—strange to say—I tore myself from him whom I had so longed to be rid of.

Established in my new quarters, for a day or two I kept the door locked, and started at every footfall in the passages. When I returned to my rooms after any little absence, I would pause at the threshold for an instant, and attentively listen, ere applying my key. But these fears were needless. Bartleby never came nigh me.

I thought all was going well, when a perturbed looking stranger visited me, inquiring whether I was the person who had recently occupied rooms at No. —— Wall Street.

Full of forebodings, I replied that I was.

"Then sir," said the stranger, who proved a lawyer, "you are responsible for the man you left there. He refuses to do any copying, he refuses to do anything; and he says he prefers not to; and he refuses to quit the premises."

"I am very sorry, sir," said I, with assumed tranquillity, but an inward tremor, "but, really, the man you allude to is nothing to me— he is no relation or apprentice of mine, that you should hold me responsible for him."

"In mercy's name, who is he?"

"I certainly cannot inform you. I know nothing about him. Formerly I employed him as a copyist; but he has done nothing for me now for some time past."

"I shall settle him then,—good morning, sir."

Several days passed, and I heard nothing more; and though I often felt a charitable prompting to call at the place and see poor Bartleby, yet a certain squeamishness of I know not what withheld me.

All is over with him, by this time, thought I at last, when through another week no further intelligence reached me. But coming to my room the day after, I found several persons waiting at my door in a high state of nervous excitement.

"That's the man—here he comes," cried the foremost one, whom I recognized as the lawyer who had previously called upon me alone.

"You must take him away, sir, at once," cried a portly person among them, advancing upon me, and whom I knew to be the landlord of No. —— Wall Street. "These gentlemen, my tenants, cannot stand it any longer; Mr. B——," pointing to the lawyer, "has turned him out of his room, and he now persists in haunting the building generally, sitting upon the banisters of the stairs by day, and sleeping in the entry by night. Everybody here is concerned; clients are leaving the offices; some fears are entertained of a mob; something you must do, and that without delay."

Aghast at this torrent, I fell back before it, and would fain have locked myself in my new quarters. In vain I persisted that Bartleby was nothing to me—no more than to any one else there. In vain:—I was the last person known to have anything to do with him, and they held me to the terrible account. Fearful then of being exposed in the papers (as one person present obscurely threatened) I considered the matter, and at length said, that if the lawyer would give me a confidential interview with the scrivener, in his (the lawyer's) own room, I would that afternoon strive my best to rid them of the nuisance they complained of.

Going up stairs to my old haunt, there was Bartleby silently sitting upon the banister at the landing.

"What are you doing here, Bartleby?" said I.

"Sitting upon the banister," he mildly replied.

I motioned him into the lawyer's room, who then left us.

"Bartleby," said I, "are you aware that you are the cause of great tribulation to me, by persisting in occupying the entry after being dismissed from the office?"

No answer.

"Now one of two things must take place. Either you must do something, or something must be done to you. Now what sort of business would you like to engage in? Would you like to re-engage in copying for some one?"

"No; I would prefer not to make any change."

"Would you like a clerkship in a dry-goods store?"

"There is too much confinement about that. No, I would not like a clerkship; but I am not particular."

"Too much confinement," I cried, "why, you keep yourself confined all the time!"

"I would prefer not to take a clerkship," he rejoined, as if to settle that little item at once.

"How would a bartender's business suit you? There is no trying of the eyesight in that."

"I would not like it at all; though, as I said before, I am not particular."

His unwonted wordiness inspirited me. I returned to the charge.

"Well then, would you like to travel through the country collecting bills for the merchants? That would improve your health."

"No, I would prefer to be doing something else."

"How then would going as a companion to Europe to entertain some young gentleman with your conversation,—how would that suit you?"

"Not at all. It does not strike me that there is anything definite about that. I like to be stationary. But I am not particular."

"Stationary you shall be then," I cried, now losing all patience, and for the first time in all my exasperating connection with him fairly flying into a passion. "If you do not go away from these premises before night, I shall feel bound—indeed I *am* bound—to—to—to quit the premises myself!" I rather absurdly concluded, knowing not with what possible threat to try to frighten his immobility into compliance. Despairing of all further efforts, I was precipitately leaving him, when a final thought occurred to me—one which had not been wholly unindulged before.

"Bartleby," said I, in the kindest tone I could assume under such exciting circumstances, "will you go home with me now—not to my office, but my dwelling—and remain there till we can conclude upon some convenient arrangement for you at our leisure? Come, let us start now, right away."

"No: at present I would prefer not to make any change at all."

I answered nothing; but effectually dodging every one by the suddenness and rapidity of my flight, rushed from the building, ran up Wall Street toward Broadway, and then jumping into the first omnibus, was soon removed from pursuit. As soon as tranquillity returned I distinctly perceived that I had now done all that I possibly could, both in respect to the demands of the landlord and his tenants, and with regard to my own desire and sense of duty, to benefit Bartleby, and shield him from rude persecution. I now strove to be entirely carefree and quiescent; and my conscience justified me in the attempt; though indeed it was not so successful as I could have wished. So fearful was I of being again hunted out by the incensed landlord and his exasperated tenants, that, surrendering my business to Nippers, for a few days I drove about the upper part of the town and through the suburbs, in my rockaway; crossed over to Jersey City and Hoboken, and paid fugitive visits to Manhattanville and Astoria. In fact I almost lived in my rockaway for the time.

When again I entered my office, lo, a note from the landlord lay upon the desk. I opened it with trembling hands. It informed me that the writer had sent to the police, and had Bartleby removed to the Tombs as a vagrant. Moreover, since I knew more about him than any one else, he wished me to appear at that place, and make a suitable statement of the facts. These tidings had a conflicting effect upon me. At first I was indignant; but at last almost approved. The landlord's energetic, summary disposition had led him to adopt a procedure which I do not think I would have decided upon myself; and yet as a last resort, under such peculiar circumstances, it seemed the only plan.

As I afterwards learned, the poor scrivener, when told that he must be conducted to the Tombs, offered not the slightest obstacle, but in his own pale, unmoving way silently acquiesced.

Some of the compassionate and curious bystanders joined the party; and headed by one of the constables, arm-in-arm with Bartleby the silent procession filed its way through all the noise, and heat, and joy of the roaring thoroughfares at noon. The same day I received the note I went to the Tombs, or, to speak more properly, the Halls of Justice. Seeking the right officer, I stated the purpose of my call, and was informed that the individual I described was indeed within. I then assured the functionary that Bartleby was a perfectly honest man, and a greatly to be compassionated (however unaccountable) eccentric. I narrated all I knew, and closed by suggesting the idea of letting him remain in as indulgent confinement as possible till something less harsh might be done—though indeed I hardly knew what. At all events, if nothing else could be decided upon, the alms-house must receive him. I then begged to have an interview.

Being under no disgraceful charge, and quite serene and harmless in all his ways, they had permitted him freely to wander about the prison, and especially in the inclosed grass-platted yards thereof. And so I found him there, standing all alone in the quietest of the yards, his face toward a high wall—while all around, from the narrow slits of the jail windows, I thought I saw peering out upon him the eyes of murderers and thieves.

"Bartleby!"

"I know you," he said, without looking round,—"and I want nothing to say to you."

"It was not I that brought you here, Bartleby," said I, keenly pained at his implied suspicion. "And to you, this should not be so vile a place. Nothing reproachful attaches to you by being here. And see, it is not so sad a place as one might think. Look, there is the sky and here is the grass."

"I know where I am," he replied, but would say nothing more, and so I left him.

As I entered the corridor again a broad, meat-like man in an apron accosted me, and jerking his thumb over his shoulder said—"Is that your friend?"

"Yes."

"Does he want to starve? If he does, let him live on the prison fare, that's all."

"Who are you?" asked I, not knowing what to make of such an unofficially speaking person in such a place.

"I am the grub-man. Such gentlemen as have friends here, hire me to provide them with something good to eat."

"Is this so?" said I, turning to the turnkey.

He said it was. "Well then," said I, slipping some silver into the grub-man's hands (for so they called him), "I want you to give particular attention to my friend there; let him have the best dinner you can get. And you must be as polite to him as possible."

"Introduce me, will you?" said the grub-man, looking at me with an expression which seemed to say he was all impatience for an opportunity to give a specimen of his breeding.

Thinking it would prove of benefit to the scrivener, I acquiesced; and asking the grub-man his name, went up with him to Bartleby.

"Bartleby, this is Mr. Cutlets; you will find him very useful to you."

"Your sarvant, sir, your sarvant," said the grub-man, making a low salutation behind his apron. "Hope you find it pleasant here, sir;—spacious grounds—cool apartments, sir—hope you'll stay with us some time—try to make it agreeable. May Mrs. Cutlets and I have the pleasure of your company to dinner, sir, in Mrs. Cutlets' private room?"

"I prefer not to dine to-day," said Bartleby, turning away. "It would disagree with me; I am unused to dinners." "So saying, he slowly moved to the other side of the inclosure and took up a position fronting the dead-wall.

"How's this?" said the grub-man, addressing me with a stare of astonishment. "He's odd, ain't he?"

"I think he is a little deranged," said I, sadly.

"Deranged? deranged is it? Well now, upon my word, I thought that friend of yourn was a gentleman forger; they are always pale and genteel-like, them forgers. I can't help pity 'em—can't help it, sir. Did you know Monroe Edwards?" he added touchingly, and paused. Then, laying his hand pityingly on my shoulder, sighed, "He died of the consumption at Sing-Sing. So you weren't acquainted with Monroe?"

"No, I was never socially acquainted with any forgers. But I cannot stop longer. Look to my friend yonder. You will not lose by it. I will see you again."

Some few days after this, I again obtained admission to the Tombs, and went through the corridors in quest of Bartleby; but without finding him.

"I saw him coming from his cell not long ago," said a turnkey, "maybe he's gone to loiter in the yards."

So I went in that direction.

"Are you looking for the silent man?" said another turnkey passing me. "Yonder he lies—sleeping in the yard there. 'Tis not twenty minutes since I saw him lie down."

The yard was entirely quiet. It was not accessible to the common prisoners. The surrounding walls, of amazing thickness, kept off all sounds behind them. The Egyptian character of the masonry weighed upon me with its gloom. But a soft imprisoned turf grew under foot. The heart of the eternal pyramids, it seemed, wherein by some strange magic, through the clefts grass-seed, dropped by birds, had sprung.

Strangely huddled at the base of the wall—his knees drawn up, and lying on his side, his head touching the cold stones—I saw the wasted Bartleby. But nothing stirred. I paused; then went close up to him; stooped over, and saw that his dim eyes were open; otherwise he seemed profoundly sleeping. Something prompted me to touch him. I felt his hand, when a tingling shiver ran up my arm and down my spine to my feet.

The round face of the grub-man peered upon me now. "His dinner is ready. Won't he dine to-day, either? Or does he live without dining?"

"Lives without dining," said I, and closed the eyes.

"Eh!—He's asleep, ain't he?"

"With kings and counsellors," murmured I.

There would seem little need for proceeding further in this history. Imagination will readily supply the meagre recital of poor Bartleby's interment. But ere parting with the reader, let me say, that if this little narrative has sufficiently interested him, to awaken curiosity as to who Bartleby was, and what manner of life he led prior to the present narrator's making his acquaintance, I can only reply, that in such curiosity I fully share—but am wholly unable to gratify it. Yet here I hardly know whether I should divulge one little item of rumour, which came to my ear a few months after the scrivener's decease. Upon what basis it rested, I could never ascertain; and hence, how true it is I cannot now tell. But inasmuch as this vague report has not been without a certain strange suggestive interest to me, however sad, it may prove the same with some others; and so I will briefly mention it. The report was this: that Bartleby had been a subordinate clerk in the Dead Letter Office at Washington, from which he had been suddenly removed by a change in the administration. When I think over this rumour I cannot adequately express the emotions which seize me. Dead letters! does it not sound like dead men? Conceive a man by nature and misfortune prone to a pallid hopelessness: can any business seem more fitted to heighten it than that of continually handling these dead letters, and assorting them for the flames? For by the cartload they are annually burned. Sometimes from out the folded paper the pale clerk takes a ring:—the finger it was meant for, perhaps, moulders in the grave; a bank-note sent in swiftest charity;—he whom it would relieve, nor eats nor hungers any more; pardon for those who died despairing; hope for those who died unhoping; good tidings for those who died stifled by unrelieved calamities. On errands of life, these letters speed to death.

Ah Bartleby! Ah humanity!

Benito Cereno (1855)

In the year 1799, Captain Amasa Delano,[1] of Duxbury, in Massachusetts, commanding a large sealer and general trader, lay at anchor, with a valuable cargo, in the harbour of St. Maria—a small, desert, uninhabited island towards the southern extremity of the long coast of Chili. There he had touched for water.

On the second day, not long after dawn, while lying in his berth, his mate came below, informing him that a strange sail was coming into the bay. Ships were then not so plenty in those waters as now. He rose, dressed, and went on deck.

The morning was one peculiar to that coast. Everything was mute and calm; everything grey. The sea, though undulated into long roods of swells, seemed fixed, and was sleeked at the surface like waved lead that has cooled and set in the smelter's mould. The sky seemed a grey mantle. Flights of troubled grey fowl, kith and kin with flights of troubled grey vapours among which they were mixed, skimmed low and fitfully over the waters, as swallows over meadows before storms. Shadows present, foreshadowing deeper shadows to come.

To Captain Delano's surprise, the stranger, viewed through the glass, showed no colours; though to do so upon entering a haven, however uninhabited in its shores, where but a single other ship might be lying, was the custom among peaceful seamen of all nations. Considering the lawlessness and loneliness of the spot, and the sort of stories, at that day, associated with those seas, Captain Delano's surprise might have deepened into some uneasiness had he not been a person of a singularly undistrustful good nature, not liable, except on extraordinary and repeated excitement, and hardly then, to indulge in personal alarms, any way involving the imputation of malign evil in man. Whether, in view of what humanity is capable, such a trait implies,

---

[1] This fictional character is based on a real person of the same name, whose *Narrative of Voyages and Travels* (1817) provides material for Melville's story.

along with a benevolent heart, more than ordinary quickness and accuracy of intellectual perception, may be left to the wise to determine.

But whatever misgivings might have obtruded on first seeing the stranger, would almost, in any seaman's mind, have been dissipated by observing that, the ship, in navigating into the harbour, was drawing too near the land, for her own safety's sake, owing to a sunken reef making out off her bow. This seemed to prove her a stranger, indeed, not only to the sealer, but the island; consequently, she could be no wonted freebooter on that ocean. With no small interest, Captain Delano continued to watch her—a proceeding not much facilitated by the vapours partly mantling the hull, through which the far matin light from her cabin streamed equivocally enough; much like the sun—by this time crescented on the rim of the horizon, and apparently, in company with the strange ship, entering the harbour—which, wimpled by the same low, creeping clouds, showed up unlike a Lima [2] intriguante's one sinister eye peering across the Plaza from the Indian loop-hole of her dusk *saya-y-manta*. [3]

It might have been but a deception of the vapours, but, the longer the stranger was watched, the more singular appeared her manœuvres. Ere long it seemed hard to decide whether she meant to come in or no—what she wanted, or what she was about. The wind, which had breezed up a little during the night, was now extremely light and baffling, which the more increased the apparent uncertainty of her movements.

Surmising, at last, that it might be a ship in distress, Captain Delano ordered his whale-boat to be dropped, and, much to the wary opposition of his mate, prepared to board her, and, at the least, pilot her in. On the night previous, a fishing-party of the seamen had gone a long distance to some detached rocks out of sight from the sealer, and, an hour or two before day-break, had returned, having met with no small success. Presuming that the stranger might have been long off soundings, the good captain put several baskets of the fish, for presents, into his boat, and so pulled away. From her continuing too near the sunken reef, deeming her in danger, calling to his men, he made all haste to apprise those on board of their situation. But, some time ere the boat came up, the wind, light though it was, having shifted, had headed the vessel off, as well as partly broken the vapours from about her.

Upon gaining a less remote view, the ship, when made signally visible on the verge of the leaden-hued swells, with the shreds of fog here and there raggedly furring her, appeared like a white-washed monastery after a thunder-storm, seen perched upon some dun cliff among the Pyrenees. But it was no purely fanciful resemblance which

[2] The capital of Peru.
[3] Skirt and shawl.

now, for a moment, almost led Captain Delano to think that nothing less than a ship-load of monks was before him. Peering over the bulwarks were what really seemed, in the hazy distance, throngs of dark cowls; while, fitfully revealed through the open port-holes, other dark moving figures were dimly descried, as of Black Friars pacing the cloisters.

Upon a still nigher approach, this appearance was modified, and the true character of the vessel was plain—a Spanish merchantman of the first class; carrying negro slaves, amongst other valuable freight, from one colonial port to another. A very large, and, in its time, a very fine vessel, such as in those days were at intervals encountered along that main; sometimes superseded Acapulco treasureships, or retired frigates of the Spanish king's navy, which, like superannuated Italian palaces, still, under a decline of masters, preserved signs of former state.

As the whale-boat drew more and more nigh, the cause of the peculiar pipe-clayed aspect of the stranger was seen in the slovenly neglect pervading her. The spars, ropes, and great part of the bulwarks, looked woolly, from long unacquaintance with the scraper, tar, and the brush. Her keel seemed laid, her ribs put together, and she launched, from Ezekiel's Valley of Dry Bones.

In the present business in which she was engaged, the ship's general model and rig appeared to have undergone no material change from their original warlike and Froissart pattern. However, no guns were seen.

The tops[4] were large, and were railed about with what had once been octagonal net-work, all now in sad disrepair. These tops hung overhead like three ruinous aviaries, in one of which was seen perched, on a ratlin, a white noddy, a strange fowl, so called from its lethargic, somnambulistic character, being frequently caught by hand at sea. Battered and mouldy, the castellated forecastle seemed some ancient turret, long ago taken by assault, and then left to decay. Towards the stern, two high-raised quarter galleries—the balustrades here and there covered with dry, tindery sea-moss—opening out from the unoccupied state-cabin, whose dead lights, for all the mild weather, were hermetically closed and caulked—these tenantless balconies hung over the sea as if it were the grand Venetian canal. But the principal relic of faded grandeur was the ample oval of the shield-like stern-piece, intricately carved with the arms of Castile and Leon,[5] medallioned about by groups of mythological or symbolical devices; uppermost and central of which was a dark satyr in a mask, holding his foot on the prostrate neck of a writhing figure, likewise masked.

Whether the ship had a figure-head, or only a plain beak, was not

4 Platforms in the mast.
5 Once Spanish kingdoms.

quite certain, owing to canvas wrapped about that part, either to protect it while undergoing a refurbishing, or else decently to hide its
decay. Rudely painted or chalked, as in a sailor freak, along the forward side of a sort of pedestal below the canvas, was the sentence,
"*Seguid vuestro jefe*" (follow your leader); while upon the tarnished
head-boards, near by, appeared, in stately capitals, once gilt, the ship's
name, "SAN DOMINICK," each letter streakingly corroded with tricklings
of cooper-spike rust; while, like mourning weeds, dark festoons of sea-
grass slimily swept to and fro over the name, with every hearse-like roll
of the hull.

As at last the boat was hooked from the bow along toward the
gangway amidship, its keel, while yet some inches separated from the
hull, harshly grated as on a sunken coral reef. It proved a huge bunch
of conglobated barnacles adhering below the water to the side like a
wen; a token of baffling airs and long calms passed somewhere in those
seas.

Climbing the side, the visitor was at once surrounded by a clamorous throng of whites and blacks, but the latter outnumbering the
former more than could have been expected, negro transportation-ship
as the stranger in port was. But, in one language, and as with one voice,
all poured out a common tale of suffering; in which the negresses, of
whom there were not a few, exceeded the others in their dolorous
vehemence. The scurvy, together with a fever, had swept off a great
part of their number, more especially the Spaniards. Off Cape Horn,
they had narrowly escaped shipwreck; then, for days together, they
had lain tranced without wind; their provisions were low; their water
next to none; their lips that moment were baked.

While Captain Delano was thus made the mark of all eager tongues,
his one eager glance took in all the faces, with every other object about
him.

Always upon first boarding a large and populous ship at sea, especially a foreign one, with a nondescript crew such as Lascars[6] or
Manilla men, the impression varies in a peculiar way from that produced by first entering a strange house with strange inmates in a
strange land. Both house and ship, the one by its walls and blinds,
the other by its high bulwarks like ramparts, hoard from view their
interiors till the last moment; but in the case of the ship there is this
addition: that the living spectacle it contains, upon its sudden and
complete disclosure, has, in contrast with the blank ocean which zones
it, something of the effect of enchantment. The ship seems unreal;
these strange costumes, gestures, and faces, but a shadowy tableau
just emerged from the deep, which directly must receive back what it
gave.

[6] East Indian sailors.

Perhaps it was some such influence as above is attempted to be described which, in Captain Delano's mind, heightened whatever, upon a staid scrutiny, might have seemed unusual; especially the conspicuous figures of four elderly, grizzled negros, their heads like black, doddered willow tops, who, in venerable contrast to the tumult below them, were couched sphynx-like, one on the starboard cat-head, another on the larboard, and the remaining pair face to face on the opposite bulwarks above the main-chains. They each had bits of unstranded old junk in their hands, and, with a sort of stoical self-content, were picking the junk into oakum, a small heap of which lay by their sides. They accompanied the task with a continuous, low, monotonous chant; droning and drooling away like so many grey-headed bag-pipers playing a funeral march.

The quarter-deck rose into an ample elevated poop, upon the forward verge of which, lifted, like the oakum-pickers, some eight feet above the general throng, sat along in a row, separated by regular spaces, the cross-legged figures of six other blacks; each with a rusty hatchet in his hand, which, with a bit of brick and a rag, he was engaged like a scullion in scouring; while between each two was a small stack of hatchets, their rusted edges turned forward awaiting a like operation. Though occasionally the four oakum-pickers would briefly address some person or persons in the crowd below, yet the six hatchet-polishers neither spoke to others, nor breathed a whisper among themselves, but sat intent upon their task, except at intervals, when, with the peculiar love in negroes of uniting industry with pastime, two-and-two they sideways clashed their hatchets together, like cymbals, with a barbarous din. All six, unlike the generality, had the raw aspect of unsophisticated Africans.

But that first comprehensive glance which took in those ten figures, with scores less conspicuous, rested but an instant upon them, as, impatient of the hubbub of voices, the visitor turned in quest of whomsoever it might be that commanded the ship.

But as if not unwilling to let nature make known her own case among his suffering charge, or else in despair of restraining it for the time, the Spanish captain, a gentlemanly, reserved-looking, and rather young man to a stranger's eye, dressed with singular richness, but bearing plain traces of recent sleepless cares and disquietudes, stood passively by, leaning against the main-mast, at one moment casting a dreary, spiritless look upon his excited people, at the next an unhappy glance toward his visitor. By his side stood a black of small stature, in whose rude face, as occasionally, like a shepherd's dog, he mutely turned it up into the Spaniard's, sorrow and affection were equally blended.

Struggling through the throng, the American advanced to the Spaniard, assuring him of his sympathies, and offering to render whatever assistance might be in his power. To which the Spaniard returned, for the present, but grave and ceremonious acknowledgments, his national formality dusked by the saturnine mood of ill health.

But losing no time in mere compliments, Captain Delano returning to the gangway, had his baskets of fish brought up; and as the wind still continued light, so that some hours at least must elapse ere the ship could be brought to the anchorage, he bade his men return to the sealer, and fetch back as much water as the whale-boat could carry, with whatever soft bread the steward might have, all the remaining pumpkins on board, with a box of sugar, and a dozen of his private bottles of cider.

Not many minutes after the boat's pushing off, to the vexation of all, the wind entirely died away, and the tide turning, began drifting back the ship helplessly seaward. But trusting this would not long last, Captain Delano sought with good hopes to cheer up the strangers, feeling no small satisfaction that, with persons in their condition he could—thanks to his frequent voyages along the Spanish main—converse with some freedom in their native tongue.

While left alone with them, he was not long in observing some things tending to heighten his first impressions, but surprise was lost in pity, both for the Spaniards and blacks, alike evidently reduced from scarcity of water and provisions; while long-continued suffering seemed to have brought out the less good-natured qualities of the negroes, besides, at the same time, impairing the Spaniard's authority over them. But, under the circumstances, precisely this condition of things was to have been anticipated. In armies, navies, cities, or families—in nature herself—nothing more relaxes good order than misery. Still, Captain Delano was not without the idea, that had Benito Cereno been a man of greater energy, misrule would hardly have come to the present pass. But the debility, constitutional or induced by the hardships, bodily and mental, of the Spanish captain, was too obvious to be overlooked. A prey to settled dejection, as if long mocked with hope he would not now indulge it, even when it had ceased to be a mock, the prospect of that day or evening at furthest, lying at anchor, with plenty of water for his people, and a brother captain to counsel and befriend, seemed in no perceptible degree to encourage him. His mind appeared unstrung, if not still more seriously affected. Shut up in these oaken walls, chained to one dull round of command, whose unconditionality cloyed him, like some hypochondriac abbot he moved slowly about, at times suddenly pausing, starting, or staring, biting his lip, biting his finger-nail, flushing, paling, twitching his beard, with other symptoms of an absent or moody mind. This distempered spirit was lodged, as before hinted, in as distempered a frame. He was rather tall, but seemed never to have been robust, and now with nervous suffering was almost worn to a skeleton. A tendency to some pulmonary complaint appeared to have been lately confirmed. His voice was like that of one with lungs half gone, hoarsely suppressed, a husky whisper. No wonder that, as in this state he tottered about, his private servant apprehensively followed him. Sometimes the negro gave his master his arm, or took his handkerchief out of his pocket for him; performing these and similar offices with that affectionate zeal which transmutes, into something filial or fraternal, acts in themselves but menial; and which has gained for the negro the repute of making the most pleasing body servant in the world; one, too, whom a master need be on no stiffly superior terms with, but may treat with familiar trust; less a servant than a devoted companion.

Marking the noisy indocility of the blacks in general, as well as what seemed the sullen inefficiency of the whites, it was not without humane satisfaction that Captain Delano witnessed the steady good conduct of Babo.

But the good conduct of Babo, hardly more than the ill-behaviour of others, seemed to withdraw the half-lunatic Don Benito from his cloudy languor. Not that such precisely was the impression made by the Spaniard on the mind of his visitor. The Spaniard's individual unrest was, for the present, but noted as a conspicuous feature in the ship's general affliction. Still, Captain Delano was not a little concerned at what he could not help taking for the time to be Don Benito's unfriendly indifference toward himself. The Spaniard's manner, too, conveyed a sort of sour and gloomy disdain, which he seemed at no pains to disguise. But this the American in charity ascribed to the harassing effects of sickness, since, in former instances, he had noted that there are peculiar natures on whom prolonged physical suffering seems to cancel every social instinct of kindness; as if forced to black bread themselves, they deemed it but equity that each person coming nigh them should, indirectly, by some slight or affront, be made to partake of their fare.

But ere long Captain Delano bethought him that, indulgent as he was at the first, in judging the Spaniard, he might not, after all, have exercised charity enough. At bottom it was Don Benito's reserve which displeased him; but the same reserve was shown toward all but his personal attendant. Even the formal reports which, according to sea-usage, were at stated times made to him by some petty underling (either a white, mulatto or black), he hardly had patience enough to listen to, without betraying contemptuous aversion. His manner upon such occasions was, in its degree, not unlike that which might be supposed to have been his imperial countryman's, Charles V., just previous to the anchoritish retirement of that monarch from the throne.

This splenetic disrelish of his place was evinced in almost every function pertaining to it. Proud as he was moody, he condescended to no personal mandate. Whatever special orders were necessary, their delivery was delegated to his body-servant, who in turn transferred them to their ultimate destination, through runners, alert Spanish boys or slave boys, like pages or pilot-fish within easy call, continually hovering round Don Benito. So that to have beheld this undemonstrative invalid gliding about, apathetic and mute, no landsman could have dreamed that in him was lodged a dictatorship beyond which, while at sea, there was no earthly appeal.

Thus, the Spaniard, regarded in his reserve, seemed as the involuntary victim of mental disorder. But, in fact, his reserve might, in some degree, have proceeded from design. If so, then in Don Benito was evinced the unhealthy climax of that icy though conscientious policy, more or less adopted by all commanders of large ships, which, except in signal emergencies, obliterates alike the manifestation of sway with every trace of sociality; transforming the man into a block, or rather into a loaded cannon, which, until there is call for thunder, has nothing to say.

Viewing him in this light, it seemed but a natural token of the perverse habit induced by a long course of such hard self-restraint, that, notwithstanding the present condition of his ship, the Spaniard should still persist in a demeanour, which, however harmless—or it may be, appropriate—in a well-appointed vessel, such as the *San Dominick* might have been at the outset of the voyage, was anything but judicious now. But the Spaniard perhaps thought that it was with captains as with gods: reserve, under all events, must still be their cue. But more probably this appearance of slumbering dominion might have been but an attempted disguise to conscious imbecility—not deep policy, but shallow device. But be all this as it might, whether Don Benito's manner was designed or not, the more Captain Delano noted its pervading reserve, the less he felt uneasiness at any particular manifestation of that reserve toward himself.

Neither were his thoughts taken up by the captain alone. Wonted to the quiet orderliness of the sealer's comfortable family of a crew, the noisy confusion of the *San Dominick's* suffering host repeatedly challenged his eye. Some prominent breaches not only of discipline but of decency were observed. These Captain Delano could not but ascribe, in the main, to the absence of those subordinate deck-officers to whom, along with higher duties, is entrusted what may be styled the police department of a populous ship. True, the old oakum-pickers appeared at times to act the part of monitorial constables to their countrymen, the blacks; but though occasionally succeeding in allaying trifling outbreaks now and then between man and man, they could do little or nothing toward establishing general quiet. The *San Dominick* was in the condition of a transatlantic emigrant ship, among whose multitude of living freight are some individuals, doubtless, as little troublesome as crates and bales; but the friendly remonstrances of such with their ruder companions are of not so much avail as the unfriendly arm of the mate. What the *San Dominick* wanted was, what the emigrant ship has, stern superior officers. But on these decks not so much as a fourth mate was to be seen.

The visitor's curiosity was roused to learn the particulars of those mishaps which had brought about such absenteeism, with its consequences; because, though deriving some inkling of the voyage from the wails which at the first moment had greeted him, yet of the details no clear understanding had been had. The best account would, doubtless, be given by the captain. Yet at first the visitor was loth to ask it, unwilling to provoke some distant rebuff. But plucking up courage, he at last accosted Don Benito, renewing the expression of his benevolent interest, adding, that did he (Captain Delano) but know the particulars of the ship's misfortunes, he would, perhaps, be better able in the end to relieve them. Would Don Benito favour him with the whole story?

Don Benito faltered; then, like some somnambulist suddenly interfered with, vacantly stared at his visitor, and ended by looking down on the deck. He maintained this posture so long, that Captain Delano, almost equally disconcerted, and involuntarily almost as rude, turned suddenly from him, walking forward to accost one of the Spanish seamen for the desired information. But he had hardly gone five paces, when with a sort of eagerness Don Benito invited him back, regretting his momentary absence of mind, and professing readiness to gratify him.

While most part of the story was being given, the two captains stood on the after part of the main-deck, a privileged spot, no one being near but the servant.

"It is now a hundred and ninety days," began the Spaniard, in his husky whisper, "that this ship, well officered and well manned, with several cabin passengers—some fifty Spaniards in all—sailed from Buenos Ayres bound to Lima, with a general cargo, Paraguay tea and the like—and," pointing forward, "that parcel of negroes, now not more than a hundred and fifty, as you see, but then numbering over three hundred souls. Off Cape Horn we had heavy gales. In one moment, by night, three of my best officers, with fifteen sailors, were lost, with the main-yard; the spar snapping under them in the slings, as they sought, with heavers, to beat down the icy sail. To lighten the hull, the heavier sacks of mata were thrown into the sea, with most of the water-pipes lashed on deck at the time. And this last necessity it was, combined with the prolonged detentions afterwards experienced, which eventually brought about our chief causes of suffering. When—"

Here there was a sudden fainting attack of his cough, brought on, no doubt, by his mental distress. His servant sustained him, and drawing a cordial from his pocket placed it to his lips. He a little revived. But unwilling to leave him unsupported while yet imperfectly restored, the black with one arm still encircled his master, at the same time keeping his eye fixed on his face, as if to watch for the first sign of complete restoration, or relapse, as the event might prove.

The Spaniard proceeded, but brokenly and obscurely, as one in a dream.

—"Oh, my God! rather than pass through what I have, with joy I would have hailed the most terrible gales; but—"

His cough returned and with increased violence; this subsiding, with reddened lips and closed eyes he fell heavily against his supporter.

"His mind wanders. He was thinking of the plague that followed the gales," plaintively sighed the servant; "my poor, poor master!" wringing one hand, and with the other wiping the mouth. "But be patient, Señor," again turning to Captain Delano, "these fits do not last long; master will soon be himself."

Don Benito reviving, went on; but as this portion of the story was very brokenly delivered, the substance only will here be set down.

It appeared that after the ship had been many days tossed in storms off the Cape, the scurvy broke out, carrying off numbers of the whites and blacks. When at last they had worked round into the Pacific, their spars and sails were so damaged, and so inadequately handled by the surviving mariners, most of whom were become invalids, that, unable to lay her northerly course by the wind, which was powerful, the unmanageable ship for successive days and nights was blown northwestward, where the breeze suddenly deserted her, in unknown waters, to sultry calms. The absence of the water-pipes now proved as fatal to life as before their presence had menaced it. Induced, or at least aggravated, by the more than scanty allowance of water, a malignant fever followed the scurvy; with the excessive heat of the lengthened calm, making such short work of it as to sweep away, as by billows, whole families of the Africans, and a yet larger number, proportionably, of the Spaniards, including, by a luckless fatality, every officer on board. Consequently, in the smart west winds eventually following the calm, the already rent sails having to be simply dropped, not furled, at need, had been gradually reduced to the beggar's rags they were now. To procure substitutes for his lost sailors, as well as supplies of water and sails, the captain at the earliest opportunity had made for Baldivia, the southernmost civilized port of Chili and South America; but upon nearing the coast the thick weather had prevented him from so much as sighting that harbour. Since which period, almost without a crew, and almost without canvas and almost without water, and at intervals giving its added dead to the sea, the *San Dominick* had been battledored about by contrary winds, inveigled by currents, or grown weedy in calms. Like a man lost in woods, more than once she had doubled upon her own track.

"But throughout these calamities," huskily continued Don Benito, painfully turning in the half embrace of his servant, "I have to thank those negroes you see, who, though to your inexperienced eyes appearing unruly, have, indeed, conducted themselves with less of restlessness than even their owner could have thought possible under such circumstances."

Here he again fell faintly back. Again his mind wandered: but he rallied, and less obscurely proceeded.

"Yes, their owner was quite right in assuring me that no fetters would be needed with his blacks; so that while, as is wont in this transportation, those negroes have always remained upon deck—not thrust below, as in the Guineamen—they have, also, from the beginning, been freely permitted to range within given bounds at their pleasure."

Once more the faintness returned—his mind roved—but, recovering, he resumed:

"But it is Babo here to whom, under God, I owe not only my own preservation, but likewise to him, chiefly, the merit is due, of pacifying his more ignorant brethren, when at intervals tempted to murmurings."

"Ah, master," sighed the black, bowing his face, "don't speak of me; Babo is nothing; what Babo has done was but duty."

"Faithful fellow!" cried Captain Delano. "Don Benito, I envy you such a friend; slave I cannot call him."

As master and man stood before him, the black upholding the white, Captain Delano could not but bethink him of the beauty of that relationship which could present such a spectacle of fidelity on the one hand and confidence on the other. The scene was heightened by the contrast in dress, denoting their relative positions. The Spaniard wore a loose Chili jacket of dark velvet; white small clothes and stockings, with silver buckles at the knee and instep; a high-crowned sombrero, of fine grass; a slender sword, silver mounted, hung from a knot in his sash; the last being an almost invariable adjunct, more for utility than ornament, of a South American gentleman's dress to this hour. Excepting when his occasional nervous contortions brought about disarray, there was a certain precision in his attire, curiously at variance with the unsightly disorder around; especially in the belittered Ghetto, forward of the main-mast, wholly occupied by the blacks.

The servant wore nothing but wide trousers, apparently, from their coarseness and patches, made out of some old top-sail; they were clean, and confined at the waist by a bit of unstranded rope, which, with his composed, deprecatory air at times, made him look something like a begging friar of St. Francis.

However unsuitable for the time and place, at least in the blunt-thinking American's eyes, and however strangely surviving in the midst of all his afflictions, the toilette of Don Benito might not, in fashion at least, have gone beyond the style of the day among South Americans of his class. Though on the present voyage sailing from Buenos Ayres, he had avowed himself a native and resident of Chili, whose inhabitants had not so generally adopted the plain coat and once plebeian

pantaloons; but, with a becoming modification, adhered to their provincial costume, picturesque as any in the world. Still, relatively to the
pale history of the voyage, and his own pale face, there seemed something so incongruous in the Spaniard's apparel, as almost to suggest the
image of an invalid courtier tottering about London streets in the time
of the plague.

The portion of the narrative which, perhaps, most excited interest,
as well as some surprise, considering the latitudes in question, was the
long calms spoken of, and more particularly the ship's so long drifting
about. Without communicating the opinion, of course, the American
could not but impute at least part of the detentions both to clumsy
seamanship and faulty navigation. Eyeing Don Benito's small, yellow
hands, he easily inferred that the young captain had not got into command at the hawse-hole but the cabin-window, and if so, why wonder
at incompetence, in youth, sickness, and aristocracy united? Such was
his democratic conclusion.

But drowning criticism in compassion, after a fresh repetition of
his sympathies, Captain Delano having heard out his story, not only
engaged, as in the first place, to see Don Benito and his people supplied
in their immediate bodily needs, but, also, now further promised to
assist him in procuring a large permanent supply of water, as well as
some sails and rigging; and, though it would involve no small embarrassment to himself, yet he would spare three of his best seamen for
temporary deck officers; so that without delay the ship might proceed
to Concepcion,[7] there fully to refit for Lima, her destined port.

Such generosity was not without its effect, even upon the invalid.
His face lighted up; eager and hectic, he met the honest glance of his
visitor. With gratitude he seemed overcome.

"This excitement is bad for master," whispered the servant, taking
his arm, and with soothing words gently drawing him aside.

When Don Benito returned, the American was pained to observe
that his hopefulness, like the sudden kindling in his cheek, was but
febrile and transient.

Ere long, with a joyless mien, looking up toward the poop, the host
invited his guest to accompany him there, for the benefit of what little
breath of wind might be stirring.

As during the telling of the story, Captail Delano had once or twice
started at the occasional cymballing of the hatchet-polishers, wondering why such an interruption should be allowed, especially in that part
of the ship, and in the ears of an invalid; and, moreover, as the
hatchets had anything but an attractive look, and the handlers of them
still less so, it was, therefore, to tell the truth, not without some lurking reluctance, or even shrinking, it may be, that Captain Delano, with
apparent complaisance, acquiesced in his host's invitation. The more

---

[7] A port in Chile.

so, since with an untimely caprice of punctilio, rendered distressing by his cadaverous aspect, Don Benito, with Castilian bows, solemnly insisted upon his guest's preceding him up the ladder leading to the elevation; where, one on each side of the last step, sat four armorial supporters and sentries, two of the ominous file. Gingerly enough stepped good Captain Delano between them, and in the instant of leaving them behind, like one running the gauntlet, he felt an apprehensive twitch in the calves of his legs.

But when, facing about, he saw the whole file, like so many organ-grinders, still stupidly intent on their work, unmindful of everything beside, he could not but smile at his late fidgeting panic.

Presently, while standing with Don Benito, looking forward upon the decks below, he was struck by one of those instances of insubordination previously alluded to. Three black boys, with two Spanish boys, were sitting together on the hatchets, scraping a rude wooden platter, in which some scanty mess had recently been cooked. Suddenly, one of the black boys, enraged at a word dropped by one of his white companions, seized a knife, and though called to forbear by one of the oakum-pickers, struck the lad over the head, inflicting a gash from which blood flowed.

In amazement, Captain Delano inquired what this meant. To which the pale Benito dully muttered, that it was merely the sport of the lad.

"Pretty serious sport, truly," rejoined Captain Delano. "Had such a thing happened on board the *Bachelor's Delight,* instant punishment would have followed."

At these words the Spaniard turned upon the American one of his sudden, staring, half-lunatic looks; then, relapsing into his torpor, answered, "Doubtless, doubtless, Señor."

Is it, thought Captain Delano, that this helpless man is one of those paper captains I've known, who by policy wink at what by power they cannot put down? I know no sadder sight than a commander who has little of command but the name.

"I should think, Don Benito," he now said, glancing toward the oakum-picker who had sought to interfere with the boys, "that you would find it advantageous to keep all your blacks employed, especially the younger ones, no matter at what useless task, and no matter what happens to the ship. Why, even with my little band, I find such a course indispensable. I once kept a crew on my quarter-deck thrumming mats for my cabin, when, for three days, I had given up my ship—mats, men, and all—for a speedy loss, owing to the violence of a gale in which we could do nothing but helplessly drive before it."

"Doubtless, doubtless," muttered Don Benito.

"But," continued Captain Delano, again glancing upon the oakum-pickers and then at the hatchet-polishers, near by, "I see you keep some at least of your host employed."

"Yes," was again the vacant response.

"Those old men there, shaking their pows from their pulpits," continued Captain Delano, pointing to the oakum-pickers, "seem to act the part of old dominies to the rest, little heeded as their admonitions are at times. Is this voluntary on their part, Don Benito, or have you appointed them shepherds to your flock of black sheep?"

"What posts they fill, I appointed them," rejoined the Spaniard in an acrid tone, as if resenting some supposed satiric reflection.

"And these others, these Ashantee [8] conjurors here," continued Captain Delano, rather uneasily eyeing the brandished steel of the hatchet-polishers, where in spots it had been brought to a shine, "this seems a curious business they are at, Don Benito?"

"In the gales we met," answered the Spaniard, "what of our general cargo was not thrown overboard was much damaged by the brine. Since coming into calm weather, I have had several cases of knives and hatchets daily brought up for overhauling and cleaning."

"A prudent idea, Don Benito. You are part owner of ship and cargo, I presume; but not of the slaves perhaps?"

"I am owner of all you see," impatiently returned Don Benito, "except the main company of blacks, who belonged to my late friend, Alexandro Aranda."

As he mentioned this name, his air was heart-broken, his knees shook; his servant supported him.

Thinking he divined the cause of such unusual emotion, to confirm his surmise, Captain Delano, after a pause, said, "And may I ask, Don Benito, whether—since awhile ago you spoke of some cabin passengers—the friend, whose loss so afflicts you, at the outset of the voyage accompanied his blacks?"

"Yes."

"But died of the fever?"

"Died of the fever.—Oh, could I but—"

Again quivering, the Spaniard paused.

"Pardon me," said Captain Delano slowly, "but I think that, by a sympathetic experience, I conjecture, Don Benito, what it is that gives the keener edge to your grief. It was once my hard fortune to lose at sea a dear friend, my own brother, then supercargo. Assured of the welfare of his spirit, its departure I could have borne like a man; but that honest eye, that honest hand—both of which had so often met mine—and that warm heart; all, all—like scraps to the dogs—to throw all to the sharks! It was then I vowed never to have for fellow-voyager a man I loved, unless, unbeknown to him, I had provided every requisite, in case of a fatality, for embalming his mortal part for interment on shore. Were your friend's remains now on board this ship, Don Benito, not thus strangely would the mention of his name affect you."

"On board this ship?" echoed the Spaniard. Then, with horrified

8 West African kingdom.

gestures, as directed against some spectre, he unconsciously fell into the ready arms of his attendant, who, with a silent appeal toward Captain Delano, seemed beseeching him not again to broach a theme so unspeakably distressing to his master.

This poor fellow now, thought the pained American, is the victim of that sad superstition which associates goblins with the deserted body of man, as ghosts with an abandoned house. How unlike are we made! What to me, in like case, would have been a solemn satisfaction, the bare suggestion, even, terrifies the Spaniard into this trance. Poor Alexandro Aranda! what would you say could you here see your friend —who, on former voyages, when you for months were left behind, has, I dare say, often longed, and longed, for one peep at you—now transported with terror at the least thought of having you anyway nigh him.

At this moment, with a dreary graveyard toll, betokening a flaw, the ship's forecastle bell, smote by one of the grizzled oakum-pickers, proclaimed ten o'clock through the leaden calm; when Captain Delano's attention was caught by the moving figure of a gigantic black, emerging from the general crowd below, and slowly advancing toward the elevated poop. An iron collar was about his neck, from which depended a chain, thrice wound round his body; the terminating links padlocked together at a broad band of iron, his girdle.

"How like a mute Atufal moves," murmured the servant.

The black mounted the steps of the poop, and, like a brave prisoner, brought up to receive sentence, stood in unquailing muteness before Don Benito, now recovered from his attack.

At the first glimpse of his approach, Don Benito had started, a resentful shadow swept over his face; and, as with the sudden memory of bootless rage, his white lips glued together.

This is some mulish mutineer, thought Captain Delano, surveying, not without a mixture of admiration, the colossal form of the negro.

"See, he waits your question, master," said the servant.

Thus reminded, Don Benito, nervously averting his glance, as if shunning, by anticipation, some rebellious response, in a disconcerted voice, thus spoke:

"Atufal, will you ask my pardon now?"

The black was silent.

"Again, master," murmured the servant, with bitter upbraiding eyeing his countryman. "Again, master; he will bend to master yet."

"Answer," said Don Benito, still averting his glance, "say but the one word *pardon*, and your chains shall be off."

Upon this, the black, slowly raising both arms, let them lifelessly fall, his links clanking, his head bowed; as much as to say, "No, I am content."

"Go," said Don Benito, with inkept emotion.

Deliberately as he had come, the black obeyed.

"Excuse me, Don Benito," said Captain Delano, "but this scene surprises me; what means it, pray?"

"It means that that negro alone, of all the band, has given me peculiar cause of offence. I have put him in chains; I—"

Here he paused; his hand to his head, as if there were a swimming there, or a sudden bewilderment of memory had come over him; but meeting his servant's kindly glance seemed reassured, and proceeded:

"I could not scourge such a form. But I told him he must ask my pardon. As yet he has not. At my command, every two hours he stands before me."

"And how long has this been?"

"Some sixty days."

"And obedient in all else? And respectful?"

"Yes."

"Upon my conscience, then," exclaimed Captain Delano, impulsively, "he has a royal spirit in him, this fellow."

"He may have some right to it," bitterly returned Don Benito; "he says he was king in his own land."

"Yes," said the servant, entering a word, "those slits in Atufal's ears once held wedges of gold; but poor Babo here, in his own land, was only a poor slave; a black man's slave was Babo, who now is the white's."

Somewhat annoyed by these conversational familiarities, Captain Delano turned curiously upon the attendant, then glanced inquiringly at his master; but, as if long wonted to these little informalities, neither master nor man seemed to understand him.

"What, pray, was Atufal's offence, Don Benito?" asked Captain Delano; "if it was not something very serious, take a fool's advice, and, in view of his general docility, as well as in some natural respect for his spirit, remit his penalty."

"No, no, master never will do that," here murmured the servant to himself, "proud Atufal must first ask master's pardon. The slave there carries the padlock, but master here carries the key."

His attention thus directed, Captain Delano now noticed for the first time that, suspended by a slender silken cord, from Don Benito's neck hung a key. At once, from the servant's muttered syllables dividing the key's purpose, he smiled and said: "So, Don Benito—padlock and key—significant symbols, truly."

Biting his lip, Don Benito faltered.

Though the remark of Captain Delano, a man of such native simplicity as to be incapable of satire or irony, had been dropped in playful allusion to the Spaniard's singularly evidenced lordship over the black; yet the hypochondriac seemed in some way to have taken it as a malicious reflection upon his confessed inability thus far to break down, at least, on a verbal summons, the entrenched will of the slave. Deploring this supposed misconception, yet despairing of correcting it, Captain

Delano shifted the subject; but finding his companion more than ever
withdrawn, as if still slowly digesting the lees of the presumed affront
above-mentioned, by-and-by Captain Delano likewise became less talkative, oppressed, against his own will, by what seemed the secret vin-
dictiveness of the morbidly sensitive Spaniard. But the good sailor himself, of a quite contrary disposition, refrained, on his part, alike from
the appearance as from the feeling of resentment, and if silent, was
only so from contagion.

Presently the Spaniard, assisted by his servant, somewhat dis-
courteously crossed over from Captain Delano; a procedure which, sensibly enough, might have been allowed to pass for idle caprice of ill-
humour, had not master and man, lingering round the corner of the
elevated skylight, begun whispering together in low voices. This was
unpleasing. And more: the moody air of the Spaniard, which at times
had not been without a sort of valetudinarian stateliness, now seemed
anything but dignified; while the menial familiarity of the servant lost
its original charm of simple-hearted attachment.

In his embarrassment, the visitor turned his face to the other side
of the ship. By so doing, his glance accidentally fell on a young Spanish
sailor, a coil of rope in his hand, just stepped from the deck to the
first round of the mizzen-rigging. Perhaps the man would not have been
particularly noticed, were it not that, during his ascent to one of the
yards, he, with a sort of covert intentness, kept his eye fixed on Captain
Delano, from whom, presently, it passed, as if by a natural sequence,
to the two whisperers.

His own attention thus redirected to that quarter, Captain Delano
gave a slight start. From something in Don Benito's manner just then,
it seemed as if the visitor had, at least partly, been the subject of the
withdrawn consultation going on—a conjecture as little agreeable to
the guest as it was little flattering to the host.

The singular alternations of courtesy and ill-breeding in the Spanish
captain were unaccountable, except on one of two suppositions—innocent lunacy, or wicked imposture.

But the first idea, though it might naturally have occurred to an
indifferent observer, and, in some respects, had not hitherto been wholly
a stranger to Captain Delano's mind, yet, now that, in an incipient way,
he began to regard the stranger's conduct something in the light of an
intentional affront, of course the idea of lunacy was virtually vacated.
But if not a lunatic, what then? Under the circumstances, would a
gentleman, nay, any honest boor, act the part now acted by his host?
The man was an impostor. Some low-born adventurer, masquerading
as an oceanic grandee; yet so ignorant of the first requisites of mere
gentlemanhood as to be betrayed into the present remarkable indeco-
rum. That strange ceremoniousness, too, at other times evinced, seemed
not uncharacteristic of one playing a part above his real level. Benito
Cereno—Don Benito Cereno—a sounding name. One, too, at that

period, not unknown, in the surname, to supercargoes and sea captains trading along the Spanish Main, as belonging to one of the most enterprising and extensive mercantile families in all those provinces; several members of it having titles; a sort of Castilian Rothschild, with a noble brother, or cousin, in every great trading town of South America. The alleged Don Benito was in early manhood, about twenty-nine or thirty. To assume a sort of roving cadetship in the maritime affairs of such a house, what more likely scheme for a young knave of talent and spirit? But the Spaniard was a pale invalid. Never mind. For even to the degree of simulating mortal disease, the craft of some tricksters had been known to attain. To think that, under the aspect of infantile weakness, the most savage energies might be couched—those velvets of the Spaniard but the velvet paw to his fangs.

From no train of thought did these fancies come; not from within, but from without; suddenly, too, and in one throng, like hoar frost; yet as soon to vanish as the mild sun of Captain Delano's good-nature regained its meridian.

Glancing over once again toward Don Benito—whose side-face, revealed above the skylight, was now turned toward him—Captain Delano was struck by the profile, whose clearness of cut was refined by the thinness incident to ill-health, as well as ennobled about the chin by the beard. Away with suspicion. He was a true off-shoot of a true hidalgo [9] Cereno.

Relieved by these and other, better thoughts, the visitor, lightly humming a tune, now began indifferently pacing the poop, so as not to betray to Don Benito that he had at all mistrusted incivility, much less duplicity; for such mistrust would yet be proved illusory, and by the event; though, for the present, the circumstance which had provoked that distrust remained unexplained. But when that little mystery should have been cleared up, Captain Delano thought he might extremely regret it, did he allow Don Benito to become aware that he had indulged in ungenerous surmises. In short, to the Spaniard's blackletter text, it was best, for a while, to leave open margin.

Presently, his pale face twitching and overcast, the Spaniard, still supported by his attendant, moved over toward his guest, when, with even more than his usual embarrassment, and a strange sort of intriguing intonation in his husky whisper, the following conversation began:

"Señor, may I ask how long you have lain at this isle?"

"Oh, but a day or two, Don Benito."

"And from what port are you last?"

"Canton."

"And there, Señor, you exchanged your seal-skins for teas and silks, I think you said?"

[9] Spanish noble.

"Yes. Silks, mostly."

"And the balance you took in specie, perhaps?"

Captain Delano, fidgeting a little, answered—

"Yes; some silver; not a very great deal, though."

"Ah—well. May I ask how many men have you on board, Señor?"

Captain Delano slightly started, but answered:

"About five-and-twenty, all told."

"And at present, Señor, all on board, I suppose?"

"All on board, Don Benito," replied the captain now with satisfaction.

"And will be to-night, Señor?"

At this last question, following so many pertinacious ones, for the soul of him Captain Delano could not but look very earnestly at the questioner, who, instead of meeting the glance, with every token of craven discomposure dropped his eyes to the deck; presenting an unworthy contrast to his servant, who, just then, was kneeling at his feet adjusting a loose shoe-buckle; his disengaged face meantime, with humble curiosity, turned openly up into his master's downcast one.

The Spaniard, still with a guilty shuffle, repeated his question:

"And—and will be to-night, Señor?"

"Yes, for aught I know," returned Captain Delano,—"but nay," rallying himself into fearless truth, "some of them talked of going off on another fishing party about midnight."

"Your ships generally go—go more or less armed, I believe, Señor?"

"Oh, a six-pounder or two, in case of emergency," was the intrepidly indifferent reply, "with a small stock of muskets, sealing-spears, and cutlasses, you know."

As he thus responded, Captain Delano again glanced at Don Benito, but the latter's eyes were averted; while abruptly and awkwardly shifting the subject, he made some peevish allusion to the calm, and then, without apology, once more, with his attendant, withdrew to the opposite bulwarks, where the whispering was resumed.

At this moment, and ere Captain Delano could cast a cool thought upon what had just passed, the young Spanish sailor before mentioned was seen descending from the rigging. In act of stooping over to spring inboard to the deck, his voluminous, unconfined frock, or shirt, of coarse woollen, much spotted with tar, opened out far down the chest, revealing a soiled under-garment of what seemed the finest linen, edged, about the neck, with a narrow blue ribbon, sadly faded and worn. At this moment the young sailor's eye was again fixed on the whisperers, and Captain Delano thought he observed a lurking significance in it, as if silent signs of some freemason sort had that instant been interchanged.

This once more impelled his own glance in the direction of Don Benito, and, as before, he could not but infer that himself formed the subject of the conference. He paused. The sound of the hatchet-polishing fell on his ears. He cast another swift side-look at the two. They had the air of conspirators. In connection with the late questionings, and the incident of the young sailor, these things now begat such return of involuntary suspicion, that the singular guilelessness of the American could not endure it. Plucking up a gay and humorous expression, he crossed over to the two rapidly, saying: "Ha, Don Benito, your black here seems high in your trust; a sort of privy-counsellor, in fact."

Upon this, the servant looked up with a good-natured grin, but the master started as from a venomous bite. It was a moment or two before the Spaniard sufficiently recovered himself to reply; which he did, at last, with cold constraint: "Yes, Señor, I have trust in Babo."

Here Babo, changing his previous grin of mere animal humor into an intelligent smile, not ungratefully eyed his master.

Finding that the Spaniard now stood silent and reserved, as if involuntarily, or purposely giving hint that his guest's proximity was inconvenient just then, Captain Delano, unwilling to appear uncivil even to incivility itself, made some trivial remark and moved off; again and again turning over in his mind the mysterious demeanour of Don Benito Cereno.

He had descended from the poop, and, wrapped in thought, was passing near a dark hatchway, leading down into the steerage, when perceiving motion there, he looked to see what moved. The same instant there was a sparkle in the shadowy hatchway, and he saw one of the Spanish sailors, prowling there, hurriedly placing his hand in the bosom of his frock, as if hiding something. Before the man could have been certain who it was that was passing, he slunk below out of sight. But enough was seen of him to make it sure that he was the same young sailor before noticed in the rigging.

What was that which so sparkled? thought Captain Delano. It was no lamp—no match—no live coal. Could it have been a jewel? But how come sailors with jewels?—or with silk-trimmed under-shirts either? Has he been robbing the trunks of the dead cabin passengers? But if so, he would hardly wear one of the stolen articles on board ship here. Ah, ah—if now that was, indeed, a secret sign I saw passing between this suspicious fellow and his captain awhile since; if I could only be certain that in my uneasiness my senses did not deceive me, then—

Here, passing from one suspicious thing to another, his mind revolved the point of the strange questions put to him concerning his ship.

By a curious coincidence, as each point was recalled, the black wizards of Ashantee would strike up with their hatchets, as in ominous comment on the white stranger's thoughts. Pressed by such enigmas and portents, it would have been almost against nature, had not, even into the least distrustful heart, some ugly misgivings obtruded.

Observing the ship now helplessly fallen into a current, with enchanted sails, drifting with increased rapidity seaward; and noting that, from a lately intercepted projection of the land, the sealer was hidden, the stout mariner began to quake at thoughts which he barely durst confess to himself. Above all, he began to feel a ghostly dread of Don Benito. And yet when he roused himself, dilated his chest, felt himself strong on his legs, and coolly considered it—what did all these phantoms amount to?

Had the Spaniard any sinister scheme, it must have reference not so much to him (Captain Delano) as to his ship (the *Bachelor's Delight*). Hence the present drifting away of the one ship from the other, instead of favouring any such possible scheme, was, for the time at least, opposed to it. Clearly any suspicion, combining such contradictions, must need be delusive. Beside, was it not absurd to think of a vessel in distress—a vessel by sickness almost dismanned of her crew— a vessel whose inmates were parched for water—was it not a thousand times absurd that such a craft should, at present, be of a piratical character; or her commander, either for himself or those under him, cherish any desire but for speedy relief and refreshment? But then, might not general distress, and thirst in particular, be affected? And might not that same undiminished Spanish crew, alleged to have perished off to a remnant, be at that very moment lurking in the hold? On heart-broken pretence of entreating a cup of cold water, fiends in human form had got into lonely dwellings, nor retired until a dark deed had been done. And among the Malay pirates, it was no unusual thing to lure ships after them into their treacherous harbours, or entice boarders from a declared enemy at sea, by the spectacle of thinly manned or vacant decks, beneath which prowled a hundred spears with yellow arms ready to upthrust them through the mats. Not that Captain Delano had entirely credited such things. He had heard of them—and now, as stories, they recurred. The present destination of the ship was the anchorage. There she would be near his own vessel. Upon gaining that vicinity, might not the *San Dominick*, like a slumbering volcano, suddenly let loose energies now hid?

He recalled the Spaniard's manner while telling his story. There was a gloomy hesitancy and subterfuge about it. It was just the manner of one making up his tale for evil purposes, as he goes. But if that story was not true, what was the truth? That the ship had unlawfully come into the Spaniard's possession? But in many of its details, especially in reference to the more calamitous parts, such as the fatalities among the seamen, the consequent prolonged beating about, the past sufferings from obstinate calms, and still continued suffering from thirst; in all these points, as well as others, Don Benito's story had corroborated not only the wailing ejaculations of the indiscriminate multitude, white and black, but likewise—what seemed impossible to be counterfeit—by the very expression and play of every human feature, which Captain Delano saw. If Don Benito's story was throughout an invention, then every soul on board, down to the youngest negress, was his carefully drilled recruit in the plot: an incredible inference. And yet, if there was ground for mistrusting the Spanish captain's veracity, that inference was a legitimate one.

In short, scarce an uneasiness entered the honest sailor's mind but, by a subsequent spontaneous act of good sense, it was ejected. At last he began to laugh at these forebodings; and laugh at the strange ship for, in its aspect some-way siding with them, as it were; and laugh, too, at the odd-looking blacks, particularly those old scissors-grinders, the Ashantees; and those bed-ridden old knitting-women, the oakum-pickers; and, in a human way, he almost began to laugh at the dark Spaniard himself, the central hobgoblin of all.

For the rest, whatever in a serious way seemed enigmatical, was now good-naturedly explained away by the thought that, for the most part, the poor invalid scarcely knew what he was about; either sulking in black vapours, or putting random questions without sense or object. Evidently, for the present, the man was not fit to be entrusted with the ship. On some benevolent plea withdrawing the command from him, Captain Delano would yet have to send her to Concepcion in charge of his second mate, a worthy person and good navigator—a plan which would prove no wiser for the *San Dominick* than for Don Benito; for— relieved from all anxiety, keeping wholly to his cabin—the sick man, under the good nursing of his servant, would probably, by the end of the passage, be in a measure restored to health and with that he should also be restored to authority.

Such were the American's thoughts. They were tranquillizing. There was a difference between the idea of Don Benito's darky pre-ordaining Captain Delano's fate, and Captain Delano's lightly arranging Don Benito's. Nevertheless, it was not without something of relief that the good seaman presently perceived his whale-boat in the distance. Its absence had been prolonged by unexpected detention at the sealer's side, as well as its returning trip lengthened by the continual recession of the goal.

The advancing speck was observed by the blacks. Their shouts attracted the attention of Don Benito, who, with a return of courtesy, approaching Captain Delano, expressed satisfaction at the coming of some supplies, slight and temporary as they must necessarily prove.

Captain Delano responded; but while doing so, his attention was drawn to something passing on the deck below: among the crowd climbing the landward bulwarks, anxiously watching the coming boat, two blacks, to all appearances accidentally incommoded by one of the sailors, flew out against him with horrible curses, which the sailor someway resenting, the two blacks dashed him to the deck and jumped upon him, despite the earnest cries of the oakum-pickers.

"Don Benito," said Captain Delano quickly, "do you see what is going on there? Look!"

But, seized by his cough, the Spaniard staggered, with both hands
to his face, on the point of falling. Captain Delano would have supported him, but the servant was more alert, who, with one hand sustaining his master, with the other applied the cordial. Don Benito
restored, the black withdrew his support, slipping aside a little, but dutifully remaining within call of a whisper. Such discretion was here
evinced as quite wiped away, in the visitor's eyes, any blemish of im-
propriety which might have attached to the attendant, from the indecorous conferences before mentioned; showing, too, that if the servant
were to blame, it might be more the master's fault than his own, since
when left to himself he could conduct thus well.

His glance thus called away from the spectacle of disorder to the
more pleasing one before him, Captain Delano could not avoid again
congratulating Don Benito upon possessing such a servant, who, though
perhaps a little too forward now and then, must upon the whole be
invaluable to one in the invalid's situation.

"Tell me, Don Benito," he added, with a smile—"I should like to
have your man here myself—what will you take for him? Would fifty
doubloons be any object?"

"Master wouldn't part with Babo for a thousand doubloons," murmured the black, overhearing the offer, and taking it in earnest, and,
with the strange vanity of a faithful slave appreciated by his master,
scorning to hear so paltry a valuation put upon him by a stranger. But
Don Benito, apparently hardly yet completely restored, and again interrupted by his cough, made but some broken reply.

Soon his physical distress became so great, affecting his mind, too,
apparently, that, as if to screen the sad spectacle, the servant gently
conducted his master below.

Left to himself, the American, to while away the time till his boat
should arrive, would have pleasantly accosted some one of the few
Spanish seamen he saw; but recalling something that Don Benito had
said touching their ill conduct, he refrained, as a ship-master indisposed
to countenance cowardice or unfaithfulness in seamen.

While, with these thoughts, standing with eye directed forward
toward that handful of sailors—suddenly he thought that some of them
returned the glance and with a sort of meaning. He rubbed his eyes,
and looked again; but again seemed to see the same thing. Under a new
form, but more obscure than any previous one, the old suspicions
recurred, but, in the absence of Don Benito, with less of panic than
before. Despite the bad account given of the sailors, Captain Delano
resolved forthwith to accost one of them. Descending the poop, he made
his way through the blacks, his movement drawing a queer cry from
the oakum-pickers, prompted by whom the negroes, twitching each
other aside, divided before him; but, as if curious to see what was the
object of this deliberate visit to their Ghetto, closing in behind, in
tolerable order, followed the white stranger up. His progress thus pro-

claimed as by mounted kings-at-arms, and escorted as by a Caffre[10] guard of honour, Captain Delano, assuming a good-humoured, off-hand air, continued to advance; now and then saying a blithe word to the negroes, and his eye curiously surveying the white faces, here and there sparsely mixed in with the blacks, like stray white pawns venturously involved in the ranks of the chessmen opposed.

While thinking which of them to select for his purpose, he chanced to observe a sailor seated on the deck engaged in tarring the strap of a large block, with a circle of blacks squatted round him inquisitively eyeing the process.

The mean employment of the man was in contrast with something superior in his figure. His hand, black with continually thrusting it into the tar-pot held for him by a negro, seemed not naturally allied to his face, a face which would have been a very fine one but for its haggardness. Whether this haggardness had aught to do with criminality, could not be determined; since, as intense heat and cold, though unlike, produce like sensations, so innocence and guilt, when, through casual association with mental pain, stamping any visible impress, use one seal—a hacked one.

Not again that this reflection occurred to Captain Delano at the time, charitable man as he was. Rather another idea. Because observing so singular a haggardness to be combined with a dark eye, averted as in trouble and shame, and then, however illogically, uniting in his mind his own private suspicions of the crew with the confessed ill-opinion on the part of their captain, he was insensibly operated upon by certain general notions, which, while disconnecting pain and abashment from virtue, as invariably link them with vice.

If, indeed, there be any wickedness on board this ship, thought Captain Delano, be sure that man there has fouled his hand in it, even as now he fouls it in the pitch. I don't like to accost him. I will speak to this other, this old Jack here on the windlass.

He advanced to an old Barcelona tar, in ragged red breeches and dirty night-cap, cheeks trenched and bronzed, whiskers dense as thorn hedges. Seated between two sleepy-looking Africans, this mariner, like his younger shipmate, was employed upon some rigging—splicing a cable—the sleepy-looking blacks performing the inferior function of holding the outer parts of the ropes for him.

Upon Captain Delano's approach, the man at once hung his head below its previous level; the one necessary for business. It appeared as if he desired to be thought absorbed, with more than common fidelity, in his task. Being addressed, he glanced up, but with what seemed a furtive, diffident air, which sat strangely enough on his weatherbeaten visage, much as if a grizzly bear, instead of growling and biting, should

---

[10] Kafiv, South African tribe.

simper and cast sheep's eyes. He was asked several questions concerning the voyage—questions purposely referring to several particulars in Don Benito's narrative—not previously corroborated by those impulsive cries greeting the visitor on first coming on board. The questions were briefly answered, confirming all that remained to be confirmed of the story. The negroes about the windlass joined in with the old sailor, but, as they became talkative, he by degrees became mute, and at length quite glum, seemed morosely unwilling to answer more questions, and yet, all the while, this ursine air was somehow mixed with his sheepish one.

Despairing of getting into unembarrassed talk with such a centaur, Captain Delano, after glancing round for a more promising countenance, but seeing none, spoke pleasantly to the blacks to make way for him; and so, amid various grins and grimaces, returned to the poop, feeling a little strange at first, he could hardly tell why, but upon the whole with regained confidence in Benito Cereno.

How plainly, thought he, did that old whiskerando yonder betray a consciousness of ill-desert. No doubt, when he saw me coming, he dreaded lest I, apprised by his captain of the crew's general misbehaviour, came with sharp words for him, and so down with his head. And yet—and yet, now that I think of it, that very old fellow, if I err not, was one of those who seemed so earnestly eyeing me here awhile since. Ah, these currents spin one's head round almost as much as they do the ship. Ha, there now's a pleasant sort of sunny sight; quite sociable, too.

His attention had been drawn to a slumbering negress, partly disclosed through the lace-work of some rigging, lying, with youthful limbs carelessly disposed, under the lee of the bulwarks, like a doe in the shade of a woodland rock. Sprawling at her lapped breasts was her wide-awake fawn, stark naked, its black little body half lifted from the deck, crosswise with its dam's; its hands, like two paws, clambering upon her; its mouth and nose ineffectually rooting to get at the mark; and meantime giving a vexatious half-grunt, blending with the composed snore of the negress.

The uncommon vigour of the child at length roused the mother. She started up, at distance facing Captain Delano. But, as if not at all concerned at the attitude in which she had been caught, delightedly she caught the child up, with maternal transports, covering it with kisses.

There's naked nature, now; pure tenderness and love, thought Captain Delano, well pleased.

This incident prompted him to remark the other negresses more particularly than before. He was gratified with their manners; like most uncivilized women, they seemed at once tender of heart and tough of constitution; equally ready to die for their infants or fight for them.

Unsophisticated as leopardesses; loving as doves. Ah! thought Captain Delano, these perhaps are some of the very women whom Mungo Park saw in Africa, and gave such a noble account of.

These natural sights somehow insensibly deepened his confidence and ease. At last he looked to see how his boat was getting on; but it was still pretty remote. He turned to see if Don Benito had returned; but he had not.

To change the scene, as well as to please himself with a leisurely observation of the coming boat, stepping over into the mizzen-chains he clambered his way into the starboard quarter-galley; one of those abandoned Venetian-looking water-balconies previously mentioned; re- treats cut off from the deck. As his foot pressed the half-damp, half- dry sea mosses matting the place, and a chance phantom cats-paw— an islet of breeze, unheralded, unfollowed—as this ghostly cats-paw came fanning his cheek, as his glance fell upon the row of small, round dead-lights, all closed like coppered eyes of the coffined, and the state- cabin door, once connecting with the gallery, even as the dead-lights had once looked out upon it, but now caulked fast like a sarcophagus lid, to a purple-black, tarred-over panel, threshold, and post; and he bethought him of the time, when that state-cabin and this state-balcony had heard the voices of the Spanish king's officers, and the forms of the Lima viceroy's daughters had perhaps leaned where he stood—as these and other images flitted through his mind, as the cats-paw through the calm, gradually he felt rising a dreamy inquietude, like that of one who alone on the prairie feels unrest from the repose of the noon.

He leaned against the carved balustrade, again looking off toward his boat; but found his eye falling upon the ribboned grass, trailing along the ship's water-line, straight as a border of green box; and parterres of sea-weed, broad ovals and crescents, floating nigh and far, with what seemed long formal alleys between, crossing the terraces of swells, and sweeping round as if leading to the grottoes below. And overhanging all was the balustrade by his arm, which, partly stained with pitch and partly embossed with moss, seemed the charred ruin of some summer-house in a grand garden long running to waste.

Trying to break one charm, he was but becharmed anew. Though upon the wide sea, he seemed in some far inland country; prisoner in some deserted château, left to stare at empty grounds, and peer out at vague roads, where never wagon or wayfarer passed.

But these enchantments were a little disenchanted as his eye fell on the corroded main-chains. Of an ancient style, massy and rusty in link, shackle and bolt, they seemed even more fit for the ship's present business than the one for which probably she had been built.

Presently he thought something moved nigh the chains. He rubbed his eyes, and looked hard. Groves of rigging were about the chains; and there, peering from behind a great stay, like an Indian from behind a hemlock, a Spanish sailor, a marlingspike in his hand, was seen, who made what seemed an imperfect gesture toward the balcony—but immediately, as if alarmed by some advancing step along the deck within, vanished into the hempen forest, like a poacher.

What meant this? Something the man had sought to communicate, unbeknown to any one, even to his captain. Did the secret involve aught unfavourable to his captain? Were those previous misgivings of Captain Delano's about to be verified? Or, in his haunted mood at the moment, had some random, unintentional motion of the man, while busy with the stay, as if repairing it, been mistaken for a significant beckoning?

Not unbewildered, again he gazed off for his boat. But it was temporarily hidden by a rocky spur of the isle. As with some eagerness he bent forward, watching for the first shooting view of its beak, the balustrade gave way before him like charcoal. Had he not clutched an outreaching rope he would have fallen into the sea. The crash, though feeble, and the fall, though hollow, of the rotten fragments, must have been overheard. He glanced up. With sober curiosity peering down upon him was one of the old oakum-pickers, slipped from his perch to an outside boom; while below the old negro—and, invisible to him, reconnoitring from a port-hole like a fox from the mouth of its den—crouched the Spanish sailor again. From something suddenly suggested by the man's air, the mad idea now darted into Captain Delano's mind; that Don Benito's plea of indisposition, in withdrawing below, was but a pretence: that he was engaged there maturing some plot, of which the sailor, by some means gaining an inkling, had a mind to warn the stranger against; incited, it may be, by gratitude for a kind word on first boarding the ship. Was it from foreseeing some possible interference like this, that Don Benito had, beforehand, given such a bad character of his sailors, while praising the negroes; though, indeed, the former seemed as docile as the latter the contrary? The whites, too, by nature, were the shrewder race. A man with some evil design, would not he be likely to speak well of that stupidity which was blind to his depravity, and malign that intelligence from which it might not be hidden? Not unlikely, perhaps. But if the whites had dark secrets concerning Don Benito, could then Don Benito be any way in complicity with the blacks? But they were too stupid. Besides, who ever heard of a white so far a renegade as to apostatize from his very species almost, by leaguing in against it with negroes? These difficulties recalled former ones. Lost in their mazes, Captain Delano, who had now regained the deck, was uneasily advancing along it, when he observed a new face; an aged sailor seated cross-legged near the main hatchway. His skin was shrunk up with wrinkles like a pelican's empty pouch; his hair frosted; his countenance grave and composed. His hands were full of ropes, which he was working into a large knot. Some blacks were about him obligingly dipping the strands for him, here and there, as the exigencies of the operation demanded.

Captain Delano crossed over to him, and stood in silence surveying the knot; his mind, by a not uncongenial transition, passed from its own entanglements to those of the hemp. For intricacy such a knot he had never seen in an American ship, or indeed any other. The old man looked like an Egyptian priest, making gordian knots for the temple of Ammon. The knot seemed a combination of double-bow-line-knot, treble-crown-knot, back-handed-well-knot, knot-in-and-out-knot, and jamming-knot.

At last, puzzled to comprehend the meaning of such a knot, Captain Delano, addressed the knotter: —

"What are you knotting there, my man?"

"The knot," was the brief reply, without looking up.

"So it seems; but what is it for?"

"For some one else to undo," muttered back the old man, plying his fingers harder than ever, the knot being now nearly completed.

While Captain Delano stood watching him, suddenly the old man threw the knot toward him, and said in broken English,—the first heard in the ship,—something to this effect—"Undo it, cut it, quick." It was said lowly, but with such condensation of rapidity, that the long, slow words in Spanish, which had preceded and followed, almost operated as covers to the brief English between.

For a moment, knot in hand, and knot in head, Captain Delano stood mute; while, without further heeding him, the old man was now intent upon other ropes. Presently there was a slight stir behind Captain Delano. Turning, he saw the chained negro, Atufal, standing quietly there. The next moment the old sailor rose, muttering, and, followed by his subordinate negroes, removed to the forward part of the ship, where in the crowd he disappeared.

An elderly negro, in a clout like an infant's, and with a pepper and salt head, and a kind of attorney air, now approached Captain Delano. In tolerable Spanish, and with a good-natured, knowing wink, he informed him that the old knotter was simple-witted, but harmless; often playing his old tricks. The negro concluded by begging the knot, for of course the stranger would not care to be troubled with it. Unconsciously, it was handed to him. With a sort of congé, the negro received it, and turning his back ferreted into it like a detective Custom House officer after smuggled laces. Soon, with some African word, equivalent to pshaw, he tossed the knot overboard.

All this is very queer now, thought Captain Delano, with a qualmish sort of emotion; but as one feeling incipient seasickness, he strove, by ignoring the symptoms, to get rid of the malady. Once more he looked off for his boat. To his delight, it was now again in view, leaving the rocky spur astern.

The sensation here experienced, after at first relieving his uneasiness, with unforeseen efficiency, soon began to remove it. The less distant sight of that well-known boat—showing it, not as before, half blended with the haze, but with outline defined, so that its individuality, like a man's, was manifest; that boat, *Rover* by name, which, though now in strange seas, had often pressed the beach of Captain Delano's home, and, brought to its threshold for repairs, had familiarly lain there, as a Newfoundland dog; the sight of that household boat evoked a thousand trustful associations, which, contrasted with previous suspicions, filled him not only with lightsome confidence, but somehow with half humorous self-reproaches at his former lack of it.

"What, I, Amasa Delano—Jack of the Beach, as they called me when a lad—I, Amasa; the same that, duck-satchel in hand, used to paddle along the waterside to the school-house made from the old hulk;—I, little Jack of the Beach, that used to go berrying with cousin Nat and the rest; I to be murdered here at the ends of the earth, on board a haunted pirate-ship by a horrible Spaniard?—Too nonsensical to think of! Who would murder Amasa Delano? His conscience is clean. There is some one above. Fie, fie, Jack of the Beach! you are a child indeed; a child of the second childhood, old boy; you are beginning to dote and drule, I'm afraid."

Light of heart and foot, he stepped aft, and there was met by Don Benito's servant, who, with a pleasing expression, responsive to his own present feelings, informed him that his master had recovered from the effects of his coughing fit, and had just ordered him to go present his compliments to his good guest, Don Amasa, and to say that he (Don Benito) would soon have the happiness to rejoin him.

There now, do you mark that? again thought Captain Delano, walking the poop. What a donkey I was. This kind gentleman who here sends me his kind compliments, he, but ten minutes ago, dark-lantern in hand, was dodging round some old grind-stone in the hold, sharpening a hatchet for me, I thought. Well, well; these long calms have a morbid effect on the mind, I've often heard, though I never believed it before. Ha! glancing toward the boat; there's *Rover;* a good dog; a white bone in her mouth. A pretty big bone through, seems to me.—What? Yes, she has fallen afoul of the bubbling tide-rip there. It sets her the other way, too, for the time. Patience.

It was now about noon, though, from the greyness of everything, it seemed to be getting toward dusk.

The calm was confirmed. In the far distance, away from the influence of land, the leaden ocean seemed laid out and leaded up, its course finished, soul gone, defunct. But the current from landward, where the ship was, increased; silently sweeping her further toward the tranced waters beyond.

Still, from his knowledge of those latitudes, cherishing hopes of a breeze, and a fair and fresh one, at any moment, Captain Delano, despite present prospects, buoyantly counted upon bringing the *San Dominick* safely to anchor ere night. The distance swept over was nothing; since, with a good wind, ten minutes' sailing would retrace more than sixty minutes' drifting. Meantime, one moment turning to mark "Rover" fighting the tide-rip, and the next to see Don Benito approaching, he continued walking the poop.

Gradually he felt a vexation arising from the delay of his boat; this soon merged into uneasiness; and at last, his eye falling continually, as from a stage-box into the pit, upon the strange crowd before and below him, and by-and-by recognizing there the face—now composed to indifference—of the Spanish sailor who had seemed to beckon from the main chains, something of his old trepidations returned.

Ah, thought he—gravely enough—this is like the ague: because it went off, it follows not that it won't come back.

Though ashamed of the relapse, he could not altogether subdue it; and so, exerting his good nature to the utmost, insensibly he came to a compromise.

Yes, this is a strange craft; a strange history, too, and strange folks on board. But—nothing more.

By way of keeping his mind out of mischief till the boat should arrive, he tried to occupy it with turning over and over, in a purely speculative sort of way, some lesser peculiarities of the captain and crew. Among others, four curious points recurred.

First, the affair of the Spanish lad assailed with a knife by the slave boy; an act winked at by Don Benito. Second, the tyranny in Don Benito's treatment of Atufal, the black; as if a child should lead a bull of the Nile by the ring in his nose. Third, the trampling of the sailor by the two negroes; a piece of insolence passed over without so much as a reprimand. Fourth, the cringing submission to their master of all the ship's underlings, mostly blacks; as if by the least inadvertence they feared to draw down his despotic displeasure.

Coupling these points, they seemed somewhat contradictory. But what then, thought Captain Delano, glancing toward his now nearing boat,—what then? Why, this Don Benito is a very capricious commander. But he is not the first of the sort I have seen; though it's true he rather exceeds any other. But as a nation—continued he in his reveries—these Spaniards are all an odd set; the very word Spaniard has a curious, conspirator, Guy-Fawkish [11] twang to it. And yet, I dare say, Spaniards in the main are as good folks as any in Duxbury, Massachusetts. Ah, good! At last "Rover" has come.

As, with its welcome freight, the boat touched the side, the oakum-pickers, with venerable gestures, sought to restrain the blacks, who, at the sight of three gurried [12] water-casks in its bottom, and a pile of wilted pumpkins in its bow, hung over the bulwarks in disorderly raptures.

[11] Guy Fawkes, an early-seventeenth-century English rebel.
[12] Gury, the offal of fish.

Don Benito with his servant now appeared; his coming, perhaps, hastened by hearing the noise. Of him Captain Delano sought permission to serve out the water, so that all might share alike, and none injure themselves by unfair excess. But sensible, and, on Don Benito's account, kind as this offer was, it was received with what seemed impatience; as if aware that he lacked energy as a commander, Don Benito, with the true jealousy of weakness, resented as an affront any interference. So, at least, Captain Delano inferred.

In another moment the casks were being hoisted in, when some of the eager negroes accidentally jostled Captain Delano, where he stood by the gangway; so that, unmindful of Don Benito, yielding to the impulse of the moment, with good-natured authority he bade the blacks stand back; to enforce his words making use of a half-mirthful, half-menacing gesture. Instantly the blacks paused, just where they were, each negro and negress suspended in his or her posture, exactly as the word had found them—for a few seconds continuing so—while, as between the responsive posts of a telegraph, an unknown syllable ran from man to man among the perched oakum-pickers. While Captain Delano's attention was fixed by this scene, suddenly the hatchet-polishers half rose, and a rapid cry came from Don Benito.

Thinking that at the signal of the Spaniard he was about to be massacred, Captain Delano would have sprung for his boat, but paused, as the oakum-pickers, dropping down into the crowd with earnest exclamations, forced every white and every negro back, at the same moment, with gestures friendly and familiar, almost jocose, bidding him, in substance, not be a fool. Simultaneously the hatchet-polishers resumed their seats, quietly as so many tailors, and at once, as if nothing had happened, the work of hoisting in the casks was resumed, whites and blacks singing at the tackle.

Captain Delano glanced toward Don Benito. As he saw his meagre form in the act of recovering itself from reclining in the servant's arms, into which the agitated invalid had fallen, he could not but marvel at the panic by which himself had been surprised on the darting supposition that such a commander, who upon a legitimate occasion, so trivial, too, as it now appeared, could lose all self-command, was, with energetic iniquity, going to bring about his murder.

The casks being on deck, Captain Delano was handed a number of jars and cups by one of the steward's aides, who, in the name of Don Benito, entreated him to do as he had proposed: dole out the water. He complied, with republican impartiality as to this republican element, which always seeks one level, serving the oldest white no better than the youngest black; excepting, indeed, poor Don Benito, whose condition, if not rank, demanded an extra allowance. To him, in the first place, Captain Delano presented a fair pitcher of the fluid; but, thirsting as he was for fresh water, Don Benito quaffed not a drop until after several grave bows and salutes: a reciprocation of courtesies which the sight-loving Africans hailed with clapping of hands.

Two of the less wilted pumpkins being reserved for the cabin table, the residue were minced up on the spot for the general regalement. But the soft bread, sugar, and bottled cider, Captain Delano would have given the Spaniards alone, and in chief Don Benito; but the latter objected; which disinterestedness, on his part, not a little pleased the American; and so mouthfuls all around were given alike to whites and blacks; excepting one bottle of cider, which Babo insisted upon setting aside for his master.

Here it may be observed that as, on the first visit of the boat, the American had not permitted his men to board the ship, neither did he now; being unwilling to add to the confusion of the decks.

Not uninfluenced by the peculiar good humour at present prevailing, and for the time oblivious of any but benevolent thoughts, Captain Delano, who from recent indications counted upon a breeze within an hour or two at furthest, despatched the boat back to the sealer with orders for all the hands that could be spared immediately to set about rafting casks to the watering-place and filling them. Likewise he bade word be carried to his chief officer, that if against present expectation the ship was not brought to anchor by sunset, he need be under no concern, for as there was to be a full moon that night, he (Captain Delano) would remain on board ready to play the pilot, should the wind come soon or late.

As the two captains stood together, observing the departing boat— the servant as it happened having just spied a spot on his master's velvet sleeve, and silently engaged rubbing it out—the American expressed his regrets that the *San Dominick* had no boats; none, at least, but the unseaworthy old hulk of the long-boat, which, warped as a camel's skeleton in the desert, and almost as bleached, lay pot-wise inverted amidships, one side a little tipped, furnishing a subterraneous sort of den for family groups of the blacks, mostly women and small children; who, squatting on old mats below, or perched above in the dark dome, on the elevated seats, were descried, some distance within, like a social circle of bats, sheltering in some friendly cave; at intervals, ebon flights of naked boys and girls, three or four years old, darting in and out of the den's mouth.

"Had you three or four boats now, Don Benito," said Captain Delano, "I think that, by tugging at the oars, your negroes here might help along matters some.—Did you sail from port without boats, Don Benito?"

"They were stove in the gales, Señor."

"That was bad. Many men, too, you lost then. Boats and men.— Those must have been hard gales, Don Benito."

"Past all speech," cringed the Spaniard.

"Tell me, Don Benito," continued his companion with increased interest, "tell me, were these gales immediately off the pitch of Cape Horn?"

"Cape Horn?—who spoke of Cape Horn?"

"Yourself did, when giving me an account of your voyage," answered Captain Delano with almost equal astonishment at this eating of his own words, even as he ever seemed eating his own heart, on the part of the Spaniard. "You yourself, Don Benito, spoke of Cape Horn," he emphatically repeated.

The Spaniard turned, in a sort of stooping posture, pausing an instant, as one about to make a plunging exchange of elements, as from air to water.

At this moment a messenger-boy, a white, hurried by, in the regular performance of his function carrying the last expired half-hour forward to the forecastle, from the cabin time-piece, to have it struck at the ship's large bell.

"Master," said the servant, discontinuing his work on the coat sleeve, and addressing the rapt Spaniard with a sort of timid apprehensiveness, as one charged with a duty, the discharge of which, it was foreseen, would prove irksome to the very person who had imposed it, and for whose benefit it was intended, "master told me never mind where he was, or how engaged, always to remind him, to a minute, when shaving-time comes. Miguel has gone to strike the half-hour afternoon. It is *now*, Master. Will master go into the cuddy?"

"Ah—yes," answered the Spaniard, starting, somewhat as from dreams into realities; then turning upon Captain Delano, he said that ere long he would resume the conversation.

"Then if master means to talk more to Don Amasa," said the servant, "why not let Don Amasa sit by master in the cuddy, and master can talk, and Don Amasa can listen, while Babo here lathers and strops."

"Yes," said Captain Delano, not unpleased with this sociable plan, "yes, Don Benito, unless you had rather not, I will go with you."

"Be it so, Señor."

As the three passed aft, the American could not but think it another strange instance of his host's capriciousness, this being shaved with such uncommon punctuality in the middle of the day. But he deemed it more than likely that the servant's anxious fidelity had something to do with the matter; inasmuch as the timely interruption served to rally his master from the mood which had evidently been coming upon him.

The place called the cuddy was a light deck-cabin formed by the poop, a sort of attic to the large cabin below. Part of it had formerly been the quarters of the officers; but since their death all the partitionings had been thrown down, and the whole interior converted into one spacious and airy marine hall; for absence of fine furniture and picturesque disarray, of odd appurtenances, somewhat answering to the wide, cluttered hall of some eccentric bachelor-squire in the country, who hangs his shooting-jacket and tobacco-pouch on deer antlers, and keeps his fishing-rod, tongs, and walking-stick in the same corner.

The similitude was heightened, if not originally suggested, by glimpses of the surrounding sea; since, in one aspect, the country and the ocean seem cousins-german.

The floor of the cuddy was matted. Overhead, four or five old muskets were stuck into horizontal holes along the beams. On one side was a claw-footed old table lashed to the deck; a thumbed missal on it, and over it a small, meagre crucifix attached to the bulkhead. Under the table lay a dented cutlass or two, with a hacked harpoon, among some melancholy old rigging, like a heap of poor friar's girdles. There were also two long, sharp-ribbed settees of malacca cane, black with age, and uncomfortable to look at as inquisitors' racks, with a large, misshapen arm-chair, which, furnished with a rude barber's crutch at the back, working with a screw, seemed some grotesque Middle Age engine of torment. A flag locker was in one corner, exposing various coloured bunting, some rolled up, others half unrolled, still others tumbled. Opposite was a cumbrous washstand, of black mahogany, all of one block, with a pedestal, like a font, and over it a railed shelf, containing combs, brushes, and other implements of the toilet. A torn hammock of stained grass swung near; the sheets tossed, and the pillow wrinkled up like a brow, as if whoever slept here slept but illy, with alternate visitations of sad thoughts and bad dreams.

The further extremity of the cuddy, overhanging the ship's stern, was pierced with three openings, windows or port holes, according as men or cannon might peer, socially or unsocially, out of them. At present neither men nor cannon were seen, though huge ring-bolts and other rusty iron fixtures of the wood-work hinted of twenty-four-pounders.

Glancing toward the hammock as he entered, Captain Delano said, "You sleep here, Don Benito?"

"Yes, Señor, since we got into mild weather."

"This seems a sort of domitory, sitting-room, sail-loft, chapel, armoury, and private closet together, Don Benito," added Captain Delano, looking round.

"Yes, Señor; events have not been favourable to much order in my arrangements."

Here the servant, napkin on arm, made a motion as if waiting his master's good pleasure. Don Benito signified his readiness, when, seating him in the malacca arm-chair, and for the guest's convenience drawing opposite it one of the settees, the servant commenced operations by throwing back his master's collar and loosening his cravat.

There is something in the negro which, in a peculiar way, fits him for avocations about one's person. Most negroes are natural valets and hair-dressers; taking to the comb and brush congenially as to the castanets, and flourishing them apparently with almost equal satisfaction. There is, too, a smooth tact about them in this employment, with a marvelous, noiseless, gliding briskness, not ungraceful in its way, singularly pleasing to behold, and still more so to be the manipulated subject of. And above all is the great gift of good humour. Not the mere grin or laugh is here meant. Those were unsuitable. But a certain easy cheerfulness, harmonious in every glance and gesture; as though God had set the whole negro to some pleasant tune.

When to all this is added the docility arising from the unaspiring contentment of a limited mind, and that susceptibility of blind attachment sometimes inhering in indisputable inferiors, one readily perceives why those hypochondriacs, Johnson and Byron—it may be something like the hypochondriac, Benito Cereno—took to their hearts, almost to the exclusion of the entire white race, their serving men, the negroes, Barber and Fletcher. But if there be that in the negro which exempts him from the inflicted sourness of the morbid or cynical mind, how, in his own prepossessing aspects, must he appear to a benevolent one? When at ease with respect to exterior things, Captain Delano's nature was not only benign, but familiarly and humorously so. At home, he had often taken rare satisfaction in sitting in his door, watching some free man of colour at his work or play. If on a voyage he chanced to have a black sailor, invariably he was on chatty, and half-gamesome terms with him. In fact, like most men of a good, blithe heart, Captain Delano took to negroes, not philanthropically, by genially, just as other men to Newfoundland dogs.

Hitherto the circumstances in which he found the *San Dominick* had repressed the tendency. But in the cuddy, relieved from his former uneasiness, and, for various reasons, more sociably inclined than at any previous period of the day, and seeing the coloured servant, napkin on arm, so debonair about his master, in a business so familiar as that of shaving, too, all his old weakness for negroes returned.

Among other things, he was amused with an odd instance of the African love of bright colours and fine shows, in the black's informally taking from the flag-locker a great piece of bunting of all hues, and lavishly tucking it under his master's chin for an apron.

The mode of shaving among the Spaniards is a little different from what it is with other nations. They have a basin, specially called a barber's basin, which on one side is scooped out, so as accurately to receive the chin, against which it is closely held in lathering; which is done, not with a brush, but with soap dipped in the water of the basin and rubbed on the face.

In the present instance salt-water was used for lack of better; and the parts lathered were only the upper lip, and low down under the throat, all the rest being cultivated beard.

These preliminaries being somewhat novel to Captain Delano he sat curiously eyeing them, so that no conversation took place, nor for the present did Don Benito appear disposed to renew any.

Setting down his basin, the negro searched among the razors, as for the sharpest, and having found it, gave it an additional edge by expertly stropping it on the firm, smooth, oily skin of his open palm; he then made a gesture as if to begin, but midway stood suspended for an instant, one hand elevating the razor, the other professionally dabbling among the bubbling suds on the Spaniard's lank neck. Not unaffected by the close sight of the gleaming steel, Don Benito nervously shuddered, his usual ghastliness was heightened by the lather, which lather, again, was intensified in its hue by the contrasting sootiness of the negro's body. Altogether the scene was somewhat peculiar, at least to Captain Delano, nor, as he saw the two thus postured, could he resist the vagary, that in the black he saw a headsman, and in the white, a man at the block. But this was one of those antic conceits, appearing and vanishing in a breath, from which, perhaps, the best regulated mind is not free.

Meantime the agitation of the Spaniard had a little loosened the bunting from around him, so that one broad fold swept curtain-like over the chair-arm to the floor, revealing, amid a profusion of armorial bars and ground-colours—black, blue and yellow—a closed castle in a blood-red field diagonal with a lion rampant in a white.

"The castle and the lion," exclaimed Captain Delano—"why, Don Benito, this is the flag of Spain you use here. It's well it's only I, and not the King, that sees this," he added with a smile, "but"—turning toward the black,—"it's all one, I suppose, so the colours be gay," which playful remark did not fail somewhat to tickle the negro.

"Now, master," he said, readjusting the flag, and pressing the head gently further back into the crotch of the chair; "now master," and the steel glanced nigh the throat.

Again Don Benito faintly shuddered.

"You must not shake so, master.—See, Don Amasa, master always shakes when I shave him. And yet master knows I never yet have drawn blood, though it's true, if master will shake so, I may some of these times. Now, master," he continued. "And now, Don Amasa, please go on with your talk about the gale, and all that, master can hear, and between times master can answer."

"Ah yes, these gales," said Captain Delano; "but the more I think of your voyage, Don Benito, the more I wonder, not at the gales, terrible as they must have been, but at the disastrous interval following them. For here, by your account, have you been these two months and more getting from Cape Horn to St. Maria, a distance which I myself, with a good wind, have sailed in a few days. True, you had calms, and long ones, but to be becalmed for two months, that is, at least, unusual. Why, Don Benito, had almost any other gentleman told me such a story, I should have been half disposed to a little incredulity."

Here an involuntary expression came over the Spaniard, similar to that just before on the deck, and whether it was the start he gave, or a sudden gawky roll of the hull in the calm, or a momentary unsteadi-

ness of the servant's hand; however it was, just then the razor drew
blood, spots of which stained the creamy lather under the throat;
immediately the black barber drew back his steel, and remaining in his
professional attitude, back to Captain Delano, and face to Don Benito,
held up the trickling razor, saying, with a sort of half humorous sorrow, "See, master,—you shook so—here's Babo's first blood."

No sword drawn before James the First of England, no assassination in that timid King's presence, could have produced a more terrified
aspect than was now presented by Don Benito.

Poor fellow, thought Captain Delano, so nervous he can't even
bear the sight of barber's blood; and this unstrung, sick man, is it
credible that I should have imagined he meant to spill all my blood,
who can't endure the sight of one little drop of his own? Surely, Amasa
Delano, you have been beside yourself this day. Tell it not when you
get home, sappy Amasa. Well, well, he looks like a murderer, doesn't
he? More like as if himself were to be done for. Well, well, this day's
experience shall be a good lesson.

Meantime, while these things were running through the honest
seaman's mind, the servant had taken the napkin from his arm, and to
Don Benito had said: "But answer Don Amasa, please, master, while I
wipe this ugly stuff of the razor, and strop it again."

As he said the words, his face was turned half round, so as to be
alike visible to the Spaniard and the American, and seemed by its
expression to hint, that he was desirous, by getting his master to go on
with the conversation, considerately to withdraw his attention from the
recent annoying accident. As if glad to snatch the offered relief, Don
Benito resumed, rehearsing to Captain Delano, that not only were the
calms of unusual duration, but the ship had fallen in with obstinate
currents, and other things he added, some of which were but repetitions
of former statements, to explain how it came to pass that the passage
from Cape Horn to St. Maria had been so exceedingly long, now and
then mingling with his words, incidental praises, less qualified than
before, to the blacks, for their general good conduct.

These particulars were not given consecutively, the servant now
and then using his razor, and so, between the intervals of shaving, the
story and panegyric went on with more than usual huskiness.

To Captain Delano's imagination, now again not wholly at rest,
there was something so hollow in the Spaniard's manner, with apparently some reciprocal hollowness in the servant's dusky comment of
silence, that the idea flashed across him, that possibly master and man,
for some unknown purpose, were acting out, both in word and deed,
nay, to the very tremor of Don Benito's limbs, some juggling play before
him. Neither did the suspicion of collusion lack apparent support, from
the fact of those whispered conferences before mentioned. But then,
what could be the object of enacting this play of the barber before him?
At last, regarding the notion as a whimsy, insensible suggested, per-

haps, by the theatrical aspect of Don Benito in his harlequin ensign, Captain Delano speedily banished it.

The shaving over, the servant bestirred himself with a small bottle of scented waters, pouring a few drops on the head, and then diligently rubbing; the vehemence of the exercise causing the muscles of his face to twitch rather strangely.

His next operation was with comb, scissors and brush; going round and round, smoothing a curl here, clipping an unruly whisker-hair there, giving a graceful sweep to the temple-lock, with other impromptu touches evincing the hand of a master; while, like any resigned gentleman in barber's hands, Don Benito bore all, much less uneasily, at least, than he had done the razoring; indeed, he sat so pale and rigid now, that the negro seemed a Nubian sculptor finishing off a white statue-head.

All being over at last, the standard of Spain removed, tumbled up, and tossed back into the flag-locker, the negro's warm breath blowing away any stray hair which might have lodged down his master's neck; collar and cravat readjusted; a speck of lint whisked off the velvet lapel; all this being done; backing off a little space, and pausing with an expression of subdued self-complacency, the servant for a moment surveyed his master, as, in toilet at least, the creature of his own tasteful hands.

Captain Delano playfully complimented him upon his achievement; at the same time congratulating Don Benito.

But neither sweet waters, nor shampooing, nor fidelity, nor sociality, delighted the Spaniard. Seeing him relapsing into forbidding gloom, and still remaining seated, Captain Delano, thinking that his presence was undesired just then, withdrew, on pretence of seeing whether, as he had prophesied, any signs of a breeze were visible.

Walking forward to the mainmast, he stood awhile thinking over the scene, and not without some undefined misgivings, when he heard a noise near the cuddy, and turning, saw the negro, his hand to his cheek. Advancing, Captain Delano perceived that the cheek was bleeding. He was about to ask the cause, when the negro's wailing soliloquy enlightened him.

"Ah, when will master get better from his sickness; only the sour heart that sour sickness breeds made him serve Babo so; cutting Babo with the razor, because, only by accident, Babo had given master one little scratch; and for the first time in so many a day, too. Ah, ah, ah," holding his hand to his face.

Is it possible, thought Captain Delano; was it to wreak in private his Spanish spite against this poor friend of his, that Don Benito, by his sullen manner, impelled me to withdraw? Ah, this slavery breeds ugly passions in man! Poor fellow!

He was about to speak in sympathy to the negro, but with a timid reluctance he now re-entered the cuddy.

Presently master and man came forth; Don Benito leaning on his servant as if nothing had happened.

But a sort of love-quarrel, after all, thought Captain Delano. He accosted Don Benito, and they slowly walked together. They had gone but a few paces, when the steward—a tall, rajah-looking mulatto, orientally set off with a pagoda turban formed by three or four Madras handkerchiefs wound about his head, tier on tier—approaching with a salaam, announced lunch in the cabin.

On their way thither, the two captains were preceded by the mulatto, who, turning round as he advanced, with continual smiles and bows, ushered them in, a display of elegance which quite completed the insignificance of the small bare-headed Babo, who, as if not unconscious of inferiority, eyed askance the graceful steward. But in part, Captain Delano imputed his jealous watchfulness to that peculiar feeling which the full-blooded African entertains for the adulterated one. As for the steward, his manner, if not bespeaking much dignity of self-respect, yet evidenced his extreme desire to please; which is doubly meritorious, as at once Christian and Chesterfieldian.[13]

Chaptain Delano observed with interest that while the complexion of the mulatto was hybrid, his physiognomy was European; classically so.

"Don Benito," whispered he, "I am glad to see this usher-of-the-golden-rod of yours; the sight refutes an ugly remark once made to me by a Barbados planter that when a mulatto has a regular European face, look out for him; he is a devil. But see, your steward here has features more regular than King George's of England; and yet there he nods, and bows, and smiles; a king, indeed—the king of kind hearts and polite fellows. What a pleasant voice he has, too."

"He has, Señor."

"But, tell me, has he not, so far as you have known him, always proved a good, worthy fellow?" said Captain Delano, pausing, while with a final genuflexion the steward disappeared into the cabin; "come, for the reason just mentioned, I am curious to know."

"Francesco is a good man," rather sluggishly responded Don Benito, like a phlegmatic appreciator, who would neither find fault nor flatter.

"Ah, I thought so. For it were strange indeed, and not very creditable to us white-skins, if a little of our blood mixed with the African's, should, far from improving the latter's quality, have the sad effect of pouring vitriolic acid into black broth; improving the hue, perhaps, but not the wholesomeness."

"Doubtless, doubtless, Señor, but"—glancing at Babo—"not to speak of negroes, your planter's remark I have heard applied to the Spanish and Indian intermixtures in our provinces. But I know nothing about the matter," he listlessly added.

13 Earl of Chesterfield (1694–1773), known for worldliness.

And here they entered the cabin.

The lunch was a frugal one. Some of Captain Delano's fresh fish and pumpkins, biscuit and salt beef, the reserved bottle of cider, and the *San Dominick's* last bottle of Canary.

As they entered, Francesco, with two or three coloured aids, was hovering over the table giving the last adjustments. Upon perceiving their master they withdrew, Francesco making a smiling congé, and the Spaniard, without condescending to notice it, fastidiously remarking to his companion that he relished not superfluous attendance.

Without companions, host and guest sat down, like a childless married couple, at opposite ends of the table, Don Benito waving Captain Delano to his place, and, weak as he was, insisting upon that gentleman being seated before himself.

The negro placed a rug under Don Benito's feet, and a cushion behind his back, and then stood behind, not his master's chair, but Captain Delano's. At first, this a little surprised the latter. But it was soon evident that, in taking his position, the black was still true to his master; since by facing him he could the more readily anticipate his slightest want.

"This is an uncommonly intelligent fellow of yours, Don Benito," whispered Captain Delano across the table.

"You say true, Señor."

During the repast, the guest again reverted to parts of Don Benito's story, begging further particulars here and there. He inquired how it was that the scurvy and fever should have committed such wholesale havoc upon the whites, while destroying less than half of the blacks. As if this question reproduced the whole scene of plague before the Spaniard's eyes, miserably reminding him of his solitude in a cabin where before he had had so many friends and officers round him, his hand shook, his face became hueless, broken words escaped; but directly the sane memory of the past seemed replaced by insane terrors of the present. With starting eyes he stared before him at vacancy. For nothing was to be seen but the hand of his servant pushing the Canary over towards him. At length a few sips served partially to restore him. He made random reference to the different constitutions of races, enabling one to offer more resistance to certain maladies than another. The thought was new to his companion.

Presently Captain Delano, intending to say something to his host concerning the pecuniary part of the business he had undertaken for him, especially—since he was strictly accountable to his owners—with reference to the new suit of sails, and other things of that sort; and naturally preferring to conduct such affairs in private, was desirous that the servant should withdraw; imagining that Don Benito for a few minutes could dispense with his attendance. He, however, waited awhile; thinking that, as the conversation proceeded, Don Benito, without being prompted, would perceive the propriety of the step.

But it was otherwise. At last catching his host's eye, Captain Delano, with a slight backward gesture of his thumb, whispered, "Don Benito, pardon me, but there is an interference with the full expression of what I have to say to you."

Upon this the Spaniard changed countenance; which was imputed to his resenting the hint, as in some way a reflection upon his servant. After a moment's pause, he assured his guest that the black's remaining with them could be of no disservice; because since losing his officers he had made Babo (whose original office, it now appeared, had been captain of the slaves) not only his constant attendant and companion, but in all things his confidant.

After this, nothing more could be said; though, indeed, Captain Delano could hardly avoid some little tinge of irritation upon being left ungratified in so inconsiderable a wish, by one, too, for whom he intended such solid services. But it is only his querulousness, thought he; and so filling his glass he proceeded to business.

The price of the sails and other matters was fixed upon. But while this was being done, the American observed that, though his original offer of assistance had been hailed with hectic animation, yet now when it was reduced to a business transaction, indifference and apathy were betrayed. Don Benito, in fact, appeared to submit to hearing the details more out of regard to common propriety, than from any impression that weighty benefit to himself and his voyage was involved.

Soon, this manner became still more reserved. The effort was vain to seek to draw him into social talk. Gnawed by his splenetic mood, he sat twitching his beard, while to little purpose the hand of his servant, mute as that on the wall, slowly pushed over the Canary.

Lunch being over, they sat down on the cushioned transom; the servant placing a pillow behind his master. The long continuance of the calm had now affected the atmosphere. Don Benito sighed heavily, as if for breath.

"Why not adjourn to the cuddy," said Captain Delano; "there is more air there." But the host sat silent and motionless.

Meantime his servant knelt before him, with a large fan of feathers. And Francesco, coming in on tiptoes, handed the negro a little cup of aromatic waters, with which at intervals he chafed his master's brow, smoothing the hair along the temples as a nurse does a child's. He spoke no word. He only rested his eye on his master's, as if, amid all Don Benito's distress, a little to refresh his spirit by the silent sight of fidelity.

Presently the ship's bell sounded two o'clock; and through the cabin-windows a slight rippling of the sea was discerned; and from the desired direction.

"There," exclaimed Captain Delano, "I told you so, Don Benito, look!"

He had risen to his feet, speaking in a very animated tone, with a view the more to rouse his companion. But though the crimson curtain of the stern-window near him that moment fluttered against his pale cheek, Don Benito seemed to have even less welcome for the breeze than the calm.

Poor fellow, thought Captain Delano, bitter experience has taught him that one ripple does not make a wind, any more than one swallow a summer. But he is mistaken for once. I will get his ship in for him, and prove it.

Briefly alluding to his weak condition, he urged his host to remain quietly where he was, since he (Captain Delano) would with pleasure take upon himself the responsibility of making the best use of the wind.

Upon gaining the deck, Captain Delano started at the unexpected figure of Atufal, monumentally fixed at the threshold, like one of those sculptured porters of black marble guarding the porches of Egyptian tombs.

But this time the start was, perhaps, purely physical. Atufal's presence, singularly attesting docility even in sullenness, was contrasted with that of the hatchet-polishers, who in patience evinced their industry; while both spectacles showed, that lax as Don Benito's general authority might be, still, whenever he chose to exert it, no man so savage or colossal but must, more or less, bow.

Snatching a trumpet which hung from the bulwarks, with a free step Captain Delano advanced to the forward edge of the poop, issuing his orders in his best Spanish. The few sailors and many negroes, all equally pleased, obediently set about heading the ship toward the harbour.

While giving some directions about setting a lower stu'n'-sail, suddenly Captain Delano heard a voice faithfully repeating his orders. Turning, he saw Babo, now for the time acting, under the pilot, his original part of captain of the slaves. This assistance proved valuable. Tattered sails and warped yards were soon brought into some trim. And no brace or halyard was pulled but to the blithe songs of the inspirited negroes.

Good fellows, thought Captain Delano, a little training would make fine sailors of them. Why see, the very women pull and sing, too. These must be some of those Ashantee negresses that make such capital soldiers, I've heard. But who's at the helm? I must have a good hand there.

He went to see.

The *San Dominick* steered with a cumbrous tiller, with large horizontal pullies attached. At each pulley-end stood a subordinate black, and between them, at the tiller-head, the responsible post, a Spanish seaman, whose countenance evinced his due share in the general hopefulness and confidence at the coming of the breeze.

He proved the same man who had behaved with so shamefaced an air on the windlass.

"Ah,—it is you, my man," exclaimed Captain Delano—"well, no more sheep's-eyes now;—look straightforward and keep the ship so. Good hand, I trust? And want to get into the harbour, don't you?"

"Sí, Señor," assented the man with an inward chuckle, grasping the tiller-head firmly. Upon this, unperceived by the American, the two blacks eyed the sailor askance.

Finding all right at the helm, the pilot went forward to the fore-castle, to see how matters stood there.

The ship now had way enough to breast the current. With the approach of evening, the breeze would be sure to freshen.

Having done all that was needed for the present, Captain Delano, giving his last orders to the sailors, turned aft to report affairs to Don Benito in the cabin; perhaps additionally incited to rejoin him by the hope of snatching a moment's private chat while his servant was engaged upon deck.

From opposite sides, there were, beneath the poop, two approaches to the cabin; one further forward than the other, and consequently communicating with a longer passage. Marking the servant still above, Captain Delano, taking the nighest entrance—the one last named, and at whose porch Atufal still stood—hurried on his way, till, arrived at the cabin threshold, he paused an instant, a little to recover from his eagerness. Then, with the words of his intended business upon his lips, he entered. As he advanced toward the Spaniard, on the transom, he heard another footstep, keeping time with his. From the opposite door, a salver in hand, the servant was likewise advancing.

"Confound the faithful fellow," thought Captain Delano; "what a vexatious coincidence."

Possibly, the vexation might have been something different, were it not for the buoyant confidence inspired by the breeze. But even as it was, he felt a slight twinge, from a sudden involuntary association in his mind of Babo with Atufal.

"Don Benito," said he, "I give you joy; the breeze will hold, and will increase. By the way, your tall man and time-piece, Atufal, stands without. By your order, of course?"

Don Benito recoiled, as if at some bland satirical touch, delivered with such adroit garnish of apparent good-breeding as to present no handle for retort.

He is like one flayed alive, thought Captain Delano; where may one touch him without causing a shrink?

The servant moved before his master, adjusting a cushion; recalled to civility, the Spaniard stiffly replied: "You are right. The slave appears where you saw him, according to my command; which is, that if at the given hour I am below, he must take his stand and abide my coming."

"Ah now, pardon me, but that is treating the poor fellow like an ex-king denied. Ah, Don Benito," smiling, "for all the license you permit in some things, I fear lest, at bottom, you are a bitter hard master."

Again Don Benito shrank; and this time, as the good sailor thought, from a genuine twinge of his conscience.

Conversation now became constrained. In vain Captain Delano

called attention to the now perceptible motion of the keel gently cleav-
ing the sea; with lack-lustre eye, Don Benito returned words few and
reserved.

By-and-by, the wind, having steadily risen, and still blowing right
into the harbour, bore the *San Dominick* swifty on. Rounding a point
of land, the sealer at distance came into open view.

Meantime Captain Delano had again repaired to the deck, remaining there some time. Having at last altered the ship's course, so as to
give the reef a wide berth, he returned for a few moments below.

I will cheer up my poor friend, this time, thought he.

"Better and better, Don Benito," he cried as he blithely re-entered;
"there will soon be an end to your cares, at least for awhile. For when,
after a long, sad voyage, you know, the anchor drops into the haven,
all its vast weight seems lifted from the captain's heart. We are getting
on famously, Don Benito. My ship is in sight. Look through this side-
light here; there she is; all a-taunt-o! The *Bachelor's Delight,* my good
friend. Ah, how this wind braces one up. Come, you must take a cup
of coffee with me this evening. My old steward will give you as fine
a cup as ever any sultan tasted. What say you, Don Benito, will you?"

At first, the Spaniard glanced feverishly up, casting a longing look
toward the sealer, while with mute concern his servant gazed into his
face. Suddenly the old ague of coldness returned, and dropping back
to his cushions he was silent.

"You do not answer. Come, all day you have been my host; would
you have hospitality all on one side?"

"I cannot go," was the response.

"What? it will not fatigue you. The ships will lie together as near
as they can, without swinging foul. It will be little more than stepping
from deck to deck; which is but as from room to room. Come, come,
you must not refuse me."

"I cannot go," decisively and repulsively repeated Don Benito.

Renouncing all but the last appearance of courtesy, with a sort of
cadaverous sullenness, and biting his thin nails to the quick, he glanced,
almost glared, at his guest; as if impatient that a stranger's presence
should interfere with the full indulgence of his morbid hour. Meantime
the sound of the parted waters came more and more gurglingly and
merrily in at the windows; as reproaching him for his dark spleen; as
telling him that, sulk as he might, and go mad with it, nature cared not
a jot; since, whose fault was it, pray?

But the foul mood was now at its depth, as the fair wind at its
height.

There was something in the man so far beyond any mere unsociality
of sourness previously evinced, that even the forbearing good-nature
of his guest could no longer endure it. Wholly at a loss to account for
such demeanour, and deeming sickness with eccentricity, however
extreme, no adequate excuse, well satisfied, too, that nothing in his

own conduct could justify it, Captain Delano's pride began to be roused. Himself became reserved. But all seemed one to the Spaniard. Quitting him, therefore, Captain Delano once more went to the deck.

The ship was now within less than two miles of the sealer. The whale-boat was seen darting over the interval.

To be brief, the two vessels, thanks to the pilot's skill, ere long in neighbourly style lay anchored together.

Before returning to his own vessel, Captain Delano had intended communicating to Don Benito the practical details of the proposed services to be rendered. But, as it was, unwilling anew to subject himself to rebuffs, he resolved, now that he had seen the *San Dominick* safely moored, immediately to quit her, without further allusion to hospitality or business. Indefinitely postponing his ulterior plans, he would regulate his future actions according to future circumstances. His boat was ready to receive him; but his host still tarried below. Well, thought Captain Delano, if he has little breeding, the more need to show mine. He descended to the cabin to bid a ceremonious, and, it may be, tacitly rebukeful adieu. But to his great satisfaction, Don Benito, as if he began to feel the weight of that treatment with which his slighted guest had, not indecorously, retaliated upon him, now supported by his servant, rose to his feet, and grasping Captain Delano's hand, stood tremulous; too much agitated to speak. But the good augury hence drawn was suddenly dashed, by his resuming all his previous reserve, with augmented gloom, as, with half-averted eyes, he silently reseated himself on his cushions. With a corresponding return of his own chilled feelings, Captain Delano bowed and withdrew.

He was hardly midway in the narrow corridor, dim as a tunnel, leading from the cabin to the stairs, when a sound, as of the tolling for execution in some jail-yard, fell on his ears. It was the echo of the ship's flawed bell, striking the hour, drearily reverberated in this subterranean vault. Instantly, by a fatality not to be withstood, his mind, responsive to the portent, swarmed with superstitious suspicions. He paused. In images far swifter than these sentences, the minutest details of all his former distrusts swept through him.

Hitherto, credulous good-nature had been too ready to furnish excuses for reasonable fears. Why was the Spaniard, so superfluously punctilious at times, now heedless of common propriety in not accompanying to the side his departing guest? Did indisposition forbid? Indisposition had not forbidden more irksome exertion that day. His last equivocal demeanour recurred. He had risen to his feet, grasped his guest's hand, motioned toward his hat; then, in an instant, all was eclipsed in sinister muteness and gloom. Did this imply one brief, repentant relenting at the final moment, from some iniquitous plot, followed by remorseless return to it? His last glance seemed to express a calamitous, yet acquiescent farewell to Captain Delano for ever. Why decline the invitation to visit the sealer that evening? Or was the Spaniard less hardened than the Jew, who refrained not from supping at the board of him whom the same night he meant to betray? What imported all those day-long enigmas and contradictions, except they were intended to mystify, preliminary to some stealthy blow? Atufal, the pretended rebel, but punctual shadow, that moment lurked by the threshold without. He seemed a sentry, and more. Who, by his own confession, had stationed him there? Was the negro now lying in wait?

The Spaniard behind—his creature before: to rush from darkness to light was the involuntary choice.

The next moment, with clenched jaw and hand, he passed Atufal, and stood unarmed in the light. As he saw his trim ship lying peacefully at her anchor, and almost within ordinary call; as he saw his household boat, with familiar faces in it, patiently rising and falling on the short waves by the *San Dominick's* side; and then, glancing about the decks where he stood, saw the oakum-pickers still gravely plying their fingers; and heard the low, buzzing whistle and industrious hum of the hatchet-polishers, still bestirring themselves over their endless occupation; and more than all, as he saw the benign aspect of Nature, taking her innocent repose in the evening; the screened sun in the quiet camp of the west shining out like the mild light from Abraham's tent; as his charmed eye and ear took in all these, with the chained figure of the black, the clenched jaw and hand relaxed. Once again he smiled at the phantoms which had mocked him, and felt something like a tinge of remorse, that, by indulging them even for a moment, he should, by implication, have betrayed an almost atheist doubt of the ever-watchful Providence above.

There was a few minutes' delay, while, in obedience to his orders, the boat was being hooked along to the gangway. During this interval, a sort of saddened satisfaction stole over Captain Delano, at thinking of the kindly offices he had that day discharged for a stranger. Ah, thought he, after good actions one's conscience is never ungrateful, however much so the benefited party may be.

Presently, his foot, in the first act of descent into the boat, pressed the first round of the side-ladder, his face presented inward upon the deck. In the same moment, he heard his name courteously sounded; and, to his pleased surprise, saw Don Benito advancing—an unwonted energy in his air, as if, at the last moment, intent upon making amends for his recent discourtesy. With instinctive good feeling, Captain Delano, revoking his foot, turned and reciprocally advanced. As he did so, the Spaniard's nervous eagerness increased, but his vital energy failed; so that, the better to support him, the servant, placing his master's hand on his naked shoulder, and gently holding it there, formed himself into a sort of crutch.

When the two captains met, the Spaniard again fervently took the hand of the American, at the same time casting an earnest glance into his eyes, but, as before, too much overcome to speak.

I have done him wrong, self-reproachfully thought Captain Delano; his apparent coldness has deceived me; in no instance has he meant to offend.

Meantime, as if fearful that the continuance of the scene might too much unstring his master, the servant seemed anxious to terminate it. And so, still presenting himself as a crutch, and walking between the two captains, he advanced with them toward the gangway; while still, as if full of kindly contrition, Don Benito would not let go the hand of Captain Delano, but retained it in his, across the black's body.

Soon they were standing by the side, looking over into the boat, whose crew turned up their curious eyes. Waiting a moment for the Spaniard to relinquish his hold, the now embarrassed Captain Delano lifted his foot, to overstep the threshold of the open gangway; but still Don Benito would not let go his hand. And yet, with an agitated tone, he said, "I can go no further; here I must bid you adieu. Adieu, my dear, dear Don Amasa. Go—go!" suddenly tearing his hand loose, "go, and God guard you better than me, my best friend."

Not unaffected, Captain Delano would now have lingered; but catching the meekly admonitory eye of the servant, with a hasty farewell he descended into his boat, followed by the continual adieus of Don Benito, standing rooted in the gangway.

Seating himself in the stern, Captain Delano, making a last salute, ordered the boat shoved off. The crew had their oars on end. The bowsman pushed the boat a sufficient distance for the oars to be lengthwise dropped. The instant that was done, Don Benito sprang over the bulwarks, falling at the feet of Captain Delano; at the same time, calling towards his ship, but in tones so frenzied, that none in the boat could understand him. But, as if not equally obtuse, three Spanish sailors, from three different and distant parts of the ship, splashed into the sea, swimming after their captain, as if intent upon his rescue.

The dismayed officer of the boat eagerly asked what this meant. To which, Captain Delano, turning a disdainful smile upon the unaccountable Benito Cereno, answered that, for his part, he neither knew nor cared; but it seemed as if the Spaniard had taken it into his head to produce the impression among his people that the boat wanted to kidnap him. "Or else—give way for your lives," he wildly added, starting at a clattering hubbub in the ship, above which rang the tocsin of the hatchet-polishers; and seizing Don Benito by the throat he added, "this plotting pirate means murder!" Here, in apparent verification of the words, the servant, a dagger in his hand, was seen on the rail overhead, poised, in the act of leaping, as if with desperate fidelity to befriend his master to the last; while, seemingly to aid the black, the three Spanish sailors were trying to clamber into the hampered bow. Meantime, the whole host of negroes, as if inflamed at the sight of their jeopardized captain, impended in one sooty avalance over the bulwarks. All this, with what preceded, and what followed, occurred with such involutions of rapidity, that past, present, and future seemed one.

Seeing the negro coming, Captain Delano had flung the Spaniard aside, almost in the very act of clutching him, and, by the unconscious recoil, shifting his place, with arms thrown up, so promptly grappled the servant in his descent, that with dagger presented at Captain Delano's heart, the black seemed of purpose to have leaped there as to his mark. But the weapon was wrenched away, and the assailant dashed down into the bottom of the boat, which now, with disentangled oars, began to speed through the sea.

At this juncture, the left hand of Captain Delano, on one side, again clutched the half-reclined Don Benito, heedless that he was in a speechless faint, while his right foot, on the other side, ground the prostrate negro; and his right arm pressed for added speed on the after oar, his eye bent forward, encouraging his men to their utmost.

But here, the officer of the boat, who had at last succeeded in beating off the towing Spanish sailors, and was now, with face turned aft, assisting the bowsman at his oar, suddenly called to Captain Delano, to see what the black was about; while a Portuguese oarsman shouted to him to give heed to what the Spaniard was saying.

Glancing down at his feet, Captain Delano saw the freed hand of the servant aiming with a second dagger—a small one, before concealed in his wool—with this he was snakishly writhing up from the boat's bottom, at the heart of his master, his countenance lividly vindictive, expressing the centred purpose of his soul; while the Spaniard, half-choked, was vainly shrinking away, with husky words, incoherent to all but the Portuguese.

That moment, across the long benighted mind of Captain Delano, a flash of revelation swept, illuminating in unanticipated clearness Benito Cereno's whole mysterious demeanour, with every enigmatic event of the day, as well as the entire past voyage of the *San Dominick*. He smote Babo's hand down, but his own heart smote him harder. With infinite pity he withdrew his hold from Don Benito. Not Captain Delano, but Don Benito, the black, in leaping into the boat, had intended to stab.

Both the black's hands were held, as, glancing up toward the *San Dominick*, Captain Delano, now with the scales dropped from his eyes, saw the negroes, not in misrule, not in tumult, not as if frantically concerned for Don Benito, but with mask torn away, flourishing hatchets and knives, in ferocious piratical revolt. Like delirious black dervishes, the six Ashantees danced on the poop. Prevented by their foes from springing into the water, the Spanish boys were hurrying up to the topmost spars, while such of the few Spanish sailors, not already in the sea, less alert, were descried, helplessly mixed in, on deck, with the blacks.

Meantime Captain Delano hailed his own vessel, ordering the ports up, and the guns run out. But by this time the cable of the *San Dominick* had been cut; and the fag-end, in lashing out, whipped away the canvas shroud about the beak, suddenly revealing, as the bleached hull swung round toward the open ocean, death for the figure-head, in a human skeleton; chalky comment on the chalked words below, *"Follow your leader."*

At the sight, Don Benito, covering his face, wailed out: " 'Tis he, Aranda! my murdered, unburied friend!"

Upon reaching the sealer, calling for ropes, Captain Delano bound the negro, who made no resistance, and had him hoisted to the deck. He would then have assisted the now almost helpless Don Benito up the side; but Don Benito, wan as he was, refused to move, or be moved, until the negro should have been first put below out of view. When, presently assured that it was done, he no more shrank from the ascent.

The boat was immediately despatched back to pick up the three swimming sailors. Meantime, the guns were in readiness, though, owing to the *San Dominick* having glided somewhat astern of the sealer, only the aftermost one could be brought to bear. With this, they fired six times; thinking to cripple the fugitive ship by bringing down her spars. But only a few inconsiderable ropes were shot away. Soon the ship was beyond the guns' range, steering broad out of the bay; the blacks thickly clustering round the bowsprit, one moment with taunting cries toward the whites, the next with upthrown gestures hailing the now dusky expanse of ocean—cawing crows escaped from the hand of the fowler.

The first impulse was to slip the cables and give chase. But, upon second thought, to pursue with whale-boat and yawl seemed more promising.

Upon inquiring of Don Benito what firearms they had on board the *San Dominick*, Captain Delano was answered that they had none that could be used; because, in the earlier stages of the mutiny, a cabin-passenger, since dead, had secretly put out of order the locks of what few muskets there were. But with all his remaining strength, Don Benito entreated the American not to give chase, either with ship or boat; for the negroes had already proved themselves such desperadoes, that, in case of a present assault, nothing but a total massacre of the whites could be looked for. But, regarding this warning as coming from one whose spirit had been crushed by misery, the American did not give up his design.

The boats were got ready and armed. Captain Delano ordered twenty-five men into them. He was going himself when Don Benito grasped his arm.

"What! have you saved my life, Señor, and are you now going to throw away your own?"

The officers also, for reasons connected with their interests and those of the voyage, and a duty owing to the owners, strongly objected against their commander's going. Weighing their remonstrances a moment, Captain Delano felt bound to remain; appointing his chief mate—an athletic and resolute man, who had been a privateer's man, and, as his enemies whispered, a pirate—to head the party. The more to encourage the sailors, they were told, that the Spanish captain considered his ship as good as lost; that she and her cargo, including some gold and silver, were worth upwards of ten thousand doubloons. Take her, and no small part should be theirs. The sailors replied with a shout.

The fugitives had now almost gained an offing. It was nearly night; but the moon was rising. After hard, prolonged pulling, the boats came up on the ship's quarters, at a suitable distance laying upon their oars to discharge their muskets. Having no bullets to return, the negroes sent their yells. But, upon the second volley, Indian-like, they hurtled their hatchets. One took off a sailor's fingers. Another struck the whaleboat's bow, cutting off the rope there, and remaining stuck in the gunwale, like a woodman's axe. Snatching it, quivering from its lodgment, the mate hurled it back. The returned gauntlet now stuck in the ship's broken quarter-gallery, and so remained.

The negroes giving too hot a reception, the whites kept a more respectful distance. Hovering now just out of reach of the hurtling hatchets, they, with a view to the close encounter which must soon come, sought to decoy the blacks into entirely disarming themselves of their most murderous weapons in a hand-to-hand fight, by foolishly flinging them, as missiles, short of the mark, into the sea. But ere long perceiving the stratagem, the negroes desisted, though not before many of them had to replace their lost hatchets with handspikes; an exchange which, as counted upon, proved in the end favourable to the assailants.

Meantime, with a strong wind, the ship still clove the water; the boats alternately falling behind, and pulling up, to discharge fresh volleys.

The fire was mostly directed toward the stern, since there, chiefly, the negroes, at present, were clustering. But to kill or maim the negroes was not the object. To take them, with the ship, was the object. To do it, the ship must be boarded; which could not be done by boats while she was sailing so fast.

A thought now struck the mate. Observing the Spanish boys still aloft, high as they could get, he called to them to descend to the yards, and cut adrift the sails. It was done. About this time, owing to causes hereafter to be shown, two Spaniards, in the dress of sailors and conspicuously showing themselves, were killed; not by volleys, but by deliberate marksman's shots; while, as it afterwards appeared, during one of the general discharges, Atufal, the black, and the Spaniard at the helm likewise were killed. What now, with the loss of the sails, and loss of leaders, the ship became unmanageable to the negroes.

With creaking masts she came heavily round to the wind; the prow slowly swinging into view of the boats, its skeleton gleaming in the horizontal moonlight, and casting a gigantic ribbed shadow upon the water. One extended arm of the ghost seemed beckoning the whites to avenge it.

"Follow your leader!" cried the mate; and, one on each bow, the boats boarded. Scaling-spears and cutlasses crossed hatchets and handspikes. Huddled upon the long-boat amidships, the negresses raised a wailing chant, whose chorus was the clash of steel.

For a time, the attack wavered; the negroes wedging themselves to beat it back; the half-repelled sailors, as yet unable to gain a footing, fighting as troopers in the saddle, one leg sideways flung over the bulwarks, and one without, plying their cutlasses like carters' whips. But in vain. They were almost overborne, when, rallying themselves into a squad as one man, with a huzza, they sprang inboard; where, entangled, they involuntarily separated again. For a few breaths' space there was a vague, muffled, inner sound as of submerged sword-fish rushing hither and thither through shoals of black-fish. Soon, in a reunited band, and joined by the Spanish seamen, the whites came to the surface, irresistibly driving the negroes toward the stern. But a barricade of casks and sacks, from side to side, had been thrown up by the mainmast. Here the negroes faced about, and though scorning peace or truce, yet fain would have had a respite. But, without pause, overleaping the barrier, the unflagging sailors again closed. Exhausted, the blacks now fought in despair. Their red tongues lolled, wolf-like, from their black mouths. But the pale sailors' teeth were set; not a word was spoken; and, in five minutes more, the ship was won.

Nearly a score of the negroes were killed. Exclusive of those by the balls, many were mangled; their wounds—mostly inflicted by the long-edged scaling-spears—resembling those shaven ones of the English at Preston Pans, made by the poled scythes of the Highlanders. On the other side, none were killed, though several were wounded; some severely, including the mate. The surviving negroes were temporarily secured, and the ship, towed back into the harbour at midnight, once more lay anchored.

Omitting the incidents and arrangements ensuing, suffice it that, after two days spent in refitting, the two ships sailed in company for Concepcion in Chili, and thence for Lima in Peru; where, before the vice-regal courts, the whole affair, from the beginning, underwent investigation.

Though, midway on the passage, the ill-fated Spaniard, relaxed from constraint, showed some signs of regaining health with free-will; yet, agreeably to his own foreboding, shortly before arriving at Lima, he relapsed, finally becoming so reduced as to be carried ashore in arms. Hearing of his story and plight, one of the many religious institutions of the City of Kings opened an hospitable refuge to him, where both physician and priest were his nurses, and a member of the order volunteered to be his own special guardian and consoler, by night and by day.

The following extracts, translated from one of the official Spanish documents, will, it is hoped, shed light on the preceding narrative, as well as, in the first place, reveal the true port of departure and true history of the *San Dominick's* voyage, down to the time of her touching at the island of Santa Maria.

But, ere the extracts come, it may be well to preface them with a remark.

The document selected, from among many others, for partial translation, contains the deposition of Benito Cereno; the first taken in the case. Some disclosures therein were, at the time, held dubious for both learned and natural reasons. The tribunal inclined to the opinion that the deponent, not undisturbed in his mind by recent events, raved of some things which could never have happened. But subsequent depositions of the surviving sailors, bearing out the revelations of their captain in several of the strangest particulars, gave credence to the rest. So that the tribunal, in its final decision, rested its capital sentences upon statements which, had they lacked confirmation, it would have deemed it but duty to reject.

I, Don José de Abos and Padilla, His Majesty's Notary for the Royal Revenue, and Register of this Province, and Notary Public of the Holy Crusade of this Bishopric, etc.

Do certify and declare, as much as is requisite in law, that, in the criminal cause commenced the twenty-fourth of the month of September, in the year seventeen hundred and ninety-nine, against the Senegal negroes of the ship *San Dominick,* the following declaration before me was made.

Declaration of the first witness, Don Benito Cereno

The same day, and month, and year, His Honour, Doctor Juan Martinez de Dozas, Councillor of the Royal Audience of this Kingdom, and learned in the law of this Intendancy, ordered the captain of the ship *San Dominick,* Don Benito Cereno, to appear; which he did in his litter, attended by the monk Infelez; of whom he received, before Don José de Abos and Padilla, Notary Public of the Holy Crusade, the oath which he took by God, our Lord, and a sign of the Cross; under which he promised to tell the truth of whatever he should know and should be asked;—and being interrogated agreeably to the tenor of the act commencing the process, he said, that on the twentieth of May last, he set sail with his ship from the Port of Valparaiso, bound to that of Callao; loaded with the produce of the country and one hundred and sixty blacks, of both sexes, mostly belonging to Don Alexandro Aranda, gentleman, of the city of Mendoza; that the crew of the ship consisted of thirty-six men, beside the persons who went as passengers; that the negroes were in part as follows:

[Here, in the original, follows a list of some fifty names, descriptions, and ages, compiled from certain recovered documents of Aranda's, and also from recollections of the deponent, from which portions only are extracted.]

—One, from about eighteen to nineteen years, named José, and this was the man that waited upon his master, Don Alexandro, and who speaks well the Spanish, having served him four or five years; . . . a mulatto, named Francesco, the cabin steward, of a good person and voice, having sung in the Valparaiso churches, native of the province of Buenos Ayres, aged about thirty-five years. . . . A smart negro, named Dago, who had been for many years a grave-digger among the Spaniards, aged forty-six years. . . . Four old negroes, born in Africa, from sixty to seventy, but sound, caulkers by trade, whose names are as follows:—the first was named Muri, and he was killed (as was also his son named Diamelo); the second, Nacta; the third, Yola, likewise killed; the fourth, Ghofan; and six full-grown negroes, aged from thirty to forty-five, all raw, and born among the Ashantees—Martinqui, Yan, Lecbe, Mapenda, Yambaio, Akim; four of whom were killed; . . . a powerful negro named Atufal, who, being supposed to have been a chief in Africa, his owners set great store by him. . . . And a small negro of Senegal, but some years among the Spaniards, aged about thirty, which negro's name was Babo; . . . that he does not remember the names of the others, but that still expecting the residue of Don Alexandro's papers will be found, will then take due account of them all, and remit to the court; . . . and thirty-nine women and children of all ages.

[After the catalogue, the deposition goes on as follows:]

. . . That all the negroes slept upon deck, as is customary in this navigation, and none wore fetters, because the owner, his friend Aranda, told him that they were all tractable; . . . that on the seventh day after leaving port, at three o'clock in the morning, all the Spaniards being asleep except the two officers on the watch, who were the boatswain, Juan Robles, and the carpenter, Juan Bautista Gayete, and the helmsman and his boy, the negroes revolted suddenly, wounded dangerously the boatswain and the carpenter, and successively killed eighteen men of those who were sleeping upon deck, some with handspikes and hatchets, and others by throwing them alive overboard, after tying them; that of the Spaniards upon deck, they left about seven, as he thinks, alive and tied, to manœuvre the ship, and three or four more who hid themselves, remained also alive. Although in the act of revolt the negroes made themselves masters of the hatchway, six or seven wounded went through it to the cockpit, without any hindrance on their part; that in the act of revolt, the mate and another person, whose name he does not recollect, attempted to come up through the hatchway, but having been wounded at the onset, they were obliged to return to the cabin; that the deponent resolved at break of day to come up the companionway, where the negro Babo was, being the ringleader, and Atufal, who assisted him, and having spoken to them, exhorted them to cease committing such atrocities, asking them, at the same time, what they wanted and intended to do, offering, himself, to obey their commands; that, notwithstanding this, they threw, in his presence, three men, alive and tied, overboard; that they told the deponent to come up, and that they would not kill him; which having done, the negro Babo asked him whether there were in those seas any negro countries where they might be carried, and he answered them. No; that the negro Babo afterwards told him to carry them to Senegal, or to the neighbouring islands of St. Nicholas; and he answered, that this was impossible, on account of the great distance, the necessity involved of rounding Cape Horn, the bad condition of the vessel, the want of provisions, sails, and water; but that the negro Babo replied to him he must carry them in any way; that they would do and conform themselves to everything the deponent should require as to eating and drinking; that after a long conference, being absolutely compelled to please them, for they threatened him to kill all the whites if they were not, at all events, carried to Senegal, he told them that what was most wanting for the voyage was water; that they would go near the coast to take it, and hence they would proceed on their course; that the negro Babo agreed to it; and the deponent steered toward the intermediate ports, hoping to meet some Spanish or foreign vessel that would save them; that within ten or eleven days they saw the land, and continued their course by it in the vicinity of Nasca; that the deponent observed that the negroes were now restless and mutinous, because he did not effect the taking in of water, the negro Babo having required, with threats, that it should be done, without fail, the following day; he told him he saw plainly that the coast was steep, and the rivers designated in the maps were not to be found, with other reasons suitable to the circumstances; that the best way would be to go to the island of Santa Maria, where they might water and victual easily, it being a desert island, as the foreigners did; that the deponent did not go to Pisco, that was near, nor make any other port of the coast, because the negro Babo had intimated to him several times, that he would kill all the whites the very moment he should perceive any city, town, or settlement of any kind on the shores to which they should be carried: that having determined to go to the island of Santa Maria, as the deponent had planned, for the purpose of trying whether, in the passage or in the island itself, they could find any vessel that should favour them, or whether he could escape from it in a boat to the neighboring coast of Arruco; to adopt the necessary means he immediately changed his course, steering for the island; that the negroes Babo and Atufal held daily conferences, in which they discussed what was necessary for their design of returning to Senegal, whether they were to kill all the Spaniards, and particularly the deponent; that eight days after parting from the coast of Nasca, the deponent being on the watch a little after daybreak, and soon after the negroes had their meeting, the negro Babo came to the place where the deponent was, and told him that he had determined to kill his master, Don Alexandro Aranda, both because he and his companions could not otherwise be sure of their liberty, and that, to keep the seamen in subjection, he wanted to prepare a warning of what road they should be made to take did they or any of them oppose him; and that, by means of the death of Don Alexandro, that warning would best be given; but, that what this last meant, the deponent did not at the time comprehend, nor could not, further than that the death of Don Alexandro was intended; and moreover, the negro Babo proposed to the deponent to call the mate, Raneds, who was sleeping in the cabin, before the thing was done, for fear, as the deponent understood it, that the mate, who was a good navigator, should be killed with Don Alexandro and the rest; that the deponent, who was the friend, from youth, of Don Alexandro, prayed and conjured, but all was useless; for the negro Babo answered him that the thing could not be prevented, and that all the Spaniards risked their death if they should attempt to frustrate his will in this matter, or any other; that, in this conflict, the deponent called the mate, Raneds, who was forced to go apart, and immediately the negro Babo commanded the Ashantee Martinqui and the Ashantee Lecbe to go and commit the murder; that those two went down with hatchets to the berth of Don Alexandro; that, yet half alive and mangled, they dragged him on deck; that they were going to throw him overboard in that state, but the negro Babo stopped them, bidding the murder be completed on the deck before him, which was done, when, by his orders, the body was carried below, forward; that nothing more was seen of it by the deponent for three days; ... that Don Alonzo Sidonia, an old man, long resident at Valparaiso, and lately appointed to a civil office in Peru, whither he had taken passage, was at the time sleeping in the berth opposite Don Alexandro's; that, awakening at his cries, surprised by them, and at the sight of the negroes with their bloody hatchets in their hands, he threw himself into the sea through a window which was near him, and was drowned, without it being in the power of the deponent to assist or take him up; ... that, a short time after killing Aranda, they brought upon deck his german-cousin, of middle-age, Don Francisco Masa, of Mendoza, and the young Don Joaquin, Marquis de Aramboalaza, then lately from Spain, with his Spanish servant Ponce, and the three young clerks of Aranda, José Mozairi, Lorenzo Bargas, and Hermenegildo Gandix, all of Cadiz; that Don Joaquin and Hermenegildo Gandix, the negro Babo, for purposes hereafter to appear, preserved alive; but Don Francisco Masa, José Mozairi, and Lorenzo Bargas, with Ponce, the servant, beside the boatswain, Juan Robles, the boatswain's mates, Manuel Viscaya and Roderigo Hurta, and four of the sailors, the negro Babo ordered to be thrown alive into the sea, although they made no resistance, nor begged for anything else but mercy; that the boatswain, Juan Robles, who knew how to swim, kept the longest above water, making acts of contrition, and, in the last words he uttered, charged this deponent to cause mass to be said for his soul to our Lady of Succour: ... that, during the three days which followed, the deponent, uncertain what fate had befallen the remains of Don Alexandro, frequently asked the negro Babo where they were, and, if still on board, whether they were to be preserved for interment ashore, entreating him so to order it; that the negro Babo answered nothing till the fourth day, when at sunrise, the deponent coming on deck, the negro Babo showed him a skeleton, which had been substituted for the ship's proper figure-head, the image of Christopher Colon, the discoverer of the New World; that the negro Babo asked him whose skeleton that was, and whether, from its whiteness, he should not think it a white's; that, upon his covering his face, the negro Babo, coming close, said words to this effect: "Keep faith with the blacks from here to Senegal, or you shall in spirit, as now in body, follow your leader," pointing to the prow; ... that the same morning the negro Babo took by succession each Spaniard forward, and asked him whose skeleton that was, and whether, from its whiteness, he should not think it a white's; that each Spaniard covered his face; that then to each the negro Babo repeated the words in the first place said to the deponent; ... that they (the Spaniards), being then assembled aft, the negro Babo harangued them, saying that he had now done all; that the deponent (as navigator for the negroes) might pursue his course, warning him and all of them that they should, soul and body, go the way of Don Alexandro if he saw them (the Spaniards) speak or plot anything against them (the negroes)—a threat which was repeated every day; that, before the events last mentioned, they had tied the cook to throw him overboard, for it is not known what thing they heard him speak, but finally the negro Babo spared his life, at the request of the deponent; that a few days after, the deponent, endeavouring not to omit any means to preserve the lives of the remaining whites, spoke to the negroes peace and tranquillity, and agreed to draw up a paper, signed by the deponent and the sailors who could write, as also by the negro Babo, for himself and all the blacks, in which the deponent obliged himself to carry them to Senegal, and they not to kill any more, and he formally to make over to them the ship, with the cargo, with which they were for that time satisfied and quieted.... But the next day, the more surely to guard against the sailors' escape, the negro Babo commanded all the boats to be destroyed but the longboat, which was unseaworthy, and another, a cutter in good condition, which, knowing it would yet be wanted for lowering the water casks, he had lowered down into the hold.

[*Various particulars of the prolonged and perplexed navigation ensuing here follow, with incidents of a calamitous calm, from which portion one passage is extracted, to wit:*]

—That on the fifth day of the calm, all on board suffering much from the heat, and want of water, and five having died in fits, and mad, the negroes became irritable, and for a chance gesture, which they deemed suspicious—though it was harmless—made by the mate, Raneds, to the deponent, in the act of handing a quadrant, they killed him; but that for this they afterwards were sorry, the mate being the only remaining navigator on board, except the deponent.

—That omitting other events, which daily happened, and which can only serve uselessly to recall past misfortunes and conflicts, after seventy-three days' navigation, reckoned from the time they sailed from Nasca, during which they navigated under a scanty allowance of water, and were afflicted with the calms before mentioned, they at last arrived at the island of Santa Maria, on the seventeenth of the month of August, at about six o'clock in the afternoon, at which hour they cast anchor very near the American ship, *Bachelor's Delight*, which lay in the same bay, commanded by the generous Captain Amasa Delano; but at six o'clock in the morning, they had already descried the port, and the negroes became uneasy, as soon as at distance they saw the ship, not having expected to see one there; that the negro Babo pacified them, assuring them that no fear need be had; that straightway he ordered the figure on the bow to be covered with canvas, as for repairs, and had the decks a little set in order; that for a time the negro Babo and the negro Atufal conferred; that the negro Atufal was for sailing away, but the negro Babo would not, and, by himself, cast about what to do; that at last he came to the deponent, proposing to him to say and do all that the deponent declares to have said and done to the American captain; ... that the negro Babo warned him that if he varied in the least, or uttered any word, or gave any look that should give the least intimation of the past events or present state, he would instantly kill him, with all his companions, showing a dagger, which he carried hid, saying something which, as he understood it, meant that that dagger would be alert as his eye; that the negro Babo then announced the plan to all his companions, which pleased them; that he then, the better to disguise the truth, devised many expedients, in some of them uniting deceit and defence; that of this sort was the device of the six Ashantees before named who were his bravos; that them he stationed on the break of the poop, as if to clean certain hatchets (in cases, which were part of the cargo), but in reality to use them, and distribute them at need, and at a given word he told them that, among other devices, was the device of presenting Atufal, his right-hand man, as chained, though in a moment the chains could be dropped; that in every particular he informed the deponent what part he was to enact in every device, and what story he was to tell on every occasion, always threatening him with instant death if he varied in the least: that, conscious that many of the negroes would be turbulent, the negro Babo appointed the four aged negroes, who were caulkers, to keep what domestic order they could on the decks; that again and again he harangued the Spaniards and his companions, informing them of his intent, and of his devices, and of the invented story that this deponent was to tell, charging them lest any of them varied from that story; that these arrangements were made and matured during the interval of two or three hours, between their first sighting the ship and the arrival on board of Captain Amasa Delano; that this happened at about half-past seven in the morning, Captain Amasa Delano coming in his boat, and all gladly receiving him; that the deponent, as well as he could force himself, acting then the part of principal owner, and a free captain of the ship, told Captain Amasa Delano, when called upon, that he came from Buenos Ayres, bound to Lima, with three hundred negroes; that off Cape Horn, and in a subsequent fever, many negroes had died; that also, by similar casualties, all the sea officers and the greatest part of the crew had died.

[And so the deposition goes on, circumstantially recounting the fictitious story dictated to the deponent by Babo, and through the deponent imposed upon Captain Delano; and also recounting the friendly offers of Captain Delano, with other things, but all of which is here omitted. After the fictitious, strange story, etc., the deposition proceeds:]

—That the generous Captain Amasa Delano remained on board all the day, till he left the ship anchored at six o'clock in the evening, deponent speaking to him always of his pretended misfortunes, under the forementioned principles, without having had it in his power to tell a single word, or give him the least hint, that he might know the truth and state of things; because the negro Babo, performing the office of an officious servant with all the appearance of submission of the humble slave, did not leave the deponent one moment; that this was in order to observe the deponent's actions and words, for the negro Babo understands well the Spanish; and besides, there were thereabout some others who were constantly on the watch, and likewise understood the Spanish; ... that upon one occasion, while deponent was standing on the deck conversing with Amasa Delano, by a secret sign the negro Babo drew him (the deponent) aside, the act appearing as if originating with the deponent; that then, he being drawn aside, the negro Babo proposed to him to gain from Amasa Delano full particulars about his ship, and crew, and arms; that the deponent asked "For what?" that the negro Babo answered he might conceive; that, grieved at the prospect of what might overtake the generous Captain Amasa Delano, the deponent at first refused to ask the desired questions, and used every argument to induce the negro Babo to give up this new design; that the negro Babo showed the point of his dagger; that, after the information had been obtained, the negro Babo again drew him aside, telling him that that very night he (the deponent) would be captain of two ships instead of one, for that, great part of the American's ship's crew being to be absent fishing, the six Ashantees, without any one else, would easily take it; that at this time he said other things to the same purpose; that no entreaties availed; that before Amasa Delano's coming on board, no hint had been given touching the capture of the American ship: that to prevent this project the deponent was powerless; . . .—that in some things his memory is confused, he cannot distinctly recall every event; . . .—that as soon as they had cast anchor at six of the clock in the evening, as has before been stated, the American captain took leave to return to his vessel; that upon a sudden impulse, which the deponent believes to have come from God and his angels, he, after the farewell had been said, followed the generous Captain Amasa Delano as far as the gunwale, where he stayed, under the pretence of taking leave, until Amasa Delano should have been seated in his boat; that on shoving off, the deponent sprang from the gunwale, into the boat, and fell into it, he knows not how, God guarding him; that—

[*Here, in the original, follows the account of what further happened at the escape, and how the "San Dominick" was retaken, and of the passage to the coast; including in the recital many expressions of "eternal gratitude" to the "generous Captain Amasa Delano." The deposition then proceeds with recapitulatory remarks, and a partial renumeration of the negroes, making record of their individual part in the past events, with a view to furnishing, according to command of the court, the data whereon to found the criminal sentences to be pronounced. From this portion is the following:*]

—That he believes that all the negroes, though not in the first place knowing to the design of revolt, when it was accomplished, approved it. . . . That the negro, José, eighteen years old, and in the personal service of Don Alexandro, was the one who communicated the information to the negro Babo, about the state of things in the cabin, before the revolt; that this is known, because, in the preceding midnight, he used to come from his berth, which was under his master's, in the cabin, to the deck where the ringleader and his associates were, and had secret conversations with the negro Babo, in which he was several times seen by the mate; that, one night, the mate drove him away twice; . . . that this same negro José, was the one who, without being commanded to do so by the negro Babo, as Lecbe and Martinqui were, stabbed his master, Don Alexandro, after he had been dragged half-lifeless to the deck; . . . that the mulatto steward, Francesco, was of

the first band of revolters, that he was, in all things, the creature and
tool of the negro Babo; that, to make his court, he, just before a repast
in the cabin, proposed, to the negro Babo, poisoning a dish for the
generous Captain Amasa Delano; this is known and believed, because
the negroes have said it; but that the negro Babo, having another design, forbade Francesco; . . . that the Ashantee Lecbe was one of the
worst of them; for that, on the day the ship was retaken, he assisted
in the defence of her, with a hatchet in each hand, with one of which
he wounded, in the breast, the chief mate of Amasa Delano, in the first
act of boarding; this all knew; that, in sight of the deponent, Lecbe
struck, with a hatchet, Don Francisco Masa when, by the negro Babo's
orders, he was carrying him to throw him overboard, alive; beside participating in the murder, before mentioned, of Don Alexandro Aranda,
and others of the cabin-passengers; that, owing to the fury with which
the Ashantees fought in the engagement with the boats, but this Lecbe
and Yan survived; that Yan was bad as Lecbe; that Yan was the man
who, by Babo's command, willingly prepared the skeleton of Don Alexandro, in a way the negroes afterwards told the deponent, but which he,
so long as reason is left him, can never divulge; that Yan and Lecbe
were the two who, in a calm by night, riveted the skeleton to the bow;
this also the negroes told him; that the negro Babo was he who traced
the inscription below it; that the negro Babo was the plotter from first
to last; he ordered every murder, and was the helm and keel of the
revolt; that Atufal was his lieutenant in all; but Atufal, with his own
hand, committed no murder; nor did the negro Babo; . . . that Atufal
was shot, being killed in the fight with the boats, ere boarding; . . .
that the negresses, of age, were knowing to the revolt, and testified
themselves satisfied at the death of their master, Don Alexandro; that,
had the negroes not restrained them, they would have tortured to death,
instead of simply killing, the Spaniards slain by command of the negro
Babo; that the negresses used their utmost influence to have the deponent made away with; that, in the various acts of murder, they sang
songs and danced—not gaily, but solemnly; and before the engagement
with the boats, as well as during the action, they sang melancholy
songs to the negroes, and that this melancholy tone was more inflaming
than a different one would have been, and was so intended; that all
this is believed, because the negroes have said it.

—That of the thirty-six men of the crew—exclusive of the passengers (all of whom are now dead), which the deponent had knowledge
of—six only remained alive, with four cabin-boys and ship-boys, included with the crew; . . .—that the negroes broke an arm of one of
the cabin-boys and gave him strokes with hatchets.

[*Then follow various random disclosures referring to various periods of time.
The following are extracted:*]

—That during the presence of Captain Amasa Delano on board, some
attempts were made by the sailors, and one by Hermenegildo Gandix,

to convey hints to him of the true state of affairs; but that these attempts were ineffectual, owing to fear of incurring death, and further-more owing to the devices which offered contradictions to the true state of affairs; as well as owing to the generosity and piety of Amasa Delano, incapable of sounding such wickedness; . . . that Luys Galgo, a sailor about sixty years of age, and formerly of the king's navy, was one of those who sought to convey tokens to Captain Amasa Delano; but his intent, though undiscovered, being suspected, he was, on a pretence, made to retire out of sight, and at last into the hold, and there was made away with. This the negroes have since said; . . . that one of the ship-boys feeling, from Captain Amasa Delano's presence, some hopes of release, and not having enough prudence, dropped some chance-word respecting his expectations, which being overheard and understood by a slave-boy with whom he was eating at the time, the latter struck him on the head with a knife, inflicting a bad wound, but of which the boy is now healing; that likewise, not long before the ship was brought to anchor, one of the seamen, steering at the time, endangered himself by letting the blacks remark a certain unconscious hopeful expression in his countenance, arising from some cause similar to the above; but this sailor, by his heedful after conduct, escaped; . . . that these state-ments are made to show the court that from the beginning to the end of the revolt, it was impossible for the deponent and his men to act otherwise than they did; . . . —that the third clerk, Hermenegildo Gandix, who before had been forced to live among the seamen, wearing a seaman's habit, and in all respects appearing to be one for the time; he, Gandix, was killed by a musket-ball fired through a mistake from the American boats before boarding; having in his fright ran up the mizzen-rigging, calling to the boats—"don't board," lest upon their boarding the negroes should kill him; that this inducing the Americans to believe he some way favoured the cause of the negroes, they fired two balls at him, so that he fell wounded from the rigging, and was drowned in the sea; . . . —that the young Don Joaquin, Marques de Arambaolaza, like Hermenegildo Gandix, the third clerk, was degraded to the office and appearance of a common seaman; that upon one occa-sion, when Don Joaquin shrank, the negro Babo commanded the Ashantee Lecbe to take tar and heat it, and pour it upon Don Joaquin's hands; . . . —that Don Joaquin was killed owing to another mistake of the Americans, but one impossible to be avoided, as upon the approach of the boats, Don Joaquin, with a hatchet tied edge out and upright to his hand, was made by the negroes to appear on the bulwarks; whereupon, seen with arms in his hands and in a questionable attitude, he was shot for a renegade seaman; . . . —that on the person of Don Joaquin was found secreted a jewel, which, by papers that were dis-covered, proved to have been meant for the shrine of our Lady of Mercy in Lima; a votive offering, beforehand prepared and guarded, to attest his gratitude, when he should have landed in Peru, his last destination, for the safe conclusion of his entire voyage from Spain;

... —that the jewel, with the other effects of the late Don Joaquin, is in the custody of the brethren of the Hospital de Sacerdotes, awaiting the decision of the honourable court; ... —that, owing to the condition of the deponent, as well as the haste in which the boats departed for the attack, the Americans were not forewarned that there were, among the apparent crew, a passenger and one of the clerks disguised by the negro Babo; ... —that, beside the negroes killed in the action, some were killed after the capture and reanchoring at night, when shackled to the ring-bolts on deck; that these deaths were committed by the sailors, ere they could be prevented. That so soon as informed of it, Captain Amasa Delano used all his authority, and, in particular with his own hand, struck down Martinez Gola, who, having found a razor in the pocket of an old jacket of his, which one of the shackled negroes had on, was aiming it at the negro's throat; that the noble Captain Amasa Delano also wrenched from the hand of Bartholomew Barlo, a dagger secreted at the time of the massacre of the whites, with which he was in the act of stabbing a shackled negro, who, the same day, with another negro, had thrown him down and jumped upon him; ... —that, for all the events, befalling through so long a time, during which the ship was in the hands of the negro Babo, he cannot here give account; but that, what he has said is the most substantial of what occurs to him at present, and is the truth under the oath which he has taken; which declaration he affirmed and ratified, after hearing it read to him.

He said that he is twenty-nine years of age, and broken in body and mind; that when finally dismissed by the court, he shall not return home to Chili, but betake himself to the monastery on Mount Agonia without; and signed with his honour, and crossed himself, and, for the time, departed as he came, in his litter, with the monk Infelez, to the Hospital de Sacerdotes.

Benito Cereno.

Doctor Rozas.

If the deposition of Benito Cereno has served as the key to fit into the lock of the complications which preceded it, then, as a vault whose door has been flung back, the *San Dominick's* hull lies open to-day.

Hitherto the nature of this narrative, besides rendering the intricacies in the beginning unavoidable, has more or less required that many things, instead of being set down in the order of occurence, should be retrospectively, or irregularly given; this last is the case with the following passages, which will conclude the account:

During the long, mild voyage to Lima, there was, as before hinted, a period during which Don Benito a little recovered his health, or, at least in some degree, his tranquillity. Ere the decided relapse which came, the two captains had many cordial conversations—their fraternal unreserve in singular contrast with former withdrawments.

Again and again, it was repeated, how hard it had been to enact the part forced on the Spaniard by Babo.

"Ah, my dear Don Amasa," Don Benito once said, "at those very times when you thought me so morose and ungrateful—nay when, as you now admit, you half thought me plotting your murder—at those very times my heart was frozen; I could not look at you, thinking of what, both on board this ship and your own, hung, from other hands, over my kind benefactor. And as God lives, Don Amasa, I know not whether desire for my own safety alone could have nerved me to that leap into your boat, had it not been for the thought that, did you, unenlightened, return to your ship, you, my best friend, with all who might be with you, stolen upon, that night, in your hammocks, would never in this world have wakened again. Do but think how you walked this deck, how you sat in this cabin, every inch of ground mined into honey-combs under you. Had I dropped the least hint, made the least advance toward an understanding between us, death, explosive death— yours as mine—would have ended the scene."

"True, true," cried Captain Delano, starting, "you saved my life, Don Benito, more than I yours; saved it, too, against my knowledge and will."

"Nay, my friend," rejoined the Spaniard, courteous even to the point of religion, "God charmed your life, but you saved mine. To think of some things you did—those smilings and chattings, rash pointings and gesturings. For less than these, they slew my mate, Raneds; but you had the Prince of Heaven's safe conduct through all ambuscades."

"Yes, all is owing to Providence, I know; but the temper of my mind that morning was more than commonly pleasant, while the sight of so much suffering—more apparent than real—added to my good nature, compassion, and charity, happily interweaving the three. Had it been otherwise, doubtless, as you hint, some of my interferences with the blacks might have ended unhappily enough. Besides that, those feelings I spoke of enabled me to get the better of momentary distrust, at times when acuteness might have cost me my life, without saving another's. Only at the end did my suspicions get the better of me, and you know how wide of the mark they then proved."

"Wide, indeed," said Don Benito, sadly; "you were with me all day; stood with me, sat with me, talked with me, looked at me, ate with me, drank with me; and yet, your last act was to clutch for a villain, not only an innocent man, but the most pitiable of all men. To such degree may malign machinations and deceptions impose. So far may even the best men err, in judging the conduct of one with the recesses of whose condition he is not acquainted. But you were forced to it; and you were in time undeceived. Would that, in both respects, it was so ever, and with all men."

"I think I understand you; you generalize, Don Benito; and mournfully enough. But the past is passed; why moralize upon it? Forget it.

See, yon bright sun has forgotten it all, and the blue sea, and the blue
sky; these have turned over new leaves."

"Because they have no memory," he dejectedly replied; "because
they are not human."

"But these mild trades that now fan your cheek, Don Benito, do
they not come with a human-like healing to you? Warm friends, stead-
fast friends are the trades."

"With their steadfastness they but waft me to my tomb, Señor,"
was the foreboding response.

"You are saved, Don Benito," cried Captain Delano, more and more
astonished and pained; "you are saved; what has cast such a shadow
upon you?"

"The negro."

There was silence, while the moody man sat, slowly and unconsciously gathering his mantle about him, as if it were a pall.

There was no more conversation that day.

But if the Spaniard's melancholy sometimes ended in muteness
upon topics like the above, there were others upon which he never
spoke at all; on which, indeed, all his old reserves were piled. Pass over
the worst and, only to elucidate, let an item or two of these be cited.
The dress so precise and costly, worn by him on the day whose events
have been narrated, had not willingly been put on. And that silver-
mounted sword, apparent symbol of despotic command, was not, indeed,
a sword, but the ghost of one. The scabbard, artificially stiffened, was
empty.

As for the black—whose brain, not body, had schemed and led the
revolt, with the plot—his slight frame, inadequate to that which it held,
had at once yielded to the superior muscular strength of his captor, in
the boat. Seeing all was over, he uttered no sound, and could not be
forced to. His aspect seemed to say: since I cannot do deeds, I will not
speak words. Put in irons in the hold, with the rest, he was carried to
Lima. During the passage Don Benito did not visit him. Nor then, nor
at any time after, would he look at him. Before the tribunal he refused.
When pressed by the judges, he fainted. On the testimony of the sailors
alone rested the legal identity of Babo. And yet the Spaniard would,
upon occasion, verbally refer to the negro, as has been shown; but
look on him he would not, or could not.

Some months after, dragged to the gibbet at the tail of a mule, the
black met his voiceless end. The body was burned to ashes; but for
many days, the head, that hive of subtlety, fixed on a pole in the Plaza,
met, unabashed, the gaze of the whites; and across the Plaza looked
toward St. Bartholomew's church, in whose vaults slept then, as now,
the recovered bones of Aranda; and across the Rimac bridge looked
toward the monastery, on Mount Agonia without; where, three months
after being dismissed by the court, Benito Cereno, borne on the bier,
did, indeed, follow his leader.

The Portent *(1866)*[1]

Hanging from the beam,
    Slowly swaying (such the law),
Gaunt the shadow on your green,
    Shenandoah!
The cut is on the crown [2]
    (Lo, John Brown),
And the stabs shall heal no more.

Hidden in the cap
    Is the anguish none can draw;
So your future veils its face,   *10*
    Shenandoah!
But the streaming beard is shown
    (Weird John Brown),
The meteor of the war.

A Utilitarian View *of the Monitor's Fight* *(1866)*[1]

Plain be the phrase, yet apt the verse,
    More ponderous than nimble;
For since grimed War here laid aside
His Orient pomp, 'twould ill befit
      Overmuch to ply
    The rhyme's barbaric cymbal.

Hail to victory without the gaud
    Of glory; zeal that needs no fans
Of banners; plain mechanic power
Plied cogently in War now placed—   *10*
    Where War belongs—
    Among the trades and artisans.

Yet this was battle, and intense—
    Beyond the strife of fleets heroic;
Deadlier, closer, calm 'mid storm;

---

[1] John Brown (1800–1859), an abolitionist leader, led a raid at Harper's Ferry, Virginia, in October, 1859, to free slaves; he was hanged December 2, 1859.
[2] Refers to a head wound received by Brown when captured, and perhaps also to the general condition of American society at the time.

---

[1] The defeat of the Confederate ironclad *Merrimac* by the armored turret ship, the *Monitor*, on March 9, 1862, marked the beginning of a new era in warfare.

No passion; all went on by crank,
     Pivot, and screw,
    And calculations of caloric.[2]

Needless to dwell; the story's known.
    The ringing of those plates on plates   20
Still ringeth round the world—
The clangor of that blacksmiths' fray.
      The anvil-din
    Resounds this message from the Fates:

War shall yet be, and to the end;
    But war-paint shows the streaks of weather;
War yet shall be, but warriors
Are now but operatives; War's made
      Less grand than Peace,
    And a singe runs through lace and feather.   30

Shiloh *(1866)*[1]

A Requiem

Skimming lightly, wheeling still,
    The swallows fly low
Over the field in clouded days,
    The forest-field of Shiloh—
Over the field where April rain
Solaced the parched ones stretched in pain
Through the pause of night
That followed the Sunday fight
    Around the church of Shiloh—
The church so lone, the log-built one,   10
That echoed to many a parting groan
      And natural prayer
    Of dying foemen mingled there—
Foeman at morn, but friends at eve—
    Fame or country least their care:
(What like a bullet can undeceive!)
    But now they lie low,
While over them the swallows skim,
    And all is hushed at Shiloh.

---

[2] Heat.

[1] A bloody but inconclusive battle in the Civil War was fought at Shiloh, Tennessee, on April 6 to 7, 1862.

Malvern Hill (*1866*)[1]

Ye elms that wave on Malvern Hill
    In prime of morn and May,
Recall ye how McClellan's men
      Here stood at bay?
While deep within yon forest dim
    Our rigid comrades lay—
Some with the cartridge in their mouth,
Others with fixed arms lifted South—
      Invoking so
The cypress glades? Ah wilds of woe!   10

The spires of Richmond, late beheld
    Through rifts in musket-haze,
Were closed from view in clouds of dust
    On leaf-walled ways,
Where streamed our wagons in caravan;
    And the Seven Nights and Days
Of march and fast, retreat and fight,
Pinched our grimed faces to gastly plight—
      Does the elm wood
Recall the haggard beards of blood?   20

The battle-smoked flag, with stars eclipsed,
    We followed (it never fell!)—
In silence husbanded our strength—
    Received their yell;
Till on this slope we patient turned
    With cannon ordered well;
Reverse we proved was not defeat;
But ah, the sod what thousands meet!—
      Does Malvern Wood
Bethink itself, and muse and brood?   30

    We elms of Malvern Hill
      Remembered every thing;
    But sap the twig will fill:
    Wag the world how it will,
      Leaves must be green in Spring.

[1] Refers to the last of Seven Days' Battles at Malvern Hill on July 1, 1862, at which General George McClellan, commander of the Northern forces, attempted an unsuccessful assault toward Richmond.

The College Colonel *(1866)*

He rides at their head;
    A crutch by his saddle just slants in view,
One slung arm is in splints, you see,
    Yet he guides his strong steed—how coldly too.
He brings his regiment home—
    Not as they filed two years before,
But a remnant half-tattered, and battered, and worn,
Like castaway sailors, who—stunned
        By the surf's loud roar,
    Their mates dragged back and seen no more—   10
Again and again breast the surge,
    And at last crawl, spent, to shore.

A still rigidity and pale—
    An Indian aloofness lones his brow;
He has lived a thousand years
Compressed in battle's pains and prayers,
    Marches and watches slow.
There are welcoming shouts, and flags;
    Old men off hat to the Boy,
Wreaths from gay balconies fall at his feet,   20
    But to *him*—there comes alloy.

It is not that a leg is lost,
    It is not that an arm is maimed,
It is not that the fever has racked—
    Self he has long disclaimed.

But all through the Seven Days' Fight,
    And deep in the Wilderness [1] grim,
And in the field-hospital tent,
    And Petersburg crater,[2] and dim
Lean brooding in Libby,[3] there came—   30
    Ah heaven!—what *truth* to him.

---

[1] Battle of the Wilderness, north of Richmond, 1864.

[2] Formed by federal mine that blew up Confederation fortifications, Petersburg, Virginia, July, 1864.

[3] Richmond prison, noted for poor conditions, where Northern officers were kept.

The Maldive Shark (1888)

About the Shark, phlegmatical one,
Pale sot of the Maldive sea,[1]
The sleek little pilot-fish, azure and slim,
How alert in attendance be.
From his saw-pit of mouth, from his charnel of maw
They have nothing of harm to dread,
But liquidly glide on his ghastly flank
Or before his Gorgonian [2] head;
Or lurk in the port of serrated teeth
In white triple tiers of glittering gates,   10
And there find a haven when peril's abroad,
An asylum in jaws of the Fates!
They are friends; and friendly they guide him to prey,
Yet never partake of the treat—
Eyes and brains to the dotard lethargic and dull,
Pale ravener of horrible meat.

To Ned (1888)[1]

Where is the world we roved, Ned Bunn?
    Hollows thereof lay rich in shade
By voyagers old involate thrown
    Ere Paul Pry [2] cruised with Pelf and Trade.
To us old lads some thoughts come home
Who roamed a world young lads no more shall roam.

Nor less the satiate year impends
    When, wearying of routine-resorts,

[1] Part of the Indian Ocean.
[2] Figures in Greek mythology, the sight of whom turned beholders to stone.

---

[1] This poem, coming late in Melville's life, is not perhaps one of his best, but it is extraordinarily interesting as it reveals the extent to which Melville's early experience in the South Pacific, and the "dream of paradise" it roused in him (see pp. 32–40 of the introduction), still remained a force within his imagination. "Ned" is the fictitious name Melville gave to Richard Tobias Greene, his companion in the South Pacific adventures related in Melville's first book *Typee,* where, however, he is called Toby.
[2] Refers, as a general type, to meddlesome people; in this instance perhaps to the missionaries about whose activities in the primitive communities of the South Pacific Melville was extremely critical. In this line he sees the prying of such figures as going together with the profit of commercial traders.

The pleasure-hunter shall break loose,
 Ned, for our Pantheistic [3] ports: —   *10*
Marquesas and glenned isles that be
Authentic Edens in a Pagan sea.

The charm of scenes untried shall lure,
 And, Ned, a legend urge the flight—
The Typee-truants under stars
 Unknown to Shakespeare's *Midsummer-Night;*
And man, if lost to Saturn's Age,[4]
Yet feeling life no Syrian pilgrimage.

But, tell, shall he, the tourist, find
 Our isles the same in violet-glow   *20*
Enamoring us what years and years—
 Ah, Ned, what years and years ago!
Well, Adam advances, smart in pace,
But scarce by violets that advance you trace.

But we, in anchor-watches calm,
 The Indian Psyche's languor [5] won,
And, musing, breathed primeval balm
 From Edens ere yet overrun;
Marvelling mild if mortal twice,
Here and hereafter, touch a Paradise.   *30*

Fragments of a Lost Gnostic Poem of the 12th Century *(1891)*

Found a family, build a state,
The pledged event is still the same:
Matter in end will never abate
His ancient brutal claim.

Indolence is heaven's ally here,
And energy the child of hell:
The Good Man pouring from his pitcher clear,
But brims the poisoned well.

---

[3] Very loose usage to suggest that when the "pleasure-hunter" who has wearied of his customary work ("routine-resorts") comes to the Marquesas, he will find them "pantheistic," that is, pleasurable and untroubled.

[4] The age of Saturn, a Roman god, that is supposed to have been one of happiness, a "golden age."

[5] Psyche, in Greek mythology, is a beautiful princess loved by Eros. Melville may be suggesting here that in the East there is a kind of erotic and languorous pleasure, at least that once there was such a pleasure before "Edens . . . overrun."

Monody (1891)[1]

To have known him, to have loved him
    After loneness long:
And then to be estranged in life,
    And neither in the wrong;
And now for death to set his seal—
    Ease me, a little ease, my song!

By wintry hills his hermit-mound
    The sheeted snow-drifts drape,
And houseless there the snow-bird flits
    Beneath the fir-trees' crape: 10
Glazed now with ice the cloistral vine
    That hid the shyest grape.

In a Garret (1891)

Gems and jewels let them heap—
    Wax sumptuous as the Sophi:
For me, to grapple from Art's deep
    One dripping trophy!

WALT WHITMAN (1819–1892)

With Walt Whitman, the face of American poetry changed forever. About the value of this change there remains significant differences to this day, but that it occurred no one would dispute.

Walt Whitman was born in West Hills, Long Island. His father, Walter, soon gave up trying to support the family by farming and moved to Brooklyn in 1823 to build houses. Walt attended public school in Brooklyn for five or six years, then he became an apprentice printer. In 1835, unable to find work in New York, he taught school for a time on Long Island, then edited and printed a newspaper, the Long Islander, *from 1838 to 1839. In 1840 he returned to New York, again working as a printer until 1845. The following year he became editor of the Brooklyn* Daily Eagle, *but his support of the Free Soil movement antagonized the conservatives who controlled the Democratic party and lost him his job. He then took a position with the New Orleans* Crescent *and spent three months there in*

---

[1] An elegy on Hawthorne, d. 1864.

1848, returning home by way of the Mississippi, the Great Lakes, and the Hudson River.

Working as a builder, journalist, store proprietor, and founder of a Free Soil paper, The Freeman, *during this period Whitman wrote the poems that he printed in 1855 as* Leaves of Grass. *Throughout the remainder of his life he kept revising and expanding that volume, and in 1891 to 1892 he approved the ninth (or "deathbed") edition. Though Whitman tried to whip up some attention for his poems by writing anonymous reviews of them, the only significant notice that came to him—but a notice of historic value—was that from Emerson: "I greet you at the beginning of a great career."*

In 1862 Whitman went to Fredericksburg to care for a brother wounded in the Civil War, and he spent the next three years nursing the wounded in hospitals in and around Washington. His Civil War poems were published in 1865 as Drum Taps. *During the war and afterward, he worked in various governmental offices until a paralytic stroke in 1873 forced him to live with a brother in Camden, New Jersey. When an 1881 edition of* Leaves of Grass *was suppressed in Boston, the resulting publicity boosted sales sufficiently for Whitman to buy a modest house in Camden. Here he remained until his death, receiving visitors and settling into the role of sage.*

Criticism, whether appreciative or depreciative, of Whitman has by now tended to settle into a number of fixed propositions, such as these:

Whitman was the first American poet to celebrate the idea of democracy, almost as if it were a kind of national religion; his democratic vision is plebeian, fraternal, and easy-going, in a way no other American writer had previously achieved. The American ethos finds its first complete expression in his verse.

Whitman's main ideas and values derive from Romanticism, but mostly through the transcendentalist notions of Emerson. "I was simmering, simmering; Emerson brought me to a boil." In his intense relationship to nature, his immersion in the idea of the self, his cultivation of the senses, his tendency to see the physical world not merely in its tangible immediacy but also as a spiritual sign, Whitman shared the values of the early nineteenth-century Romantics.

Whitman was a poet of personal and sexual liberation. He broke past the fearful inhibitions and restraints of the genteel tradition; he celebrated the human body as beautiful and innocent; he shook off the Puritan fears of sexuality and treated it as a source of pleasure and a rite of mystery.

Whitman brought a new language and a new rhythm into poetry. He abandoned the set rhetoric of "poetic diction," he did not hesitate to use the language of the street in his poems. He abandoned, also, the regular

*meters and stanzaic patterns of traditional English poetry, preferring
instead to employ lines of irregular length, presumably dependent on the
unfixed rhythms of speech and incantation, a kind of cadenced verse
that lent itself at times to oratory and at other times to chanting.*

Now all such statements are true, but not true enough or not the whole
truth; they do Whitman the injustice of making him seem simpler
than he actually was. For the more one reads Whitman, the clearer
it becomes that he was an elusive figure. He is hard to pin down,
partly because he engaged in a variety of self-mystifications, partly
because he became the object of a tiresome cult of adulation, and
partly because critics can find in his work almost anything they
want: nationalist war whoops, expressions of indeterminate sexuality, democratic sentiment, pantheist religiosity, and much else.

One main line of Whitman criticism has stressed his role as public
spokesman, thereby accepting his claim to embody the collective
spirit of American democracy within his rather eccentric and furtive personality. Thereby, too, this approach to Whitman has been
forced to place its greatest stress on his more grandiose program-
matic poems, usually not his best. A second major line of Whitman
criticism has exalted him as a sexual champion, a sort of linsey-
woolsey D. H. Lawrence.

No lack of inducements exists for seeing Whitman in these vatic postures, but such arguments tend to obscure what is best in the poems
themselves. As a national poet Whitman now seems inadequate
because he so cheerfully lacks a full sense of social complexity.
In some of his later prose, notably "Democratic Vistas," he does
begin to see the problems and troubles corroding the American
experiment in democracy, especially at the point where it enters
the economy of industrial capitalism. But in most of his declamatory poems he tends to write about democracy in too grandiose and
unhistorical a way, as if it were some sort of abstract deity untouched by the contaminations of real life. As a sexual prophet,
however, Whitman suffers from an opposite difficulty: he has done
his work too well, no one is now likely to be shocked by his
"Calamus" or "Children of Adam" poems. Some of these charm us,
others are troubling because of the abstractness and diffuseness
with which they celebrate the need for concrete experience. After
reading them one may wish that Whitman had indicated some faint
awareness that the sexual liberation he proclaimed might bring new
troubles of its own.

That the one poet Americans accept as their national bard should lack
the accredited national virtues seems something of a joke. Whitman
himself knew this, and if the reader comes to see Whitman's own
awareness of the ambiguities in his chosen role, it becomes easier

to appreciate his irony and humor—Whitman staring in amusement at the sheer oddity of declaring himself Walt a kosmos, or Whitman announcing that

Having pried through the strata, analyz'd to a hair, counsel'd with doctors and calculated close,
I find no sweeter fat than sticks to my own bones.

Whitman speaks for the national ethos, the divine average, the En Masse (as he calls it), but he is actually a solitary, a secretive watcher, and sometimes a rather precious esthete. He calls himself "one of the toughs," but the greatest esthetic pleasure he knows is the opera. He puffs out his chest with democratic vanity, but his vision of the democratic life has nothing in common with the emphasis on success or the "rugged individualism" which has dominated American society.

Whitman is a poet of many selves, a stranger in our midst, who at one point may celebrate collective aspirations and, at another, individual tastes. He is a poet at once remarkably close to, and extremely alien from, American culture. In his greatest work, "Song of Myself," the self of the poem is fluid, a kind of reservoir of undiscovered and untested possibilities, like America itself. The self is here defined by its unwillingness to rest in familiar definition. At times it seems, in certain portions of the poem, to expand toward the condition of a protean demigod who absorbs all human creatures into its folds; at other times, the self sinks to an almost mineral tranquility, a quasi-mystical dissolution of individual consciousness. The famous "oceanic" impulse that Whitman shares with other romantic poets—the impulse to merge himself with, lose himself in, the whole of creation—is made more acceptable by the evidence that the self of the poem also acts from deep anxiety and loneliness, a fear of annihilation prompting the appetite for cosmic expansiveness.

But what finally matters is not the variety of postures the self assumes in Whitman's poetry as much as the charm and wit and openness to passion with which the poet assumes them. Occasionally Whitman yields to rhetorical bluster and a kind of inane benignity. Yet between the extremes of his cosmic megalomania and the disintegration of self, there remain the rich substance of his poetry, the elegiac gravity that lends it so exquisitely dignified a tone, the quiet comedy that keeps appearing and reappearing.

Not words, not music or rhyme I want, not custom or lecture, not even the best
Only the lull I like, the hum of your valved voice.

Agonies are one of my changes of garments.

Speech is the twin of my vision, it is unequal to measure itself,
It provokes me forever, it says sarcastically,
Walt you contain enough, why don't you let it out then?

I am the man, I suffer'd, I was there.

*At his best Whitman is a master of phrasing, a master of the precise,
delicate, and epigrammatic statement, a master of the kind of
writing which brings us to the surprise of a new insight. At times,
in his not quite successful poems, his catalogs of objects and places
become boring, his declamations become grandiose. But anyone
who even glances at "Song of Myself," who turns to the descriptive
power with which section 5 ends ("And mossy scabs of the wormfence, and heaped stones, and elder and mullen and pokeweed"),
or to the very next section in which the grass is "the flag of my disposition" and then a few lines later is "the beautiful uncut hair of
graves," or to the final sections where death ("You bitter hug of
mortality") is approached and accepted and yet parried—anyone
who comes to such writing should see that it is the work of a poet
with a great gift for language.*

*There are passages in Whitman where the struggle of the self to locate
a principle of change comes to a momentary stop. A quietness
begins; the language becomes hushed and controlled; the poet, not
Walt the kosmos but Whitman the solitary, exposes himself in all
his vulnerability. It is the moment after the struggle between the
self and everything that resists and hurts and destroys the self,
the blessed moment when anxiety has not been suppressed or dispelled, but brought to proper subordination. Whitman reaches such
moments in occasional passages of "Song of Myself" and for almost
the whole of "Crossing Brooklyn Ferry." One thinks of them as
moments of twilight, somewhat similar to those shadowy intervals
between sleeping and waking, when the unconscious is still active
and free, yet we are not without some capacity to extricate ourselves from it. These are moments of rare psychic balance, and few
writers have managed to create verbal equivalents as beautiful as
those of Whitman.*

*It is in these moments that he writes most remarkably of death. When
Whitman acknowledges in "Crossing Brooklyn Ferry" the certainty
of his "non-being" in the future, it is in order to take on the being
of those who, like himself, will stand and muse upon the continuity
and tragic finality of life.*

FURTHER READING

In 1959 Malcolm Cowley reprinted the first edition of *Leaves of Grass*,
and in 1961 Roy Harvey Pearce reprinted the third edition. The

standard biography, not very useful for literary criticism, is Gay
Wilson Allen's *The Solitary Singer* (1955). Roger Asselineau's *The
Evolution of Walt Whitman* (1960) is a good scholarly study, and
Richard Chase's *Walt Whitman Reconsidered* (1955) is one of the
best critical introductions.

Song of Myself (1855)[1]

1

I celebrate myself,
And what I assume you shall assume,
For every atom belonging to me as good belongs to you.

I loafe and invite my soul,
I lean and loafe at my ease . . . . observing a spear of summer grass.

[1] In the several editions of *Leaves of Grass* Whitman kept changing and adding to
his poems. Readers and editors have long held to different opinions about which
version of a particular Whitman poem is the better, and there is no reason, short of
bibliographical fanaticism, to insist on one edition to the absolute exclusion of
another. The editor of this anthology has chosen to use the first edition of "'Song
of Myself," which appeared in 1855, the earliest printing of *Leaves of Grass*,
though in that edition the poem did not yet have its present name, but was entitled
"A Poem of Walt Whitman, an American." In the 1855 edition Whitman's punctuation is more eccentric but, in this editor's opinion, more effective than in the later
editions. In 1855 Whitman used four dots to mark pronounced pauses—breaks
which in later editions were changed to conventional punctuation such as commas,
semicolons, and periods. The use of the dots has been felt by many readers a very
effective device for suggesting the alternation of speech and silence, phrase and
pause, which seems organic to Whitman's poetic method. Thus, "I am the man . . . .
I suffered . . . . I was there" tends to get rammed together when printed, "I am the
man, I suffer'd, I was there."

But there are other, perhaps more urgent reasons for using the 1855 edition.
As he kept reworking his poems, he sometimes dropped striking images and phrases
that had appeared in the early edition, and later, in 1867, he inserted some allusions
to the Civil War which do not seem in keeping with the poem as written.

The section numbers did not appear in the 1855 edition, but have been
supplied from the final version of the poem.

The editor wishes only to add that he recognizes the value of the arguments
made by those who prefer later versions of this poem—in whatever edition, a great
masterpiece.

2

Houses and rooms are full of perfumes .... the shelves are crowded
   with perfumes,
I breathe the fragrance myself, and know it and like it,
The distillation would intoxicate me also, but I shall not let it.

The atmosphere is not a perfume .... it has no taste of the distillation
   .... it is odorless,
It is for my mouth forever .... I am in love with it,   10
I will go to the bank by the wood and become undisguised and naked,
I am mad for it to be in contact with me.

The smoke of my own breath,
Echoes, ripples, and buzzed whispers .... loveroot, silkthread, crotch
   and vine,
My respiration and inspiration .... the beating of my heart .... the
   passing of blood and air through my lungs,
The sniff of green leaves and dry leaves, and of the shore and dark-
   colored sea-rocks, and of hay in the barn,
The sound of the belched words of my voice .... words loosed to the
   eddies of the wind,
A few light kisses .... a few embraces .... a reaching around of arms,
The play of shine and shade on the trees as the supple boughs wag,
The delight alone or in the rush of the streets, or along the fields and
   hillsides,   20
The feeling of health .... the full-noon trill .... the song of me rising
   from bed and meeting the sun.

Have you reckoned a thousand acres much? Have you reckoned the
   earth much?
Have you practiced so long to learn to read?
Have you felt so proud to get at the meaning of poems?

Stop this day and night with me and you shall possess the origin of all
   poems,
You shall possess the good of the earth and sun .... there are millions
   of suns left,
You shall no longer take things at second or third hand .... nor look
   through the eyes of the dead .... nor feed on the spectres in books,
You shall not look through my eyes either, nor take things from me,
You shall listen to all sides and filter them from yourself.

3

I have heard what the talkers were talking .... the talk of the beginning
   and the end,   30
But I do not talk of the beginning or the end.

There was never any more inception than there is now,
Nor any more youth or age than there is now;
And will never be any more perfection than there is now,
Nor any more heaven or hell than there is now.

Urge and urge and urge,
Always the procreant urge of the world.

Out of the dimness opposite equals advance . . . . Always substance and
    increase,
Always a knit of identity . . . . always distinction . . . . always a breed of
    life.

To elaborate is no avail . . . . Learned and unlearned feel that it is so.   40

Sure as the most certain sure . . . . plumb in the uprights, well entretied,
    braced in the beams,
Stout as a horse, affectionate, haughty, electrical,
I and this mystery here we stand.

Clear and sweet is my soul . . . . and clear and sweet is all that is not
    my soul.

Lack one lacks both . . . . and the unseen is proved by the seen,
Till that becomes unseen and receives proof in its turn.

Showing the best and dividing it from the worst, age vexes age,
Knowing the perfect fitness and equanimity of things, while they discuss
    I am silent, and go bathe and admire myself.

Welcome is every organ and attribute of me, and of any man hearty and
    clean,
Not an inch nor a particle of an inch is vile, and none shall be less
    familiar than the rest.   50

I am satisfied . . . . I see, dance, laugh, sing;
As God comes a loving bedfellow and sleeps at my side all night and
    close on the peep of the day,
And leaves for me baskets covered with white towels bulging the house
    with their plenty,
Shall I postpone my acceptation and realization and scream at my eyes,
That they turn from gazing after and down the road,
And forthwith cipher and show me to a cent,
Exactly the contents of one, and exactly the contents of two, and which
    is ahead?

4

Trippers and askers surround me,
People I meet . . . the effect upon me of my early life . . . . of the ward
    and city I live in . . . . of the nation,

The latest news . . . . discoveries, inventions, societies . . . . authors old
    and new,   60
My dinner, dress, associates, looks, business, compliments, dues,
The real or fancied indifference of some man or woman I love,
The sickness of one of my folks—or of myself . . . . or ill-doing . . . . or
    loss or lack of money . . . . or depressions or exaltations,
They come to me days and nights and go from me again,
But they are not the Me myself.

Apart from the pulling and hauling stands what I am,
Stands amused, complacent, compassionating, idle, unitary,
Looks down, is erect, bends an arm on an impalpable certain rest,
Looks with its sidecurved head curious what will come next,
Both in and out of the game, and watching and wondering at it.   70

Backward I see in my own days where I sweated through fog with
    linguists and contenders,
I have no mockings or arguments . . . . I witness and wait.

    5
I believe in you my soul . . . . the other I am must not abase itself to you,
And you must not be abased to the other.

Loafe with me on the grass . . . . loose the stop from your throat,
Not words, not music or rhyme I want . . . . not custom or lecture, not
    even the best,
Only the lull I like, the hum of your valved voice.

I mind how we lay in June, such a transparent summer morning;
You settled your head athwart my hips and gently turned over upon
    me,
And parted the shirt from by bosom-bone, and plunged your tongue to
    my barestript heart,   80
And reached till you felt my beard, and reached till you held my feet.

Swiftly arose and spread around me the peace and joy and knowledge
    that pass all the art and argument of the earth;
And I know that the hand of God is the elderhand of my own,
And I know that the spirit of God is the eldest brother of my own,
And that all the men ever born are also my brothers . . . . and the
    women my sisters and lovers,
And that a kelson [2] of the creation is love;
And limitless are leaves stiff or drooping in the fields,
And brown ants in the little wells beneath them,
And mossy scabs of the wormfence, and heaped stones, and elder and
    mullen and pokeweed.

2 A line of timbers, joined by bolts.

6

A child said, What is the grass? fetching it to me with full hands;   *90*
How could I answer the child? . . . . I do not know what it is any more
    than he.

I guess it must be the flag of my disposition, out of hopeful green stuff
    woven.

Or I guess it is the handkerchief of the Lord,
A scented gift and remembrancer designedly dropped,
Bearing the owner's name someway in the corners, that we may see and
    remark, and say Whose?

Or I guess the grass is itself a child . . . . the produced babe of the
    vegetation.

Or I guess it is a uniform hieroglyphic,
And it means, Sprouting alike in broad zones and narrow zones,
Growing among black folks as among white,
Kanuck, Tuckahoe, Congressman, Cuff, I give them the same, I receive
    them the same.   *100*

And now it seems to me the beautiful uncut hair of graves.

Tenderly will I use you curling grass,
It may be you transpire from the breasts of young men,
It may be if I had known them I would have loved them;
It may be you are from old people and from women, and from offspring
    taken soon out of their mothers' laps,
And here you are the mothers' laps.

This grass is very dark to be from the white heads of old mothers,
Darker than the colorless beards of old men,
Dark to come from under the faint red roofs of mouths.

O I perceive after all so many uttering tongues!   *110*
And I perceive they do not come from the roofs of mouths for nothing.

I wish I could translate the hints about the dead young men and
    women,
And the hints about old men and mothers, and the offspring taken soon
    out of their laps.

What do you think has become of the young and old men?
And what do you think has become of the women and children?

They are alive and well somewhere;
The smallest sprout shows there is really no death,
And if ever there was it led forward life, and does not wait at the end
    to arrest it,
And ceased the moment life appeared.

All goes onward and outward . . . . and nothing collapses,   *120*
And to die is different from what any one supposed, and luckier.

7

Has any one supposed it lucky to be born?
I hasten to inform him or her it is just as lucky to die, and I know it.

I pass death with the dying, and birth with the new-washed babe . . . .
    and am not contained between my hat and boots,
And peruse manifold objects, no two alike, and every one good,
The earth good, and the stars good, and their adjuncts all good.

I am not an earth nor an adjunct of an earth,
I am the mate and companion of people, all just as immortal and
    fathomless as myself;
They do not know how immortal, but I know.

Every kind for itself and its own . . . . for me mine male and female,   *130*
For me all that have been boys and that love women,
For me the man that is proud and feels how it stings to be slighted,
For me the sweetheart and the old maid . . . . for me mothers and the
    mothers of mothers,
For me lips that have smiled, eyes that have shed tears,
For me children and the begetters of children.

Who need be afraid of the merge?
Undrape . . . . you are not guilty to me, nor stale nor discarded,
I see through the broadcloth and gingham whether or no,
And am around, tenacious, acquisitive, tireless . . . . and can never be
    shaken away.

8

The little one sleeps in its cradle,   *140*
I lift the gauze and look a long time, and silently brush away flies with
    my hand.

The youngster and the redfaced girl turn aside up the bushy hill,
I peeringly view them from the top.

The suicide sprawls on the bloody floor of the bedroom,
It is so . . . . I witnessed the corpse . . . . there the pistol had fallen.

The blab of the pave . . . . the tires of carts and sluff of bootsoles and
    talk of the promenaders,
The heavy omnibus, the driver with his interrogating thumb, the clank
    of the shod horses on the granite floor,

The carnival of sleighs, the clinking and shouted jokes and pelts of
  snowballs;
The hurrahs for popular favorites . . . . the fury of roused mobs,
The flap of the curtained litter—the sick man inside, borne to the
  hospital,   150
The meeting of enemies, the sudden oath, the blows and fall,
The excited crowd—the policeman with his star quickly working his
  passage to the centre of the crowd;
The impressive stones that receive and return so many echoes,
The souls moving along . . . . are they invisible while the least atom of
  the stones is visible?
What groans of overfed or half-starved who fall on the flags sunstruck
  or in fits,
What exclamations of women taken suddenly, who hurry home and
  give birth to babes,
What living and buried speech is always vibrating here . . . . what howls
  restrained by decorum,
Arrests of criminals, slights, adulterous offers made, acceptances, rejec-
  tions with convex lips,
I mind them or the resonance of them . . . . I come again and again.

9
The big doors of the country-barn stand open and ready,   160
The dried grass of the harvest-time loads the slow-drawn wagon,
The clear light plays on the brown gray and green intertinged,
The armfuls are packed to the sagging mow:
I am there . . . . I help . . . . I came stretched atop of the load,
I felt its soft jolts . . . . one leg reclined on the other,
I jump from the crossbeams, and seize the clover and timothy,
And roll head over heels, and tangle my hair full of wisps.

10
Alone far in the wilds and mountains I hunt,
Wandering amazed at my own lightness and glee,
In the late afternoon choosing a safe spot to pass the night,   170
Kindling a fire and broiling the freshkilled game,
Soundly falling asleep on the gathered leaves, my dog and gun by my
  side.

The Yankee clipper is under her three skysails . . . . she cuts the sparkle
  and scud,
My eyes settle the land . . . . I bend at her prow or shout joyously from
  the deck.

The boatmen and clamdiggers arose early and stopped for me,
I tucked my trowser-ends in my boots and went and had a good time,
You should have been with us that day round the chowder-kettle.

I saw the marriage of the trapper in the open air in the far-west . . . .
    the bride was a red girl,
Her father and his friends sat near by crosslegged and dumbly smoking
    . . . . they had moccasins to their feet and large thick blankets
    hanging from their shoulders;
On a bank lounged the trapper . . . . he was dressed mostly in skins . . . .
    his luxuriant beard and curls protected his neck,   *180*
One hand rested on his rifle . . . . the other hand held firmly the wrist
    of the red girl,
She had long eyelashes . . . . her head was bare . . . . her coarse straight
    locks descended upon her voluptuous limbs and reached to her feet.

The runaway slave came to my house and stopped outside,
I heard his motions crackling the twigs of the woodpile,
Through the swung half-door of the kitchen I saw him limpsey and
    weak,
And went where he sat on a log, and led him in and assured him,
And brought water and filled a tub for his sweated body and bruised
    feet,
And gave him a room that entered from my own, and gave him some
    coarse clean clothes,
And remember perfectly well his revolving eyes and his awkwardness,
And remember putting plasters on the galls of his neck and ankles;   *190*
He staid with me a week before he was recuperated and passed north,
I had him sit next me at table . . . . my firelock leaned in the corner.

11

Twenty-eight young men bathe by the shore,
Twenty-eight young men, and all so friendly,
Twenty-eight years of womanly life, and all so lonesome.

She owns the fine house by the rise of the bank,
She hides handsome and richly drest aft the blinds of the window.

Which of the young men does she like the best?
Ah the homeliest of them is beautiful to her.

Where are you off to, lady? for I see you,
You splash in the water there, yet stay stock still in your room.   *200*

Dancing and laughing along the beach came the twenty-ninth bather,
The rest did not see her, but she saw them and loved them.

The beards of the young men glistened with wet, it ran from their long
    hair,
Little streams passed all over their bodies.

An unseen hand also passed over their bodies,
It descended tremblingly from their temples and ribs.

The young men float on their backs, their white bellies swell to the sun
. . . . they do not ask who seizes fast to them,
They do not know who puffs and declines with pendant and bending
arch,
They do not think whom they souse with spray.   *210*

12

The butcher-boy puts off his killing-clothes, or sharpens his knife at the
stall in the market,
I loiter enjoying his repartee and his shuffle and breakdown.

Blacksmiths with grimed and hairy chests environ the anvil,
Each has his main-sledge . . . . they are all out . . . . there is a great heat
in the fire.

From the cinder-strewed threshold I follow their movements,
The lithe sheer of their waists plays even with their massive arms,
Overhand the hammers roll—overhand so slow—overhand so sure,
They do not hasten, each man hits in his place.

13

The negro holds firmly the reins of his four horses . . . . the block swags
underneath on its tied-over chain,
The negro that drives the huge dray of the stoneyard . . . . steady and
tall he stands poised on one leg on the stringpiece,   *220*
His blue shirt exposes his ample neck and breast and loosens over his
hipband,
His glance is calm and commanding . . . . he tosses the slouch of his
hat away from his forehead,
The sun falls on his crispy hair and moustache . . . . falls on the black
of his polish'd and perfect limbs.

I behold the picturesque giant and love him . . . . and I do not stop there,
I go with the team also.

In me the caresser of life wherever moving . . . . backward as well as
forward slueing,
To niches aside and junior bending.

Oxen that rattle the yoke or halt in the shade, what is that you express
in your eyes?
It seems to me more than all the print I have read in my life.

My tread scares the wood-drake and wood-duck on my distant and day-
long ramble,   *230*
They rise together, they slowly circle around.
. . . . I believe in those winged purposes,

And acknowledge the red yellow and white playing within me,
And consider the green and violet and the tufted crown intentional;
And do not call the tortoise unworthy because she is not something else,
And the mocking bird in the swamp never studied the gamut,[3] yet trills
    pretty well to me,
And the look of the bay mare shames silliness out of me.

14

The wild gander leads his flock through the cool night,
Ya-honk! he says, and sounds it down to me like an invitation;
The pert may suppose it meaningless, but I listen closer,   240
I find its purpose and place up there toward the November sky.

The sharphoofed moose of the north, the cat on the housesill, the
    chickadee, the prairie-dog,
The litter of the grunting sow as they tug at her teats,
The brood of the turkeyhen, and she with her halfspread wings,
I see in them and myself the same old law.

The press of my foot to the earth springs a hundred affections,
They scorn the best I can do to relate them.

I am enamoured of growing outdoors,
Of men that live among cattle or taste of the ocean or woods,
Of the builders and steerers of ships, of the wielders of axes and mauls,
    of the drivers of horses,   250
I can eat and sleep with them week in and week out.

What is commonest and cheapest and nearest and easiest is Me,
Me going in for my chances, spending for vast returns,
Adorning myself to bestow myself on the first that will take me,
Not asking the sky to come down to my goodwill,
Scattering it freely forever.

15

The pure contralto sings in the organloft,
The carpenter dresses his plank . . . . the tongue of his foreplane
    whistles its wild ascending lisp,
The married and unmarried children ride home to their thanksgiving
    dinner,
The pilot seizes the king-pin, he heaves down with a strong arm,   260
The mate stands braced in the whaleboat, lance and harpoon are ready,
The duck-shooter walks by silent and cautious stretches,
The deacons are ordained with crossed hands at the altar,

---

[3] Of the musical scale.

The spinning-girl retreats and advances to the hum of the big wheel,
The farmer stops by the bars of a Sunday and looks at the oats and rye,
The lunatic is carried at last to the asylum a confirmed case,
He will never sleep any more as he did in the cot in his mother's
    bedroom;
The jour printer [4] with gray head and gaunt jaws works at his case,
He turns his quid of tobacco, his eyes get blurred with the manuscript;
The malformed limbs are tied to the anatomist's table,   270
What is removed drops horribly in a pail;
The quadroon girl is sold at the stand . . . . the drunkard nods by the
    barroom stove,
The machinist rolls up his sleeves. . . . the policeman travels his beat
    . . . . the gatekeeper marks who pass,
The young fellow drives the express-wagon . . . . I love him though I do
    not know him;
The half-breed straps on his light boots to compete in the race,
The western turkey-shooting draws old and young . . . . some lean on
    their rifles, some sit on logs,
Out from the crowd steps the marksman and takes his position and
    levels his piece;
The groups of newly-come immigrants cover the wharf or levee,
The woollypates hoe in the sugarfield, the overseer views them from
    his saddle;
The bugle calls in the ballroom, the gentlemen run for their partners,
    the dancers bow to each other;   280
The youth lies awake in the cedar-roofed garret and harks to the
    musical rain,
The Wolverine sets traps on the creek that helps fill the Huron,
The reformer ascends the platform, he spouts with his mouth and nose,
The company returns from its excursion, the darkey brings up the rear
    and bears the well-riddled target,
The squaw wrapt in her yellow-hemmed cloth is offering moccasins and
    beadbags for sale,
The connoisseur peers along the exhibition-gallery with halfshut eyes
    bent sideways,
The deckhands make fast the steamboat, the plank is thrown for the
    shoregoing passengers,
The young sister holds out the skein, the elder sister winds it off in a
    ball and stops now and then for the knots,
The one-year wife is recovering and happy, a week ago she bore her
    first child,
The cleanhaired Yankee girl works with her sewing-machine or in the
    factory or mill,   290
The nine months gone is in the parturition chamber, her faintness and
    pains are advancing;

---

[4] Employee, one who works by the day.

The pavingman leans on his twohanded rammer—the reporter's lead
   flies swiftly over the notebook—the signpainter is lettering with red
   and gold,
The canal-boy trots on the towpath—the bookkeeper counts at his
   desk—the shoemaker waxes his thread,
The conductor beats time for the band and all the performers follow
   him,
The child is baptised—the convert is making the first professions,
The regatta is spread on the bay . . . . how the white sails sparkle!
The drover watches his drove, he sings out to them that would stray,
The pedlar sweats with his pack on his back—the purchaser higgles
   about the odd cent,
The camera and plate are prepared, the lady must sit for her
   daguerreotype,
The bride unrumples her white dress, the minutehand of the clock
   moves slowly,   *300*
The opium eater reclines with rigid head and just-opened lips,
The prostitute draggles her shawl, her bonnet bobs on her tipsy and
   pimpled neck,
The crowd laughs at her blackguard oaths, the men jeer and wink to
   each other,
(Miserable! I do not laugh at your oaths nor jeer you,)
The President holds a cabinet council, he is surrounded by the great
   secretaries,
On the piazza walk five friendly matrons with twined arms;
The crew of the fish-smack pack repeated layers of halibut in the hold,
The Missourian crosses the plains toting his wares and his cattle,
The fare-collector goes through the train—he gives notice by the jingling
   of loose change,
The floormen are laying the floor—the tinners are tinning the roof—
   the masons are calling for mortar,   *310*
In single file each shouldering his hod pass onward the laborers;
Seasons pursuing each other the indescribable crowd is gathered . . . .
   it is the Fourth of July . . . . what salutes of cannon and small arms!
Seasons pursuing each other the plougher ploughs and the mower mows
   and the wintergrain falls in the ground;
Off on the lakes the pikefisher watches and waits by the hole in the
   frozen surface,
The stumps stand thick round the clearing, the squatter strikes deep
   with his axe,
The flatboatmen make fast toward dusk near the cottonwood or
   pekantrees,
The coon-seekers go now through the regions of the Red river, or
   through those drained by the Tennessee, or through those of the
   Arkansas,
The torches shine in the dark that hangs on the Chattahoochee or
   Altamahaw;

Patriarchs sit at supper with sons and grandsons and great grandsons
    around them,
In walls of adobie, in canvas tents, rest hunters and trappers after their
    day's sport.   320
The city sleeps and the country sleeps,
The living sleep for their time . . . . the dead sleep for their time,
The old husband sleeps by his wife and the young husband sleeps by
    his wife;
And these one and all tend inward to me, and I tend outward to them,
And such as it is to be of these more or less I am.

16
I am of old and young, of the foolish as much as the wise,
Regardless of others, ever regardful of others,
Maternal as well as paternal, a child as well as a man,
Stuffed with the stuff that is coarse, and stuffed with the stuff that is
    fine,
One of the great nations, the nation of many nations—the smallest the
    same and the largest the same,   330
A southerner soon as a northerner, a planter nonchalant and hospitable,
A Yankee bound my own way . . . . ready for trade . . . . my joints
    the limberest joints on earth and the sternest joints on earth,
A Kentuckian walking the vale of the Elkhorn in my deerskin leggings,
A boatman over the lakes or bays or along coasts . . . . a Hoosier, a
    Badger, a Buckeye,
A Louisianian or Georgian, a poke-easy from sandhills and pines,
At home on Canadian snowshoes or up in the bush, or with fishermen
    off Newfoundland,
At home in the fleet of iceboats, sailing with the rest and tacking,
At home on the hills of Vermont or in the woods of Maine or the Texan
    ranch,
Comrade of Californians . . . . comrade of free northwesterners, loving
    their big proportions,
Comrade of raftsmen and coalmen—comrade of all who shake hands
    and welcome to drink and meat;   340
A learner with the simplest, a teacher of the thoughtfulest,
A novice beginning experient of myriads of seasons,
Of every hue and trade and rank, of every caste and religion,
Not merely of the New World but of Africa Europe or Asia . . . . a
    wandering savage,
A farmer, mechanic, or artist . . . . a gentleman, sailor, lover or quaker,
A prisoner, fancy-man, rowdy, lawyer, physician or priest.

I resist anything better than my own diversity,
And breathe the air and leave plenty after me,
And am not stuck up, and am in my place.

The moth and the fisheggs are in their place,   *350*
The suns I see and the suns I cannot see are in their place,
The palpable is in its place and the impalpable is in its place.

17

These are the thoughts of all men in all ages and lands, they are not
    original with me,
If they are not yours as much as mine they are nothing or next to
    nothing,
If they do not enclose everything they are next to nothing,
If they are not the riddle and the untying of the riddle they are nothing,
If they are not just as close as they are distant they are nothing.

This is the grass that grows wherever the land is and the water is,
This is the common air that bathes the globe.

This is the breath of laws and songs and behaviour,   *360*
This is the tasteless water of souls . . . . this is the true sustenance,
It is for the illiterate . . . . it is for the judges of the supreme court . . . .
    it is for the federal capitol and the state capitols,
It is for the admirable communes of literary men and composers and
    singers and lecturers and engineers and savans,
It is for the endless races of working people and farmers and seamen.

18

This is the trill of a thousand clear cornets and scream of the octave
    flute and strike of triangles.
I play not a march for victors only . . . . I play great marches for con-
    quered and slain persons.

Have you heard that it was good to gain the day?
I also say it is good to fall . . . . battles are lost in the same spirit in
    which they are won.

I sound triumphal drums for the dead . . . . I fling through my em-
    bouchures [5] the loudest and gayest music to them,
Vivas to those who have failed, and to those whose war-vessels sank in
    the sea, and those themselves who sank in the sea,   *370*
And to all generals that lost engagements, and all overcome heroes, and
    the numberless unknown heroes equal to the greatest heroes known.

19

This is the meal pleasantly set . . . . this is the meat and drink for
    natural hunger,

[5] Mouthpiece of a musical instrument, an instance of Whitman's perhaps excessive
fondness for foreign phrases.

It is for the wicked just the same as the righteous . . . . I make appoint-
ments with all,
I will not have a single person slighted or left away,
The keptwoman and sponger and thief are hereby invited . . . . the
heavy-lipped slave is invited . . . . the venerealee is invited,
There shall be no difference between them and the rest.

This is the press of a bashful hand . . . . this is the float and odor of
hair,
This is the touch of my lips to yours . . . . this is the murmur of
yearning,
This is the far-off depth and height reflecting my own face,
This is the thoughtful merge of myself and the outlet again.   380

Do you guess I have some intricate purpose?
Well I have . . . . for the April rain has, and the mica on the side of a
rock has.

Do you take it I would astonish?
Does the daylight astonish? or the early redstart twittering through
the woods?
Do I astonish more than they?

This hour I tell things in confidence,
I might not tell everybody but I will tell you.

20

Who goes there! hankering, gross, mystical, nude?
How is it I extract strength from the beef I eat?

What is a man anyhow? What am I? and what are you?   390
All I mark as my own you shall offset it with your own,
Else it were time lost listening to me.

I do not snivel that snivel the world over,
That months are vacuums and the ground but wallow and filth,
That life is a suck and a sell, and nothing remains at the end but
threadbare crape and tears.

Whimpering and truckling fold with powders for invalids . . . . conformity goes to the fourth-removed,
I cock my hat as I please indoors or out.

Shall I pray? Shall I venerate and be ceremonious?
I have pried through the strata and analyzed to a hair,
And counselled with doctors and calculated close and found no sweeter
fat than sticks to my own bones.   400

In all people I see myself, none more and not one a barleycorn less,
And the good or bad I say of myself I say of them.

And I know I am solid and sound,
To me the converging objects of the universe perpetually flow,
All are written to me, and I must get what the writing means.

And I know I am deathless,
I know this orbit of mine cannot be swept by a carpenter's compass,
I know I shall not pass like a child's carlacue cut with a burnt stick at
    night.

I know I am august,
I do not trouble my spirit to vindicate itself or be understood,   410
I see that the elementary laws never apologize,
I reckon I behave no prouder than the level I plant my house by after
    all.

I exist as I am, that is enough,
If no other in the world be aware I sit content,
And if each and all be aware I sit content.

One world is aware, and by far the largest to me, and that is myself,
And whether I come to my own today or in ten thousand or ten million
    years,
I can cheerfuly take it now, or with equal cheerfulness I can wait.

My foothold is tenoned and mortised in granite,
I laugh at what you call dissolution,   420
And I know the amplitude of time.

21

I am the poet of the body,
And I am the poet of the soul.

The pleasures of heaven are with me, and the pains of hell are with me,
The first I graft and increase upon myself . . . . the latter I translate
    into a new tongue.

I am the poet of the woman the same as the man,
And I say it is as great to be a woman as to be a man,
And I say there is nothing greater than the mother of men.

I chant a new chant of dilation or pride,
We have had ducking and deprecating about enough,   430
I show that size is only development.

Have you outstript the rest? Are you the President?
It is a trifle . . . . they will more than arrive there every one, and still
    pass on.

I am he that walks with the tender and growing night;
I call to the earth and sea half-held by the night.

Press close barebosomed night! Press close magnetic nourishing night!
Night of south winds! Night of the large few stars!
Still nodding night! Mad naked summer night!

Smile O voluptuous coolbreathed earth!
Earth of the slumbering and liquid trees!   440
Earth of departed sunset! Earth of the mountains misty-topt!
Earth of the vitreous pour of the full moon just tinged with blue!
Earth of shine and dark mottling the tide of the river!
Earth of the limpid gray of clouds brighter and clearer for my sake!
Far-swooping elbowed earth! Rich apple-blossomed earth!
Smile, for your lover comes!

Prodigal! you have given me love! . . . . therefore I to you give love!
O unspeakable passionate love!

Thruster holding me tight and that I hold tight!
We hurt each other as the bridegroom and the bride hurt each other.   450

22
You sea! I resign myself to you also . . . . I guess what you mean,
I behold from the beach your crooked inviting fingers,
I believe you refuse to go back without feeling of me;
We must have a turn together . . . . I undress . . . . hurry me out of sight
    of the land,
Cushion me soft . . . . rock me in billowy drowse,
Dash me with amorous wet . . . . I can repay you.

Sea of stretched ground-swells!
Sea breathing broad and convulsive breaths!
Sea of the brine of life! Sea of unshovelled and always-ready graves!
Howler and scooper of storms! Capricious and dainty sea!   460
I am integral with you . . . . I too am of one phase and of all phases.

Partaker of influx and efflux . . . . extoller of hate and conciliation,
Extoller of amies and those that sleep in each others' arms.

I am he attesting sympathy;
Shall I make my list of things in the house and skip the house that
    supports them?

I am the poet of commonsense and of the demonstrable and of
    immortality;
And am not the poet of goodness only . . . . I do not decline to be the
    poet of wickedness also.

Washes and razors for foofoos .... for me freckles and a bristling
    beard.

What blurt is it about virtue and about vice?
Evil propels me, and reform of evil propels me .... I stand indifferent,   470
My gait is no faultfinder's or rejector's gait,
I moisten the roots of all that has grown.

Did you fear some scrofula out of the unflagging pregnancy?
Did you guess the celestial laws are yet to be worked over and rectified?

I step up to say that what we do is right and what we affirm is right
    .... and some is only the ore of right,
Witnesses of us .... one side a balance and the antipodal side a
    balance,
Soft doctrine as steady help as stable doctrine,
Thoughts and deeds of the present our rouse and early start.

This minute that comes to me over the past decillions,
There is no better than it and now.   480

What behaved well in the past or behaves well today is not such a
    wonder,
The wonder is always and always how there can be a mean man or an
    infidel.

23
Endless unfolding of words of ages!
And mine a word of the modern .... a word en masse.[6]

A word of the faith that never balks,
One time as good as another time .... here or henceforward it is all
    the same to me.

A word of reality .... materialism first and last imbuing.

Hurrah for positive science! Long live exact demonstration!
Fetch stonecrop and mix it with cedar and branches of lilac;
This is the lexicographer or chemist .... this made a grammar of the
    old cartouches,   490
These mariners put the ship through dangerous unknown seas,
This is the geologist, and this works with the scalpel, and this is a
    mathematician.

Gentlemen I receive you, and attach and clasp hands with you,
The facts are useful and real .... they are not my dwelling .... I enter
    by them to an area of the dwelling.

[6] Another Whitman Gallicism, meaning the whole of humanity.

I am less the reminder of property or qualities, and more the reminder
　of life,
And go on the square for my own sake and for other's sake,
And make short account of neuters and geldings, and favor men and
　women fully equipped,
And beat the gong of revolt, and stop with fugitives and them that plot
　and conspire.

24

Walt Whitman, an American, one of the roughs, a kosmos,
Disorderly fleshy and sensual . . . . eating drinking and breeding,   *500*
No sentimentalist . . . . no stander above men and women or apart from
　them . . . . no more modest than immodest.

Unscrew the locks from the doors!
Unscrew the doors themselves from their jambs!

Whoever degrades another degrades me . . . . and whatever is done or
　said returns at last to me,
And whatever I do or say I also return.

Through me the afflatus surging and surging . . . . through me the cur-
　rent and index.

I speak the password primeval . . . . I give the sign of democracy;
By God! I will accept nothing which all cannot have their counterpart
　of on the same terms.

Through me many long dumb voices,
Voices of the interminable generations of slaves,   *510*
Voices of prostitutes and of deformed persons,
Voices of the diseased and despairing, and of thieves and dwarfs,
Voices of cycles of preparation and accretion,
And of the threads that connect the stars—and of wombs, and of the
　Fatherstuff,
And of the rights of them the others are down upon,
Of the trivial and flat and foolish and despised,
Of fog in the air and beetles rolling balls of dung.

Through me forbidden voices,
Voices of sexes and lusts . . . . voices veiled, and I remove the veil,
Voices indecent by me clarified and transfigured.   *520*

I do not press my finger across my mouth,
I keep as delicate around the bowels as around the head and heart,
Copulation is no more rank to me than death is.

I believe in the flesh and the appetites,
Seeing hearing and feeling are miracles, and each part and tag of me
　is a miracle.

Divine am I inside and out, and I make holy whatever I touch or am
    touched from;
The scent of these arm-pits is aroma finer than prayer,
This head is more than churches or bibles or creeds.

If I worship any particular thing it shall be some of the spread of my
    body;
Translucent mould of me it shall be you.   530
Shaded ledges and rests, firm masculine coulter, it shall be you,
Whatever goes to the tilth of me it shall be you,
You my rich blood, your milky stream pale strippings of my life;
Breast that presses against other breasts it shall be you,
My brain it shall be your occult convolutions,
Root of washed sweet-flag, timorous pond-snipe, nest of guarded dupli-
    cate eggs, it shall be you,
Mixed tussled hay of head and beard and brawn it shall be you,
Trickling sap of maple, fibre of manly wheat, it shall be you;
Sun so generous it shall be you,
Vapors lighting and shading my face it shall be you,   540
You sweaty brooks and dews it shall be you,
Winds whose soft-tickling genitals rub against me it shall be you,
Broad muscular fields, branches of liveoak, loving lounger in my wind-
    ing paths, it shall be you,
Hands I have taken, face I have kissed, mortal I have ever touched,
    it shall be you.

I dote on myself . . . . there is that lot of me, and all so luscious,
Each moment and whatever happens thrills me with joy.

I cannot tell how my ankles bend . . . . nor whence the cause of my
    faintest wish,
Nor the cause of the friendship I emit . . . . nor the cause of the
    friendship I take again.

To walk up my stoop is unaccountable . . . . I pause to consider if it
    really be,
That I eat and drink is spectacle enough for the great authors and
    schools,   550
A morning-glory at my window satisfies me more than the metaphysics
    of books.

To behold the daybreak!
The little light fades the immense and diaphanous shadows,
The air tastes good to my palate.

Hefts of the moving world at innocent gambols, silently rising, freshly
    exuding,
Scooting obliquely high and low.

Something I cannot see puts upward libidinous prongs,
Seas of bright juice suffuse heaven.

The earth by the sky staid with . . . . the daily close of their junction,
The heaved challenge from the east that moment over my head, 560
The mocking taunt, See then whether you shall be master!

25

Dazzling and tremendous how quick the sunrise would kill me,
If I could not now and always send sunrise out of me.

We also ascend dazzling and tremendous as the sun,
We found our own my soul in the calm and cool of the daybreak.

My voice goes after what my eyes cannot reach,
With the twirl of my tongue I encompass worlds and volumes of
    worlds.

Speech is the twin of my vision . . . . it is unequal to measure itself.
It provokes me forever,
It says sarcastically, Walt, you understand enough . . . . why don't you
    let it out then? 570
Come now I will not be tantalized . . . . you conceive too much of articu-
    lation.

Do you not know how the buds beneath are folded?
Waiting in gloom protected by frost,
The dirt receding before my prophectical screams,
I underlying causes to balance them at last,
My knowledge my live parts . . . . it keeping tally with the meaning of
    things,
Happiness . . . . which whoever hears me let him or her set out in search
    of this day.

My final merit I refuse you . . . . I refuse putting from me the best I am.

Encompass worlds but never try to encompass me,
I crowd your noisiest talk by looking toward you. 580

Writing and talk do not prove me,
I carry the plenum of proof and every thing else in my face,
With the hush of my lips I confound the topmost skeptic.

26

I think I will do nothing for a long time but listen,
And accrue what I hear into myself . . . . and let sounds contribute
    toward me.

I hear the bravuras of birds . . . . the bustle of growing wheat . . . .
gossip of flames . . . . clack of sticks cooking my meals.

I hear the sound of the human voice . . . . a sound I love,
I hear all sounds as they are tuned to their uses . . . . sounds of the city
and sounds out of the city . . . . sounds of the day and night;
Talkative young ones to those that like them . . . . the recitative of
fish-pedlars and fruit-pedlars . . . . the loud laugh of workpeople at
their meals,
The angry base of disjointed friendship . . . . the faint tones of the
sick,   *590*
The judge with hands tight to the desk, his shaky lips pronouncing a
death-sentence,
The heave'e'yo of stevedores unlading ships by the wharves . . . . the
refrain of the anchor-lifters;
The ring of alarm-bells . . . . the cry of fire . . . . the whir of swift-
streaking engines and hose-carts with premonitory tinkles and
colored lights,
The steam-whistle . . . . the solid roll of the train of approaching cars;
The slow-march played at night at the head of the association,
They go to guard some corpse . . . . the flag-tops are draped with black
muslin.

I hear the violincello or man's heart complaint,
And hear the keyed cornet or else the echo of sunset.

I hear the chorus . . . . it is a grand-opera . . . . this indeed is music!

A tenor large and fresh as the creation fills me,   *600*
The orbic flex of his mouth is pouring and filling me full.

I hear the trained soprano . . . . she convulses me like the climax of
my love-grip;
The orchestra whirls me wider than Uranus flies,
It wrenches unnamable ardors from my breast,
It throbs me to gulps of the farthest down horror,
It sails me . . . . I dab with bare feet . . . . they are licked by the indolent
waves,
I am exposed . . . . cut by bitter and poisoned hail,
Steeped amid honeyed morphine . . . . my windpipe squeezed in the
fakes of death,
Let up again to feel the puzzle of puzzles,
And that we call Being.   *610*

27
To be in any form, what is that?
If nothing lay more developed the quahaug and its callous shell were
enough.

Mine is no callous shell,
I have instant conductors all over me whether I pass or stop,
They seize every object and lead it harmlessly through me.

I merely stir, press, feel with my fingers, and am happy,
To touch my person to some one else's is about as much as I can stand.

28

Is this then a touch? . . . . quivering me to a new identity,
Flames and ether making a rush for my veins,
Treacherous tip of me reaching and crowding to help them,   620
My flesh and blood playing out lightning, to strike what is hardly
    different from myself,
On all sides prurient provokers stiffening my limbs,
Straining the udder of my heart for its withheld drip,
Behaving licentious toward me, taking no denial,
Depriving me of my best as for a purpose,
Unbuttoning my clothes and holding me by the bare waist,
Deluding my confusion with the calm of the sunlight and pasture fields,
Immodestly sliding the fellow-senses away,
They bribed to swap off with touch, and go and graze at the edges
    of me,
No consideration, no regard for my draining strength or my anger,   630
Fetching the rest of the herd around to enjoy them awhile,
Then all uniting to stand on a headland and worry me.

The sentries desert every other part of me,
They have left me helpless to a red marauder,
They all come to the headland to witness and assist against me.

I am given up by traitors;
I talk wildly . . . . I have lost my wits . . . . I and nobody else am the
    greatest traitor,
I went myself first to the headland . . . . my own hands carried me
    there.

You villain touch! what are you doing? . . . . my breath is tight in its
    throat;
Unclench your floodgates! you are too much for me.   640

29

Blind loving wrestling touch! Sheathed hooded sharptoothed touch!
Did it make you ache so leaving me?

Parting tracked by arriving . . . . perpetual payment of the perpetual
    loan,
Rich showering rain, and recompense richer afterward.

Sprouts take and accumulate . . . . stand by the curb prolific and vital,
Landscapes projected masculine full-sized and golden.

30

All truths wait in all things,
They neither hasten their own delivery nor resist it,
They do not need the obstetric forceps of the surgeon,
The insignificant is as big to me as any,   650
What is less or more than a touch?

Logic and sermons never convince,
The damp of the night drives deeper into my soul.

Only what proves itself to every man and woman is so,
Only what nobody denies is so.

A minute and a drop of me settle my brain;
I believe the soggy clods shall become lovers and lamps,
And a compend of compends is the meat of a man or woman,
And a summit and flower there is the feeling they have for each other,
And they are to branch boundlessly out of that lesson until it becomes
    omnific,[7]   660
And until every one shall delight us, and we them.

31

I believe a leaf of grass is no less than the journeywork of the stars,
And the pismire is equally perfect, and a grain of sand, and the egg of
    the wren,
And the tree-toad is a chef-d'œuvre for the highest,
And the running blackberry would adorn the parlors of heaven,
And the narrowest hinge in my hand puts to scorn all machinery,
And the cow crunching with depressed head surpasses any statue,
And a mouse is miracle enough to stagger sextillions of infidels,
And I could come every afternoon of my life to look at the farmer's girl
    boiling her iron tea-kettle and baking shortcake.

I find I incorporate gneiss and coal and long-threaded moss and fruits
    and grains and esculent roots,   670
And am stucco'd with quadrupeds and birds all over,
And have distanced what is behind me for good reasons,
And call any thing close again when I desire it.

In vain the speeding or shyness,
In vain the plutonic rocks send their old heat against my approach,
In vain the mastodon retreats beneath its own powdered bones,
In vain objects stand leagues off and assume manifold shapes,

[7] All-creating.

In vain the ocean settling in hollows and the great monsters lying low,
In vain the buzzard houses herself with the sky,
In vain the snake slides through the creepers and logs,   680
In vain the elk takes to the inner passes of the woods,
In vain the razorbilled auk sails far north to Labrador,
I follow quickly . . . . I ascend to the nest in the fissure of the cliff.

32
I think I could turn and live awhile with the animals . . . . they are so
    placid and self-contained,
I stand and look at them sometimes half the day long.

They do not sweat and whine about their condition,
They do not lie awake in the dark and weap for their sins,
They do not make me sick discussing their duty to God,
Not one is dissatisfied . . . . not one is demented with the mania of own-
    ing things,
Not one kneels to another nor to his kind that lived thousands of years
    ago,   690
Not one is respectable or industrious over the whole earth.

So they show their relations to me and I accept them;
They bring me tokens of myself . . . . they evince them plainly in their
    possession.

I do not know where they got those tokens,
I must have passed that way untold times ago and negligently dropt
    them,
Myself moving forward then and now and forever,
Gathering and showing more always and with velocity,
Infinite and omnigenous and the like of these among them;
Not too exclusive toward the reachers of my remembrancers,
Picking out here one that shall be my amie,   700
Choosing to go with him on brotherly terms.

A gigantic beauty of a stallion, fresh and responsive to my caresses,
Head high in the forehead and wide between the ears,
Limbs glossy and supple, tail dusting the ground,
Eyes well apart and full of sparking wickedness . . . . ears finely cut
    and flexibly moving.

His nostrils dilate . . . . my heels embrace him . . . . his well built limbs
    tremble with pleasure . . . . we speed around and return.

I but use you a moment and then I resign you stallion . . . . and do
    not need your paces, and outgallop them,
And myself as I stand or sit pass faster than you.

33

Swift wind! Space! My Soul! Now I know it is true what I guessed at; 710
What I guessed when I loafed on the grass,
What I guessed while I lay alone in my bed .... and again as I walked
    the beach under the paling stars of the morning.

My ties and ballasts leave me .... I travel .... I sail .... my elbows
    rest in the sea-gaps,
I skirt the sierras .... my palms cover continents,
I am afoot with my vision.

By the city's quadrangular houses .... in log-huts, or camping with
    lumbermen,
Along the ruts of the turnpike .... along the dry gulch and rivulet bed,
Hoeing my onion-patch, and rows of carrots and parsnips .... crossing
    savannas .... trailing in forests,
Prospecting .... gold-digging .... girdling the trees of a new purchase,
Scorched ankle-deep by the hot sand .... hauling my boat down the
    shallow river;
Where the panther walks to and fro on a limb overhead .... where the
    buck turns furiously at the hunter, 720
Where the rattlesnake suns his flabby length on a rock .... where the
    otter is feeding on fish,
Where the alligator in his tough pimples sleeps by the bayou,
Where the black bear is searching for roots or honey .... where the
    beaver pats the mud with his paddle-tail;
Over the growing sugar .... over the cottonplant .... over the rice in
    its low moist field;
Over the sharp-peaked farmhouse with its scalloped scum and slender
    shoots from the gutters;
Over the western persimmon .... over the longleaved corn and the
    delicate blue-flowered flax;
Over the white and brown buckwheat, a hummer and a buzzer there
    with the rest,
Over the dusky green of the rye as it ripples and shades in the breeze;
Scaling mountains .... pulling myself cautiously up .... holding on by
    low scragged limbs,
Walking the path worn in the grass and beat through the leaves of the
    brush; 730
Where the quail is whistling betwixt the woods and the wheatlot,
Where the bat flies in the July eve .... where the great goldbug drops
    through the dark;
Where the flails keep time on the barn floor,
Where the brook puts out of the roots of the old tree and flows to the
    meadow,
Where cattle stand and shake away flies with the tremulous shuddering
    of their hides,

Where the cheese-cloth hangs in the kitchen, and andirons straddle the
 hearth-slab, and cobwebs fall in festoons from the rafters;
Where triphammers crash . . . . where the press is whirling its cylinders;
Wherever the human heart beats with terrible throes out of its ribs;
Where the pear-shaped balloon is floating aloft . . . . floating in it myself
 and looking composedly down;
Where the life-car is drawn on the slipnoose . . . . where the heat
 hatches pale-green eggs in the dented sand,   740
Where the she-whale swims with her calves and never forsakes them,
Where the steamship trails hindways its long pennant of smoke,
Where the ground-shark's fin cuts like a black chip out of the water,
Where the half-burned brig is riding on unknown currents,
Where shells grow to her slimy deck, and the dead are corrupting below;
Where the striped and starred flag is borne at the head of the regiments;
Approaching Manhattan, up by the long-stretching island,
Under Niagara, the cataract falling like a veil over my countenance;
Upon a door-step . . . . upon the horse-block of hard wood outside,
Upon the race-course, or enjoying pic-nics or jigs or a good game of
 base-ball,   750
At he-festivals with blackguard jibes and ironical license and bull-
 dances and drinking and laughter,
At the cider-mill, tasting the sweet of the brown sqush . . . . sucking the
 juice through a straw,
At apple-peelings, wanting kisses for all the red fruit I find,
At musters and beach-parties and friendly bees and huskings and house-
 raisings;
Where the mockingbird sounds his delicious gurgles, and cackles and
 screams and weeps,
Where the hay-rick stands in the barnyard, and the dry-stalks are scat-
 tered, and the brood cow waits in the hovel,
Where the bull advances to do his masculine work, and the stud to the
 mare, and the cock is treading the hen,
Where the heifers browse, and the geese nip their food with short jerks;
Where the sundown shadows lengthen over the limitless and lonesome
 prairie,
Where the herds of buffalo make a crawling spread of the square miles
 far and near;   760
Where the hummingbird shimmers . . . . where the neck of the long-
 lived swan is curving and winding;
Where the laughing-gull scoots by the slappy shore and laughs her near-
 human laugh;
Where beehives range on a gray bench in the garden half-hid by the
 high weeds;
Where the band-necked partridges roost in a ring on the ground with
 their heads out;
Where burial coaches enter the arched gates of a cemetery;
Where winter wolves bark amid wastes of snow and icicled trees;

Where the yellow-crowned heron comes to the edge of the marsh at
    night and feeds upon small crabs;
Where the splash of swimmers and divers cools the warm noon;
Where the katydid works her chromatic reed on the walnut-tree over
    the well;
Through patches of citrons and cucumbers with silver-wired leaves,   770
Through the salt-lick or orange glade . . . . or under conical firs;
Through the gymnasium . . . . through the curtained saloon . . . . through
    the office or public hall;
Pleased with the native and pleased with the foreign . . . . pleased with
    the new and old,
Pleased with women, the homely as well as the handsome,
Pleased with the quakeress as she puts off her bonnet and talks
    melodiously,
Pleased with the primitive tunes of the choir of the whitewashed church,
Pleased with the earnest words of the sweating Methodist preacher, or
    any preacher . . . . looking seriously at the camp-meeting;
Looking in at the shop-windows in Broadway the whole forenoon . . . .
    pressing the flesh of my nose to the thick plate-glass,
Wandering the same afternoon with my face turned up to the clouds;
My right and left arms round the sides of two friends and I in the
    middle;   780
Coming home with the bearded and dark-cheeked bush-boy . . . . riding
    behind him at the drape of the day;
Far from the settlements studying the print of animals' feet, or the
    moccasin print;
By the cot in the hospital reaching lemonade to a feverish patient,
By the coffined corpse when all is still, examining with a candle;
Voyaging to every port to dicker and adventure;
Hurrying with the modern crowd, as eager and fickle as any,
Hot toward one I hate, ready in my madness to knife him;
Solitary at midnight in my back yard, my thoughts gone from me a
    long while,
Walking the old hills of Judea with the beautiful gentle god by my
    side;
Speeding through space . . . . speeding through heaven and the stars,   790
Speeding amid the seven satellites and the broad ring and the diameter
    of eighty thousand miles,
Speeding with tailed meteors . . . . throwing fire-balls like the rest,
Carrying the crescent child that carries its own full mother in its belly:
Storming enjoying planning loving cautioning,
Backing and filling, appearing and disappearing,
I tread day and night such roads.

I visit the orchards of God and look at the spheric product,
And look at quintillions ripened, and look at quintillions green.

I fly the flight of the fluid and swallowing soul,

My course runs below the soundings of plummets.   *800*

I help myself to material and immaterial,
No guard can shut me off, no law can prevent me.

I anchor my ship for a little while only,
My messengers continually cruise away or bring their returns to me.

I go hunting polar furs and the seal . . . . leaping chasms with a pike-
    pointed staff . . . . clinging to topples of brittle and blue.

I ascend to the foretruck . . . . I take my place late at night in the crow's
    nest . . . . we sail through the arctic sea . . . . it is plenty light enough,
Through the clear atmosphere I stretch around on the wonderful beauty,
The enormous masses of ice pass me and I pass them . . . . the scenery
    is plain in all directions,
The white-topped mountains point up in the distance . . . . I fling out
    my fancies toward them;
We are about approaching some great battlefield in which we are soon
    to be engaged,   *810*
We pass the colossal outposts of the encampment . . . . we pass with still
    feet and caution;
Or we are entering by the suburbs some vast and ruined city . . . . the
    blocks and fallen architecture more than all the living cities of the
    globe.

I am a free companion . . . . I bivouac by invading watchfires.

I turn the bridegroom out of bed and stay with the bride myself,
And tighten her all night to my thighs and lips.

My voice is the wife's voice, the screech by the rail of the stairs,
They fetch my man's body up dripping and drowned.

I understand the large hearts of heroes,
The courage of present times and all times;
How the skipper saw the crowded and rudderless wreck of the steam-
    ship, and death chasing it up and down the storm,   *820*
How he knuckled tight and gave not back one inch, and was faithful
    of days and faithful of nights,
And chalked in large letters on a board, Be of good cheer, We will not
    desert you;
How he saved the drifting company at last,
How the lank loose-gowned women looked when boated from the side
    of their prepared graves,
How the silent old-faced infants, and the lifted sick, and the sharp-
    lipped unshaved men;
All this I swallow and it tastes good . . . . I like it well, and it becomes
    mine,
I am the man . . . . I suffered . . . . I was there.

The disdain and calmness of martyrs,
The mother condemned for a witch and burnt with dry wood, and her
    children gazing on;
The hounded slave that flags in the race and leans by the fence, blow-
    ing and covered with sweat,   *830*
The twinges that sting like needles his legs and neck,
The murderous buckshot and the bullets,
All these I feel or am.

I am the hounded slave . . . . I wince at the bite of the dogs,
Hell and despair are upon me . . . . crack and again crack the
    marksmen,
I clutch the rails of the fence . . . . my gore dribs thinned with the ooze
    of my skin,
I fall on the weeds and stones,
The riders spur their unwilling horses and haul close,
They taunt my dizzy ears . . . . they beat me violently over the head with
    their whip-stocks.

Agonies are one of my changes of garments;   *840*
I do not ask the wounded person how he feels . . . . I myself become the
    wounded person,
My hurt turns livid upon me as I lean on a cane and observe.

I am the mashed fireman with breastbone broken . . . . tumbling walls
    buried me in their debris,
Heat and smoke I inspired . . . . I heard the yelling shouts of my
    comrades,
I heard the distant click of their picks and shovels;
They have cleared the beams away . . . . they tenderly lift me forth.

I lie in the night air in my red shirt . . . . the pervading hush is for my
    sake,
Painless after all I lie, exhausted but not so unhappy,
White and beautiful are the faces around me . . . . the heads are bared
    of their fire-caps,
The kneeling crowd fades with the light of the torches.   *850*

Distant and dead resuscitate,
They show as the dial or move as the hands of me . . . . and I am the
    clock myself.

I am an old artillerist, and tell of some fort's bombardment . . . . and
    am there again.

Again the reveille of drummers . . . . again the attacking cannon and
    mortars and howitzers,
Again the attacked send their cannon responsive.

I take part . . . . I see and hear the whole,
The cries and curses and roar . . . . the plaudits for well aimed shots,

The ambulanza slowly passing and trailing its red drip,
Workmen searching after damages and to make indispensable repairs,
The fall of grenades through the rent roof . . . . the fan-shaped explosion,   *860*
The whizz of limbs heads stone wood and iron high in the air.

Again gurgles the mouth of my dying general . . . . he furiously waves
     with his hand,
He gasps through the clot . . . . Mind not me . . . . mind . . . . the
     entrenchments.

34

I tell not the fall of Alamo . . . . not one escaped to tell the fall of
     Alamo,
The hundred and fifty [8] are dumb yet at Alamo.
Hear now the tale of a jetblack sunrise,
Hear of the murder in cold blood of four hundred and twelve young
     men.

Retreating they had formed in a hollow square with their baggage for
     breastworks,
Nine hundred lives out of the surrounding enemy's nine times their
     number was the price they took in advance,
Their colonel was wounded and their ammunition gone,   *870*
They treated for an honorable capitulation, received writing and seal,
     gave up their arms, and marched back prisoners of war.

They were the glory of the race of rangers,
Matchless with a horse, a rifle, a song, a supper or a courtship,
Large, turbulent, brave, handsome, generous, proud and affectionate,
Bearded, sunburnt, dressed in the free costume of hunters,
Not a single one over thirty years of age.

The second Sunday morning they were brought out in squads and
     massacred . . . . it was beautiful early summer,
The work commenced about five o'clock and was over by eight.

None obeyed the command to kneel,
Some made a mad and helpless rush . . . . some stood stark and straight,   *880*
A few fell at once, shot in the temple or heart . . . . the living and dead
     lay together,
The maimed and mangled dug in the dirt . . . . the new-comers saw
     them there;
Some half-killed attempted to crawl away,
These were dispatched with bayonets or battered with the blunts of
     muskets;

[8] A reference to the shooting of American prisoners of war by the Mexicans in
March 1836.

A youth not seventeen years old seized his assassin till two more came
    to release him,
The three were all torn, and covered with the boy's blood.

At eleven o'clock began the burning of the bodies;
And that is the tale of the murder of the four hundred and twelve
    young men,
And that was a jetblack sunrise.

35

Did you read in the seabooks of the oldfashioned frigate-fight?   *890*
Did you learn who won by the light of the moon and stars?

Our foe was no skulk in his ship, I tell you,
His was the English pluck, and there is no tougher or truer, and never
    was, and never will be;
Along the lowered eve he came, horribly raking us.

We closed with him .... the yards entangled .... the cannon touched,
My captain lashed fast with his own hands.

We had received some eighteen-pound shots under the water,
On our lower-gun-deck two large pieces had burst at the first fire, killing
    all around and blowing up overhead.

Ten o'clock at night, and the full moon shining and the leaks on the
    gain, and five feet of water reported,
The master-at-arms loosing the prisoners confined in the after-hold to
    give them a chance for themselves.   *900*

The transit to and from the magazine was now stopped by the sentinels,
They saw so many strange faces they did not know whom to trust.

Our frigate was afire .... the other asked if we demanded quarters? if
    our colors were struck and the fighting done?

I laughed content when I heard the voice of my little captain,
We have not struck, he composedly cried, We have just begun our part
    of the fighting.

Only three guns were in use,
One was directed by the captain himself against the enemy's mainmast,
Two well-served with grape and canister silenced his musketry and
    cleared his decks.

The tops alone seconded the fire of this little battery, especially the
    maintop,
They all held out bravely during the whole of the action.   *910*

Not a moment's cease,
The leaks gained fast on the pumps . . . . the fire eat toward the powder-
    magazine,
One of the pumps was shot away . . . . it was generally thought we were
    sinking.

Serene stood the little captain,
He was not hurried . . . . his voice was neither high nor low,
His eyes gave more light to us than our battle-lanterns.

Toward twelve at night, there in the beams of the moon they sur-
    rendered to us.

36

Stretched and still lay the midnight,
Two great hulls motionless on the breast of the darkness,
Our vessel riddled and slowly sinking . . . . preparations to pass to the
    one we had conquered,   920
The captain on the quarter deck coldly giving his orders through a
    countenance white as a sheet,
Near by the corpse of the child that served in the cabin,
The dead face of an old salt with long white hair and carefully curled
    whiskers,
The flames spite of all that could be done flickering aloft and below,
The husky voices of the two or three officers yet fit for duty,
Formless stacks of bodies and bodies by themselves . . . . dabs of flesh
    upon the masts and spars,
The cut of cordage and dangle of rigging . . . . the slight shock of the
    soothe of waves,
Black and impressive guns, and litter of powder-parcels, and the strong
    scent,
Delicate sniffs of the seabreeze . . . . smells of sedgy grass and fields
    by the shore . . . . death-messages given in charge to survivors,
The hiss of the surgeon's knife and the gnawing teeth of his saw,   930
The wheeze, the cluck, the swash of falling blood . . . . the short wild
    scream, the long dull tapering groan,
These so . . . . these irretrievable.

37

O Christ! My fit is mastering me!
What the rebel said gaily adjusting his throat to the rope-noose,
What the savage at the stump, his eye-sockets empty, his mouth spirt-
    ing whoops and defiance,
What stills the traveler come to the vault at Mount Vernon,

What sobers the Brooklyn boy as he looks down the shores of the Wall-
    about and remembers the prison ships,
What burnt the gums of the redcoat at Saratoga when he surrendered
    his brigades,
These become mine and me every one, and they are but little,

I become as much more as I like.   940
I become any presence or truth of humanity here,
And see myself in prison shaped like another man,
And feel the dull unintermitted pain.

For me the keepers of convicts shoulder their carbines and keep watch,
It is I let out in the morning and barred at night.

Not a mutineer walks handcuffed to the jail, but I am handcuffed to
him and walk by his side,
I am less the jolly one there, and more the silent one with sweat on my
    twitching lips.

Not a youngster is taken for larceny, but I go too and am tried and
    sentenced.

Not a cholera patient lies at the last gasp, but I also lie at the last gasp,
My face is ash-colored, my sinews gnarl . . . . away from me people
    retreat.   950

Askers embody themselves in me, and I am embodied in them,
I project my hat and sit shamefaced and beg.

I rise extatic through all, and sweep with the true gravitation,
The whirling and whirling is elemental within me.

38
Somehow I have been stunned. Stand back!
Give me a little time beyond my cuffed head and slumbers and dreams
    and gaping,
I discover myself on a verge of the usual mistake.

That I could forget the mockers and insults!
That I could forget the trickling tears and the blows of the bludgeons
    and hammers!
That I could look with a separate look on my own crucifixion and
    bloody crowning!   960

I remember . . . . I resume the overstaid fraction,
The grave of rock multiplies what has been confided to it . . . . or to any
    graves,
The corpses rise . . . . the gashes heal . . . . the fastenings roll away.

I troop forth replenished with supreme power, one of an average un-
    ending procession,
We walk the roads of Ohio and Massachusetts and Virginia and Wiscon-
    sin and New York and New Orleans and Texas and Montreal and
    San Francisco and Charleston and Savannah and Mexico,
Inland and by the seacoast and boundary lines .... and we pass the
    boundary lines.

Our swift ordinances are on their way over the whole earth,
The blossoms we wear in our hats are the growth of two thousand years.

Eleves[9] I salute you,
I see the approach of your numberless gangs .... I see you understand
    yourselves and me,   970
And know that they who have eyes are divine, and the blind and lame
    are equally divine,
And that my steps drag behind yours yet go before them,
And are aware how I am with you no more than I am with everybody.

39

The friendly and flowing savage .... Who is he?
Is he waiting for civilization or past it and mastering it?

Is he some southwesterner raised outdoors? Is he Canadian?
Is he from the Mississippi country? or from Iowa, Oregon or California?
    or from the mountain? or prairie life or bush-life? or from the sea?

Wherever he goes men and women accept and desire him,
They desire he should like them and touch them and speak to them and
    stay with them.

Behaviour lawless as snow-flakes .... words simple as grass .... un-
    combed head and laughter and naivete;   980
Slowstepping feet and the common features, and the common modes
    and emanations,
They descend in new forms from the tips of his fingers,
They are wafted with the odor of his body or breath .... they fly out
    of the glance of his eyes.

40

Flaunt of the sunshine I need not your bask .... lie over,
You light surfaces only .... I force the surfaces and the depths also.

Earth! you seem to look for something at my hands,
Say old topknot! what do you want?

9 French for students; here perhaps followers.

Man or woman! I might tell how I like you, but cannot,
And might tell what it is in me and what it is in you, but cannot,
And might tell the pinings I have . . . . the pulse of my nights and days.   *990*

Behold I do not give lectures or a little charity,
What I give I give out of myself.

You there, impotent, loose in the knees, open your scarfed chops till
    I blow grit within you,
Spread your palms and lift the flaps of your pockets,
I am not to be denied . . . . I compel . . . . I have stores plenty and to
    spare,
And any thing I have I bestow.

I do not ask who you are . . . . that is not important to me,
You can do nothing and be nothing but what I will infold you.

To a drudge of the cottonfields or emptiér of privies I lean . . . . on his
    right cheek I put the family kiss,
And in my soul I swear I never will deny him.   *1000*

On women fit for conception I start bigger and nimbler babes,
This day I am jetting the stuff of far more arrogant republics.

To any one dying . . . . thither I speed and twist the knob of the door,
Turn the bedclothes toward the foot of the bed,
Let the physician and the priest go home.

I seize the descending man . . . . I raise him with resistless will.

O despairer, here is my neck,
By God! you shall not go down! Hang your whole weight upon me.

I dilate you with tremendous breath . . . . I buoy you up;
Every room of the house do I fill with an armed force . . . . lovers of me,
    bafflers of graves: *1010*
Sleep! I and they keep guard all night;
Not doubt, not decease shall dare to lay finger upon you,
I have embraced you, and henceforth possess you to myself,
And when you rise in the morning you will find what I tell you is so.

41
I am he bringing help for the sick as they pant on their backs,
And for strong upright men I bring yet more needed help.

I heard what was said of the universe,
Heard it and heard of several thousand years;
It is middling well as far as it goes . . . . but is that all?

Magnifying and applying come I,   1020
Outbidding at the start the old cautious hucksters,
The most they offer for mankind and eternity less than a spirit of my
    own seminal wet,
Taking myself the exact dimensions of Jehovah and laying them away,
Lithographing Kronos and Zeus his son, and Hercules his grandson,
Buying drafts of Osiris and Isis and Belus and Brahma and Adonai,
In my portfolio placing Manito loose, and Allah on a leaf, and the
    crucifix engraved,
With Odin, and the hideous-faced Mexitli, and all idols and images,
Honestly taking them all for what they are worth, and not a cent more,
Admitting they were alive and did the work of their day,
Admitting they bore mites as for unfledged birds who have now to rise
    and fly and sing for themselves,   1030
Accepting the rough deific sketches to fill out better in myself . . . .
    bestowing them freely on each man and woman I see,
Discovering as much or more in a framer framing a house,
Putting higher claims for him there with his rolled-up sleeves, driving
    the mallet and chisel;
Not objecting to special revelations . . . . considering a curl of smoke
    or a hair on the back of my hand as curious as any revelation;
Those ahold of fire-engines and hook-and-ladder ropes more to me than
    the gods of the antique wars,
Minding their voices peal through the crash of destruction,
Their brawny limbs passing safe over charred laths . . . . their white
    foreheads whole and unhurt out of the flames;
By the mechanic's wife with her babe at her nipple interceding for
    every person born;
Three scythes at harvest whizzing in a row from three lusty angels with
    shirts bagged out at their waists;
The snag-toothed hostler with red hair redeeming sins past and to come,   1040
Selling all he possesses and traveling on foot to fee lawyers for his
    brother and sit by him while he is tried for forgery:
What was strewn in the amplest strewing the square rod about me, and
    not filling the square rod then;
The bull and the bug never worshipped half enough,
Dung and dirt more admirable than was dreamed,
The supernatural of no account . . . . myself waiting my time to be one
    of the supremes,
The day getting ready for me when I shall do as much good as the best,
    and be as prodigious,
Guessing when I am it will not tickle me much to receive puffs out of
    pulpit or print;
By my life-lumps! becoming already a creator!
Putting myself here and now to the ambushed womb of the shadows!

42

.... A call in the midst of the crowd,   *1050*
My own voice, orotund sweeping and final.

Come my children,
Come my boys and girls, and my women and household and intimates,
Now the performer launches his nerve .... he has passed his prelude
    on the reeds within.

Easily written loosefingered chords! I feel the thrum of their climax and
    close.

My head evolves on my neck,
Music rolls, but not from the organ .... folks are around me, but they
    are no household of mine.

Ever the hard and unsunk ground,
Ever the eaters and drinkers .... ever the upward and downward sun
    .... ever the air and the ceaseless tides,
Ever myself and my neighbors, refreshing and wicked and real,   *1060*
Ever the old inexplicable query .... ever that thorned thumb—that
    breath of itches and thirsts,
Ever the vexer's hoot! hoot! till we find where the sly one hides and
    bring him forth;
Ever love .... ever the sobbing liquid of life,
Ever the bandage under the chin .... ever the trestles of death.

Here and there with dimes on the eyes walking,
To feed the greed of the belly the brains liberally spooning,
Tickets buying or taking or selling, but in to the feast never once going;
Many sweating and ploughing and thrashing, and then the chaff for
    payment receiving,
A few idly owning, and they the wheat continually claiming.

This is the city .... and I am one of the citizens;   *1070*
Whatever interests the rest interests me .... politics, churches, news-
    papers, schools,
Benevolent societies, improvements, banks, tariffs, steamships, factories,
    markets,
Stocks and stores and real estate and personal estate.

They who piddle and patter here in collars and tailed coats .... I am
    aware who they are .... and that they are not worms or fleas,
I acknowledge the duplicates of myself under all the scrape-lipped and
    pipe-legged concealments.

The weakest and shallowest is deathless with me,
What I do and say the same waits for them,
Every thought that flounders in me the same flounders in them.

I know perfectly well my own egotism,
And know my omnivorous words, and cannot say any less, 1080
And would fetch you whoever you are flush with myself.

My words are words of a questioning, and to indicate reality;
This printed and bound book . . . . but the printer and the printing-office boy?
The marriage estate and settlement . . . . but the body and mind of the bridegroom? also those of the bride?
The panorama of the sea . . . . but the sea itself?
The well-taken photographs . . . . but your wife or friend close and solid in your arms?
The fleet of ships of the line and all the modern improvements . . . . but the craft and pluck of the admiral?
The dishes and fare and furniture . . . . but the host and hostess, and the look out of their eyes?
The sky up there . . . . yet here or next door or across the way?
The saints and sages in history . . . . but you yourself? 1090
Sermons and creeds and theology . . . . but the human brain, and what is called reason, and what is called love, and what is called life?

43
I do not despise you priests;
My faith is the greatest of faiths and the least of faiths,
Enclosing all worship ancient and modern, and all between ancient and modern,
Believing I shall come again upon the earth after five thousand years,
Waiting responses from oracles . . . . honoring the gods . . . . saluting the sun,
Making a fetish of the first rock or stump . . . . powowing with sticks in the circle of obis,[10]
Helping the lama or brahmin as he trims the lamps of the idols,
Dancing yet through the streets in a phallic procession . . . . rapt and austere in the woods, a gymnosophist,[11]
Drinking mead from the skull-cup . . . . to shasta and vedas admirant . . . . minding the koran, 1100
Walking the teokallis,[12] spotted with gore from the stone and knife— beating the serpent-skin drum;
Accepting the gospels, accepting him that was crucified, knowing assuredly that he is divine,
To the mass kneeling—to the puritan's prayer rising—sitting patiently in a pew,

[10] Magical amulets.
[11] Refers to mystical Hindu sect.
[12] Mexican temples.

Ranting and frothing in my insane crisis—waiting dead-like till my
   spirit arouses me;
Looking forth on pavement and land, and outside of pavement and land,
Belonging to the winders of the circuit of circuits.

One of that centripetal and centrifugal gang,
I turn and talk like a man leaving charges before a journey.

Down-hearted doubters, dull and excluded,
Frivolous sullen moping angry affected disheartened atheistical,   *1110*
I know every one of you, and know the unspoken interrogatories,
By experience I know them.

How the flukes splash!
How they contort rapid as lightning, with spasms and spouts of blood!

Be at peace bloody flukes of doubters and sullen mopers,
I take my place among you as much as among any;
The past is the push of you and me and all precisely the same,
And the day and night are for you and me and all,
And what is yet untried and afterward is for you and me and all.

I do not know what is untried and afterward,   *1120*
But I know it is sure and alive and sufficient.

Each who passes is considered, and each who stops is considered, and
   not a single one can it fail.
It cannot fail the young man who died and was buried,
Nor the young woman who died and was put by his side,
Nor the little child that peeped in at the door and then drew back and
   was never seen again,
Nor the old man who has lived without purpose, and feels it with bit-
   terness worse than gall,
Nor him in the poorhouse tubercled by rum and the bad disorder,
Nor the numberless slaughtered and wrecked . . . . nor the brutish
   koboo,[13] called the ordure of humanity,
Nor the sacs merely floating with open mouths for food to slip in,
Nor any thing in the earth, or down in the oldest graves of the earth,   *1130*
Nor any thing in the myriads of spheres, nor one of the myriads of
   myriads that inhabit them,
Nor the present, nor the least wisp that is known.

44
It is time to explain myself . . . . let us stand up.

What is known I strip away . . . . I launch all men and women forward
   with me into the unknown.

[13] Wild creatures.

The clock indicates the moment . . . . but what does eternity indicate?

Eternity lies in bottomless reservoirs . . . . its buckets are rising forever
    and ever,
They pour and they pour and they exhale away.

We have thus far exhausted trillions of winters and summers;
There are trillions ahead, and trillions ahead of them.

Births have brought us richness and variety,
And other births will bring us richness and variety.   *1140*

I do not call one greater and one smaller,
That which fills its period and place is equal to any.

Were mankind murderous or jealous upon you my brother or my sister?
I am sorry for you . . . . they are not murderous or jealous upon me;
All has been gentle with me . . . . I keep no account with lamentation;
What have I to do with lamentation?

I am an acme of things accomplished, and I an encloser of things to be.

My feet strike an apex of the apices of the stairs,
On every step bunches of ages, and larger bunches between the steps,   *1150*
All below duly traveled—and still I mount and mount.

Rise after rise bow the phantoms behind me,
Afar down I see the huge first Nothing, the vapor from the nostrils of
    death,
I know I was even there . . . . I waited unseen and always,
And slept while God carried me through the lethargic mist,
And took my time . . . . and took no hurt from the fœtid carbon.

Long I was hugged close . . . . long and long.

Immense have been the preparations for me,
Faithful and friendly the arms that have helped me.

Cycles ferried my cradle, rowing and rowing like cheerful boatmen;   *1160*
For room to me stars kept aside in their own rings,
They sent influences to look after what was to hold me.

Before I was born out of my mother generations guided me,
My embryo has never been torpid . . . . nothing could overlay it;
For it the nebula cohered to an orb . . . . the long slow strata piled to
    rest it on . . . . vast vegetables gave it sustenance,
Monstrous sauroids[14] transported it in their mouths and deposited it
    with care.

All forces have been steadily employed to complete and delight me,
Now I stand on this spot with my soul.

[14] An extinct species of fish.

45

Span of youth! Ever-pushed elasticity! Manhood balanced and florid
and full!

My lovers suffocate me!   *1170*
Crowding my lips, and thick in the pores of my skin,
Jostling me through streets and public halls . . . . coming naked to me
at night,
Crying by day Ahoy from the rocks of the river . . . . swinging and
chirping over my head,
Calling my name from flowerbeds or vines or tangled underbrush,
Or while I swim in the bath . . . . or drink from the pump at the corner
. . . . or the curtain is down at the opera . . . . or I glimpse at a
woman's face in the railroad car;
Lighting on every moment of my life,
Bussing my body with soft and balsamic busses,
Noiselessly passing handfuls out of their hearts and giving them to be
mine.

Old age superbly rising! Ineffable grace of dying days!

Every condition promulges not only itself . . . . it promulges what grows
after and out of itself,
And the dark hush promulges as much as any.   *1180*

I open my scuttle at night and see the far-sprinkled systems,
And all I see, multiplied as high as I can cipher, edge but the rim of
the farther systems.

Wider and wider they spread, expanding and always expanding,
Outward and outward and forever outward.

My sun has his sun, and round him obediently wheels,
He joins with his partners a group of superior circuit,
And greater sets follow, making specks of the greatest inside them.

There is no stoppage, and never can be stoppage;
If I and you and the worlds and all beneath or upon their surfaces, and
all the palpable life, were this moment reduced back to a pallid
float, it would not avail in the long run,   *1190*
We should surely bring up again where we now stand,
And as surely go as much farther, and then farther and farther.

A few quadrillions of eras, a few octillions of cubic leagues, do not
hazard the span, or make it impatient,
They are but parts . . . . any thing is but a part.

See ever so far . . . . there is limitless space outside of that,
Count ever so much . . . . there is limitless time around that.

Our rendezvous is fitly appointed . . . . God will be there and wait till
we come.

46

I know I have the best of time and space—and that I was never measured, and never will be measured.

I tramp a perpetual journey,
My signs are a rain-proof coat and good shoes and a staff cut from the
    woods;   1200
No friend of mine takes his ease in my chair,
I have no chair, nor church nor philosophy;
I lead no man to a dinner-table or library or exchange,
But each man and each woman of you I lead upon a knoll,
My left hand hooks you round the waist,
My right hand points to landscapes of continents, and a plain public
    road.

Not I, not any one else can travel that road for you,
You must travel it for yourself.

It is not far . . . . it is within reach,
Perhaps you have been on it since you were born, and did not know,   1210
Perhaps it is every where on water and on land.

Shoulder your duds, and I will mine, and let us hasten forth;
Wonderful cities and free nations we shall fetch as we go.

If you tire, give me both burdens, and rest the chuff of your hand on
    my hip,
And in due time you shall repay the same service to me;
For after we start we never lie by again.

This day before dawn I ascended a hill and looked at the crowded
    heaven,
And I said to my spirit, When we become the enfolders of those orbs
    and the pleasure and knowledge of every thing in them, shall we
    be filled and satisfied then?
And my spirit said No, we level that lift to pass and continue beyond.

You are also asking me questions, and I hear you;   1220
I answer that I cannot answer . . . . you must find out for yourself.

Sit awhile wayfarer,
Here are biscuits to eat and here is milk to drink,
But as soon as you sleep and renew yourself in sweet clothes I will
    certainly kiss you with my goodbye kiss and open the gate for your
    egress hence.

Long enough have you dreamed contemptible dreams,
Now I wash the gum from your eyes,
You must habit yourself to the dazzle of the light and of every moment
    of your life.

Long have you timidly waded, holding a plank by the shore,
Now I will you to be a bold swimmer,
To jump off in the midst of the sea, and rise again and nod to me and
    shout, and laughingly dash with your hair.   *1230*

47

I am the teacher of athletes,
He that by me spreads a wider breast than my own proves the width
    of my own,
He most honors my style who learns under it to destroy the teacher.

The boy I love, the same becomes a man not through derived power
    but in his own right,
Wicked, rather than virtuous out of conformity or fear,
Fond of his sweetheart, relishing well his steak,
Unrequited love or a slight cutting him worse than a wound cuts,
First rate to ride, to fight, to hit the bull's eye, to sail a skiff, to sing a
    song or play on the banjo,
Preferring scars and faces pitted with smallpox over all latherers and
    those that keep out of the sun.

I teach straying from me, yet who can stray from me?   *1240*
I follow you whoever you are from the present hour;
My words itch at your ears till you understand them.

I do not say these things for a dollar, or to fill up the time while I wait
    for a boat;
It is you talking just as much as myself . . . . I act as the tongue of you,
It was tied in your mouth . . . . in mine it begins to be loosened.

I swear I will never mention love or death inside a house,
And I swear I never will translate myself at all, only to him or her who
    privately stays with me in the open air.

If you would understand me go to the heights or water-shore,
The nearest gnat is an explanation and a drop or the motion of waves
    a key,
The maul the oar and the handsaw second my words.   *1250*

No shuttered room or school can commune with me.
But roughs and little children better than they.

The young mechanic is closest to me . . . . he knows me pretty well,
The woodman that takes his axe and jug with him shall take me with
    him all day,
The farmboy ploughing in the field feels good at the sound of my voice,
In vessels that sail my words must sail . . . . I go with fishermen and
    seamen, and love them,

My face rubs to the hunter's face when he lies down alone in his
    blanket,
The driver thinking of me does not mind the jolt of his wagon,
The young mother and old mother shall comprehend me,
The girl and the wife rest the needle a moment and forget where they
    are,   *1260*
They and all would resume what I have told them.

48

I have said that the soul is not more than the body,
And I have said that the body is not more than the soul,
And nothing, not God, is greater to one than one's-self is,
And whoever walks a furlong without sympathy walks to his own
    funeral, dressed in his shroud,
And I or you pocketless of a dime may purchase the pick of the earth,
And to glance with an eye or show a bean in its pod confounds the
    learning of all times,
And there is no trade or employment but the young man following it
    may become a hero,
And there is no object so soft but it makes a hub for the wheeled
    universe,
And any man or woman shall stand cool and supercilious before a
    million universes.   *1270*

And I call to mankind, Be not curious about God,
For I who am curious about each am not curious about God,
No array of terms can say how much I am at peace about God and
    about death.

I hear and behold God in every object, yet I understand God not in the
    least,
Nor do I understand who there can be more wonderful than myself.

Why should I wish to see God better than this day?
I see something of God each hour of the twenty-four, and each moment
    then,
In the faces of men and women I see God, and in my own face in the
    glass;
I find letters from God dropped in the street, and every one is signed
    by God's name,
And I leave them where they are, for I know that others will punctually
    come forever and ever.   *1280*

49

And as to you death, and you bitter hug of mortality . . . . it is idle to
    try to alarm me.

To his work without flinching the accoucheur comes,
I see the elderhand pressing receiving supporting,
I recline by the sills of the exquisite flexible doors . . . . and mark the
    outlet, and mark the relief and escape.

And as to you corpse I think you are good manure, but that does not
    offend me,
I smell the white roses sweetscented and growing,
I reach to the leafy lips . . . . I reach to the polished breasts of melons.

And as to you life, I reckon you are the leavings of many deaths,
No doubt I have died myself ten thousand times before.

I hear you whispering there O stars of heaven,   *1290*
O suns . . . . O grass of graves . . . . O perpetual transfers and promo-
    tions . . . . if you do not say anything how can I say anything?

Of the turbid pool that lies in the autumn forest,
Of the moon that descends the steeps of the soughing twilight,
Toss, sparkles of day and dusk . . . . toss on the black stems that decay
    in the muck,
Toss to the moaning gibberish of the dry limbs.

I ascend from the moon . . . . I ascend from the night,
And perceive of the ghastly glitter the sunbeams reflected,
And debouch [15] to the steady and central from the offspring great or
    small.

   50
There is that in me . . . . I do not know what it is . . . . but I know it is
    in me.

Wrenched and sweaty . . . . calm and cool then my body becomes; I
    sleep . . . . I sleep long.   *1300*

I do not know it . . . . it is without name . . . . it is a word unsaid,
It is not in any dictionary or utterance or symbol.

Something it swings on more than the earth I swing on,
To it the creation is the friend whose embracing awakes me.

Perhaps I might tell more . . . . Outlines! I plead for my brothers and
    sisters.

Do you see O my brothers and sisters?
It is not chaos or death . . . . it is form and union and plan . . . . it is
    eternal life . . . . it is happiness.

15 Military term meaning break out of confinement.

51

The past and present wilt . . . . I have filled them and emptied them,
And proceed to fill my next fold of the future.   *1310*

Listener up there! Here you . . . . what have you to confide to me?
Look in my face while I snuff the sidle of evening,
Talk honestly, for no one else hears you, and I stay only a minute
    longer.

Do I contradict myself?
Very well then . . . . I contradict myself;
I am large . . . . I contain multitudes.

I concentrate toward them that are nigh . . . . I wait on the door-slab.

Who has done his day's work and will soonest be through with his
    supper?
Who wishes to walk with me?

Will you speak before I am gone? Will you prove already too late?   *1320*

52

The spotted hawk swoops by and accuses me . . . . he complains of my
    gab and my loitering.

I too am not a bit tamed . . . . I too am untranslatable,
I sound my barbaric yawp over the roofs of the world.

The last scud of day holds back for me,
It flings my likeness after the rest and true as any on the shadowed
    wilds,
It coaxes me to the vapor and the dusk.

I depart as air . . . . I shake my white locks at the runaway sun,
I effuse my flesh in eddies and drift it in lacy jags.

I bequeath myself to the dirt to grow from the grass I love,
If you want me again look for me under your bootsoles.   *1330*

You will hardly know who I am or what I mean,
But I shall be good health to you nevertheless,
And filter and fibre your blood.

Failing to fetch me at first keep encouraged,
Missing me one place search another,
I stop some where waiting for you.

Crossing Brooklyn Ferry *(1856, 1881)*[1]

1

Flood-tide below me! I see you face to face!
Clouds of the west—sun there half an hour high—I see you also face
 to face.

Crowds of men and women attired in the usual costumes, how curious
 you are to me!
On the ferry-boats the hundreds and hundreds that cross, returning
 home, are more curious to me than you suppose,
And you that shall cross from shore to shore years hence are more to
 me, and more in my meditations, than you might suppose.

2

The impalpable sustenance of me from all things at all hours of the day,
The simple, compact, well-join'd scheme, myself disintegrated, every
 one disintegrated yet part of the scheme,
The similitudes of the past and those of the future,
The glories strung like beads on my smallest sights and hearings, on the
 walk in the street and the passage over the river,
The current rushing so swiftly and swimming with me far away,   10
The others that are to follow me, the ties between me and them,
The certainty of others, the life, love, sight, hearing of others.

Others will enter the gates of the ferry and cross from shore to shore,
Others will watch the run of the flood-tide,
Others will see the shipping of Manhattan north and west, and the
 heights of Brooklyn to the south and east,
Others will see the islands large and small;
Fifty years hence, others will see them as they cross, the sun half an
 hour high,
A hundred years hence, or ever so many hundred years hence, others
 will see them,
Will enjoy the sunset, the pouring-in of the flood-tide, the falling-back
 to the sea of the ebb-tide.

3

It avails not, time nor place—distance avails not,   20
I am with you, you men and women of a generation, or ever so many
 generations hence,

[1] This poem first appeared in the second edition of *Leaves of Grass* printed in 1856,
then entitled "Sun-down Poem." In 1860 Whitman gave it its present title. He
made major revisions in 1881, and that is the edition here used.

Just as you feel when you look on the river and sky, so I felt,
Just as any of you is one of a living crowd, I was one of a crowd,
Just as you are refresh'd by the gladness of the river and the bright
    flow, I was refresh'd,
Just as you stand and lean on the rail, yet hurry with the swift current,
    I stood yet was hurried,
Just as you look on the numberless masts of ships and the thick-
    stemm'd pipes of steamboats, I look'd.

I too many and many a time cross'd the river of old,
Watched the Twelfth-month sea-gulls, saw them high in the air floating
    with motionless wings, oscillating their bodies,
Saw how the glistening yellow lit up parts of their bodies and left the
    rest in strong shadow,
Saw the slow-wheeling circles and the gradual edging toward the south,   30
Saw the reflection of the summer sky in the water,
Had my eyes dazzled by the shimmering track of beams,
Look'd at the fine centrifugal spokes of light round the shape of my
    head in the sunlit water,
Look'd on the haze on the hills southward and south-westward,
Look'd on the vapor as it flew in fleeces tinged with violet,
Look'd toward the lower bay to notice the vessels arriving,
Saw their approach, saw aboard those that were near me,
Saw the white sails of schooners and sloops, saw the ships at anchor,
The sailors at work in the rigging or out astride the spars,
The round masts, the swinging motion of the hulls, the slender ser-
    pentine pennants,   40
The large and small steamers in motion, the pilots in their pilot-houses,
The white wake left by the passage, the quick tremulous whirl of the
    wheels,
The flags of all nations, the falling of them at sunset,
The scallop-edged waves in the twilight, the ladled cups, the frolicsome
    crests and glistening,
The stretch afar growing dimmer and dimmer, the gray walls of the
    granite storehouses by the docks,
On the river the shadowy group, the big steam-tug closely flank'd on
    each side by the barges, the hay-boat, the belated lighter,
On the neighboring shore the fires from the foundry chimneys burning
    high and glaringly into the night,
Casting their flicker of black contrasted with wild red and yellow light
    over the tops of houses, and down into the clefts of streets.

4

These and all else were to me the same as they are to you,
I loved well those cities, loved well the stately and rapid river,   50
The men and women I saw were all near to me,

Others the same—others who look back on me because I look'd forward
    to them,
(The time will come, though I stop here to-day and to-night.)

5
What is it then between us?
What is the count of the scores or hundreds of years between us?

Whatever it is, it avails not—distance avails not, and place avails not,
I too lived, Brooklyn of ample hills was mine,
I too walk'd the streets of Manhattan island, and bathed in the waters
    around it,
I too felt the curious abrupt questionings stir within me.
In the day among crowds of people sometimes they came upon me,   60
In my walks home late at night or as I lay in my bed they came upon
    me,
I too had been struck from the float forever held in solution,
I too had receiv'd identity by my body,
That I was I knew was of my body, and what I should be I knew I
    should be of my body.

6
It is not upon you alone the dark patches fall,
The dark threw its patches down upon me also,
The best I had done seem'd to me blank and suspicious,
My great thoughts as I supposed them, were they not in reality meagre?
Nor is it you alone who know what it is to be evil,
I am he who knew what it was to be evil,   70
I too knitted the old knot of contrariety,
Blabb'd, blush'd, resented, lied, stole, grudg'd,
Had guile, anger, lust hot wishes I dared not speak,
Was wayward, vain, greedy, shallow, sly, cowardly malignant,
The wolf the snake, the hog, not wanting in me,
The cheating look, the frivolous word, the adulterous wish, not wanting,
Refusals, hates, postponements, meanness, laziness, none of these
    wanting,
Was one with the rest, the days and haps of the rest,
Was call'd by my nighest name by clear loud voices of young men as
    they saw me approaching or passing,
Felt their arms on my neck as I stood, or the negligent leaning of their
    flesh against me as I sat,   80
Saw many I loved in the street or ferry-boat or public assembly, yet
    never told them a word,
Lived the same life with the rest, the same old laughing, gnawing,
    sleeping,

Play'd the part that still looks back on the actor or actress,
The same old role, the role that is what we make it, as great as we like,
Or as small as we like, or both great and small.

7

Closer yet I approach you,
What thought you have of me now, I had as much of you—I laid in
    my stores in advance,
I consider'd long and seriously of you before you were born.
Who was to know what should come home to me?
Who knows but I am enjoying this?   90
Who knows, for all the distance, but I am as good as looking at you
    now, for all you cannot see me?

8

Ah, what can ever be more stately and admirable to me than mast-
    hemm'd Manhattan?
River and sunset and scallop-edg'd waves of flood-tide?
The sea-gulls oscillating their bodies, the hay-boat in the twilight, and
    the belated lighter?
What gods can exceed these that clasp me by the hand, and with voices
    I love call me promptly and loudly by my nighest name as I
    approach?

What is more subtle than this which ties me to the woman or man that
    looks in my face?
Which fuses me into you now, and pours my meaning into you?

We understand then de we not?
What I promis'd without mentioning it, have you not accepted?
What the study could not teach—what the preaching could not accom-
    plish is accomplish'd, is it not?   100

9

Flow on, river! flow with the flood-tide, and ebb with the ebb-tide!
Frolic on, crested and scallop-edg'd waves!
Gorgeous clouds of the sunset! drench with your splendor me, or the
    men and women generations after me!
Cross from shore to shore, countless crowds of passengers!
Stand up, tall masts of Mannahatta! stand up, beautiful hills of
    Brooklyn!
Throb, baffled and curious brain! throw out questions and answers!
Suspend here and everywhere, eternal float of solution!

Gaze, loving and thirsting eyes, in the house or street or public
    assembly!
Sound out, voices of young men! loudly and musically call me by my
    nighest name!
Live, old life! play the part that looks back on the actor or actress!   *110*
Play the old role, the role that is great or small according as one
    makes it!
Consider, you who peruse me, whether I may not in unknown ways be
    looking upon you;
Be firm, rail over the river, to support those who lean idly, yet haste
    with the hasting current;
Fly on, sea-birds! fly sideways, or wheel in large circles high in the air;
Receive the summer sky, you water, and faithfully hold it till all down-
    cast eyes have time to take it from you!
Diverge, fine spokes of light, from the shape of my head, or any one's
    head, in the sunlit water!
Come on, ships from the lower bay! pass up or down, white-sail'd
    schooners, sloops, lighters!
Flaunt away, flags of all nations! be duly lower'd at sunset!
Burn high your fires, foundry chimneys! cast black shadows at night-
    fall! cast red and yellow light over the tops of the houses!
Appearances, now or henceforth, indicate what you are,   *120*
You necessary film, continue to envelop the soul,
About my body for me, and your body for you, be hung our divinest
    aromas,
Thrive, cities—bring your freight, bring your shows, ample and suffi-
    cient rivers,
Expand, being than which none else is perhaps more spiritual,
Keep your places, objects than which none else is more lasting.

You have waited, you always wait, you dumb, beautiful ministers,
We receive you with free sense at last, and are insatiate henceforward,
Not you any more shall be able to foil us, or withhold yourselves from
    us,
We use you, and do not cast you aside—we plant you permanently
    within us,
We fathom you not—we love you—there is perfection in you also,   *130*

You furnish your parts toward eternity,
Great or small, you furnish your parts toward the soul.

Out of the Cradle
Endlessly Rocking *(1859, 1881)*[1]

Out of the cradle endlessly rocking,
Out of the mocking-bird's throat, the musical shuttle,
Out of the Ninth-month midnight,
Over the sterile sands and the fields beyond, where the child leaving his
    bed wander'd alone, bareheaded, barefoot,
Down from the shower'd halo,
Up from the mystic play of shadows twining and twisting as if they were
    alive,
Out from the patches of briers and blackberries,
From the memories of the bird that chanted to me,
From your memories sad brother, from the fitful risings and fallings I
    heard,
From under that yellow half-moon late-risen and swollen as if with tears,   *10*
From those beginning notes of yearning and love there in the mist,
From the thousand responses of my heart never to cease,
From the myriad thence-arous'd words,
From the word stronger and more delicious than any,
For such as now they start the scene revisiting,
As a flock, twittering, rising, or overhead passing,
Borne hither, ere all eludes me, hurriedly,
A man, yet by these tears a little boy again,
Throwing myself on the sand, confronting the waves,
I, chanter of pains and joys, uniter of here and hereafter,   *20*
Taking all hints to use them, but swiftly leaping beyond them,
A reminiscence sing.

Once Paumanok,
When the lilac-scent was in the air and Fifth-month grass was growing,
Up this seashore in some briers,
Two feather'd guests from Alabama, two together,
And their nest, and four light-green eggs spotted with brown,
And every day the he-bird to and fro near at hand,
And every day the she-bird crouch'd on her nest, silent, with bright eyes,
And every day I, a curious boy, never too close, never disturbing them,   *30*
Cautiously peering, absorbing, translating.

Shine! shine! shine!
Pour down your warmth, great sun!
While we bask, we two together.

---

[1] First published in the New York *Saturday Press* on December 24, 1859, this poem
appeared in the 1860 edition of *Leaves of Grass* under the title "A Word Out of the
Sea." The present title he adopted in 1871. The edition here used is that of 1881.

Two together!
Winds blow south, or winds blow north,
Day come white, or night come black,
Home, or rivers and mountains from home,
Singing all time, minding no time,
While we two keep together.   40

Till of a sudden,
May-be kill'd, unknown to her mate,
One forenoon the she-bird crouch'd not on the nest,
Nor return'd that afternoon, nor the next,
Nor ever appear'd again.

And thenceforward all summer in the sound of the sea,
And at night under the full of the moon in calmer weather,
Over the hoarse surging of the sea,
Or flitting from brier to brier by day,
I saw, I heard at intervals the remaining one, the he-bird,   50
The solitary guest from Alabama.

Blow! blow! blow!
Blow up sea-winds along Paumanok's shore;
I wait and I wait till you blow my mate to me.

Yes, when the stars glisten'd,
All night long on the prong of a moss-scallop'd stake,
Down almost amid the slapping waves,
Sat the lone singer wonderful causing tears.

He call'd on his mate,
He pour'd forth the meanings which I of all men know.   60

Yes my brother I know,
The rest might not, but I have treasur'd every note,
For more than once dimly down to the beach gliding,
Silent, avoiding the moonbeams, blending myself with the shadows,
Recalling now the obscure shapes, the echoes, the sounds and sights
    after their sorts,
The white arms out in the breakers tirelessly tossing,
I, with bare feet, a child, the wind wafting my hair,
Listen'd long and long.

Listen'd to keep, to sing, now translating the notes,
Following you my brother.   70

Soothe! soothe! soothe!
Close on its wave soothes the wave behind,
And again another behind embracing and lapping, every one close,
But my love soothes not me, not me.

Low hangs the moon, it rose late,
It is lagging—O I think it is heavy with love, with love.

O madly the sea pushes upon the land,
With love, with love.

O night! do I not see my love fluttering out among the breakers?
What is that little black thing I see there in the white?   80

Loud! loud! loud!
Loud I call to you, my love!

High and clear I shoot my voice over the waves,
Surely you must know who is here, is here,
You must know whom I am, my love.

Low-hanging moon!
What is that dusky spot in your brown yellow?
O it is the shape, the shape of my mate!
O moon do not keep her from me any longer.

Land! land! O land!   90
Whichever way I turn, O I think you could give me my mate back again
*   if you only would,*
For I am almost sure I see her dimly whichever way I look.

O rising stars!
Perhaps the one I want so much will rise, will rise with some of you.

O throat! O trembling throat!
Sound clearer through the atmosphere!
Pierce the woods, the earth,
Somewhere listening to catch you must be the one I want.

Shake out carols!
Solitary here, the night's carols!   100
Carols of lonesome love! death's carols!
Carols under that lagging, yellow, waning moon!
O under that moon where she droops almost down into the sea!
O reckless despairing carols.

But soft! sink low!
Soft! let me just murmur,
And do you wait a moment you husky-nois'd sea,
For somewhere I believe I heard my mate responding to me,
So faint, I must be still, be still to listen,
But not altogether still, for then she might not come immediately to me.   110

Hither my love!
Here I am! here!
With this just-sustain'd note I announce myself to you,
This gentle call is for you my love, for you.

Do not be decoy'd elsewhere,
That is the whistle of the wind, it is not my voice,
That is the fluttering, the fluttering of the spray,
Those are the shadows of leaves.

O darkness! O in vain!
O I am very sick and sorrowful.   120
O brown halo in the sky near the moon, drooping upon the sea!
O troubled reflection in the sea!

O throat! O throbbing heart!
And I singing uselessly, uselessly all the night.

O past! O happy life! O songs of joy!
In the air, in the woods, over fields,
Loved! loved! loved! loved! loved!
But my mate no more, no more with me!
We two together no more.

The aria sinking,   130
All else continuing, the stars shining,
The winds blowing, the notes of the bird continuous echoing,
With angry moans the fierce old mother incessantly moaning,
On the sands of Paumanok's shore gray and rustling,
The yellow half-moon enlarged, sagging down, drooping, the face of the
      sea almost touching
The boy ecstatic, with his bare feet the waves, with his hair the atmos-
      phere dallying,
The love in the heart long pent, now loose, now at last tumultuously
      bursting,
The aria's meaning, the ears, the soul, swiftly depositing,
The strange tears down the cheeks coursing,
The colloquy there, the trio, each uttering,   140
The undertone, the savage old mother incessantly crying,
To the boy's soul's questions sullenly timing, some drown'd secret hissing,
To the outsetting bard.

Demon or bird! (said the boy's soul,)
Is it indeed toward your mate you sing? or is it really to me?
For I, that was a child, my tongue's use sleeping, now I have heard you,
Now in a moment I know what I am for, I awake,
And already a thousand singers, a thousand songs, clearer, louder and
      more sorrowful than yours,
A thousand warbling echoes have started to life within me, never to die.

O you singer solitary, singing by yourself, projecting me,   150
O solitary me listening, never more shall I cease perpetuating you,
Never more shall I escape, never more the reverberations,
Never more the cries of unsatisfied love be absent from me,

Never again leave me to be the peaceful child I was before what there
    in the night,
By the sea under the yellow and sagging moon,
The messenger there arous'd, the fire, the sweet hell within,
The unknown want, the destiny of me.

O give me the clew! (it lurks in the night here somewhere,)
O if I am to have so much, let me have more!

A word then, (for I will conquer it,)   160
The word final, superior to all,
Subtle, sent up—what is it?—I listen;

Are you whispering it, and have been all the time, you sea waves?
Is that it from your liquid rims and wet sands?

Whereto answering, the sea,
Delaying not, hurrying not,
Whisper'd me through the night, and very plainly before daybreak,
Lisp'd to me the low and delicious word death,
And again death, death, death, death,
Hissing melodious, neither like the bird nor like my arous'd child's heart,   170
But edging near as privately for me rustling at my feet,
Creeping thence steadily up to my ears and laving me softly all over,
Death, death, death, death, death.

Which I do not forget,
But fuse the song of my dusky demon and brother,
That he sang to me in the moonlight on Paumanok's gray beach,
With the thousand responsive songs at random,
My own songs awaked from that hour,
And with them the key, the word up from the waves,
The word of the sweetest song and all songs,   180
The strong and delicious word which, creeping to my feet,
(Or like some old crone rocking the cradle, swathed in sweet garments,
    bending aside,)
The sea whisper'd me.

Hours Continuing Long, Sore and Heavy-hearted (1860)

Hours continuing long, sore and heavy-hearted,
Hours of the dusk, when I withdraw to a lonesome and unfrequented
    spot, seating myself, leaning my face in my hands;
Hours sleepless, deep in the night, when I go forth, speeding swiftly
    the country roads, or through the city streets, or pacing miles and
    miles, stifling plaintive cries;

Hours discouraged, distracted—for the one I cannot content myself
    without, soon I saw him content himself without me;
Hours when I am forgotten, (O weeks and months are passing, but I
    believe I am never to forget!)
Sullen and suffering hours! (I am ashamed—but it is useless—I am
    what I am;)
Hours of my torment—I wonder if other men ever have the like, out of
    the like feelings?
Is there even one other like me—distracted—his friend, his lover, lost
    to him?
Is he too as I am now? Does he still rise in the morning, dejected, think-
    ing who is lost to him? and at night, awaking, think who is lost?
Does he too harbor his friendship silent and endless? harbor his anguish
    and passion?   10
Does some stray reminder, or the casual mention of a name, bring the
    fit back upon him, taciturn and deprest?
Does he see himself reflected in me? In these hours, does he see the face
    of his hours reflected?

Cavalry Crossing a Ford (1865, 1871)

A line in long array where they wind betwixt green islands,
They take a serpentine course, their arms flash in the sun—hark to the
    musical clank,
Behind the silvery river, in it the splashing horses loitering stop to drink,
Behold the brown-faced men, each group, each person a picture, the
    negligent rest on the saddles,
Some emerge on the opposite bank, others are just entering the ford—
    while,
Scarlet and blue and snowy white,
The guidon flags flutter gayly in the wind.

When Lilacs Last in the Dooryard Bloom'd *(1865, 1881)*[1]

1

When lilacs last in the dooryard bloom'd,
And the great star early droop'd in the western sky in the night,
I mourn'd, and yet shall mourn with ever-returning spring.

Ever-returning spring, trinity sure to me you bring,
Lilac blooming perennial and drooping star in the west,
And thought of him I love.

2

O powerful western fallen star!
O shades of night—O moody, tearful night!
O great star disappear'd—O the black murk that hides the star!
O cruel hands that hold me powerless—O helpless soul of me!   10
O harsh surrounding cloud that will not free my soul.

3

In the dooryard fronting an old farm-house near the white-wash'd
    palings,
Stands the lilac-bush tall-growing with heart-shaped leaves of rich green,
With many a pointed blossom rising delicate, with the perfume strong
    I love,
With every leaf a miracle—and from this bush in the dooryard,
With delicate-color'd blossoms and heart-shaped leaves of rich green,
A sprig with its flower I break.

4

In the swamp in secluded recesses,
A shy and hidden bird is warbling a song.

Solitary the thrush,   20
The hermit withdrawn to himself, avoiding the settlements,
Sings by himself a song.
Song of the bleeding throat,
Death's outlet song of life, (for well dear brother I know,
If thou wast not granted to sing thou would'st surely die.)

[1] This elegy for Abraham Lincoln first appeared in sequel to *Drum-Taps*, a part of
the second edition of *Drum-Taps* (1865). It was then printed in the fourth, or
1867, edition of *Leaves of Grass*, with extensive revisions. The version here offered
includes these, as well as the 1881, revisions.

5

Over the breast of the spring, the land, amid cities,
Amid lanes and through old woods, where lately the violets peep'd from
    the ground, spotting the gray debris,
Amid the grass in the fields each side of the lanes, passing the endless
    grass,
Passing the yellow-spear'd wheat, every grain from its shroud in the
    dark-brown fields uprisen,
Passing the apple-tree blows of white and pink in the orchards,   *30*
Carrying a corpse to where it shall rest in the grave,
Night and day journeys a coffin.

6

Coffin that passes through lanes and streets,
Through day and night with the great cloud darkening the land,
With the pomp of the inloop'd flags with the cities draped in black,
With the show of the States themselves as of crape-veil'd women
    standing,
With processions long and winding and the flambeaus of the night,
With the countless torches lit, with the silent sea of faces and the un-
    bared heads,
With the waiting depot, the arriving coffin, and the sombre faces,
With dirges through the night, with the thousand voices rising strong,
    and solemn,   *40*
With all the mournful voices of the dirges pour'd around the coffin,
The dim-lit churches and the shuddering organs—where amid these you
    journey,
With the tolling tolling bells' perpetual clang,
Here, coffin that slowly passes,
I give you my sprig of lilac.

7

(Nor for you, for one alone,
Blossoms and branches green to coffins all I bring,
For fresh as the morning, thus would I chant a song for you O sane and
    sacred death.

All over bouquets of roses,
O death, I cover you over with roses and early lilies,   *50*
But mostly and now the lilac that blooms the first,
Copious I break, I break the sprigs from the bushes,
With loaded arms I come, pouring for you,
For you and the coffins all of you O death.)

8

O western orb sailing the heaven,
Now I know what you must have meant as a month since I walk'd,
As I walk'd in silence the transparent shadowy night,
As I saw you had something to tell as you bent to me night after night,
As you droop'd from the sky low down as if to my side, (while the other
    stars all look'd on,)
As we wander'd together the solemn night, (for something I know not
    what kept me from sleep,)   60
As the night advanced, and I saw on the rim of the west how full you
    were of woe,
As I stood on the rising ground in the breeze in the cool transparent
    night,
As I watch'd where you pass'd and was lost in the netherward black of
    the night,
As my soul in its trouble dissatisfied sank, as where you sad orb,
Concluded, dropt in the night, and was gone.

9

Sing on there in the swamp,
O singer bashful and tender, I hear your notes, I hear your call,
I hear, I come presently, I understand you,
But a moment I linger, for the lustrous star has detain'd me,
The star my departing comrade holds and detains me.   70

10

O how shall I warble myself for the dead one there I loved?
And how shall I deck my song for the large sweet soul that has gone?
And what shall my perfume be for the grave of him I love?

Sea-winds blown from east and west,
Blown from the Eastern sea and blown from the Western sea, till there
    on the prairies meeting,
These and with these and the breath of my chant,
I'll perfume the grave of him I love.

11

O what shall I hang on the chamber walls?
And what shall the pictures be that I hang on the walls,
To adorn the burial-house of him I love?   80
Pictures of growing spring and farms and homes,
With the Fourth-month eve at sundown, and the gray smoke lucid and
    bright,

With floods of the yellow gold of the gorgeous, indolent, sinking sun,
   burning, expanding the air,
With the fresh sweet herbage under foot, and the pale green leaves of
   the trees prolific,
In the distance the flowing glaze, the breast of the river, with a wind-
   dapple here and there,
With ranging hills on the banks, with many a line against the sky, and
   shadows,
And the city at hand with dwellings so dense, and stacks of chimneys,
And all the scenes of life and the workshops, and the workmen homeward returning.

12

Lo, body and soul—this land,
My own Manhattan with spires, and the sparkling and hurrying tides,
   and the ships,   90
The varied and ample land, the South and the North in the light, Ohio's
   shores and flashing Missouri,
And ever the far-spreading prairies cover'd with grass and corn.

Lo, the most excellent sun so calm and haughty,
The violet and purple morn with just-felt breezes,
The gentle soft-born measureless light,
The miracle spreading bathing all, the fulfill'd noon,
The coming eve delicious, the welcome night and the stars,
Over my cities shining all, enveloping man and land.

13

Sing on, sing on you gray-brown bird,
Sing from the swamps, the recesses, pour your chant from the bushes,   100
Limitless out of the dusk, out of the cedars and pines.

Sing on dearest brother, warble your reedy song,
Loud human song, with voice of uttermost woe.

O liquid and free and tender!
O wild and loose to my soul—O wondrous singer!
You only I hear—yet the star holds me, (but will soon depart,)
Yet the lilac with mastering odor holds me.

14

Now while I sat in the day and look'd forth,
In the close of the day with its light and the fields of spring, and the
   farmers preparing their crops,

In the large unconscious scenery of my land with its lakes and forests,   *110*
In the heavenly aerial beauty, (after the perturb'd winds and the storms,)
Under the arching heavens of the afternoon swift passing, and the voices of children and women,
The many-moving sea-tides, and I saw the ships how they sail'd,
And the summer approaching with richness, and the fields all busy with labor,
And the infinite separate houses, how they all went on, each with its meals and minutia of daily usages,
And the streets how their throbbings throbb'd, and the cities pent—lo, then and there,
Falling upon them all and among them all, enveloping me with the rest,
Appear'd the cloud, appear'd the long black trail,
And I knew death, its thought, and the sacred knowledge of death.

Then with the knowledge of death as walking one side of me,   *120*
And the thought of death close-walking the other side of me,
And I in the middle as with companions, and as holding the hands of companions,
I fled forth to the hiding receiving night that talks not,
Down to the shores of the water, the path by the swamp in the dimness,
To the solemn shadowy cedars and ghostly pines so still.

And the singer so shy to the rest receiv'd me,
The gray-brown bird I know receiv'd us comrades three,
And he sang the carol of death, and a verse for him I love.

From deep secluded recesses,
From the fragrant cedars and the ghostly pines so still,   *130*
Came the carol of the bird.

And the charm of the carol rapt me,
As I held as if by their hands my comrades in the night,
And the voice of my spirit tallied the song of the bird.

Come lovely and soothing death,
Undulate round the world, serenely arriving, arriving,
In the day, in the night, to all, to each,
Sooner or later delicate death.

Prais'd be the fathomless universe,
For life and joy, and for objects and knowledge curious,   *140*
And for love, sweet love—but praise! praise! praise!
For the sure-enwinding arms of cool-enfolding death.

Dark mother always gliding near with soft feet,
Have none chanted for thee a chant of fullest welcome?
Then I chant it for thee, I glorify thee above all,

I bring thee a song that when thou must indeed come, come unfalter-
*   ingly.*

Approach strong deliveress,
When it is so, when thou hast taken them I joyously sing the dead,
Lost in the loving floating ocean of thee,
Laved in the flood of thy bliss O death.   150

From me to thee glad serenades,
Dances for thee I propose saluting thee, adornments and feastings for
*   thee,*
And the sights of the open landscape and the high-spread sky are fitting,
And life and the fields, and the huge and thoughtful night.

The night in silence under many a star,
The ocean shore and the husky whispering wave whose voice I know,
And the soul turning to thee O vast and well-veil'd death,
And the body gratefully nestling close to thee.

Over the tree-tops I float thee a song,
Over the rising and sinking waves, over the myriad fields and the
*   prairies wide,*   160
Over the dense-pack'd cities all and the teeming wharves and ways,
I float this carol with joy, with joy to thee O death.

15
To the tally of my soul,
Loud and strong kept up the gray-brown bird,
With pure deliberate notes spreading filling the night.

Loud in the pines and cedars dim,
Clear in the freshness moist and the swamp-perfume,
And I with my comrades there in the night.

While my sight that was bound in my eyes unclosed,
As to long panoramas of visions.   170

And I saw askant the armies,
I saw as in noiseless dreams hundreds of battle-flags,
Borne through the smoke of the battles and pierc'd with missiles I saw
    them,
And carried hither and yon through the smoke, and torn and bloody,
And at last but a few shreds left on the staffs, (and all in silence,)
And the staffs all splinter'd and broken.

I saw battle-corpses, myriads of them,
And the white skeletons of young men, I saw them,
I saw the debris and debris of all the slain soldiers of the war,
But I saw they were not as was thought,   180

They themselves were fully at rest, they suffer'd not,
The living remain'd and suffer'd, the mother suffer'd,
And the wife and the child and the musing comrade suffer'd,
And the armies that remain'd suffer'd.

16

Passing the visions, passing the night,
Passing, unloosing the hold of my comrades' hands,
Passing the song of the hermit bird and the tallying song of my soul,
Victorious song, death's outlet song, yet varying ever-altering song,
As low and wailing, yet clear the notes, rising and falling, flooding the
    night,
Sadly sinking and fainting, as warning and warning, and yet again
    bursting with joy,   190
Covering the earth and filling the spread of the heaven,
As that powerful psalm in the night I heard from recesses,
Passing, I leave thee lilac with heart-shaped leaves,
I leave thee there in the door-yard, blooming, returning with spring.

I cease from my song for thee,
From my gaze on thee in the west, fronting the west, communing with
    thee,
O comrade lustrous with silver face in the night.

Yet each to keep and all, retrievements out of the night,
The song, the wondrous chant of the gray-brown bird,
And the tallying chant, the echo arous'd in my soul,   200
With the lustrous and drooping star with the countenance full of woe,
With the holders holding my hand nearing the call of the bird,
Comrades mine and I in the midst, and their memory ever to keep, for
    the dead I loved so well,
For the sweetest, wisest soul of all my days and lands—and this for his
    dear sake,
Lilac and star and bird twined with the chant of my soul,
There in the fragrant pines and the cedars dusk and dim.

A Glimpse (1867)

A glimpse through an interstice caught,
Of a crowd of workmen and drivers in a bar-room around the stove late
    of winter night, and I unremark'd seated in a corner,
Of a youth who loves me and whom I love, silently approaching and
    seating himself near, that he may hold me by the hand,

A long while amid the noises of coming and going, of drinking and oath
    and smutty jest,
There we two, content, happy in being together, speaking little, perhaps
    not a word.

A Noiseless Patient Spider *(1871, 1881)*

A noiseless patient spider,
I mark'd where on a little promontory it stood isolated,
Mark'd how to explore the vacant vast surrounding,
It launch'd forth filament, filament, filament, out of itself,
Ever unreeling them, ever tirelessly speeding them.

And you O my soul where you stand,
Surrounded, detached, in measureless oceans of space,
Ceaselessly musing, venturing, throwing, seeking the spheres to connect
    them,
Till the bridge you will need be form'd, till the ductile anchor hold,
Till the gossamer thread you fling catch somewhere, O my soul. 10

Democracy *(1867)*[1]

    After the rest is said—after many time-honored and really true
things for subordination, experience, rights of property, etc., have been
listened to, and acquiesced in—after the valuable and well-settled statement of our duties and relations in society is thoroughly conned over
and exhausted—it remains to bring forward and modify everything else
with the idea of that Something a man is, standing apart from all else,
divine in his own right, and a woman in hers, sole and untouchable
by any canons of religion, politics, or what is called modesty or art.
    The radiation of this truth, practically a modern one, is the history
and key of the most significant doings of our immediately preceding
three centuries, and has been the political genesis and life of America.
Advancing visibly, it still more advances invisibly. Underneath the fluc-
tuations of the expressions of society, as well as the movements of the
politics of the leading nations, we see steadily pressing ahead, and
strengthening itself, even in the midst of immense tendencies toward
aggregation, this image of completeness in separatism, of individual
personal dignity, of a single person, either male or female, character-

[1] This essay first appeared in *The Galaxy*; it is an early, more concise version of
"Democratic Vistas."

ized in the main, not from extrinsic acquirements or position, but in the pride of himself or herself alone; and, as an eventual conclusion and summing-up, the simple, but tremendous and revolutionary, idea that the last, best dependence is to be upon Humanity itself, and its own inherent, normal, full-grown qualities, without any superstitious support whatever.

The purpose of Democracy—supplanting old belief in the necessary absoluteness of established dynastic rulership, temporal, ecclesiastical, and scholastic, as furnishing the only security against chaos, crime, and ignorance—is, through many transmigrations, and amid endless ridicules, arguments, and ostensible failures, to illustrate, at all hazards, this doctrine of the sovereignty and sacredness of the individual, co-ëqual with the balance-doctrine that man, properly trained, may and must become a law, and series of laws, unto himself, surrounding and providing for, not only his own personal control, but all his relations to other individuals, and to the State; and that, while other theories, as in the past histories of nations, have proved wise enough, and indispensable perhaps for their conditions, *this*, as matters now stand in our civilized world, is the only Scheme worth working from, as warranting results like those of Nature's laws, reliable, when once established, to carry on themselves.

With such for outset, and a silent, momentary prayer that we may be enabled to tell what is worthy the faith within us, we follow on.

Leaving unsaid much that should properly prepare the way for the treatment of this many-sided matter of Democracy—leaving the whole history and consideration of the Feudal Plan and its products, embodying Humanity, its politics and civilization, through the retrospect of past time (which Plan and products, indeed, make up all of the past, and a major part of the present)—leaving unanswered, at least by any specific and local answer, many a well-wrought argument and instance, and many a conscientious declamatory cry and warning—as, very lately, from an eminent and venerable person abroad—things, problems, full of doubt, dread, suspense, (not new to me, but old occupiers of many an anxious hour in city's din, or night's silence), we still may give a paragraph or so, whose drift is opportune. Time alone can finally answer these things. But as a substitute in passing let us, even if fragmentarily, throw forth a thought or two—a short direct or indirect suggestion of the premises of the theory, that other Plan, in the new spirit, under the new forms, started here in our America.

As to the political section of Democracy, which introduces and breaks ground for further and vaster sections, few probably are the minds, even in these republican States, that fully comprehend the aptness of that phrase, " THE GOVERNMENT OF THE PEOPLE, BY THE PEOPLE, FOR THE PEOPLE," which we inherit from the lips of Abraham Lincoln; a formula whose verbal shape is homely wit, but whose scope includes both the totality and all minutiæ of the lesson.

The People! Like our huge earth itself, which, to ordinary scansion, is full of vulgar contradictions and offence, Man, viewed in the lump, displeases, and is a constant puzzle and affront to the merely educated classes. The rare, cosmical, artist-mind, lit with the Infinite, alone confronts his manifold and oceanic qualities; but taste, intelligence and culture (so-called), have been against the masses, and remain so. There is plenty of glamour about the most damnable crimes and hoggish meannesses, special and general, of the Feudal and dynastic world, with its *personnel* of lords and queens and courts, so well-dressed and so handsome. But the People are ungrammatical, untidy, and their sins are gaunt and ill-bred.

Literature has never recognized the People, and, whatever may be said, does not to-day. Speaking generally, the tendencies of literature, as pursued, are to make mostly critical and querulous men. It seems as if, so far, there were some natural repugnance between a literary and professional life, and the rude spirit of the Democracies. There is, in later literature, a treatment of benevolence, a charity business, rife enough; but I know nothing more rare, even in this country, than a fit scientific estimate and reverent appreciation of the People—of their measureless wealth of latent power and capacity, their vast, artistic contrasts of lights and shades—and in America, their entire reliability in emergencies, and a certain breadth of historic grandeur, of peace or war, surpassing all the vaunted samples of the personality of book-heroes, in all the records of the world.

The movements of the late war, and their results, to any sense that studies well and comprehends them, show that Popular Democracy practically justifies itself beyond the proudest claims and wildest hopes of its enthusiasts. Probably no future age can know, as we well know, how the gist of this fiercest and most resolute of the world's warlike contentions resided exclusively in the unnamed, unknown rank and file; and how the brunt of its labor of death was, to all essential purposes, Volunteered. The People, of their own choice, fighting, dying for their own idea, insolently attacked by the Secession-Slave-Power, and its very existence imperilled. Descending to detail, entering any of the armies, and mixing with the private soldiers, we see and have seen august spectacles.We have seen the alacrity with which the American-born populace, the peaceablest and most good-natured race in the world, and the most personally independent and intelligent, and the least fitted to submit to the irksomeness and exasperation of regimental discipline, sprang, at the first tap of the drum, to arms—not for gain, nor even glory, nor to repel invasion—but for an emblem, a mere abstraction— for the life, *the safety of the Flag.* We have seen the unequalled docility and obedience of these soldiers. We have seen them tried long and long by hopelessness, mismanagement, and by defeat; have seen the incredible slaughter toward or through which the armies (as at first Fredericksburg, and afterward at the Wilderness), still unhesitatingly obeyed orders to advance. We have seen them in trench, or crouching behind breastwork, or tramping in deep mud, or amid pouring rain or snow, or under forced marches in hottest Summer (as on the road to get to Gettysburg), vast suffocating swarms, divisions, corps, with every single man so grimed and black with sweat and dust, his own mother would not have known him; his clothes all dirty, stained and torn, with sour, accumulated sweat for perfume, many a comrade, perhaps a brother, sun-struck, staggering out, dying, by the roadside, of exhaustion—yet the great bulk bearing steadily on, cheery enough, hollow-bellied from hunger, but sinewy with unconquerable resolution.

We have seen this race proved by wholesale by drearier, yet more fearful tests—the wound, the amputation, the shattered face or limb, the slow, hot fever, long, impatient anchorage in bed, and all the forms of maiming, operation and disease. Alas! America have we seen, though only in her early youth, already to hospital brought. There have we watched these soldiers, many of them only boys in years—marked their decorum, their religious nature and fortitude, and their sweet affection. Wholesale, truly! For at the front, and through the camps, in countless tents, stood the regimental, brigade and division hospitals; while everywhere amid the land, in or near cities, rose clusters of huge, whitewashed, crowded, wooden barracks, (Washington City alone, at one period, containing in her Army hospitals of this kind, 50,000 wounded and sick men)—and there ruled Agony with bitter scourge, yet seldom brought a cry; and there stalked Death by day and night along the narrow aisles between the rows of cots, or by the blankets on the ground, and touched lightly many a poor sufferer, often with blessed, welcome touch.

I know not whether I shall be understood, but I realize that it is finally from what I learned in such scenes that I am now penning this article. One night in the gloomiest period of the war, in the Patent Office Hospital, as I stood by the bedside of a Pennsylvania soldier, who lay, conscious of quick approaching death, yet perfectly calm, and with noble, spiritual manner, the veteran surgeon, Dr. Stone (Horatio Stone, the sculptor), turning aside, said to me that though he had witnessed many, many deaths of soldiers, and had been a worker at Bull Run, Antietam, Fredericksburg, etc., he had not seen yet the first case of man or boy that met the approach of dissolution with cowardly qualms or terror. My own observation fully bears out the remark.

What have we here, if not, towering above all talk and argument, the plentifully-supplied, last-needed proof of Democracy, in its personalities?

Grand, common stock! to me the accomplished and convincing growth, prophetic of the future; proof undeniable to sharpest sense, of perfect beauty, tenderness and pluck, that never Feudal lord, nor Greek nor Roman breed, yet rivalled. Let no tongue ever speak in disparagement of the American races, North or South, to one who has been through the war in the great Army hospitals.

—Meantime, Humanity (for we will not shirk anything) has always, in every department, been full of perverse maleficence, and is so yet. In downcast hours the Soul thinks it always will be—but soon recovers from such sickly moods. I, as Democrat, see clearly enough (none more clearly), the crude, defective streaks in all the strata of the common people; the specimens and vast collections of the ignorant, the credulous, the unfit and uncouth, the incapable and the very low and poor. The eminent person, in his conscientious cry just mentioned, sneerlingly asks whether we expect to elevate and improve politics by absorbing such morbid collections and qualities therein. The point is a formidable one, and there will doubtless always be numbers of solid citizens who will never get over it. Our answer is general, and is involved in the scope and letter of this article. We believe the object of political and all other government (having, of course, provided for the police, the safety of life, property, and the basic common and civil law, always first in order) to be, among the rest, not merely to rule, to repress disorder, etc., but to develop, to open up to cultivation, to encourage the possibilities of all beneficent and manly outcroppage, and of that aspiration for independence, and the pride and self-respect latent in all characters. (Or, if there be exceptions, we cannot, fixing our eyes on them alone, make theirs the rule for all.)

The mission of government, henceforth, in civilized lands, is not authority alone, not even of law, nor by that favorite standard of the eminent writer, the rule of the best men, the born heroes and captains of the race (as if such ever, or one time out of a hundred, got into the big places, elective or dynastic!)—but, higher than the highest arbitrary rule, to train communities through all their grades, beginning with individuals and ending there again, to rule themselves.

What Christ appeared for in the moral-spiritual field for Humankind, namely, that in respect to the absolute Soul, there is in the possession of such by each single individual, something so transcendent, so incapable of gradations (like life), that, to that extent, it places all beings on a common level, utterly regardless of the distinctions of intellect, station, or any height or lowliness whatever—is tallied in like manner, in this other field, by Democracy's rule that men, the Nation, as a common aggregate of living identities, affording in each a separate and complete subject for freedom, worldly thrift and happiness, and for a fair chance for growth, and for protection, in citizenship, etc., must, to the political extent of the suffrage or vote, if no further, be placed, in each and in the whole, on one broad, primary, universal, common platform.

The purpose is not altogether direct; perhaps it is more indirect. To be a voter with the rest is not so much; and this, like every institute, will have its imperfections. But to become an enfranchised man, and now to stand and start without humiliation, and equal with the rest; to commence, or have the road cleared to commence, the grand experiment of development, whose end, perhaps requiring several generations, may be the forming of a full-grown manly or womanly Personality—that *is* something. To ballast the state is also secured, and in our times is to be secured, in no other way.

We do not (at any rate I do not) put it either so much on the ground that the People, the masses, even the best of them are, in their latent or exhibited qualities, essentially sensible and good—nor on the ground of their rights; but that, good or bad, rights or no rights, the Democratic formula is the only safe and preservative one for coming times. We endow the masses with the suffrage for their own sake, no doubt; then, still more, from another point of view, for community's sake. Leaving the rest to the sentimentalists, we present Freedom as sufficient in its scientific aspects, cold as ice, reasoning, clear and passionless as crystal.

Democracy too is law, and of the strictest, amplest kind. Many suppose (and often in its own ranks the error) that it means a throwing aside of law, and running riot. But, briefly, it is the superior law, not alone that of physical force, the body, which, adding to, it supersedes with that of the spirit. Law is the unshakable order of the universe forever; and the law over all, and law of laws, is the law of successions; that of the superior law, in time, gradually supplanting and overwhelming the inferior one. (While, for myself, I would cheerfully agree—first covenanting that the formative tendencies shall be administered in favor, or, at least not against it, and that this reservation be closely construed—that until the individual or community show due signs, or be so minor and fractional as not to endanger the State, the condition of tutelage may continue, and self-government must abide its time.)

—Nor is the esthetic point, always an important one, without fascination for highest aiming souls. The common ambition strains for common elevations, to become some privileged exclusive. The master sees greatness and health in being part of the mass. Nothing will do as well as common ground. Would you have in yourself the divine, vast, general law? Then merge yourself in it.

And, topping Democracy, this most alluring record, that it alone can bind, and ever seeks to bind, all nations, all men, of however various and distant lands, into a brotherhood, a family. It is the old, yet ever-modern dream of Earth, out of her eldest and her youngest, her fond philosophers and poets. Not this half only, this Individualism, which isolates. There is another half, which is Adhesiveness or Love, that fuses, ties and aggregates, making the races comrades, and fraternizing all. Both are to be vitalized by Religion (sole worthiest elevator of man or State) breathing into the proud, material tissues, the breath of life. For at the core of Democracy, finally, is the Religious element. All the Religions, old and new, are there. Nor may the Scheme step forth, clothed in resplendent beauty and command, till these, bearing the best, the latest fruit, the Spiritual, the aspirational, shall fully appear.

—Portions of our pages we feel to indite with reference toward Europe more than our own land, and thus, perhaps not absolutely needed for the home reader. But the whole question hangs together, and fastens and links all peoples. The Liberalist of to-day has this advantage over antique or medieval times, that his doctrine seeks both to universalize as well as individualize. The great word Solidarity has arisen.

How, then (for in that shape forebodes the current deluge)—how shall we, good-class folk, meet the rolling, mountainous surges of "swarmery" that already beat upon and threaten to overwhelm us? What disposal, short of wholesale throat-cutting and extermination (which seems not without its advantages), offers, for the countless herds of "hoofs and hobnails," that will somehow, and so perversely get themselves born, and grow up to annoy and vex us? What under heaven is to become of "nigger Cushee," that imbruted and lazy being— now, worst of all, preposterously free? etc. Never before such a yawning gulf; never such danger as now from incarnated Democracy advancing, with the laboring classes at its back. Woe the day; woe the doings, the prospects thereof! England, or any respectable land, giving the least audience to these "servants of the mud gods," or, utterly infatuate, extending to them the suffrage, takes swift passage therewith, bound for the infernal pit. Ring the alarum bell! Put the flags at half mast! Or, rather, let each man spring for the nearest loose spar or plank. The ship is going down!

Be not so moved, not to say distraught, my venerable friend. Spare those spasms of dread and disgust. England, after her much-widened suffrage, as she did before, will still undergo troubles and tribulations, without doubt; but they will be as nothing to what (in the judgment of all heads not quite careened and addled), would certainly follow the spirit, carried out in any modern nation, these days, of your appeal or diatribe. Neither by berating them, nor twitting them with their low condition of ignorance and misery, nor by leaving them as they are, nor by turning the screws still tighter, nor by taking even the most favorable chances for "the noble Few" to come round with relief, will the demon of that "unanimous vulgar" (paying very heavy taxes) be pacified and made harmless any more. Strangely enough, about the only way to really lay the fiend appears to be this very way—the theme of these your ravings. A sort of fate and antique Nemesis, of the highest old Greek tragedy sort, is in it (as in our own Play, or affair, rapidly played of late here in the South, through all the acts—indeed a regular, very wondrous Eschuylean piece—to that old part First, that bound and chained unkillable Prometheus, now, after twenty-three hundred years, very grandly and epico-dramatically supplementing and fully supplying the lost, or never before composed, Second and Third parts). Your noble, hereditary, Anglo-Saxon-Norman institutions (still here so loudly championed and battled for in your argument) having been, through some seven or eight centuries, thriftily engaged in cooking up this mess, have now got to eat it. The only course eligible, it is plain, is to plumply confront, embrace, absorb, swallow (O, big and bitter pill!) the entire British "swarmery," demon, "loud roughs" and all. These ungrateful men, not satisfied with the poor-house for their old age, and the charity-school for their infants, evidently mean business—may-be of bloody kind. By all odds, my friend, the thing to do is to make a flank movement, surround them, disarm them, give them their first degree, incorporate them in the State as voters, and then—wait for the next emergency.

Nor may I permit myself to dismiss this utterance of the eminent person without pronouncing its laboriously-earned and fully-deserved credit for about the highest eminence attained yet, in a certain direction, of any linguistic product, written or spoken, to me known. I have had occasion in my past life (being born, as it were, with propensities, from my earliest years, to attend popular American speech-gatherings, conventions, nominations, camp-meetings, and the like, and also as a reader of newspapers, foreign and domestic)—I therefore know that trial to one's ears and brains from divers creatures, alluded to by sample, and well-hetchelled in this diatribe, crow-cawing the words Liberty, loyalty, human rights, constitutions, etc. I, too, have heard the ceaseless braying, screaming blatancy (on behalf of my own side), making noisiest threats and clatter stand for sense. But I must now affirm that such a comic-painful hullabaloo and vituperative cat-squalling as this about "the Niagara leap," "swarmery," "Orsonism," etc. (meaning, in point, as I make out, simply extending to full-grown British working-folk, farmers, mechanics, clerks, and so on—the "industrial aristocracy," indeed, there named—the privilege of the ballot, or vote, deciding, by popular majorities, who shall be designated to sit in one of the two Houses of Parliament, if it mean anything), I never yet encountered; no, not even in extremest hour of midnight, in whooping Tennessee revival, or Bedlam let loose in crowded, colored Carolina bush-meeting.

But to proceed, and closer to our text.

The curse and canker of Nations politically has been—or, at any rate, will be, as things have come to exist in our day—the having of certain portions of the people set off from the rest by a line drawn—they not privileged as others, but degraded, humiliated, made of no account. We repeat it, the question is, finally, one of Science—the science of the present and the future. Much quackery teems, of course, yet does not really affect the orbic quality of the matter. To work in, if we may so term it, and justify God, his divine aggregate, the People (or, the veritable horned and fluketailed Devil, *his* aggregate, then, since you so convulsively insist upon it, O eminence!)—this, without doubt, is what Democracy is for; and this is what our America means, and is doing—may I not say, has done? If not, she means nothing more, and does nothing more than any other land. And as, by virtue of its cosmical, antiseptic power, Nature's stomach is fully strong enough not only to digest the morbific matter always presented, not to be turned aside, and perhaps, indeed, intuitively gravitating thither— but even to change such contributions into nutriment for highest use and life—so American Democracy's. That is the lesson we, these days, send over to European lands by every western breeze.

And, truly, whatever may be said in the way of abstract argument, for or against the theory of a wider democratizing of institutions in any civilized country, much trouble might well be saved to those European lands by recognizing this palpable fact (for a palpable fact it is), that some form of such democratizing is about the only resource now left. *That,* or chronic dissatisfaction continued, mutterings which grow annually louder and louder, till, in due course, and pretty swiftly in most cases, the inevitable crisis, crash, dynastic ruin. Anything worthy to be called statesmanship in the Old World, I should say, among the advanced students, adepts, or men of any brains, does not debate to-day whether to hold on, attempting to lean back and monarchize, or to look forward and democratize—but *how,* and in what degree and part, most prudently to democratize. The difficulties of the transfer may be fearful; perhaps none here in our America can truly know them. I, for one, fully acknowledge them, and sympathize deeply. But there is Time, and must be Faith; and Opportunities, though gradual and slow, will everywhere be born. And beaming like a star, to any and to all, whatever else may for a while be quenched, shines not the eternal signal in the West?

—There is (turning home again) a thought, or fact, I must not forget—subtle and vast, dear to America, twin-sister of its Democracy— so ligatured indeed to it, that either's death, if not the other's also, would make that other live out life, dragging a corpse, a loathsome, horrid tag and burden forever at its feet. What the idea of Messiah was to the ancient race of Israel, through storm and calm, through public glory and their name's humiliation, tenacious, refusing to be argued with, shedding all shafts of ridicule and disbelief, undestroyed by captivities, battles, deaths—for neither the scalding blood of war, nor the rotted ichor of peace could ever wash it out, nor has yet—a great Idea, bedded in Judah's heart—source of the loftiest Poetry the world yet knows—continuing on the same, though all else varies—the spinal thread of the incredible romance of that people's career along five thousand years—so runs this thought, this fact, amid our own land's race and history. It is the thought of Oneness, averaging, including all; of Identity—the indissoluble Union of These States.

—The eager and often inconsiderate appeals of reformers and revolutionists are indispensable to counterbalance the inertness and fossilism making so large a part of human institutions. The latter will always take care of themselves. The former is to be treated with indulgence, and even respect. As circulation to air, so is agitation and a plentiful degree of speculative license to political and moral sanity.

Indirectly, but surely, goodness, virtue, law (of the very best) follow Freedom. These, to Democracy, are what the keel is to the ship, or saltness to the ocean.

The gravitation-hold of Liberalism will be a more universal owner-ship of property, general homesteads, general comfort—a vast, inter-twining reticulation of wealth. No community furnished throughout with homes, and substantial, however moderate, incomes, commits suicide, or "shoots Niagara." As the human frame, or, indeed, any object in this manifold Universe, is best kept together by the simple miracle of its own cohesion, and the necessity and profit thereof, so a great and varied Nationality, occupying millions of square miles, were firmest held and knit by the principle of the safety and endurance of the aggregate of its middling property owners.

So that, from another point of view, ungracious as it may sound, and a paradox after what we have been saying, Democracy looks with suspicious, ill-satisfied eye upon the very poor, and on the ignorant. She asks for men and women well-off, owners of houses and acres, and with cash in the bank—and with some cravings for literature, too; and must have them, and hastens to make them. Luckily, the seed is already well-sown, and has taken ineradicable root.

—Huge and mighty are our Days, our republican lands—and most in their rapid shiftings, their changes, all in the interest of the Cause. As I write, the din of disputation rages around me. Acrid the temper of the parties, vital the pending questions. Congress convenes; the President sends his Message; Reconstruction is still in abeyance; the nominations and the contest for the twenty-first Presidentiad draw close, with the loudest threat and bustle. Of these, and all the like of these, the eventuations I know not; but well I know that behind them, and whatever their eventuations, the really vital things remain safe and certain, and all the needed work goes on. Time, with soon or later superciliousness, disposes of Presidents, Congressmen, party platforms, and such. Anon, it clears the stage of each and any mortal shred that thinks itself so potent to its day; and at and after which (with precious, golden exceptions once or twice in a century), all that relates to sir potency is flung to moulder in a burial-vault, and no one bothers him-self the least bit about it afterward. But the People ever remains, ten-dencies continue, and all the idiocratic transfers in unbroken chain go on. In a few years the dominion-heart of America will be far inland, toward the West. Our future National Capitol will not be where the present one is. I should say that certainly, in less than fifty years, it will migrate a thousand or two miles, will be re-founded, and every thing belonging to it made on a different plan, original, far more superb. The main social, political spine-character of The States will probably run along the Ohio, Missouri and Mississippi Rivers, and west and north of them, including Canada. Those regions, with the group of powerful brothers toward the Pacific (destined to the mastership of that sea and its countless Paradises of islands), will compact and settle the traits of America, with all the old retained, but more expanded, grafted on newer, hardier, purely native stock. A giant growth, composite from the rest, getting their contribution, absorbing it to make it more illustrious. From the North, Intellect, the sun of things—also the idea of unswayable Justice, anchor amid the last, the wildest tempests. From the South, the living Soul, the animus of good and bad, haughtily admitting no demonstration but its own. While from the West itself comes solid Personality, with blood and brawn, and the deep quality of all-accepting fusion.

Political Democracy, as it exists and practically works in America, supplies a training-school for making grand young men. It is life's gymnasium, not of good only, but of all. We try often, though we fall back often. A brave delight, fit for freedom's athletes, fills these arenas, and fully satisfies, out of the action in them, irrespective of success. Whatever we do not attain, we at any rate attain the experiences of the fight, the hardening of the strong campaign, and throb with currents of attempt at least. Time is ample. Let the victors come after us. Not for nothing does evil play its part among men. *Vive,* the attack—the perennial assault! *Vive,* the unpopular cause—the spirit that audaciously aims—the courage that dies not—the never-abandoned efforts, pursued the same amid opposing proofs and precedents.

—Once, before the war, I, too, was filled with doubt and gloom. A traveller, an acute and good man, had impressively said to me, that day—putting in form, indeed, my own observations: I have traveled much in the United States, and watched their politicians, and listened to the speeches of the candidates, and read the journals, and gone into the public houses, and heard the unguarded talk of men. And I have found your vaunted America honey-combed from top to toe with infidelism, even to itself and its own programme. I have marked the brazen hell-faces of secession and slavery gazing defiantly from all the windows and doorways. I have everywhere found, primarily, thieves and scalliwags arranging the nominations to offices, and sometimes filling the offices themselves. I have found the North just as full of bad stuff as the South. Of the holders of public office in the Nation, or in the States, or their municipalities, I have found that not one in a hundred has been chosen by any spontaneous selection of the outsiders, the people, but all have been nominated and put through by little or large caucuses of the politicians, and have got in by electioneering, not desert. I have noticed how the millions of sturdy farmers and mechanics are thus the helpless supple-jacks of comparatively few politicians. And I have noticed more and more, the alarming spectacle of parties usurping the Government, and openly and shamelessly wielding it for party purposes.

Sad, serious, deep truths. Yet are there other, still deeper, amply confronting, dominating truths. Over those politicians, and over all their insolence and wiles, and over the powerfulest parties, looms a Power, too sluggish may-be, but ever holding decisions and decrees in hand, ready, with stern process to execute them as soon as plainly needed, and at times, indeed, summarily crushing to atoms the mightiest parties, even in the hour of their pride.

Far different are the amounts of these things from what, at first sight, they appear. Though it is no doubt important who is elected President or Governor, Mayor or Legislator, there are other, quieter contingencies, infinitely more important. Shams, etc., will always be the show, like ocean's scum; enough if waters deep and clear make up the rest. Enough, that while the piled embroidered shoddy gaud and fraud spreads to the superficial eye, the hidden warp and weft are genuine, and will wear forever. Enough, in short, that the race, the land which could raise such as the late rebellion, could also put it down.

The average man of a land at last only is important. He, in These States, remains immortal owner and boss, deriving good uses, somehow, out of any sort of servant in office, even the basest; because (certain universal requisites, and their settled regularity and protection, being first secured), a Nation like ours, in the formation state, trying continually new experiments, choosing new delegations, is not served by the best men only, but sometimes more by those that provoke it—by the combats they arouse. Thus national rage, fury, discussion, etc., sublimer than content. Thus, also, the warning signals, invaluable for after times.

What is more dramatic than the spectacle we have seen repeated, and doubtless long shall see—the popular judgment taking the successful candidates on trial in the offices—standing off, as it were, and observing them and their doings for a while, and always giving, finally, the fit, exactly due reward.

—When I pass to and fro, different latitudes, different seasons, beholding the crowds of the great cities, New York, Boston, Philadelphia, Cincinnati, Chicago, St. Louis, San Francisco, New Orleans, Baltimore—when I mix with these interminable swarms of alert, turbulent, good-natured, independent citizens, mechanics, clerks, young persons— at the the idea of this mass of men, so fresh and free, so loving and so proud, a singular awe falls upon me. I feel, with dejection and amazement, that among our geniuses and talented writers or speakers, few or none have yet really spoken to this people, or obsorbed the central spirit and the idiosyncrasies which are theirs, and which, thus, in highest ranges, so far remain entirely uncelebrated, unexpressed.

Dominion strong is the body's; dominion stronger is the mind's. What has filled, and fills to-day our intellect, our fancy, furnishing the standards therein, is yet foreign. The great poems, Shakespeare included, are poisonous to the idea of the pride and dignity of the common people, the life-blood of Democracy. The models of our literature, as we get it from other lands, ultramarine, have had their birth originally in courts, and basked and grown in castle sunshine; all smells of princes' favors. For esthetic Europe is yet exclusively feudal.

The literature of These States, a new projection, when it comes, must be the born outcrop, through all rich and luxuriant forms, but stern and exclusive, of the sole Idea of The States, belonging here alone. Of course, of workers of a certain sort, we have already plenty, contributing after their kind; many elegant, many learned, all complacent. But, touched by the National test, they wither to ashes. I say I have not seen one single writer, artist, lecturer, or what not, that has confronted the voiceless but ever erect and active, pervading, underlying will and typic Aspiration of the land, in a spirit kindred to itself. Do you call those genteel little creatures American poets? Do you term that perpetual, pistareen, pasteboard work, American art, American opera, drama, taste, verse? I think I hear, echoed as from some mountain-top afar in the West, the scornful laugh of the Genius of These States.

—Democracy, in silence, biding its time, ponders its own ideals, not of men only, but of women. The idea of the women of America (extricated from this daze, this fossil and unhealthy air which hangs about the word, Lady), developed, raised to become the robust equals, workers, and even practical and political deciders with the men— greater than man, we may admit, through their divine maternity, always their towering, emblematical attribute—but great, at any rate, as man, in all departments; or, rather, capable of being so, soon as they realize it, and can bring themselves to give up toys and fictions, and launch forth, as men do, amid real, independent, stormy life.

—Then, as toward finale (and, in that, overarching the true scholar's lesson), we have to say there can be no complete or epical presentation of Democracy, or any thing like it, at this day, because its doctrines will only be effectually incarnated in any one branch, when, in all, their spirit is at the root and centre. How much is still to be disentangled, freed! How long it takes to make this world see that it is, in itself, the final authority and reliance!

Did you, too, suppose Democracy was only for elections, for politics, and for a party name? I say Democracy is only of use there that it may pass on and come to its flower and fruits in manners, in the highest forms of interaction between men, and their beliefs—Democracy in all public and private life, and in the Army and Navy. I have intimated that, as a paramount scheme, it has yet few or no full realizers and believers. I do not see, either, that it owes any serious thanks to noted propagandists or champions, or has been essentially helped, though often harmed, by them. It has been and is carried on by all the moral forces, and by trade, finance, machinery, intercommunications, etc., and can no more be stopped than the tides, or the earth in its orbit. Doubtless, also, it resides, crude and latent, well down in the hearts of the fair average of the American-born people, mainly in the agricultural regions. But it is not yet, there or anywhere, the fully-received, the fervid, the absolute faith.

I submit, therefore, that the fruition of Democracy, on aught like a grand scale, resides altogether in the future. As, under any profound and comprehensive view of the gorgeous-composite Feudal world, we see in it, through the long ages and cycles of ages, the results of a deep, integral, human and divine principle, or fountain, from which issued law, ecclesia, manners, institutes, costumes, personalities, poems (hitherto unequalled), faithfully partaking of their source, and indeed only arising either to betoken it, or to furnish parts of that varied-flowing display, whose centre was one and absolute—so, long ages hence, shall the due historian or critic make at least an equal retrospect, an equal History for the Democratic principle. It, too, must be adorned, credited with its results; then, when it, with imperial power, through amplest time, has dominated mankind—has been the source and test of all the moral, esthetic, social, political, and religious expressions and institutes of the civilized world—has begotten them in spirit and in form, and carried them to its own unprecedented heights—has had monastics and ascetics, more numerous, more devout than the monks and priests of all previous creeds—has swayed the ages with a breadth and rectitude tallying Nature's own—has fashioned, systematized, and triumphantly finished and carried out, in its own interest, and with unparalleled success, a New Earth and a New Man.

—Thus we presume to write, as it were, upon things that exist not, and travel by maps yet unmade, and a blank. But the throes of birth are upon us; and we have something of this advantage in seasons of strong formations, doubts, suspense—for then the afflatus of such themes haply may fall upon us, more or less; and then, hot from surrounding revolution, our speech, though without polished coherence, and a failure by the standard called criticism, comes forth, real at least, as the lightnings.

And may-be we, these days, have, too, our own reward (for there are yet some, in all lands, worthy to be so encouraged.) Though not for us the joy of entering at the last the conquered city—nor ours the chance ever to see with our own eyes the peerless power and splendid *eclat* of the Democratic principle, arrived at meridian, filling the world with effulgence and majesty far beyond those of past history's kings, or all dynastic sway; there is yet, to whoever is eligible among us, the prophetic vision, the joy of being tossed in the brave turmoil of these times—the promulgation and the path, obedient, lowly reverent to the voice, the gesture of the god, or holy ghost, which others see not, hear not—with the proud consciousness that amid whatever clouds, seductions, or heart-wearying postponements, we have never deserted, never despaired, never abandoned the Faith.

EMILY DICKINSON (1830–1866)

There was something about Emily Dickinson's private little drama that invited quantities of nonsense from her biographers. Emily the "New England nun"; Emily the broken-hearted lover; Emily the quaint little lady tossing poems and flowers across her fence to the neighbors; Emily the oracle in quatrains; Emily the subject of more saccharine books than any other American writer. Here, however, we start with the assumption that the only Emily Dickinson who matters is the author of 1,775 poems, most of them bad, a goodly number fine, and a few dozen great.

Emily Dickinson was born in Amherst, Massachusetts, and except for a trip to Washington and Philadelphia, and two or three visits to Boston, she never left home. Even Mount Holyoke College, which she attended for a year, was only a few miles away.

She lived in a small compass but with great concentration. The few people she knew loomed large. First, there was her father, a man whose heart she described as "pure and terrible," a lawyer, treasurer of Amherst College, a Congressman, and pillar of the First Church. Both at church, which the family attended twice on Sundays, and at college, where the students were grouped according to their professions of Christianity, Emily Dickinson, unable to believe, knew the experience of "fleeing from Sacrament." Yet those who have once lived within its reach can rarely flee sacrament entirely: what she rebelled against would nevertheless be the main influence upon, and the unavoidable setting of, her work.

"I don't know anything more about affairs in the world than if I was in a trance," said Emily Dickinson at the age of sixteen. Her first link with the world was a lawyer named Benjamin Newton, who apparently gave her some religious and literary guidance and whom she described as "a friend who taught me Immortality." Charles Wadsworth, a spotless Presbyterian minister with wife and children, was Emily Dickinson's first and great love; when he accepted a call to Calvary Church in San Francisco, she began to dress immaculately in white and to write copiously, averaging a poem a day in 1862.

A few of these she sent to Thomas Wentworth Higginson, a Unitarian clergyman and influential critic, who became for Miss Dickinson just about the only public audience she had. He encouraged, he sympathized with, and sometimes he understood. In the last decade of her life, Miss Dickinson is said again to have fallen in love, this time with Judge Otis P. Lord. But the ways of the recluse were by now irrevocable and she died as she had lived: "I do not cross my

*father's ground to any house or town." At her death seven of her
poems had appeared in print, and only in the 1890s, when her relatives and Higginson began to publish her work, did she receive any
public attention.*

To feel sorry for Emily Dickinson is as foolish as it is presumptuous.
"When she went upstairs and closed the door," writes Allen Tate,
"she mastered life by rejecting it. Others in their way had done it
before; still others did it later. If we suppose—which is to suppose
the improbable—that the love affair precipitated the seclusion, it
was only a pretext; she would have found another. Mastery of the
world by rejecting the world was the doctrine, even if not always
the practise, of Jonathan Edwards and Cotton Mather."

By the standards of the late nineteenth century, both the decades in
which she wrote and the one in which she was first published, Miss
Dickinson's poems were eccentric, amateurish, and barbaric. They
were metrically unpolished; they relied on odd verbal coinages;
they were often difficult to understand; and when understood, they
betrayed ideas both shocking and perverse. It was hard to think of
Emily Dickinson as "refined" in the sense that Elizabeth Barrett
Browning was.

Technically, Miss Dickinson's poems follow a cluster of simple patterns.
They are derived from the English hymn, notably from Isaac Watt's
collection, The Psalms, Hymns and Spiritual Songs, which was a
standard item in every New England household. English hymns
consisted of quatrains arranged in four lines of eight syllables each
(long meter), or four lines alternating eight and six syllables each
(common meter), or four lines with two of six syllables each, one
of eight, and then one of six (short meter). Having been shrewdly
taught by the hymnals that long meter bears the risk of monotony,
Miss Dickinson used it sparingly; most of her poems are in common meter, and a few—but among the most splendid—are in short
meter. Naturally, she varied these patterns a good deal, sometimes
dropping a syllable, sometimes substituting trochaic and dactylic
for iambic stresses. Her major innovations concerned diction and
rhyme. She allowed herself coinages—some brilliant, some merely
impudent—as well as elliptical phrases compressed to the gnomic
and metaphors of incongruity and shock. She rhymed with a freedom unknown in her day, though common enough in the twentieth
century, using eye rhymes, imperfect rhymes, and suspended
rhymes. Some of these experiments (it is not clear whether she
thought of them as experiments) will strike modern readers as successful, and others as evidence of the cost a writer must pay who
works in too great an isolation from the traditions of her culture.

About Emily Dickinson's intellectual background—which is mostly to say, her relationship to the Christianity of New England—there has been much dispute. It is not a matter to be settled in this note. One thing does seem clear: she lived within the ambience of Calvinism and experienced both the power and chaos of its decline; she knew the heritage of doctrine and the imperiousness of a morality received down the generations. The evidence suggests, however, that she was neither a practicing nor an orthodox Christian. Poems can be brought as evidence for almost any religious position. She wrote some that are explicitly in rebellion against Christianity; some that express her dislike for the "punishing" aspect of religion; some in which she quarrels with Christ; some which even flirt with Satanism; and some, of course, that could be written only by a person with a strong religious consciousness or, still more, a person familiar with that state of religious surrender we call "transport." Emily Dickinson was not, in any serious sense of the term, a mystic: there is no evidence that she sought or reached a direct communion with the godhead. Nor was she, like Jones Very, a devotional poet. Yet Christ was a constant and looming presence in her world; thoughts of sin, grace, and redemption were real to her, whether in the acceptance or denying. Austin Warren has written well on this side of her:

> Her rearing was in Trinitarian Congregationalism, often in New England villages referred to as—in contrast to Unitarian heresy—the Orthodox Church. Unlike the rest of her family . . . Emily never "joined the church," never would fix the content of her belief; but she knew what her neighbors and her pastor believed, and like Emerson in his attacks on Harvard College, had the personal comfort and poetic license of cherishing favorite skepticisms without supposing that they would undermine, and hence render impossible of attack, the solid faith of others. . . . She lacks Hawthorne's sense of sin, and isolation for privacy is hardly an evil to her; the analogy to Hawthorne lies rather in her obsession with death and futurity—still more the sense of mystery. . . . Her deepest poems are metaphysical or tragic; her mode of vision symbolist—thinking in analogies. Emerson (whose Essays an early "tutor" gave her) may have flexed her mind, encouraged her speculations and her questionings of orthodoxy; but her mythology remains—what Hawthorne's was and Emerson's never—Biblical and Trinitarian. She is a rebel—but not, like Emerson, a schismatic.

Let us try briefly to describe the kinds of poems she wrote. They seldom sing; nor can they be chanted in a large rhetorical style; and the best of them are rarely charming or sweet. Primarily they are poems of statement and linked perception—statement condensed to wit and epigram, perception brought to brilliance by her capacity for *yoking together incongruous elements of experience, from the quid-dities of housework to the immensities of Christian doctrine. Some-times her poems follow the pattern of the riddle—"Tell all the truth but tell it slant"—though not, at her best, in behalf of verbal display or dazzle. In her best poems Emily Dickinson penetrates to a version of truth and seeks to quicken the common perceptions of daily life into a widening awareness of the pleasures and terrors of mortality. She is a "wisdom poet," but her wisdom is quirky, tangential, odd. In her inferior poems, it is eccentric, countrified, cute.*

The few dozen great poems Emily Dickinson wrote are notable for the way in which she combines the sensation of surprise with the im-pression of inevitability. "After great pain, a formal feeling comes/ The nerves sit ceremonious, like tombs." We read these lines and may at first be slightly bewildered by the use of "formal" in the first one, though we probably guess that everything depends on it. We then decide that the very unusualness is here a brilliant stroke, for what Miss Dickinson is saying here can partly be paraphrased as follows: After great suffering we find it necessary and restorative to return to fixed and even ritualized ways of behavior, for they bring a sort of peace, or at least a measure of relief. Though still wrought up (they "sit"), the nerves can thereby achieve an equilib-rium in tension, so that the pain which continues is experienced in a somewhat more bearable fashion (the nerves are "like tombs," the places where the causes and sensations of pain are interred and thereby kept at some distance.) After scrutinizing lines like these, the sense of surprise they yield is heightened when we also acknowledge the inevitability of the perception they contain—that feeling of yes, we have known the experience too, though have never been able to describe it so well.

Through such dramatic images and contrasts of incongruity, Emily Dickinson achieves the inner motion of her poems. Brief and seem-ingly uneventful, they often race through the very span of mor-tality, achieving through generalization, example, and ironic quali-fication a life span in a few stanzas.

The central areas of concern in Miss Dickinson's poems are these: the natural world, stirred by her impatient eye into animation, but seldom sentimentalized or seen in Emersonian terms as a spiritual emblem or an object of pantheistic immersion; then poems about the experience of love, but so far as we know, seldom directed toward a particular person and instead focused on the generalized dynamic of love, that is, on desiring, yielding, connecting; then poems that deal with the convolutions of moral experience; and finally a group pinning down moments of ecstacy or what we have called "transport."

This division is, of course, arbitrary, since many of Miss Dickinson's poems, especially the best ones, overlap these categories and evade them. Their strength is in releasing the energies and hungers of the human soul, especially as it must subsist on itself, "making do"—as New Englanders would put it—with the inevitabilities of isolation and loss. Alone in her garden or her room, Emily Dickinson seems to have experienced her life with greater intensity than most other human beings, or at least to have reported it with greater intensity. She learned that precisely through isolation—one of her obsessive themes—could the universe be reached. And death too is a major preoccupation in her poems. Sometimes it is the common experience of loss such as we all know; sometimes as an element quickening life; and most strangely of all, as a state of potential being foreseen and experienced. There are a number of remarkable poems ("Because I could not stop for death" is one) in which Emily Dickinson writes as if she were already dead and sending messages back—telegrams of fate—to the world of the living.

If the bulk of her poems fail, as the bulk of most writers' work must fail, the best are among the greatest in the English language. Her voice is unmistakable: she writes like no one else, before or after. The circumference of her experience is narrow but its content marvelously full, for she writes out of an organic experience. In one of her best poems, "There's a certain slant of life," she compares the light of a winter afternoon, in its capacity to oppress (depress) us, with "the heft of cathedral tunes." It is a bold simile, the force of which depends on our having some sense of how oppressive listening to "cathedral tunes" can be for a young girl, or a mature woman, like Emily Dickinson. By way of comparison, one thinks of a passage in the work of a writer utterly different from Miss Dickinson—the Yiddish story writer Sholom Aleichem who remarks in one of his stories that the voice of a cantor was as hoarse as if he had just finished the Yom Kippur services. Here too one must have some sense of the reference in its cultural context, behind which, as in Emily Dickinson's comparison, there is the whole weight of an organic culture.

Emily Dickinson's progress is summed up by a distinguished twentieth-century American poet, Louise Bogan:

> We see the young poet moving away, by gradual degrees, from her early slight addiction to graveyardism, to an Emersonian belief in the largeness and harmony of nature. Step by step, she advances into the terror and anguish of her destiny; she is frightened, but she holds fast and describes

her fright. She is driven to the verge of sanity, but manages to remain, in
some fashion, the observer and recorder of her extremity. Nature is no
longer a friend, but often an inimical presence. Nature is a haunted house.
And—a truth even more terrible—the inmost self can be haunted.

FURTHER READING

Biographical and critical studies include Charles Anderson's *Emily*
   Dickinson's Poetry: Stairway of Surprise (1960); Richard Chase's
   Emily Dickinson (1951); Thomas H. Johnson's *Emily Dickinson:*
   An Interpretative Biography (1955); and George F. Whicher's *This*
   Was a Poet: A Critical Biography of Emily Dickinson (1938).

A Note on the Texts

The textual status of Emily Dickinson's poems is enormously compli-
   cated and, as this anthology is being prepared, still a matter of
   some scholarly dispute. During her lifetime Emily Dickinson pub-
   lished, as far as we know, only seven of her poems, and these were
   printed anonymously. After her death, the remaining manuscripts
   were turned over by her sister, Lavinia, to a neighbor, Mrs. Mabel
   Loomis Todd, who, together with Emily Dickinson's old friend
   Thomas Wentworth Higginson, published in 1890 Poems by Emily
   Dickinson. *A Second Series appeared in 1891, and a* Third Series
   in 1896. In 1914 Martha Dickinson Bianchi, Emily's niece, issued
   still another collection of previously unpublished poems, The Single
   Hound, *and in 1924 she issued* The Complete Poems of Emily
   Dickinson—*which, as it turned out, was anything but complete.*
   And so it went until 1945 when Mrs. Todd and her daughter, Milli-
   cent Todd Bingham, brought out 668 still unpublished poems in
   Bolts of Melody. *Understandably, there was dismay among both*
   admirers of Emily Dickinson and scholars of American literature
   that the work of one of our greatest poets should be made available
   in this piecemeal way and by editors not perhaps fully trained for
   the task.

Finally, in 1955, Thomas H. Johnson published The Poems of Emily
   Dickinson *in three volumes, containing all 1,775 of her known*
   poems, their chronology, and their variants. Professor Johnson
   printed these poems in what purports to be the style first used by
   Emily Dickinson: a great many capitalizations and a highly indi-
   vidual (probably eccentric and private) mode of punctuation, with
   dashes of various lengths and angles replacing commas, semicolons,
   and periods.

For scholarly purposes Professor Johnson's edition is remarkably valu-
   able, though since its appearance it has been criticized by various

colleagues in matters of detail. Since 1955 it has become customary for many anthologists and editors to use Emily Dickinson's poems in the form presented by Professor Johnson.

Yet *it may be seriously doubted that, for ordinary readers not concerned with the fine points of textual variation, the Johnson edition is the most accessible or the most pleasing. Even in terms of literal accuracy of transcription, Professor Johnson simply could not reproduce the bewildering variety of punctuation symbols Emily Dickinson employed; nor do we have any reason to suppose that she regarded these as integral to final drafts—assuming that she thought in terms of final drafts.*

The *truth would therefore seem to be that we will never know exactly how Emily Dickinson wanted her poems finally to read and look. That being so, the responsibility of a future editor will be to provide texts that are as faithful as possible to the original, yet, through normalization of spelling and punctuation, do not distract attention from the matter of the poems. As Professor Johnson himself has recognized, his edition does not give us a satisfactory reading text: the eye rebels against the plethora of dashs, which make the page look like a battlefield strewn with bunkers and foxholes. Fortunately, some of the necessary editing has been done by the English poet James Reeves, who has issued a volume of selected Dickinson poems based on the Johnson text but with the spelling and punctuation normalized.*

So *that the reader can judge for himself the relative merits between versions of Emily Dickinson's poetry, in this anthology we offer two—that of Professor Johnson and that which follows his text but uses normalized spelling and punctuation. Left-hand pages present the work of Professor Johnson, and right-hand pages offer, with the exceptions of the last four poems, the editing of Mr. Reeves.*

Success Is Counted Sweetest

Success is counted sweetest
By those who ne'er succeed.
To comprehend a nectar
Requires sorest need.

Not one of all the purple Host
Who took the Flag today
Can tell the definition
So clear of Victory

As he defeated—dying—
On whose forbidden ear   *10*
The distant strains of triumph
Burst agonized and clear!

Exultation Is the Going

Exultation is the going
Of an inland soul to sea,
Past the houses—past the headlands—
Into deep Eternity—

Bred as we, among the mountains,
Can the sailor understand
The divine intoxication
Of the first league out from land?

What Inn Is This

What Inn is this
Where for the night
Peculiar Traveller comes?
Who is the Landlord?
Where the maids?
Behold, what curious rooms!
No ruddy fires on the hearth—
No brimming Tankards flow—
Necromancer! Landlord!
Who are these below?   *10*

Success Is Counted Sweetest

Success is counted sweetest
By those who ne'er succeed.
To comprehend a nectar
Requires sorest need.

Not one of all the purple host
Who took the flag today
Can tell the definition
So clear of victory

As he defeated, dying,
On whose forbidden ear   10
The distant strains of triumph
Burst agonized and clear.

Exultation Is the Going

Exultation is the going
Of an inland soul to sea,
Past the houses, past the headlands,
Into deep eternity.

Bred as we, among the mountains,
Can the sailor understand
The divine intoxication
Of the first league out from land?

What Inn Is This

What inn is this
Where for the night
Peculiar traveller comes?
Who is the landlord?
Where the maids?
Behold, what curious rooms!
No ruddy fires on the hearth—
No brimming tankards flow.
Necromancer! Landlord!
Who are these below?   10

Safe in Their Alabaster Chambers

Safe in their Alabaster Chambers—
Untouched by Morning—
And untouched by Noon—
Lie the meek members of the Resurrection—
Rafter of Satin—and Roof of Stone!

Grand go the Years—in the Crescent—above them—
Worlds scoop their Arcs—
And Firmaments—row—
Diadems—drop—and Doges—surrender—
Soundless as dots—on a Disc of Snow—   10
version of 1861

Wild Nights—Wild Nights!

Wild Nights—Wild Nights!
Were I with thee
Wild Nights should be
Our luxury!

Futile—the Winds—
To a Heart in port—
Done with the Compass—
Done with the Chart!

Rowing in Eden—
Ah, the Sea!   10
Might I but moor—Tonight—
In Thee!

There's a Certain Slant of Light

There's a certain Slant of light,
Winter Afternoons—
That oppresses, like the Heft
Of Cathedral Tunes—

Heavenly Hurt, it gives us—
We can find no scar,
But internal difference,
Where the Meanings, are—   *(continued on page 680)*

Safe in Their Alabaster Chambers

Safe in their alabaster chambers,
Untouched by morning
And untouched by noon,
Sleep the meek members of the resurrection—
Rafter of satin,
And roof of stone.

Grand go the years in the crescent above them,
Worlds scoop their arcs
And firmaments row,
Diadems drop and Doges surrender,   10
Soundless as dots on a disc of snow.

Wild Nights—Wild Nights!

Wild nights—wild nights!
Were I with thee,
Wild nights should be
Our luxury.

Futile the winds
To a heart in port
Done with the compass,
Done with the chart.

Rowing in Eden—
Ah, the sea!   10
Might I but moor tonight
In thee.

There's a Certain Slant of Light

There's a certain slant of light,
Winter afternoons,
That oppresses like the heft
Of cathedral tunes.

Heavenly hurt it gives us.
We can find no scar
But internal difference
Where the meanings are.   *(continued on page 681)*

(continued from page 678)
None may teach it—Any—
'Tis the Seal Despair—   *10*
An imperial affliction
Sent us of the Air—

When it comes, the Landscape listens—
Shadows—hold their breath—
When it goes, 'tis like the Distance
On the look of Death—

I Felt a Funeral in My Brain

I felt a Funeral, in my Brain,
And Mourners to and fro
Kept treading—treading—till it seemed
That Sense was breaking through—

And when they all were seated,
A Service, like a Drum—
Kept beating—beating—till I thought
My Mind was going numb—

And then I heard them lift a Box
And creak across my Soul   *10*
With those same Boots of Lead, again,
Then Space—began to toll,

As all the Heavens were a Bell,
And Being, but an Ear,
And I, and Silence, some strange Race
Wrecked, solitary, here—

And then a Plank in Reason, broke,
And I dropped down, and down—
And hit a World, at every plunge,
And Finished knowing—then—   *20*

The Soul Selects Her Own Society

The Soul selects her own Society—
Then—shuts the Door—
To her divine Majority—
Present no more—

Unmoved—she notes the Chariots—pausing—
At her low Gate—   *(continued on page 682)*

(continued from page 679)
None may teach it any—
'Tis the seal despair,   10
An imperial affliction
Sent us of the air.

When it comes the landscape listens,
Shadows hold their breath.
When it goes 'tis like the distance
On the look of death.

I Felt a Funeral in My Brain

I felt a funeral in my brain,
And mourners to and fro
Kept treading, treading, till it seemed
That sense was breaking through.

And when they all were seated,
A service like a drum
Kept beating, beating, till I thought
My mind was going numb.

And then I heard them lift a box
And creak across my soul   10
With those same boots of lead again,
Then space began to toll,

As all the Heavens were a bell,
And being but an ear,
And I and silence some strange race
Wrecked solitary here.

And then a plank in reason broke,
And I dropped down and down
And hit a world at every plunge,
And finished knowing then.   20

The Soul Selects Her Own Society

The soul selects her own society,
Then shuts the door.
To her divine majority
Present no more.

Unmoved she notes the chariots pausing
At her low gate;   *(continued on page 683)*

(continued from page 680)
Unmoved—an Emperor be kneeling
Upon her Mat—

I've known her—from an ample nation—
Choose One—   10
Then—close the Valves of her attention—
Like Stone—

It Might Be Lonelier

It might be lonelier
Without the Loneliness—
I'm so accustomed to my Fate—
Perhaps the Other—Peace—

Would interrupt the Dark—
And crowd the little Room—
Too scant—by Cubits—to contain
The Sacrament—of Him—

I am not used to Hope—
It might intrude upon—   10
Its sweet parade—blaspheme the place—
Ordained to Suffering—

It might be easier
To fail—with Land in Sight—
Than gain—My Blue Peninsula—
To perish—of Delight—

After Great Pain a Formal Feeling Comes

After great pain, a formal feeling comes—
The Nerves sit ceremonious, like Tombs—
The stiff Heart questions was it He, that bore,
And Yesterday, or Centuries before?

The Feet, mechanical, go round—
Of Ground, or Air, or Ought—
A Wooden way
Regardless grown,
A Quartz contentment, like a stone—

This is the Hour of Lead—   10
Remembered, if outlived,
As Freezing persons, recollect the Snow—
First—Chill—then Stupor—then the letting go—

(continued from page 681)
Unmoved, an Emperor be kneeling
Upon her mat.

I've known her from an ample nation
Choose one,   *10*
Then close the valves of her attention
Like stone.

It Might Be Lonelier

It might be lonelier
Without the loneliness.
I'm so accustomed to my fate,
Perhaps the other peace

Would interrupt the dark
And crowd the little room
To scant by cubits to contain
The sacrament of him.

I am not used to hope.
It might intrude upon   *10*
Its sweet parade, blaspheme the place
Ordained to suffering.

It might be easier
To fail with land in sight
Than gain my blue peninsula
To perish of delight.

After Great Pain a Formal Feeling Comes

After great pain, a formal feeling comes.
The nerves sit ceremonious, like tombs;
The stiff Heart questions was it He that bore?
And yesterday, or centuries before?

The feet, mechanical, go round
Of ground, or air, or ought,
A wooden way
Regardless grown,
A quartz contentment, like a stone.

This is the hour of lead   *10*
Remembered, if outlived,
As freezing persons recollect the snow—
First chill, then stupor, then the letting go.

Much Madness Is Divinest Sense

Much Madness is divinest Sense—
To a discerning Eye—
Much Sense—the starkest Madness—
'Tis the Majority
In this, as All, prevail—
Assent—and you are sane—
Demur—you're straightway dangerous—
And handled with a Chain—

This Is My Letter to the World

This is my letter to the World
That never wrote to Me—
The simple News that Nature told—
With tender Majesty

Her Message is committed
To Hands I cannot see—
For love of Her—Sweet—countrymen—
Judge tenderly—of Me

I Heard a Fly Buzz When I Died

I heard a Fly buzz—when I died—
The Stillness in the Room
Was like the Stillness in the Air—
Between the Heaves of Storm—

The Eyes around—had wrung them dry—
And Breaths were gathering firm
For that last Onset—when the King
Be witnessed—in the Room—

I willed my Keepsakes—Signed away
What portion of me be   10
Assignable—and then it was
There interposed a Fly—

With Blue—uncertain stumbling Buzz—
Between the light—and me—
And then the Windows failed—and then
I could not see to see—

Much Madness Is Divinest Sense

Much madness is divinest sense
To a discerning eye—
Much sense the starkest madness.
'Tis the majority
In this, as all, prevail.
Assent and you are sane;
Demur, you're straightway dangerous
And handled with a chain.

This Is My Letter to the World

This is my letter to the world
That never wrote to me,
The simple news that nature told
With tender majesty.

Her message is committed
To hands I cannot see.
For love of her, sweet countrymen,
Judge tenderly of me.

I Heard a Fly Buzz When I Died

I heard a fly buzz when I died.
The stillness in the room
Was like the stillness in the air
Between the heaves of storm.

The eyes around had wrung them dry,
And breaths were gathering firm
For that last onset when the king
Be witnessed in the room.

I willed my keepsakes, signed away
What portion of me be   10
Assignable; and then it was
There interposed a fly

With blue uncertain stumbling buzz
Between the light and me;
And then the windows failed; and then
I could not see to see.

It Was Not Death, for I Stood Up

It was not Death, for I stood up,
And all the Dead, lie down—
It was not Night, for all the Bells
Put out their Tongues, for Noon.

It was not Frost, for on my Flesh
I felt Siroccos—crawl—
Nor Fire—for just my Marble feet
Could keep a Chancel, cool—

And yet, it tasted, like them all,
The Figures I have seen   10
Set orderly, for Burial,
Reminded me, of mine—

As if my life were shaven,
And fitted to a frame,
And could not breathe without a key,
And 'twas like Midnight, some—

When everything that ticked—has stopped—
And Space stares all around—
Or Grisly frosts—first Autumn morns,
Repeal the Beating Ground—   20

But, most, like Chaos—Stopless—cool—
Without a Chance, or Spar—
Or even a Report of Land—
To justify—Despair.

I Started Early, Took My Dog

I started Early—Took my Dog—
And visited the Sea—
The Mermaids in the Basement
Came out to look at me—

And Frigates—in the Upper Floor
Extended Hempen Hands—
Presuming Me to be a Mouse—
Aground—upon the Sands—

But no Man moved Me—till the Tide
Went past my simple Shoe—   10
And past my Apron—and my Belt
And past my Bodice—too—   *(continued on page 688)*

It Was Not Death, for I Stood Up

It was not death, for I stood up,
And all the dead lie down.
It was not night, for all the bells
Put out their tongues for noon.

It was not frost, for on my flesh
I felt siroccos crawl;
Nor fire, for just my marble feet
Could keep a chancel cool—

And yet it tasted like them all.
The figures I have seen　　　　　　　　　　*10*
Set orderly for burial
Reminded me of mine,

As if my life were shaven
And fitted to a frame
And could not breathe without a key;
And 'twas like midnight some

When everything that ticked has stopped
And space stares all around,
Or grisly frosts, first Autumn morns,
Repeal the beating ground,　　　　　　　　*20*

But most like chaos—stopless, cool,
Without a chance or spar,
Or even a report of land
To justify despair.

I Started Early, Took My Dog

I started early, took my dog,
And visited the sea.
The mermaids in the basement
Came out to look at me

And frigates in the upper floor
Extended hempen hands,
Presuming me to be a mouse
Aground upon the sands,

But no man moved me till the tide
Went past my simple shoe　　　　　　　　*10*
And past my apron and my belt
And past my bodice too,　　　*(continued on page 689)*

(continued from page 686)
And made as He would eat me up—
As wholly as a Dew
Upon a Dandelion's Sleeve—
And then—I started—too—

And He—He followed—close behind—
I felt His Silver Heel
Upon my Ankle—Then my Shoes
Would overflow with Pearl—   20

Until We met the Solid Town—
No One He seemed to know—
And bowing—with a Mighty look—
At me—The Sea withdrew—

The Heart Asks Pleasure First

The Heart asks Pleasure—first—
And then—Excuse from Pain—
And then—those little Anodynes
That deaden suffering—

And then—to go to sleep—
And then—if it should be
The will of its Inquistor
The privilege to die—

Our Journey Had Advanced

Our journey had advanced—
Our feet were almost come
To that odd Fork in Being's Road—
Eternity—by Term—

Our pace took sudden awe—
Our feet—reluctant—led—
Before—were Cities—but Between—
The Forest of the Dead—

Retreat—was out of Hope—
Behind—a Sealed Route—   10
Eternity's White Flag—Before—
And God—at every Gate—

(*continued from page 687*)
And made as he would eat me up
As wholly as a dew
Upon a dandelion's sleeve;
And then I started too

And he, he followed close behind;
I felt his silver heel
Upon my ankle, then my shoes
Would overflow with pearl,   20

Until we met the solid town.
No one he seemed to know
And bowing with a mighty look
At me, the sea withdrew.

The Heart Asks Pleasure First

The heart asks pleasure first,
And then excuse from pain,
And then those little anodynes
That deaden suffering,

And then to go to sleep,
And then if it should be
The will of its inquisitor
The privilege to die.

Our Journey Had Advanced

Our journey had advanced,
Our feet were almost come
To that odd fork in being's road,
Eternity by term.

Our pace took sudden awe,
Our feet reluctant led;
Before were cities, but between,
The forest of the dead.

Retreat was out of hope;
Behind, a sealed route,   10
Eternity's white flag before,
And God at every gate.

Pain Has an Element of Blank

Pain—has an Element of Blank—
It cannot recollect
When it begun—or if there were
A time when it was not—

It has no Future—but itself—
Its Infinite contain
Its Past—enlightened to perceive
New Periods—of Pain.

Because I Could Not Stop for Death

Because I could not stop for Death—
He kindly stopped for me—
The Carriage held but just Ourselves—
And Immortality.

We slowly drove—He knew no haste
And I had put away
My labor and my leisure too,
For His Civility—

We passed the School, where Children strove
At Recess—in the Ring—   *10*
We passed the Fields of Gazing Grain—
We passed the Setting Sun—

Or rather—He passed Us—
The Dews drew quivering and chill—
For only Gossamer, my Gown—
My Tippet—only Tulle—

We paused before a House that seemed
A Swelling of the Ground—
The Roof was scarcely visible—
The Cornice—in the Ground—   *20*

Since then—'tis Centuries—and yet
Feels shorter than the Day
I first surmised the Horses' Heads
Were toward Eternity—

Pain Has an Element of Blank

Pain has an element of blank.
It cannot recollect
When it begun or if there were
A time when it was not.

It has no future but itself;
Its infinite contain
Its past, enlightened to perceive
New periods of pain.

Because I Could Not Stop for Death

Because I could not stop for Death
He kindly stopped for me.
The carriage held but just ourselves
And immortality.

We slowly drove. He knew no haste,
And I had put away
My labour and my leisure too
For his civility.

We passed the school where children strove
At recess in the ring.   10
We passed the fields of gazing grain;
We passed the setting sun—

Or rather, he passed us.
The dews drew quivering and chill,
For only gossamer my gown,
My tippet only tulle.

We paused before a house that seemed
A swelling of the ground.
The roof was scarcely visible,
The cornice in the ground.   20

Since then 'tis centuries, and yet
Feels shorter than the day
I first surmised the horses' heads
Were toward Eternity.

A Light Exists in Spring

A Light exists in Spring
Not present on the Year
At any other period—
When March is scarcely here

A Color stands abroad
On Solitary Fields
That Science cannot overtake
But Human Nature feels.

It waits upon the Lawn,
It shows the furthest Tree   10
Upon the furthest Slope you know
It almost speaks to you.

Then as Horizons step
Or Noons report away
Without the Formula of sound
It passes and we stay—

A quality of loss
Affecting our Content
As Trade had suddenly encroached
Upon a Sacrament.   20

The Missing All Prevented Me

The Missing All—prevented Me
From missing minor Things.
If nothing larger than a World's
Departure from a Hinge—
Or Sun's extinction, be observed—
'Twas not so large that I
Could lift my Forehead from my work
For Curiosity.

A Light Exists in Spring

A light exists in spring
Not present on the year
At any other period.
When March is scarcely here

A color stands abroad
On solitary fields
That science cannot overtake,
But human nature feels.

It waits upon the lawn;
It shows the furthest tree   10
Upon the furthest slope you know;
It almost speaks to you.

Then, as horizons step,
Or noons report away,
Without the formula of sound,
It passes, and we stay:

A quality of loss
Affecting our content,
As trade had suddenly encroached
Upon a sacrament.   20

The Missing All Prevented Me

The Missing All prevented me
From missing minor things.
If nothing larger than a world's
Departure from a hinge
Or sun's extinction be observed,
'Twas not so large that I
Could lift my forehead from my work
For curiosity.

At Half Past Three, a Single Bird

At Half past Three, a single Bird
Unto a silent Sky
Propounded but a single term
Of cautious melody.

At Half past Four, Experiment
Had subjugated test
And lo, Her silver Principle
Supplanted all the rest.

At Half past Seven, Element
Nor Implement, be seen—   10
And Place was where the Presence was
Circumference between.

The Last Night that She Lived

The last Night that She lived
It was a Common Night
Except the Dying—this to Us
Made Nature different

We noticed smallest things—
Things overlooked before
By this great light upon our Minds
Italicized—as 'twere.

As We went out and in
Between Her final Room   10
And Rooms where Those to be alive
Tomorrow were, a Blame

That Others could exist
While She must finish quite
A jealousy for Her arose
So nearly infinite—

We waited while She passed—
It was a narrow time—
Too jostled were Our Souls to speak
At length the notice came.   20

She mentioned, and forgot—
Then lightly as a Reed
Bent to the Water, struggled scarce—
Consented, and was dead—   *(continued on page 696)*

At Half Past Three, a Single Bird

At half past three a single bird
Unto a silent sky
Propounded but a single term
Of cautious melody.

At half past four experiment
Had subjugated test,
And lo, her silver principle
Supplanted all the rest.

At half past seven element
Nor implement be seen,   *10*
And place was where the presence was,
Circumference between.

The Last Night that She Lived

The last night that she lived,
It was a common night
Except the dying—this to us
Made nature different.

We noticed smallest things,
Things overlooked before,
By this great light upon our minds
Italicised, as 'twere.

As we went out and in
Between her final room   *10*
And rooms where those to be alive
Tomorrow were, a blame

That others could exist
While she must finish quite,
A jealousy for her arose
So nearly infinite.

We waited while she passed;
It was a narrow time.
Too jostled were our souls to speak.
At length the notice came.   *20*

She mentioned, and forgot;
Then lightly as a reed
Bent to the water, struggled scarce,
Consented, and was dead.   *(continued on page 697)*

(continued from page 694)
And We—We placed the Hair—
And drew the Head erect—
And then an awful leisure was
Belief to regulate—

After a Hundred Years

After a hundred years
Nobody knows the Place
Agony that enacted there
Motionless as Peace

Weeds triumphant ranged
Strangers strolled and spelled
At the lone Orthography
Of the Elder Dead

Winds of Summer Fields
Recollect the way—   10
Instinct picking up the Key
Dropped by memory—

Great Streets of Silence Led Away

Great Streets of silence led away
To Neighborhoods of Pause—
Here was no Notice—no Dissent
No Universe—no Laws—

By Clocks, 'twas Morning, and for Night
The Bells at Distance called—
But Epoch had no basis here
For Period exhaled.

As Imperceptibly as Grief

As imperceptibly as Grief
The Summer lapsed away—
Too imperceptible at last
To seem like Perfidy—
A Quietness distilled
As Twilight long begun,   *(continued on page 698)*

(continued from page 695)
And we, we placed the hair
And drew the head erect;
And then an awful leisure was,
Belief to regulate.

After a Hundred Years

After a hundred years
Nobody knows the place,
Agony that enacted there
Motionless as peace.

Weeds triumphant ranged.
Strangers strolled and spelled
At the lone orthography
Of the elder dead.

Winds of summer fields
Recollect the way,   10
Instinct picking up the key
Dropped by memory.

Great Streets of Silence Led Away

Great streets of silence led away
To neighborhoods of pause.
Here was no notice, no dissent,
No universe, no laws.

By clocks 'twas morning, and for night
The bells at distance called,
But epoch had no basis here
For period exhaled.

As Imperceptibly as Grief

As imperceptibly as grief
The summer lapsed away,
Too imperceptible, at last,
To seem like perfidy.
A quietness distilled,
As twilight long begun,   (continued on page 699)

(continued from page 696)
Or Nature spending with herself
Sequestered Afternoon—
The Dusk drew earlier in—
The Morning foreign shone—　　　　　*10*
A courteous, yet harrowing Grace,
As Guest, that would be gone—
And thus, without a Wing
Or service of a Keel
Our Summer made her light escape
Into the Beautiful.

There Came a Wind Like a Bugle

There came a Wind like a Bugle—
It quivered through the Grass
And a Green Chill upon the Heat
So ominous did pass
We barred the Windows and the Doors
As from an Emerald Ghost—
The Doom's electric Moccasin
That very instant passed—
On a strange Mob of panting Trees
And Fences fled away　　　　　*10*
And Rivers where the Houses ran
Those looked that lived—that Day—
The Bell within the steeple wild
The flying tidings told—
How much can come
And much can go,
And yet abide the World!

My Life Closed Twice before Its Close

My life closed twice before its close—
It yet remains to see
If Immortality unveil
A third event to me

So huge, so hopeless to conceive
As these that twice befell.
Parting is all we know of heaven,
And all we need of hell.

(continued from page 697)
Or nature, spending with herself
Sequestered afternoon.
The dusk drew earlier in,
The morning foreign shone,—   *10*
A courteous, yet harrowing grace,
As guest that would be gone.
And thus, without a wing
Or service of a keel,
Our summer made her light escape
Into the beautiful.

There Came a Wind Like a Bugle

There came a wind like a bugle.
It quivered through the grass,
And a green chill upon the heat
So ominous did pass.
We barred the windows and the doors
As from an emerald ghost.
The doom's electric moccasin
That very instant passed.
On a strange mob of panting trees
And fences fled away   *10*
And rivers where the houses ran
Those looked that lived that day.
The bell within the steeple wild
The flying tidings told—
How much can come
And much can go,
And yet abide the world.

My Life Closed Twice before Its Close

My life closed twice before its close.
It yet remains to see
If immortality unveil
A third event to me,

So huge, so hopeless to conceive
As these that twice befell.
Parting is all we know of heaven,
And all we need of hell.

The Civil War: Fiction and Memoir

Introduction

Precisely what the Civil War signified in American history, or even why it was fought at all, has remained a subject of intense debate among our historians. With time and the objectivity that time sometimes brings, most earlier notions about the war have been abandoned—that it was simply a noble crusade of the righteous North to end the Southern evil of slavery, that it was a heroic defense by the South to defend the principle of states' rights or the reality of its distinctive way of life. We are not now inclined toward simple-minded or monolithic explanations for complex historical events.

The Civil War has been subjected to a wide range of interpretations. Some regard it primarily as a socioeconomic conflict—industrial-capitalist North versus slave-agrarian South—in which moral issues, such as slavery, are at best mere ideological rationales for class interest. Others see it primarily in national-political terms, as a struggle over the destiny of the Union and the right of states to secede at will. The Civil War figures in the lives of American writers who lived through it mainly as a profound emotional trauma: a fratricidal conflict which threatened the survival—the very idea—of the young nation. Apart from the skeptical Hawthorne, who distrusted all politics, the Northern writers were actively committed to the Union cause: some because they were passionately eager for the abolition of slavery, others because they were idealistically devoted to the idea of the United States as a democratic nation.

During the war itself, debate had already begun about its meaning and value, and more reflective people experienced considerable disquiet. The veteran Abolitionist leader Wendell Phillips, who had previously excoriated his country for permitting slavery and had even assaulted the Stars and Stripes as a symbol of oppression, now said that the Northern cause embodied "sovereignity and justice." Another Abolitionist leader, Lydia Maria Child, was far more skeptical or far more open in her skepticism than Phillips: she wrote that there was little "of either right principle or good feeling at the foundation of this unanimous Union sentiment." Lincoln himself, for all the moral grandeur with which he has been invested by his countrymen, kept repeating during the early years of the war that its purpose was not the liberation of blacks but the preservation of the Union. In August 1962 he wrote to Horace Greeley:

My paramount objective in this struggle is to save the Union, and it is not either to save or destroy slavery. If I could save the Union without freeing any slaves I would do it, and if I could do it by freeing all the slaves I would do it; and if I could save it by freeing some and leaving others alone I would also do that.

Yet it was only five months later that the Emancipation Proclamation, at once a moral statement and a political gesture, came out under Lincoln's name. And still more remarkable, the above disheartening passage from the letter to Greeley was written a month *after* Lincoln had composed the first draft of the Emancipation Proclamation—a fact from which we should conclude not that he was hypocrital or cynical, but that the course of historical change is difficult and the problems Lincoln faced in trying to hold together sharply conflicting interests and opinions in the North were overwhelming. Perhaps the most realistic contemporary analysts of the Civil War were those Northerners who rallied to the Union flag not because they had illusions about the motives of many of their leaders or thought the North was engaged in a holy crusade, but because they believed it likely that in order to win the war it would be necessary for Lincoln to come out in favor of freeing the slaves. They felt that, in this as in so many other real-life circumstances, the moral issue had become dependent on the political one. At the same time, however, the dismal results of the decades following the Civil War—the decades in which a Southern white oligarchy gradually reestablished its domination over the blacks—vindicated, at least in part, those skeptics like Lydia Child who questioned the moral credentials of the North.

For some of our major writers, like Whitman and Melville, the Civil War figures not so much in political terms—though both detested slavery—but as a collective tragedy, the first major event in the history of the nation that could be described as tragic. Melville was struck by the sheer terribleness of the war, the way it became impersonal and mechanical, a kind of machine created for devouring the young. Whitman was struck by the vulnerability and innocence of the young soldiers he visited in hospitals, as he was also by the shattering of the American dream that we were a pacific nation unstained by the guilts and crimes of Europe. In their war poetry— in this anthology, it appears in the previous section so that their work can be kept together—both writers express a kind of awe at the spectacle of human destructiveness and a helplessness before the magnitude of uncontrollable events.

Most of the material in this section consists of memoirs and personal accounts. Apparently, it was hard to use the experience of fratricide for imaginative literary purposes immediately after men had lived through it, and by far the best writing about the Civil War in the years directly following it is nonfictional in character. The addresses by Lincoln stand in a class by themselves, so finely eloquent and gravely humane do they still seem. But even the lesser materials such as the memoirs of Grant and Sherman are well written in an austere and distant way. At least as well written are the excerpts from the autobiographies of the ex-slave Frederick Douglas, who seems almost instinctively to have absorbed, despite the handicaps imposed on him during his youth, the stately periods and soaring rhetoric which nineteenth-century public men liked to employ. The South is also represented here, in the touching ode by a gifted but little-known poet, Henry Timrod, and in the brilliant diary of Mary Chestnut.

Only two items of fiction appear in this section, those by Ambrose Bierce and Hamlin Garland. Both of these are efforts at a realistic evocation of the experience of war. The terribleness of the first "modern" war in history—the first war in which slaughter was carried through on a large-scale, scientific basis—was not quickly captured by writers of fiction. Not until 1895, when the young Stephen Crane published *The Red Badge of Courage*, did the great novel about the Civil War finally come into being. It may tell us something about the workings of the literary imagination that what the survivors of the war could not do, a young writer who had never fought could.

HARRIET BEECHER STOWE (1811–1896)

*Daughter of one eminent clergyman, wife of another, and sister of
Henry Ward Beecher, the most famous pulpit orator of his day,
Harriet Beecher Stowe was born in Connecticut. Her father's appointment as head of a theological seminary in 1832 caused the
family to move to Cincinnati, on the edge of the slave states. Four
years later, she married Calvin Stowe, the seminary's professor of
Biblical literature.*

*Urgently in need of money and encouraged to write about slavery by
her family, Mrs. Stowe composed* Uncle Tom's Cabin *as a serial for
an antislavery weekly in Washington. When it ran at great length,
from June, 1851, to April, 1852, the editor asked Mrs. Stowe to cut
it short; but the paper's readers protested so vigorously, it became
clear that the story had the makings of a great popular success.
Within its first year after publication in book form,* Uncle Tom's
Cabin *sold over 300,000 copies in the United States and 2,500,000
abroad. It came just at the right time, when antislavery sentiment
had become popular in the North: highly moralistic, it satisfied the
tastes of many readers; extremely melodramatic, it provided
surface preachments with a strong base of narrative excitement.
Meeting its author, Abraham Lincoln said, "So this is the little lady
who made this big war."*

*In later years Mrs. Stowe continued to write voluminously, for the most
part stories and sketches, based partly on her own experience, about
the distinctive qualities of New England life.* The Minister's Wooing,
The Pearl of Orr's Island, *and* Oldtown Folks *were all written in
the decade between 1859 and 1869; and despite a weakness for
stock situations and moralistic sentiment, they all have strong passages and sections evoking the details of regional experience.*

It was fashionable, earlier in this century, to dismiss Uncle Tom's Cabin
*as a crude propaganda novel which had served its—noble or nefar-
ious—purpose. But in recent years critical interest in the book has
steadily grown. James Baldwin, the distinguished Negro writer,
attacked* Uncle Tom's Cabin *in a 1949 essay entitled "Everybody's
Protest Novel." Describing Mrs. Stowe's novel as "sentimental," he
charged that the whole category of "social protest fiction" to which
it belongs ends by debasing the very people it claims to be concerned about because it insists that ". . . it is [man's] categorization
alone which is real and which cannot be transcended." Mrs. Stowe,
wrote Baldwin, "was not so much a novelist as an impassioned
pamphleteer; her book was not intended to do anything more than
prove that slavery was wrong; was, in fact, perfectly horrible. This
makes material for a pamphlet but it is hardly enough for a
novel . . ."*

A very different judgment has been offered by the leading American critic Edmund Wilson in his study of Civil War literature, Patriotic Gore (1962). Wilson finds Uncle Tom's Cabin *a work of "eruptive force" and remarks that "the farther one reads . . ., the more one becomes aware that a critical mind is at work, which has the complex situation in a very firm grip and which, no matter how vehement the characters become, is controlling and coordinating their interrelations." What Mrs. Stowe offers, in this view, is not so much a historically accurate picture of slavery as it actually existed, but an enormously powerful projection of the impact slavery made on a strong and sensitive American mind in the middle of the nineteenth century. Through the conventions of melodrama there burst shattering images of the horrors that follow, and must follow, when men are allowed to own other men.*

FURTHER READING

A useful biography is Forrest Wilson's *Crusader in Crinoline: The Life of Harriet Beecher Stowe* (1941). Baldwin's essay, eminently worth reading, appears in *Notes of a Native Son* (1955); Edmund Wilson's equally valuable essay, in *Patriotic Gore* (1962).

FROM *Uncle Tom's Cabin; or, Life Among the Lowly* (1851, 1852)

A little before the sale commenced, a short, broad, muscular man, in a checked shirt considerably open at the bosom, and pantaloons much the worse for dirt and wear, elbowed his way through the crowd, like one who is going actively into a business; and, coming up to the group, began to examine them systematically. From the moment that Tom saw him approaching, he felt an immediate and revolting horror at him, that increased as he came near. He was evidently, though short, of gigantic strength. His round, bullet head, large, light-gray eyes, with their shaggy, sandy eye-brows, and stiff, wiry, sunburned hair, were rather unprepossessing items, it is to be confessed; his large, coarse mouth was distended with tobacco, the juice of which, from time to time, he ejected from him with great decision and explosive force; his hands were immensely large, hairy, sunburned, freckled, and very dirty, and garnished with long nails, in a very foul condition. This man proceeded to a very free personal examination of the lot. He seized Tom by the jaw, and pulled open his mouth to inspect his teeth; made him strip up to his sleeve, to show his muscle; turned him round, made him jump and spring, to show his paces.

"Where was you raised?" he added, briefly, to these investigations.

"In Kintuck, Mas'r," said Tom, looking about, as if for deliverance.

"What have you done?"

"Had care of Mas'r's farm," said Tom.

"Likely story!" said the other, shortly, as he passed on. He paused a moment before Dolph; then spitting a discharge of tobacco-juice on his well-blacked boots, and giving a contemptuous umph, he walked on. Again he stopped before Susan and Emmeline. He put out his heavy, dirty hand, and drew the girl towards him; passed it over her neck and bust, felt her arms, looked at her teeth, and then pushed her back against her mother, whose patient face showed the suffering she had been going through at every motion of the hideous stranger.

The girl was frightened, and began to cry.

"Stop that, you minx!" said the salesman; "no whimpering here,— the sale is going to begin." And accordingly the sale begun.

Adolph was knocked off, at a good sum, to the young gentleman who had previously stated his intention of buying him; and the other servants of the St. Clare lot went to various bidders.

"Now, up with you, boy! d'ye hear?" said the autioneer to Tom.

Tom stepped upon the block, gave a few anxious looks round; all seemed mingled in a common, indistinct noise,—the clatter of the saleman crying off his qualifications in French and English, the quick fire of French and English bids; and almost in a moment came the final thump of the hammer, and the clear ring on the last syllable of the word "*dollars*" as the auctioneer announced his price, and Tom was made over.—He had a master!

He was pushed from the block;—the short, bullet-headed man seizing him roughly by the shoulder, pushed him to one side, saying, in a harsh voice, "Stand there, *you!*"

Tom hardly realized anything; but still the bidding went on,— rattling, clattering, now French, now English. Down goes the hammer again,—Susan is sold! She goes down from the block, stops, looks wistfully back,—her daughter stretches her hands towards her. She looks with agony in the face of the man who has bought her,—a respectable middle-aged man, of benevolent countenance.

"O, Mas'r, please do buy my daughter!"

"I'd like to, but I'm afraid I can't afford it!" said the gentleman, looking, with painful interest, as the young girl mounted the block, and looked around her with a frightened and timid glance.

The blood flushes painfully in her otherwise colorless cheek, her eye has a feverish fire, and her mother groans to see that she looks more beautiful than she ever saw her before. The auctioneer sees his advantage, and expatiates volubly in mingled French and English, and bids rise in rapid succession.

"I'll do anything in reason," said the benevolent-looking gentleman, pressing in and joining with the bids. In a few moments they have run beyond his purse. He is silent; the auctioneer grows warmer; but bids gradually drop off. It lies now between an aristocratic old citizen and our bullet-headed acquaintance. The citizen bids for a few turns, contemptuously measuring his opponent; but the bullet-head has the advantage over him, both in obstinacy and concealed length of purse, and the controversy lasts but a moment; the hammer falls,—he has got the girl, body and soul, unless God help her!

Her master is Mr. Legree, who owns a cotton plantation on the Red river. She is pushed along into the same lot with Tom and two other men, and goes off, weeping as she goes.

The benevolent gentleman is sorry; but, then, the thing happens every day! One sees girls and mothers crying, at these sales, *always!* it can't be helped, &c.; and he walks off, with his acquisition, in another direction.

Two days after, the lawyer of the Christian firm of B. & Co., New York, sent on their money to them. On the reverse of that draft, so obtained, let them write these words of the great Paymaster, to whom they shall make up their account in a future day: *"When he maketh inquisition for blood, he forgetteth not the cry of the humble!"*

FREDERICK DOUGLASS (1817?–1895)

Frederick Douglass has long been recognized as an important figure in nineteenth-century American history, and the time has now come for recognition of his large gifts as a writer.

Douglass was born a slave in Talbot County, Maryland. As a young man, in 1838 he escaped from bondage and made his way north, where he became the leading American Negro in the antislavery movement and, after the Civil War, in the fight for the black man's rights. Impressive for his courage and for the guidance he gave to a crucified race, Douglass first made his mark as an orator in the Abolitionist cause. During the Civil War he helped recruit black soldiers for Massachusetts regiments, and afterward he struggled hard, if mostly without success, to win for the ex-slaves those rights which legally should have been theirs. In his later years Douglass held various offices in the government, including that of Minister to Haiti.

During his lifetime Douglass wrote three autobiographies, each of the latter two drawing upon and elaborating what he had written earlier. The first of these volumes, Narrative of the Life of Frederick Douglass, an American Slave, *appeared in 1845 under the auspices of the Antislavery Office in Boston. It was in this volume that he recalled his experiences as a slave with the greatest vividness. Ten years later appeared* My Bondage and My Freedom, *an enlarged version of his* Narrative. *And in 1881 he issued* Life and

Times of Frederick Douglass, *which he then published in a final, reworked version in 1892. As he kept rewriting the story of his life, Douglass lost something in keenness of memory, but gained in intellectual breadth and reflectiveness.*

Apart from his range of humane sympathies and an objectivity which enabled him even to imagine the responses and dilemmas of the white slaveowners who had mistreated him, Douglass's work is remarkable for its stylistic composure. He seems to have absorbed naturally the capacity for writing that stately and rounded prose which many of our best nineteenth-century American writers took over from Johnsonian England, and though rarely considered in traditional histories of our literature, his work deserves to be honored as a classic of our prose.

FURTHER READING

Arna Bontemps, *Frederick Douglass, Fighter, Freeman* (1959); Philip Sterling and Raylord Logan, *Four Took Freedom* (1967); Philip S. Foner, *Frederick Douglass* (1964).

FROM *Narrative of the Life of Frederick Douglass, an American Slave* (1845)

Chapter 1

I was born in Tuckahoe, near Hillsborough, and about twelve miles from Easton, in Talbot county, Maryland. I have no accurate knowledge of my age, never having seen any authentic record containing it. By far the larger part of the slaves know as little of their ages as horses know of theirs, and it is the wish of most masters within my knowledge to keep their slaves thus ignorant. I do not remember to have ever met a slave who could tell of his birthday. They seldom come nearer to it than planting-time, harvest-time, cheery-time, spring-time, or fall-time. A want of information concerning my own was a source of unhappiness to me even during childhood. The white children could tell their ages. I could not tell why I ought to be deprived of the same privilege. I was not allowed to make any inquiries of my master concerning it. He deemed all such inquiries on the part of a slave improper and impertinent, and evidence of a restless spirit. The nearest estimate I can give makes me now between twenty-seven and twenty-eight years of age. I come to this, from hearing my master say, some time during 1835, I was about seventeen years old.

My mother was named Harriet Bailey. She was the daughter of Isaac and Betsey Bailey, both colored, and quite dark. My mother was of a darker complexion than either my grandmother or grandfather.

My father was a white man. He was admitted to be such by all I ever heard speak of my parentage. The opinion was also whispered that my master was my father; but of the correctness of this opinion, I know nothing; the means of knowing was withheld from me. My mother and I were separated when I was but an infant—before I knew her as my mother. It is a common custom, in the part of Maryland from which I ran away, to part children from their mothers at a very early age. Frequently, before the child has reached its twelfth month, its mother is taken from it, and hired out on some farm a considerable distance off, and the child is placed under the care of an old woman, too old for field labor. For what this separation is done, I do not know, unless it be to hinder the development of the child's affection toward its mother, and to blunt and destroy the natural affection of the mother for the child. This is the inevitable result.

I never saw my mother, to know her as such, more than four or five times in my life; and each of these times was very short in duration, and at night. She was hired by a Mr. Stewart, who lived about twelve miles from my home. She made her journeys to see me in the night, travelling the whole distance on foot, after the performance of her day's work. She was a field hand, and a whipping is the penalty of not being in the field at sunrise, unless a slave has special permission from his or her master to the contrary—a permission which they seldom get, and one that gives to him that gives it the proud name of being a kind master. I do not recollect of ever seeing my mother by the light of day. She was with me in the night. She would lie down with me, and get me to sleep, but long before I waked she was gone. Very little communication ever took place between us. Death soon ended what little we could have while she lived, and with it her hardships and suffering. She died when I was about seven years old, on one of my master's farms near Lee's Mill. I was not allowed to be present during her illness, at her death, or burial. She was gone long before I knew any thing about it. Never having enjoyed, to any considerable extent, her soothing presence, her tender and watchful care, I received the tidings of her death with much the same emotions I should have probably felt at the death of a stranger.

Called thus suddenly away, she left me without the slightest intimation of who my father was. The whisper that my master was my father, may or may not be true; and, true or false, it is of but little consequence to my purpose whilst the fact remains, in all its glaring odiousness, that slaveholders have ordained, and by law established, that the children of slave women shall in all cases follow the condition of their mothers; and this is done too obviously to administer to their own lusts, and make a gratification of their wicked desires profitable as well as pleasurable; for by this cunning arrangement, the slaveholder, in cases not a few, sustains to his slaves the double relation of master and father.

I know of such cases; and it is worthy of remark that such slaves invariably suffer greater hardships, and have more to contend with, than others. They are, in the first place, a constant offence to their mistress. She is ever disposed to find fault with them; they can seldom do any thing to please her; she is never better pleased than when she sees them under the lash, especially when she suspects her husband of showing to his mulatto children favors which he withholds from his black slaves. The master is frequently compelled to sell this class of his slaves, out of deference to the feelings of his white wife; and, cruel as the deed may strike any one to be, for a man to sell his own children to human flesh-mongers, it is often the dictate of humanity for him to do so; for, unless he does this, he must not only whip them himself, but must stand by and see one white son tie up his brother, of but few shades darker complexion than himself, and ply the gory lash to his naked back; and if he lisp one word of disapproval, it is set down to his parental partiality, and only makes a bad matter worse, both for himself and the slave whom he would protect and defend.

Every year brings with it multitudes of this class of slaves. It was doubtless in consequence of a knowledge of this fact, that one great statesman of the south predicted the downfall of slavery by the inevitable laws of population. Whether this prophecy is ever fulfilled or not, it is nevertheless plain that a very different-looking class of people are springing up at the south, and are now held in slavery, from those originally brought to this country from Africa; and if their increase will do no other good, it will do away the force of the argument, that God cursed Ham, and therefore American slavery is right. If the lineal descendants of Ham are alone to be scripturally enslaved, it is certain that slavery at the south must soon become unscriptural; for thousands are ushered into the world, annually, who, like myself, owe their existence to white fathers, and those fathers most frequently their own masters.

I have had two masters. My first master's name was Anthony. I do not remember his first name. He was generally called Captain Anthony—a title which, I presume, he acquired by sailing a craft on the Chesapeake Bay. He was not considered a rich slaveholder. He owned two or three farms, and about thirty slaves. His farms and slaves were under the care of an overseer. The overseer's name was Plummer. Mr. Plummer was a miserable drunkard, a profane swearer, and a savage monster. He always went armed with a cowskin and a heavy cudgel. I have known him to cut and slash the women's heads so horribly, that even master would be enraged at his cruelty, and would threaten to whip him if he did not mind himself. Master, however, was not a humane slaveholder. It required extraordinary barbarity on the part of an overseer to affect him. He was a cruel man, hardened by a long life of slaveholding. He would at times seem to take great pleasure in whipping a slave. I have often been awakened at the dawn of day by the most heart-rending shrieks of an own aunt of mine, whom he used to tie up to a joist, and whip upon her naked back till she was literally covered with blood. No words, no tears, no prayers, from his gory victim, seemed to move his iron heart from its bloody purpose. The louder she screamed, the harder he whipped; and where the blood ran fastest, there he whipped longest. He would whip her to make her scream, and whip her to make her hush; and not until overcome by fatigue, would he cease to swing the blood-clotted cowskin. I remember the first time I ever witnessed this horrible exhibition. I was quite a child, but I well remember it. I never shall forget it whilst I remember any thing. It was the first of a long series of such outrages, of which I was doomed to be a witness and a participant. It struck me with awful force. It was the blood-stained gate, the entrance to the hell of slavery, through which I was about to pass. It was a most terrible spectacle. I wish I could commit to paper the feelings with which I beheld it.

This occurrence took place very soon after I went to live with my old master, and under the following circumstances. Aunt Hester went out one night,—where or for what I do not know,—and happened to be absent when my master desired her presence. He had ordered her not to go out evenings, and warned her that she must never let him catch her in company with a young man, who was paying attention to her belonging to Colonel Lloyd. The young man's name was Ned Roberts, generally called Lloyd's Ned. Why master was so careful of her, may be safely left to conjecture. She was a woman of noble form, and of graceful proportions, having very few equals, and fewer superiors, in personal appearance, among the colored or white women of our neighborhood.

Aunt Hester had not only disobeyed his orders in going out, but had been found in company with Lloyd's Ned; which circumstance, I found, from what he said while whipping her, was the chief offence. Had he been a man of pure morals himself, he might have been thought interested in protecting the innocence of my aunt; but those who knew him will not suspect him of any such virtue. Before he commenced whipping Aunt Hester, he took her into the kitchen, and stripped her from neck to waist, leaving her neck, shoulders, and back, entirely naked. He then told to her to cross her hands, calling her at the same time a d——d b——h. After crossing her hands, he tied them with a strong rope, and led her to a stool under a large hook in the joist, put in for the purpose. He made her get upon the stool, and tied her hands to the hook. She now stood fair for his infernal purpose. Her arms were stretched up at their full length, so that she stood upon the ends of her toes. He then said to her, "Now, you d——d b——h, I'll learn you how to disobey my orders!" and after rolling up his sleeves, he com-

menced to lay on the heavy cowskin, and soon the warm, red blood
(amid heart-rending shrieks from her, and horrid oaths from him)
came dripping to the floor. I was so terrified and horror-stricken at the
sight, that I hid myself in a closet, and dared not venture out till long
after the bloody transaction was over. I expected it would be my turn
next. It was all new to me. I have never seen any thing like it before.
I had always lived with my grandmother on the outskirts of the plantation, where she was put to raise the children of the younger women.
I had therefore been, until now, out of the way of the bloody scenes
that often occurred on the plantation.

Chapter 6

My new mistress proved to be all she appeared when I first met her
at the door,—a woman of the kindest heart and finest feelings. She had
never had a slave under her control previously to myself, and prior to
her marriage she had been dependent upon her own industry for a
living. She was by trade a weaver; and by constant application to her
business, she had been in a good degree preserved from the blighting
and dehumanizing effects of slavery. I was utterly astonished at her
goodness. I scarcely knew how to behave towards her. She was entirely
unlike any other white woman I had ever seen. I could not approach
her as I was accustomed to approach other white ladies. My early
instruction was all out of place. The crouching servility, usually so
acceptable a quality in a slave, did not answer when manifested toward
her. Her favor was not gained by it; she seemed to be disturbed by it.
She did not deem it impudent or unmannerly for a slave to look her
in the face. The meanest slave was put fully at ease in her presence,
and none left without feeling better for having seen her. Her face was
made of heavenly smiles, and her voice of tranquil music.

But, alas! this kind heart had but a short time to remain such. The
fatal poison of irresponsible power was already in her hands, and soon
commenced its infernal work. That cheerful eye, under the influence
of slavery, soon became red with rage; that voice, made all of sweet
accord, changed to one of harsh and horrid discord; and that angelic
face gave place to that of a demon.

Very soon after I went to live with Mr. and Mrs. Auld, she very
kindly commenced to teach me the A, B, C. After I had learned this,
she assisted me in learning to spell words of three or four letters. Just
at this point of my progress, Mr. Auld found out what was going on,
and at once forbade Mrs. Auld to instruct me further, telling her,
among other things, that it was unlawful, as well as unsafe, to teach
a slave to read. To use his own words, further, he said, "If you give a
nigger an inch, he will take an ell. A nigger should know nothing but
to obey his master—to do as he is told to do. Learning would *spoil* the
best nigger in the world. Now," said he, "if you teach that nigger (speak-

ing of myself) how to read, there would be no keeping him. It would forever unfit him to be a slave. He would at once become unmanageable, and of no value to his master. As to himself, it could do him no good, but a great deal of harm. It would make him discontented and unhappy." These words sank deep into my heart, stirred up sentiments within that lay slumbering, and called into existence an entirely new train of thought. It was a new and special revelation, explaining dark and mysterious things, with which my youthful understanding had struggled, but struggled in vain. I now understood what had been to me a most perplexing difficulty—to wit, the white man's power to enslave the black man. It was a grand achievement, and I prized it highly. From that moment, I understood the pathway from slavery to freedom. It was just what I wanted, and I got it at a time when I the least expected it. Whilst I was saddened by the thought of losing the aid of my kind mistress, I was gladdened by the invaluable instruction which, by the merest accident, I had gained from my master. Though conscious of the difficulty of learning without a teacher, I set out with high hope, and a fixed purpose, at whatever cost of trouble, to learn how to read. The very decided manner with which he spoke, and strove to impress his wife with the evil consequences of giving me instruction, served to convince me that he was deeply sensible of the truths he was uttering. It gave me the best assurance that I might rely with the utmost confidence on the results which, he said, would flow from teaching me to read. What he most dreaded, that I most desired. What he most loved, that I most hated. That which to him was a great evil, to be carefully shunned, was to me a great good, to be diligently sought; and the argument which he so warmly urged, against my learning to read, only served to inspire me with a desire and determination to learn. In learning to read, I owe almost as much to the bitter opposition of my master, as to the kindly aid of my mistress. I acknowledge the benefit of both.

I had resided but a short time in Baltimore before I observed a marked difference, in the treatment of slaves, from that which I had witnessed in the country. A city slave is almost a freeman, compared with a slave on the plantation. He is much better fed and clothed, and enjoys privileges altogether unknown to the slave on the plantation. There is a vestige of decency, a sense of shame, that does much to curb and check those outbreaks of atrocious cruelty so commonly enacted upon the plantation. He is a desperate slaveholder, who will shock the humanity of his non-slaveholding neighbors with the cries of his lacerated slave. Few are willing to incur the odium attaching to the reputation of being a cruel master; and above all things, they would not be known as not giving a slave enough to eat. Every city slaveholder is anxious to have it known of him, that he feeds his slaves well; and it is due to them to say, that most of them do give their slaves enough to eat. There are, however, some painful exceptions to this rule. Directly

opposite to us, on Philpot Street, lived Mr. Thomas Hamilton. He owned
two slaves. Their names were Henrietta and Mary. Henrietta was about
twenty-two years of age, Mary was about fourteen; and of all the
mangled and emaciated creatures I ever looked upon, these two were
the most so. His heart must be harder than stone, that could look upon
these unmoved. The head, neck, and shoulders of Mary were literally
cut to pieces. I have frequently felt her head, and found it nearly covered with festering sores, caused by the lash of her cruel mistress. I
do not know that her master ever whipped her, but I have been an
eye-witness to the cruelty of Mrs. Hamilton. I used to be in Mr. Hamilton's house nearly every day. Mrs. Hamilton used to sit in a large chair
in the middle of the room, with a heavy cowskin always by her side,
and scarce an hour passed during the day but was marked by the blood
of one of these slaves. The girls seldom passed her without her saying,
"Move faster, you *black gip!*" at the same time giving them a blow with
the cowskin over the head or shoulders, often drawing the blood. She
would then say, "Take that, you *black gip!*"—continuing, "If you don't
move faster, I'll move you!" Added to the cruel lashings to which these
slaves were subjected, they were kept nearly half-starved. They seldom
knew what it was to eat a full meal. I have seen Mary contending with
the pigs for the offal thrown into the street. So much was Mary kicked
and cut to pieces, that she was oftener called *"pecked"* than by her
name.

FROM **Life and Times of Frederick Douglass** (1892)

Chapter 6   A Child's Reasoning

. . . Why am I a slave? Why are some people slaves and others
masters? These were perplexing questions and very troublesome to
my childhood. I was very early told by some one that "*God up in the
sky*" had made all things, and had made black people to be slaves
and white people to be masters. I was told too that God was good, and
that He knew what was best for everybody. This was, however, less
satisfactory than the first statement. It came point blank against all
my notions of goodness. The case of Aunt Esther was in my mind.
Besides, I could not tell how anybody could know that God made black
people to be slaves. Then I found, too, that there were puzzling exceptions to this theory of slavery, in the fact that all black people were
not slaves, and all white people were not masters. . . .

For the present we will attend to a further description of the busi-
nesslike aspect of Col. Lloyd's "Great House" farm. There was always
much bustle and noise here on the two days at the end of each month,
for then the slaves belonging to the different branches of this great

estate assembled here by their representatives to obtain their monthly allowances of cornmeal and pork. These were gala days for the slaves of the outlying farms, and there was much rivalry among them as to who should be elected to go up to the Great House farm for the "Allowances," and indeed to attend to any other business at this great place, to them the capital of a little nation. Its beauty and grandeur, its immense wealth, its numerous population, and the fact that uncles Harry, Peter, and Jake, the sailors on board the sloop, usually kept on sale trinkets which they bought in Baltimore to sell to their less fortunate fellow-servants, made a visit to the Great House farm a high privilege, and eagerly sought. It was valued, too, as a mark of distinction and confidence, but probably the chief motive among the competitors for the office was the opportunity it afforded to shake off the monotony of the field and to get beyond the overseer's eye and lash. Once on the road with an oxteam and seated on the tongue of the cart, with no overseer to look after him, one felt comparatively free.

Slaves were expected to sing as well as to work. A silent slave was not liked, either by masters or overseers. "Make a noise there! Make a noise there!" and "bear a hand," were words usually addressed to slaves when they were silent. This, and the natural disposition of the Negro to make a noise in the world, may account for the almost constant singing among them when at their work. There was generally more or less singing among the teamsters, at all times. It was a means of telling the overseer in the distance, where they were and what they were about. But on the allowance days those commissioned to the Great House farm were peculiarly vocal. While on the way they would make the grand old woods for miles around reverberate with their wild and plaintive notes. They were indeed both merry and sad. Child as I was, these wild songs greatly depressed my spirits. Nowhere outside of dear old Ireland, in the days of want and famine, have I heard sounds so mournful.

In all these slave songs there was some expression of praise of the Great House farm—something that would please the pride of the Lloyds.

I am going to the Great House farm,
      O, yea! O, yea! O, yea!
My old master is a good old master,
      O, yea! O, yea! O, yea!

These words would be sung over and over again, with others, improvised as they went along—jargon, perhaps, to the reader, but full of meaning to the singers. I have sometimes thought that the mere hearing of these songs would have done more to impress the good people of the North with the soul-crushing character of slavery than whole volumes exposing the physical cruelties of the slave system, for the heart has no language like song. Many years ago, when recollecting my experience in this respect, I wrote of these slave songs in the following strain:

"I did not, when a slave, fully understand the deep meaning of those rude and apparently incoherent songs. I was, myself, within the circle, so that I could then neither hear nor see as those without might see and hear. They breathed the prayer and complaint of souls overflowing with the bitterest anguish. They depressed my spirits and filled my heart with ineffable sadness."

The remark in the olden time was not unfrequently made, that slaves were the most contented and happy laborers in the world, and their dancing and singing were referred to in proof of this alleged fact; but it was a great mistake to suppose them happy because they sometimes made those joyful noises. The songs of the slaves represented their sorrows, rather than their joys. Like tears, they were a relief to aching hearts. It is not inconsistent with the constitution of the human mind that it avails itself of one and the same method for expressing opposite emotions. Sorrow and desolation have their songs, as well as joy and peace.

It was the boast of slaveholders that their slaves enjoyed more of the physical comforts of life than the peasantry of any country in the world. My experience contradicts this. The men and the women slaves on Col. Lloyd's farm received, as their monthly allowance of food, eight pounds of pickled pork, or its equivalent in fish. The pork was often tainted, and the fish were of the poorest quality. With their pork or fish, they had given them one bushel of Indian meal, unbolted, of which quite fifteen per cent was more fit for pigs than for men. With this, one pint of salt was given, and this was the entire monthly allowance of a full-grown slave, working constantly in the open field from morning till night every day in the month except Sunday. There is no kind of work which really requires a better supply of food to prevent physical exhaustion than the field-work of a slave. The yearly allowance of clothing was not more ample than the supply of food. It consisted of two tow-linen shirts, one pair of trousers of the same coarse material, for summer, and a woolen pair of trousers and a woolen jacket for winter, with one pair of yarn stockings and a pair of shoes of the coarsest description. Children under ten years old had neither shoes, stockings, jackets, nor trousers. They had two coarse tow-linen shirts per year, and when these were worn out they went naked till the next allowance day—and this was the condition of the little girls as well as of the boys.

As to beds, they had none. One coarse blanket was given them, and this only to the men and women. The children stuck themselves in holes and corners about the quarters, often in the corners of huge chimneys, with their feet in the ashes to keep them warm. The want of beds, however, was not considered a great privation by the field hands. Time to sleep was of far greater importance. For when the day's work was done most of these had their washing, mending, and cooking to do, and having few or no facilities for doing such things, very many of their needed sleeping hours were consumed in necessary preparations for the labors of the coming day. The sleeping apartments, if they could have been properly called such, had little regard to comfort or decency. Old and young, male and female, married and single, dropped down upon the common clay floor, each covering up with his or her blanket, their only protection from cold or exposure. The night, however, was shortened at both ends. The slaves worked often as long as they could see, and were late in cooking and mending for the coming day, and at the first gray streak of the morning they were summoned to the field by the overseer's horn. They were whipped for oversleeping more than for any other fault. Neither age nor sex found any favor. The overseer stood at the quarter door, armed with stick and whip, ready to deal heavy blows upon any who might be a little behind time. When the horn was blown there was a rush for the door, for the hindermost one was sure to get a blow from the overseer. Young mothers who worked in the field were allowed an hour about ten o'clock in the morning to go home to nurse their children. This was when they were not required to take them to the field with them, and leave them upon "turning row," or in the corner of the fences.

As a general rule the slaves did not come to their quarters to take their meals, but took their ashcake (called thus because baked in the ashes) and piece of pork, or their salt herrings, where they were at work.

But let us now leave the rough usage of the field, where vulgar coarseness and brutal cruelty flourished as rank as weeds in the tropics and where a vile wretch, in the shape of a man, rides, walks, and struts about, with whip in hand, dealing heavy blows and leaving deep gashes on the flesh of men and women, and turn our attention to the less repulsive slave life as it existed in the home of my childhood. Some idea of the splendor of that place sixty years ago has already been given. The contrast between the condition of the slaves and that of their masters was marvelously sharp and striking. There were pride, pomp, and luxury on the one hand, servility, dejection, and misery on the other.

ABRAHAM LINCOLN (1809–1865)

The most revered of all American Presidents was born in Hardin County, Kentucky, and as he later said, "was raised to farm work." At the age of twenty-one he went to Illinois and worked for a time in the town of New Salem, until a company of volunteers elected him their captain for the Black Hawk War.

Lincoln was defeated when he first tried for the Illinois state legislature in 1832, but he won the next four elections—and kept studying law on the side. "I was losing interest in politics," he later recalled, "when the repeal of the Missouri Compromise aroused me again." His debates with Douglas were held during the Illinois Senatorial campaign of 1858, and though Lincoln lost the election, he was nominated for the Presidency at the Republican national convention of 1860. Inaugurated for a second term in 1865, he was assassinated five days after Lee's surrender at Appomatox.

At the peak of his career, Lincoln became a master of English prose. The Gettysburg Address and the Second Inaugural Address are models of pure and elevated English which, unlike the speeches of many later Presidents, were written by Lincoln himself; one feels about them that the absolute rightness of language is a mirror to an absolute rightness of feeling. Never before had Lincoln achieved such compactness of phrase and command of rhythm; apparently, it was his sense of an overwhelming historical responsibility that released his gift for language, his engagement with sublimity.

Lincoln's formal education was skimpy, but from his boyhood until his death he was passionately fond of reading. He knew the Bible, he knew Bunyan's Pilgrim's Progress, *he knew Milton, Gibbon, and Shakespeare—a sufficient basis for the development of a mature prose style. And Lincoln cared about language, he worked hard at getting precisely the modulation or nuance he wanted. Mostly, Lincoln had only a self-education, but his mastery of language suggests that it was a true education.*

FURTHER READING

Roy P. Basler edited *Abraham Lincoln: His Speeches and Writings* (1946) with a useful introduction. Carl Sandburg's two-volume *Abraham Lincoln: The Prairie Years* (1926) and his four-volume *Abraham Lincoln: The War Years* (1939) were abridged in one volume in 1954. Sandburg's biography is loving and rhapsodic; cooler treatments can be found in Benjamin Thomas's *Abraham Lincoln* (1952), David Donald's *Lincoln Reconsidered* (1956), and Richard Hofstadter's *The American Political Tradition* (1948).

Letter to Horace Greeley

Executive Mansion, Washington,
August 22, 1862

Hon. Horace Greely:

Dear Sir:

I have just read yours of the 19th. addressed to myself through the New-York Tribune. If there be in it any statements, or assumptions of fact, which I may know to be erroneous, I do not, now and here, controvert them. If there be in it any inferences which I may believe to be falsely drawn, I do not now and here, argue against them. If there be perceptable in it an impatient and dictatorial tone, I waive it in deference to an old friend, whose heart I have always supposed to be right.

As to the policy I "seem to be pursuing" as you say, I have not meant to leave any one in doubt.

I would save the Union. I would save it the shortest way under the Constitution. The sooner the national authority can be restored; the nearer the Union will be "the Union as it was." If there be those who would not save the Union, unless they could at the same time *save* slavery, I do not agree with them. If there be those who would not save the Union unless they could at the same time *destroy* slavery, I do not agree with them. My paramount object in this struggle *is* to save the Union, and is *not* either to save or to destroy slavery. If I could save the Union without freeing *any* slave I would do it; and if I could save it by freeing some and leaving others alone I would also do that. What I do about slavery, and the colored race, I do because I believe it helps to save the Union; and what I forbear, I forbear because I do *not* believe it would help to save the Union. I shall do *less* whenever I shall believe what I am doing hurts the cause, and I shall do *more* whenever I shall believe doing more will help the cause. I shall try to correct errors when shown to be errors; and I shall adopt new views so fast as they shall appear to be true views.

I have here stated my purpose according to my view of *official* duty; and I intend no modification of my oft-expressed *personal* wish that all men every where could be free.

Yours,
A. Lincoln

The Gettysburg Address (1863)[1]

Four score and seven years ago our fathers brought forth on this continent, a new nation, conceived in Liberty, and dedicated to the proposition that all men are created equal.

Now we are engaged in a great civil war; testing whether that nation, or any nation so conceived and so dedicated, can long endure. We are met on a great battlefield of that war. We have come to dedicate a portion of that field as a final resting-place for those who here gave their lives that that nation might live. It is altogether fitting and proper that we should do this.

---

[1] Several days before delivering the Gettysburg Address, Lincoln saw the full text of the featured speaker of the occasion, Edward Everett, and as if by ironic contrast, told a newspaperman that his own speech would be "short, short, short." It consists of ten sentences and can be spoken in five minutes.

But, in a larger sense, we cannot dedicate—we cannot consecrate—we cannot hallow—this ground. The brave men, living and dead, who struggled here have consecrated it, far above our poor power to add or detract. The world will little note, nor long remember, what we say here, but it can never forget what they did here. It is for us the living, rather, to be dedicated here to the unfinished work which they who fought here have thus far so nobly advanced. It is rather for us to be here dedicated to the great task remaining before us—that from these honored dead we take increased devotion to that cause for which they gave the last full measure of devotion; that we here highly resolve that these dead shall not have died in vain; that this nation, under God, shall have a new birth of freedom; and that government of the people, by the people, for the people, shall not perish from the earth.

Second Inaugural Address (1865)

Fellow Countrymen:

At this second appearing to take the oath of the presidential office, there is less occasion for an extended address than there was at the first. Then a statement, somewhat in detail, of a course to be pursued, seemed fitting and proper. Now, at the expiration of four years, during which public declarations have been constantly called forth on every point and phase of the great contest which still absorbs the attention and engrosses the energies of the nation, little that is new could be presented. The progress of our arms, upon which all else chiefly depends, is as well known to the public as to myself; and it is, I trust, reasonably satisfactory and encouraging to all. With high hope for the future, no prediction in regard to it is ventured.

On the occasion corresponding to this four years ago, all thoughts were anxiously directed to an impending civil war. All dreaded it—all sought to avert it. While the inaugural address was being delivered from this place, devoted altogether to saving the Union without war, insurgent agents were in the city seeking to destroy it without war—seeking to dissolve the Union, and divide effects, by negotiation. Both parties deprecated war; but one of them would make war rather than let the nation survive; and the other would accept war rather than let it perish. And the war came.

One-eighth of the whole population were colored slaves, not distributed generally over the Union, but localized in the southern part of it. These slaves constituted a peculiar and powerful interest. All knew that this interest was, somehow, the cause of the war. To strengthen, perpetuate, and extend this interest was the object for which the insurgents would rend the Union, even by war; while the government claimed no right to do more than to restrict the territorial enlargement of it.

Neither party expected for the war the magnitude or the duration which it has already attained. Neither anticipated that the cause of the conflict might cease with, or even before, the conflict itself should cease. Each looked for an easier triumph, and a result less fundamental and astounding. Both read the same Bible, and pray to the same God; and each invokes His aid against the other. It may seem strange that any men should dare to ask a just God's assistance in wringing their bread from the sweat of other's men's faces; but let us judge not, that we be not judged. The prayers of both could not be answered—that of neither has been answered fully.

The Almighty has his own purposes. "Woe unto the world because of offenses! for it must needs be that offenses come; but woe to that man by whom the offense cometh." If we shall suppose that American slavery is one of those offenses which, in the providence of God, must needs come, but which, having continued through His appointed time. He now wills to remove, and that He gives to both North and South this terrible war, as the woe due to those by whom the offense came, shall we discern therein any departure from those divine attributes which the believers in a living God always ascribe to Him? Fondly do we hope—fervently do we pray—that this mighty scourge of war may speedily pass away. Yet, if God wills that it continue until all the wealth piled by the bondman's two hundred and fifty years of unrequited toil shall be sunk, and until every drop of blood drawn with the lash shall be paid by another drawn with the sword, as was said three thousand years ago, so still it must be said, "The judgments of the Lord are true and righteous altogether."

With malice toward none; with charity for all; with firmness in the right, as God gives us to see the right, let us strive on to finish the work we are in; to bind up the nation's wounds; to care for him who shall have borne the battle, and for his widow, and his orphan—to do all which may achieve and cherish a just and lasting peace among ourselves, and with all nations.

ULYSSES S. GRANT (1822–1885)

In 1881, when Mark Twain met ex-President Grant, he urged the old soldier to compose his memoirs. Grant, as Twain remembered later,

wouldn't listen to the suggestion. He had no confidence in his ability to write well; whereas we all know now that he possessed an admirable literary gift and style. He was also sure that the book would have no sale, and of course that would be a humility, too. I argued that the book would have an enormous sale. . . .

It did. Three years later, hard-pressed for money and suffering from the cancer of the throat that soon would kill him, Grant set about to write the book. It took him slightly less than a year, and he died a week after his manuscript was finished. The Memoirs *sold three hundred thousand copies in the first two years after their appearance and earned close to half a million dollars for Grant's destitute family. Though a major achievement, the* Memoirs *came gradually to be neglected, perhaps because Grant himself came to be regarded as an unattractive figure: a ruthless general, an incompetent President, a native philistine. Only since Edmund Wilson wrote with great respect about the* Memoirs *in his* Patriotic Gore *have they regained the place of honor they deserve in American writing.*

Grant was born in a log cabin in a small Ohio town. Though not inclined to the military life, he found his way to West Point from which he graduated in 1843. He served in the Mexican war, which he had the good sense to regard as an unjust war on our part, and remained in the army for several years more, with a record far from distinguished. Asked to leave the army because of his excessive drinking in the seven years that intervened before he reentered at the outset of the Civil War, Grant's life was downright pitiable. He failed totally at every civilian job he undertook, and in St. Louis, where he lived for a time, people avoided him as a down-and-outer.

The story of Grant's achievements in the Union army is too familiar to repeat: his military genius, his absolute calm under fire, his ability to inspire loyalty among officers and men. Elected President in 1868, he served two terms, surely one of the least competent and most bewildered chief executives this nation has ever had. (For a devastating portrait of Grant as President, see The Education of Henry Adams, *chapter 17, on p. 1113 in this anthology.)*

The Memoirs *themselves, lapidary in structure and dynamic in pace, are first rate. Grant wrote with an objectivity, a disregard for self-justification, and a "hard limpidity" of phrase (to use Henry James's term) which few of our professional writers could match. We must again marvel at the native excellence of the prose employed by at least some Americans in public life during the nineteenth century.*

The English critic Matthew Arnold, a cultivated humanist whom one would not supposed naturally inclined toward a man like Grant, nevertheless wrote a lengthy essay on the Memoirs. *He found Grant himself dull and mystifying, "touched by no divine light and giving out none"; yet in the* Memoirs *themselves, despite a prose "all astray" and a lamentable confusion of "shall" and "will," he found "a language straightforward, nervous, firm, possessing in general the high merit of saying clearly in the fewest possible words what had to be said, and saying it, frequently, with shrewd and unexpected turns of expression."*

FURTHER READING

William Hesseltine, *Ulysses S. Grant: Politician* (1935).

FROM *Personal Memoirs of U. S. Grant* (1885)

Some two or three miles from Pittsburg landing was a log meeting-house called Shiloh. It stood on the ridge which divides the waters of Snake and Lick creeks, the former emptying into the Tennessee just north of Pittsburg landing, and the latter south. This point was the key to our position and was held by Sherman. His division was at that time wholly raw, no part of it ever having been in an engagement; but I thought this deficiency was more than made up by the superiority of the commander. McClernand was on Sherman's left, with troops that had been engaged at forts Henry and Donelson and were therefore veterans so far as western troops had become such at that stage of the war. Next to McClernand came Prentiss with a raw division, and on the extreme left, Stuart with one brigade of Sherman's division. Hurlbut was in rear of Prentiss, massed, and in reserve at the time of the onset. The division of General C. F. Smith was on the right, also in reserve. General Smith was still sick in bed at Savannah, but within hearing of our guns. His services would no doubt have been of inestimable value had his health permitted his presence. The command of his division devolved upon Brigadier-General W. H. L. Wallace, a most estimable and able officer; a veteran too, for he had served a year in the Mexican war and had been with his command at Henry and Donelson. Wallace was mortally wounded in the first day's engagement, and with the change of commanders thus necessarily effected in the heat of battle the efficiency of his division was much weakened.

The position of our troops made a continuous line from Lick Creek on the left to Owl Creek, a branch of Snake Creek, on the right, facing nearly south and possibly a little west. The water in all these streams was very high at the time and contributed to protect our flanks. The enemy was compelled, therefore, to attack directly in front. This he did with great vigor, inflicting heavy losses on the National side, but suffering much heavier on his own.

The Confederate assaults were made with such a disregard of losses on their own side that our line of tents soon fell into their hands. The ground on which the battle was fought was undulating, heavily timbered with scattered clearings, the woods giving some protection to the troops on both sides. There was also considerable underbrush. A number of attempts were made by the enemy to turn our right flank, where Sherman was posted, but every effort was repulsed with heavy loss. But the front attack was kept up so vigorously that, to prevent the success of these attempts to get on our flanks, the National troops were compelled, several times, to take positions to the rear nearer Pittsburg landing. When the firing ceased at night the National line was all of a mile in rear of the position it had occupied in the morning.

In one of the backward moves, on the 6th, the division commanded by General Prentiss did not fall back with the others. This left his flanks exposed and enabled the enemy to capture him with about 2,200 of his officers and men. General Badeau gives four o'clock of the 6th as about the time this capture took place. He may be right as to the time, but my recollection is that the hour was later. General Prentiss himself gave the hour as half-past five. I was with him, as I was with each of the division commanders that day, several times, and my recollection is that the last time I was with him was about half-past four, when his division was standing up firmly and the General was as cool as if expecting victory. But no matter whether it was four or later, the story that he and his command were surprised and captured in their camps is without any foundation whatever. If it had been true, as currently reported at the time and yet believed by thousands of people, that Prentiss and his division had been captured in their beds, there would not have been an all-day struggle, with the loss of thousands killed and wounded on the Confederate side.

With the single exception of a few minutes after the capture of Prentiss, a continuous and unbroken line was maintained all day from Snake Creek or its tributaries on the right to Lick Creek or the Tennessee on the left above Pittsburg. There was no hour during the day when there was not heavy firing and generally hard fighting at some point on the line, but seldom at all points at the same time. It was a case of Southern dash against Northern pluck and endurance. Three of the five divisions engaged on Sunday were entirely raw, and many of the men had only received their arms on the way from their States to the field. Many of them had arrived but a day or two before and were hardly able to load their muskets according to the manual. Their officers were equally ignorant of their duties. Under these circumstances it is not astonishing that many of the regiments broke at the first fire. In two cases, as I now remember, colonels led their regiments from the field on first hearing the whistle of the enemy's bullets. In these cases the colonels were constitutional cowards, unfit for any military position; but not so the officers and men led out of danger by them. Better troops never went upon a battle-field than many of these, officers and men, afterwards proved themselves to be, who fled panic-stricken at the first whistle of bullets and shell at Shiloh.

During the whole of Sunday I was continuously engaged in passing from one part of the field to another, giving directions to division commanders. In thus moving along the line, however, I never deemed it important to stay long with Sherman. Although his troops were then under fire for the first time, their commander, by his constant presence with them, inspired a confidence in officers and men that enabled them to render services on that bloody battle-field worthy of the best of veterans. McClernand was next to Sherman, and the hardest fighting was in front of these two divisions. McClernand told me on that day, the 6th, that he profited much by having so able a commander supporting him. A casualty to Sherman that would have taken him from the field that day would have been a sad one for the troops engaged at Shiloh. And how near we came to this! On the 6th Sherman was shot twice, once in the hand, once in the shoulder, the ball cutting his coat and making a slight wound, and a third ball passed through his hat. In addition to this he had several horses shot during the day.

The nature of this battle was such that cavalry could not be used in front; I therefore formed ours into line in rear, to stop stragglers— of whom there were many. When there would be enough of them to make a show, and after they had recovered from their fright, they would be sent to reinforce some part of the line which needed support, without regard to their companies, regiments or brigades.

On one occasion during the day I rode back as far as the river and met General Buell, who had just arrived; I do not remember the hour, but at that time there probably were as many as four or five thousand stragglers lying under cover of the river bluff, panic-stricken, most of whom would have been shot where they lay, without resistance, before they would have taken muskets and marched to the front to protect themselves. This meeting between General Buell and myself was on the dispatch-boat used to run between the landing and Savannah. It was brief, and related specially to his getting his troops over the river. As we left the boat together, Buell's attention was attracted by the men lying under cover of the river bank. I saw him berating them and trying to shame them into joining their regiments. He even threatened them with shells from the gunboats near by. But it was all to no effect. Most of these men afterward proved themselves as gallant as any of those who saved the battle from which they had deserted. I have no doubt that this sight impressed General Buell with the idea that a line of retreat would be a good thing just then. If he had come in by the front instead of through the stragglers in the rear, he would have thought and felt differently. Could he have come through the Confederate rear, he would have witnessed there a scene similar to that at our own. The distant rear of an army engaged in battle is not the best place from which to judge correctly what is going on in front. Later in the war, while occupying the country between the Tennessee and the Mississippi, I learned that the panic in the Confederate lines had not differed much from that within our own. Some of the country people estimated the stragglers from Johnston's army as high as 20,000. Of course this was an exaggeration. . . .

There was, as I have said, a deep ravine in front of our left. The Tennessee River was very high and there was water to a considerable depth in the ravine. Here the enemy made a last desperate effort to turn our flank, but was repelled. The gunboats *Tyler* and *Lexington,* Gwin and Shirk commanding, with the artillery under Webster, aided the army and effectually checked their further progress. Before any of Buell's troops had reached the west bank of the Tennessee, firing had almost entirely ceased; anything like an attempt on the part of the enemy to advance had absolutely ceased. There was some artillery firing from an unseen enemy, some of his shells passing beyond us; but I do not remember that there was the whistle of a single musket-ball heard. As his troops arrived in the dusk General Buell marched several of his regiments part way down the face of the hill where they fired briskly for some minutes, but I do not think a single man engaged in this firing received an injury. The attack had spent its force.

General Lew. Wallace, with 5,000 effective men, arrived after firing had ceased for the day, and was placed on the right. Thus night came, Wallace came, and the advance of Nelson's division came; but none— unless night—in time to be of material service to the gallant men who saved Shiloh on that first day against large odds. Buell's loss on the 6th of April was two men killed and one wounded, all members of the 36th Indiana infantry. The Army of the Tennesse lost on that day at least 7,000 men. The presence of two or three regiments of Buell's army on the west bank before firing ceased had not the slightest effect in preventing the capture of Pittsburg landing.

So confident was I before firing had ceased on the 6th that the next day would bring victory to our arms if we could only take the initiative, that I visited each division commander in person before any reinforcements had reached the field. I directed them to throw out heavy lines of skirmishers in the morning as soon as they could see, and push them forward until they found the enemy, following with their entire divisions in supporting distance, and to engage the enemy as soon as found. To Sherman I told the story of the assault at Fort Donelson, and said that the same tactics would win at Shiloh. Victory was assured when Wallace arrived, even if there had been no other support. I was glad, however, to see the reinforcements of Buell and credit them with doing all there was for them to do. During the night of the 6th the remainder of Nelson's division, Buell's army, crossed the river and were ready to advance in the morning, forming the left wing. Two other divisions, Crittenden's and McCook's, came up the river from Savannah in the transports and were on the west bank early on the 7th. Buel commanded them in person. My command was thus nearly doubled in numbers and efficiency.

During the night rain fell in torrents and our troops were exposed to the storm without shelter. I made my headquarters under a tree a few hundred yards back from the river bank. My ankle was so much swollen from the fall of my horse the Friday night preceding, and the bruise was so painful, that I could get no rest. The drenching rain would have precluded the possibility of sleep without this additional cause. Some time after midnight, growing restive under the storm and the continuous pain, I moved back to the log-house under the bank. This had been taken as a hospital, and all night wounded men were being brought in, their wounds dressed, a leg or an arm amputated as the case might require, and everything being done to save life or alleviate suffering. The sight was more unendurable than encountering the enemy's fire, and I returned to my tree in the rain.

The advance on the morning of the 7th developed the enemy in the camps occupied by our troops before the battle began, more than a mile back from the most advanced position of the Confederates on the day before. It is known now that they had not yet learned of the arrival of Buell's command. Possibly they fell back so far to get the shelter of our tents during the rain, and also to get away from the shells that were dropped upon them by the gunboats every fifteen minutes during the night.

The position of the Union troops on the morning of the 7th was as follows: General Lew. Wallace on the right; Sherman on his left; then McClernand and then Hurlbut. Nelson, of Buell's army, was on our extreme left, next to the river. Crittendon was next in line after Nelson and on his right; McCook followed and formed the extreme right of Buell's command. My old command thus formed the right wing, while the troops directly under Buell constituted the left wing of the army. These relative positions were retained during the entire day, or until the enemy was driven from the field.

In a very short time the battle became general all along the line. This day everything was favorable to the Union side. We had now become the attacking party. The enemy was driven back all day, as we had been the day before, until finally he beat a precipitate retreat. The last point held by him was near the road leading from the landing to Corinth, on the left of Sherman and right of McClernand. About three o'clock, being near that point and seeing that the enemy was giving way everywhere else, I gathered up a couple of regiments, or parts of regiments, from troops near by, formed them in line of battle and marched them forward, going in front myself to prevent premature or long-range firing. At this point there was a clearing between us and the enemy favorable for charging, although exposed. I knew the enemy were ready to break and only wanted a little encouragement from us to go quickly and join their friends who had started earlier. After marching to within musket-range I stopped and let the troops pass. The command, *Charge*, was given, and was executed with loud cheers and with a run; when the last of the enemy broke. . . .

During this second day of the battle I had been moving from right to left and back, to see for myself the progress made. In the early part of the afternoon, while riding with Colonel McPherson and Major Hawkins, then my chief commissary, we got beyond the left of our troops. We were moving along the northern edge of a clearing, very leisurely, toward the river above the landing. There did not appear to be an enemy to our right, until suddenly a battery with musketry opened upon us from the edge of the woods on the other side of the clearing. The shells and balls whistled about our ears very fast for about a minute. I do not think it took us longer than that to get out of range and out of sight. In the sudden start we made, Major Hawkins lost his hat. He did not stop to pick it up. When we arrived at a perfectly safe position we halted to take an account of damages. McPherson's horse was panting as if ready to drop. On examination it was found that a ball had struck him forward of the flank just back of the saddle, and had gone entirely through. In a few minutes the poor beast dropped dead; he had given no sign of injury until we came to a stop. A ball had struck the metal scabbard of my sword, just below the hilt, and broken it nearly off; before the battle was over it had broken off entirely. There were three of us: one had lost a horse, killed; one a hat and one a sword-scabbard. All were thankful that it was no worse.

After the rain of the night before and the frequent and heavy rains for some days previous, the roads were almost impassable. The enemy carrying his artillery and supply trains over them in his retreat, made them still worse for troops following. I wanted to pursue, but had not the heart to order the men who had fought desperately for two days, lying in the mud and rain whenever not fighting, and I did not feel disposed to positively order Buell, or any part of his command, to pursue. Although the senior in rank at the time I had been so only a few weeks. Buell was, and had been for some time past, a department commander, while I commanded only a district. I did not meet Buell in person until too late to get troops ready and pursue with effect; but had I seen him at the moment of the last charge I should have at least requested him to follow.

I rode forward several miles the day after the battle, and found that the enemy had dropped much, if not all, of their provisions, some ammunition and the extra wheels of their caissons, lightening their loads to enable them to get off their guns. About five miles out we found their field hospital abandoned. An immediate pursuit must have resulted in the capture of a considerable number of prisoners and probably some guns.

Shiloh was the severest battle fought at the West during the war, and but few in the East equalled it for hard, determined fighting. I saw an open field, in our possession on the second day, over which the Confederates had made repeated charges the day before, so covered with dead that it would have been possible to walk across the clearing, in any direction, stepping on dead bodies, without a foot touching the ground. On our side National and Confederate troops were mingled together in about equal proportions; but on the remainder of the field nearly all were Confederates. On one part, which had evidently not been ploughed for several years, probably because the land was poor, bushes had grown up, some to the height of eight or ten feet. There was not one of these left standing unpierced by bullets. The smaller ones were all cut down.

Contrary to all my experience up to that time, and to the experience of the army I was then commanding, we were on the defensive. We were without intrenchments or defensive advantages of any sort, and more than half the army engaged the first day was without experience or even drill as soldiers. The officers with them, except the division commanders and possibly two or three of the brigade commanders, were equally inexperienced in war. The result was a Union victory that gave the men who achieved it great confidence in themselves ever after.

The enemy fought bravely, but they had started out to defeat and destroy an army and capture a position. They failed in both, with very heavy loss in killed and wounded, and must have gone back discouraged and convinced that the "Yankee" was not an enemy to be despised.

WILLIAM TECUMSEH SHERMAN (1820–1891)

Like his colleague Ulysses S. Grant, General Sherman was born in Ohio and served in the Mexican war. His early life included some vivid adventures as a young officer in California and then as a banker in St. Louis and San Francisco. He first saw action in the Civil War as a colonel of infantry at Bull Run. In the spring of 1864, when Grant was appointed General-in-chief of the Union armies, Sherman, now a brigadier general, took command of the Division of the Mississippi. During the remainder of that year he made his famous "March to the Sea" which culminated in the burning of Atlanta and transformed Sherman into one of the most hated men in Southern history. This early version of the blitzkrieg was later acknowledged as a tactical innovation in warfare. Sherman himself, in his usual blunt fashion, had no inclination to romanticize his achievement; years later, in 1880, he made his famous remark, "... there is many a boy here today who looks on war as all glory, but boys, it is all hell."

In one of his letters Sherman described General Grant as "guarded" and "prudent," and himself as "outspoken" and "careless." Some such difference also holds between their memoirs of the war. Each is remarkably well written, especially when one considers that neither general had any pretensions to being a professional literary man;

but they are well written in very different ways. Grant's memoirs are impersonal and cool, Sherman's personal and warm. Mark Twain was right when he said that Sherman was a born master of narrative: he can draw lively pictures of men in battle, he knows how to spin off an anecdote which illuminates some larger issue, and he is very good at arranging his material so as to highlight dramatic moments and bring everything to a strong climax. His account of the march through the South is a masterpiece of storytelling in which nothing of the horror is minimized nor any effort made to deny the ruthlessness with which Sherman subdued the enemy. There is not a touch of hypocrisy or piety in Sherman's Memoirs; he does not paint himself any prettier than he is; and even those readers who recoil in disgust must respect his frankness.

FURTHER READING

The *Memoirs* were published in two volumes in 1875. Sherman's letters were edited by M. A. DeWolfe Howe in 1909, and recent studies include Earl Schenck Miers' *The General Who Marched to the Sea* (1951) and R. G. Ahearn's *W. L. Sherman and the Settlement of the West* (1956).

FROM *Memoirs* (1875)[1]

. . . All hands were kept busy tearing up the railroad, and it was not until toward evening of the 1st day of September that the Fourteenth Corps (Davis) closed down on the north front of Jonesboro', connecting on his right with Howard, and his left reaching the railroad, along which General Stanley was moving, followed by Schofield. General Davis formed his divisions in line about 4 P. M., swept forward over some old cotton fields in full view, and went over the rebel parapet handsomely, capturing the whole of Govan's brigade, with two field-batteries of ten guns. Being on the spot, I checked Davis's movement, and ordered General Howard to send the two divisions of the Seventeenth Corps (Blair) round by his right rear, to get below Jonesboro', and to reach the railroad, so as to cut off retreat in that direction. I also dispatched orders after orders to hurry forward Stanley, so as to lap around Jonesboro' on the east, hoping thus to capture the whole of Hardee's corps. I sent first Captain Audenried (aide-de-camp), then Colonel Poe, of the Engineers, and lastly General Thomas himself (and that is the only time during the campaign I can recall seeing General

[1] These selections describe the capture of Atlanta by Northern troops and their march to the sea.

Thomas urge his horse into a gallop). Night was approaching, and the country on the farther side of the railroad was densely wooded. General Stanley had come up on the left of Davis, and was deploying, though there could not have been on his front more than a skirmish-line. Had he moved straight on by the flank, or by a slight circuit to his left, he would have inclosed the whole ground occupied by Hardee's corps, and that corps could not have escaped us; but night came on, and Hardee did escape.

Meantime General Slocum had reached his corps (the Twentieth), stationed at the Chattahoochee bridge, had relieved General A. S. Williams in command, and orders had been sent back to him to feel forward occasionally toward Atlanta, to observe the effect when we had reached the railroad. That night I was so restless and impatient that I could not sleep, and about midnight there arose toward Atlanta sounds of shells exploding, and other sound like that of musketry. I walked to the house of a farmer close by my bivouac, called him out to listen to the reverberations which came from the direction of Atlanta (twenty miles to the north of us), and inquired of him if he had resided there long. He said he had, and that these sounds were just like those of a battle. An interval of quiet then ensued, when again, about 4 A. M., arose other similar explosions, but I still remained in doubt whether the enemy was engaged in blowing up his own magazines, or whether General Slocum had not felt forward, and become engaged in a real battle.

The next morning General Hardee was gone, and we all pushed forward along the railroad south, in close pursuit, till we ran up against his lines at a point just above Lovejoy's Station. While bringing forward troops and feeling the new position of our adversary, rumors came from the rear that the enemy had evacuated Atlanta, and that General Slocum was in the city. Later in the day I received a note in Slocum's own handwriting, stating that he had heard during the night the very sounds that I have referred to; that he had moved rapidly up from the bridge about daylight, and had entered Atlanta unopposed. His letter was dated inside the city, so there was no doubt of the fact. General Thomas's bivouac was but a short distance from mine, and, before giving notice to the army in general orders, I sent one of my staff-officers to show him the note. In a few minutes the officer returned, soon followed by Thomas himself, who again examined the note, so as to be perfectly certain that it was genuine. The news seemed to him too good to be true. He snapped his fingers, whistled, and almost danced, and, as the news spread to the army, the shouts that arose from our men, the wild hallooing and glorious laughter, were to us a full recompense for the labor and toils and hardships through which we had passed in the previous three months.

A courier-line was at once organized, messages were sent back and forth from our camp at Lovejoy's to Atlanta, and to our telegraph-station at the Chattahoochee bridge. Of course, the glad tidings flew on the wings of electricity to all parts of the North, where the people had patiently awaited news of their husbands, sons, and brothers, away down in "Dixie Land;" and congratulations came pouring back full of good-will and patriotism. This victory was most opportune; Mr. Lincoln himself told me afterward that even he had previously felt in doubt, for the summer was fast passing away; that General Grant seemed to be checkmated about Richmond and Petersburg, and my army seemed to have run up against an impassable barrier, when, suddenly and unexpectedly, came the news that "Atlanta was ours, and fairly won." On this text many a fine speech was made, but none more eloquent than that by Edward Everett, in Boston. A presidential election then agitated the North. Mr. Lincoln represented the national cause, and General McClellan had accepted the nomination of the Democratic party, whose platform was that the war was a failure, and that it was better to allow the South to go free to establish a separate government, whose corner-stone should be slavery. Success to our arms at that instant was therefore a political necessity; and it was all-important that something startling in our interest should occur before the election in November. The brilliant success at Atlanta filled that requirement, and made the election of Mr. Lincoln certain. Among the many letters of congratulation received, those of Mr. Lincoln and General Grant seem most important:

Executive Mansion,
Washington, D.C., September 3, 1864
The national thanks are rendered by the President to Major-General W. T. Sherman and the gallant officers and soldiers of his command before Atlanta, for the distinguished ability and perseverance displayed in the campaign in Georgia, which, under Divine favor, has resulted in the capture of Atlanta. The marches, battles, sieges, and other military operations, that have signalized the campaign, must render it famous in the annals of war, and have entitled those who have participated therein to the applause and thanks of the nation.

Abraham Lincoln,
President of the United States

City Point, Virginia, September 4, 1864—9 P.M.
Major-General Sherman:
I have just received your dispatch announcing the capture of Atlanta. In honor of your great victory, I have ordered a salute to be fired with *shotted* guns from every battery bearing upon the enemy. The salute will be fired within an hour, amid great rejoicing.

U. S. Grant,
Lieutenant-General

These dispatches were communicated to the army in general orders, and we all felt duly encouraged and elated by the praise of those competent to bestow it.

The army still remained where the news of success had first found us, viz., Lovejoy's; but, after due reflection, I resolved not to attempt at that time a further pursuit of Hood's army, but slowly and deliberately to move back, occupy Atlanta, enjoy a short period of rest, and to think well over the next step required in the progress of events. Orders for this movement were made on the 5th September, and three days were given for each army to reach the place assigned it, viz.: the Army of the Cumberland in and about Atlanta; the Army of the Tennessee at East Point; and the Army of the Ohio at Decatur.

Personally I rode back to Jonesboro' on the 6th, and there inspected the rebel hospital, full of wounded officers and men left by Hardee in his retreat. The next night we stopped at Rough and Ready, and on the 8th of September we rode into Atlanta, then occupied by the Twentieth Corps (General Slocum). In the Court-House Square was encamped a brigade, embracing the Massachusetts Second and Thirty-third Regiments, which had two of the finest bands of the army, and their music was to us all a source of infinite pleasure during our sojourn in that city. I took up my headquarters in the house of Judge Lyons, which stood opposite one corner of the Court-House Square, and at once set about a measure already ordered, of which I had thought much and long, viz., to remove the entire civil population, and to deny to all civilians from the rear the expected profits of civil trade. Hundreds of sutlers and traders were waiting at Nashville and Chattanooga, greedy to reach Atlanta with their wares and goods, with which to drive a profitable trade with the inhabitants. I gave positive orders that none of these traders, except three (one for each separate army), should be permitted to come nearer than Chattanooga; and, moreover, I peremptorily required that all the citizens and families resident in Atlanta should go away, giving to each the option to go south or north, as their interests or feelings dictated. I was resolved to make Atlanta a pure military garrison or depot, with no civil population to influence military measures. I had seen Memphis, Vicksburg, Natchez, and New Orleans, all captured from the enemy, and each at once was garrisoned by a full division of troops, if not more; so that success was actually crippling our armies in the field by detachments to guard and protect the interests of a hostile population.

I gave notice of this purpose, as early as the 4th of September, to General Halleck, in a letter concluding with these words:

If the people raise a howl against my barbarity and cruelty, I will answer that war is war, and not popularity-seeking. If they want peace, they and their relatives must stop the war.

I knew, of course, that such a measure would be strongly criticised, but made up my mind to do it with the absolute certainty of its justness, and that time would sanction its wisdom. I knew that the people of the South would read in this measure two important conclusions: one, that we were in earnest; and the other, if they were sincere in their common and popular clamor "to die in the last ditch," that the opportunity would soon come.

Soon after our reaching Atlanta, General Hood had sent in by a flag of truce a proposition, offering a general exchange of prisoners, saying that he was authorized to make such an exchange by the Richmond authorities, out of the vast number of our men then held captive at Andersonville, the same whom General Stoneman had hoped to rescue at the time of his raid. Some of these prisoners had already escaped and got in, had described the pitiable condition of the remainder, and, although I felt a sympathy for their hardships and sufferings as deeply as any man could, yet as nearly all the prisoners who had been captured by us during the campaign had been sent, as fast as taken, to the usual depots North, they were then beyond my control. There were still about two thousand, mostly captured at Jonesboro', who had been sent back by cars, but had not passed Chattanooga. These I ordered back, and offered General Hood to exchange them for Stoneman, Buell, and such of my own army as would make up the equivalent; but I would not exchange for his prisoners *generally*, because I knew these would have to be sent to their own regiments, away from my army, whereas all we could give him could at once be put to duty in his immediate army.

About 7 A.M. of November 16th we rode out of Atlanta by the Decatur road, filled by the marching troops and wagons of the Fourteenth Corps; and reaching the hill, just outside of the old rebel works, we naturally paused to look back upon the scenes of our past battles. We stood upon the very ground whereon was fought the bloody battle of July 22d, and could see the copse of wood where McPherson fell. Behind us lay Atlanta, smouldering and in ruins, the black smoke rising high in air, and hanging like a pall over the ruined city. Away off in the distance, on the McDonough road, was the rear of Howard's column, the gun-barrels glistening in the sun, the white-topped wagons stretching away to the south; and right before us the Fourteenth Corps, marching steadily and rapidly, with a cheery look and swinging pace, that made light of the thousand miles that lay between us and Richmond. Some band, by accident, struck up the anthem of "John Brown's soul goes marching on;" the men caught up the strain, and never before or since have I heard the chorus of "Glory, glory, hallelujah!" done with more spirit, or in better harmony of time and place.

Then we turned our horses' heads to the east; Atlanta was soon lost behind the screen of trees, and became a thing of the past. Around it clings many a thought of desperate battle, of hope and fear, that now seem like the memory of a dream; and I have never seen the place since. The day was extremely beautiful, clear sunlight, with bracing air, and an unusual feeling of exhilaration seemed to pervade all minds—a feeling of something to come, vague and undefined, still full of venture and intense interest. Even the common soldiers caught the inspiration, and many a group called out to me as I worked my way past them, "Uncle Billy, I guess Grant is waiting for us at Richmond!" Indeed, the general sentiment was that we were marching for Richmond, and that there we should end the war, but how and when they seemed to care not; nor did they measure the distance, or count the cost in life, or bother their brains about the great rivers to be crossed, and the food required for man and beast, that had to be gathered by the way. There was a "devil-may-care" feeling pervading officers and men, that made me feel the full load of responsibility, for success would be accepted as a matter of course, whereas, should we fail, this "march" would be adjudged the wild adventure of a crazy fool. I had no purpose to march direct for Richmond by way of Augusta and Charlotte, but always designed to reach the sea-coast first at Savannah or Port Royal, South Carolina, and even kept in mind the alternative of Pensacola.

The first night out we camped by the road-side near Lithonia. Stone Mountain, a mass of granite, was in plain view, cut out in clear outline against the blue sky; the whole horizon was lurid with the bonfires of rail-ties, and groups of men all night were carrying the heated rails to the nearest trees, and bending them around the trunks. Colonel Poe had provided tools for ripping up the rails and twisting them when hot; but the best and easiest way is the one I have described, of heating the middle of the iron-rails on bonfires made of the cross-ties, and then winding them around a telegraph-pole or the trunk of some convenient sapling. I attached much importance to this destruction of the railroad, gave it my own personal attention, and made reiterated orders to others on the subject.

The next day we passed through the handsome town of Covington, the soldiers closing up their ranks, the color-bearers unfurling their flags, and the bands striking up patriotic airs. The white people came out of their houses to behold the sight, spite of their deep hatred of the invaders, and the negroes were simply frantic with joy. Whenever they heard my name, they clustered about my horse, shouted and prayed in their peculiar style, which had a natural eloquence that would have moved a stone. I have witnessed hundreds, if not thousands, of such scenes; and can now see a poor girl, in the very ecstasy of the Methodist "shout," hugging the banner of one of the regiments, and jumping up to the "feet of Jesus."

I remember, when riding around by a by-street in Covington, to avoid the crowd that followed the marching column, that some one brought me an invitation to dine with a sister of Sam. Anderson, who was a cadet at West Point with me; but the messenger reached me after we had passed the main part of the town. I asked to be excused, and rode on to a place designated for camp, at the crossing of the Ulcofauhachee River, about four miles to the east of the town. Here we made our bivouac, and I walked up to a plantation-house close by, where were assembled many negroes, among them an old, gray-haired man, of as fine a head as I ever saw. I asked him if he understood about the war and its progress. He said he did; that he had been looking for the "angel of the Lord" ever since he was knee-high, and, though we professed to be fighting for the Union, he supposed that slavery was the cause, and that our success was to be his freedom. I asked him if all the negro slaves comprehended this fact, and he said they surely did. I then explained to him that we wanted the slaves to remain where they were, and not to load us down with useless mouths, which would eat up the food needed for our fighting-men; that our success was their assured freedom; that we could receive a few of their young, hearty men as pioneers; but that, if they followed us in swarms of old and young, feeble and helpless, it would simply load us down and cripple us in our great task. I think Major Henry Hitchcock was with me on that occasion, and made a note of the conversation, and I believe that old man spread this message to the slaves, which was carried from mouth to mouth, to the very end of our journey, and that it in part saved us from the great danger we incurred of swelling our numbers so that famine would have attended our progress. It was at this very plantation that a soldier passed me with a ham on his musket, a jug of sorghum-molasses under his arm, and a big piece of honey in his hand, from which he was eating, and, catching my eye, he remarked *sotto voce* and carelessly to a comrade, "Forage liberally on the country," quoting from my general orders. On this occasion, as on many others that fell under my personal observation, I reproved the man, explained that foraging must be limited to the regular parties properly detailed, and that all provisions thus obtained must be delivered to the regular commissaries, to be fairly distributed to the men who kept their ranks.

From Covington the Fourteenth Corps (Davis's), with which I was traveling, turned to the right for Milledgeville, *via* Shady Dale. General Slocum was ahead at Madison, with the Twentieth Corps, having torn up the railroad as far as that place, and thence had sent Geary's division on to the Oconee, to burn the bridges across that stream, when this corps turned south by Eatonton, for Milledgeville, the common "objective" for the first stage of the "march." We found abundance of corn, molasses, meal, bacon, and sweet-potatoes. We also took a good many cows and oxen, and a large number of mules. In all these the country was quite rich, never before having been visited by a hostile army; the recent crop had been excellent, had been just gathered and laid by for the winter. As a rule, we destroyed none, but kept our wagons full, and fed our teams bountifully.

The skill and success of the men in collecting forage was one of the features of this march. Each brigade commander had authority to detail a company of foragers, usually about fifty men, with one or two commissioned officers selected for their boldness and enterprise. This party would be dispatched before daylight with a knowledge of the intended day's march and camp; would proceed on foot five or six miles from the route traveled by their brigade, and then visit every plantation and farm within range. They would usually procure a wagon or family carriage, load it with bacon, corn-meal, turkeys, chickens, ducks, and every thing that could be used as food or forage, and would then regain the main road, usually in advance of their train. When this came up, they would deliver to the brigade commissary the supplies thus gathered by the way. Often would I pass these foraging-parties at the roadside, waiting for their wagons to come up, and was amused at their strange collections—mules, horses, even cattle, packed with old saddles and loaded with hams, bacon, bags of cornmeal, and poultry of every character and description. Although this foraging was attended with great danger and hard work, there seemed to be a charm about it that attracted the soldiers, and it was a privilege to be detailed on such a party. Daily they returned mounted on all sorts of beasts, which were at once taken from them and appropriated to the general use; but the next day they would start out again on foot, only to repeat the experience of the day before. No doubt, many acts of pillage, robbery, and violence, were committed by these parties of foragers, usually called "bummers;" for I have since heard of jewelry taken from women, and the plunder of articles that never reached the commissary; but these acts were exceptional and incidental. I never heard of any cases of murder or rape; and no army could have carried along sufficient food and forage for a march of three hundred miles; so that foraging in some shape was necessary. The country was sparsely settled, with no magistrates or civil authorities who could respond to requisitions, as is done in all the wars of Europe; so that this system of foraging was simply indispensable to our success. By it our men were well supplied with all the essentials of life and health, while the wagons retained enough in case of unexpected delay, and our animals were well fed. Indeed, when we reached Savannah, the trains were pronounced by experts to be the finest in flesh and appearance ever seen with any army. . . .

Mr. Stanton[2] staid in Savannah several days, and seemed very curious about matters and things in general. I walked with him through the city, especially the bivouacs of the several regiments that occupied the vacant squares, and he seemed particularly pleased at the ingenuity of the men in constructing their temporary huts. Four of the "dog-tents," or *tentes d'abri*, buttoned together, served for a roof, and the sides were made of clapboards, or rough boards brought from demolished houses or fences. I remember his marked admiration for the hut of a soldier

---

[2] Edwin M. Stanton (1814–1869), Secretary of War in Lincoln's cabinet. Sherman is here expressing the military man's resentment of policies determined by national considerations beyond the range of the commander in the field.

who had made his door out of a handsome parlor mirror, the glass gone and its gilt frame serving for his door.

He talked to me a great deal about the negroes, the former slaves, and I told him of many interesting incidents, illustrating their simple character and faith in our arms and progress. He inquired particularly about General Jeff C. Davis, who, he said, was a Democrat, and hostile to the negro. I assured him that General Davis was an excellent soldier, and I did not believe he had any hostility to the negro; that in our army we had no negro soldiers, and, as a rule, we preferred white soldiers, but that we employed a large force of them as servants, teamsters, and pioneers, who had rendered admirable service. He then showed me a newspaper account of General Davis taking up his pontoon-bridge across Ebenezer Creek, leaving sleeping negro men, women, and children, on the other side, to be slaughtered by Wheeler's cavalry. I had heard such a rumor, and advised Mr. Stanton, before becoming prejudiced, to allow me to send for General Davis, which he did, and General Davis explained the matter to his entire satisfaction. The truth was, that, as we approached the seaboard, the freedmen in droves, old and young, followed the several columns to reach a place of safety. It so happened that General Davis's route into Savannah followed what was known as the "River-road," and he had to make constant use of his pontoon-train—the head of his column reaching some deep, impassable creek before the rear was fairly over another. He had occasionally to use the pontoons both day and night. On the occasion referred to, the bridge was taken up from Ebenezer Creek while some of the camp-followers remained asleep on the farther side, and these were picked up by Wheeler's cavalry. Some of them, in their fright, were drowned in trying to swim over, and others may have been cruelly killed by Wheeler's men, but this was a mere supposition. At all events, the same thing might have resulted to General Howard, or to any other of the many most humane commanders who filled the army. General Jeff C. Davis was strictly a soldier, and doubtless hated to have his wagons and columns encumbered by these poor negroes, for whom we all felt sympathy, but a sympathy of a different sort from that of Mr. Stanton, which was not of pure humanity, but of *politics*. The negro question was beginning to loom up among the political eventualities of the day, and many foresaw that not only would the slaves secure their freedom, but that they would also have votes. I did not dream of such a result then, but knew that slavery, as such, was dead forever, and did not suppose that the former slaves would be suddenly, without preparation, manufactured into voters, equal to all others, politically and socially. . . .

It certainly was a strange fact that the great War Secretary should have catechized negroes concerning the character of a general who had commanded a hundred thousand men in battle, had captured cities, conducted sixty-five thousand men successfully across four hundred miles of hostile territory, and had just brought tens of thousands of freedmen to a place of security; but because I had not loaded down my army by other hundreds of thousands of poor negroes, I was construed by others as hostile to the black race. I had received from General Halleck, at Washington, a letter warning me that there were certain influential parties near the President who were torturing him with suspicions of my fidelity to him and his negro policy; but I shall always believe that Mr. Lincoln, though a civilian, knew better, and appreciated my motives and character. . . .

There is no doubt that Mr. Stanton, when he reached Savannah, shared these thoughts, but luckily the negroes themselves convinced him that he was in error, and that they understood their own interests far better than did the men in Washington, who tried to make political capital out of this negro question. The idea that such men should have been permitted to hang around Mr. Lincoln, to torture his life by suspicions of the officers who were toiling with the single purpose to bring the war to a successful end, and thereby to liberate *all* slaves, is a fair illustration of the influences that poison a political capital.

My aim then was, to whip the rebels, to humble their pride, to follow them to their inmost recesses, and make them fear and dread us. "Fear of the Lord is the beginning of wisdom." I did not want them to cast in our teeth what General Hood had once done in Atlanta, that we had to call on *their* slaves to help us to subdue them. But, as regards kindness to the race, encouraging them to patience and forbearance, procuring them food and clothing, and providing them with land whereon to labor, I assert that no army ever did more for that race than the one I commanded in Savannah. . . .

To say that I was merely angry at the tone and substance of published bulletins of the War Department, would hardly express the state of my feelings. I was outraged beyond measure, and was resolved to resent the insult, cost what it might. I went to the Wayanda and showed them to Mr. Chase, with whom I had a long and frank conversation, during which he explained to me the confusion caused in Washington by the assassination of Mr. Lincoln, the sudden accession to power of Mr. Johnson, who was then supposed to be bitter and vindictive in his feelings toward the South, and the wild pressure of every class of politicians to enforce on the new President their pet schemes. He showed me a letter of his own, which was in print, dated Baltimore, April 11th, and another of April 12th, addressed to the President, urging him to recognize the freedmen as equal in all respects to the whites. He was the first man, of any authority or station, who ever informed me that the Government of the United States would insist on extending to the former slaves of the South the elective franchise, and he gave as a reason the fact that the slaves, grateful for their freedom, for which they were indebted to the armies and Government of the North, would, by their votes, offset the disaffected and rebel element of the white population of the South. At that time quite a storm was prevailing at sea, outside, and our two vessels lay snug at the wharf at Morehead City. I saw a good deal of Mr. Chase, and several notes passed between us, of which I have the originals yet. Always claiming that the South had herself freed all her slaves by rebellion, and that Mr. Lincoln's proclamation of freedom (of September 22, 1862) was binding on all officers of the General Government, I doubted the wisdom of at once clothing them with the elective franchise, without some previous preparation and qualification; and then realized the national loss in the death at that critical moment of Mr. Lincoln, who had long pondered over the difficult questions involved, who, at all events, would have been honest and frank, and would not have withheld from his army commanders at least a hint that would have been to them a guide. It was plain to me, therefore, that the manner of his assassination had stampeded the civil authorities in Washington, had unnerved them, and that they were then undecided as to the measures indispensably necessary to prevent anarchy at the South.

JOHN WILLIAM DE FOREST (1826–1906)

As with so many other writers of his generation, De Forest's best work bears the heavy stamp of his war experience, an experience which led him, despite strong Northern sympathies, to deflate and de-romanticize everything connected with warfare. De Forest is one of those post-Civil War writers who bring a cloud of honest grey-ness and prosiness to our literary landscape.

Born in Connecticut of a well-to-do family, he spent several years abroad because of poor health, and began his career as a writer in the 1850s. He served in the Union army for more than six years, first as a captain in the infantry and then with the Freedman's Bureau in South Carolina. His best-known novel, Miss Ravenal's Conversion from Secession to Loyalty, *came out in 1867. It is competent, earnest, and complex, a believable picture of Northern and Southern society during the war years, but like most of De Forest's fiction, it finally seems lacklustre, deficient in imaginative flavor and stylistic verve. In the history of American fiction, however, this novel is important for the utterly unheroic and stubbornly honest way in which it describes battle. Here is De Forest's striking picture of a field hospital:*

In the center of this mass of suffering stood several operating tables, each burdened by a grievously wounded man and surrounded by surgeons and their assistants. Underneath were great pools of clotted blood, amidst which lay amputated fingers, hands, arms, feet and legs, only a little more ghastly in color than the faces of those who waited their turn on the table. The surgeons, who never ceased their awful labor, were daubed with blood to the elbows . . . .

Speculation goes that De Forest's war scenes influenced Stephen Crane in writing A Red Badge of Courage.

Throughout the Civil War De Forest wrote long, extremely objective and detailed letters about his experiences to his wife. From these and some articles he wrote during the war, he put together two volumes called A Volunteer's Adventures *and* A Union Officer in the Reconstruction. *Though quite remarkable as records of what he saw and suffered in the war, and still more remarkable for the stoical detachment with which he recorded his observations even during the worst moments of combat, these volumes were, for some unknown reason, not published during De Forest's lifetime; they first appeared in 1946 and 1948 respectively.*

FURTHER READING

James F. Light, *John De Forest*, 1965.

FROM **A Volunteer's Adventures**

The letters printed in this volume were mostly to my wife. Of course many more were written, but a certain number have naturally disappeared, and others were mere scraps on ammunition paper, etc. Those here included might have been reduced to a narrative; but it seems to me that they show camp life clearly and naturally; hence I leave them as they are.

Steam transport Fulton, *March 6, 1862*

Did you receive the note which I sent you by the pilot? If so you know that the *Fulton* carries five companies of the Fourteenth Maine besides the ten companies of the Twelfth Connecticut, in all some fifteen hundred military greenhorns.

We are still rolling and splashing southward without a chance to mail you a letter. I was disappointed when we passed Fortress Monroe, and surprised as well as disappointed when we passed Charleston. It became clear then that we were to go to Ship Island or some other point in the Gulf, far from you and from all possibility of learning promptly of your welfare.

With the exception of one moderate gale, lasting barely eighteen hours, the passage has been a smooth one, and since we reached the latitude of Georgia, delightful. Light breezes, a calm sea, a bright sun, a temperature which makes the men take off their coats have accompanied us around Florida and into the Gulf. The coughs and colds that worried us in camp at Hartford have disappeared. Not one of the swarming men on board has died or seems likely to for a good while to come.

Personally I am more comfortably situated than I expected to be. I have got out of the hole where I was lodged at first, and am in a tolerable stateroom beside the stairway, only objectionable as being too near the boiler and also not quite large enough for three. Even the soldiers are much better accommodated than I supposed when I last wrote you; there is room enough below for every man to stretch himself at full length in his blanket or overcoat. Some of them were comically surprised and indignant when they learned that they were not to be made free of the after part of the ship. "That's a pooty way to treat a poor soldier!" whined one gawky lout as the sergeant of the guard, an old regular, routed him out of a seat on the quarter-deck and hustled him forward.

Not a woman on board; the ship is as the world was before Eve was created; the most jealous of wives need not be afraid to have her husband here. I am as indolent as passengers usually are; I cannot even study my drill book and the regulations. I smoke like a Turk; I walk the deck till the broiling sun sends me up to the breezy top of the wheelhouse; I load my revolver and shoot at gulls or floating tufts of seaweed; in my best estate I play at checkers on the quarter-deck. The cabin is so hot and close that it is not pleasant to linger there.

The general indifference to our future is curious and makes me wonder if we are beginning to be heroes. Nobody knows where we are ultimately going, and nobody appears to care. We vaguely expect to follow Porter's mortar fleet and occupy some place which has been shelled into submission. It seems impossible as yet to believe that we peaceful burghers are going to fight. You must not suppose that this tremulous handwriting results from terror of coming battle. It is merely the ship's engine shaking the table. . . .

New Orleans, May 2, 1862

We had a charming sail from Fort Jackson to New Orleans through scenery which surpasses the Connecticut River valley and is not inferior to that of the Hudson, though quite different in character.

It is a continuous flat, generally below the level of the Mississippi, but richly beautiful and full of variety. The windings of the mighty river, the endless cypress forests in the background, the vast fields of cane and corn, the abundant magnolias and orange groves and bananas, the plantation houses showing white through dark-green foliage furnished an uninterrupted succession of lovely pictures. Of course the verdure was a fascinating novelty to men who came last from the white sands of Ship Island, and previously from the snows of New England.

Apparently this paradise had been nearly deserted by its inhabitants. Between Fort Jackson and Chalmette, a few miles below New Orleans, we saw hardly fifty white people on the banks, and the houses had the look of having been closed and abandoned. Even the Negroes were far from being as numerous as we had expected. None of the whites signalled to us, or took any other notice of us, or seemed to see us. One elderly man, driving northward with a rockaway full of women, kept along with us for a quarter of a mile or so, without once turning his white-bearded face toward us.

The blacks, as might be expected, were more communicative and more friendly. They gathered to stare at us, and when there were no whites near, they gave enthusiastic evidence of good will, dancing at us, waving hats or branches and shouting welcome. One old mauma, who spoke English and had perhaps once been "sold down de ribber," capered vigorously on the levee, screaming, "Bress de Lawd! I knows dat ar flag. I knew it would come. Praise de Lawd!"

Perhaps some of the planters had fled the region in fear of a slave insurrection; but, as we had learned at Fort Jackson, they had another reason for seeking a place of safety. The fleet had come up the river like an angel of destruction, hurling shells and broadsides into thickets which sheltered ambuscades, and knocking to pieces dwellings occupied by guerrillas. Seventeen miles below New Orleans it pitched into Fort Leon, and sent the garrison flying across the flats to the cypress forest. Then the town surrendered, and with it all the fortifications in the vicinity, while the Rebel troops scurried up the river.

Our tug dragged the *Farley* to dock during the evening of April 30th. The city was dark and quiet; not a soul came near us; we slept on board. During the following morning we were towed further up the levee to make a landing. Thousands of people gathered along the docks to stare in silence at the passing transports. The first troops ashore were the Fourth Wisconsin, Thirty-first Massachusetts, Ninth Connecticut and part of a battery. Then came the turn of the Twelfth Connecticut. Company by company we formed on the quarter-deck, each man carrying his arms, knapsack, havresack and canteen, the whole kit weighing near fifty pounds.

Down the ladder we crept and fell into line fronting the city, surrounded by male and female roughs and ragged urchins, who hooted and sneered and swore. Some of them stared angrily at Weber, my veteran first sergeant, as his monotonous orders cracked out, "Lhoad at will, lhoad! Order aharms! Carry aharms! Pr's'nt aharms!"

Thereupon, as the presentation is to me, I shout, "Shoulder arms! Order arms! In place, rest!"

The regimental line forms slowly, for the transport towers high above the low wharf, and it is uneasy work descending the long, slip-

pery ladder. The roughs, the low women and the ragged urchins continue to hoot, jeer, swear and call us evil names. The soldiers (who
had learned discipline at Ship Island) stand like statues, without replying by word or look. The mob becomes more excited when it learns
that we have really loaded with ball. A red-nosed man, addressing me
personally, declares with many oaths, "We don't want you here, damn
it! You haven't come among friends, not by a damn sight. We don't
want you, d'ye understand? We wouldn't give you a cup of water."

I don't want a cup of water, and I make no reply. But a ragged
Irishman emerges from the crowd with a shillelah four feet long, which
he holds by the middle and whirls around his wolfish head, meanwhile
damning and God-damning and God-damning-to-hell the red-nosed man,
who hastily departs around the nearest corner. Then the Irishman
salutes me in military style, takes off his shabby hat to the colors and
makes them a low bow.

Other and better dressed people follow his example. One man gives
Lieutenant Potter an *Evening Delta,* begging him in a whisper not to
mention it. Another mutters to Captain Dickinson that, if we want re-
cruits, there will be plenty. A handsome, grey-whiskered gentleman and
a very handsome young lady, evidently his daughter, study our faces
sympathetically and then salute the flag with an expression of solemn
joy.

Obviously there are two parties in the city, and for aught we yet
know, ours may be the strongest. In any case there is no danger of a
popular insurrection. Our fleet, with guns run out and howitzers in the
tops, commands various points along the levee and could suppress New
Orleans without help from the army.

New Orleans, September 29, 1862

I saw last evening something very curious and interesting to me.
I saw a new race; a race which is seeking to win a respectable footing
in human society; a race which holds such a footing in Europe though
scorned by us. One of our lieutenants, a dandified, pleasant youngster,
fell ill a few weeks since and was sent to a city hospital, not far from
the barracks of one of Butler's newly raised colored regiments. When
he got strong enough for duty he volunteered to act as adjutant of this
corps and held the position for about a fortnight. There was not an
officer in it who was not a whiter man than himself; hence he treated
them like white men, and so won their exceeding good will. The consequence is that, since he returned to our camp, they invite him to dinners
and suppers.

Yesterday he asked me to join him at an entertainment given by a
wealthy business man named Dumas, whose brother is captain in the
First Colored and will be major of the Second. The ladies were very
pretty, he said, and had not a trace of the African in their faces. So

down to the city I went with the lieutenant and our regimental adjutant. At Dumas' house we found six other officers, three of them from white regiments and three from colored. Our entertainer is a man of about thirty who looks like a West Indian; his brother has the complexion of an Italian and features which remind one of the first Napolean. Both of them, although natives of New Orleans, have spent a great part of their lives in Paris, and speak good French, but nothing else. They did not differ in air and manners from the young Frenchmen whom I used to know abroad. One of the three officers present, of this mixed blood, was an extremely blond youth with curly yellow locks.

Madame Dumas, about twenty years old, with regular features, handsome dark eyes, wavy black hair and a pale but healthy color, looks like a Jewess of southern Europe. Her sister, a few years older, resembles a Jewess of the swarthy, heavy type. Then there were two girl-cousins of sixteen, lately from convent schools in Paris, two jolly little brunettes with slim figures and lively French manners. What a happy evening they passed with our dandy lieutenant and adjutant! It was giggle and jabber for two hours in their end of the room, all the funnier because the two boys spoke no French and only one of the girls knew a little English. Being the only linguist in the party, I had to do not a little interpreting. The supper was a collation of cakes, confectionery, creams, ices and champagne, followed by *café noir*, cognac and delicious cigars.

Then came the piano, with French songs and American patriotic songs, followed by dancing. How enchanted the girls were to waltz and polk with our two youngsters! It was really delightful to gaze once more upon coquetry and courting; it was pleasant also to speak to an intelligent woman without being repelled by an angry stare. Since my arrival here until last evening I had not uttered a word to one of your sex, barring my charcoal-tinted washerwoman and the cocoanut-brown damsel who waits at our mess-table.

New Orleans, October 1, 1862

I have been looking into the way of life of our garrison in this city. It seems outrageous that, while we of the field regiments have been stick-in-the-muds for months, badly fed and so vilely lodged that I would have been grateful for a stable to sleep in, these fellows should have elegant houses, cellars full of choice wines, encouragement to plunder, and generous promotions. I dined with one of the colonels and passed the night with his adjutant. Of course I was not indignantly surprised to find the field officer grandly lodged and abounding in foraged claret. But I really was disgusted at receiving an even more luxurious hospitality from a mere lieutenant.

The adjutant's house is small, but it is a treasure box. Bills found in a secretary prove that the furniture, all of Parisian make, cost fifteen thousand dollars. The bedsteads are lofty four-posters, elaborately carved and of solid mahogany. The washing set of my bedroom is a cream-colored ground glass, very pretty and curious if not expensive. One of the most valuable articles is a small bureau encrusted with patterns of gilt enamel set in tortoise shell. . . .

The adjutant and the lieutenant who lodges with him are making themselves at home; for instance, I heard the latter say, "I think I shall send this thing to my wife." He held in his hand a large tortoise-shell fan which I judged must have cost fully one hundred dollars. I suspect that he had no idea of its value and had never heard of fans worth more than a dollar or two.

The cellar is well stocked with madeira and burgundy, some of the vintages being twenty years old, if one may credit the invoices. As there was no champagne in it, the adjutant plundered two other private wine cellars, one of them belonging to Soulé. He told me that in one day he and his friends drank forty-six bottles. I found the burgundy soured and corky, although he did not know it, the barbarian; but the sauterne, which he served iced for breakfast, was in good condition and of superior quality. The breakfast was exquisite, and no wonder, for the cook is a noted *artiste*, a handsome quadroon named Alick, formerly chief in one of the best restaurants here.

Now all this looting and foraging is a disorder and a shame. Of course it is General Butler who is chiefly in fault for it. He could stop it at once, but he leaves the doors open for it, and the officers understand that he likes to see it. So they use what they want, and pack up the residue to carry away, and believe that they are doing right.

It is a very different regime from that of our old general, Phelps, who would not take a private house for himself and fretted over the theft of a sweet potato.

Near Thibodeaux, November 20, 1862

Brigade officer of the day yesterday; rode something like thirty miles visiting pickets; ten miles in the morning, ten in the afternoon and ten at midnight. Miserable horses; saddle went to smash miles from camp; had to draw my sword on plantation dogs. I would rather have marched thirty miles on foot. One result of this wearing job will be a short letter.

I have lately been on a "military commission," trying various kinds of bad subjects, wandering soldiers, ornary Southerners and loose Negroes. It is necessary to do something to put down the multifarious anarchy which we and the rebellion have brought upon this region. A stolid plantation hand (with less intellect than a learned pig) who had criminally assaulted a white girl was condemned and hung. Being recorder of the court, I have had much writing to do, and also some translating from the French, for several of the witnesses were Cajuns and knew not a word of English. You must understand that the Cajuns are descendants of the exiled Acadians celebrated in Longfellow's *Evangeline*. Judging by the specimens thus far known to me, they are ignorant, stupid and unpoetic.

Near Thibodeaux, December 7, 1862

I have received your comments on our Lilliputian battle at Labadieville. You must understand that I took post in the front rank during the charge for a good reason. As my men had never been under fire before, I was afraid they might get startled and disordered, and I wanted to set them an example in facing danger. I can trust them now and shall hereafter march in rear of the company, where a captain should be according to the drill book.

I have discovered why officers are in general braver than soldiers. The soldier is responsible for himself alone, and so is apt to think of himself alone. The officer is responsible for his company, and so partially forgets his own peril. His whole soul is occupied with the task of keeping his ranks in order, and it is only now and then that he takes serious note of the bullets and shells. It would demand a good deal of courage, I think, to be a mere looker-on in a battle.

An officer of the ——th gave me an amusing account of the chaplain of his regiment; sitting his horse calmly in rear of the charging, yelling line and peering after it through his specs with an expression of enlightened curiosity; now glancing at the rolls of smoke which marked the Rebels' position and now at the tufts of dust thrown up by their shot; the whole man as bland and content as if he were in a prayer meeting. He is a terrible forager, this valiant young son of the prophets. He makes frequent pilgrimages after provisions for his flock and helps personally towards devouring the substance of the enemy. Some days ago he presented himself at regimental headquarters and said, "Colonel, the health of this battalion requires sweet potatoes, and I should like permission to take up a contribution. By the way, it is Sunday, I believe. If I get back early enough, I shall preach this afternoon."

Off he went with a couple of soldiers, impressed a plough and a pair of mules at a plantation, and returned with a load of vegetables.

But we have nearly worn out the foraging business. The land for miles around is as bare of pigs as if a legion of devils had run away with them all. Meantime I am nourished at a moderate cost in an honest fashion. One of my men has been detailed as guard over two large plantations, his duty being to drive off plunderers and to make the Negroes get in the sugar crop. The owners are humbly thankful for his protection; they have given him a pony, a hogshead of sugar and a barrel of syrup; and they allow him to bring me poultry at fair prices and vegetables for nothing. . . .

Skirmishing is not nearly so trying as charging or line fighting. In the first place, you generally have cover; in the second, if you are shot at you can also shoot. Now to fire at a person who is firing at you is somehow wonderfully consolatory and sustaining; more than that, it is exciting and produces in you the so-called joy of battle. I was presently shouting with enthusiasm, cheering my men with jokes and laughter, jumping over fallen trees instead of crawling under them, and running about regardless of exposure. Then the close whistle of bullets, or their loud *whack* as they buried themselves in the stumps near me, would drive me temporarily to shelter. Such is skirmishing when it goes nicely, or, in other words, when the enemy is not too numerous. As to being slaughtered and driven back and scared to death, you can not make it pleasant under any circumstances. . . .

FROM *Letters Written from Port Hudson*

Now came forty days and nights in the wilderness of death. Before we left that diminutive gully fifty or sixty men of the regiment had stained it with their blood, and several of the trees, which filled it with shade, had been cut asunder by cannon shot, while others were dying under the scars of innumerable bullets. The nuisance of trench duty does not consist in the overwhelming amount of danger at any particular moment, but in the fact that danger is perpetually present. The spring its always bent; the nerves never have a chance to recuperate; the elasticity of courage is slowly worn out. Every morning I was awakened by the popping of rifles and the whistling of balls; hardly a day passed that I did not hear the loud exclamations of the wounded, or see corpses borne to the rear; and the gamut of my good-night lullaby varied all the way from Minié rifles to sixty-eight pounders.

In one respect our gully was detestable. Well covered in front, it was open at one end, and this end was exposed to the enemy. I often wished that I could turn the wretched hole around. From a distance of nearly half a mile the Rebel sharpshooters drew a bead on us with a precision which deserved the highest commendation of their officers, but which made us curse the day they were born. One incident proves, I think, that they were able to hit an object farther off than they could distinguish its nature. A rubber blanket, hung over the stump of a sapling five feet high, which stood in the centre of our bivouac, was pierced by a bullet from this quarter. A minute later a second bullet passed directly over the object and lodged in a tree behind it. I ordered the blanket to be taken down, and then the firing ceased. Evidently the invisible marksman, eight hundred yards away, had mistaken it for a Yankee. Several men were hit upon this same hillock, or immediately in rear of it; and I for one never crossed it without wondering whether I should get safely to the other side.

Another fatal spot was an exposed corner in the narrow terrace which our men had made in the bank, as a standing place whence to fire over the knoll.

"Don't go there, Captain," a soldier said to me when I first approached the place. "That's Dead Man's Corner. Five men have been killed there already." . . .

We lost eight or ten men during that first day, partly from not knowing these dangerous localities, and partly from excess of zeal. Our fellows attempted to advance the position, leaped the knoll without orders, and took to the trees on the outer slope, and were only driven back after sharp fighting.

"Served me right. I'd no business there," said a suddenly enlightened Irishman, as he came in with a hole through his shoulder.

As the siege drew on and we found that there was plenty of danger without running after it, we all became more or less illuminated by this philosophy. It is a remark as old as sieges that trench duty has a tendency to unfit men for field fighting. The habit of taking cover becomes stronger than the habit of moving in unison; and, moreover, the health is enfeebled by confinement, and the nervous system shaken by incessant peril. . . .

The garrison gave us full as good as we sent. Several of our men were shot in the face through the portholes as they were taking aim. One of these unfortunates, I remember, drew his rifle back, set the butt on the ground, leaned the muzzle against the parapet, turned around, and fell lifeless. He had fired at the moment he was hit, and two or three eye-witnesses asserted that his bullet shivered the edge of the opposite porthole, so that in all probability he and his antagonist died together.

New Iberia, Louisiana, December 4, 1863

We are still doing nothing but attending to our health and taking wholesome exercise in the way of drill. The cold weather has had a wonderful effect in freshening up our fever-wilted constitutions. Perhaps that result was the real end and aim of our seemingly purposeless military promenade.

You would be amazed to see the swarming mulattoes and quadroons and octoroons who possess this region and call themselves Americans. Some of the richest planters, men of really great wealth, are of mixed descent. When we march through a town the people who gather to stare at us remind me of the Negro quarters of Philadelphia and New York. I understand that very few of them speak English and that they are nearly all extremely ignorant. These are not the former slaves, observe, but the former masters.

Near Charles Town, [West] Virginia, August 21, 1864

Well, we tramped down the Shenandoah Valley, and we tramped back again. If ever I volunteer again I shall remember this vale of sorrows and shall specify that I am not to make war in it. Blazing hot marches, heavy guard duty, a diet of green corn and green apples have made a rough campaign of it thus far.

In the way of scenery the valley is charming and surpasses that of the Connecticut. The mountains are lofty enough to be striking, and their contours of advance and retreat have much variety. The streams too are fine, and the many oak groves are lovely. We frequently halted in them, and once we had the luck to camp in one. Just now our Corps is posted in a long belt of forest which serves it both as shelter and as ambush. The weather has changed to rain, and on one of our late marches we got soaking wet, a circumstance which seems never to hurt anybody who wears a uniform.

Thus far General Sheridan is cautious about fighting, perhaps because of instructions from high political authority. With so many elections at hand, including the presidential, it would not do to have this army beaten and the North invaded. So, whenever Early is re-enforced, Sheridan retreats to a strong position and waits to be attacked. It is to the enemy's interest just now to take the offensive, but we doubt if Early has men enough to risk it.

An order to fall in may come at any moment. Such orders generally arrive at night in the awkwardest moment possible. Then we march like fury for hours; and then nothing comes of it; we march back again. Of course the general understands it all, and perhaps Omniscience does, but nobody else.

Well, this is soldiering of course, to do as we are ordered, and ask no explanations.

FROM *"The Battle of Cedar Creek"* **Letters**

Allow me here a digression concerning fugitives, a class much misrepresented by novelists and poets. Defeated and retreating soldiers do not fly at full speed for any considerable distance. After a run of a hundred yards or less, even though the bullets are still whizzing around them, they drop into a walk, perhaps from lack of breath, perhaps from shame. Thenceforward they tramp steadily rearward, not in the least wild with fright, but discreetly selecting the best cover, slipping through hollows and woods, halting for rest and discourse behind buildings, and in short taking care of themselves with provoking intelligence. But, although they are so cool, you will find it no easy task to rally them. Try it; they will stare at you and straggle on; their faces seem to say, "We have done our best and without avail; now let somebody else face the music."

Draw your sword on them, and they will halt; but turn away, and they will begin to sidle rearward. The chief trouble with them seems to be that they have got out of their places in the military machine. If one of them finds his own company, he will probably rejoin it; he will also join another company of the same regiment; but another regiment he has no use for. An officer who loses his command appears similarly bewildered. He rarely attempts to rally any but his own men and wanders about in search of them, letting the battle go. But if a superior officer seizes upon this lost being and puts him in command of a squad of rallied men, he will lead them back among the bullets, his morale restored by the authority and responsibility which have been thrust upon him. . . .

What with starving, freezing, swamp fever, forced marches and being shot, war is glorious fun, merely glorious, not comfortable. Perhaps the Chinese are right in holding that it is not worthy of the admiration and attention of a civilized people.

But to the great mass of mankind, cultured as well as barbarous, it has a strange fascination. Hungry as the Twelfth was, and heavily as it had suffered from the enemy, it was in good spirits because the enemy had been whipped.

MARY BOYKIN CHESTNUT (1823?–1886)

Daughter of a onetime governor of South Carolina, Mrs. Chestnut went to Washington as a young girl, when her father served as a member of Congress in the pre-Civil War period. Her acquaintance with political figures on both sides of the war dates from this period.

At seventeen, she married James Chestnut Jr., who, after a brief political career, became a Confederate general and aide to President Jefferson Davis. Mrs. Chestnut was therefore close to the center of the Confederate government during the time she kept her diary.

This diary, which in its complete version comes to about 400,000 words, was published in a sharply condensed version in 1904. Many years later Ben Ames Williams, a popular novelist looking for material about the Old South, came across Mrs. Chestnut's complete diary. He took it to be a major document both for historical and literary reasons, and in 1949 he issued an edition of it containing about 300,000 words.

Mrs. Chestnut was a shrewd observer, entirely free of magnolia sentiment and political self-deception. Though committed to the South, she could write: "God forgive us, but ours is a monstrous system, a wrong and an iniquity!. . . Any lady is ready to tell you who is the father of all the mulatto children in everybody's household but her own." Such cutting observations, together with her capacity to describe public figures in a sharp sentence or two, make her diaries one of the most realistic and entertaining accounts we have of the Confederacy as it went down to defeat.

FURTHER READING

There is a fine portrait of Mrs. Chestnut, as well as of her work, in Edmund Wilson's *Patriotic Gore.* (1962).

FROM **A Diary from Dixie** *(1904, 1949)*

February 15th, 1861

I came to Charleston on November 7th and then went to Florida to see my mother. On the train, just before we reached Fernandina, a woman called out: "That settles the hash!" Tanny touched me on the shoulder and said: "Lincoln's elected." "How do you know?" "The man over there has a telegram." Someone cried: "Now that the black radical Republicans have the power I suppose they will Brown [1] us all."

I have always kept a journal, with notes and dates and a line of poetry or prose, but from today forward I will write more. I now wish I had a chronicle of the two delightful and eventful years that have just passed. Those delights have fled, and one's breath is taken away to think what events have since crowded in. . . .

It is hard for me to believe these people are in earnest. They are not putting the young, active, efficient, in place anywhere. Whenever there is an election, they hunt up some old fossil who was ages ago laid on the shelf. There never was such a resurrection of the dead and forgotten. This does not look like business. My first doubts came when I saw who were elected to any office and that efficiency was never thought of but political maneuvering still ruled. My father was a South Carolina nullifier, Governor of the state at the time of the nullification row, and then United States Senator; so I was of necessity a rebel born. My husband's family being equally pledged to the Union party rather exasperated my zeal. Yet I felt a nervous dread and horror of this break with so great a power as the United States, but I was ready and willing. South Carolina had been rampant for years. She was the torment of herself and everybody else. Nobody could live in this state unless he were a fire-eater. Come what would, I wanted them to fight and stop talking. South Carolinians had exasperated and heated themselves into a fever that only blood-letting could ever cure. It was the inevitable remedy. So I was a seceder.

[1] A reference to John Brown, abolitionist leader, meaning the South would be placed under severe pressures.

March 4th, (1861)

The Washington Congress, they say, has passed peace measures. . . .

I have seen a Negro woman sold upon the block at auction. I was walking. The woman on the block overtopped the crowd. I felt faint, seasick. The creature looked so like my good little Nancy. She was a bright mulatto, with a pleasant face. She was magnificently gotten up in silks and satins. She seemed delighted with it all, sometimes ogling the bidders, sometimes looking quite coy and modest; but her mouth never relaxed from its expanded grin of excitement. I dare say the poor thing knew who would buy her. My very soul sickened. It was too dreadful. I tried to reason. "You know how women sell themselves and are sold in marriage, from queens downwards, eh? You know what the Bible says about slavery, and marriage. Poor women, poor slaves."

March 5th, (1861)

We stood on the balcony to see our Confederate Flag go up. Roar of cannon. Miss Sanders complained, and so did Captain Ingraham, of the deadness of the mob. "It was utterly spiritless," she said. "No cheering, or so little; no enthusiasm." Captain Ingraham suggested: "Gentlemen are apt to be quiet. This was a thoughtful crowd. The true mob element with us just now is hoeing corn." And yet, it is uncomfortable that the idea has gone abroad that we have no joy, no pride in this thing. The Band was playing "Massa's in the Cold, Cold Ground."

Miss Tyler, daughter of ex-President Tyler, ran up our Flag.

I read Lincoln's Inaugural. Comes he in Peace, or comes he in War? Or to tread but one measure as young Lochinvar?

March 14th, (1861)

"Now this is positive," they say. "Fort Sumter is to be relieved, and we are to have no war." Poor Sumter. Relieved? Not half as much as we would be! After all, this is far too good to be true. If there be no war, how triumphant Mr. Chestnut will be. He is the only man who has persisted from the first that this would be a peaceful revolution. Heaven grant it may be so!

Mr. Browne told us that in the interest of peace, Lincoln came through Baltimore locked up in an Adams Express car. A noble entrance into the government of a free people! He wore a Scotch cap. Baltimore "Plug Uglies" have a bad name.

April 20th, 1861

Mulberry. Home again. In those last days of my stay in Charleston I did not find time to write a word. And so we took Fort Sumter, *nous autres*. We, Mrs. Frank Hampton and others and I, took it in the passageway of the Mills House, between the reception room and the draw-ing-room. There we held a sofa against all comers. That was after we found out that bombarding did not kill anybody. Before that we wept and prayed and took our tea in groups, in our rooms away from the haunts of men.

Captain Ingraham and his kind took Fort Sumter from the Battery, with field glasses, and figures made with ten sticks in the sand to show what ought to be done.

Wigfall, Chestnut, Miles, Manning; they took it rowing about in the Harbour in small boats from Fort to Fort under the enemy's guns, bombs bursting in air.

And the boys and men who worked those guns so faithfully at the Forts; they took it too, their way.

Old Colonel Beaufort Watts told me many stories of the *jeunesse dorée* under fire. They took it easily as they do most things. They had cotton bag bomb-proofs at Fort Moultrie, and when Anderson's shot knocked them about someone called out: "Cotton is falling." Down went the kitchen chimney and loaves of bread flew out. They cheered gaily: "Bread stuffs are rising." Willie Preston fired the shot which broke Anderson's flagstaff. Mrs. Hampton from Columbia telegraphed him: "Well done, Willie!" She is his grandmother, the wife or widow of General Hampton of the Revolution, and the mildest, sweetest, gentlest of old ladies. It shows how the war spirit is waking us all up.

Colonel Miles (who won his spurs in a boat, so William Gilmore Simms said) gave us this characteristic anecdote. They met a Negro out in the Bay rowing towards the city with some plantation supplies. "Are you not afraid of Colonel Anderson's cannon?" "No, sar, Marse Ander-son ain't dars'nt to hit me. He know Marster wouldn't 'low it."

I have been sitting idly today looking out upon this beautiful lawn, wondering if this can be the same world I was in a few days ago. After the smoke and the din of the battle, a calm.

June 28th, 1861

In Mrs. Davis's drawing-room last night, the President took a seat by me on the sofa where I sat. He talked for nearly an hour. He laughed at our faith in our own prowess. We are like the British; we think every Southerner equal to three Yankees at least, but we will have to be equivalent to a dozen now. After his experience of the fighting qualities of Southerners in Mexico, Mr. Davis believes that we will do all that can be done by pluck and muscle, endurance and dogged courage, dash and red-hot patriotism, and yet his tone was not sanguine. There was a sad refrain running through it all. For one thing, either way, he thinks it will be a long war. That floored me at once. It has been too long for me already. Then he said that before the end came we would have many a bitter experience. He said only fools doubted the courage of the

Yankees, or their willingness to fight when they saw fit. And now we have stung their pride, we have roused them till they will fight like devils. He said Mr. Chestnut's going as aide-de-camp to Beauregard was a mistake, and that he ought to raise a regiment of his own. . . .

Mr. Lamar, who does not love slavery any more than Sumner does—nor more than I do—laughs at the compliment New England pays us. We want to separate from them, to be rid of Yankees forever, at any price; and they hate us so. Yet they would clasp us—or hook us, as Polonius has it—to their bosoms with hooks of steel. We are an unwilling bride. I think incompatibility of temper began when it was made plain to us that we get all the opprobrium of slavery while they, with their tariff, get the money there is in it. . . .

I told Lamar how Mr. Chestnut laughed when he remembered the Town and Gown fights (Students and Snobs, so called then) at Princeton, and now heard our people say that Northern men would not fight. Lamar said Yankees did not fight for the fun of it; they always made it pay or let it alone. Wigfall said to the Pennsylvania Cameron in the Senate, who announced himself as furiously out on a war path: "The profit will accrue."

July 7th, 1861

Lincoln wants four hundred millions of money, and men in proportion. Can he get them? He will find us a heavy handfull.

Midnight. I hear Maria's guns.

We are always picking up some good thing of the rough Illinoisian's saying. Lincoln objects to some man: "Oh, he is too *interruptious*." That is a horrid style of man or woman. The Interruptious! I know the thing, but had no name for it before. . . .

Mary Hammy, having a fiancé in the wars, is inclined at times to be sad and tearful. Mrs. Preston quoted her Negro nurse to her. "Never take any more trouble in your heart than you can kick off at the end of your toes."

July 27th, 1861

Captain Ingraham told Captain Smith Lee: "Don't be so conceited about your looks. Mrs. Chestnut thinks your brother Robert a handsomer man than you." I did not contradict the statement, and yet it was false. This is how I saw Robert E. Lee for the first time. I had heard of him, strange to say, in this wise. Though his family, who then lived at Arlington, called to see me in Washington because of Mrs. Chestnut's intimacy with Nelly Custis in the old Philadelphia days, and because Mrs. Lee was Nelly Custis's niece, I had not known the head of the Lee family. He was somewhere with the Army. Last summer at the White Sulphur, I met Roony Lee and his wife, that sweet little Charlotte Wickham, and

I spoke of Roony with great praise. Mrs. Izard said: "Don't waste your admiration on him. Wait till you see his father! He is the nearest to a perfect man I ever saw." "How?" "Every way. Handsome, clever, agreeable, high bred!" Now, here in Richmond, Mrs. Stanard came for Mrs. Preston and me, to drive to the camp. She was in an open carriage. A man riding a beautiful horse joined us. He wore a hat with somehow a military look to it. He sat his horse gracefully, and he was so distinguished at all points that I very much regretted not catching the name as Mrs. Stanard gave it to us. He, however, heard ours, and bowed as gracefully as he rode; and the few remarks he made to each of us showed he knew all about us. But Mrs. Stanard was in ecstacies of pleasurable excitement. I felt she had bagged a big fish, since just then they abounded in Richmond. We chatted lightly and I enjoyed it, since the man and horse and everything about them was perfection. As he left us, I said eagerly: "Who is he?" "You did not know? Why, that was Robert E. Lee, the first gentleman of Virginia."

All the same, I like Smith Lee better; and I like his looks too. Besides, I know him well. Can anyone say they know his brother? I doubt it! He looks so cold, quiet and grand. . . .

The Northern papers say we hung and quartered a Zouave, cut him in four pieces, and that we tie prisoners to a tree and bayonet them. In other words, we are savages! It ought to teach us not to credit what our papers say of them. We are absolutely treating their prisoners as well as our own men. In fact it is complained of here. I am going to the hospitals here for the enemy's sick and wounded to see for myself.

August 3rd, 1861

Ransom Calhoun, Willie Preston and Dr. Nott's boys are here. These foolish, rash, hair-brained Southern lads have been within an ace of a fight over their camping ground with a Maryland company. That is too Irish, to be so ready to fight anybody, friend or foe. They are thrilling with fiery ardor. The red-hot Southern martial spirit is in the air. These young men, however, were all educated abroad; and it is French or German ideas that they are filled with. The Marylanders were as rash and reckless as themselves, and had their coattails ready for anybody to tread on, Donnybrook Fair fashion. One would think there were Yankees enough and to spare for any killing that was to be done. It all began about picketing their horses. These quarrelsome young soldiers have lovely manners. They are so sweet tempered here among us at the Arlington.

Captain Ingraham's . . . heart is torn in twain. The United States Navy has been his supreme affection, his first thought and duty. Patriotism now calls him to turn and fight against his first love. When I tell him he ought to have brought his ships in with him, he is amazed. "That would have been treason," he cries. I say: "Not so, not more than coming yourself. The ships were ours, as much as you were ours. Half of everything was ours. We paid our taxes, kept up the revenue." He smiles in pity at a woman pretending to understand things; but I say: "We were a co-partnership. When we dissolved it, we had a right to divide assets. Our money helped to build ships, and the tariff in some inscrutable way took all our money. We had a right to share and share alike all public property."

August 18th, 1861

The New York Tribune [2] is so unfair. It began howling to get rid of us. We were so wicked. Now that we are so willing to leave them to their over-righteous self-consciousness, they cry "crush our enemy or they will subjugate us." The idea, that we want to invade or to subjugate! We would only be too grateful to be left alone. Only let us alone. We ask no more, of Gods or men.

A general belief says: "This war is an attempt to extend the area of slavery." Can that be? When not one third of our volunteer army are slave owners? And not one third of that third fail to dislike slavery as much as Mrs. Stowe, or Horace Greeley. [3] And few have found their hatred or love of it remunerative as an investment.

August 27th, 1861

I hate slavery. You say there are no more fallen women on a plantation than in London, in proportion to numbers; but what do you say to this? A magnate who runs a hideous black harem with its consequences under the same roof with his lovely white wife, and his beautiful and accomplished daughters? He holds his head as high and poses as the model of all human virtues to these poor women whom God and the laws have given him. From the height of his awful majesty, he scolds and thunders at them, as if he never did wrong in his life. Fancy such a man finding his daughter reading "Don Juan." "You with that immoral book!" And he orders her out of his sight. You see, Mrs. Stowe did not hit the sorest spot. She makes Legree a bachelor.

November 28th, (1861)

"Ye who listen with credulity to the whispers of fancy"—pause, and look on this picture and that.

On one side Mrs. Stowe, Greeley, Thoreau, Emerson, Sumner, [4] They

---

[2] A strongly pro-Northern newspaper.

[3] Horace Greeley (1811–1872) was editor of the *New York Tribune.*

[4] Charles Sumner (1811–1874), United States Senator from Massachusetts, strongly opposed to slavery.

live in nice New England homes, clean, sweet-smelling, shut up in libraries, writing books which ease their hearts of their bitterness against us. What self-denial they do practice is to tell John Brown to come down here and cut our throats in Christ's name. Now consider what I have seen of my mother's life, my grandmother's, my mother-in-law's. These people were educated at Northern schools, they read the same books as their Northern contemporaries, the same daily papers, the same Bible. They have the same ideas of right and wrong, are high-bred, lovely, good, pious, doing their duty as they conceive it. They live in Negro villages. They do not preach and teach hate as a gospel, and the sacred duty of murder and insurrection; but they strive to ameliorate the condition of these Africans in every particular. They set them the example of a perfect life, a life of utter self-abnegation. Think of these holy New Englanders forced to have a Negro village walk through their houses whenever they see fit, dirty, slatternly, idle, ill-smelling by nature. These women I love have less chance to live their own lives in peace than if they were African missionaries. They have a swarm of blacks about them like children under their care, not as Mrs. Stowe's fancy painted them, and they hate slavery worse than Mrs. Stowe does. Book-making which leads you to a round of visits among crowned heads is an easier way to be a saint than martyrdom down here, doing unpleasant duty among the Negroes with no reward but the threat of John Brown hanging like a drawn sword over your head in this world, and threats of what is to come to you from blacker devils in the next.

The Mrs. Stowes have the plaudits of crowned heads; we take our chances, doing our duty as best we may among the woolly heads. My husband supported his plantation by his law practice. Now it is running him in debt. Our people have never earned their own bread. Take this estate, what does it do, actually? It all goes back in some shape to what are called slaves here, called operatives, or tenants, or peasantry elsewhere. I doubt if ten thousand in money ever comes to this old gentleman's hands. When Mrs. Chestnut married South, her husband was as wealthy as her brothers-in-law. How is it now? Their money has accumulated for their children. This old man's goes to support a horde of idle dirty Africans, while he is abused as a cruel slave owner. I say we are no better than our judges in the North, and no worse. We are human beings of the nineteenth century and slavery has to go, of course. All that has been gained by it goes to the North and to Negroes. The slave owners, when they are good men and women, are the martyrs. I hate slavery. I even hate the harsh authority I see parents think it their duty to exercise toward their children.

But what good does it do to write all that? I have before me a letter I wrote to Mr. Chestnut while he was on our plantation in Mississippi in 1842. It is the most fervid abolition document I have ever read. I came across it while burning letters the other day, but that letter I did not burn.

June 9th, (1862)

Bratten, who married Miss Mann, is taken prisoner; Beverly Mann killed; his mother-in-law a few days ago found stone dead in her bed. Misfortunes enough for one family surely. When we read of the battles in India, in Italy, in the Crimea, what did we care? It was only an interesting topic, like any other, to look for in the paper. Now, you hear of a battle with a thrill and a shudder. It has come home to us. Half the people that we know in the world are under the enemy's guns. A telegram comes to you and you leave it on your lap. You are pale with fright. You handle it, or dread to touch it, as you would a rattlesnake, or worse; for a snake could only strike you. How many, many of your friends or loved ones this scrap of paper may tell you have gone to their death.

When you meet people, sad and sorrowful is the greeting. They press your hand, and tears stand in their eyes or roll down their cheeks as they happen to have more or less self-control. They have brothers, fathers, or sons as the case may be in the battle; and this thing now seems never to stop. We have no breathing time given us. It cannot be so at the North, for the papers say gentlemen do not go in the ranks there. They are officers, or clerks of departments. That is why we see so many foreign regiments represented among our prisoners; Germans, Irish, Scotch. But with us, every company in the field is filled with our nearest and dearest as rank and file, common soldiers.

July 8th, 1862

Our table talk today: this war was undertaken by us to shake off the yoke of foreign invaders, so we consider our cause righteous. The Yankees, since the war began, have discovered it is to free the slaves they are fighting, so their cause is noble. They also expect to make the war pay. Yankees do not undertake anything that does not pay. They think we belong to them. We have been good milk cows, milked by the tariff—or skimmed. We let them have all of our hard earnings. We bore the ban of slavery; they got the money. Cotton pays everybody who handles it, sells it, manufactures it; but it rarely pays the men who make it. Second-hand, the Yankees received the wages of slavery. They grew rich; we grew poor. The receiver of stolen goods is as bad as the thief. That applies to us too. We received the savages they stole from Africa and brought to us in their slave ships.

July 21st, 1862

I have letters from Harriet Grant and from Mary DeSaussure: The one pitifully asks that my husband try to get some news of Mrs. Brownfield's son, who is reported dead, but whom Mrs. Brownfield still hopes may be alive; the other thanks me for my letter of sympathy and tells me how to send Mr. DeSaussure's watch. Recalling all the ties it dissolves, all the blood it commands to flow, all the healthy industry it arrests, all the mad men it arms, all the victims that it creates, I question whether one man really honest, pure, and humane who has gone through such an ordeal could ever hazard it again unless he is assured victory is secure; yes, and that the object for which he fights will not be wrested from his hands amidst the uproar of the elements that the battle has released.

December 5th, 1863

General Lawton was here last night. He superseded Colonel Myers last winter, in spite of Miles with the Congress at his heels. He was one of Stonewall's generals, so I listened with all my ears. "Stonewall could not sleep, so every two or three nights you were waked up by orders to have your brigade in marching order before daylight, and to report in person to the Commander. Then you were marched a few miles out and then a few miles in again." "A little different from the western stories, and some generals nearer Richmond asleep several hours after they have been expected to attack." General Lawton said: "The restless, discontented spirits move the world. All this of Stonewall's was to make us always ready, ever on the alert; and the end of it was this. Jackson's men had gone half a day's march before Pete Longstreet waked and breakfasted." He added: "I think there is a popular delusion about the amount of praying Jackson did. He certainly preferred a fight on Sunday to a sermon. Failing to manage a fight, he loved next best a long Presbyterian sermon, Calvinistic to the core.

"He had no sympathy with human infirmity. He was a one-idea man. He looked upon broken-down men and stragglers as the same thing. He classed all who were weak and weary, who fainted by the wayside, as men wanting in patriotism. If a man's face was white as cotton and his pulse so low that you could not feel it, he merely looked upon him impatiently as an inefficient soldier, and rode off out of patience. He was the true type of all great soldiers. He did not value human life where he had an object to accomplish. He could order men to their death as a matter of course. Napoleon's French conscription could not have kept him supplied with men, he used up his command so rapidly. Hence, while he was alive there was more pride than truth in the talk of his soldiers' love for him. They feared him, and obeyed him to the death; faith they had in him, a faith stronger than death. But I doubt if he had their love, though their respect he did command. And now that they begin to see that a few years more of Stonewall Jackson would have freed them from the yoke of the hateful Yankee, they deify him. They are proud to have been one of the famous Stonewall Brigade, to have been a brick in that wall.

"But be ye sure, it was bitter hard work to keep up with Stonewall

Jackson, as all know who ever served with him. He gave his orders rapidly and distinctly, and rode away without allowing answer or remonstrance. When you failed, you were apt to be put under arrest. When you succeeded, he only said 'good.' "

January 1st, 1864

General Edward Johnston says he got Grant a place because he could not bear to see an old army man driving a wagon. That was when he found him out west. Grant had been put out of the army for habitual drunkenness. He is their best man. . . . He don't care a snap if his men fall like the leaves. He fights to win, that chap; he is not distracted by a thousand side issues; he does not see them. He sees only in a straight line. Like Louis Napoleon, from a battle in the gutter he goes straight up.

And like Lincoln, we have ceased to carp at him because he is a rough clown, no gentleman, etc. You never hear now of his nasty fun, but only of his wisdom. It doesn't take much soap and water to wash the hands that hold the rod of empire. They once talked of Lincoln's drunkenness too. Now, since Vicksburg, they have not a word to say against Grant's habits. He has the disagreeable habit of not retreating before our irresistible veterans! You need not be afraid of a little dirt on the hands which wield a Field Marshall's baton, either.

Thus runs our table-talk. General Lee and Albert Sydney Johnston; they show blood and breeding; they are of the Bayard, the Philip Sydney order of soldier. But if General Lee had Grant's resources, he would have bagged the last Yankee or had them all safe back in Massachusetts. You mean, if he had not the weight of the Negro question on his shoulders? No, I mean if he had Grant's unlimited allowance of the powers of war, men, money, ammunition, arms. . . .

The Examiner gives this pleasant information to the enemy; that we are not ready, and we cannot be before spring, and that now is their time. Our safeguard, our hope, our trust is in beneficient mud! Impossible mud! So I hail with delight these long, long, rainy days, and longer nights. Things are deluging, sloppy, and up to the ankles in water and dirt, enough to satisfy the muddiest-minded croaker of us all.

March 18th, 1864

General Lee had tears in his eyes when he spoke of his daughter-in-law, now dead; that lovely little Charlotte Wickham, Mrs. Roony Lee. Roony Lee says "Beast" Butler was very kind to him while he was a prisoner; and the "Beast" has sent him back his war horse. The Lees are men enough to speak the truth of friend or enemy, not fearing consequences.

September 1st, (1864)

The battle is raging at Atlanta, our fate hanging in the balance.

September 2nd

Atlanta is gone. Well that agony is over. Like David, when the child was dead, I will get up from my knees, will wash my face and comb my hair. There is no hope, but we will try to have no fear.

September 21st, (1864)

The President has gone West. He sent for Mr. Chestnut.

I went with Mrs. Rhett to hear Dr. Palmer. I did not know before how utterly hopeless was our situation. This man is so eloquent; it was hard to listen and not give way. Despair was his word, and martyrdom. He offered us nothing more in this world than the martyr's crown. He is not for slavery, he says; he is for freedom, the freedom to govern our own country as we see fit. He is against foreign interference in our state matters. That is what Mr. Palmer went to war for, it appears. Every day shows that slavery is doomed the world over. For that he thanked God. He spoke of this time of our agony; and then came the cry: "Help us, Oh God! Vain is the help of man." So we came away shaken to the depths.

November 28th, 1864

The Yankees have just got things shipshape; a splendid army, perfectly disciplined, and new levies coming in day and night to them. Their gentry do not go into the ranks. They pile up shoddy fortunes cheating their government; they dwell in their comfortable cities, tranquil, in no personal fear. The war is to them only a pleasurable excitement.

Someone said: "If we had only freed the Negroes at first, and put them in the Army, that would have trumped their trick." I remember when Mr. Chestnut spoke to his Negroes about it, his head men were keen to go in the Army, to be free and get a bounty after the War. Now they say coolly that they don't want freedom if they have to fight for it. That means they are pretty sure of having it anyway.

February 16th, 1865

My ideas of those last days in Columbia are confused. The Martins left the Friday before I did, and their Mammy refused to go with them. That daunted me. Then Mrs. McCord, who was to send her girls with me, changed her mind. She sent them upstairs in her house and actually took away the staircase; at least that was her plan.

Then I met Christopher Hampton arranging to take away his sisters. They were flitting, but only as far as Yorkville. He said it was time to move on. Sherman was at Orangeburg, barely a day's journey from Columbia, and he left a track as blackened as a fire in the prairies.

April 22nd, 1865

Colonel Cadwallader Jones came with a dispatch, sealed and secret. It was for General Chestnut. I opened it. Lincoln, Old Abe Lincoln, killed, murdered! Seward wounded! Why? By whom? It is simply maddening. I sent off messenger after messenger for General Chestnut. I have not the faintest idea where he is, but I know this foul murder will bring down worse miseries on us.

Mary Darby says: "But they murdered him themselves! There are no Confederates in Washington." "But if they see fit to accuse us of instigating it?" . . .

Now look out for bands of marauders, black and white; lawless, disbanded soldiers, from both armies.

An armistice, they say, is agreed on.

May 2nd, 1865

I am writing from the roadside below Blackstock's, *en route* to Camden. Since we left Chester, solitude; nothing but tall, blackened chimneys to show that any man has ever trod this road before us. This is Sherman's track! It is hard not to curse him.

I wept incessantly at first. "The roses of the gardens are already hiding the ruins," said Mr. Chestnut, trying to say something. Then I made a vow. If we are a crushed people, I will never be a whimpering, pining slave. . . .

May 16th, (1865)

We are scattered, stunned, the remnant of heart left alive in us filled with brotherly hate. We sit and wait until the drunken tailor who rules the United States of America issues a proclamation and defines our anomalous position.

Such a hue and cry, everybody blamed by somebody else. Only the dead heroes left stiff and stark on the battle field escape. I cry: "Blame every man who stayed at home and did not fight, but not one word against those who stood out until the bitter end, and stacked muskets at Appomattox."

June 4th, 1865

President Davis [5] is in a dungeon, and in chains. Men watch him day and night. By orders of Andy, the bloody-minded tailer, [6] nobody above the rank of colonel can take the amnesty oath, and nobody who owns over twenty thousand dollars, or who has assisted the Confederates. Howell Cobb and R. M. T. Hunter are arrested. Our turn next, maybe. Not among the Negroes does fear dwell now, nor uncertainty nor anxiety. It dwells here, haunting us, tracking us, running like an accursed discord through all the music tones of our existence.

June 12th, (1865)

Andy, made lord of all by the madman Booth, [7] says "destruction only to the wealthy classes." Better teach the Negroes to stand alone, before they break up all they leaned on. After all, the number of us who own over $20,000 is comparatively small.

My husband will remain quietly at home. He has done nothing that he had not a right to do, nor anything that he is ashamed of. He will not fly his country, nor hide anywhere in it; these are his words. He has a huge volume of Macaulay, which seems to absorb him.

I have been ill, since I wrote last. I had a letter from Serena. They have been visited by bushwhackers, the roughs who always follow in the wake of an army. My sister Kate, they forced back against the wall. She had Katie, the baby, in her arms. Miller, the brave boy, clung to his mother, though he could do no more. They tried to force brandy down her throat. They knocked Mary down with the butt end of a pistol, and Serena they struck with open hand, leaving the mark on her cheek for weeks. When they struck Mary, Serena seized the Captain's arm. "Do you let your men do that?" and she showed Mary's bleeding head. "No, no!" he said. "That's too bad. You keep all together, and I will get them away for tonight, and then you go off at once." They went that night to the Kings', the next day to Greenville. Next day, while Mary had her head bound up, Confederate prisoners passed. "What is the matter with your head?" "A soldier struck me." All the blood in the man rushed up into his face. "Struck you!" That there could be men found on this earth so brutal as to strike either of these two!

Colonel Chestnut's bank stock, his bonds, his railroad stocks as well as his hundreds of Negroes are now all given up. Nothing but land remains, and debts.

[5] Jefferson Davis (1808–1889), head of the Confederacy.

[6] A reference to Andrew Johnson (1808–1875), who became President of the United States when Lincoln was assassinated.

[7] John Wilkes Booth (1838–1865), the assassin of Lincoln.

HENRY TIMROD (1828–1867)

Laureate of the Confederacy, as he came to be called, Henry Timrod was born of poor parents in Charleston, South Carolina. He attended the University of Georgia, where he studied the classical writers; his early poems include imitations of Catullus and exercises in the manner of Wordsworth.

Though never in robust health, Timrod served as a war correspondent with the Confederate army. For a while he edited a paper in Columbia, South Carolina, until Sherman's army captured and burned the town. Suffering from malnutrition and unable even to raise the fare for a trip to New York, where a publisher had expressed interest in his work, Timrod died without seeing the bulk of his work in print.

A minor but authentic poet, Timrod found his voice during the war:

> At last, we are
> A nation among nations; and the world
> Shall soon behold in many a distant port
> Another flag unfurled!
> Now, come what may, whose favor need we court?
> And, under God, whose thunder need we fear?

The poems he wrote during the war express with some ardor and force the spirit of the Confederacy. His "Ode" for the Confederate dead is written in a lower key, but with a more humane tone, and its touching final lines can apply to the dead of any army.

FURTHER READING

Poems of Henry Timrod, edited by P. H. Hayne (1873); Guy A. Cardwell, Jr., *The Uncollected Poems of Henry Timrod* (1942); J. B. Hubbell, *The Last Days of Henry Timrod* (1941).

Ode (1866)

Sung at the Occasion of Decorating the Graves of the Confederate Dead, at Magnolia Cemetery, Charleston, S.C., June 16, 1866

Sleep sweetly in your humble graves,
    Sleep, martyrs of a fallen cause;
Though yet no marble column craves
    The pilgrim here to pause.

In seeds of laurel in the earth
    The blossom of your fame is blown,
And somewhere, waiting for its birth,
    The shaft is in the stone!

Meanwhile, behalf the tardy years
    Which keep in trust your storied tombs,   *10*
Behold! your sisters bring their tears.
    And these memorial blooms.

Small tributes! but your shades will smile
    More proudly on these wreaths today,
Than when some cannon-molded pile
    Shall overlook this bay.

Stoop, angels, hither from the skies!
    There is no holier spot of ground
Than where defeated valor lies,
    By mourning beauty crowned!   *20*

AMBROSE BIERCE (1842–1914?)

Born in Ohio, the ninth child of sternly religious and constantly im-
poverished parents, Bierce had only one year of formal schooling.
His harsh childhood can hardly have stimulated him to warm feel-
ings about humanity, and his experience in the Civil War, even less
so. Immediately after the war broke out, he enlisted in the Union
army. He took part in the battle of Shiloh, where he conducted him-
self with courage but was profoundly shaken by the carnage to which
he was witness. By the war's end he had been mentioned fifteen
or sixteen times for gallantry and was discharged a brevet major.
Horrible as war seemed to him, he yet found the atmosphere of the
army congenial, perhaps because it was an atmosphere without the
hypocritical pretensions to humaneness which he detested in the
civilian world.

Moving to San Francisco, Bierce became a newspaper columnist, editor,
and central figure in a literary group that included Bret Harte,
Joaquin Miller, and Mark Twain. He wrote stories, poems, and
journalism throughout the next few decades. In 1891 he issued his
best collection of stories, Tales of Soldiers and Civilians; *in 1906,*
his bitter and sometimes merely sour epigrams, The Cynic's Word
Book. *"Bitter" Bierce, as he came to be called, disappeared in Mexico*
in 1914, under circumstances that have never been unravelled.

The Civil War was the decisive experience shaping Bierce's work, which
has something in common with the "black humor" that has become

fashionable in American writing during the 1960s. In his most characteristic work, everything is overshadowed by the presence of death. Death grins, it mocks, and then triumphs. Death reigns in battle, death appears through the mockery of accident, but to Bierce's eye, it is always gratuitous, meaningless, and without dignity. His best stories are sharply plotted, with an eye toward a shock of surprise at the end; they are written in a cool, almost clinical style, as if he were a cosmic physician coping with endless numbers of patients.

Read in large number, Bierce's stories pall, and their accumulated horrors come to seem mechanical, even unfrightening. They are ruled too compulsively by the homicidal theme and lack that tragic implication or humane compassion which redeems the greatest war fiction. But a few of his stories seem certain to survive: "An Occurrence at Owl Creek Bridge" and "A Major's Tale" are examples which yield mordant insights into the outrage of war.

FURTHER READING

Early biographies include Vincent Starrett, *Ambrose Bierce* (1920), and Carey McWilliams, *Ambrose Bierce* (1929). The most recent and definitive biography is Paul Fatout's *Ambrose Bierce, the Devil's Lexicographer* (1951).

An Occurrence at Owl Creek Bridge *(1891)*

I

A man stood upon a railroad bridge in northern Alabama, looking down into the swift water twenty feet below. The man's hands were behind his back, the wrists bound with a cord. A rope closely encircled his neck. It was attached to a stout crosstimber above his head and the slack fell to the level of his knees. Some loose boards laid upon the sleepers supporting the metals of the railway supplied a footing for him and his executioners—two private soldiers of the Federal army, directed by a sergeant who in civil life may have been a deputy sheriff. At a short remove upon the same temporary platform was an officer in the uniform of his rank, armed. He was a captain. A sentinel at each end of the bridge stood with his rifle in the position known as "support," that is to say, vertical in front of the left shoulder, the hammer resting on the forearm thrown straight across the chest—a formal and unnatural position, enforcing an erect carriage of the body. It did not appear to be the duty of these two men to know what was occurring at the center of the bridge; they merely blockaded the two ends of the foot planking that traversed it.

Beyond one of the sentinels nobody was in sight; the railroad ran straight away into a forest for a hundred yards, then, curving, was lost to view. Doubtless there was an outpost farther along. The other bank of the stream was open ground—a gentle aclivity topped with a stockade of vertical tree trunks, loop-holed for rifles, with a single embrasure through which protruded the muzzle of a brass cannon commanding the bridge. Midway of the slope between bridge and fort were the spectators—a single company of infantry in line, at "parade rest," the butts of the rifles on the ground, the barrels inclining slightly backward against the right shoulder, the hands crossed upon the stock. A lieutenant stood at the right of the line, the point of his sword upon the ground, his left hand resting upon his right. Excepting the group of four at the center of the bridge, not a man moved. The company faced the bridge, staring stonily, motionless. The sentinels, facing the banks of the stream, might have been statues to adorn the bridge. The captain stood with folded arms, silent, observing the work of his subordinates, but making no sign. Death is a dignitary who when he comes announced is to be received with formal manifestations of respect, even by those most familiar with him. In the code of military etiquette silence and fixity are forms of deference.

The man who was engaged in being hanged was apparently about thirty-five years of age. He was a civilian, if one might judge from his habit, which was that of a planter. His features were good—a straight nose, firm mouth, broad forehead, from which his long, dark hair was combed straight back, falling behind his ears to the collar of his well-fitting frock-coat. He wore a mustache and pointed beard, but no whiskers; his eyes were large and dark gray, and had a kindly expression which one would hardly have expected in one whose neck was in the hemp. Evidently this was no vulgar assassin. The liberal military code makes provision for hanging many kinds of persons, and gentlemen are not excluded.

The preparations being complete, the two private soldiers stepped side and each drew away the plank upon which he had been standing. The sergeant turned to the captain, saluted and placed himself immediately behind that officer, who in turn moved apart one pace. These movements left the condemned man and the sergeant standing on the two ends of the same plank, which spanned three of the crossties of the bridge. The end upon which the civilian stood almost, but not quite, reached a fourth. This plank had been held in place by the weight of the captain; it was now held by that of the sergeant. At a signal from the former the latter would step aside, the plank would tilt and the condemned man go down between two ties. The arrangement commended itself to his judgment as simple and effective. His face had not been covered nor his eyes bandaged. He looked a moment at his "unsteadfast footing," then let his gaze wander to the swirling water of the stream racing madly beneath his feet. A piece of dancing driftwood caught his attention and his eyes followed it down the current. How slowly it appeared to move! What a sluggish stream!

He closed his eyes in order to fix his last thoughts upon his wife and children. The water, touched to gold by the early sun, the brooding mists under the banks at some distance down the stream, the fort, the soldiers, the piece of drift—all had distracted him. And now he became conscious of a new disturbance. Striking through the thought of his dear ones was a sound which he could neither ignore nor understand, a sharp, distinct, metallic percussion like the stroke of a blacksmith's hammer upon the anvil; it had the same ringing quality. He wondered what it was, and whether immeasurably distant or near by—it seemed both. Its recurrence was regular, but as slow as the tolling of a death knell. He awaited each stroke with impatience and he knew not why—apprehension. The intervals of silence grew progressively longer; the delays became maddening. With their greater infrequency the sounds increased in strength and sharpness. They hurt his ear like the thrust of a knife; he feared he would shriek. What he heard was the ticking of his watch.

He unclosed his eyes and saw again the water below him. "If I could free my hands," he thought, "I might throw off the noose and spring into the stream. By diving I could evade the bullets and, swimming vigorously, reach the bank, take to the woods and get away home. My home, thank God, is as yet outside their lines; my wife and little ones are still beyond the invader's farthest advance."

As these thoughts, which have here to be set down in words, were flashed into the doomed man's brain rather than evolved from it, the captain nodded to the sergeant. The sergeant stepped aside.

II

Peyton Farquhar was a well-to-do planter, of an old and highly respected Alabama family. Being a slave owner and, like other slave owners, a politician he was naturally an original secessionist and ardently devoted to the Southern cause. Circumstances of an imperious nature, which it is unnecessary to relate here, had prevented him from taking service with the gallant army that had fought the disastrous campaigns ending with the fall of Corinth, and he chafed under the inglorious restraint, longing for the release of his energies, the larger life of the soldier, the opportunity for distinction. That opportunity, he felt, would come, as it comes to all in war time. Meanwhile he did what he could. No service was too humble for him to perform in aid of the South, no adventure too perilous for him to undertake if consistent with the character of a civilian who was at heart a soldier, and who in good faith and without too much qualification assented to at least a part of the frankly villainous dictum that all is fair in love and war.

One evening while Farquhar and his wife were sitting on a rustic bench near the entrance to his grounds, a gray-clad soldier rode up to the gate and asked for a drink of water. Mrs. Farquhar was only too happy to serve him with her own white hands. While she was fetching the water her husband approached the dusty horseman and inquired eagerly for news from the front.

"The Yanks are repairing the railroads," said the man, "and are getting ready for another advance. They have reached the Owl Creek bridge, put it in order and built a stockade on the north bank. The commandant has issued an order, which is posted everywhere, declaring that any civilian caught interfering with the railroad, its bridges, tunnels or trains will be summarily hanged. I saw the order."

"How far is it to the Owl Creek bridge?" Farquhar asked.

"About thirty miles."

"Is there no force on this side the creek?"

"Only a picket post half a mile out, on the railroad, and a single sentinel at this end of the bridge."

"Suppose a man—a civilian and student of hanging—should delude the picket post and perhaps get the better of the sentinel," said Farquhar, smiling, "what could he accomplish?"

The soldier reflected. "I was there a month ago," he replied. "I observed that the flood of last winter had lodged a great quantity of driftwood against the wooden pier at this end of the bridge. It is now dry and would burn like tow."

The lady had now brought the water, which the soldier drank. He thanked her ceremoniously, bowed to her husband and rode away. An hour later, after nightfall, he repassed the plantation, going northward in the direction from which he had come. He was a Federal scout.

III

As Peyton Farquhar fell straight downward through the bridge he lost consciousness and was as one already dead. From this state he was awakened—ages later, it seemed to him—by the pain of a sharp pressure upon his throat, followed by a sense of suffocation. Keen, poignant agonies seemed to shoot from his neck downward through every fibre of his body and limbs. These pains appeared to flash along well-defined lines of ramification and to beat with an inconceivably rapid periodicity. They seemed like streams of pulsating fire heating him to an intolerable temperature. As to his head, he was conscious of nothing but a feeling of fulness—of congestion. These sensations were unaccompanied by thought. The intellectual part of his nature was already effaced; he had power only to feel, and feeling was torment. He was conscious of motion. Encompassed in a luminous cloud, of which he was now merely the fiery heart, without material substance, he swung through unthinkable arcs of oscillation, like a vast pendulum.

Then all at once, with terrible suddenness, the light about him shot upward with the noise of a loud plash; a frightful roaring was in his ears, and all was cold and dark. The power of thought was restored; he knew that the rope had broken and he had fallen into the stream. There was no additional strangulation; the noose about his neck was already suffocating him and kept the water from his lungs. To die of hanging at the bottom of a river!—the idea seemed to him ludicrous. He opened his eyes in the darkness and saw above him a gleam of light, but how distant, how inaccessible! He was still sinking, for the light became fainter and fainter until it was a mere glimmer. Then it began to grow and brighten, and he knew that he was rising toward the surface—knew it with reluctance, for he was now very comfortable. "To be hanged and drowned," he thought, "that is not so bad; but I do not wish to be shot. No; I will not be shot; that is not fair."

He was not conscious of an effort, but a sharp pain in his wrist apprised him that he was trying to free his hands. He gave the struggle his attention, as an idler might observe the feat of a juggler, without interest in the outcome. What splendid effort! What magnificent, what superhuman strength! Ah, that was a fine endeavor! Bravo! The cord fell away; his arms parted and floated upward, the hands dimly seen on each side in the growing light. He watched them with a new interest as first one and then the other pounced upon the noose at his neck. They tore it away and thrust it fiercely aside, its undulations resembling those of a water-snake. "Put it back, put it back!" He thought he shouted these words to his hands, for the undoing of the noose had been succeeded by the direst pang that he had yet experienced. His neck ached horribly; his brain was on fire; his heart, which had been fluttering faintly, gave a great leap, trying to force itself out at his mouth. His whole body was racked and wrenched with an insupportable anguish! But his disobedient hands gave no heed to the command. They beat the water vigorously with quick, downward strokes, forcing him to the surface. He felt his head emerge; his eyes were blinded by the sunlight; his chest expanded convulsively, and with a supreme and crowning agony his lungs engulfed a great draught of air, which instantly he expelled in a shriek!

He was now in full possession of his physical senses. They were, indeed, preternaturally keen and alert. Something in the awful disturbance of his organic system had so exalted and refined them that they made record of things never before perceived. He felt the ripples upon his face and heard their separate sounds as they struck. He looked at the forest on the bank of the stream, saw the individual trees, the leaves and the veining of each leaf—saw the very insects upon them: the locusts, the brilliant-bodied flies, the gray spiders stretching their webs from twig to twig. He noted the prismatic colors in all the dewdrops upon a million blades of grass. The humming of the gnats that danced above the eddies of the stream, the beating of the dragon-flies' wings, the strokes of the water-spiders' legs, like oars which had lifted their boat—all these made audible music. A fish slid along beneath his eyes and he heard the rush of its body parting the water.

He had come to the surface facing down the stream; in a moment the visible world seemed to wheel slowly round, himself the pivotal point, and he saw the bridge, the fort, the soldiers upon the bridge, the captain, the sergeant, the two privates, his executioners. They were in silhouette against the blue sky. They shouted and gesticulated, pointing at him. The captain had drawn his pistol, but did not fire; the others were unarmed. Their movements were grotesque and horrible, their forms gigantic.

Suddenly he heard a sharp report and something struck the water smartly within a few inches of his head, spattering his face with spray. He heard a second report, and saw one of the sentinels with his rifle at his shoulder, a light cloud of blue smoke rising from the muzzle. The man in the water saw the eye of the man on the bridge gazing into his own through the sights of the rifle. He observed that it was a gray eye and remembered having read that gray eyes were keenest, and that all famous marksmen had them. Nevertheless, this one had missed.

A counter-swirl had caught Farquhar and turned him half round; he was again looking into the forest on the bank opposite the fort. The sound of a clear, high voice in a monotonous singsong now rang out behind him and came across the water with a distinctness that pierced and subdued all other sounds, even the beating of the ripples in his ears. Although no soldier, he had frequented camps enough to know the dread significance of that deliberate, drawling, aspirated chant; the lieutenant on shore was taking a part in the morning's work. How coldly and pitilessly—with what an even, calm intonation, presaging and enforcing tranquillity in the men—with what accurately measured intervals fell those cruel words:

"Attention, company! . . . Shoulder arms! . . . Ready! . . . Aim! . . . Fire!"

Farquhar dived—dived as deeply as he could. The water roared in his ears like the voice of Niagara, yet he heard the dulled thunder of the volley and, rising again toward the surface, met shining bits of metal, singularly flattened, oscillating slowly downward. Some of them touched him on the face and hands, then fell away, continuing their descent. One lodged between his collar and neck; it was uncomfortably warm and he snatched it out.

As he rose to the surface, gasping for breath, he saw that he had been a long time under water; he was perceptibly farther down stream—nearer to safety. The soldiers had almost finished reloading; the metal ramrods flashed all at once in the sunshine as they were drawn from the barrels, turned in the air, and thrust into their sockets. The two sentinels fired again, independently and ineffectually.

The hunted man saw all this over his shoulder; he was now swimming vigorously with the current. His brain was as energetic as his arms and legs; he thought with the rapidity of lightning.

The officer," he reasoned, "will not make that martinet's error a second time. It is as easy to dodge a volley as a single shot. He has probably already given the command to fire at will. God help me, I cannot dodge them all!"

An appalling plash within two yards of him was followed by a loud, rushing sound, *diminuendo*, which seemed to travel back through the air to the fort and died in an explosion which stirred the very river to its deeps! A rising sheet of water curved over him, fell down upon him, blinded him, strangled him! The cannon had taken a hand in the game. As he shook his head free from the commotion of the smitten water he heard the deflected shot humming through the air ahead, and in an instant it was cracking and smashing the branches in the forest beyond.

"They will not do that again," he thought, "the next time they will use a charge of grape. I must keep my eye upon the gun; the smoke will apprise me—the report arrives too late; it lags behind the missile. That is a good gun."

Suddenly he felt himself whirled round and round—spinning like a top. The water, the banks, the forests, the now distant bridge, fort and men—all were commingled and blurred. Objects were represented by their colors only; circular horizontal streaks of color—that was all he saw. He had been caught in a vortex and was being whirled on with a velocity of advance and gyration that made him giddy and sick. In a few moments he was flung upon the gravel at the foot of the left bank of the stream—the southern bank—and behind a projecting point which concealed him from his enemies. The sudden arrest of his motion, the abrasion of one of his hands on the gravel, restored him, and he wept with delight. He dug his fingers into the sand, threw it over himself in handfuls and audibly blessed it. It looked like diamonds, rubies, emeralds; he could think of nothing beautiful which it did not resemble. The trees upon the bank were giant garden plants; he noted a definite order in their arrangement, inhaled the fragrance of their blooms. A strange, roseate light shone through the spaces among their trunks and the wind made in their branches the music of æolian harps. He had no wish to perfect his escape—was content to remain in that enchanting spot until retaken.

A whiz and rattle of grapeshot among the branches high above his head roused him from his dream. The baffled cannoneer had fired him a random farewell. He sprang to his feet, rushed up the sloping bank, and plunged into the forest.

All that day he traveled, laying his course by the rounding sun. The forest seemed interminable; nowhere did he discover a break in it, not even a woodman's road. He had not known that he lived in so wild a region. There was something uncanny in the revelation.

By nightfall he was fatigued, footsore, famishing. The thought of his wife and children urged him on. At last he found a road which led him in what he knew to be the right direction. It was as wide and straight as a city street, yet it seemed untraveled. No fields bordered it, no dwelling anywhere. Not so much as the barking of a dog suggested human habitation. The black bodies of the trees formed a straight wall on both sides, terminating on the horizon in a point, like a diagram in a lesson in perspective. Overhead, as he looked up through this rift in the wood, shone great golden stars looking unfamiliar and grouped in strange constellations. He was sure they were arranged in some order which had a secret and malign significance. The wood on either side was full of singular noises, among which—once, twice, and again—he distinctly heard whispers in an unknown tongue.

His neck was in pain and lifting his hand to it he found it horribly swollen. He knew that it had a circle of black where the rope had bruised it. His eyes felt congested; he could no longer close them. His tongue was swollen with thirst; he relieved its fever by thrusting it forward from between his teeth into the cold air. How softly the turf had carpeted the untraveled avenue—he could no longer feel the roadway beneath his feet!

Doubtless, despite his suffering, he had fallen asleep while walking, for now he sees another scene—perhaps he has merely recovered from a delirium. He stands at the gate of his own home. All is as he left it, and all bright and beautiful in the morning sunshine. He must have traveled the entire night. As he pushes open the gate and passes up the wide white walk, he sees a flutter of female garments; his wife, looking fresh and cool and sweet, steps down from the veranda to meet him. At the bottom of the steps she stands waiting, with a smile of ineffable joy, an attitude of matchless grace and dignity. Ah, how beautiful she is! He springs forward with extended arms. As he is about to clasp her he feels a stunning blow upon the back of the neck; a blinding white light bazes all about him with a sound like the shock of a cannon—then all is darkness and silence!

Peyton Farquhar was dead; his body, with a broken neck, swung gently from side to side beneath the timbers of the Owl Creek bridge.

HAMLIN GARLAND (1860–1940)

Garland was born on the western border of Wisconsin, but as a boy he moved with his family to Iowa and then to the Dakota Territory, where at twenty-three he homesteaded a farm. At every step, in every state, poverty dogged him and his parents. Selling his homestead rights for two hundred dollars, Garland went to Boston to get an education, but he was rejected—a Jude the Obscure from the West—at Harvard University. He then tried, as best he could, to educate himself in the Boston Public Library. In 1884 he enrolled as a student at the Boston School of Oratory, and through his work there he met William Dean Howells, who would be helpful and receptive to this young man.

After a trip west in 1887, during which he saw the Western farmer in a period of depression and debt, Garland returned to Boston to write fiction. What he saw in the West, Garland would recall, was "the ugliness, the endless drudgery, and the loneliness of the farmer's lot . . . [it] smote me with stern insistence." His one commanding and fruitful subject was the life of the American farmer in the Western states, no longer treated as romantic idyll, but in terms harshly realistic and compassionate. Garland's sympathies were genuine, and despite notable literary failings—his ear for language was poor—he managed to evoke the "mechanical daily routine of these lives." Says one of Garland's farmers: "A man like me is helpless. Just like a fly in a pan of molasses. . . . The more he tears around the more liable he is to rip his legs off."

Garland was not the first American writer of fiction to portray the West through the coarse lens of realism. Edward Eggleston in The Hoosier School-master *(1871) and Ed Howe in* The Story of a Country Town *(1883) had torn away the romantic trappings from the life of the Western towns. In one of his essays declaring the program of the new realism, Garland sardonically asked: "Shall we sit down and copy the last epics of feudalism, and repeat the dying Echoes of Romance?" His answer was a fiction he described as "veritism," by which he meant that he stood somewhere between the mild realism of Howells, which he knew to be too weak for his subject, and the deterministic naturalism of Zola, which he was still enough of an American to find shocking.*

Garland proved to be a one-book author: his small but authentic contribution to American literature is concentrated in his volume of stories, Main-travelled Roads *(1891). He wrote a good many more books but they are either preachy, in behalf of Populism and the single tax proposals of Henry George, or syrupy lapses into the kind of romanticism he had earlier attacked.*

FURTHER READING

Jean Halloway, *Hamlin Garland* (1960); Lars Ahrenbrink, *The Beginnings of Naturalism in American Fiction* (1950); Charles Child Walcutt, *American Literary Naturalism: A Divided Stream* (1956).

The Return of a Private (1891)

On the road leading "back to God's country" and wife and babies

I

The nearer the train drew toward La Crosse, the soberer the little group of "vets" became. On the long way from New Orleans they had beguiled tedium with jokes and friendly chaff; or with planning with elaborate detail what they were going to do now, after the war. A long journey, slowly, irregularly, yet persistently pushing northward. When they entered on Wisconsin Territory they gave a cheer, and another when they reached Madison, but after that they sank into a dumb expectancy. Comrades dropped off at one or two points beyond, until there were only four or five left who were bound for La Crosse County.

Three of them were gaunt and brown, the fourth was gaunt and pale, with signs of fever and ague upon him. One had a great scar down his temple; one limped; and they all had unnaturally large bright eyes, showing emaciation. There were no bands greeting them at the stations, no banks of gaily dressed ladies waving handkerchiefs and shouting "Bravo!" as they came in on the caboose of a freight train into the towns that had cheered and blared at them on their way to war. As they looked out or stepped upon the platform for a moment, as the train stood at the station, the loafers looked at them indifferently. Their blue coats, dusty and grimy, were too familiar now to excite notice, much less a friendly word. They were the last of the army to return, and the loafers were surfeited with such sights.

The train jogged forward so slowly that it seemed likely to be midnight before they should reach La Crosse. The little squad of "vets" grumbled and swore, but it was no use, the train would not hurry; and as a matter of fact, it was nearly two o'clock when the engine whistled "down brakes."

Most of the group were farmers, living in districts several miles out of the town, and all were poor.

"Now, boys," said Private Smith, he of the fever and ague, "we are landed in La Crosse in the night. We've got to stay somewhere till mornin'. Now, I ain't got no two dollars to waste on a hotel, I've got a wife and children, so I'm goin' to roost on a bench and take the cost of a bed out of my hide."

"Same here," put in one of the other men. "Hide'll grow on again, dollars come hard. It's goin' to be mighty hot skirmishin' to find a dollar these days."

"Don't think they'll be a deputation of citizens waitin' to 'scort us to a hotel, eh?" said another. His sarcasm was too obvious to require an answer.

Smith went on: "Then at daybreak we'll start f'r home; at least I will."

"Well, I'll be dummed if I'll take two dollars out o' *my* hide," one of the younger men said. "I'm goin' to a hotel, ef I don't never lay up a cent."

"That'll do f'r you," said Smith; "but if you had a wife an' three young 'uns dependin' on yeh—"

"Which I ain't, thank the Lord! and don't intend havin' while the court knows itself."

The station was deserted, chill, and dark, as they came into it at exactly a quarter to two in the morning. Lit by the oil lamps that flared a dull red light over the dingy benches, the waiting room was not an inviting place. The younger man went off to look up a hotel, while the rest remained and prepared to camp down on the floor and benches. Smith was attended to tenderly by the other men, who spread their blankets on the bench for him, and by robbing themselves made quite a comfortable bed, though the narrowness of the bench made his sleeping precarious.

It was chill, though August, and the two men sitting with bowed heads grew stiff with cold and weariness, and were forced to rise now and again, and walk about to warm their stiffened limbs. It didn't occur to them, probably, to contrast their coming home with their going forth, or with the coming home of the generals, colonels, or even captains— but to Private Smith, at any rate, there came a sickness at heart almost deadly, as he lay there on his hard bed and went over his situation.

In the deep of the night, lying on a board in the town where he had enlisted three years ago, all elation and enthusiasm gone out of him, he faced the fact that with the joy of homecoming was mingled the bitter juice of care. He saw himself sick, worn out, taking up the work on his half-cleared farm, the inevitable mortgage standing ready with open jaw to swallow half his earnings. He had given three years of his life for a mere pittance of pay, and now—

Morning dawned at last, slowly, with a pale yellow dome of light rising silently above the bluffs which stand like some huge battle-mented castle, just east of the city. Out to the left the great river swept on its massive yet silent way to the south. Jays called across the river from hillside to hillside, through the clear, beautiful air, and hawks began to skim the tops of the hills. The two vets were astir early, but Private Smith had fallen at last into a sleep, and they went out without waking him. He lay on his knapsack, his gaunt face turned toward the ceiling, his hands clasped on his breast, with a curious pathetic effect of weakness and appeal.

An engine switching near woke him at last, and he slowly sat up and stared about. He looked out of the window and saw that the sun was lightening the hills across the river. He rose and brushed his hair as well as he could, folded his blankets up, and went out to find his companions. They stood gazing silently at the river and at the hills.

"Looks nat'cherl, don't it?" they said as he came out.

"That's what it does," he replied. "An' it looks good. D'yeh see that peak?" He pointed at a beautiful symmetrical peak, rising like a slightly truncated cone, so high that it seemed the very highest of them all. It was lighted by the morning sun till it glowed like a beacon, and a light scarf of gray morning fog was rolling up its shadowed side.

"My farm's just beyond that. Now, ef I can only ketch a ride, we'll be home by dinnertime."

"I'm talkin' about breakfast," said one of the others.

"I guess it's one more meal o' hardtack f'r me," said Smith.

They foraged around, and finally found a restaurant with a sleepy old German behind the counter, and procured some coffee, which they drank to wash down their hardtack.

"Time'll come," said Smith, holding up a piece by the corner, "when this'll be a curiosity."

"I hope to God it will! I bet I've chawed hardtack enough to shingle every house in the coulee. I've chawed it when my lampers was down, and when they wasn't. I've took it dry, soaked, and mashed. I've had it wormy, musty, sour, and blue-moldy. I've had it in little bits and big bits; 'fore coffee an' after coffee. I'm ready f'r a change. I'd like t' git hol't jest about now o' some of the hot biscuits my wife c'n make when she lays herself out f'r company."

"Well, if you set there gablin', you'll never *see* yer wife."

"Come on," said Private Smith. "Wait a moment, boys; less take suthin'. It's on me." He led them to the rusty tin dipper which hung on a nail beside the wooden water pail, and they grinned and drank. (Things were primitive in La Crosse then.) Then, shouldering their blankets and muskets, which they were "taking home to the boys," they struck out on their last march.

"They called that coffee 'Jayvy'," grumbled one of them, "but it never went by the road where government Jayvy resides. I reckon I know coffee from peas."

They kept together on the road along the turnpike, and up the winding road by the river, which they followed for some miles. The river was very lovely, curving down along its sandy beds, pausing now and then under broad basswood trees, or running in dark, swift, silent currents under tangles of wild grapevines, and drooping alders, and haw trees. At one of these lovely spots the three vets sat down on the thick green sward to rest, "on Smith's account." The leaves of the trees were as fresh and green as in June, the jays called cheery greetings to them, and kingfishers darted to and fro, with swooping, noiseless flight.

"I tell yeh, boys, this knocks the swamps of Loueesiana into kingdom come."

"You bet. All they c'n raise down there is snakes, niggers, and p'rticler hell."

"An' fightin' men," put in the older man.

"An' fightin' men. If I had a good hook an' line I'd sneak a pick'rel out o' that pond. Say, remember that time I shot that alligator—"

"I guess we'd better be crawlin' along," interrupted Smith, rising and shouldering his knapsack, with considerable effort, which he tried to hide.

"Say, Smith, lemme give you a lift on that."

"I guess I c'n manage," said Smith grimly.

" 'Course. But, yeh see, I may not have a chance right off to pay yeh back for the times ye've carried my gun and hull caboodle. Say, now, gimme that gun, anyway."

"All right, if yeh feel like it, Jim," Smith replied, and they trudged along doggedly in the sun, which was getting higher and hotter each half mile.

"Ain't it queer there ain't no teams comin' along."

"Well, no, seein's it's Sunday."

"By jinks, that's a fact! It *is* Sunday. I'll git home in time f'r dinner, sure. She don't hev dinner usually till about *one* on Sundays." And he fell into a muse, in which he smiled.

"Well, I'll git home jest about six o'clock, jest about when the boys are milkin' the cows," said old Jim Cranby. "I'll step into the barn an' then I'll say, 'He*ah!* why ain't this milkin' done before this time o' day? An' then won't they yell!" he added, slapping his thigh in great glee.

Smith went on. "I'll jest go up the path. Old Rover'll come down the road to meet me. He won't bark; he'll know me, an' he'll come down waggin' his tail an' shonin' his teeth. That's his way of laughin'. An' so I'll walk up to the kitchen door, an' I'll say '*Dinner* f'r a hungry man!' An' then she'll jump up, an'—"

He couldn't go on. His voice choked at the thought of it. Saunders, the third man, hardly uttered a word. He walked silently behind the others. He had lost his wife the first year he was in the army. She died of pneumonia caught in the autumn rains, while working in the fields in his place.

They plodded along till at last they came to a parting of the ways. To the right the road continued up the main valley; to the left it went over the ridge.

"Well, boys," began Smith as they grounded their muskets and looked away up the valley, "here's where we shake hands. We've marched together a good many miles, an' now I s'pose we're done."

"Yes, I don't think we'll do any more of it f'r a while. I don't want to, I know."

"I hope I'll see yeh once in a while, boys, to talk over old times."

"Of course," said Saunders, whose voice trembled a little, too. "It ain't *exactly* like dyin'."

"But we'd ought'r go home with you," said the younger man. "You never'll climb that ridge with all them things on yer back."

"Oh, I'm all right! Don't worry about me. Every step takes me nearer home, yeh see. Well, goodbye, boys."

They shook hands. "Goodbye. Good luck!"

"Same to you. Lemme know how you find things at home."

He turned once before they passed out of sight and waved his cap, and they did the same, and all yelled. Then all marched away with their long, steady, loping, veteran step. The solitary climber in blue walked on for a time, with his mind filled with the kindness of his comrades, and musing upon the many jolly days they had had together in camp and field.

He thought of his chum, Billy Tripp. Poor Billy! A "minie" ball fell into his breast one day, fell wailing like a cat, and tore a great ragged hole in his heart. He looked forward to a sad scene with Billy's mother and sweetheart. They would want to know all about it. He tried to recall all that Billy had said, and the particulars of it, but there was little to remember, just that wild wailing sound high in the air, a dull slap, a short, quick, expulsive groan, and the boy lay with his face in the dirt in the plowed field they were marching across.

That was all. But all the scenes he had since been through had not dimmed the horror, the terror of that moment, when his boy comrade fell, with only a breath between a laugh and a death groan. Poor handsome Billy! Worth millions of dollars was his young wife.

These somber recollections gave way at length to more cheerful feelings as he began to approach his home coulee. The fields and houses grew familiar, and in one or two he was greeted by people seated in the doorway. But he was in no mood to talk, and pushed on steadily, though he stopped and accepted a drink of milk once at the well-side of a neighbor.

The sun was getting hot on that slope, and his step grew slower, in spite of his iron resolution. He sat down several times to rest. Slowly he crawled up the rough, reddish-brown road, which wound along the hillside, under great trees, through dense groves of jack oaks, with treetops far below him on his left hand, and the hills far above him on his right. He crawled along like some minute wingless variety of fly.

He ate some hardtack, sauced with wild berries, when he reached the summit of the ridge, and sat there for some time, looking down into his home coulee.

Somber, pathetic figure! His wide, round, gray eyes gazing down into the beautiful valley, seeing and not seeing, the splendid cloudshadows sweeping over the western hills and across the green and yellow wheat far below. His head drooped forward on his palm, his shoulders took on a tired stoop, his cheekbones showed painfully. An observer might have said, "He is looking down upon his own grave."

II

Sunday comes in a Western wheat harvest with such sweet and sudden relaxation to man and beast that it would be holy for that reason, if for no other. And Sundays are usually fair in harvesttime. As one goes out into the field in the hot morning sunshine, with no sound abroad save the crickets and the indescribably pleasant, silken rustling of the ripened grain, the reaper and the very sheaves in the stubble seem to be resting, dreaming.

Around the house, in the shade of the trees, the men sit, smoking, dozing, or reading the papers, while the women, never resting, move about at the housework. The men eat on Sundays about the same as on other days, and breakfast is no sooner over and out of the way than dinner begins.

But at the Smith farm there were no men dozing or reading. Mrs. Smith was alone with her three children, Mary, nine, Tommy, six, and little Ted, just past four. Her farm, rented to a neighbor, lay at the head of a coulee or narrow gulley, made at some far-off postglacial period by the vast and angry floods of water which gullied these tremendous furrows in the level prairie—furrows so deep that undisturbed portions of the original level rose like hills on either side—rose to quite considerable mountains.

The chickens wakened her as usual that Sabbath morning from dreams of her absent husband, from whom she had not heard for weeks. The shadows drifted over the hills, down the slopes, across the wheat, and up the opposite wall in leisurely way, as if, being Sunday, they could "take it easy," also. The fowls clustered about the housewife as she went out into the yard. Fuzzy little chickens swarmed out from the coops where their clucking and perpetually disgruntled mothers tramped about, petulantly thrusting their heads through the spaces between the slats.

A cow called in a deep, musical bass, and a calf answered from a little pen nearby, and a pig scurried guiltily out of the cabbages. Seeing all this, seeing the pig in the cabbages, the tangle of grass in the garden, the broken fence which she had mended again and again—the little woman, hardly more than a girl, sat down and cried. The bright Sabbath morning was only a mockery without him!

A few years ago they had bought this farm, paying part, mortgaging the rest in the usual way. Edward Smith was a man of terrible energy. He worked "nights and Sundays," as the saying goes, to clear the farm of its brush and of its insatiate mortgage. In the midst of his Herculean struggle came the call for volunteers, and with the grim and unselfish devotion to his country which made the Eagle Brigade able to "whip its weight in wildcats," he threw down his scythe and his grub ax, turned his cattle loose, and became a blue-coated cog in a vast machine for killing men, and not thistles. While the millionnaire sent his money to England for safekeeping, this man, with his girl-wife and three babies, left them on a mortgaged farm and went away to fight for an idea. It was foolish, but it was sublime for all that.

That was three years before, and the young wife, sitting on the well curb on this bright Sabbath harvest morning, was righteously rebellious. It seemed to her that she had borne her share of the country's sorrow.

Two brothers had been killed, the renter in whose hands her husband had left the farm had proved a villain, one year the farm was without crops, and now the overripe grain was waiting the tardy hand of the neighbor who had rented it, and who was cutting his own grain first.

About six weeks before, she had received a letter saying, "We'll be discharged in a little while." But no other word had come from him. She had seen by the papers that his army was being discharged, and from day to day other soldiers slowly percolated in blue streams back into the state and county, but still *her* private did not return.

Each week she had told the children that he was coming, and she had watched the road so long that it had become unconscious, and as she stood at the well, or by the kitchen door, her eyes were fixed unthinkingly on the road that wound down the coulee. Nothing wears on the human soul like waiting. If the stranded mariner, searching the sun-bright seas, could once give up hope of a ship, that horrible grinding on his brain would cease. It was this waiting, hoping, on the edge of despair, that gave Emma Smith no rest.

Neighbors said, with kind intentions, "He's sick, maybe, an' can't start North just yet. He'll come along one o' these days."

"Why don't he write?" was her question, which silenced them all. This Sunday morning it seemed to her as if she couldn't stand it any longer. The house seemed intolerably lonely. So she dressed the little ones in their best calico dresses and homemade jackets, and closing up the house, set off down the coulee to old Mother Gray's.

"Old Widder Gray" lived at the "mouth of the coulee." She was a widow woman with a large family of stalwart boys and laughing girls. She was the visible incarnation of hospitality and optimistic poverty. With Western openheartedness she fed every mouth that asked food of her, and worked herself to death as cheerfully as her girls danced in the neighborhood harvest dances.

She waddled down the path to meet Mrs. Smith with a smile on her face that would have made the countenance of a convict expand.

"Oh, you little dears! Come right to yer granny. Gimme a kiss! Come right in, Mis' Smith. How are yeh, anyway? Nice mornin', ain't it? Come in an' set down. Everything's in a clutter, but that won't scare you any."

She led the way into the "best room," a sunny, square room, carpeted with a faded and patched rag carpet, and papered with a horrible white-and-green-striped wallpaper, where a few ghastly effigies of dead members of the family hung in variously sized oval walnut frames. The house resounded with singing, laughter, whistling, tramping of boots, and scufflings. Half-grown boys came to the door and crooked their fingers at the children, who ran out, and were soon heard in the midst of the fun.

"Don't s'pose you've heard from Ed?" Mrs. Smith shook her head. "He'll turn up some day, when you ain't lookin' for 'm." The good old soul had said that so many times that poor Mrs. Smith derived no comfort from it any longer.

"Liz heard from Al the other day. He's comin' some day this week. Anyhow, they expect him."

"Did he say anything of—"

"No, he didn't," Mrs. Gray admitted. "But then it was only a short letter, anyhow. Al ain't much for ritin', anyhow. But come out and see my new cheese. I tell yeh, I don't believe I ever had better luck in my life. If Ed should come, I want you should take him up a piece of this cheese."

It was beyond human nature to resist the influence of that noisy, hearty, loving household, and in the midst of the singing and laughing the wife forgot her anxiety, for the time at least, and laughed and sang with the rest.

About eleven o'clock a wagon load more drove up to the door, and Bill Gray, the widow's oldest son, and his whole family from Sand Lake Coulee piled out amid a good-natured uproar, as characteristic as it was ludicrous. Everyone talked at once, except Bill, who sat in the wagon with his wrists on his knees, a straw in his mouth, and an amused twinkle in his blue eyes.

"Ain't heard nothin' o' Ed, I s'pose?" he asked in a kind of bellow. Mrs. Smith shook her head. Bill, with a delicacy very striking in such a great giant, rolled his quid in his mouth and said:

"Didn't know but you had. I hear two or three of the Sand Lake boys are comin'. Left New Orleenes some time this week. Didn't write nothin' about Ed, but no news is good news in such cases, Mother always says."

"Well, go put out yer team," said Mrs. Gray, "an' go'n bring me in some taters, an', Sim, you go see if you c'n find some corn. Sadie, you put on the water to b'ile. Come now, hustle yer boots, all o' yeh. If I feed this yer crowd, we've got to have some raw materials. If y' think I'm goin' to feed yeh on pie—"

The children went off into the fields, the girls put dinner on to "b'ile," and then went to change their dresses and fix their hair. "Somebody might come," they said.

"Land sakes, I *hope* not! I don't know where in time I'd set 'em, 'less they'd eat at the secont table," Mrs. Gray laughed in pretended dismay.

The two older boys, who had served their time in the army, lay out on the grass before the house, and whittled and talked desultorily about the war and the crops, and planned buying a threshing machine. The older girls and Mrs. Smith helped enlarge the table and put on the dishes, talking all the time in that cheery, incoherent, and meaningful way a group of such women have—a conversation to be taken for its spirit rather than for its letter, though Mrs. Gray at last got the ear of them all and dissertated at length on girls.

"Girls in love ain't no use in the whole blessed week," she said. "Sundays they're a-lookin' down the road, expectin' he'll *come*. Sunday afternoons they can't think o' nothin' else, 'cause he's *here*. Monday mornin's they're sleepy and kind o' dreamy and slimpsy, and good f'r nothin' on Tuesday and Wednesday. Thursday they git absent-minded, an' begin to look off toward Sunday agin, an' mope aroun' and let the dishwater git cold, right under their noses. Friday they break dishes, and go off in the best room an' snivel, an' look out o' the winder. Saturdays they have queer spurts o' workin' like all p'ssessed, an' spurts o' frizzin' their hair. An' Sunday they begin it all over agin."

The girls giggled and blushed all through this tirade from their mother, their broad faces and powerful frames anything but suggestive of lackadaisical sentiment. But Mrs. Smith said:

"Now, Mrs. Gray, I hadn't ought to stay to dinner. You've got—"

"Now you set right down! If any of them girls' beaus comes, they'll have to take what's left, that's all. They ain't s'posed to have much appetite, nohow. No, you're goin' to stay if they starve, an' they ain't no danger o' that."

At one o'clock the long table was piled with boiled potatoes, cords of boiled corn on the cob, squash and pumpkin pies, hot biscuit, sweet pickles, bread and butter, and honey. Then one of the girls took down a conch shell from a nail and, going to the door, blew a long, fine, free blast, that showed there was no weakness of lungs in her ample chest.

Then the children came out of the forest of corn, out of the crick, out of the loft of the barn, and out of the garden. The men shut up their jackknives, and surrounded the horse trough to souse their faces in the cold, hard water, and in a few moments the table was filled with a merry crowd, and a row of wistful-eyed youngsters circled the kitchen wall, where they stood first on one leg and then on the other, in impatient hunger.

"They come to their feed f'r all the world jest like the pigs when y' holder 'poo—ee!" See 'em scoot!" laughed Mrs. Gray, every wrinkle on her face shining with delight. "Now pitch in, Mrs. Smith," she said, presiding over the table. "You know these men critters. They'll eat every grain of it, if yeh give 'em a chance. I swan, they're made o' Indian rubber, their stomachs is, I know it."

"Haft to eat to work," said Bill, gnawing a cob with a swift, circular motion that rivaled a corn sheller in results.

"More like workin' to eat," put in one of the girls with a giggle. "More eat 'n' work with you."

"*You* needn't say anything, Net. Anyone that'll eat seven ears—"

"I didn't, no such thing. You piled your cobs on my plate."

"That'll do to tell Ed Varney. It won't go down here, where we know yeh."

"Good land! Eat all yeh want! They's plenty more in the fiel's, but I can't afford to give you young 'uns tea. The tea is for us womenfolks, and 'specially f'r Mis' Smith an' Bill's wife. We're agoin' to tell fortunes by it."

One by one the men filled up and shoved back, and one by one the children slipped into their places, and by two o'clock the women alone remained around the debris-covered table, sipping their tea and telling fortunes.

As they got well down to the grounds in the cup, they shook them with a circular motion in the hand, and then turned them bottom-side-up quickly in the saucer, then twirled them three or four times one way, and three or four times the other, during a breathless pause. Then Mrs. Gray lifted the cup and, gazing into it with profound gravity, pronounced the impending fate.

It must be admitted that, to a critical observer, she had abundant preparation for hitting close to the mark; as when she told the girls that "somebody was coming." "It is a man," she went on gravely. "He is cross-eyed—"

"Oh, you hush!"

"He has red hair, and is death on b'iled corn and hot biscuit."

The others shrieked with delight.

"But he's goin' to get the mitten, that redheaded feller is, for I see a feller comin' up behind him."

"Oh, lemme see, lemme see!" cried Nettie.

"Keep off," said the priestess with a lofty gesture. "His hair is black. He don't eat so much, and he works more."

The girls exploded in a shriek of laughter and pounded their sister on the back.

At last came Mrs. Smith's turn, and she was trembling with excitement as Mrs. Gray again composed her jolly face to what she considered a proper solemnity of expression.

"Somebody is comin' to *you*," she said after a long pause. "He's got a musket on his back. He's a soldier. He's almost here. See?"

She pointed at two little tea stems, which formed a faint suggestion of a man with a musket on his back. He had climbed nearly to the edge of the cup. Mrs. Smith grew pale with excitement. She trembled so she could hardly hold the cup in her hand as she gazed into it.

"It's Ed," cried the old woman. "He's on the way home. Heavens an' earth! There he is now!" She turned and waved her hand out toward the road. They rushed to the door and looked where she pointed.

A man in a blue coat, with a musket on his back, was toiling slowly up the hill, on the sun-bright, dusty road, toiling slowly, with bent head half-hidden by a heavy knapsack. So tired it seemed that walking was indeed a process of falling. So eager to get home he would not stop, would not look aside, but plodded on, amid the cries of the locusts, the welcome of the crickets, and the rustle of the yellow wheat. Getting back to God's country, and his wife and babies!

Laughing, crying, trying to call him and the children at the same

time, the little wife, almost hysterical, snatched her hat and ran out into
the yard. But the soldier had disappeared over the hill into the hollowy
beyond, and, by the time she had found the children, he was too far
away for her voice to reach him. And besides, she was not sure it was
her husband, for he had not turned his head at their shouts. This
seemed so strange. Why didn't he stop to rest at his old neighbor's
house? Tortured by hope and doubt, she hurried up the coulee as fast
as she could push the baby wagon, the bluecoated figure just ahead
pushing steadily, silently forward up the coulee.

When the excited, panting little group came in sight of the gate, they
saw the blue-coated figure standing, leaning upon the rough rail fence,
his chin on his palms, gazing at the empty house. His knapsack, canteen, blankets, and musket lay upon the dusty grass at his feet.

He was like a man lost in a dream. His wide, hungry eyes devoured
the scene. The rough lawn, the little unpainted house, the field of clear
yellow wheat behind it, down across which streamed the sun, now
almost ready to touch the high hill to the west, the crickets crying
merrily, a cat on the fence nearby, dreaming, unmindful of the stranger
in blue.

How peaceful it all was. O God! How far removed from all camps,
hospitals, battlelines. A little cabin in a Wisconsin coulee, but it was
majestic in its peace. How did he ever leave it for those years of tramping, thirsting, killing?

Trembling, weak with emotion, her eyes on the silent figure, Mrs.
Smith hurried up to the fence. Her feet made no noise in the dust and
grass, and they were close upon him before he knew of them. The
oldest boy ran a little ahead. He will never forget that figure, that face.
It will always remain as something epic, that return of the private. He
fixed his eyes on the pale face, covered with a ragged beard.

"Who *are* you, sir?" asked the wife, or, rather, started to ask, for
he turned, stood a moment, and then cried:

"Emma!"

"Edward!"

The children stood in a curious row to see their mother kiss this
bearded, strange man, the elder girl sobbing sympathetically with her
mother. Illness had left the soldier partly deaf, and this added to the
strangeness of his manner.

But the boy of six years stood away, even after the girl had recognized her father and kissed him. The man turned then to the baby and
said in a curiously unpaternal tone:

"Come here, my little man; don't you know me?" But the baby
backed away under the fence and stood peering at him critically.

"My little man!" What meaning in those words! This baby seemed
like some other woman's child, and not the infant he had left in his
wife's arms. The war had come between him and his baby—he was only
"a strange man, with big eyes, dressed in blue, with Mother hanging to
his arm, and talking in a loud voice."

"And this is Tom," he said, drawing the oldest boy to him. "*He'll* come and see me. *He* knows his poor old pap when he comes home from the war."

The mother heard the pain and reproach in his voice and hastened to apologize.

"You've changed so, Ed. He can't know yeh. This is Papa, Teddy; come and kiss him—Tom and Mary do, Come, won't you?" But Teddy still peered through the fence with solemn eyes, well out of reach. He resembled a half-wild kitten that hesitates, studying the tones of one's voice.

"I'll fix him," said the soldier, and sat down to undo his knapsack, out of which he drew three enormous and very red apples. After giving one to each of the older children, he said:

"*Now* I guess he'll come. Eh, my little man? Now come see your pap."

Teddy crept slowly under the fence, assisted by the overzealous Tommy, and a moment later was kicking and squalling in his father's arms. Then they entered the house, into the sitting room, poor, bare, art-forsaken little room, too, with its rag carpet, its square clock, and its two or three chromos and pictures from *Harper's Weekly* pinned about.

"Emma, I'm all tired out," said Private Smith as he flung himself down on the carpet as he used to do, while his wife brought a pillow to put under his head, and the children stood about, munching their apples.

"Tommy, you run and get me a pan of chips; and Mary, you get the teakettle on, and I'll go and make some biscuit."

And the soldier talked. Question after question he poured forth about the crops, the cattle, the renter, the neighbors. He slipped his heavy government brogan shoes off his poor, tired, blistered feet, and lay out with utter, sweet relaxation. He was a free man again, no longer a soldier under command. At supper he stopped once, listened, and smiled. "That's old Spot. I know her voice. I s'pose that's her calf out there in the pen. I can't milk her tonight, though, I'm too tired; but I tell you, I'd like a drink o' her milk. What's become of old Rove?"

"He died last winter. Poisoned, I guess." There was a moment of sadness for them all. It was some time before the husband spoke again, in a voice that trembled a little.

"Poor old feller! He'd a known me a half a mile away. I expected him to come down the hill to meet me. It 'ud 'a' been more like comin' home if I could 'a' seen him comin' down the road an' waggin' his tail, an' laughin' that way he has, I tell yeh, it kin' o' took hold o' me to see the blinds down an' the house shut up."

"But, yeh see, we—we expected you'd write again 'fore you started. And then we thought we'd see you if you *did* come," she hastened to explain.

"Well, I ain't worth a cent on writin'. Besides, it's just as well yeh didn't know when I was comin'. I tell yeh, it sounds good to hear them chickens out there, an' turkeys, an' the crickets. Do you know they don't

have just the same kind o' crickets down South. Who's Sam hired t'
help cut yer grain?"

"The Ramsey boys."

"Looks like a good crop; but I'm afraid I won't do much gettin' it
cut. This cussed fever an' ague has got me down pretty low. I don't
know when I'll get red of it. I'll bet I've took twenty-five pounds of
quinine, if I've taken a bit. Gimme another biscuit. I tell yeh, they taste
good, Emma. I ain't had anything like it—Say, if you'd 'a' heard me
braggin' to th' boys about your butter 'n' biscuits, I'll bet your ears 'ud
'a' burnt."

The private's wife colored with pleasure. "Oh, you're always
a-braggin' about your things. Everybody makes good butter."

"Yes; old lady Snyder, for instance."

"Oh, well, she ain't to be mentioned. She's Dutch."

"Or old Mis' Snively. One more cup o' tea, Mary. That's my girl! I'm
feeling better already. I just b'lieve the matter with me is, I'm *starved*."

This was a delicious hour, one long to be remembered. They were
like lovers again. But their tenderness, like that of a typical American,
found utterance in tones, rather than in words. He was praising her
when praising her biscuit, and she knew it. They grew soberer when he
showed where he had been struck, one ball burning the back of his
hand, one cutting away a lock of hair from his temple, and one passing
through the calf of his leg. The wife shuddered to think how near she
had come to being a soldier's widow. Her waiting no longer seemed
hard. This sweet, glorious hour effaced it all.

Then they rose and all went out into the garden and down to the
barn. He stood beside her while she milked old Spot. They began to
plan fields and crops for next year. Here was the epic figure which
Whitman has in mind, and which he calls the "common American
soldier." With the livery of war on his limbs, this man was facing his
future, his thoughts holding no scent of battle. Clean, clear-headed, in
spite of physical weakness, Edward Smith, private, turned future-ward
with a sublime courage.

His farm was mortgaged, a rascally renter had run away with his
machinery, "departing between two days," his children needed clothing,
the years were coming upon him, he was sick and emaciated, but his
heroic soul did not quail. With the same courage with which he faced
his southern march, he entered upon a still more hazardous future.

Oh, that mystic hour! The pale man with big eyes standing there by
the well, with his young wife by his side. The vast moon swinging above
the eastern peaks; the cattle winding down the pasture slopes with
jangling bells; the crickets singing; the stars blooming out sweet and
far and serene; the katydids rhythmically calling; the little turkeys crying querulously as they settled to roost in the poplar tree near the open
gate. The voices at the well drop lower, the little ones nestle in their
father's arms at last, and Teddy falls asleep there.

The common soldier of the American volunteer army had returned. His war with the South was over, and his fight, his daily running fight, with nature and against the injustice of his fellow men was begun again. In the dusk of that far-off valley his figure looms vast, his personal peculiarities fade away, he rises into a magnificent type.

He is a gray-haired man of sixty now, and on the brown hair of his wife the white is also showing. They are fighting a hopeless battle, and must fight till God gives them furlough.

FRANCIS GRIERSON (1848–1927)

When Benjamin Henry Jesse Francis Shepard began to write in 1889, he took his mother's family name of Grierson, both because he was proud of the name (a cousin had distinguished himself in the Civil War) and because he wished to keep his two careers, music and writing, separate. Born in England and brought to the United States when he was six months old, Grierson lived in a log cabin in Sangamon County, Illinois, until the family moved to the St. Louis area. He sang in the choir of a Catholic church in St. Louis, then made his way to Paris in 1869. His genius for piano improvisation and his amazing voice (which had a range of four octaves) enabled him to make triumphant tours of France and Russia. When he returned to the United States, the citizens of San Diego gave him, in 1887, a city block and the money to build a house on it if he would settle there. The San Diego boom died in 1889, however, and Grierson sold the house and returned to Europe to commence his second career, as writer.

Grierson considered himself a mystic, and his works include essays on mysticism as well as literary and musical criticism. But his best work by far is The Valley of Shadows *(1909), a memoir of the Middle West just before the Civil War. Though the subject matter of this book is the rough and crude life of illiterate pioneers, Grierson writes about it with a refinement of detail and precision of language which one might associate with French literature.*

Grierson's work was all but forgotten, until Edmund Wilson, in preparation for Patriotic Gore, *his monumental study of Civil War literature, rediscovered it. "No other book," writes Wilson about* The Valley of Shadows, *"so gives us the sense of the imminence of the national crisis for which people dimly felt they were being prepared without having been given the power to control it—not so much a storm that was going to burst as a drama, a sacred drama, in which they would have to perform."*

FROM *The Valley of Shadows* (1909)

Chapter 4   Socrates Gives Advice

On stormy nights in the autumn the north wind brought with it voices that moaned and sighed. Every sweep of the wind came with a chorus of lamentations that moved round and round, first on one side then on the other, and the intervals of silence between the gusts came as respites before some final disaster. The big locust, that stood alone, had an ominous whistle, while the trees and bushes at the front and back swayed under the low, swooping gusts, until the Log-House seemed once more a part of the wild and primitive forest.

At times streaks of cold light from the semi-circling moon would fall through the window on the old rag-carpet. Old, because each strip had belonged to garments worn long before the carpet was put together. It needed the moonlight or the soft rays of the setting sun to bring out all its romance and mystery. Then the stripes of saffron evoked the presence of Kezia Jordan, and the darker hues memories of the Load-Bearer, Socrates, and Minerva Wagner. What romantic adventure these patches suggested! I would sit and count the pieces and compare one colour with another, for each seemed imbued with a personality of its own. Here, in the common sitting-room, filled with chimeras about to vanish, each strip of cloth was as a pillow for some dead thing of the past, some greeting or regret. There were strips worn when the wearer set sail from the old country, others had faced a hail of bullets at Buena Vista, passed through an Indian rising, or the first stormy meetings of the Abolitionists in Illinois. Once all these strips of cloth had stood for life and action; they wrapped a world of dreams and moods, but now they covered a rough floor in a house of logs. They humanised the interior as graves humanise a plot of earth. And never did sacred carpet of Mecca contain so much of the magic of life; for here, too, daily prayers were said on bended knee, and the carpet seemed one with the religious aspirations of the occupants, with all our hopes and fears, joys and sorrows.

How genial and home-like it was! It belonged to the order of the wild roses and flowering weeds, the corn and clover, the morning-glories, the gympsum, the sumac, and the red-winged blackbirds that soared in circles around and above the house.

If its shreds and patches suggested things of the past, the Log-House life it represented was palpitating with the present: full of human dreams and ambitions, of the voiceless sentiments that make a home in the bosom of the prairie. It invited the tired wayfarer of the lonely roads to come in and be refreshed with steaming coffee and hot biscuits, pound-cake, and dainty pies made from the products of the loamy soil; it invited all to step in and listen to words of encouragement if in trouble, and words of sympathy if in affliction; for the rag-carpet was made for the Log-House, and the Log-House was made for Man.

The day Socrates made his first call at the Log-House I happened to be at home, instead of fishing, a mile away, or wandering about in my accustomed haunts among the squirrels, birds and rabbits. He brought Ebenezer Hicks with him.

Socrates entertained me with some simple stories of his experience as a hunter and trapper twenty or thirty years earlier: how he killed big game during the winters of the great snows, his buffalo hunts in Missouri and Iowa, his strange devices for snaring the mink, the fox, and the raccoon.

I devoured every word with eager excitement: here was the actual romance of the wild woods.

"And have you killed many bitterns and owls?" I inquired.

"I don't b'lieve in killin' things ye cain't eat or skin."

It seemed to me that this Socrates of the wilderness had something of the look of a big horned owl, with his bushy eyebrows and short scraggy beard. Over his sparsely-covered head the years had cast a halo of experience and wisdom, and I began to respect this man who united in himself so much adventure and common-sense. He seemed strong as a lion and harmless as a lamb, free as the winds of the prairie, yet methodical and never in doubt. He brought with him into the Log-House—where our family had gathered like a flock of sheep in a strange land—a feeling of security and a renewal of faith and courage.

"There's not much need of raising stock in this part of the country," said my father jokingly; "game is so plentiful."

"The new settlers air givin' tharselves a heap o' trouble jes' fer the fun o' ploughin' en reapin'. They snap the bow-strings. They air tryin' te kill big game with a shot-gun, en the shot scatters all over the kintry. It air good 'nough fer rabbits en squirrels, but it don't stop a buck jumpin' er a b'ar from browsin'. I see a heap o' hard work fer some o' these here settlers what's comin' in from the ole kintries over East. 'Tain't wisdom.

"Some folks air too good fer this world 'thout bein' plumb ready fer the nex'. Accordin' te thar reasonin', a prairie-chicken settin' on the fence air better'n two birds o' paradise over yander. The world air a sorrowin' vale, kase folks hez too many stakes in the groun'. Ez fer me, I kin shoot en trap all I ken eat, jes' plantin' 'nough corn fer hoe-cakes en a leetle fodder, en some taters en turnips en pum'kins; en I hev a sight more smoked venison en b'ar meat in winter than I kin eat ez a single man with on'y one stommick; en I 'low I kin give a traveller hoe-cakes en fried chicken all he wants to fill up on."

Socrates sat like a lump of hewn adamant, his look alone being sufficient guarantee of his ability to take care of himself without the slightest trouble or worry.

"Thar be folks that air trampin' over these prairies a-spadin' up trouble like thar warn't none te be hed by settin' down in the city en lettin' other folks bring it to 'em. Thar's a heap too much corn en wheat, a durned sight too many kyows en hosses; en the four-legged critters chaws up what the two-legged critters gathers in. It air wus nor dog eat dog, seein' ez how the four-legged critters air livin' on the fat o' the land while the pore planters air livin' on spar' ribs en hens with sinoos ez tough ez b'iled owels."

"But it makes a great difference when a man has a family to support and educate," remarked my mother, thinking of the responsibility of parents.

"I allow readin' en writin' air a good thing if ye've got any figurin' to do; but cipherin's a drefful load on the mind. Thar's Si Jordan yander; he sets figurin' o' nights, en calculatin' te see jes' how he'll come out at the end o' the year; but I allers say to myself he's like the groun'-hog, he won't come out."

"Still, it would be awkward to have to calculate with nothing but your fingers," observed my father, smiling.

"Fingers or no fingers, book-larnin' don't make a man no better than he war in a state o' natur'. Them as reads newspapers knows too much 'bout other folks's sins en not 'nough 'bout thar own. Over Decatur en Fancy Creek way they built meetin'-houses with steeples on 'em, en the wimin-folks tuck te wearin' store clothes en the men-folks put on b'iled shirts. But when the comet come into view the wimin put on their ole sun-bonnets, allowin' pink calico te be more'n enough te be jedged in."

My mother, as she looked up from her knitting, thought his round grey eyes seemed bigger and rounder than ever. She noticed in his face an expression of naïve irony and unconscious satire which she had not remarked before. But later there radiated from his face a sense of pity when he thought of all the hard work she would have to do. In some unaccountable way he had come into touch with the unexpressed hopes and fears of the silent man sitting before him, and the pale, passive face of his wife, who was knitting.

Then, as if struck with a sudden, new idea, he said: —

"Ye kin divide the day's doin's into two passels—the happenin's en the fac's; en thar ain't but two leadin' fac's in all creation—bein' born en bein' dead. Howsomever, right in betwixt 'em thar's some purty lively happenin's a steppin' roun' on all fours, ez when a panther takes a notion te drap on a pig's back; it's a shore thing fer the panther but a dead loss fer the owner. En it air jest ez sartin the fact air plumb agin the pig, but he don't live long 'nough te know it. Thar's been a suddin burial, en the mourner kin see the fact, but he ain't never see the corpse. Anyhow, it's an argimint thet'll work itself out ez easy ez a groun'-worm arter rain, en it don't make no pertickler difference which end comes up fust, heads en tails bein' purty nigh ekil."

My father enjoyed a hearty laugh, and my mother stopped knitting and eyed Socrates as if trying to fathom the secret of his strange originality.

"It beats my time all holler," he went on, "te see folks so kind o' waverin' en onsartin. Instead o' waitin' fer the last hour they make fer it with thar heads down like a bull agin a red flag, en no tail-twistin' 'll stop 'em. Thar's skasely a settler among the new uns but what'll tell ye they air workin' te live. It air workin' te die, thet's what I call it."

"Thar's a good many workin' land they ain't got no title to," remarked Ebenezer Hicks.

"When I go te meetin' en hear some o' these settlers sing about readin' thar title cl'ar te mansions in the skies I allers feel like askin' 'em how they're holdin' on te the land they got; kase thar ain't but two kyinds o' settlers—them ez buys right out, and them ez squats right down, en I've allers found thet hymn air a dead favourite among the people thet set right down jes whar thar feet begin te swell.

"What I know 'bout Bible-teachin' air plumb agin' squatters takin' up land t'other side Jordan. The Lord God hez issued a writ statin' His objections. I ain't never knowed a real live Yankee thet war any good at squattin'. They come from below the Ohio, whar they hev seen the niggers do all the work. En when they come up to this kintry they sing about readin' thar title cl'ar te big slices o' land in the nex' world! I tell ye what it is, if thar's ever goin' te be war it'll be betwix' them thet wants the land fer nothin' en them thet wants it fer sunthin', if it ain't fer more'n shootin' snipe en plover. The squatters air lazy; en t'other folks, like the Squar hyar, air killin' tharselves by doin' too much.

"My ole daddy larnt me te go through this sorrowin' vale like the varmints do—easy en nat'ral like, never gallopin' when ye kin lope, en never lopin' when ye kin lay down. It's a heap easier. Thar ain't a hog but knows he kin root fer a livin' if ye give him a fair show; thar ain't a squirrel but knows how te stow away 'nough te nibble on when he wakes up en finds his blood's kinder coolin' down en things is p'intin' te zero."

After a pause he looked hard at my father, and put the question abruptly:

"What'll ye do, Squar, when ye plough up the prairie thar nex' year, en sow it with corn ez ye calc'late on doin'? How d'ye 'low ye'll git all the work done 'thout extry hands?"

It was an unexpected query that left my father without an immediate answer. He had never given the subject any serious thought.

Socrates continued without waiting for explanations:

"Ye'll hev a heap o' corn-huskin' te do, en ye suttinly ain't a-goin' te reckon on thet leetle lady with them hands o' her'n doin' much corn-huskin' en sech. 'Pears like she'll hev more'n enough te keep her a-goin' right in the house."

My mother was thinking: "The Lord's will be done. He had a reason for sending us here; some day we may know why."

Socrates resumed:

"Hirin' extry hands means payin' out a lot o' money; mebbe yer purse-strings air like yer latch-string, en mebbe ye got a plenty te last ye till nex' harvest time. Things ain't like they war; folks useter come

twenty mile to a corn-huskin', en the doin's ud end up with eatin' en
drinkin' en dancin'. Now people air too busy with thar own funerals.
They useter help other people work tharselves to death; now they stay
at home en dig thar own graves 'thout borrowing shovels er sendin' fer
a fiddler te help 'em mourn with thar tired feet. I keep sayin' the comet
may pass over 'thout drappin'; but if the politicioners, en the lawyers,
en them ez sez they don't know nothin', en the hordes o' settlers thet
cain't tell the difference betwix' a yaller dog en a long-eared rabbit ain't
a-bringin' the world to a spot stop, then Zack Caverly hez missed fire,
en it'll be the fust time."

"As for that," said my father, "it certainly does look as if some great
change would soon come over the country. Many are turning to religion
for consolation, while others predict civil war."

"I see some cussed mean folks pretendin' te hev religion. Some on
'em air thet deceivin' I allers feel like watchin' 'em with a spy-glass till
they git into the woods en then sendin' my ole hound arter 'em te see
they don't commit bigamy er hang themselves right on my diggin's."

"Wal," said Ebenezer Hicks, who had been listening attentively, "I
'low ye've tetched a festern sore when ye say some on 'em air ekil te
committin' treason en blasphemy, but ez fer me I hev allers been a
church member; but some folks ain't never satisfied te leave things ez
they wur. It's my opinion all the trouble hez come about in the Church
by them busy-bodies mixin' up religion with politics. Abolition hez been
a bone o' contention en a skewer through both wings o' the Methodists.
You war thar when Azariah James preached thet sermon, windin' up
by h'istin' the Abolition flag, en you too, Squar, en you heared what he
said."

"Ye'll allow he hed all creation te h'ist on," remarked Socrates; "the
stars en stripes te begin with, two kyinds o' lawyers en four kyinds o'
preachers—all on 'em off'n whisky. T'other party ain't got no flag, but
thar whisky makes 'em see the stars en they make the niggers feel the
stripes."

Ebenezer Hicks, wishing to turn the conversation, simply observed:
"Over at Bloomington en Springfield the people air all fer Lincoln."

But Socrates held to the subject and went on:

"What beats my time is te know what you folks hez te do with
the nigger question anyway. Did ye ever own any slaves?"

"Nary a one."

"Wal, then, what difference does it make te you whether they work
ez slaves er work ez we uns work? Looks like ye belong te them thet's
pinin' away kase ye ain't got sorrers enough o' yer own te hitch to.
When we all heared Azariah James preach—the on'y time the meetin'-
house hez been open all summer—I see right away we'd got plumb
into the middle o' the Abolition circus en someone ud turn a somerset
afore he got through. Fact is, the people o' this here State air a-gittin'

ready te send Abe Lincoln te Washington, en ole Buchanan's jes' keepin' the presidential cheer from warpin' till Abe comes."

"That preacher, Azariah James," said my father, "was not such a fool as some of the congregation thought he was."

"Not nigh," returned Socrates, as he rose from his seat and took his leave.

A few days after his visit my mother remarked:

"Now, I suppose, we shall not have any more visitors for a long time. There are days when I wish someone would call, and somehow I have been thinking a good deal of Mrs. Jordan lately. I should like a visit from her more than from anyone else I know just at present."

That same afternoon, as I was returning to the house from the hollow where I had been gathering hazel-nuts, I thought I could discern a stranger through the window. I entered the house and found Kezia Jordan seated in the rocking-chair.

Once more her presence opened the door to a world that transcended all the familiar forms of speech; for it was not what she said, but what she looked, that impressed me so profoundly.

Moulded and subdued by the lonely days, the monotonous weeks, the haunting hush of the silent nights, and the same thoughts and images returning again and again, she appeared as one who had conquered the world of silence. Elihu Gest partly explained himself by his explanation of others, but Kezia Jordan made few comments, and they were rarely personal. She never talked for the sake of talking. As she sat there she might have been a statue, for to-day she brought with her an inexorable detachment from worldly thoughts and influences.

The sentiments she inspired in me were like those produced by the motion of clouds on a calm moonlight night, or the falling of leaves on a still, dreamy day of Indian summer. There were moments when her presence seemed to possess something preternatural, when she imparted to others an extraordinary and superhuman quietude. Her spirit, freed for ever from the trammels and tumults of the world, seemed heedless of the passing moments, resigned to every secret and mandate of destiny; for hers was a freedom which was not attained in a single battle— the conflict was begun by her ancestors when they landed at Plymouth Rock. In the tribulations that followed the successsive generations were stripped of the superfluities of life. One by one vanities and illusions fell from the fighters like shattered muskets and tattered garments. Each generation, stripped of the tinsel, became acquainted with the folly of plaints and the futility of protests. Little by little the pioneers began to understand, and in the last generation of all there resulted a knowledge too deep for discussion and a wisdom too great for idle misgivings.

Where was the hurried visitor from foreign lands who could sound the depths of such a soul?

The influences were different when Mrs. Busby came to the Log-

House. She brought with her pleasant maxims about her bakings, her messes, and herb-medicines, and talked on and on without caring what the subject was. She created commotion and movement, and under her hands the kettle hissed and spouted.

Mrs. Jordan handled things as if they had life and feeling, and without being conscious of influencing others she brought with her a power that penetrated to the core of things. She had passed the time when her duties had to be accomplished by the aid of a strenuous use of the reasoning faculties. She had arrived at that stage when religion was not a thing of reason, but a state of perpetual feeling. Circumstances altered, conditions changed and found her the same, unaltered and unalterable.

Yet she had her day-dreams, moments of rapt meditation which bordered on forgetfulness, when the formless visions and homely realities of kitchen, meeting-house, and prairie became one, and the song of the blackbird and the chirping of the cricket seemed a part of her own life and feeling. She possessed the dominant influence of an abiding power with a total absence of self-assertion, for hers was that true power of the soul, an influence that penetrates to depths which intellect alone can never reach.

I thought the rocking-chair was made for Kezia Jordan, and the ragcarpet too, and somehow I could never quite free my mind from the impression that the flowers about the house were hers as well.

Soon after my arrival a rap was heard at the door, and in walked Minerva Wagner, proud, lean, wrinkled, and unbending. She came within the category of those who, according to Zack Caverly, were labouring under the necessity of borrowing trouble. She had not yet recovered from the shock produced by the Abolition sermon of the preacher, Azariah James. Mrs. Wagner was our nearest neighbour to the north, and every time I glanced in that direction I would marvel at the listless, lonely life of the family in the little frame house stuck like a white speck on the brow of the prairie, ten times more lonely and isolated than the Log-House we inhabited. Whenever I saw someone moving about over there I thought of a tomb opening its doors and letting out an imprisoned ghost; for every member of the family looked and walked and talked alike, except, perhaps, old Minerva Wagner, who stood to-day facing the inexorable present, stern, relentless, unable to account for anything she saw or heard, but choking with prejudice against what she persisted in calling "the Yankee trash of Indianny and Illinoise."

After some talk about pickles and bacon and apple-butter, and some allusion to the awful state of the country, brought on by the Anti-Slavery agitation, Mrs. Wagner took her departure, and once more the room assumed the calm, peaceful aspect commensurate with Kezia Jordan's presence. My mother made tea, and the moments passed as if there were no clock ticking the time away and no regrets for the old days that would never return; and when at last Mrs. Jordan rose from her seat she looked more slender than ever in her simple dress of copperas-coloured jean; and when the clouds parted and the setting sun shone full on the windows, her spare figure cast a shadow that fell across the rag-carpet, and there, under her feet, were strips of coloured cloth, the counterpart of her own dress, and it seemed as if she had always belonged to the Log-House and ought never to leave it.

Chapter 16   Abraham Lincoln

It was the 15th day of October, 1858. Crowds were pouring into Alton. For some days people had been arriving by the steam-packets from up and down the river, the up-boats from St. Louis, bringing visitors with long, black hair, goatees, and stolid, Indian-like faces, slave-owners and slave-dealers, from the human marts of Missouri and Kentucky; the northern visitors arriving by boat or rail, Abolitionists and Republicans, with a cast of features distinctly different from the types coming from the south.

They came from villages, townships, the prairies, from all the adjoining counties, from across the Mississippi, from far-away cities, from representative societies north and south, from congressional committees in the east, from leading journals of all political parties, and from every religious denomination within hundreds of miles, filling the broad space in front of the Town Hall, eager to see and hear the now famous debaters—the popular Stephen A. Douglas, United States Senator, nicknamed the "Little Giant," and plain Abraham Lincoln, nicknamed the "Rail-Splitter."

The great debate had begun on the 21st of August at another town, and to-day the long-discussed subject would be brought to a close. Douglas stood for the doctrine that slavery was nationalised by the Constitution, that Congress had no authority to prevent its introduction in the new Territories like Kansas and Nebraska, and that the people of each State could alone decide whether they should be slave States or free. Lincoln opposed the introduction of slavery into the new Territories.

On this memorable day the "irrepressible conflict" predicted by Seward actually began, and it was bruited about that Lincoln would be mobbed or assassinated if he repeated here the words he used in some of his speeches delivered in the northern part of the State. From the surging sea of faces thousands of anxious eyes gazed upward at the group of politicians on the balcony like wrecked mariners scanning the horizon for the smallest sign of a white sail of hope.

This final debate resembled a duel between two men-of-war, the pick of a great fleet, all but these two sunk or abandoned in other waters, facing each other in the open, the Little Giant hurling at his opponent, from his flagship of slavery, the deadliest missiles, Lincoln calmly waiting to sink his antagonist by one simple broadsider. Alton had seen nothing so exciting since the assassination of Lovejoy, the fearless Abolitionist, many years before.

In the earlier discussions Douglas seemed to have the advantage. A past-master in tact and audacity, skilled in the art of rhetorical skirmishing, he had no equal on the "stump," while in the Senate he was feared by the most brilliant debaters for his ready wit and his dashing eloquence.

Regarded in the light of historical experience, reasoned about in the light of spiritual reality, and from the point of view that nothing can happen by chance, it seems as if Lincoln and Douglas were predestined to meet side by side in this discussion, and unless I dwell in detail on the mental and physical contrast the speakers presented it would be impossible to give an adequate idea of the startling difference in the two temperaments: Douglas—short, plump, and petulant; Lincoln—long, gaunt, and self-possessed; the one white-haired and florid, the other black-haired and swarthy; the one educated and polished, the other unlettered and primitive. Douglas had the assurance of a man of authority, Lincoln had moments of deep mental depression, often bordering on melancholy, yet controlled by a fixed, and, I may say, predestined will, for it can no longer be doubted that without the marvellous blend of humour and stolid patience so conspicuous in his character, Lincoln's genius would have turned to madness after the defeat of the Northern Army at Bull-Run, and the world would have had something like a repetition of Napoleon's fate after the burning of Moscow. Lincoln's humour was the balance-pole of his genius that enabled him to cross the most giddy heights without losing his head. Judge Douglas opened the debate in a sonorous voice plainly heard throughout the assembly, and with a look of mingled defiance and confidence he marshalled his facts and deduced his arguments. To the vigour of his attack there was added the prestige of the Senate Chamber, and for some moments it looked as if he would carry the majority with him, a large portion of the crowd being Pro-Slavery men, while many others were "on the fence" waiting to be persuaded.

At last, after a great oratorical effort, he brought his speech to a close amidst the shouts and yells of thousands of admirers.

And now Abraham Lincoln, the man who, in 1830, undertook to split for Mrs. Nancy Miller four hundred rails for every yard of brown jean dyed with walnut bark that would be required to make him a pair of trousers, the flat boatman, local stump-speaker and country lawyer, rose from his seat, stretched his long bony limbs upward as if to get them into working order, and stood like some solitary pine on a lonely summit, very tall, very dark, very gaunt, and very rugged, his swarthy features stamped with a sad serenity, and the instant he began to speak the ungainly mouth lost its heaviness, the half-listless eyes attained a wondrous power, and the people stood bewildered and breathless under the natural magic of the strangest, most original personality known to the English-speaking world since Robert Burns. There were other very tall and dark men in the heterogeneous assembly, but not one who resembled the speaker. Every movement of his long, muscular frame denoted inflexible earnestness, and a something issued forth, elemental and mystical, that told what the man had been, what he was, and what he would do in the future. There were moments when he seemed all legs and feet, and again he appeared all head and neck; yet every look of the deep-set eyes, every movement of the prominent jaw, every wave of the hard-gripping hand, produced an impression, and before he had spoken twenty minutes the conviction took possession of thousands that here was the prophetic man of the present and the political saviour of the future. Judges of human nature saw at a glance that a man so ungainly, so natural, so earnest, and so forcible, had no place in his mental economy for the thing called vanity.

Douglas had been theatrical and scholarly, but this tall, homely man was creating by his very looks what the brilliant lawyer and experienced Senator had failed to make people see and feel. The Little Giant had assumed striking attitudes, played tricks with his flowing white hair, mimicking the airs of authority with patronising allusions; but these affectations, usually so effective when he addressed an audience alone, went for nothing when brought face to face with realities. Lincoln had no genius for gesture and no desire to produce a sensation. The failure of Senator Douglas to bring conviction to critical minds was caused by three things: a lack of logical sequence in argument, a lack of intuitional judgment, and a vanity that was caused by too much intellect and too little heart. Douglas had been arrogant and vehement, Lincoln was now logical and penetrating. The Little Giant was a living picture of ostentatious vanity; from every feature of Lincoln's face there radiated the calm, inherent strength that always accompanies power. He relied on no props. With a pride sufficient to protect his mind and a will sufficient to defend his body, he drank water when Douglas, with all his wit and rhetoric, could begin or end nothing without stimulants. Here, then, was one man out of all the millions who believed in himself, who did not consult with others about what to say, who never for a moment respected the opinion of men who preached a lie. My old friend, Don Piatt, in his personal impressions of Lincoln, whom he knew well and greatly esteemed, declares him to be the homeliest man he ever saw; but serene confidence and self-poise can never be ugly. What thrilled the people who stood before Abraham Lincoln on that day was the sight of a being who, in all his actions and habits, resembled themselves, gentle as he was strong, fearless as he was honest, who towered above them all in that psychic radiance that penetrates in some mysterious way every fibre of the hearer's consciousness.

The enthusiasm created by Douglas was wrought out of smart epigram thrusts and a facile superficial eloquence. He was a match for the politicians born within the confines of his own intellectual circle: witty, brilliant, cunning and shallow, his weight in the political balance was purely materialistic; his scales of justice tipped to the side of cotton, slavery and popular passions, while the man who faced him now brought to the assembly cold logic in place of wit, frankness in place of cunning, reasoned will and judgment in place of chicanery and sophistry. Lincoln's presence infused into the mixed and uncertain throng something spiritual and supernormal. His looks, his words, his voice, his attitude were like a magical essence dropped into the seething cauldron of politics, reacting against the foam, calming the surface and letting the people see to the bottom. It did not take him long.

"Is it not a false statesmanship," he asked, "that undertakes to build up a system of policy upon the basis of caring nothing about the very thing that everybody does care the most about? Judge Douglas may say he cares not whether slavery is voted up or down, but he must have a choice between a right thing and a wrong thing. He contends that whatever community wants slaves has a right to have them. So they have, if it is not a wrong; but if it is a wrong he cannot say people have a right to do wrong. He says that upon the score of equality slaves should be allowed to go into a new Territory like other property. This is strictly logical if there is no difference between it and other property. If it and other property are equal his argument is entirely logical; but if you insist that one is wrong and the other right there is no use to institute a comparison between right and wrong."

This was the broadsider. The great duel on the high seas of politics was over. The Douglas ship of State Sovereignty was sinking. The debate was a triumph that would send Lincoln to Washington as President in a little more than two years from that date.

People were fascinated by the gaunt figure, in long, loose garments, that seemed like a "huge skeleton in clothes," attracted by the homely face, and mystified, yet proud of the fact that a simple denizen of their own soil should wield so much power.

When Lincoln sat down Douglas made one last feeble attempt at an answer; but Lincoln, in reply to a spectator who manifested some apprehension as to the outcome, rose, and spreading out his great arms at full length, like a condor about to take wing, exclaimed, with humorous indifference, "Oh! let him go it!" These were the last words he uttered in the greatest debate of the *ante-bellum* days.

The victor bundled up his papers and withdrew, the assembly shouting, "Hurrah for Abe Lincoln as next President!" "Bully for old Abe!" "Lincoln for ever!" etc., etc. Excited crowds followed him about, reporters caught his slightest word, and by night time the bar-rooms, hotels, street corners and prominent stores were filled with his admirers, fairly intoxicated with the exciting triumph of the day.

From Vernacular to Sophisticated Art

Introduction

In the two or three decades after the Civil War, a number of our greatest nineteenth-century writers continued with their work, often their best work. Some of them lived in circumstances of extreme isolation (Melville and Emily Dickinson, for example), others as public figures receiving enormous public approval (Whitman and Twain). Melville, a popular writer in the prewar years, now entered a phase of almost complete public obscurity, suffering neglect from both readers and critics, but quietly continuing to write works of poetry and fiction. Emily Dickinson, living in Amherst, Massachusetts, and seemingly deaf to the affairs of ordinary American society, wrote her poems during these years but insisted on keeping most of them out of public print. Mark Twain, the one American writer of the nineteenth century whom the ordinary reading public recognized as its cultural spokesman, composed his best work during these postwar years. And it was also in these decades that the young Henry James wrote a number of his sophisticated and artful novels. (Because James's literary career cuts across the nineteenth and twentieth centuries and reaches its fulfillment in the latter, his work is presented and discussed in the third volume of this anthology.)

Apart from these major figures, however, a whole series of new literary schools and impulses during the 1870s and 1880s began to appear: first, local-color writing, then the realistic novel, and after that, the beginnings of naturalist and impressionist fiction. The writings in this section illustrate some of these trends—though by its very nature the realistic novel cannot be adequately represented in an anthology.

It would be a mistake to suppose that the Civil War is some sort of Chinese wall completely separating the literature composed before it from that composed after it. In retrospect we can see that the Civil War did mark a major turning point for the people who lived through it, including many of the writers who appear in this section, but their lives do demonstrate a considerable amount of continuity. That is one reason this section covers writing which spans the war— from pre-Civil War humor playing with the manners and vocabulary of a regional culture (Longstreet) to post-Civil War fiction delicately investigating the details of a regional experience (Sarah Orne Jewett); from writings meant to record the common speech of an area faithfully or for purposes of comic exaggeration (Crockett, the early Twain) to writings tensed and complicated into a new American style (the later Twain, Stephen Crane).

In the General Introduction one section (pages 12 to 15) discusses the
importance of regionalism in nineteenth-century American culture
and literature. The point is made there that during the 1830s and
1840s, when American literary men were strongly preoccupied with
the need to forge a national consciousness and create a distinctively
American literature, regionalism was really the major force (or at
least one major force) shaping the poetry and fiction of the time.
After the Civil War, however, a curious twist takes place. As a result
of the nationalistic sentiment created by the war, and also because
of the growth of industrialism and the remarkable improvement in
transportation and communications, the United States as a nation
takes on a much more unified character than it had previously had,
yet at the same time there flourishes a popular kind of writing,
usually called "local color," that tries deliberately to exploit the distinctive traits and idiosyncracies of the slowly vanishing ways of
regional life. Perhaps there is a causal connection here. Precisely as
the country becomes more homogenous, precisely as the differences
among the various regions begin to fade in importance and vividness, there occurs a strong outburst of popular nostalgia, quickly
seized upon by many writers, for everything in the American past
that is disappearing.

Is there a difference between regional and local-color writing? Some
literary historians and critics have tried to draw a sharp distinction
between the two, and as long as we remember that it is a convenience of analysis more than a reality of history, this line of distinction can be very useful. It runs something like this: Regional
writing is authentic, often naïve in character, close to folk experience. As it emerges from that experience, it can exhibit the charm
and shrewdness of life in preindustrial America, especially its varieties of humor. Often it employs precisely shaded regional dialects
for effects of credibility and color—also, to get away from the
formalities and stiffness of literary prose. Regional writers publish
their work in books and magazines, which means they may earn
money from doing so; but by and large they are not, or not mainly,
concerned with a conscious *exploitation* of nostalgia for passing
ways of life; they are not intent primarily on cooking up a confec-
tion of quaintness for middle-class urban audiences indulging their
nostalgia in the safety of living rooms. Regional writers are often
quite modest in their ambition, trying simply to capture the surface
tones and colors of a limited arc of our national experience. But a
few of them, precisely through the accuracy with which they do this,
succeed in breaking through to larger ends. The particular detail can
yield universal significance.

Local color, by contrast, is often seen as a kind of fiction which has become self-conscious, slick, and exploitative in regard to the region

about which the writer tells his stories. He may know a great deal about the region; he may himself have emerged from it; but he now is writing with an eye toward the magazine public. The local colorist tries to make the life of the region picturesque, even if that means evading unpleasant details; he draws his picture with a glow of deceit, sometimes self-deceit; he inclines toward set formulas of narrative rather than truthful depictions of experience. These and other weaknesses of local-color writing are well described by Carlos Baker:

> the curious pursuit of the unique, idiosyncratic, or grotesque in local character ... a noticeable though not universal tendency to gloss over the uglier aspects of the human predicament; a reactionary glorification and sentimentalization of a wealthy and powerful plantation aristocracy ... an equally deplorable tendency to overdo the "common man" motif ... an attempt to petrify and monumentalize that which in all classes and castes was petering out through its own internal weakness or decadence ... The predilection for dialect ... in which authors played at amateur phonetics under the mistaken impression that the use of heavily apostrophized contractions, barbaric misspellings, and other desperate expedients would be useful to future linguistic historians, is distressing. . . .

Yet the analytic distinction between regional writing and local-color writing soon breaks down under the pressures of historical examination. Some regional writing at its best—like the exquisite cameo art of Sarah Orne Jewett and some of the more ambitious fiction of George Washington Cable—avoids the characteristic faults of local-color writing. But the truth is that regionalism always contains within itself the temptation of the quaint provincial and the expansive picturesque, while local color contains the possibility of transcending its own limitations and moving toward a modest and intimate realism. Bernard Bowron has made this point very well:

> American realism owes a good deal to the literature of local color, ambivalently realistic though it was. In its pure form, best represented by Bret Harte's sentimental tales, it falsified experience unconscionably. Hearts of gold appear with monotonous regularity under the unlikeliest exteriors, to the moral uplift of a happy, tear-drenched audience. No deviation from the correct sentiments is allowed; a local milieu is exploited simply for its "exotic" qualities, which means that it is neither rendered fully nor organically related to the characters who move within it. Everything is innocent and meaningless. Still, even at the worst, this is not the whole story. Except for its Southern offshoot, which could not let go the myth of a "befo' de war" aristocracy, local-color fiction based itself on the important assumption that the proper material for literature was the life of common people. . . .

Moreover, though magazine editors of the seventies and eighties may have favored and promoted a sentimental pattern for the local-color story or novel, by no means all local colorists confined themselves strictly to such a pattern. From the beginning, serious writers sought out, or at least could not avoid, the play of environmental influences upon local character. This certainly holds true for Harriet Beecher Stowe, whose New England novels of the sixties set the stage for the local-color movement of the following decades. Beneath her tireless didacticism one discovers a durable core of realistic observation. *The Minister's Wooing, The Pearl of Orr's Island*, and especially *Old Town Folks* pay considerable attention to the details of New England domestic life, customs, and theology and to the geographical rather than the mere "landscape" qualities of the region. To the extent that Mrs. Stowe brings these elements to bear upon the shaping of character, her people appeal to a reader's sense of "the probable and ordinary course of man's experience."

The same—with all due allowance for romantic and sentimental excrescences—must be said for such later writers as Eggleston, Kirkland, Cable, Freeman, and Jewett. Their stories may have sold themselves to editors and readers as local color, but they were something more than that, something far more promising for realism; in them, region as exotic backdrop for an improbable didactic drama gives way to region as an actor and force *within* the drama of everyday life. Thus the local-color movement served to establish an audience for a more serious treatment of commonplace existence, and at the same time gave rise to an occasional piece of honest and persuasive regionalism.

About the term *realism* there has been endless discussion and dispute among literary historians and critics—indeed, among all readers of literature. It is a difficult and tricky term, yet we find that in discussing literature we really cannot do without it. We can banish the word but not the ideas surrounding it.

In the last two or so decades of the nineteenth century, realism in American literature signified at least the following elements:

A desire to represent in works of fiction the immediate, commonplace experience of ordinary Americans as it could be observed in a recognizable social locale and at a specific historical moment. Not legendary white whales, not ladies with scarlet letters on their bosoms, not mythical pathfinders in mythical Western prairies; but the kinds of people who might actually be found in a Midwestern small town, or in a Maine fishing village, or in an upstate New York city, men who worked on farms or ran little stores—these were now the favored characters for writers like William Dean Howells, Hamlin Garland, Ed Howe, Joseph Kirkland, Harold Frederic, and Sarah Orne Jewett.

A wish no longer to indulge in rosy self-idealization, and instead a readiness to show the drabness of life in a small town, the poverty of life in a large city. And this signified an intention not only to expose the faults and evils of society, but also to show the psychic and moral costs of those faults and evils.

A strong need to exorcise—to get out of their system— the small towns from which many American writers had come and which had traditionally been celebrated as the seat of American virtue and innocence. Now, instead, the new realistic novelists turned with wrath or bitterness, often with disillusionment, on the life of their origins. The same held true for those who came from rural America: their disenchantment proved a strong incentive toward realistic portraiture of what life had been like on the farm.

A new readiness to confront the sensual nature of human beings. No longer were such matters to be avoided or glossed over; instead, in the work of writers like Howe and Frederic, as to a lesser extent Howells, there was a frank recognition of the power of sexuality in human affairs and a strong interest in the ways that power could be made into a major motif in a work of fiction.

A new perspective upon American society, no longer seen as a homogeneous Jeffersonian community, but as a locale in which many of the class conflicts and ideological disputes of European society could more or less be found.

Realism, then, meant both a way of looking at human experience and a way of writing a work of fiction. Ian Watt offers an excellent brief description of the realistic novel:

[It works on] the premise, or primary convention, that the novel is a full and authentic report of human experience and is therefore under an obligation to satisfy its reader with such details of the story as the individuality of the actors concerned, the particulars of the times and places of their actions, details which are presented through a more largely referential use of language than is common in other literary forms.

These remarks are only the barest beginnings of an enormously complicated problem in the history and criticism of literature; and in regard to late-nineteenth-century American writing, they do no more than point toward new possibilities, gathering energies, and only partially realized hopes. A sustained discussion of the development of realistic fiction in the United States could not break off with the turn of the century for it is only at the beginning of the twentieth century, with the work of Theodore Dreiser and Edith Wharton, that the realistic novel comes into its own. Meanwhile, however, the realistic movement in fiction branches out into other directions: the complex psychological fictions of Henry James which contain elements not only of realism but of fable and of fantasy; the brilliant novels and stories of Stephen Crane, which move into the kinds of fiction commonly described as naturalism and impressionism. But perhaps the most useful hint is this: labels like realism, naturalism, impressionism, and the like, can help us to find common elements in the works of different writers; but finally, these labels should not to be taken too solemnly; they are like scaffolds—to be discarded once the building is up. What matters most is our relationship to, our sense of, our involvement with, a particular work of literature.

DAVY CROCKETT (1786–1836)

*Half mortal, half myth, Davy Crockett was born in a log cabin. It could
hardly have been otherwise.*

*Master hunter, Indian fighter, living emblem of the frontier, spinner of
tall tales, homespun humorist, Davy Crockett grew up in Tennessee
at a time when it was still part of the Far West. He wasted little time
with "book-larnin'," because everything he needed to know he could
find out in the woods and from the old trappers. He fought in the
Creek War (1813 to 1814) under Andrew Jackson, and was then
elected to the state legislature and twice to Congress (1827 to 1831,
1833 to 1835). Helping the Texans defend the Alamo, he died a
hero.*

*Even during his lifetime Davy had become a figure of folklore, and with
the shrewdness of such figures, he decided to cast far his wit and
wisdom—as well as gain the material awards that might come
from the casting—by issuing his autobiography in 1834,* Narrative
of the Life of David Crockett of West Tennessee. *By then, hundreds
of Davy Crockett stories had been spread by the richly imaginative
liars who were making the hard life of early settlements a little more
cheerful. Davy became a superman in coonskins, doing great feats
of bravery and telling stories that expanded in repetition. When he
died, Davy was already a figure somewhat larger than life, and after
death he slipped happily into a paradise of legend.*

FURTHER READING

Constance Rourke's biography *Davy Crockett* (1934) is superb. See also
Richard Dorson's *Davy Crockett: American Comic Legend* (1939)
and J. A. Shackford's *David Crockett: The Man and the Legend*
(1955).

Narrative of the Life of
David Crockett of West Tennessee *(1834)*

Chapter 5

I was living ten miles below Winchester when the Creek war commenced; and as military men are making so much fuss in the world
at this time, I must give an account of the part I took in the defence of
the country. If it should make me president, why I can't help it; such
things will sometimes happen; and my pluck is, never "to seek, nor
decline office."

It is true, I had a little rather not; but yet, if the government can't get on without taking another president from Tennessee, to finish the work of "retrenchment and reform," why, then, I reckon I must go in for it. But I must begin about the war, and leave the other matter for the people to begin on.

The Creek Indians had commenced their open hostilities by a most bloody butchery at Fort Mimms. There had been no war among us for so long, that but few, who were not too old to bear arms, knew any thing about the business. I, for one, had often thought about war, and had often heard it described; and I did verily believe in my own mind, that I couldn't fight in that way at all; but my after experience convinced me that this was all a notion. For when I heard of the mischief which was done at the fort, I instantly felt like going, and I had none of the dread of dying that I expected to feel. In a few days a general meeting of the militia was called for the purpose of raising volunteers; and when the day arrived for that meeting, my wife, who had heard me say I meant to go to the war, began to beg me not to turn out. She said she was a stranger in the parts where we lived, had no connexions living near her, and that she and our little children would be left in a lonesome and unhappy situation if I went away. It was mighty hard to go against such arguments as these; but my countrymen had been murdered, and I knew that the next thing would be, that the Indians would be scalping the women and the children all about there, if we didn't put a stop to it. I reasoned the case with her as well as I could, and told her, that if every man would wait till his wife got willing for him to go to war, there would be no fighting done, until we would all be killed in our own houses; that I was as able to go as any man in the world; and that I believed it was a duty I owed to my country. Whether she was satisfied with this reasoning or not, she did not tell me; but seeing I was bent on it, all she did was to cry a little, and turn about to her work. The truth is, my dander was up, and nothing but war could bring it right again. . . .

About eight hundred of the volunteers, and of that number I was one, were now sent back, crossing the Tennessee river, and on through Huntsville, so as to cross the river again at another place, and to get on the Indians in another direction. After we passed Huntsville, we struck on the river at the Muscle Shoals, and at a place on them called Melton's Bluff. This river is here about two miles wide, and a rough bottom; so much so, indeed, in many places, as to be dangerous; and in fording it this time, we left several of the horses belonging to our men, with their feet fast in the crevices of the rocks. The men, whose horses were thus left, went ahead on foot. We pushed on till we got to what was called the Black Warrior's town, which stood near the very spot where Tuscaloosa now stands, which is the seat of government for the state of Alabama.

This Indian town was a large one; but when we arrived we found the Indians had all left it. There was a large field of corn standing out, and a pretty good supply in some cribs. There was also a fine quantity of dried beans, which were very acceptable to us; and without delay we secured them as well as the corn, and then burned the town to ashes; after which we left the place. . . .

We then marched to a place, which we called Camp Wills; and here it was that Captain Cannon was promoted to a colonel, and Colonel Coffee to a general. We then marched to the Ten Islands, on the Coosa river, where we established a fort; and our spy companies were sent out. They soon made prisoners of Bob Catala and his warriors, and, in a few days afterwards, we heard of some Indians in a town about eight miles off. So we mounted our horses, and put out for that town, under the direction of two friendly Creeks we had taken for pilots. We had also a Cherokee colonel, Dick Brown, and some of his men with us. When we got near the town we divided; one of our pilots going with each division. And so we passed on each side of the town, keeping near to it, until our lines met on the far side. We then closed up at both ends, so as to surround it completely; and then we sent Captain Hammond's company of rangers to bring on the affray. He had advanced near the town, when the Indians saw him, and they raised the yell, and came running at him like so many red devils. The main army was now formed in a hollow square around the town, and they pursued Hammond till they came in reach of us. We then gave them a fire, and they returned it, and then ran back into their town. We began to close on the town by making our files closer and closer, and the Indians soon saw they were our property. So most of them wanted us to take them prisoners; and their squaws and all would run and take hold of any of us they could, and give themselves up. I saw seven squaws have hold of one man, which made me think of the Scriptures. So I hollered out the Scriptures was fulfilling; that there was seven women holding to one man's coat tail. But I believe it was a hunting-shirt all the time. We took them all prisoners that came out to us in this way; but I saw some warriors run into a house, until I counted forty-six of them. We pursued them until we got near the house, when we saw a squaw sitting in the door, and she placed her feet against the bow she had in her hand, and then took an arrow, and, raising her feet, she drew with all her might, and let fly at us, and she killed a man, whose name, I believe, was Moore. He was a lieutenant, and his death so enraged us all, that she was fired on, and had at least twenty balls blown through her. This was the first man I ever saw killed with a bow and arrow. We now shot them like dogs; and then set the house on fire, and burned it up with the forty-six warriors in it. I recollect seeing a boy who was shot down near the house. His arm and thigh was broken, and he was so near the burning house that the grease was stewing out of him. In this situation he was still trying to crawl along; but not a murmur escaped him, though he was only about twelve years old. So sullen is the Indian, when his dander is up, that he had sooner die than make a noise, or ask for quarters.

The number that we took prisoners, being added to the number we killed, amounted one hundred and eighty-six; though I don't remember the exact number of either. We had five of our men killed. We then returned to our camp, at which our fort was erected, and known by the name of Fort Strother. No provisions had yet reached us, and we had now been for several days on half rations. However we went back to our Indian town on the next day, when many of the carcasses of the Indians were still to be seen. They looked very awful, for the burning had not entirely consumed them, but given them a very terrible appearance, at least what remained of them. It was, somehow or other, found out that the house had a potatoe cellar under it, and an immediate examination was made, for we were all as hungry as wolves. We found a fine chance of potatoes in it, and hunger compelled us to eat them, though I had a little rather not; if I could have helped it, for the oil of the Indians we had burned up on the day before had run down on them, and they looked like they had been stewed with fat meat. We then again returned to the army, and remained there for several days almost starving, as all our beef was gone. We commenced eating the beef-hides, and continued to eat every scrap we could lay our hands on. . . .

I continued at home now, working my farm for two years, as the war finally closed soon after I quit the service. The battle at New Orleans had already been fought, and treaties were made with the Indians which put a stop to their hostilities.

But in this time, I met with the hardest trial which ever falls to the lot of man. Death, that cruel leveller of all distinctions,—to whom the prayers and tears of husbands, and of even helpless infancy, are addressed in vain,—entered my humble cottage, and tore from my children an affectionate good mother, and from me a tender and loving wife. . . .

There lived in the neighbourhood, a widow lady whose husband had been killed in the war. She had two children, a son and daughter, and both quite small, like my own. I began to think, that as we were both in the same situation, it might be that we could do something for each other; and I therefore began to hint a little around the matter, as we were once and a while together. She was a good industrious woman, and owned a snug little farm, and lived quite comfortable. I soon began to pay my respects to her in real good earnest; but I was as sly about it as a fox when he is going to rob a hen-roost. I found that my company wasn't at all disagreeable to her; and I thought I could treat her children with so much friendship as to make her a good stepmother to mine, and in this I wan't mistaken, as we soon bargained, and got married, and then went ahead. In a great deal of peace we raised our first crop of children, and they are all married and doing well. But we had a second crop together; and I shall notice them as I go along, as my wife and myself both had a hand in them, and they therefore belong to the history of my second marriage. . . .

The place on which I lived was sickly, and I was determined to leave it. I therefore set out the next fall to look at the country which had been purchased of the Chickasaw tribe of Indians. I went on to a place called Shoal Creek, about eighty miles from where I lived, and here again I got sick. I took the ague and fever, which I supposed was brought on me by camping out. I remained here for some time, as I was unable to go farther; and in that time, I became so well pleased with the country about there, that I resolved to settle in it. It was just only a little distance in the purchase, and no order had been established there; but I thought I could get along without order as well as any body else. And so I moved and settled myself down on the head of Shoal Creek. We remained here some two or three years, without any law at all; and so many bad characters began to flock in upon us, that we found it necessary to set up a sort of temporary government of our own. I don't mean that we made any president, and called him the "government," but we met and made what we called a corporation; and I reckon we called *it* wrong, for it wa'n't a bank, and hadn't any deposites; and now they call the bank a corporation. But be this as it may, we lived in the back-woods, and didn't profess to know much, and no doubt used many wrong words. But we met, and appointed magistrates and constables to keep order. We didn't fix any laws for them, tho': for we supposed they would know law enough, whoever they might be; and so we left it to themselves to fix the laws.

I was appointed one of the magistrates; and when a man owed a debt, and wouldn't pay it, I and my constable ordered our warrant, and then he would take the man, and bring him before me for trial. I would give judgment against him, and then an order of an execution would easily scare the debt out of him. If any one was charged with marking his neighbour's hogs, or with stealing any thing, which happened pretty often in those days,—I would have him taken, and if there was tolerable grounds for the charge, I would have him well whip'd and cleared. . . .

Next morning, being the first day of May, I went to some of the newspaper offices, read the news, and returned to take a ride with Colonel S. D. Jackson, in an elegant barouche. We drove up the city [New York] and took a view of the improvements and beautiful houses in the new part. By the time we returned down Broadway, it seemed to me that the city was flying before some awful calamity. "Why," said I, "colonel, what under heaven is the matter? Everybody appears to be pitching out their furniture, and packing it off." He laughed, and said this was the general "mooving day." Such a sight nobody ever saw, unless it was in this same city. It seemed a kind of frolic, as if they were changing houses just for fun. Every street was crowded with carts, drays, and people. So the world goes. It would take a good deal to get me out of my log house; but here, I understand, many persons "moove" every year.

Having alighted, and taken some refreshment, I asked Colonel Webb to go with me to the "Fivepoints," a noted place near the centre of the city. This is the place where Van Buren's warriors came from during the election, when the wild Irish, with their clubs and bludgeons, knocked down every one they could find that would not huzza for Jackson. However, I had a great curiosity to see them; and on we went, the major and me, and in the midst of that great city we came to a place where five streets all come together; and from this it takes the name of the "Five-points." The buildings are little, old, frame houses, and looked like some little country village. The houses all had cellars; and as that day was fashionable to moove, they were mooving too. The streets looked like a *clearing*, in my part of the world, as they were emptying and burning the straw out of their beds. It appeared as if the cellars was jam full of people; and such fidling and dancing nobody ever saw before in this world. I thought they were the true "heaven-borns." Black and white, white and black, all hug-em-snug together, happy as lords and ladies, sitting sometimes round in a ring, with a jug of liquor between them: and I do think I saw more drunk folks, men and women, that day, than I ever saw before. This is part of what is called by the Regency the "glorious sixth ward"—the regular Van Buren ground-floor. I thought I would rather risque myself in an Indian fight than venture among these creatures after night. I said to the colonel, "God deliver me from such constituents, or from a party supported by such. In my country, when you meet an Irishman, you find a first-rate gentleman; but these are worse than savages; they are too mean to swab hell's kitchen." He took me to the place where the election was held. It appeared to me that all the place round was made ground, and that there was more room in the houses under-ground than above; and I suppose there must have been a flood of rain during the election, which forced those rats out of their holes. There is more people stowed away together here than any place I ever saw. I heard a story, and it is asserted to be true, that about here, some years ago, a committee visited all the houses, to see how they were coming on. One house, that was four stories high, and four rooms on a floor, had sixteen families in it, and four in the garret, which was divided into four parts by a streak of charcoal. An old lady, that was spinning up there, was asked how they made out. She said, pretty well; and that they would be quiet enough if it was not for the old woman in the opposite corner, and she took boarders, and they often made a noise. I believe it is true. What a miserable place a city is for poor people: they are half starved, poorly clothed, and perished for fire. I sometimes wonder they don't clear out to a new country, where every skin hangs by its own tail; but I suppose they think an hour's indulgence in vice is sweet enough for the bitter of the rest.

AUGUSTUS BALDWIN LONGSTREET (1790–1870)

Born in Augusta, Georgia, Longstreet—like many upper-class Southern boys of his time—was sent North to Yale University for his higher education. In 1815 he was admitted to the Georgia bar, and in 1822 he became a judge. In 1839 he was chosen to be president of what is now Emory University; later he became president of the Universities of Mississippi (1848 to 1856) and of South Carolina (from 1858 to the Civil War.)

In his later, eminently respectable, years Longstreet was somewhat embarrassed by the humorous sketches he had written in the early 1830s. Originally published in Southern newspapers and journals, these sketches proved so popular that he collected them under the title of Georgia Scenes, Characters, Incidents etc. in the First Half Century of the Republic *(1835). The older Longstreet need not have felt this book beneath his dignity, for it has assured him a modest place in American literary history.*

Longstreet's sketches follow a pattern characteristic of much early American humor. The writer is obviously a well-educated man. Through hints of erudition, attitudes expressed by a phrase here and there, and above all a rather formal style, he makes it perfectly clear that he should not be confused with the country roughs he writes about. But some impulse toward realism gets the better of his vanity, and he employs the vernacular when he has his characters speak. The lively speech of the characters, if it does not become so faithful to local dialect as to be undecipherable, almost always proves more interesting than the writer's stuffy prose. In "The Horse Swap" this contrast of style is very noticeable, as is the contrast between the two horse traders, each of whom represents a tradition— wanton overstatement and sly understatement—in folk speech.

FURTHER READING

J. D. Wade's *Augustus Baldwin Longstreet* (1924) is a standard biography. Brief critical discussions can be found in Constance Rourke's *American Humor* (1931), Bernard De Voto's *Mark Twain's America* (1932), and Walter Blair's *Native American Humor* (1937).

FROM *Georgia Scenes* (1835)

The Horse Swap

During the session of the Superior Court in the village of ———,
about three weeks ago, when a number of people were collected in the
principal street of the village, I observed a young man riding up and
down the street, as I supposed, in a violent passion. He galloped this
way, then that, and then the other; spurred his horse to one group of
citizens, then to another; then dashed off at half-speed, as if fleeing from
danger; and, suddenly checking his horse, returned—first in a pace,
then in a trot, and then in a canter. While he was performing these
various evolutions he cursed, swore, whooped, screamed, and tossed
himself in every attitude which man could assume on horseback. In
short, he cavorted most magnanimously (a term which, in our tongue,
expresses all that I have described, and a little more), and seemed to
be setting all creation at defiance. As I like to see all that is passing, I
determined to take a position a little nearer to him, and to ascertain, if
possible, what it was that affected him so sensibly. Accordingly I approached a crowd before which he had stopped for a moment, and examined it with the strictest scrutiny. But I could see nothing in it that
seemed to have anything to do with the cavorter. Every man appeared
to be in good humor, and all minding their own business. Not one so
much as noticed the principal figure. Still he went on. After a semicolon
pause, which my appearance seemed to produce (for he eyed me closely
as I approached), he fetched a whoop, and swore that "he could out-
swap any live man, woman, or child that ever walked these hills, or that
ever straddled horseflesh since the days of old daddy Adam." "Stranger,"
said he to me, "did you ever see the *Yallow* Blossom from Jasper?"

"No," said I, "but I have often heard of him."

"I'm the boy," continued he; "perhaps a *leetle*, jist a *leetle* of the
best man at horse-swap that ever trod shoe-leather."

I began to feel my situation a little awkward, when I was relieved
by a man somewhat advanced in years, who stepped up and began to
survey the Yellow Blossom's horse with much apparent interest. This
drew the rider's attention, and he turned the conversation from me to
the stranger.

"Well, my old coon," said he, "do you want to swap *hosses?*"

"Why, I don't know," replied the stranger; "I believe I've got a beast
I'd trade with you for that one, if you like him."

"Well, fetch up your nag, my old cock; you're jist the lark I wanted
to get hold of. I am perhaps a *leetle*, jist a *leetle*, of the best man at a
horse swap that ever stole *cracklins* out of his mammy's fat gourd.
Where's your *hoss?*"

"I'll bring him presently; but I want to examine your horse a little."

"Oh, look at him," said the Blossom, alighting and hitting him a cut—"look at him! He's the best piece of *hoss*-flesh in the thirteen united universal worlds. There's no sort o' mistake in little Bullet. He can pick up miles on his feet, and fling 'em behind him as fast as the next man's *hoss,* I don't care where he comes from. And he can keep at it as long as the sun can shine without resting."

During this harangue little Bullet looked as if he understood it all, believed it, and was ready at any moment to verify it. He was a horse of goodly countenance, rather expressive of vigilance than fire; though an unnatural appearance of fierceness was thrown into it by the loss of his ears, which had been cropped pretty close to his head. Nature had done but little for Bullet's head and neck; but he managed, in a great measure, to hid their defects by bowing perpetually. He had obviously suffered severely for corn; but if his ribs and hip bones had not disclosed the fact, *he* never would have done it; for he was in all respects as cheerful and happy as if he commanded all the corn-cribs and fodder-stacks in Georgia. His height was about twelve hands; but as his shape partook somewhat of that of the giraffe, his haunches stood much lower. They were short, strait, peaked, and concave. Bullet's tail, however, made amends for all his defects. All that the artist could do to beautify it had been done; and all that horse could do to compliment the artist, Bullet did. His tail was nicked in superior style, and exhibited the line of beauty in so many directions that it could not fail to hit the most fastidious taste in some of them. From the root it dropped into a graceful festoon, then rose in a handsome curve, then resumed its first direction, and then mounted suddenly upward like a cypress knee to a perpendicular of about two and a half inches. The whole had a careless and bewitching inclination to the right. Bullet obviously knew where his beauty lay, and took all occasions to display it to the best advantage. If a stick cracked, or if any one moved suddenly about him, or coughed, or hawked, or spoke a little louder than common, up went Bullet's tail like lightning; and if the *going up* did not please, the *coming down* must of necessity, for it was as different from the other movement as was its direction. The first was a bold and rapid flight upward, usually to an angle of forty-five degrees. In this position he kept his interesting appendage until he satisfied himself that nothing in particular was to be done; when he commenced dropping it by half inches, in second beats, then in triple time, then faster and shorter, and faster and shorter still, until it finally died away imperceptibly into its natural position. If I might compare sights to sounds, I should say its *settling* was more like the note of a locust than anything else in nature.

Either from native sprightliness of disposition, from uncontrollable activity, or from an unconquerable habit of removing flies by the stamping of the feet, Bullet never stood still, but always kept up a gentle fly-scaring movement of his limbs, which was peculiarly interesting.

"I tell you, man," proceeded the Yellow Blossom, "he's the best live hoss that ever trod the grit of Georgia. Bob Smart knows the hoss. Come here, Bob, and mount this hoss, and show Bullet's motion." Here Bullet bristled up, and looked as if he had been hunting for Bob all day long, and had just found him. Bob sprang on his back. "Boo-oo-oo!" said Bob, with a fluttering noise of the lips, and away went Bullet as if in a quarter race, with all his beauties spread in handsome syle.

"Now fetch him back," said Blossom. Bullet turned and came in pretty much as he went out.

"Now trot him by." Bullet reduced his tail to *customary*, sidled to the right and left airily, and exhibited at least three varieties of trot in the short space of fifty yards.

"Make him pace!" Bob commenced twitching the bridle and kicking at the same time. These inconsistent movements obviously (and most naturally) disconcerted Bullet; for it was impossible for him to learn from them whether he was to proceed or stand still. He started to trot, and was told that wouldn't do. He attempted a canter, and was checked again. He stopped, and was urged to go on. Bullet now rushed into the wide field of experiment, and struck out a gait of his own that completely turned the tables upon his rider, and certainly deserved a patent. It seemed to have derived its elements from the jig, the minuet, and the cotillion. If it was not a pace, it certainly had *pace* in it, and no man would venture to call it anything else; so it passed off to the satisfaction of the owner.

"Walk him!" Bullet was now at home again, and he walked as if money were staked on him.

The stranger, whose name I afterwards learned was Peter Ketch, having examined Bullet to his heart's content, ordered his son Neddy to go and bring up Kit. Neddy soon appeared upon Kit, a well-formed sorrel of the middle size, and in good order. His *tout-ensemble* threw Bullet entirely in the shade, though a glance was sufficient to satisfy any one that Bullet had the decided advantage of him in point of intellect.

"Why, man," said Blossom, "do you bring such a hoss as that to trade for Bullet? Oh, I see, you've no notion of trading!"

"Ride him off, Neddy!" said Peter. Kit put off at a handsome lope.

"Trot him back!" Kit came in at a long sweeping trot, and stopped suddenly at the crowd.

"Well," said Blossom, "let me look at him; maybe he'll do to plough."

"Examine him," said Peter, taking hold the bridle close to the mouth; "he's nothing but a tacky. He ain't as *pretty* a horse as Bullet, I know, but he'll do. Start 'em together for a hundred and fifty *mile*, and if Kit ain't twenty mile ahead of him at the coming out, any man may take Kit for nothing. But he's a monstrous mean horse, gentlemen; any man may see that. He's the scariest horse, too, you ever saw. He won't do to hunt on, nohow. Stranger, will you let Neddy have your rifle to shoot off him? Lay the rifle between his ears, Neddy, and shoot at the blaze in that stump. Tell me when his head is high enough."

Ned fired and hit the blaze, and Kit did not move a hair's breadth.

"Neddy, take a couple of sticks, and beat on that hogs-head at Kit's tail."

Ned made a tremendous rattling, at which Bullet took fright, broke his bridle, and dashed off in grand style, and would have stopped all farther negotiations by going home in disgust, had not a traveller arrested him and brought him back; but Kit did not move.

"I tell you, gentlemen," continued Peter, "he's the scariest horse you ever saw. He ain't as gentle as Bullet, but he won't do any harm if you watch him. Shall I put him in a cart, gig, or wagon for you, stranger? He'll cut the same capers there he does here. He's a monstrous mean horse."

During all this time Blossom was examining him with the nicest scrutiny. Having examined his frame and limbs, he now looked at his eyes.

"He's got a curious look out of his eyes," said Blossom.

"Oh yes, sir," said Peter, "just as blind as a bat. Blind horses always have clear eyes. Make a motion at his eyes, if you please, sir."

Blossom did so, and Kit threw up his head rather as if something pricked him under the chin than as if fearing a blow. Blossom repeated the experiment, and Kit jerked back in considerable astonishment.

"Stone-blind, you see, gentlemen," proceeded Peter; "but he's just as good to travel of a dark night as if he had eyes."

"Blame my buttons," said Blossom, "if I like them eyes!"

"No," said Peter, "nor I neither. I'd rather have 'em made of diamonds; but they'll do—if they don't show as much white as Bullet's."

"Well," said Blossom, "make a pass at me."

"No," said Peter, "you made the banter, now make your pass."

"Well, I'm never afraid to price my hosses. You must give me twenty-five dollars boot."

"Oh, certainly; say fifty, and my saddle and bridle in. Here, Neddy, my son, take away daddy's horse."

"Well," said Blossom, "I've made my pass, now you make yours."

"I'm for short talk in a horse swap, and therefore always tell a gentleman at once what I mean to do. You must give me ten dollars."

Blossom swore absolutely, roundly, and profanely that he never would give boot.

"Well," said Peter, "I didn't care about trading; but you cut such high shines that I thought I'd like to back you out, and I've done it. Gentlemen, you see I've brought him to a back."

"Come, old man," said Blossom, "I've been joking with you. I begin to think you do want to trade; therefore, give me five dollars and take Bullet. I'd rather lose ten dollars any time than not make a trade, though I hate to fling away a good hoss."

"Well," said Peter, "I'll be as clever as you are. Just put the five dollars on Bullet's back, and hand him over; it's a trade."

Blossom swore again, as roundly as before, that he would not give boot; and, said he, "Bullet wouldn't hold five dollars on his back, no how. But, as I bantered you, if you say an even swap, here's at you."

"I told you," said Peter, "I'd be as clever as you; therefore, here goes two dollars more, just for trade sake. Give me three dollars, and it's a bargain."

Blossom repeated his former assertion; and here the parties stood for a long time, and the by-standers (for many were now collected) began to taunt both parties. After some time, however, it was pretty unanimously decided that the old man had backed Blossom out.

At length Blossom swore he "never should be backed out for three dollars after bantering a man"; and, accordingly, they closed the trade.

"Now," said Blossom, as he handed Peter the three dollars, "I'm a man that, when he makes a bad trade, makes the most of it until he can make a better. I'm for no rues and after-claps."

"That's just my way," said Peter; "I never goes to law to mend my bargains."

"Ah, you're the kind of boy I love to trade with. Here's your hoss, old man. Take the saddle and bridle off him, and I'll strip yours; but lift up the blanket easy from Bullet's back, for he's a mighty tender-backed hoss."

The old man removed the saddle, but the blanket stuck fast. He attempted to raise it, and Bullet bowed himself, switched his tail, danced a little, and gave signs of biting.

"Don't hurt him, old man," said Blossom, archly; "take it off easy. I am, perhaps, leetle of the best man at a horse-swap that ever catched a coon."

Peter continued to pull at the blanket more and more roughly, and Bullet became more and more *cavortish*, insomuch that, when the blanket came off, he had reached the *kicking* point in good earnest.

The removal of the blanket disclosed a sore on Bullet's back that seemed to have defied all medical skill. It measured six full inches in length and four in breadth, and had as many features as Bullet had motions. My heart sickened at the sight; and I felt that the brute who had been riding him in that situation deserved the halter.

The prevailing feeling, however, was that of mirth. The laugh became loud and general at the old man's expense, and rustic witticisms were liberally bestowed upon him and his late purchase. These Blossom continued to provoke by various remarks. He asked the old man "if he thought Bullet would let five dollars lie on his back." He declared most seriously that he had owned that horse three months, and had never discovered before that he had a sore back, "or he never should have thought of trading him," etc., etc.

The old man bore it all with the most philosophic composure. He evinced no astonishment at his late discovery, and made no replies. But his son Neddy had not disciplined his feelings quite so well. His eyes opened wider and wider from the first to the last pull of the blanket, and when the whole sore burst upon his view, astonishment and fright seemed to contend for the mastery of his countenance. As the blanket disappeared, he stuck his hands in his breeches pockets, heaved a deep sigh, and lapsed into a profound reverie, from which he was only roused by the cuts at his father. He bore them as long as he could; and, when he could contain himself no longer, he began, with a certain wildness of expression which gave a peculiar interest to what he uttered: "His back's mighty bad off; but dod drot my sould if he's put it to daddy as bad as he thinks he has, for old Kit's both blind and *deef*, I'll be dod drot if he eint!"

"The devil he is!" said Blossom.

"Yes, dod drot my soul if he *eint!*" You walk him, and see if he *eint*. His eyes don't look like it; but he's *jist as leve go agin the* house with you, or in a ditch, as anyhow. Now you go try him." The laugh was now turned on Blossom, and many rushed to test the fidelity of the little boy's report. A few experiments established its truth beyond controversy.

"Neddy," said the old man, "you oughtn't to try and make people discontented with their things. Stranger, don't mind what the little boy says. If you can only get Kit rid of them little failings you'll find him all sorts of a horse. You are a *leetle* the best man at a horse-swap that ever I got hold of but don't fool away Kit. Come, Neddy, my son, let's be moving; the stranger seems to be getting snappish."

GEORGE WASHINGTON CABLE (1844–1925)

The split in American experience which brought the nation to civil strife was strongly visible in the family background of George Washington Cable: his mother came from a New England Puritan line, his father from slave-holding Virginians. Cable himself, in later life, would blend moral earnestness with an intense interest in Southern folkways.

Born in New Orleans, Cable had to leave school at fifteen when his father died. He worked in a custom-house supporting his penniless family until the Civil War, and then, despite his physical frailty, he fought with the Mississippi cavalry. Dutifully praying every night, as his mother had instructed him to, and studying Latin and mathematics when he had a spare moment, the studious young Cable remained in the cavalry, despite two wounds, until General Forrest surrendered in May 1865.

After the war, Cable worked as a surveyor, bookkeeper, and reporter for the New Orleans Picayune. *His true interest, however, lay not in journalism but in local history. He soon became a recognized authority in Creole culture and Louisiana history; and as he deepened his*

*sense of the past, he also began to question his commitments in the
present, rethinking his loyalty to the Southern cause and concluding
that it had little justice on its side. With remarkable courage, and
at a time when few white men in either the South or North cared
or dared to speak out, Cable became a spokesman for Negro rights
in the South. Meanwhile, he was also writing vivid short stories
about the entanglements of whites and blacks in Louisiana society.
A number of these stories appeared in* Scribner's *and other magazines, bringing him a national reputation, but somewhat mislead-
ingly, since it was that of a regional writer or local colorist.*

*Though he used real situations and characters in composing his stories
("The Story of Bras-Coupé," which appears on pp. 825 to 844, was
told to him by a porter in his office), Cable had little interest in, or
taste for, the quaint effects and special pleading characteristics of
local-color fiction. Cable wanted to portray the social confusions and
psychic torments of Southern life with as much honesty, realism,
and moral complexity as he could summon; and like a greater
Southern writer to follow him, William Faulkner, he chose as the
focus of his stories the mixture of white and Negro blood and the
way two races living side by side, but trying to pretend they were
distinct, necessarily failed one another in humanity and compassion.
His writings are strong, sometimes too complicated and melodramatic in plot; they have nothing in common with Old South
magnolia romanticism or local-color pastel. The qualities of Cable's
fiction have been well described by Edmund Wilson:*

*What is unique in the work of this Southerner is the exercise of a Protes-
tant conscience in a meridional and partly Catholic community, in which
it is, however, completely at home. The violence and the scandal he writes
about are the conditions of the world he lives in, but presented from a
point of view that is quite distinct from the point of view of those who
commit them or suffer them. It is also undoubtedly true that Cable had
derived certain benefits from growing up in this mixed milieu. The
lucidity and accuracy of French had, both in style and thought, served
him well, and New Orleans had a regional culture such as no other
Southern city possessed. . . . And the piquant variety in New Orleans of
races, religions and nationalities had given Cable a kind of international
experience which he could hardly, in the pre-war period, have got anywhere else in the United States.*

*Unpopular in his native region because he spoke out for the oppressed
Negroes, Cable could only make a precarious living as a writer. He
supplemented his income by platform readings, touring in 1884 to
1886 with Mark Twain, who admired Cable's ability and integrity.*

Cable's most important books are Old Creole Days *(1879), a collection
of his best stories;* The Grandissimes *(1880), a novel; and* The Negro

Question *(1890), a fine sociological study and plea for civil rights for Negroes. The last forty years of his life Cable spent in Northampton, Massachusetts, where he was now somewhat more at home than in New Orleans.*

FURTHER READING

The standard and excellent biography is Arlin Turner's *George Washington Cable* (1956). There are good critical discussions of his work in Edmund Wilson's *Patriotic Gore* (1962) and Richard Chase's *The American Novel and its Tradition* (1957).

FROM *The Grandissimes* (1880)

The Story of Bras-Coupé [1]

. . . Bras-Coupé . . . had been, in Africa and under another name, a prince among his people. In a certain war of conquest, to which he had been driven by *ennui*, he was captured, stripped of his royalty, marched down upon the beach of the Atlantic, and, attired as a true son of Adam, with two goodly arms intact, became a commodity. Passing out of first hands in barter for a looking glass, he was shipped in good order and condition on board the good schooner *Egalité*, whereof Blank was master, to be delivered without delay at the port of Nouvelle Orleans (the dangers of fire and navigation excepted), unto Blank Blank. In witness whereof, He that made men's skins of different colors, but all blood of one, hath entered the same upon His book, and sealed it to the day of judgment.

Of the voyage little is recorded—here below; the less the better. Part of the living merchandise failed to keep; the weather was rough, the cargo large, the vessel small. However, the captain discovered there was room over the side, and there—all flesh is grass—from time to time during the voyage he jettisoned the unmerchantable.

Yet, when the reopened hatches let in the sweet smell of the land, Bras-Coupé had come to the upper—the favored—the buttered side of the world; the anchor slid with a rumble of relief down through the muddy fathoms of the Mississippi, and the prince could hear through the schooner's side the savage current of the river, leaping and licking

[1] "The Story of Bras-Coupé" is based on a true story told to George Washington Cable by an old French-speaking Negro. Rejected by one magazine editor after another, the tale became a part of *The Grandissimes*, Cable's first novel. There are two Honore Grandissimes in the story. One is a pure white Creole loved by the mulatto slave, Palmyre; the other, his mulatto half brother, loves Palmyre.

about the bows, and whimpering low welcomes home. A splendid picture to the eyes of the royal captive, as his head came up out of the hatchway, was the little Franco-Spanish-American city that lay on the low, brimming bank. There were little forts that showed their whitewashed teeth; there was a green parade ground, and yellow barracks, and cabildo, and hospital, and cavalry stables, and customhouse, and a most inviting jail, convenient to the cathedral—all of dazzling white and yellow, with a black stripe marking the track of the conflagration of 1794, and here and there among the low roofs a lofty one with round-topped dormer windows and a breezy belvedere looking out upon the plantations of coffee and indigo beyond the town.

When Bras-Coupé staggered ashore, he stood but a moment among a drove of "likely boys," before Agricola Fusilier, managing the business adventures of the Grandissime estate, as well as the residents thereon, and struck with admiration for the physical beauties of the chieftain (a man may even fancy a Negro—as a Negro), bought the lot, and, loth to resell him with the rest to some unappreciative 'Cadian, induced Don José Martinez' overseer to become his purchaser.

Down in the rich parish of St. Bernard (whose boundary line now touches that of the distended city) lay the plantation, known before Bras-Coupé passed away, as La Renaissance. Here it was that he entered at once upon a chapter of agreeable surprises. He was humanely met, presented with a clean garment, lifted into a cart drawn by oxen, taken to a whitewashed cabin of logs, finer than his palace at home, and made to comprehend that it was a free gift. He was also given some clean food, whereupon he fell sick. At home it would have been the part of piety for the magnate next the throne to launch him heavenward at once; but now, healing doses were administered, and to his amazement he recovered. It reminded him that he was no longer king.

His name, he replied to an inquiry touching that subject, was ——
——, something in the Jaloff tongue, which he by and by condescended to render into Congo: Mioko-Koanga, in French, Bras-Coupé, the Arm Cut off. Truly it would have been easy to admit, had this been his meaning, that his tribe, in losing him, had lost its strong right arm close off at the shoulder; not so easy for his high-paying purchaser to allow, if this other was his intent; that the arm which might no longer shake the spear or swing the wooden sword, was no better than a useless stump never to be lifted for aught else. But whether easy to allow or not, that was his meaning. He made himself a type of all Slavery, turning into flesh and blood the truth that all Slavery is maiming.

He beheld more luxury in a week than all his subjects had seen in a century. Here Congo girls were dressed in cottons and flannels worth, where he came from, an elephant's tusk apiece. Everybody wore clothes —children and lads alone excepted. Not a lion had invaded the settlement since his immigration. The serpents were as nothing; an occasional one coming up through the floor—that was all. True, there was more emaciation than unassisted conjecture could explain—a profusion of enlarged joints and diminished muscles, which, thank God, was even then confined to a narrow section and disappeared with Spanish rule. He had no experimental knowledge of it; nay, regular meals, on the contrary, gave him anxious concern, yet had the effect—spite of his apprehension that he was being fattened for a purpose—of restoring the herculian puissance which formerly in Africa had made him the terror of the battle.

When one day he had come to be quite himself, he was invited out into the sunshine, and, escorted by the driver (a sort of foreman to the overseer), went forth dimly wondering. They reached a field where some men and women were hoeing. He had seen men and women—subjects of his—labor—a little—in Africa. The driver handed him a hoe; he examined it with silent interest—until by signs he was requested to join the pastime.

"What?"

He spoke, not with his lips, but with the recoil of his splendid frame and the ferocious expansion of his eyes. This invitation was a cataract of lightning leaping down an ink-black sky. In one instant of all-pervading clearness he read his sentence—WORK.

Bras-Coupé was six feet five. With a sweep as quick as instinct the back of the hoe smote the driver full in the head. Next, the prince lifted the nearest Congo crosswise, brought thirty-two teeth together in his wildly kicking leg and cast him away as a bad morsel; then, throwing another into the branches of a willow, and a woman over his head into a draining-ditch, he made one bound for freedom, and fell to his knees, rocking from side to side under the effect of a pistol ball from the overseer. It had struck him in the forehead, and, running around the skull in search of a penetrable spot, tradition—which sometimes jests—says, came out despairingly, exactly where it had entered.

It so happened that, except the overseer, the whole company were black. Why should the trivial scandal be blabbed? A plaster or two made everything even in a short time, except in the driver's case—for the driver died. The woman whom Bras-Coupé had thrown over his head lived to sell calas to Joseph Frowenfeld.

Don José, young and austere, knew nothing about agriculture and cared as much about human nature. The overseer often thought this, but never said it; he would not trust even himself with the dangerous criticism. When he ventured to reveal the foregoing incidents to the Señor, he laid all the blame possible upon the man whom death had removed beyond the reach of correction, and brought his account to a climax by hazarding the assertion that Bras-Coupé was an animal that could not be whipped.

"*Caramba!*" exclaimed the master, with gentle emphasis, "how so?"

"Perhaps Señor had better ride down to the quarters," replied the overseer.

It was a great sacrifice of dignity, but the master made it.

"Bring him out."

They brought him out—chains on his feet, chains on his wrists, an iron yoke on his neck. The Spanish-Creole master had often seen the bull, with his long, keen horns and blazing eye, standing in the arena; but this was as though he had come face to face with a rhinoceros.

"This man is not a Congo," he said.

"He is a Jaloff," replied the encouraged overseer. "See his fine, straight nose; moreover, he is a *candio*—a prince. If I whip him he will die."

The dauntless captive and fearless master stood looking into each other's eyes until each recognized in the other his peer in physical courage, and each was struck with an admiration for the other which no after difference was sufficient entirely to destroy. Had Bras-Coupé's eye quailed but once—just for one little instant—he would have got the lash; but, as it was——

"Get an interpreter," said Don José; then, more privately, "and come to an understanding. I shall require it of you."

Where might one find an interpreter—one not merely able to render a Jaloff's meaning into Creole French, or Spanish, but with such a turn for diplomatic correspondence as would bring about an "understanding" with this African buffalo? The overseer was left standing and thinking, and Clemence, who had not forgotten who threw her into the draining-ditch, cunningly passed by.

"Ah, Clemence——"

"*Mo pas capabe! Mo pas capabe!* (I cannot, I cannot!) *Ya, ya, ya! 'oir Miché Agricol' Fusilier! ouala yune bon monture, oui!*"—which was to signify that Agricolo could interpret the very Papa Lébat.

"Agricola Fusilier! The last man on earth to make peace."

But there seemed to be no choice, and to Agricola the overseer went. It was but a little ride to the Grandissime place.

"I, Agricola Fusilier, stand as an interpreter to a Negro? H-sir!"

"But I thought you might know of some person," said the weakening applicant, rubbing his ear with his hand.

"Ah!" replied Agricola, addressing the surrounding scenery, "if I did not—who would? You may take Palmyre."

The overseer softly smote his hands together at the happy thought.

"Yes," said Agricola, "take Palmyre; she has picked up as many Negro dialects as I know European languages."

And she went to the don's plantation as interpretress, followed by Agricola's prayer to Fate that she might in some way be overtaken by disaster. The two hated each other with all the strength they had. He knew not only her pride, but her passion for the absent Honoré. He hated her, also, for her intelligence, for the high favor in which she stood with her mistress, and for her invincible spirit, which was more offensively patent to him than to others, since he was himself the chief object of her silent detestation.

It was Palmyre's habit to do nothing without painstaking. "When Mademoiselle comes to be Señora," thought she—she knew that her mistress and the don were affianced—"it will be well to have Señor's esteem. I shall endeavor to succeed." It was from this motive, then, that with the aid of her mistress she attired herself in a resplendence of scarlet and beads and feathers that could not fail the double purpose of connecting her with the children of Ethiopia and commanding the captive's instant admiration.

Alas for those who succeed too well! No sooner did the African turn his tiger glance upon her than the fire of his eyes died out; and when she spoke to him in the dear accents of his native tongue, the matter of strife vanished from his mind. He loved.

He sat down tamely in his irons and listened to Palmyre's argument as a wrecked mariner would listen to ghostly church bells. He would give a short assent, feast his eyes, again assent, and feast his ears; but when at length she made bold to approach the actual issue, and finally uttered the loathed word, *Work*, he rose up, six feet five, and statue of indignation in black marble.

And then Palmyre, too, rose up, glorying in him, and went to explain to master and overseer. Bras Coupé understood, she said, that he was a slave—it was the fortune of war, and he was a warrior; but, according to a generally recognized principle in African international law, he could not reasonably be expected to work.

"As Señor will remember I told him," remarked the overseer; "how can a man expect to plow with a zebra?"

Here he recalled a fact in his early experience. An African of this stripe had been found to answer admirably as a "driver" to make others work. A second and third parley, extending through two or three days, were held with the prince, looking to his appointment to the vacant office of driver; yet what was the master's amazement to learn at length that his Highness declined the proffered honor.

"Stop!" spoke the overseer again, detecting a look of alarm in Palmyre's face as she turned away, "he doesn't do any such thing. If Señore will let me take the man to Agricola——"

"No!" cried Palmyre, with an agonized look, " I will tell. He will take the place and fill it if you will give me to him for his own—but oh, messieurs, for the love of God—I do not want to be his wife!"

The overseer looked at the Señor, ready to approve whatever he should decide. Bras-Coupé's intrepid audacity took the Spaniard's heart by irresistible assault.

"I leave it entirely with Señor Fusilier," he said.

"But he is not my master; he has no right——"

"Silence!"

And she was silent; and so, sometimes, is fire in the wall.

Agricola's consent was given with malicious promptness, and as Bras-Coupé's fetters fell off it was decreed that, should he fill his office efficiently, there should be a wedding on the rear veranda of the Grandissime mansion simultaneously with the one already appointed to take place in the grand hall of the same house six months from that present day. In the meanwhile Palmyre should remain with Mademoiselle, who had promptly but quietly made up her mind that Palmyre should not be wed unless she wished to be. Bras-Coupé made no objection, was royally worthless for a time, but learned fast, mastered the "gumbo" dialect in a few weeks, and in six months was the most valuable man ever bought for gourde dollars. Nevertheless, there were but three persons within as many square miles who were not most vividly afraid of him.

The first was Palmyre. His bearing in her presence was ever one of solemn, exalted respect, which, whether from pure magnanimity in himself, or by reason of her magnetic eye, was something worth being there to see. "It was royal!" said the overseer.

The second was not that official. When Bras-Coupé said—as, at stated intervals, he did say—"*Mo courri c'ez Agricole Fusilier 'pou oir' n'amourouse*" (I go to Agricola Fusilier to see my betrothed), the overseer would sooner have intercepted a score of painted Chickasaws than that one lover. He would look after him and shake a prophetic head. "Trouble coming; better not deceive that fellow"; yet that was the very thing Palmyre dared do. Her admiration for Bras-Coupé was almost boundless. She rejoiced in his stature; she reveled in the contemplation of his untamable spirit; he seemed to her the gigantic embodiment of her own dark, fierce will, the expanded realization of her lifetime longing for terrible strength. But the single deficiency in all this impassioned regard was—what so many fairer loves have found impossible to explain to so many gentler lovers—an entire absence of preference; her heart she could not give him—she did not have it. Yet after her first prayer to the Spaniard and his overseer for deliverance, to the secret surprise and chagrin of her young mistress, she simulated content. It was artifice; she knew Agricola's power, and to seem to consent was her one chance with him. He might thus be beguiled into withdrawing his own consent. That failing, she had Mademoiselle's promise to come to the rescue, which she could use at the last moment; and that failing, there was a dirk in her bosom, for which a certain hard breast was not too hard. Another element of safety, of which she knew nothing, was a letter from the Cannes Brulées. The word had reached there that love had conquered—that, despite all hard words, and rancor, and positive injury, the Grandissime hand—the fairest of Grandissime hands— was about to be laid into that of one who without much stretch might be called a De Grapion; that there was, moreover, positive effort being made to induce a restitution of old gaming-table spoils. Honoré and Mademoiselle, his sister, one on each side of the Atlantic, were striving for this end. Don José sent this intelligence to his kinsman as glad tidings (a lover never imagines there are two sides to that which makes him happy), and, to add a touch of humor, told how Palmyre, also, was given to the chieftain. the letter that came back to the young Spaniard did not blame him so much: *he* was ignorant of all the facts; but a very formal one to Agricola begged to notify him that if Palmyre's union with Bras-Coupé should be completed, as sure as there was a God in heaven, the writer would have the life of the man who knowingly had thus endeavored to dishoner one who *shared the blood of the De Grapions.* Thereupon Agricola, contrary to his general character, began to drop hints to Don José that the engagement of Bras-Coupé and Palmyre need not be considered irreversible; but the don was not desirous of disappointing his terrible pet. Palmyre, unluckily, played her game a little too deeply. She thought the moment had come for herself to insist on the match, and thus provoke Agricola to forbid it. To her incalculable dismay she saw him a second time reconsider and become silent.

The second person who did not fear Bras-Coupé was Mademoiselle. On one of the giant's earliest visits to see Palmyre he obeyed the summons which she brought him, to appear before the lady. A more artificial man might have objected on the score of dress, his attire being a single gaudy garment tightly enveloping the waist and thighs. As his eyes fell upon the beautiful white lady, he prostrated himself upon the ground, his arms outstretched before him. He would not move till she was gone. Then he arose like a hermit who has seen a vision. *"Bras-Coupé 'n pas oulé oir zombis."* (Bras-Coupé dares not look upon a spirit.) From that hour he worshiped. He saw her often; every time, after one glance at her countenance, he would prostrate his gigantic length with his face in the dust.

The third person who did not fear him was—Agricola? Nay, it was the Spaniard—a man whose capability to fear anything in nature or beyond had never been discovered.

Long before the end of his probation Bras-Coupé would have slipped the entanglements of bondage, though as yet he felt them only as one feels a spider's web across the face, had not the master, according to a little affectation of the times, promoted him to be his gamekeeper. Many a day did these two living magazines of wrath spend together in the dismal swamps and on the meager intersecting ridges, making war upon deer and bear and wildcat; or on the Mississippi after wild goose and pelican; when even a word misplaced would have made either the slayer of the other. Yet the months ran smoothly round and the wedding night drew nigh.[2] A goodly company had assembled. All things were ready. The bride was dressed, the bridegroom had come. On the great back piazza, which had been enclosed with sailcloth and lighted with lanterns, was Palmyre, full of a new and deep design and playing her

[2] An over-zealous Franciscan once complained bitterly to the bishop of Havana, that people were being married in Louisiana in their own houses after dark and thinking nothing of it. It is not certain that he had reference to the Grandissime mansion; at any rate he was tittered down by the whole community. *Au.*

deceit to the last, robed in costly garments to whose beauty was added the charm of their having been worn once, and once only, by her beloved Mademoiselle.

But where was Bras-Coupé?

The question was asked of Palmyre by Agricola with a gaze that meant in English, "No tricks, girl!"

Among the servants who huddled at the windows and door to see the inner magnificence a frightened whisper was already going round.

"We have made a sad discovery, Miché Fusilier," said the overseer. "Bras-Coupé is here; we have him in a room just yonder. But—the truth is, sir, Bras-Coupé is a voodoo."

"Well, and suppose he is; what of it? Only hush; do not let his master know it. It is nothing; all the blacks are voodoos, more or less."

"But he declines to dress himself—has painted himself all rings and stripes, antelope fashion."

"Tell him Agricola Fusilier says, 'dress immediately!' "

"Oh, Miché, we have said that five times already, and his answer— you will pardon me—his answer is—spitting on the ground—that you are a contemptible *dotchian*" (white trash).

There is nothing to do but privily to call the very bride—the lady herself. She comes forth in all her glory, small, but oh, so beautiful! Slam! Bras-Coupé is upon his face, his finger tips touching the tips of her snowy slippers. She gently bids him go and dress, and at once he goes.

Ah! now the question may be answered without whispering. There is Bras-Coupé, towering above all heads, in ridiculous red and blue regimentals, but with a look of savage dignity upon him that keeps everyone from laughing. The murmur of admiration that passed along the thronged gallery leaped up into a shout in the bosom of Palmyre. Oh, Bras-Coupé—heroic soul! She would not falter. She would let the silly priest say his say—then her cunning should help her *not to be* his wife, yet to show his mighty arm how and when to strike.

"He is looking for Palmyre," said some, and at that moment he saw her.

"Ho-o-o-o-o!"

Agricola's best roar was a penny trumpet to Bras-Coupé's note of joy. The whole masculine half of the indoor company flocked out to see what the matter was. Bras-Coupé was taking her hand in one of his and laying his other upon her head; and as someone made an unnecessary gesture for silence, he sang, beating slow and solemn time with his naked foot and with the hand that dropped hers to smite his breast:

"*En haut la montagne, zami,*
  Mo pé coupé canne, zami,
  Pou' fé i'a'zen' zami,
  Pou' mo baille Palmyre.

Ah! Palmyre, Palmyre, mo c'ere,
Mo l'aimé 'ou'—mo l'aimé 'ou'."

"*Montagne?*" asked one slave of another, "*qui ce çà, montagne? gnia pas quiç' ose comme çà dans la Louisiana?*" (What's a mountain? We haven't such things in Louisiana).
"*Mein ye gagnein plein montagnes dans l'Afrique*, listen!"

"*Ah! Palmyre, Palmyre, mo' piti zozo,*
Mo l'aimé 'ou'—mo l'aimé l'aimé 'ou'."

"*Bravissimo!*"—but just then a counterattraction drew the white company back into the house. An old French priest with sandaled feet and a dirty face had arrived. There was a moment of handshaking with the good father, then a moment of palpitation and holding of the breath, and then—you would have known it by the turning away of two or three feminine heads in tears—the lily hand became the don's, to have and to hold, by authority of the Church and the Spanish king. And all was merry, save that outside there was coming up as villainous a night as ever cast black looks in through snug windows.

It was just as the newly wed Spaniard, with Agricola and all the guests, were concluding the byplay of marrying the darker couple, that the hurricane struck the dwelling. The holy and jovial father had made faint pretense of kissing this second bride; the ladies, colonels, dons, etc.—though the joke struck them as a trifle coarse—were beginning to laugh and clap hands again and the gowned jester to bow to right and left, when Bras-Coupé, tardily realizing the consummation of his hopes, stepped forward to embrace his wife.

"Bras-Coupé!"

The voice was that of Palmyre's mistress. She had not been able to comprehend her maid's behavior, but now Palmyre had darted upon her an appealing look.

The warrier stopped as if a javelin had flashed over his head and stuck in the wall.

"Bras-Coupé must wait till I give him his wife."

He sank, with hidden face, slowly to the floor.

"Bras-Coupé hears the voice of zombis; the voice is sweet, but the words are very strong; from the same sugar cane comes *sirop* and *tafia;* Bras-Coupé says to zombis, 'Bras-Coupé will wait; but if the *dotchians* deceive Bras-Coupé' "—he rose to his feet with his eyes closed and his great black fist lifted over his head—"Bras-Coupé will call Voodo-Magnan!"

The crowd retreated, and the storm fell like a burst of infernal applause. A whiff like fifty witches flouted up the canvas curtain of the gallery, and a fierce black cloud, drawing the moon under its cloak, belched forth a stream of fire that seemed to flood the ground; a peal of thunder followed as if the sky had fallen in, the house quivered, the great oaks groaned, and every lesser thing bowed down before the awful blast. Every lip held its breath for a minute—or an hour, no one knew— there was a sudden lull of the wind, and the floods came down. Have you heard it thunder and rain in those Louisiana lowlands? Every clap seems to crack the world. It has rained a moment; you peer through the black pane—your house is an island, all the land is sea.

However, the supper was spread in the hall, and in due time the guests were filled. Then a supper was spread in the big hall in the basement, below stairs, the sons and daughters of Ham came down like the fowls of the air upon a rice field, and Bras-Coupé, throwing his heels about with the joyous carelessness of a smutted Mercury, for the first time in his life tasted the blood of the grape. A second, a fifth, a tenth time he tasted it, drinking more deeply each time, and would have taken it ten times more had not his bride cunningly concealed it. It was like stealing a tiger's kittens.

The moment quickly came when he wanted his eleventh bumper. As he presented his request a silent shiver of consternation ran through the dark company; and when, in what the prince meant as a remonstrative tone, he repeated the petition—splitting the table with his fist by way of punctuation—there ensued a hustling up staircases and a cramming into dim corners that left him alone at the banquet.

Leaving the table, he strode upstairs and into the chirruping and dancing of the grand salon. There was a halt in the cotillion and a hush of amazement like the shutting off of steam. Bras-Coupé strode straight to his master, laid his paw upon his fellow bridegroom's shoulder and in a thunder-tone demanded:

"More!"

The master swore a Spanish oath, lifted his hand and—fell, beneath the terrific fist of his slave, with a bang that jingled the candelabras. Dolorous stroke!—for the dealer of it. Given, apparently to him—poor, tipsy savage—in self-defense, punishable, in a white offender, by a small fine or a few days' imprisonment, it assured Bras-Coupé the death of a felon; such was the old *Code Noir.* (We have a *Code Noir* now, but the new one is a mental reservation, not an enactment.)

The guests stood for an instant as if frozen, smitten stiff with the instant expectation of insurrection, conflagration, and rapine (just as we do today whenever some poor swaggering Pompey rolls up his fist and gets a ball through his body), while, singlehanded and naked-fisted in a room full of swords, the giant stood over his master, making strange signs and passes and rolling out in wrathful words of his mother tongue what it needed no interpreter to tell his swarming enemies was a voodoo malediction.

"*Nous sommes grigis!*" screamed two or three ladies. (We are bewitched!)

"Look to your wives and daughters!" shouted a Brahman-Mandarin.

"Shoot the black devils without mercy!" cried a Mandarin-Fusilier, unconsciously putting into a single outflash of words the whole Creole treatment of race troubles.

With a single bound Bras-Coupé reached the drawing-room door; his gaudy regimentals made a red and blue streak down the hall; there was a rush of frilled and powdered gentlemen to the rear veranda, an avalanche of lightning with Bras-Coupé in the midst, making for the swamp, and then all without was blackness of darkness and all within was a wild commingled chatter of Creole, French, and Spanish tongues —in the midst of which the reluctant Agricola returned his dress sword to its scabbard.

While the wet lanterns swung on crazily in the trees along the way by which the bridegroom was to have borne his bride; while Madame Grandissime prepared an impromptu bridal chamber; while the Spaniard bathed his eye and the blue gash on his cheekbone; while Palmyre paced her room in a fever and wild tremor of conflicting emotions throughout the night and the guests splashed home after the storm as best they could, Bras-Coupé was practically declaring his independence on a slight rise of ground hardly sixty feet in circumference and lifted scarce above the water in the inmost depths of the swamp.

And what surroundings! Endless colonnades of cypresses; long, motionless drapings of gray moss; broad sheets of noisome waters, pitchy black, resting on bottomless ooze; cypress knees studding the surface; patches of floating green, gleaming brilliantly here and there; yonder where the sunbeams wedge themselves in, constellations of water lilies, the many-hued iris, and a multitude of flowers that no man had named; here, too, serpents great and small, of wonderful colorings, and the dull and loathsome moccasin sliding warily off the dead tree; in dimmer recesses the cow alligator, with her nest hard by; turtles a century old; owls and bats, raccoons, opossums, rats, centipedes and creatures of like vileness; great vines of beautiful leaf and scarlet fruit in deadly clusters; maddening mosquitoes, parasitic insects, gorgeous dragonflies and pretty water lizards; the blue heron, the snowy crane, the redbird, the moss-bird, the nighthawk and the chuck-will's-widow; a solemn stillness and stifled air only now and then disturbed by the call or whir of the summer duck, the dismal ventriloquous note of the rain crow, or the splash of a dead branch falling into the clear but lifeless bayou.

The pack of Cuban hounds that howl from Don José's kennels cannot snuff the trail of the stolen canoe that glides through the somber blue vapors of the African's fastnesses. His arrows send no tell-tale reverberations to the distant clearing. Many a wretch in his native wilderness has Bras-Coupé himself, in palmier days, driven to just such

an existence, to escape the chains and horrors of the barracoons; therefore not a whit broods he over man's inhumanity, but, taking the affair
as a matter of course, casts about him for a future.

Bras-Coupé let the autumn pass, and wintered in his den.

Don José, in a majestic way, endeavored to be happy. He took his
señora to his hall, and under her rule it took on for a while a look and
feeling which turned it from a hunting lodge into a home. Wherever the
lady's steps turned—or it is as correct to say wherever the proud tread
of Palmyre turned—the features of bachelor's hall disappeared; guns,
dogs, oars, saddles, nets, went their way into proper banishment, and
the broad halls and lofty chambers—the floors now muffled with mats
of palmetto leaf—no longer re-echoed the tread of a lonely master, but
breathed a redolence of flowers and a rippling murmur of well-contented
song.

But the song was not from the throat of Bras-Coupé's "*piti zozo.*"
Silent and severe by day, she moaned away whole nights heaping re-
proaches upon herself for the impulse—now to her, because it had
failed, inexplicable in its folly—which had permitted her hand to lie in
Bras-Coupé's and the priest to bind them together.

For in the audacity of her pride, or, as Agricola would have said, in
the immensity of her impudence, she had held herself consecrate to a
hopeless love. But now she was a black man's wife! and even he unable
to sit at her feet and learn the lesson she had hoped to teach him. She
had heard of San Domingo, and for months the fierce heart within her
silent bosom had been leaping and shouting and seeing visions of fire
and blood, and when she brooded over the nearness of Agricola and the
remoteness of Honoré these visions got from her a sort of mad consent.
The lesson she would have taught the giant was Insurrection. But it was
too late. Letting her dagger sleep in her bosom, and with an undefined
belief in imaginary resources, she had consented to join hands with her
giant hero before the priest; and when the wedding had come and gone,
like a white sail, she was seized with a lasting, fierce despair. A wild
aggressiveness that had formerly characterized her glance in moments
of anger—moments which had grown more and more infrequent under
the softening influence of her Mademoiselle's nature—now came back
intensified and blazed in her eye perpetually. Whatever her secret love
may have been in kind, its sinking beyond hope below the horizon had
left her fifty times the mutineer she had been before—the mutineer who
has nothing to lose.

"She loves her *candio*, said the Negroes.

"Simple creatures!" said the overseer, who prided himself on his dis-
cernment, "she loves nothing; she hates Agricola; it's a case of hate at
first sight—the strongest kind."

Both were partly right; her feelings were wonderfully knit to the
African; and she now dedicated herself to Agricola's ruin.

The Señor, it has been said, endeavored to be happy; but now his heart conceived and brought forth its first-born fear, sired by superstition—the fear that he was bewitched. The Negroes said that Bras-Coupé had cursed the land. Morning after morning the master looked out with apprehension toward his fields, until one night the worm came upon the indigo and between sunset and sunrise every green leaf had been eaten up, and there was nothing left for either insect or apprehension, to feed upon.

And then he said—and the echo came back from the Cannes Brulées—that the very bottom culpability of this thing rested on the Grandissimes, and specifically on their fugleman Agricola, through his putting the hellish African upon him. Moreover, fever and death, to a degree unknown before, fell upon his slaves. Those to whom life was spared—but to whom strength did not return—wandered about the place like scarecrows, looking for shelter, and made the very air dismal with the reiteration, *"No' ouanga."* (We are bewitched.) *"Bras-Coupé fe moi des grigis."* (The voodoo's spells are on me.) The ripple of song was hushed and the flowers fell upon the floor.

"I have heard an English maxim," wrote Colonel De Grapion to his kinsman, "which I would recommend you to put into practice—'Fight the devil with fire.'"

No, he would not recognize devils as belligerents.

But if Rome commissioned exorcists, could not he employ one?

No, he would not! If his hounds could not catch Bras-Coupé, why, let him go. The overseer tried the hounds once more and came home with the best one across his saddlebow, an arrow run half through its side.

Once the blacks attempted by certain familiar rum-pourings and nocturnal charm-singing to lift the curse; but the moment the master heard the wild monotone of their infernal worship, he stopped it with a word.

Early in February came the spring, and with it some resurrection of hope and courage. It may have been—it certainly was, in part—because young Honoré Grandissime had returned. He was like the sun's warmth wherever he went; and the other Honoré was like his shadow. The fairer one quickly saw the meaning of these things, hastened to cheer the young don with hopes of a better future, and to effect, if he could, the restoration of Bras-Coupé to his master's favor. But this latter effort was an idle one. He had long sittings with his uncle Agricola to the same end, but they always ended fruitless and often angrily.

His dark half brother had seen Palmyre and loved her. Honoré would gladly have solved one or two riddles by effecting their honorable union in marriage. The previous ceremony on the Grandissime back piazza need be no impediment; all slave owners understood those things. Following Honoré's advice, the f.m.c., who had come into possession of his paternal portion, sent to Cannes Brulées a written offer, to buy Palmyre at any price that her master might name, stating his intention to free her and make her his wife. Colonel De Grapion could hardly hope to settle Palmyre's fate more satisfactorily, yet he could not forego an opportunity to indulge his pride by following up the threat he had hung over Agricola to kill whosoever should give Palmyre to a black man. He referred the subject and the would-be purchaser to him. It would open up to the old braggart a line of retreat, thought the planter of the Cannes Brulées.

But the idea of retreat had left Citizen Fusilier.

"She is already married," said he to M. Honoré Grandissime, f.m.c. "She is the lawful wife of Bras-Coupé; and what God has joined together let no man put asunder. You know it, sirrah. You did this for impudence, to make a show of your wealth. You intended it as an insinuation of equality. I overlook the impertinence for the sake of the man whose white blood you carry; but h-mark you, if ever you bring your Parisian airs and self-sufficient face on a level with mine again, h-I will slap it."

The quadroon, three nights after, was so indiscreet as to give him the opportunity, and he did it—at that quadroon ball, to which Dr. Keene alluded in talking to Frowenfeld.

But Don José, we say, plucked up new spirit.

"Last year's disasters were but fortune's freaks," he said. "See, others' crops have failed all about us."

The overseer shook his head.

"*C'est ce maudit cocodri' là bas.*" (It is that accursed alligator, Bras-Coupé, down yonder in the swamp.)

And by and by the master was again smitten with the same belief. He and his neighbors put in their crops afresh. The spring waned, summer passed, the fevers returned, the year wore round, but no harvest smiled. "Alas!" cried the planters. "We are all poor men!" The worst among the worst were the fields of Bras-Coupé's master—parched and shriveled. "He does not understand planting," said his neighbors; "neither does his overseer. Maybe, too, it is true as he says, that he is voodooed."

One day at high noon the master was taken sick with fever.

The third noon after—the sad wife sitting by the bedside—suddenly, right in the center of the room, with the open door behind him, stood the magnificent, half-nude form of Bras-Coupé. He did not fall down as the mistress's eyes met his, though all his flesh quivered. The master was lying with his eyes closed. The fever had done a fearful three days' work.

"*Mioko-koanga oulé so' femme.*" (Bras-Coupé wants his wife.)

The master started wildly and stared upon his slave.

"*Bras-Coupé oulé so' femme!*" repeated the black.

"Seize him!" cried the sick man, trying to rise.

But, though several servants had ventured in with frightened faces, none dared molest the giant. The master turned his entreating eyes upon his wife, but she seemed stunned, and only covered her face with her hands and sat as if paralyzed by a foreknowledge of what was coming.

Bras-Coupé lifted his great, black palm and commenced:

"Mo cé voudrai que la maison ci là et tout ça qui pas femme' ici s'raient encore maudits!" (May this house and all in it who are not women be accursed!)

The master fell back upon his pillow with a groan of helpless wrath.

The African pointed his finger through the open window.

"May its fields not know the plow nor nourish the cattle that overrun it."

The domestics, who had thus far stood their ground, suddenly rushed from the room like stampeded cattle, and at that moment appeared Palmyre.

"Speak to him," faintly cried the panting invalid.

She went firmly up to her husband and lifted her hand. With an easy motion, but quick as lightning, as a lion sets foot on a dog, he caught her by the arm.

"Bras-Coupé oulé so' femme," he said, and just then Palmyre would have gone with him to the equator.

"You shall not have her!" gasped the master.

The African seemed to rise in height and, still holding his wife at arm's length, resumed his malediction:

"May weeds cover the ground until the air is full of their odor and the wild beasts of the forest come and lie down under their cover."

With a frantic effort the master lifted himself upon his elbow and extended his clenched fish in speechless defiance; but his brain reeled, his sight went out, and when again he saw, Palmyre and her mistress were bending over him, the overseer stood awkwardly by, and Bras-Coupé was gone.

The plantation became an invalid camp. The words of the voodoo found fulfillment on every side. The plow went not out; the herds wandered through broken hedges from field to field and came up with staring bones and shrunken sides; a frenzied mob of weeds and thorns wrestled and throttled each other in a struggle for standing room—ragweed, smartweed, sneezeweed, bindweed, ironweed—until the burning skies of midsummer checked their growth and crowned their unshorn tops with rank and dingy flowers.

"Why in the name of—St. Francis," asked the priest of the overseer, "didn't the Señora use her power over the black scoundrel when he stood and cursed, that day?"

"Why, to tell you the truth, Father," said the overseer, in a discreet whisper, "I can only suppose she thought Bras-Coupé had half a right to do it."

"Ah, ah, I see; like her brother Honoré—looks at both sides of a question—a miserable practice; but why couldn't Palmyre use *her* eyes? They would have stopped him."

"Palmyre? Why Palmyre has become the best *monture* (Plutonian medium) in the parish. Agricola Fusilier himself is afraid of her. Sir, I think sometimes Bras-Coupé is dead and his spirit has gone into Palmyre. She would rather add to his curse than take from it."

"Ah!" said the jovial divine, with a fat smile, "castigation would help her case; the whip is a great sanctifier. I fancy it would even make a Christian of the inexpugnable Bras-Coupé."

But Bras-Coupé kept beyond the reach alike of the lash and of the Latin Bible.

By and by came a man with a rumor, whom the overseer brought to the master's sickroom, to tell that an enterprising Frenchman was attempting to produce a new staple in Louisiana, one that worms would not annihilate. It was that year of history when the despairing planters saw ruin hovering so close over them that they cried to heaven for succor. Providence raised up Etienne de Boré. "And if Etienne is successful," cried the newsbearer, "and gets the juice of the sugar cane to crystallize, so shall all of us, after him, and shall yet save our lands and homes. Oh, Señor, it will make you strong again to see these fields all cane and the long rows of Negroes and Negresses cutting it, while they sing their song of those droll African numerals, counting the canes they cut," and the bearer of good tidings sang them for very joy:

An - o - qué, An - o - bia, Bia - tail - la, Que - re - que,

Hal - lo - oua, Au - mon - dé, Au - tap - o - té, Au -

pa - to - té, Au - qué - ré - qué, Bo.

"And Honoré Grandissime is going to introduce it on his lands," said Don José.

"That is true," said Agricola Fusilier, coming in. Honoré, the indefatigable peacemaker, had brought his uncle and his brother-in-law for the moment not only to speaking but to friendly terms.

The Señor smiled.

"I have some good tidings, too," he said; "my beloved lady has borne me a son."

"Another scion of the house of Grand—— I mean Martinez!" exclaimed Agricola. "And now, Don José, let me say that *I* have an item of rare intelligence!"

The don lifted his feeble head and opened his inquiring eyes with a sudden, savage light in them.

"No," said Agricola, "he is not exactly taken yet, but they are on his track."

"Who?"

"The police. We may say he is virtually in our grasp."

It was on a Sabbath afternoon that a band of Choctaws, having just played a game of racquette behind the city and a similar game being bout to end between the white champions of two rival *faubourgs,* the beating of tom-toms, rattling of mules' jawbones and sounding of wooden horns drew the populace across the fields to a spot whose present name of Congo Square still preserves a reminder of its old barbaric pastimes. On a grassy plain under the ramparts, the performers of these hideous discords sat upon the ground facing each other, and in their midst the dancers danced. They gyrated in couples, a few at a time, throwing their bodies into the most startling attitudes and the wildest contortions, while the whole company of black lookers-on, incited by the tones of the weird music and the violent posturing of the dancers, swayed and writhed in passionate sympathy, beating their breasts, palms and thighs in time with the bones and drums, and at frequent intervals lifting, in that wild African unison no more to be described than forgotten, the unutterable songs of the Babouille and Counjaille dances, with their ejaculatory burdens of *"Aie! Aie! Voudou Magnan!"* and *Aie Calinda! Dancé Calinda!"* The volume of sound rose and fell with the augmentation of diminution of the dancers' extravagances. Now a fresh man, young and supple, bounding into the ring, revived the flagging rattlers, drummers and trumpeters; now a wearied dancer, finding his strength going, gathered all his force at the cry of *"Dancé zisqu'a mort!"* rallied to a grand finale and with one magnificent antic, fell, foaming at the mouth.

The amusement had reached its height. Many participants had been lugged out by the neck to avoid their being danced on, and the enthusiasm had risen to a frenzy, when there bounded into the ring the blackest of black men, an athlete of superb figure, in breeches of *indienne—* the stuff used for slave women's best dresses—jingling with bells, his feet in moccasins, his tight, crisp hair decked out with feathers, a necklace of alligator's teeth rattling on his breast and a living serpent twined about his neck.

It chanced that but one couple was dancing. Whether they had been sent there by advice of Agricola is not certain. Snatching a tambourine from a bystander as he entered, the stranger thrust the male dancer aside, faced the woman and began a series of saturnalian antics, compared with which all that had gone before was tame and sluggish; and as he finally leaped, with tinkling heels, clean over his bewildered partner's head, the multitude howled with rapture.

Ill-starred Bras-Coupé. He was in that extra-hazardous and irresponsible condition of mind and body known in the undignified present as "drunk again."

By the strangest fortune, if not, as we have just hinted, by some design, the man whom he had once deposited in the willow bushes, and the woman Clemence, were the very two dancers, and no other, whom he had interrupted. The man first stupidly regarded, next admiringly gazed upon, and then distinctly recognized, his whilom driver. Five minutes later the Spanish police were putting their heads together to devise a quick and permanent capture; and in the midst of the sixth minute, as the wonderful fellow was rising in a yet more astounding leap than his last, a lasso fell about his neck and brought him, crashing like a burnt tree, face upward upon the turf.

"The runaway slave," said the old French code, continued in force by the Spaniards, "the runaway slave who shall continue to be so for one month from the day of his being denounced to the officers of justice, shall have his ears cut off and shall be branded with the flower-de-luce on the shoulder; and on a second offense of the same nature, persisted in during one month of his being denounced, he shall be hamstrung, and marked with the flower-de-luce on the other shoulder. On the third offense he shall die." Bras-Coupé had run away only twice. "But," said Agricola, "these 'bossals' must be taught their place. Besides, there is Article 27 of the same code: 'The slave who, having struck his master, shall have produced a bruise, shall suffer capital punishment'—a very necessary law!" He concluded with a scowl upon Palmyre, who shot back a glance which he never forgot.

The Spaniard showed himself very merciful—for a Spaniard; he spared the captive's life. He might have been more merciful still; but Honoré Grandissime said some indignant things in the African's favor, and as much to teach the Grandissimes a lesson as to punish the runaway, he would have repented his clemency, as he repented the momentary truce with Agricola, but for the tearful pleading of the Señora and the hot, dry eyes of her maid. Because of these he overlooked the offense against his person and estate, and delivered Bras-Coupé to the law to suffer only the penalties of the crime he had committed against society by attempting to be a free man.

We repeat it for the credit of Palmyre, that she pleaded for Bras-Coupé. But what it cost her to make that intercession, knowing that his death would leave her free, and that if he lived she must be his wife, let us not attempt to say.

In the midst of the ancient town, in a part which is now crumbling away, stood the Calaboza, with its humid vaults, grated cells, iron cages and its whips; and there, soon enough, they strapped Bras-Coupé face downward and laid on the lash. And yet not a sound came from the mutilated and unconquered African to annoy the ear of the sleeping city.

("And you suffered this thing to take place?" asked Joseph Frowenfeld of Honoré Grandissime.

"My-de'-seh!" exclaimed the Creole, "they lied to me—said they would not harm him!")

He was brought at sunrise to the plantation. The air was sweet with the smell of the weed-grown fields. The long-horned oxen that drew him and the naked boy that drove the team stopped before his cabin.

"You cannot put that creature in there," said the thoughtful overseer. "He would suffocate under a roof—he has been too long out-of-doors for that. Put him on my cottage porch." There, at last, Palmyre burst into tears and sank down, while before her on a soft bed of dry grass rested the helpless form of the captive giant, a cloth thrown over his galled back, his ears shorn from his head, and the tendons behind his knees severed. His eyes were dry, but there was in them that unspeakable despair that fills the eye of the charger when, fallen in battle, he gazes with sidewise-bended neck upon the ruin wrought upon him. His eye turned sometimes slowly to his wife. He need not demand her now—she was always by him.

There was much talk over him—much idle talk; no power or circumstance has ever been found that will keep a Creole from talking. He merely lay still under it with a fixed frown; but once some incautious tongue dropped the name of Agricola. The black man's eyes came so quickly round to Palmyre that she thought he would speak; but no; his words were all in his eyes. She answered their gleam with a fierce affirmative glance, whereupon he slowly bent his head and spat upon the floor.

There was yet one more trial of his wild nature. The mandate came from his master's sickbed that he must lift the curse.

Bras-Coupé merely smiled. God keep thy enemy from such a smile! The overseer, with a policy less Spanish than his master's, endeavored to use persuasion. But the fallen prince would not so much as turn one glance from his parted hamstrings. Palmyre was then besought to intercede. She made one poor attempt, but her husband was nearer doing her an unkindness than ever he had been before; he made a slow sign for silence—with his fist; and every mouth was stopped.

At midnight following, there came, on the breeze that blew from the mansion, a sound of running here and there, of wailing and sobbing—another Bridegroom was coming, and the Spaniard, with much such a lamp in hand as most of us shall be found with, neither burning brightly nor wholly gone out, went forth to meet Him.

"Bras Coupé," said Palmyre, next evening, speaking low in his mangled ear, "the master is dead; he is just buried. As he was dying, Bras-Coupé, he asked that you would forgive him."

The maimed man looked steadfastly at his wife. He had not spoken since the lash struck him, and he spoke not now; but in those large, clear eyes, where his remaining strength seemed to have taken refuge as in a citadel, the old fierceness flared up for a moment, and then, like an expiring beacon, went out.

"Is your mistress well enough by this time to venture here?" whispered the overseer to Palmyre. "Let her come. Tell her not to fear, but to bring the babe—in her own arms, tell her—quickly!"

The lady came, her infant boy in her arms, knelt down beside the bed of sweet grass and set the child within the hollow of the African's arm. Bras-Coupé turned his gaze upon it; it smiled, its mother's smile, and put its hand upon the runaway's face, and the first tears of Bras-Coupé's life, the dying testimony of his humanity, gushed from his eyes and rolled down his check upon the infant's hand. He laid his own tenderly upon the babe's forehead, then removing it, waved it abroad, inaudibly moved his lips, dropped his arm, and closed his eyes. The curse was lifted.

"*Le pauv' dgiab'!*" said the overseer, wiping his eyes and looking fieldward. "Palmyre, you must get the priest."

The priest came, in the identical gown in which he had appeared the night of the two weddings. To the good father's many tender questions Bras-Coupé turned a failing eye that gave no answers; until, at length:

"Do you know where you are going?" asked the holy man.

"Yes," answered his eyes, brightening.

"Where?"

He did not reply; he was lost in contemplation, and seemed looking far away.

So the question was repeated.

"Do you know where you are going?"

And again the answer of the eyes. He knew.

"Where?"

The overseer at the edge of the porch, the widow with her babe, and Palmyre and the priest bending over the dying bed turned an eager ear to catch the answer.

"To——" The voice failed a moment; the departing hero essayed again; again it failed; he tried once more, lifted his hand, and with an ecstatic, upward smile, whispered, "To—Africa"—and was gone.

KATE CHOPIN (1851–1904)

*Born Katherine O'Flaherty in St. Louis of a French mother and Irish
father, Kate Chopin married a New Orleans banker and, at the age
of nineteen, went to live among the Acadians of Louisiana. One of
the Chopin plantations had belonged to a New Englander notorious
for brutality to his slaves, a man who had been the model for Simon
Legree in* Uncle Tom's Cabin. *Kate found herself stirred and horrified by this sense of past wrongs hanging over the place she had
come to, and she used this setting in her first novel,* At Fault *(1890).*

*The Chopin family spent much of its time in France, but Kate immersed
herself in Louisiana customs and legends and produced some very
fine short stories. After her husband's death in the early 1880s she
returned to St. Louis and horrified the city by publishing in 1899 a
novel,* The Awakening, *which is notable for the frankness with
which its sensuous heroine follows her desires.*

*"Désirée's Baby" gives further evidence that Kate Chopin was free of
many of the shibboleths of her age. This compactly plotted story
portrays the miseries and deceits attendant on a racially segregated
society, and especially those which follow from notions of racial
superiority. Miss Chopin's materials will strike some readers as an
anticipation, on a miniature scale, of William Faulkner's great novel*
Absalom, Absalom.

FURTHER READING

Daniel S. Rankin, *Kate Chopin and Her Creole Stories* (1932).

Désirée's Baby (1894)

As the day was pleasant, Madame Valmondé drove over to L'Abri to
see Désirée and the baby.

It made her laugh to think of Désirée with a baby. Why, it seemed
but yesterday that Désirée was little more than a baby herself; when
Monsieur in riding through the gateway of Valmondé had found her
lying asleep in the shadow of the big stone pillar.

The little one awoke in his arms and began to cry for "Dada." That
was as much as she could do or say. Some people thought she might have
strayed there of her own accord, for she was of the toddling age. The
prevailing belief was that she had been purposely left by a party of
Texans, whose canvas-covered wagon, late in the day, had crossed the
ferry that Coton Maïs kept, just below the plantation. In time Madame
Valmondé abandoned every speculation but the one that Désirée had

been sent to her by a beneficent Providence to be the child of her affection, seeing that she was without child of the flesh. For the girl grew to
be beautiful and gentle, affectionate and sincere,—the idol of Valmondé.

It was no wonder, when she stood one day against the stone pillar
in whose shadow she had lain asleep, eighteen years before, that Armand
Aubigny riding by and seeing her there, had fallen in love with her.
That was the way all the Aubignys fell in love, as if struck by a pistol
shot. The wonder was that he had not loved her before; for he had
known her since his father brought him home from Paris, a boy of eight,
after his mother died there. The passion that awoke in him that day,
when he saw her at the gate, swept along like an avalanche, or like a
prairie fire, or like anything that drives headlong over all obstacles.

Monsieur Valmondé grew practical and wanted things well considered: that is, the girl's obscure origin. Armand looked into her eyes
and did not care. He was reminded that she was nameless. What did it
matter about a name when he could give her one of the oldest and
proudest in Louisiana? He ordered the *corbeille* from Paris, and contained himself with what patience he could until it arrived; then they
were married.

Madame Valmondé had not seen Désirée and the baby for four
weeks. When she reached L'Abri she shuddered at the first sight of it,
as she always did. It was a sad looking place, which for many years
had not known the gentle presence of a mistress, old Monsieur Aubigny
having married and buried his wife in France, and she having loved
her own land too well ever to leave it. The roof came down steep and
black like a cowl, reaching out beyond the wide galleries that encircled
the yellow stuccoed house. Big, solemn oaks grew close to it, and their
thick-leaved, far-reaching branches shadowed it like a pall. Young
Aubigny's rule was a strict one, too, and under it his negroes had forgotten how to be gay, as they had been during the old master's easy-
going and indulgent lifetime.

The young mother was recovering slowly, and lay full length, in her
soft white muslins and laces, upon a couch. The baby was beside her,
upon her arm, where he had fallen asleep, at her breast. The yellow
nurse woman sat beside a window fanning herself.

Madame Valmondé bent her portly figure over Désirée and kissed
her, holding her an instant tenderly in her arms. Then she turned to the
child.

"This is not the baby!" she exclaimed, in startled tones. French was
the language spoken at Valmondé in those days.

"I knew you would be astonished," laughed Désirée, "at the way he
has grown. The little *cochon de lait!* Look at his legs, mamma, and his
hands and fingernails,—real finger-nails. Zandrine had to cut them this
morning. Isn't it true, Zandrine?"

The woman bowed her turbaned head majestically, "Mais si,
Madame."

"And the way he cries," went on Désirée, "is deafening. Armand heard him the other day as far away as La Blanche's cabin."

Madame Valmondé had never removed her eyes from the child. She lifted it and walked with it over to the window that was lightest. She scanned the baby narrowly, then looked as searchingly at Zandrine, whose face was turned to gaze across the fields.

"Yes, the child has grown, has changed;" said Madame Valmondé, slowly, as she replaced it beside its mother. "What does Armand say?"

Désirée's face became suffused with a glow that was happiness itself.

"Oh, Armand is the proudest father in the parish, I believe, chiefly because it is a boy, to bear his name; though he says not,—that he would have loved a girl as well. But I know it isn't true. I know he says that to please me. And mamma," she added, drawing Madame Valmondé's head down to her, and speaking in a whisper, "he hasn't punished one of them—not one of them—since baby is born. Even Négrillon, who pretended to have burnt his leg that he might rest from work —he only laughed, and said Négrillon was a great scamp. Oh, mamma, I'm so happy! it frightens me."

What Désirée said was true. Marriage, and later the birth of his son, had softened Armand Aubigny's imperious and exacting nature greatly. This was what made the gentle Désirée so happy, for she loved him desperately. When he frowned she trembled, but loved him. When he smiled, she asked no greater blessing of God. But Armand's dark, handsome face had not often been disfigured by frowns since the day he fell in love with her.

When the baby was about three months old, Désirée awoke one day to the conviction that there was something in the air menacing her peace. It was at first too subtle to grasp. It had only been a disquieting suggestion; an air of mystery among the blacks; unexpected visits from far-off neighbors who could hardly account for their coming. Then a strange, an awful change in her husband's manner, which she dared not ask him to explain. When he spoke to her, it was with averted eyes, from which the old love-light seemed to have gone out. He absented himself from home; and when there, avoided her presence and that of her child, without excuse. And the very spirit of Satan seemed suddenly to take hold of him in his dealings with the slaves. Désirée was miserable enough to die.

She sat in her room, one hot afternoon, in her *peignoir*, listlessly drawing through her fingers the strands of her long, silky brown hair that hung about her shoulders. The baby, half naked, lay asleep upon her own great mahogany bed, that was like a sumptuous throne, with its satin-lined half-canopy. One of La Blanche's little quadroon boys— half naked too—stood fanning the child slowly with a fan of peacock feathers. Désirées eyes had been fixed absently and sadly upon the baby, while she was striving to penetrate the threatening mist that she felt closing about her. She looked from her child to the boy who stood beside him, and back again; over and over. "Ah!" It was a cry that she could not help; which she was not conscious of having uttered. The blood turned like ice in her veins, and a clammy moisture gathered upon her face.

She tried to speak to the little quadroon boy; but no sound would come, at first. When he heard his name uttered, he looked up, and his mistress was pointing to the door. He laid aside the great, soft fan, and obediently stole away, over the polished floor, on his bare tiptoes.

She stayed motionless, with gaze riveted upon her child, and her face the picture of fright.

Presently her husband entered the room, and without noticing her, went to a table and began to search among some papers which covered it.

"Armand," she called to him, in a voice which must have stabbed him, if he was human. But he did not notice. "Armand," she said again. Then she rose and tottered towards him. "Armand," she panted once more, clutching his arm, "look at our child. What does it mean? tell me."

He coldly but gently loosened her fingers from about his arm and thrust the hand away from him. "Tell me what it means!" she cried despairingly.

"It means," he answered lightly, "that the child is not white; it means that you are not white."

A quick conception of all that this accusation meant for her nerved her with unwonted courage to deny it. "It is a lie; it is not true, I am white! Look at my hair, it is brown; and my eyes are gray, Armand, you know they are gray. And my skin is fair," seizing his wrist. "Look at my hand; whiter than yours, Armand," she laughed hysterically.

"As white as La Blanche's," he returned cruelly; and went away leaving her alone with their child.

When she could hold a pen in her hand, she sent a despairing letter to Madame Valmondé.

"My mother, they tell me I am not white. Armand has told me I am not white. For God's sake tell them it is not true. You must know it is not true. I shall die. I must die. I cannot be so unhappy, and live."

The answer that came was as brief:

"My own Désirée: Come home to Valmondé; back to your mother who loves you. Come with your child."

When the letter reached Désirée she went with it to her husband's study, and laid it open upon the desk before which he sat. She was like a stone image: silent, white, motionless after she placed it there.

In silence he ran his cold eyes over the written words. He said nothing. "Shall I go, Armand?" she asked in tones sharp with agonized suspense.

"Yes, go."

"Do you want me to go?"

"Yes, I want you to go."

He thought Almighty God had dealt cruelly and unjustly with him; and felt, somehow, that he was paying Him back in kind when he stabbed thus into his wife's soul. Moreover he no longer loved her, because of the unconscious injury she had brought upon his home and his name.

She turned away like one stunned by a blow, and walked slowly towards the door, hoping he would call her back.

"Good-by, Armand," she moaned.

He did not answer her. That was his last blow at fate.

Désirée went in search of her child. Zandrine was pacing the sombre gallery with it. She took the little one from the nurse's arms with no word of explanation, and descending the steps, walked away, under the live-oak branches.

It was an October afternoon; the sun was just sinking. Out in the still fields the negroes were picking cotton.

Désirée had not changed the thin white garment nor the slippers which she wore. Her hair was uncovered and the sun's rays brought a golden gleam from its brown meshes. She did not take the broad, beaten road which led to the far-off plantation of Valmondé. She walked across a deserted field, where the stubble bruised her tender feet, so delicately shod, and tore her thin gown to shreds.

She disappeared among the reeds and willows that grew thick along the banks of the deep, sluggish bayou; and she did not come back again.

Some weeks later there was a curious scene enacted at L'Abri. In the centre of the smoothly swept back yard was a great bonfire. Armand Aubigny sat in the wide hallway that commanded a view of the spectacle; and it was he who dealt out to a half dozen negroes the material which kept this fire ablaze.

A graceful cradle of willow, with all its dainty furbishings, was laid upon the pyre, which had already been fed with the richness of a priceless *layette*. Then there were silk gowns, and velvet and satin ones added to these; laces, too, and embroideries; bonnets and gloves; for the *corbeille* had been of rare quality.

The last thing to go was a tiny bundle of letters; innocent little scribblings that Désirée had sent to him during the days of their espousal. There was the remnant of one back in the drawer from which he took them. But it was not Désirée's; it was part of an old letter from his mother to his father. He read it. She was thanking God for the blessing of her husband's love: —

"But, above all," she wrote, "night and day, I thank the good God for having so arranged our lives that our dear Armand will never know that his mother, who adores him, belongs to the race that is cursed with the brand of slavery."

SARAH ORNE JEWETT (1849–1909)

Born in South Berwick, Maine, Miss Jewett accompanied her father, a cultivated and humane country doctor, as he made the rounds of his patients' homes. For a writer who evokes the verities and surfaces of life along the Maine coast, this was an ideal preparation: she met a wide range of characters, and even while being charmed by their saltiness, she was persuaded of their humanity. As a girl Miss Jewett also read, and loved, Harriet Beecher Stowe's The Pearl of Orr's Island, *a fiction portraying Maine life, though with more concessions to the melodrama and self-indulgence of local color than Miss Jewett would ever allow.*

At the age of twenty Miss Jewett began to publish her stories, and in 1877, encouraged by William Dean Howells, she collected them in a volume called Deephaven. *Her finest book, from which "The Hiltons' Holiday" is taken, is* The Country of the Pointed Firs (1896), *a masterpiece in miniature.*

Miss Jewett wrote:

> When I was perhaps fifteen, the first city boarders began to make their appearance near Berwick, and the way they misconstrued the country people and made game of their peculiarities fired me with indignation. I determined to teach the world that country people were not the awkward, ignorant set these people seemed to think. I wanted the world to know their grand, simple lives; and, as far as I had a mission, when I first began to write, I think that was it.

But Miss Jewett had more than a mission, she had a keen awareness of the problems of literary craft. She knew the special problems pertaining to her special kind of fiction: "It is difficult to report the great events of New England; expression is so slight, and those few words which escape us in moments of deep feeling look meager on the printed page."

The usual perspective of Miss Jewett's stories is retrospective. A sensitive observer, clearly a version of the author herself, looks back upon the decline of the once thriving Maine country; the past is recaptured through delicate cameos of character and incident that owe their success to the utmost purity of phrasing; the tone is nostalgic yet highly disciplined, at once tender, amused, and respectful. And while the narrator is clearly no longer quite at one with these people, she is also deeply involved with them and knows from the inside their speech, their customs, and their emotions. (It is interesting to compare Miss Jewett's stories with somewhat similar ones in the lovely little book Cranford, *published in 1853, about a small and declining English town by the novelist Elizabeth Gaskell.)*

*If Miss Jewett's stories are occasionally wistful, they are rarely senti-
mental. She enjoys the Maine people, and rarely does she indulge
in the habitual fault of local-color writing, which is to hold up
provincial oddities to cosmopolitan inspection. She can be brisk
about Maine faults and sharp about Maine limitations because she
looks upon her characters as both special in cultural qualities and
universal in human traits. And she is always in control, a craftsman
choosing her words with New England frugality and scrupulousness.*

*It has been customary to speak of Miss Jewett's work as "minor," but it
is time that this misapprehension came to an end. She precisely and
faithfully rendered life in the small, with imaginative care. Why
should we condescend with words like "minor"? Sarah Orne Jewett
was one of the finest writers this country has had.*

FURTHER READING

Willa Cather, the distinguished twentieth-century novelist, edited a two-
volume edition, *The Best Stories of Sarah Orne Jewett* (1925). F. O.
Matthiessen's *Sarah Orne Jewett* (1929) is an affectionate study.

The Hiltons' Holiday (1896)

1

There was a bright, full moon in the clear sky, and the sunset was
still shining faintly in the west. Dark woods stood all about the old
Hilton farmhouse, save down the hill, westward, where lay the shadowy
fields which John Hilton, and his father before him, had cleared and
tilled with much toil,—the small fields to which they had given the
industry and even affection of their honest lives.

John Hilton was sitting on the doorstep of his house. As he moved
his head in and out of the shadows, turning now and then to speak to
his wife, who sat just within the doorway, one could see his good face,
rough and somewhat unkempt, as if he were indeed a creature of the
shady woods and brown earth, instead of the noisy town. It was late in
the long spring evening, and he had just come from the lower field as
cheerful as a boy, proud of having finished the planting of his potatoes.

"I had to do my last row mostly by feelin'," he said to his wife. "I'm
proper glad I pushed through, an' went back an' ended off after supper.
'T would have taken me a good part o' to-morrow mornin', an' broke my
day."

"'T ain't no use for ye to work yourself all to pieces, John," answered
the woman quickly. "I declare it does seem harder than ever that we

couldn't have kep' our boy; he'd been comin' fourteen years old this fall, most a grown man, and he'd work right 'longside of ye now the whole time."

"'T was hard to lose him; I do seem to miss little John," said the father sadly. "I expect there was reasons why 't was best. I feel able an' smart to work; my father was a girt strong man, an' a monstrous worker afore me. 'T ain't that; but I was thinkin' by myself to-day what a sight o' company the boy would ha' been. You know, small's he was, how I could trust to leave him anywheres with the team, and how he'd beseech to go with me wherever I was goin'; always right in my tracks I used to tell 'em. Poor little John, for all he was so young he had a great deal o' judgment; he'd ha' made a likely man."

The mother sighed heavily as she sat within the shadow.

"But then there's the little girls, a sight o' help an' company," urged the father eagerly, as if it were wrong to dwell upon sorrow and loss. "Katy, she's most as good as a boy, except that she ain't very rugged. She's a real little farmer, she's helped me a sight this spring; an' you've got Susan Ellen, that makes a complete little housekeeper for ye as far as she's learnt. I don't see but we're better off than most folks, each on us having a work-mate."

"That's so, John," acknowledged Mrs. Hilton wistfully, beginning to rock steadily in her straight, splint-bottomed chair. It was always a good sign when she rocked.

"Where be the little girls so late?" asked their father. "'T is gettin' long past eight o'clock. I don't know when we've all set up so late, but it's so kind o' summer-like an' pleasant. Why, where be they gone?"

"I've told ye; only over to Becker's folks," answered the mother. "I don't see myself what keeps 'em so late; they beseeched me after supper till I let 'em go. They're all in a dazzle with the new teacher; she asked 'em to come over. They say she's unusual smart with 'rethmetic, but she has a kind of gorpen look to me. She's goin' to give Katy some pieces for her doll, but I told Katy she ought to be ashamed wantin' dolls' pieces, big as she's gettin' to be. I don't know's she ought, though; she ain't but nine this summer."

"Let her take her comfort," said the kind-hearted man. "Them things draws her to the teacher, an' makes them acquainted. Katy's shy with new folks, more so 'n Susan Ellen, who's of the business kind. Katy's shy-feelin' and wishful."

"I don't know but she is," agreed the mother slowly. "Ain't it sing'lar how well acquainted you be with that one, an' I with Susan Ellen? 'T was always so from the first. I'm doubtful sometimes our Katy ain't one that'll be like to get married—anyways not about here. She lives right with herself, but Susan Ellen ain't nothin' when she's alone, she's always after company; all the boys is waitin' on her a'ready. I ain't afraid but she'll take her pick when the time comes. I expect to see Susan Ellen well settled,—she feels grown up now,—but Katy don't care one mite 'bout none o' them things. She wants to be rovin' out o' doors. I do believe she'd stand an' hark to a bird the whole forenoon."

"Perhaps she'll grow up to be a teacher," suggested John Hilton. "She takes to her book more 'n the other one. I should like one on 'em to be a teacher same's my mother was. They're good girls as anybody's got."

"So they be," said the mother, with unusual gentleness, and the creak of her rocking-chair was heard, regular as the ticking of a clock. The night breeze stirred in the great woods, and the sound of a brook that went falling down the hillside grew louder and louder. Now and then one could hear the plaintive chirp of a bird. The moon glittered with whiteness like a winter moon, and shone upon the low-roofed house until its small window-panes gleamed like silver, and one could almost see the colors of a blooming bush of lilac that grew in a sheltered angle by the kitchen door. There was an incessant sound of frogs in the lowlands.

"Be you sound asleep, John?" asked the wife presently.

"I don't know but what I was a'most," said the tired man, starting a little. "I should laugh if I was to fall sound asleep right here on the step; 't is the bright night, I expect, makes my eyes feel heavy, an' 't is so peaceful. I was up an' dressed a little past four an' out to work. Well, well!" and he laughed sleepily and rubbed his eyes. "Where's the little girls? I'd better step along an' meet 'em."

"I wouldn't just yet; they'll get home all right, but 't is late for 'em certain. I don't want 'em keepin' Mis' Becker's folks up neither. There, le' 's wait a few minutes," urged Mrs. Hilton.

"I've be'n a-thinkin' all day I'd like to give the child'n some kind of a treat," said the father, wide awake now. "I hurried up my work 'cause I had it so in mind. They don't have the opportunities some do, an' I want 'em to know the world, an' not stay right here on the farm like a couple o'bushes."

"They're a sight better off not to be so full o' notions as some is," protested the mother suspiciously.

"Certain," answered the farmer; "but they're good, bright child'n, an' commencin' to take a sight o' notice. I want 'em to have all we can give 'em. I want 'em to see how other folks does things."

"Why, so do I,"—here the rocking-chair stopped ominously,—"but so long 's they're contented"—

"Contented ain't all in this world; hopper-toads may have that quality an' spend all their time a-blinkin'. I don't know's bein' contented is all there is to look for in a child. Ambition's somethin' to me."

"Now you've got your mind on to some plot or other." (The rocking-chair began to move again.) "Why can't you talk right out?"

"'T ain't nothin' special," answered the good man, a little ruffled; he was never prepared for his wife's mysterious powers of divination. "Well there, you do find things out the master! I only thought perhaps I'd take 'em to-morrow, an' go off somewhere if 't was a good day. I've been promisin' for a good while I'd take 'em to Topham Corners; they've never been there since they was very small."

"I believe you want a good time yourself. You ain't never got over bein' a boy." Mrs. Hilton seemed much amused. "There, go if you want to an' take 'em; they've got their summer hats an' new dresses. I don't know o' nothin' that stands in the way. I should sense it better if there was a circus or anythin' to go to. Why don't you wait an' let the girls pick 'em some strawberries or nice ros'berries, and then they could take an' sell 'em to the stores?"

John Hilton reflected deeply. "I should like to get me some good yellow-turnip seed to plant late. I ain't more 'n satisfied with what I've been gettin' o' late years o' Ira Speed. An I'm goin' to provide me with a good hoe; mine's gettin' wore out an' all shackly. I can't seem to fix it good."

"Them's excuses," observed Mrs. Hilton, with friendly tolerance. "You just cover up the hoe with somethin', if you get it—I would. Ira Speed's so jealous he'll remember it of you this twenty year, your goin' an' buyin' a new hoe o' anybody but him."

"I've always thought 't was a free country," said John Hilton soberly. "I don't want to vex Ira neither; he favors us all he can in trade. 'T is difficult for him to spare a cent, but he's as honest as daylight."

At this moment there was a sudden sound of young voices, and a pair of young figures came out from the shadow of the woods into the moonlighted open space. An old cock crowed loudly from his perch in the shed, as if he were a herald of royalty. The little girls were hand in hand, and a brisk young dog capered about them as they came.

"Wa'n't it dark gittin' home through the woods this time o' night?" asked the mother hastily, and not without reproach.

"I don't love to have you gone so late; mother an' me was timid about ye, and you've kep' Mis' Becker's folks up, I expect," said their father regretfully. "I don't want to have it said that my little girls ain't got good manners."

"The teacher had a party," chirped Susan Ellen, the elder of the two children. "Goin' home from school she asked the Grover boys, an' Mary an' Sarah Speed. An' Mis' Becker was real pleasant to us: she passed round some cake, an' handed us sap sugar on one of her best plates, an' we played games an' sung some pieces too. Mis' Becker thought we did real well. I can pick out most of a tune on the cabinet organ; teacher says she'll give me lessons."

"I want to know, dear!" exclaimed John Hilton.

"Yes, an' we played Copenhagen, an' took sides spellin', an' Katy beat everybody spellin' there was there."

Katy had not spoken; she was not so strong as her sister, and while Susan Ellen stood a step or two away addressing her eager little audience, Katy had seated herself close to her father on the doorstep. He put his arm around her shoulders, and drew her close to his side, where she stayed.

"Ain't you got nothin' to tell, daughter?" he asked, looking down fondly; and Katy gave a pleased little sigh for answer.

"Tell 'em what's goin' to be the last day o' school, and about our trimmin' the schoolhouse," she said; and Susan Ellen gave the programme in most spirited fashion.

"'T will be a great time," said the mother, when she had finished. "I don't see why folks wants to go trapesin' off to strange places when such things is happenin' right about 'em." But the children did not observe her mysterious air. "Come, you must step yourselves right to bed!"

They all went into the dark, warm house; the bright moon shone upon it steadily all night, and the lilac flowers were shaken by no breath of wind until the early dawn.

2

The Hiltons always waked early. So did their neighbors, the crows and song-sparrows and robins, the lightfooted foxes and squirrels in the woods. When John Hilton waked, before five o'clock, an hour later than usual because he had sat up so late, he opened the house door and came out into the yard, crossing the short green turf hurriedly as if the day were too far spent for any loitering. The magnitude of the plan for taking a whole day of pleasure confronted him seriously, but the weather was fair, and his wife, whose disapproval could not have been set aside, had accepted and even smiled upon the great project. It was inevitable now, that he and the children should go to Topham Corners. Mrs. Hilton had the pleasure of waking them, and telling the news.

In a few minutes they came frisking out to talk over the great plans. The cattle were already fed, and their father was milking. The only sign of high festivity was the wagon pulled out into the yard, with both seats put in as if it were Sunday; but Mr. Hilton still wore his every-day clothes, and Susan Ellen suffered instantly from disappointment.

"Ain't we goin', father?" she asked complainingly; but he nodded and smiled at her, even though the cow, impatient to get to pasture, kept whisking her rough tail across his face. He held his head down and spoke cheerfully, in spite of this vexation.

"Yes, sister, we're goin' certain', an' goin' to have a great time too." Susan Ellen thought that he seemed like a boy at that delightful moment, and felt new sympathy and pleasure at once. "You go an' help mother about breakfast an' them things; we want to get off quick 's we can. You coax mother now, both on ye, an' see if she won't go with us."

"She said she wouldn't be hired to," responded Susan Ellen. "She says it's goin' to be hot, an' she's laid out to go over an' see how her aunt Tamsen Brooks is this afternoon."

The father gave a little sigh; then he took heart again. The truth was that his wife made light of the contemplated pleasure, and, much as he usually valued her companionship and approval, he was sure that they should have a better time without her. It was impossible, however, not to feel guilty of disloyalty at the thought. Even though she might be completely unconscious of his best ideals, he only loved her and the ideals the more, and bent his energies to satisfying her indefinite expectations. His wife still kept much of that youthful beauty which Susan Ellen seemed likely to reproduce.

An hour later the best wagon was ready, and the great expedition set forth. The little dog sat apart, and barked as if it fell entirely upon him to voice the general excitement. Both seats were in the wagon, but the empty place testified to Mrs. Hilton's unyielding disposition. She had wondered why one broad seat would not do, but John Hilton meekly suggested that the wagon looked better with both. The little girls sat on the back seat dressed alike in their Sunday hats of straw with blue ribbons, and their little plaid shawls pinned neatly about their small shoulders. They wore gray thread gloves, and sat very straight. Susan Ellen was half a head the taller, but otherwise, from behind, they looked much alike. As for their father, he was in his Sunday best,—a plain black coat, and a winter hat of felt, which was heavy and rusty-looking for that warm early summer day. He had it in mind to buy a new straw hat at Topham, so that this with the turnip seed and the hoe made three important reasons for going.

"Remember an' lay off your shawls when you get there, an' carry them over your arms," said the mother, clucking like an excited hen to her chickens. "They'll do to keep the dust off your new dresses goin' an' comin'. An' when you eat your dinners don't get spots on you, an' don't point at folks as you ride by, an' stare, or they'll know you come from the country. An' John, you call into Cousin Ad'line Marlow's an' see how they all be, an' tell her I expect her over certain to stop awhile before hayin'. It always eases her phthisic to git up here on the highland, an I've got a new notion about doin' over her best-room carpet sence I see her that'll save rippin' one breadth. An' don't come home all wore out; an', John, don't you go an' buy me no kick-shaws to fetch home. I ain't a child, an' you ain't got no money to waste. I expect you'll go, like 's not, an' buy you some kind of a foolish boy's hat; do look an' see if it's reasonable good straw, an' won't splinter all off round the edge. An' you mind, John"—

"Yes, yes, hold on!" cried John impatiently; then he cast a last affectionate, reassuring look at her face, flushed with the hurry and responsibility of starting them off in proper shape. "I wish you was goin' too," he said, smiling. "I do so!" Then the old horse started, and they went out at the bars, and began the careful long descent of the hill. The young dog, tethered to the lilac-bush, was frantic with piteous appeals; the little girls piped their eager good-bys again and again, and their father turned many times to look back and wave his hand. As for their mother, she stood alone and watched them out of sight.

There was one place far out on the high-road where she could catch a last glimpse of the wagon, and she waited what seemed a very long time until it appeared and then was lost to sight again behind a low hill. "They're nothin' but a pack o' child'n together," she said aloud; and then felt lonelier than she expected. She even stooped and patted the unresigned little dog as she passed him, going into the house.

The occasion was so much more important than any one had foreseen that both the little girls were speechless. It seemed at first like going to church in new clothes, or to a funeral; they hardly knew how to behave at the beginning of a whole day of pleasure. They made grave bows at such persons of their acquaintance as happened to be straying in the road. Once or twice they stopped before a farmhouse, while their father talked an inconsiderately long time with some one about the crops and the weather, and even dwelt upon town business and the doings of the select-men, which might be talked of at any time. The explanations that he gave of their excursion seemed quite unnecessary. It was made entirely clear that he had a little business to do at Topham Corners, and thought he had better give the little girls a ride; they had been very steady at school, and he had finished planting, and could take the day as well as not. Soon, however, they all felt as if such an excursion were an every-day affair, and Susan Ellen began to ask eager questions, while Katy silently sat apart enjoying herself as she never had done before. She liked to see the strange houses, and the children who belonged to them; it was delightful to find flowers that she knew growing all along the road, no matter how far she went from home. Each small homestead looked its best and pleasantest, and shared the exquisite beauty that early summer made,—shared the luxury of greenness and floweriness that decked the rural world. There was an early peony or a late lilac in almost every dooryard.

It was seventeen miles to Topham. After a while they seemed very far from home, having left the hills far behind, and descended to a great level country with fewer tracts of woodland, and wider fields where the crops were much more forward. The houses were all painted, and the roads were smoother and wider. It had been so pleasant driving along that Katy dreaded going into the strange town when she first caught sight of it, though Susan Ellen kept asking with bold fretfulness if they were not almost there. They counted the steeples of four churches, and their father presently showed them the Topham Academy, where their grandmother once went to school, and told them that perhaps some day they would go there too. Katy's heart gave a strange leap; it was such a tremendous thing to think of, but instantly the suggestion was transformed for her into one of the certainties of life. She looked with solemn awe at the tall belfry, and the long rows of windows in the front of the academy, there where it stood high and white among the clustering trees. She hoped that they were going to drive by, but something forbade her taking the responsibility of saying so.

Soon the children found themselves among the crowded village houses. Their father turned to look at them with affectionate solicitude.

"Now sit up straight and appear pretty," he whispered to them. "We're among the best people now, an' I want folks to think well of you."

"I guess we're as good as they be," remarked Susan Ellen, looking at some innocent passers-by with dark suspicion, but Katy tried indeed to sit straight, and folded her hands prettily in her lap, and wished with all her heart to be pleasing for her father's sake. Just then an elderly woman saw the wagon and the sedate party it carried, and smiled so kindly that it seemed to Katy as if Topham Corners had welcomed and received them. She smiled back again as if this hospitable person were an old friend, and entirely forgot that the eyes of all Topham had been upon her.

"There, now we're coming to an elegant house that I want you to see; you'll never forget it," said John Hilton. "It's where Judge Masterson lives, the great lawyer; the handsomest house in the county, everybody says."

"Do you know him, father?" asked Susan Ellen.

"I do," answered John Hilton proudly. "Him and my mother went to school together in their young days, and were always called the two best scholars of their time. The judge called to see her once; he stopped to our house to see her when I was a boy. An' then, some years ago— you've heard me tell how I was on the jury, an' when he heard my name spoken he looked at me sharp, and asked if I wa'n't the son of Catharine Winn, an' spoke most beautiful of your grandmother, an' how well he remembered their young days together."

"I like to hear about that," said Katy.

"She had it pretty hard, I'm afraid, up on the old farm. She was keepin' school in our district when father married her—that's the main reason I backed 'em down when they wanted to tear the old schoolhouse all to pieces," confided John Hilton, turning eagerly. "They all say she lived longer up here on the hill than she could anywhere, but she never had her health. I wa'n't but a boy when she died. Father an' me lived alone afterward till the time your mother come; 't was a good while, too; I wa'n't married so young as some. 'T was lonesome, I tell you; father was plumb discouraged losin' of his wife, an' her long sickness an' all set him back, an' we'd work all day on the land an' never say a word. I s'pose 't is bein' so lonesome early in life that makes me so pleased to have some nice girls growin' up round me now."

There was a tone in her father's voice that drew Katy's heart toward him with new affection. She dimly understood, but Susan Ellen was less interested. They had often heard this story before, but to one child it was always new and to the other old. Susan Ellen was apt to think it tiresome to hear about her grandmother, who, being dead, was hardly worth talking about.

"There's Judge Masterson's place," said their father in an every-day manner, as they turned a corner, and came into full view of the beautiful old white house standing behind its green trees and terraces and lawns. The children had never imagined anything so stately and fine, and even Susan Ellen exclaimed with pleasure. At that moment they saw an old gentleman, who carried himself with great dignity, coming slowly down the wide box-bordered path toward the gate.

"There he is now, there's the judge!" whispered John Hilton excitedly, reining his horse quickly to the green roadside. "He's goin' downtown to his office; we can wait right here an' see him. I can't expect him to remember me; it's been a good many years. Now you are goin' to see the great Judge Masterson!"

There was a quiver of expectation in their hearts. The judge stopped at his gate, hesitating a moment before he lifted the latch, and glanced up the street at the country wagon with its two prim little girls on the back seat, and the eager man who drove. They seemed to be waiting for something; the old horse was nibbling at the fresh roadside grass. The Judge was used to being looked at with interest, and responded now with a smile as he came out to the sidewalk, and unexpectedly turned their way. Then he suddenly lifted his hat with grave politeness, and came directly toward them.

"Good-morning, Mr. Hilton," he said. "I am very glad to see you, sir;" and Mr. Hilton, the little girls' own father, took off his hat with equal courtesy, and bent forward to shake hands.

Susan Ellen cowered and wished herself away, but little Katy sat straighter than ever, with joy in her father's pride and pleasure shining in her pale, flower-like little face.

"These are your daughters, I am sure," said the old gentleman kindly, taking Susan Ellen's limp and reluctant hand; but when he looked at Katy, his face brightened. "How she recalls your mother!" he said with great feeling. "I am glad to see this dear child. You must come to see me with your father, my dear," he added, still looking at her. "Bring both the little girls, and let them run about the old garden; the cherries are just getting ripe," said Judge Masterson hospitably. "Perhaps you will have time to stop this afternoon as you go home?"

"I should call it a great pleasure if you would come and see us again some time. You may be driving our way, sir," said John Hilton.

"Not very often in these days," answered the old judge. "I thank you for the kind invitation. I should like to see the fine view again from your hill westward. Can I serve you in any way while you are in town? Good-by, my little friends!"

Then they parted, but not before Katy, the shy Katy, whose hand the judge still held unconsciously while he spoke, had reached forward as he said good-by, and lifted her face to kiss him. She could not have told why, except that she felt drawn to something in the serious, worn face. For the first time in her life the child had felt the charm of manners; perhaps she owned a kinship between that which made him what

he was, and the spark of nobleness and purity in her own simple soul.
She turned again and again to look back at him as they drove away.

"Now you have seen one of the first gentlemen in the country," said
their father. "It was worth comin' twice as far"—but he did not say any
more, nor turn as usual to look in the children's faces.

In the chief business street of Topham a great many country wagons like
the Hiltons' were fastened to the posts, and there seemed to our holiday-
makers to be a great deal of noise and excitement.

"Now I've got to do my errands, and we can let the horse rest and
feed," said John Hilton. "I'll slip his headstall right off, an' put on his
halter. I'm goin' to buy him a real good treat o' oats. First we'll go an'
buy me my straw hat; I feel as if this one looked a little past to wear
in Topham. We'll buy the things we want, an' then we'll walk all along
the street, so you can look in the windows an' see the han'some things,
same's your mother likes to. What was it mother told you about your
shawls?"

"To take 'em off an' carry 'em over our arms," piped Susan Ellen,
without comment, but in the interest of alighting and finding themselves
afoot upon the pavement the shawls were forgotten. The children stood
at the doorway of a shop while their father went inside, and they tried
to see what the Topham shapes of bonnets were like, as their mother
had advised them; but everything was exciting and confusing, and they
could arrive at no decision. When Mr. Hilton came out with a hat in his
hand to be seen in a better light, Katy whispered that she wished he
would buy a shiny one like Judge Masterson's; but her father only smiled
and shook his head, and said that they were plain folks, he and Katy.
There were dry-goods for sale in the same shop, and a young clerk who
was measuring linen kindly pulled off some pretty labels with gilded
edges and gay pictures, and gave them to the little girls, to their exceeding joy. He may have had small sisters at home, this friendly lad, for
he took pains to find two pretty blue boxes besides, and was rewarded
by their beaming gratitude.

It was a famous day; they even became used to seeing so many people
pass. The village was full of its morning activity, and Susan Ellen gained
a new respect for her father, and an increased sense of her own consequence, because even in Topham several persons knew him and called
him familiarly by name. The meeting with an old man who had once
been a neighbor seemed to give Mr. Hilton the greatest pleasure. The
old man called to them from a house doorway as they were passing, and
they all went in. The children seated themselves wearily on the wooden
step, but their father shook his old friend eagerly by the hand, and declared that he was delighted to see him so well and enjoying the fine
weather.

"Oh, yes," said the old man, in a feeble, quavering voice, "I'm astonishin' well for my age. I don't complain, John, I don't complain."

They talked long together of people whom they had known in the past, and Katy, being a little tired, was glad to rest, and sat still with her hands folded, looking about the front yard. There were some kinds of flowers that she never had seen before.

"This is the one that looks like my mother," her father said, and touched Katy's shoulder to remind her to stand up and let herself be seen. "Judge Masterson saw the resemblance; we met him at his gate this morning."

"Yes, she certain does look like your mother, John," said the old man, looking pleasantly at Katy, who found that she liked him better than at first. "She does, certain; the best of young folks is, they remind us of the old ones. 'T is nateral to cling to life, folks say, but for me, I git impatient at time. Most everybody's gone now, an' I want to be goin'. 'T is somethin' before me, an' I want to have it over with. I want to be there 'long o' the rest o' the folks. I expect to last quite a while though; I may see ye couple o' times more, John."

John Hilton responded cheerfully, and the children were urged to pick some flowers. The old man awed them with his impatience to be gone. There was such a townful of people about him, and he seemed as lonely as if he were the last survivor of a former world. Until that moment they had felt as if everything were just beginning.

"Now I want to buy somethin' pretty for your mother," said Mr. Hilton, as they went soberly away down the street, the children keeping fast hold of his hands. "By now the old horse will have eat his dinner and had a good rest, so pretty soon we can jog along home. I'm goin' to take you round by the academy, and the old North Meetinghouse where Dr. Barstow used to preach. Can't you think o' somethin' that your mother'd want?" he asked suddenly, confronted by a man's difficulty of choice.

"She was talkin' about wantin' a new pepper-box, one day; the top o' the old one won't stay on," suggested Susan Ellen, with delightful readiness. "Can't we have some candy, father?"

"Yes, ma'am," said John Hilton, smiling and swinging her hand to and fro as they walked. "I feel as if some would be good myself. What's all this?" They were passing a photographer's doorway with its enticing array of portraits. "I do declare!" he exclaimed excitedly, "I'm goin' to have our pictures taken; 't will please your mother more 'n a little."

This was, perhaps, the greatest triumph of the day, except the delightful meeting with the judge; they sat in a row, with the father in the middle, and there was no doubt as to the excellence of the likeness. The best hats had to be taken off because they cast a shadow, but they were not missed, as their owners had feared. Both Susan Ellen and Katy looked their brightest and best; their eager young faces would forever shine there; the joy of the holiday was mirrored in the little picture. They did not know why their father was so pleased with it; they would not know until age had dowered them with the riches of association and remembrance.

Just at nightfall the Hiltons reached home again, tired out and happy. Katy had climbed over into the front seat beside her father, because that was always her place when they went to church on Sundays. It was a cool evening, there was a fresh sea wind that brought a light mist with it, and the sky was fast growing cloudy. Somehow the children looked different; it seemed to their mother as if they had grown older and taller since they went away in the morning, and as if they belonged to the town now as much as to the country. The greatness of their day's experience had left her far behind; the day had been silent and lonely without them, and she had had their supper ready, and been watching anxiously, ever since five o'clock. As for the children themselves they had little to say at first—they had eaten their luncheon early on the way to Topham. Susan Ellen was childishly cross, but Katy was pathetic and wan. They could hardly wait to show the picture, and their mother was as much pleased as everybody had expected.

"There, what did make you wear your shawls?" she exclaimed a moment afterward, reproachfully. "You ain't been an' wore 'em all day long? I wanted folks to see how pretty your new dresses was, if I did make 'em. Well, well! I wish more'n ever now I'd gone an' seen to ye!"

"An here's the pepper-box!" said Katy, in a pleased, unconscious tone.

"That really is what I call beautiful," said Mrs. Hilton, after a long and doubtful look. "Our other one was only tin. I never did look so high as a chiny one with flowers, but I can get us another any time for every day. That's a proper hat, as good as you could have got, John. Where's your new hoe?" she asked as he came toward her from the barn, smiling with satisfaction.

"I declare to Moses if I didn't forget all about it," meekly acknowledged the leader of the great excursion. "That an' my yellow-turnip seed, too; they went clean out o' my head, there was so many other things to think of. But 't ain't no sort o' matter; I can get a hoe just as well to Ira Speed's."

His wife could not help laughing. "You an' the little girls have had a great time. They was full o' wonder to me about everything, and I expect they'll talk about it for a week. I guess we was right about havin' 'em see somethin' more o' the world."

"Yes," answered John Hilton, with humility, "yes, we did have a beautiful day. I didn't expect so much. They looked as nice as anybody, and appeared so modest an' pretty. The little girls will remember it perhaps by an' by. I guess they won't never forget this day they had 'long o' father."

It was evening again, the frogs were piping in the lower meadows, and in the woods, higher up the great hill, a little owl began to hoot. The sea air, salt and heavy, was blowing in over the country at the end of the hot bright day. A lamp was lighted in the house, the happy children were talking together, and supper was waiting. The father and mother lingered for a moment outside and looked down over the shadowy fields; then they went in, without speaking. The great day was over, and they shut the door.

JOHN HAY (1838–1905)

Born in Pike County, Illinois, Hay graduated from Brown University, then practiced law in Springfield in an office next door to Lincoln's. When Lincoln was elected President, Hay went along as his assistant. After the war, he served as legation secretary in Paris, Vienna, and Madrid.

Returning to the United States, he joined the staff of the New York Tribune, where some of his Pike County ballads were first published. Hay employed a strong and swinging ballad meter to tell the tales of Jim Bludso, a Mississippi steamboat captain, and other rough-and-tumble Midwestern characters. He also tried to simulate local dialects. Later, when he became United States Ambassador to Great Britain and then Secretary of State under McKinley and Theodore Roosevelt, Hay was embarrassed by the widespread popularity of these ballads, sometimes quoted to him even by literary figures in Europe.

FURTHER READING
Tyler Dennett, *John Hay from Poetry to Politics* (1934).

Jim Bludso (1899)

Of the Prairie Belle

Wall, no! I can't tell whar he lives,
    Because he don't live, you see;
Leastways, he's got out of the habit
    Of livin' like you and me.
Whar have you been for the last three year
    That you have n't heard folks tell
How Jimmy Bludso passed in his checks
    The night of the Prairie Belle?

He were n't no saint,—them engineers
    Is all pretty much alike,—
One wife in Natchez-under-the-Hill   *10*
    And another one here, in Pike;
A keerless man in his talk was Jim,
    And an awkward hand in a row,
But he never flunked, and he never lied,—
    I reckon he never knowed how.

And this was all the religion he had,—
    To treat his engine well;
Never be passed on the river;
    To mind the pilot's bell;   *20*
And if ever the Prairie Belle took fire,—
    A thousand times he swore,
He'd hold her nozzle agin the bank
    Till the last soul got ashore.

All boats has their day on the Mississip,
    And her day come at last,—
The Movastar was a better boat,
    But the Belle she *would n't* be passed.
And so she come tearin' along that night—
    The oldest craft on the line—   *30*
With a nigger squat on her safety-valve,
    And her furnace crammed, rosin and pine.

The first bust out as she clared the bar,
    And burnt a hole in the night,
And quick as a flash she turned, and made
    For that willer-bank on the right.
There was runnin' and cursin', but Jim yelled out,
    Over all the infernal roar,
"I'll hold her nozzle agin the bank
    Till the last galoot's ashore."   *40*

Through the hot, black breath of the burnin' boat
    Jim Bludso's voice was heard,
And they all had trust in his cussedness,
    And knowed he would keep his word.
And, sure's you're born, they all got off
    Afore the smokestacks fell,—
And Bludso's ghost went up alone
    In the smoke of the Prairie Belle.

He were n't no saint,—but at jedgment
    I'd run my chance with Jim,   *50*
'Longside of some pious gentlemen
    That would n't shook hands with him.

He seen his duty, a dead-sure thing,—
    And went for it thar and then;
And Christ ain't a-going to be too hard
    On a man that died for men.

Little Breeches *(1899)*

I don't go much on religion,
    I never ain't had no show;
But I've got a middlin' tight grip, sir,
    On the handful o' things I know.
I don't pan out on the prophets
    And free-will, and that sort of thing,—
But I b'lieve in God and the angels,
    Ever sence one night last spring.

I come into town with some turnips,
    And my little Gabe come along,—   *10*
No four-year-old in the county
    Could beat him for pretty and strong,
Peart and chipper and sassy,
    Always ready to swear and fight,—
And I'd larnt him to chaw terbacker
    Jest to keep his milk-teeth white.

The snow come down like a blanket
    As I passed by Taggart's store;
I went in for a jug of molasses
    And left the team at the door.   *20*
They scared at something and started,—
    I heard one little squall,
And hell-to-split over the prairie
    Went team, Little Breeches, and all.

Hell-to-split over the prairie!
    I was almost froze with skeer;
But we rousted up some torches,
    And sarched for 'em far and near.
At last we struck hosses and wagon,
    Snowed under a soft white mound,   *30*
Upsot, dead beat,—but of little Gabe
    No hide nor hair was found.

And here all hope soured on me,
    Of my fellow-critter's aid,—
I jest flopped down on my marrow-bones,
    Crotch-deep in the snow, and prayed.

By this, the torches was played out,
    And me and Isrul Parr
Went off for some wood to a sheepfold
    That he said was somewhar thar.   *40*

We found it at last, and a little shed
    Where they shut up the lambs at night.
We looked in and seen them huddled thar,
    So warm and sleepy and white;
And thar sot Little Breeches and chirped,
    As peart as ever you see,
"I want a chaw of terbacker,
    And that's what's the matter of me."

How did he git thar? Angels.
    He could never have walked in that storm;   *50*
They jest scooped down and toted him
    To whar it was safe and warm.
And I think that saving a little child,
    And fotching him to his own,
Is a derned sight better business
    Than loafing around the Throne.

MARK TWAIN (1835–1910)

*In the life and work of a good many American writers there is a pattern
so recurrent it cannot be dismissed as merely accidental: the career
that begins with buoyant energy, full of pleasure and democratic
optimism, ends despairingly, full of bitterness and misanthropy.
Sometimes, as in Melville's* Billy Budd, *there is a culminating resolution: the old writer, weary of his earlier struggles and skepticisms,
comes to accept the world as it is; he makes his peace. But with a
writer like Mark Twain, who in his best fiction is the master of the
American idyll, the final vision of life is bleak, angry, unreconciled.*

*Samuel Clemens (Mark Twain was his pen name, adopted while working
on a Nevada newspaper) was born in Florida, Missouri, then a frontier settlement of a few log cabins. When he was four years old, the
family moved to Hannibal, Missouri, a river town boasting 500
souls and sharing in the prosperity of the Mississippi. For the next
six or seven years the Clemens's lived in Hannibal, and it was from
those years that Twain would draw his most precious memories.
From them he would recall the melancholy and loneliness of the
woods, the idleness of loafers on sleepy streets, the residual pieties
of transplanted New Englanders trying to live right, the hustle and
noise when boats would stop at the town wharf.*

*He was eleven when his father died, and to keep the family afloat he
was apprenticed to a printer. Shortly afterward he began almost two
years of personal wandering—and, it turned out, literary preparation. He was a printer in river towns (Keokuk, Iowa, St. Louis, and
Cincinnati), as well as in New York, Philadelphia, and Washington.
He learned to pilot a steamboat between St. Louis and New Orleans,
a skill that enabled him to earn good money and of which he would
always be extremely proud. During the Civil War he spent a few
weeks in a Confederate unit, but he clearly had little enthusiasm
for the South (he always spoke with horror of slavery) and less for
soldiering. So he headed West, prospecting in Nevada and becoming
a reporter for the Virginia City* Territorial Enterprise.

*By now Twain had been apprenticed to three trades—printing, piloting,
and mining—and each would contribute something to his career as
writer. In those days printers were often men of quasiliterary incli-
nations, from whom one could learn more than just how to set a
line of type. Piloting was an occupation for men of independence, a
craft and maybe an art, which Twain would later celebrate in one
of his best books. The days he spent out West helped him too, for
he got to know a wide range of native types, to say nothing of home-
grown eccentrics, whom he would depict in his books. And the raw
journalism of the West could teach a young man to compose with
speed and economy.*

*In 1870 Twain married Olivia Langdon, a wealthy and genteel young
lady from Elmira, New York. Over the decades Olivia has been given
rough treatment by some of Twain's biographers and critics who
have blamed her for censoring Twain's language, bringing him into
a world of Eastern swells uncongenial to his talent and character,
and in effect, taming his native genius. Twain's own conventional
adoration of his wife—"I would quit wearing socks if she thought
them immoral"—contributed to this impression. Mostly, however,
these biographers and critics are wrong. Twain's language remained
firmly under his own command and he had quite as great a distaste
for the off-color phrase (at least in print) as did his wife. He himself
wanted to enter the company of the Eastern swells, both financial
and cultural—for if he was sometimes a caustic rebel against commercial standards, he could also be uncritically subservient to the
values of "success." It is not clear that being lionized in Boston really
hurt Twain as a writer, but if it did, Olivia is hardly to blame. And
as for taming him, he was in this respect the archetypal American
husband: he wanted, he demanded to be tamed. Instead of wondering whether his wife kept Twain from writing more great books
than he did, it might be profitable to wonder how, or whether, she
helped him write the great books that he did.*

After their marriage the couple moved to Hartford in 1871 and, encour-

aged by the success of his early books, built an enormous and expensive house. There Twain lived—prosperous, happy, and productive—until the panic of 1893 caught him financially overextended. Having invested heavily in a typesetting machine and in his own printing firm, Twain faced ruin until a Standard Oil executive took over and straightened out his affairs. By prolonged lecturing abroad, Twain then earned enough to repay his creditors.

The final years were hard. One of his daughters suffered from epileptic seizures, another died suddenly of spinal meningitis. Olivia died in 1904 after a long illness, and Twain, a dedicated family man, found himself lonely and adrift. He was famous, he was comfortable, he was honored (he went to Oxford for a degree and found pleasure in the scarlet robes: "I like the degree well enough, but I'm crazy about the clothes."). But he still had to face the common lot of weary bones and failing powers. His last writings, many of them left in fragmentary form, are explosions of wrath, sometimes merely of irritation, against the stupidity of the human race; fierce denunciations of American imperialist policies at the turn of the century; and exercises in a rather crude philosophical determinism not always to be distinguished from cracker-barrel agnosticism.

Mark Twain's triumphant entry into our literature marks the cultural emergence of a new area of American life, the midcontinental heartland. As a distinctive region, the Mississippi Valley represented something sharply different from the Eastern seaboard. Its economy, its social relationships, its geographic sense, its cultural tone, its very use of the English language—all were more insular and plebeian, rough and self-sufficient than those of the New England or mid-Atlantic states. The mark of the pioneer was still visible, the memory of the Indians still strong. And the literature that began to be composed in this part of the country was naturally distinctive, too. One of Twain's best critics, Bernard De Voto, has remarked:

It is absurd to speak of this as the first American literature that was independent of European influences, for our literature had obediently divorced itself from Europe as soon as Emerson ordered it to. The humorous core of Innocents Abroad was not independence of Europe, but indifference to it. Thoreau and Emerson and Poe were detached from Europe but completely aware of being heirs to it, but here was a literature which had grown up in disregard of Europe—which had looked inward toward the Mississippi and not outward toward the Atlantic.

Twain's first book, Innocents Abroad *(1869), is a humorous, sometimes raucously slapstick, account of a travel journey undertaken by a group of Americans innocently persuaded that no marvel of the Old World can compare with the comforts of the New. Its irreverent, even disdainful, tone toward European culture marks it as a book no Bostonian or New Yorker could have written.* Innocents Abroad *contains a wide streak of philistinism, reflecting a bit too accurately the values of the region from which Twain derived, but there is also, it must be admitted, a kind of relief to be gained from its happy-go-lucky dismissal of Europe.*

The work of the early Twain is marked above all by exuberance, the energy and gaiety of a man who does not feel the weight of the past heavy on his shoulders, who believes implicitly in the good nature of himself, his characters, and his readers, and who, almost unawares, exudes the self-delight of a burgeoning young culture. Between Twain's early—and to a lesser extent, his late—work one can detect several subliterary traditions:

The humor of the old Southwest (discussed in the General Introduction, pages 14 to 15), which provided him with some of his basic materials and techniques—the tall tale, the deadpan spinner of the tall tale whose glum manner serves to accentuate the extravagance of what he is recounting, the contrast between the accomplished prose the author is capable of employing, and the picturesque dialect of his backwoods characters

The tradition of Western story telling, with its pleasure in physical experience, its easy-going acceptance of rogues and worse, its mockery of the tenderfoot from back East, its friendly commerce with the natural world, and its freedom from Eastern nail-biting moralism

The work of the professional humorists like Artemus Ward and Josh Billings, skillful vaudevillians touring the lecture circuits and doing pieces for the newspapers in which they would pose as semiliterates running a seven-year war against traditional spelling, but still notable for their shrewd common sense

Twain soon moved beyond these cultural sources. Roughing It *(1872), a lively book about the old West, still employs the formulas of the popular humorists; Twain can clown with the best of them, and his account of a visit to a Mormon elder besieged by wives and noisy children is one of the funniest pieces ever written by an American. But he is also developing new resources, touches of ironic observation about the mores and manners of the West, passages of nostalgia for earlier pioneer days unsullied by money grubbing, and a prose style notable for its freshness and clarity.*

Early in his career Twain became the darling of the American public, the kind of writer often called a "culture hero." By this we mean a writer who speaks both for and to an entire culture, articulating its deepest values and winning the adoration of its entire range of audiences. What Twain expressed in his earlier writing with both good nature and ironic sharpness was the notion, deeply grounded in American folklore, that in the West life was more "natural" and

*men more unspoiled than in the effete and "cultured" East. West-
erners of course loved this, feeling that after all those decades of
Boston tyranny, their day in American writing had finally come.
Easterners liked it too, for it spoke to their nostalgia for a simpler—
and did not simpler mean better?—America, no longer to be found
along the Atlantic but movingly evoked in Twain's books.*

*Twain wrote a lot, and much of what he wrote is second rate or worse.
He had uncertain critical faculties in regard to his own work, and
to the end of his life he believed that his soupy book on Joan of Arc
was his best. But in addition to a pleasing book like* Roughing It *and
a distinguished near-miss like* Puddn'head Wilson *(1894), there are
three volumes on which his claim to greatness finally rests.*

The first is Old Times on the Mississippi *(1875) a recollection of the
pre-Civil War Mississippi Valley which De Voto has rightly called
"a study in pure ecstacy." There are few books in American or any
other literature which describe so well the state of human contentment with a job well done, which celebrate so finely the values of
craft and work. And few books use the English language to such
disciplined effect—here indeed is the beginning of the American
style, colloquial but not scrappy, relaxed but not sprawling, vivid
but not exhibitionist. It is a style that derives from but transcends
speech: it has the directness and ease we like to associate with,
though in fact are rarely present in, speech. Anyone who wants to
learn to write English well could do no better than to study* Old
Times on the Mississippi.

The second is Tom Sawyer *(1876), a boy's book but also an American
masterpiece: the idyll of the average boy, geared to the nostalgia,
fantasies, and decent limitations of the average man.*

The third of Twain's major achievements is of course Huckleberry Finn
*(1884), by common consent one of the world's great books. Discussed
in the General Introduction (pages 37 to 39,* Huckleberry Finn
*is a novel at once transparent as clear water and endlessly complex
and subtle. It is an idyll of boyhood, a parable of fraternity breaking
past the social obsessions of the race, a deadly accurate portrait of
the society of the Mississippi, an account of a boy's initiation into
the entanglements of moral judgment, a stirring dream of a moment
of perfect freedom, and a moral fable about the conflict between
friendship and conscience, humane impulse and law. The painful
contrast between the arcadian promise of early American democracy
and the disappointments brought about by its phase of industrial
and financial power would haunt Twain through all his later years;
and in* Huckleberry Finn *this theme finds oblique but unforgettable
representation. It is above all a beautiful book, and no one has
written more attractively about its language than Richard Chase:*

The book makes a music of words which is beautifully sustained and modu-

lated to the very end. The language is original and it has proved to be one of the most important discoveries—for it was discovered and adapted rather than being created out of the whole cloth—that have occurred in American literature. Hemingway's well-known pronouncement that "all modern American literature comes from one book by Mark Twain . . ." states a large truth. . . . Wherever we find, in writers such as Stephen Crane, Sherwood Anderson, Sinclair Lewis, Faulkner, or Hemingway himself, a style that flows with the easy grace of colloquial speech and gets its directness and simplicity by leaving out subordinate words and clauses, we will be right in thinking that this is the language of Mark Twain. . . . The language of Huckleberry Finn is a kind of joyous exorcism of traditional literary English, but this ritual act allies it irrevocably with what it exorcises. But it is also literary because, unlike ordinary spoken language, it is always conscious of the traditional English—notably of the Bible and Shakespeare—from which it is departing.

Of Twain's work in his late period, the period of determinism and despair, "The Man Who Corrupted Hadleyburg" (1898) is an efficient example. One should read such things with an awareness in mind of how greatly the young Twain had once hoped, how joyously he had expressed the ethos of early America. Only then can the bitterness of the late work be fully tasted.

FURTHER READING

William M. Gibson and Henry Nash Smith edited the *Mark Twain-Howells* letters in 1960. The single best critical study is Henry Nash Smith, *Mark Twain: The Development of a Writer* (1962); a fine introduction is Bernard De Voto, *The Portable Mark Twain* (1946). Also: Kenneth R. Andrew, *Nook Farm: Mark Twain's Hartford Years* (1950); Walter Blair, *Mark Twain and Huck Finn* (1960); Bernard De Voto, *Mark Twain at Work* (1942); DeLancey Ferguson, *Mark Twain: Man and Legend* (1943); Dixon Wecter, *Sam Clemens of Hannibal* (1952).

The Notorious Jumping Frog of Calaveras County (1865)

In compliance with the request of a friend of mine, who wrote me from the East, I called on good-natured, garrulous old Simon Wheeler, and inquired after my friend's friend, Leonidas W. Smiley, as requested to do, and I hereunto append the result. I have a lurking suspicion that *Leonidas* W. Smiley is a myth; that my friend never knew such a personage; and that he only conjectured that if I asked old Wheeler about him, it would remind him of his infamous *Jim* Smiley, and he would go to work and bore me to death with some exasperating reminiscence of him as long and as tedious as it should be useless to me. If that was the design, it succeeded.

I found Simon Wheeler dozing comfortably by the barroom stove of the dilapidated tavern in the decayed mining camp of Angel's, and I noticed that he was fat and bald-headed, and had an expression of winning gentleness and simplicity upon his tranquil countenance. He roused up, and gave me good day. I told him that a friend of mine had commissioned me to make some inquiries about a cherished companion of his boyhood named *Leonidas* W. Smiley—*Rev. Leonidas* W. Smiley, a young minister of the Gospel, who he had heard was at one time a resident of Angel's Camp. I added that if Mr. Wheeler could tell me anything about this Rev. Leonidas W. Smiley, I would feel under many obligations to him.

Simon Wheeler backed me into a corner and blockaded me there with his chair, and then sat down and reeled off the monotonous narrative which follows this paragraph. He never smiled, he never frowned, he never changed his voice from the gentle-flowing key to which he tuned his initial sentence, he never betrayed the slightest suspicion of enthusiasm; but all through the interminable narrative there ran a vein of impressive earnestness and sincerity, which showed me plainly that, so far from his imagining that there was anything ridiculous or funny about his story, he regarded it as a really important matter, and admired its two heroes as men of transcendent genius in *finesse*. I let him go on in his own way, and never interrupted him once.

"Rev. Leonidas W. H'm, Reverend Le—well, there was a feller here once by the name of *Jim* Smiley, in the winter of '49—or maybe it was the spring of '50—I don't recollect exactly, somehow, though what makes me think it was one or the other is because I remember the big flume warn't finished when he first come to the camp; but anyway, he was the curiousest man about always betting on anything that turned up you ever see, if he could get anybody to bet on the other side; and if he couldn't he'd change sides. Any way that suited the other man would suit *him*—any way just so's he got a bet, *he* was satisfied. But still he was lucky, uncommon lucky; he most always come out winner. He was always ready and laying for a chance; there couldn't be no solit'ry thing mentioned but that feller'd offer to bet on it, and take ary side you please, as I was just telling you. If there was a horse-race, you'd find him flush or you'd find him busted at the end of it; if there was a dog-fight, he'd bet on it; if there was a cat-fight, he'd bet on it; if there was a chicken-fight, he'd bet on it; why, if there was two birds setting on a fence, he would bet you which one would fly first; or if there was a camp-meeting, he would be there reg'lar to bet on Parson Walker, which he judged to be the best exhorter about here, and so he was too, and a good man. If he even see a straddle-bug start to go anywheres, he would bet you how long it would take him to get to—to wherever he was going to, and if you took him up, he would foller that straddle-bug to Mexico but what he would find out where he was bound for and how long he was on the road. Lots of the boys here has seen that Smiley, and can tell you about him. Why, it never made no difference to *him*—he'd bet on *any* thing—the dangdest feller. Parson Walker's wife laid very sick once, for a good while, and it seemed as if they warn't going to save her; but one morning he come in, and Smiley up and asked him how she was, and he said she was considerable better—thank the Lord for his inf'nite mercy—and coming on so smart that with the blessing of Prov'dence she'd get well yet; and Smiley, before he thought, says, 'Well, I'll resk two-and-a-half she don't anyway.'

"Thish-yer Smiley had a mare—the boys called her the fifteen-minute nag, but that was only in fun, you know, because of course she was faster than that—and he used to win money on that horse, for all she was so slow and always had the asthma, or the distemper, or the consumption, or something of that kind. They used to give her two or three hundred yards' start, and then pass her under way; but always at the fag end of the race she'd get excited and desperate like, and come cavorting and straddling up, and scattering her legs around limber, sometimes in the air, and sometimes out to one side among the fences, and kicking up m-o-r-e dust and raising m-o-r-e racket with her coughing and sneezing and blowing her nose—and *always* fetch up at the stand just about a neck ahead, as near as you could cipher it down.

"And he had a little small bull-pup, that to look at him you'd think he warn't worth a cent but to set around and look ornery and lay for a chance to steal something. But as soon as money was up on him he was a different dog; his under-jaw'd begin to stick out like the fo'castle of a steamboat, and his teeth would uncover and shine like the furnaces. And a dog might tackle him and bully-rag him, and bite him, and throw him over his shoulder two or three times, and Andrew Jackson—which was the name of the pup—Andrew Jackson would never let on but what *he* was satisfied, and hadn't expected nothing else—and the bets being doubled and doubled on the other side all the time, till the money was all up; and then all of a sudden he would grab that other dog jest by the j'int of his hind leg and freeze to it—not chaw, you understand, but only just grip and hang on till they throwed up the sponge, if it was a year. Smiley always come out winner on that pup, till he harnessed a dog once that didn't have no hind legs, because they'd been sawed off in a circular saw, and when the thing had gone along far enough, and the money was all up, and he come to make a snatch for his pet holt, he see in a minute how he'd been imposed on, and how the other dog had him in the door, so to speak, and he 'peared surprised, and then he looked sorter discouraged-like, and didn't try no more to win the fight, and so he got shucked out bad. He give Smiley a look, as much as to say his heart was broke, and it was *his* fault, for putting up a dog that hadn't no hind legs for him to take holt of, which was his main dependence in a fight, and then he limped off a piece and laid down and died. It was a good pup, was that Andrew Jackson, and would have made a name for hisself if he'd lived, for the stuff was in him and he had genius—I know it, because he hadn't no opportunities to speak of, and it don't stand to reason that a dog could make such a fight as he could under them circumstances if he hadn't no talent. It always makes me feel sorry when I think of that last fight of his'n, and the way it turned out.

"Well, thish-yer Smiley had rat-tarriers, and chicken cocks, and tomcats and all them kind of things, till you couldn't rest, and you couldn't fetch nothing for him to bet on but he'd match you. He ketched a frog one day, and took him home, and said he cal'lated to educate him; and so he never done nothing for three months but set in his back yard and learn that frog to jump. And you bet you he *did* learn him, too. He'd give him a little punch behind, and the next minute you'd see that frog whirling in the air like a doughnut—see him turn one summer-set, or maybe a couple, if he got a good start, and come down flat-footed and all right, like a cat. He got him up so in the matter of ketching flies, and kep' him in practice so constant, that he'd nail a fly every time as fur as he could see him. Smiley said all a frog wanted was education, and he could do 'most anything—and I believe him. Why, I've seen him set Dan'l Webster down here on this floor—Dan'l Webster was the name of the frog—and sing out, 'Flies, Dan'l, flies!' and quicker'n you could wink he'd spring straight up and snake a fly off'n the counter there, and flop down on the floor ag'in as solid as a gob of mud, and fall to scratching the side of his head with his hind foot as indifferent as if he hadn't no idea he'd been doin' any more'n any frog might do. You never see a frog so modest and straight-for'ard as he was, for all he was so gifted. And when it come to fair and square jumping on a dead level, he could get over more ground at one straddle than any animal of his breed you ever see. Jumping on a dead level was his strong suit, you understand; and when it come to that, Smiley would ante up money on him as long as he had a red. Smiley was monstrous proud of his frog, and well he might be, for fellers that had traveled and been everywheres all said he laid over any frog that ever *they* see.

"Well, Smiley kep' the beast in a little lattice box, and he used to fetch him downtown sometimes and lay for a bet. One day a feller—a stranger in the camp, he was—come acrost him with his box, and says:

"'What might it be that you've got in the box?'

"And Smiley says, sorter indifferent-like, 'It might be a parrot, or it might be a canary, maybe, but it ain't—it's only just a frog.'

"And the feller took it, and looked at it careful, and turned it round this way and that, and says, 'H'm—so 'tis. Well, what's *he* good for?'

"'Well,' Smiley says, easy and careless, 'he's good enough for *one* thing, I should judge—he can outjump any frog in Calaveras County.'

"The feller took the box again, and took another long, particular look, and give it back to Smiley, and says, very deliberate, 'Well,' he says, 'I don't see no p'ints about that frog that's any better'n any other frog.'

"'Maybe you don't,' Smiley says. 'Maybe you understand frogs and maybe you don't understand 'em; maybe you've had experience, and maybe you ain't only a amature, as it were. Anyways, I've got *my* opinion, and I'll resk forty dollars that he can outjump any frog in Calaveras County.'

"And the feller studied a minute, and then says, kinder sad-like, 'Well, I'm only a stranger here, and I ain't got no frog; but if I had a frog, I'd bet you.'

"And then Smiley says, 'That's all right—that's all right—if you'll hold my box a minute, I'll go and get you a frog.' And so the feller took the box, and put up his forty dollars along with Smiley's, and set down to wait.

"So he set there a good while thinking and thinking to himself, and then he got the frog out and prized his mouth open and took a teaspoon and filled him full of quail-shot—filled him pretty near up to his chin—and set him on the floor. Smiley he went to the swamp and slopped around in the mud for a long time, and finally he ketched a frog, and fetched him in, and give him to this feller, and says:

"'Now, if you're ready, set him alongside of Dan'l, with his fore paws just even with Dan'ls, and I'll give the word.' Then he says, 'One—two—three—*git!*' and him and the feller touched up the frogs from behind, and the new frog hopped off lively, but Dan'l give a heave, and hysted up his shoulders—so—like a Frenchman, but it warn't no use—he couldn't budge; he was planted as solid as a church, and he couldn't no more stir than if he was anchored out. Smiley was a good deal surprised, and he was digusted too, but he didn't have no idea what the matter was, of course.

"The feller took the money and started away; and when he was going out at the door, he sorter jerked his thumb over his shoulder—so—at Dan'l, and says again, very deliberate, 'Well,' he says, '*I* don't see no p'ints about that frog that's any better'n any other frog.'

"Smiley he stood scratching his head and looking down at Dan'l a long time, and at last he says, 'I do wonder what in the nation that frog throw'd off for—I wonder if there ain't something the matter with him—he 'pears to look mighty baggy, somehow.' And he ketched Dan'l by the nap of the neck, and hefted him, and says, 'Why blame my cats if he don't weigh five pound!' and turned him upside down and he belched out a double handful of shot. And then he see how it was, and he was the maddest man—he set the frog down and took out after that feller, but he never ketched him. And——"

[Here Simon Wheeler heard his name called from the front yard, and got up to see what was wanted.] And turning to me as he moved away, he said: "Just set where you are, stranger, and rest easy—I ain't going to be gone a second."

But, by your leave, I did not think that a continuation of the history of the enterprising vagabond *Jim* Smiley would be likely to afford me much information concerning the Rev. *Leonidas* W. Smiley, and so I started away.

At the door I met the sociable Wheeler returning, and he button-holed me and recommenced:

"Well, thish-year Smiley had a yaller one-eyed cow that didn't have no tail, only just a short stump like a bannanner, and——"

However, lacking both time and inclination, I did not wait to hear about the afflicted cow, but took my leave.

FROM **Old Times on the Mississippi** *(1875)*[1]

The Boys' Ambition

When I was a boy, there was but one permanent ambition among my comrades in our village[2] on the west bank of the Mississippi River. That was, to be a steamboatman. We had transient ambitions of other sorts, but they were only transient. When a circus came and went, it left us all burning to become clowns; the first negro minstrel show that ever came to our section left us all suffering to try that kind of life; now and then we had a hope that, if we lived and were good, God would permit us to be pirates. These ambitions faded out, each in its turn: but the ambition to be a steamboatman always remained.

Once a day a cheap, gaudy packet arrived upward from St. Louis, and another downward from Keokuk. Before these events, the day was glorious with expectancy; after them, the day was a dead and empty thing. Not only the boys, but the whole village, felt this. After all these years I can picture that old time to myself now, just as it was then: the white town drowsing in the sunshine of a summer's morning; the streets empty or pretty nearly so; one or two clerks sitting in front of the Water Street

---

[1] In 1875 Mark Twain published in *The Atlantic Monthly* a series of reminiscences about "old Mississippi days of steamboating glory and grandeur as I saw them (during 5 years) *from the pilot house.*" Eight years later he enlarged—and diluted— the original work, publishing it as a book under the title *Life on the Mississippi.* It is an all but universal critical judgment that the earlier work, *Old Times on the Mississippi,* is superior, more compact, more coherent, more evocative.

What follows here is the bulk of *Old Times on the Mississippi,* minus only some concluding pages which drop the narrative line and offer journalistic information about piloting.

[2] Hannibal, Missouri. *Au.*

stores, with their splint-bottomed chairs tilted back against the wall, chins on breasts, hats slouched over their faces, asleep—with shingle-shavings enough around to show what broke them down; a sow and a litter of pigs loafing along the sidewalk, doing a good business in watermelon rinds and seeds; two or three lonely little freight piles scattered about the "levee;" a pile of "skids"[3] on the slope of the stone-paved wharf, and the fragrant town drunkard asleep in the shadow of them; two or three wood flats at the head of the wharf, but nobody to listen to the peaceful lapping of the wavelets against them; the great Mississippi, the majestic, the magnificent Mississippi, rolling its mile-wide tide along, shining in the sun; the dense forest away on the other side; the "point" above the town, and the "point" below, bounding the river-glimpse and turning it into a sort of sea, and withal a very still and brilliant and lonely one. Presently a film of dark smoke appears above one of those remote "points;" instantly a negro drayman, famous for his quick eye and prodigious voice, lifts up the cry, "S-t-e-a-m-boat a-comin'!" and the scene changes! The town drunkard stirs, the clerks wake up, a furious clatter of drays follows, every house and store pours out a human contribution, and all in a twinkling the dead town is alive and moving. Drays, carts, men, boys, all go hurrying from many quarters to a common centre, the wharf. Assembled there, the people fasten their eyes upon the coming boat as upon a wonder they are seeing for the first time. And the boat *is* rather a handsome sight, too. She is long and sharp and trim and pretty; she has two tall fancy-topped chimneys, with a gilded device of some kind swung between them; a fanciful pilot-house, all glass and "ginger-bread," perched on top of the "texas" deck behind them; the paddle-boxes are gorgeous with a picture or with gilded rays above the boat's name; the boiler deck, the hurricane deck, and the texas deck are fenced and ornamented with clean white railings; there is a flag gallantly flying from the jack-staff; the furnace doors are open and the fires glaring bravely; the upper decks are black with passengers; the captain stands by the big bell, calm, imposing, the envy of all; great volumes of the blackest smoke are rolling and tumbling out of the chimneys—a husbanded grandeur created with a bit of pitch pine just before arriving at a town; the crew are grouped on the forecastle; the broad stage is run far out over the port bow, and an envied deck-hand stands picturesquely on the end of it with a coil of rope in his hand; the pent steam is screaming through the gauge-cocks; the captain lifts his hand, a bell rings, the wheels stop; then they turn back, churning the water to foam, and the steamer is at rest. Then such a scramble as there is to get aboard, and to get ashore, and to take in freight and to discharge freight, all at one and the same time; and such a yelling and cursing as the mates facilitate it all with! Ten minutes later the steamer is under way again, with

---

[3] Wooden fenders hung over the side of a boat to protect it while taking cargo on and off.

no flag on the jack-staff and no black smoke issuing from the chimneys. After ten more minutes the town is dead again, and the town drunkard asleep by the skids once more.

My father was a justice of the peace, and I supposed he possessed the power of life and death over all men and could hang anybody that offended him. This was distinction enough for me as a general thing; but the desire to be a steamboatman kept intruding, nevertheless. I first wanted to be a cabin-boy, so that I could come out with a white apron on and shake a table-cloth over the side, where all my old comrades could see me; later I thought I would rather be the deck-hand who stood on the end of the stage-plank with the coil of rope in his hand, because he was particularly conspicuous. But these were only day-dreams,—they were too heavenly to be contemplated as real possibilities. By and by one of our boys went away. He was not heard of for a long time. At last he turned up as apprentice engineer or "striker" on a steamboat. This thing shook the bottom out of all my Sunday-school teachings. That boy had been notoriously worldy, and I just the reverse; yet he was exalted to this eminence, and I left in obscurity and misery. There was nothing generous about this fellow in his greatness. He would always manage to have a dusty bolt to scrub while his boat tarried at our town, and he would sit on the inside guard and scrub it, where we all could see him and envy him and loathe him. And whenever his boat was laid up he would come home and swell around the town in his blackest and greasiest clothes, so that nobody could help remembering that he was a steamboatman; and he used all sorts of steamboat technicalities in his talk, as if he were so used to them that he forgot common people could not understand them. He would speak of the "labboard" side of a horse in an easy, natural way that would make one wish he was dead. And he was always talking about "St. Looey" like an old citizen; he would refer casually to occasions when he was "coming down Fourth Street," or when he was "passing by the Planter's House," or when there was a fire and he took a turn on the brakes [4] of "the old Big Missouri;" and then he would go on and lie about how many towns the size of ours were burned down there that day. Two or three of the boys had long been persons of consideration among us because they had been to St. Louis once and had a vague general knowledge of its wonders, but the day of their glory was over now. They lapsed into a humble silence, and learned to disappear when the ruthless "cub"-engineer approached. This fellow had money, too, and hair oil. Also an ignorant silver watch and a showy brass watch-chain. He wore a leather belt and used no suspenders. If ever a youth was cordially admired and hated by his comrades, this one was. No girl could withstand his charms. He "cut out" every boy in the village. When his boat blew up at last, it diffused a tranquil contentment among us such as we had not known for months. But when he came

[4] The handles of a pump.

home the next week, alive, renowned, and appeared in church all battered up and bandaged, a shining hero, stared at and wondered over by
everybody, it seemed to us that the partiality of Providence for an unde-
serving reptile had reached a point where it was open to criticism.

This creature's career could produce but one result, and it speedily
followed. Boy after boy managed to get on the river. The minister's son
became an engineer. The doctor's and the postmaster's sons became
"mud clerks;" the wholesale liquor dealer's son became a barkeeper on
a boat; four sons of the chief merchant, and two sons of the county
judge, became pilots. Pilot was the grandest position of all. The pilot,
even in those days of trivial wages, had a princely salary—from a hundred and fifty to two hundred and fifty dollars a month, and no board
to pay. Two months of his wages would pay a preacher's salary for a
year. Now some of us were left disconsolate. We could not get on the
river—at least our parents would not let us.

So by and by I ran away. I said I would never come home again till
I was a pilot and could come in glory. But somehow I could not manage
it. I went meekly aboard a few of the boats that lay packed together like
sardines at the long St. Louis wharf, and very humbly inquired for the
pilots, but got only a cold shoulder and short words from mates and
clerks. I had to make the best of this sort of treatment for the time
being, but I had comforting day-dreams of a future when I should be a
great and honored pilot, with plenty of money, and could kill some of
these mates and clerks and pay for them.

I Want to Be a Cub-Pilot

Months afterward the hope within me struggled to a reluctant death,
and I found myself without an ambition. But I was ashamed to go home.
I was in Cincinnati, and I set to work to map out a new career. I had
been reading about the recent exploration of the river Amazon by an
expedition sent out by our government. It was said that the expedition,
owing to difficulties, had not thoroughly explored a part of the country
lying about the head-waters, some four thousand miles from the mouth
of the river. It was only about fifteen hundred miles from Cincinnati to
New Orleans, where I could doubtless get a ship. I had thirty dollars left;
I would go and complete the exploration of the Amazon. This was all
the thought I gave to the subject. I never was great in matters of detail.
I packed my valise, and took passage on an ancient tub called the "Paul
Jones," for New Orleans. For the sum of sixteen dollars I had the scarred
and tarnished splendor of "her" main saloon principally to myself, for
she was not a creature to attract the eye of wiser travelers.

When we presently got under way and went poking down the broad
Ohio, I became a new being, and the subject of my own admiration. I
was a traveller! A word never had tasted so good in my mouth before. I
had an exultant sense of being bound for mysterious lands and distant

climes which I never have felt in so uplifting a degree since. I was in such a glorified condition that all ignoble feelings departed out of me, and I was able to look down and pity the untravelled with a compassion that had hardly a trace of contempt in it. Still, when we stopped at villages and wood-yards, I could not help lolling carelessly upon the railings of the boiler deck to enjoy the envy of the country boys on the bank. If they did not seem to discover me, I presently sneezed to attract their attention, or moved to a position where they could not help seeing me. And as soon as I knew they saw me I gaped and stretched, and gave other signs of being mightily bored with travelling.

I kept my hat off all the time, and stayed where the wind and the sun could strike me, because I wanted to get the bronzed and weather-beaten look of an old traveller. Before the second day was half gone, I experienced a joy which filled me with the purest gratitude; for I saw that the skin had begun to blister and peel off my face and neck. I wished that the boys and girls at home could see me now.

We reached Louisville in time—at least the neighborhood of it. We stuck hard and fast on the rocks in the middle of the river, and lay there four days. I was now beginning to feel a strong sense of being a part of the boat's family, a sort of infant son to the captain and younger brother to the officers. There is no estimating the pride I took in this grandeur, or the affection that began to swell and grow in me for those people. I could not know how the lordly steamboatman scorns that sort of presumption in a mere landsman. I particularly longed to acquire the least trifle of notice from the big stormy mate, and I was on the alert for an opportunity to do him a service to that end. It came at last. The riotous powwow of setting a spar was going on down on the forecastle, and I went down there and stood around in the way—or mostly skipping out of it—till the mate suddenly roared a general order for somebody to bring him a capstan bar. I sprang to his side and said: "Tell me where it is—I 'll fetch it!"

If a rag-picker had offered to do a diplomatic service for the Emperor of Russia, the monarch could not have been more astounded than the mate was. He even stopped swearing. He stood and stared down at me. It took him ten seconds to scrape his disjointed remains together again. Then he said impressively: "Well, if this don't beat hell!" and turned to his work with the air of a man who had been confronted with a problem too abstruse for solution.

I crept away, and courted solitude for the rest of the day. I did not go to dinner; I stayed away from supper until everybody else had finished. I did not feel so much like a member of the boat's family now as before. However, my spirits returned, in instalments, as we pursued our way down the river. I was sorry I hated the mate so, because it was not in (young) human nature not to admire him. He was huge and muscular, his face was bearded and whiskered all over; he had a red woman and a blue woman tattooed on his right arm,—one on each side of a blue anchor with a red rope to it; and in the matter of profanity he was sublime. When he was getting out cargo at a landing, I was always where I could see and hear. He felt all the majesty of his great position, and made the world feel it, too. When he gave even the simplest order, he discharged it like a blast of lightning, and sent a long, reverberating peal of profanity thundering after it. I could not help contrasting the way in which the average landsman would give an order, with the mate's way of doing it. If the landsman should wish the gang-plank moved a foot farther forward, he would probably say: "James, or William, one of you push the plank forward, please;" but put the mate in his place, and he would roar out: "Here, now, start that gangplank for'ard! Lively, now! *What* 're you about! Snatch it! *snatch* it! There! there! Aft again! aft again! Don't you hear me? Dash it to dash! are you going to *sleep* over it! 'Vast heaving. 'Vast heaving, I tell you! Going to heave it clear astern? WHERE 're you going with the barrel! *for'ard* with it 'fore I make you swallow it, you dash-dash-dash-*dashed* split between a tired mud-turtle and a crippled hearse-horse!"

I wished I could talk like that.

When the soreness of my adventure with the mate had somewhat worn off, I began timidly to make up to the humblest official connected with the boat—the night watchman. He snubbed my advances at first, but I presently ventured to offer him a new chalk pipe, and that softened him. So he allowed me to sit with him by the big bell on the hurricane deck, and in time he melted into conversation. He could not well have helped it, I hung with such homage on his words and so plainly showed that I felt honored by his notice. He told me the names of dim capes and shadowy islands as we glided by them in the solemnity of the night, under the winking stars, and by and by got to talking about himself. He seemed over-sentimental for a man whose salary was six dollars a week—or rather he might have seemed so to an older person than I. But I drank in his words hungrily, and with a faith that might have moved mountains if it had been applied judiciously. What was it to me that he was soiled and seedy and fragrant with gin? What was it to me that his grammar was bad, his construction worse, and his profanity so void of art that it was an element of weakness rather than strength in his conversation? He was a wronged man, a man who had seen trouble, and that was enough for me. As he mellowed into his plaintive history his tears dripped upon the lantern in his lap, and I cried, too, from sympathy. He said he was the son of an English nobleman—either an earl or an alderman, he could not remember which, but believed he was both; his father, the nobleman, loved him, but his mother hated him from the cradle; and so while he was still a little boy he was sent to "one of them old, ancient colleges"—he couldn't remember which; and by and by his father died and his mother seized the property and "shook" him, as he phrased it. After his mother shook him, members of the nobility with whom he was acquainted used their influence to get him

the position of "loblolly-boy in a ship;" and from that point my watchman threw off all trammels of date and locality and branched out into
a narrative that bristled all along with incredible adventures; a narrative
that was so reeking with bloodshed, and so crammed with hair-breadth
escapes and the most engaging and unconscious personal villanies, that
I sat speechless, enjoying, shuddering, wondering, worshipping.

It was a sore blight to find out afterwards that he was a low, vulgar,
ignorant, sentimental, half-witted humbug, an untravelled native of the
wilds of Illinois, who had absorbed wildcat literature and appropriated
its marvels, until in time he had woven odds and ends of the mess into
this yarn, and then gone on telling it to fledglings like me, until he had
come to believe it himself.

A Cub-Pilot's Experience

What with lying on the rocks four days at Louisville, and some other
delays, the poor old "Paul Jones" fooled away about two weeks in making the voyage from Cincinnati to New Orleans. This gave me a chance
to get acquainted with one of the pilots, and he taught me how to steer
the boat, and thus made the fascination of river life more potent than
ever for me.

It also gave me a chance to get acquainted with a youth who had
taken deck passage—more's the pity; for he easily borrowed six dollars
of me on a promise to return to the boat and pay it back to me the day
after we should arrive. But he probably died or forgot, for he never
came. It was doubtless the former, since he had said his parents were
wealthy, and he only travelled deck passage [5] because it was cooler.

I soon discovered two things. One was that a vessel would not be
likely to sail for the mouth of the Amazon under ten or twelve years;
and the other was that the nine or ten dollars still left in my pocket
would not suffice for so impossible an exploration as I had planned,
even if I could afford to wait for a ship. Therefore it followed that I
must contrive a new career. The "Paul Jones" was now bound for St.
Louis. I planned a siege against my pilot, and at the end of three hard
days he surrendered. He agreed to teach me the Mississippi River from
New Orleans to St. Louis for five hundred dollars, payable out of the
first wages I should receive after graduation. I entered upon the small
enterprise of "learning" twelve or thirteen hundred miles of the great
Mississippi River with the easy confidence of my time of life. If I had
really known what I was about to require of my faculties, I should not
have had the courage to begin. I supposed that all a pilot had to do was
to keep his boat in the river, and I did not consider that that could be
much of a trick, since it was so wide.

The boat backed out from New Orleans at four in the afternoon, and

[5] "Deck" passage—i.e., steerage passage. *Au.*

it was "our watch" until eight. Mr. Bixby, my chief, "straightened her up," plowed her along past the sterns of the other boats that lay at the Levee, and then said, "Here, take her; shave those steamships as close as you 'd peel an apple." I took the wheel, and my heart-beat fluttered up into the hundreds; for it seemed to me that we were about to scrape the side off every ship in the line, we were so close. I held my breath and began to claw the boat away from the danger; and I had my own opinion of the pilot who had known no better than to get us into such peril, but I was too wise to express it. In half a minute I had a wide margin of safety intervening between the "Paul Jones" and the ships; and within ten seconds more I was set aside in disgrace, and Mr. Bixby was going into danger again and flaying me alive with abuse of my cowardice. I was stung, but I was obliged to admire the easy confidence with which my chief loafed from side to side of his wheel, and trimmed the ships so closely that disaster seemed ceaselessly imminent. When he had cooled a little he told me that the easy water was close ashore and the current outside, and therefore we must hug the bank, up-stream, to get the bene-fit of the former, and stay well out, down-stream, to take advantage of the latter. In my own mind I resolved to be a down-stream pilot and leave the up-streaming to people dead to prudence.

Now and then Mr. Bixby called my attention to certain things. Said he, "This is Six-Mile Point." I assented. It was pleasant enough informa-tion, but I could not see the bearing of it. I was not conscious that it was a matter of any interest to me. Another time he said, "This is Nine-Mile Point." Later he said, "This is Twelve-Mile Point." They were all about level with the water's edge; they all looked about alike to me; they were monotonously unpicturesque. I hoped Mr. Bixby would change the sub-ject. But no; he would crowd up around a point, hugging the shore with affection, and then say: "The slack water ends here, abreast this bunch of China trees; now we cross over." So he crossed over. He gave me the wheel once or twice, but I had no luck. I either came near chipping the edge of a sugar-plantation, or I yawed too far from shore, and so dropped back into disgrace again and got abused.

The watch was ended at last, and we took supper and went to bed. At midnight the glare of a lantern shone in my eyes, and the night watchman said: —

"Come! turn out!"

And then he left. I could not understand this extraordinary proce-dure; so I presently gave up trying to, and dozed off to sleep. Pretty soon the watchman was back again, and this time he was gruff. I was annoyed. I said: —

"What do you want to come bothering around here in the middle of the night for? Now, as like as not, I 'll not get to sleep again to-night."

The watchman said: —

"Well, if this an't good, I 'm blest."

The "off-watch" was just turning in, and I heard some brutal laughter from them and such remarks as "Hello, watchman! an't the new cub turned out yet? He 's delicate, likely. Give him some sugar in a rag, and send for the chambermaid to sing rock-a-by-baby to him."

About this time Mr. Bixby appeared on the scene. Something like a minute later I was climbing the pilot-house steps with some of my clothes on and the rest in my arms. Mr. Bixby was close behind, commenting. Here was something fresh—this thing of getting up in the middle of the night to go to work. It was a detail in piloting that had never occurred to me at all. I knew that boats ran all night, but somehow I had never happened to reflect that somebody had to get up out of a warm bed to run them. I began to fear that piloting was not quite so romantic as I had imagined it was; there was something very real and work-like about this new phase of it.

It was a rather dingy night, although a fair number of stars were out. The big mate was at the wheel, and he had the old tub pointed at a star and was holding her straight up the middle of the river. The shores on either hand were not much more than half a mile apart, but they seemed wonderfully far away and ever so vague and indistinct. The mate said:—

"We've got to land at Jones's plantation, sir."

The vengeful spirit in me exulted. I said to myself, I wish you joy of your job, Mr. Bixby; you'll have a good time finding Mr. Jones's plantation such a night as this; and I hope you never *will* find it as long as you live.

Mr. Bixby said to the mate:—

"Upper end of the plantation, or the lower?"

"Upper."

"I can't do it. The stumps there are out of water at this stage. It's no great distance to the lower, and you 'll have to get along with that."

"All right, sir. If Jones don't like it, he'll have to lump it, I reckon."

And then the mate left. My exultation began to cool and my wonder to come up. Here was a man who not only proposed to find this plantation on such a night, but to find either end of it you preferred. I dreadfully wanted to ask a question, but I was carrying about as many short answers as my cargo-room would admit of, so I held my peace. All I desired to ask Mr. Bixby was the simple question whether he was ass enough to really imagine he was going to find that plantation on a night when all plantations were exactly alike and all of the same color. But I held in. I used to have fine inspirations of prudence in those days.

Mr. Bixby made for the shore and soon was scraping it, just the same as if it had been daylight. And not only that, but singing—

"Father in heaven, the day is declining," etc.

It seemed to me that I had put my life in the keeping of a peculiarly reckless outcast. Presently he turned on me and said:—

"What's the name of the first point above New Orleans?"

I was gratified to be able to answer promptly, and I did. I said I did n't know.

"Don't *know*?"

This manner jolted me. I was down at the foot again, in a moment. But I had to say just what I had said before.

"Well, you 're a smart one," said Mr. Bixby. "What 's the name of the *next* point?"

Once more I did n't know.

"Well, this beats anything. Tell me the name of *any* point or place I told you."

I studied a while and decided that I could n't.

"Look here! What do you start out from, above Twelve-Mile Point, to cross over?"

"I—I—don't know."

"You—you—don't know?" mimicking my drawling manner of speech. "What *do* you know?"

"I—I—nothing, for certain."

"By the great Caesar's ghost, I believe you! You 're the stupidest dunderhead I ever saw or heard of, so help me Moses! The idea of *you* being a pilot—*you!* Why, you don't know enough to pilot a cow down a lane."

Oh, but his wrath was up! He was a nervous man, and he shuffled from one side of his wheel to the other as if the floor was hot. He would boil awhile to himself, and then overflow and scald me again.

"Look here! What do you suppose I told you the names of those points for?"

I tremblingly considered a moment, and then the devil of temptation provoked me to say: —

"Well to—to—be entertaining, I thought."

This was a red rag to the bull. He raged and stormed so (he was crossing the river at the time) that I judged it made him blind, because he ran over the steering-oar of a trading-scow. Of course the traders sent up a volley of red-hot profanity. Never was a man so grateful as Mr. Bixby was: because he was brim ful, and here were subjects who would *talk back.* He threw open a window, thrust his head out, and such an irruption followed as I never had heard before. The fainter and farther away the scowmen's curses drifted, the higher Mr. Bixby lifted his voice and the weightier his adjectives grew. When he closed the window he was empty. You could have drawn a seine through his system and not caught curses enough to disturb your mother with. Presently he said to me in the gentlest way: —

"My boy, you must get a little memorandum-book; and every time I tell you a thing, put it down right away. There 's only one way to be a pilot, and that is to get this entire river by heart. You have to know it just like A B C."

That was a dismal revelation to me; for my memory was never

loaded with anything but blank cartridges. However, I did not feel discouraged long. I judged that it was best to make some allowances, for
doubtless Mr. Bixby was "stretching." Presently he pulled a rope and
struck a few strokes on the big bell. The stars were all gone now, and the
night was as black as ink. I could hear the wheels churn along the bank,
but I was not entirely certain that I could see the shore. The voice of the
invisible watchman called up from the hurricane deck:—

"What 's this, sir?"

"Jones's plantation."

I said to myself, I wish I might venture to offer a small bet that it
is n't. But I did not chirp. I only waited to see. Mr. Bixby handled the
engine bells, and in due time the boat's nose came to the land, a torch
glowed from the forecastle, a man skipped ashore, a darky's voice on the
bank said, "Gimme de k'yarpet-bag, Mars' Jones," and the next moment
we were standing up the river again, all serene. I reflected deeply a
while, and then said,—but not aloud,—Well, the finding of that plantation was the luckiest accident that ever happened; but it could n't
happen again in a hundred years. And I fully believed it *was* an accident,
too.

By the time we had gone seven or eight hundred miles up the river,
I had learned to be a tolerably plucky upstream steersman, in daylight,
and before we reached St. Louis I had made a trifle of progress in night-
work, but only a trifle. I had a note-book that fairly bristled with the
names of towns, "points," bars, islands, bends, reaches, etc.; but the
information was to be found only in the note-book—none of it was in
head. It made my heart ache to think I had only got half of the river
set down; for as our watch was four hours off and four hours on, day
and night, there was a long four-hour gap in my book for every time
I had slept since the voyage began.

My chief was presently hired to go on a big New Orleans boat, and
I packed my satchel and went with him. She was a grand affair. When
I stood in her pilot-house I was so far above the water that I seemed
perched on a mountain; and her decks stretched so far away, fore and
aft, below me, that I wondered how I could ever have considered the
little "Paul Jones" a large craft. There were other differences, too. The
"Paul Jones's" pilot-house was a cheap, dingy, battered rattle-trap,
cramped for room: but here was a sumptuous glass temple; room
enough to have a dance in; showy red and gold window-curtains; an
imposing sofa; leather cushions and a back to the high bench where
visiting pilots sit, to spin yarns and "look at the river;" bright, fanciful
"cuspadores," instead of a broad wooden box filled with sawdust; nice
new oilcloth on the floor; a hospitable big stove for winter; a wheel as
high as my head, costly with inlaid work; a wire tiller-rope; bright brass
knobs for the bells; and a tidy, white-aproned, black "texas-tender," to
bring up tarts and ices and coffee during mid-watch, day and night.
Now this was "something like;" and so I began to take heart once more

to believe that piloting was a romantic sort of occupation after all. The moment we were under way I began to prowl about the great steamer and fill myself with joy. She was as clean and as dainty as a drawing-room; when I looked down her long, gilded saloon, it was like gazing through a splendid tunnel; she had an oil-picture, by some gifted sign-painter, on every stateroom door; she glittered with no end of prism-fringed chandeliers; the clerk's office was elegant, the bar was marvellous, and the bar-keeper had been barbered and upholstered at incredible cost. The boiler deck (*i.e.*, the second story of the boat, so to speak), was as spacious as a church, it seemed to me; so with the forecastle; and there was no pitiful handful of deck-hands, firemen, and roustabouts down there, but a whole battalion of men. The fires were fiercely glaring from a long row of furnaces, and over them were eight huge boilers! This was unutterable pomp. The mighty engines—but enough of this. I had never felt so fine before. And when I found that the regiment of natty servants respectfully "sir'd" me, my satisfaction was complete.

A Daring Deed

When I returned to the pilot-house St. Louis was gone, and I was lost. Here was a piece of river which was all down in my book, but I could make neither head nor tail of it: you understand, it was turned around. I had seen it when coming upstream, but I had never faced about to see how it looked when it was behind me. My heart broke again, for it was plain that I had got to learn this troublesome river *both ways*.

The pilot-house was full of pilots, going down to "look at the river." What is called the "upper river" (the two hundred miles between St. Louis and Cairo, where the Ohio comes in) was low; and the Mississippi changes its channel so constantly that the pilots used to always find it necessary to run down to Cairo to take a fresh look, when their boats were to lie in port a week; that is, when the water was at a low stage. A deal of this "looking at the river" was done by poor fellows who seldom had a berth, and whose only hope of getting one lay in their being always freshly posted and therefore ready to drop into the shoes of some reputable pilot, for a single trip, on account of such pilot's sudden illness, or some other necessity. And a good many of them constantly ran up and down inspecting the river, not because they ever really hoped to get a berth, but because (they being guests of the boat) it was cheaper to "look at the river" than stay ashore and pay board. In time these fellows grew dainty in their tastes, and only infested boats that had an established reputation for setting good tables. All visiting pilots were useful, for they were always ready and willing, winter or summer, night or day, to go out in the yawl and help buoy the channel or assist the boat's pilot in any way they could. They were likewise welcome because all pilots are tireless talkers, when gathered together, and as they talk only about the river they are always understood and are always interesting. Your true pilot cares nothing about anything on earth but the river, and his pride in his occupation surpasses the pride of kings.

We had a fine company of these river inspectors along this trip. There were eight or ten; and there was abundance of room for them in our great pilot-house. Two or three of them wore polished silk hats, elaborate shirt-fronts, diamond breastpins, kid gloves, and patent-leather boots. They were choice in their English, and bore themselves with a dignity proper to men of solid means and prodigious reputation as pilot. The others were more or less loosely clad, and wore upon their heads tall felt cones that were suggestive of the days of the Commonwealth.

I was a cipher in this august company, and felt subdued, not to say torpid. I was not even of sufficient consequence to assist at the wheel when it was necessary to put the tiller hard down in a hurry; the guest that stood nearest did that when occasion required—and this was pretty much all the time, because of the crookedness of the channel and the scant water. I stood in a corner; and the talk I listened to took the hope all out of me. One visitor said to another:—

"Jim, how did you run Plum Point, coming up?"

"It was in the night, there, and I ran it the way one of the boys on the 'Diana' told me; started out about fifty yards above the wood pile on the false point, and held on the cabin under Plum Point till I raised the reef—quarter less twain—then straightened up for the middle bar till I got well abreast the old one-limbed cotton-wood in the mend, then got my stern on the cotton-wood and head on the low place above the point, and came through a-booming—nine and a half."

"Pretty square crossing, ain't it?"

"Yes, but the upper bar's working down fast."

Another pilot spoke up and said:—

"I had better water than that, and ran it lower down; started out from the false point—mark twain—raised the second reef abreast the big snag in the bend, and had quarter less twain."

One of the gorgeous ones remarked:—

"I don't want to find fault with your leadsmen, but that 's a good deal of water for Plum Point, it seems to me."

There was an approving nod all around as this quiet snub dropped on the boaster and "settled" him. And so they went on talk-talk-talking. Meantime, the thing that was running in my mind was, "Now, if my ears hear aright, I have not only to get the names of all the towns and islands and bends, and so on, by heart, but I must even get up a warm personal acquaintanceship with every old snag and one-limbed cotton-wood and obscure wood pile that ornaments the banks of this river for twelve hundred miles; and more than that, I must actually know where these things are in the dark, unless these guests are gifted with eyes that can pierce through two miles of solid blackness. I wish the piloting business was in Jericho and I had never thought of it."

At dusk Mr. Bixby tapped the big bell three times (the signal to land), and the captain emerged from his drawing-room in the forward end of the texas, and looked up inquiringly. Mr. Bixby said: —

"We will lay up here all night, captain."

"Very well, sir."

That was all. The boat came to shore and was tied up for the night. It seemed to me a fine thing that the pilot could do as he pleased, without asking so grand a captain's permission. I took my supper and went immediately to bed, discouraged by my day's observations and experiences. My late voyage's note-booking was but a confusion of meaningless names. It had tangled me all up in a knot every time I had looked at it in the daytime. I now hoped for respite in sleep; but no, it revelled all through my head till sunrise again, a frantic and tireless nightmare.

Next morning I felt pretty rusty and low-spirited. We went booming along, taking a good many chances, for we were anxious to "get out of the river" (as getting out to Cairo was called) before night should overtake us. But Mr. Bixby's partner, the other pilot, presently grounded the boat, and we lost so much time getting her off that it was plain the darkness would overtake us a good long way above the mouth. This was a great misfortune, especially to certain of our visiting pilots, whose boats would have to wait for their return, no matter how long that might be. It sobered the pilot-house talk a good deal. Coming up-stream, pilots did not mind low water or any kind of darkness; nothing stopped them but fog. But down-stream work was different; a boat was too nearly helpless, with a stiff current pushing behind her; so it was not customary to run down-stream at night in low water.

There seemed to be one small hope, however: if we could get through the intricate and dangerous Hat Island crossing before night, we could venture the rest, for we would have plainer sailing and better water. But it would be insanity to attempt Hat Island at night. So there was a deal of looking at watches all the rest of the day, and a constant ciphering upon the speed we were making; Hat Island was the eternal subject; sometimes hope was high and sometimes we were delayed in a bad crossing, and down it went again. For hours all hands lay under the burden of this suppressed excitement; it was even communicated to me, and I got to feeling so solicitous about Hat Island, and under such an awful pressure of responsibility, that I wished I might have five minutes on shore to draw a good, full, relieving breath, and start over again. We were standing no regular watches. Each of our pilots ran such portions of the river as he had run when coming up-stream, because of his greater familiarity with it; but both remained in the pilot-house constantly.

An hour before sunset Mr. Bixby took the wheel, and Mr. W——

stepped aside. For the next thirty minutes every man held his watch in his hand and was restless, silent, and uneasy. At last somebody said, with a doomful sigh,—

"Well yonder's Hat Island—and we can't make it."

All the watches closed with a snap, everybody sighed and muttered something about its being "too bad, too bad—ah, if we could *only* have got here half an hour sooner!" and the place was thick with the atmosphere of disappointment. Some started to go out, but loitered, hearing no bell-tap to land. The sun dipped behind the horizon, the boat went on. Inquiring looks passed from one guest to another; and one who had his hand on the door-knob and had turned it, waited, then presently took away his hand and let the knob turn back again. We bore steadily down the bend. More looks were exchanged, and nods of surprised admiration—but no words. Insensibly the men drew together behind Mr. Bixby, as the sky darkened and one or two dim stars came out. The dead silence and sense of waiting became oppressive. Mr. Bixby pulled the cord, and two deep, mellow notes from the big bell floated off on the night. Then a pause, and one more note was struck. The watchman's voice followed, from the hurricane-deck:—

"Labboard lead, there! Stabboard lead!"

The cries of the leadsmen began to rise out of the distance, and were gruffly repeated by the word-passers on the hurricane deck.

"M-a-r-k three! . . . . M-a-r-k three! . . . . Quarter-less-three! . . . . Half twain! . . . . Quarter twain! . . . . M-a-r-k twain! . . . . Quarter-less"—

Mr. Bixby pulled two bell-ropes, and was answered by faint jinglings far below in the engine room, and our speed slackened. The steam began to whistle through the gauge-cocks. The cries of the leadsmen went on—and it is a wierd sound, always, in the night. Every pilot in the lot was watching now, with fixed eyes, and talking under his breath. Nobody was calm and easy but Mr. Bixby. He would put his wheel down and stand on a spoke, and as the steamer swung into her (to me) utterly invisible marks—for we seemed to be in the midst of a wide and gloomy sea—he would meet and fasten her there. Out of the mumur of half-audible talk, one caught a coherent sentence now and then—such as:

"There; she's over the first reef all right!

After a pause, another subdued voice:—

"Her stern's coming down just *exactly* right, by *George!*"

"Now she's in the marks; over she goes!"

Somebody else muttered:—

"Oh, it was done beautiful—*beautiful!*"

Now the engines were stopped altogether, and we drifted with the current. Not that I could see the boat drift, for I could not, the stars being all gone by this time. This drifting was the dismalest work; it held one's heart still. Presently I discovered a blacker gloom than that which surrounded us. It was the head of the island. We were closing right down upon it. We entered its deeper shadow, and so imminent seemed the peril that I was likely to suffocate; and I had the strongest impulse to do *something*, anything, to save the vessel. But still Mr. Bixby stood by his wheel, silent, intent as a cat, and all the pilots stood shoulder to shoulder at his back.

She'll not make it!" somebody whispered.

The water grew shoaler and shoaler, by the leadsman's cries, till it was down to: —

"Eight-and-a-half! .... E-i-g-h-t feet! .... E-i-g-h-t feet! .... Seven-and"—

Mr. Bixby said warningly through his speaking-tube to the engineer: —

"Stand by, now!"

"Aye-aye, sir!"

"Seven-and-a-half! Seven feet! *Six* and"—

We touched bottom! Instantly Mr. Bixby set a lot of bells ringing, shouted through the tube, *"Now,* let her have it—every ounce you 've got!" then to his partner, "Put her hard down! snatch her! snatch her!" The boat rasped and ground her way through the sand, hung upon the apex of disaster a single tremendous instant, and then over she went! And such a shout as went up at Mr. Bixby's back never loosened the roof of a pilot-house before!

There was no more trouble after that. Mr. Bixby was a hero that night; and it was some little time, too, before his exploit ceased to be talked about by river men.

Fully to realize the marvellous precision required in laying the great steamer in her marks in that mirky waste of water, one should know that not only must she pick her intricate way through snags and blind reefs, and then shave the head of the island so closely as to brush the overhanging foliage with her stern, but at one place she must pass almost within arm's reach of a sunken and invisible wreck that would snatch the hull timbers from under her if she should strike it, and destroy a quarter of a million dollars' worth of steamboat and cargo in five minutes, and maybe a hundred and fifty human lives into the bargain.

The last remark I heard that night was a compliment to Mr. Bixby, uttered in soliloquy and with unction by one of our guests. He said: —

"By the Shadow of Death, but he's a lightning pilot!"

Perplexing Lessons

At the end of what seemed a tedious while, I had managed to pack my head full of islands, towns, bars, "points," and bends; and a curiously inanimate mass of lumber it was, too. However, inasmuch as I could shut my eyes and reel off a good long string of these names without leaving out more than ten miles of river in every fifty, I began to

feel that I could make her skip those little gaps. But of course my complacency could hardly get start enough to lift my nose a trifle into the
air, before Mr. Bixby would think of something to fetch it down again.
One day he turned on me suddenly with this settler: —

"What is the shape of Walnut Bend?"

He might as well have asked me my grandmother's opinion of
protoplasm. I reflected respectfully, and then said I did n't know it
had any particular shape. My gunpowdery chief went off with a bang,
of course, and then went on loading and firing until he was out of
adjectives.

I had learned long ago that he only carried just so many rounds of
ammunition, and was sure to subside into a very placable and even
remorseful old smooth-bore as soon as they were all gone. That word
"old" is merely affectionate; he was not more than thirty-four. I waited.
By and by he said: —

"My boy, you 've got to know the *shape* of the river perfectly. It is
all there is left to steer by on a very dark night. Everything else is
blotted out and gone. But mind you, it has n't the same shape in the
night that it has in the day-time."

"How on earth am I ever going to learn it, then?"

"How do you follow a hall at home in the dark? Because you know
the shape of it. You can't see it."

"Do you mean to say that I 've got to know all the million trifling
variations of shape in the banks of this interminable river as well as I
know the shape of the front hall at home?"

"On my honor, you 've got to know them *better* than any man ever
did know the shapes of the halls in his own house."

"I wish I was dead!"

"Now I don't want to discourage you, but"—

"Well, pile it on me; I might as well have it now as another time."

"You see, this has got to be learned; there is n't any getting around
it. A clear starlight night throws such heavy shadows that, if you did
n't know the shape of a shore perfectly, you would claw away from
every bunch of timber, because you would take the black shadow of
it for a solid cape; and you see you would be getting scared to death
every fifteen minutes by the watch. You would be fifty yards from shore
all the time when you ought to be within fifty feet of it. You can't see
a snag in one of those shadows, but you know exactly where it is, and
the shape of the river tells you when you are coming to it. Then there
's your pitch-dark night; the river is a very different shape on a pitch-
dark night from what it is on a starlight night. All shores seem to be
straight lines, then, and mighty dim ones, too; and you 'd *run* them
for straight lines, only you know better. You boldly drive your boat right
into what seems to be a solid, straight wall (you knowing very well that
in reality there is a curve there), and that wall falls back and makes
way for you. Then there 's your gray mist. You take a night when

there 's one of these grisly, drizzly, gray mists, and then there is n't *any* particular shape to a shore. A gray mist would tangle the head of the oldest man that ever lived. Well, then different kinds of *moonlight* change the shape of the river in different ways. You see"—

"Oh, don't say any more, please! Have I got to learn the shape of the river according to all these five hundred thousand different ways? If I tried to carry all that cargo in my head it would make me stoop-shouldered."

"*No!* you only learn *the* shape of the river; and you learn it with such absolute certainty that you can always steer by the shape that 's *in your head*, and never mind the one that 's before your eyes."

"Very well, I 'll try it; but, after I have learned it, can I depend on it? Will it keep the same form and not go fooling around?"

Before Mr. Bixby could answer, Mr. W—— came in to take the watch, and he said,—

"Bixby, you 'll have to look out for President's Island, and all that country clear away up above the Old Hen and Chickens. The banks are caving and the shape of the shores changing like everything. Why, you would n't know the point above 40. You can go up inside the old sycamore snag, now." [6]

So that question was answered. Here were leagues of shore changing shape. My spirits were down in the mud again. Two things seemed pretty apparent to me. One was, that in order to be a pilot a man had got to learn more than any one man ought to be allowed to know; and the other was, that he must learn it all over again in a different way every twenty-four hours.

That night we had the watch until twelve. Now it was an ancient river custom for the two pilots to chat a bit when the watch changed. While the relieving pilot put on his gloves and lit his cigar, his partner, the retiring pilot, would say something like this: —

"I judge the upper bar is making down a little at Hale's Point; had quarter twain with the lower lead and mark twain [7] with the other."

"Yes, I thought it was making down a little, last trip. Meet any boats?"

"Met one abreast the head of 21, but she was away over hugging the bar, and I couldn't make her out entirely. I took her for the 'Sunny South'—had n't any skylight forward of the chimneys."

And so on. And as the relieving pilot took the wheel his partner [8] would mention that we were in such-and-such a bend, and say we were abreast of such-and-such a man's wood-yard or plantation. This was

[6] It may not be necessary, but still it can do no harm to explain that "inside" means between the snag and the shore. *Au.*

[7] Two fathoms. Quarter twain is 2¼ fathoms, 13½ feet. Mark three is three fathoms. *Au.*

[8] "Partner" is technical for "the other pilot." *Au.*

courtesy; I supposed it was *necessity*. But Mr. W—— came on watch full twelve minutes late on this particular night,—a tremendous breach of etiquette; in fact, it is the unpardonable sin among pilots. So Mr. Bixby gave him no greeting whatever, but simply surrendered the wheel and marched out of the pilot-house without a word. I was appalled; it was a villanous night for blackness, we were in a particularly wide and blind part of the river, where there was no shape or substance to anything, and it seemed incredible that Mr. Bixby should have left that poor fellow to kill the boat trying to find out where he was. But I resolved that I would stand by him any way. He should find that he was not wholly friendless. So I stood around, and waited to be asked where we were. But Mr. W—— plunged on serenely through the solid firmament of black cats that stood for an atmosphere, and never opened his mouth. Here is a proud devil, thought I; here is a limb of Satan that would rather send us all to destruction than put himself under obligations to me, because I am not yet one of the salt of the earth and privileged to snub captains and lord it over everything dead and alive in a steamboat. I presently climbed up on the bench; I did not think it was safe to go to sleep while this lunatic was on watch.

However, I must have gone to sleep in the course of time, because the next thing I was aware of was the fact that day was breaking, Mr. W—— gone, and Mr. Bixby at the wheel again. So it was four o'clock and all well—but me; I felt like a skinful of dry bones and all of them trying to ache at once.

Mr. Bixby asked me what I had stayed up there for. I confessed that it was to do Mr. W—— a benevolence,—tell him where he was. It took five minutes for the entire preposterousness of the thing to filter into Mr. Bixby's system, and then I judge it filled him nearly up to the chin; because he paid me a compliment—and not much of a one either. He said,—

"Well, taking you by-and-large, you do seem to be more different kinds of an ass than any creature I ever saw before. What did you suppose he wanted to know for?"

I said I thought it might be a convenience to him.

"Convenience! D–nation! Did n't I tell you that a man's got to know the river in the night the same as he'd know his own front hall?"

"Well, I can follow the front hall in the dark if I know it *is* the front hall; but suppose you set me down in the middle of it in the dark and not tell me which hall it is; how am *I* to know?"

"Well, you've *got* to, on the river!"

"All right. Then I 'm glad I never said anything to Mr. W——"

"I should say so! Why, he'd have slammed you through the window and utterly ruined a hundred dollars' worth of windowsash and stuff."

I was glad this damage had been saved, for it would have made me unpopular with the owners. They always hated anybody who had the name of being careless, and injuring things.

I went to work now to learn the shape of the river; and of all the eluding and ungraspable objects that ever I tried to get mind or hands on, that was the chief. I would fasten my eyes upon a sharp, wooden point that projected far into the river some miles ahead of me, and go to laboriously photographing its shape upon my brain; and just as I was beginning to succeed to my satisfaction, we would draw up toward it and the exasperating thing would begin to melt away and fold back into the bank; If there had been a conspicuous dead tree standing upon the very point of the cape, I would find that tree inconspicuously merged into the general forest, and occupying the middle of a straight shore, when I got abreast of it! No prominent hill would stick to its shape long enough for me to make up my mind what its form really was, but it was as dissolving and changeful as if it had been a mountain of butter in the hottest corner of the tropics. Nothing ever had the same shape when I was coming down-stream that it had borne when I went up. I mentioned these little difficulties to Mr. Bixby. He said,—

"That 's the very main virtue of the thing. If the shapes did n't change every three seconds they would n't be of any use. Take this place where we are now, for instance. As long as that hill over yonder is only one hill, I can boom right along the way I 'm going; but the moment it splits at the top and forms a V, I know I 've got to scratch to starboard in a hurry, or I 'll bang this boat's brains out against a rock; and then the moment one of the prongs of the V swings behind the other, I 've got to waltz to larboard again, or I 'll have a misunderstanding with a snag that would snatch the keelson out of this steamboat as neatly as if it were a sliver in your hand. If that hill did n't change its shape on bad nights there would be an awful steamboat grave-yard around here inside of a year."

It was plain that I had got to learn the shape of the river in all the different ways that could be thought of,—upside down, wrong end first, inside out, fore-and-aft, and "thort-ships,"—and then know what to do on gray nights when it had n't any shape at all. So I set about it. In the course of time I began to get the best of this knotty lesson, and my self-complacency moved to the front once more. Mr. Bixby was all fixed, and ready to start it to the rear again. He opened on me after this fashion: —

"How much water did we have in the middle crossing at Hole-in-the-Wall, trip before last?"

I considered this an outrage. I said: —

"Every trip, down and up, the leadsmen are singing through that tangled place for three quarters of an hour on a stretch. How do you reckon I can remember such as mess as that?"

"My boy, you 've got to remember it. You 've got to remember the exact spot and the exact marks the boat lay in when we had the shoalest water, in every one of the five hundred shoal places between St. Louis and New Orleans; and you must n't get the shoal soundings and marks of one trip mixed up with the shoal soundings and marks of another, either, for they're not often twice alike. You must keep them separate."

When I came to myself again, I said,—

"When I get so that I can do that, I 'll be able to raise the dead, and then I won't have to pilot a steamboat to make a living. I want to retire from this business. I want a slush-bucket and a brush; I'm only fit for a roustabout. I have n't got brains enough to be a pilot; and if I had I would n't have strength enough to carry them around, unless I went on crutches."

"Now drop that! When I say I 'll learn [9] a man the river, I mean it. And you can depend on it, I 'll learn him or kill him."

Continued Perplexities

There was no use in arguing with a person like this. I promptly put such a strain on my memory that by and by even the shoal water and the countless crossing-marks began to stay with me. But the result was just the same. I never could more than get one knotty thing learned before another presented itself. Now I had often seen pilots gazing at the water and pretending to read it as if it were a book; but it was a book that told me nothing. A time came at last, however, when Mr. Bixby seemed to think me far enough advanced to bear a lesson on water-reading. So he began: —

"Do you see that long, slanting line on the face of the water? Now, that 's a reef. Moreover, it 's a bluff reef. There is a solid sandbar under it that is nearly as straight up and down as the side of a house. There is plenty of water close up to it, but mighty little on top of it. If you were to hit it you would knock the boat's brains out. Do you see where the line fringes out at the upper end and begins to fade away?"

"Yes, sir."

"Well, that is a low place; that is the head of the reef. You can climb over there, and not hurt anything. Cross over, now, and follow along close under the reef—easy water there—not much current."

I followed the reef along till I approached the fringed end. Then Mr. Bixby said,—

"Now get ready. Wait till I give the word. She won't want to mount the reef; a boat hates shoal water. Stand by—wait—*wait*—keep her well in hand. *Now* cramp her down! Snatch her! snatch her!"

He seized the other side of the wheel and helped to spin it around until it was hard down, and then we held it so. The boat resisted, and refused to answer for a while, and next she came surging to starboard, mounted the reef, and sent a long, angry ridge of water foaming away from her bows.

---

[9] "Teach" is not in the river vocabulary. *Au.*

"Now watch her; watch her like a cat, or she 'll get away from you. When she fights strong and the tiller slips a little, in a jerky, greasy sort of way, let up on her a trifle; it is the way she tells you at night that the water is too shoal; but keep edging her up, little by little, toward the point. You are well up on the bar, now; there is a bar under every point, because the water that comes down around it forms an eddy and allows the sediment to sink. Do you see those fine lines on the face of the water that branch out like the ribs of a fan? Well, those are little reefs; you want to just miss the ends of them, but run them pretty close. Now look out—look out! Don't you crowd that slick, greasy-looking place; there ain't nine feet there; she won't stand it. She begins to smell it; look sharp, I tell you! Oh, blazes, there you go! Stop the starboard wheel! Quick! Ship up to back! Set her back!"

The engine bells jingled and the engines answered promptly, shooting white columns of steam far aloft out of the 'scape pipes, but it was too late. The boat had "smelt" the bar in good earnest; the foamy ridges that radiated from her bows suddenly disappeared, a great dead swell came rolling forward, and swept ahead of her, she careened far over to larboard, and went tearing away toward the other shore as if she were about scared to death. We were a good mile from where we ought to have been, when we finally got the upper hand of her again.

During the afternoon watch the next day, Mr. Bixby asked me if I knew how to run the next few miles. I said:—

"Go inside the first snag above the point, outside the next one, start out from the lower end of Higgins's wood-yard, make a square crossing, and"—

"That 's all right. I 'll be back before you close up on the next point."

But he was n't. He was still below when I rounded it and entered upon a piece of the river which I had some misgivings about. I did not know that he was hiding behind a chimney to see how I would perform. I went gayly along, getting prouder and prouder, for he had never left the boat in my sole charge such a length of time before. I even got to "setting" her and letting the wheel go, entirely, while I vaingloriously turned my back and inspected the stern marks and hummed a tune, a sort of easy indifference which I had prodigiously admired in Bixby and other great pilots. Once I inspected rather long, and when I faced to the front again my heart flew into my mouth so suddenly that if I had n't clapped my teeth together I should have lost it. One of those frightful bluff reefs was stretching its deadly length right across our bows! My head was gone in a moment; I did not know which end I stood on; I gasped and could not get my breath; I spun the wheel down with such rapidity that it wove itself together like a spider's web; the boat answered and turned square away from the reef, but the reef followed her! I fled, but still it followed still it kept—right across my bows! I never looked to see where I was going, I only fled. The awful crash was imminent. Why did n't that villain come? If I committed the crime of ringing a bell, I might get thrown overboard. But better that than kill the boat. So in blind desperation I started such a rattling "shivaree" down below as never had astounded an engineer in this world before, I fancy. Amidst the frenzy of the bells the engines began to back and fill in a furious way, and my reason forsook its throne— we were about to crash into the woods on the other side of the river. Just then Mr. Bixby stepped calmly into view on the hurricane deck. My soul went out to him in gratitude. My distress vanished; I would have felt safe on the brink of Niagara, with Mr. Bixby on the hurricane deck. He blandly and sweetly took his tooth-pick out of his mouth between his fingers, as if it were a cigar,—we were just in the act of climbing an overhanging big tree, and the passengers were scudding astern like rats,—and lifted up these commands to me ever so gently: —

"Stop the starboard. Stop the larboard. Set her back on both."

The boat hesitated, halted, pressed her nose among the boughs a critical instant, then reluctantly began to back away.

"Stop the larboard. Come ahead on it. Stop the starboard. Come ahead on it. Point her for the bar."

I sailed away as serenely as a summer's morning. Mr. Bixby came in and said, with mock simplicity,—

"When you have a hail, my boy, you ought to tap the big bell three times before you land, so that the engineers can get ready."

I blushed under the sarcasm, and said I had n't had any hail.

"Ah! Then it was for wood, I suppose. The officer of the watch will tell you when he wants to wood up."

I went on consuming, and said I was n't after wood.

"Indeed? Why, what could you want over here in the bend, then? Did you ever know of a boat following a bend up-stream at this stage of the river?"

"No, sir,—and I was n't trying to follow it. I was getting away from a bluff reef."

"No, it was n't a bluff reef; there is n't one within three miles of where you were."

"But I saw it. It was as bluff as that one yonder."

"Just about. Run over it!"

"Do you give it as an order?"

"Yes, Run over it!"

"If I don't, I wish I may die."

"All right; I am taking the responsibility."

I was just as anxious to kill the boat, now, as I had been to save it before. I impressed my orders upon my memory, to be used at the inquest, and made a straight break for the reef. As it disappeared under our bows I held my breath; but we slid over it like oil.

"Now, don't you see the difference? It was n't anything but a *wind* reef. The wind does that."

So I see. But it is exactly like a bluff reef. How am I ever going to tell them apart?"

"I can't tell you. It is an instinct. By and by you will just naturally *know* one from the other, but you never will be able to explain why or how you know them apart."

It turned out to be true. The face of the water, in time, became a wonderful book—a book that was a dead language to the uneducated passenger, but which told its mind to me without reserve, delivering its most cherished secrets as clearly as if it uttered them with a voice. And it was not a book to be read once and thrown aside, for it had a new story to tell every day. Throughout the long twelve hundred miles there was never a page that was void of interest, never one that you could leave unread without loss, never one that you would want to skip, thinking you could find higher enjoyment in some other thing. There never was so wonderful a book written by man; never one whose interest was so absorbing, so unflagging, so sparklingly renewed with every re-perusal. The passenger who could not read it was charmed with a peculiar sort of faint dimple on its surface (on the rare occasions when he did not overlook it altogether); but to the pilot that was an *italicized* passage; indeed, it was more than that, it was a legend of the largest capitals, with a string of shouting exclamation points at the end of it; for it meant that a wreck or a rock was buried there that could tear the life out of the strongest vessel that ever floated. It is the faintest and simplest expression the water ever makes, and the most hideous to a pilot's eye. In truth, the passenger who could not read this book saw nothing but all manner of pretty pictures in it, painted by the sun and shaded by the clouds, whereas to the trained eye these were not pictures at all, but the grimmest and most dead-earnest of reading-matter.

Now when I had mastered the language of this water and had come to know every trifling feature that bordered the great river as familiarly as I knew the letters of the alphabet, I had made a valuable acquisition. But I had lost something, too. I had lost something which could never be restored to me while I lived. All the grace, the beauty, the poetry, had gone out of the majestic river! I still keep in mind a certain wonderful sunset which I witnessed when steamboating was new to me. A broad expanse of the river was turned to blood; in the middle distance the red hue brightened into gold, through which a solitary log came floating, black and conspicuous; in one place a long, slanting mark lay sparkling upon the water; in another the surface was broken by boiling, tumbling rings, that were as many-tinted as an opal; where the ruddy flush was faintest, was a smooth spot that was covered with graceful circles and radiating lines, ever so delicately traced; the shore on our left was densely wooded, and the sombre shadow that fell from this forest was broken in one place by a long ruffled trail that shone like silver; and high above the forest wall a clean-stemmed dead tree waved a single leafy bough that glowed like a flame in the unobstructed splendor that was flowing from the sun. There were graceful curves, reflected images, woody heights, soft distances; and over the whole scene, far and near, the dissolving lights drifted steadily, enriching it, every passing moment, with new marvels of coloring.

I stood like one bewitched. I drank it in, in a speechless rapture. The world was new to me, and I had never seen anything like this at home. But as I have said, a day came when I began to cease from noting the glories and the charms which the moon and the sun and the twilight wrought upon the river's face; another day came when I ceased altogether to note them. Then, if that sunset scene had been repeated, I should have looked upon it without rapture, and should have commented upon it, inwardly, after this fashion: This sun means that we are going to have wind to-morrow; that floating log means that the river is rising, small thanks to it; that slanting mark on the water refers to a bluff reef which is going to kill somebody's steamboat one of these nights, if it keeps on stretching out like that; those tumbling "boils" show a dissolving bar and a changing channel there; the lines and circles in the slick water over yonder are a warning that that troublesome place is shoaling up dangerously; that silver streak in the shadow of the forest is the "break" from a new snag, and he has located himself in the very best place he could have found to fish for steamboats; that tall dead tree, with a single living branch, is not going to last long, and then how is a body ever going to get through this blind place at night without the friendly old landmark?

No, the romance and beauty were all gone from the river. All the value any feature of it had for me now was the amount of usefulness it could furnish toward compassing the safe piloting of a steamboat. Since those days, I have pitied doctors from my heart. What does the lovely flush in a beauty's cheek mean to a doctor but a "break" that ripples above some deadly disease? Are not all her visible charms sown thick with what are to him the signs and symbols of hidden decay? Does he ever see her beauty at all, or does n't he simply view her professionally, and comment upon her unwholesome condition all to himself? And does n't he sometimes wonder whether he has gained most or lost most by learning his trade?

Completing My Education

Whosoever has done me the courtesy to read my chapters which have preceded this may possibly wonder that I deal so minutely with piloting as a science. It was the prime purpose of those chapters; and I am not quite done yet. I wish to show, in the most patient and painstaking way, what a wonderful science it is. Ship channels are buoyed and lighted, and therefore it is a comparatively easy undertaking to learn to run them; clear-water rivers, with gravel bottoms, change their channels very gradually, and therefore one needs to learn them but once; but piloting becomes another matter when you apply it to vast streams like the Mississippi and the Missouri, whose alluvial banks cave and change constantly, whose snags are always hunting up new quarters, whose sand-bars are never at rest, whose channels are forever dodging and shirking, and whose obstructions must be confronted in all nights and all weathers without the aid of a single lighthouse or a single buoy; for there is neither light nor buoy to be found anywhere in all this three or four thousand miles of villainous river.[10] I feel justified in enlarging upon this great science for the reason that I feel sure no one has ever yet written a paragraph about it who had piloted a steamboat himself, and so had a practical knowledge of the subject. If the theme were hackneyed, I should be obliged to deal gently with the reader; but since it is wholly new, I have felt at liberty to take up a considerable degree of room with it.

When I had learned the name and position of every visible feature of the river; when I had so mastered its shape that I could shut my eyes and trace it from St. Louis to New Orleans; when I had learned to read the face of the water as one would cull the news from the morning paper; and finally, when I had trained my dull memory to treasure up an endless array of soundings and crossing-marks, and keep fast hold of them, I judged that my education was complete: so I got to tilting my cap to the side of my head, and wearing a toothpick in my mouth at the wheel. Mr. Bixby had his eye on these airs. One day he said,—

"What is the height of that bank yonder, at Burgess's?"

"How can I tell, sir? It is three quarters of a mile away."

"Very poor eye—very poor. Take the glass."

I took the glass and presently said,—

"I can't tell. I suppose that that bank is about a foot and a half high."

"Foot and a half! That's a six-foot bank. How high was the bank along here last trip?"

"I don't know; I never noticed."

"You did n't? Well, you must always do it hereafter."

"Why?"

"Because you 'll have to know a good many things that it tells you. For one thing, it tells you the stage of the river—tells you whether there 's more water or less in the river along here than there was last trip."

"The leads tell me that." I rather thought I had the advantage of him there.

"Yes, but suppose the leads lie? The bank would tell you so, and

[10] True at the time referred to, not true now (1882). *Au.*

then you 'd stir those leadsmen up a bit. There was a ten-foot bank here last trip, and there is only a six-foot bank now. What does that signify?"

"That the river is four feet higher than it was last trip."

"Very good. Is the river rising or falling?"

"Rising."

"No it ain't."

"I guess I am right, sir. Yonder is some driftwood floating down the stream."

"A rise *starts* the drift-wood, but then it keeps on floating a while after the river is done rising. Now the bank will tell you about this. Wait till you come to a place where it shelves a little. Now here; do you see this narrow belt of fine sediment? That was deposited while the water was higher. You see the drift-wood begins to strand, too. The bank helps in other ways. Do you see that stump on the false point?"

"Ay, ay, sir."

"Well, the water is just up to the roots of it. You must make a note of that."

"Why?"

"Because that means that there 's seven feet in the chute of 103."

"But 103 is a long way up the river yet."

"That's where the benefit of the bank comes in. There is water enough in 103 *now*, yet there may not be by the time we get there, but the bank will keep us posted all along. You don't run close chutes on a falling river, up-stream, and there are precious few of them that you are allowed to run at all down-stream. There 's a law of the United States against it. The river may be rising by the time we get to 103, and in that case we 'll run it. We are drawing—how much?"

"Six feet aft,—six and a half forward."

"Well, you do seem to know something."

"But what I particularly want to know is, if I have got to keep up an everlasting measuring of the banks of this river, twelve hundred miles, month in and month out?"

"Of course!"

My emotions were too deep for words for a while. Presently I said,—

"And how about these chutes? Are there many of them?"

"I should say so. I fancy we shan't run any of the river this trip as you 've seen it run before—so to speak. If the river begins to rise again, we 'll go up behind bars that you 've always seen standing out of the river, high and dry like a roof of a house; we 'll cut across low places that you 've never noticed at all, right through the middle of bars that cover three hundred acres of river; we 'll creep through cracks where you 've always thought was solid land; we 'll dart through the

woods and leave twenty-five miles of river off to one side; we 'll see the
hind side of every island between New Orleans and Cairo."

"Then I 've got to go to work and learn just as much more river
as I already know."

"Just about twice as much more, as near as you can come at it."

"Well, one lives to find out. I think I was a fool when I went into
this business."

"Yes, that is true. And you are yet. But you 'll not be when you 've
learned it."

"Ah, I never can learn it."

"I will see that you *do*."

By and by I ventured again: —

"Have I got to learn all this thing just as I know the rest of the
river—shapes and all—and so I can run it at night?"

"Yes. And you 've got to have good fair marks from one end of the
river to the other, that will help the bank tell you when there is water
enough in each of these countless places—like that stump, you know.
When the river first begins to rise, you can run half a dozen of the
deepest of them; when it rises a foot more you can run another dozen;
the next foot will add a couple of dozen, and so on: so you see you
have to know your banks and marks to a dead moral certainty, and
never get them mixed; for when you start through one of those cracks,
there 's no backing out again, as there is in the big river; you 've got
to go through, or stay there six months if you get caught on a falling
river. There are about fifty of these cracks which you can't run at all
except when the river is brim full and over the banks."

"This new lesson is a cheerful prospect."

"Cheerful enough. And mind what I 've just told you; when you
start into one of those places you 've got to go through. They are too
narrow to turn around in, too crooked to back out of, and the shoal
water is always *up at the head;* never elsewhere. And the head of them
is always likely to be filling up, little by little, so that the marks you
reckon their depth by, this season, may not answer for next."

"Learn a new set, then, every year?"

"Exactly. Cramp her up to the bar! What are you standing up
through the middle of the river for?"

The next few months showed me strange things. On the same day
that we held the conversation above narrated, we met a great rise
coming down the river. The whole vast face of the stream was black
with drifting dead logs, broken boughs, and great trees that had caved
in and been washed away. It required the nicest steering to pick one's
way through this rushing raft, even in the day-time, when crossing
from point to point; and at night the difficulty was mightily increased;
every now and then a huge log, lying deep in the water, would sud-

denly appear right under our bows, coming head-on; no use to try to avoid it then; we could only stop the engines, and one wheel would walk over that log from one end to the other, keeping up a thundering racket and careening the boat in a way that was very uncomfortable to passengers. Now and then we would hit one of these sunken logs a rattling bang, dead in the center, with a full head of steam, and it would stun the boat as if she had hit a continent. Sometimes this log would lodge, and stay right across our nose, and back the Mississippi up before it; we would have to do a little crawfishing, then, to get away from the obstruction. We often hit *white* logs in the dark, for we could not see them till we were right on them, but a black log is a pretty distinct object at night. A white snag is an ugly customer when the daylight is gone.

Of course, on the great rise, down came a swarm of prodigious timber-rafts from the headwaters of the Mississippi, coal-barges from Pittsburgh, little trading scows from everywhere, and broadhorns from "Posey County," Indiana, freighted with "fruit and furniture"—the usual term for describing it, though in plain English the freight thus aggrandized was hoop-poles and pumpkins. Pilots bore a mortal hatred to these craft, and it was returned with usury. The law required all such helpless traders to keep a light burning, but it was a law that was often broken. All of a sudden, on a murky night, a light would hop up, right under our bows, almost, and an agonized voice, with the back-woods "whang" to it, would wail out:—

"Whar 'n the —— you goin' to! Cain 't you see nothin', you dash-dashed aig-suckin', sheep-stealin', one-eyed son of a stuffed monkey!"

Then for an instant, as we whistled by, the red glare from our fur-naces would reveal the scow and the form of the gesticulating orator, as if under a lightning-flash, and in that instant our firemen and deck-hands would send and receive a tempest of missiles and profanity, one of our wheels would walk off with the crashing fragments of a steering-oar, and down the dead blackness would shut again. And that flatboat-man would be sure to go into New Orleans and sue our boat, swearing stoutly that he had a light burning all the time, when in truth his gang had the lantern down below to sing and lie and drink and gamble by, and no watch on deck. Once, at night, in one of those forest-bordered crevices (behind an island) which steamboatmen intensely describe with the phrase "as dark as the inside of a cow," we should have eaten up a Posey County family, fruit, furniture, and all, but that they hap-pened to be fiddling down below and we just caught the sound of the music in time to sheer off, doing no serious damage, unfortunately, but coming so near it that we had good hopes for a moment. These people brought up their lantern, then, of course; and as we backed and filled to get away, the precious family stood in the light of it—both sexes and various ages—and cursed us till everything turned blue. Once a coal-

boatman sent a bullet through our pilot-house, when we borrowed a
steering-oar of him in a very narrow place.

The River Rises

During this big rise these small-fry craft were an intolerable nuisance. We were running chute after chute,—a new world to me,—and
if there was a particularly cramped place in a chute, we would be pretty
sure to meet a broad-horn there; and if he failed to be there, we would
find him in a still worse locality, namely, the head of the chute, on the
shoal water. And then there would be no end of profane cordialities
exchanged.

Sometimes, in the big river, when we would be feeling our way
cautiously along through a fog, the deep hush would suddenly be broken
by yells and a clamor of tin pans, and all in an instant a log raft would
appear vaguely through the webby veil, close upon us; and then we
did not wait to swap knives, but snatched our engine bells out by the
roots and piled on all the steam we had, to scramble out of the way!
One does n't hit a rock or a solid log raft with a steamboat when he
can get excused.

You will hardly believe it, but many steamboat clerks always carried a large assortment of religious tracts with them in those old departed steamboating days. Indeed they did. Twenty times a day we
would be cramping up around a bar, while a string of these small-fry
rascals were drifting down into the head of the bend away above and
beyond us a couple of miles. Now a skiff would dart away from one of
them, and come fighting its laborious way across the desert of water.
It would "ease all," in the shadow of our forecastle, and the panting
oarsmen would shout, "Gimme a pa-a-per!" as the skiff drifted swiftly
astern. The clerk would throw over a file of New Orleans journals. If
these were picked up *without comment,* you might notice that now a dozen
other skiffs had been drifting down upon us without saying anything.
You understand, they had been waiting to see how No. 1 was going to
fare. No. 1 making no comment, all the rest would bend to their oars
and come on, now; and as fast as they came the clerk would heave
over neat bundles of religious tracts, tied to shingles. The amount of
hard swearing which twelve packages of religious literature will command when impartially divided up among twelve raftsmen's crews, who
have pulled a heavy skiff two miles on a hot day to get them, is simply
incredible.

As I have said, the big rise brought a new world under my vision.
By the time the river was over its banks we had forsaken our old paths
and were hourly climbing over bars that had stood ten feet out of water
before; we were shaving stumpy shores, like that at the foot of Madrid
Bend, which I had always seen avoided before; we were clattering through

chutes like that of 82, where the opening at the foot was an unbroken wall of timber till our nose was almost at the very spot. Some of these chutes were utter solitudes. The dense, untouched forest overhung both banks of the crooked little crack, and one could believe that human creatures had never intruded there before. The swinging grape-vines, the grassy nooks and vistas glimpsed as we swept by, the flowering creepers waving their red blossoms from the tops of dead trunks, and all the spendthrift richness of the forest foliage, were wasted and thrown away there. The chutes were lovely places to steer in; they were deep, except at the head; the current was gentle; under the "points" the water was absolutely dead, and the invisible banks so bluff that where the tender willow thickets projected you could bury your boat's broadside in them as you tore along, and then you seemed fairly to fly.

Behind other islands we found wretched little farms, and wretcheder little log-cabins; there were crazy rail fences sticking a foot or two above the water, with one or two jeans-clad, chills-racked, yellow-faced male miserables roosting on the top-rail, elbows on knees, jaws in hands, grinding tobacco and discharging the result at floating chips through crevices left by lost teeth; while the rest of the family and the few farm-animals were huddled together in an empty wood-flat riding at her moorings close at hand. In this flatboat the family would have to cook and eat and sleep for a lesser or greater number of days (or possibly weeks), until the river should fall two or three feet and let them get back to their log-cabins and their chills again—chills being a merciful provision of an all-wise Providence to enable them to take exercise without exertion. And this sort of watery camping out was a thing which these people were rather liable to be treated to a couple of times a year: by the December rise out of the Ohio, and the June rise out of the Mississippi. And yet these were kindly dispensations, for they at least enabled the poor things to rise from the dead now and then, and look upon life when a steamboat went by. They appreciated the blessing, too, for they spread their mouths and eyes wide open and made the most of these occasions. Now what *could* these banished creatures find to do to keep from dying of the blues during the low-water season!

Once, in one of these lovely island chutes, we found our course completely bridged by a great fallen tree. This will serve to show how narrow some of the chutes were. The passengers had an hour's recreation in a virgin wilderness, while the boat-hands chopped the bridge away; for there was no such thing as turning back, you comprehend.

From Cairo to Baton Rouge, when the river is over its banks, you have no particular trouble in the night; for the thousand-mile wall of dense forest that guards the two banks all the way is only gapped with a farm or wood-yard opening at intervals, and so you can't "get out of the river" much easier than you could get out of a fenced lane; but from Baton Rouge to New Orleans it is a different matter. The river is more than a mile wide, and very deep—as much as two hundred feet, in places. Both banks, for a good deal over a hundred miles, are shorn of their timber and bordered by continuous sugar plantations, with only here and there a scattering sapling or row of ornamental China-trees. The timber is shorn off clear to the rear of the plantations, from two to four miles. When the first frost threatens to come, the planters snatch off their crops in a hurry. When they have finished grinding the cane, they form the refuse of the stalks (which they call *bagasse*) into great piles and set fire to them, though in other sugar countries the bagasse is used for fuel in the furnaces of the sugar mills. Now the piles of damp bagasse burn slowly, and smoke like Satan's own kitchen.

An embankment ten or fifteen feet high guards both banks of the mississippi all the way down that lower end of the river, and this embankment is set back from the edge of the shore from ten to perhaps a hundred feet, according to circumstances; say thirty or forty feet, as a general thing. Fill that whole region with an impenetrable gloom of smoke from a hundred miles of burning bagasse piles, when the river is over the banks, and turn a steamboat loose along there at midnight and see how she will feel. And see how you will feel, too! You find yourself away out in the midst of a vague dim sea that is shoreless, that fades out and loses itself in the murky distances; for you cannot discern the thin rib of embankment, and you are always imagining you see a straggling tree when you don't. The plantations themselves are transformed by the smoke, and look like a part of the sea. All through your watch you are tortured with the exquisite misery of uncertainty. You hope you are keeping in the river, but you do not know. All that you are sure about is that you are likely to be within six feet of the bank *and* destruction, when you think you are a good half-mile from shore. And you are sure, also, that if you chance suddenly to fetch up against the embankment and topple your chimneys overboard, you will have the small comfort of knowing that it is about what you were expecting to do. One of the great Vicksburg packets darted out into a sugar plantation one night, at such a time, and had to stay there a week. But there was no novelty about it; it had often been done before.

I thought I had finished this chapter, but I wish to add a curious thing, while it is in my mind. It is only relevant in that it is connected with piloting. There used to be an excellent pilot on the river, a Mr. X., who was a somnambulist. It was said that if his mind was troubled about a bad piece of river, he was pretty sure to get up and walk in his sleep and do strange things. He was once fellow-pilot for a trip or two with George Ealer, on a great New Orleans passenger packet. During a considerable part of the first trip George was uneasy, but got over it by and by, as X. seemed content to stay in his bed when asleep. Late one night the boat was approaching Helena, Arkansas; the water was low, and the crossing above the town in a very blind and tangled condition. X. had seen the crossing since Ealer had, and as the night was particularly drizzly, sullen, and dark, Ealer was considering whether he had not better have X. called to assist in running the place, when the door opened and X. walked in. Now on very dark nights, light is a deadly enemy to piloting; you are aware that if you stand in a lighted room, on such a night, you cannot see things in the street to any purpose; but if you put out the lights and stand in the gloom you can make out objects in the street pretty well. So, on very dark nights, pilots do not smoke; they allow no fire in the pilot-house stove, if there is a crack which can allow the least ray to escape; they order the furnaces to be curtained with huge tarpaulins and the sky-lights to be closely blinded. Then no light whatever issues from the boat. The undefinable shape that now entered the pilot-house had Mr. X.'s voice. This said,—

"Let me take her, George; I 've seen this place since you have, and it is so crooked that I reckon I can run it myself easier than I could tell you how to do it."

"It is kind of you, and I swear *I* am willing. I have n't got another drop of perspiration left in me. I have been spinning around and around the wheel like a squirrel. It is so dark I can't tell which way she is swinging till she is coming around like a whirligig."

So Ealer took a seat on the bench, panting and breathless. The black phantom assumed the wheel without saying anything, steadied the waltzing steamer with a turn or two, and then stood at ease, coaxing her a little to this side and then to that, as gently and as sweetly as if the time had been noonday. When Ealer observed this marvel of steering, he wished he had not confessed! He stared, and wondered, and finally said,—

"Well, I thought I knew how to steer a steamboat, but that was another mistake of mine."

X. said nothing, but went serenely on with his work. He rang for the leads; he rang to slow down the steam; he worked the boat carefully and neatly into invisible marks, then stood at the centre of the wheel and peered blandly out into the blackness, fore and aft, to verify his position; as the leads shoaled more and more, he stopped the engines entirely, and the dead silence and suspense of "drifting" followed; when the shoalest water was struck, he cracked on the steam, carried her handsomely over, and then began to work her warily into the next system of shoal marks; the same patient, heedful use of leads and engines followed, the boat slipped through without touching bottom, and entered upon the third and last intricacy of the crossing; imperceptibly she moved through the gloom, crept by inches into her marks, drifted tediously till the shoalest water was cried, and then, under a tremendous head of steam, went swinging over the reef and away into deep water and safety!

Ealer let his long-pent breath pour in a great relieving sigh, and said:—

"That 's the sweetest piece of piloting that was ever done on the Mississippi River! I would n't believe it could be done, if I had n't seen it."

There was no reply, and he added: —

"Just hold her five minutes longer, partner, and let me run down and get a cup of coffee."

A minute later Ealer was biting into a pie, down in the "texas," and comforting himself with coffee. Just then the night watchman happened in, and was about to happen out again, when he noticed Ealer and exclaimed,—

"Who is at the wheel, sir?"

"X."

"Dart for the pilot-house, quicker than lightning!"

The next moment both men were flying up the pilot-house companion-way, three steps at a jump! Nobody there! The great steamer was whistling down the middle of the river at her own sweet will! The watchman shot out of the place again; Ealer seized the wheel, set an engine back with power, and held his breath while the boat reluctantly swung away from a "towhead" which she was about to knock into the middle of the Gulf of Mexico!

By and by the watchman came back and said,—

"Did n't that lunatic tell you he was asleep, when he first came up here?"

"No."

"Well, he was. I found him walking along on top of the railings, just as unconcerned as another man would walk a pavement; and I put him to bed; now just this minute there he was again, away astern, going through that sort of tight-rope deviltry the same as before."

"Well, I think I 'll stay by next time he has one of those fits. But I hope he 'll have them often. You just ought to have seen him take this boat through Helena crossing. *I* never saw anything so gaudy before. And if he can do such gold-leaf, kid-glove, diamond-breastpin piloting when he is sound asleep, what *could n't* he do if he was dead!"

Sounding

When the river is very low, and one's steamboat is "drawing all the water" there is in the channel,—or a few inches more, as was often the case in the old times,—one must be painfully circumspect in his piloting. We used to have to "sound" a number of particularly bad places almost every trip when the river was at a very low stage.

Sounding is done in this way. The boat ties up at the shore, just above the shoal crossing; the pilot not on watch takes his "cub" or steersman and a picked crew of men (sometimes an officer also), and goes out in the yawl—provided the boat has not that rare and sumptuous luxury, a regularly devised "sounding-boat"—and proceeds to hunt for the best water, the pilot on duty watching his movements through a spy-glass, meantime, and in some instances assisting by signals of the boat's whistle, signifying "try higher up" or "try lower down;" for the surface of the water, like an oil-painting, is more expressive and intelligible when inspected from a little distance than very close at hand. The whistle signals are seldom necessary, however, never, perhaps, except when the wind confuses the significant ripples upon the water's surface. When the yawl has reached the shoal place, the speed is slackened, the pilot begins to sound the depth with a pole ten or twelve feet long, and the steersman at the tiller obeys the order to "hold her up to starboard;" or "let her fall off to larboard;"[11] or "steady —steady as you go."

When the measurements indicate that the yawl is approaching the shoalest part of the reef, the command is given to "ease all!" Then the men stop rowing and the yawl drifts with the current. The next order is, "Stand by with the buoy!" The moment the shallowest point is reached, the pilot delivers the order, "Let go the buoy!" and over she goes. If the pilot is not satisfied, he sounds the place again; if he finds better water higher up or lower down, he removes the buoy to that place. Being finally satisfied, he gives the order, and all the men stand their oars straight up in the air, in line; a blast from the boat's whistle indicates that the signal has been seen; then the men "give way" on their oars and lay the yawl alongside the buoy; the steamer comes creeping carefully down, is pointed straight at the buoy, husbands her power for the coming struggle, and presently, at the critical moment, turns on all her steam and goes grinding and wallowing over the buoy and the sand, and gains the deep water beyond. Or maybe she doesn't; maybe she "strikes and swings." Then she has to while away several hours (or days) sparring herself off.

Sometimes a buoy is not laid at all, but the yawl goes ahead, hunting the best water, and the steamer follows along in its wake. Often there is a deal of fun and excitement about sounding, especially if it is a glorious summer day, or a blustering night. But in winter the cold and the peril take most of the fun out of it.

A buoy is nothing but a board four or five feet long, with one end turned up; it is a reversed school-house bench, with one of the supports left and the other removed. It is anchored on the shoalest part of the reef by a rope with a heavy stone made fast to the end of it. But for the resistance of the turned-up end of the reversed bench, the current would pull the buoy under water. At night, a paper lantern with a candle in it is fastened on top of the buoy, and this can be seen a mile or more, a little glimmering spark in the waste of blackness.

Nothing delights a cub so much as an opportunity to go out sounding. There is such an air of adventure about it; often there is danger; it is so gaudy and man-of-war-like to sit up in the stern-sheets and steer a swift yawl; there is something fine about the exultant spring of the boat when an experienced old sailor crew throw their souls into the oars; it is lovely to see the white foam stream away from the bows;

[11] The term "'larboard" is never used at sea, now, to signify the left hand; but was always used on the river in my time. *Au.*

there is music in the rush of the water; it is deliciously exhilarating, in summer, to go speeding over the breezy expanses of the river when the world of wavelets is dancing in the sun. It is such grandeur, too, to the cub, to get a chance to give an order; for often the pilot will simply say, "Let her go about;" and leave the rest to the cub, who instantly cries, in his sternest tone of command, "Ease starboard! Strong on the larboard! Starboard give way! With a will, men!" The cub enjoys sounding for the further reason that the eyes of the passengers are watching all the yawl's movements with absorbing interest if the time be daylight; and if it be night he knows that those same wondering eyes are fastened upon the yawl's lantern as it glides out into the gloom and dims away in the remote distance.

One trip a pretty girl of sixteen spent her time in our pilot-house with her uncle and aunt, every day and all day long. I fell in love with her. So did Mr. Thornburg's cub, Tom G——. Tom and I had been bosom friends until this time; but now a coolness began to arise. I told the girl a good many of my river adventures, and made myself out a good deal of a hero; Tom tried to make himself appear to be a hero, too, and succeeded to some extent, but then he always had a way of embroidering. However, virtue is its own reward, so I was a barely perceptible trifle ahead in the contest. About this time something happened which promised handsomely for me: the pilots decided to sound the crossing at the head of 21. This would occur about nine or ten o'clock at night, when the passengers would be still up; it would be Mr. Thornburg's watch, therefore my chief would have to do the sounding. We had a perfect love of a sounding-boat—long, trim, graceful, and as fleet as a greyhound; her thwarts were cushioned; she carried twelve oarsmen; one of the mates was always sent in her to transmit orders to her crew, for ours was a steamer where no end of "style" was put on.

We tied up at the shore above 21, and got ready. It was a foul night, and the river was so wide, there, that a landsman's uneducated eye could discern no opposite shore through such a gloom. The passengers were alert and interested; everything was satisfactory. As I hurried through the engine-room, picturesquely gotten up in storm toggery, I met Tom, and could not forbear delivering myself of a mean speech:—

"Ain't you glad *you* don't have to go out sounding?"

Tom was passing on, but he quickly turned, and said,—

"Now just for that, you can go and get the sounding-pole yourself. I was going after it, but I 'd see you in Halifax, now, before I 'd do it."

"Who wants you to get it? *I* don't. It 's in the sounding-boat."

"It ain't, either. It 's been new-painted; and it 's been up on the ladies cabin guards two days, drying."

I flew back, and shortly arrived among the crowd of watching and wondering ladies just in time to hear the command:

"Give way, men!"

I looked over, and there was the gallant sounding-boat booming away, the unprincipled Tom presiding at the tiller, and my chief sitting by him with the sounding-pole which I had been sent on a fool's errand to fetch. Then that young girl said to me,—

"Oh, how awful to have to go out in that little boat on such a night! Do you think there is any danger?"

I would rather have been stabbed. I went off, full of venom, to help in the pilot-house. By and by the boat's lantern disappeared, and after an interval a wee spark glimmered upon the face of the water a mile away. Mr. Thornburg blew the whistle in acknowledgment, backed the steamer out, and made for it. We flew along for a while, then slackened steam and went cautiously gliding toward the spark. Presently Mr. Thornburg exclaimed,—

"Hello, the buoy-lantern's out!"

He stopped the engines. A moment or two later he said,—

"Why, there it is again!"

So he came ahead on the engines once more, and rang for the leads. Gradually the water shoaled up, and then began to deepen again! Mr. Thornburg muttered:—

"Well, I don't understand this. I believe that buoy has drifted off the reef. Seems to be a little too far to the left. No matter, it is safest to run over it, anyhow."

So, in that solid world of darkness we went creeping down on the light. Just as our bows were in the act of plowing over it, Mr. Thornburg seized the bell-ropes, rang a startling peal, and exclaimed,—

"My soul, it's the sounding-boat!"

A sudden chorus of wild alarms burst out far below—a pause—and then a sound of grinding and crashing followed. Mr. Thornburg exclaimed,—

"There! the paddle-wheel has ground the sounding-boat to lucifer matches! Run! See who is killed!"

I was on the main deck in the twinkling of an eye. My chief and the third mate and nearly all the men were safe. They had discovered their danger when it was too late to pull out of the way; then, when the great guards overshadowed them in a moment later, they were prepared and knew what to do; at my chief's order they sprang at the right instant, seized the guard, and were hauled aboard. The next moment the sounding-yawl swept aft to the wheel and was struck and splintered to atoms. Two of the men and the cub Tom, were missing—a fact which spread like wildfire over the boat. The passengers came flocking to the forward gangway, ladies and all, anxious-eyed, white-faced, and talked in awed voices of the dreadful thing. And often and again I heard them say, "Poor fellows! poor boy, poor boy!"

By this time the boat's yawl was manned and away, to search for the missing. Now a faint call was heard, off to the left. The yawl had disappeared in the other direction. Half the people rushed to one side to encourage the swimmer with their shouts; the other half rushed the other way to shriek to the yawl to turn about. By the callings, the swimmer was approaching, but some said the sound showed failing strength. The crowd massed themselves against the boiler-deck railings, leaning over and staring into the gloom; and every faint and fainter cry wrung from them such words as "Ah, poor fellow, poor fellow! is there *no* way to save him?"

But still the cries held out, and drew nearer, and presently the voice said pluckily,—

"I can make it! Stand by with a rope!"

What a rousing cheer they gave him! The chief mate took his stand in the glare of a torch-basket, a coil of rope in his hand, and his men grouped about him. The next moment the swimmer's face appeared in the circle of light, and in another one the owner of it was hauled aboard, limp and drenched, while cheer on cheer went up. It was that devil Tom.

The yawl crew searched everywhere, but found no sign of the two men. They probably failed to catch the guard, tumbled back, and were struck by the wheel and killed. Tom had never jumped for the guard at all, but had plunged head-first into the river and dived under the wheel. It was nothing; I could have done it easy enough, and I said so; but everybody went on just the same, making a wonderful to-do over that ass, as if he had done something great. That girl could n't seem to have enough of that pitiful "hero" the rest of the trip; but little I cared; I loathed her, any way.

The way we came to mistake the sounding-boat's lantern for the buoy-light was this. My chief said that after laying the buoy he fell away and watched it till it seemed to be secure; then he took up a position a hundred yards below it and a little to one side of the steamer's course, headed the sounding-boat up-stream, and waited. Having to wait some time, he and the officer got to talking; he looked up when he judged that the steamer was about on the reef; saw that the buoy was gone, but supposed that the steamer had already run over it; he went on with his talk; he noticed that the steamer was getting very close down to him, but that was the correct thing; it was her business to shave him closely, for convenience in taking him aboard; he was expecting to sheer off, until the last moment; then it flashed upon him that she was trying to run him down, mistaking his lantern for the buoy light; so he sang out, "Stand by to spring for the guard, men!" and the next instant the jump was made.

A Pilot's Needs

But I am wandering from what I was intending to do; that is, make plainer than perhaps appears in the previous chapters some of the peculiar requirements of the science of piloting. First of all, there is one faculty which a pilot must incessantly cultivate until he has brought it to absolute perfection. Nothing short of perfection will do. That faculty is memory. He cannot stop with merely thinking a thing is so and so; he must *know* it; for this is eminently one of the "exact" sciences. With what scorn a pilot was looked upon, in the old times, if he ever ventured to deal in that feeble phrase "I think," instead of the vigorous one "I know!" One cannot easily realize what a tremendous thing it is to know every trivial detail of twelve hundred miles of river and know it with absolute exactness. If you will take the longest street in New York, and travel up and down it, conning its features patiently until you know every house and window and lamp-post and big and little sign by heart, and know them so accurately that you can instantly name the one you are abreast of when you are set down at random in that street in the middle of an inky black night, you will then have a tolerable notion of the amount and the exactness of a pilot's knowledge who carries the Mississippi River in his head. And then if you will go on until you know every street crossing, the character, size, and position of the crossing-stones, and the varying depth of mud in each of these numberless places, you will have some idea of what the pilot must know in order to keep a Mississippi steamer out of trouble. Next, if you will take half of the signs in that long street, and *change their places* once a month, and still manage to know their new positions accurately on dark nights, and keep up with these repeated changes without making any mistakes, you will understand what is required of a pilot's peerless memory by the fickle Mississippi.

I think a pilot's memory is about the most wonderful thing in the world. To know the Old and New Testaments by heart, and be able to recite them glibly, forward or backward, or begin at random anywhere in the book and recite both ways and never trip or make a mistake, is no extravagant mass of knowledge, and no marvellous facility, compared to a pilot's massed knowledge of the Mississippi and his marvellous facility in the handling of it. I make this comparison deliberately, and believe I am not expanding the truth when I do it. Many will think my figure too strong, but pilots will not.

And how easily and comfortably the pilot's memory does its work; how placidly effortless is its way; how *unconsciously* it lays up its vast stores, hour by hour, day by day, and never loses or mislays a single valuable package of them all! Take an instance. Let a leadsman cry, "Half twain! half twain! half twain! half twain! half twain!" until it becomes as monotonous as the ticking of a clock; let conversation be going on all the time, and the pilot be doing his share of the talking, and no longer consciously listening to the leadsman; and in the midst of this endless string of half twains let a single "quarter twain" be interjected, without emphasis, and then the half twain cry go on again, just as before: two or three weeks later that pilot can describe with precision the boat's position in the river when that quarter twain was uttered, and give you such a lot of head-marks, stern-marks, and side-marks to guide you, that you ought to be able to take the boat there and put her in that same spot again yourself! The cry of "quarter twain" did not really take his mind from his talk, but his trained faculties instantly photographed the bearings, noted the change of depth, and laid up the important details for future reference without requiring any assistance from *him* in the matter. If you were walking and talking with a friend, and another friend at your side kept up a monotonous repetition of the vowel sound A, for a couple of blocks, and then in the midst interjected an R, thus A, A, A, A, A, R, A, A, A, etc., and gave the R no emphasis, you would not be able to state, two or three weeks afterward, that the R had been put in, nor be able to tell what objects you were passing at the moment it was done. But you could if your memory had been patiently and laboriously trained to do that sort of thing mechanically.

Give a man a tolerably fair memory to start with, and piloting will develop it into a very colossus of capability. But *only in the matters it is daily drilled in*. A time would come when the man's faculties could not help noticing landmarks and soundings, and his memory could not help holding on to them with the grip of a vice; but if you asked that same man at noon what he had had for breakfast, it would be ten chances to one that he could not tell you, Astonishing things can be done with the human memory if you will devote it faithfully to one particular line of business.

At the time that wages soared so high on the Missouri River, my chief, Mr. Bixby, went up there and learned more than a thousand miles of that stream with an ease and rapidity that were astonishing. When he had seen each division *once* in the daytime and *once* at night, his education was so nearly complete that he took out a "daylight" license; a few trips later he took out a full license, and went to piloting day and night,—and he ranked A 1, too.

Mr. Bixby placed me as steersman for a while under a pilot whose feats of memory were a constant marvel to me. However, his memory was born in him, I think, not built. For instance, somebody would mention a name. Instantly Mr. Brown would break in:—

"Oh, I knew *him*. Sallow-faced, red-headed fellow, with a little scar on the side of his throat, like a splinter under the flesh. He was only in the Southern trade six months. That was thirteen years ago. I made a trip with him. There was five feet in the upper river then; the 'Henry Blake' grounded at the foot of Tower Island drawing four and a half; the 'George Elliott' unshipped her rudder on the wreck of the 'Sunflower' "—

"Why, the 'Sunflower' did n't sink until"—

"I know when she sunk; it was three years before that, on the 2d of December; Asa Hardy was captain of her, and his brother John was first clerk; and it was his first trip in her, too; Tom Jones told me these things a week afterward in New Orleans; he was first mate of the 'Sunflower.' Captain Hardy stuck a nail in his foot the 6th of July of the next year, and died of the lockjaw on the 15th. His brother John died two years after,—3d of March,—erysipelas. I never saw either of the Hardys,—they were Alleghany River men,—but people who knew them told me all these things. And they said Captain Hardy wore yarn socks winter and summer just the same, and his first wife's name was Jane Shook,—she was from New England,—and his second one died in a lunatic asylum. It was in the blood. She was from Lexington, Kentucky. Name was Horton before she was married."

And so on, by the hour, the man's tongue would go. He could *not* forget anything. It was simply impossible. The most trivial details remained as distinct and luminous in his head, after they had lain there for years, as the most memorable events. His was not simply a pilot's memory; its grasp was universal. If he were talking about a trifling letter he had received seven years before, he was pretty sure to deliver you the entire screed from memory. And then without observing that he was departing from the true line of his talk, he was more than likely to hurl in a long-drawn parenthetical biography of the writer of that letter; and you were lucky indeed, if he did not take up that writer's relatives, one by one, and give you their biographies, too.

Such a memory as that is a great misfortune. To it, all occurrences are of the same size. Its possessor cannot distinguish an interesting circumstance from an uninteresting one. As a talker, he is bound to clog his narrative with tiresome details and make himself an insufferable bore. Moreover, he cannot stick to his subject. He picks up every little grain of memory he discerns in his way, and so is led aside. Mr. Brown would start out with the honest intention of telling you a vastly funny anecdote about a dog. He would be "so full of laugh" that he could hardly begin; then his memory would start with the dog's breed and personal appearance; drift into a history of his owner; of his owner's family, with descriptions of weddings and burials that had occurred in it, together with recitals of congratulatory verses and obituary poetry provoked by the same; then this memory would recollect that one of these events occurred during the celebrated "hard winter" of such and such a year, and a minute description of that winter would follow, along with the names of people who were frozen to death, and statistics showing the high figures which pork and hay went up to. Pork and hay would suggest corn and fodder; corn and fodder would suggest cows and horses; cows and horses would suggest the circus and certain celebrated bareback rides; the transition from the circus to the menagerie was easy and natural; from the elephant to equatorial Africa was but a step; then of course the heathen savages would suggest religion; and at the end of three or four hours' tedious jaw, the watch would change, and Brown would go out of the pilot-house muttering extracts from sermons he had heard years before about the efficacy of prayer as a means of grace. And the original first mention would be all you had learned about that dog, after all this waiting and hungering.

A pilot must have a memory; but there are two higher qualities which he must also have. He must have good and quick judgment and decision, and a cool, calm courage that no peril can shake. Give a man the merest trifle of pluck to start with, and by the time he has become a pilot he cannot be unmanned by any danger a steamboat can get into; but one cannot quite say the same for judgment. Judgment is a matter of brains, and a man must *start* with a good stock of that article or he will never succeed as a pilot.

The growth of courage in the pilot-house is steady all the time, but it does not reach a high and satisfactory condition until some time after the young pilot has been "standing his own watch," alone and under the staggering weight of all the responsibilities connected with the position. When the apprentice has become pretty thoroughly acquainted with the river, he goes clattering along so fearlessly with his steamboat, night or day, that he presently begins to imagine that it is *his* courage that animates him; but the first time the pilot steps out and leaves him to his own devices he finds out it was the other man's. He discovers that the article has been left out of his own cargo altogether. The whole river is bristling with exigencies in a moment; he is not prepared for them; he does not know how to meet them; all his knowledge forsakes him; and within fifteen minutes he is as white as a sheet and scared almost to death. Therefore pilots wisely train these cubs by various strategic tricks to look danger in the face a little more calmly. A favorite way of theirs is to play a friendly swindle upon the candidate.

Mr. Bixby served me in this fashion once, and for years afterward I used to blush even in my sleep when I thought of it. I had become a good steersman; so good, indeed, that I had all the work to do on our watch, night and day; Mr. Bixby seldom made a suggestion to me; all he ever did was to take the wheel on particularly bad nights or in particularly bad crossings, land the boat when she needed to be landed, play gentleman of leisure nine tenths of the watch, and collect the wages. The lower river was about bank-full, and if anybody had questioned my ability to run any crossing between Cairo and New Orleans without help or instruction, I should have felt irreparably hurt. The idea of being afraid of any crossing in the lot, in the *day-time*, was a thing too preposterous for contemplation. Well, one matchless summer's day I was bowling down the bend above Island 66, brimful of self-conceit and carrying my nose as high as a giraffe's, when Mr. Bixby said,—

"I am going below a while. I suppose you know the next crossing?"

This was almost an affront. It was about the plainest and simplest crossing in the whole river. One could n't come to any harm, whether he ran it right or not; and as for depth, there never had been any bottom there. I knew all this, perfectly well.

"Know how to *run* it? Why, I can run it with my eyes shut."

"How much water is there in it?"

"Well, that is an old question. I could n't get bottom there with a church steeple."

"You think so, do you?"

The very tone of the question shook my confidence. That was what Mr. Bixby was expecting. He left, without saying anything more. I began to imagine all sorts of things. Mr. Bixby, unknown to me, of course, sent somebody down to the forecastle with some mysterious instructions to the leadsmen, another messenger was sent out to whisper among the officers, and then Mr. Bixby went into hiding behind a smoke-stack where he could observe results. Presently the captain stepped out on the hurricane deck; next the chief mate appeared; then a clerk. Every moment or two a straggler was added to my audience; and before I got to the head of the island I had fifteen or twenty people assembled down there under my nose. I began to wonder what the trouble was. As I started across, the captain glanced aloft at me and said, with a sham uneasiness in his voice,—

"Where is Mr. Bixby?"

"Gone below, sir."

But that did the business for me. My imagination began to construct dangers out of nothing, and they multiplied faster than I could keep the run of them. All at once I imagined I saw shoal water ahead! The wave of coward agony that surged through me then came near dislocating every joint in me. All my confidence in that crossing vanished. I seized the bell-rope; dropped it, ashamed; seized it again; dropped it once more; clutched it tremblingly once again, and pulled it so feebly that I could hardly hear the stroke myself. Captain and mate sang out instantly, and both together,—

"Starboard lead there! and quick about it!"

This was another shock. I began to climb the wheel like a squirrel; but I would hardly get the boat started to port before I would see new dangers on that side, and away I would spin to the other; only to find perils accumulating to starboard, and be crazy to get to port again. Then came the leadsman's sepulchral cry: —

"D-e-e-p four!"

Deep four in a bottomless crossing! The terror of it took my breath away.

"M-a-r-k three! ... M-a-r-k three! ... Quarter less three! ... Half twain!"

This was frightful! I seized the bell-ropes and stopped the engines.

"Quarter twain! Quarter twain! *Mark* twain!"

I was helpless. I did not know what in the world to do. I was quaking from head to foot, and I could have hung my hat on my eyes, they stuck out so far.

"Quarter *less* twain! Nine and a *half!*"

We were *drawing* nine! My hands were in a nerveless flutter. I could not ring a bell intelligibly with them. I flew to the speaking-tube and shouted to the engineer,—

"Oh, Ben, if you love me, *back* her! Quick, Ben! Oh, back the immortal *soul* out of her!"

I heard the door close gently. I looked around, and there stood Mr. Bixby, smiling a bland, sweet smile. Then the audience on the hurricane deck sent up a thundergust of humiliating laughter. I saw it all, now, and I felt meaner than the meanest man in human history. I laid in the lead, set the boat in her marks, came ahead on the engines, and said: —

"It was a fine trick to play on an orphan, *was n't* it? I suppose I 'll never hear the last of how I was ass enough to heave the lead at the head of 66."

"Well, no, you won't, maybe. In fact I hope you won't; for I want you to learn something by that experience. Did n't you *know* there was no bottom in that crossing?"

"Yes, sir, I did."

"Very well, then. You should n't have allowed me or anybody else to shake your confidence in that knowledge. Try to remember that. And another thing: when you get into a dangerous place, don't turn coward. That is n't going to help matters any."

It was a good enough lesson, but pretty hardly learned. Yet about the hardest part of it was that for months I so often had to hear a phrase which I had conceived a particular distaste for. It was, "Oh, Ben, if you love me, back her!"

Rank and Dignity of Piloting

In my preceding chapters I have tried, by going into the minutiæ of the science of piloting, to carry the reader step by step to a comprehension of what the science consists of; and at the same time I have tried to show him that it is a very curious and wonderful science, too, and very worthy of his attention. If I have seemed to love my subject, it is no surprising thing, for I loved the profession far better than any I have followed since, and I took a measureless pride in it. The reason is plain: a pilot, in those days, was the only unfettered and entirely independent human being that lived in the earth. Kings are but the hampered servants of parliament and the people; parliaments sit in chains forged by their constituency; the editor of a newspaper cannot be independent, but must work with one hand tied behind him by party and patrons, and be content to utter only half or two thirds of his mind; no clergyman is a free man and may speak the whole truth, regardless of his parish's opinions; writers of all kinds are manacled servants of the public. We write frankly and fearlessly, but then we "modify" before we print. In truth, every man and woman and child has a master, and worries and frets in servitude; but in the day I write of, the Mississippi pilot had *none*. The captain could stand upon the hurricane deck, in the pomp of a very brief authority, and give him five or six orders while the vessel backed into the stream, and then that skipper's reign was over. The moment that the boat was under way in the river, she was under the sole and unquestioned control of the pilot. He could do with her exactly as he pleased, run her when and whither he chose, and tie her up to the bank whenever his judgment said that that course was best. His movements were entirely free; he consulted no one, he received commands from nobody, he promptly resented even the merest suggestions. Indeed, the law of the United States forbade him to listen to commands or suggestions, rightly considering that the pilot necessarily knew better how to handle the boat than anybody could tell him. So here was the novelty of a king without a keeper, an absolute monarch who was absolute in sober truth and not by a fiction of words. I have seen a boy of eighteen taking a great steamer serenely into what seemed almost certain destruction, and the aged captain standing mutely by, filled with apprehension but powerless to interfere. His interference, in that particular instance, might have been an excellent thing, but to permit it would have been to establish a most pernicious precedent. It will easily be guessed, considering the pilot's boundless authority, that he was a great personage in the old steamboating days. He was treated with marked courtesy by the captain and with marked deference by all officers and servants; and this deferential spirit was quickly communicated to the passengers, too. I think pilots were about the only people I ever knew who failed to show, in some degree, embarrassment in the presence of travelling foreign princes. But then, people in one's own grade of life are not usually embarrassing objects.

By long habits, pilots came to put all their wishes in the form of commands. It "gravels" me, to this day, to put my will in the weak shape of a request, instead of launching it in the crisp language of an order.

In those old days, to load a steamboat at St. Louis, take her to New Orleans and back, and discharge cargo, consumed about twenty-five days, on an average. Seven or eight of these days the boat spent at the wharves of St. Louis and New Orleans, and every soul on board was hard at work, except the two pilots; *they* did nothing but play gentleman up town, and receive the same wages for it as if they had been on duty. The moment the boat touched the wharf at either city, they were ashore; and they were not likely to be seen again till the last bell was ringing and everything in readiness for another voyage.

When a captain got hold of a pilot of particularly high reputation, he took pains to keep him. When wages were four hundred dollars a month on the Upper Mississippi, I have known a captain to keep such a pilot in idleness, under full pay, three months at a time, while the river was frozen up. And one must remember that in those cheap times four hundred dollars was a salary of almost inconceivable splendor. Few men on shore got such pay as that, and when they did they were mightily looked up to. When pilots from either end of the river wandered into our small Missouri village, they were sought by the best and the fairest, and treated with exalted respect. Lying in port under wages was a thing which many pilots greatly enjoyed and appreciated; especially if they belonged in the Missouri River in the heyday of that trade (Kansas times [12]), and got nine hundred dollars a trip, which was equivalent to about eighteen hundred dollars a month. Here is a conversation of that day. A chap out of the Illinois River, with a little stern-wheel tub, accosts a couple of ornate and gilded Missouri River pilots: —

"Gentlemen, I 've got a pretty good trip for the up-country, and shall want you about a month. How much will it be?"

"Eighteen hundred dollars apiece."

"Heavens and earth! You take my boat, let me have your wages, and I 'll divide!"

I will remark, in passing, that Mississippi steamboatmen were important in landsmen's eyes (and in their own, too, in a degree) according to the dignity of the boat they were on. For instance, it was a proud thing to be of the crew of such stately craft as the "Aleck Scott" or the "Grand Turk." Negro firemen, deck hands, and barbers belonging to those boats were distinguished personages in their grade of life, and they were well aware of that fact, too. A stalwart darkey once gave offense at a negro ball in New Orleans by putting on a good many airs. Finally one of the managers bustled up to him and said, —

"Who *is* you, any way? Who *is* you? dat's what *I* wants to know!"

The offender was not disconcerted in the least, but swelled himself up and threw that into his voice which showed that he knew he was not putting on all those airs on a stinted capital.

"Who *is* I? Who *is* I? I let you know mighty quick who I is! I want you niggers to understan' dat I fires de middle do' [13] on de 'Aleck Scott!' "

That was sufficient.

The barber of the "Grand Turk" was a spruce young negro, who aired his importance with balmy complacency, and was greatly courted by the circle in which he moved. The young colored population of New Orleans were much given to flirting, at twilight, on the banquettes of the back streets. Somebody saw and heard something like the following, one evening, in one of those localities. A middle-aged negro woman projected her head through a broken pane and shouted (very willing that the neighbors should hear and envy), "You Mary Ann, come in de house dis minute! Stannin' out dah foolin' 'long wid dat low trash, an' heah's de barber off'n de 'Gran' Turk' wants to conwerse wid you!"

My reference, a moment ago, to the fact that a pilot's peculiar official position placed him out of the reach of criticism or command, brings Stephen W—— naturally to my mind. He was a gifted pilot, a good fellow, a tireless talker, and had both wit and humor in him. He had a most irreverent independence, too, and was deliciously easy-

---

[12] In the late 1850s there was a heavy migration into Kansas.
[13] Door. *Au.*

going and comfortable in the presence of age, official dignity, and even
the most august wealth. He always had work, he never saved a penny,
he was a most persuasive borrower, he was in debt to every pilot on the
river, and to the majority of the captains. He could throw a sort of
splendor around a bit of harum-scarum, devil-may-care piloting, that
made it almost fascinating—but not to everybody. He made a trip with
good old Captain Y—— once, and was "relieved" from duty when the
boat got to New Orleans. Somebody expressed surprise at the discharge.
Captain Y—— shuddered at the mere mention of Stephen. Then his
poor, thin old voice piped out something like this:

"Why, bless me! I would n't have such a wild creature on my boat
for the world—not for the whole world! He swears, he sings, he
whistles, he yells—I never saw such an Injun to yell. All times of the
night—it never made any difference to him. He would just yell that
way, not for anything in particular, but merely on account of a kind
of devilish comfort he got out of it. I never could get into a sound sleep
but he would fetch me out of bed, all in a cold sweat, with one of those
dreadful war-whoops. A queer being,—very queer being; no respect for
anything or anybody. Sometimes he called me 'Johnny.' And he kept a
fiddle, and a cat. He played execrably. This seemed to distress the cat,
and so the cat would howl. Nobody could sleep where that man—and
his family—was. And reckless? There never was anything like it. Now
you may believe it or not, but as sure as I am sitting here, he brought
my boat a-tilting down through those awful snags at Chicot under a
rattling head of steam, and the wind a-blowing like the very nation, at
that! My officers will tell you so. They saw it. And, sir, while he was
a-tearing right down through those snags, and I a-shaking in my shoes
and praying, I wish I may never speak again if he didn't pucker up his
mouth and go to *whistling!* Yes, sir; whistling 'Buffalo gals, can't you
come out to-night, can't you come out to-night, can't you come out
to-night;' and doing it as calmly as if we were attending a funeral and
were n't related to the corpse. And when I remonstrated with him about
it, he smiled down on me as if I was his child, and told me to run in
the house and try to be good, and not be meddling with my superiors!"[14]

Once a pretty mean captain caught Stephen in New Orleans out of
work and as usual out of money. He laid steady siege to Stephen, who
was in a very "close place," and finally persuaded him to hire with him
at one hundred and twenty-five dollars per month, just half wages, the
captain agreeing not to divulge the secret and so bring down the contempt of all the guild upon the poor fellow. But the boat was not more
than a day out of New Orleans before Stephen discovered that the captain was boasting of his exploit, and that all the officers had been told.

[14] Considering a captain's ostentatious but hollow chieftainship, and a pilot's real
authority, there was something impudently apt and happy about that way of
phrasing it. *Au.*

Shephen winced, but said nothing. About the middle of the afternoon the captain stepped out on the hurricane deck, cast his eye around, and looked a good deal surprised. He glanced inquiringly aloft at Stephen, but Stephen was whistling placidly, and attending to business. The captain stood around a while in evident discomfort, and once or twice seemed about to make a suggestion; but the etiquette of the river taught him to avoid that sort of rashness, and so he managed to hold his peace. He chafed and puzzled a few minutes longer, then retired to his apartments. But soon he was out again, and apparently more perplexed than ever. Presently he ventured to remark with deference,—

"Pretty good stage of the river now, ain't it, sir?"

"Well, I should say so! Bank-full *is* a pretty liberal stage."

"Seems to be a good deal of current here."

"Good deal don't describe it! It's worse than a mill-race."

"Is n't it easier in toward shore than it is out here in the middle?"

"Yes, I reckon it is; but a body can't be too careful with a steamboat. It's pretty safe out here; can't strike any bottom here, you can depend on that."

The captain departed, looking rueful enough. At this rate, he would probably die of old age before his boat got to St. Louis. Next day he appeared on deck and again found Stephen faithfully standing up the middle of the river, fighting the whole vast force of the Mississippi, and whistling the same placid tune. This thing was becoming serious. In by the shore was a slower boat clipping along in the easy water and gaining steadily; she began to make for an island chute; Stephen stuck to the middle of the river. Speech was *wrung* from the captain. He said,—

"Mr. W——., don't that chute cut off a good deal of distance?"

"I think it does, but I don't know."

"Don't know! Well, is n't there water enough in it now to go through?"

"I expect there is, but I am not certain."

"Upon my word this is odd! Why, those pilots on that boat yonder are going to try it. Do you mean to say that you don't know as much as they do?"

"*They!* Why, *they* are two-hundred-and-fifty-dollar pilots! But don't you be uneasy; I know as much as any man can afford to know for a hundred and twenty-five!"

The captain surrendered.

Five minutes later Stephen was bowling through the chute and showing the rival boat a two-hundred-and-fifty-dollar pair of heels.

FROM **A Tramp Abroad** (1880)

Jim Baker's Blue-jay Yarn

Animals talk to each other, of course. There can be no question about that; but I suppose there are very few people who can understand them. I never knew but one man who could. I knew he could, however, because he told me so himself. He was a middle-aged, simple-hearted miner, who had lived in a lonely corner of California, among the woods and mountains, a good many years, and had studied the ways of his only neighbors, the beasts and the birds, until he believed he could accurately translate any remark which they made. This was Jim Baker. According to Jim Baker, some animals have only a limited education, and use only very simple words, and scarcely ever a comparison or a flowery figure; whereas, certain other animals have a large vocabulary, a fine command of language and a ready and fluent delivery; consequently these latter talk a great deal; they like it; they are conscious of their talent, and they enjoy "showing off." Baker said, that after long and careful observation, he had come to the conclusion that the blue-jays were the best talkers he had found among birds and beasts. Said he:

"There's more *to* a blue-jay than any other creature. He has got more moods and more different kinds of feelings than other creatures; and, mind you, whatever a blue-jay feels, he can put into language. And no mere commonplace language, either, but rattling, out-and-out book-talk—and bristling with metaphor, too—just bristling! And as for command of language—why, *you* never see a blue-jay stuck for a word. No man ever did. They just boil out of him! And another thing: I've noticed a good deal, and there's no bird, or cow, or anything that uses as good grammar as a blue-jay. You may say a cat uses good grammar. Well, a cat does—but you let a cat get excited, once; you let a cat get to pulling fur with another cat on a shed, nights, and you'll hear grammar that will give you the lockjaw. Ignorant people think it's the *noise* which fighting cats make that is so aggravating, but it ain't so; it's the sickening grammar they use. Now I've never heard a jay use bad grammar but very seldom; and when they do, they are as ashamed as a human; they shut right down and leave.

"You may call a jay a bird. Well, so he is, in a measure—because he's got feathers on him, and don't belong to no church, perhaps; but otherwise he is just as much a human as you be. And I'll tell you for why. A jay's gifts, and instincts, and feelings, and interests, cover the whole ground. A jay hasn't got any more principle than a Congressman. A jay will lie, a jay will steal, a jay will deceive, a jay will betray; and four times out of five, a jay will go back on his solemnest promise. The sacredness of an obligation is a thing which you can't cram into no blue-jay's head. Now, on top of all this, there's another thing: a jay can outswear any gentleman in the mines. You think a cat can swear. Well, a cat can; but you give a blue-jay a subject that calls for his reserve powers, and where is your cat? Don't talk to *me*—I know too much about this thing. And there's yet another thing; in the one little particular of scolding—just good, clean, out-and-out scolding—a blue jay can lay over anything, human or divine. Yes, sir, a jay is everything that a man is. A jay can cry, a jay can laugh, a jay can feel shame, a jay can reason and plan and discuss, a jay likes gossip and scandal, a jay has got a sense of humor, a jay knows when he is an ass just as well as you do—maybe better. If a jay ain't human, he better take in his sign, that's all. Now I'm going to tell you a perfectly true fact about some blue-jays.

"When I first begun to understand jay language correctly, there was a little incident that happened here. Seven years ago, the last man in this region but me moved away. There stands his house—been empty ever since; a log house, with a plank roof—just one big room, and no more; no ceiling—nothing between the rafters and the floor. Well, one Sunday morning I was sitting out here in front of my cabin with my cat, taking the sun, and looking at the blue hills, and listening to the leaves rustling so lonely in the trees, and thinking of the home away yonder in the States, that I hadn't heard from in thirteen years, when a blue-jay lit on that house, with an acorn in his mouth, and says, 'Hello, I reckon I've struck something!' When he spoke, the acorn dropped out of his mouth and rolled down the roof, of course, but he didn't care; his mind was all on the thing he had struck. It was a knot-hole in the roof. He cocked his head to one side, shut one eye and put the other one to the hole, like a possum looking down a jug; then he glanced up with his bright eyes, gave a wink or two with his wings— which signifies gratification, you understand—and says, 'It looks like a hole, it's located like a hole—blamed if I don't believe it *is* a hole!'

"Then he cocked his head down and took another look; he glances up perfectly joyful this time; winks his wings and his tail both, and says, 'Oh, no, this ain't no fat thing, I reckon! If I ain't in luck!—why it's a perfectly elegant hole!' So he flew down and got that acorn, and fetched it up and dropped it in, and was just tilting his head back with the heavenliest smile on his face, when all of a sudden he was paralyzed into a listening attitude, and that smile faded gradually out of his countenance like breath off'n a razor, and the queerest look of surprise took its place. Then he says, 'Why I didn't hear it fall!' He cocked his eye at the hole again, and took a long look; raised up and shook his head; stepped around to the other side of the hole, and took another look from that side; shook his head again. He studied a while, then he just went into the *de*tails—walking round and round the hole, and spied into it from every point of the compass. No use. Now he took a thinking attitude on the comb of the roof, and scratched the back of his head and with his right foot for a minute, and finally says, 'Well, it's too many for *me*, that's certain; must be a mighty long hole; however, I ain't got no time to fool around here, I got to 'tend to business; I reckon it's all right—chance it, anyway!'

"So he flew off and fetched another acorn and dropped it in, and tried to flirt his eye to the hole quick enough to see what become of it, but he was too late. He held his eye there as much as a minute; then he raised up and sighed, and says, 'Consound it, I don't seem to understand this thing, no way; however, I'll tackle her again.' He fetched another acorn and done his level best to see what become of it, but he couldn't. He says, 'Well, *I* never struck no such a hole as this before; I'm of the opinion it's a totally new kind of hole.' Then he begun to get mad. He held in for a spell, walking up and down the comb of the roof, and shaking his head and muttering to himself; but his feelings got the upper hand of him presently, and he broke loose and cussed himself black in the face. I never see a bird take on so about a little thing. When he got through he walks to the hole and looks in again for half a minute; then he says, 'Well, you're a long hole, and a deep hole, and a mighty singular hole altogether—but I've started to fill you, and I'm d—d if I *don't* fill you, if it takes a hundred years!'

"And with that, away he went. You never see a bird work so since you was born. He laid into his work like a nigger, and the way he hove acorns into that hole for about two hours and a half was one of the most exciting and astonishing spectacles I ever struck. He never stopped to take a look any more—he just hove 'em in, and went for more. Well, at last he could hardly flop his wings, he was so tuckered out. He comes a-drooping down, once more, sweating like an ice-pitcher, drops his acorn in and says, '*Now* I guess I've got the bulge on you by this time!' So he bent down for a look. If you'll believe me, when his head come up again he was just pale with rage. He says, 'I've shoveled acorns enough in there to keep the family thirty years, and if I can see a sign of one of 'em, I wish I may land in a museum with a belly full of sawdust in two minutes!'

"He just had strength enough to crawl up on to the comb and lean his back agin the chimbly, and then he collected his impressions and begun to free his mind. I see in a second that what I had mistook for profanity in the mines was only just the rudiments, as you may say.

"Another jay was going by, and heard him doing his devotions, and stops to inquire what was up. The sufferer told him the whole circumstances, and says, 'Now younder's the hole, and if you don't believe me, go and look for yourself.' So this fellow went and looked, and comes back and says, 'How many did you say you put in there?' 'Not any less than two tons,' says the sufferer. The other jay went and looked again. He couldn't seem to make it out, so he raised a yell, and three more jays come. They all examined the hole, they all made the sufferer tell it over again, then they all discussed it, and got off as many leather-headed opinions about it as an average crowd of humans could have done.

"They called in more jays; then more and more, till pretty soon this whole region 'peared to have a blue flush about it. There must have been five thousand of them; and such another jawing and disputing and ripping and cussing, you never heard. Every jay in the whole lot put his eye to the hole, and delivered a more chuckled-headed opinion about the mystery than the jay that went there before him. They examined the house all over, too. The door was standing half-open, and at last one old jay happened to go and light on it and look in. Of course, that knocked the mystery galley-west in a second. There lay the acorns, scattered all over the floor. He flopped his wings and raised a whoop. 'Come here!' he says, 'Come here, everybody; hang'd if this fool hasn't been trying to fill up a house with acorns!' They all came a-swooping down like a blue cloud, and as each fellow lit on the door and took a glance, the whole absurdity of the contract that the first jay had tackled hit him home and he fell over backwards suffocating with laughter, and the next jay took his place and done the same.

"Well, sir, they roosted around here on the house-top and the trees for an hour, and guffawed over that thing like human beings. It ain't no use to tell me a blue-jay hasn't got a sense of humor, because I know better. And memory too. They brought jays here from all over the United States to look down that hole, every summer for three years. Other birds too. And they could all see the point, except an owl that came from Nova Scotia to visit the Yo Semite, and he took this thing in on his way back. He said he couldn't see anything funny in it. But then, he was a good deal disappointed about Yo Semite, too."

The Man That Corrupted Hadleyburg (1898)

I

It was many years ago. Hadleyburg was the most honest and upright town in all the region around about. It had kept that reputation unsmirched during three generations, and was prouder of it than of any other of its possessions. It was so proud of it, and so anxious to insure its perpetuation, that it began to teach the principles of honest dealing to its babies in the cradle, and made the like teachings the staple of their culture thenceforward through all the years devoted to their education. Also, throughout the formative years temptations were kept out of the way of the young people, so that their honesty could have every chance to harden and solidify, and become a part of their very bone. The neighboring towns were jealous of this honorable supremacy, and affected to sneer at Hadleyburg's pride in it and call it vanity; but all the same they were obliged to acknowledge that Hadleyburg was in reality an incorruptible town; and if pressed they would also acknowledge that the mere fact that a young man hailed from Hadleyburg was all the recommendation he needed when he went forth from his natal town to seek for responsible employment.

But at last, in the drift of time, Hadleyburg had the ill luck to offend a passing stranger—possibly without knowing it, certainly without caring, for Hadleyburg was sufficient unto itself, and cared not a rap for strangers or their opinions. Still, it would have been well to make an exception in this one's case, for he was a bitter man and revengeful. All through his wanderings during a whole year he kept his injury in mind, and gave all his leisure moments to trying to invent a compensating satisfaction for it. He contrived many plans, and all of them were good, but none of them was quite sweeping enough; the poorest of them would hurt a great many individuals, but what he wanted was a plan which would comprehend the entire town, and not let so much as one person escape unhurt. At last he had a fortunate idea, and when it fell into his brain it lit up his whole head with an evil joy. He began to form a plan at once, saying to himself, "That is the thing to do—I will corrupt the town."

Six months later he went to Hadleyburg, and arrived in a buggy at the house of the old cashier of the bank about ten at night. He got a sack out of the buggy, shouldered it, and staggered with it through the cottage yard, and knocked at the door. A woman's voice said "Come in," and he entered, and set his sack behind the stove in the parlor, saying politely to the old lady who sat reading the *Missionary Herald* by the lamp:

"Pray keep your seat, madam, I will not disturb you. There—now it is pretty well concealed; one would hardly know it was there. Can I see your husband a moment, madam?"

No, he was gone to Brixton, and might not return before morning.

"Very well, madam, it is no matter. I merely wanted to leave that sack in his care, to be delivered to the rightful owner when he shall be found. I am a stranger; he does not know me; I am merely passing through the town tonight to discharge a matter which has been long in my mind. My errand is now completed, and I go pleased and a little proud, and you will never see me again. There is a paper attached to the sack which will explain everything. Good night, madam."

The old lady was afraid of the mysterious big stranger, and was glad to see him go. But her curiosity was roused, and she went straight to the sack and brought away the paper. It began as follows:

TO BE PUBLISHED; *or, the right man sought out by private inquiry—either will answer. This sack contains gold coin weighing a hundred and sixty pounds four ounces—*

"Mercy on us, and the door not locked!"

Mrs. Richards flew to it all in a tremble and locked it, then pulled down the window-shades and stood frightened, worried, and wondering if there was anything else she could do toward making herself and the

money more safe. She listened awhile for burglars, then surrendered to
curiosity and went back to the lamp and finished reading the paper:

*I am a foreigner, and am presently going back to my own country, to remain
there permanently. I am grateful to America for what I have received at her
hands during my long stay under her flag; and to one of her citizens—a
citizen of Hadleyburg—I am especially grateful for a great kindness done me
a year or two ago. Two great kindnesses, in fact. I will explain. I was a
gambler. I say I was. I was a ruined gambler. I arrived in this village at night,
hungry and without a penny. I asked for help—in the dark; I was ashamed
to beg in the light. I begged of the right man. He gave me twenty dollars—
that is to say, he gave me life, as I considered it. He also gave me fortune;
for out of that money I have made myself rich at the gaming-table. And
finally, a remark which he made to me has remained with me to this day, and
has at last conquered me; and in conquering has saved the remnant of my
morals; I shall gamble no more. Now I have no idea who that man was, but I
want him found, and I want him to have this money, to give away, throw
away, or keep, as he pleases. It is merely my way of testifying my gratitude
to him. If I could stay, I would find him myself; but no matter, he will be
found. This is an honest town, an incorruptible town, and I know I can trust
it without fear. This man can be identified by the remark which he made to
me; I feel persuaded that he will remember it.*

*And now my plan is this: If you prefer to conduct the inquiry privately, do so.
Tell the contents of this present writing to any one who is likely to be the
right man. If he shall answer, 'I am the man; the remark I made was
so-and-so,' apply the test—to wit: open the sack, and in it you will find a
sealed envelope containing that remark. If the remark mentioned by the
candidate tallies with it, give him the money, and ask no further questions,
for he is certainly the right man.*

*But if you shall prefer a public inquiry, then publish this present writing in
the local paper—with these instructions added, to wit: Thirty days from now,
let the candidate appear at the town-hall at eight in the evening (Friday), and
hand his remark, in a sealed envelope, to the Rev. Mr. Burgess (if he will be
kind enough to act); and let Mr. Burgess there and then destroy the seals of the
sack, open it, and see if the remark is correct; if correct, let the money be
delivered, with my sincere gratitude, to my benefactor thus identified.*

Mrs. Richards sat down, gently quivering with excitement, and was
soon lost in thinkings—after this pattern: "What a strange thing it is!
... And what a fortune for that kind man who set his bread afloat upon
the waters! ... If it had only been my husband that did it!—for we are
so poor, so old and poor! ..." Then, with a sigh—"But it was not my
Edward; no, it was not he that gave a stranger twenty dollars. It is a
pity, too; I see it now. ..." Then, with a shudder—"But it is *gambler's*
money! the wages of sin: we couldn't take it; we couldn't touch it. I
don't like to be near it; it seems a defilement." She moved to a farther
chair. ... "I wish Edward would come and take it to the bank; a burglar
might come at any moment; it is dreadful to be here all alone with it."

At eleven Mr. Richards arrived, and while his wife was saying, "I am *so* glad you've come!" he was saying, "I'm so tired—tired clear out; it is dreadful to be poor, and have to make these dismal journeys at my time of life. Always at the grind, grind, grind, on a salary—another man's slave, and he sitting at home in his slippers, rich and comfortable."

"I am so sorry for you, Edward, you know that; but be comforted: we have our livelihood; we have our good name—"

"Yes, Mary, and that is everything. Don't mind my talk—it's just a moment's irritation and doesn't mean anything. Kiss me—there, it's all gone now, and I am not complaining any more. What have you been getting? What's in the sack?"

Then his wife told him the great secret. It dazed him for a moment; then he said:

"It weighs a hundred and sixty pounds? Why, Mary, it's for-ty thousand dollars—think of it—a whole fortune! Not ten men in this village are worth that much. Give me the paper."

He skimmed through it and said:

"Isn't it an adventure! Why, it's a romance; it's like the impossible things one reads about in books, and never sees in life." He was well stirred up now; cheerful, even gleeful. He tapped his old wife on the cheek, and said, humorously, "Why, we're rich, Mary, rich; all we've got to do is to bury the money and burn the papers. If the gambler ever comes to inquire, we'll merely look coldly upon him and say: 'What is this nonsense you are talking? We have never heard of you and your sack of gold before'; and then he would look foolish, and—"

"And in the meantime, while you are running on with your jokes, the money is still here, and it is fast getting along toward burglar-time."

"True. Very well, what shall we do—make the inquiry private? No, not that; it would spoil the romance. The public method is better. Think what a noise it will make! And it will make all the other towns jealous; for no stranger would trust such a thing to any town but Hadleyburg, and they know it. It's a great card for us. I must get to the printing-office now, or I shall be too late."

"But stop—stop—don't leave me here alone with it, Edward!"

But he was gone. For only a little while, however. Not far from his own house he met the editor-proprietor of the paper, and gave him the document, and said, "Here is a good thing for you, Cox—put it in."

"It may be too late, Mr. Richards, but I'll see."

At home again he and his wife sat down to talk the charming mystery over; they were in no condition for sleep. The first question was, Who could the citizen have been who gave the stranger the twenty dollars? It seemed a simple one; both answered it in the same breath:

"Barclay Goodson."

"Yes," said Richards, "he could have done it, and it would have been like him, but there's not another in the town."

"Everybody will grant that, Edward—grant it privately, anyway. For six months, now, the village has been its own proper self once more—honest, narrow, self-righteous, and stingy."

"It is what he always called it, to the day of his death—said it right out publicly, too."

"Yes, and he was hated for it."

"Oh, of course; but he didn't care. I reckon he was the best-hated man among us, except the Reverend Burgess."

"Well, Burgess deserves it—he will never get another congregation here. Mean as the town is, it knows how to estimate *him*. Edward, doesn't it seem odd that the stranger should appoint Burgess to deliver the money?"

"Well, yes—it does. That is—that is—"

"Why so much that-*is*-ing? Would *you* select him?"

"Mary, maybe the stranger knows him better than this village does."

"Much *that* would help Burgess!"

The husband seemed perplexed for an answer; the wife kept a steady eye upon him, and waited. Finally Richards said, with the hesitancy of one who is making a statement which is likely to encounter doubt:

"Mary, Burgess is not a bad man."

His wife was certainly surprised.

"Nonsense!" she exclaimed.

"He is not a bad man. I know. The whole of his unpopularity had its foundation in that one thing—the thing that made so much noise."

"That 'one thing,' indeed! As if that 'one thing' wasn't enough, all by itself."

"Plenty. Plenty. Only he wasn't guilty of it."

"How you talk! Not guilty of it! Everybody knows he *was* guilty."

"Mary, I give you my word—he was innocent."

"I can't believe it, and I don't. How do you know?"

"It is a confession. I am ashamed, but I will make it. I was the only man who knew he was innocent. I could have saved him, and—and—well, you know how the town was wrought up—I hadn't the pluck to do it. It would have turned everybody against me. I felt mean, ever so mean; but I didn't dare; I hadn't the manliness to face that."

Mary looked troubled, and for a while was silent. Then she said, stammeringly:

"I—I don't think it would have done for you to—to—One mustn't—er—public opinion—one has to be so careful—so—" It was a difficult road, and she got mired; but after a little she got started again. "It was a great pity, but—Why, we couldn't afford it, Edward—we couldn't indeed. Oh, I wouldn't have had you do it for anything!"

"It would have lost us the good will of so many people, Mary; and then—and then—"

"What troubles me now is, what *he* thinks of us, Edward."

"He? *He* doesn't suspect that I could have saved him."

"Oh," exclaimed the wife, in a tone of relief, "I am glad of that! As long as he doesn't know that you could have saved him, he—he— well, that makes it a great deal better. Why, I might have known he didn't know, because he is always trying to be friendly with us, as little encouragement as we give him. More than once people have twitted me with it. There's the Wilsons, and the Wilcoxes, and the Harknesses, they take a mean pleasure in saying, '*Your friend* Burgess,' because they know it pesters me. I wish he wouldn't persist in liking us so; I can't think why he keeps it up."

"I can explain it. It's another confession. When the thing was new and hot, and the town made a plan to ride him on a rail, my conscience hurt me so that I couldn't stand it, and I went privately and gave him notice, and he got out of the town and staid out till it was safe to come back."

"Edward! If the town had found it out—"

"*Don't!* It scares me yet, to think of it. I repented of it the minute it was done; and I was even afraid to tell you, lest your face might betray it to somebody. I didn't sleep any that night, for worrying. But after a few days I saw that no one was going to suspect me, and after that I got to feeling glad I did it, And I feel glad yet, Mary—glad through and through."

"So do I, now, for it would have been a dreadful way to treat him. Yes, I'm glad; for really you did owe him that, you know. But, Edward, suppose it should come out yet, some day!"

"It won't."

"Why?"

"Because everybody thinks it was Goodson."

"Of course they would!"

"Certainly. And of course *he* didn't care. They persuaded poor old Sawlsberry to go and charge it on him, and he went blustering over there and did it. Goodson looked him over, like as if he was hunting for a place on him that he could despise the most, then he says, 'So you are the Committee of Inquiry, are you?' Sawlsberry said that was about what he was. 'Hm. Do they require particulars, or do you reckon a kind of a *general* answer will do?' 'If they require particulars, I will come back, Mr. Goodson; I will take the general answer first.' 'Very well, then, tell them to go to hell—I reckon that's general enough. And I'll give you some advice, Sawlsberry; when you come back for the particulars, fetch a basket to carry the relics of yourself home in.' "

"Just like Goodson; it's got all the marks. He had only one vanity: he thought he could give advice better than any other person."

"It settled the business, and saved us, Mary. The subject was dropped."

"Bless you, I'm not doubting *that*."

Then they took up the gold-sack mystery again, with strong interest. Soon the conversation began to suffer breaks—interruptions caused by absorbed thinkings. The breaks grew more and more frequent. At last Richards lost himself wholly in thought. He sat long, gazing vacantly at the floor, and by and by he began to punctuate his thoughts with little nervous movements of his hands that seemed to indicate vexation. Meantime his wife too had relapsed into a thoughtful silence, and her movements were beginning to show a troubled discomfort. Finally Richards got up and strode aimlessly about the room, plowing his hands through his hair, much as a somnambulist might do who was having a bad dream. Then he seemed to arrive at a definite purpose; and without a word he put on his hat and passed quickly out of the house. His wife sat brooding, with a drawn face, and did not seem to be aware that she was alone. Now and then she murmured, "Lead us not into t— . . . but—but—we are so poor, so poor! . . . Lead us not into . . . Ah, who would be hurt by it?—and no one would ever know. . . . Lead us . . ." The voice died out in mumblings. After a little she glanced up and muttered in a half-frightened, half-glad way:

"He is gone! But, oh dear, he may be too late—too late. . . . Maybe not—maybe there is still time." She rose and stood thinking, nervously clasping and unclasping her hands. A slight shudder shook her frame, and she said, out of a dry throat, "God forgive me—it's awful to think such things—but . . . Lord, how we are made—how strangely we are made!"

She turned the light low, and slipped stealthily over and kneeled down by the sack and felt of its ridgy sides with her hands, and fondled them lovingly; and there was a gloating light in her poor old eyes. She fell into fits of absence; and came half out of them at times to mutter, "If we had only waited!—oh, if we had only waited a little, and not been in such a hurry!"

Meantime Cox had gone home from his office and told his wife all about the strange thing that had happened, and they had talked it over eagerly, and guessed that the late Goodson was the only man in the town who could have helped a suffering stranger with so noble a sum as twenty dollars. Then there was a pause, and the two became thoughtful and silent. And by and by nervous and fidgety. At last the wife said, as if to herself:

"Nobody knows this secret but the Richardses . . . and us . . . nobody."

The husband came out of his thinkings with a slight start, and gazed wistfully at his wife, whose face was become very pale; then he hestitatingly rose, and glanced furtively at his hat, then at his wife—a sort of mute inquiry. Mrs. Cox swallowed once or twice, with her hand at her throat, then in place of speech she nodded her head. In a moment she was alone, and mumbling to herself.

And now Richards and Cox were hurrying through the deserted streets, from opposite directions. They met, panting, at the foot of the printing-office stairs; by the night light there they read each other's face. Cox whispered:

"Nobody knows about this but us?"

The whispered answer was,

"Not a soul—on honor, not a soul!"

"If it isn't too late to—"

The men were starting up-stairs; at this moment they were overtaken by a boy, and Cox asked:

"Is that you, Johnny?"

"Yes, sir."

"You needn't ship the early mail—nor *any* mail; wait till I tell you."

"It's already gone, sir."

"Gone?" It had the sound of an unspeakable disappointment in it.

"Yes, sir. Time-table for Brixton and all the towns beyond changed to-day, sir—had to get the papers in twenty minutes earlier than common. I had to rush; if I had been two minutes later—"

The men turned and walked slowly away, not waiting to hear the rest. Neither of them spoke during ten minutes; then Cox said, in a vexed tone:

"What possessed you to be in such a hurry, *I* can't make out."

The answer was humble enough:

"I see it now, but somehow I never thought, you know, until it was too late. But the next time—"

"Next time be hanged! It won't come in a thousand years."

Then the friends separated without a good night, and dragged themselves home with the gait of mortally stricken men. At their homes their wives sprang up with an eager "Well?"—then saw the answer with their eyes and sank down sorrowing, without waiting for it to come in words. In both houses a discussion followed of a heated sort—a new thing; there had been discussions before, but not heated ones, not ungentle ones. The discussions to-night were a sort of seeming plagiarisms of each other. Mrs. Richards said,

"If you had only waited, Edward—if you had only stopped to think; but no, you must run straight to the printing-office and spread it all over the world."

"It *said* publish it."

"That is nothing; it also said do it privately, if you liked. There, now—is that true, or not?"

"Why, yes—yes, it is true; but when I thought what a stir it would make, and what a compliment it was to Hadleyburg that a stranger should trust it so—"

"Oh, certainly, I know all that; but if you had only stopped to think, you would have seen that you *couldn't* find the right man, because he is in his grave, and hasn't left chick nor child nor relation behind him;

and as long as the money went to somebody that awfully needed it, and nobody would be hurt by it, and—and—"

She broke down, crying. Her husband tried to think of some comforting thing to say, and presently came out with this:

"But after all, Mary, it must be for the best—it *must* be; we know that. And we must remember that it was so ordered—"

"Ordered! Oh, everything's *ordered*, when a person has to find some way out when he has been stupid. Just the same, it was *ordered* that the money should come to us in this special way, and it was you that must take it on yourself to go meddling with the designs of Providence—and who gave you the right? It was wicked, that is what it was—just blasphemous presumption, and no more becoming to a meek and humble professor of—"

"But, Mary, you know how we have been trained all our lives long, like the whole village, till it is absolutely second nature to us to stop not a single moment to think when there's an honest thing to be done—"

"Oh, I know it, I know it—it's been one everlasting training and training and training in honesty—honesty shielded, from the very cradle, against every possible temptation, and so it's *artificial* honesty, and weak as water when temptation comes, as we have seen this night. God knows I never had shade nor shadow of a doubt of my petrified and indestructible honesty until now—and now, under the very first big and real temptation, I—Edward, it is my belief that this town's honesty is as rotten as mine is; as rotten as yours is. It is a mean town, a hard, stingy town, and hasn't a virtue in the world but this honesty it is so celebrated for and so conceited about; and so help me, I do believe that if ever the day comes that its honesty falls under great temptation, its grand reputation will go to ruin like a house of cards. There, now, I've made confession, and I feel better; I am a humbug, and I've been one all my life, without knowing it. Let no man call me honest again—I will not have it."

"I—well, Mary, I feel a good deal as you do; I certainly do. It seems strange, too, so strange. I never could have believed it—never."

A long silence followed; both were sunk in thought. At last the wife looked up and said:

"I know what you are thinking, Edward."

Richards had the embarrassed look of a person who is caught.

"I am ashamed to confess it, Mary, but—"

"It's no matter, Edward, I was thinking the same question myself."

"I hope so. State it."

"You were thinking, if a body could only guess out *what the remark was* that Goodson made to the stranger."

"It's perfectly true. I feel guilty and ashamed. And you?"

"I'm past it. Let us make a pallet here; we've got to stand watch till the bank vault opens in the morning and admits the sack. . . . Oh dear, oh dear—if we hadn't made the mistake!"

The pallet was made, and Mary said:

"The open sesame—what could it have been? I do wonder what that remark could have been? But come; we will get to bed now."

"And sleep?"

"No: think."

"Yes, think."

By this time the Coxes too had completed their spat and their reconciliation, and were turning in—to think, to think, and toss, and fret, and worry over what the remark could possibly have been which Goodson made to the stranded derelict; that golden remark; that remark worth forty thousand dollars, cash.

The reason that the village telegraph-office was open later than usual that night was this: The foreman of Cox's paper was the local representative of the Associated Press. One might say its honorary representative, for it wasn't four times a year that he could furnish thirty words that would be accepted. But this time it was different. His despatch stating what he had caught got an instant answer:

Send the whole thing—all the details—twelve hundred words.

A colossal order! The foreman filled the bill; and he was the proudest man in the State. By breakfast-time the next morning the name of Hadleyburg the Incorruptible was on every lip in America, from Montreal to the Gulf, from the glaciers of Alaska to the orange-groves of Florida; and millions and millions of people were discussing the stranger and his money-sack, and wondering if the right man would be found, and hoping some more news about the matter would come soon—right away.

II

Hadleyburg village woke up world-celebrated—astonished—happy—vain. Vain beyond imagination. Its nineteen principal citizens and their wives went about shaking hands with each other, and beaming, and smiling, and congratulating, and saying *this* thing adds a new word to the dictionary—*Hadleyburg,* synonym for *incorruptible*—destined to live in dictionaries forever! And the minor and unimportant citizens and their wives went around acting in much the same way. Everybody ran to the bank to see the gold-sack; and before noon grieved and envious crowds began to flock in from Brixton and all neighboring towns; and that afternoon and next day reporters began to arrive from everywhere to verify the sack and its history and write the whole thing up anew, and make dashing free-hand pictures of the sack, and of Richards's house, and the bank, and the Presbyterian church, and the Baptist church, and the public square, and the town-hall where the test would be applied and the money delivered; and damnable portraits of the Richardses, and Pinkerton the banker, and Cox, and the foreman, and Reverend Burgess, and the postmaster—and even of Jack Halliday, who was the loafing, good-natured, no-account, irreverent fisherman, hunter, boys' friend, stray-dogs' friend, typical "Sam Lawson" of the town. The little, mean, smirking, oily Pinkerton showed the sack to all comers, and rubbed his sleek palms together pleasantly, and enlarged upon the town's fine old reputation for honesty and upon this wonderful indorsement of it, and hoped and believed that the example would now spread far and wide over the American world, and be epoch-making in the matter of moral regeneration. And so on, and so on.

By the end of a week things had quieted down again; the wild intoxication of pride and joy had sobered to a soft, sweet, silent delight—a sort of deep, nameless, unutterable content. All faces bore a look of peaceful, holy happiness.

Then a change came. It was a gradual change: so gradual that its beginnings were hardly noticed; maybe were not noticed at all, except by Jack Halliday, who always noticed everything; and always made fun of it, too, no matter what it was. He began to throw out chaffing remarks about people not looking quite so happy as they did a day or two ago; and next he claimed that the new aspect was deepening to positive sadness; next, that it was taking on a sick look; and finally he said that everybody was become so moody, thoughtful, and absent-minded that he could rob the meanest man in town of a cent out of the bottom of his breeches pocket and not disturb his revery.

At this stage—or at about this stage—a saying like this was dropped at bedtime—with a sigh, usually—by the head of each of the nineteen principal households: "Ah, what *could* have been the remark that Goodson made?"

And straightway—with a shudder—came this, from the man's wife:

"Oh, *don't!* What horrible thing are you mulling in your mind? Put it away from you, for God's sake!"

But that question was wrung from those men again the next night—and got the same retort. But weaker.

And the third night the men uttered the question yet again—with anguish, and absently. This time—and the following night—the wives fidgeted feebly, and tried to say something. But didn't.

And the night after that they found their tongues and responded—longingly:

"Oh, if we *could* only guess!"

Halliday's comments grew daily more and more sparklingly disagreeable and disparaging. He went diligently about, laughing at the town, individually and in mass. But his laugh was the only one left in the village: it fell upon a hollow and mournful vacancy and emptiness. Not even a smile was findable anywhere. Halliday carried a cigar-box around on a tripod, playing that it was a camera, and halted all passers and aimed the thing and said, "Ready!—now look pleasant, please," but not even this capital joke could surprise the dreary faces into any softening.

So three weeks passed—one week was left. It was Saturday evening—after supper. Instead of the aforetime Saturday-evening flutter and bustle and shopping and larking, the streets were empty and desolate. Richards and his old wife sat apart in their little parlor—miserable and thinking. This was become their evening habit now: the lifelong habit which had preceded it, of reading, knitting, and contented chat, or receiving or paying neighborly calls, was dead and gone and forgotten, ages ago—two or three weeks ago; nobody talked now, nobody read, nobody visited—the whole village sat at home, sighing, worrying, silent. Trying to guess out that remark.

The postman left a letter. Richards glanced listlessly at the superscription and the postmark—unfamiliar, both—and tossed the letter on the table and resumed his might-have-beens and his hopeless dull miseries where he had left them off. Two or three hours later his wife got wearily up and was going away to bed without a good night— custom now—but she stopped near the letter and eyed it awhile with a dead interest, then broke it open, and began to skim it over. Richards, sitting there with his chair tilted back against the wall and his chin between his knees, heard something fall. It was his wife. He sprang to her side, but she cried out:

"Leave me alone, I am too happy. Read the letter—read it!"

He did. He devoured it, his brain reeling. The letter was from a distant state, and it said:

I am a stranger to you, but no matter: I have somehting to tell. I have just arrived home from Mexico, and learned about that episode. Of course you do not know who made that remark, but I know, and I am the only person living who does know. It was GOODSON. *I knew him well, many years ago. I passed through your village that very night, and was his guest till the midnight train came along. I overheard him make that remark to the stranger in the dark— it was in Hale Alley. He and I talked of it the rest of the way home, and while smoking in his house. He mentioned many of your villagers in the course of his talk—most of them in a very uncomplimentary way, but two or three favorably; among these latter yourself. I say "favorably"—nothing stronger. I remember his saying he did not actually* LIKE *any person in the town—not one; but that you—I* THINK *he said you—am almost sure—had done him a very great service once, possibly without knowing the full value of it, and he wished he had a fortune, he would leave it to you when he died, and a curse apiece for the rest of the citizens. Now, then, if it was you that did him that service, you are his legitimate heir, and entitled to the sack of gold. I know that I can trust to your honor and honesty, for in a citizen of Hadleyburg these virtues are an unfailing inheritance, and so I am going to reveal to you the remark, well satisfied that if you are not the right man you will seek and find the right one and see that poor Goodson's debt of gratitude for the service referred to is paid. This is the remark:* "YOU ARE FAR FROM BEING A BAD MAN: GO, AND REFORM."

Howard L. Stephenson.

"Oh, Edward, the money is ours, and I am so grateful, *oh,* so grateful—kiss me, dear, it's forever since we kissed—and we needed it so—the money—and now you are free of Pinkerton and his bank, and nobody's slave any more; it seems to me I could fly for joy."

It was a happy half-hour that the couple spent there on the settee caressing each other; it was the old days come again—days that had begun with their courtship and lasted without a break till the stranger brought the deadly money. By and by the wife said:

"Oh, Edward, how lucky it was you did him that grand service, poor Goodson! I never liked him, but I love him now. And it was fine and beautiful of you never to mention it or brag about it." Then, with a touch of reproach, "But you ought to have told *me,* Edward, you ought to have told your wife, you know."

"Well, I—er—well, Mary, you see—"

"Now stop hemming and hawing, and tell me about it, Edward. I always loved you, and now I'm proud of you. Everybody believes there was only one good generous soul in this village, and now it turns out that you—Edward, why don't you tell me?"

"Well—er—er—Why, Mary, I can't!"

"You *can't? Why* can't you?"

"You see, he—well, he—he made me promise I wouldn't."

The wife looked him over, and said, very slowly:

"Made—you—promise? Edward, what do you tell me that for?"

"Mary, do you think I would lie?"

She was troubled and silent for a moment, then she laid her hand within his and said:

"No . . . no. We have wandered far enough from our bearings—God spare us that! In all your life you have never uttered a lie. But now—now that the foundations of things seem to be crumbling from under us, we—we—" She lost her voice for a moment, then said, brokenly, "Lead us not into temptation. . . . I think you made the promise, Edward. Let it rest so. Let us keep away from that ground. Now—that is all gone by; let us be happy again; it is no time for clouds."

Edward found it something of an effort to comply, for his mind kept wandering—trying to remember what the service was that he had done Goodson.

The couple lay awake the most of the night, Mary happy and busy, Edward busy but not so happy. Mary was planning what she would do with the money. Edward was trying to recall that service. At first his conscience was sore on account of the lie he had told Mary—if it was a lie. After much reflection—suppose it *was* a lie? What then? Was it such a great matter? Aren't we always *acting* lies? Then why not *tell* them? Look at Mary—look what she had done. While he was hurrying off on his honest errand, what was she doing? Lamenting because the papers hadn't been destroyed and the money kept! Is theft better than lying?

That point lost its sting—the lie dropped into the background and left comfort behind it. The next point came to the front: *Had* he rendered that service? Well, here was Goodson's own evidence as reported in Stephenson's letter; there could be no better evidence than that— it was even *proof* that he had rendered it. Of course. So that point was settled. . . . No, not quite. He recalled with a wince that this unknown Mr. Stephenson was just a trifle unsure as to whether the performer of it was Richards or some other—and, oh dear, he had put Richards on his honor! He must himself decide whither that money must go— and Mr. Stephenson was not doubting that if he was the wrong man he would go honorably and find the right one. Oh, it was odious to put a man in such a situation—ah, why couldn't Stephenson have left out that doubt! What did he want to intrude that for?

Further reflection. How did it happen that *Richards's* name remained in Stephenson's mind as indicating the right man, and not some other man's name? That looked good. Yes, that looked very good. In fact, it went on looking better and better, straight along—until by and by it grew into positive *proof*. And then Richards put the matter at once out of his mind, for he had a private instinct that a proof once established is better left so.

He was feeling reasonably comfortable now, but there was still one other detail that kept pushing itself on his notice: of course he had done that service—that was settled; but what *was* that service? He must recall it—he would not go to sleep till he had recalled it; it would make his peace of mind perfect. And so he thought and thought. He thought of a dozen things—possible services, even probable services— but none of them seemed adequate, none of them seemed large enough, none of them seemed worth the money—worth the fortune Goodson had wished he could leave in his will. And besides, he couldn't remember having done them, anyway. Now, then—now, then—what *kind* of a service would it be that would make a man so inordinately grateful? Ah—the saving of his soul! That must be it. Yes, he could remember, now, how he once set himself the task of converting Goodson, and labored at it as much as—he was going to say three months; but upon closer examination it shrunk to a month, then to a week, then to a day, then to nothing. Yes, he remembered now, and with unwelcome vividness, that Goodson had told him to go to thunder and mind his own business—*he* wasn't hankering to follow Hadleyburg to heaven!

So that solution was a failure—he hadn't saved Goodson's soul. Richards was discouraged. Then after a little came another idea: had he saved Goodson's property? No, that wouldn't do—he hadn't any. His life? That is it! Of course. Why, he might have thought of it before. This time he was on the right track, sure. His imagination-mill was hard at work in a minute, now.

Thereafter during a stretch of two exhausting hours he was busy saving Goodson's life. He saved it in all kinds of difficult and perilous ways. In every case he got it saved satisfactorily up to a certain point; then, just as he was beginning to get well persuaded that it had really happened, a troublesome detail would turn up which made the whole thing impossible. As in the matter of drowning, for instance. In that case he had swum out and tugged Goodson ashore in an unconscious state with a great crowd looking on and applauding, but when he had got it all thought out and was just beginning to remember all about it, a whole swarm of disqualifying details arrived on the ground: the town would have known of the circumstance, Mary would have known of it, it would glare like a limelight in his own memory instead of being an inconspicuous service which he had possibly rendered "without knowing its full value." And at this point he remembered that he couldn't swim, anyway.

Ah—*there* was a point which he had been overlooking from the start: it had to be a service which he had rendered "possibly without knowing the full value of it." Why, really, that ought to be an easy hunt—much easier than those others. And sure enough, by and by he found it. Goodson, years and years ago, came near marrying a very sweet and pretty girl, named Nancy Hewitt, but in some way or other the match had been broken off; the girl died, Goodson remained a bachelor, and by and by became a soured one and a frank despiser of the human species. Soon after the girl's death the village found out, or thought it had found out, that she carried a spoonful of negro blood in her veins. Richards worked at these details a good while, and in the end he thought he remembered things concerning them which must have gotten mislaid in his memory through long neglect. He seemed to dimly remember that it was *he* that found out about the negro blood; that it was he that told the village; that the village told Goodson where they got it; that he thus saved Goodson from marrying the tainted girl; that he had done him this great service "without knowing the full value of it," in fact without knowing that he *was* doing it; but that Goodson knew the value of it, and what a narrow escape he had had, and so went to his grave grateful to his benefactor and wishing he had a fortune to leave him. It was all clear and simple now, and the more he went over it the more luminous and certain it grew; and at last, when he nestled to sleep satisfied and happy, he remembered the whole thing just as if it had been yesterday. In fact, he dimly remembered Goodson's *telling* him his gratitude once. Meantime Mary had spent six thousand dollars on a new house for herself and a pair of slippers for her pastor, and then had fallen peacefully to rest.

That same Saturday evening the postman had delivered a letter to each of the other principal citizens—nineteen letters in all. No two of the envelopes were alike, and no two of the superscriptions were in the same hand, but the letters inside were just like each other in every detail but one. They were exact copies of the letters received by Richards—handwriting and all—and were all signed by Stephenson, but in place of Richards's name each receiver's own name appeared.

All night long eighteen principal citizens did what their caste-brother Richards was doing at the same time—they put in their energies trying to remember what notable service it was that they had unconsciously done Barclay Goodson. In no case was it a holiday job; still they succeeded.

And while they were at this work, which was difficult, their wives put in the night spending the money, which was easy. During that one night the nineteen wives spent an average of seven thousand dollars each out of the forty thousand in the sack—a hundred and thirty-three thousand altogether.

Next day there was a surprise for Jack Halliday. He noticed that the faces of the nineteen chief citizens and their wives bore that expression of peaceful and holy happiness again. He could not understand it, neither was he able to invent any remarks about it that could damage it or disturb it. And so it was his turn to be dissatisfied with life. His private guesses at the reasons for the happiness failed in all instances, upon examination. When he met Mrs. Wilcox and noticed the placid ecstasy in her face, he said to himself, "Her cat has had kittens"—and went and asked the cook: it was not so; the cook had detected the happiness, but did not know the cause. When Halliday found the duplicate ecstasy in the face of "Shadbelly" Billson (village nickname), he was sure some neighbor of Billson's had broken his leg, but inquiry showed that this had not happened. The subdued ecstasy in Gregory Yates's face could mean but one thing—he was a mother-in-law short: it was another mistake. "And Pinkerton—Pinkerton—he has collected ten cents that he thought he was going to lose." And so on, and so on. In some cases the guesses had to remain in doubt, in the others they proved distinct errors. In the end Halliday said to himself, "Anyway it foots up that there's nineteen Hadleyburg families temporarily in heaven: I don't know how it happened; I only know Providence is off duty to-day."

An architect and builder from the next state had lately ventured to set up a small business in this unpromising village, and his sign had now been hanging out a week. Not a customer yet; he was a discouraged man, and sorry he had come. But his weather changed suddenly now. First one and then another chief citizen's wife said to him privately:

"Come to my house Monday week—but say nothing about it for the present. We think of building."

He got eleven invitations that day. That night he wrote his daughter and broke off her match with her student. He said she could marry a mile higher than that.

Pinkerton the banker and two or three other well-to-do men planned country-seats—but waited. That kind don't count their chickens until they are hatched.

The Wilsons devised a grand new thing—a fancy-dress ball. They made no actual promises, but told all their acquaintanceship in confidence that they were thinking the matter over and thought they should give it—"and if we do, you will be invited, of course." People were surprised, and said, one to another, "Why, they are crazy, those poor Wilsons, they can't afford it." Several among the nineteen said privately to their husbands, "It is a good idea: we will keep still till their cheap thing is over, then *we* will give one that will make it sick."

The days drifted along, and the bill of future squanderings rose higher and higher, wilder and wilder, more and more foolish and reckless. It began to look as if every member of the nineteen would not only spend his whole forty thousand dollars before receiving-day, but be actually in debt by the time he got the money. In some cases lightheaded people did not stop with planning to spend, they really spent— on credit. They bought land, mortgages, farms, speculative stocks, fine clothes, horses, and various other things, paid down the bonus, and made themselves liable for the rest—at ten days. Presently the sober second thought came, and Halliday noticed that a ghastly anxiety was beginning to show up in a good many faces. Again he was puzzled, and didn't know what to make of it. "The Wilcox kittens aren't dead, for they weren't born; nobody's broken a leg; there's no shrinkage in mother-in-laws; *nothing* has happened—it is an unsolvable mystery."

There was another puzzled man, too—the Rev. Mr. Burgess. For days, wherever he went, people seemed to follow him or to be watching out for him; and if he ever found himself in a retired spot, a member of the nineteen would be sure to appear, thrust an envelope privately into his hand, whisper "To be opened at the town-hall Friday evening," then vanish away like a guilty thing. He was expecting that there might be one claimant for the sack—doubtful, however, Goodson being dead— but it never occurred to him that all this crowd might be claimants. When the great Friday came at last, he found that he had nineteen envelopes.

III

The town hall had never looked finer. The platform at the end of it was backed by a showy draping of flags; at intervals along the walls were festoons of flags; the gallery fronts were clothed in flags; the supporting columns were swathed in flags; all this was to impress the stranger, for he would be there in considerable force, and in a large degree he would be connected with the press. The house was full. The

412 fixed seats were occupied; also the 68 extra chairs which had been packed into the aisles; the steps of the platform were occupied; some distinguished strangers were given seats on the platform; at the horse-shoe of tables which fenced the front and sides of the platform sat a strong force of special correspondents who had come from everywhere. It was the best-dressed house the town had ever produced. There were some tolerably expensive toilets there, and in several cases the ladies who wore them had the look of being unfamiliar with that kind of clothes. At least the town thought they had that look, but the notion could have arisen from the town's knowledge of the fact that these ladies had never inhabited such clothes before.

The gold-sack stood on a little table at the front of the platform where all the house could see it. The bulk of the house gazed at it with a burning interest, a mouth-watering interest, a wistful and pathetic interest; a minority of nineteen couples gazed at it tenderly, lovingly, proprietarily, and the male half of this minority kept saying over to themselves the moving little impromptu speeches of thankfulness for the audience's applause and congratulations which they were presently going to get up and deliver. Every now and then one of these got a piece of paper out of his vest pocket and privately glanced at it to refresh his memory.

Of course there was a buzz of conversation going on—there always is; but at last when the Rev. Mr. Burgess rose and laid his hand on the sack he could hear his microbes gnaw, the place was so still. He related the curious history of the sack, then went on to speak in warm terms of Hadleyburg's old and well-earned reputation for spotless honesty, and of the town's just pride in this reputation. He said that this reputation was a treasure of priceless value; that under Providence its value had now become inestimably enhanced, for the recent episode had spread this fame far and wide, and thus had focused the eyes of the American world upon this village, and made its name for all time, as he hoped and believed, a synonym for commercial incorruptibility. [*Applause.*] "And who is to be the guardian of this noble treasure—the community as a whole? Not! The responsibility is individual, not com-munal. From this day forth each and every one of you is in his own person its special guardian, and individually responsible that no harm shall come to it. Do you—does each of you—accept this great trust? [*Tumultuous assent.*] Then all is well. Transmit it to your children and to your children's children. To-day your purity is beyond reproach—see to it that it shall remain so. To-day there is not a person in your com-munity who could be beguiled to touch a penny not his own—see to it that you abide in this grace. ["*We will! we will!*"] This is not the place to make comparisons between ourselves and other communities—some of them ungracious toward us; they have their ways, we have ours; let us be content. [*Applause.*] I am done. Under my hand, my friends, rests a stranger's eloquent recognition of what we are; through him the world will always henceforth know what we are. We do not know who he is, but in your name I utter your gratitude, and ask you to raise your voices in indorsement."

The house rose in a body and made the walls quake with the thunders of its thankfulness for the space of a long minute. Then it sat down, and Mr. Burgess took an envelope out of his pocket. The house held its breath while he slit the envelope open and took from it a slip of paper. He read its contents—slowly and impressively—the audience listening with tranced attention to this magic document, each of whose words stood for an ingot of gold:

" *'The remark which I made to the distressed stranger was this: "You are very far from being a bad man: go, and reform."'*" Then he continued:

"We shall know in a moment now whether the remark here quoted corresponds with the one concealed in the sack; and if that shall prove to be so—and it undoubtedly will—this sack of gold belongs to a fellow-citizen who will henceforth stand before the nation as the symbol of the special virtue which has made our town famous throughout the land—Mr. Billson!"

The house had gotten itself all ready to burst into the proper tornado of applause; but instead of doing it, it seemed stricken with a paralysis; there was a deep hush for a moment or two, then a wave of whispered murmurs swept the place—of about this tenor: *"Billson!* oh, come, this is *too* thin! Twenty dollars to a stranger—or *anybody—Billson!* tell it to the marines!" And now at this point the house caught its breath all of a sudden in a new access of astonishment, for it discovered that whereas in one part of the hall Deacon Billson was standing up with his head meekly bowed, in another part of it Lawyer Wilson was doing the same. There was a wondering silence now for a while.

Everybody was puzzled, and nineteen couples were surprised and indignant.

Billson and Wilson turned and stared at each other. Billson asked, bitingly:

"Why do *you* rise, Mr. Wilson?"

"Because I have a right to. Perhaps you will be good enough to explain to the house why *you* rise?"

"With great pleasure. Because I wrote that paper.

"It is an impudent falsity! I wrote it myself."

It was Burgess's turn to be paralyzed. He stood looking vacantly at first one of the men and then the other, and did not seem to know what to do. The house was stupefied. Lawyer Wilson spoke up, now, and said,

"I ask the Chair to read the name signed to that paper."

That brought the Chair to itself, and it read out the name:

" 'John Wharton *Billson.*' "

"There!" shouted Billson, "what have you got to say for yourself, now? And what kind of apology are you going to make to me and to this insulted house for the imposture which you have attempted to play here?"

"No apologies are due, sir; and as for the rest of it, I publicly charge you with pilfering my note from Mr. Burgess and substituting a copy of it signed with your own name. There is no other way by which you could have gotten hold of the test-remark; I alone, of living men, possessed the secret of its wording."

There was likely to be a scandalous state of things if this went on; everybody noticed with distress that the short-hand scribes were scribbling like mad; many people were crying "Chair, Chair! Order! order!" Burgess rapped with his gavel, and said:

"Let us not forget the proprieties due. There has evidently been a mistake somewhere, but surely that is all. If Mr. Wilson gave me an envelope—and I remember now that he did—I still have it."

He took one out of his pocket, opened it, glanced at it, looked surprised and worried, and stood silent a few moments. Then he waved his hand in a wandering and mechanical way, and made an effort or two to say something, then gave it up, despondently. Several voices cried out:

"Read it! read it! What is it?"

So he began in a dazed and sleep-walker fashion:

" *'The remark which I made to the unhappy stranger was this: "You are far from being a bad man.* [The house gazed at him, marveling.] *Go, and reform.'* " [*Murmurs:* "Amazing! what can this mean?"] "This one," said the Chair, "is signed Thurlow G. Wilson."

"There!" cried Wilson. "I reckon that settles it! I knew perfectly well my note was purloined."

"Purloined!" retorted Billson, "I'll let you know that neither you nor any man of your kidney must venture to—"

The Chair. "Order, gentlemen, order! Take your seats, both of you, please."

They obeyed, shaking their heads and grumbling angrily. The house was profoundly puzzled; it did not know what to do with this curious emergency. Presently Thompson got up. Thompson was the hatter. He would have liked to be a Nineteener; but such was not for him: his stock of hats was not considerable enough for the position. He said:

"Mr. Chairman, if I may be permitted to make a suggestion, can both of these gentlemen be right? I put it to you, sir, can both have happened to say the very same words to the stranger? It seems to me—"

The tanner got up and interrupted him. The tanner was a disgruntled man; he believed himself entitled to be a Nineteener, but he couldn't get recognition. It made him a little unpleasant in his ways and speech. Said he:

"Sho, *that's* not the point! *That* could happen—twice in a hundred

years—but not the other thing. *Neither* of them gave the twenty
dollars!

[*A ripple of applause.*]

Billson. "I did!"

Wilson. "I did!"

Then each accused the other of pilfering.

The Chair. "Order! Sit down, if you please—both of you. Neither of
the notes has been out of my possession at any moment."

A Voice. "Good—that settles *that!*"

The Tanner. "Mr. Chairman, one thing is now plain: one of these
men has been eavesdropping under the other one's bed, and filching
family secrets. If it is not unparliamentary to suggest it, I will remark
that both are equal to it. [*The Chair.* "Order! order!"] I withdraw the
remark, sir, and will confine myself to suggesting that *if* one of them
has overheard the other reveal the test-remark to his wife, we shall catch
him now."

A Voice. "How?"

The Tanner. "Easily. The two have not quoted the remark in exactly
the same words. You would have noticed that, if there hadn't been a
considerable stretch of time and an exciting quarrel inserted between
the two readings."

A Voice. "Name the difference."

The Tanner. "The word *very* is in Billson's note, and not in the
other."

Many Voices. "That's so—he's right!"

The Tanner. "And so, if the Chair will examine the test-remark in
the sack, we shall know which of these two frauds—[*The Chair.*
"Order!"]—which of these two adventurers—[*The Chair.* "Order!
order!"]—which of these two gentlemen—[*laughter and applause*]—is
entitled to wear the belt as being the first dishonest blatherskite ever
bred in this town—which he has dishonored, and which will be a sultry
place for him from now out!" [*Vigorous applause.*]

Many Voices. "Open it!—open the sack!"

Mr. Burgess made a slit in the sack, slid his hand in and brought
out an envelope. In it were a couple of folded notes. He said:

"One of these is marked, 'Not to be examined until all written communications which have been addressed to the Chair—if any—shall
have been read. The other is marked 'The Test.' Allow me. It is worded
—to wit:

" 'I do not require that the first half of the remark which was made
to me by my benefactor shall be quoted with exactness, for it was not
striking, and could be forgotten; but its closing fifteen words are quite
striking, and I think easily rememberable; unless *these* shall be accurately reproduced, let the applicant be regarded as an impostor. My
benefactor began by saying he seldom gave advice to any one, but that

it always bore the hall-mark of high value when he did give it. Then
he said this—and it has never faded from my memory: *"You are far
from being a bad man*—"'"

Fifty Voices. "That settles it—the money's Wilson's! Wilson! Wilson! Speech! Speech!"

People jumped up and crowded around Wilson, wringing his hand
and congratulating fervently—meantime the Chair was hammering with
the gavel and shouting:

"Order, gentlemen! Order! Order! Let me finish reading, please."
When quiet was restored, the reading was resumed—as follows:

"'"Go, and reform—or, mark my words—some day, for your sins,
you will die and go to hell or Hadleyburg—TRY AND MAKE IT THE
FORMER."'"

A ghastly silence followed. First an angry cloud began to settle
darkly upon the faces of the citizenship; after a pause the cloud began
to rise, and a tickled expression tried to take its place; tried so hard
that it was only kept under with great and painful difficulty; the reporters, the Brixtonites, and other strangers bent their heads down and
shielded their faces with their hands, and managed to hold in by main
strength and heroic courtesy. At this most inopportune time burst upon
the stillness the roar of a solitary voice—Jack Halliday's:

"That's got the hall-mark on it!"

Then the house let go, strangers and all. Even Mr. Burgess's gravity
broke down presently, then the audience considered itself officially
absolved from all restraint, and it made the most of its privilege. It
was a good long laugh, and a tempestuously whole-hearted one, but it
ceased at last—long enough for Mr. Burgess to try to resume, and for
the people to get their eyes partially wiped; then it broke out again; and
afterward yet again; then at last Burgess was able to get out these
serious words:

It is useless to try to disguise the fact—we find ourselves in the
presence of a matter of grave import. It involves the honor of your
town, it strikes at the town's good name. The difference of a single word
between the test-remarks offered by Mr. Wilson and Mr. Billson was
itself a serious thing, since it indicated that one or the other of these
gentlemen had committed a theft—"

The two men were sitting limp, nerveless, crushed; but at these
words both were electrified into movement, and started to get up—

"Sit down!" said the Chair, sharply, and they obeyed. "That, as I
have said, was a serious thing. And it was—but for only one of them.
But the matter has become graver; for the honor of *both* is now in
formidable peril. Shall I go even further, and say in inextricable peril?
Both left out the crucial fifteen words." He paused. During several moments he allowed the pervading stillness to gather and deepen its
impressive effects, then added: "There would seem to be but one way

whereby this could happen. I ask these gentlemen—Was there *collu-sion?—agreement?"*

A low murmur sifted through the house; its import was, "He's got them both."

Billson was not used to emergencies; he sat in a helpless collapse. But Wilson was a lawyer. He struggled to his feet, pale and worried, and said:

"I ask the indulgence of the house while I explain this most painful matter. I am sorry to say what I am about to say, since it must inflict irreparable injury upon Mr. Billson, whom I have always esteemed and respected until now, and in whose invulnerability to temptation I entirely believed—as did you all. But for the preservation of my own honor I must speak—and with frankness. I confess with shame—and I now beseech your pardon for it—that I said to the ruined stranger all of the words contained in the test-remark, including the disparaging fifteen. [*Sensation.*] When the late publication was made I recalled them, and I resolved to claim the sack of coin, for by every right I was entitled to it. Now I will ask you to consider this point, and weigh it well: that stranger's gratitude to me that night knew no bounds; he said himself that he could find no words for it that were adequate, and that if he should ever be able he would repay me a thousandfold. Now, then, I ask you this: Could I expect—could I believe—could I even remotely imagine—that, feeling as he did, he would do so ungrateful a thing as to add those quite unnecessary fifteen words to his test?—set a trap for me?—expose me as a slanderer of my own town before my own people assembled in a public hall? It was preposterous; it was impossible. His test would contain only the kindly opening clause of my remark. Of that I had no shadow of doubt. You would have thought as I did. You would not have expected a base betrayal from one whom you had befriended and against whom you had committed no offense. And so, with perfect confidence, perfect trust, I wrote on a piece of paper the opening words—ending with 'Go, and reform,'—and signed it. When I was about to put it in an envelope I was called into my back office, and without thinking I left the paper lying open on my desk." He stopped, turned his head slowly toward Billson, waited a moment, then added: "I ask you to note this: when I returned, a little later, Mr. Billson was retiring by my street door." [*Sensation.*]

In a moment Billson was on his feet and shouting:

"It's a lie! It's an infamous lie!"

The Chair. "Be seated, sir! Mr. Wilson has the floor."

Billson's friends pulled him into his seat and quieted him, and Wilson went on:

"Those are the simple facts. My note was now lying in a different place on the table from where I had left it. I noticed that, but attached no importance to it, thinking a draught had blown it there. That Mr.

Billson would read a private paper was a thing which could not occur to me; he was an honorable man, and he would be above that. If you will allow me to say it, I think his extra word *'very'* stands explained; it is attributable to a defect of memory. I was the only man in the world who could furnish here any detail of the test-remark—by *honorable* means. I have finished."

There is nothing in the world like a persuasive speech to fuddle the mental apparatus and upset the convictions and debauch the emotions of an audience not practised in the tricks and delusions of oratory. Wilson sat down victorious. The house submerged him in tides of approving applause; friends swarmed to him and shook him by the hand and congratulated him, and Billson was shouted down and not allowed to say a word. The Chair hammered and hammered with its gavel, and kept shouting:

"But let us proceed, gentlemen, let us proceed!"

At last there was a measurable degree of quiet, and the hatter said:

"But what is there to proceed with, sir, but to deliver the money?"

Voices. "That's it! That's it! Come forward, Wilson!"

The Hatter. "I move three cheers for Mr. Wilson, Symbol of the special virtue which—"

The cheers burst forth before he could finish; and in the midst of them—and in the midst of the clamor of the gavel also—some enthusiasts mounted Wilson on a big friend's shoulder and were going to fetch him in triumph to the platform. The Chair's voice now rose above the noise—

"Order! To your places! You forget that there is still a document to be read." When quiet had been restored he took up the document, and was going to read it, but laid it down again saying, "I forgot; this is not to be read until all written communications received by me have first been read." He took an envelope out of his pocket, removed its inclosure, glanced at it—seemed astonished—held it out and gazed at it— stared at it.

Twenty or thirty voices cried out:

"What is it? Read it! read it!"

And he did—slowly, and wondering:

" 'The remark which I made to the stranger—[*Voices.* "Hello! how's this?"]—was this: "You are far from being a bad man. [*Voices.* "Great Scott!"] Go, and reform." ' [*Voice.* "Oh, saw my leg off!"] Signed by Mr. Pinkerton, the banker."

The pandemonium of delight which turned itself loose now was of a sort to make the judicious weep. Those whose withers were unwrung laughed till the tears ran down; the reporters, in throes of laughter, set down disordered pot-hooks which would never in the world be decipherable; and a sleeping dog jumped up, scared out of its wits, and barked itself crazy at the turmoil. All manner of cries were scattered through the din: "We're getting rich—*two* Symbols of Incorruptibility!—without counting Billson!" *"Three!"*—count Shadbelly in—we can't have too many!" "All right—Billson's elected!" "Alas, poor Wilson—victim of *two* thieves!"

A Powerful Voice. "Silence! The Chair's fished up something more out of its pocket."

Voices. "Hurrah! Is it something fresh? Read it! read! read!"

The Chair [reading]. " 'The remark which I made,' etc.: ' "You are far from being a bad man. Go," ' etc. Signed 'Gregory Yates.' "

Tornado of Voices. "Four Symbols!" " 'Rah for Yates!" "Fish again!"

The house was in a roaring humor now, and ready to get all the fun out of the occasion that might be in it. Several Nineteeners, looking pale and distressed, got up and began to work their way toward the aisles, but a score of shouts went up:

"The doors, the doors—close the doors; no Incorruptible shall leave this place! Sit down, everybody!"

The mandate was obeyed.

"Fish again! Read! read!"

The Chair fished again, and once more the familiar words began to fall from its lips—" 'You are far from being a bad man.' "

"Name! name! What's his name?"

" 'L. Ingoldsby Sargent.' "

"Five elected! Pile up the Symbols! Go on, go on!"

" 'You are far from being a bad—' "

"Name! name!"

" 'Nicholas Whitworth.' "

"Hooray! hooray! it's a symbolical day!"

Somebody wailed in, and began to sing this rhyme (leaving out "it's") to the lovely "Mikado" tune of "When a man's afraid, a beautiful maid—"; the audience joined in, with joy; then, just in time, somebody contributed another line—

And don't this you forget—

The house roared it out. A third line was at once furnished—

Corruptibles far from Hadleyburg are—

The house roared that one too. As the last note died, Jack Halliday's voice rose high and clear, freighted with a final line—

But the Symbols are here, you bet!

That was sung, with booming enthusiasm. Then the happy house started in at the beginning and sang the four lines through twice, with immense swing and dash, and finished up with a crashing three-times-three and a tiger for "Hadleyburg the Incorruptible and all Symbols of it which we shall find worthy to receive the hall-mark to-night."

Then the shouting at the Chair began again, all over the place:

"Go on! go on! Read! read some more! Read all you've got!"

"That's it—go on! We are winning eternal celebrity!"

A dozen men got up now and began to protest. They said that this farce was the work of some abandoned joker, and was an insult to the whole community. Without a doubt these signatures were all forgeries—

"Sit down! sit down! Shut up! You are confessing. We'll find *your* names in the lot."

"Mr. Chairman, how many of those envelopes have you got?"

The Chair counted.

"Together with those that have been already examined, there are nineteen."

A storm of derisive applause broke out.

"Perhaps they all contain the secret. I move that you open them all and read every signature that is attached to a note of that sort—and read also the first eight words of the note."

"Second the motion!"

It was put and carried—uproariously. Then poor old Richards got up, and his wife rose and stood at his side. Her head was bent down, so that none might see that she was crying. Her husband gave her his arm, and so supporting her, he began to speak in a quavering voice:

"My friends, you have known us two—Mary and me—all our lives, and I think you have liked us and respected us—"

The Chair interrupted him:

"Allow me. It is quite true—that which you are saying, Mr. Richards: this town *does* know you two; it *does* like you; it *does* respect you; more—it honors you and *loves* you—"

Halliday's voice rang out:

"That's the hall-marked truth, too! If the Chair is right, let the house speak up and say it. Rise! Now, then—hip! hip! hip!—all together!"

The house rose in mass, faced toward the old couple eagerly, filled the air with a snow-storm of waving handkerchiefs, and delivered the cheers with all its affectionate heart.

The Chair then continued:

"What I was going to say is this: We know your good heart, Mr. Richards, but this is not a time for the exercise of charity toward offenders. [*Shouts of "Right! right!"*] I see your generous purpose in your face, but I cannot allow you to plead for these men—"

"But I was going to—"

"Please take your seat, Mr. Richards. We must examine the rest of these notes—simple fairness to the men who have already been exposed requires this. As soon as that has been done—I give you my word for this—you shall be heard."

Many Voices. "Right!—the Chair is right—no interruption can be permitted at this stage! Go on!—the names! the names!—according to the terms of the motion!"

The old couple sat reluctantly down, and the husband whispered to the wife, "It is pitifully hard to have to wait; the shame will be greater than ever when they find we were only going to plead for *ourselves.*"

Straightway the jollity broke loose again with the reading of the names.

" 'You are far from being a bad man—' Signature, 'Robert J. Titmarsh.'

" 'You are far from being a bad man—' Signature, 'Eliphalet Weeks.'

" 'You are far from being a bad man—' Signature, 'Oscar B. Wilder.' "

At this point the house lit upon the idea of taking the eight words out of the Chairman's hands. He was not unthankful for that. Thenceforward he held up each note in its turn, and waited. The house droned out the eight words in a massed and measured and musical deep volume of sound (with a daringly close resemblance to a well-known church chant)—" 'You are f-a-r from being a b-a-a-a-d man.' " Then the Chair said, "Signature, 'Archibald Willcox.' ".And so on, and so on, name after name, and everybody had an increasingly and gloriously good time except the wretched Nineteen. Now and then, when a particularly shining name was called, the house made the Chair wait while it chanted the whole of the test-remark from the beginning to the closing words, "And go to hell or Hadleyburg—try and make it the for-or-m-e-r!" and in these special cases they added a grand and agonized and imposing "A-a-a-*men!*"

The list dwindled, dwindled, dwindled, poor old Richards keeping tally of the count, wincing when a name resembling his own was pronounced, and waiting in miserable suspense for the time to come when it would be his humiliating privilege to rise with Mary and finish his plea, which he was intending to word thus: ". . . for until now we have never done any wrong thing, but have gone our humble way unreproached. We are very poor, we are old, and have no chick nor child to help us; we were sorely tempted, and we fell. It was my purpose when I got up before to make confession and beg that my name might not be read out in this public place, for it seemed to us that we could not bear it; but I was prevented. It was just; it was our place to suffer with the rest. It has been hard for us. It is the first time we have ever heard our name fall from any one's lips—sullied. Be merciful—for the sake of the better days; make our shame as light to bear as in your charity you can." At this point in his revery Mary nudged him, perceiving that his mind was absent. The house was chanting, "You are f-a-r," etc.

"Be ready," Mary whispered. "Your name comes now; he has read eighteen."

The chant ended.

"Next! next! next!" came volleying from all over the house.

Burgess put his hand into his pocket. The old couple, trembling, began to rise. Burgess fumbled a moment, then said,

"I find I have read them all."

Faint with joy and surprise, the couple sank into their seats, and Mary whispered:

"Oh, bless God, we are saved!—he has lost ours—I wouldn't give this for a hundred of those sacks!"

The house burst out with its "Mikado" travesty, and sang it three times with ever-increasing enthusiasm, rising to its feet when it reached for the third time the closing line—

But the Symbols are here, you bet!

and finishing up with cheers and a tiger for "Hadleyburg purity and our eighteen immortal representatives of it."

Then Wingate, the saddler, got up and proposed cheers "for the cleanest man in town, the one solitary important citizen in it who didn't try to steal that money—Edward Richards."

They were given with great and moving heartiness; then somebody proposed that Richards be elected sole guardian and Symbol of the now Sacred Hadleyburg Tradition, with power and right to stand up and look the whole sarcastic world in the face.

Passed, by acclamation; then they sang the "Mikado" again, and ended it with:

And there's *one* Symbol left, you bet!

There was a pause; then—

A Voice. "Now, then who's to get the sack?"

The Tanner (with bitter sarcasm). "That's easy. The money has to be divided among the eighteen Incorruptibles. They gave the suffering stranger twenty dollars apiece—and that remark—each in his turn—it took twenty-two minutes for the procession to move past. Staked the stranger—total contribution, $360. All they want is just the loan back—and interest—forty thousand dollars altogether."

Many Voices [derisively]. "That's it! Divvy! divvy! Be kind to the poor—don't keep them waiting!"

The Chair. "Order! I now offer the stranger's remaining document. It says: 'If no claimant shall appear [*grand chorus of groans*] I desire that you open the sack and count out the money to the principal citizens of your town, they to take it in trust [*cries of "Oh! Oh! Oh!"*], and use it in such ways as to them shall seem best for the propagation and preservation of your community's noble reputation for incorruptible honesty [*more cries*]—a reputation to which their names and their efforts will add a new and far-reaching luster.' [*Enthusiastic outburst of sarcastic applause.*] That seems to be all. No—here is a postscript:

" 'P. S.—CITIZENS OF HADLEYBURG: There *is* no test-remark— nobody made one. [*Great sensation.*] There wasn't any pauper stranger, nor any twenty-dollar contribution, nor any accompanying benediction and compliment—these are all inventions. [*General buzz and hum of astonishment and delight.*] Allow me to tell my story—it will take but a word or two. I passed through your town at a certain time, and received a deep offense which I had not earned. Any other man would have been content to kill one or two of you and call it square, but to me that would have been a trivial revenge, and inadequate; for the dead do not *suffer.* Besides, I could not kill you all—and, anyway, made as I am, even that would not have satisfied me. I wanted to damage every man in the place, and every woman—and not in their bodies or in their estate, but in their vanity—the place where feeble and foolish people are most vulnerable. So I disguised myself and came back and studied you. You were easy game. You had an old and lofty reputation for honesty, and naturally you were proud of it—it was your treasure of treasures, the very apple of your eye. As soon as I found out that you carefully and vigilantly kept yourselves and your children *out of temptation,* I knew how to proceed. Why, you simple creatures, the weakest of all weak things is a virtue which has not been tested in the fire. I laid a plan, and gathered a list of names. My project was to corrupt Hadleyburg the Incorruptible. My idea was to make liars and thieves of nearly half a hundred smirchless men and women who had never in their lives uttered a lie or stolen a penny. I was afraid of Goodson. He was neither born nor reared in Hadleyburg. I was afraid that if I started to operate my scheme by getting my letter laid before you, you would say to yourselves, "Goodson is the only man among us who would give away twenty dollars to a poor devil"—and then you might not bite at my bait. But Heaven took Goodson; then I knew I was safe, and I set my trap and baited it. It may be that I shall not catch all the men to whom I mailed the pretended test secret, but I shall catch the most of them, if I know Hadleyburg nature. [*Voices.* "Right—he got every last one of them."] I believe they will even steal ostensible *gamble*-money, rather than miss, poor, tempted, and mistrained fellows. I am hoping to eternally and everlastingly squelch your vanity and give Hadleyburg a new renown—one that will *stick*—and spread far. If I have succeeded, open the sack and summon the Committee on Propagation and Preservation of the Hadleyburg Reputation.' "

A *Cyclone of Voices.* "Open it! Open it! The Eighteen to the front! Committee on Propagation of the Tradition! Forward—the Incorruptibles!"

The Chair ripped the sack wide, and gathered up a handful of bright, broad, yellow coins, shook them together, then examined them—

"Friends, they are only gilded disks of lead!"

There was a crashing outbreak of delight over this news, and when the noise had subsided, the tanner called out:

"By right of apparent seniority in this business, Mr. Wilson is Chairman of the Committee on Propagation of the Tradition. I suggest that he step forward on behalf of his pals, and receive in trust the money."

A *Hundred Voices.* "Wilson! Wilson! Wilson! Speech! Speech!"

Wilson [*in a voice trembling with anger*]. "You will allow me to say, and without apologies for my language, *damn* the money!"

A Voice. "Oh, and him a Baptist!"

A Voice. "Seventeen Symbols left! Step up, gentlemen, and assume your trust!"

There was a pause—no response.

The Saddler. "Mr. Chairman, we've got *one* clean man left, anyway, out of the late aristocracy; and he needs money, and deserves it. I move that you appoint Jack Halliday to get up there and auction off that sack of gilt twenty-dollar pieces, and give the result to the right man—the man whom Hadleyburg delights to honor—Edward Richards."

This was received with great enthusiasm, the dog taking a hand again; the saddler started the bids at a dollar, the Brixton folk and Barnum's representative fought hard for it, the people cheered every jump that the bids made, the excitement climbed moment by moment higher and higher, the bidders got on their mettle and grew steadily more and more daring, more and more determined, the jumps went from a dollar up to five, then to ten, then to twenty, then fifty, then to a hundred, then—

At the beginning of the auction Richards whispered in distress to his wife: "O Mary, can we allow it? It—it—you see, it is an honor-reward, a testimonial to purity of character, and—and—can we allow it? Hadn't I better get up and—O Mary, what ought we to do?—what do you think we—[*Halliday's voice.* "Fifteen I'm bid!—fifteen for the sack!—twenty!—ah, thanks!—thirty—thanks again! Thirty, thirty, thirty!—do I hear forty?—forty it is! Keep the ball rolling, gentlemen, keep it rolling!—fifty! thanks, noble Roman! going at fifty, fifty, fifty!— seventy!—ninety!—splendid!— a hundred!—pile it up, pile it up!— hundred and twenty—forty!—just in time!—hundred and fifty!—TWO hundred!—superb! Do I hear two h— thanks!—two hundred and fifty!—"]*

"It is another temptation, Edward—I'm all in a tremble—but, oh, we've escaped *one* temptation, and that ought to warn us to— ["*Six did I hear?—thanks!—six-fifty, six-f—SEVEN hundred!*"] And yet, Edward, when you think—nobody susp— ["*Eight hundred dollars!—hurrah!— make it nine!—Mr. Parsons, did I hear you say—thanks—nine!—this noble sack of virgin lead going at only nine hundred dollars, gilding and all—come! do I hear—a thousand!—gratefully yours!—did some one say eleven?—a sack which is going to be the most celebrated in the whole Uni—*"] O Edward" (beginning to sob), "we are *so* poor!—but— but—do as you think best—do as you think best."

Edward fell—that is, he sat still; sat with a conscience which was not satisfied, but which was overpowered by circumstances.

Meantime a stranger, who looked like an amateur detective gotten up as an impossible English earl, had been watching the evening's proceedings with manifest interest, and with a contented expression in his face; and he had been privately commenting to himself. He was now soliloquizing somewhat like this: "None of the Eighteen are bidding; that is not satisfactory; I must change that—the dramatic unities require it; they must buy the sack they tried to steal; they must pay a heavy price, too—some of them are rich. And another thing, when I make a mistake in Hadleyburg nature the man that puts that error upon me is entitled to a high honorarium, and some one must pay it. This poor old Richards has brought my judgment to shame; he is an honest man:—I don't understand it, but I acknowledge it. Yes, he saw my deuces *and* with a straight flush, and by rights the pot is his. And it shall be a jackpot, too, if I can manage it. He disappointed me, but let that pass."

He was watching the bidding. At a thousand, the market broke; the prices tumbled swiftly. He waited—and still watched. One competitor dropped out; then another, and another. He put in a bid or two, now. When the bids had sunk to ten dollars, he added a five; some one raised him a three; he waited a moment, then flung in a fifty-dollar jump, and the sack was his—at $1,282. The house broke out in cheers—then stopped; for he was on his feet, and had lifted his hand. He began to speak.

"I desire to say a word, and ask a favor. I am a speculator in rarities, and I have dealings with persons interested in numismatics all over the world. I can make a profit on this purchase, just as it stands; but there is a way, if I can get your approval, whereby I can make every one of these leaden twenty-dollar pieces worth its face in gold, and perhaps more. Grant me that approval, and I will give part of my gains to your Mr. Richards, whose invulnerable probity you have so justly and so cordially recognized tonight; his share shall be ten thousand dollars, and I will hand him the money to-morrow. [*Great applause from the house.* But the "invulnerable probity" made the Richardses blush prettily; however, it went for modesty, and did no harm.] If you will pass my proposition by a good majority—I would like a two-thirds vote—I will regard that as the town's consent, and that is all I ask. Rarities are always helped by any device which will rouse curiosity and compel remark. Now if I may have your permission to stamp upon the faces of each of these ostensible coins the names of the eighteen gentlemen who—"

Nine-tenths of the audience were on their feet in a moment—dog and all—and the proposition was carried with a whirlwind of approving applause and laughter.

They sat down, and all the Symbols except "Dr." Clay Harkness got up, violently protesting against the proposed outrage, and threatening to—

"I beg you not to threaten me," said the stranger, calmly. "I know my legal rights, and am not accustomed to being frightened at bluster." [*Applause.*] He sat down. "Dr." Harkness saw an opportunity here. He was one of the two very rich men of the place, and Pinkerton was the other. Harkness was proprietor of a mint; that is to say, a popular patent medicine. He was running for the legislature on one ticket, and Pinkerton on the other. It was a close race and a hot one, and getting hotter every day. Both had strong appetites for money; each had bought a great tract of land, with a purpose; there was going to be a new railway, and each wanted to be in the legislature and help locate the route to his own advantage; a single vote might make the decision, and with it two or three fortunes. The stake was large, and Harkness was a daring speculator. He was sitting close to the stranger. He leaned over while one or another of the other Symbols was entertaining the house with protests and appeals, and asked, in a whisper:

"What is your price for the sack?"

"Forty thousand dollars."

"I'll give you twenty."

"No."

"Twenty-five."

"No."

"Say thirty."

"The price is forty thousand dollars; not a penny less."

"All right, I'll give it. I will come to the hotel at ten in the morning. I don't want it known: will see you privately."

"Very good." Then the stranger got up and said to the house:

"I find it late. The speeches of these gentlemen are not without merit, not without interest, not without grace; yet if I may be excused I will take my leave. I thank you for the great favor which you have shown me in granting my petition. I ask the Chair to keep the sack for me until to-morrow, and to hand these three five-hundred-dollar notes to Mr. Richards." They were passed up to the Chair. "At nine I will call for the sack, and at eleven will deliver the rest of the ten thousand to Mr. Richards in person, at his home. Good night."

Then he slipped out, and left the audience making a vast noise, which was composed of a mixture of cheers, the "Mikado" song, dog-disapproval, and the chant, "You are f-a-r from being a b-a-a-d man— a-a-a-a-men!"

IV

At home the Richardses had to endure congratulations and compliments until midnight. Then they were left to themselves. They looked a little sad, and they sat silent and thinking. Finally Mary sighed and said,

"Do you think we are to blame, Edward—*much* to blame?" and her eyes wandered to the accusing triplet of big bank-notes lying on the table, where the congratulators had been gloating over them and reverently fingering them. Edward did not answer at once; then he brought out a sigh and said, hesitatingly:

"We—we couldn't help it, Mary. It—well, it was ordered. *All* things are."

Mary glanced up and looked at him steadily, but he didn't return the look. Presently she said:

"I thought congratulations and praises always tasted good. But—it seems to me, now—Edward?"

"Well?"

"Are you going to stay in the bank?"

"N-no."

"Resign?"

"In the morning—by note."

"It does seem best."

Richards bowed his head in his hands and muttered:

"Before, I was not afraid to let oceans of people's money pour through my hands, but—Mary, I am so tired, so tired—"

"We will go to bed."

At nine in the morning the stranger called for the sack and took it to the hotel in a cab. At ten Harkness had a talk with him privately. The stranger asked for and got five checks on a metropolitan bank—drawn to "Bearer"—four for $1,500 each, and one for $34,000. He put one of the former in his pocketbook, and the remainder, representing $38,500, he put in an envelope, and with these he added a note, which he wrote after Harkness was gone. At eleven he called at the Richards house and knocked. Mrs. Richards peeped through the shutters, then went and received the envelope, and the stranger disappeared without a word. She came back flushed and a little unsteady on her legs, and gasped out:

"I am sure I recognized him! Last night it seemed to me that maybe I had seen him somewhere before."

"He is the man that brought the sack here?"

"I am almost sure of it."

"Then he is the ostensible Stephenson, too, and sold every important citizen in this town with his bogus secret. Now if he has sent checks instead of money, we are sold, too, after we thought we had escaped. I was beginning to feel fairly comfortable once more, after my night's rest, but the look of that envelope makes me sick. It isn't fat enough; $8,500 in even the largest bank-notes makes more bulk than that."

"Edward, why do you object to checks?"

"Checks signed by Stephenson! I am resigned to take the $8,500 if it could come in bank-notes—for it does seem that it was so ordered, Mary—but I have never had much courage, and I have not the pluck to try to market a check signed with that disastrous name. It would be a trap. That man tried to catch me; we escaped somehow or other; and now he is trying a new way. If it is checks—"

"Oh, Edward, it is *too* bad!" and she held up the checks and began to cry.

"Put them in the fire! quick! we mustn't be tempted. It is a trick to make the world laugh at *us*, along with the rest, and—Give them to *me*, since you can't do it!" He snatched them and tried to hold his grip till he could get to the stove; but he was human, he was a cashier, and he stopped a moment to make sure of the signature. Then he came near to fainting.

"Fan me, Mary, fan me! They are the same as gold!"

"Oh, how lovely, Edward! Why?"

"Signed by Harkness. What can the mystery of that be, Mary?"

"Edward, do you think—"

"Look here—look at this! Fifteen—fifteen—fifteen—thirty-four. Thirty-eight thousand five hundred! Mary, the sack isn't worth twelve dollars, and Harkness—apparently—has paid about par for it."

"And does it all come to us, do you think—instead of the ten thousand?"

"Why, it looks like it. And the checks are made to 'Bearer,' too."

"Is that good, Edward? What is it for?"

"A hint to collect them at some distant bank, I reckon. Perhaps Harkness doesn't want the matter known. What is that—a note?"

"Yes. It was with the checks."

It was in the "Stephenson" handwriting, but there was no signature. It said:

I am a disappointed man. Your honesty is beyond the reach of temptation. I had a different idea about it, but I wronged you in that, and I beg pardon, and do its sincerely. I honor you—and that is sincere too. This town is not worthy to kiss the hem of your garment. Dear sir, I made a square bet with myself that there were nineteen debauchable men in your self-righteous community. I have lost. Take the whole pot, you are entitled to it.

Richards drew a deep sigh, and said:

"It seems written with fire—it burns so. Mary—I am miserable again."

"I, too. Ah, dear, I wish—"

"To think, Mary—he *believes* in me."

"Oh, don't, Edward—I can't bear it."

"If those beautiful words were deserved, Mary—and God knows I believed I deserved them once—I think I could give the forty thousand dollars for them. And I would put that paper away, as representing more than gold and jewels, and keep it always. But now— We could not live in the shadow of its accusing presence, Mary."

He put it in the fire.

A messenger arrived and delivered an envelope.

Richards took from it a note and read it; it was from Burgess.

You saved me, in a difficult time. I saved you last night. It was at cost of a lie, but I made the sacrifice freely, and out of a grateful heart. None in this village knows so well as I know how brave and good and noble you are. At bottom you cannot respect me, knowing as you do of that matter of which I am accused, and by the general voice condemned; but I beg that you will at least believe that I am a grateful man; it will help me to bear my burden.

                              [Signed]   *"Burgess."*

"Saved, once more. And on such terms!" He put the note in the fire. "I—I wish I were dead, Mary, I wish I were out of it all."

"Oh, these are bitter, bitter days, Edward. The stabs, through their very generosity, are so deep—and they come so fast!"

Three days before the election each of two thousand voters suddenly found himself in possession of a prized memento—one of the renowned bogus double-eagles. Around one of its faces was stamped these words: "THE REMARK I MADE TO THE POOR STRANGER WAS—" Around the other face was stamped these: "GO, AND REFORM. [SIGNED] PINKERTON." Thus the entire remaining refuse of the renowned joke was emptied upon a single head, and with calamitous effect. It revived the recent vast laugh and concentrated it upon Pinkerton; and Harkness's election was a walkover.

Within twenty-four hours after the Richardses had received their checks their consciences were quieting down, discouraged; the old couple were learning to reconcile themselves to the sin which they had committed. But they were to learn, now, that a sin takes on new and real terrors when there seems a chance that it is going to be found out. This gives it a fresh and most substantial and important aspect. At church the morning sermon was of the usual pattern; it was the same old things said in the same old way; they had heard them a thousand times and found them innocuous, next to meaningless, and easy to sleep under; but now it was different: the sermon seemed to bristle with accusations; it seemed aimed straight and specially at people who were concealing deadly sins. After church they got away from the mob of congratulators as soon as they could, and hurried homeward, chilled to the bone at they did not know what—vague, shadowy, indefinite fears. And by chance they caught a glimpse of Mr. Burgess as he turned a corner. He paid no attention their nod of recognition! He hadn't seen it; but they did not know that. What could his conduct mean? It might mean—it might mean—oh, a dozen dreadful things. Was it possible that he knew that Richards could have cleared him of guilt in that bygone time, and had been silently waiting for a chance to even up accounts? At home, in their distress they got to imagining that their servant might have been in the next room listening when Richards revealed the secret to his wife that he knew of Burgess's innocence; next, Richards began to imagine that he had heard the swish of a gown in there at that time; next, he was sure he *had* heard it. They would call Sarah in, on a pretext, and watch her face: if she had been betraying them to Mr. Burgess, it would show in her manner. They asked her some questions—questions which were so random and incoherent and seemingly purposeless that the girl felt sure that the old people's minds had been affected by their sudden good fortune; the sharp and watchful gaze which they bent upon her frightened her, and that completed the business. She blushed, she became nervous and confused, and to the old people these were plain signs of guilt—guilt of some fearful sort or other—without doubt she was a spy and a traitor. When they were alone again they began to piece many unrelated things together and get horrible results out of the combination. When things had got about to the worst, Richards was delivered of a sudden gasp, and his wife asked:

"Oh, what is it?—what is it?"

"The note—Burgess's note! Its language was sarcastic, I see it now." He quoted: " 'At bottom you cannot respect me, *knowing*, as you do, of *that matter* of which I am accused'—oh, it is perfectly plain, now, God help me! He knows that I know! You see the ingenuity of the phrasing. It was a trap—and like a fool, I walked into it. And Mary—?"

"Oh, it is dreadful—I know what you are going to say—he didn't return your transcript of the pretended test-remark."

"No—kept it to destroy us with. Mary, he has exposed us to some already. I know it—I know it well. I saw it in a dozen faces after church. Ah, he wouldn't answer our nod of recognition—*he* knew what he had been doing!"

In the night the doctor was called. The news went around in the morning that the old couple were rather seriously ill—prostrated by the exhausting excitement growing out of their great windfall, the congratulations, and the late hours, the doctor said. The town was sincerely distressed; for these old people were about all it had left to be proud of, now.

Two days later the news was worse. The old couple were delirious, and were doing strange things. By witness of the nurses, Richards had exhibited checks—for $8,500? No—for an amazing sum—$38,500! What could be the explanation of this gigantic piece of luck?

The following day the nurses had more news—and wonderful. They had concluded to hide the checks, lest harm come to them; but when they searched they were gone from under the patient's pillow—vanished away. The patient said:

"Let the pillow alone; what do you want?"

"We thought it best that the checks—"

"You will never see them again—they are destroyed. They came from Satan. I saw the hell-brand on them, and I knew they were sent to betray me to sin." Then he fell to gabbling strange and dreadful things which were not clearly understandable, and which the doctor admonished them to keep to themselves.

Richards was right; the checks were never seen again.

A nurse must have talked in her sleep, for within two days the forbidden gabblings were the property of the town; and they were of a surprising sort. They seemed to indicate that Richards had been a claimant for the sack himself, and that Burgess had concealed that fact and then maliciously betrayed it.

Burgess was taxed with this and stoutly denied it. And he said it was not fair to attach weight to the chatter of a sick old man who was out of his mind. Still, suspicion was in the air, and there was much talk.

After a day or two it was reported that Mrs. Richards's delirious deliveries were getting to be duplicates of her husband's. Suspicion flamed up into conviction, now, and the town's pride in the purity of its one undiscredited important citizen began to dim down and flicker toward extinction.

Six days passed, then came more news. The old couple were dying. Richards's mind cleared in his latest hour, and he sent for Burgess. Burgess said:

"Let the room be cleared. I think he wishes to say something in privacy."

"No!" said Richards: "I want witnesses. I want you all to hear my confession, so that I may die a man, and not a dog. I was clean—artificially—like the rest; and like the rest I fell when temptation came. I signed a lie, and claimed the miserable sack. Mr. Burgess remembered that I had done him a service, and in gratitude (and ignorance) he suppressed my claim and saved me. You know the thing that was charged against Burgess years ago. My testimony, and mine alone, could have cleared him, and I was a coward, and left him to suffer disgrace—"

"No—no—Mr. Richards, you—"

"My servant betrayed my secret to him—"

"No one has betrayed anything to me—"

—"and then he did a natural and justifiable thing, he repented of the saving kindness which he had done me, and he *exposed* me—as I deserved—"

"Never!—I make oath—"

"Out of my heart I forgive him."

Burgess's impassioned protestations fell upon deaf ears; the dying man passed away without knowing that once more he had done poor Burgess a wrong. The old wife died that night.

The last of the sacred Nineteen had fallen a prey to the fiendish sack; the town was stripped of the last rag of its ancient glory. Its mourning was not showy, but it was deep.

By act of the Legislature—upon prayer and petition—Hadleyburg was allowed to change its name to (never mind what—I will not give it away), and leave one word out of the motto that for many generations had graced the town's official seal.

It is an honest town once more, and the man will have to rise early that catches it napping again.

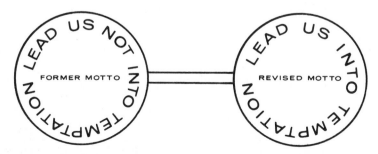

WILLIAM DEAN HOWELLS (1837–1920)

*For many years William Dean Howells was the central figure—which is
not to say the greatest writer—in the literary life of the United
States. A man of wide cultural and humane sympathies, Howells
helped introduce a new realism into late-nineteenth-century American writing both through his own fiction and as a champion of the
European masters who were then being translated into English.*

*The son of a newspaperman, Howells was born in Ohio and lived there
for most of his boyhood, moving from town to town as his father
changed jobs. While still a youth he went to work on the Columbus
paper,* Ohio State Journal, *and by the time he was twenty-three he
had published two books (one, a campaign biography of Lincoln)
and some poems in the* Atlantic Monthly. *In 1860 he took a journey
to Boston which marked his entry into the literary world of the
East, and at a famous dinner attended by Holmes and Lowell, there
occurred what Holmes would describe as "the apostolic succession
. . . the laying on of hands."*

*Largely as the result of the Lincoln book, Howells was appointed United
States consul in Venice; a series of travel letters from there, repub-
lished as* Venetian Life *(1866), enhanced his reputation, and by the
time he was thirty-five, he was editor of the* Atlantic. *While maintaining his cordial relations with the Brahmins of Boston, he also
encouraged such writers as Henry James, Mark Twain, and Sarah
Orne Jewett. He would, in fact, be a life-long friend of both James
and Twain, symbolically centered between these great figures at the
opposite poles of our culture. During this period Howells began to
evolve his theories of realistic fiction and to portray the "poor Real
Life, which I love" in such novels as* Their Wedding Journey *(1872),*
A Modern Instance *(1882),* The Rise of Silas Lapham *(1885), and*
A Hazard of New Fortunes *(1890). Howells explained his literary
views:*

> *I feel more and more persuaded that we have only to study American life
> with the naked eye in order to find it infinitely various and entertaining.
> The trouble has always been that we have looked at it through somebody
> else's confounded literary telescope. I find it hard work myself to trust my
> eyes, and I catch myself feeling for the telescope, but I hope to do with-
> out it, altogether, by and by.*

*Toward the end of the century Howells began to write literary and
social criticism that reflected his deepening humanitarian interests
and his turn, influenced by a reading of Tolstoy, toward a mild form
of socialism. Meanwhile he kept lending his warm-hearted support
to new writers such as Crane, Garland, and Frank Norris.*

Howells's reputation has rested mainly on his realistic social novels. Their realism depends on an intimate knowledge of the surface details—the manners, speech, dress, appearances—of late-nineteenth-century American life. No other American novelist has known so well, or written with such a mixture of sympathy and ironic distance, about the life of the American middle class. Howells was one of the first Americans to write novels in the way nineteenth-century English and Continental writers did—that is, to write works of fiction dealing with commonplace social life, set in familiar places and populated with recognizable characters. Yet Howells's realism, though always earnest, was rarely whole-hearted; there were aspects of life from which he flinched, even though his honesty as a writer forced him to approach them. His realism was inhibited by a native prudishness and by a failure to cope with those drives in human existence which cannot be understood, let alone contained, by goodwill and common sense.

Those of Howells's novels dealing with social problems—the decline of the small businessman, the conflict between labor and employer— are now likely to seem a little tepid. They lack fire, dramatic concentration, boldness of imagination. They are attenuated by the very gentility which Howells in his conscious mind wanted to leave behind—at least, leave behind in part. By contrast, some of Howells's less ambitious novels, mostly his novels of social comedy, are notable for a quiet shrewdness of observation and now seem livelier. Such works as Indian Summer *(1886),* The Landlord at Lion's Head *(1897), and* The Vacation of the Kelwyns *(1910) retain their point and sparkle. Howells's books of reminiscence have also stood the test of time:* A Boy's Town *(1890) is a classic portrait of small-town American life in the mid-nineteenth century, and* My Mark Twain *(1910) is a lovely summoning of things past.*

Howells, like Cooper, is a writer who does not lend himself to anthologizing, for his best effects are secured in his books as a whole. The selections from his nonfiction that appear below should yield a glimpse of his talents as critic and memorialist, while "Editha," a story with a shade more tartness than one usually finds in Howells's novels, shows his capacity for evoking certain modes of feminine psychology.

FURTHER READING

Edwin Cady, *The Road to Realism* (1956) and *The Realist at War* (1958), a two-volume work tracing Howells's career; Everett Carter, *Howells and the Age of Realism* (1954).

FROM *The Smiling Aspects*
of American Life (1886)[1]

... While *The Crime and the Punishment*[2] may be read with the
deepest sympathy and interest, and may enforce with unique power the
lessons which it teaches, it is to be praised only in its place, and its
message is to be received with allowances by readers exterior to the
social and political circumstances in which it was conceived. It used to
be one of the disadvantages of the practice of romance in America,
which Hawthorne more or less whimsically lamented, that there were
so few shadows and inequalities in our broad level of prosperity; and
it is one of the reflections suggested by Dostoïevsky's book that whoever
struck a note so profoundly tragic in American fiction would do a false
and mistaken thing—as false and as mistaken in its way as dealing in
American fiction with certain nudities which the Latin peoples seem to
find edifying. Whatever their deserts, very few American novelists have
been led out to be shot, or finally exiled to the rigors of a winter at
Duluth; one might make Herr Most[3] the hero of a labor-question
romance with perfect impunity; and in a land where journeyman
carpenters and plumbers strike for four dollars a day the sum of hunger
and cold is certainly very small, and the wrong from class to class is
almost inappreciable. We invite our novelists, therefore, to concern
themselves with the more smiling aspects of life, which are the more
American, and to seek the universal in the individual rather than the
social interests. It is worth while, even at the risk of being called commonplace, to be true to our well-to-do actualities; the very passions
themselves seem to be softened and modified by conditions which cannot be said to wrong any one, to cramp endeavor, or to cross lawful
desire. Sin and suffering and shame there must always be in the world,
we suppose, but we believe that in this new world of ours it is mainly
from one to another one, and oftener still from one to one's self. We have
death too in America, and a great deal of disagreeable and painful disease, which the multiplicity of our patent medicines does not seem to
cure; but this is tragedy that comes in the very nature of things, and
is not peculiarly American, as the large, cheerful average of health and
success and happy life is. It will not do to boast, but it is well to be
true to the facts, and to see that, apart from these purely mortal
troubles, the race here enjoys conditions in which most of the ills that
have darkened its annals may be averted by honest work and unselfish
behavior.

---

[1] First published in *Harper's Magazine*, 1886, this essay, slightly modified, was reprinted by Howells in his book *Criticism and Fiction* (1891).

[2] The novel by Fyodor Dostœvsky (1821–1881).

[3] Johann Most (1846–1906), anarchist leader who spent his later years in the
United States.

It is only now and then, when some dark shadow of our shameful past appears, that we can believe there ever was a tragic element in our prosperity. Even then, when we read such an artlessly impressive sketch as Mrs. Sarah Bradford[4] writes of Harriet Tubman[5]—once famous as the Moses of her people—the self-freed bondwoman who led three hundred of her brethren out of slavery, and with a price set upon her head, risked her life and liberty nineteen times in this cause; even then it affects us like a tale

Of old, unhappy, far-off things,
And battles long ago,

and nothing within the date of actual history. We cannot realize that most of the men and women now living were once commanded by the law of the land to turn and hunt such fugitives back into slavery, and to deliver such an outlaw as Harriet over to her owner; that those who abetted such outlaws were sometimes mulcted to the last dollar of their substance in fines. We can hardly imagine such things now for the purposes of fiction; all troubles that now hurt and threaten us are as crumpled rose leaves in our couch. But we may nevertheless read Dostoïevsky, and especially our novelists may read him, to advantage, for in spite of his terrible picture of a soul's agony he is hopeful and wholesome, and teaches in every page patience, merciful judgment, humble helpfulness, and that brotherly responsibility, that duty of man to man, from which not even the Americans are emancipated.

FROM *Criticism and Fiction* (1891)

Chapter 18   Pernicious Fiction

In General Grant's confession of novel-reading there is a sort of inference that he had wasted his time, or else the guilty conscience of the novelist in me imagines such an inference. But however this may be, there is certainly no question concerning the intention of a correspondent who once wrote to me after reading some rather bragging claims I had made for fiction as a mental and moral means. "I have very grave doubts," he said, "as to the whole list of magnificent things that you seem to think novels have done for the race, and can witness in myself many evil things which they have done for me. Whatever in my mental make-up is wild and visionary, whatever is untrue, whatever

---

[4] *Sarah Bradford* , an American author.

[5] Born a slave, Harriet Tubman (1821–1913) escaped to the North and became active in the Underground Railroad, which helped escaping slaves, and in the abolitionist movement.

is injurious, I can trace to the perusal of some work of fiction. Worse than that, they beget such high-strung and super-sensitive ideas of life that plain industry and plodding perseverance are despised, and matter-of-fact poverty, or every-day, commonplace distress, meets with no sympathy, if indeed noticed at all, by one who has wept over the impossibly accumulated sufferings of some gaudy hero or heroine."

I am not sure that I had the controversy with this correspondent that he seemed to suppose; but novels are now so fully accepted by everyone pretending to cultivated taste—and they really form the whole intellectual life of such immense numbers of people, without question of their influence, good or bad, upon the mind—that it is refreshing to have them frankly denounced, and to be invited to revise one's ideas and feelings in regard to them. A little honesty, or a great deal of honesty, in this quest will do the novel, as we hope yet to have it, and as we have already begun to have it, no harm; and for my own part I will confess that I believe fiction in the past to have been largely injurious, as I believe the stage play to be still almost wholly injurious, through its falsehood, its folly, its wantonness, and its aimlessness. It may be safely assumed that most of the novel-reading which people fancy an intellectual pastime is the emptiest dissipation, hardly more related to thought or the wholesome exercise of the mental faculties than opium-eating; in either case the brain is drugged, and left weaker and crazier for the debauch. If this may be called the negative result of the fiction habit, the positive injury that most novels work is by no means so easily to be measured in the case of young men whose character they help so much to form or deform, and the women of all ages whom they keep so much in ignorance of the world they misrepresent. Grown men have little harm from them, but in the other cases, which are the vast majority, they hurt because they are not true—not because they are malevolent, but because they are idle lies about human nature and the social fabric, which it behooves us to know and to understand, that we may deal justly with ourselves and with one another. One need not go so far as our correspondent, and trace to the fiction habit "whatever is wild and visionary, whatever is untrue, whatever is injurious," in one's life; bad as the fiction habit is it is probably not responsible for the whole sum of evil in its victims, and I believe that if the reader will use care in choosing from this fungus-growth with which the fields of literature teem every day, he may nourish himself as with the true mushroom, at no risk from the poisonous species.

The tests are very plain and simple, and they are perfectly infallible. If a novel flatters the passions, and exalts them above the principles, it is poisonous; it may not kill, but it will certainly injure; and this test will alone exclude an entire class of fiction, of which eminent examples will occur to all. Then the whole spawn of so-called unmoral romances, which imagine a world where the sins of sense are unvisited by the penalties following, swift or slow, but inexorably sure, in the real world,

are deadly poison: these do kill. The novels that merely tickle our prejudices and lull our judgment, or that coddle our sensibilities or pamper
our gross appetite for the marvelous are not so fatal, but they are innu-
tritious, and clog the soul with unwholesome vapors of all kinds. No
doubt they too help to weaken the moral fibre, and make their readers
indifferent to "plodding perseverance and plain industry," and to "matter-of-fact poverty and commonplace distress."

Without taking them too seriously, it still must be owned that the
"gaudy hero and heroine" are to blame for a great deal of harm in the
world. That heroine long taught by example, if not precept, that Love,
or the passion or fancy she mistook for it, was the chief interest of a
life, which is really concerned with a great many other things; that it
was lasting in the way she knew it; that it was worthy of every sacrifice,
and was altogether a finer thing than prudence, obedience, reason; that
love alone was glorious and beautiful, and these were mean and ugly
in comparison with it. More lately she has begun to idolize and illustrate Duty, and she is hardly less mischievous in this new role, opposing duty, as she did love, to prudence, obedience, and reason. The stock
hero, who, if we met him, we could not fail to see was a most deplorable person, has undoubtedly imposed himself upon the victims of the
fiction habit as admirable. With him, too, love was and is the great
affair, whether in its old romantic phase of chivalrous achievement or
manifold suffering for love's sake, or its more recent development of
the "virile," the bullying, and the brutal, or its still more recent agonies
of self-sacrifice, as idle and useless as the moral experiences of the
insane asylums. With his vain posturings and his ridiculous splendor
he is really a painted barbarian, the prey of his passions and his delusions, full of obsolete ideals, and the motives and ethics of a savage,
which the guilty author of his being does his best—or his worst—in
spite of his own light and knowledge, to foist upon the reader as something generous and noble. I am not merely bringing this charge against
that sort of fiction which is beneath literature and outside of it, "the
shoreless lakes of ditch-water," whose miasms fill the air below the
empyrean where the great ones sit; but I am accusing the work of
some of the most famous, who have, in this instance or in that, sinned
against the truth, which can alone exalt and purify men. I do not say
that they have constantly done so, or even commonly done so; but that
they have done so at all marks them as of the past, to be read with
the due historical allowance for their epoch and their conditions. For
I believe that, while inferior writers will and must continue to imitate
them in their foibles and their errors, no one hereafter will be able to
achieve greatness who is false to humanity, either in its facts or its
duties. The light of civilization has already broken even upon the novel,
and no conscientious man can now set about painting an image of
life without perpetual question of the verity of his work, and without
feeling bound to distinguish so clearly that no reader of his may be

misled, between what is right and what is wrong, what is noble and what is base, what is health and what is perdition, in the actions and the characters he portrays.

The fiction that aims merely to entertain—the fiction that is to serious fiction as the opera-bouffe, the ballet, and the pantomime are to the true drama—need not feel the burden of this obligation so deeply; but even such fiction will not be gay or trivial to any reader's hurt, and criticism will hold it to account if it passes from painting to teaching folly.

More and more not only the criticism which prints its opinions, but the infinitely vaster and powerfuler criticism which things and feels them merely, will make this demand. I confess that I do not care to judge any work of the imagination without first of all applying this test to it. We must ask ourselves before we ask anything else, Is it true?—true to the motives, the impulses, the principles that shape the life of actual men and women? This truth, which necessarily includes the highest morality and the highest artistry—this truth given, the book cannot be wicked and cannot be weak; and without it all graces of style and feats of invention and cunning of construction are so many super-fluities of naughtiness. It is well for the truth to have all these, and shine in them, but for falsehood they are merely meretricious, the bedizenment of the wanton; they atone for nothing, they account for nothing. But in fact they come naturally of truth, and grace it without solicitation; they are added unto it. In the whole range of fiction we know of no true picture of life—that is, of human nature—which is not also a masterpiece of literature, full of divine and natural beauty. It may have no touch or tint of this special civilization or of that; it had better have this local color well ascertained; but the truth is deeper and finer than aspects, and if the book is true to what men and women know of one another's souls it will be true enough, and it will be great and beautiful. It is the conception of literature as something apart from life, superfinely aloof, which makes it really unimportant to the great mass of mankind, without a message or a meaning for them; and it is the notion that a novel may be false in its portrayal of causes and effects that makes literary art contemptible even to those whom it amuses, that forbids them to regard the novelist as a serious or right-minded person. If they do not in some moment of indignation cry out against all novels, as my correspondent does, they remain besotted in the fume of the delusions purveyed to them, with no higher feeling for the author than such maudlin affection as the habitué of an opium-joint perhaps knows for the attendant who fills his pipe with the drug.

Or, as in the case of another correspondent who writes that in his youth he "read a great many novels, but always regarded it as an amusement, like horse-racing and card-playing," for which he had no time when he entered upon the serious business of life, it renders them merely contemptuous. His view of the matter may be commended to the brotherhood and sisterhood of novelists as full of wholesome if bitter suggestion; and we urge them not to dismiss it with high literary scorn as that of some Boeotian dull to the beauty of art. Refuse it as we may, it is still the feeling of the vast majority of people for whom life is earnest, and who find only a distorted and misleading likeness of it in our books. We may fold ourselves in our scholars' gowns, and close the doors of our studies, and affect to despise this rude voice; but we cannot shut it out. It comes to us from wherever men are at work, from wherever they are truly living, and accuses us of unfaithfulness, of triviality, of mere stage-play; and none of us can escape conviction except he prove himself worthy of his time—a time in which the great masters have brought literature back to life, and filled its ebbing veins with the red tides of reality. We cannot all equal them; we need not copy them; but we can all go to the sources of their inspiration and their power; and to draw from these no one need go far—no one need really go out of himself.

Fifty years ago, Carlyle,[1] in whom the truth was always alive, but in whom it was then unperverted by suffering, by celebrity, and by despair, wrote in his study of Diderot[2]: "Were it not reasonable to prophesy that this exceeding great multitude of novel-writers and such like must, in a new generation, gradually do one of two things: either retire into the nurseries, and work for children, minors, and semi-fatuous persons of both sexes, or else, what were far better, sweep their novel-fabric into the dust-cart, and betake themselves with such faculty as they have to understand and record what is true, of which surely there is, and will forever be, a whole infinitude unknown to us of infinite importance to us? Poetry, it will more and more come to be understood, is nothing but higher knowledge; and the genuine Romance (for grown persons), Reality."

If, after half a century, fiction still mainly works for "children, minors, and semi-fatuous persons of both sexes," it is nevertheless one of the hopefulest signs of the world's progress that it has begun to work for "grown persons," and if not exactly in the way that Carlyle might have solely intended in urging its writers to compile memoirs instead of building the "novel-fabric," still it has, in the highest and widest sense, already made Reality its Romance. I cannot judge it, I do not not even care for it, except as it has done this; and I can hardly conceive of a literary self-respect in these days compatible with the old trade of make-believe, with the production of the kind of fiction which is too much honored by classification with card-playing and horse-racing. But let fiction cease to lie about life; let it portray men and women as they are, actuated by the motives and the passions in the measure we all know; let it leave off painting dolls and working them by springs and

---

[1] Thomas Carlyle (1795–1881), English essayist and historian.
[2] Denis Diderot (1713–1784), French philosopher and writer.

wires; let it show the different interests in their true proportions; let it forbear to preach pride and revenge, folly and insanity, egotism and prejudice, but frankly own these for what they are, in whatever figures and occasions they appear; let it not put on fine literary airs; let it speak the dialect, the language, that most Americans know—the language of unaffected people everywhere—and there can be no doubt of an unlimited future, not only of delightfulness but of usefulness, for it.

FROM *My Mark Twain* (1910)

At the time of our first meeting, which must have been well toward the winter, Clemens (as I must call him instead of Mark Twain, which seemed always somehow to mask him from my personal sense) was wearing a sealskin coat, with the fur out, in the satisfaction of a caprice, or the love of strong effect which he was apt to indulge through life. I do not know what droll comment was in Fields's mind with respect to this garment, but probably he felt that here was an original who was not to be brought to any Bostonian book in the judgment of his vivid qualities. With his crest of dense red hair, and the wide sweep of his flaming mustache, Clemens was not discordantly clothed in that sealskin coat, which afterward, in spite of his own warmth in it, sent the cold chills through me when I once accompanied it down Broadway, and shared the immense publicity it won him. He had always a relish for personal effect, which expressed itself in the white suit of complete serge which he wore in his last years, and in the Oxford gown which he put on for every possible occasion, and said he would like to wear all the time. That was not vanity in him, but a keen feeling for costume which the severity of our modern tailoring forbids men, though it flatters women to every excess in it; yet he also enjoyed the shock, the offence, the pang which it gave the sensibilities of others. . . .

To the period of Clemens's residence in Fifth Avenue belongs his efflorescence in white serge. He was always rather aggressively indifferent about dress, and at a very early date in our acquaintance Aldrich and I attempted his reform by clubbing to buy him a cravat. But he would not put away his stiff little black bow, and until he imagined the suit of white serge, he wore always a suit of black serge, truly deplorable in the cut of the sagging frock. After his measure had once been taken he refused to make his clothes the occasion of personal interviews with his tailor; he sent the stuff by the kind elderly woman who had been in the service of the family from the earliest days of his marriage, and accepted the result without criticism. But the white serge was an inspiration which few men would have had the courage to act upon. The first time I saw him wear it was at the authors' hearing before the

Congressional Committee on Copyright in Washington. Nothing could have been more dramatic than the gesture with which he flung off his long loose overcoat, and stood forth in white from his feet to the crown of his silvery head. It was a magnificent *coup*, and he dearly loved a *coup;* but the magnificent speech which he made, tearing to shreds the venerable farrago of nonsense about non-property in ideas which had formed the basis of all copyright legislation, made you forget even his spectacularity.

It is well known how proud he was of his Oxford gown, not merely because it symbolized the honor in which he was held by the highest literary body in the world, but because it was so rich and so beautiful. The red and the lavender of the cloth flattered his eyes as the silken black of the same degree of Doctor of Letters, given him years before at Yale, could not do. His frank, defiant happiness in it, mixed with a due sense of burlesque, was something that those lacking his poet-soul could never imagine; they accounted it vain, weak; but that would not have mattered to him if he had known it. In his London sojourn he had formed the top-hat habit, and for a while he lounged splendidly up and down Fifth Avenue in that society emblem; but he seemed to tire of it, and to return kindly to the soft hat of his Southwestern tradition. . . .

Once when I came on from Cambridge he followed me to my room to see that the water was not frozen in my bath, or something of the kind, for it was very cold weather, and then hospitably lingered. Not to lose time in banalities I began at once from the thread of thought in my mind. "I wonder why we hate the past so," and he responded from the depths of his own consciousness, "It's so damned humiliating," which is what any man would say of his past if he were honest; but honest men are few when it comes to themselves. Clemens was one of the few, and the first of them among all the people I have known. I have known, I suppose, men as truthful, but not so promptly, so absolutely, so positively, so almost aggressively truthful. He could lie, of course, and did to save others from grief or harm; he was not stupidly truthful; but his first impulse was to say out the thing and everything that was in him. To those who can understand it will not be contradictory of his sense of humiliation from the past, that he was not ashamed for anything he ever did to the point of wishing to hide it. He could be, and he was, bitterly sorry for his errors, which he had enough of in his life, but he was not ashamed in that mean way. What he had done he owned to, good, bad, or indifferent, and if it was bad he was rather amused than troubled as to the effect in your mind. He would not obtrude the fact upon you, but if it were in the way of personal history he would not dream of withholding it, far less of hiding it.

He was the readiest of men to allow an error if he were found in it. . . .

Fully half our meetings were at my house in Cambridge, where he made himself as much at home as in Hartford. He would come ostensibly to stay at the Parker House, in Boston, and take a room, where he would light the gas and leave it burning, after dressing, while he drove out to Cambridge and stayed two or three days with us. Once, I suppose it was after a lecture, he came in evening dress and passed twenty-four hours with us in that guise, wearing an overcoat to hide it when we went for a walk. Sometimes he wore the slippers which he preferred to shoes at home, and if it was muddy, as it was wont to be in Cambridge, he would put a pair of rubbers over them for our rambles. He like the lawlessness and our delight in allowing it, and he rejoiced in the confession of his hostess, after we had once almost worn ourselves out in our pleasure with the intense talk, with the stories and the laughing, that his coming almost killed her, but it was worth it.

In those days he was troubled with sleeplessness, or, rather, with reluctant sleepiness, and he had various specifics for promoting it. At first it had been champagne just before going to bed, and we provided that, but later he appeared from Boston with four bottles of lager-beer under his arms; lager-beer, he said now, was the only thing to make you go to sleep, and we provided that. Still later, on a visit I paid him at Hartford, I learned that hot Scotch was the only soporific worth considering, and Scotch whiskey duly found its place on our sideboard. One day, very long afterward, I asked him if he were still taking hot Scotch to make him sleep. He said he was not taking anything. For a while he had found going to bed on the bath-room floor a soporific; then one night he went to rest in his own bed at ten o'clock, and had gone promptly to sleep without anything. He had done the like with the like effect ever since. Of course, it amused him; there were few experiences, of life, grave or gay, which did not amuse him, even when they wronged him.

He came on to Cambridge in April, 1875, to go with me to the centennial ceremonies at Concord in celebration of the battle of the Minute Men with the British troops a hundred years before. We both had special invitations, including passage from Boston; but I said, Why bother to go into Boston when we could just as well take the train for Concord at the Cambridge station? He equally decided that it would be absurd; so we breakfasted deliberately, and then walked to the station, reasoning of many things as usual. When the train stopped, we found it packed inside and out. People stood dense on the platforms of the cars; to our startled eyes they seemed to project from the windows, and unless memory betrays me they lay strewn upon the roofs like brake-men slain at the post of duty. Whether this was really so or not, it is certain that the train presented an impenetrable front even to our imagination, and we left it to go its way without the slightest effort to board. We remounted the fame-worn steps of Porter's Station, and began exploring North Cambridge for some means of transportation overland to Concord, for we were that far on the road by which the British went and came on the day of the battle. The liverymen whom we appealed to received us, some with compassion, some with derision, but in either mood convinced us that we could not have hired a cat to attempt our conveyance, must less a horse, or vehicle of any description. It was a raw, windy day, very unlike the exceptionally hot April day when the routed redcoats, pursued by the Colonials, fled panting back to Boston, with "their tongues hanging out like dogs," but we could not take due comfort in the vision of their discomfiture; we could almost envy them, for they had at least got to Concord. A swift procession of coaches, carriages, and buggies, all going to Concord, passed us, inert and helpless, on the sidewalk in the peculiarly cold mud of North Cambridge. We began to wonder if we might not stop one of them and bribe it to take us, but we had not the courage to try, and Clemens seized the opportunity to begin suffering with an acute indigestion, which gave his humor a very dismal cast. I felt keenly the shame of defeat, and the guilt of responsibility for our failure, and when a gay party of students came toward us on the top of a tally-ho, luxuriously empty inside, we felt that our chance had come, and our last chance. He said that if I would stop them and tell them who I was they would gladly, perhaps proudly, give us passage; I contended that if with his far vaster renown he would approach them, our success would be assured. While we stood, lost in this "contest of civilities," the coach passed us, with gay notes blown from the horns of the students, and then Clemens started in pursuit, encouraged with shouts from the merry party who could not imagine who was trying to run them down, to a rivalry in speed. The unequal match could end only in one way, and I am glad I cannot recall what he said when he came back to me. Since then I have often wondered at the grief which would have wrung those blithe young hearts if they could have known that they might have had the company of Mark Twain to Concord that day and did not.

We hung about, unavailingly, in the bitter wind a while longer, and then slowly, very slowly, made our way home. We wished to pass as much time as possible, in order to give probability to the deceit we intended to practise, for we could not bear to own ourselves baffled in our boasted wisdom of taking the train at Porter's Station, and had agreed to say that we had been to Concord and got back. Even after coming home to my house, we felt that our statement would be wanting in verisimilitude without further delay, and we crept quietly into my library, and made up a roaring fire on the hearth, and thawed ourselves out in the heat of it before we regained our courage for the undertaking. With all these precautions we failed, for when our statement was imparted to the proposed victim she instantly pronounced it unreliable, and we were left with it on our hands intact. I think the humor of this situation was finally a greater pleasure to Clemens than an actual visit to Concord would have been; only a few weeks before his death he laughed our defeat over with one of my family in Bermuda, and exulted in our prompt detection.

Editha (1905)

The air was thick with the war feeling, like the electricity of a storm which has not yet burst. Editha sat looking out into the hot spring afternoon, with her lips parted, and panting with the intensity of the question whether she could let him go. She had decided that she could not let him stay, when she saw him at the end of the still leafless avenue, making slowly up towards the house, with his head down and his figure relaxed. She ran impatiently out on the veranda, to the edge of the steps, and imperatively demanded greater haste of him with her will before she called aloud to him: "George!"

He had quickened his pace in mystical response to her mystical urgence, before he could have heard her; now he looked up and answered, "Well?"

"Oh, how united we are!" she exulted, and then she swooped down the steps to him. "What is it?" she cried.

"It's war," he said, and he pulled her up to him and kissed her.

She kissed him back intensely, but irrelevantly, as to their passion, and uttered from deep in her throat. "How glorious!"

"It's war," he repeated, without consenting to her sense of it; and she did not know just what to think at first. She never knew what to think of him; that made his mystery, his charm. All through their courtship, which was contemporaneous with the growth of the war feeling, she had been puzzled by his want of seriousness about it. He seemed to despise it even more than he abhorred it. She could have understood his abhorring any sort of bloodshed; that would have been a survival of his old life when he thought he would be a minister, and before he changed and took up the law. But making light of a cause so high and noble seemed to show a want of earnestness at the core of his being. Not but that she felt herself able to cope with a congenital defect of that sort, and make his love for her save him from himself. Now perhaps the miracle was already wrought in him. In the presence of the tremendous fact that he announced, all triviality seemed to have gone out of him; she began to feel that. He sank down on the top step, and wiped his forehead with his handkerchief, while she poured out upon him her question of the origin and authenticity of his news.

All the while, in her duplex emotioning, she was aware that now at the very beginning she must put a guard upon herself against urging him, by any word or act, to take the part that her whole soul willed him to take, for the completion of her ideal of him. He was very nearly perfect as he was, and he must be allowed to perfect himself. But he was peculiar, and he might very well be reasoned out of his peculiarity. Before her reasoning went her emotioning: her nature pulling upon his nature, her womanhood upon his manhood, without her knowing the means she was using to the end she was willing. She had always supposed that the man who won her would have done something to win her; she did not know what, but something. George Gearson had simply asked her for her love, on the way home from a concert, and she gave her love to him, without, as it were, thinking. But now, it flashed upon her, if he could do something worthy to *have* won her—be a hero, *her* hero—it would be even better than if he had done it before asking her; it would be grander. Besides, she had believed in the war from the beginning.

"But don't you see, dearest," she said, "that it wouldn't have come to this if it hadn't been in the order of Providence? And I call any war glorious that is for the liberation of people who have been struggling for years against the cruelest oppression. Don't you think so, too?"

"I suppose so," he returned, languidly. "But war! Is it glorious to break the peace of the world?"

"That ignoble peace! It was no peace at all, with that crime and shame at our very gates." She was conscious of parroting the current phrases of the newspapers, but it was no time to pick and choose her words. She must sacrifice anything to the high ideal she had for him, and after a good deal of rapid argument she ended with the climax: "But now it doesn't matter about the how or why. Since the war has come, all that is gone. There are no two sides any more. There is nothing now but our country."

He sat with his eyes closed and his head leant back against the veranda, and he remarked, with a vague smile, as if musing aloud, "Our country—right or wrong."

"Yes, right or wrong!" she returned, fervidly. "I'll go and get you some lemonade." She rose rustling, and whisked away; when she came back with two tall glasses of clouded liquid on a tray, and the ice clucking in them, he still sat as she had left him, and she said, as if there had been no interruption: "But there is no question of wrong in this case. I call it a sacred war. A war for liberty and humanity, if ever there was one. And I know you will see it just as I do, yet."

He took half the lemonade at a gulp, and he answered as he set the glass down: "I know you always have the highest ideal. When I differ from you I ought to doubt myself."

A generous sob rose in Editha's throat for the humility of a man, so very nearly perfect, who was willing to put himself below her.

Besides, she felt, more subliminally, that he was never so near slipping through her fingers as when he took that meek way.

"You shall not say that! Only, for once I happen to be right." She seized his hand in her two hands, and poured her soul from her eyes into his. "Don't you think so?" she entreated him.

He released his hand and drank the rest of his lemonade, and she added, "Have mine, too," but he shook his head in answering, "I've no business to think so, unless I act so, too."

Her heart stopped a beat before it pulsed on with leaps that she felt in her neck. She had noticed that strange thing in men: they seemed to feel bound to do what they believed, and not think a thing was finished when they said it, as girls did. She knew what was in his mind, but she pretended not, and she said, "Oh, I am not sure," and then faltered.

He went on as if to himself, without apparently heeding her: "There's only one way of proving one's faith in a thing like this."

She could not say that she understood, but she did understand.

He went on again. "If I believed you—if I felt as you do about this war—Do you wish me to feel as you do?"

Now she was really not sure; so she said: "George, I don't know what you mean."

He seemed to muse away from her as before. "There is a sort of fascination in it. I suppose that at the bottom of his heart every man would like at times to have his courage tested, to see how he would act."

"How can you talk in that ghastly way?"

"It *is* rather morbid. Still, that's what it comes to, unless you're swept away by ambition or driven by conviction. I haven't the conviction or the ambition, and the other thing is what it comes to with me. I ought to have been a preacher, after all; then I couldn't have asked it of myself, as I must, now I'm a lawyer. And you believe it's a holy war, Editha?" he suddenly addressed her. "Oh, I know you do! But you wish me to believe so, too?"

She hardly knew whether he was mocking or not, in the ironical way he always had with her plainer mind. But the only thing was to be outspoken with him.

"George, I wish you to believe whatever you think is true, at any and every cost. If I've tried to talk you into anything, I take it all back."

"Oh, I know that, Editha. I know how sincere you are, and how— I wish I had your undoubting spirit! I'll think it over; I'd like to believe as you do. But I don't, now; I don't, indeed. It isn't this war alone; though this seems peculiarly wanton and needless; but it's every war— so stupid; it makes me sick. Why shouldn't this thing have been settled reasonably?"

"Because," she said, very throatily again, "God meant it to be war."

"You think it was God? Yes, I suppose that is what people will say."

"Do you suppose it would have been war if God hadn't meant it?"

"I don't know. Sometimes it seems as if God had put this world into men's keeping to work it as they pleased."

"Now, George, this is blasphemy."

"Well, I won't blaspheme. I'll try to believe in your pocket Providence," he said, and then he rose to go.

"Why don't you stay to dinner?" Dinner at Balcom's Works was at one o'clock.

"I'll come back to supper, if you'll let me. Perhaps I shall bring you a convert."

"Well, you may come back, on that condition."

"All right. If I don't come, you'll understand."

He went away without kissing her, and she felt it a suspension of their engagement. It all interested her intensely; she was undergoing a tremendous experience, and she was being equal to it. While she stood looking after him, her mother came out through one of the long windows onto the veranda, with a catlike softness and vagueness.

"Why didn't he stay to dinner?"

"Because—because—war has been declared," Editha pronounced, without turning.

Her mother said, "Oh, my!" and then said nothing more until she had sat down in one of the large Shaker chairs and rocked herself for some time. Then she closed whatever tacit passage of thought there had been in her mind with the spoken words: "Well, I hope *he* won't go."

"And *I* hope he *will*," the girl said, and confronted her mother with a stormy exaltation that would have frightened any creature less unimpressionable than a cat.

Her mother rocked herself again for an interval of cogitation. What she arrived at in speech was: "Well, I guess you've done a wicked thing, Editha Balcom."

The girl said, as she passed indoors through the same window her mother had come out by: "I haven't done anything—yet."

In her room, she put together all her letters and gifts from Gearson, down to the withered petals of the first flower he had offered, with that timidity of his veiled in that irony of his. In the heart of the packet she enshrined her engagement ring which she had restored to the pretty box he had brought it her in. Then she sat down, if not calmly yet strongly, and wrote:

GEORGE:—I understood when you left me. But I think we had better emphasize your meaning that if we cannot be one in everything we had better be one in nothing. So I am sending these things for your keeping till you have made up your mind.

I shall always love you, and therefore I shall never marry any one else. But the man I marry must love his country first of all, and be able to say to me, "I Could not love thee, dear, so much,
Loved I not honor more."

There is no honor above America with me. In this great hour there is no other honor.

Your heart will make my words clear to you. I had never expected to say so much, but it has come upon me that I must say the utmost.   EDITHA.

She thought she had worded her letter well, worded it in a way that could not be bettered; all had been implied and nothing expressed.

She had it ready to send with the packet she had tied with red, white, and blue ribbon, when it occurred to her that she was not just to him, that she was not giving him a fair chance. He had said he would go and think it over, and she was not waiting. She was pushing, threatening, compelling. That was not a woman's part. She must leave him free, free, free. She could not accept for her country or herself a forced sacrifice.

In writing her letter she had satisfied the impulse from which it sprang; she could well afford to wait till he had thought it over. She put the packet and the letter by, and rested serene in the consciousness of having done what was laid upon her by her love itself to do, and yet used patience, mercy, justice.

She had her reward. Gearson did not come to tea, but she had given him till morning, when, late at night there came up from the village the sound of a fife and drum, with a tumult of voices, in shouting, singing, and laughing. The noise drew nearer and nearer; it reached the street end of the avenue; there it silenced itself, and one voice, the voice she knew best, rose over the silence. It fell; the air was filled with cheers; the fife and drum struck up, with the shouting, singing, and laughing again, but now retreating; and a single figure came hurrying up the avenue.

She ran down to meet her lover and clung to him. He was very gay, and he put his arm around her with a boisterous laugh. "Well, you must call me Captain now; or Cap, if you prefer; that's what the boys call me. Yes, we've had a meeting at the town-hall, and everybody has volunteered; and they selected me for captain, and I'm going to the war, the big war, the glorious war, the holy war ordained by the pocket Providence that blesses butchery. Come along; let's tell the whole family about it. Call them from their downy beds, father, mother, Aunt Hitty, and all the folks!"

But when they mounted the veranda steps he did not wait for a larger audience; he poured the story out upon Editha alone.

"There was a lot of speaking, and then some of the fools set up a shout for me. It was all going one way, and I thought it would be a good joke to sprinkle a little cold water on them. But you can't do that with a crowd that adores you. The first thing I knew I was sprinkling hell-fire on them. 'Cry havoc, and let slip the dogs of war.' That was the style. Now that it had come to the fight, there were no two parties; there was one country, and the thing was to fight to a finish as quick as possible. I suggested volunteering then and there, and I wrote my name first of all on the roster. Then they elected me—that's all. I wish I had some ice-water."

She left him walking up and down the veranda, while she ran for the ice-pitcher and a goblet, and when she came back he was still walking up and down, shouting the story he had told her to her father and mother, who had come out more sketchily dressed than they commonly were by day. He drank goblet after goblet of the ice-water without noticing who was giving it, and kept on talking, and laughing through his talk wildly. "It's astonishing," he said, "how well the worse reason looks when you try to make it appear the better. Why, I believe I was the first convert to the war in that crowd tonight! I never thought I should like to kill a man; but now I shouldn't care; and the smokeless powder lets you see the man drop that you kill. It's all for the country! What a thing it is to have a country that *can't* be wrong, but if it is, is right, anyway!"

Editha had a great, vital thought, an inspiration. She set down the ice-pitcher on the veranda floor, and ran up-stairs and got the letter she had written him. When at last he noisily bade her father and mother, "Well, good-night. I forgot I woke you up; I sha'n't want any sleep myself," she followed him down the avenue to the gate. There, after the whirling words that seemed to fly away from her thoughts and refuse to serve them, she made a last effort to solemnize the moment that seemed so crazy, and pressed the letter she had written upon him.

"What's this?" he said. "Want me to mail it?"

"No, no. It's for you. I wrote it after you went this morning. Keep it—keep it—and read it sometime—" She thought, and then her inspiration came: "Read it if ever you doubt what you've done, or fear that I regret your having done it. Read it after you've started."

They strained each other in embraces that seemed as ineffective as their words, and he kissed her face with quick, hot breaths that were so unlike him, that made her feel as if she had lost her old lover and found a stranger in his place. The stranger said: "What a gorgeous flower you are, with your red hair, and your blue eyes that look black now, and your face with the color painted out by the white moonshine! Let me hold you under the chin, to see whether I love blood, you tiger-lily!" Then he laughed Gearson's laugh, and released her, scared and giddy. Within her wilfulness she had been frightened by a sense of subtler force in him, and mystically mastered as she had never been before.

She ran all the way back to the house, and mounted the steps panting. Her mother and father were talking of the great affair. Her mother said: "Wa'n't Mr. Gearson in rather of an excited state of mind? Didn't you think he acted curious?"

"Well, not for a man who'd just been elected captain and had set 'em up for the whole of Company A," her father chuckled back.

"What in the world do you mean, Mr. Balcom? Oh! There's Editha!" She offered to follow the girl indoors.

"Don't come mother!" Editha called, vanishing.

Mrs. Balcom remained to reproach her husband. "I don't see much of anything to laugh at."

"Well, it's catching. Caught it from Gearson. I guess it won't be much of a war, and I guess Gearson don't think so, either. The other fellows will back down as soon as they see we mean it. I wouldn't lose any sleep over it. I'm going back to bed, myself."

Gearson came again next afternoon, looking pale and rather sick, but quite himself, even to his languid irony. "I guess I'd better tell you,

Editha, that I consecrated myself to your god of battles last night by pouring too many libations to him down my own throat. But I'm all right now. One has to carry off the excitement, somehow."

"Promise me," she commanded, "that you'll never touch it again!"

"What! Not let the cannikin clink? Not let the soldier drink? Well, I promise."

"You don't belong to yourself now; you don't even belong to *me*. You belong to your country, and you have a sacred charge to keep yourself strong and well for your country's sake. I have been thinking, thinking all night and all day long."

"You look as if you had been crying a little, too," he said, with his queer smile.

"That's all past. I've been thinking, and worshipping *you*. Don't you suppose I know all that you've been through, to come to this? I've followed you every step from your old theories and opinions."

"Well, you've had a long row to hoe."

"And I know you've done this from the highest motives—"

"Oh, there won't be much pettifogging to do till this cruel war is—"

"And you haven't simply done it for my sake. I couldn't respect you if you had."

"Well, then we'll say I haven't. A man that hasn't got his own respect intact wants the respect of all the other people he can corner. But we won't go into that. I'm in for the thing now, and we've got to face our future. My idea is that this isn't going to be a very protracted struggle; we shall just scare the enemy to death before it comes to a fight at all. But we must provide for contingencies, Editha. If anything happens to me—"

"Oh, George!" She clung to him, sobbing.

"I don't want you to feel foolishly bound to my memory. I should hate that, wherever I happened to be."

"I am yours, for time and eternity—time and eternity." She liked the words; they satisfied her famine for phrases.

"Well, say eternity; that's all right; but time's another thing; and I'm talking about time. But there is something! My mother! If anything happens—"

She winced, and he laughed. "You're not the bold soldier-girl of yesterday!" Then he sobered. "If anything happens, I want you to help my mother out. She won't like my doing this thing. She brought me up to think war a fool thing as well as a bad thing. My father was in the Civil War; all through it; lost his arm in it." She thrilled with the sense of the arm round her; what if that should be lost? He laughed as if divining her: "Oh, it doesn't run in the family, as far as I know!" Then he added, gravely: "He came home with misgivings about war, and they grew on him. I guess he and mother agreed between them that I was to be brought up in his final mind about it; but that was before my time. I only knew him from my mother's report of him and his opinions; I don't know whether they were hers first; but they were hers last. This will be a blow to her. I shall have to write and tell her—"

He stopped, and she asked: "Would you like me to write, too, George?"

"I don't believe that would do. No, I'll do the writing. She'll understand a little if I say that I thought the way to minimize it was to make war on the largest possible scale at once—that I felt I must have been helping on the war somehow if I hadn't helped keep it from coming, and I knew I hadn't; when it came, I had no right to stay out of it."

Whether his sophistries satisfied him or not, they satisfied her. She clung to his breast, and whispered, with closed eyes and quivering lips: "Yes, yes, yes!"

"But if anything should happen, you might go to her and see what you could do for her. You know? It's rather far off; she can't leave her chair—"

"Oh, I'll go, if it's the ends of the earth! But nothing will happen! Nothing *can!* I—"

She felt herself lifted with his rising, and Gearson was saying, with his arm still round her, to her father: "Well, we're off at once, Mr. Balcom. We're to be formally accepted at the capital, and then bunched up with the rest somehow, and sent into camp somewhere, and got to the front as soon as possible. We all want to be in the van, of course; we're the first company to report to the Governor. I came to tell Editha, but I hadn't got round to it."

She saw him again for a moment at the capital, in the station, just before the train started southward with his regiment. He looked well, in his uniform, and very soldierly, but somehow girlish, too, with his clean-shaven face and slim figure. The manly eyes and the strong voice satisfied her, and his preoccupation with some unexpected details of duty flattered her. Other girls were weeping and bemoaning themselves, but she felt a sort of noble distinction in the abstraction, the almost unconsciousness, with which they parted. Only at the last moment he said: "Don't forget my mother. It mayn't be such a walk-over as I supposed," and he laughed at the notion.

He waved his hand to her as the train moved off—she knew it among a score of hands that were waved to other girls from the platform of the car, for it held a letter which she knew was hers. Then he went inside the car to read it, doubtless, and she did not see him again. But she felt safe for him through the strength of what she called her love. What she called her God, always speaking the name in a deep voice and with the implication of a mutual understanding, would watch over him and keep him and bring him back to her. If with an empty sleeve, then he should have three arms instead of two, for both of hers should be his for life. She did not see, though, why she should always be thinking of the arm his father had lost.

There were not many letters from him, but they were such as she could have wished, and she put her whole strength into making hers such as she imagined he could have wished, glorifying and supporting him. She wrote to his mother glorifying him as their hero, but the brief answer she got was merely to the effect that Mrs. Gearson was not well enough to write herself, and thanking her for her letter by the hand of some one who called herself, "Yrs truly, Mrs. W. J. Andrews."

Editha determined not to be hurt, but to write again quite as if the answer had been all she expected. Before it seemed as if she could have written, there came news of the first skirmish, and in the list of the killed, which was telegraphed as a trifling loss on our side, was Gearson's name. There was a frantic time of trying to make out that it might be, must be, some other Gearson; but the name and the company and the regiment and the State were too definitely given.

Then there was a lapse into depths out of which it seemed as if she never could rise again; then a lift into clouds far above all grief, black clouds, that blotted out the sun, but where she soared with him, with George—George! She had the fever that she expected of herself, but she did not die in it; she was not even delirious, and it did not last long. When she was well enough to leave her bed, her one thought was of George's mother, of his strangely worded wish that she should go to her and see what she could do for her. In the exaltation of the duty laid upon her—it buoyed her up instead of burdening her—she rapidly recovered.

Her father went with her on the long railroad journey from northern New York to western Iowa; he had business out at Davenport, and he said he could just as well go then as any other time; and he went with her to the little country town where George's mother lived in a little house on the edge of the illimitable cornfields, under trees pushed to a top of the rolling prairie. George's father had settled there after the Civil War, as so many other old soldiers had done; but they were Eastern people, and Editha fancied touches of the East in the June rose overhanging the front door, and the garden with early summer flowers stretching from the gate of the paling fence.

It was very low inside the house, and so dim, with the closed blinds, that they could scarcely see one another: Editha tall and black in her crapes which filled the air with the smell of their dyes; her father standing decorously apart with his hat on his forearm, as at funerals; a woman rested in a deep arm-chair, and the woman who had let the strangers in stood behind the chair.

The seated woman turned her head round and up, and asked the woman behind her chair: "*Who* did you say?"

Editha, if she had done what she expected of herself, would have gone down on her knees at the feet of the seated figure and said, "I am George's Editha," for answer.

But instead of her own voice she heard that other woman's voice, saying: "Well, I don't know as I *did* get the name just right. I guess I'll have to make a little more light in here," and she went and pushed two of the shutters ajar.

Then Editha's father said, in his public will-now-address-a-few-remarks tone: "My name is Balcom, ma'am—Junius H. Balcom, of Balcom's Works, New York; my daughter—"

"Oh!" the seated woman broke in, with a powerful voice, the voice that always surprised Editha from Gearson's slender frame. "Let me see you. Stand round where the light can strike on your face," and Editha dumbly obeyed. "So, you're Editha Balcom," she sighed.

"Yes," Editha said, more like a culprit than a comforter.

"What did you come for?" Mrs. Gearson asked.

Editha's face quivered and her knees shook. "I came—because—because George—" She could go no further.

"Yes," the mother said, "he told me he had asked you to come if he got killed. You didn't expect that, I suppose, when you sent him."

"I would rather have died myself than done it!" Editha said, with more truth in her deep voice than she ordinarily found in it. "I tried to leave him free—"

"Yes, that letter of yours, that came back with his other things, left him free."

Editha saw now where George's irony came from.

"It was not to be read before—unless—until— I told him so," she faltered.

"Of course, he wouldn't read a letter of yours, under the circumstances, till he thought you wanted him to. Been sick?" the woman abruptly demanded.

"Very sick," Editha said, with self-pity.

"Daughter's life," her father interposed, "was almost despaired of, at one time."

Mrs. Gearson gave him no heed. "I suppose you would have been glad to die, such a brave person as you! I don't believe *he* was glad to die. He was always a timid boy, that way; he was afraid of a good many things; but if he was afraid he did what he made up his mind to. I suppose he made up his mind to go, but I knew what it cost him by what it cost me when I heard of it. I had been through *one* war before. When you sent him you didn't expect he would get killed."

The voice seemed to compassionate Editha, and it was time. "No," she huskily murmured.

"No, girls don't; women don't, when they give their men up to their country. They think they'll come marching back, somehow, just as gay as they went, or if it's an empty sleeve, or even an empty pantaloon, it's all the more glory, and they're so much the prouder of them, poor things!"

The tears began to run down Editha's face; she had not wept till then; but it was now such a relief to be understood that the tears came.

"No, you didn't expect him to get killed," Mrs. Gearson repeated, in a voice which was startlingly like George's again. "You just expected him to kill some one else, some of those foreigners, that weren't there because they had any say about it, but because they had to be there, poor wretches—conscripts, or whatever they call 'em. You thought it would be all right for my George, *your* George, to kill the sons of those miserable mothers and the husbands of those girls that you would never see the faces of." The woman lifted her powerful voice in a psalmlike note. "I thank my God he didn't live to do it! I thank my God they killed him first, and that he ain't livin' with their blood on his hands!" She dropped her eyes, which she had raised with her voice, and glared at Editha. "What you got that black on for?" She lifted herself by her powerful arms so high that her helpless body seemed to hang limp its full length. "Take it off, take it off, before I tear it from your back!"

The lady who was passing the summer near Balcom's Works was sketching Editha's beauty, which lent itself wonderfully to the effects of a colorist. It had come to that confidence which is rather apt to grow between artist and sitter, and Editha had told her everything.

"To think of your having such a tragedy in your life!" the lady said. She added: I suppose there are people who feel that way about war. But when you consider the good this war has done—how much it has done for the country! I can't understand such people, for my part. And when you had come all the way out there to console her—got up out of a sick-bed! Well!"

"I think," Editha said, magnanimously, "she wasn't quite in her right mind; and so did papa."

"Yes," the lady said, looking at Editha's lips in nature and then at her lips in art, and giving an empirical touch to them in the picture. "But how dreadful of her! How perfectly—excuse me—how *vulgar!*"

A light broke upon Editha in the darkness which she felt had been without a gleam of brightness for weeks and months. The mystery that had bewildered her was solved by the word; and from that moment she rose from grovelling in shame and self-pity, and began to live again in the ideal.

STEPHEN CRANE (1871–1900)

That genius—so Henry James is reported to have murmured after hearing the news of Stephen Crane's death. It is a phrase of recognition that seems to occur spontaneously to people when they first experience the shock of his fiction. For almost all readers, including those who dislike or are unnerved by it, feel that in his novels and stories, sometimes in his poems, there resides that mysterious quality—inspiration, power, technical mastery—we call "genius." Crane did not live long enough to leave behind him a large body of major writing, but in his brilliant novel The Red Badge of Courage *(1895) and in half a dozen or so stories (including the three in this anthology), he showed himself a writer of the first rank, as well as a precursor of the literary modernism that would flower in the twentieth century.*

Stephen Crane was the fourteenth child of a Methodist minister, Jonathan Townley Crane. Though in his mature life Crane would reject both the dogmas and solaces of religion, preferring instead to struggle with a view of the universe as determined by laws both unknowable and hostile, the heritage of Methodism nevertheless shows itself in his writings. His stories are laced with religious imagery and allusion; he sometimes rebels openly and sardonically against the watery comforts of late-nineteenth-century religiosity; and at a still deeper level he returns to a sense of those ineradicable cruelties and perversities in the human psyche which has an oblique kinship with the Christian doctrine of Original Sin.

In 1879 the Crane family settled in Port Jervis, New York, after moving from one New Jersey town to another. Two years later the father died, and in a short while Stephen was contributing to the family income by doing legwork for the news agency run in Asbury Park, New Jersey, by his brother Townley. His formal education was sparse: he spent a semester at Lafayette College and another at Syracuse. His literary culture was thin, and it would remain so till the end of his career. Deciding that "humanity was a more interesting study" than the college curriculum, he quit school to become a full-time reporter for his brother's agency. But that job, like the agency itself, quickly came to an end, when Crane wrote a caustic report of a workingmen's parade in Asbury Park, a resort town frequented by the wealthy. Good citizens were shocked at his social sacrilege and newspaper editors apologized to their readers. Townley's agency was finished.

Here is a sentence from Crane's report which shows the beginnings of his terse, ironic, even cruel style: "The bona fide Asbury Parker is a man to whom a dollar, when held close to his eye, often shuts out any impression he may have that other people possess rights." A twenty-one-year-old novice who could turn out that kind of sentence wasn't likely to remain an ordinary reporter for long.

He didn't. Crane moved to New York City and became a free-lance writer, experiencing poverty for a time and starting what he would call his "artistic education on the Bowery." In 1892—after publishers had refused it—he put out his first novel, Maggie, A Girl of the Streets. *Uneven in quality but strikingly powerful in parts, this naturalistic novel brought friendly reviews from William Dean*

Howells and Hamlin Garland. A forerunner of the harsh portraits of slum life that would later be composed by writers like Theodore Dreiser and James T. Farrell, Maggie, said Crane, was meant

to show that environment is a tremendous thing in the world and frequently shapes lives regardless. If one proves that theory, one makes room in Heaven for all sorts of souls (notably an occasional street girl) who are not confidently expected to be there by many excellent people. . . .

In 1895 came The Red Badge of Courage, *one of the finest novels ever written by an American. Though Crane himself had never "smelled even the powder of battle," this story of a young soldier facing his first test under fire in the Civil War pulsates with the atmosphere of the battlefield. Crane's imagination, which allowed him to enter the tangle of fears experienced by his young soldier, served him better than the experience of many other writers. "A psychological portrait of fear," as Crane called it,* The Red Badge of Courage *depicts the initiation of a youth into terror, and then that fortitude of will and solidarity of men by means of which terror can be confronted. It is also a work radically original both in method and language, one of the first American ventures into literary impressionism. Upon its appearance, Crane achieved immediate and deserved international fame.*

Fame brought problems. Young as he was, Crane could see

the majestic forces which are arrayed against man's true success—not the world—the world is silly, changeable, any of its decisions can be reversed—but man's own colossal impulses more strong than chains, and I perceived that the fight was not going to be with the world but with myself.

In his few remaining years Crane traveled a great deal as a newspaper correspondent. He went to the West and to Mexico, he endured shipwreck off the Florida coast, he covered wars in Greece and Cuba, he became the friend in England of the great writers Henry James and Joseph Conrad. He lived recklessly, he wasted his energies and talents. To fulfill his role as journalist, he underwent constant ordeals and dangers—perhaps also to fulfill his image of what a writer should be, a writer who lives on the brink of danger and personally encounters all the sensations of life. Wherever he went, he saw violence. And violence, he felt, was the outer sign of an inner condition; violence was the condition of man. Crane wore himself out, though not before entering domesticity of a sort. In 1896 he met Cora Taylor, a Jacksonville madam with not merely a heart of gold but a headful of brains, who cared for him after his shipwreck, followed him to wars in Europe, and lived as his common-law wife.

Exhausted from overwork and exposure, Crane succumbed in 1899 to the final stages of tuberculosis. In the spring of 1900 Cora arranged for him to take a rest cure in the Black Forest in Germany, but a week after their arrival he died. Crane's life, like his best work, was brief, violent and brilliant; it seemed to follow the nineteenth-century pattern of romantic excess and self-destruction, but together with these there was a tough discipline and a hard, ironic spirit. He was never a shattered butterfly.

In speaking about his novels we have used the literary terms naturalism *and* impressionism. *By their very nature these cannot be entirely precise, yet they can be useful, if only in illuminating certain qualities Crane's work shared with other late-nineteenth-century writers. Naturalism is an extreme version of realism, often associated with the French novelist Émile Zola. Zola believed he was composing his novels on scientific principles, according to laws of natural inheritance and social determinism. Most naturalistic novelists have since been inclined to write about men and women, usually those of the lower classes sunk in poverty and degradation, as helpless agents and victims of forces beyond their control. Sometimes these forces are seen as inherent in the very nature of existence, sometimes as conditioned by an oppressive social system; the first view leads to resignation, the second to radicalism. In their effort to show how human life is shaped and misshaped—then broken—by these external forces, naturalistic novelists often use a method of accumulation, patiently piling on detail after detail to create the impression that the story they tell has an internal and inexorable logic. Now, to some extent,* Maggie *follows the naturalistic pattern, especially in Crane's use of the slum setting and his bias toward social determinism; but in his literary methods Crane is quite far from the naturalists, since usually he is fiercely selective rather than coldly accumulative, nervously rapid rather than ploddingly slow.*

The term impressionism *makes more sense in describing Crane's work. Ford Madox Ford, himself a distinguished novelist, has said about impressionism:*

> *We saw that Life did not narrate, but made impressions on our brains. We in turn, if we wished to produce on you an effect of life, must not narrate but render . . . impressions.*

The same idea has been developed by an Italian critic, Sergio Perosa, with greater detail:

> *the basic canons of impressionistic writing [are] the apprehension of life through the play of perceptions, the significant montage of sense impressions, the reproduction of chromatic touches by colorful and precise*

notations, the reduction of elaborate syntax to the correlation of sentences, which leads to a sketchy, and at the same time evocative, kind of writing.

But even when useful, such critical categories as naturalism and impressionism do not yet tell us what is distinctive about a writer's work; they only help us approach it. All of Crane's important fiction is a fiction of extreme situations. It portrays men at the point where civilized norms begin to break down and the structure of human character buckles under the thrust of primitive drives. The norms of civilization are tested—perhaps, suggests Crane, they can really be tested only—by experiences in which all the energies and emotions swirling beneath civilized life are mobilized.

Men are thrust into situations of danger. Being men, they cannot avoid the sensations of fear and sometimes panic. They discover, when forced to confront such terrors in common, that they can now reach a kind of brotherhood. But this brotherhood is likely to be maintained only for a moment, at the peak of danger, when it seems too frightful to be alone. And even then, it is viewed by Crane with strong ironic qualifications, for once the threat comes to an end, either because it has been met successfully or has engulfed its victims, men revert to their "normal" condition of vanity, self-deceit and loneliness. Only at the edge of fear can they discover the color of their souls. Only then can they know the distance, large or small, between the codes of behavior by which they would like to live and the inner natures with which they must live. Toward these men—as Crane's best critic, John Berryman, has remarked— Crane is both ally and enemy: he burrows into their consciousness, he shares their ordeals, he becomes one of them, yet he also stands apart at a cold distance, sardonically watching their pitiful efforts to maintain their dignity, excuse their failures, and regain their pomposity. A contemporary of Stephen Crane, the critic Edward Garnett, had already observed these qualities in his work, praising

his wonderful insight into and mastery of the primary passions, and his irony deriding the swelling emotions of the self. . . . It is the perfect fusion of these two forces of passion and irony that creates Crane's spiritual background, and raises his work, at its finest, into the higher zone of man's tragic conflict with the universe.

Crane's stories of initiation and test vary, of course, from one another and in the degree to which they follow the pattern described above. "The Open Boat" comes the closest to conforming to the pattern of an elemental testing of untried men under circumstances which both reveal and disintegrate their characters. "The Blue Hotel" presents a major and brilliant variation: the Swede brings to the action his own preconceived panic, a result of excessive imagination and weak nerves, and through the uncontainable workings of this panic he provokes a situation in which the threat he had feared now *materializes and the doom he had expected overwhelms him. "The Bride Comes to Yellow Sky" represents a charmingly comic variant: a dangerous confrontation builds up, but the social circumstances and rituals to which the actors are accustomed have changed, and as a result they no longer know how to act out their conflict—the Old West is no longer the Old West, the sheriff will no longer have to play dangerous games with Scratchy, and everyone can go home relieved.*

What interests Crane in these stories is not so much the internal history of human character nor the familiar external social relations of the ordinary world. What interests him is the response to extreme crisis, the possibility that Ernest Hemingway would later call "grace under pressure"—or the absence of grace under pressure. John Berryman lists some of the literary consequences:

> *Crane's stories are as unlike earlier stories as his poems are unlike earlier poems. He threw away, thoughtfully, plot; outlawed juggling and arrangement of material (Poe, Bierce, O'Henry); excluded the whole usual mechanism of society; banished equally sex (Maupassant) and romantic love (Chekhov—unknown to him); decided not to develop his characters; decided not to have any conflicts between them as characters; resolved not to have any characters at all in the usual sense; simplified everything that remained and, watching intently, tenderly, and hopelessly, blew Fate through it—saying with inconceivable rapidity and an air of immense deliberation what he saw.*

Inevitably, the kind of story Crane wrote had to be brief, cutting away the history and background of crisis in order to focus on crisis itself. Inevitably, the tone had to be tense, violent, seemingly barbaric. And inevitably, the language had to be stripped of the orotundness, decorations, and qualifications of earlier American prose. It had to be a language that would come at the reader like a blow, ferocious in its primary impact, violent in its imagery, venturing all kinds of unexpected mixtures of impression, and shocking the reader into a fresh apprehension of the strangeness of the world. In The Red Badge of Courage *the columns of troops are "like two serpents crawling out of the cavern of the night." The red sun is "pasted in the sky like a wafer." When its central character runs from the battle, "There was the law, he said. Nature had given him a sign. The squirrel, immediately upon recognizing danger, had taken to his legs without ado." And examine, for an effect of power and surprise, the opening sentence of "The Open Boat."*

FURTHER READING

Crane's letters have been edited by R. W. Stallman and Lilian Gilkes, *Stephen Crane: Letters* (1960). An early vivid but not always reli-

able biography is Thomas Beer, *Shephen Crane: A Study in American Letters* (1923). The best critical biography is John Berryman,
Stephen Crane (1950). The poetry is studied in Daniel Hoffman,
The Poetry of Stephen Crane (1957). An excellent early criticism
is H. G. Wells, "Stephen Crane from an English Standpoint," reprinted in Edmund Wilson, *The Shock of Recognition.*

An Experiment in Misery (1894)[1]

It was late at night, and a fine rain was swirling softly down, causing the pavements to glisten with hue of steel and blue and yellow in
the rays of the innumerable lights. A youth was trudging slowly, without enthusiasm, with his hands buried deep in his trousers pockets,
toward the downtown places where beds can be hired for coppers. He
was clothed in an aged and tattered suit, and his derby was a marvel
of dust-covered crown and torn rim. He was going forth to eat as the
wanderer may eat, and sleep as the homeless sleep. By the time he had
reached City Hall Park he was so completely plastered with yells of
"bum" and "hobo," and with various unholy epithets that small boys
had applied to him at intervals, that he was in a state of the most
profound dejection. The sifting rain saturated the old velvet collar of
his overcoat, and as the wet cloth pressed against his neck, he felt that
there no longer could be pleasure in life. He looked about him searching for an outcast of highest degree that they two might share miseries,
but the lights threw a quivering glare over rows and circles of deserted
benches that glistened damply, showing patches of wet sod behind
them. It seemed that their usual freights had fled on this night to better things. There were only squads of well-dressed Brooklyn people who
swarmed toward the bridge.

The young man loitered about for a time and then went shuffling
off down Park Row. In the sudden descent in style of the dress of the
crowd he felt relief, and as if he were at last in his own country. He
began to see tatters that matched his tatters. In Chatham Square there
were aimless men strewn in front of saloons and lodging-houses, standing sadly, patiently, reminding one vaguely of the attitudes of chickens
in a storm. He aligned himself with these men, and turned slowly to
occupy himself with the flowing life of the great street.

Through the mists of the cold and storming night, the cable cars
went in silent procession, great affairs shining with red and brass, moving with formidable power, calm and irresistible, dangerful and gloomy,
breaking silence only by the loud fierce cry of the gong. Two rivers of

[1] This story is one of a group of short fictions Crane wrote about the Bowery, the
section of lower Manhattan where derelicts, tramps, and paupers have traditionally
congregated.

people swarmed along the sidewalks, spattered with black mud which made each shoe leave a scarlike impression. Overhead, elevated trains with a shrill grinding of the wheels stopped at the station, which upon its leg-like pillars seemed to resemble some monstrous kind of crab squatting over the street. The quick fat puffings of the engines could be heard. Down an alley there were somber curtains of purple and black, on which street lamps dully glittered like embroidered flowers.

A saloon stood with a voracious air on a corner. A sign leaning against the front of the doorpost announced "Free hot soup to-night!" The swing doors, snapping to and fro like ravenous lips, made gratified smacks as the saloon gorged itself with plump men, eating with astounding and endless appetite, smiling in some indescribable manner as the men came from all directions like sacrifices to a heathenish superstition.

Caught by the delectable sign, the young man allowed himself to be swallowed. A bartender placed a schooner of dark and portentous beer on the bar. Its monumental form upreared until the froth atop was above the crown of the young man's brown derby.

"Soup over there, gents," said the bartender affably. A little yellow man in rags and the youth grasped their schooners and went with speed toward a lunch-counter, where a man with oily but imposing whiskers ladled genially from a kettle until he had furnished his two mendicants with a soup that was steaming hot, and in which there were little floating suggestions of chicken. The young man, sipping his broth, felt the cordiality expressed by the warmth of the mixture, and he beamed at the man with oily but imposing whiskers, who was presiding like a priest behind an altar. "Have some more gents?" he inquired of the two sorry figures before him. The little yellow man accepted with a swift gesture, but the youth shook his head and went out, following a man whose wondrous seediness promised that he would have a knowledge of cheap lodging-houses.

On the sidewalk he accosted the seedy man. "Say, do you know a cheap place to sleep?"

The other hesitated for a time, gazing sideways. Finally he nodded in the direction of the street. "I sleep up there," he said, "when I've got the price."

"How much?"

"Ten cents."

The young man shook his head dolefully. "That's too rich for me."

At that moment there approached the two a reeling man in strange garments. His head was a fuddle of bushy hair and whiskers, from which his eyes peered with a guilty slant. In a close scrutiny it was possible to distinguish the cruel lines of a mouth which looked as if its lips had just closed with satisfaction over some tender and piteous morsel. He appeared like an assassin steeped in crimes performed awkwardly.

But at this time his voice was tuned to the coaxing key of an affectionate puppy. He looked at the men with wheedling eyes, and began to sing a little melody for charity. "Say, gents, can't yeh give a poor feller a couple of cents t' git a bed? I got five, an' I gits anudder two I gits me a bed. Now, on th' square, gents, can't yeh jest gimme two cents t' git a bed? Now, yeh know how a respecterble gentlem'n feels when he's down on his luck, an' I—"

The seedy man, staring with imperturbable countenance at a train which clattered overhead, interrupted in an expressionless voice: "Ah, go t'hell!"

But the youth spoke to the prayerful assassin in tones of astonishment and inquiry. "Say, you must be crazy! Why don't yeh strike somebody that looks as if they had money?"

The assassin, tottering about on his uncertain legs, and at intervals brushing imaginary obstacles from before his nose, entered into a long explanation of the psychology of the situation. It was so profound that it was unintelligible.

When he had exhausted the subject, the young man said to him: "Let's see th' five cents."

The assassin wore an expression of drunken woe at this sentence, filled with suspicion of him. With a deeply pained air he began to fumble in his clothing, his red hands trembling. Presently he announced in a voice of bitter grief, as if he had been betrayed: "There's on'y four."

"Four," said the young man thoughtfully. "Well, look-a here, I'm a stranger here, an' if ye'll steer me to your cheap joint I'll find the other three."

The assassin's countenance became instantly radiant with joy. His whiskers quivered with the wealth of his alleged emotions. He seized the young man's hand in a transport of delight and friendliness.

"B' Gawd," he cried, "if ye'll do that, b' Gawd, I'd say yeh was a damned good fellow, I would, an' I'd remember yeh all m' life, I would, b' Gawd, an' if I ever got a chance I'd return the compliment"—he spoke with drunken dignity—"b' Gawd, I'd treat yeh white, I would, an' I'd allus remember yeh."

The young man drew back, looking at the assassin coldly. "Oh, that's all right," he said. "You show me th' joint—that's all you've got t' do."

The assassin, gesticulating gratitude, led the young man along a dark street. Finally he stopped before a little dusty door. He raised his hand impressively. "Look-a here," he said, and there was a thrill of deep and ancient wisdom upon his face, "I've brought yeh here, an' that's my part, ain't it? If th' place don't suit yeh, yeh needn't git mad at me, need yeh? There won't be no bad feelin', will there?"

"No," said the young man.

The assassin waved his arm tragically, and led the march up the steep stairway. On the way the young man furnished the assassin with three pennies. At the top a man with benevolent spectacles looked at them through a hole in a board. He collected their money, wrote some names on a register, and speedily was leading the two men along a gloom-shrouded corridor.

Shortly after the beginning of this journey the young man felt his liver turn white, for from the dark and secret places of the building there suddenly came to his nostrils strange and unspeakable odors, that assailed him like malignant diseases with wings. They seemed to be from human bodies closely packed in dens; the exhalations from a hundred pairs of reeking lips; the fumes from a thousand bygone debauches; the expression of a thousand present miseries.

A man, naked save for a little snuff-colored undershirt, was parading sleepily along the corridor. He rubbed his eyes and, giving vent to a prodigious yawn, demanded to be told the time.

"Half-past one."

The man yawned again. He opened a door, and for a moment his form was outlined against a black, opaque interior. To this door came the three men, and as it was again opened the unholy odors rushed out like fiends, so that the young man was obliged to struggle as against an overpowering wind.

It was some time before the youth's eyes were good in the intense gloom within, but the man with benevolent spectacles led him skilfully, pausing but a moment to deposit the limp assassin upon a cot. He took the youth to a cot that lay tranquilly by the window, and showing him a tall locker for clothes that stood near the head with the ominous air of a tombstone, left him.

The youth sat on his cot and peered about him. There was a gas-jet in a distant part of the room, that burned a small flickering orange-hued flame. It caused vast masses of tumbled shadows in all parts of the place; save where, immediately about it, there was a little gray haze. As the young man's eyes became used to the darkness, he could see upon the cots that thickly littered the floor the forms of men sprawled out, lying in death-like silence, or heaving and snoring with tremendous effort, like stabbed fish.

The youth locked his derby and his shoes in the mummy-case near him, and then lay down with an old and familiar coat around his shoulders. A blanket he handled gingerly, drawing it over part of the coat. The cot was covered with leather, and as cold as melting snow. The youth was obliged to shiver for some time on this affair, which was like a slab. Presently, however, his chill gave him peace, and during this period of leisure from it he turned his head to stare at his friend the assassin, whom he could dimly discern where he lay sprawled on a cot in the abandon of a man filled with drink. He was snoring with incredible vigor. His wet hair and beard dimly glistened, and his inflamed nose shone with subdued luster like a red light in a fog.

Within reach of the youth's hand was one who lay with yellow breast and shoulders bare to the cold draughts. One arm hung over the side of the cot, and the fingers lay full length upon the wet cement floor of the room. Beneath the inky brows could be seen the eyes of the man, exposed by the partly opened lids. To the youth it seemed that he and this corpse-like being were exchanging a prolonged stare, and that the other threatened with his eyes. He drew back, watching his neighbor from the shadows of his blanket-edge. The man did not move once through the night, but lay in this stillness as of death like a body stretched out expectant of the surgeon's knife.

And all through the room could be seen the tawny hues of naked flesh, limbs thrust into the darkness, projecting beyond the cots, up-reared knees, arms hanging long and thin over the cot-edges. For the most part they were statuesque, carven, dead. With the curious lockers standing all about like tombstones, there was a strange effect of a graveyard where bodies were merely flung.

Yet occasionally could be seen limbs wildly tossing in fantastic nightmare gestures, accompanied by guttural cries, grunts, oaths. And there was one fellow off in a gloomy corner, who in his dreams was oppressed by some frightful calamity, for of a sudden he began to utter long wails that went almost like yells from a hound, echoing wailfully and weird through this chill place of tombstones where men lay like the dead.

The sound, in its high piercing beginnings that dwindled to final melancholy moans, expressed a red and grim tragedy of the unfathomable possibilities of the man's dreams. But to the youth these were not merely the shrieks of a vision-pierced man: they were an utterance of the meaning of the room and its occupants. It was to him the protest of the wretch who feels the touch of the imperturbable granite wheels, and who then cries with an impersonal eloquence, with a strength not from him, giving voice to the wail of a whole section, a class, a people. This, weaving into the young man's brain, and mingling with his views of the vast and somber shadows that, like mighty black fingers, curled around the naked bodies, made the young man so that he did not sleep, but lay carving the biographies for these men from his meager experience. At times the fellow in the corner howled in a writhing agony of his imaginations.

Finally a long lance-point of gray light shot through the dusty panes of the window. Without, the young man could see roofs drearily white in the dawning. The point of light yellowed and grew brighter, until the golden rays of the morning sun came in bravely and strong. They touched with radiant color the form of a small fat man who snored in stuttering fashion. His round and shiny bald head glowed suddenly with the valor of a decoration. He sat up, blinked at the sun, swore fretfully, and pulled his blanket over the ornamental spendors of his head.

The youth contentedly watched this rout of the shadows before the bright spears of the sun, and presently he slumbered. When he awoke he heard the voice of the assassin raised in valiant curses. Putting up his head, he perceived his comrade seated on the side of the cot engaged in scratching his neck with long fingernails that rasped like files.

"Hully Jee, dis is a new breed. They've got canopeners on their feet." He continued in a violent tirade.

The young man hastily unlocked his closet and took out his shoes and hat. As he sat on the side of the cot lacing his shoes, he glanced about and saw that daylight had made the room comparatively commonplace and uninteresting. The men, whose faces seemed stolid, serene, or absent, were engaged in dressing, while a great crackle of bantering conversation arose.

A few were parading in unconcerned nakedness. Here and there were men of brawn, whose skins shone clear and ruddy. They took splendid poses, standing massively like chiefs. When they had dressed in their ungainly garments there was an extraordinary change. They then showed bumps and deficiencies of all kinds.

There were others who exhibited many deformities. Shoulders were slanting, humped, pulled this way and pulled that way. And notable among these latter men was the little fat man who had refused to allow his head to be glorified. His pudgy form, builded like a pear, bustled to and fro, while he swore in fishwife fashion. It appeared that some article of his apparel had vanished.

The young man attired himself speedily, and went to his friend the assassin. At first the latter looked dazed at the sight of the youth. This face seemed to be appealing to him through the cloudwastes of his memory. He scratched his neck and reflected. At last he grinned, a broad smile gradually spreading until his countenance was a round illumination. "Hello, Willie," he cried cheerily.

"Hello," said the young man. "Are yeh ready t' fly?"

"Sure." The assassin tied his shoe carefully with some twine and came ambling.

When he reached the street the young man experienced no sudden relief from unholy atmospheres. He had forgotten all about them, and had been breathing naturally, and with no sensation of discomfort or distress.

He was thinking of these things as he walked along the street, when he was suddenly startled by feeling the assassin's hand, trembling with excitement, clutching his arm, and when the assassin spoke, his voice went into quavers from a supreme agitation.

"I'll be hully, bloomin' blowed if there wasn't a feller with a nightshirt on up there in that joint."

The youth was bewildered for a moment, but presently he turned to smile indulgently at the assassin's humor. "Oh, you're a damned liar," he merely said.

Whereupon the assassin began to gesture extravagantly and take oath by strange gods. He frantically placed himself at the mercy of remarkable fates if his tale were not true. "Yes, he did! I cross m' heart thousan' times!" he protested, and at the moment his eyes were large with amazement, his mouth wrinkled in unnatural glee. "Yessir! A nightshirt! A hully white nightshirt!"

"You lie!"

"No, sir! I hope ter die b'fore I kin git anudder ball if there wasn't a jay wid a hully, bloomin' white nightshirt!"

His face was filled with the infinite wonder of it. "A hully white nightshirt," he continually repeated.

The young man saw the dark entrance to a basement restaurant. There was a sign which read "No mystery about our hash!" and there were other age-stained and world-battered legends which told him that the place was within his means. He stopped before it and spoke to the assassin. "I guess I'll git somethin' t' eat."

At this the assassin, for some reason, appeared to be quite embarrassed. He gazed at the seductive front of the eating-place for a moment. Then he started slowly up the street. "Well, good-bye, Willie," he said bravely.

For an instant the youth studied the departing figure. Then he called out, "Hol' on a minnet." As they came together he spoke in a certain fierce way, as if he feared that the other would think him to be charitable. "Look-a here, if yeh wanta git some breakfas' I'll lend yeh three cents t' do it with. But say, look-a here, you've gotta git out an' hustle. I ain't goin' t' support yeh, or I'll go broke b'fore night. I ain't no millionaire."

"I take me oath, Willie," said the assassin earnestly, "th' on'y thing I really needs is a ball. Me t'roat feels like a fryin'-pan. But as I can't get a ball, why, th' next bes' thing is breakfast, an' if yeh do that for me, b' Gawd, I say yeh was th' whitest lad I ever see."

They spent a few moments in dexterous exchanges of phrases, in which they each protested that the other was, as the assassin had originally said, "a respecterble gentlem'n." And they concluded with mutual assurances that they were the souls of intelligence and virtue. Then they went into the restaurant.

There was a long counter, dimly lighted from hidden sources. Two or three men in soiled white aprons rushed here and there.

The youth bought a bowl of coffee for two cents and a roll for one cent. The assassin purchased the same. The bowls were webbed with brown seams, and the tin spoons wore an air of having emerged from the first pyramid. Upon them were black moss-like encrustations of age, and they were bent and scarred from the attacks of long-forgotten teeth. But over their repast the wanderers waxed warm and mellow. The assassin grew affable as the hot mixture went soothingly down his parched throat, and the young man felt courage flow in his veins.

Memories began to throng in on the assassin, and he brought forth long tales, intricate, incoherent, delivered with a chattering swiftness as from an old woman. "—great job out 'n Orange. Boss keep yeh hustlin', though, all time. I was there three days, and then I went an' ask 'im t' lend me a dollar. 'G-g-go ter the devil,' he says, an' I lose me job.

"South no good. Damn niggers work for twenty-five an' thirty cents a day. Run white man out. Good grub, though. Easy livin'.

"Yas; useter work little in Toledo, raftin' logs. Make two or three dollars er day in the spring. Lived high. Cold as ice, though, in the winter.

"I was raised in northern N' York. O-o-oh, yeh jest oughto live there. No beer ner whisky, though, 'way off in the woods. But all th' good hot grub yeh can eat. B' Gawd, I hung around there long as I could till th' ol' man fired me. 'Git t' hell outa here, yeh wuthless skunk, git t' hell outa here, an' go die,' he says. 'You're a hell of a father,' I says, 'you are,' an' I quit 'im."

As they were passing from the dim eating-place, they encountered an old man who was trying to steal forth with a tiny package of food, but a tall man with an indomitable moustache stood dragon-fashion, barring the way of escape. They heard the old man raise a plaintive protest. "Ah, you always want to know what I take out, and you never see that I usually bring a package in here from my place of business."

As the wanderers trudged slowly along Park Row, the assassin began to expand and grow blithe. "B' Gawd, we've been livin' like kings," he said, smacking appreciative lips.

"Look out, or we'll have t' pay fer it t'-night," said the youth with gloomy warning.

But the assassin refused to turn his gaze toward the future. He went with a limping step, into which he injected a suggestion of lamb-like gambols. His mouth was wreathed in a red grin.

In City Hall Park the two wanderers sat down in the little circle of benches sanctified by traditions of their class. They huddled in their old garments, slumbrously conscious of the march of the hours which for them had no meaning.

The people of the street hurrying hither and thither made a blend of black figures, changing, yet frieze-like. They walked in their good clothes as upon important missions, giving no gaze to the two wanderers seated upon the benches. They expressed to the young man his infinite distance from all that he valued. Social position, comfort, the pleasures of living were unconquerable kingdoms. He felt a sudden awe.

And in the background a multitude of buildings, of pitiless hues and sternly high, were to him emblematic of a nation forcing its regal head into the clouds, throwing no downward glances; in the sublimity of its aspirations ignoring the wretches who may flounder at its feet. The roar of the city in his ear was to him the confusion of strange tongues, babbling heedlessly; it was the clink of coin, the voice of the city's hopes, which were to him no hopes.

He confessed himself an outcast, and his eyes from under the lowered rim of his hat began to glance guiltily, wearing the criminal expression that comes with certain convictions.

The Open Boat (1897)[1]

A Tale Intended to be after the Fact: Being the Experience of Four Men from the Sunk Steamer "Commodore"

I

None of them knew the color of the sky. Their eyes glanced level, and were fastened upon the waves that swept toward them. These waves were of the hue of slate, save for the tops, which were of foaming white, and all of the men knew the colors of the sea. The horizon narrowed and widened, and dipped and rose, and at all times its edge was jagged with waves that seemed thrust up in points like rocks.

Many a man ought to have a bathtub larger than the boat which here rode upon the sea. These waves were most wrongfully and barbarously abrupt and tall, and each froth-top was a problem in small-boat navigation.

The cook squatted in the bottom, and looked with both eyes at the six inches of gunwale which separated him from the ocean. His sleeves were rolled over his fat forearms, and the two flaps of his unbuttoned vest dangled as he bent to bail out the boat. Often he said, "Gawd! that was a narrow clip." As he remarked it he invariably gazed eastward over the broken sea.

The oiler, steering with one of the two oars in the boat, sometimes raised himself suddenly to keep clear of water that swirled in over the stern. It was a thin little oar, and it seemed often ready to snap.

The correspondent, pulling at the other oar, watched the waves and wondered why he was there.

The injured captain, lying in the bow, was at this time buried in that profound dejection and indifference which comes, temporarily at least, to even the bravest and most enduring when, willy-nilly, the firm fails, the army loses, the ship goes down. The mind of the master of a vessel is rooted deep in the timbers of her, though he command for a day or a decade; and this captain had on him the stern impression of a scene in the grays of dawn of seven turned faces, and later a stump of a topmast with a white ball on it, that slashed to and fro at the waves, went low and lower, and down. Thereafter there was something strange in his voice. Although steady, it was deep with mourning, and of a quality beyond oration or tears.

[1] Crane sailed as a correspondent on the *Commodore*, an American steamer, which on January 1, 1897, left Jacksonville, Florida, with munitions and men for Cuban rebels. That night the steamer sank; there were suspicions of sabotage. With four others, Crane got back to Daytona Beach in a ten-foot dinghy. In June, 1897, he published his fictional account, *The Open Boat*, in *Scribner's Magazine*.

"Keep 'er a little more south, Billie," said he.

"A little more south, sir," said the oiler in the stern.

A seat in this boat was not unlike a seat upon a bucking broncho, and, by the same token, a broncho is not much smaller. The craft pranced and reared and plunged like an animal. As each wave came, and she rose for it, she seemed like a horse making at a fence outrageously high. The manner of her scramble over these walls of water is a mystic thing, and, moreover, at the top of them were ordinarily these problems in white water, the foam racing down from the summit of each wave requiring a new leap, and a leap from the air. Then, after scornfully bumping a crest, she would slide and race and splash down a long incline, and arrive bobbing and nodding in front of the next menace.

A singular disadvantage of the sea lies in the fact that, after successfully surmounting one wave, you discover that there is another behind it just as important and just as nervously anxious to do something effective in the way of swamping boats. In a ten-foot dinghy one can get an idea of the resources of the sea in the line of waves that is not probable to the average experience, which is never at sea in a dinghy. As each slaty wall of water approached, it shut all else from the view of the men in the boat, and it was not difficult to imagine that this particular wave was the final outburst of the ocean, the last effort of the grim water. There was a terrible grace in the move of the waves, and they came in silence, save for the snarling of the crests.

In the wan light the faces of the men must have been gray. Their eyes must have glinted in strange ways as they gazed steadily astern. Viewed from a balcony, the whole thing would, doubtless, have been weirdly picturesque. But the men in the boat had no time to see it, and if they had had leisure, there were other things to occupy their minds. The sun swung steadily up the sky, and they knew it was broad day because the color of the sea changed from slate to emerald-green streaked with amber lights, and the foam was like tumbling snow. The process of the breaking day was unknown to them. They were aware only of this effect upon the color of the waves that rolled toward them.

In disjointed sentences the cook and the correspondent argued as to the difference between a life-saving station and a house of refuge. The cook had said: "There's a house of refuge just north of the Mosquito Inlet Light, and as soon as they see us they'll come off in their boat and pick us up."

"As soon as who see us?" said the correspondent.

"The crew," said the cook.

"Houses of refuge don't have crews," said the correspondent. "As I understand them, they are only places where clothes and grub are stored for the benefit of shipwrecked people. They don't carry crews."

"Oh, yes, they do," said the cook.

"No, they don't," said the correspondent.

"Well, we're not there yet, anyhow," said the oiler in the stern.

"Well," said the cook, "perhaps it's not a house of refuge that I'm thinking of as being near Mosquito Inlet Light; perhaps it's a life-saving station."

"We're not there yet," said the oiler in the stern.

II

As the boat bounced from the top of each wave the wind tore through the hair of the hatless men, and as the craft plopped her stern down again the spray slashed past them. The crest of each of these waves was a hill, from the top of which the men surveyed for a moment a broad, tumultuous expanse, shining and wind-riven. It was probably splendid, it was probably glorious, this play of the free sea, wild with lights of emerald and white and amber.

"Bully good thing it's an on-shore wind," said the cook. "If not, where would we be? Wouldn't have a show."

"That's right," said the correspondent.

The busy oiler nodded his assent.

Then the captain, in the bow, chuckled in a way that expressed humor, contempt, tragedy, all in one. "Do you think we've got much of a show now, boys?" said he.

Whereupon the three were silent, save for a trifle of hemming and hawing. To express any particular optimism at this time they felt to be childish and stupid, but they all doubtless possessed this sense of the situation in their minds. A young man thinks doggedly at such times. On the other hand, the ethics of their condition was decidedly against any open suggestion of hopelessness. So they were silent.

"Oh, well," said the captain, soothing his children, "we'll get ashore all right."

But there was that in his tone which made them think; so the oiler quoth, "Yes! if this wind holds."

The cook was bailing. "Yes! if we don't catch hell in the surf."

Canton-flannel gulls flew near and far. Sometimes they sat down on the sea, near patches of brown seaweed that rolled over the waves with a movement like carpets on a line in a gale. The birds sat comfortably in groups, and they were envied by some in the dinghy, for the wrath of the sea was no more to them than it was to a covey of prairie chickens a thousand miles inland. Often they came very close and stared at the men with black, bead-like eyes. At these times they were uncanny and sinister in their unblinking scrutiny, and the men hooted angrily at them, telling them to be gone. One came, and evidently decided to alight on the top of the captain's head. The bird flew parallel to the boat and did not circle, but made short sidelong jumps in the air in chicken fashion. His black eyes were wistfully fixed upon the captain's head. "Ugly brute," said the oiler to the bird. "You look as if you were made with a jackknife." The cook and the correspondent swore darkly at the creature. The captain naturally wished to knock it away with the end of the heavy painter, but he did not dare do it, because anything resembling an emphatic gesture would have capsized this freighted boat; and so, with his open hand, the captain gently and carefully waved the gull away. After it had been discouraged from the pursuit the captain breathed easier on account of his hair, and others breathed easier because the bird struck their minds at this time as being somehow gruesome and ominous.

In the meantime the oiler and the correspondent rowed; and also they rowed. They sat together in the same seat, and each rowed an oar. Then the oiler took both oars; then the correspondent took both oars, then the oiler; then the correspondent. They rowed and they rowed. The very ticklish part of the business was when the time came for the reclining one in the stern to take his turn at the oars. By the very last star of truth, it is easier to steal eggs from under a hen than it was to change seats in the dinghy. First the man in the stern slid his hand along the thwart and moved with care, as if he were of Sèvres. Then the man in the rowing-seat slid his hand along the other thwart. It was all done with the most extraordinary care. As the two sidled past each other, the whole party kept watchful eyes on the coming wave, and the captain cried: "Look out, now! Steady, there!"

The brown mats of seaweed that appeared from time to time were like islands, bits of earth. They were travelling, apparently, neither one way nor the other. They were, to all intents, stationary. They informed the men in the boat that it was making progress slowly toward the land.

The captain, rearing cautiously in the bow after the dinghy soared on a great swell, said that he had seen the lighthouse at Mosquito Inlet. Presently the cook remarked that he had seen it. The correspondent was at the oars then, and for some reason he too wished to look at the lighthouse; but his back was toward the far shore, and the waves were important, and for some time he could not seize an opportunity to turn his head. But at last there came a wave more gentle than the others, and when at the crest of it he swifty scoured the western horizon.

"See it?" said the captain.

"No," said the correspondent, slowly; "I didn't see anything."

"Look again," said the captain. He pointed. "It's exactly in that direction."

At the top of another wave the correspondent did as he was bid, and this time his eyes chanced on a small, still thing on the edge of the swaying horizon. It was precisely like the point of a pin. It took an anxious eye to find a lighthouse so tiny.

"Think we'll make it, Captain?"

"If this wind holds and the boat don't swamp, we can't do much else," said the captain.

The little boat, lifted by each towering sea and splashed viciously by the crests, made progress that in the absence of seaweed was not apparent to those in her. She seemed just a wee thing wallowing, miraculously top up, at the mercy of five oceans. Occasionally a great spread of water, like white flames, swarmed into her.

"Bail her, cook," said the captain, serenely.

"All right, Captain," said the cheerful cook.

III

It would be difficult to describe the subtle brotherhood of men that was here established on the seas. No one said that it was so. No one mentioned it. But it dwelt in the boat, and each man felt it warm him. They were a captain, an oiler, a cook, and a correspondent, and they were friends—friends in a more curiously iron-bound degree than may be common. The hurt captain, lying against the water jar in the bow, spoke always in a low voice and calmly; but he could never command a more ready and swiftly obedient crew than the motley three of the dinghy. It was more than a mere recognition of what was best for the common safety. There was surely in it a quality that was personal and heartfelt. And after this devotion to the commander of the boat, there was this comradeship, that the correspondent, for instance, who had been taught to be cynical of men, knew even at the time was the best experience of his life. But no one said that it was so. No one mentioned it.

"I wish we had a sail," remarked the captain. "We might try my overcoat on the end of an oar, and give you two boys a chance to rest." So the cook and the correspondent held the mast and spread wide the overcoat; the oiler steered; and the little boat made good way with her new rig. Sometimes the oiler had to scull sharply to keep a sea from breaking into the boat, but otherwise sailing was a success.

Meanwhile the lighthouse had been growing slowly larger. It had now almost assumed color, and appeared like a little gray shadow on the sky. The man at the oars could not be prevented from turning his head rather often to try for a glimpse of this little gray shadow.

At last, from the top of each wave, the men in the tossing boat could see land. Even as the lighthouse was an upright shadow on the sky, this land seemed but a long black shadow on the sea. It certainly was thinner than paper. "We must be about opposite New Smyrna," said the cook, who had coasted this shore often in schooners. "Captain, by the way, I believe they abandoned that life-saving station there about a year ago."

"Did they?" said the captain.

The wind slowly died away. The cook and the correspondent were not now obliged to slave in order to hold high the oar, but the waves continued their old impetuous swooping at the dinghy, and the little craft, no longer under way, struggled woundily over them. The oiler or the correspondent took the oars again.

Shipwrecks are *apropos* of nothing. If men could only train for them and have them occur when the men had reached pink condition, there would be less drowning at sea. Of the four in the dinghy none had slept any time worth mentioning for two days and two nights previous to embarking in the dinghy, and in the excitement of clambering about the deck of a foundering ship they had also forgotten to eat heartily.

For these reasons, and for others, neither the oiler nor the correspondent was fond of rowing at this time. The correspondent wondered ingenuously how in the name of all that was sane could there be people who thought it amusing to row a boat. It was not an amusement; it was a diabolical punishment, and even a genius of mental aberrations could never conclude that it was anything but a horror to the muscles and a crime against the back. He mentioned to the boat in general how the amusement of rowing struck him, and the weary-faced oiler smiled in full sympathy. Previously to the foundering, by the way, the oiler had worked double watch in the engine-room of the ship.

"Take here easy now boys," said the captain. "Don't spend yourselves. If we have to run a surf you'll need all your strength, because we'll sure have to swim for it. Take your time."

Slowly the land arose from the sea. From a black line it became a line of black and a line of white—trees and sand. Finally the captain said that he could make out a house on the shore. "That's the house of refuge, sure," said the cook. "They'll see us before long, and come out after us."

The distant lighthouse reared high. "The keeper ought to be able to make us out now, if he's looking through a glass," said the captain. "He'll notify the life-saving people."

"None of those other boats could have got ashore to give word of the wreck," said the oiler, in a low voice, "else the life boat would be out hunting us."

Slowly and beautifully the land loomed out of the sea. The wind came again. It had veered from the northeast to the southeast. Finally a new sound struck the ears of the men in the boat. It was the low thunder of the surf on the shore. "We'll never be able to make the lighthouse now," said the captain. "Swing her head a little more north, Billie."

"A little more north, sir," said the oiler.

Whereupon the little boat turned her nose once more down the wind, and all but the oarsman watched the shore grow. Under the influence of this expansion doubt and direful apprehension were leaving the minds of the men. The management of the boat was still most absorbing, but it could not prevent a quiet cheerfulness. In an hour, perhaps, they would be ashore.

Their backbones had become thoroughly used to balancing in the boat, and they now rode this wild colt of a dinghy like circus men. The correspondent thought that he had been drenched to the skin, but happening to feel in the top of his coat, he found therein eight cigars. Four of them were soaked with sea water; four were perfectly scatheless. After a search, somebody produced three dry matches; thereupon the four waifs rode in their little boat and, with an assurance of an impending rescue shining in their eyes, puffed at the big cigars, and judged well and ill of all men. Everybody took a drink of water.

IV

"Cook," remarked the captain, "there don't seem to be any signs of life about your house of refuge."

"No," replied the cook. "Funny they don't see us!"

A broad stretch of lowly coast lay before the eyes of the men. It was of low dunes topped with dark vegetation. The roar of the surf was plain, and sometimes they could see the white lip of a wave as it spun up the beach. A tiny house was blocked out black upon the sky. Southward, the slim lighthouse lifted its little gray length.

Tide, wind, and waves were swinging the dinghy northward. "Funny they don't see us," said the men.

The surf's roar was here dulled, but its tone was nevertheless thunderous and mighty. As the boat swam over the great rollers the men sat listening to this roar. "We'll swamp sure," said everybody.

It is fair to say here that there was not a life-saving station within twenty miles in either direction; but the men did not know this fact, and in consequence they made dark and opprobrious remarks concerning the eyesight of the nation's life savers. Four scowling men sat in the dinghy and surpassed records in the invention of epithets.

"Funny they don't see us."

The light-heartedness of a former time had completely faded. To their sharpened minds it was easy to conjure pictures of all kinds of incompetency and blindness and, indeed, cowardice. There was the shore of the populous land, and it was bitter and bitter to them that from it came no sign.

"Well," said the captain, ultimately, "I suppose we'll have to make a try for ourselves. If we stay out here too long, we'll none of us have strength left to swim after the boat swamps."

And so the oiler, who was at the oars, turned the boat straight for the shore. There was a sudden tightening of muscles. There was some thinking.

"If we don't all get ashore," said the captain—"If we don't all get ashore, I suppose you fellows know where to send news of my finish?"

They then briefly exchanged some addresses and admonitions. As for the reflections of the men, there was a great deal of rage in them. Perchance they might be formulated thus: "If I am going to be drowned —if I am going to be drowned—if I am going to be drowned, why, in the name of the seven mad gods who rule the sea, was I allowed to come thus far and contemplate sand and trees? Was I brought here merely to have my nose dragged away as I was about to nibble the sacred cheese of life? It is preposterous! If this old ninny woman, Fate, cannot do better than this, she should be deprived of the management of men's fortunes. She is an old hen who knows not her intention. If she has decided to drown me, why did she not do it in the beginning and save me all this trouble? The whole affair is absurd. . . . But no; she cannot mean to drown me. She dare not drown me. She cannot drown me. Not after all this work!" Afterward the man might have had an impulse to shake his fist at the clouds. "Just you drown me, now, and then hear what I call you!"

The billows that came at this time were more formidable. They seemed always just about to break and roll over the little boat in a turmoil of foam. There was a preparatory and long growl in the speech of them. No mind unused to the sea would have concluded that the dinghy could ascend these sheer heights in time. The shore was still afar. The oiler was a wily surfman. "Boys," he said swifty, "she won't live three minutes more, and we're too far out to swim. Shall I take her to sea again, Captain?"

"Yes; go ahead!" said the captain.

This oiler, by a series of quick miracles and fast and steady oarsmanship, turned the boat in the middle of the surf and took her safely to sea again.

There was a considerable silence as the boat bumped over the furrowed sea to deeper water. Then somebody in gloom spoke: "Well, anyhow, they must have seen us from the shore by now."

The gulls went in slanting flight up the wind toward the gray, desolate east. A squall, marked by dingy clouds and clouds brick-red, like smoke from a burning building, appeared from the southeast.

"What do you think of those life-saving people? Ain't they peaches?"

"Funny they haven't seen us."

"Maybe they think we're out here for sport! Maybe they think we're fishin'. Maybe they think we're damned fools."

It was a long afternoon. A changed tide tried to force them southward, but wind and wave said northward. Far ahead, where coast-line, sea, and sky formed their mighty angle, there were little dots which seemed to indicate a city on the shore.

"St. Augustine?"

The captain shook his head. "Too near Mosquito Inlet."

And the oiler rowed, and then the correspondent rowed; then the oiler rowed. It was a weary business. The human back can become the seat of more aches and pains than are registered in books for the composite anatomy of a regiment. It is a limited area, but it can become the theater of innumerable muscular conflicts, tangles, wrenches, knots, and other comforts.

"Did you ever like to row, Billie?" asked the correspondent.

"No," said the oiler; "hang it!"

When one exchanged the rowing-seat for a place in the bottom of

the boat, he suffered a bodily depression that caused him to be careless
of everything save an obligation to wiggle one finger. There was cold
sea water swashing to and fro in the boat, and he lay in it. His head,
pillowed on a thwart, was within an inch of the swirl of a wave crest,
and sometimes a particularly obstreperous sea came inboard and
drenched him once more. But these matters did not annoy him. It is
almost certain that if the boat had capsized he would have tumbled
comfortably out upon the ocean as if he felt sure that it was a great,
soft mattress.

"Look! There's a man on the shore!"

"Where?"

"There! See 'im? See 'im?"

"Yes, sure! He's walking along."

"Now he's stopped. Look! He's facing us!"

"He's waving at us!"

"So he is! By thunder!"

"Ah, now we're all right! Now we're all right! There'll be a boat out
here for us in half an hour."

"He's going on. He's running. He's going up to that house there."

The remote beach seemed lower than the sea, and it required a
searching glance to discern the little black figure. The captain saw a
floating stick, and they rowed to it. A bath towel was by some weird
chance in the boat, and, tying this on the stick, the captain waved it.
The oarsman did not dare turn his head, so he was obliged to ask
questions.

"What's he doing now?"

"He's standing still again. He's looking, I think. . . . There he goes
again—toward the house. . . . Now he's stopped again."

"Is he waving at us?"

"No, not now; he was though."

"Look! There comes another man!"

"He's running."

"Look at him go, would you!"

"Why, he's on a bicycle. Now he's met the other man. They're both
waving at us. Look!"

"There comes something up the beach."

"What the devil is that thing?"

"Why, it looks like a boat."

"Why, certainly, it's a boat."

"No; it's on wheels."

"Yes, so it is. Well, that must be the life boat. They drag them
along shore on a wagon."

"That's the life boat, sure."

"No, by —— , it's—it's an omnibus."

"I tell you it's a life boat."

"It is not! It's an omnibus. I can see it plain. See? One of these big
hotel omnibuses."

"By thunder, you're right. It's an omnibus, sure as fate. What do you suppose they are doing with an omnibus? Maybe they are going around collecting the life crew, hey?"

"That's it, likely. Look! There's a fellow waving a little black flag. He's standing on the steps of the omnibus. There come those other two fellows. Now they're all talking together. Look at the fellow with the flag. Maybe he ain't waving it!"

"That ain't a flag, is it? That's his coat. Why, certainly, that's his coat."

"So it is; it's his coat. He's taken it off and is waving it around his head. But would you look at him swing it!"

"Oh, say, there isn't any life-saving station there. That's just a winter-resort hotel omnibus that has brought over some of the boarders to see us drown."

"What's that idiot with the coat mean? What's he signalling, any-how?"

"It looks as if he were trying to tell us to go north. There must be a life-saving station up there."

"No; he thinks we're fishing. Just giving us a merry hand. See? Ah, there, Willie!"

"Well, I wish I could make something out of those signals. What do you suppose he means?"

"He don't mean anything; he's just playing."

"Well, if he'd just signal us to try the surf again, or to go to sea and wait, or go north, or south, or go to hell, there would be some reason in it. But look at him! He just stands there and keeps his coat revolving like a wheel. The ass!"

"There come more people."

"Now there's quite a mob. Look! Isn't that a boat?"

"Where? Oh, I see where you mean. No, that's no boat."

"That fellow is still waving his coat."

"He must think we like to see him do that. Why don't he quit it? It don't mean anything."

"I don't know. I think he is trying to make us go north. It must be that there's a life-saving station there somewhere."

"Say, he ain't tired yet. Look at 'im wave!"

"Wonder how long he can keep that up. He's been revolving his coat ever since he caught sight of us. He's an idiot. Why aren't they getting men to bring a boat out? A fishing boat—one of those big yawls—could come out here all right. Why don't he do something?"

"Oh, it's all right now."

"They'll have a boat out here for us in less than no time, now that they've seen us."

A faint yellow tone came into the sky over the low land. The shadows on the sea slowly deepened. The wind bore coldness with it, and the men began to shiver.

"Holy smoke!" said one, allowing his voice to express his impious mood, "if we keep on monkeying out here! If we've got to flounder out here all night!"

"Oh, we'll never have to say here all night! Don't you worry. They've seen us now, and it won't be long before they'll come chasing out after us."

The shore grew dusky. The man waving a coat blended gradually into this gloom, and it swallowed in the same manner the omnibus and the group of people. The spray, when it dashed uproariously over the side, made the voyagers shrink and swear like men who were being branded.

"I'd like to catch the chump who waved the coat. I feel like soaking him one, just for luck."

"Why? What did he do?"

"Oh, nothing, but then he seemed so damned cheerful."

In the meantime the oiler rowed, and then the correspondent rowed, and then the oiler rowed. Gray-faced and bowed forward, they mechanically, turn by turn, plied the leaden oars. The form of the lighthouse had vanished from the southern horizon, but finally a pale star appeared, just lifting from the sea. The streaked saffron in the west passed before the all-merging darkness, and the sea to the east was black. The land had vanished, and was expressed only by the low and drear thunder of the surf.

"If I am going to be drowned—if I am going to be drowned—If I am going to be drowned, why, in the name of the seven mad gods who rule the sea, was I allowed to come thus far and contemplate sand and trees? Was I brought here merely to have my nose dragged away as I was about to nibble the sacred cheese of life?"

The patient captain, drooped over the water jar, was sometimes obliged to speak to the oarsman.

"Keep her head up! Keep her head up!"

"Keep her head up, sir." The voices were weary and low.

This was surely a quiet evening. All save the oarsman lay heavily and listlessly in the boat's bottom. As for him, his eyes were just capable of noting the tall black waves that swept forward in a most sinister silence, save for an occasional subdued growl of a crest.

The cook's head was on a thwart, and he looked without interest at the water under his nose. He was deep in other scenes. Finally he spoke. "Billie," he murmured dreamfully, "what kind of pie do you like best?"

V

"Pie!" said the oiler and the correspondent, agitatedly. "Don't talk about those things, blast you!"

"Well," said the cook, "I was just thinking about ham sandwiches, and—"

A night on the sea in an open boat is a long night. As darkness settled finally, the shine of the light, lifting from the sea in the south, changed to full gold. On the northern horizon a new light appeared, a small bluish gleam on the edge of the waters. These two lights were the furniture of the world. Otherwise there was nothing but waves.

Two men huddled in the stern, and distances were so magnificent in the dinghy that the rower was enabled to keep his feet partly warm by thrusting them under his companions. Their legs indeed extended far under the rowing-seat until they touched the feet of the captain forward. Sometimes, despite the efforts of the tired oarsman, a wave came piling into the boat, an icy wave of the night, and the chilling water soaked them anew. They would twist their bodies for a moment and groan, and sleep the dead sleep once more, while the water in the boat gurgled about them as the craft rocked.

The plan of the oiler and the correspondent was for one to row until he lost the ability, and then arouse the other from his sea-water couch in the bottom of the boat.

The oiler plied the oars until his head drooped forward and the overpowering sleep blinded him; and he rowed yet afterward. Then he touched a man in the bottom of the boat, and called his name. "Will you spell me for a little while?" he said meekly.

"Sure, Billie," said the correspondent, awaking and dragging himself to a sitting position. They exchanged places carefully, and the oiler, cuddling down in the sea water at the cook's side, seemed to go to sleep instantly.

The particular violence of the sea had ceased. The waves came without snarling. The obligation of the man at the oars was to keep the boat headed so that the tilt of the rollers would not capsize her, and to preserve her from filling when the crests rushed past. The black waves were silent and hard to be seen in the darkness. Often one was almost upon the boat before the oarsman was aware.

In a low voice the correspondent addressed the captain. He was not sure that the captain was awake, although this iron man seemed to be always awake. "Captain, shall I keep her making for that light north, sir?"

The same steady voice answered him. "Yes. Keep it about two points off the port bow."

The cook had tied a life belt around himself in order to get even the warmth which this clumsy cork contrivance could donate, and he seemed almost stove-like when a rower, whose teeth invariably chattered wildly as soon as he ceased his labor, dropped down to sleep.

The correspondent, as he rowed, looked down at the two men sleeping underfoot. The cook's arm was around the oiler's shoulders, and, with their fragmentary clothing and haggard faces, they were the babes of the sea—a grotesque rendering of the old babes in the wood.

Later he must have grown stupid at his work, for suddenly there was a growling of water, and a crest came with a roar and a swash into the boat, and it was a wonder that it did not set the cook afloat in his life belt. The cook continued to sleep, but the oiler sat up, blinking his eyes and shaking with the new cold.

"Oh, I'm awful sorry, Billie," said the correspondent, contritely.

"That's all right, old boy," said the oiler, and lay down again and was asleep.

Presently it seemed that even the captain dozed, and the correspondent thought that he was the one man afloat on all the oceans. The wind had a voice as it came over the waves, and it was sadder than the end.

There was a long, loud swishing astern of the boat, and a gleaming trail of phosphorescence, like blue flame, was furrowed on the black waters. It might have been made by a monstrous knife.

Then there came a stillness, while the correspondent breathed with open mouth and looked at the sea.

Suddenly there was another swish and another long flash of bluish light, and this time it was alongside the boat, and might almost have been reached with an oar. The correspondent saw an enormous fin speed like a shadow through the water, hurling the crystalline spray and leaving the long glowing trail.

The correspondent looked over his shoulder at the captain. His face was hidden, and he seemed to be asleep. He looked at the babes of the sea. They certainly were asleep. So, being bereft of sympathy, he leaned a little way to one side and swore softly into the sea.

But the thing did not then leave the vicinity of the boat. Ahead or astern, on one side or the other, at intervals long or short, fled the long sparkling streak, and there was to be heard the *whiroo* of the dark fin. The speed and power of the thing was greatly to be admired. It cut the water like a gigantic and keen projectile.

The presence of this biding thing did not affect the man with the same horror that it would if he had been a picnicker. He simply looked at the sea dully and swore in an undertone.

Nevertheless, it is true that he did not wish to be alone with the thing. He wished one of his companions to awake by chance and keep him company with it. But the captain hung motionless over the water jar, and the oiler and the cook in the bottom of the boat were plunged in slumber.

VI

"If I am going to be drowned—if I am going to be drowned—if I am going to be drowned, why, in the name of the seven mad gods who rule the sea, was I allowed to come thus far and contemplate sand and trees?"

During this dismal night, it may be remarked that a man would conclude that it was really the intention of the seven mad gods to drown him, despite the abominable injustice of it. For it was certainly an abominable injustice to drown a man who had worked so hard, so hard. The man felt it would be a crime most unnatural. Other people had drowned at sea since galleys swarmed with painted sails, but still—

When it occurs to a man that nature does not regard him as important, and that she feels she would not maim the universe by disposing of him, he at first wishes to throw bricks at the temple, and he hates deeply the fact that there are no bricks and no temples. Any visible expression of nature would surely be pelleted with his jeers.

Then, if there be no tangible thing to hoot, he feels, perhaps, the desire to confront a personification and indulge in pleas, bowed to one knee, and with hands supplicant, saying, "Yes, but I love myself."

A high cold star on a winter's night is the word he feels that she says to him. Thereafter he knows the pathos of his situation.

The men in the dinghy had not discussed these matters, but each had, no doubt, reflected upon them in silence and according to his mind. there was seldom any expression upon their faces save the general one of complete weariness. Speech was devoted to the business of the boat.

To chime the notes of his emotion, a verse mysteriously entered the correspondent's head. He had even forgotten that he had forgotten this verse, but it suddenly was in his mind.

A soldier of the Legion lay dying in Algiers;
There was lack of woman's nursing, there was dearth of woman's tears;
But a comrade stood beside him, and he took the comrade's hand,
And he said, "I never more shall see my own, my native land."

In his childhood the correspondent had been made acquainted with the fact that a soldier of the Legion lay dying in Algiers, but he had never regarded it as important. Myriads of his school-fellows had informed him of the soldier's plight, but the dinning had naturally ended by making him perfectly indifferent. He had never considered it his affair that a soldier of the Legion lay dying in Algiers, nor had it appeared to him as a matter for sorrow. It was less to him than breaking a pencil's point.

Now, however, it quaintly came to him as a human, living thing. It was no longer merely a picture of a few throes in the breast of a poet, meanwhile drinking tea and warming his feet at the grate; it was an actuality—stern, mournful, and fine.

The correspondent plainly saw the soldier. He lay on the sand with his feet out straight and still. While his pale left hand was upon his chest in an attempt to thwart the going of his life, the blood came between his fingers. In the far Algerian distance, a city of low square forms was set against a sky that was faint with the last sunset hues. The correspondent, plying the oars and dreaming of the slow and slower movements of the lips of the soldier, was moved by a profound and perfectly impersonal comprehension. He was sorry for the soldier of the Legion who lay dying in Algiers.

The thing which had followed the boat and waited had evidently grown bored at the delay. There was no longer to be heard the slash of the cutwater, and there was no longer the flame of the long trail. The light in the north still glimmered, but it was apparently no nearer to the boat. Sometimes the boom of the surf rang in the correspondent's ears, and he turned the craft seaward then and rowed harder. Southward, some one had evidently built a watch fire on the beach. It was too low and too far to be seen, but it made a shimmering, roseate reflection upon the bluff back of it, and this could be discerned from the boat. The wind came stronger, and sometimes a wave suddenly raged out like a mountain cat, and there was to be seen the sheen and sparkle of a broken crest.

The captain, in the bow, moved on his water jar and sat erect. "Pretty long night," he observed to the correspondent. He looked at the shore. "Those life-saving people take their time."

"Did you see that shark playing around?"

"Yes, I saw him. He was a big fellow, all right."

"Wish I had known you were awake."

Later the correspondent spoke into the bottom of the boat. "Billie!" There was a slow and gradual disentanglement. "Billie, will you spell me?"

"Sure," said the oiler.

As soon as the correspondent touched the cold, comfortable sea water in the bottom of the boat and had huddled close to the cook's life belt he was deep in sleep, despite the fact that his teeth played all the popular airs. This sleep was so good to him that it was but a moment before he heard a voice call his name in a tone that demonstrated the last stages of exhaustion. "Will you spell me?"

"Sure, Billie."

The light in the north had mysteriously vanished, but the correspondent took his course from the wide-awake captain.

Later in the night they took the boat farther out to sea, and the captain directed the cook to take one oar at the stern and keep the boat facing the seas. He was to call out if he should hear the thunder of the surf. This plan enabled the oiler and the correspondent to get respite together. "We'll give those boys a chance to get into shape again," said the captain. They curled down and, after a few preliminary chatterings and trembles, slept once more the dead sleep. Neither knew they had bequeathed to the cook the company of another shark, or perhaps the same shark.

As the boat caroused on the waves, spray occasionally bumped over the side and gave them a fresh soaking, but this had no power to break their repose. The ominous slash of the wind and the water affected them as it would have affected mummies.

"Boys," said the cook, with the notes of every reluctance in his voice, "She's drifted in pretty close. I guess one of you had better take her to sea again." The correspondent, aroused, heard the crash of the toppled crests.

As he was rowing, the captain gave him some whiskey and water, and this steadied the chills out of him. "If I ever get ashore and anybody shows me even a photograph of an oar—"

At last there was a short conversation.

"Billie! . . . Billie, will you spell me?"

"Sure," said the oiler.

VII

When the correspondent again opened his eyes, the sea and the sky were each of the gray hue of the dawning. Later, carmine and gold was painted upon the waters. The morning appeared finally, in its splendor, with a sky of pure blue, and the sunlight flamed on the tips of the waves.

On the distant dunes were set many little black cottages, and a tall white windmill reared above them. No man, nor dog, nor bicycle appeared on the beach. The cottages might have formed a deserted village.

The voyagers scanned the shore. A conference was held in the boat. "Well," said the captain, "if no help is coming, we might better try a run through the surf right away. If we stay out here much longer we will be too weak to do anything for ourselves at all." The others silently acquiesced in this reasoning. The boat was headed for the beach. The correspondent wondered if none ever ascended the tall wind-tower, and if then they never looked seaward. This tower was a giant, standing with its back to the plight of the ants. It represented in a degree, to the correspondent, the serenity of nature amid the struggles of the individual—nature in the wind, and nature in the vision of men. She did not seem cruel to him then, nor beneficent, nor treacherous, nor wise. But she was indifferent, flatly indifferent. It is, perhaps, plausible that a man in this situation, impressed with the unconcern of the universe, should see the innumerable flaws of his life and have them taste wickedly in his mind, and wish for another chance. A distinction between right and wrong seems absurdly clear to him, then, in this new ignorance of the grave-edge, and he understands that if he were given another opportunity he would mend his conduct and his words, and be better and brighter during an introduction or at a tea.

"Now, boys," said the captain, "she is going to swamp sure. All we can do is to work her in as far as possible, and then when she swamps, pile out and scramble for the beach. Keep cool now, and don't jump until she swamps sure."

The oiler took the oars. Over his shoulders he scanned the surf. "Captain," he said, "I think I'd better bring her about and keep her head-on to the seas, and back her in."

"All right, Billie," said the captain. "Back her in." The oiler swung the boat then, and, seated in the stern, the cook and the correspondent were obliged to look over their shoulders to contemplate the lonely and indifferent shore.

The monstrous inshore rollers heaved the boat high until the men were again enabled to see the white sheets of water scudding up the slanted beach. "We won't get in very close," said the captain. Each time a man could wrest his attention from the roller, he turned his glance towards the shore, and in the expression of the eyes during this contemplation there was a singular quality. The correspondent, observing the others, knew that they were not afraid, but the full meaning of their glances was shrouded.

As for himself, he was too tired to grapple fundamentally with the fact. He tried to coerce his mind into thinking of it, but the mind was dominated at this time by the muscles, and the muscles said they did not care. It merely occurred to him that if he should drown it would be a shame.

There were no hurried words, no pallor, no plain agitation. The men simply looked at the shore. "Now, remember to get well clear of the boat when you jump," said the captain.

Seaward the crest of a roller suddenly fell with a thunderous crash, and the long white comber came roaring down upon the boat.

"Steady now," said the captain. The men were silent. They turned their eyes from the shore to the comber and waited. The boat slid up the incline, leaped at the furious top, bounced over it, and swung down the long back of the wave. Some water had been shipped, and the cook bailed it out.

But the next crest crashed also. The tumbling, boiling flood of white water caught the boat and whirled it almost perpendicular. Water swarmed in from all sides. The correspondent had his hands on the gunwale at this time, and when the water entered at that place he swiftly withdrew his fingers, as if he objected to wetting them.

The little boat, drunken with this weight of water, reeled and snuggled deeper into the sea.

"Bail her out, cook! Bail her out!" said the captain.

"All right, Captain," said the cook.

"Now, boys, the next one will do for us sure," said the oiler. "Mind to jump clear of the boat."

The third wave moved forward, huge, furious, implacable. It fairly swallowed the dinghy, and almost simultaneously the men tumbled into the sea. A piece of life belt had lain in the bottom of the boat, and as the correspondent went overboard he held this to his chest with his left hand.

The January water was icy, and he reflected immediately that it was colder than he had expected to find it off the coast of Florida. This appeared to his dazed mind as a fact important enough to be noted at the time. The coldness of the water was sad; it was tragic. This fact was somehow mixed and confused with his opinion of his own situation so that it seemed almost a proper reason for tears. The water was cold.

When he came to the surface he was conscious of little but the noisy water. Afterward he saw his companions in the sea. The oiler was ahead in the race. He was swimming strongly and rapidly. Off to the correspondent's left, the cook's great white and corked back bulged out of the water; and in the rear the captain was hanging with one good hand to the keel of the overturned dinghy.

There is a certain immovable quality to a shore, and the correspondent wondered at it amid the confusion of the sea.

It seemed also very attractive; but the correspondent knew that it was a long journey, and he paddled leisurely. The piece of life preserver lay under him, and sometimes he whirled down the incline of a wave as if he were on a hand-sled.

But finally he arrived at a place in the sea where the travel was beset with difficulty. He did not pause swimming to inquire what manner of current had caught him, but there his progress ceased. The shore was set before him like a bit of scenery on a stage, and he looked at it, and understood with his eyes each detail of it.

As the cook passed, much farther to the left, the captain was calling to him, "Turn over on your back, cook! Turn over on your back and use the oar."

"All right, sir." The cook turned on his back, and, paddling with an oar, went ahead as if he were a canoe.

Presently the boat also passed to the left of the correspondent, with the captain clinging with one hand to the keel. He would have appeared like a man raising himself to look over a board fence if it were not for the extraordinary gymnastics of the boat. The correspondent marvelled that the captain could still hold to it.

They passed on nearer to shore—the oiler, the cook, the captain— and following them went the water jar, bouncing gaily over the seas.

The correspondent remained in the grip of this strange new enemy, a current. The shore, with its white slope of sand and its green bluff, topped with little silent cottages, was spread like a picture before him. It was very near to him then, but he was impressed as one who, in a gallery, looks at a scene from Britanny or Algiers.

He thought: "I am going to drown? Can it be possible? Can it be possible? Can it be possible?" Perhaps an individual must consider his own death to be the final phenomenon of nature.

But later a wave perhaps whirled him out of this small deadly current, for he found suddenly that he could again make progress towards the shore. Later still he was aware that the captain, clinging with one hand to the keel of the dinghy, had his face turned away from the shore and towards him and was calling his name. "Come to the boat! Come to the boat!"

In his struggle to reach the captain and the boat, he reflected that when one gets properly wearied drowning must really be a comfortable arrangement—a cessation of hostilities accompanied by a large degree of relief; and he was glad of it, for the main thing in his mind for some moments had been horror of the temporary agony; he did not wish to be hurt.

Presently he saw a man running along the shore. He was undressing with most remarkable speed. Coat, trousers, shirt, everything flew magically off him.

"Come to the boat!" called the captain.

"All right, Captain." As the correspondent paddled, he saw the captain let himself down to bottom and leave the boat. Then the correspondent performed his one little marvel of the voyage. A large wave caught him and flung him with ease and supreme speed completely over the boat and far beyond it. It struck him even then as an event in gymnastics and a true miracle of the sea. An overturned boat in the surf is not a plaything to a swimming man.

The correspondent arrived in water that reached only to his waist, but his condition did not enable him to stand for more than a moment. Each wave knocked him into a heap, and the undertow pulled at him.

Then he saw the man who had been running and undressing, and undressing and running, come bounding into the water. He dragged ashore the cook, and then waded toward the captain; but the captain waved him away and sent him to the correspondent. He was naked— naked as a tree in winter; but a halo was about his head, and he shone like a saint. He gave a strong pull, and a long drag, and a bully heave at the correspondent's hand. The correspondent, schooled in the minor formulae, said, "Thanks, old man." But suddenly the man cried, "What's that?" He pointed a swift finger. The correspondent said, "Go."

In the shallows, face downward, lay the oiler. His forehead touched sand that was periodically, between each wave, clear of the sea.

The correspondent did not know all that transpired afterward. When he achieved safe ground he fell, striking the sand with each particular part of his body. It was as if he had dropped from a roof, but the thud was grateful to him.

It seems that instantly the beach was populated with men with blankets, clothes, and flasks, and women with coffee pots and all the remedies sacred to their minds. The welcome of the land to the men from the sea was warm and generous; but a still and dripping shape was carried slowly up the beach, and the land's welcome for it could only be the different and sinister hospitality of the grave.

When it came night, the white waves paced to and fro in the moonlight, and the wind brought the sound of the great sea's voice to the men on the shore, and they felt that they could then be interpreters.

The Blue Hotel (1898)

I

The Palace Hotel at Fort Romper was painted a light blue, a shade that is on the legs of a kind of heron, causing the bird to declare its position against any background. The Palace Hotel, then, was always screaming and howling in a way that made the dazzling winter landscape of Nebraska seem only a gray swampish hush. It stood alone on the prairie, and when the snow was falling the town two hundred yards away was not visible. But when the traveller alighted at the railway station he was obliged to pass the Palace Hotel before he could come upon the company of low clapboard houses which composed Fort Romper, and it was not to be thought that any traveller could pass the Palace Hotel without looking at it. Pat Scully, the proprietor, had proved himself a master of strategy when he chose his paints. It is true that on clear days, when the great transcontinental expresses, long lines of swaying Pullmans, swept through Fort Romper, passengers were overcome at the sight, and the cult that knows the brown-reds and the subdivisions of the dark greens of the East expressed shame, pity, horror, in a laugh. But to the citizens of this prairie town and to the people who would naturally stop there, Pat Scully had performed a feat. With this opulence and splendor, these creeds, classes, egotisms, that streamed through Romper on the rails day after day, they had no color in common.

As if the displayed delights of such a blue hotel were not sufficiently enticing, it was Scully's habit to go every morning and evening to meet the leisurely trains that stopped at Romper and work his seductions upon any man that he might see wavering, gripsack in hand.

One morning, when a snow-crusted engine dragged its long string of freight cars and its one passenger coach to the station, Scully performed the marvel of catching three men. One was a shaky and quick-eyed Swede, with a great shining cheap valise; one was a tall bronzed cowboy, who was on his way to a ranch near the Dakota line; one was a little silent man from the East, who didn't look it, and didn't announce it. Scully practically made them prisoners. He was so nimble and merry and kindly that each probably felt it would be the height of brutality to try to escape. They trudged off over the creaking board sidewalks in the wake of the eager little Irishman. He wore a heavy fur cap squeezed tightly down on his head. It caused his two red ears to stick out stiffly, as if they were made of tin.

At last, Scully, elaborately, with boisterous hospitality, conducted them through the portals of the blue hotel. The room which they entered was small. It seemed to be merely a proper temple for an enormous stove, which, in the center, was humming with godlike violence. At various points on its surface the iron had become luminous and glowed yellow from the heat. Beside the stove Scully's son Johnnie was playing High-Five with an old farmer who had whiskers both gray and sandy. They were quarrelling. Frequently the old farmer turned his face towards a box of sawdust—colored brown from tobacco juice—that was behind the stove, and spat with an air of great impatience and irritation. With a loud flourish of words Scully destroyed the game of cards, and bustled his son upstairs with part of the baggage of new guests. He himself conducted them to three basins of the coldest water in the world. The cowboy and the Easterner burnished themselves fiery red with this water, until it seemed to be some kind of a metal polish. The Swede, however, merely dipped his fingers gingerly and with trepidation. It was notable that throughout this series of small ceremonies the three travellers were made to feel that Scully was very benevolent. He was conferring great favors upon them. He handed the towel from one another with an air of philanthropic impulse.

Afterward they went to the first room, and, sitting about the stove, listened to Scully's officious clamor at his daughters, who were preparing the midday meal. They reflected in the silence of experienced men who tread carefully amid new people. Nevertheless, the old farmer, stationary, invincible in his chair near the warmest part of the stove, turned his face from the sawdust box frequently and addressed a glowing commonplace to the strangers. Usually he was answered in short but adequate sentences by either the cowboy or the Easterner. The Swede said nothing. He seemed to be occupied in making furtive estimates of each man in the room. One might have thought that he had the sense of silly suspicion which comes to guilt. He resembled a badly frightened man.

Later, at dinner, he spoke a little, addressing his conversation entirely to Scully. He volunteered that he had come from New York, where for ten years he had worked as a tailor. These facts seemed to strike Scully as fascinating, and afterward he volunteered that he had lived at Romper for fourteen years. The Swede asked about the crops and the price of labor. He seemed barely to listen to Scully's extended replies. His eyes continued to rove from man to man.

Finally, with a laugh and a wink, he said that some of these Western communities were very dangerous; and after his statement he straightened his legs under the table, tilted his head, and laughed again, loudly. It was plain that the demonstration had no meaning to the others. They looked at him wondering and in silence.

II

As the men trooped heavily back into the front room, the two little windows presented views of a turmoiling sea of snow. The huge arms of the wind were making attempts—mighty, circular, futile—to embrace the flakes as they sped. A gate-post like a still man with a blanched face stood aghast amid this profligate fury. In a hearty voice Scully announced the presence of a blizzard. The guests of the blue hotel, lighting their pipes, assented with grunts of lazy masculine contentment. No island of the sea could be exempt in the degree of this little room with its humming stove. Johnnie, son of Scully, in a tone which defined his opinion of his ability as a card player, challenged the old farmer of both gray and sandy whiskers to a game of High-Five. The farmer agreed with a contemptuous and bitter scoff. They sat close to the stove, and squared their knees under a wide board. The cowboy and the Easterner watched the game with interest. The Swede remained near the window, aloof, but with a countenance that showed signs of an inexplicable excitement.

The play of Johnnie and the gray-beard was suddenly ended by another quarrel. The old man arose while casting a look of heated scorn at his adversary. He slowly buttoned his coat, and then stalked with fabulous dignity from the room. In the discreet silence of all the other men the Swede laughed. His laughter rang somehow childish. Men by this time had begun to look at him askance, as if they wished to inquire what ailed him.

A new game was formed jocosely. The cowboy volunteered to become the partner of Johnnie, and they all then turned to ask the Swede to throw in his lot with the little Easterner. He asked some questions about the game, and, learning that it wore many names, and that he had played it when it was under an alias, he accepted the invitation. He strode towards the men nervously, as if he expected to be assaulted. Finally, seated, he gazed from face to face and laughed shrilly. This laugh was so strange that the Easterner looked up quickly, the cowboy sat intent and with his mouth open, and Johnnie paused, holding the cards with still fingers.

Afterward there was a short silence. Then Johnnie said, "Well, let's get at it. Come on now!" They pulled their chairs forward until their knees were bunched under the board. They began to play, and their interest in the game caused the others to forget the manner of the Swede.

The cowboy was a board-whacker. Each time that he held superior cards he whanged them, one by one, with exceeding force, down upon the improvised table, and took the tricks with a glowing air of prowess and pride that sent thrills of indignation into the hearts of his opponents. A game with a board-whacker in it is sure to become intense. The countenances of the Easterner and the Swede were miserable whenever the cowboy thundered down his aces and kings, while Johnnie, his eyes gleaming with joy, chuckled and chuckled.

Because of the absorbing play none considered the strange ways of the Swede. They paid strict heed to the game. Finally, during a lull caused by a new deal, the Swede suddenly addressed Johnnie: "I suppose there have been a good many men killed in this room." The jaws of the others dropped and they looked at him.

"What in hell are you talking about?" said Johnnie.

The Swede laughed again his blatant laugh, full of a kind of false courage and defiance. "Oh, you know what I mean all right," he answered.

"I'm a liar if I do!" Johnnie protested. The card game was halted, and the men stared at the Swede. Johnnie evidently felt that as the son of the proprietor he should make a direct inquiry. "Now, what might you be drivin' at, mister?" he asked. The Swede winked at him. It was a wink full of cunning. His fingers shook on the edge of the board. "Oh, maybe you think I have been to nowheres. Maybe you think I'm a tenderfoot?"

"I don't know nothin' about you," answered Johnnie, "and I don't give a damn where you've been. All I got to say is that I don't know what you're driving at. There hain't never been nobody killed in this room."

The cowboy, who had been steadily gazing at the Swede, then spoke: "What's wrong with you, mister?"

Apparently it seemed to the Swede that he was formidably menaced. He shivered and turned white near the corners of his mouth. He sent an appealing glance in the direction of the little Easterner. During these moments he did not forget to wear his air of advanced pot-valor. "They say they don't know what I mean," he remarked mockingly to the Easterner.

The latter answered after prolonged and cautious reflection. "I don't understand you," he said, impassively.

The Swede made a movement then which announced that he thought he had encountered treachery from the only quarter where he had expected sympathy, if not help. "Oh, I see you are all against me. I see—"

The cowboy was in a state of deep stupefaction. "Say," he cried, as he tumbled the deck violently down upon the board "—say, what are you gittin' at, hey?"

The Swede sprang up with the celerity of a man escaping from a snake on the floor. "I don't want to fight!" he shouted. "I don't want to fight!"

The cowboy stretched his long legs indolently and deliberately. His hands were in his pockets. He spat into the sawdust box. "Well, who the hell thought you did?" he inquired.

The Swede backed rapidly toward a corner of the room. His hands were out protectingly in front of his chest, but he was making an obvious struggle to control his fright. "Gentlemen," he quavered, "I suppose I am going to be killed before I can leave this house! I suppose I am going to be killed before I can leave this house!" In his eyes was the dying-swan look. Through the windows could be seen the snow turning blue in the shadow of dusk. The wind tore at the house and some loose thing beat regularly against the clapboards like a spirit tapping.

A door opened, and Scully himself entered. He paused in surprise as he noted the tragic attitude of the Swede. Then he said, "What's the matter here?"

The Swede answered him swiftly and eagerly: "These men are going to kill me."

"Kill you!" ejaculated Scully. "Kill you! What are you talkin'?"

The Swede made the gesture of a martyr.

Scully wheeled sternly upon his son. "What is this, Johnnie?"

The lad had grown sullen. "Damned if I know," he answered. "I can't make no sense to it." He began to shuffle the cards, fluttering them together with an angry snap. "He says a good many men have been killed in this room, or something like that. And he says he's goin' to be killed here too. I don't know what ails him. He's crazy, I shouldn't wonder."

Scully then looked for explanation to the cowboy, but the cowboy simply shrugged his shoulders.

"Kill you?" said Scully again to the Swede. "Kill you? Man, you're off your nut."

"Oh, I know," burst out the Swede. "I know what will happen. Yes, I'm crazy—yes. Yes, of course, I'm crazy—yes. But I know one thing—" There was a sort of sweat of misery and terror upon his face. "I know I won't get out of here alive."

The cowboy drew a deep breath, as if his mind was passing into the last stages of dissolution. "Well, I'm doggoned," he whispered to himself.

Scully wheeled suddenly and faced his son. "You've been troublin' this man!"

Johnnie's voice was loud with its burden of grievance. "Why, good Gawd, I ain't done nothin' to 'im."

The Swede broke in. "Gentlemen, do not disturb yourselves. I will leave this house. I will go away, because"—he accused them dramatically with his glance—"because I do not want to be killed."

Scully was furious with his son. "Will you tell me what is the matter, you young divil? What's the matter, anyhow? Speak out!"

"Blame it!" cried Johnnie in despair, "don't I tell you I don't know? He—he says we want to kill him, and that's all I know. I can't tell what ails him."

The Swede continued to repeat: "Never mind, Mr. Scully; never mind. I will leave this house. I will go away, because I do not wish to be killed. Yes, of course, I am crazy—yes. But I know one thing! I will go away. I will leave this house. Never mind, Mr. Scully; never mind. I will go away."

"You will not go 'way," said Scully. "You will not go 'way until I hear the reason of this business. If anybody has troubled you I will take care of him. This is my house. You are under my roof, and I will not allow any peaceable man to be troubled here." He cast a terrible eye upon Johnnie, the cowboy, and the Easterner.

"Never mind, Mr. Scully; never mind. I will go away. I do not wish to be killed." The Swede moved towards the door which opened upon the stairs. It was evidently his intention to go at once for his baggage.

"No, no," shouted Scully peremptorily; but the white-faced man slid by him and disappeared. "Now," said Scully severely, "what does this mane?"

Johnnie and the cowboy cried together: "Why, we didn't do nothin' to 'im!"

Scully's eyes were cold. "No," he said, "you didn't?"

Johnnie swore a deep oath. "Why, this is the wildest loon I ever see. We didn't do nothin' at all. We were jest sittin' here playin' cards, and he—"

The father suddenly spoke to the Easterner. "Mr. Blanc," he asked, "what has these boys been doin'?"

The Easterner reflected again. "I didn't see anything wrong at all," he said at last slowly.

Scully began to howl. "But what does it mane?" He stared ferociously at his son. "I have a mind to lather you for this, me boy."

Johnnie was frantic. "Well, what have I done?" he bawled at his father.

III

"I think you are tongue-tied," said Scully finally to his son, the cowboy, and the Easterner; and at the end of this scornful sentence he left the room.

Upstairs the Swede was swiftly fastening the straps of his great valise. Once his back happened to be half turned towards the door, and, hearing a noise there, he wheeled and sprang up, uttering a loud cry. Scully's wrinkled visage showed grimly in the light of the small lamp he carried. This yellow effulgence, streaming upward, colored only his prominent features, and left his eyes, for instance, in mysterious shadow. He resembled a murderer.

"Man! man!" he exclaimed, "have you gone daffy?"

"Oh, no! Oh, no!" rejoined the other. "There are people in this world who know pretty nearly as much as you do—understand?"

For a moment they stood gazing at each other. Upon the Swede's deathly pale cheeks were two spots brightly crimson and sharply edged, as if they had been carefully painted. Scully placed the light on the table and sat himself on the edge of the bed. He spoke ruminatively. "By cracky, I never heard of such a thing in my life. It's a complete muddle. I can't, for the soul of me, think how you ever got this idea into your head." Presently he lifted his eyes and asked: "And did you sure think they were going to kill you?"

The Swede scanned the old man as if he wished to see into his mind. "I did," he said at last. He obviously suspected that this answer might precipitate an outbreak. As he pulled on a strap his whole arm shook, the elbow wavering like a bit of paper.

Scully banged his hand impressively on the footboard of the bed. "Why, man, we're goin' to have a line of ilictric street cars in this town next spring."

"'A line of electric street cars,'" repeated the Swede, stupidly.

"And," said Scully, "there's a new railroad goin' to be built down from Broken Arm to here. Not to mintion the four churches and the smashin' big brick schoolhouse. Then there's the big factory, too. Why, in two years Romper'll be a met-tro-*pol*-is."

Having finished the preparation of his baggage, the Swede straightened himself. "Mr. Scully," he said, with sudden hardihood, "how much do I owe you?"

"You don't owe me anythin'," said the old man, angrily.

"Yes, I do," retorted the Swede. He took seventy-five cents from his pocket and tendered it to Scully; but the latter snapped his fingers in disdainful refusal. However, it happened that they both stood gazing in a strange fashion at three silver pieces on the Swede's open palm.

"I'll not take your money," said Scully at last. "Not after what's been goin' on here." Then a plan seemed to strike him. "Here," he cried, picking up his lamp and moving towards the door. "Here! Come with me a minute."

"No," said the Swede, in overwhelming alarm.

"Yes," urged the old man. "Come on! I want you to come and see a picter—just across the hall—in my room."

The Swede must have concluded that his hour was come. His jaw dropped and his teeth showed like a dead man's. He ultimately followed Scully across the corridor, but he had the step of one hung in chains.

Scully flashed the light high on the wall of his own chamber. There was revealed a ridiculous photograph of a little girl. She was leaning against a balustrade of gorgeous decoration, and the formidable bang to her hair was prominent. The figure was as graceful as an upright sled-stake, and, withal, it was of the hue of lead. "There," said Scully, tenderly, "that's the picter of my little girl that died. Her name was Carrie. She had the purtiest hair you ever saw! I was that fond of her, she—"

Turning then, he saw that the Swede was not contemplating the picture at all, but, instead, was keeping keen watch on the gloom in the rear.

"Look, man!" cried Scully, heartily. "That's the picter of my little gal that died. Her name was Carrie. And then here's the picter of my oldest boy, Michael. He's a lawyer in Lincoln, an' doin' well. I gave that boy a grand eddication, and I'm glad for it now. He's a fine boy. Look at 'im now. Ain't he bold as blazes, him there in Lincoln, an honored an' respicted gintleman! An honored and respicted gintleman," concluded Scully with a flourish. And, so saying, he smote the Swede jovially on the back.

The Swede faintly smiled.

"Now," said the old man, "there's only one more thing." He dropped suddenly to the floor and thrust his head beneath the bed. The Swede could hear his muffled voice. "I'd keep it under me piller if it wasn't for that boy Johnnie. Then there's the old woman—Where is it now? I never put it twice in the same place. Ah, now come out with you!"

Presently he backed clumsily from under the bed, dragging with him an old coat rolled into a bundle. "I've fetched him," he muttered. Kneeling on the floor, he unrolled the coat and extracted from its heart a large yellow-brown whiskey bottle.

His first manœuver was to hold the bottle up to the light. Reassured, apparently, that nobody had been tampering with it, he thrust it with a generous movement towards the Swede.

The weak-kneed Swede was about to eagerly clutch this element of strength, but he suddenly jerked his hand away and cast a look of horror upon Scully.

"Drink," said the old man affectionately. He had risen to his feet, and now stood facing the Swede.

There was a silence. Then again Scully said: "Drink!"

The Swede laughed wildly. He grabbed the bottle, put it to his mouth; and as his lips curled absurdly around the opening and his throat worked, he kept his glance, burning with hatred, upon the old man's face.

IV

After the departure of Scully the three men, with the card board still upon their knees, preserved for a long time an astounded silence. Then Johnnie said: "That's the doddangedest Swede I ever see."

"He ain't no Swede," said the cowboy, scornfully.

"Well, what is he then?" cried Johnnie. "What is he then?"

"It's my opinion," replied the cowboy deliberately, "he's some kind of a Dutchman." It was a venerable custom of the country to entitle as Swedes all light-haired men who spoke with a heavy tongue. In consequence the idea of the cowboy was not without its daring. "Yes, sir," he repeated. "It's my opinion this feller is some kind of a Dutchman."

"Well, he says he's a Swede, anyhow," muttered Johnnie, sulkily. He turned to the Easterner: "What do you think, Mr. Blanc?"

"Oh, I don't know," replied the Easterner.

"Well, what do you think makes him act that way?" asked the cowboy.

"Why, he's frightened." The Easterner knocked his pipe against a rim of the stove. "He's clear frightened out of his boots."

"What at?" cried Johnnie and the cowboy together.

The Easterner reflected over his answer.

"What at?" cried the others again.

"Oh, I don't know, but it seems to me this man has been reading dime novels, and he thinks he's right out in the middle of it—the shootin' and stabbin' and all."

"But," said the cowboy, deeply scandalized, "this ain't Wyoming, ner none of them places. This is Nebrasker."

"Yes," added Johnnie, "an' why don't he wait till he gits *out West?*"

The travelled Easterner laughed. "It isn't different there even—not in these days. But he thinks he's right in the middle of hell."

Johnnie and the cowboy mused long.

"It's awful funny," remarked Johnnie at last.

"Yes," said the cowboy. "This is a queer game. I hope we don't git snowed in, because then we'd have to stand this here man bein' around with us all the time. That wouldn't be no good."

"I wish pop would throw him out," said Johnnie.

Presently they heard a loud stamping on the stairs, accompanied by ringing jokes in the voice of old Scully, and laughter, evidently from the Swede. The men around the stove stared vacantly at each other. "Gosh!" said the cowboy. The door flew open, and old Scully, flushed and anecdotal, came into the room. He was jabbering at the Swede, who followed him, laughing bravely. It was the entry of two roisterers from a banquet hall.

"Come now," said Scully sharply to the three seated men, "move up and give us a chance at the stove." The cowboy and the Easterner obediently sidled their chairs to make room for the newcomers. Johnnie, however, simply arranged himself in a more indolent attitude, and then remained motionless.

"Come! Git over, there," said Scully.

"Plenty of room on the other side of the stove," said Johnnie.

"Do you think we want to sit in the draught?" roared the father.

But the Swede here interposed with a grandeur of confidence. "No, no. Let the boy sit where he likes," he cried in a bullying voice to the father.

"All right! All right!" said Scully, deferentially. The cowboy and the Easterner exchanged glances of wonder.

The five chairs were formed in a crescent about one side of the stove. The Swede began to talk; he talked arrogantly, profanely, angrily. Johnnie, the cowboy, and the Easterner maintained a morose silence, while old Scully appeared to be receptive and eager, breaking in constantly with sympathetic ejaculations.

Finally the Swede announced that he was thirsty. He moved in his chair, and said that he would go for a drink of water.

"I'll git it for you," cried Scully at once.

"No," said the Swede, contemptuously. "I'll get it for myself." He arose and stalked with the air of on owner off into the executive parts of the hotel.

As soon as the Swede was out of hearing Scully sprang to his feet and whispered intensely to the others: "Upstairs he thought I was tryin' to poison 'im."

"Say," said Johnnie, "this makes me sick. Why don't you throw 'im out in the snow?"

"Why, he's all right now," declared Scully. "It was only that he was from the East, and he thought this was a tough place. That's all. He's all right now."

The cowboy looked with admiration upon the Easterner. "You were straight," he said. "You were on to that there Dutchman."

"Well," said Johnnie to his father, "he may be all right now, but I don't see it. Other time he was scared, but now he's too fresh."

Scully's speech was always a combination of Irish brogue and idiom, Western twang and idiom, and scraps of curiously formal diction taken from the story-books and newspapers. He now hurled a strange mass of language at the head of his son. "What do I keep? What do I keep? What do I keep?" he demanded, in a voice of thunder. He slapped his knee impressively, to indicate that he himself was going to make reply, and that all should heed. "I keep a hotel," he shouted. "A hotel, do you mind? A guest under my roof has sacred privileges. He is to be intimidated by none. Not one word shall he hear that would prijudice him in favor of goin' away. I'll not have it. There's no place in this here town where they can say they iver took in a guest of mine because he was afraid to stay here." He wheeled suddenly upon the cowboy and the Easterner. "Am I right?"

"Yes, Mr. Scully," said the cowboy, "I think you're right."

"Yes, Mr. Scully," said the Easterner, "I think you're right."

V

At six-o'clock supper, the Swede fizzed like a fire-wheel. He sometimes seemed on the point of bursting into riotous song, and in all his madness he was encouraged by old Scully. The Easterner was encased in reserve; the cowboy sat in wide-mouthed amazement, forgetting to eat, while Johnnie wrathily demolished great plates of food. The daughters of the house, when they were obliged to replenish the biscuits, approached as warily as Indians, and, having succeeded in their purpose, fled with ill-concealed trepidation. The Swede domineered the whole feast, and he gave it the appearance of a cruel bacchanal. He seemed to have grown suddenly taller; he gazed, brutally disdainful, into every face. His voice rang through the room. Once when he jabbed out harpoon-fashion with his fork to pinion a biscuit, the weapon nearly impaled the hand of the Easterner, which had been stretched quietly out for the same biscuit.

After supper, as the men filed towards the other room, the Swede smote Scully ruthlessly on the shoulder. "Well, old boy, that was a good, square meal." Johnnie looked hopefully at his father; he knew that shoulder was tender from an old fall; and, indeed, it appeared for a moment as if Scully was going to flame out over the matter, but in the end he smiled a sickly smile and remained silent. The others understood from his manner that he was admitting his responsibility for the Swede's new viewpoint.

Johnnie, however, addressed his parent in an aside. "Why don't you license somebody to kick you downstairs?" Scully scowled darkly by way of reply.

When they were gathered about the stove, the Swede insisted on another game of High-Five. Scully gently deprecated the plan at first, but the Swede turned a wolfish glare upon him. The old man subsided, and the Swede canvassed the others. In his tone there was always a great threat. The cowboy and the Easterner both remarked indifferently that they would play. Scully said that he would presently have to go to meet the 6:58 train, and so the Swede turned menacingly upon Johnnie. For a moment their glances crossed like blades, and then Johnnie smiled and said, "Yes, I'll play."

They formed a square, with the little board on their knees. The Easterner and the Swede were again partners. As the play went on, it was noticeable that the cowboy was not board-whacking as usual. Meanwhile, Scully, near the lamp, had put on his spectacles and, with an appearance curiously like an old priest, was reading a newspaper. In time he went out to meet the 6:58 train, and, despite his precautions, a gust of polar wind whirled into the room as he opened the door. Besides scattering the cards, it chilled the players to the marrow. The Swede cursed frightfully. When Scully returned, his entrance disturbed a cosy and friendly scene. The Swede again cursed. But presently they were once more intent, their heads bent forward and their hands moving swiftly. The Swede had adopted the fashion of board-whacking.

Scully took up his paper and for a long time remained immersed in matters which were extraordinarily remote from him. The lamp burned badly, and once he stopped to adjust the wick. The newspaper, as he turned from page to page, rustled with a slow and comfortable sound. Then suddenly he heard three terrible words: "You are cheatin'!"

Such scenes often prove that there can be little of dramatic import in environment. Any room can present a tragic front; any room can be comic. This little den was now hideous as a torture-chamber. The new faces of the men themselves had changed it upon the instant. The Swede held a huge fist in front of Johnnie's face, while the latter looked steadily over it into the blazing orbs of his accuser. The Easterner had grown pallid; the cowboy's jaw had dropped in that expression of bovine amazement which was one of his important mannerisms. After the three words, the first sound in the room was made by Scully's paper as it floated forgotten to his feet. His spectacles had also fallen from his nose, but by a clutch he had saved them in air. His hand, grasping the spectacle, now remained poised awkwardly and near his shoulder. He stared at the card-players.

Probably the silence was while a second elapsed. Then, if the floor had been suddenly twiched out from under the men they could not have moved quicker. The five had projected themselves headlong towards a common point. It happened that Johnnie, in rising to hurl himself upon the Swede, had stumbled slightly because of his curiously instinctive care for the cards and the board. The loss of the moment allowed time for the arrival of Scully, and also allowed the cowboy time to give the Swede a great push which sent him staggering back. The men found tongue together, and hoarse shouts of rage, appeal, or fear burst from every throat. The cowboy pushed and jostled feverishly at the Swede, and the Easterner and Scully clung wildly to Johnnie; but through the smoky air, above the swaying bodies of the peace-controllers, the eyes of the two warriors ever sought each other in glances of challenge that were at once hot and steely.

Of course the board had been overturned, and now the whole company of cards was scattered over the floor, where the boots of the men trampled the fat and painted kings and queens as they gazed with their silly eyes at the war that was waging above them.

Scully's voice was dominating the yells. "Stop now! Stop, I say! Stop, now—"

Johnnie, as he struggled to burst through the rank formed by Scully and the Easterner, was crying, "Well, he says I cheated! He says I cheated! I won't allow no man to say I cheated! If he says I cheated, he's a —— ——!"

The cowboy was telling the Swede, "Quit, now! Quit, d'ye hear—"

The screams of the Swede never ceased: "He did cheat! I saw him! I saw him—"

As for the Easterner, he was importuning in a voice that was not heeded: "Wait a moment, can't you? Oh, wait a moment. What's the good of a fight over a game of cards? Wait a moment—"

In this tumult no complete sentences were clear. "Cheat"—"Quit"—"He says"—these fragments pierced the uproar and rang out sharply. It was remarkable that, whereas Scully undoubtedly made the most noise, he was the least heard of any of the riotous band.

Then suddenly there was a great cessation. It was as if each man had paused for breath; and although the room was still lighted with the anger of men, it could be seen that there was no danger of immediate conflict, and at once Johnnie, shouldering his way forward, almost succeeded in confronting the Swede, "What did you say I cheated for? What did you say I cheated for? I don't cheat, and I won't let no man say I do?"

The Swede said, "I saw you! I saw you!"

"Well," cried Johnnie, "I'll fight any man what says I cheat!"

"No, you won't," said the cowboy. "Not here."

"Ah, be still, can't you?" said Scully, coming between them.

The quiet was sufficient to allow the Easterner's voice to be heard. He was repeating, "Oh, wait a moment, can't you? What's the good of a fight over a game of cards? Wait a moment!"

Johnnie, his red face appearing above his father's shoulder, hailed the Swede again. "Did you say I cheated?"

The Swede showed his teeth. "Yes."

"Then," said Johnnie, "we must fight."

"Yes, fight," roared the Swede. He was like a demoniac. "Yes, fight! I'll show you what kind of a man I am! I'll show you who you want to fight! Maybe you think I can't fight! Maybe you think I can't! I'll show you, you skin, you card-sharp! Yes, you cheated! You cheated!"

"Well, let's go at it, then, mister," said Johnnie, coolly.

The cowboy's brow was beaded with sweat from his efforts in intercepting all sorts of raids. He turned in despair to Scully. "What are you goin' to do now?"

A change had come over the Celtic visage of the old man. He now seemed all eagerness; his eyes glowed.

"We'll let them fight," he answered, stalwartly. "I can't put up with it any longer. I've stood this damned Swede till I'm sick. We'll let them fight."

VI

The men prepared to go out-of-doors. The Easterner was so nervous that he had great difficulty in getting his arms into the sleeves of his new leather coat. As the cowboy drew his fur cap down over his ears his hands trembled. In fact, Johnnie and old Scully were the only ones who displayed no agitation. These preliminaries were conducted without words.

Scully threw open the door. "Well, come on," he said. Instantly a terrific wind caused the flame of the lamp to struggle at its wick, while a puff of black smoke sprang from the chimney-top. The stove was in midcurrent of the blast, and its voice swelled to equal the roar of the storm. Some of the scarred and bedabbled cards were caught up from the floor and dashed helplessly against the farther wall. The men lowered their heads and plunged into the tempest as into a sea.

No snow was falling, but great whirls and clouds of flakes, swept up from the ground by the frantic winds, were streaming southward with the speed of bullets. The land was blue with the sheen of bullets. The covered land was blue with the sheen of an unearthly satin, and there was no other hue save where, at the low, black railway station—which seemed incredibly distant—one light gleamed like a tiny jewel. As the men floundered into a thigh-deep drift, it was known that the Swede was bawling out something. Scully went to him, put a hand on his shoulder, and projected an ear. "What's that you say?" he shouted.

"I say," bawled the Swede again, "I won't stand much show against this gang. I know you'll all pitch on me."

Scully smote him reproachfully on the arm. "Tut, man!" he yelled. The wind tore the words from Scully's lips and scattered them far alee.

"You are all a gang of—" boomed the Swede, but the storm also seized the remainder of this sentence.

Immediately turning their backs upon the wind, the men had swung around a corner to the sheltered side of the hotel. It was the function of the little house to preserve here, amid this great devastation of snow, an irregular V-shape of heavily encrusted grass, which crackled beneath the feet. One could imagine the great drifts piled against the windward side. When the party reached the comparative peace of this spot it was found that the Swede was still bellowing.

"Oh, I know what kind of a thing this is! I know you'll all pitch on me. I can't lick you all!"

Scully turned upon him panther-fashion. "You'll not have to whip all of us. You'll have to whip my son Johnnie. An' the man what troubles you durin' that time will have me to deal with."

The arrangements were swiftly made. The two men faced each other, obedient to the harsh commands of Scully, whose face, in the subtly luminous gloom, could be seen set in the austere impersonal lines that are pictured on the countenances of the Roman veterans. The Easterner's teeth were chattering, and he was hopping up and down like a mechanical toy. The cowboy stood rock-like.

The contestants had not stripped off any clothing. Each was in his ordinary attire. Their fists were up, and they eyed each other in a calm that had the elements of leonine cruelty in it.

During this pause, the Easterner's mind, like a film, took lasting impressions of three men—the iron-nerved master of the ceremony; the Swede, pale, motionless, terrible; and Johnnie, serene yet ferocious, brutish yet heroic. The entire prelude had in it a tragedy greater than the tragedy of action, and this aspect was accentuated by the long, mellow cry of the blizzard, as it sped the tumbling and wailing flakes into the black abyss of the south.

"Now!" said Scully.

The two combatants leaped forward and crashed together like bullocks. There was heard the cushioned sound of blows, and of a curse squeezing out from between the tight teeth of one.

As for the spectators, the Easterner's pent-up breath exploded from him with a pop of relief, absolute relief from the tension of the preliminaries. The cowboy bounded into the air with a yowl. Scully was immovable as from supreme amazement and fear at the fury of the fight which he himself had permitted and arranged.

For a time the encounter in the darkness was such a perplexity of flying arms that it presented no more detail than would a swiftly revolving wheel. Occasionally a face, as if illumined by a flash of light, would shine out, ghastly and marked with pink spots. A moment later, the men might have been known as shadows, if it were not for the involuntary utterance of oaths that came from them in whispers.

Suddenly a holocaust of warlike desire caught the cowboy, and he bolted forward with the speed of a broncho. "Go it. Johnnie! go it! Kill him! Kill him!"

Scully confronted him. "Kape back," he said; and by his glance the cowboy could tell that this man was Johnnie's father.

To the Easterner there was a monotony of unchangeable fighting that was an abomination. This confused mingling was eternal to his sense, which was concentrated in a longing for the end, the priceless end. Once the fighters lurched near him, and as he scrambled hastily backward he heard them breathe like men on the rack.

"Kill him, Johnnie! Kill him! Kill him! Kill him!" The cowboy's face was contorted like one of those agony masks in museums.

"Keep still," said Scully, icily.

Then there was a sudden loud grunt, incomplete, cut short, and Johnnie's body swung away from the Swede and fell with sickening heaviness to the grass. The cowboy was barely in time to prevent the mad Swede from flinging himself upon his prone adversary. "No, you don't," said the cowboy, interposing an arm. "Wait a second."

Scully was at his son's side. "Johnnie! Johnnie, me boy!" His voice had a quality of melancholy tenderness. "Johnnie! Can you go on with it?" He looked anxiously down into the bloody, pulpy face of his son.

There was a moment of silence, and then Johnnie answered in his ordinary voice, "Yes, I—it—yes."

Assisted by his father he struggled to his feet. "Wait a bit now till you git your wind," said the old man.

A few paces away the cowboy was lecturing the Swede. "No, you don't! Wait a second!"

The Easterner was plucking at Scully's sleeve. "Oh, this is enough," he pleaded. "This is enough! Let it go as it stands. This is enough!"

"Bill," said Scully, "git out of the road." The cowboy stepped aside. "Now." The combatants were actuated by a new caution as they advanced towards collision. They glared at each other, and then the Swede aimed a lightning blow that carried with it his entire weight. Johnnie was evidently half stupid from weakness, but he miraculously dodged, and his fist sent the over-balanced Swede sprawling.

The cowboy, Scully, and the Easterner burst into a cheer that was like a chorus of triumphant soldiery, but before its conclusion the Swede had scuffled agilely to his feet and come in berserk abandon at his foe. There was another perplexity of flying arms, and Johnnie's body again swung away and fell, even as a bundle might fall from a roof. The Swede instantly staggered to a little wind-waved tree and leaned upon it, breathing like an engine, while his savage and flame-lit eyes roamed from face to face as the men bent over Johnnie. There was a splendor of isolation in his situation at this time which the Easterner felt once when, lifting his eyes from the man on the ground, he beheld that mysterious and lonely figure, waiting.

"Are you any good yet, Johnnie?" asked Scully in a broken voice.

The son gasped and opened his eyes languidly. After a moment he answered, "No—I ain't—any good—any—more." Then, from shame and bodily ill, he began to weep, the tears furrowing down through the blood-stains on his face. "He was too—too—too heavy for me."

Scully straightened and addressed the waiting figure. "Stranger," he said, evenly, "it's all up with our side." Then his voice changed into that vibrant huskiness which is commonly the tone of the most simple and deadly announcements. "Johnnie is whipped."

Without replying, the victor moved off on the route to the front door of the hotel.

The cowboy was formulating new and unspellable blasphemies. The Easterner was startled to find that they were out in a wind that seemed to come direct from the shadowed arctic floes. He heard again the wail of the snow as it was flung to its grave in the south. He knew now that all this time the cold had been sinking into him deeper and deeper, and he wondered that he had not perished. He felt indifferent to the condition of the vanquished man.

"Johnnie, can you walk?" asked Scully.

"Did I hurt—hurt him any?" asked the son.

"Can you walk, boy? Can you walk?"

Johnnie's voice was suddenly strong. There was a robust impatience in it. "I asked you whether I hurt him any!"

"Yes, yes, Johnnie," answered the cowboy, consolingly; "he's hurt a good deal."

They raised him from the ground, and as soon as he was on his feet he went tottering off, rebuffing all attempts at assistance. When the party rounded the corner they were fairly blinded by the pelting of the snow. It burned their faces like fire. The cowboy carried Johnnie through the drift to the door. As they entered, some cards again rose from the floor and beat against the wall.

The Easterner rushed to the stove. He was so profoundly chilled that he almost dared to embrace the glowing iron. The Swede was not in the room. Johnnie sank into a chair and, folding his arms on his knees, buried his face in them. Scully, warming one foot and then the other at a rim of the stove, muttered to himself with Celtic mournfulness. The cowboy had removed his fur cap, and with a dazed and rueful air he was running one hand through his tousled locks. From overhead they could hear the creaking of boards, as the Swede tramped here and there in his room.

The sad quiet was broken by the sudden flinging open of a door that led toward the kitchen. It was instantly followed by an inrush of women. They precipitated themselves upon Johnnie amid a chorus of lamentation. Before they carried their prey off to the kitchen, there to be bathed and harangued with that mixture of sympathy and abuse which is a feat of their sex, the mother straightened herself and fixed old Scully with an eye of stern reproach. "Shame be upon you, Patrick Scully!" she cried. "Your own son, too. Shame be upon you!"

"There, now! Be quiet, now!" said the old man, weakly.

"Shame be upon you, Patrick Scully!" The girls, rallying to this slogan, sniffled disdainfully in the direction of those trembling accomplices, the cowboy and the Easterner. Presently they bore Johnnie away, and left the three men to dismal reflection.

VII

"I'd like to fight this here Dutchman myself," said the cowboy, breaking a long silence.

Scully wagged his head sadly. "No, that wouldn't do. It wouldn't be right. It wouldn't be right."

"Well, why wouldn't it?" argued the cowboy. "I don't see no harm in it."

"No," answered Scully, with mournful heroism. "It wouldn't be right. It was Johnnie's fight, and now we mustn't whip the man just because he whipped Johnnie."

"Yes, that's true enough," said the cowboy; "but—he better not get fresh with me, because I couldn't stand no more of it."

"You'll not say a word to him," commanded Scully, and even then they heard the tread of the Swede on the stairs. His entrance was made theatric. He swept the door back with a bang and swaggered to the middle of the room. No one looked at him. "Well," he cried, insolently, at Scully, "I s'pose you'll tell me now how much I owe you?"

The old man remained stolid, "You don't owe me nothin'."

"Huh!" said the Swede, "huh! Don't owe 'im nuthin'."

The cowboy addressed the Swede. "Stranger, I don't see how you come to be so gay around here."

Old Scully was instantly alert. "Stop!" he shouted, holding his hand forth, fingers upward. "Bill, you shut up!"

The cowboy spat carelessly into the sawdust box. "I didn't say a word, did I?" he asked.

"Mr. Scully," called the Swede, "how much do I owe you?" It was seen that he was attired for departure, and that he had his valise in his hand.

"You don't owe me nothin'," repeated Scully in the same imperturbable way.

"Huh!" said the Swede. "I guess you're right. I guess if it was any way at all, you'd owe me somethin'. That's what I guess." He turned to the cowboy. "Kill him! Kill him! Kill him!'" he mimicked, and then guffawed victoriously. "'Kill him!'" He was convulsed with ironical humor.

But he might have been jeering the dead. The three men were immovable and silent, staring with glassy eyes at the stove.

The Swede opened the door and passed into the storm, giving one dirisive glance backward at the still group.

As soon as the door was closed, Scully and the cowboy leaped to their feet and began to curse. They tramped to and fro, waving their arms and smashing into the air their fists. "Oh, but that was a hard minute!" wailed Scully. "That was a hard minute! Him there leerin' and scoffin'! One bang at his nose was worth forty dollars to me that minute! How did you stand it, Bill?"

"How did I stand it?" cried the cowboy in a quivering voice. "How did I stand it? Oh!"

The old man burst into sudden brogue. "I'd loike to take that Swade," he wailed, "and hould 'im down on a shtone flure and bate 'im to a jelly wid a shtick!"

The cowboy groaned in sympathy. "I'd like to git him by the neck and ha-ammer him"—he brought his hand down on a chair with a noise like a pistol-shot—"hammer that there Dutchman until he couldn't tell himself from a dead coyote!"

"I'd bate 'im until he—"

"I'd show *him* some things—"

And then together they raised a yearning, fanatic cry—"Oh-o-oh! if we only could—"

"Yes!"

"Yes!"

"And then I'd—"

"O-o-oh!"

VIII

The Swede, tightly gripping his valise, tacked across the face of the storm as if he carried sails. He was following a line of little naked, gasping trees which, he knew, must mark the way of the road. His face, fresh from the pounding of Johnnie's fists, felt more pleasure than pain in the wind and the driving snow. A number of square shapes loomed upon him finally, and he knew them as the houses of the main body of the town. He found a street and made travel along it, leaning heavily upon the wind whenever, at a corner, a terrific blast caught him.

He might have been in a deserted village. We picture the world as thick with conquering and elate humanity, but here, with the bugles of the tempest pealing, it was hard to imagine a peopled earth. One viewed the existence of man then as a marvel, and conceded a glamor of wonder to these lice which were caused to cling to a whirling, fire-smote, ice-locked, disease-stricken, space-lost bulb. The conceit of man was explained by this storm to be the very engine of life. One was a coxcomb not to die in it. However, the Swede found a saloon.

In front of it an indomitable red light was burning, and the snow-flakes were made blood-color as they flew through the circumscribed territory of the lamp's shining. The Swede pushed open the door of the saloon and entered. A sanded expanse was before him, and at the end of it four men sat about a table drinking. Down one side of the room extended a radiant bar, and its guardian was leaning upon his elbows listening to the talk of the men at the table. The Swede dropped his valise upon the floor and, smiling fraternally upon the barkeeper, said, "Gimme some whiskey, will you?" The man placed a bottle, a whiskey-glass, and a glass of ice-thick water upon the bar. The Swede poured himself an abnormal portion of whiskey and drank it in three gulps. "Pretty bad night," remarked the bartender, indifferently. He was making the pretension of blindness which is usually a distinction of his class; but it could have been seen that he was furtively studying the half-erased blood stains on the face of the Swede, "Bad night," he said again.

"Oh, it's good enough for me," replied the Swede, hardily, as he poured himself some more whiskey. The barkeeper took his coin and manœvered it through its reception by the highly nickelled cash-machine. A bell rang; a card labelled "20 cts." had appeared.

"No," continued the Swede, "this isn't too bad weather. It's good enough for me."

"So?" murmured the barkeeper, languidly.

The copious drams made the Swede's eyes swim, and he breathed a trifle heavier. "Yes, I like this weather. It suits me." It was apparently his design to impart a deep significance to these words.

"So?" murmured the bartender again. He turned to gaze dreamily at the scroll-like birds and bird-like scrolls which had been drawn with soap upon the mirrors in back of the bar.

"Well, I guess I'll take another drink," said the Swede, presently. "Have something?"

"No, thanks; I'm not drinkin'," answered the bartender. Afterward he asked, "How did you hurt your face?"

The Swede immediately began to boast loudly. "Why, in a fight. I thumped the soul out of a man down here at Scully's hotel."

The interest of the four men at the table was at last aroused.

"Who was it?" said one.

"Johnnie Scully," blustered the Swede. "Son of the man what runs it. He will be pretty near dead for some weeks, I can tell you. I made a nice thing of him. I did. He couldn't get up. They carried him in the house. Have a drink?"

Instantly the men in some subtle way encased themselves in reserve. "No, thanks," said one. The group was of curious formation. Two were prominent local business men; one was the district attorney; and one was a professional gambler of the kind known as "square." But a scrutiny of the group would not have enabled an observer to pick the gambler from the men of more reputable pursuits. He was, in fact, a man so delicate in manner, when among people of fair class, and so judicious in his choice of victims, that in the strictly masculine part of the town's life he had come to be explicitly trusted and admired. People called him a thoroughbred. The fear and contempt with which his craft was regarded were undoubtedly the reason why his quiet dignity shone conspicuous above the quiet dignity of men who might be merely hatters, billiard-markers, or grocery-clerks. Beyond an occasional unwary traveller who came by rail, this gambler was supposed to prey solely upon reckless and senile farmers, who, when flush with good crops, drove into town in all the pride and confidence of an absolutely invulnerable stupidity. Hearing at times in circuitous fashion of the despoilment of such a farmer, the important men of Romper invariably laughed in contempt of the victim, and if they thought of the wolf at all, it was with a kind of pride at the knowledge that he would never dare think of attacking their wisdom and courage. Besides, it was popular that this gambler had a real wife and two real children in a neat cottage in a suburb, where he led an exemplary home life; and when any one even suggested a discrepancy in his character, the crowd immediately vociferated descriptions of this virtuous family circle. Then men who led exemplary home lives, and men who did not lead exemplary home lives, all subsided in a bunch, remarking that there was nothing more to be said.

However, when a restriction was placed upon him—as, for instance, when a strong clique of members of the new Pollywog Club refused to permit him, even as a spectator, to appear in the rooms of the organization—the candor and gentleness with which he accepted the judgment disarmed many of his foes and made his friends more desperately partisan. He invariably distinguished between himself and a respectable Romper man so quickly and frankly that his manner actually appeared to be a continual broadcast compliment.

And one must not forget to declare the fundamental fact of his entire position in Romper. It is irrefutable that in all affairs outside his business, in all matters that occur eternally and commonly between man and man, this thieving card-player was so generous, so just, so moral, that, in a contest, he could have put to flight the consciences of nine-tenths of the citizens of Romper.

And so it happened that he was seated in this saloon with the two prominent local merchants and the district attorney.

The Swede continued to drink raw whiskey, meanwhile babbling at the barkeeper and trying to induce him to indulge in potations. "Come on. Have a drink. Come on. What—no? Well, have a little one, then. By gawd, I've whipped a man to-night, and I want to celebrate. I whipped him good, too. Gentlemen," the Swede cried to the men at the table. "have a drink?"

"Ssh!" said the barkeeper.

The group at the table, although furtively attentive, had been pretending to be deep in talk, but now a man lifted his eyes towards the Swede and said, shortly, "Thanks. We don't want any more."

At this reply the Swede ruffled out his chest like a rooster. "Well," he exploded, "It seems I can't get anybody to drink with me in this town. Seems so, don't it? Well!"

"Ssh!" said the barkeeper.

"Say," snarled the Swede, "don't you try to shut me up. I won't have it. I'm a gentleman, and I want people to drink with me. And I want 'em to drink with me now. *Now*—do you understand?" He rapped the bar with his knuckles.

Years of experience had calloused the bartender. He merely grew sulky. "I hear you," he answered.

"Well," cried the Swede, "listen hard then. See those men over there? Well, they're going to drink with me, and don't you forget it. Now you watch."

"Hi!" yelled the barkeeper, "this won't do!"

"Why won't it?" demanded the Swede. He stalked over to the table, and by chance laid his hand upon the shoulder of the gambler. "How about this?" he asked wrathfully. "I asked you to drink with me."

The gambler simply twisted his head and spoke over his shoulder. "My friend, I don't know you."

"Oh, hell!" answered the Swede, "come and have a drink."

"Now, my boy," advised the gambler, kindly, "take your hand off my shoulder and go 'way and mind your own business." He was a little, slim man, and it seemed strange to hear him use this tone of heroic patronage to the burly Swede. The other men at the table said nothing.

"What! You won't drink with me, you little dude? I'll make you, then! I'll make you!" The Swede had grasped the gambler frenziedly at the throat, and was dragging him from his chair. The other men sprang up. The barkeeper dashed around the corner of his bar. There was a great tumult, and then was seen a long blade in the hand of the gambler. It shot forward, and a human body, this citadel of virtue, wisdom, power, was pierced as easily as if it had been a melon. The Swede fell with a cry of supreme astonishment.

The prominent merchants and the district attorney must have at once tumbled out of the place backward. The bartender found himself hanging limply to the arm of a chair and gazing into the eyes of a murderer.

"Henry," said latter, as he wiped his knife on one of the towels that hung beneath the bar rail, "you tell 'em where to find me. I'll be home, waiting for 'em." Then he vanished. A moment afterward the barkeeper was in the street dinning through the storm for help and, moreover, companionship.

The corpse of the Swede, alone in the saloon, had its eyes fixed upon a dreadful legend that dwelt atop of the cash-machine: "This registers the amount of your purchase."

IX

Months later, the cowboy was frying pork over the stove of a little ranch near the Dakota line, when there was a quick thud of hoofs outside, and presently the Easterner entered with the letters and the papers.

"Well," said the Easterner at once, "the chap that killed the Swede has got three years. Wasn't much, was it?"

"He has? Three years?" The cowboy poised his pan of pork, while he ruminated upon the news. "Three years. That ain't much."

"No. It was light sentence," replied the Easterner as he unbuckled his spurs. "Seems there was a good deal of sympathy for him in Romper."

"If the bartender had been any good," observed the cowboy, thoughtfully, "he would have gone in and cracked that there Dutchman on the head with a bottle in the beginnin' of it and stopped all this here murderin'."

"Yes, a thousand things might have happened," said the Easterner, tartly.

The cowboy returned his pan of pork to the fire, but his philosophy continued. "It's funny, ain't it? If he hadn't said Johnnie was cheatin' he'd be alive this minute. He was an awful fool. Game played for fun, too. Not for money. I believe he was crazy."

"I feel sorry for that gambler," said the Easterner.

"Oh, so do I," said the cowboy. "He don't deserve none of it for killin' who he did."

"The Swede might not have been killed if everything had been square."

"Might not have been killed?" exclaimed the cowboy. "Everythin' square? Why, when he said that Johnnie was cheatin' and acted like such a jackass? And then in the saloon he fairly walked up to git hurt?" With these arguments the cowboy browbeat the Easterner and reduced him to rage.

"You're a fool!" cried the Easterner, viciously. "You're a bigger jackass than the Swede by a million majority. Now let me tell you one thing. Let me tell you something. Listen! Johnnie *was* cheating!"

" 'Johnnie,' " said the cowboy, blankly. There was a minute of silence, and then he said, robustly, "Why, no. The game was only for fun."

"Fun or not," said the Easterner, "Johnnie was cheating. I saw him.

I know it. I saw him. And I refused to stand up and be a man. I let the Swede fight it out alone. And you—you were simply puffing around the place and wanting to fight. And then old Scully himself! We are all in it! This poor gambler isn't even a noun. He is a kind of an adverb. Every sin is the result of a collaboration. We, five of us, have collaborated in the murder of this Swede. Usually there are from a dozen to forty women really involved in every murder, but in this case it seems to be only five men—you, I, Johnnie, old Scully; and that fool of an unfortunate gambler came merely as a culmination, the apex of a human movement, and gets all the punishment."

The cowboy, injured and rebellious, cried out blindly into this fog of mysterious theory: "Well, I didn't do anythin', did I?"

The Bride Comes to Yellow Sky (1898)

I

The great Pullman was whirling onward with such dignity of motion that a glance from the window seemed simply to prove that the plains of Texas were pouring eastward. Vast flats of green grass, dull-hued spaces of mesquit and cactus, little groups of frame houses, woods of light and tender trees, all were sweeping into the east, sweeping over the horizon, a precipice.

A newly married pair had boarded this coach at San Antonio. The man's face was reddened from many days in the wind and sun, and a direct result of his new black clothes was that his brick-colored hands were constantly performing in a most conscious fashion. From time to time he looked down respectfully at his attire. He sat with a hand on each knee, like a man waiting in a barber's shop. The glances he devoted to other passengers were furtive and shy.

The bride was not pretty, nor was she very young. She wore a dress of blue cashmere, with small reservations of velvet here and there, and with steel buttons abounding. She continually twisted her head to regard her puff sleeves, very stiff, straight, and high. They embarrassed her. It was quite apparent that she had cooked, and that she expected to cook, dutifully. The blushes caused by the careless scrutiny of some passengers as she had entered the car were strange to see upon this plain, under-class countenance, which was drawn in placid, almost emotionless lines.

They were evidently very happy. "Ever been in a parlor-car before?" he asked, smiling with delight.

"No," she answered; "I never was. It's fine, ain't it?"

"Great! And then after a while we'll go forward to the diner, and get a big lay-out. Finest meal in the world. Charge a dollar."

"Oh, do they?" cried the bride. "Charge a dollar? Why, that's too much—for us—ain't it, Jack?"

"Not this trip, anyhow," he answered bravely. "We're going to go the whole thing."

Later he explained to her about the trains. "You see, it's a thousand miles from one end of Texas to the other; and this train runs right across it, and never stops but for four times." He had the pride of an owner. He pointed out to her the dazzling fittings of the coach; and in truth her eyes opened wider as she contemplated the sea-green figured velvet, the shining brass, silver, and glass, the wood that gleamed as darkly brilliant as the surface of a pool of oil. At one end a bronze figure sturdily held a support for a separated chamber, and at convenient places on the ceiling were frescoes in olive and silver.

To the minds of the pair, their surroundings reflected the glory of their marriage that morning in San Antonio; this was the environment of their new estate; and the man's face in particular beamed with an elation that made him appear ridiculous to the negro porter. This individual at times surveyed them from afar with an amused and superior grin. On other occasions he bullied them with skill in ways that did not make it exactly plain to them that they were being bullied. He subtly used all the manners of the most unconquerable kind of snobbery. He oppressed them; but of this oppression they had small knowledge, and they speedily forgot that infrequently a number of travellers covered them with stares of derisive enjoyment. Historically there was supposed to be something infinitely humorous in their situation.

"We are due in Yellow Sky at 3:42," he said, looking tenderly into her eyes.

"Oh, are we?" she said, as if she had not been aware of it. To evince surprise at her husband's statement was part of her wifely amiability. She took from a pocket a little silver watch; and as she held it before her, and stared at it with a frown of attention, the new husband's face shone.

"I bought it in San Anton' from a friend of mine," he told her gleefully.

"It's seventeen minutes past twelve," she said, looking up at him with a kind of shy and clumsy coquetry. A passenger, noting this play, grew excessively sardonic, and winked at himself in one of the numerous mirrors.

At last they went to the dining-car. Two rows of negro waiters, in glowing white suits, surveyed their entrance with the interest, and also the equanimity, of men who had been forewarned. The pair fell to the lot of a waiter who happened to feel pleasure in steering them through their meal. He viewed them with the manner of a fatherly pilot, his countenance radiant with benevolence. The patronage, entwined with the ordinary deference, was not plain to them. And yet, as they returned to their coach, they showed in their faces a sense of escape.

To the left, miles down a long purple slope, was a little ribbon of mist where moved the keening Rio Grande. The train was approaching it at an angle, and the apex was Yellow Sky. Presently it was apparent that, as the distance from Yellow Sky grew shorter, the husband became commensurately restless. His brick-red hands were more insistent in their prominence. Occasionally he was even rather absent-minded and far-away when the bride leaned forward and addressed him.

As a matter of truth, Jack Potter was beginning to find the shadow of a deed weigh upon him like a leaden slab. He, the town marshal of Yellow Sky, a man known, liked, and feared in his corner, a prominent person, had gone to San Antonio to meet a girl he believed he loved, and there, after the usual prayers, had actually induced her to marry him, without consulting Yellow Sky for any part of the transaction. He was now bringing his bride before an innocent and unsuspecting community.

Of course people in Yellow Sky married as it pleased them, in accordance with a general custom; but such was Potter's thought of his duty to his friends, or of their idea of his duty, or of an unspoken form which does not control men in these matters, that he felt he was heinous. He had committed an extraordinary crime. Face to face with this girl in San Antonio, and spurred by his sharp impulse, he had gone headlong over all the social hedges. At San Antonio he was like a man hidden in the dark. A knife to sever any friendly duty, any form, was easy to his hand in that remote city. But the hour of Yellow Sky—the hour of daylight—was approaching.

He knew full well that his marriage was an important thing to his town. It could only be exceeded by the burning of the new hotel. His friends could not forgive him. Frequently he had reflected on the advisability of telling them by telegraph, but a new cowardice had been upon him. He feared to do it. And now the train was hurrying him toward a scene of amazement, glee, and reproach. He glanced out of the window at the line of haze swinging slowly in toward the train.

Yellow Sky had a kind of brass band, which played painfully, to the delight of the populace. He laughed without heart as he thought of it. If the citizens could dream of his prospective arrival with his bride, they would parade the band at the station and escort them, amid cheers and laughing congratulations, to his adobe home.

He resolved that he would use all the devices of speed and plainscraft in making the journey from the station to his house. Once within that safe citadel, he could issue some sort of vocal bulletin, and then not go among the citizens until they had time to wear off a little of their enthusiasm.

The bride looked anxiously at him. "What's worrying you, Jack?"

He laughed again. "I'm not worrying, girl; I'm only thinking of Yellow Sky."

She flushed in comprehension.

A sense of mutual guilt invaded their minds and developed a finer tenderness. They looked at each other with eyes softly aglow. But Potter often laughed the same nervous laugh; the flush upon the bride's face seemed quite permanent.

The traitor to the feelings of Yellow Sky narrowly watched the speeding landscape. "We're nearly there," he said.

Presently the porter came and announced the proximity of Potter's home. He held a brush in his hand, and, with all his airy superiority gone, he brushed Potter's new clothes as the latter slowly turned this way and that way. Potter fumbled out a coin and gave it to the porter, as he had seen others do. It was a heavy and muscle-bound business, as that of a man shoeing his first horse.

The porter took their bag, and as the train began to slow they moved forward to the hooded platform of the car. Presently the two engines and their long string of coaches rushed into the station of Yellow Sky.

"They have to take water here," said Potter, from a constricted throat and in mournful cadence, as one announcing death. Before the train stopped his eye had swept the length of the platform, and he was glad and astonished to see there was none upon it but the station-agent, who, with a slightly hurried and anxious air, was walking toward the water-tanks. When the train had halted, the porter alighted first, and placed in position a little temporary step.

"Come on, girl," said Potter, hoarsely. As he helped her down they each laughed on a false note. He took the bag from the negro, and bade his wife cling to his arm. As they slunk rapidly away, his hang-dog glance perceived that they were unloading the two trunks, and also that the station agent, far ahead near the baggage car, had turned and was running towards him, making gestures. He laughed, and groaned as he laughed, when he noted the first effect of his marital bliss upon Yellow Sky. He gripped his wife's arm firmly to his side, and they fled. Behind them the porter stood, chuckling fatuously.

II

The California express on the Southern Railway was due at Yellow Sky in twenty-one minutes. There were six men at the bar of the Weary Gentleman Saloon. One was a drummer who talked a great deal and rapidly; three were Texans who did not care to talk at that time; and two were Mexican sheep-herders, who did not talk as a general practice in the Weary Gentleman Saloon. The barkeeper's dog lay on the board walk that crossed in front of the door. His head was on his paws, and he glanced drowsily here and there with the constant vigilance of a dog that is kicked on occasion. Across the sandy street were some vivid green grass-plots, so wonderful in appearance, amid the sands that burned near them in a blazing sun, that they caused a doubt in the mind. They exactly resembled the grass mats used to represent lawns on the stage. At the cooler end of the railway station, a man without a coat sat in a tilted chair and smoked his pipe. The fresh-cut bank of the Rio Grande circled near the town, and there could be seen beyond it a great plum-colored plain of mesquit.

Save for the busy drummer and his companions in the saloon, Yellow Sky was dozing. The newcomer leaned gracefully upon the bar, and recited many tales with the confidence of a bard who has come upon a new field.

"—and at the moment that the old man fell downstairs with the bureau in his arms, the old woman was coming up with two scuttles of coal, and of course—"

The drummer's tale was interrupted by a young man who suddenly appeared in the open door. He cried: "Scratchy Wilson's drunk, and has turned loose with both hands." The two Mexicans at once set down their glasses and faded out of the rear entrance of the saloon.

The drummer, innocent and jocular, answered: "All right, old man. S'pose he has? Come in and have a drink, anyhow."

But the information had made such an obvious cleft in every skull in the room that the drummer was obliged to see its importance. All had become instantly solemn. "Say," said he, mystified, "what is this?" His three companions made the introductory gesture of eloquent speech; but the young man at the door forestalled them.

"It means, my friend," he answered, as he came into the saloon, "that for the next two hours this town won't be a health resort."

The barkeeper went to the door, and locked and barred it; reaching out of the window, he pulled in heavy wooden shutters, and barred them. Immediately a solemn, chapel-like gloom was upon the place. The drummer was looking from one to another.

"But say," he cried, "what is this anyhow? You don't mean there is going to be a gun-fight?"

"Don't know whether there'll be a fight or not," answered one man, grimly; "but there'll be some shootin'—some good shootin'."

The young man who had warned them waved his hand. "Oh, there'll be a fight fast enough, if any one wants it. Anybody can get a fight out there in the street. There's a fight just waiting."

The drummer seemed to be swayed between the interest of a foreigner and a perception of personal danger.

"What did you say his name was?" he asked.

"Scratchy Wilson," they answered in chorus.

"And will he kill anybody? What are you going to do? Does this happen often? Does he rampage around like this once a week or so? Can he break in that door?"

"No; he can't break down that door," replied the barkeeper. "He's tried it three times. But when he comes you'd better lay down on the floor, stranger. He's dead sure to shoot at it, and a bullet may come through."

Thereafter the drummer kept a strict eye upon the door. The time had not yet been called for him to hug the floor, but, as a minor precaution, he sidled near to the wall. "Will he kill anybody?" he said again.

The men laughed low and scornfully at the question.

"He's out to shoot, and he's out for trouble. Don't see any good in experimentin' with him."

"But what do you do in a case like this? What do you do?"

A man responded: "Why, he and Jack Potter—"

"But," in chorus the other men interrupted, "Jack Potter's in San Anton'."

"Well, who is he? What's he got to do with it?"

"Oh, he's the town marshal. He goes out and fights Scratchy when he gets on one of these tears."

"Wow!" said the drummer, mopping his brow. "Nice job he's got."

The voices had toned away to mere whisperings. The drummer wished to ask further questions, which were born of an increasing anxiety and bewilderment; but when he attempted them, the men merely looked at him in irritation and motioned him to remain silent. A tense waiting hush was upon them. In the deep shadows of the room their eyes shone as they listened for sounds from the street. One man made three gestures at the barkeeper; and the latter moving like a ghost, handed him a glass and a bottle. The man poured a full glass of whiskey, and set down the bottle noiselessly. He gulped the whiskey in a swallow, and turned again toward the door in immovable silence. The drummer saw that the barkeeper, without a sound, had taken a Winchester from beneath the bar. Later he saw this individual beckoning to him, so he tiptoed across the room.

"You better come with me back of the bar."

"No, thanks," said the drummer, perspiring; "I'd rather be where I can make a break for the back door."

Whereupon the man of bottles made a kindly but peremptory gesture. The drummer obeyed it, and, finding himself seated on a box with his head below the level of the bar, balm was laid upon his soul at sight of various zinc and copper fittings that bore a resemblance to armor-plate. The barkeeper took a seat comfortably upon an adjacent box.

"You see," he whispered, "this here Scratchy Wilson is a wonder with a gun—a perfect wonder; and when he goes on the war-trail, we hunt our holes—naturally. He's about the last one of the old gang that used to hang out along the river here. He's a terror when he's drunk. When he's sober he's all right—kind of simple—wouldn't hurt a fly— nicest fellow in town. But when he's drunk—whoo!"

There were periods of stillness. "I wish Jack Potter was back from San Anton'," said the barkeeper. "He shot Wilson up once—in the leg— and he would sail in and pull out the kinks in this thing."

Presently they heard from a distance the sound of a shot, followed by three wild yowls. It instantly removed a bond from the men in the darkened saloon. There was a shuffling of feet. They looked at each other. "Here he comes," they said.

III

A man in a maroon-colored flannel shirt, which had been purchased for purposes of decoration, and made principally by some Jewish women on the East Side of New York, rounded a corner and walked into the middle of the main street of Yellow Sky. In either hand the man held a long, heavy, blue-black revolver. Often he yelled, and these cries rang through a semblance of a deserted village, shrilly flying over the roofs in a volume that seemed to have no relation to the ordinary vocal strength of a man. It was as if the surrounding stillness formed the arch of a tomb over him. These cries of ferocious challenge rang against walls of silence. And his boots had red tops with gilded imprints, of the kind beloved in winter by little sledding boys on the hillsides of New England.

The man's face flamed in a rage begot of whiskey. His eyes, rolling, and yet keen for ambush, hunted the still doorways and windows. He walked with the creeping movement of the midnight cat. As it occurred to him, he roared menacing information. The long revolvers in his hands were as easy as straws; they were moved with an electric swiftness. The little fingers of each hand played sometimes in a musician's way. Plain from the low collar of the shirt, the cords of his neck straightened and sank, straightened and sank as passion moved him. The only sounds were his terrible invitations. The calm adobes preserved their demeanor at the passing of this small thing in the middle of the street.

There was no offer of fight—no offer of fight. The man called to the sky. There were no attractions. He bellowed and fumed and swayed his revolvers here and everywhere.

The dog of the barkeeper of the Weary Gentleman Saloon had not appreciated the advance of events. He yet lay dozing in front of his master's door. At sight of the dog, the man paused and raised his revolver humorously. At sight of the man, the dog sprang up and walked diagonally away, with a sullen head, and growling. The man yelled, and the dog broke into a gallop. As it was about to enter an alley, there was a loud noise, a whistling, and something spat the ground directly before it. The dog screamed, and, wheeling in terror, galloped headlong in a new direction. Again there was a noise, a whistling, and sand was kicked viciously before it. Fear-stricken, the dog turned and flurried like an animal in a pen. The man stood laughing, his weapons at his hips.

Ultimately the man was attracted by the closed door of the Weary Gentleman Saloon. He went to it and, hammering with a revolver, demanded drink.

The door remaining imperturbable, he picked a bit of paper from the walk, and nailed it to the framework with a knife. He then turned his

back contemptuously upon this popular resort, and, walking to the opposite side of the street and spinning there on his heel quickly and lithely,
fired at the bit of paper. He missed it by a half-inch. He swore at himself, and went away. Later he comfortably fusilladed the windows of his
most intimate friend. The man was playing with this town; it was a toy
for him.

But still there was no offer of fight. The name of Jack Potter, his
ancient antagonist, entered his mind, and he concluded that it would
be a glad thing if he should go to Potter's house, and by bombardment
induce him to come out and fight. He moved in the direction of his
desire, chanting Apache scalp-music.

When he arrived at it, Potter's house presented the same still front
as had the other adobes. Taking up a strategic position, the man howled
a challenge. But this house regarded him as might a great stone god.
It gave no sign. After a decent wait, the man howled further challenges,
mingling with them wonderful epithets.

Presently there came the spectacle of a man churning himself into
deepest rage over the immobility of a house. He fumed at it as the
winter wind attacks a prairie cabin in the North. To the distance there
should have gone the sound of a tumult like the fighting of two hundred
Mexicans. As necessity bade him, he paused for breath or to reload his
revolvers.

IV

Potter and his bride walked sheepishly and with speed. Sometimes
they laughed together shamefacedly and low.

"Next corner, dear," he said finally.

They put forth the efforts of a pair walking bowed against a strong
wind. Potter was about to raise a finger to point the first appearance of
the new home when, as they circled the corner, they came face to face
with a man in a maroon-colored shirt, who was feverishly pushing cartridges into a large revolver. Upon the instant the man dropped his
revolver to the ground, and, like lightning, whipped another from its
holster. The second weapon was aimed at the bridegroom's chest.

There was a silence. Potter's mouth seemed to be merely a grave for
his tongue. He exhibited an instinct to at once loosen his arm from the
woman's grip, and he dropped the bag to the sand. As for the bride, her
face had gone as yellow as old cloth. She was a slave to hideous rites,
gazing at the apparitional snake.

The two men faced each other at a distance of three paces. He of
the revolver smiled with a new and quiet ferocity.

"Tried to sneak up on me," he said. "Tried to sneak up on me!" His
eyes grew more baleful. As Potter made a slight movement, the man
thrust his revolver venomously forward. "No; don't you do it, Jack
Potter. Don't you move a finger toward a gun just yet. Don't you move

an eyelash. The time has come for me to settle with you, and I'm goin' to do it my own way, and loaf along with no interferin'. So if you don't want a gun bent on you, just mind what I tell you."

Potter looked at his enemy. "I ain't got a gun on me, Scratchy." he said. "Honest, I ain't." He was stiffening and steadying, but yet somewhere at the back of his mind a vision of the Pullman floated: the sea-green figured velvet, the shining brass, silver, and glass, the wood that gleamed as darkly brilliant as the surface of a pool of oil—all the glory of the marriage, the environment of the new estate. "You know I fight when it comes to fighting, Scratchy Wilson; but I ain't got a gun on me. You'll have to do all the shootin' yourself."

His enemy's face went livid. He stepped forward, and lashed his weapon to and fro before Potter's chest. "Don't you tell me you ain't got no gun on you, you whelp. Don't tell me no lie like that. There ain't a man in Texas ever seen you without no gun. Don't take me for no kid." His eyes blazed with light, and his throat worked like a pump.

"I ain't takin' you for no kid," answered Potter. His heels had not moved an inch backward. "I'm takin' you for a —— fool. I tell you I ain't got a gun, and I ain't. If you're goin' to shoot me up, you better begin now; you'll never get a chance like this again."

So much enforced reasoning had told on Wilson's rage; he was calmer. "If you ain't got a gun, why ain't you got a gun?" he sneered. "Been to Sunday school?"

"I ain't got a gun because I've just come from San Anton' with my wife. I'm married," said Potter. "And if I'd thought there was going to be any galoots like you prowling around when I brought my wife home, I'd had a gun, and don't you forget it."

"Married!" said Scratchy, not at all comprehending.

"Yes, married. I'm married," said Potter, distinctly.

"Married?" said Scratchy. Seemingly for the first time, he saw the drooping, drowning woman at the other man's side. "No!" he said. He was like a creature allowed a glimpse of another world. He moved a pace backward, and his arm, with the revolver, dropped to his side. "Is this the lady?" he asked.

"Yes; this is the lady," answered Potter.

There was another period of silence.

"Well," said Wilson at last, slowly, "I s'pose it's all off now."

"It's all off if you say so, Scratchy. You know I didn't make the trouble." Potter lifted his valise.

"Well, I 'low it's off, Jack," said Wilson. He was looking at the ground. "Married!" He was not a student of chivalry; it was merely that in the presence of this foreign condition he was a simple child of the earlier plains. He picked up his starboard revolver, and, placing both weapons in their holsters, he went away. His feet made funnel-shaped tracks in the heavy sand.

Black Riders Came from the Sea *(1895)*

Black riders came from the sea.
There was clang and clang of spear and shield,
And clash and clash of hoof and heel,
Wild shouts and the wave of hair
In the rush upon the wind:
Thus the ride of Sin.

In the Desert *(1895?)*

In the desert
I saw a creature, naked, bestial,
Who, squatting upon the ground,
Held his heart in his hands,
And ate of it.
I said, "Is it good, friend?"
"It is bitter—bitter," he answered;
"But I like it
Because it is bitter,
And because it is my heart."   10

War Is Kind *(1899)*

Do not weep, maiden, for war is kind.
Because your lover threw wild hands toward the sky
And the affrighted steed ran on alone,
Do not weep.
War is kind.

Hoarse, booming drums of the regiment,
Little souls who thirst for fight,
These men were born to drill and die.
The unexplained glory flies above them,
Great is the battle-god, great, and his kingdom—   10
A field where a thousand corpses lie.

Do not weep, babe, for war is kind.
Because your father tumbled in the yellow trenches,
Raged at his breast, gulped and died,
Do not weep.
War is kind.

Swift blazing flag of the regiment,
Eagle with crest of red and gold,
These men were born to drill and die.
Point for them the virtue of slaughter,   20
Make plain to them the excellence of killing
And a field where a thousand corpses lie.
Mother whose heart hung humble as a button
On the bright splendid shroud of your son,
Do not weep.
War is kind.

A Man Said to the Universe *(1899)*

A man said to the universe:
"Sir, I exist!"
"However," replied the universe,
"The fact has not created in me
A sense of obligation."

A Man Adrift on a Slim Spar (POSTHUMOUS)

A man adrift on a slim spar
A horizon smaller than the rim of a bottle.
Tented waves rearing lashy dark points
The near whine of froth in circles.
                     God is cold.

The incessant raise and swing of the sea
And the growl after growl of crest
The sinkings, green, seething, endless
The upheaval half-completed.
                     God is cold.   10

The seas are in the hollow of Thy Hand;
Oceans may be turned to a spray
Raising down through the stars
Because of a gesture of pity toward a babe.
Oceans may become gray ashes
Die with a long moan and roar
Amid the tumult of the fishes
And the cries of the ships,
Because The Hand beckons the mice.

A horizon smaller than a doomed assassin's cap,   20
Inky, surging tumults
A reeling, drunken sky and no sky
A pale hand sliding from a polished spar.
                    God is cold.

The puff of a coat imprisoning air:
A face kissing the water-death
A weary slow sway of a lost hand
And the sea, the moving sea, the sea.
                    God is cold.

American Historians as Artists

Introduction

Only in the last decade or two has a group of distinguished nineteenth-century American historians—William Prescott, John Motley, and Francis Parkman—come to be regarded as writers whose work should be treated not merely as history but also as literature. This trend in judgment was brought to a climax in 1959 when David Levin published a fine study, *History as Romantic Art*, in which the major writings of these historians—Prescott's *History of the Conquest of Mexico*, Motley's *The Rise of the Dutch Republic*, and Parkman's *The Oregon Trail* and *Montcalm and Wolfe*—are analyzed not merely as historical narratives but also as works of the literary imagination.

All of them scions of wealthy Boston families, all of them Brahmins in their politics and cultural tastes (conservative in opinion, suspicious of popular democracy, aloof from both the vitality and vulgarity of ninetenth-century American life), Prescott, Motley, and Parkman looked for subjects that would enable them to display a grand design of human action, rather than what they took to be the paltriness of ordinary American life. They wanted to describe heroic sweeps of historical change in which great men could act out a drama of will and endurance. Prescott wrote about the Spanish conquerors of the American continent, Cortes and Pizarro; Motley about the struggle of the Protestant Dutch to free themselves from Spanish domination, with William of Orange figuring as a hero of overwhelming nobility; and Parkman about the majesty of the American continent and the struggle between two formidable military men, Montcalm and Wolfe, during the war between England and France for the possession of Canada.

All three of these historians did enormous amounts of research, so much so that at least some of Prescott and more of Parkman can still stand up as serious historical investigation; but finally what interested them most was the internal design, color, and vividness of their books. For this among other reasons, they are called romantic historians.

Influenced both by Carlyle's theory that history is shaped primarily by the imagination and will of great men and by Walter Scott's brilliantly tinted historical novels, they were concerned with composing history as art rather than history as science. They wanted their works to be dramatically telling in overall design, richly immediate in the portraiture of great figures, and picturesquely authentic in local detail. Prescott, for example, wrote in his notebook about his conception of the *History of the Conquest of Mexico:*

> The true way of conceiving the subject is, not as a philosophical theme, but as an epic in prose, a romance of chivalry; as romantic and chivalrous as any which Boiardo or Ariesto ever fabled . . . ; and which, while it combines all the picturesque features of the romantic school, is borne onward on a tide of destiny, like that which broods over the fiction of the Grecian poets; for surely there is nothing in the compass of Grecian epic or tragic fable, in which the resistless march of destiny is more discernible, than in the sad fortunes of the dynasty of Montezuma. It is, without doubt, the most poetic subject ever offered to the pen of the historian.

Historians devoted to such a conception of history—Parkman, the youngest of the three, modified his views toward greater sobriety, yet did not fundamentally abandon this conception—would naturally be concerned with language and rhythm, with verbal metaphor and dramatic set piece, in a way that more orthodox historians might not. Somewhat like eighteenth-century Dutch genre painters or like those French painters, from David to Delacroix, who loved to do large canvasses full of swirling and highly colored figures, the New England historians were extremely self-conscious in the way they balanced off one strand of historical narrative against another and in the effort they made to paint starkly chromatic and chiaroscuroed word pictures at the climaxes of their work. Here, for example, is a brilliant passage from Prescott's *History of the Conquest of Mexico,* in which he describes, with a fine mixture of precise detail and narrative thrust, a sacrificial ceremony among the Aztecs:

> As the sad procession wound up the sides of the pyramid, the unhappy victim threw away his gay chaplets of flowers, and broke in pieces the musical instruments with which he had solaced the hours of captivity. On the summit he was received by six priests, whose long and matted locks flowed disorderly from their sable robes, covered with hieroglyphic scrolls of mystic import. They led him to the sacrificial stone, a huge block of jasper, with its upper surface somewhat convex. On this the prisoner was stretched. Five priests secured his head and his limbs; while the sixth, clad in a scarlet mantle, emblematic of his bloody office, dexterously opened the breast with a sharp razor of *itzli,*—a volcanic substance, hard as flint,—and, inserting his hand in the wound, tore out the palpitating heart. The minister of death, first holding this up towards the sun, an object of worship through Anahuac, cast it at the feet of the diety to whom the temple was devoted, while the multitudes below prostrated themselves in humble adoration. The tragic story of this prisoner was expounded by the priests as the type of human destiny, which, brilliant in its commencement, too often closes in sorrow and disaster.

And here is a passage from Parkman's *Montcalm and Wolfe* describing a British attack at Ticonderoga in a style that is somewhat more restrained, certainly more tense, than that of Prescott:

> The scene was frightful: masses of infuriated men who could not go forward and would not go back; straining for an enemy they could not reach, and firing on an enemy they could not see; caught in the entanglement of fallen trees; tripped by briars, stumbling over logs, tearing through boughs; shouting, yelling, cursing, and pelted all the while with bullets that killed them by scores, stretched them on the ground, or hung them on jagged branches in strange attitudes of death.

Only in occasional passages, of course, did Prescott and Parkman write this well. Their effort at the deliberate picturesque and the planned dramatic sometimes had a way of slipping into stock phrasing and overly elaborate scenes; too often their most ambitious effects now seem artificial; and almost all of their books are too long and overwritten.

In still another respect are these historians properly called romantic. Sons of New England, they could not approach the historical past with the ethical neutrality or scientific detachment to which some historians aspire; for them history was a record of moral struggle and moral growth; with varying degrees of sophistication, they shared in the cult of progress which had spread through Europe during the late-eighteenth and early-nineteenth centuries. Professor Levin summarizes their outlook:

> The basic assumption was human progress. Motley went so far as to say that were it not for progress, history would be the most "contemptible" subject to study. Human progress had proceeded westward, from the Middle East to North America. And all along the way, whether they knew it or not, the people of the vanguard had carried with them a new principle: Christianity in the "German woods," nationality in the Iberian peninsula, the Reformation in the Netherlands and England, Democracy (or Liberty) in the American colonies. In the grand design of Providence the victories of these principles were the most meaningful advances in history; moreover, a nation owed her successes to her adherence to the progressive principle—a principle which, by definition (had there been a definition), agreed with natural law.

By contrast, Henry Adams, composing in 1889 to 1891 his magnificent *History of the United States During the Administration of Jefferson and Madison*, found the commonplace life of the young nation full of interest and drama; he sought not for picturesque effects but for a sinewy, rapid prose; and he wished, as he said, to create "a necessary sequence of human movement" by the "severest process of stating, with the least possible comment, such facts as seemed sure, in such order as seemed rigorously consequent." This statement put Adams well onto the path of "scientific history," though his intellectual powers and stylistic command were far beyond what most of the later practitioners of "scientific history" could display. Adams's great *History* brings together the best in the competing notions of history as art and history as science. In the work of a master, the distinction collapses.

WILLIAM HICKLING PRESCOTT (1796–1859)

In a quiet but profound way, the life of the historian William Prescott is a story of heroism. From late adolescence until death, he struggled against the handicap of damaged eyesight. As a junior at Harvard, the young Prescott was hit in the left eye by a hard piece of bread thrown during an undergraduate brawl. The accident, nearly fatal, left the eye permanently damaged.

Prescott was born into a distinguished and wealthy Boston family. As a boy he discovered his lifelong passion for books and spent many hours reading in the Athenaeum library. But only at Harvard did he begin the regimen of devoted scholarly labor that would mark his life.

After his terrible accident Prescott went to England for medical care for by 1815 his other eye had also begun to fail. For a time he feared he would become totally blind: "As to the future," he wrote a friend, "it is too evident I shall never be able to pursue a profession." Yet on his return to Boston, he again threw himself into intellectual work, for a time literary studies and, after about 1825, historical research. Though still badly handicapped by his poor sight, Prescott collected books and documents, used his wealth to employ secretaries who helped him, and gained the friendship of foreign scholars who provided him with clues and material.

When Prescott published his first major work, the painstaking and vivid History of Ferdinand and Isabella *(1838), he became a famous author overnight. He continued his labors, this time on the work that would be his masterpiece,* History of the Conquest of Mexico *(1843), in which he provided the richest account then available of Mexican antiquities and the most dramatic narrative of Cortes's adventures. His last years were devoted to still other historical projects.*

When close to death, Prescott asked to be taken to his study, there to say farewell to the books with which he had spent his life. His biographer and friend, George Ticknor, presents the scene with rhetorical sweep:

> There he lay in unmoved, inaccessible peace, and the lettered dead of all the ages and climes and countries collected there seemed to look down upon him in their earthly immortality and claim that his name should hereafter be imperishably associated with theirs.

Prescott's work as a romantic historian is discussed in the introduction to this section.

FURTHER READING

The first and still most useful of the biographies is by George Ticknor
(1864). David Levin's *History as Romantic Art* (1959) is a fine
study of Prescott, Motley, and Parkman.

FROM *History of the Conquest of Mexico* (1843)[1]

Book III, Chapters 6 and 7

On the following morning he made his entrance at the head of his
army into Cholula, attended by no other Indians than those from Cem-
poalla, and a handful of Tlascalans to take charge of the baggage. His
allies, at parting, gave him many cautions respecting the people he was
to visit, who, while they affected to despise them as a nation of traders,
employed the dangerous arms of perfidy and cunning. As the troops
drew near the city, the road was lined with swarms of people of both
sexes and every age—old men tottering with infirmity, women with
children in their arms—all eager to catch a glimpse of the strangers,
whose persons, weapons, and horses were objects of intense curiosity to
eyes which had not hitherto ever encountered them in battle. The Spaniards, in turn, were filled with admiration at the aspect of the Cholulans,
much superior in dress and general appearance to the nations they had
hitherto seen. They were particularly struck with the costume of the
higher classes, who wore fine embroidered mantles, resembling the
graceful *albornoz*, or Moorish cloak, in their texture and fashion. They
showed the same delicate taste for flowers as the other tribes of the
plateau, decorating their persons with them and tossing garlands and
bunches among the soldiers. An immense number of priests mingled
with the crowd, swinging their aromatic censers, while music from various kinds of instruments gave a lively welcome to the visitors and made
the whole scene one of gay, bewildering enchantment. If it did not have
the air of a triumphal procession so much as at Tlascala, where the
melody of instruments was drowned by the shouts of the multitude, it
gave a quiet assurance of hospitality and friendly feeling not less
grateful.

The Spaniards were also struck with the cleanliness of the city, the
width and great regularity of the streets, which seemed to have been
laid out on a settled plan, with the solidity of the houses, and the num-

[1] This selection describes the way, in August, 1519, Hernando Cortes, with slightly
more than 400 Spanish soldiers, marched toward Tenochtitlan, the Aztec capital,
defeating some Indians, winning others over as allies through guile and threats,
and gradually taking control of Mexico.

ber and size of the pyramidal temples. In the court of one of these, and its surrounding buildings, they were quartered.

They were soon visited by the principal lords of the place, who seemed solicitous to provide them with accommodations. Their table was plentifully supplied, and, in short, they experienced such attentions as were calculated to dissipate their suspicions, and made them impute those of their Tlascalan friends to prejudice and old national hostility.

In a few days the scene changed. Messengers arrived from Montezuma, who, after a short and unpleasant intimation to Cortes that his approach occasioned much disquietude to their master, conferred separately with the Mexican ambassadors still in the Castilian camp and then departed, taking one of the latter along with them. From this time, the deportment of their Cholulan hosts underwent a visible alteration. They did not visit the quarters as before and, when invited to do so, excused themselves on pretence of illness. The supply of provisions was stinted, on the ground that they were short of maize. These symptoms of alienation, independently of temporary embarrassment, caused serious alarm in the breast of Cortes for the future. His apprehensions were not allayed by the reports of the Cempoallans, who told him that in wandering round the city they had seen several streets barricaded, the *azoteas,* or flat roofs of the houses, loaded with huge stones and other missiles, as if preparatory to an assault, and in some places they had found holes covered over with branches, and upright stakes planted within, as if to embarrass the movements of the cavalry. Some Tlascalans coming in, also, from their camp informed the general that a great sacrifice, mostly of children, had been offered up in a distant quarter of the town to propitiate the favor of the gods, apparently for some intended enterprise. They added that they had seen numbers of the citizens leaving the city with their women and children, as if to remove them to a place of safety. These tidings confirmed the worst suspicions of Cortes, who had no doubt that some hostile scheme was in agitation. If he had felt any, a discovery by Marina,[2] the good angel of the expedition, would have turned these doubts into certainty.

The amiable manners of the Indian girl had won her the regard of the wife of one of the caciques, who repeatedly urged Marina to visit her house, darkly intimating that in this way she would escape the fate that awaited the Spaniards. The interpreter, seeing the importance of obtaining further intelligence at once, pretended to be pleased with the proposal and affected, at the same time, great discontent with the white men, by whom she was detained in captivity. Thus throwing the credulous Cholulan off her guard, Marina gradually insinuated herself into her confidence so far as to draw from her a full account of the conspiracy.

[2] An Indian girl given to Cortes as a slave in Tabasco on his first arrival in Yucatan. She became an interpreter for him and bore him a son.

It originated, she said, with the Aztec emperor, who had sent rich bribes to the great caciques, and to her husband among others, to secure them in his views. The Spaniards were to be assaulted as they marched out of the capital, when entangled in its streets, in which numerous impediments had been placed to throw the cavalry into disorder. A force of twenty thousand Mexicans was already quartered at no great distance from the city, to support the Cholulans in the assault. It was confidently expected that the Spaniards, thus embarrassed in their movements, would fall an easy prey to the superior strength of their enemy. A sufficient number of prisoners was to be reserved to grace the sacrifices of Cholula; the rest were to be led in fetters to the capital of Montezuma.

While this conversation was going on, Marina occupied herself with putting up such articles of value and wearing apparel as she proposed to take with her in the evening, when she could escape unnoticed from the Spanish quarters to the house of her Cholulan friend, who assisted her in the operation. Leaving her visitor thus employed, Marina found an opportunity to steal away for a few moments and, going to the general's apartment, disclosed to him her discoveries. He immediately caused the cacique's wife to be seized, and on examination she fully confirmed the statement of his Indian mistress.

The intelligence thus gathered by Cortes filled him with the deepest alarm. He was fairly taken in the snare. To fight or to fly seemed equally difficult. He was in a city of enemies, where every house might be converted into a fortress, and where such embarrassments were thrown in the way as might render the maneuvers of his artillery and horse nearly impracticable. In addition to the wily Cholulans, he must cope, under all these disadvantages, with the redoubtable warriors of Mexico. He was like a traveller who has lost his way in the darkness among precipices, where any step may dash him to pieces and where to retreat or to advance is equally perilous.

He was desirous to obtain still further confirmation and particulars of the conspiracy. He accordingly induced two of the priests in the neighborhood, one of them a person of much influence in the place, to visit his quarters. By courteous treatment and liberal largesses of the rich presents he had received from Montezuma—thus turning his own gifts against the giver—he drew from them a full confirmation of the previous report. The emperor had been in a state of pitiable vacillation since the arrival of the Spaniards. His first orders to the Cholulans were to receive the strangers kindly. He had recently consulted his oracles anew and obtained for answer that Cholula would be the grave of his enemies; for the gods would be sure to support him in avenging the sacrilege offered to the Holy City. So confident were the Aztecs of success that numerous manacles, or poles with thongs which served as such, were already in the place to secure the prisoners.

Cortes, now feeling himself fully possessed of the facts, dismissed the priests with injunctions of secrecy, scarcely necessary. He told them

it was his purpose to leave the city on the following morning and requested that they would induce some of the principal caciques to grant
him an interview in his quarters. He then summoned a council of his
officers, though, as it seems, already determined as to the course he was
to take.

The members of the council were differently affected by the startling
intelligence according to their different characters. The more timid, disheartened by the prospect of obstacles which seemed to multiply as they
drew nearer the Mexican capital, were for retracing their steps and
seeking shelter in the friendly city of Tlascala. Others, more persevering
but prudent, were for taking the more northerly route originally recommended by their allies. The greater part supported the general, who was
ever of opinion that they had no alternative but to advance. Retreat
would be ruin. Halfway measures were scarcely better and would infer a
timidity which must discredit them with both friend and foe. Their true
policy was to rely on themselves—to strike such a blow as should intimi-
date their enemies and show them that the Spaniards were as incapable
of being circumvented by artifice as of being crushed by weight of numbers and courage in the open field.

When the caciques, persuaded by the priests, appeared before Cortes,
he contented himself with gently rebuking their want of hospitality and
assured them the Spaniards would be no longer a burden to their city,
as he proposed to leave it early on the following morning. He requested,
moreover, that they would furnish a reinforcement of two thousand men
to transport his artillery and baggage. The chiefs, after some consultation, acquiesced in a demand which might in some measure favor their
own designs.

On their departure, the general summoned the Aztec ambassadors
before him. He briefly acquainted them with his detection of the treacherous plot to destroy his army, the contrivance of which, he said, was
imputed to their master, Montezuma. It grieved him much, he added, to
find the emperor implicated in so nefarious a scheme and that the Spaniards must now march as enemies against the prince whom they had
hoped to visit as a friend.

The ambassadors, with earnest protestations, asserted their entire
ignorance of the conspiracy and their belief that Montezuma was equally
innocent of a crime which they charged wholly on the Cholulans. It was
clearly the policy of Cortes to keep on good terms with the Indian
monarch, to profit as long as possible by his good offices and to avail
himself of his fancied security—such feelings of security as the general
could inspire him with—to cover his own future operations. He affected
to give credit, therefore, to the assertion of the envoys and declared his
unwillingness to believe that a monarch who had rendered the Spaniards
so many friendly offices would now consummate the whole by a deed
of such unparalleled baseness. The discovery of their twofold duplicity,
he added, sharpened his resentment against the Cholulans, on whom

he would take such vengeance as should amply requite the injuries done both to Montezuma and the Spaniards. He then dismissed the ambassadors, taking care, notwithstanding this show of confidence, to place a strong guard over them to prevent communication with the citizens.

That night was one of deep anxiety to the army. The ground they stood on seemed loosening beneath their feet, and any movement might be the one marked for their destruction. Their vigilant general took all possible precautions for their safety, increasing the number of the sentinels and posting his guns in such a manner as to protect the approaches to the camp. His eyes, it may well be believed, did not close during the night. Indeed every Spaniard lay down in his arms, and every horse stood saddled and bridled, ready for instant service. But no assault was meditated by the Indians, and the stillness of the hour was undisturbed except by the occasional sounds heard in a populous city, even when buried in slumber, and by the hoarse cries of the priests from the turrets of the *teocallis*,[3] proclaiming through their trumpets the watches of the night.

With the first streak of morning light, Cortes was seen on horseback, directing the movements of his little band. The strength of his forces he drew up in the great square or court, surrounded partly by buildings, as before noticed, and in part by a high wall. There were three gates of entrance, at each of which he placed a strong guard. The rest of his troops, with his great guns, he posted without the enclosure in such a manner as to command the avenues and secure those within from interruption in their bloody work. Orders had been sent the night before to the Tlascalan chiefs to hold themselves ready, at a concerted signal, to march into the city and join the Spaniards.

The arrangements were hardly completed before the Cholulan caciques appeared, leading a body of levies, *tamanes*, even more numerous than had been demanded. They were marched at once into the square commanded, as we have seen, by the Spanish infantry, which was drawn up under the walls. Cortes then took some of the caciques aside. With a stern air, he bluntly charged them with the conspiracy, showing that he was well acquainted with all the particulars. He had visited their city, he said, at the invitation of their emperor; had come as a friend; had respected the inhabitants and their property; and, to avoid all cause of umbrage, had left a great part of his forces without the walls. They had received him with a show of kindness and hospitality, and, reposing on this, he had been decoyed into the snare and found this kindness only a mask to cover the blackest perfidy.

The Cholulans were thunderstruck at the accusation. An undefined awe crept over them as they gazed on the mysterious strangers and felt themselves in the presence of beings who seemed to have the power of reading the thoughts scarcely formed in their bosoms. There was no use

---

3 Temples.

in prevarication or denial before such judges. They confessed the whole and endeavored to excuse themselves by throwing the blame on Montezuma. Cortes, assuming an air of higher indignation at this, assured them that the pretence should not serve, since, even if well founded, it would be no justification; and he would now make such an example of them for their treachery that the report of it should ring throughout the wide borders of Anahuac![4]

The fatal signal, the discharge of an arquebuse, was then given. In an instant every musket and crossbow was levelled at the unfortunate Cholulans in the court-yard, and a frightful volley poured into them as they stood crowded together like a herd of deer in the center. They were taken by surprise, for they had not heard the preceding dialogue with the chiefs. They made scarcely any resistance to the Spaniards, who followed up the discharge of their pieces by rushing on them with their swords; and, as the half-naked bodies of the natives afforded no protection, they hewed them down with as much ease as the reaper mows down the ripe corn in harvest time. Some endeavored to scale the walls, but only afforded a surer mark to the arquebusiers and archers. Others threw themselves into the gateways, but were received on the long pikes of the soldiers who guarded them. Some few had better luck in hiding themselves under the heaps of slain with which the ground was soon loaded.

While this work of death was going on, the countrymen of the slaughtered Indians, drawn together by the noise of the massacre, had commenced a furious assault on the Spaniards from without. But Cortes had placed his battery of heavy guns in a position that commanded the avenues, and swept off the files of the assailants as they rushed on. In the intervals between the discharges, which, in the imperfect state of the science in that day, were much longer than in ours, he forced back the press by charging with the horse into the midst. The steeds, the guns, the weapons of the Spaniards were all new to the Cholulans. Notwithstanding the novelty of the terrific spectacle, the flash of fire-arms mingling with the deafening roar of the artillery as its thunders reverberated among the buildings, the despairing Indians pushed on to take the places of their fallen comrades.

While this fierce struggle was going forward, the Tlascalans, hearing the concerted signal, had advanced with quick pace into the city. They had bound, by order of Cortes, wreaths of sedge round their heads that they might the more surely be distinguished from the Cholulans. Coming up in the very heat of the engagement, they fell on the defenceless rear of the townsmen, who, trampled down under the heels of the Castilian cavalry on one side and galled by their vindictive enemies on the other, could no longer maintain their ground. They gave way, some taking refuge in the nearest buildings, which, being partly of wood, were

[4] *Anahuac* means "near the water."

speedily set on fire. Others fled to the temples. One strong party, with a number of priests at its head, got possession of the great *teocalli*. There was a vulgar tradition, already alluded to, that, on removal of part of the walls, the god would send forth an inundation to overwhelm his enemies. The superstitious Cholulans with great difficulty succeeded in wrenching away some of the stones in the walls of the edifice. But dust, not water, followed. Their false gods deserted them in the hour of need. In despair they flung themselves into the wooden turrets that crowned the temple, and poured down stones, javelins, and burning arrows on the Spaniards as they climbed the great staircase, which, by a flight of one hundred and twenty steps, scaled the face of the pyramid. But the fiery shower fell harmless on the steel bonnets of the Christians, while they availed themselves of the burning shafts to set fire to the wooden citadel, which was speedily wrapt in flames. Still the garrison held out, and though quarter, it is said, was offered, only one Cholulan availed himself of it. The rest threw themselves headlong from the parapet or perished miserably in the flames.

All was now confusion and uproar in the fair city which had so lately reposed in security and peace. The groans of the dying, the frantic supplications of the vanquished for mercy were mingled with the loud battle-cries of the Spaniards as they rode down their enemy, and with the shrill whistle of the Tlascalans, who gave full scope to the long-cherished rancor of ancient rivalry. The tumult was still further swelled by the incessant rattle of musketry and the crash of falling timbers, which sent up a volume of flame that outshone the ruddy light of morning, making altogether a hideous confusion of sights and sounds that converted the Holy City into a pandemonium. As resistance slackened, the victors broke into the houses and sacred places, plundering them of whatever valuables they contained, plate, jewels, which were found in some quantity, wearing-apparel and provisions, the two last coveted even more than the former by the simple Tlascalans, thus facilitating a division of the spoil, much to the satisfaction of their Christian confederates. Amidst this universal license, it is worthy of remark, the commands of Cortes were so far respected that no violence was offered to women or children, though these, as well as numbers of the men, were made prisoners, to be swept into slavery by the Tlascalans. These scenes of violence had lasted some hours, when Cortes, moved by the entreaties of some Cholulan chiefs who had been reserved from the massacre, backed by the prayers of the Mexican envoys, consented, out of regard, as he said, to the latter, the representatives of Montezuma, to call off the soldiers and put a stop, as well as he could, to further outrage. Two of the caciques were also permitted to go to their countrymen with assurances of pardon and protection to all who would return to their obedience.

These measures had their effect. By the joint efforts of Cortes and the caciques, the tumult was with much difficulty appeased. The assailants, Spaniards and Indians, gathered under their respective banners, and the Cholulans, relying on the assurance of their chiefs, gradually returned to their homes.

The first act of Cortes was to prevail on the Tlascalan chiefs to liberate their captives. Such was their deference to the Spanish commander that they acquiesced, though not without murmurs, contenting themselves, as they best could, with the rich spoil rifled from the Cholulans, consisting of various luxuries long since unknown in Tlascala. His next care was to cleanse the city from its loathsome impurities, particularly from the dead bodies which lay festering in heaps in the streets and great square. The general, in his letter to Charles the Fifth, admits three thousand slain; most accounts say six, and some swell the amount yet higher. As the eldest and principal cacique was among the number, Cortes assisted the Cholulans in installing a successor in his place. By these pacific measures, confidence was gradually restored. The people in the environs, reassured, flocked into the capital to supply the place of the diminished population. The markets were again opened, and the usual avocations of an orderly, industrious community were resumed. Still, the long piles of black and smoldering ruins proclaimed the hurricane which had so lately swept over the city, and the walls surrounding the scene of slaughter in the great square, which were standing more than fifty years after the event, told the sad tale of the Massacre of Cholula.

This passage in their history is one of those that have left a dark stain on the memory of the Conquerors. Nor can we contemplate at this day, without a shudder, the condition of this fair and flourishing capital thus invaded in its privacy and delivered over to the excesses of a rude and ruthless soldiery. But, to judge the action fairly, we must transport ourselves to the age when it happened. The difficulty that meets us in the outset is to find a justification of the right of conquest at all. But it should be remembered that religious infidelity, at this period, and till much later, was regarded—no matter whether founded on ignorance or education, whether hereditary or acquired, heretical or pagan—as a sin to be punished with fire and fagot in this world and eternal suffering in the next. This doctrine, monstrous at it is, was the creed of the Romish, in other words, of the Christian Church—the basis of the Inquisition and of those other species of religious persecutions which have stained the annals, at some time or other, of nearly every nation in Christendom. Under this code, the territory of the heathen, wherever found, was regarded as a sort of religious waif, which, in default of a legal proprietor, was claimed and taken possession of by the Holy See, and as such was freely given away by the head of the church to any temporal potentate whom he pleased that would assume the burden of conquest. Thus, Alexander the Sixth generously granted a large portion of the Western Hemisphere to the Spaniards, and of the Eastern to the Portuguese. These lofty pretensions of the successors of the humble fisherman of Galilee, far from being nominal, were acknowledged and appealed to as conclusive in controversies between nations.

   With the right of conquest thus conferred, came also the obligation, on which it may be said to have been founded, to retrieve the nations sitting in darkness from eternal perdition. This obligation was acknowledged by the best and the bravest, the gownsman in his closet, the missionary, and the warrior in the crusade. However much it may have been debased by temporal motives and mixed up with worldly considerations of ambition and avarice, it was still active in the mind of the Christian conqueror. We have seen how far paramount it was to every calculation of personal interest in the breast of Cortes. The concession of the pope then, founded on and enforcing the imperative duty of conversion, was the assumed basis—and, in the apprehension of that age, a sound one—of the right of conquest.

   The right could not, indeed, be construed to authorize any unnecessary act of violence to the natives. The present expedition, up to the period of its history at which we are now arrived, had probably been stained with fewer of such acts than almost any similar enterprise of the Spanish discoverers in the New World. Throughout the campaign, Cortes had prohibited all wanton injuries to the natives in person or property and had punished the perpetrators of them with exemplary severity. He had been faithful to his friends and, with perhaps a single exception, not unmerciful to his foes. Whether from policy or principle, it should be recorded to his credit; though, like every sagacious mind, he may have felt that principle and policy go together.

   He had entered Cholula as a friend, at the invitation of the Indian emperor, who had a real, if not avowed, control over the state. He had been received as a friend, with every demonstration of good will; when, without any offence of his own or his followers, he found they were to be the victims of an insidious plot, that they were standing on a mine which might be sprung at any moment and bury them all in its ruins. His safety, as he truly considered, left no alternative but to anticipate the blow of his enemies. Yet who can doubt that the punishment thus inflicted was excessive, that the same end might have been attained by directing the blow against the guilty chiefs, instead of letting it fall on the ignorant rabble, who but obeyed the commands of their masters? But when was it ever seen that fear, armed with power, was scrupulous in the exercise of it, or that the passions of a fierce soldiery, inflamed by conscious injuries, could be regulated in the moment of explosion?

   We shall, perhaps, pronounce more impartially on the conduct of the Conquerors if we compare it with that of our own contemporaries under somewhat similar circumstances. The atrocities of Cholula were not so bad as those inflicted on the descendants of these very Spaniards, in the late war of the Peninsula, by the most polished nations of our time; by the British at Badajoz, for example—at Taragona, and a hundred other places, by the French.[5] The wanton butchery, the ruin of

[5] Prescott refers here to the war of the British against the French in Portugal and Spain, 1808 to 1814.

property, and, above all, those outrages worse than death, from which the female part of the population were protected at Cholula, show a catalogue of enormities quite as black as those imputed to the Spaniards and without the same apology for resentment—with no apology indeed, but that afforded by a brave and patriotic resistance. The consideration of these events, which, from their familiarity, make little impression on our senses, should render us more lenient in our judgments of the past, showing, as they do, that man in a state of excitement, savage or civilized, is much the same in every age. It may teach us—it is one of the best lessons of history—that, since such are the inevitable evils of war, even among the most polished people, those who hold the destinies of nations in their hands, whether rulers or legislators, should submit to every sacrifice, save that of honor, before authorizing an appeal to arms. The extreme solicitude to avoid these calamities, by the aid of peaceful congresses and impartial mediation, is, on the whole, the strongest evidence, stronger than that afforded by the progress of science and art, of our boasted advance in civilization.

It is far from my intention to vindicate the cruel deeds of the old Conquerors. Let them lie heavy on their heads. They were an iron race, who perilled life and fortune in the cause; and, as they made little account of danger and suffering for themselves, they had little sympathy to spare for their unfortunate enemies. But, to judge them fairly, we must not do it by the lights of our own age. We must carry ourselves back to theirs and take the point of view afforded by the civilization of their time. Thus only can we arrive at impartial criticism in reviewing the generations that are past. We must extend to them the same justice which we shall have occasion to ask from posterity, when, by the light of a higher civilization, it surveys the dark or doubtful passages in our own history, which hardly arrest the eye of the contemporary.

But whatever be thought of this transaction in a moral view, as a stroke of policy it was unquestionable. The nations of Anahuac had beheld, with admiration mingled with awe, the little band of Christian warriors steadily advancing along the plateau in face of every obstacle, overturning army after army with as much ease, apparently, as the good ship throws off the angry billows from her bows; or rather like the lava, which, rolling from their own volcanoes, holds on its course unchecked by obstacles, rock, tree, or building, bearing them along or crushing and consuming them in its fiery path. The prowess of the Spaniards—"the white goods," as they were often called—made them to be thought invincible. But it was not till their arrival at Cholula that the natives learned how terrible was their vengeance; and they trembled!

None trembled more than the Aztec emperor on his throne among the mountains. He read in these events the dark characters traced by the finger of Destiny. He felt his empire melting away like a morning mist. He might well feel so. Some of the most important cities in the neighborhood of Cholula, intimidated by the fate of that capital, now sent their envoys to the Castilian camp, tendering their allegiance and propitiating the favor of the strangers by rich presents of gold and slaves. Montezuma, alarmed at these signs of defection, took counsel again of his impotent deities; but, although the altars smoked with fresh hecatombs of human victims, he obtained no cheering response. He determined, therefore, to send another embassy to the Spaniards, disavowing any participation in the conspiracy of Cholula.

FRANCIS PARKMAN (1823–1893)

The Parkmans were one of those old New England families, going back to Puritan times, who had risen to comfortable wealth through commerce and social prominence through the church. Young Francis Parkman was educated at Harvard, where he took a law degree and concluded that pretty girls and horses were "the 'first-ratest' things in nature." These amiable distractions notwithstanding, Parkman had already set upon the major project of his life, an extended history of the "Old French War" which would allow him to combine his literary ambitions with his love of the forest. Later the mature Parkman would remember that as a boy "his thoughts were always in the forests" and "possessed his waking and sleeping dreams, filling him with vague cravings impossible to satisfy." What had been a somewhat romantic passion in his boyhood was transformed, however, into an active intellectual interest when he studied at Harvard with the noted historian Jared Sparks, who communicated to Parkman his excitement over the subject of exploration.

After leaving Harvard Parkman was a dedicated traveler, first through the New England woods and Canada, and then, in 1846, through the old Northwest, where he explored the wild country and lived for a time with the Sioux Indians. "One season on the prairies," he wrote in a letter to his father, "will teach a man more than a half a dozen in the settlements. There is no place on earth where he is thrown more completely on his own resources." But this visit to the Western prairies almost cost Parkman his life, for he suffered from eye troubles caused by the glare of the sun and dysentery caused by a poor diet. Only through enormous exertions of his will did he manage to complete his journey.

In 1849 Parkman published his classic Oregon Trail, *one of the first books to celebrate the saga of American exploration. Two years later came his first historical work,* History of the Conspiracy of Pontiac, *an account of the struggles between France and England in the New World—the theme that would dominate his remaining historical writings.*

As a result of his Western travels, Parkman was reduced to a state of semi-invalidism, a peculiarly galling fate for a man as dedicated as he to the creed of manliness and activism. In 1858, some eight years after his marriage, he was further stricken by the death of his wife, and he now entered a stage, recurrent through his life, of depression and sickness. It has been suggested by recent students of Parkman's life that he suffered from hypochondria and a neurotic need, carried out at great physical and psychic cost, to play the role of the vigorous man. Modelling himself on William Prescott, the somewhat older Boston historian whom he admired, Parkman nevertheless completed a series of historical volumes on the period in American colonial history dominated by the imperial rivalries between England and France.

Though enchanted with the forest, Parkman did not share in either the romanticism about nature or the idealization of "coonskin democracy" which was popular in his day. Like the scion of the Federalists that he was, he believed in the need for an aristocracy of selflessness and intelligence which would keep democratic societies from falling into mediocrity or worse.

Parkman's work as historian and writer is discussed in the introduction to this section.

FURTHER READING

Otis Pease, *Parkman's History: The Historian as Literary Artist* (1953); David Levin, *History as Romantic Art* (1959).

FROM **Montcalm and Wolfe** (1899)[1]

Ticonderoga

The peninsula of Ticonderoga consists of a rocky plateau, with low grounds on each side, bordering Lake Champlain on the one hand, and the outlet of Lake George on the other. The fort stood near the end of the peninsula, which points towards the southeast. Thence, as one goes westward, the ground declines a little, and then slowly rises, till, about half a mile from the fort, it reaches its greatest elevation, and begins still more gradually to decline again. Thus a ridge is formed across the

[1] This historical volume covers the struggle between England and France that is commonly known to us as the French and Indian War. Louis Joseph de Montcalm (1712–1759) was the commander of the French forces, and James Wolfe (1727–1759) was the commander of the British.

plateau between the steep declivities that sink to the low grounds on right and left. Some weeks before, a French officer named Hugues had suggested the defence of this ridge by means of an abattis. Montcalm approved his plan; and now, at the eleventh hour, he resolved to make his stand here. The two engineers, Pontleroy and Desandrouin, had already traced the outline of the works, and the soldiers of the battalion of Berry had made some progress in constructing them. At dawn of the seventh, while Abercromby, fortunately for his enemy, was drawing his troops back to the landing-place, the whole French army fell to their task. The regimental colors were planted along the line, and the officers, stripped to the shirt, took axe in hand and labored with their men. The trees that covered the ground were hewn down by thousands, the tops lopped off, and the trunks piled one upon another to form a massive breastwork. The line followed the top of the ridge, along which it zig-zagged in such a manner that the whole front could be swept by flank-fires of musketry and grape. Abercromby describes the wall of logs as between eight and nine feet high; in which case there must have been a rude *banquette*, or platform to fire from, on the inner side. It was certainly so high that nothing could be seen over it but the crowns of the soldiers' hats. The upper tier was formed of single logs, in which notches were cut to serve as loopholes; and in some places sods and bags of sand were piled along the top, with narrow spaces to fire through. From the central part of the line the ground sloped away like a natural glacis; while at the sides, and especially on the left, it was undulating and broken. Over this whole space, to the distance of a musket-shot from the works, the forest was cut down, and the trees left lying where they fell among the stumps, with tops turned outwards, forming one vast abattis, which, as a Massachusetts officer says, looked like a forest laid flat by a hurricane. But the most formidable obstruction was immediately along the front of the breastwork, where the ground was covered with heavy boughs, overlapping and interlaced, with sharpened points bristling into the face of the assailant like the quills of a porcupine. As these works were all of wood, no vestige of them remains. The earthworks now shown to tourists as the lines of Montcalm are of later construction; and though on the same ground, are not on the same plan.

Here, then, was a position which, if attacked in front with musketry alone, might be called impregnable. But would Abercromby so attack it? He had several alternatives. He might attempt the flank and rear of his enemy by way of the low grounds on the right and left of the plateau, a movement which the precautions of Montcalm had made difficult, but not impossible. Or, instead of leaving his artillery idle on the strand of Lake George, he might bring it to the front and batter the breastwork, which, though impervious to musketry, was worthless against heavy cannon. Or he might do what Burgoyne did with success a score of years later, and plant a battery on the heights of Rattlesnake Hill, now called Mount Defiance, which commanded the position of the French, and whence the inside of their breastwork could be scoured with round-shot from end to end. Or, while threatening the French front with a part of his army, he could march the rest a short distance through the woods on his left to the road which led from Ticonderoga to Crown Point, and which would soon have brought him to the place called Five-Mile Point, where Lake Champlain narrows to the width of an easy rifle-shot, and where a battery of field-pieces would have cut off all Montcalm's supplies and closed his only way of retreat. As the French were provisioned for but eight days, their position would thus have been desperate. They plainly saw the danger; and Doreil declares that had the movement been made, their whole army must have surrendered. Montcalm had done what he could; but the danger of his position was inevitable and extreme. His hope lay in Abercromby; and it was a hope well founded. The action of the English general answered the utmost wishes of his enemy.

Abercromby had been told by his prisoners that Montcalm had six thousand men, and that three thousand more were expected every hour. Therefore he was in haste at attack before these succors could arrive. As was the general, so was the army. "I believe," writes an officer, "we were one and all infatuated by a notion of carrying every obstacle by a mere *coup de mousqueterie.*" Leadership perished with Lord Howe, and nothing was left but blind, headlong valor.

Clerk, chief engineer, was sent to reconnoitre the French works from Mount Defiance; and came back with the report that, to judge from what he could see, they might be carried by assault. Then, without waiting to bring up his cannon, Abercromby prepared to storm the lines.

The French finished their breastwork and abattis on the evening of the seventh, encamped behind them, slung their kettles, and rested after their heavy toil. Lévis had not yet appeared; but at twilight one of his officers, Captain Pouchot, arrived with three hundred regulars, and announced that his commander would come before morning with a hundred more. The reinforcement, though small, was welcome, and Lévis was a host in himself. Pouchot was told that the army was half a mile off. Thither he repaired, made his report to Montcalm, and looked with amazement at the prodigious amount of work accomplished in one day. Lévis himself arrived in the course of the night, and approved the arrangement of the troops. They lay behind their lines till daybreak; then the drums beat, and they formed in order of battle. The battalions of La Sarre and Languedoc were posted on the left, under Bourlamaque, the first battalion of Berry with that of Royal Roussillon in the centre, under Montcalm, and those of La Reine, Béarn, and Guienne on the right, under Lévis. A detachment of volunteers occupied the low grounds between the breastwork and the outlet of Lake George; while, at the foot of the declivity on the side towards Lake Champlain, were stationed four hundred and fifty colony regulars and Canadians, behind an abattis which they had made for themselves; and as they were covered by the cannon of the fort, there was some hope that they would check any flank movement which the English might attempt on that side. Their posts being thus assigned, the men fell to work again to strengthen their defences. Including those who came with Lévis, the total force of effective soldiers was now thirty-six hundred.

Soon after nine o'clock a distant and harmless fire of small-arms began on the slopes of Mount Defiance. It came from a party of Indians who had just arrived with Sir William Johnson, and who, after amusing themselves in this manner for a time, remained for the rest of the day safe spectators of the fight. The soldiers worked undisturbed till noon, when volleys of musketry were heard from the forest in front. It was the English light troops driving in the French pickets. A cannon was fired as a signal to drop tools and form for battle. The white uniforms lined the breastwork in a triple row, with the grenadiers behind them as a reserve, and the second battalion of Berry watching the flanks and rear.

Meanwhile the English army had moved forward from its camp by the saw-mill. First came the rangers, the light infantry, and Bradstreet's armed boatmen, who, emerging into the open space, began a spattering fire. Some of the provincial troops followed, extending from left to right, and opening fire in turn; then the regulars, who had formed in columns of attack under cover of the forest, advanced their solid red masses into the sunlight, and passing through the intervals between the provincial regiments, pushed forward to the assault. Across the rough ground, with its maze of fallen trees whose leaves hung withering in the July sun, they could see the top of the breastwork, but not the men behind it; when, in an instant, all the line was obscured by a gush of smoke, a crash of exploding firearms tore the air, and grapeshot and musket-balls swept the whole space like a tempest; "a damnable fire," says an officer who heard them screaming about his ears. The English had been ordered to carry the works with the bayonet; but their ranks were broken by the obstructions through which they struggled in vain to force their way, and they soon began to fire in turn. The storm raged in full fury for an hour. The assailants pushed close to the breastwork; but there they were stopped by the bristling mass of sharpened branches, which they could not pass under the murderous cross-fires that swept them from front and flank. At length they fell back, exclaiming that the works were impregnable. Abercromby, who was at the saw-mill, a mile and a half in the rear, sent order to attack again, and again they came on as before.

The scene was frightful: masses of infuriated men who could not go forward and would not go back; straining for an enemy they could not reach, and firing on an enemy they could not see; caught in the entanglement of fallen trees; tripped by briers, stumbling over logs, tearing through boughs; shouting, yelling, cursing, and pelted all the while with bullets that killed them by scores, stretched them on the ground, or hung them on jagged branches in strange attitudes of death. The provincials supported the regulars with spirit, and some of them forced their way to the foot of the wooden wall.

The French fought with the intrepid gayety of their nation, and shouts of *Vive le Roi!* and *Vive notre Général!* mingled with the din of musketry. Montcalm, with his coat off, for the day was hot, directed the defence of the centre, and repaired to any part of the line where the danger for the time seemed greatest. He is warm in praise of his enemy, and declares that between one and seven o'clock they attacked him six successive times. Early in the action Abercromby tried to turn the French left by sending twenty bateaux, filled with troops, down the outlet of Lake George. They were met by the fire of the volunteers stationed to defend the low grounds on that side, and, still advancing, came within range of the cannon of the fort, which sank two of them and drove back the rest. . . .

Toward five o'clock two English columns joined in a most determined assault on the extreme right of the French, defended by the battalions of Guienne and Béarn. The danger for a time was imminent. Montcalm hastened to the spot with the reserves. The assailants hewed their way to the foot of the breastwork; and though again and again repulsed, they again and again renewed the attack. The Highlanders fought with stubborn and unconquerable fury. "Even those who were mortally wounded," writes one of their lieutenants, "cried to their companions not to lose a thought upon them, but to follow their officers and mind the honor of their country. Their ardor was such that it was difficult to bring them off." Their major, Campbell of Inverawe, found his foreboding true. He received a mortal shot, and his clansmen bore him from the field. Twenty-five of their officers were killed or wounded, and half the men fell under the deadly fire that poured from the loopholes. Captain John Campbell and a few followers tore their way through the abattis, climbed the breastwork, leaped down among the French, and were bayoneted there.

As the colony troops and Canadians on the low ground were left undisturbed, Lévis sent them an order to make a sortie and attack the left flank of the charging columns. They accordingly posted themselves among the trees along the declivity, and fired upwards at the enemy, who presently shifted their position to the right, out of the line of shot. The assault still continued, but in vain; and at six there was another effort, equally fruitless. From this time till half-past seven a lingering fight was kept up by the rangers and other provincials, firing from the edge of the woods and from behind the stumps, bushes, and fallen trees in front of the lines. Its only objects were to cover their comrades, who were collecting and bringing off the wounded, and to protect the retreat of the regulars, who fell back in disorder to the Falls. As twilight came on, the last combatant withdrew, and none were left but the dead. Abercromby had lost in killed, wounded, and missing, nineteen hundred and forty-four officers and men. The loss of the French, not counting that of Langy's detachment, was three hundred and seventy-seven. Bourlamaque was dangerously wounded; Bouganville slightly; and the hat of Lévis was twice shot through.

Montcalm, with a mighty load lifted from his soul, passed along the lines, and gave the tired soldiers the thanks they nobly deserved. Beer, wine, and food were served out to them, and they bivouacked for the night on the level ground between the breastwork and the fort. The enemy had met a terrible rebuff; yet the danger was not over. Abercromby still had more than thirteen thousand men, and he might renew the attack with cannon. But, on the morning of the ninth, a band of volunteers who had gone out to watch him brought back the report that he was in full retreat. The saw-mill at the Falls was on fire, and the last English soldier was gone. On the morning of the tenth, Lévis, with a strong detachment, followed the road to the landing-place, and found signs that a panic had overtaken the defeated troops. They had left behind several hundred barrels of provisions and a large quantity of baggage; while in a marshy place that they had crossed was found a considerable number of their shoes, which had stuck in the mud, and which they had not stopped to recover. They had embarked on the morning after the battle, and retreated to the head of the lake in a disorder and dejection woefully contrasted with the pomp of their advance. A gallant army was sacrificed by the blunders of its chief.

With the Peace of Paris ended the checkered story of New France; a story which would have been a history if faults of constitution and the bigotry and folly of rulers had not dwarfed it to an episode. Yet it is a noteworthy one in both its lights and its shadows; in the disinterested zeal of the founder of Quebec, the self-devotion of the early missionary martyrs, and the daring enterprise of explorers; in the spiritual and temporal vassalage from which the only escape was to the savagery of the wilderness; and in the swarming corruptions which were the natural result of an attempt to rule, by the absolute hand of a master beyond the Atlantic, a people bereft of every vestige of civil liberty. Civil liberty was given them by the British sword; but the conqueror left their religious system untouched, and through it they have imposed upon themselves a weight of ecclesiastical tutelage that finds few equals in the most Catholic countries of Europe. Such guardianship is not without certain advantages. When faithfully exercised it aids to uphold some of the tamer virtues, if that can be called a virtue which needs the constant presence of a sentinel to keep it from escaping: but it is fatal to mental robustness and moral courage; and if French Canada would fulfil its aspirations it must cease to be one of the most priest-ridden communities of the modern world.

Scarcely were they free from the incubus of France when the British provinces showed symptoms of revolt. The measures on the part of the mother-country which roused their resentment, far from being oppressive, were less burdensome than the navigation laws to which they had long submitted; and they resisted taxation by Parliament simply because it was in principle opposed to their rights as freemen. They did not, like the American provinces of Spain at a later day, sunder themselves from a parent fallen into decrepitude; but with astonishing audacity they affronted the wrath of England in the hour of her triumph, forgot their jealousies and quarrels, joined hands in the common cause, fought, endured, and won. The disunited colonies became the United States. The string of discordant communities along the Atlantic coast has grown to a mighty people, joined in a union which the earthquake of civil war served only to compact and consolidate. Those who in the weakness of their dissensions needed help from England against the savage on their borders have become a nation that may defy every foe but that most dangerous of all foes, herself, destined to a majestic future if she will shun the excess and perversion of the principles that made her great, prate less about the enemies of the past and strive more against the enemies of the present, resist the mob and the demagogue as she resisted Parliament and King, rally her powers from the race for gold and the delirium of prosperity to make firm the foundations on which that prosperity rests, and turn some fair proportion of her vast mental forces to other objects than material progress and the game of party politics. She has tamed the savage continent, peopled the solitude, gathered wealth untold, waxed potent, imposing, redoubtable; and now it remains for her to prove, if she can, that the rule of the masses is consistent with the highest growth of the individual; that democracy can give the world a civilization as mature and pregnant, ideas as energetic and vitalizing, and types of manhood as lofty and strong, as any of the systems which it boasts to supplant.

HENRY ADAMS (1838–1918)

As a young man Henry Adams dreamed of "a national set of young men like ourselves or better, to start new influences not only in politics, but in literature, in law, in society, and throughout the whole social organization of the country—a national school of our own generation." In part he was expressing here that ideal of disinterested public service which had inspired the best of the Bostonians during the nineteenth century and had found its most brilliant embodiment in the history of his own family. Adams's great-grandfather, John, had been a founding father of the republic and second President of the United States; his grandfather, John Quincy, had also been a President of the United States; his father, Charles Francis, had served in the crucial post of United States Ambassador to England during the Civil War; and other relatives had occupied prominent places in the government of their country. Henry Adams thus grew up in a milieu where public office, public power, and public influence were taken for granted. If one can speak of an American aristocracy or patriciate resting upon wealth and cultivation, patriotism and intelligence, then the Adams family stood at its very center.

Yet together with this tradition the family shared in the experience of another, one that began with the defeat of grandfather John Quincy Adams by Andrew Jackson in 1828. This second tradition, still a minor one, was that of responding to the growing democratization and urbanization of American society by an act of withdrawal, sometimes hard to distinguish from Brahmin snobbishness but always founded in the Adams's sense of moral principle. With the years, it would prove to be the special fate of Henry Adams that he would be the most extreme representative of this impulse to withdraw.

As a boy Henry Adams had been reared in the most simulating and cultivated of circumstances. A brilliant student at Harvard, already displaying his formidable powers for assimilating quantities of knowledge, he began, after his graduation in 1858, a career as both world traveler and world scholar, continuing his researches in Germany, Switzerland, France, and Italy. He also began to write regularly for leading American periodicals, though in a letter to his brother Charles he growled in a style that anticipates his later attitudes: "I will not go down into the rough-and-tumble, nor mix with the crowd, nor write anonymously. . . . You like the strife of the world. I detest and despise it. . . . You like roughness and strength; I like taste and dexterity."

After a number of his muckraking pieces made advancement under the Grant administration seem unlikely, Adams abandoned journalism and became a professor of history at Harvard. He was, by all accounts, a superb teacher, employing a version of the Socratic method in his lectures and training his students to use original documents in his seminars. Meanwhile, in 1872, he had married Marian Hooper, an attractive and intelligent woman, and when the Adams's moved to Washington in 1877, their house became a center of social and intellectual life.

It is roughly at this point that his major achievements as historian and writer begin. There were two novels, Democracy *(1880), a biting if somewhat thin depiction of jungle politics in Washington, and* Esther *(1884), a sensitive if also thin depiction of intellectual and private life among cultivated Americans. In 1879 Adams had published a distinguished biography of Albert Gallatin, Jefferson's Secretary of the Treasury, whom Adams saw as a prototype of the selfless and high-minded public servant undone by the degradation of democratic society. And in 1882 he issued a life of John Randolph, whom Adams saw as the prototype of the selfless and high-minded public servant undone by weaknesses of character. Adams grew increasingly dubious about the democratic experiment which his own family had done so much to promote: he wrote a friend in 1885*

*that he was "struck by the remarkable way in which politics dete-
riorates the moral tone of everyone who mixes in them."*

Adams's greatest historical work, a masterpiece of its kind, is the History of the United States of America during the Administrations of
Jefferson and Madison *(1889 to 1891), which brought him fame and
approval. It is a work in which his emotions are deeply committed,
since it deals with a period of our national history he most admired
and felt not yet fatally corrupted; it is a work, as well, in which he
develops on a full scale his talents for narrative excitement and
character portraiture, without, however, imposing those insistently
pessimistic theories that would later shape—and as some critics
believe, misshape—his views of history.*

*Despite these enormous achievements and the acclaim they brought
him, Adams felt, or kept publicly saying that he felt, more and more
a stranger in his native land. He denied himself the pleasures of
success, he withdrew from the applause of all but a tiny circle of
cultivated friends. In 1885 his wife took her life, and this catastro-
phe shattered him emotionally, persuading him that he was a failure
not only publicly but privately. Adams became a wanderer across
the continents, a man of great intellectual power and personal force
but without social or national roots. Traveling in Europe, he found
himself increasingly drawn to the medieval period, in which he saw
a harmony and comeliness of life, above all a unity of values and
belief, that was sadly absent from all subsequent centuries. In 1904
he published* Mont-Saint-Michel and Chartres, *an historical* tour de
force *in which he painted a glowing picture of the way medieval
man, through his worship of the Virgin Mary, achieved a moral and
psychic integration containing "the highest idea of himself as a
unit in a unified universe." Since that high point of civilization,
roughly in the eleventh century, the life of Western man had
crumbled—Adams thought—into chaos, uncertainty, disbelief, and
multiplicity: man no longer knew who he was, why he lived, nor
what impulsions led him to act. The great myth of the Virgin had
been replaced by the lifeless energy of the Dynamo.*

*With this sense of a catastrophic relativization of values, Adams was to
live for the rest of his life. The actuality of his experience, as a spry
and greatly honored intellectual figure, was not nearly so grim as
he would make it out; there was in Adams a tendency to self-
dramatization that cannot always be distinguished from self-pity.
But that he agonized over his predicament is not to be denied, even
if seen as the predicament of a cultural persona at least as much
as that of an actual person: this son of the Boston great who felt
repelled by American public life, this intellectual who grew increasingly alienated from the course of history, this amateur philosopher*

who could find no moral purpose or meaning in the universe and now concluded that there was a steady running-down of energies in human affairs that soon would lead to an atomic apocalypse.

In 1907 Adams privately printed his autobiography, The Education of Henry Adams, *in its way as remarkable a book as his* History. *The* Education, *which was not made available to the general public until his death in 1918, is a classical record of the self-torment—but also, it should be noticed, the self-mockery—of a romantic sensibility. Writing about himself in the third person, Adams tries to see himself not only as a cultural prototype but also as a slightly preposterous fellow: the mixture of self-importance and self-deprecation is fluid, changing from section to section, and not always easy to measure precisely.*

The earliest and best parts of the Education *deal with Adams's childhood in Quincy, Massachusetts, and these pages offer an incomparable evocation of life in early republican America, at least that life as it was experienced by the New England patriciate. Adams's years as secretary to his father when the latter was Ambassador to England during the Civil War are treated caustically. And the sections on the Grant administration and the Chicago Exposition, each crucial to the transformation of American civilization that Adams meant indirectly to portray in his autobiography, are fine examples of Adams's abilities as social satirist and historical analyst. Throughout the* Education *there are passages of reflection, sometimes introspection, in which Adams assays his own role as representative intellectual, a figure of failure and futility, unable to affect the course of events. Perhaps the dominant social motif in the book is Adams's profound disillusionment with the United States in the years after the Civil War. The hopes that had once been held for a Jeffersonian democracy, preindustrial and without extreme differences in wealth and power, now lay shattered; and instead, as Adams saw it, the country had entered a degeneration symbolized by such names as Gould and Fisk, Vanderbilt and Rockefeller.*

Like many intellectuals to come after him, Adams also felt himself homeless on a larger, more "cosmic," scale. In a world deprived of God and the unifying dignities of religion, a world that science could measure and to some extent control but not make any the more intelligible or bearable, Adams wondered where men would now find the values by which to live—indeed, whether they would now care to look for them. Everything seemed to have crumbled into multiplicity and relativism; there were no objective criteria for judgment. Society was headed for an ice age of materialism, or a crackup of warfare. All that remained for men of conscience and perception was to keep a clear vision, to insist upon standards of

*excellence, to defend the lonely bulwarks of truth. It was a posture
at once heroic and peevish, and for many younger writers soured
by the betrayals of the First World War Adams naturally came to
seem a culture hero, a model of clear-sightedness in a false world.*

*Whatever one may feel about Adams's final views, there can hardly be
any doubt that in the* Education *he composed a book of the first
order. Gripping in its account of intellectual drama, rich with portraits of notable times and men, enormously complex in its circling
of the narrator's self, the book is one of the major texts in the history
of modern intellectual life.*

FURTHER READING

Ernest Samuels's *The Young Henry Adams* (1948) and his *Henry
Adams: The Middle Years* (1958) compose the first two volumes of
a three-volume standard biography; the last volume is in progress.
Four volumes of Adams's letters have been edited by Worthington
C. Ford (1920, 1930, 1938). J. C. Levenson's *The Mind and Art of
Henry Adams* (1957) is a good critical study.

To John Gorham Palfrey

London, 15th April, 1864

. . . Time rattles along so fast that this letter will scarcely reach you
before the third anniversary of our departure. We are settled here now
nearly as much at home as though we were in Boston, so far as familiarity with our surroundings go, and yet London never seems to me to
allow any homelike feelings. I never quit it even for an afternoon at
Richmond or a Sunday at Walton, without feeling a sort of shudder at
returning, to be struck as freshly as ever with the solemnity, the gloom,
the squalor and the horrible misery and degradation that seem to me to
brood over the place. The magnificence I know and can appreciate. It
has done its best to make me a socialist and has nearly succeeded. The
society I think dull, and the art and literature poor. So that you see I am
well suited to return to Boston unspoiled by my travels, a sadder and a
wiser man.

Our great event just now is the arrival of Garibaldi, and his reception. Of all curious events, this is the most extraordinary. You know
what Garibaldi is; the companion of Mazzini;[1] the representative of the
"cosmopolitan revolution"; a regular "child of Nature," unintellectual,

---

[1] Giusseppi Mazzini (1805–1872), Italian nationalist leader.

uncultivated; but enthusiastic and a genius. Every Government in
Europe dreads him, or rather his party, and he is the enemy of them
all and of none more, whether he will or no, than of England. Suddenly
he drops down here, and the people, the real "dangerous classes" go out
to meet him with such a reception as never was known before. It was a
regular uprising of democracy. But then to our delight, the young Duke
and Duchess of Sutherland get hold of him, and at once compromise
the whole English aristocracy, and give a hoist to the *rouges* and the
democracy throughout Europe, by bringing him to Stafford House and
making themselves co-conspirators with every refugee in England, to
murder Napoleon, destroy Victor Emmanuel, and proclaim equality and
division of property. I don't think I exaggerate the moral effect of this
affair on the minds of the democrats. I am a real Garibaldian, and
ready to accept, if necessary, his views, at the same time that I think
hero-worship, as such, is a precious dangerous thing to meddle with.
But here is the whole Clan Sutherland, with the young Duke dancing
about at its head, forcing Garibaldi down the throats of the English
nobility, who daren't openly say no, and who make the worst faces at
the process, you can conceive. A few nights since, Stafford House was
thrown open for a reception in honor of the General. By the way, what
a glorious palace it is. I would like to have such a one at Quincy. We
went; the only diplomats there except the Turk. Garibaldi was there;
quantum mutatus ab illo Garibaldio that I saw four years ago, surrounded by a yelling mob in Palermo, with a few hundred guerilla
troops, and not a nobleman among them. The beautiful young Duchess
had him by the arm; she glittering with *the* diamonds; he in a military,
loose poncho, or cape. The Duke pirouetted before, behind, and on either
side. The Duchess Dowager sailed majestically alongside, battling
fiercely for the honor of being chief-keeper, but kept silent by her splendid daughter-in-law. In a tangled and promiscuous medley followed the
Argylls, Tauntons, Howards, Blantyres, and every Leveson-Gower that
draws breath. They paraded through the apartments, as well as Garibaldi could limp along, and we poor lookers-on drew aside and formed
a passage for the procession triumphant to pass through. It was superb!
And yet almost the last great occasion that Stafford House was open,
was to allow this perfect nobility to do honor to Mrs. Beecher Stowe, and
both then and now the whole thing too strongly resembles a desperate
humbug for me to be much impressed by it. Sentimental liberalism is
pretty, but it won't hold. Garibaldi is pretty safe to suffer the fate of
Mrs. Stowe, and American anti-slavery, whenever he stands in need of
aristocratic aid. Meanwhile he sits at the feet of the beautiful Duchess
(and there he is indeed to be envied) and smokes his cigars in her
boudoir, and goes to bed immediately after dinner, and smokes in bed;
and has two shirts (the famous red flannel) and a light blue cape lined
with red (*rouge*, you see, always), which constitute his entire wardrobe.
And in short, I rather doubt whether the good hero yet quite knows

where he is, or has any clear idea of how it happens that he who has declared war to the knife against aristocracy and privilege everywhere, has become himself an aristocrat so suddenly. Meanwhile the non-Sutherland aristocracy growl fiercely, but are regularly over-sloughed by the popular wave, and we outsiders think it all as good a practical joke as ever was got up.

When shall we come home? After this season is over, we shall become very restless and if the war is over, as we strongly hope, we must leave here. I wonder whether Sumner wouldn't take the place. I suppose he might get it if he wanted it, on our departure. Then Gov. Andrew could replace him in the Senate, which would be an improvement. I hope to find you and yours, including Frank, well and prosperous at my return; and for my own part am ready to leave the Society of Courts to those that are courtiers, and rest awhile at the law-school in Cambridge or elsewhere. . . .

To Charles Francis Adams, Jr.

Friday, 21 May, 1869

. . . I see you are getting back to your old dispute with me on the purpose of life, by means of an attack on my self-esteem. You are quite right in the point you make. I do think too much about my own productions and myself generally. Stick to that and you may kick me all day long. I will not go down into the rough-and-tumble, nor mix with the crowd, nor write anonymously, except for mere literary practice. My path is a different one; and was never chosen in order to suit other people's tastes, but my own. Of course a man can't do this without appearing to think a great deal about himself, and perhaps doing so in fact. The very line he draws requires care to observe, and is invidious to everyone else. In America there is no such class, and the tendency is incessant to draw everyone into the main current. I have told you before that I mean to be unpopular, and do it because I must do it, or do as other people do and give up the path I chose for myself years ago. Your ideas and mine don't agree, but they never have agreed. You like the strife of the world. I detest it and despise it. You work for power. I work for my own satisfaction. You like roughness and strength; I like taste and dexterity. For God's sake, let us go our ways and not try to be like each other.

To William James

Beverly Farms, Mass., 27 July, 1882

I have read your two papers with that attention which, etc., etc., etc., and am partially prepared to discuss them with you. As I understand your Faith, your X, your reaction of the individual on the cosmos, it is the old question of Free Will over again. You *choose* to assume that the will is free. Good! Reason proves that the Will cannot be free. Equally good! Free or not, the mere fact that a doubt can exist, proves that X must be a very microscopic quantity. If the orthodox are grateful to you for such gifts, the world has indeed changed, and we have much to thank God for, if there is a God, that he should have left us unable to decide whether our thoughts, if we have thoughts, are our own or his'n.

Although your gift to the church seems to me a pretty darned mean one, I admire very much your manner of giving it, which magnifies the crumb into at least forty loaves and fishes. My wife is quite converted by it. She enjoyed the paper extremely. Since she read it she has talked of giving five dollars to Russell Sturgis's church for napkins. As the impression fades, she talks less of the napkins.

With hero-worship like Carlyle's, I have little patience. In history heroes have neutralysed each other, and the result is no more than would have been reached without them. Indeed in military heroes I suspect that the ultimate result has been retardation. Nevertheless you could doubtless at any time stop the entire progress of human thought by killing a few score of men. So far I am with you. A few hundred men represent the entire intellectual activity of the whole thirteen hundred millions. What then? They drag us up the cork-screw stair of thought, but they can no more get their brains to run out of their especial convolutions than a railway train (with a free will of half an inch on three thousand miles) can run free up Mount Shasta. Not one of them has ever got so far as to tell us a single fact worth knowing. We can't prove even that we are.

Meanwhile I enclose your letter to Monrod.

Pleasant voyage and happy return. Our love to Harry.

FROM *History of the United States of America during the Administration of Thomas Jefferson* (1889 to 1891)[1]

Volume 1, Chapter 6   American Ideals

Nearly every foreign traveller who visited the United States during these early years, carried away an impression sober if not sad. A thousand miles of desolate and dreary forest, broken here and there by settlements; along the sea-coast a few flourishing towns devoted to commerce; no arts, a provincial literature, a cancerous disease of negro slavery, and differences of political theory fortified within geographical lines—what could be hoped for such a country except to repeat the story of violence and brutality which the world already knew by heart, until repetition for thousands of years had wearied and sickened mankind? Ages must probably pass before the interior could be thoroughly settled; even Jefferson, usually a sanguine man, talked of a thousand years with acquiescence, and in his first Inaugural Address, at a time when the Mississippi River formed the Western boundary, spoke of the country as having "room enough for our descendants to the hundredth and thousandth generation." No prudent person dared to act on the certainty that when settled, one government could comprehend the whole; and when the day of separation should arrive, and America should have her Prussia, Austria, and Italy, as she already had her England, France, and Spain, what else could follow but a return to the old conditions of local jealousies, wars, and corruption which had made a slaughter-house of Europe?

The mass of Americans were sanguine and self-confident, partly by temperament, but partly also by reason of ignorance; for they knew little of the difficulties which surrounded a complex society. The Duc de Liancourt,[2] like many critics, was struck by this trait. Among other instances, he met with one in the person of a Pennsylvania miller, Thomas Lea, "a sound American patriot, persuading himself that nothing good is done, and that no one has any brains, except in America; that the wit, the imagination, the genius of Europe are already in decrepitude"; and the duke added: "This error is to be found in almost all Americans,—legislators, administrators, as well as millers, and is less innocent there." In the year 1796 the House of Representatives debated

---

[1] Adams's nine-volume work was published in the years between 1889 and 1891. In his great work Adams was one of the first American historians to attempt an historical work along "scientific" principles, though this chapter is actually an example of Adams's powers as a literary artist.

[2] Francois Alexandre Frédéric de la Rochefoucauld-Liancourt (1747–1827), a French royalist who, after the abolition of the monarch in 1792, spent some time in the United States.

whether to insert in the Reply to the President's Speech a passing remark that the nation was "the freest and most enlightened in the
world,"—a nation as yet in swaddling-clothes, which had neither literature, arts, sciences, nor history; nor even enough nationality to be sure
that it was a nation. The moment was peculiarly ill-chosen for such a
claim, because Europe was on the verge of an outburst of genius. Goethe
and Schiller, Mozart and Haydn, Kant and Fichte, Cavendish and
Herschel were making way for Walter Scott, Wordsworth, and Shelley,
Heine and Balzac, Beethoven and Hegel, Oersted and Cuvier, great
physicists, biologists, geologists, chemists, mathematicians, meta-
physicians, and historians by the score. Turner was painting his earliest
landscapes, and Watt completing his latest steam-engine; Napoleon was
taking command of the French armies, and Nelson of the English fleets;
investigators, reformers, scholars, and philosophers swarmed, and the
influence of enlightenment, even amid universal war, was working with
an energy such as the world had never before conceived. The idea that
Europe was in her decrepitude proved only ignorance and want of
enlightenment, if not of freedom, on the part of Americans, who could
only excuse their error by pleading that notwithstanding these objections, in matters which for the moment most concerned themselves
Europe was a full century behind America. If they were right in thinking that the next necessity of human progress was to lift the average
man upon an intellectual and social level with the most favored, they
stood at least three generations nearer than Europe to their common
goal. The destinies of the United States were certainly staked, without
reserve or escape, on the soundness of this doubtful and even improbable principle, ignoring or overthrowing the institutions of church,
aristocracy, family, army, and political intervention, which long experience had shown to be needed for the safety of society. Europe might be
right in thinking that without such safeguards society must come to an
end; but even Europeans must concede that there was a chance, if no
greater than one in a thousand, that America might, at least for a time,
succeed. If this stake of temporal and eternal welfare stood on the
winning card; if man actually should become more virtuous and enlightened, by mere process of growth, without church or paternal authority;
if the average human being could accustom himself to reason with the
logical processes of Descartes and Newton!—what then?

Then, no one could deny that the United States would win a stake
such as defied mathematics. With all the advantages of science and
capital, Europe must be slower than America to reach the common goal.
American society might be both sober and sad, but except for negro
slavery it was sound and healthy in every part, Stripped for the hardest
work, every muscle firm and elastic, every ounce of brain ready for use,
and not a trace of superfluous flesh on his nervous and supple body, the
American stood in the world a new order of man. From Maine to Florida,
society was in this respect the same, and was so organized as to use its
human forces with more economy than could be approached by any

society of the world elsewhere. Not only were artificial barriers carefully removed, but every influence that could appeal to ordinary ambition was applied. No brain or appetite active enough to be conscious of stimulants could fail to answer the intense incentive. Few human beings, however sluggish, could long resist the temptation to acquire power; and the elements of power were to be had in America almost for the asking. Reversing the old-world system, the American stimulant increased in energy as it reached the lowest and most ignorant class, dragging and whirling them upward as in the blast of a furnace. The penniless and homeless Scotch or Irish immigrant was caught and consumed by it; for every stroke of the axe and the hoe made him a capitalist, and made gentlemen of his children. Wealth was the strongest agent for moving the mass of mankind; but political power was hardly less tempting to the more intelligent and better-educated swarms of American-born citizens, and the instinct of activity, once created, seemed heritable and permanent in the race.

Compared with this lithe young figure, Europe was actually in decrepitude. Mere class distinctions, the *patois* or dialect of the peasantry, the fixity of residence, the local costumes and habits marking a history that lost itself in the renewal of identical generations, raised from birth barriers which paralyzed half the population. Upon this mass of inert matter rested the Church and the State, holding down activity of thought. Endless wars withdrew many hundred thousand men from production, and changed them into agents of waste; huge debts, the evidence of past wars and bad government, created interests to support the system and fix its burdens on the laboring class; courts, with habits of extravagance that shamed common-sense, helped to consume private economics. All this might have been borne; but behind this stood aristocracies, sucking their nourishment from industry, producing nothing themselves, employing little or no active capital or intelligent labor, but pressing on the energies and ambition of society with the weight of an incubus. Picturesque and entertaining as these social anomalies were, they were better fitted for the theatre or for a museum of historical costumes than for an active workshop preparing to compete with such machinery as America would soon command. From an economical point of view, they were as incongruous as would have been the appearance of a mediæval knight in helmet and armor, with battle-axe and shield, to run the machinery of Arkwright's cotton-mill; but besides their bad economy they also tended to prevent the rest of society from gaining a knowledge of its own capacities. In Europe, the conservative habit of mind was fortified behind power. During nearly a century Voltaire himself—the friend of kings, the wit and poet, historian and philosopher of his age—had carried on, in daily terror, in exile and excommunication, a protest against an intellectual despotism contemptible even to its own supporters. Hardly was Voltaire dead, when Priestley,[3] as great a

[3] Joseph Priestley (1733–1804), English scientist.

man if not so great a wit, trying to do for England what Voltaire tried to do for France, was mobbed by the people of Birmingham and driven to America. Where Voltaire and Priestley failed, common men could not struggle; the weight of society stifled their thought. In America the balance between conservative and liberal forces was close; but in Europe conservatism held the physical power of government. In Boston a young Buckminster[4] might be checked for a time by his father's prayers or commands in entering the path that led toward freer thought; but youth beckoned him on, and every reward that society could offer was dangled before his eyes. In London or Paris, Rome, Madrid, or Vienna, he must have sacrificed the worldly prospects of his life.

Granting that the American people were about to risk their future on a new experiment, they naturally wished to throw aside all burdens of which they could rid themselves. Believing that in the long run interest, not violence, would rule the world, and that the United States must depend for safety and success on the interests they could create, they were tempted to look upon war and preparations for war as the worst of blunders; for they were sure that every dollar capitalized in industry was a means of overthrowing their enemies more effective than a thousand dollars spent on frigates or standing armies. The success of the American system was, from this point of view, a question of economy. If they could relieve themselves from debts, taxes, armies, and government interference with industry, they must succeed in outstripping Europe in economy of production; and Americans were even then partly aware that if their machine were not so weakened by these economics as to break down in the working, it must of necessity break down every rival. If their theory was sound, when the day of competition should arrive, Europe might choose between American and Chinese institutions, but there would be no middle path; she might become a confederated democracy, or a wreck.

Whether these ideas were sound or weak, they seemed self-evident to those Northern democrats who, like Albert Gallatin, were comparatively free from slave-owning theories, and understood the practical forces of society. If Gallatin wished to reduce the interference of government to a minimum, and cut down expenditures to nothing, he aimed not so much at saving money as at using it with the most certain effect. The revolution of 1800 was in his eyes chiefly political, because it was social; but as a revolution of society, he and his friends hoped to make it the most radical that had occurred since the downfall of the Roman empire. Their ideas were not yet cleared by experience, and were confused by many contradictory prejudices, but wanted neither breadth nor shrewdness.

Many apparent inconsistencies grew from this undeveloped form of

---

[4] Joseph Buckminster (1784–1812), a prominent liberal Unitarian clergyman in New England.

American thought, and gave rise to great confusion in the different estimates of American character that were made both at home and abroad.

That Americans should not be liked was natural; but that they should not be understood was more significant by far. After the downfall of the French republic they had no right to expect a kind word from Europe, and during the next twenty years they rarely received one. The liberal movement of Europe was cowed, and no one dared express democratic sympathies until the Napoleonic tempest had passed. With this attitude Americans had no right to find fault, for Europe cared less to injure them than to protect herself. Nevertheless, observant readers could not but feel surprised that none of the numerous Europeans who then wrote or spoke about America seemed to study the subject seriously. The ordinary traveller was apt to be little more reflective than a bee or an ant, but some of these critics possessed powers far from ordinary; yet Talleyrand alone showed that had he but seen America a few years later than he did, he might have suggested some sufficient reason for apparent contradictions that perplexed him in the national character. The other travellers—great and small, from the Duc de Liancourt to Basil Hall,[5] a long and suggestive list—were equally perplexed. They agreed in observing the contradictions, but all, including Talleyrand, saw only sordid motives. Talleyrand expressed extreme astonishment at the apathy of Americans in the face of religious sectarians; but he explained it by assuming that the American ardor of the moment was absorbed in money-making. The explanation was evidently insufficient, for the Americans were capable of feeling and showing excitement, even to their great pecuniary injury, as they frequently proved; but in the foreigner's range of observation, love of money was the most conspicuous and most common trait of American character. "There is, perhaps, no civilized country in the world," wrote Félix de Beaujour,[6] soon after 1800, "where there is less generosity in the souls, and in the heads fewer of those illusions which make the charm or the consolation of life. Man here weighs everything, calculates everything, and sacrifices everything to his interest." An Englishman named Fearon,[7] in 1818, expressed the same idea with more distinctness: "In going to America, I would say generally, the emigrant must expect to find, not an economical or cleanly people; not a social or generous people; not a people of enlarged ideas; not a people of liberal opinions, or toward whom you can express your thoughts free as air; not a people friendly to the advocates of liberty in Europe; not a people who understand liberty from investigation and principle; not a people who comprehend the meaning of the words

---

[5] Basil Hall (1788–1844), British travel writer.

[6] Félix de Beaujour (1765–1836), French consul general to the United States in 1804, who wrote *Sketch of the United States* (1814).

[7] Henry Fearon (1770–1825), author of *Sketches of America* (1818).

With abject mind—from a tyrannic lord
Inviting penance, fruitlessly endured.
So, like a fugitive whose feet have cleared
Some boundary which his followers may not cross
In prosecution of their deadly chase,
Respiring, I looked round. How bright the sun,
The breeze how soft! Can anything produced
In the Old World compare, thought I, for power
And majesty, with this tremendous stream
Sprung from the desert? And behold a city
Fresh, youthful, and aspiring! . . .
                                          Sooth to say,
On nearer view, a motley spectacle
Appeared, of high pretensions—unreproved
But by the obstreperous voice of higher still;
Big passions strutting on a petty stage,
Which a detached spectator may regard
Not unamused. But ridicule demands
Quick change of objects; and to laugh alone,
. . . in the very centre of the crowd
To keep the secret a poignant scorn,
                                     . . . is least fit
For the gross spirit of mankind.[11]

Thus Wordsworth, although then at his prime, indulging in what sounded like a boast that he alone had felt the sense sublime of something interfused, whose dwelling is the light of setting suns, and the round ocean, and the living air, and the blue sky, and in the mind of man,— even he, whose moods the heavy and the weary weight of all this unintelligible world was lightened by his deeper sympathies with nature and the soul, could do no better, when he stood in the face of American democracy, than "keep the secret of a poignant scorn."

Possibly the view of Wordsworth and Moore, of Weld, Dennie, and Dickens was right. The American democrat possessed little art of expression, and did not watch his own emotions with a view of uttering them either in prose or verse; he never told more of himself than the world might have assumed without listening to him. Only with diffidence could history attribute to such a class of men a wider range of thought or feeling than they themselves cared to proclaim. Yet the difficulty of denying or even ignoring the wider range was still greater, for no one questioned the force or the scope of an emotion which caused the poorest peasant in Europe to see what was invisible to poet and philosopher,—the dim outline of a mountain-summit across the ocean, rising high above the mist and mud of American democracy. As though to call

[11] These lines come from William Wordsworth's *The Excursion*, III, 870.

attention to some such difficulty, European and American critics, while affirming that Americans were a race without illusions or enlarged ideas, declared in the same breath that Jefferson was a visionary whose theories would cause the heavens to fall upon them. Year after year, with endless iteration, in every accent of contempt, rage, and despair, they repeated this charge against Jefferson. Every foreigner and Federalist agreed that he was a man of illusions, dangerous to society and unbounded in power of evil; but if this view of his character was right, the same visionary qualities seemed also to be a national trait, for every one admitted that Jefferson's opinions, in one form or another, were shared by a majority of the American people.

Illustrations might be carried much further, and might be drawn from every social class and from every period in national history. Of all presidents, Abraham Lincoln has been considered the most typical representative of American society, chiefly because his mind, with all its practical qualities, also inclined, in certain directions, to idealism. Lincoln was born in 1809, the moment when American character stood in lowest esteem. Ralph Waldo Emerson, a more distinct idealist, was born in 1803. William Ellery Channing, another idealist, was born in 1780. Men like John Fitch, Oliver Evans, Robert Fulton, Joel Barlow, John Stevens, and Eli Whitney were all classed among visionaries. The whole society of Quakers belonged in the same category. The records of the popular religious sects abounded in examples of idealism and illusion to such an extent that the masses seemed hardly to find confort or hope in any authority, however old or well established. In religion as in politics, Americans seemed to require a system which gave play to their imagination and their hopes.

Some misunderstanding must always take place when the observer is at cross-purposes with the society he describes. Wordsworth might have convinced himself by a moment's thought that no country could act on the imagination as America acted upon the instincts of the ignorant and poor, without some quality that deserved better treatment than poignant scorn; but perhaps this was only one among innumerable cases in which the unconscious poet breathed an atmosphere which the self-conscious poet could not penetrate. With equal reason he might have taken the opposite view,—that the hard, practical, money-getting American democrat, who had neither generosity nor honor nor imagination, and who inhabited cold shades where fancy sickened and where genius died, was in truth living in a world of dream, and acting a drama more instinct with poetry than all the avatars of the East, walking in gardens of emerald and rubies, in ambition already ruling the world and guiding Nature with a kinder and wiser hand than had ever yet been felt in human history. From this point his critics never approached him,—they stopped at a stone's throw; and at the moment when they declared that the man's mind had no illusions, they added that he was a knave or a lunatic. Even on his practical and sordid side, the American might easily have been represented as a victim to illusion. If the Englishman had lived as the American speculator did,—in the future,—the hyperbole of enthusiasm would have seemed less monstrous. "Look at my wealth!" cried the American to his foreign visitor. "See these solid mountains of salt and iron, of lead, copper, silver, and gold! See these magnificent cities scattered broadcast to the Pacific! See my cornfields rustling and waving in the summer breeze from ocean to ocean, so far that the sun itself is not high enough to mark where the distant mountains bound by golden seas! Look at this continent of mine, fairest of created worlds, as she lies turning up to the sun's never-failing caress her broad and exuberant breasts, overflowing with milk for her hundred million children! See how she glows with youth, health, and love!" Perhaps it was not altogether unnatural that the foreigner, on being asked to see what needed centuries to produce, should have looked about him with bewilderment and indignation. "Gold! cities! cornfields! continents! Nothing of the sort! I see nothing but tremendous wastes, where sickly men and women are dying of home-sickness or are scalped by savages! mountain-ranges a thousand miles long, with no means of getting to them, and nothing in them when you get there! swamps and forests choked with their own rotten ruins! nor hope of better for a thousand years! Your story as a fraud, and you are a liar and swindler!"

Met in this spirit, the American, half perplexed and half defiant, retaliated by calling his antagonist a fool, and by mimicking his heavy tricks of manner. For himself he cared little, but his dream was his whole existence. The men who denounced him admitted that they left him in his forest-swamp quaking with fever, but clinging in the delirium of death to the illusions of his dazzled brain. No class of men could be required to support their convictions with a steadier faith, or pay more devotedly with their persons for the mistakes of their judgment. Whether imagination or greed led them to describe more than actually existed, they still saw no more than any inventor or discoverer must have seen in order to give him the energy of success. They said to the rich as to the poor, "Come and share our limitless riches! Come and help us bring to light these unimaginable stores of wealth and power!" The poor came, and from them were seldom heard complaints of deception or delusion. Within a moment, by the mere contact of a moral atmosphere, they saw the gold and jewels, the summer cornfields and the glowing continent. The rich for a long time stood aloof,—they were timid and narrow-minded; but this was not all,—between them and the American democrat was a gulf.

The charge that Americans were too fond of money to win the confidence of Europeans was a curious inconsistency; yet this was a common belief. If the American deluded himself and led others to their death by baseless speculations; if he buried those he loved in a gloomy forest where they quaked and died while he persisted in seeing there a splendid, healthy, and well-built city,—no one could deny that he sacrificed wife and child to his greed for gain, that the dollar was his god, and a sordid avarice his demon. Yet had this been the whole truth, no European capitalist would have hesitated to make money out of his grave; for, avarice against avarice, no more sordid or meaner type existed in America than could be shown on every 'Change in Europe. With much more reason Americans might have suspected that in America Englishmen found everywhere a silent influence, which they found nowhere in Europe, and which had nothing to do with avarice or with the dollar, but, on the contrary, seemed likely at any moment to sacrifice the dollar in a cause and for an object so illusory that most Englishmen could not endure to hear it discussed. European travellers who passed through America noticed that everywhere, in the White House at Washington and in log-cabins beyond the Alleghanies, except for a few Federalists, every American, from Jefferson and Gallatin down to the poorest squatter, seemed to nourish an idea that he was doing what he could to overthrow the tyranny which the past had fastened on the human mind. Nothing was easier than to laugh at the ludicrous expressions of this simple-minded conviction, or to cry out against its coarseness, or grow angry with its prejudices; to see its nobler side, to feel the beatings of a heart underneath the sordid surface of a gross humanity, was not so easy. Europeans seemed seldom or never conscious that the sentiment could possess a noble side, but found only matter for complaint in the remark that every American democrat believed himself to be working for the overthrow of tyranny, aristocracy, hereditary privilege, and priesthood, wherever they existed. Even where the American did not openly proclaim this conviction in words, he carried so dense an atmosphere of the sentiment with him in his daily life as to give respectable Europeans an uneasy sense of remoteness.

Of all historical problems, the nature of a national character is the most difficult and the most important. Readers will be troubled, at almost every chapter of the coming narrative, by the want of some formula to explain what share the popular imagination bore in the system pursued by government. The acts of the American people during the administrations of Jefferson and Madison were judged at the time by no other test. According as bystanders believed American character to be hard, sordid, and free from illusion, they were severe and even harsh in judgment. This rule guided the governments of England and France. Federalists in the United States, knowing more of the circumstances, often attributed to the democratic instinct a visionary quality which they regarded as sentimentality, and charged with many bad consequences. If their view was correct, history could occupy itself to no better purpose than in ascertaining the nature and force of the quality which was charged with results so serious; but nothing was more elusive than the spirit of American democracy. Jefferson, the literary representative of the class, spoke chiefly for Virginians, and dreaded so greatly his own reputation as a visionary that he seldom or never uttered his whole thought. Gallatin and Madison were still more cautious. The press in no country could give shape to a mental condition so shadowy. The people themselves, although millions in number, could not have expressed their finer instincts had they tried, and might not have recognized them if expressed by others.

In the early days of colonization, every new settlement represented an idea and proclaimed a mission. Virginia was founded by a great, liberal movement aiming at the spread of English liberty and empire. The Pilgrims of Plymouth, the Puritans of Boston, the Quakers of Pennsylvania, all avowed a moral purpose, and began by making institutions that consciously reflected a moral idea. No such character belonged to the colonization of 1800. From Lake Erie to Florida, in long, unbroken line, pioneers were at work, cutting into the forests with the energy of so many beavers, and with no more express moral purpose than the beavers they drove away. The civilization they carried with them was rarely illumined by an idea; they sought room for no new truth, and aimed neither at creating, like the Puritans, a government of saints, nor, like the Quakers, one of love and peace; they left such experiments behind them, and wrestled only with the hardest problems of frontier life. No wonder that foreign observers, and even the educated, well-to-do Americans of the sea-coast, could seldom see anything to admire in the ignorance and brutality of frontiersmen, and should declare that virtue and wisdom no longer guided the United States! What they saw was not encouraging. To a new society, ignorant and semi-barbarous, a mass of demagogues insisted on applying every stimulant that could inflame its worst appetites, while at the same instant taking away every influence that had hitherto helped to restrain its passions. Greed for wealth, lust for power, yearning for the blank void of savage freedom such as Indians and wolves delighted in,—these were the fires that flamed under the caldron of American society, in which, as conservatives believed, the old, well-proven, conservative crust of religion, government, family, and even common respect for age, education, and experience was rapidly melting away, and was indeed already broken into fragments, swept about by the seething mass of scum ever rising in greater quantities to the surface.

Against this Federalist and conservative view of democratic tendencies, democrats protested in a thousand forms, but never in any mode of expression which satisfied them all, or explained their whole character. Probably Jefferson came nearest to the mark, for he represented the hopes of science as well as the prejudices of Virginia; but Jefferson's writings may be searched from beginning to end without revealing the whole measure of the man, far less of the movement. Here and there in his letters a suggestion was thrown out, as though by chance, revealing larger hopes,—as in 1815, at a moment of despondency, he wrote: "I fear from the experience of the last twenty-five years that morals do not of necessity advance hand in hand with the sciences." In 1800, in the flush of triumph, he believed that his task in the world was to establish a democratic republic, with the sciences for an intellectual field, and physical and moral advancement keeping pace with their advance. Without an excessive introduction of more recent ideas, he might be imagined to define democratic progress, in the somewhat affected precision of his French philosophy: "Progress is either physical or intellectual. If we can bring it about that men are on the average an inch taller in the next generation than in this; if they are an inch larger round the chest; if their brain is an ounce or two heavier, and their life a year or two longer,—that is progress. If fifty years hence the average man shall invariably argue from two ascertained premises where he now jumps to a conclusion from a single supposed revelation,—that is progress! I expect it to be made here, under our democratic stimulants, on a great scale, until every man is potentially an athlete in body and an Aristotle in mind." To this doctrine the New Englander [John Adams] replied, "What will you do for moral progress?" Every possible answer to this question opened a chasm. No doubt Jefferson held the faith that men would improve morally with their physical and intellectual growth; but he had no idea of any moral improvement other than that which came by nature. He could not tolerate a priesthood, a state church, or revealed religion. Conservatives, who could tolerate no society without such pillars of order, were, from their point of view, right in answering, "Give us rather the worst despotism of Europe,—there our souls at least may have a chance of salvation!" To their minds vice and virtue were not relative, but fixed terms. The Church was a divine institution. How could a ship hope to reach port when the crew threw overboard sails, spars, and compass, unshipped their rudder, and all the long day thought only of eating and drinking. Nay, even should the new experiment succeed in a wordly sense, what was a man profited if he gained the whole world, and lost his own soul? The Lord God was a jealous God, and visited the sins of the parents upon the children; but what worse sin could be conceived than for a whole nation to join their chief in chanting the strange hymn with which Jefferson, a new false prophet, was deceiving and betraying his people: "It does me no injury for my neighbor to say there are twenty Gods or no God!"

On this ground conservatism took its stand, as it had hitherto done with success in every similar emergency in the world's history, and fixing its eyes on moral standards of its own, refused to deal with the subject as further open to argument. The two parties stood facing opposite ways, and could see no common ground of contact.

Yet even then one part of the American social system was proving itself to be rich in results. The average American was more intelligent than the average European, and was becoming every year still more active-minded as the new movement of society caught him up and swept him through a life of more varied experiences. On all sides the national mind responded to its stimulants. Deficient as the American was in the machinery of higher instruction; remote, poor; unable by any exertion to acquire the training, the capital, or even the elementary textbooks he needed for a fair development of his natural powers,—his native energy and ambition already responded to the spur applied to them. Some of his triumphs were famous throughout the world; for Benjamin Franklin had raised high the reputation of American printers, and the actual President of the United States, who signed with Franklin the treaty of peace with Great Britain, was the son of a small farmer, and had himself kept a school in his youth. In both these cases social recognition followed success; but the later triumphs of the American mind were becoming more and more popular. John Fitch was not only one of the poorest, but one of the least-educated Yankees who ever made a name; he could never spell with tolerable correctness, and his life ended as it began,—in the lowest social obscurity. Eli Whitney was better educated than Fitch, but had neither wealth, social influence, nor patron to back his ingenuity. In the year 1800 Eli Terry, another Connecticut Yankee of the same class, took into his employ two young men to help him make wooden clocks, and this was the capital on which the greatest clock-manufactory in the world began its operations. In 1797 Asa Whittemore, a Massachusetts Yankee, invented a machine to make cards for carding wool, which "operated as if it had a soul," and became the foundation for a hundred subsequent patents. In 1790 Jacob Perkins, of Newbury-port, invented a machine capable of cutting and turning out two hundred thousand nails a day; and then invented a process for transferring engraving from a very small steel cylinder to copper, which revolutionized cotton-printing. The British traveller Weld, passing through Wilmington, stopped, as Liancourt had done before him, to see the great flour-mills on the Brandywine. "The improvements," he said, "which have been made in the machinery of the flour-mills in America are very great. The chief of these consist in a new application of the screw, and the introduction of what are called elevators, the idea of which was evidently borrowed from the chain-pump." This was the invention of Oliver Evans, a native of Delaware, whose parents were in very humble life, but who was himself, in spite of every disadvantage, an inventive genius of the first order. Robert Fulton, who in 1800 was in Paris with Joel Barlow, sprang from the same source in Pennsylvania. John Stevens, a native of New York, belonged to a more favored class, but followed the same impulses. All these men were the outcome of typical American society, and all their inventions transmuted the democratic instinct into a practical and tangible shape. Who would undertake to say that there was a limit to the fecundity of this teeming source? Who that saw only the narrow, practical, money-getting nature of these devices could venture to assert that as they wrought their end and raised the standard of millions, they would not also raise the creative power of those millions to a higher plane? If the priests and barons who set their names to Magna Charta had been told that in a few centuries every swine-herd and cobbler's apprentice would write and read with an ease such as few kings could then command, and reason with better logic than any university could then practise, the priest and baron would have been more incredulous than any man who was told in 1800 that within another five centuries the ploughboy would go a-field whistling a sonata of Beethoven, and figure out in quarternions the relation of his furrows. The American democrat knew so little of art that among his popular illusions he could not then nourish artistic ambition; but leaders like Jefferson, Gallatin, and Barlow might without extravagance count upon a coming time when diffused ease and education should bring the masses into familiar contact with higher forms of human achievement, and their vast creative power, turned toward a nobler culture, might rise to the level of that democratic genius which found expression in the Parthenon; might revel in the delights of a new Buonarotti and a richer Titan; might create for five hundred million people the America of thought and art which alone could satisfy their omnivorous ambition.

Whether the illusions, so often affirmed and so often denied to the American people, took such forms or not, there were in effect the problems that lay before American society: Could it transmute its social power into the higher forms of thought? Could it provide for the moral and intellectual needs of mankind? Could it take permanent political shape? Could it give new life to religion and art? Could it create and maintain in the mass of mankind those habits of mind which had hitherto belonged to men of science alone? Could it physically develop the convolutions of the human brain? Could it produce, or was it compatible with the differentiation of a higher variety of the human race? Nothing less than this was necessary for its complete success.

FROM **The Education of Henry Adams** (*1907*)

Chapter 1   Quincy (1838–1848)

Under the shadow of Boston State House, turning its back on the house of John Hancock, the little passage called Hancock Avenue runs, or ran, from Beacon Street, skirting the State House grounds, to Mount Vernon Street, on the summit of Beacon Hill; and there, in the third house below Mount Vernon Place, February 16, 1838, a child was born, and christened later by his uncle, the minister of the First Church after the tenets of Boston Unitarianism, as Henry Brooks Adams.

Had he been born in Jerusalem under the shadow of the Temple and circumcised in the Synagogue by his uncle the high priest, under the name of Israel Cohen, he would scarcely have been more distinctly branded, and not much more heavily handicapped in the races of the coming century, in running for such stakes as the century was to offer;

but, on the other hand, the ordinary traveller, who does not enter the field of racing, finds advantage in being, so to speak, ticketed through life, with the safeguards of an old, established traffic. Safeguards are often irksome, but sometimes convenient, and if one needs them at all, one is apt to need them badly. A hundred years earlier, such safeguards as his would have secured any young man's success; and although in 1838 their value was not very great compared with what they would have had in 1738, yet the mere accident of starting a twentieth-century career from a nest of associations so colonial—to troglodytic—as the First Church, the Boston State House, Beacon Hill, John Hancock and John Adams, Mount Vernon Street and Quincy, all crowding on ten pounds of unconscious babyhood, was so queer as to offer a subject of curious speculation to the baby long after he had witnessed the solution. What could become of such a child of the seventeenth and eighteenth centuries, when he should wake up to find himself required to play the game of the twentieth? Had he been consulted, would he have cared to play the game at all, holding such cards as he held, and suspecting that the game was to be one of which neither he nor any one else back to the beginning of time knew the rules or the risks or the stakes? He was not consulted and was not responsible, but had he been taken into the confidence of his parents, he would certainly have told them to change nothing as far as concerned him. He would have been astounded by his own luck. Probably no child, born in the year, held better cards than he. Whether life was an honest game of chance, or whether the cards were marked and forced, he could not refuse to play his excellent hand. He could never make the usual plea of irresponsibility. He accepted the situation as though he had been a party to it, and under the same circumstances would do it again, the more readily for knowing the exact values. To his life as a whole he was a consenting, contracting party and partner from the moment he was born to the moment he died. Only with that understanding—as a consciously assenting member in full partnership with the society of his age—had his education an interest to himself or to others.

As it happened, he never got to the point of playing the game at all; he lost himself in the study of it, watching the errors of the players; but this is the only interest in the story, which otherwise has no moral and little incident. A story of education—seventy years of it—the practical value remains to the end in doubt, like other values about which men have disputed since the birth of Cain and Abel; but the practical value of the universe has never been stated in dollars. Although every one cannot be a Gargantua-Napoleon-Bismarck and walk off with the great bells of Notre Dame, every one must bear his own universe, and most persons are moderately interested in learning how their neighbors have managed to carry theirs.

This problem of education, started in 1838, went on for three years, while the baby grew, like other babies, unconsciously, as a vegetable, the outside world working as it never had worked before, to get his new universe ready for him. Often in old age he puzzled over the question whether, on the doctrine of chances, he was at liberty to accept himself or his world as an accident. No such accident had ever happened before in human experience. For him, alone, the old universe was thrown into the ash heap and a new one created. He and his eighteenth-century, troglodytic Boston were suddenly cut apart—separated forever—in act if not in sentiment, by the opening of the Boston and Albany Railroad; the appearance of the first Cunard steamers in the bay; and the telegraphic messages which carried from Baltimore to Washington the news that Henry Clay and James K. Polk were nominated for the Presidency. This was in May, 1844; he was six years old; his new world was ready for use, and only fragments of the old met his eyes.

Of all this that was being done to complicate his education, he knew only the color of yellow. He first found himself sitting on a yellow kitchen floor in strong sunlight. He was three years old when he took this earliest step in education; a lesson of color. The second followed soon; a lesson of taste. On December 3, 1841, he developed scarlet fever. For several days he was as good as dead, reviving only under the careful nursing of his family. When he began to recover strength, about January 1, 1842, his hunger must have been stronger than any other pleasure or pain, for while in after life he retained not the faintest recollection of his illness, he remembered quite clearly his aunt entering the sick-room bearing in her hand a saucer with a baked apple.

The order of impressions retained by memory might naturally be that of color and taste, although one would rather suppose that the sense of pain would be first to educate. In fact, the third recollection of the child was that of discomfort. The moment he could be removed, he was bundled up in blankets and carried from the little house in Hancock Avenue to a larger one which his parents were to occupy for the rest of their lives in the neighboring Mount Vernon Street. The season was midwinter, January 10, 1842, and he never forgot his acute distress for want of air under his blankets, or the noises of moving furniture.

As a means of variation from a normal type, sickness in childhood ought to have a certain value not to be classed under any fitness or unfitness of natural selection; and especially scarlet fever affected boys seriously, both physically and in character, though they might through life puzzle themselves to decide whether it had fitted or unfitted them for success; but this fever of Henry Adams took greater and greater importance in his eyes, from the point of view of education, the longer he lived. At first, the effect was physical. He fell behind his brothers two or three inches in height, and proportionally in bone and weight. His character and processes of mind seemed to share in this fining-down process of scale. He was not good in a fight, and his nerves were more delicate than boys' nerves ought to be. He exaggerated these weaknesses as he grew older. The habit of doubt; of distrusting his own judgment and of totally rejecting the judgment of the world; the tendency to regard every question as open; the hesitation to act except as a choice of evils; the shirking of responsibility; the love of line, form, quality; the horror of ennui; the passion for companionship and the antipathy to society—all these are well-known qualities of New England character in no way peculiar to individuals but in this instance they seemed to be stimulated by the fever, and Henry Adams could never make up his mind whether, on the whole, the change of character was morbid or healthy, good or bad for his purpose. His brothers were the type; he was the variation.

As far as the boy knew, the sickness did not affect him at all, and he grew up in excellent health, bodily and mental, taking life as it was given; accepting its local standards without a difficulty, and enjoying much of it as keenly as any other boy of his age. He seemed to himself quite normal, and his companions seemed always to think him so. Whatever was peculiar about him was education, not character, and came to him, directly and indirectly, as the result of that eighteenth-century inheritance which he took with his name.

The atmosphere of education in which he lived was colonial, revolutionary, almost Cromwellian, as though he were steeped, from his greatest grandmother's birth, in the odor of political crime. Resistance to something was the law of New England nature; the boy looked out on the world with the instinct of resistance; for numberless generations his predecessors had viewed the world chiefly as a thing to be reformed, filled with evil forces to be abolished, and they saw no reason to suppose that they had wholly succeeded in the abolition; the duty was unchanged. That duty implied not only resistance to evil, but hatred of it. Boys naturally look on all force as an enemy, and generally find it so, but the New Englander, whether boy or man, in his long struggle with stingy or hostile universe, had learned also to love the pleasure of hating; his joys were few.

Politics, as a practice, whatever its professions, had always been the systematic organization of hatreds, and Massachusetts politics had been as harsh as the climate. The chief charm of New England was harshness of contrasts and extremes of sensibility—a cold that froze the blood, and a heat that boiled it—so that the pleasure of hating—one's self if no better victim offered—was not its rarest amusement; but the charm was a true and natural child of the soil, not a cultivated weed of the ancients. The violence of the contrast was real and made the strongest motive of education. The double exterior nature gave life its relative values. Winter and summer, cold and heat, town and country, force and freedom, marked two modes of life and thought, balanced like lobes of the brain. Town was winter confinement, school, rule, discipline; straight, gloomy streets, piled with six feet of snow in the middle; frosts that made the snow sing under wheels or runners; thaws when the streets became dangerous to cross; society of uncles, aunts, and cousins who

expected children to behave themselves, and who were not always gratified; above all else, winter represented the desire to escape and go free.
Town was restraint, law, unity. Country, only seven miles away, was
liberty, diversity, outlawry, the endless delight of mere sense impressions given by nature for nothing, and breathed by boys without knowing it.

Boys are wild animals, rich in the treasures of sense, but the New
England boy had a wider range of emotions than boys of more equable
climates. He felt his nature crudely, as it was meant. To the boy Henry
Adams, summer was drunken. Among senses, smell was the strongest—
smell of hot pine-woods and sweet-fern in the scorching summer noon;
of new-mown hay; of ploughed earth; of box hedges; of peaches, lilacs,
syringas; of stables, barns, cow-yards; of salt water and low tide on the
marshes; nothing came amiss. Next to smell came taste, and the children knew the taste of everything they saw or touched, from pennyroyal
and flagroot to the shell of a pignut and the letters of a spelling-book—
the taste of A-B, AB, suddenly revived on the boy's tongue sixty years
afterwards. Light, line, and color as sensual pleasures, came later and
were as crude as the rest. The New England light is glare, and the
atmosphere harshens color. The boy was a full man before he ever knew
what was meant by atmosphere; his idea of pleasure in light was the
blaze of a New England sun. His idea of color was a peony, with the
dew of early morning on its petals. The intense blue of the sea, as he
saw it a mile or two away, from the Quincy hills; the cumuli in a June
afternoon sky; the strong reds and greens and purples of colored prints
and children's picture-books, as the American colors then ran; these
were ideals. The opposites or antipathies, were the cold grays of November evenings, and the thick, muddy thaws of Boston winter. With such
standards, the Bostonian could not but develop a double nature. Life
was a double thing. After a January blizzard, the boy who could look
with pleasure into the violent snow-glare of the cold white sunshine,
with its intense light and shade, scarcely knew what was meant by tone.
He could reach it only by education.

Winter and summer, then, were two hostile lives, and bred two
separate natures. Winter was always the effort to live; summer was
tropical license. Whether the children rolled in the grass, or waded in
the brook, or swam in the salt ocean, or sailed in the bay, or fished for
smelts in the creeks, or netted minnows in the salt-marshes, or took to
the pine-woods and the granite quarries, or chased muskrats and hunted
snapping-turtles in the swamps, or mushrooms or nuts on the autumn
hills, summer and country were always sensual living, while winter was
always compulsory learning. Summer was the multiplicity of nature;
winter was school.

The bearing of the two seasons on the education of Henry Adams
was no fancy; it was the most decisive force he ever knew; it ran
through life, and made the division between its perplexing, warring,

irreconcilable problems, irreducible opposites, with growing emphasis to the last year of study. From earliest childhood the boy was accustomed to feel that, for him, life was double. Winter and summer, town and country, law and liberty, were hostile, and the man who pretended they were not, was in his eyes a schoolmaster—that is, a man employed to tell lies to little boys. Though Quincy was but two hours' walk from Beacon Hill, it belonged in a different world. For two hundred years, every Adams, from father to son, had lived within sight of State Street,[1] and sometimes had lived in it, yet none had ever taken kindly to the town, or been taken kindly by it. The boy inherited his double nature. He knew as yet nothing about his great-grandfather, who had died a dozen years before his own birth: he took for granted that any great-grandfather of his must have always been good, and his enemies wicked; but he divined his great-grandfather's character from his own. Never for a moment did he connect the two ideas of Boston and John Adams; they were separate and antagonistic; the idea of John Adams went with Quincy. He knew his grandfather John Quincy Adams only as an old man of seventy-five or eighty who was friendly and gentle with him, but except that he heard his grandfather always called "the President," and his grandmother "the Madam," he had no reason to suppose that his Adams grandfather differed in character from his Brooks grandfather who was equally kind and benevolent. He like the Adams side best, but for no other reason than that it reminded him of the country, the summer, and the absence of restraint. Yet he felt also that Quincy was in a way inferior to Boston, and that socially Boston looked down on Quincy. The reason was clear enough even to a five-year old child. Quincy had no Boston style. Little enough style had either; a simpler manner of life and thought could hardly exist, short of cave-dwelling. The flint-and-steel with which his grandfather Adams used to light his own fires in the early morning was still on the mantel-piece of his study. The idea of a livery or even a dress for servants or of an evening toilette, was next to blasphemy. Bathrooms, water-supplies, lighting, heating, and the whole array of domestic comforts, were unknown at Quincy. Boston had already a bathroom, a water-supply, a furnace, and gas. The superiority of Boston was evident, but a child liked it no better for that.

The magnificence of his grandfather Brooks's house in Pearl Street or South Street has long ago disappeared, but perhaps his country house at Medford may still remain to show what impressed the mind of a boy in 1845 with the idea of city splendor. The President's place at Quincy was the larger and older and far the more interesting of the two; but a boy felt at once its inferiority in fashion. It showed plainly enough its want of wealth. It smacked of colonial age, but not of Boston style or plush curtains. To the end of his life he never quite overcame the prejudice thus drawn in with his childish breath. He never could compel

[1] The financial district of Boston.

himself to care for nineteenth-century style. He was never able to adopt it, any more than his father or grandfather or great-grandfather had done. Not that he felt it as particularly hostile, for he reconciled himself to much that was worse; but because, for some remote reason, he was born an eighteenth-century child. The old house at Quincy was eighteenth century. What style it had was in its Queen Anne mahogany panels and its Louis Seize chairs and sofas. The panels belonged to an old colonial Vassall who built the house; the furniture had been brought back from Paris in 1789 or 1801 or 1817, along with porcelain and books and much else of old diplomatic remnants; and neither of the two eight-eenth-century styles—neither English Queen Anne nor French Louis Seize—was comfortable for a boy, or for any one else. The dark mahog-any had been painted white to suit daily life in winter gloom. Nothing seemed to favor, for a child's objects, the older forms. On the contrary, most boys, as well as grown-up people, preferred the new, with good reason, and the child felt himself distinctly at a disadvantage for the taste.

Nor had personal preference any share in his bias. The Brooks grandfather was as amiable and as sympathetic as the Adams grand-father. Both were born in 1767, and both died in 1848. Both were kind to children, and both belonged rather to the eighteenth than to the nine-teenth centuries. The child knew no difference between them except that one was associated with winter and the other with summer; one with Boston, the other with Quincy. Even with Medford, the association was hardly easier. Once as a very young boy he was taken to pass a few days with his grandfather Brooks under charge of his aunt, but became so violently homesick that within twenty-four hours he was brought back in disgrace. Yet he could not remember ever being seriously homesick again.

The attachment to Quincy was not altogether sentimental or wholly sympathetic. Quincy was not a bed of thornless roses. Even there the curse of Cain set its mark. There as elsewhere a cruel universe com-bined to crush a child. As though three or four vigorous brothers and sisters, with the best will, were not enough to crush any child, every one else conspired towards an education which he hated. From cradle to grave this problem of running order through chaos, direction through space, discipline through freedom, unity through multiplicity, has always been, and must always be, the task of education, as it is the moral of religion, philosophy, science, art, politics, and economy; but a boy's will is his life, and he dies when it is broken, as the colt dies in harness, taking a new nature in becoming tame. Rarely has the boy felt kindly towards his tamers. Between him and his master has always been war. Henry Adams never knew a boy of his generation to like a master, and the task of remaining on friendly terms with one's own family, in such a relation, was never easy.

All the more singular it seemed afterwards to him that his first serious contact with the President should have been a struggle of will, in which the old man almost necessarily defeated the boy, but instead of leaving, as usual in such defeats, a lifelong sting, left rather an impression of as fair treatment as could be expected from a natural enemy. The boy met seldom with such restraint. He could not have been much more than six years old at the time—seven at the utmost—and his mother had taken him to Quincy for a long stay with the President during the summer. What became of the rest of the family he quite forgot; but he distinctly remembered standing at the house door one summer morning in a passionate outburst of rebellion against going to school. Naturally his mother was the immediate victim of his rage; that is what mothers are for, and boys also; but in this case the boy had his mother at unfair disadvantage, for she was a guest, and had no means of enforcing obedience. Henry showed a certain tactical ability by refusing to start, and he met all efforts at compulsion by successful, though too vehement protest. He was in fair way to win, and was holding his own, with sufficient energy, at the bottom of the long staircase which led up to the door of the President's library, when the door opened, and the old man slowly came down. Putting on his hat, he took the boy's hand without a word, and walked with him, paralyzed by awe, up the road to the town. After the first moments of consternation at this interference in a domestic dispute, the boy reflected that an old gentleman close on eighty would never trouble himself to walk near a mile on a hot summer morning over a shadeless road to take a boy to school, and that it would be strange if a lad imbued with the passion of freedom could not find a corner to dodge around, somewhere before reaching the school door. Then and always, the boy insisted that this reasoning justified his apparent submission; but the old man did not stop, and the boy saw all his strategical points turned, one after another, until he found himself seated inside the school, and obviously the centre of curious if not malevolent criticism. Not till then did the President release his hand and depart.

The point was that this act, contrary to the inalienable rights of boys, and nullifying the social compact, ought to have made him dislike his grandfather for life. He could not recall that it had this effect even for a moment. With a certain maturity of mind, the child must have recognized that the President, though a tool of tyranny, had done his disreputable work with a certain intelligence. He had shown no temper, no irritation, no personal feeling, and had made no display of force. Above all, he had held his tongue. During their long walk he had said nothing; he had uttered no syllable of revolting cant about the duty of obedience and the wickedness of resistance to law; he had shown no concern in the matter; hardly even a consciousness of the boy's existence. Probably his mind at that moment was actually troubling itself little about his grandson's iniquities, and much about the iniquities of President Polk, but the boy could scarcely at that age feel the whole satisfaction of thinking that President Polk was to be the vicarious victim of his own sins, and he gave his grandfather credit for intelligent silence. For this forbearance he felt instinctive respect. He admitted force as a form of right; he admitted even temper, under protest; but the seeds of a moral education would at that moment have fallen on the stoniest soil in Quincy, which is, as every one knows, the stoniest glacial and tidal drift known in any Puritan land.

Neither party to this momentary disagreement can have felt rancor, for during these three or four summers the old President's relations with the boy were friendly and almost intimate. Whether his older brothers and sisters were still more favored he failed to remember, but he was himself admitted to a sort of familiarity which, when in his turn he had reached old age, rather shocked him, for it must have sometimes tried the President's patience. He hung about the library; handled the books; deranged the papers; ransacked the drawers; searched the old purses and pocket-books for foreign coins; drew the sword-cane; snapped the travelling-pistols; upset everything in the corners, and penetrated the President's dressing-closet where a row of tumblers, inverted on the shelf, covered caterpillars which were supposed to become moths or butterflies, but never did. The Madam bore with fortitude the loss of the tumblers which her husband purloined for these hatcheries; but she r ade protest when he carried off her best cut-glass bowls to plant with ; corns or peachstones that he might see the roots grow, but which, she said, he commonly forgot like the caterpillars.

At that time the President rode the hobby of tree-culture, and some fine old trees should still remain to witness it, unless they have been improved off the ground; but his was a restless mind, and although he took his hobbies seriously and would have been annoyed had his grandchild asked whether he was bored like an English duke, he probably cared more for the processes than for the results, so that his grandson was saddened by the sight and smell of peaches and pears, the best of their kind, which he brought up from the garden to rot on his shelves for seed. With the inherited virtues of his Puritan ancestors, the little boy Henry conscientiously brought up to him in his study the finest peaches he found in the garden, and ate only the less perfect. Naturally he ate more by way of compensation, but the act showed that he bore no grudge. As for his grandfather, it is even possible that he may have felt a certain self-reproach for his temporary rôle of schoolmaster—seeing that his own career did not offer proof of the worldly advantages of docile obedience—for there still exists somewhere a little volume of critically edited Nursery Rhymes with the boy's name in full written in the President's trembling hand on the fly-leaf. Of course there was also the Bible, given to each child at birth, with the proper inscription in the President's hand on the fly-leaf; while their grandfather Brooks supplied the silver mugs.

So many Bibles and silver mugs had to be supplied, that a new house, or cottage, was built to hold them. It was "on the hill," five minutes' walk above "the old house," with a far view eastward over Quincy Bay, and northward over Boston. Till his twelfth year, the child passed his summers there, and his pleasures of childhood mostly centered in it. Of education he had as yet little to complain. Country schools were not very serious. Nothing stuck to the mind except home impressions, and the sharpest were those of kindred children; but as influences that warped a mind, none compared with the mere effect of the back of the President's bald head, as he sat in his pew on Sundays, in line with that of President Quincy, who, though some ten years younger, seemed to children about the same age. Before railways entered the New England town, every parish church showed half-a-dozen of these leading citizens, with gray hair, who sat on the main aisle in the best pews, and had sat there, or in some equivalent dignity, since the time of St. Augustine, if not since the glacial epoch. It was unusual for boys to sit behind a President grandfather, and to read over his head the tablet in memory of a President great-grandfather, who had "pledged his life, his fortune, and his sacred honor" to secure the independence of his country and so forth; but boys naturally supposed, without much reasoning, that other boys had the equivalent of President grandfathers, and that churches would always go on, with the bald-headed leading citizens on the main aisle, and Presidents or their equivalents on the walls. The Irish gardener once said to the child: "You'll be thinkin' you'll be President too!" The casualty of the remark made so strong an impression on his mind that he never forgot it. He could not remember ever to have thought on the subject; to him, that there should be a doubt of his being President was a new idea. What had been would continue to be. He doubted neither about Presidents nor about Churches, and no one suggested at that time a doubt whether a system of society which had lasted since Adam would outlast one Adams more.

The Madam was a little more remote than the President, but more decorative. She stayed much in her own room with the Dutch tiles, looking out on her garden with the box walks, and seemed a fragile creature to a boy who sometimes brought her a note or a message, and took distinct pleasure in looking at her delicate face under what seemed to him very becoming caps. He liked her refined figure; her gentle voice and manner; her vague effect of not belonging there, but to Washington or to Europe, like her furniture, and writing-desk with little glass doors above and little eighteenth-century volumes in old binding, labelled "Peregrine Pickle" or "Tom Jones" or "Hannah More." Try as she might, the Madam could never be Bostonian, and it was her cross in life, but to the boy it was her charm. Even at that age, he felt drawn to it. The Madam's life had been in truth far from Boston. She was born in London in 1775, daughter of Joshua Johnson, an American merchant, brother of Governor Thomas Johnson of Maryland; and Catherine Nuth, of an English family in London. Driven from England by the Revolutionary

War, Joshua Johnson took his family to Nantes, where they remained till the peace. The girl Louisa Catherine was nearly ten years old when brought back to London, and her sense of nationality must have been confused; but the influence of the Johnsons and the services of Joshua obtained for him from President Washington the appointment of Consul in London on the organization of the Government in 1790. In 1794 President Washington appointed John Quincy Adams Minister to The Hague. He was twenty-seven years old when he returned to London, and found the Consul's house a very agreeable haunt. Louisa was then twenty.

At that time, and long afterwards, the Consul's house, far more than the Minister's, was the centre of contact for travelling Americans, either official or other. The Legation was a shifting point, between 1785 and 1815; but the Consulate, far down in the City, near the Tower, was convenient and inviting; so inviting that it proved fatal to young Adams. Louisa was charming, like a Romney portrait, but among her many charms that of being a New England woman was not one. The defect was serious. Her future mother-in-law, Abigail, a famous New England woman whose authority over her turbulent husband, the second President, was hardly so great as that which she exercised over her son, the sixth to be, was troubled by the fear that Louisa might not be made of stuff stern enough, or brought up in conditions severe enough, to suit a New England climate, or to make an efficient wife for her paragon son, and Abigail was right on that point, as on most others where sound judgment was involved; but sound judgment is sometimes a source of weakness rather than of force, and John Quincy already had reason to think that his mother held sound judgments on the subject of daughters-in-law which human nature, since the fall of Eve, made Adams helpless to realize. Being three thousand miles away from his mother, and equally far in love, he married Louisa in London, July 26, 1797, and took her to Berlin to be the head of the United States Legation. During three or four exciting years, the young bride lived in Berlin; whether she was happy or not, whether she was content or not, whether she was socially successful or not, her descendants did not surely know; but in any case she could by no chance have become educated there for a life in Quincy or Boston. In 1801 the overthrow of the Federalist Party [2] drove her and her husband to America, and she became at last a member of the Quincy household, but by that time her children needed all her attention, and she remained there with occasional winters in Boston and Washington, till 1809. Her husband was made Senator in 1803, and in 1809 was appointed Minister to Russia. She went with him to St. Petersburg, taking her baby, Charles Francis, born in 1807; but broken-hearted at having to leave her two older boys behind. The life at St. Petersburg was hardly gay for her; they were far too poor to shine in that extravagant

[2] This refers to the election of Thomas Jefferson to the Presidency.

society; but she survived it, though her little girl baby did not, and in the winter of 1814–15, alone with the boy of seven years old, crossed Europe from St. Petersburg to Paris, in her travelling-carriage, passing through the armies, and reaching Paris in the *Cent Jours* [3] after Napoleon's return from Elba. Her husband next went to England as Minister, and she was for two years at the Court of the Regent. In 1817 her husband came home to be Secretary of State, and she lived for eight years in F Street, doing her work of entertainer for President Monroe's administration. Next she lived four miserable years in the White House. When that chapter was closed in 1829, she had earned the right to be tired and delicate, but she still had fifteen years to serve as wife of a Member of the House, after her husband went back to Congress in 1833. Then it was that the little Henry, her grandson, first remembered her, from 1843 to 1848, sitting in her panelled room, at breakfast, with her heavy silver teapot and sugar-bowl and cream-jug, which still exist somewhere as an heirloom of the modern safety-vault. By that time she was seventy years old or more, and thoroughly weary of being beaten about a stormy world. To the boy she seemed singularly peaceful, a vision of silver gray, presiding over her old President and her Queen Anne mahogany; an exotic, like her Sèvres china; an object of deference to every one, and of great affection to her son Charles; but hardly more Bostonian than she had been fifty years before, on her wedding-day, in the shadow of the Tower of London.

Such a figure was even less fitted than that of her old husband, the President, to impress on a boy's mind, the standards of the coming century. She was Louis Seize, like the furniture. The boy knew nothing of her interior life, which had been, as the venerable Abigail, long since at peace, foresaw, one of severe stress and little pure satisfaction. He never dreamed that from her might come some of those doubts and self-questionings, those hesitations, those rebellions against law and discipline, which marked more than one of her descendants; but he might even then have felt some vague instinctive suspicion that he was to inherit from her the seeds of the primal sin, the fall from grace, the curse of Abel, that he was not of pure New England stock, but half exotic. As a child of Quincy he was not a true Bostonian, but even as a child of Quincy he inherited a quarter taint of Maryland blood. Charles Francis, half Marylander by birth, had hardly seen Boston till he was ten years old, when his parents left him there at school in 1817, and he never forgot the experience. He was to be nearly as old as his mother had been in 1845, before he quite accepted Boston, or Boston quite accepted him.

A boy who began his education in these surroundings, with physical strength inferior to that of his brothers, and with a certain delicacy of

---

[3] Hundred days, refers to Napoleon's restoration to power, ending with his destruction at Waterloo.

mind and bone, ought rightly to have felt at home in the eighteenth century and should, in proper self-respect, have rebelled against the standards of the nineteenth. The atmosphere of his first ten years must have been very like that of his grandfather at the same age, from 1767 till 1776, barring the battle of Bunker Hill, and even as late as 1846, the battle of Bunker Hill remained actual. The tone of Boston society was colonial. The true Bostonian always knelt in self-abasement before the majesty of English standards; far from concealing it as a weakness, he was proud of it as his strength. The eighteenth century ruled society long after 1850. Perhaps the boy began to shake it off rather earlier than most of his mates.

Indeed this prehistoric stage of education ended rather abruptly with his tenth year. One winter morning he was conscious of a certain confusion in the house in Mount Vernon Street, and gathered, from such words as he could catch, that the President, who happened to be then staying there, on his way to Washington, had fallen and hurt himself. Then he heard the word paralysis. After that day he came to associate the word with the figure of his grandfather, in a tall-backed, invalid armchair, on one side of the spare bedroom fireplace, and one of his old friends, Dr. Parkman or P. P. F. Degrand, on the other side, both dozing.

The end of this first, or ancestral and Revolutionary, chapter came on February 21, 1848—and the month of February brought life and death as a family habit—when the eighteenth century, as an actual and living companion, vanished. If the scene on the floor of the House, when the old President fell, struck the still simple-minded American public with a sensation unusually dramatic, its effect on a ten-year-old boy, whose boy-life was fading away with the life of his grandfather, could not be slight. One had to pay for Revolutionary patriots; grandfathers and grandmothers; Presidents; diplomats; Queen Anne mahogany and Louis Seize chairs, as well as for Stuart portraits. Such things warp young life. Americans commonly believed that they ruined it, and perhaps the practical common-sense of the American mind judged right. Many a boy might be ruined by much less than the emotions of the funeral service in the Quincy church, with its surroundings of national respect and family pride. By another dramatic chance it happened that the clergyman of the parish, Dr. Lunt, was an unusual pulpit orator, the ideal of a somewhat austere intellectual type, such as the school of Buckminster and Channing inherited from the old Congregational clergy. His extraordinarily refined appearance, his dignity of manner, his deeply cadenced voice, his remarkable English and his fine appreciation, gave to the funeral service a character that left an overwhelming impression on the boy's mind. He was to see many great functions— funerals and festivals—in after-life, till his only thought was to see no more, but he never again witnessed anything nearly so impressive to him as the last services at Quincy over the body of one President and the ashes of another.

The effect of the Quincy service was deepened by the official ceremony which afterwards took place in Faneuil Hall[4]; when the boy was taken to hear his uncle, Edward Everett, deliver a Eulogy. Like all Mr. Everett's orations, it was an admirable piece of oratory, such as only an admirable orator and scholar could create; too good for a ten-year-old boy to appreciate at its value; but already the boy knew that the dead President could not be in it, and had even learned why he would have been out of place there; for knowledge was beginning to come fast. The shadow of the War of 1812 still hung over State Street; the shadow of the Civil War to come had already begun to darken Faneuil Hall. No rhetoric could have reconciled Mr. Everett's audience to his subject. How could he say there, to an assemblage of Bostonians in the heart of mercantile Boston, that the only distinctive mark of all the Adamses, since old Sam Adams's father a hundred and fifty years before, had been their inherited quarrel with State Street, which had again and again broken out into riot, bloodshed, personal feuds, foreign and civil war, wholesale banishments and confiscations, until the history of Florence was hardly more turbulent than that of Boston? How could he whisper the word Hartford Convention[5] before the men who had made it? What would have been said had he suggested the chance of Secession and Civil War?

Thus already, at ten years old, the boy found himself standing face to face with a dilemma that might have puzzled an early Christian. What was he?—where was he going? Even then he felt that something was wrong, but he concluded that it must be Boston. Quincy had always been right, for Quincy represented a moral principle—the principle of resistance to Boston. His Adams ancestors must have been right, since they were always hostile to State Street. If State Street was wrong, Quincy must be right! Turn the dilemma as he pleased, he still came back on the eighteenth century and the law of Resistance; of Truth; of Duty, and of Freedom. He was a ten-year-old priest and politician. He could under no circumstances have guessed what the next fifty years had in store, and no one could teach him; but sometimes, in his old age, he wondered—and could never decide—whether the most clear and certain knowledge would have helped him. Supposing he had seen a New York stock-list of 1900, and had studied the statistics of railways, telegraphs, coal, and steel—would he have quitted his eighteenth-century, his ancestral prejudices, his abstract ideals, his semi-clerical training, and the rest, in order to perform an expiatory pilgrimage to State Street, and ask for the fatted calf of his grandfather Brooks and a clerkship in the Suffolk Bank?

[4] Meeting place for American revolutionaries in Boston, known as "cradle of liberty."

[5] A secret meeting of Federalists in 1814, opposing war with England.

Sixty years afterwards he was still unable to make up his mind. Each course had its advantages, but the material advantages, looking back, seemed to lie wholly in State Street.

Chapter 17   President Grant (1869)

. . . At least four-fifths of the American people—Adams among the rest—had united in the election of General Grant to the Presidency,[6] and probably had been more or less affected in their choice by the parallel they felt between Grant and Washington. Nothing could be more obvious. Grant represented order. He was a great soldier, and the soldier always represented order. He might be as partisan as he pleased, but a general who had organized and commanded half a million or a million men in the field, must know how to administer. Even Washington, who was, in education and experience, a mere cave-dweller, had known how to organize a government, and had found Jeffersons and Hamiltons to organize his departments. The task of bringing the Government back to regular practices, and of restoring moral and mechanical order to administration, was not very difficult; it was ready to do it itself, with a little encouragement. No doubt the confusion, especially in the old slave States and in the currency, was considerable, but the general disposition was good, and every one had echoed the famous phrase: "Let us have peace."

Adams was young and easily deceived, in spite of his diplomatic adventures, but even at twice his age he could not see that this reliance on Grant was unreasonable. Had Grant been a Congressman one would have been on one's guard, for one knew the type. One never expected from a Congressman more than good intentions and public spirit. Newspaper-men as a rule had no great respect for the lower House; Senators had less; and Cabinet officers had none at all. Indeed, one day when Adams was pleading with a Cabinet officer for patience and tact in dealing with Representatives, the Secretary impatiently broke out: "You can't use tact with a Congressman! A Congressman is a hog! You must take a stick and hit him on the snout!" Adams knew far too little, compared with the Secretary, to contradict him, though he thought the phrase somewhat harsh and even as applied to the average Congressman of 1869—he saw little or nothing of later ones—but he knew a shorter way of silencing criticism. He had but to ask: "If a Congressman is a hog, what is a Senator?" This innocent question, put in a candid spirit, petrified any executive officer that ever sat a week in his office. Even Adams admitted that Senators passed belief. The comic side of their egotism partly disguised its extravagance, but faction had gone so far under Andrew Johnson that at times the whole Senate seemed to

[6] In 1868.

catch hysterics of nervous bucking without apparent reason. Great leaders, like Sumner[7] and Conkling,[8] could not be burlesqued; they were more grotesque than ridicule could make them; even Grant, who rarely sparkled in epigram, became witty on their account; but their egotism and factiousness were no laughing matter. They did permanent and terrible mischief, as Garfield[9] and Blaine,[10] and even McKinley[11] and John Hay,[12] were to feel. The most troublesome task of a reform President was that of bringing the Senate back to decency.

Therefore no one, and Henry Adams less than most, felt hope that any President chosen from the ranks of politics or politicians would raise the character of government; and by instinct if not by reason, all the world united on Grant. The Senate understood what the world expected, and waited in silence for a struggle with Grant more serious than that with Andrew Johnson. Newspaper-men were alive with eagerness to support the President against the Senate. The newspaper-man is, more than most men, a double personality; and his person feels best satisfied in its double instincts when writing in one sense and thinking in another. All newspaper-men, whatever they wrote, felt alike about the Senate. Adams floated with the stream. He was eager to join in the fight which he foresaw as sooner or later inevitable. He meant to support the executive in attacking the Senate and taking away its two-thirds vote and power of confirmation, nor did he much care how it should be done, for he thought it safer to effect the revolution in 1870 than to wait till 1920.

With this thought in mind, he went to the Capitol to hear the names announced which should reveal the carefully guarded secret of Grant's Cabinet. To the end of his life, he wondered at the suddenness of the revolution which actually, within five minutes, changed his intended future into an absurdity so laughable as to make him ashamed of it. He was to hear a long list of Cabinet announcements not much weaker or more futile than that of Grant, and none of them made him blush, while Grant's nominations had the singular effect of making the hearer ashamed, not so much of Grant, as of himself. He had made another total misconception of life—another inconceivable false start. Yet, unlikely as it seemed, he had missed his motive narrowly, and his intention had been more than sound, for the Senators made no secret of saying with senatorial frankness that Grant's nominations betrayed his

[7] Charles Sumner (1811–1874), United States Senator from Massachusetts.

[8] Roscoe Conkling (1829–1888), United States Senator from New York.

[9] James Garfield (1831–1881), twentieth President of the United States, assassinated four months after his inauguration.

[10] James Blaine (1830–1893), United States political leader.

[11] William McKinley (1843–1902), twenty-fifth President of the United States (1897–1901).

[12] John Hay (1838–1905), Secretary of State under McKinley.

intent as plainly as they betrayed his incompetence. A great soldier might be a baby politician.

Adams left the Capitol, much in the same misty mental condition that he recalled as marking his railway journey to London on May 13, 1861; he felt in himself what Gladstone [13] bewailed so sadly, "the incapacity of viewing things all round." He knew, without absolutely saying it, that Grant had cut short the life which Adams had laid out for himself in the future. After such a miscarriage, no thought of effectual reform could revive for at least one generation, and he had no fancy for ineffectual politics. What course could he sail next? He had tried so many, and society had barred them all! For the moment, he saw no hope but in following the stream on which he had launched himself. The new Cabinet, as individuals, were not hostile. Subsequently Grant made changes in the list which were mostly welcome to a Bostonian— or should have been—although fatal to Adams. The name of Hamilton Fish, as Secretary of State, suggested extreme conservatism and probable deference to Sumner. The name of George S. Boutwell, as Secretary of the Treasury, suggested only a somewhat lugubrious joke; Mr. Boutwell could be described only as the opposite of Mr. McCulloch, and meant inertia; or, in plain words, total extinction for any one resembling Henry Adams. On the other hand, the name of Jacob D. Cox, as Secretary of the Interior, suggested help and comfort; while that of Judge Hoar, as Attorney-General, promised friendship. On the whole, the personal outlook, merely for literary purposes, seemed fairly cheerful, and the political outook, though hazy, still depended on Grant himself. No one doubted that Grant's intention had been one of reform; that his aim had been to place his administration above politics; and until he should actually drive his supporters away, one might hope to support him. One's little lantern must therefore be turned on Grant. One seemed to know him so well, and really knew so little.

By chance it happened that Adam Badeau [14] took the lower suite of rooms at Dohna's, and, as it was convenient to have one table, the two men dined together and became intimate. Badeau was exceedingly social, though not in appearance imposing. He was stout; his face was red, and his habits were regularly irregular; but he was very intelligent, a good newspaper-man, and an excellent military historian. His life of Grant was no ordinary book. Unlike most newspaper-men, he was a friendly critic of Grant, as suited an officer who had been on the General's staff. As a rule, the newspaper correspondents in Washington were unfriendly, and the lobby sceptical. From that side one heard tales that made one's hair stand on end, and the old West Point army officers were no more flattering. All described him as vicious, narrow, dull, and vindictive. Badeau, who had come to Washington for a consulate which

13 William Gladstone (1809–1898), British statesman.
14 Adam Badeau (1831–1895), a close friend of Adams.

was slow to reach him, resorted more or less to whiskey for encouragement, and became irritable, besides being loquacious. He talked much about Grant, and showed a certain artistic feeling for analysis of character, as a true literary critic would naturally do. Loyal to Grant, and still more so to Mrs. Grant, who acted as his patroness, he said nothing, even when far gone, that was offensive about either, but he held that no one except himself and Rawlins understood the General. To him, Grant appeared as an intermittent energy, immensely powerful when awake, but passive and plastic in repose. He said that neither he nor the rest of the staff knew why Grant succeeded; they believed in him because of his success. For stretches of time, his mind seemed torpid. Rawlins and the others would systematically talk their ideas into it, for weeks, not directly, but by discussion among themselves, in his presence. In the end, he would announce the idea as his own, without seeming conscious of the discussion; and would give the orders to carry it out with all the energy that belonged to his nature. They could never measure his character or be sure when he would act. They could never follow a mental process in his thought. They were not sure that he did think.

In all this, Adams took deep interest, for although he was not, like Badeau, waiting for Mrs. Grant's power of suggestion to act on the General's mind in order to germinate in a consulate or a legation, his portrait gallery of great men was becoming large, and it amused him to add an authentic likeness of the greatest general the world had seen since Napoleon. Badeau's analysis was rather delicate; infinitely superior to that of Sam Ward [15] or Charles Nordhoff. [16]

Badeau took Adams to the White House one evening and introduced him to the President and Mrs. Grant. First and last, he saw a dozen Presidents at the White House, and the most famous were by no means the most agreeable, but he found Grant the most curious object of study among them all. About no one did opinions differ so widely. Adams had no opinion, or occasion to make one. A single word with Grant satisfied him that, for his own good, the fewer words he risked, the better. Thus far in life he had met with but one man of the same intellectual or unintellectual type—Garibaldi. [17] Of the two, Garibaldi seemed to him a trifle the more intellectual, but, in both, the intellect counted for nothing; only the energy counted. The type was pre-intellectual, archaic, and would have seemed so even to the cave-dwellers. Adam, according to legend, was such a man.

In time one came to recognize the type in other men, with differences and variations, as normal; men whose energies were the greater, the less they wasted on thought; men who sprang from the soil to power;

[15] Sam Ward (1814–1884), an American author.
[16] Charles Nordhoff (1830–1901), an American author.
[17] Giuseppi Garibaldi (1807–1882), Italian nationalist revolutionary.

apt to be distrustful of themselves and of others; shy; jealous; sometimes vindictive; more or less dull in outward appearance; always needing stimulants; but for whom action was the highest stimulant—the instinct of fight. Such men were forces of nature, energies of the prime, like the *Pteraspis*,[18] but they made short work of scholars. They had commanded thousands of such and saw no more in them than in others. The fact was certain; it crushed argument and intellect at once.

Adams did not feel Grant as a hostile force; like Badeau he saw only an uncertain one. When in action he was superb and safe to follow; only when torpid he was dangerous. To deal with him one must stand near, like Rawlins, and practice more or less sympathetic habits. Simpleminded beyond the experience of Wall Street or State Street, he resorted, like most men of the same intellectual calibre, to commonplaces when at a loss for expression: "Let us have peace!" or, "The best way to treat a bad law is to execute it"; or a score of such reversible sentences generally to be gauged by their sententiousness; but sometimes he made one doubt his good faith; as when he seriously remarked to a particularly bright young woman that Venice would be a fine city if it were drained. In Mark Twain, this suggestion would have taken rank among his best witticisms; in Grant it was a measure of simplicity not singular. Robert E. Lee betrayed the same intellectual commonplace, in a Virginian form, not to the same degree, but quite distinctly enough for one who knew the American. What worried Adams was not the commonplace; it was, as usual, his own education. Grant fretted and irritated him, like the *Terebratula*,[19] as a defiance of first principles. He had no right to exist. He should have been extinct for ages. The idea that, as society grew older, it grew one-sided, upset evolution, and made of education a fraud. That, two thousand years after Alexander the Great and Julius Cæsar, a man like Grant should be called—and should actually and truly be—the highest product of the most advanced evolution, made evolution ludicrous. One must be as commonplace as Grant's own commonplaces to maintain such an absurdity. The progress of evolution from President Washington to President Grant, was alone evidence enough to upset Darwin.

Chapter 22   Chicago (1893)

    . . . By the time he got back to Washington on September 19, the storm having partly blown over, life had taken on a new face, and one so interesting that he set off to Chicago to study the Exposition again, and stayed there a fortnight absorbed in it. He found matter of study to fill a hundred years, and his education spread over chaos. Indeed, it seemed to him as though, this year, education went mad. The silver

[18] A fossil form of fish, the most ancient known.
[19] A bivalved mollusk that attaches itself to rocks, etc.

question, thorny as it was, fell into relations as simple as words of one syllable, compared with the problems of credit and exchange that came to complicate it; and when one sought rest at Chicago, educational game started like rabbits from every building, and ran out of sight among thousands of its kind before one could mark its burrow. The Exposition itself defied philosophy. One might find fault till the last gate closed, one could still explain nothing that needed explanation. As a scenic display, Paris had never approached it, but the inconceivable scenic display consisted in its being there at all—more surprising, as it was, than anything else on the continent, Niagara Falls, the Yellowstone Geysers, and the whole railway system thrown in, since these were all natural products in their place; while, since Noah's Ark, no such Babel of loose and ill-joined, such vague and ill-defined and unrelated thoughts and half-thoughts and experimental outcries as the Exposition, had ever ruffled the surface of the Lakes.

The first astonishment became greater every day. That the Exposition should be a natural growth and product of the Northwest offered a step in evolution to startle Darwin; but that it should be anything else seemed an idea more startling still; and even granting it were not—admitting it to be a sort of industrial, speculative growth and product of the Beaux Arts [20] artistically induced to pass the summer on the shore of Lake Michigan—could it be made to seem at home there? Was the American made to seem at home in it? Honestly, he had the air of enjoying it as though it were all his own; he felt it was good; he was proud of it; for the most part, he acted as though he had passed his life in landscape gardening and architectural decoration. If he had not done it himself, he had known how to get it done to suit him, as he knew how to get his wives and daughters dressed at Worth's or Paquin's. Perhaps he could not do it again; the next time he would want to do it himself and would show his own faults; but for the moment he seemed to have leaped directly from Corinth and Syracuse and Venice, over the heads of London and New York, to impose classical standards on plastic Chicago. Critics had no trouble in criticising the classicism, but all trading cities had always shown traders' taste, and, to the stern purist of religious faith, no art was thinner than Venetian Gothic. All traders' taste smelt of bric-à-brac; Chicago tried at least to give her taste a look of unity.

One sat down to ponder on the steps beneath Richard Hunt's [21] dome almost as deeply as on the steps of Ara Cœli,[22] and much to the same purpose. Here was a breach of continuity—a rupture in historical sequence! Was it real, or only apparent? One's personal universe hung on the answer, for, if the rupture was real and the new American world

[20] The main and conservative art academy of Paris.

[21] Richard Hunt (1827–1895), American architect, designed main building at Chicago Fair of 1893.

[22] An ancient church in Rome which Adams especially liked.

could take this sharp and conscious twist towards ideals, one's personal friends would come in, at last, as winners in the great American chariot-race for fame. If the people of the Northwest actually knew what was good when they saw it, they would some day talk about Hunt and Richardson,[23] La Farge[24] and St. Gaudens,[25] Burnham[26] and McKim,[27] and Stanford White[28] when their politicians and millionaires were otherwise forgotten. The artists and architects who had done the work offered little encouragement to hope it; they talked freely enough, but not in terms that one cared to quote; and to them the Northwest refused to look artistic. They talked as though they worked only for themselves; as though art, to the Western people, was a stage decoration; a diamond shirt-stud; a paper collar; but possibly the architects of Pæstum and Girgenti had talked in the same way, and the Greek had said the same thing of Semitic Carthage two thousand years ago.

Jostled by these hopes and doubts, one turned to the exhibits for help, and found it. The industrial schools tried to teach so much and so quickly that the instruction ran to waste. Some millions of other people felt the same helplessness, but few of them were seeking education, and to them helplessness seemed natural and normal, for they had grown up in the habit of thinking a steam-engine or a dynamo as natural as the sun, and expected to understand one as little as the other. For the historian alone the Exposition made a serious effort. Historical exhibits were common, but they never went far enough; none were thoroughly worked out. One of the best was that of the Cunard steamers, but still a student hungry for results found himself obliged to waste a pencil and several sheets of paper trying to calculate exactly when, according to the given increase of power, tonnage, and speed, the growth of the ocean steamer would reach its limits. His figures brought him, he thought, to the year 1927; another generation to spare before force, space, and time should meet. The ocean steamer ran the surest line of triangulation into the future, because it was the nearest of man's products to a unity; railroads taught less because they seemed already finished except for mere increase in number; explosives taught most, but needed a tribe of chemists, physicists, and mathematicians to explain; the dynamo taught least because it had barely reached infancy, and, if its progress was to be constant at the rate of the last ten years, it would result in infinite costly energy within a generation. One lingered long among the dynamos, for they were new, and they gave to history a new phase. Men of science could never understand the ignorance and naïveté of the historian, who, when he came suddenly on a new power, asked

---

[23] Henry Richardson (1838–1886), American architect.

[24] John La Farge (1835–1910), American artist, much admired by Adams.

[25] Augustus St. Gaudens (1848–1907), American sculptor.

[26] Daniel Burnham (1846–1912), leading architect of Chicago World's Fair.

[27] Charles McKim (1847–1909), architect of Boston Public Library.

[28] Stanford White (1853–1906), a leading American architect.

naturally what it was; did it pull or did it push? Was it a screw or thrust? Did it flow or vibrate? Was it a wire or a mathematical line? And a score of such questions to which he expected answers and was astonished to get none.

Education ran riot at Chicago, at least for retarded minds which had never faced in concrete form so many matters of which they were ignorant. Men who knew nothing whatever—who had never run a steam-engine, the simplest of forces—who had never put their hands on a lever—had never touched an electric battery—never talked through a telephone, and had not the shadow of a notion what amount of force was meant by a *watt* or an *ampère* or an *erg*, or any other term of measurement introduced within a hundred years—had no choice but to sit down on the steps and brood as they had never brooded on the benches of Harvard College, either as student or professor, aghast at what they had said and done in all these years, and still more ashamed of the childlike ignorance and babbling futility of the society that let them say and do it. The historical mind can think only in historical processes, and probably this was the first time since historians existed, that any of them had sat down helpless before a mechanical sequence. Before a metaphysical or a theological or a political sequence, most historians had felt helpless, but the single clue to which they had hitherto trusted was the unity of natural force.

Did he himself quite know what he meant? Certainly not! If he had known enough to state his problem, his education would have been complete at once. Chicago asked in 1893 for the first time the question whether the American people knew where they were driving. Adams answered, for one, that he did not know, but would try to find out. On reflecting sufficiently deeply, under the shadow of Richard Hunt's architecture, he decided that the American people probably knew no more than he did; but that they might still be driving or drifting unconsciously to some point in thought, as their solar system was said to be drifting towards some point in space; and that, possibly, if relations enough could be observed, this point might be fixed. Chicago was the first expression of American thought as a unity. . . .

Chapter 25   *The Dynamo and the Virgin (1900)*

Until the Great Exposition of 1900 [29] closed its doors in November, Adams haunted it, aching to absorb knowledge, and helpless to find it. He would have liked to know how much of it could have been grasped by the best-informed man in the world. While he was thus meditating chaos, Langley [30] came by, and showed it to him. At Langley's behest,

[29] In Paris.

[30] Samuel Langley (1834–1906), astronomer, inventor of instrument for measuring solar heat, flew first model airplane in 1896.

the Exhibition dropped its superfluous rags and stripped itself to the skin. For Langley knew what to study, and why, and how; while Adams might as well have stood outside in the night, staring at the Milky Way. Yet Langley said nothing new, and taught nothing that one might not have learned from Lord Bacon, three hundred years before; but though one should have known the "Advancement of Science" as well as one knew the "Comedy of Errors," the literary knowledge counted for nothing until some teacher should show how to apply it. Bacon took a vast deal of trouble in teaching King James I and his subjects, American or other, towards the year 1620, that true science was the development or economy of forces; yet an elderly American in 1900 knew neither the formula nor the forces; or even so much as to say to himself that his historical business in the Exposition concerned only the economies or developments of force since 1893, when he began the study at Chicago.

Nothing in education is so astonishing as the amount of ignorance it accumulates in the form of inert facts. Adams had looked at most of the accumulations of art in the storehouses called Art Museums; yet he did not know how to look at the art exhibits of 1900. He had studied Karl Marx and his doctrines of history with profound attention, yet he could not apply them at Paris. Langley, with the ease of a great master of experiment, threw out of the field every exhibit that did not reveal a new application of force, and naturally threw out, to begin with, almost the whole art exhibit. Equally, he ignored almost the whole industrial exhibit. He led his pupil directly to the forces. His chief interest was in new motors to make his airship feasible, and he taught Adams the astonishing complexities of the new Daimler [31] motor, and of the automobile, which, since 1893, had become a nightmare at a hundred kilometres an hour, almost as destructive as the electric tram which was only ten years older; and threatening to become as terrible as the locomotive steam-engine itself, which was almost exactly Adams's own age.

Then he showed his scholar the great hall of dynamos, and explained how little he knew about electricity or force of any kind, even of his own special sun, which spouted heat in inconceivable volume, but which, as far as he knew, might spout less or more, at any time, for all the certainty he felt in it. To him, the dynamo itself was but an ingenious channel for conveying somewhere the heat latent in a few tons of poor coal hidden in a dirty engine-house carefully kept out of sight; but to Adams the dynamo became a symbol of infinity. As he grew accustomed to the great gallery of machines, he began to feel the forty-foot dynamos as a moral force, much as the early Christians felt the Cross. The planet itself seemed less impressive, in its old-fashioned, deliberate, annual or daily revolution, than this huge wheel, revolving within arm's-length at some vertiginous speed, and barely murmuring—scarcely humming an audible warning to stand a hair's-breadth further for respect of

[31] Gottlieb Daimler (1834–1900), pioneer inventor of the automobile.

power—while it would not wake the baby lying close against its frame. Before the end, one began to pray for it; inherited instinct taught the natural expression of man before silent and infinite force. Among the thousand symbols of ultimate energy, the dynamo was not so human as some, but it was the most expressive.

Yet the dynamo, next to the steam-engine, was the most familiar of exhibits. For Adams's objects its value lay chiefly in its occult mechanism. Between the dynamo in the gallery of machines and the engine-house outside, the break of continuity amounted to abysmal fracture for a historian's objects. No more relation could he discover between the steam and the electric current than between the Cross and the cathedral. The forces were interchangeable if not reversible, but he could see only an absolute *fiat* in electricity as in faith. Langley could not help him. Indeed, Langley seemed to be worried by the same trouble, for he constantly repeated that the new forces were anarchical, and specially that he was not responsible for the new rays, that were little short of parricidal in their wicked spirit towards science. His own rays, with which he had doubled the solar spectrum, were altogether harmless and beneficent; but Radium [32] denied its God—or, what was to Langley the same thing, denied the truths of his Science. The force was wholly new.

A historian who asked only to learn enough to be as futile as Langley or Kelvin,[33] made rapid progress under this teaching, and mixed himself up in the tangle of ideas until he achieved a sort of Paradise of ignorance vastly consoling to his fatigued senses. He wrapped himself in vibrations and rays which were new, and he would have hugged Marconi and Branly had he met them, as he hugged the dynamo; while he lost his arithmetic in trying to figure out the equation between the discoveries and economies of force. The economies, like the discoveries, were absolute, supersensual, occult; incapable of expression in horse-power. What mathematical equivalent could he suggest as the value of a Branly [34] coherer? Frozen air, or the electric furnace, had some scale of measurement, no doubt, if somebody could invent a thermometer adequate to the purpose; but X-rays had played no part whatever in man's consciousness, and the atom itself had figured only as a fiction of thought. In these seven years man had translated himself into a new universe which had no common scale of measurement with the old. He had entered a supersensual world, in which he could measure nothing except by chance collisions of movements imperceptible to his senses, perhaps even imperceptible to his instruments, but perceptible to each other, and so to some known ray at the end of the scale. Langley seemed prepared for anything, even for an indeterminable number of universes interfused—physics stark mad in metaphysics.

[32] Recently discovered, in 1898, by Mme. Curie.
[33] Lord Kelvin (1824–1907), pioneer in thermodynamics.
[34] Edouard Branley (1846–1940), French scientist who invented an instrument for detecting radio waves.

Historians undertake to arrange sequences,—called stories, or histories—assuming in silence a relation of cause and effect. These assumptions, hidden in the depths of dusty libraries, have been astounding, but commonly unconscious and childlike; so much so, that if any captious critic were to drag them to light, historians would probably reply, with one voice, that they had never supposed themselves required to know what they were talking about. Adams, for one, had toiled in vain to find out what he meant. He had even published a dozen volumes of American history for no other purpose than to satisfy himself whether, by the severest process of stating, with the least possible comment, such facts as seemed sure, in such order as seemed rigorously consequent, he could fix for a familiar moment a necessity sequence of human movement. The result had satisfied him as little as at Harvard College. Where he saw sequence, other men saw something quite different, and no one saw the same unit of measure. He cared little about his experiments and less about his statesmen, who seemed to him quite as ignorant as himself and as a rule, no more honest; but he insisted on a relation of sequence, and if he could not reach it by one method, he would try as many methods as science knew. Satisfied that the sequence of men led to nothing and that the sequence of their society could lead no further, while the mere sequence of time was artificial, and the sequence of thought was chaos, he turned at last to the sequence of force; and thus it happened that, after ten years' pursuit, he found himself lying in the Gallery of Machines at the Great Exposition of 1900, his historical neck broken by the sudden irruption of forces totally new.

Since no one else showed much concern, an elderly person without other cares had no need to betray alarm. The year 1900 was not the first to upset schoolmasters. Copernicus and Galileo had broken many professorial necks about 1600; Columbus had stood the world on its head towards 1500; but the nearest approach to the revolution of 1900 was that of 310, when Constantine [35] set up the Cross. The rays that Langley disowned, as well as those which he fathered, were occult, supersensual, irrational; they were what, in terms of medieval science, were called immediate modes of the divine substance.

The historian was thus reduced to his last resources. Clearly if he was bound to reduce all these forces to a common value, this common value could have no measure but that of their attraction on his own mind. He must treat them as they had been felt; as convertible, reversible, interchangeable attractions on thought. He made up his mind to venture it; he would risk translating rays into faith. Such a reversible process would vastly amuse a chemist, but the chemist could not deny that he, or some of his fellow physicists, could feel the force of both. When Adams was a boy in Boston, the best chemist in the place had probably never heard of Venus except by way of scandal, or of the Virgin except as idolatry;

[35] Constantine I (c. 280–337), reported to have seen a cross in the sky indicating victory for him in battle.

neither had he heard of dynamos or automobiles or radium; yet his mind was ready to feel the force of all, though the rays were unborn and the women were dead.

Here opened another totally new education, which promised to be by far the most hazardous of all. The knife-edge along which he must crawl, like Sir Lancelot in the twelfth century, divided two kingdoms of force which had nothing in common but attraction. They were as different as a magnet is from gravitation, supposing one knew what a magnet was, or gravitation, or love. The force of the Virgin was still felt at Lourdes, and seemed to be as potent as X-rays but in America neither Venus nor Virgin ever had value as a force—at most as sentiment. No American had ever truly been afraid of either.

This problem in dynamics gravely perplexed an American historian. The Woman had once been supreme; in France she still seemed potent, not merely as a sentiment, but as a force. Why was she unknown in America? For evidently America was ashamed of her, and she was ashamed of herself, otherwise they would not have strewn fig-leaves so profusely all over her. When she was a true force, she was ignorant of fig-leaves, but the monthly-magazine-made American female had not a feature that would have been recognized by Adam. The trait was notorious, and often humorous, but any one brought up among Puritans knew that sex was a sin. In any previous age, sex was strength. Neither art nor beauty was needed. Every one, even among Puritans, knew that neither Diana of the Ephesians nor any of the Oriental goddesses was worshipped for her beauty. She was goddess because of her force; she was the animated dynamo; she was reproduction—the greatest and most mysterious of all energies; all she needed was to be fecund. Singularly enough, not one of Adams's many schools of education had ever drawn his attention to the opening lines of Lucretius, though they were perhaps the finest in all Latin literature, where the poet invoked Venus exactly as Dante invoked the Virgin: —

Quae quoniam rerum naturam sola *gubernas.*[36]

The Venus of Epicurean philosophy survived in the Virgin of the Schools: —

Donna, sei tanto grande, e tanto vali,
Che qual vuol grazia, e a te non ricorre,
Sua disianza vuol volar senz' ali.[37]

All this was to American thought as though it had never existed. The true American knew something of the facts, but nothing of the feelings; he read the letter, but he never felt the law. Before this historical chasm,

---

[36] "Since thou art, above all, sole mistress of the nature of things, . . ." (from *de Rerum Natura*).

[37] "Lady, thou art so great in all things/That he who wishes grace and seeks thee not/His desires fly upwards without wings" (from *The Divine Comedy*).

a mind like that of Adams felt itself helpless; he turned from the Virgin to the Dynamo as though he were a Branly coherer. On one side, at the Louvre and at Chartres, as he knew by the record of work actually done and still before his eyes, was the highest energy ever known to man, the creator of four-fifths of his noblest art, exercising vastly more attraction over the human mind than all the steam-engines and dynamos ever dreamed of; and yet this energy was unknown to the American mind. An American Virgin would never dare command; an American Venus would never dare exist.

The question, which to any plain American of the nineteenth century seemed as remote as it did to Adams, drew him almost violently to study, once it was posed; and on this point Langleys were as useless as though they were Herbert Spencers [38] or dynamos. The idea survived only as art. There one turned as naturally as though the artist were himself a woman. Adams began to ponder, asking himself whether he knew of any American artist who had ever insisted on the power of sex, as every classic had always done; but he could think only of Walt Whitman; Bret Harte, as far as the magazines would let him venture; and one or two painters, for the flesh-tones. All the rest had used sex for sentiment, never for force; to them, Eve was a tender flower, and Herodias an unfeminine horror. American art, like the American language and American education, was as far as possible sexless. Society regarded this victory over sex as its greatest triumph, and the historian readily admitted it, since the moral issue, for the moment, did not concern one who was studying the relations of unmoral force. He cared nothing for the sex of the dynamo until he could measure its energy.

Vaguely seeking a clue, he wandered through the art exhibit, and, in his stroll, stopped almost every day before St. Gaudens's General Sherman, which had been given the central post of honor. St. Gaudens himself was in Paris, putting on the work his usual interminable last touches, and listening to the usual contradictory suggestions of brother sculptors. Of all the American artists who gave to American art whatever life it breathed in the seventies, St. Gaudens was perhaps the most sympathetic, but certainly the most inarticulate. General Grant or Don Cameron had scarcely less instinct of rhetoric than he. All the others—the Hunts, Richardson, John La Farge, Stanford White—were exuberant; only St. Gaudens could never discuss or dilate on an emotion, or suggest artistic arguments for giving to his work the forms that he felt. He never laid down the law, or affected the despot, or became brutalized like Whistler by the brutalities of his world. He required no incense; he was no egoist; his simplicity of thought was excessive; he could not imitate, or give any form but his own to the creations of his hand. No one felt more strongly than he the strength of other men, but the idea that they could affect him never stirred an image in his mind.

This summer his health was poor and his spirits were low. For such

[38] Herbert Spencer (1820–1903), British philosopher and sociologist.

a temper, Adams was not the best companion, since his own gaiety was not *folle;* [39] but he risked going now and then to the studio on Mont Parnasse to draw him out for a stroll in the Bois de Boulogne, or dinner as pleased his moods, and in return St. Gaudens sometimes let Adams go about in his company.

Once St. Gaudens took him down to Amiens, with a party of Frenchmen, to see the cathedral. Not until they found themselves actually studying the sculpture of the western portal, did it dawn on Adams's mind that, for his purposes, St. Gaudens on that spot had more interest to him than the cathedral itself. Great men before great monuments express great truths, provided they are not taken too solemnly. Adams never tired of quoting the supreme phrase of his idol Gibbon, before the Gothic cathedrals; "I darted a contemptuous look on the stately monuments of superstition." Even in the footnotes of his history Gibbon had never inserted a bit of humor more human than this, and one would have paid largely for a photograph of the fat little historian, on the background of Notre Dame of Amiens, trying to persuade his readers—perhaps himself—that he was darting a contemptuous look on the stately monument, for which he felt in fact the respect which every man of his vast study and active mind always feels before objects worthy of it; but besides the humor, one felt also the relation. Gibbon ignored the Virgin, because in 1789 religious monuments were out of fashion. In 1900 his remark sounded fresh and simple as the green fields to ears that had heard a hundred years of other remarks, mostly no more fresh and certainly less simple. Without malice, one might find it more instructive than a whole lecture of Ruskin. One sees what one brings, and at that moment Gibbon brought the French Revolution. Ruskin brought reaction against the Revolution. St. Gaudens had passed beyond all. He liked the stately monuments much more than he liked Gibbon or Ruskin; he loved their dignity; their unity; their scale; their lines; their lights and shadows; their decorative sculpture; but he was even less conscious than they of the force that created it all—the Virgin, the Woman—by whose genius "the stately monuments of superstition" were built, through which she was expressed. He would have seen more meaning in Isis [40] with the cow's horns, at Edfoo, who expressed the same thought. The art remained, but the energy was lost even upon the artist.

Yet in mind and person St. Gaudens was a survival of the 1500; he bore the stamp of the Renaissance, and should have carried an image of the Virgin round his neck, or stuck in his hat, like Louis XI. In mere time he was a lost soul that had strayed by chance into the twentieth century, and forgotten where it came from. He writhed and cursed at his ignorance, much as Adams did at his own, but in the opposite sense. St. Gaudens was a child of Benvenuto Cellini, smothered in an Ameri-

[39] Wild.
[40] Egyptian fertility goddess.

can cradle. Adams was a quintessence of Boston, devoured by curiosity to think like Benvenuto. St. Gaudens's art was starved from birth, and Adams's instinct was blighted from babyhood. Each had but half of a nature, and when they came together before the Virgin of Amiens they ought both to have felt in her the force that made them one; but it was not so. To Adams she became more than ever a channel of force; to St. Gaudens she remained as before a channel of taste.

For a symbol of power, St. Gaudens instinctively preferred the horse, as was plain in his horse and Victory of the Sherman monument. Doubtless Sherman also felt it so. The attitude was so American that, for at least forty years, Adams had never realized that any other could be in sound taste. How many years had he taken to admit a notion of what Michael Angelo and Rubens were driving at? He could not say; but he knew that only since 1895 had he begun to feel the Virgin or Venus as force, and not everywhere even so. At Chartres—perhaps at Lourdes—possibly at Cnidos [41] if one could still find there the divinely naked Aphrodite of Praxiteles—but otherwise one must look for force to the goddesses of Indian mythology. The idea died out long ago in the German and English stock. St. Gaudens at Amiens was hardly less sensitive to the force of the female energy than Matthew Arnold at the Grande Chartreuse. [42] Neither of them felt goddesses as power—only as reflected emotion, human expression, beauty, purity, taste, scarcely even as sympathy. They felt a railway train as power; yet they, and all other artists, constantly complained that the power embodied in a railway train could never be embodied in art. All the steam in the world could not, like the Virgin, build Chartres.

Yet in mechanics, whatever the mechanicians might think, both energies acted as interchangeable forces on man, and by action on man all known force may be measured. Indeed, few men of science measured force in any other way. After once admitting that a straight line was the shortest distance between two points, no serious mathematician cared to deny anything that suited his convenience, and rejected no symbol, unproved or unproveable, that helped him to accomplish work. The symbol was force, as a compass-needle or a triangle was force, as the mechanist might prove by losing it, and nothing could be gained by ignoring their value. Symbol or energy, the Virgin had acted as the greatest force the Western world ever felt, and had drawn man's activities to herself more strongly than any other power, natural or supernatural, had ever done; the historian's business was to follow the track of the energy; to find where it came from and where it went to; its complex

[41] Shrine to Aphrodite in Asia Minor.
[42] An old Carthusian monastery near Grenoble, France. Adams invokes the name of Matthew Arnold because Arnold had written a poem, "Stanzas from the Grand Chartreuse" which Adams liked to quote, especially the famous lines: "Wandering between two worlds, one dead/The other powerless to be born."

source and shifting channels; its values, equivalents, conversions. It could scarcely be more complex than radium; it could hardly be deflected, diverted, polarized, absorbed more perplexingly than other radiant matter. Adams knew nothing about any of them, but as a mathematical problem of influence on human progress, though all were occult, all reacted on his mind, and he rather inclined to think the Virgin easiest to handle.

The pursuit turned out to be long and tortuous, leading at last into the vast forests of scholastic science. From Zeno to Descartes, hand in hand with Thomas Aquinas, Montaigne, and Pascal, one stumbled as stupidly as though one were still a German student of 1860. Only with the instinct of despair could one force one's self into this old thicket of ignorance after having been repulsed at a score of entrances more promising and more popular. Thus far, no path had led anywhere, unless perhaps to an exceedingly modest living. Forty-five years of study had proved to be quite futile for the pursuit of power; one controlled no more force in 1900 than in 1850, although the amount of force controlled by society had enormously increased. The secret of education still hid itself somewhere behind ignorance, and one fumbled over it as feebly as ever. In such labyrinths, the staff is a force almost more necessary than the legs; the pen becomes a sort of blind-man's dog, to keep him from falling into the gutters. The pen works for itself, and acts like a hand, modelling the plastic material over and over again to the form that suits it best. The form is never arbitrary, but is a sort of growth like crystallization, as any artist knows too well; for often the pencil or pen runs into side-paths and shapelessness, loses its relations, stops or is bogged. Then it has to return on its trail, and recover, if it can, its line of force. The result of a year's work depends more on what is struck out than on what is left in; on the sequence of the main lines of thought, than on their play or variety. Compelled once more to lean heavily on this support, Adams covered more thousands of pages with figures as formal as though they were algebra, laboriously striking out, altering, burning, experimenting, until the year had expired, the Exposition had long been closed, and winter drawing to its end before he sailed from Cherbourg, on January 19, 1901 for home.

Index of Authors and Titles

Index of First Lines of Poetry